WORLD PHYSICAL MAP

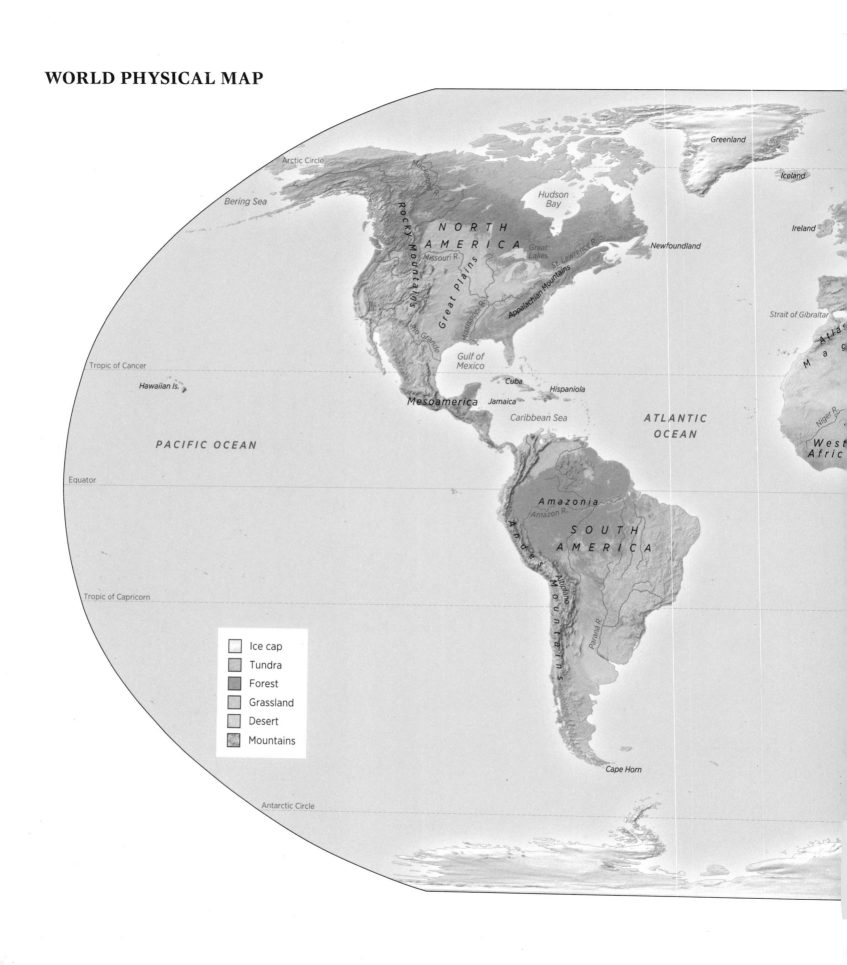

Greenland

Iceland

Arctic Circle

Bering Sea

Mackenzie R.

Hudson Bay

Ireland

NORTH AMERICA

Rocky Mountains

Missouri R.

Great Lakes

St. Lawrence R.

Newfoundland

Great Plains

Appalachian Mountains

Mississippi R.

Strait of Gibraltar

Atlas

Ma

Rio Grande

Tropic of Cancer

Gulf of Mexico

Hawaiian Is.

Cuba

Hispaniola

Mesoamerica

Jamaica

Niger R.

West Africa

Caribbean Sea

ATLANTIC OCEAN

PACIFIC OCEAN

Equator

Amazonia

Amazon R.

SOUTH AMERICA

Andes Mountains

Altiplano

Tropic of Capricorn

Paraná R.

	Ice cap
	Tundra
	Forest
	Grassland
	Desert
	Mountains

Cape Horn

Antarctic Circle

ARCTIC OCEAN

Scandinavia

North
a

Baltic Sea

Volga R.

Ob R.

Yenisei R.

S i b e r i a

Lena R.

Bering Sea

EUROPE

E u r a s i a n   S t e p p e

A S I A

Alps

Danube R.

Black Sea

Caspian Sea

L. Balkhash

C e n t r a l
A s i a

Manchuria

Sea of
Japan

t s.

Sicily

Anatolia

Tigris R.

Zagros Mts.

Southwest Asia

Euphrates R.

Tarim
Basin

Gobi Desert

Huang
He

Yellow
Sea

r e b

Mediterranean Sea

Syrian
Desert

Persian
Gulf

H i m a l a y a   M o u n t a i n s

E a s t   A s i a

Yangzi R.

Strait of
Hormuz

Indus R.

a   h   a   r   a

Nile R.

Red Sea

Arabian
Desert

S o u t h
A s i a

Ganges R.

South
China
Sea

Philippines

PACIFIC OCEAN

h   e   l

Arabian
Sea

Deccan

Bay of
Bengal

Southeast
Asia

Bab al-Mandab

A F R I C A

Ethiopian
Highlands

Sri Lanka

Mekong R.

C e n t r a l
A f r i c a

Straits of
Malacca

Congo R.

L. Victoria

E a s t
A f r i c a

Sumatra

Borneo

New
Guinea

Java

Zambezi R.

INDIAN
OCEAN

Coral Sea

Madagascar

S o u t h e r n
A f r i c a

Great Sandy
Desert

A U S T R A L I A

Cape of
Good Hope

New
Zealand

Tasmania

0		1,000		2,000 mi

0		1,000		2,000 km

A N T A R C T I C A

J. R. McNEILL

THE WEBS *of* HUMANKIND

A WORLD HISTORY

SECOND EDITION

VOLUME TWO

W. W. NORTON & COMPANY
Celebrating a Century of Independent Publishing

W. W. NORTON & COMPANY has been independent since its founding in 1923, when William Warder Norton and Mary D. Herter Norton first published lectures delivered at the People's Institute, the adult education division of New York City's Cooper Union. The firm soon expanded its program beyond the Institute, publishing books by celebrated academics from America and abroad. By midcentury, the two major pillars of Norton's publishing—trade books and college texts—were firmly established. In the 1950s, the Norton family transferred control of the company to its employees, and today—with a staff of five hundred and hundreds of trade, college, and professional titles published each year—W. W. Norton & Company stands as the largest and oldest publishing house owned wholly by its employees.

Editor in Chief, Social Sciences: Justin Cahill
Associate Managing Editor: Melissa Atkin
Associate Editor: Angie Merila
Copyeditors: Scott Sugarman, Alice Vigliani
Production Manager: Jane Searle
Senior Managing Editor, College: Marian Johnson
Managing Editors, College: Carla Talmadge and Kim Yi
Media Editor: Carson Russell
Media Project Editor: Rachel Mayer
Media Associate Editor: Jennifer Jussel
Media Editorial Assistant: Clara Drimmer
Photo Editor: Thomas Persano
Associate Art Director: Anne-Michelle Gallero
Permissions Specialist: Joshua Garvin
Marketing Manager: Sarah England Bartley
Layout Artist: Brad Walrod/Kenoza Type, Inc.
Cartographer and Illustrator: Mapping Specialists—Fitchburg, WI
Manufacturing: Transcontinental Interglobe Inc.—Beauceville, QC

ISBN: 978-1-324-06127-4

Library of Congress Control Number: 2023947999

W. W. Norton & Company, Inc., 500 Fifth Avenue, New York, NY 10110

wwnorton.com

W. W. Norton & Company Ltd., 15 Carlisle Street, London W1D 3BS

1 2 3 4 5 6 7 8 9 0

This book is dedicated to families: especially the one into which
I was born, the one that Julie and I created, and the one that
is the community of historians at Georgetown University—
students and teachers, past and present.

ABOUT THE AUTHOR

J. R. McNEILL studied at Swarthmore College and Duke University, where he completed a PhD in 1981. Since 1985, he has taught at Georgetown University, in the History Department and School of Foreign Service, where he held the Cinco Hermanos Chair in Environmental and International Affairs before becoming University Professor in 2006. He has taught roughly 3,000 Georgetown students in courses on world history, international-relations history, and environmental history.

McNeill's books include *Atlantic Empires of France and Spain: Louisbourg and Havana, 1700–1763* (1985); *The Mountains of the Mediterranean World: An Environmental History* (1992); *Something New under the Sun: An Environmental History of the Twentieth-Century World* (2000), cowinner of the World History Association book prize and the Forest History Society book prize; *The Human Web: A Bird's-Eye View of World History* (2003), coauthored with his father, William McNeill; and *Mosquito Empires: Ecology and War in the Greater Caribbean, 1620–1914* (2010), which won the Beveridge Prize from the American Historical Association. His latest book, *The Great Acceleration: An Environmental History of the Anthropocene since 1945*, appeared in 2016. He has edited or coedited 15 other books, including two volumes of *The Cambridge World History* (2015).

In 2010, McNeill was awarded the Toynbee Prize for "academic and public contributions to humanity." In 2014, the World History Association awarded him its annual prize for achievement in that field; in 2019, the American Society for Environmental History presented him with its Distinguished Scholar Award. The Royal Netherlands Academy of Arts and Sciences awarded him the Heineken Prize for history in 2018. In 2011–2013, he served as president of the American Society for Environmental History, and in 2019 as president of the American Historical Association. He is a member of the American Academy of Arts and Sciences.

CONTENTS IN BRIEF

PART 4   WEAVING THE GLOBAL WEB, 1400 TO 1800   498

15. Convergence: The Discovery of the Oceans and Biological Globalization, 1400 to 1800   501
16. Disruption: Africa, the Americas, Siberia, and Oceania, 1492 to 1850   535
17. Cultural Upheavals: Religious and Intellectual Movements, 1500 to 1750   573
18. University of War: Empires and Power, 1450 to 1800   605
19. The First Global Economy, 1500 to 1800   641

PART 5   REVOLUTIONS, 1640 TO 1920   672

20. The Best and Worst of Times: Atlantic Revolutions, 1640 to 1830   675
21. Fossil Fuels and Mass Production: Industrial Revolutions around the World, 1780 to 1914   709
22. Two Liberations: The Vital Revolution and the Abolitions of Slavery and Serfdom, 1750 to 1950   747
23. Nationalism and Imperialism: Tightening the Global Web, 1800 to 1930   783
24. Making the World Modern: Confronting Industrialization, Nationalism, and Imperialism, 1850 to 1920   821

PART 6   THE GLOBAL WEB SINCE 1870   850

25. International Politics: War, Peace, and Ideologies, 1870 to 1940   853
26. World War II, Global War in the Global Web, 1937 to 1945   893
27. The Cold War and Decolonization, 1945 to 1991   931
28. Rebalancing the Global Web: Africa, Latin America, and the Rise of East Asia since 1960   971
29. A Shrinking World: Globalization since 1980   1007

CONTENTS

PART 4   WEAVING THE GLOBAL WEB, 1400 TO 1800   498

15.   Convergence: The Discovery of the Oceans and Biological Globalization, 1400 to 1800   501

THE WORLD'S WEBS IN THE FIFTEENTH CENTURY   502

The Old World Web   502

   Interactions within the Old World Web | A Thickening Web

Local Webs   504

Webs in the Americas   504

Webs in Africa   505

PREVAILING WINDS AND THE OPEN SEA   505

The Ming Voyages, 1405–1433   506

European Voyaging, 1400–1700   509

   European Mariners' Motives | Learning the Atlantic | African Coasts | Columbus Crosses the Atlantic | Da Gama Sails to India | Magellan Crosses the Pacific

CONSIDERING THE EVIDENCE Portuguese Reasoning about Skin Color   517

Weaving a Maritime Web   518

BIOLOGICAL GLOBALIZATION, 1492–1800   519

Deadly Diseases   521

Useful Animals   522

Key Crops   522

   Maize | Cassava

THE HUMAN WEB The Columbian Exchange, 1492–1800   524–25

Biological Globalization in the Pacific   526

The Impact of Biological Exchange   526

THE BEGINNINGS OF A GLOBAL WEB   527

CONCLUSION   528

CHAPTER REVIEW   529

FURTHER READING   529

MAKING CONNECTIONS Biological Globalization: Movement, Disease, and Impacts   530

16. **Disruption: Africa, the Americas, Siberia, and Oceania, 1492 to 1850**   **535**

AFRICA AND THE GLOBAL WEB   **537**
Islam in Africa   538
European and Christian Influences on Coastal Africa   540
  Kongo and Angola
  CONSIDERING THE EVIDENCE The Perils of Trade in Kongo   541
  Mozambique | The Cape of Good Hope
The Transatlantic Slave Trade   543
  Dimensions of the Trade | The Slaving Business |
  Consequences in Africa

THE AMERICAS JOIN THE GLOBAL WEB   **548**
Disease and Depopulation: Regional Variations   548
  The Caribbean | Mesoamerica and the Andes | Ecological,
  Social, and Economic Factors | Effect on Climate
New Empires   551
Settlement and Transoceanic Economies   553
  Fisheries and Furs | The Plantation Zone | Silver | Agriculture
Hybrid Societies   555
  Creole Languages and Cultures | Shifting Social Hierarchies |
  Independent Groups

SIBERIA ABSORBED   **557**
Fur: A Lucrative Export   558
The Russification of Siberia   559

OCEANIA AND AUSTRALIA ENMESHED   **560**
Another Disease Disaster   560
Christianity and Trade Goods   561
Australia   561
New Zealand   563
Hawaii   564

CONCLUSION   **565**

CHAPTER REVIEW   **566**

FURTHER READING   **566**

MAKING CONNECTIONS Firsthand Accounts from the
Middle Passage and Life in Slavery, ca. 1770–1830   567

17. **Cultural Upheavals: Religious and Intellectual Movements, 1500 to 1750**   **573**

INFORMATION FLOWS AND INTELLECTUAL FERMENTS   **575**
Information Technology: The Printing Press   575

EUROPE: EXTREME TURBULENCE   **577**

The Renaissance   577

Religion: Protestant and Catholic Reformations   578

Luther and Protestantism | The Catholic Reformation |
Witch Hunts

The Scientific Revolution   583

Astronomy and Heliocentrism | Chemistry and
Experimentation | Medicine | Institutions and Connections

THE WORLD OF ISLAM: A SHI'A REFORMATION   **587**

Shi'ism   587

Safavids and Shi'ism in Iran   588

Shi'ism under the Safavids | The Wider Islamic World

SIKHISM IN INDIA: THE BIRTH OF A NEW RELIGION   **590**

Nanak's Teachings   591

The Development of Sikhism   591

**CHINA AND JAPAN: CONFUCIAN REFORMATION AND
IMPORTED CHRISTIANITY**   **592**

Wang Yangming   592

CONSIDERING THE EVIDENCE A Hymn by Kabir in the *Adi Granth*   593

Christianity in China and Japan   594

REPRESSION AND PERSECUTION   **595**

INTELLECTUAL UPHEAVAL: PARALLELS AND CONTRASTS   **596**

CONCLUSION   **597**

CHAPTER REVIEW   **599**

FURTHER READING   **599**

MAKING CONNECTIONS New Paths to Truth and Wisdom   600

18. **University of War: Empires and Power, 1450 to 1800**   **604**

EARLY MODERN EMPIRE IN GLOBAL PERSPECTIVE   **607**

WARFARE AND ITS PRICE: THE MILITARY REVOLUTION   **608**

Bigger Battalions, Higher Taxes   608

Navies and Artillery   609

Standing Armies   610

THE TOKUGAWA CONSOLIDATION OF POWER IN JAPAN   **611**

The Introduction of Firearms   611

Nobunaga and Hideyoshi   611

Establishing the Tokugawa Shogunate   612

THE QING CONSOLIDATION IN CHINA — 613
The Fall of the Ming — 613
The Qing Conquest — 613
Statecraft and Military Innovation — 615

THE MUGHAL EMPIRE IN INDIA — 616
Mughal Might — 616
Mughal Consolidation — 617
Mughal Decline — 618

THE OTTOMAN EMPIRE — 619
Ottoman Expansion — 619
Ottoman Consolidation — 621
The Tax System — 621
  CONSIDERING THE EVIDENCE An Ottoman Register in Ukraine — 622
    The Millet System

IMPERIAL CONSOLIDATION IN RUSSIA — 623
Ivan IV — 623
Peter the Great — 623

THE HABSBURG EMPIRE: THE FIRST GLOBAL POWER — 624
Soft Power — 625
Hard Power — 625
A Patchwork Empire — 625

THE UNIVERSITY OF WAR AND THE RISE OF EUROPE — 627
Military Competition and State Power — 627
Political Fragmentation and Global Reach — 627
The Rise of Big States: Leadership or Circumstance? — 628

RESPONSES OF SMALLER POWERS — 628
Iran and Southeast Asia — 628
Kongo and Morocco — 628
The Costs of Maintaining Tradition: Poland and Egypt's Mamluk Sultanate — 629

NOMADS AND PIRATES IN A WORLD OF EXPANDING STATES — 630
Nomad Power — 630
Pirates — 631
    The Caribbean and Indian Ocean | The Barbary Pirates

CONCLUSION — 632

CHAPTER REVIEW — 634

FURTHER READING — 634

MAKING CONNECTIONS The Exercise of Power — 635

19. The First Global Economy, 1500 to 1800   640

WORLD POPULATION AND THE GLOBAL ECONOMY   643
A Population Landmark   644
The Size of the World Economy   645

THE DISTRIBUTION OF ECONOMIC BENEFITS   645
Incredible Shrinking Humans   645
Falling Incomes for Wage Laborers   647

TRADE   647
Spices and the Spice Trade   648
Cotton and the Cotton Trade   650
Silver and the Silver Trade   652
     Financing the Spanish and Japanese States | Promoting
     Economic Growth in China and India

NEW BUSINESS FORMATS: PLANTATIONS, COMPANIES, BANKS   655
Plantations   655
     The Spread of the Sugar Plantation | Sugar and
     Plantation Slavery
Chartered Joint-Stock Companies   658
     Company Origins | The Dutch East India Company (VOC)
Banks   660
     Lending at Interest
   CONSIDERING THE EVIDENCE On the Circulation of Blood
and Money   661
     Bank Notes and Credit

GLOBAL LINKS AND COMMERCIAL REVOLUTIONS   662
China   663
Atlantic Europe   664
Other Regions in the Global Economy   664

CONCLUSION   665

CHAPTER REVIEW   667

FURTHER READING   667

MAKING CONNECTIONS The Global Coffee Trade   668

PART 5   REVOLUTIONS, 1640 TO 1920   672

20. The Best and Worst of Times: Atlantic Revolutions, 1640 to 1830   675

THE ATLANTIC WORLD IN GLOBAL PERSPECTIVE   676

KONGO AND BRITAIN, 1640–1709   677

Civil War and Revolution in Kongo, 1640–1709   677
Monarchy and the Slave Trade | Fragmentation of Power | Beatriz Kimpa Vita's Movement for Reunification

The British Civil Wars and Revolution, 1640–1707   679
King versus Parliament | The Commonwealth | The Restoration | The Glorious Revolution

NORTH AMERICA, 1750–1790   682

Growing Tensions with Britain   683
Indigenous Lands | British Taxes

The American Revolution   685
Keys to American Victory

Outcomes of the Revolution   686
Women's Rights | Compromising on Slavery

FRANCE, 1780–1815   687

Origins of the French Revolution   687
The Enlightenment | Socioeconomic Changes | Other Pressures

The Early Revolution   689
The Declaration of the Rights of Man and Citizen | Targeting Church and Monarchy

A Radical Turn   690
Jacobin Reforms | The Committee of Public Safety

Napoleon Bonaparte: Expansion and Overreach   691

HAITI, 1780–1804   693

A Plantation Colony: Sugar, Coffee, Slaves   693

Toussaint and the Haitian Revolution   693
French Intervention | Aftermath

SPANISH AMERICA, 1765–1825   695

A Diverse Society   695

The Bourbon Reforms   695
Túpac Amaru's Revolt | Tensions over Trade

Geopolitical Shifts   698

Bolívar and the Spanish American Republics   698

THE ATLANTIC REVOLUTIONS IN BROADER PERSPECTIVE   699

Atlantic Connections   699

CONSIDERING THE EVIDENCE A Revolutionary's Letter from Jamaica   700

CONCLUSION   **775**

CHAPTER REVIEW   **777**

FURTHER READING   **777**

MAKING CONNECTIONS Smallpox and Inoculation   778

23. **Nationalism and Imperialism: Tightening the
Global Web, 1800 to 1930**   **782**

NATIONALISM AND NATION-STATES   **784**

France   785

Japan   786

Canada   787

First Nations and Assimilation | Canadian Nationalism,
Britain, and the United States

Germany   788

Bismarck and German Unification

Nationalism as a Source of State Power   789

Nationalism and Multiethnic Empires   790

The Habsburg Empire | The Russian Empire | The Ottoman
Empire | Minority Nationalisms

IMPERIALISM   **792**

Technologies and Imperialism   792

Nationalism in Support of Imperialism   794

Cultures of Imperialism   795

Social Darwinism and Pseudoscientific Racism | Concepts
of Manliness and Muscular Christianity | Intellectual Responses

The British in India, 1818–1914   798

Imperial Strategy: Divide and Rule | Economic Effects

The French in Algeria, 1830–1914   799

Colons and French Rule | Economic Impact

Forms of Imperialism: Settler Colonies   801

The Partition and Conquest of Africa, 1874–1914   801

The Berlin Conference | Military Conquest and Cattle Disease

Colonial Africa to 1930   803

Economic Exploitation | Christianity in Africa | Islam in Africa

European Imperialism in Southeast Asia and the Pacific   805

Imperial Latecomers: Italy, Japan, and the United States   806

LAND EMPIRES   **807**

Russia: The World's Biggest Land Empire   807

Secondary Empires: Comanche Texas and Ethiopia   808

Comanche Texas, 1730–1870 | Ethiopia, 1870–1913

CONSIDERING THE EVIDENCE Ethiopian Imperialism through
Russian Eyes   811

Other Secondary Empires   812

NATIONALISM, IMPERIALISM, AND THE GLOBAL WEB   812

CONCLUSION   813

CHAPTER REVIEW   814

FURTHER READING   814

MAKING CONNECTIONS The Heyday of Eugenics   815

24. Making the World Modern: Confronting Industrialization, Nationalism, and Imperialism, 1850 to 1920   820

MILLENARIAN VISIONS: THE GHOST DANCE AND CANUDOS   823

The Ghost Dance in the Western United States   823

Wovoka's Prophecy | Wounded Knee

Canudos in Northeastern Brazil   825

CONSIDERING THE EVIDENCE Messengers of the Ghost Dance   826

Antônio Conselheiro's Quest for Justice

GIANT REBELLIONS, 1850–1864: CHINA AND INDIA   827

The Taiping Rebellion, 1850–1864   828

The Plight of the Qing | Jesus's Younger Brother | Rebellion

The Indian Rebellion, 1857–1858   830

Grievances | Rebellion | Aftermath

Rebellions as Global and Local   833

REVOLUTIONS, 1870s–1920: CHINA AND MEXICO   834

The Chinese Revolution, 1880s–1910s   835

Pressures and Grievances | Foreign Pressure and Internal Revolt | Sun Yatsen, Revolutionary | Revolution and Republic, 1911–1916

The Mexican Revolution, 1870s–1920   839

The Porfiriato, 1876–1910 | Revolution, 1910–1920 | Outcome and Aftermath

Revolutions and Global Forces, 1900–1920   843

CONCLUSION   843

CHAPTER REVIEW   845

FURTHER READING   845

MAKING CONNECTIONS The Steam Engine, River Gunboats, and Global Imperialism   846

PART 6   THE GLOBAL WEB SINCE 1870 850

25. International Politics: War, Peace, and Ideologies, 1870 to 1940   852

WORLD WAR I AND ITS LEGACIES   854
The Great Powers, 1870–1914   854
Origins of the War   856
The Course of the War   857
The Human Cost   860
The Russian Revolution of 1917   862
   Grievances and Reforms | War, Defeat, and Revolution | Lenin | The October Revolution and Early Bolshevik Rule
Versailles and Postwar Partitions   864
   Remaking Europe | Remaking the Middle East
Suffragism to 1939   867
   Prewar Suffrage Movements | Early Suffrage | Suffrage and World War I
The Rise of the United States   870
The Great Depression   871

FASCISM AND COMMUNISM, 1919–1939   872
Fascism to 1939   872
   Italian Fascism and Mussolini | German Fascism and Hitler
Communism to 1939   876
   Soviet Communism and Stalin

ANTICOLONIALISM TO 1939   879
China and the May Fourth Movement   879
India   880
   Gandhi
CONSIDERING THE EVIDENCE Satyagraha: Gandhi's Strategy of Resistance   882
Africa, the Caribbean, and Pan-Africanism   882
   Pan-Africanism
Anticolonialism and the Global Web   884

CONCLUSION   884

CHAPTER REVIEW   886

FURTHER READING   886

MAKING CONNECTIONS Pan-Africanism, Pan-Arabism, and Pan-Turkism   887

26. World War II: Global War in the Global Web, 1937 to 1945   892

ORIGINS   894
Fascism and Historical Fantasies   895
Japanese Aggression in Asia to 1937   896
German Aggression in Europe to 1939   896

THE COURSE OF THE WAR   898
Japanese Advances in Asia and the Pacific   898
The War in China | The War in the Pacific to 1943
Axis Advances in Europe   901
War in the West | Operation Barbarossa and Stalingrad | War in North Africa and Italy
The Final Years, 1943–1945   904

WHY THE ALLIES WON   905
Coalition War   905
Economic War   906
Material Advantages | Mobilization and Manufacturing
Scientific War   909

HOME FRONTS AND MILITARY OCCUPATIONS   911
Home Fronts   911
Axis Powers
CONSIDERING THE EVIDENCE Propaganda for the Japanese Home Front   912
The Allies | Race and War Efforts
Military Occupations and Resistance Movements   915
Europe | Asia | Maltreatment of Women

THE HUMAN COST   917
War Crimes   917
Bombing of Cities   918
The Holocaust   918
The Scale of Genocide | Defiance

AFTERMATH   921
Refugees, Vengeance, Justice | Human Rights | Postwar Adjustments
PUZZLES IN WORLD HISTORY How Much Do People of Prominence Influence World History?   922

CONCLUSION   923

CHAPTER REVIEW   925

FURTHER READING   925

MAKING CONNECTIONS The Holocaust, Genocide, and Concentration Camps   926

27. **The Cold War and Decolonization, 1945 to 1991**   **930**

**COLD WAR ORIGINS: FRACTURES IN THE
WORLD WAR II ALLIANCE**   **933**

Security Concerns   933

    Soviet Security and Eastern Europe | The U.S. Vision
of Security | Clashing Visions

The World Economy   934

THE CHARACTER AND COURSE OF THE WAR   **935**

Strategies   935

Nuclear Weapons   936

Propaganda   937

A Divided Europe   938

    Crises in Berlin, 1948 and 1961 | Uprisings in 1953, 1956,
and 1968

East Asia and the Communist Victory in China   941

    Mao Zedong and the Chinese Civil War | War in Korea |
War in Vietnam

Regional Conflicts and the Cold War   944

    War in Angola | War in Afghanistan | War in Latin America |
The Costs of War | The Cold War in the Arctic

THE DECLINE AND COLLAPSE OF THE USSR   **947**

The Sino-Soviet Rift   947

The Soviet Economy and Oil   948

    Gorbachev's Gambles

Eastern Europe in the 1980s   949

Collapse   949

DECOLONIZATION AS A GLOBAL MOVEMENT   **950**

Overview of Decolonization, 1776–1991   950

The Big Pulse, 1947–1975   950

    The Shifting Balance of Power | Inspiration: Dien Bien Phu,
Suez, Bandung | The Global Web and Decolonization

Asian Decolonization: India and Indonesia   953

    India | Indonesia

African Decolonization   956

    Ghana | Algeria

VIOLENCE AND LEGACIES OF DECOLONIZATION   **960**

Violent and Peaceful Decolonizations   960

Postcolonial Borders   961

Neocolonialism   961

CONSIDERING THE EVIDENCE Sankara Condemns Neocolonialism   962

Peasants, Population, and Decolonization   963

CONCLUSION   **963**

CHAPTER REVIEW   **965**

FURTHER READING   **965**

MAKING CONNECTIONS Global Politics During the Cold War   966

28. Rebalancing the Global Web: Africa, Latin America, and the Rise of East Asia since 1960   970

GROWTH SINCE 1960: A GLOBAL CHANGE   972
CONSIDERING THE EVIDENCE Measuring Growth and Inequality   973

THE RISE OF EAST ASIA   974
Sources of Economic Growth   974
Demographic Change | Technology, the Open Economy, and Labor

Japan   976
The U.S. Occupation and Strategic Support | *Zaibatsu* and *Keiretsu*

South Korea   978
Industrial Policy and U.S. Support | Economic and Social Change

China   979
The Economy under Maoism | The Cultural Revolution | Deng Xiaoping | Deng's Economic Reforms | Economic Effects and Global Reach | Sources of China's Economic Surge

Environmental and Social Problems   985
PUZZLES IN WORLD HISTORY How Many Children per Family?   986
Rebalancing in the Global Web   986

THE GLOBAL SOUTH SINCE 1960   987
Africa in the Global Web since 1960   987
Perspectives on Economic Performance | Stifled Economies | Fragmented Politics

Latin America in the Global Web since 1960   993
Population and Migration | Economy and Inequality | Politics and Democratization | Latin America in the Global Web

CONCLUSION   1000

CHAPTER REVIEW   1001

FURTHER READING   1001

MAKING CONNECTIONS Economic Shifts in the 1970s and 1980s   1002

29. A Shrinking World: Globalization since 1980   1006

ENVIRONMENTAL CHANGE: INTO THE ANTHROPOCENE?   1008
Climate Change and Climate Politics   1009
Environmental Turbulence   1010

POPULATION TRENDS SINCE 1950   1013
Population and Public Health   1013
Countercurrents in Public Health: Emerging Diseases   1014
Fertility Declines   1015
THE HUMAN WEB The COVID-19 Pandemic   1016–1017

Urbanization in Overdrive   1018
International Migration   1018

POLITICS AND THE GLOBAL WEB   **1020**
International Institutions   1020
Revivals of Religious Politics   1021
    Political Islam | Other Religions
Democracy Cresting   1024
    Contributing Conditions | Authoritarian Responses
CONSIDERING THE EVIDENCE Social Media in the Arab Spring   1025
    The Role of Social Media
War and Peace in the Twenty-First Century   1027

THE GLOBAL ECONOMY SINCE 1980   **1028**
The Growth of International Trade   1028
    Free Trade Policy | Information Technology
Global Finance   1029
    Deregulation and Economic Instability | The Great Recession
Heightened Inequality   1031

CULTURAL GLOBALIZATION   **1032**
Music   1032
Sports   1034

GLOBAL COMMUNITY AND ITS LIMITS   **1035**
    Indigenous Peoples Make Common Cause |
    Imaginary Globalization

CONCLUSION   **1038**

CHAPTER REVIEW   **1039**

FURTHER READING   **1039**

MAKING CONNECTIONS Indigenous Peoples and
Politics since 1963   1040

ACKNOWLEDGMENTS   **A-1**

GLOSSARY OF KEY TERMS
AND PRONUNCIATION GUIDE   **G-4**

TEXT CREDITS   **TC-19**

PHOTO CREDITS   **PC-21**

INDEX   **I-25**

MAPS

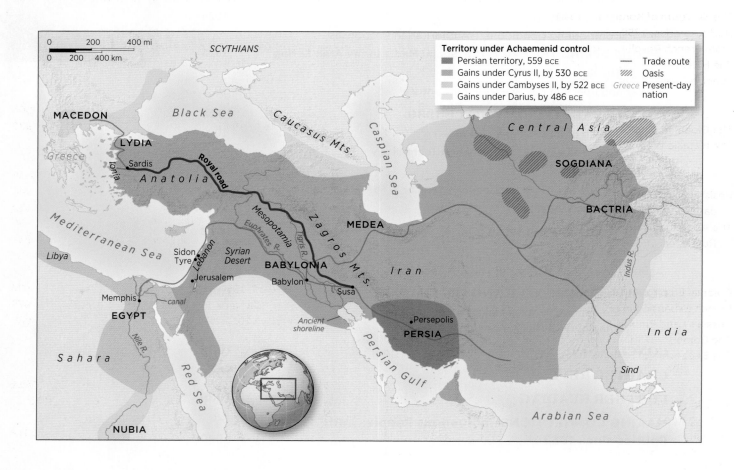

CHAPTER 15

Prevailing Winds and Ocean Currents   506
Voyages of Zheng He, 1405–1433   507
Early Exploration of the Atlantic, 1400–1480   510
Navigation in the Atlantic and Indian Oceans, 1492–1500   515
The Columbian Exchange, 1492–1800   524–25

CHAPTER 16

Africa: The Spread of Islam and the European Presence,
    1450–1800   539
African Slave Trades, 1400–1900   546–47
European Presence in the Americas, ca. 1750   552
Muscovy, Russia, and Siberia, 1400–1800   559
Australia and New Zealand, ca. 1770–1900   562

CHAPTER 17

Religious Geography of Europe, 1555–1650   581
Safavid Iran, 1500–1630   589

CHAPTER 18

The Unification of Tokugawa Japan, 1580–1603   612
The Qing Empire, ca. 1600–1800   614
The Mughal Empire, ca. 1500–1707   618
The Expansion of the Ottoman Empire, ca. 1320s–1683   620
The Growth of Habsburg Territories, Thirteenth through
    Sixteenth Centuries   626

CHAPTER 19

The Spice Trade, ca. 1600	649
The Cotton Trade, ca. 1700	651
The Silver Trade, ca. 1600	653
The Sugar Industry, ca. 1750	656

CHAPTER 20

The Kingdom of Kongo, ca. 1640	677
North America, 1750–1783	683
From French Revolution to French Empire, 1789–1814	692
The Haitian Revolution, 1791–1804	693
Spanish America, 1800–1830	697

CHAPTER 21

The Global Impact of Industrialization, ca. 1914	722–23
The Metallic Web, 1800–1920	730–31

CHAPTER 22

Resistance to Slavery and Abolition of Slavery, ca. 1750–1950	758–59
The Abolition of Serfdom in Eastern Europe and Russia, ca. 1800–1861	771

CHAPTER 23

Colonial Empires in 1830 and 1914	794–95
French Expansion in North Africa, 1830–1914	800
Russia's Land Empire, 1800–1900	808
The Comanche Empire, ca. 1800–1850	809
The Expansion of Ethiopia, 1850–1910	810

CHAPTER 24

Indigenous North America: Devastation and Response, 1850–1900	824
Foreign Incursions and the Taiping Rebellion, 1842–1860	828
The Indian Rebellion, 1857–1858	831
The Chinese Revolution, 1905–1911	836
The Mexican Revolution, 1910–1920	841

CHAPTER 25

European Alliance Systems and the Ottoman Empire, 1914	857
World War I, 1914–1918	859
A New Political Geography: Europe, the Middle East, and Africa, 1922	865
The Indian Independence Movement, 1915–1935	880

CHAPTER 26

Territorial Aggressions in Europe, 1936–1939	897
Japanese Expansion and World War II in Asia and the Pacific, 1931–1945	899
World War II in Europe, North Africa, and the Middle East, 1940–1945	903
The Holocaust, 1939–1945	920

CHAPTER 27

The Cold War World, 1946–1991	938–39
The Arctic Cold War and Its Legacies	946
Decolonization in South and Southeast Asia	952
Decolonization in Africa and the Middle East	958
Decolonization in the Greater Caribbean Region	961

CHAPTER 28

Share of World GDP, 1960–2020	974
The Rise of East Asia since 1960	975
African Railroads in 2017	989

CHAPTER 29

Climate Change: Emissions and Sea Level Rise, 1751–2016	1011
The COVID-19 Pandemic	1016–17
International Migration and Refugee Flows, ca. 2015–2020	1019

FEATURES

The Webs of Humankind offers four text features that reinforce and enrich the book's presentation of world history. They are meant to support student work with primary sources and strengthen their engagement with world history questions.

The first is a primary source feature called **Considering the Evidence**, which appears in every chapter. Authored by Daren Ray (Auburn University), Considering the Evidence presents text documents and images of art and artifacts for analysis by students. Each box includes a contextual headnote and study questions. The primary sources all shed light on the events and developments of each chapter.

The second feature, **Puzzles in World History**, comprises short essays by J. R. McNeill on compelling world history questions that emerge from the text discussions. There are seven Puzzles features integrated throughout the book. They can be used to key class discussion and/or student writing.

The third, **The Human Web**, is an infographic feature that combines images, text, and maps to illustrate webs of interaction at key periods. Each volume of the textbook offers three Human Web features. Each one is built around a central map of an important web, with images and text reflecting the goods, technology, beliefs, and material culture shared by peoples across the web. Each includes an introductory headnote by J. R. McNeill and study questions based on the feature and the chapter reading.

The fourth and newest feature, **Making Connections**, gathers around four to six sources from diverse global perspectives centered on a particular theme. These new features include introductory headnotes, reflection questions before each source, and Making Connections questions that help students compare the sources. This new feature appears at the end of every chapter and includes a mixture of textual and visual primary sources.

FEATURE CONTENTS

CHAPTER 15   **Convergence: The Discovery of the Oceans and Biological Globalization, 1400 to 1800**

CONSIDERING THE EVIDENCE Portuguese Reasoning about Skin Color

THE HUMAN WEB The Columbian Exchange, 1492–1800

MAKING CONNECTIONS Biological Globalization: Movement, Disease, and Impacts

CHAPTER 16   **Disruption: Africa, the Americas, Siberia, and Oceania, 1492 to 1850**

CONSIDERING THE EVIDENCE The Perils of Trade in Kongo

MAKING CONNECTIONS Firsthand Accounts from the Middle Passage and Life in Slavery, ca. 1770–1830

CHAPTER 17   **Cultural Upheavals: Religious and Intellectual Movements, 1500 to 1750**

CONSIDERING THE EVIDENCE A Hymn by Kabir in the *Adi Granth*

MAKING CONNECTIONS New Paths to Truth and Wisdom

CHAPTER 18   **University of War: Empires and Power, 1450 to 1800**

CONSIDERING THE EVIDENCE An Ottoman Register in Ukraine

MAKING CONNECTIONS The Exercise of Power

CHAPTER 19   **The First Global Economy, 1500 to 1800**

CONSIDERING THE EVIDENCE On the Circulation of Blood and Money

MAKING CONNECTIONS The Global Coffee Trade

CHAPTER 20   **The Best and Worst of Times: Atlantic Revolutions, 1640 to 1830**

CONSIDERING THE EVIDENCE A Revolutionary's Letter from Jamaica

MAKING CONNECTIONS Women and Atlantic Revolutions

CHAPTER 21   **Fossil Fuels and Mass Production: Industrial Revolutions around the World, 1780 to 1914**

CONSIDERING THE EVIDENCE Rage against the Machines

THE HUMAN WEB The Metallic Web, 1800–1920

MAKING CONNECTIONS The Emergence of the Industrial Working Class in Britain

CHAPTER 22   **Two Liberations: The Vital Revolution and the Abolitions of Slavery and Serfdom, 1750 to 1950**

CONSIDERING THE EVIDENCE Demanding Freedom and Dignity in West Africa

PUZZLES IN WORLD HISTORY Why Do Humans Live So Long?

MAKING CONNECTIONS Smallpox and Inoculation

CHAPTER 23   **Nationalism and Imperialism: Tightening the Global Web, 1800 to 1930**

CONSIDERING THE EVIDENCE Ethiopian Imperialism through Russian Eyes

MAKING CONNECTIONS The Heyday of Eugenics

CHAPTER 24   **Making the World Modern: Confronting Industrialization, Nationalism, and Imperialism, 1850 to 1920**

CONSIDERING THE EVIDENCE Messengers of the Ghost Dance

MAKING CONNECTIONS The Steam Engine, River Gunboats, and Global Imperialism

CHAPTER 25   **International Politics: War, Peace, and Ideologies, 1870 to 1940**

CONSIDERING THE EVIDENCE Satyagraha: Gandhi's Strategy of Resistance

MAKING CONNECTIONS Pan-Africanism, Pan-Arabism, and Pan-Turkism

CHAPTER 26   **World War II: Global War in the Global Web, 1937 to 1945**

CONSIDERING THE EVIDENCE Propaganda for the Japanese Home Front

PUZZLES IN WORLD HISTORY How Much Do People of Prominence Influence World History?

MAKING CONNECTIONS The Holocaust, Genocide, and Concentration Camps

CHAPTER 27   **The Cold War and Decolonization, 1945 to 1991**

CONSIDERING THE EVIDENCE Sankara Condemns Neocolonialism

MAKING CONNECTIONS Global Politics During the Cold War

CHAPTER 28   **Rebalancing the Global Web: Africa, Latin America, and the Rise of East Asia since 1960**

CONSIDERING THE EVIDENCE Measuring Growth and Inequality

PUZZLES IN WORLD HISTORY How Many Children per Family?

MAKING CONNECTIONS Economic Shifts in the 1970s and 1980s

CHAPTER 29   **A Shrinking World: Globalization since 1980**

CONSIDERING THE EVIDENCE Social Media in the Arab Spring

THE HUMAN WEB The COVID-19 Pandemic

MAKING CONNECTIONS Indigenous Peoples and Politics since 1963

PEDAGOGY

The Webs of Humankind presents a set of pedagogical features intended to guide introductory students through the chapters and support their understanding of world history.

All chapters open with a list of **Focus Questions** that correspond to the major section headings in the chapter. These questions, which appear also in the relevant running heads at the tops of pages, are meant to alert students to the key developments in each section. All chapters also open with a **Chronology** of major events and an **immersive narrative vignette** to draw students into the reading.

The chapters end with a summary **Conclusion** and a **Chapter Review** page that includes **Review Questions**, a list of the **Key Terms** (with page references) that appear in bold in the chapter, and a **Further Reading** list compiled and annotated by J. R. McNeill. A **Glossary** at the end of the book includes definitions of all key terms and a pronunciation guide.

The author also collaborated on the art program, which includes more than 700 images, and on the more than 150 original maps, all with captions by the author.

DIGITAL RESOURCES FOR TEACHING AND LEARNING

W. W. Norton has a long history of delivering robust and carefully designed digital resources to support teaching and learning. The resources described here have been built from the ground up—with guidance and input from active world history instructors—specifically for use with *The Webs of Humankind*, Second Edition, by J. R. McNeill.

NEW FOR THE SECOND EDITION

THE NORTON ILLUMINE EBOOK

Norton's high-quality content shines brighter through engaging and motivational features that illuminate core concepts for all students in a supportive, accessible, and low-stakes environment. The active reading experience includes the ability to highlight, take notes, search, read offline, and more. Instructors can embed their own content into the text and promote student accountability through easy-to-use assignment tools in their LMS.

"A Bird's-Eye View" Author Videos

In a series of videos embedded at the start of each chapter, J. R. McNeill discusses the significant webs that will be explored in the pages that follow.

Check Your Understanding Questions

At the end of each section of the ebook, embedded Check Your Understanding questions reinforce key topics to take away from the reading. Rich feedback explains why each answer is correct or incorrect.

RESOURCES FOR STUDENTS

Each of the following courseware tools can be integrated directly into your existing learning management system for easy student access.

INQUIZITIVE

InQuizitive is Norton's award-winning adaptive learning tool that personalizes the learning experience for students and enhances their understanding of the key themes and objectives from each chapter. InQuizitive features hundreds of interactive questions tagged to each chapter's **Focus Questions**—including questions based on maps, historical images, and primary source documents—all of which are delivered in an engaging gamelike environment with detailed, answer-specific feedback.

HISTORY SKILLS TUTORIALS

The History Skills Tutorials are interactive, online modules that support student development of key skills for the world history course—such as analysis and interpretation of primary source documents, images, and maps. With interactive practice assessments, helpful guiding feedback, and videos with J. R. McNeill, these tutorials teach students the critical analysis skills that they will put to use in their academic and professional careers.

PRIMARY SOURCE AND MAP EXERCISES

Building from the critical analysis skills developed in the History Skills Tutorials (above), a series of assignable Primary Source Exercises and Map Exercises provide students the opportunity to practice these skills in every week of the course. Each exercise includes 5 to 10 interactive questions based on documents, images, and maps found in the chapter reading.

ADDITIONAL CONTENT

This website offers additional study and review materials for students to use outside of class:

- An **Online Reader** features dozens of additional primary source documents and images, with brief headnotes and sample questions for analysis.
- **Flashcards** invite students to review the key terms from the textbook.
- **Chapter Outlines** give students a detailed snapshot of the key topics of each chapter.

RESOURCES FOR INSTRUCTORS

All instructor resources are available for download after free registration at wwnorton.com/catalog/instructor-resources

RESOURCES FOR YOUR LMS

Easily add high-quality Norton digital resources to your online, hybrid, or lecture courses. Get started building your course with our easy-to-use integrated resources; all activities can be accessed right within your existing learning management system. The downloadable file includes integration links to the following resources, organized by chapter:

- The Norton Illumine Ebook
- InQuizitive
- History Skills Tutorials
- Primary Source Exercises and Map Exercises
- Additional Content

TEST BANK

The Test Bank features more than 1,500 questions—including multiple choice, true-false, and short-answer questions—aligned with the chapter's Focus Questions. This bank of quiz and exam content provides multiple avenues for comprehension and skill assessment.

Norton Testmaker brings Norton's high-quality testing materials online. Create assessments from anywhere with an Internet connection without downloading files or installing specialized software. Search and filter test bank questions by chapter, type, difficulty, learning objectives, and other criteria. You can also customize questions to fit your course. Then, easily export your tests to Microsoft Word or Common Cartridge files for import into your LMS.

INSTRUCTOR'S MANUAL

The Instructor's Manual contains:

- Detailed chapter summaries
- Chapter outlines
- Discussion/forum prompts
- Lecture ideas
- Sample responses to Questions for Analysis in the text, and more

LECTURE AND ART POWERPOINT SLIDES

The lecture PowerPoint slides combine chapter review, images, maps, and lecture notes, and are easily customizable. Art PowerPoint slides and JPEGs are available separately for every image and map in the text. Alt-text is provided for each item.

First Day of Class slides, new to the Second Edition, support instructors in delivering transparent assignments, an approach that has been shown to lead to more equitable outcomes. Designed to be shared with students or shown in the classroom early in the semester, the slides focus on how each Norton product works, what is expected of students, the purpose and relevance of each resource, and strategies for student success.

PREFACE

How did our world get to be the way it is? Why are some parts of the world so much richer than others? Is gender inequality universal, or have societies ever existed without it? Why are empires, so common in the past, so rare today? Why in both the Americas and Eurasia—which developed in near-complete isolation from each other—did many early cities feature monumental architecture, grid patterns, and open public spaces? When and why did slavery begin, and why, after thousands of years, was it abolished almost everywhere in the nineteenth century? What role has climate change played in history, and has that role changed in recent decades?

The study of world history can provide answers to big questions like these. Almost any variety of history can help explain how and why societies have changed over time. However, world history (or global history—I make no distinction between the two terms) is a special kind of history. It is not the sum of all history: it is in fact more than the sum of its parts.

What Is Distinctive about World History?

World history is comparative: it helps distinguish what is common from what is distinctive about societies. In the early chapters of this book, we will notice that places where people raised crops that store well were much more likely to develop kingdoms, empires, and other states than places where people relied on crops that spoil too quickly to be stored and distributed. An important pattern like this would be harder to see if we were looking at the histories of China, India, Africa, and South America separately, without comparison. So too with several religious movements of the sixteenth and seventeenth centuries. The Protestant Reformation in Europe, the birth of the Sikh religion in India, and the Shi'a Islamic revival in seventeenth-century Iran all emphasized personal relationships with divinity and valued intuition over institutions in matters of faith. Comparing these (as Chapter 17 does) suggests a common pattern despite the different contexts.

World history is also selective. Because the past is virtually infinite, all historians must choose what to include in their accounts and what to leave out. World historians must be more selective to avoid burying their subject beneath a giant jumble of facts. World history tends to foreground parallels, contrasts, and connections among societies more than the details of each one. So, for example, Chapter 8 considers the impact of iron working on both northern Europe and sub-Saharan Africa after 1000 BCE. In Africa, iron making and iron tools tended to bring societies closer through trade, but in northern Europe they had the opposite effect, weakening existing linkages. A world historical lens on international politics similarly shows that on every continent in the sixteenth and seventeenth centuries, a handful of big empires grew much larger, eliminating hundreds of smaller states. In Chapter 18, we see that this was not an accident but a result of faster flows of new technologies and techniques of warfare through a globalizing world.

In the process of being selective, world history can also highlight the global trends that are distinctive across long

stretches of time. For thousands of years, powerful states saw fit to build and maintain empires as long as their vigor lasted. But after 1960 or so, the idea of empire lost its appeal, and ever since the powerful have preferred to avoid formal empires. That is a historically unique development, although not necessarily a permanent change. On even longer time scales, we can see, as Chapter 29 explains, that the modern rise in greenhouse gas concentrations in the atmosphere has been faster—by far—than any other such rise in the historical or geological record. These two examples of distinctive aspects of our own time are best understood in the long sweep of world history.

The Approach of This Textbook

This book differs from most world history textbooks in a few ways. It has one author, not several, which has been hard on that author but might be good for the reader because it raises the odds of achieving a consistent viewpoint and framework. I hope I have achieved that, because it might compensate for the chief disadvantage of a single-authored world history: no author can know everything. I do not have the same command of human evolution, ancient Chinese history, medieval Russian history, or modern U.S. history that specialists in these fields have. However, I have taught world history for decades and learned a fair bit along the way, not least from my students. I've also written global-scale histories before, mainly environmental histories. This book reflects my own background as a historian, giving frequent attention to matters of geography, health, and environment.

With a sole author, it is easier to sustain a single framework for understanding world history. Having an effective framework is essential because it helps organize information and put it into a context—avoiding that giant jumble of facts. The framework here is based on the concept of webs of social interaction. It's an approach that, I hope, will provide readers with a strong sense of the connectedness, but also the contrasts, of world history—in an easily accessible way.

The Webs of Humankind: An Overview

People always and everywhere have been connected to others. These connections have taken many forms, ranging from kinship and friendship to economic exchange and military confrontation. In all such relationships, people exchanged information and used it to guide their future behavior. They often also exchanged technologies, religious beliefs, artistic visions, trade goods, food crops, violent threats, lethal infections, and much else. These exchanges shaped what people could do and could imagine. When exchanges and connections between groups became regular, I call them webs of interaction.

For most of human history—from the dawn of our species' existence some 300,000 years ago until roughly 13,000 years ago—our ancestors lived in a very loose, far-flung human web. Their communities were normally small migratory bands that only occasionally mixed with others. That way of life rarely presented them with the stimuli of new ideas and objects to consider. By later standards, the pace of change in arenas such as technology or social organization was glacially slow. This doesn't mean nothing happened, though: this was the time when humans invented religion and language, and migrated from their place of origin in Africa to settle every habitable continent. These were all momentous changes, even if they happened extremely slowly.

Beginning around 13,000 years ago (or roughly 11,000 BCE), a handful of changes occurred that encouraged the weaving of much tighter webs of interaction. While the loose and far-flung human web continued in the background, new, tighter webs developed where people began to settle into permanent, sedentary communities. Sedentary life in those times worked best beside a seashore with abundant edible marine life (as on the coasts of Japan, for example) or amid wild grasses that yielded reliable and nutritious seeds (as in what is now southeastern Turkey). Some of these now-sedentary people domesticated wild animals and plants, converting them genetically into livestock and crops, respectively. Farming, the first evidence of which comes from Southwest Asia, encouraged larger communities, denser populations, and more vibrant, if still local, interactive webs—*local* here meaning several villages and a few thousand people. Changes in technology and social organization now came more rapidly than before.

Around 5,500 years ago (3500 BCE), much bigger and tighter webs formed when people first clustered together into cities and then built networks of cities linked by regular trade and communication. This too happened first in Southwest Asia, specifically in what is now southern Iraq. But it didn't take long—a thousand years at most—before cities and regional webs linking multiple cities emerged elsewhere—in Northeast Africa, South Asia, and East Asia. By 200 CE such webs appeared in the Americas too, especially in Mesoamerica and the Andes region of South America. Each of these regional webs, between roughly 2500 BCE and 200 CE, would grow to contain a few million people, dozens of cities, and thousands of villages. Within these emerging webs, changes in ideas, technologies, and social structures came faster than before, and faster than among people not connected to webs. Cities—where people with different outlooks, religions, skills, and technologies rubbed shoulders every day—became hothouses of innovation and adaptation. They were nodes in the regional webs.

Mainly through the expansion of long-distance trade, those urban-based webs gradually linked up to one another. The biggest one formed between the Nile and the Ganges, and the next biggest in East Asia. By roughly 200 CE, sprawling webs of interaction spanned continents. By far the biggest, called the Old World web in this book, was anchored at either end by China and Egypt, stretching over most of Eurasia and North Africa. (Scholars often refer to Eurasia and Africa as the Old World, a usage I adopt because human occupation of those continents predates that anywhere else.) In 200 CE, it encompassed tens of millions of people living in cities and villages, especially along rivers such as the Huang He (Yellow River), the Yangzi, the Ganges, the Indus, the Tigris and Euphrates, and the Nile. All of these rivers served as sources of irrigation water and arteries of transport, permitting more productive farming, larger food supplies, more people, more trade—and more frequent and sustained interaction of all sorts. The Old World web eventually—by 1400 CE—grew to include almost everyone living within a space bounded by Japan and Java in the east and Iceland and West Africa in the west. At the time, that area included at least three-quarters of humankind, or more than 200 million people.

Smaller but still sizeable regional webs grew up elsewhere. In Africa, the northeastern region along the Nile and the Red Sea coast was enmeshed in the Old World web early on—by 1500 BCE, if not before. Elsewhere in Africa, much smaller webs developed, especially along the Niger River in West Africa. That one merged with the Old World web by about 800 CE, mainly via trans-Saharan trade routes that linked North Africa and West Africa as never before.

In the Americas, as in the Old World, irrigation agriculture nourished local webs, the first of them starting as early as 3000 BCE in the Andes. Bigger regional webs formed in the Andes by about 100 CE and in Mesoamerica by about 200 CE. Both the Mesoamerican and Andean webs grew over time, but intermittently, with many reversals. The outer threads of these two webs by 1450 CE extended far across the Americas and linked both continents very loosely through trade and migrations.

In Oceania, as people sailed from what is now Indonesia out to remote Pacific islands, a process that began around 2000 BCE, they formed thin webs linking island communities. These loose webs brought thousands—not millions—of people into contact with one another over vast distances.

In character, these smaller webs bore many similarities to the Old World web: they were held together by trade, travel, and communication, and clusters of people—whether in cities or tightly packed villages—served as key nodes for the transmission of ideas, goods, and everything else. But in size, the Old World web, from its beginning around 200 CE, always outstripped all others.

A Global Web

Beginning in the fifteenth century, breakthroughs in transport and communication fused all these webs into a single global one. Breakthroughs in ship design and in information storage, especially printing technology, contributed to a bigger breakthrough: sailors accumulated enough information to crack the code of the planet's winds and currents, enabling them to navigate the deep oceans much more securely than ever before. That launched an era of intercontinental voyaging that wove the world's coastlands together into a global web. Beginning with Chapter 15, which overlaps both volumes of the text, this Global web is the main story of the book.

This new Global web triggered thoroughgoing and accelerating changes in the sixteenth through the eighteenth centuries, the first of which I call biological globalization. Infectious diseases such as measles and smallpox spread to populations with no acquired immunities, especially in the Americas and on Pacific islands, cutting populations by 50 to 95 percent. Sailors and ships also carried crops to new environments. Potatoes, for example, native to the Andes, gradually became part of the diet in northern Europe, and eventually in China and north India as well. Maize, originally from Mexico, became Africa's most important crop.

The Global web brought changes that extended far beyond biological transfers. New information and ideas from the four corners of the Earth led people to reconsider long-cherished beliefs, altering religious landscapes in Europe and Asia, as Chapter 17 explains. The variety of political formats in which people lived diminished as small polities gave way to growing empires. The productive techniques and technologies that underpinned industrialization spread widely within decades after their introduction during the eighteenth and nineteenth centuries, reflecting the accelerating flow of information characteristic of the Global web. So too with new ideas about freedom, justice, and sovereignty that underlaid political revolutions around the world, from the United States and France in the late eighteenth century to Mexico, Russia, and China in the early twentieth.

Throughout the last 150 years, with telegraphs, telephones, and networked computers, the Global web has grown tighter, its communications faster, its linkages stronger. Cities, which were home to about 10 percent of humankind in 1800, by 2010 accounted for more than half of the world's population. Today, almost everyone lives within a single, unified, global-scale web of interaction, competition, and cooperation. Different people experience this differently, but almost no one (aside from a few thousand people deep in rain forests) lives outside it.

Web Making: A Globalizing Process

The long process of web making over thousands of years is in effect a globalizing one. The first webs launched a long-term trend—with reversals—toward greater connectedness. In this sense, world history has direction to it. Several motors drove the web-making process. Among them were the economic advantages of specialization and exchange, which inspired trade. The desire of powerful monarchs, whether Macedonian kings such as Alexander the Great or Chinese emperors such as Han Wudi, to expand their influence also extended the reach of webs. So did the ambition of missionaries to spread their religions. Merchants, monarchs, and missionaries weren't trying to extend webs—they didn't think in these terms at all. But their ambitions and actions had that effect. So did the routine movements of anonymous travelers, pilgrims, refugees, soldiers, sailors,

pastoral nomads, and everyone else who traveled, interacted with strangers, and—unintentionally—helped to build sustained webs of interaction.

The long-term trend of webs growing, tightening, and consolidating was far from consistent. At times, when empires fell apart, plagues swept through, or trade routes shifted, contacts and connections would languish and webs unravel. This happened after the fifth century CE in western Europe when half of the Roman Empire fell. Webs might also fray as a result of deliberate choices, as in East Asia in the late eighth century CE when the rulers of China's Tang dynasty decided to reduce foreign contacts of all sorts. The complete disappearance of webs occurred often on local scales, probably more often in the Americas than elsewhere. Typically, it happened after a demographic collapse that reduced population density and gave more people the option of moving to empty land and becoming self-sufficient, far away from rulers, taxes, forced labor, and conscription. But bigger webs, although they often frayed or shrank, rarely disappeared altogether and normally

MAJOR WEBS OF WORLD HISTORY

NAME AND EXPLANATION	LOCATION	APPROXIMATE DATES
Human web This refers to the faint and intermittent ties that have linked all, or almost all, humans throughout our species' entire career. But its connections have been weak compared to the tighter local and regional webs and to the Global web of the last five centuries.	Everywhere people have lived, except in the few cases where groups became genuinely isolated	From human origins ca. 300,000 years ago until today
Southwest Asian web This formed in the Tigris-Euphrates valley beginning around 5000 BCE. It extended into surrounding uplands by 3500 BCE, lasting until 2500 BCE, when it was subsumed into the Nile-Indus web.	Mesopotamia and neighboring areas	5000 BCE to 2500 BCE
Nile-Indus web This was an expansion of the Southwest Asian web to both the east and the west.	From Egypt, and at times its southern neighbor Nubia, across Southwest Asia to the Indus valley	2500 BCE to 1500 BCE
Nile-Ganges web A further expansion across north India.	From Egypt and Nubia across Southwest Asia and north India	1500 BCE to 200 CE
East Asian web This originated in China but extended to neighboring societies.	North and central China, with strands reaching into Korea, Japan, Central Asia, and northernmost Vietnam	1000 BCE to 200 CE
Old World web This is the fusion of the East Asian web and the Nile-Ganges web, with extensions into Europe and Africa.	From Senegal and Scotland in the west to Japan and Java in the east, including the Indian Ocean world	200 CE to 1500 CE
Andean web This formed in South America from the Moche and Tiwanaku cultures.	From the Altiplano in Bolivia to the coasts of Peru, straddling the high Andes	100 CE to 1500 CE
Mesoamerican web This developed with the interactions among the Maya, the Zapotecs, and Teotihuacán.	Central and southern Mexico and the Maya lands of Yucatán and northern Guatemala	200 CE to 1500 CE
Global web This is the fusion of the Old World web, the American webs, and all other local and regional webs.	Global, but tiny uncontacted communities deep in rain forests such as Amazonia remain outside it	1500 CE to the present; it began to take shape with oceanic voyagers in the fifteenth and sixteenth centuries and is still tightening in the twenty-first.

rebounded within a century or two, as happened in East Asia after new dynasties replaced the Tang.

The expansion of webs was often a brutal process. It frequently involved warfare and epidemics. Both occurred at once in many cases—as, for example, after Christopher Columbus's voyages of the 1490s. Newly introduced diseases in combination with warfare killed tens of millions of people in the Americas. Peoples who had formerly lived outside of webs, such as much of the indigenous populations of the Americas, Australia, Polynesia, and Siberia, often suffered heavily for a century or more once they became entangled in webs.

As a rule, the expansion of webs, especially the Global web in recent centuries, has reduced cultural diversity. The number of languages spoken has fallen by about half since 1500, while English, Spanish, Hindi, Arabic, Chinese, and a few others have acquired more speakers. The number of legal traditions too has declined: more and more people live under fewer and fewer legal systems, many of them now based on English common law, Roman law, or Islam's code of shari'a. Farmers' fields feature fewer strains of wheat, maize, and rice than they did 500 years ago, partly because farmers now have more information about which crop varieties yield best in their environments.

The table at left summarizes the main webs featured in this book. Many smaller ones that involved thousands, but not millions, of people are left out of the table. The dates are given in round numbers and are approximate because webs formed and merged gradually, with no sharp beginnings or end points.

New in the Second Edition: A Focus on Indigeneity and on the Modern Era

Among the virtues of world history is seeing commonalities among peoples' experiences around the world. This Second Edition adds a new focus on the history of indigenous peoples. Just who counts as Indigenous is controversial today, as explained in Chapter 29 (a new glossary definition in that chapter also explains why in this book we have chosen to capitalize *Indigenous* when it is used as an identity label, as it has come into usage in the twentieth and twenty-first centuries, but as lowercase *indigenous* when it is being used as a descriptive term). In this book, the term *indigenous* is used to refer to original populations in lands settled after about 1500 CE by (usually) Europeans. These include First Nations in Canada, Native Americans in the United States, various groups usually called *Indios* in Latin America, Maori in New Zealand, Aboriginals in Australia, Pacific Islanders, dozens of communities in Siberia, and a few others as well. But they also include peoples in, for example, Taiwan and Hokkaido, whose islands were conquered and settled by Chinese and Japanese, respectively. Indigenous peoples are diverse.

The book attends to the histories of all these populations going back many thousands of years to the first human settlements of Australia and the Americas. Discussions in these chapters are devoted to their experiences in the millennia before they came in contact with strangers from other continents. In the Second Edition, in response partly to instructor feedback and partly to emerging trends within the historical profession, the history of their role in the Global web after 1500 receives new emphasis.

That history shows some of the complexity and ambiguity of life inside of webs. At first, as mentioned above, entanglement in the Global web proved catastrophic for indigenous peoples. Yet in time, they found ways to take advantage of web connections to strengthen their cultures, revive their languages, solidify their identities, and recover some of their autonomy. In some cases, they used

these connections to build empires, as in the case of the Comanche in the early nineteenth century (Chapter 24). Since the 1970s, as Chapter 29 explains, Indigenous communities around the world have linked up with one another, finding allies, making common cause, and advancing their agendas. They have also made use of international institutions, such as the United Nations. The additional focus on Indigenous peoples brings out the fact that involvement in webs brought both dangers and opportunities to all humans enmeshed in them.

The Second Edition, also in response to instructor feedback, expands the treatment of twentieth- and twenty-first century world history. World War II now gets a chapter unto itself, emphasizing the long shadow it continues to cast over global politics today. The Cold War and decolonization are put side-by-side to emphasize their connections to one another. The political economy of the Global South since roughly 1960 is the subject of a full chapter, emphasizing the participation of East Asia, Latin America, and Africa in the Global web. And, since history never stops happening, new discussions appear of recent developments such as the war in Ukraine or the responses to COVID-19.

The Second Edition also includes a new feature called Making Connections. This is the equivalent of a world history sourcebook built into the text. Every chapter now is followed by a set of documents or images, usually of artwork or archeological remains, chosen to reflect one or more of the chapter's themes. Brief introductions help students to make sense of the cluster as a whole and of each individual piece of evidence. Questions for reflection provided for each document or image help students think about the possible meanings of the evidence. Wrestling with ambiguous and inconclusive evidence is a large part of what historians do. It is also a large part of what every citizen, employer, employee, and consumer does every day, so there is every reason to get better at it. The Making Connections feature is intended to help in that regard and to make each student's experience with the study of world history more participatory.

Regionalization and Organization

With the globalizing process of web making at work throughout, this book takes a largely regional organization in Volume 1 and a global one in Volume 2. The schemes of regionalization it adopts change as the world changed, reflecting the formation, and occasional decay, of webs. So, for example, "Africa" in some periods is treated as a continental unit, but at other times regions of Africa appear as parts of larger maritime webs. In Chapter 12, the coasts of

East Africa are presented as a key element of a region called the Indian Ocean world. In Chapter 20, other parts of Africa appear as components of a different region, the Atlantic world, united by trade, travel, and exchanges among the coastlands of the Americas, Europe, and Africa.

The book often avoids the vocabulary of regions as we typically see them today. A conventional regionalization of the world takes the continents as regions, with a few additions such as *Middle East* and, lately, *Asia-Pacific*. In emphasizing webs of interaction, this book minimizes the projection onto the past of today's conventional regions. So there is no *Middle East* until the twentieth century here, and no *Latin America* until the nineteenth century. It is worth noting too that in this world history some of the most important regions are defined by water, not land. There is no perfect way to regionalize the globe for all time periods. The different regionalization schemes used in this book reflect the changing reality of web connections among people in the past.

Parts and Periods

This book is divided into six parts, each of which corresponds to a period of time.

Part 1 (Chapters 1–2) takes on the longest sweep of time, from human origins to about 1500 BCE. For most of this period, all people lived in Africa. When some migrated to other continents, beginning about 70,000–100,000 years ago, we follow them wherever they went, which included every habitable continent by 14,000 years ago. Part 1 is global in the sense that it considers the experience of the entire human population. The very thin and faint web uniting our entire species endured despite the intercontinental wanderings of peoples.

Part 2 (Chapters 3–9) deals mainly with the period between 3500 BCE AND 200 CE and shifts to a regional scheme of

organization. It addresses the emergence of regional webs in parts of Eurasia, Africa, and the Americas, as outlined in the table above. In doing so, it examines the rise of cities, states, organized religions, and stratified, hierarchical societies. In places such as China, India, or Egypt—among others—these millennia also saw the formation of durable cultural traditions anchored in religion. By 200 CE, several regional webs in Eurasia and North Africa had fused into the single, sprawling Old World web. Chapter 8 pairs two places not often drawn together for comparison: northern Europe and sub-Saharan Africa. They were similar in that they stood on the frontiers of the big webs in the millennia before 200 CE. As a result, they had smaller polities, a slower pace of technological change, and better health than did people living in the larger webs. Slowly, though, they too became entangled in the Nile-Ganges web and, eventually, the full Old World web. The Americas and Oceania, the focus of Chapter 9, remained worlds unto themselves, unaffected by the formation of the Old World web until well beyond 200 CE. So this chapter continues up to 1000 CE, by which time a big web linking both North and South America had taken shape.

Part 3 (Chapters 10–14) maintains a regional organization and takes up the centuries between 200 CE and 1400 CE. Most of Part 3 is devoted to developments within the Old World web, in East and South Asia, Africa, and Europe. It deals with several aspects of the maturation of regional webs—such as improvements in transport and navigation and the accelerated spread of cultural traditions such as Buddhism, Christianity, and Islam. The final chapter of Part 3 returns to the Americas and Oceania. It stretches beyond 1400 CE because each of them still stood apart with no significant links to one another or to the Old World web until 1492 in the Americas and about 1770 in Oceania. Both built, or extended, webs of their own, which developed in accordance with prevailing conditions: the vast distances of the Pacific, for example, rewarded the navigational skills that islanders developed, while the paucity of domesticable animals in the Americas encouraged agriculture that did not require plowing. Yet strong, thought-provoking parallels existed between the societies in the Old World web and those of the Americas—for example, in the relationships between religious and political power, or the prevalence of gender inequality.

With **Part 4** (Chapters 15–19), the book becomes global in scope again because the links connecting every large population strengthened so much between 1400 and 1800 with the weaving of the Global web. Chapter 15, a pivotal chapter that ends Volume 1 and begins Volume 2, focuses on the convergence of the world's webs into a single Global web and the wave of biological exchanges that followed. This biological globalization set some of the basic conditions for world history in the next centuries, mainly through major shifts in agriculture and population. The connections of the Global web meant that the oceans no longer separated peoples as much as before. The histories of Angola and Brazil, as we see in Chapter 16, were firmly linked by a transatlantic slave trade that established African culture in much of Brazil. In Chapter 19, we see that the histories of China and Mexico developed a tie through transpacific trades in silver, silk, and porcelain routed through the Philippines. Part 4 considers the comparatively sudden changes resulting from this surge of globalization in the realms of ecology, ideas and culture, economies, and political competition.

With one exception, the chapters of **Part 5** (20–24) are also global in scope and organized by theme. They span the centuries between 1620 and 1920. The exception is Chapter 20, which is devoted to political revolutions in the Atlantic world—Africa, Europe, and the Americas. Collectively, these Atlantic revolutions were momentous enough, and their legacies global enough, to merit treatment as a unit unto themselves. The balance of Part 5 considers fundamental changes such as industrialization, the near-elimination of slavery and other forms of forced labor, improvements in human health, and the rise of such political trends as nationalism and imperialism. It also treats some major political revolutions—in part, efforts to resist imperialism and industrialization—in India, China, Mexico, and Russia. Its main theme is the many political and social realignments and revolutions encouraged by the formation, and tightening, of the Global web. It seeks to find some balance between global currents and local factors in explaining these turbulent times.

Part 6 (Chapters 25–29) takes on a mere century and a half, from 1870 to the present—an era of accelerating globalization and episodes of fierce resistance against it. Part 6 takes up international politics more thoroughly than earlier parts of the book do, but it also explores the global economy, particularly the rapid rise of East Asia and its contrasts with Africa and Latin America; global ecological shifts including recent climate change; and social and cultural transformations such as migration, urbanization, and the rise of globalized popular music and sports. Politics, for example, predominates in Chapter 25, on World War I and its aftermath, which included political movements such as fascism, communism, anticolonialism and suffragism. Acute political struggles feature in Chapter 26, now entirely devoted to World War II, and in Chapter 27, on the intertwined processes of decolonization and the Cold War. Chapters 28 and 29, while not ignoring politics, shift the focus mainly to the world economy, the environment, and culture. The pace and scope of global integration in this last century and a half is extraordinary, and many peoples and communities found the rapidity of changes wrenching or the direction of change unwelcome. Part 6 explains why the pace was so fast and the process so disruptive.

Considering the Evidence of World History

One last point to bear in mind before the story begins. Understanding history is like assembling a challenging jigsaw puzzle. Some of the pieces clearly fit together in obvious ways. Most of them don't, and it is not easy to know what to make of them. Many of the pieces are missing, hidden under the rugs of time. All this means that history is an exercise in creating plausible interpretations from incomplete and sometimes contradictory evidence.

One needs to use imagination disciplined by evidence to arrive at a reliable reconstruction of the past. It is evidence—written texts, works of art, archeology, oral traditions, historical linguistics, and now also genetic analysis—that helps us figure out what is plausible and what isn't, what arguments to accept and what to reject. Among the skills history teaches are the abilities to assess evidence thoughtfully and to recognize when the evidence is insufficient or contradictory, making strong conclusions difficult.

When multiple pieces of evidence seem to be saying the same thing, and especially when different types of evidence harmonize, we can be more confident of our conclusions. So, for example, when linguistic evidence, genetic evidence, and pottery fragments all suggest that people from West Africa filtered into central and southern Africa beginning in roughly 1500 BCE, we can be confident that something historians call the Bantu migration took place—even though there is not a single written document of the time that says anything about it. If pottery were the only evidence, we could not be sure about the migration—people can trade pots over long distances, one person to the next, without migrating. If we had only the genetic or the linguistic evidence, we would have only the fuzziest idea about when the migration occurred.

For the deeper past, we have fewer written records, and none more than about 5,000 years old. In some places—the Americas, Oceania, and most of sub-Saharan Africa, for example—written records are nonexistent or at best extremely rare until 500 years ago. In these situations, other forms of evidence such as archeological remains or genetic analysis become much more important to underpinning interpretations of the past.

Keep in mind too that written documents usually reflect the viewpoints of adults rather than children, men rather than women, the rich rather than the poor, the powerful rather than the weak, and the literate rather than the illiterate. In archeology, as well, we are likelier to find the remains of royal palaces built of stone than peasant huts made of thatched reeds. Historians (and other scholars) have shown ingenuity in overcoming these inherent biases, "reading against the grain," as historians often put it. But these asymmetries of information remain, and it is important to remain aware of them.

Sifting, evaluating, and interpreting incomplete and sometimes contradictory evidence, and evidence of different types, are crucial intellectual skills. The study of history, and especially world history, hones those skills. The new Making Connections feature, added to every chapter in the Second Edition, invites you to develop your abilities to evaluate imperfect evidence by interpreting original sources. Interpreting such variable evidence is often challenging, but it is the kind of task that helps us learn to navigate the real world, with all its confusing, confounding, and contradictory information. As Ziauddin Barani, a scholar of the fourteenth century writing in Persian but working in India, said: "I have not observed such advantages from any branch of learning as I have from history." The branches of learning have changed since his day, as a grounding in history would lead you to expect, but he could still be right.

Various labels on the map (partial, as legible):

Cciaus articus:

Tropicus cacri

Linha equinocialis:

Mare barbaricus:

Occanus yndicus meridionalis.

Cciaus capricorni

Linha equinocialis:

Os pontes daues em affrica

Cam boa   Castello damina.

Mate oceanus:

Mores tiune

Mare per duan

Mare oceanus:

Pollus antarcticus:

Pollus antarcticus.

PART 4

WEAVING THE GLOBAL WEB

1400 TO 1800

Chapters 15 through 19 cover world history between 1400 and 1800. During that span, which historians often call the early modern period, human history became genuinely global for the first time. Events in South America, such as a discovery of silver, affected China, and changes in Chinese tax policies affected silver miners in South America. The regional webs featured in Part 3 fused into a single Global web.

The great economist Adam Smith in his famous work, *The Wealth of Nations* (1776), wrote that:

The Cantino Planisphere This Portuguese map was drawn by hand in 1502. Its rendering of the African coastline is especially detailed, an indication of how quickly and how well Portuguese mapmakers and navigators accumulated geographical information.

The discovery of America, and that of a passage to the East Indies by the Cape of Good Hope, are the two greatest and most important events recorded in the history of mankind.... By uniting, in some measure, the most distant parts of the world, by enabling them to relieve one another's wants, to increase one another's enjoyments, and to encourage one another's industry, their general tendency would seem to be beneficial.

Now, two and a half centuries after Adam Smith, it's a bit easier to see the full significance of "uniting, in some measure, the most distant parts of the world." In Part 4, we focus on just how this "uniting" happened, and on its consequences—economic, political, intellectual, social, and biological. From here on in the book, as history becomes more globalized, our portrayal of it also becomes more global in scope.

THE FIRST PULSE OF GLOBALIZATION

Before starting in, one further point is worth establishing. Although Smith refers to the discovery of America, in fact America—the Western Hemisphere—already had tens of millions of people in it, and neither the Vikings nor Columbus actually discovered it. What Columbus did discover was a practical route between Europe and America. He and dozens of other mariners collectively learned how to sail the world's oceans by exploiting the prevailing winds and currents. Before the fifteenth century, almost all sailors except Polynesians and Vikings hugged the shorelines. Polynesians in the tropical Pacific and Vikings in the North Atlantic had learned how to navigate and survive at sea for many weeks without sighting land. But even they did not establish enduring routes over the seas they sailed.

Between 1400 and 1800, mariners traversed all the world's seas and linked all the world's inhabited coastlines and hinterlands. They discovered oceanic routes, unlocked the secrets of the globe's wind patterns, and, armed with this knowledge, spun the first genuinely global web of humankind. That was the first pulse of true globalization, and its events belong—just as Smith said—among the most important in history.

NEW CROSSROADS

One aspect of the new global connections deserves underlining at the start. For thousands of years before the 1490s, the best place on Earth in which to learn about other places was Southwest Asia. Its connections, by land and sea, brought its peoples into at least intermittent touch with others in Africa, Europe, South Asia, and to a lesser extent Southeast and East Asia as well. Southwest Asian societies enjoyed access to the Mediterranean, Black, and Red Seas; the Indian Ocean world; and the overland routes of the Eurasian steppe. Southwest Asia was the land bridge connecting world regions, the closest thing to a center of the Old World web. This geographical position put Southwest Asian societies in a situation that was sometimes dangerous but often advantageous. Their position exposed them at times to more epidemics and perhaps more invasions than most peoples elsewhere. But it also enabled them to learn more from more places, and this they could turn to their advantage.

Southwest Asia gradually lost this dangerous but privileged position after the 1490s. Seaborne communications and trade enabled Atlantic Europeans gradually to take over this role. Increasingly, they, rather than Southwest Asians, learned more about technologies in use around the world. Atlantic Europeans could now adopt useful technologies from a larger menu of options than others had done. And now they, rather than Arabs, Armenians, and Persians, knew more about relative prices in different markets, enabling them to make money in trade more reliably, buying low and selling high in different parts of the world.

GLOBAL HISTORY

In Part 3, the chapters each addressed a separate region, but they shared common themes. Here, in Part 4, with the world drawing together into a single web, the chapters address separate themes with a global scope. Chapter 15 explores the navigation advances that wove the world together and the biological exchanges among regions that resulted. Chapter 16 considers the impacts of the newly formed Global web on societies previously enmeshed in smaller webs. All of these societies faced severe challenges that some survived but others did not. Chapters 17 through 19 deal with the cultural, political, and economic implications, respectively, of weaving a Global web.

So how did all this weaving start? The answer lies with sailors.

CHRONOLOGY

1291
Italian sailors attempt
to circumnavigate Africa

1368–1644
Ming dynasty in China

ca. 1300–1400
European and Moroccan
sailors reach the Canary
Islands

1415
Portuguese army
captures Moroccan
port of Ceuta

1405–1433
Zheng He
organizes and
leads seven
maritime voyages

1497
Vasco da Gama embarks on expedition to
India; John Cabot makes round-trip from
England to Newfoundland

1494
Spain and Portugal sign
the Treaty of Tordesillas

ca. 1480
Knowledge of how to make great
ships is lost in China; Portuguese
sailors establish a fort in
West Africa

By 1570
The Pacific Ocean wind
system is deciphered

ca. 1550–1750
Maize becomes a food
staple in Atlantic Africa

1402–1424
Reign of Yongle Emperor

1402–1496
Spanish conquest of the Guanches
in the Canary Islands

ca. 1430–1460
Henry the Navigator organizes systematic
voyaging along the coasts of Atlantic Africa

1492
Christopher Columbus
lands in the Bahamas

1492–1650
Populations in the Americas
fall by 70 to 95 percent

1519–1522
Ferdinand Magellan's
surviving crew members
circumnavigate the globe

1500
Pedro Álvares Cabral claims
Brazil for Portugal

Convergence

THE DISCOVERY OF THE OCEANS AND BIOLOGICAL GLOBALIZATION

1400 to 1800

ca. 1670
Military expansion
of Asante kingdom
begins

ca. 1650
Population of the
Americas begins
to recover

O n the morning of October 11, 1492, indigenous Americans living on an island in the Bahamas (probably Watlings Island) walked to the beach and, to their astonishment, discovered Christopher Columbus. Few if any Bahamians had ever seen men wearing clothes, which was not done in their islands, let alone men in metal armor. None had ever seen ships. Columbus's ships far eclipsed the dugout canoes that plied Bahamian waters. What those astonished people made of the strangers on their shores we will never know, although it's a reasonable guess that some were curious and some were terrified. Columbus, for his part, thought he stood on an island off the coast of China.

Nearly six years later, in 1498, residents of the Indian port city of Calicut, strolling along the harbor, were almost as astonished to discover Portuguese ships approaching. Some of them had surely seen Europeans before, although not many. But they had never seen European ships anywhere in the Indian Ocean, nor any ships carrying big cannon as these did. The ships' commander,

Maize Comes to Asia This Japanese screen from the mid-seventeenth century was probably produced in Kyoto, where aristocrats valued finely detailed ink drawings of exotic plants. It shows the Mesoamerican food crop of maize, which together with potatoes and cassava spread from the Americas to the rest of the world in a surge of biological globalization after 1492. The screen is among the earliest evidence of maize in Japan.

FOCUS QUESTIONS

1. What were the major contours of world history in 1400, as shown in the regional webs of the time?

2. What were the main differences in oceanic voyaging conducted by China's Ming dynasty and the Atlantic Europeans?

3. What were the most important effects of the biological globalization initiated by the oceanic voyaging of Atlantic Europeans?

4. Why was the first Global web to extend across the world a significant development?

Vasco da Gama, soon found occasion to use the big cannon.

These two encounters in the 1490s symbolize the opening of a new era in world history. Before the 1490s, the Americas and Afro-Eurasia remained essentially separate hemispheres. Before the 1490s, the American web and the Old World web relied heavily on overland connections together with short-distance maritime links. Long sea voyages in either hemisphere were very rare. After the 1490s, sailors linked the world's coastlands as never before. Indeed, the world's populated coasts, with scant exceptions, came to form the first genuinely Global web of human interaction, channeling the flow of ideas, technologies, goods, crops, diseases, and much else.

But before we get to the story of sailors and the seven seas, let's pause and look at the lands on which people lived as of the fifteenth century, and specifically, the webs of interaction within which they lived. Before examining the formation of a Global web, it helps to remember its constituent parts.

THE WORLD'S WEBS IN THE FIFTEENTH CENTURY

As of 1400, the 350 to 450 million people on Earth spoke several thousand languages, followed several hundred religions, and recognized several hundred political rulers. (A few tens of millions of them recognized no rulers at all, although with each passing year fewer and fewer lived in so-called stateless societies.) Despite nearly 5,000 years of states, cities, and empires, and some 2,000 years of expanding, proselytizing religions, the human race remained politically and culturally fragmented. It was in no deep sense a community. Even within the Old World web, spectacular diversity prevailed—from the refined world of Confucian scholars in urban China, with its leisured philosophy and gorgeous calligraphy, to the poor and dangerous world of illiterate fisherfolk (such as my ancestors) on the coasts of Scotland.

THE OLD WORLD WEB

That diversity resulted partly from the sheer size of the Old World web. Its frontiers, in 1400, stretched from Greenland to Japan and from Indonesia to West Africa. Three-fourths of humanity lived within it. Thousands of caravan tracks, navigable rivers, and sea routes held the web together. It included hubs or nodes, such as Malacca, Calicut, Hormuz, Cairo, Constantinople, or Venice, where people routinely heard many languages and where the silks of China crossed paths with the ivory of East Africa or the amber of Scandinavia. But it also included spaces where people kept to themselves, deep in the forests of Siberia or high in the Himalaya mountains, minimally connected to empires, trade routes, or major religions. These people, comparatively few in number, lived within the Old World web's frontiers, but they were not part of its fabric—at least, not yet in 1400.

INTERACTIONS WITHIN THE OLD WORLD WEB
The Old World web had two main trunk routes. The overland caravan routes, collectively known as the Silk Road, linked eastern and western Eurasia. The caravan routes flourished in times of peace, when strong empires kept brigands in check and prevented dozens of local rulers from demanding payment from traders in exchange for safe passage. The best example is the Pax

Overland and Seaborne Trade These two 15th-century images show contrasting sides of the long-distance trade circuits of the Old World Web. The Chinese image at left shows overland transport of Chinese ceramics to Southwest Asia, only part of which would have taken place in a donkey cart. The image at right, from a Portuguese manuscript of 1497, shows Portuguese ships, called carracks, that undertook oceanic voyages along the coasts of Africa and into the Indian Ocean.

Mongolica (ca. 1260–1350), when the short-lived Mongol Empire stamped out brigandage almost everywhere along routes between Korea and Iraq, making travel safer for merchants.

The second main trunk route, also in reality a series of shorter routes, was by sea. It extended from the East Asian ports through the waters of Southeast Asia and into the Indian Ocean, as far west as the coasts of Africa. Via a short overland passage in Egypt, these routes connected to the Mediterranean. Mastery of the monsoon winds had opened this trunk route in ancient times.

The traffic within the Old World web, along these trunk routes and countless lesser ones, served as a homogenizing force. Cultural interaction and political conquests reduced the number of different languages spoken. Meanwhile, more and more people chose (sometimes under duress) to follow fewer and fewer religions, and so Buddhism, Hinduism, Christianity, and Islam (some people would include Confucianism as a religion too) each acquired tens of millions of believers, while many other religions disappeared. Of course, at the same time, the big religions fractured, developing internal splits such as the Sunni–Shi'a divide in Islam or the Orthodox–Catholic schism in Christianity. And the big languages fractured too, although slowly. They developed dialects, so the Arabic spoken in Morocco gradually came to seem strange to Arabs in Iraq because it sounded so different from their own. So the process of homogenization in the Old World web had its limits and countercurrents.

A THICKENING WEB During the fifteenth century, the eastern and western edges of the Old World web were rapidly consolidating and thickening as a result of maritime trade. In earlier centuries, mastery of the arts of camel management had boosted the connectivity of the central regions of the Old World web, making desert crossings in Central Asia, Arabia, and Africa much more practical. Mastery of the monsoon winds had given sea traders in the Indian Ocean world a precocious start in developing long-distance networks. But now, from at least 1200 onward, improving ship design and navigational skill in both western Europe and eastern Asia were fast accumulating, reducing the risks of sea travel and making trade and economic specialization yet more rewarding. Sailing the western Pacific waters from Japan to Java, or the eastern Atlantic from Scandinavia to Morocco, was dangerous indeed. Both seas featured frequent, furious storms, not to mention (especially in the western Pacific) bold, enterprising pirates. But bigger and better ships helped sailors overcome their understandable fears of these hazards.

The rewards to risking one's life and cargo at sea were genuine and growing. Both western Europe and eastern Asia produced a wide diversity of resources and goods. Markets had sprung up offering tempting prices at which to sell scarce goods from afar, whether Spanish wine in the Netherlands or Moluccan spices in China. At times, even bulk goods such as rice, salt, and timber could justify sea voyages in these regions.

Comparing Currencies Strange as it seems, both these images show money. The coins at left come from the Southeast Asian kingdom of Srivijaya (seventh to thirteenth centuries) and look a good deal like money in circulation across the Old World web, where several centuries previously millions of people came to agree that small discs of gold, silver, or copper were valuable. The giant limestone disc at right served as money in the Caroline Islands of the western Pacific, especially the island of Yap, where money was used only for major transactions. The stones themselves, which might weigh a few tons, did not need to move. Instead, everyone agreed the stones had new owners after a transaction. Srivijayan society was much more trade- and market-oriented than Yap's.

Both these emerging maritime worlds drew additional traffic from networks of navigable rivers. In Europe, the big rivers flow fairly evenly throughout the year and permit ship or barge traffic well inland. In East and Southeast Asia, the big rivers are more seasonal because of the pattern of summer monsoon rain. But with painstaking construction of canals, dikes, and dams, these rivers too served as reliable avenues of commerce, linking interior regions with the sea.

So, in 1400, the eastern and western edges of the Old World web were humming with riverine and seaborne trade. Knowledge of geography, winds, and currents; of ship design, cartography, and navigation; of goods, markets, and prices was growing at ever faster rates. Both regions were developing a more maritime and commercial culture. Population levels were recovering from the disease and climate disasters of the fourteenth century, and cities were expanding rapidly.

LOCAL WEBS

In 1400, some 60 to 120 million people in Oceania, the Americas, and the southern third of Africa lived outside the Old World web altogether. They too, of course, took part in trade networks, military conquests, and the same sorts of activities as people in the Old World web. But their scales of operations were smaller. In Oceania, people in Polynesia and Micronesia had built their own small webs of interaction. Archipelagoes like that of Hawaii,

or Tonga and Fiji, hosted constant interactions among hundreds of thousands of people. In the Caroline Islands of Micronesia by 1400 or 1450, a well-integrated exchange network had grown up, using big stone discs as money—some of them heavier than a car. But this little web probably involved at most tens of thousands of people. In demographic terms, these Oceanic networks were tiny compared to the Old World web.

WEBS IN THE AMERICAS

In the Americas, as we saw in Chapter 14, much larger webs had developed around the dense populations in the Andes and in Mesoamerica. In 1400, perhaps 40 to 70 million people lived in the Americas, and about half were in either the Andes or Mesoamerica. Most indigenous Americans, and all those in the Andes or Mesoamerica, took part in interactive webs. In the absence of pack animals (outside of llamas and alpacas in the high Andes), goods traveled mainly by watercraft or human porters, although on North America's Great Plains, dogs dragged sleds—called travois—laden with gear. Canoes and rafts linked peoples on riverbanks and shorelines. Elsewhere, people had to carry everything themselves.

So the character of the American webs was slightly different from that of the Old World web, with less bulk commerce in transit. Crops such as maize diffused widely within this web, and so did some cultural practices such as ball games and mound building. But the volume and intensity of the exchanges of goods over long distances were modest compared to what occurred in the Old World web, with its camel and donkey caravans and its shipping. Buzzing local markets did exist, as in the Basin of Mexico, the region around today's Mexico City. As in the Old World web, those societies enmeshed in the American web featured more specialization and exchange, greater wealth, greater inequality, and greater military power, than those societies outside the web.

Like its counterparts, the American webs left some people untouched. In the far south of South America and in the northern reaches of North America, scattered populations lived essentially subsistence lives, with little wealth or social hierarchy, free from the grasping hands of kings and emperors. In pockets of Central American or Amazonian rain forest too, there were some people living substantially in isolation.

WEBS IN AFRICA

Most of the northern half of Africa, by 1400, lay within the Old World web. Egypt had long been one of the web's linchpins. Trade and cultural exchange, most notably the spread of Islam, tied the East African coast as far south as Kilwa and Sofala, the Mediterranean lands, and the West African Sahel firmly to the rest of the Old World web. Where rivers made travel easy, as along the Nile and Niger, tendrils of the Old World web reached further still.

But the southern third of Africa, like sizeable parts of the Americas, or Siberia, stood apart from any big web. People there were not importing shiploads of luxury goods from Egypt or India; they were not sending young men to study Islam in Cairo or Baghdad. They were not experimenting with Indian Ocean–world technology such as sugar mills or lateen-rigged sails. Instead, they were producing food and clothing for themselves or for local use, they were following their own religions, and they were using the same technologies—perhaps with minor alterations—that their ancestors had employed for many generations. They lived outside the Old World web, but within much smaller webs of their own making.

As in the Americas, these little webs in southern Africa were better for circulating ideas than goods. Without pack animals, wheeled vehicles, or ships, people here had to move everything on their backs, on their heads, or in canoes.

So, in 1400, the world included one giant interactive web in Eurasia and the northern half of Africa, a large one in the Americas, and small, local ones elsewhere. The Old World web was home to most of the world's people, and to its most formidable states and societies. It alone had sailing ships capable of carrying hundreds of tons of cargo. It alone had many kinds of pack animals suited to almost any terrain. It alone had wheeled vehicles. By 1400, it had fewer obstacles to interaction, especially to trade, than did the other, smaller webs around the world.

The Old World web was not necessarily a pleasant place to live—certainly not if life expectancy or social equality are the measures—but it was where people had built the most powerful militaries, the most efficient communications networks, and the most sophisticated technologies. Therefore, it comes as no surprise that the people who forged the first truly global web, came from the edges of the Old World web.

PREVAILING WINDS AND THE OPEN SEA

Before 1400, as earlier chapters explained, several peoples had developed maritime cultures. The most extraordinary of these was the Polynesian, which carried colonists throughout the archipelagoes of the tropical Pacific and as far south as New Zealand. However, by 1400 its farthest outposts had become cut off, and sea traffic took place mainly within archipelagoes. The Vikings, too, had a seafaring history several centuries long, although by 1400 they had stopped exploring the North Atlantic and their Greenland colony was on the verge of extinction. Many other peoples sailed routinely on more protected seas, such as the Mediterranean, the Arabian Gulf, the Bay of Bengal, the South China Sea, or the Sea of Japan. The islands of Indonesia, and adjacent coasts of Southeast Asia, hosted sizeable regular traffic by 1000 CE. The traffic in all these seas was much thicker and more regular than in the Polynesian Pacific or the Viking North Atlantic. The vessels were often larger, and some could carry hundreds of tons of cargo. The routes were well established and studded with commercial seaports. Those who plied these routes usually hugged the shores, although certain passages, such as from East Africa to India and back, took sailors far from land for a week or two.

Sailors had accumulated a considerable, if fragmented,

Prevailing Winds and Ocean Currents Mariners of the fifteenth and sixteenth centuries figured out the global system of winds and ocean currents, enabling them to plot the routes of sailing ships that tied the Global web together.

knowledge of winds and currents. Polynesians knew how to ride the currents and the trade winds of the Pacific. People all around the Indian Ocean knew how to use the monsoon to sail north in the summer and south in the winter. Everywhere, sailors had mastered the local tides, currents, and winds for the short voyages that made up the great majority of seafaring. But no one knew the overall pattern of the planet's winds. No one knew how it might be possible, in the Atlantic and Pacific as well as the Indian Ocean, to find winds that would reliably take ships far out to sea, thousands of miles from land, and then safely home again. In the fifteenth and sixteenth centuries, people learned where to find these winds, unlocking the secrets of oceanic navigation.

The ocean winds form gigantic merry-go-rounds. In the North Atlantic, for example, the prevailing winds spin in a clockwise fashion. Its westerlies (winds are named for the direction *from* which they blow, unlike ocean currents; so a westerly wind and an easterly current are going the same way) whip across from North America to Europe. Further south, the trade winds blow along the northwestern coasts of Africa and then whistle across to the Caribbean. In the South Atlantic, the merry-go-round spins counterclockwise, so the westerlies lie far to the south and the trade winds cross from Angola to Brazil. The North and South Pacific have their own spinning wheels, as does the southern Indian Ocean. (The winds of the northern part of the Indian Ocean are governed by the monsoon.) The whole system slides north by a few

hundred miles from April to August and slips back south from September to March. So there is a general pattern to the world's winds. But nobody knew that in 1400.

THE MING VOYAGES, 1405–1433

In 1400, the biggest ships and perhaps the best navigators were Chinese. Under the Song, the Yuan, and then the Ming (1368–1644) dynasties, the Chinese had rapidly developed ship and navigation technology, and Chinese merchants had taken a large role in the booming trade between East and Southeast Asia. The Ming maintained a state shipyard that employed between 20,000 and 30,000 workers. Their biggest ships carried a thousand people. Chinese tinkerers had invented the magnetic compass, and Chinese navigators used it more than sailors elsewhere. Their maritime culture was developing rapidly, thanks to constant voyaging to the islands of Southeast Asia, to Japan, and to every coast in between. By 1400, that maritime culture and Ming finances had reached a point at which they could support large, expensive, showy voyages to overawe just about everyone from Vietnam to East Africa.

Two crucial components of that maturing maritime culture were ship design and navigational tools. Chinese mariners had long used sternpost rudders and double-hulled construction. Rudders improved the steering of ships, and double hulls usually saved them from sinking if rammed or smashed on rocks. Chinese sailors also used the space between hulls to carry fresh water. During the Song dynasty, their seaborne trade links to the Indian Ocean had acquainted them with new rigging and sails—particularly the lateen sail common in Arab shipping, good for sailing into the wind. Shipbuilders used these features, old and new, to design seagoing ships of 2,500 tons. They also put small cannon on these huge ships. As for navigation, Chinese sailors were already using printed sea manuals with star charts, as well as the compass, during the Song dynasty. A new emperor soon put Chinese maritime culture to new uses.

In 1402, after a bloody succession struggle, a crafty uncle ousted his nephew and became emperor of Ming China. Like all Chinese emperors, he took a reign name upon ascending the throne: the Yongle Emperor. To help consolidate his position, he promoted loyal eunuchs into positions of power, one of whom, **Zheng He**, became Yongle's indispensable adviser and political fixer. Ruling with an iron fist, Yongle moved the capital from the south to Beijing, rebuilt the Grand Canal, launched campaigns against the Mongols (in which Zheng He distinguished himself), invaded and annexed part of Vietnam, and chased down and executed everyone loyal to his nephew.

Yongle also made his devoted aide Zheng He an admiral. Even though he had probably never smelled the sea,

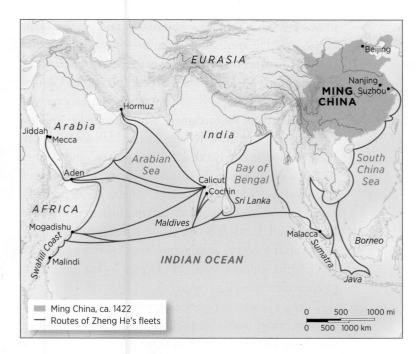

Voyages of Zheng He, 1405–1433 The Chinese admiral Zheng He led seven massive fleets into the Indian Ocean, following routes long familiar to merchants in these waters. Zheng He and his captains knew how to ride the monsoon winds, navigate with star charts, and find safe harbors. His routes extended to the far edges of the Indian Ocean world, the Arabian Peninsula and the Swahili coast.

Zheng He's Flagship No contemporary image of Zheng He's fleet survives. This is a modern artist's rendition of one of his flagships. Textual descriptions mention ships with nine masts, an overall length of 44 zhang or 440 feet (134m), a beam (or width) of 18 zhang (180 feet or 55m), which is substantially larger than an American football field. Modern scholars are uncertain whether or not to take these texts at their word. But if the sources exaggerate the dimensions of Zheng He's biggest ships, it is probably not by much—to judge by the size of the Nanjing drydocks where they were built and from the remains of a stern rudder post found there. The Nanjing yards built about 50 such giant ships for Zheng He's expeditions between 1405 and 1433.

Zheng He organized massive maritime expeditions the likes of which China—and the world—had never seen. A possible purpose was to find and capture Yongle's nephew, who according to rumor had escaped his uncle's extermination campaign. But the scale of the undertaking indicates that Yongle had additional motives. As one contemporary put it, the emperor wanted to send his soldiers to "strange lands in order to make manifest the wealth and power" of China. In 1405, Zheng He set sail from Suzhou with roughly 300 ships, newly built in the shipyards of Nanjing along the Yangzi. They carried 28,000 men, both sailors and soldiers, a crew larger than the population of any city they would visit. His biggest ships, if we can believe the Chinese sources, were gigantic, about 400 feet (120 m) by 160 feet (50 m) and displacing 20,000 tons—far larger than any yet built anywhere and 10 times the size of Columbus's flagship. They were the largest wooden ships ever built.

Zheng He sailed well-traveled seas from China into the Indian Ocean. He used persuasion, intimidation, and military power to oust unfriendly rulers in Sumatra and Sri Lanka and install replacements more willing to acknowledge Yongle's overlordship and pay him tribute. Zheng He annihilated pirates—or maybe just merchant princes who failed to show proper enthusiasm for the emperor and so earned the title "pirate" in Chinese accounts. According to one Ming scholar-bureaucrat with typical contempt for foreigners, while stopped at Sri Lanka's coast on the third voyage Zheng He's soldiers "ravaged and made captive that entire country" and cleaned "out in a single sweep those noxious pests" and "insignificant worms." On a later voyage, Zheng He deposited a giant stone slab in Sri Lanka with inscriptions in Chinese, Persian, and Tamil (a South Asian language in use in Sri Lanka after 1000 CE) commemorating his visit as an emissary of "the supreme overlord of kings"—lest anyone fail to appreciate Yongle's stature.

Zheng He was not exploring new routes. On his first six expeditions (1405–1424) he commanded gigantic fleets with large armies aboard. On three voyages, they went as far as the East African coast. But in every case, they visited ports and coasts well known to the maritime merchants of the Indian Ocean world, places where the occasional Chinese trader and certainly Chinese goods were familiar.

It was a traditional priority of Chinese statecraft to defend the empire's landward frontiers. Yongle mounted and personally led many expeditions into the Mongolian steppe and sent several embassies to Central Asia to improve the political situation on his frontiers. Overawing distant foreigners by sea ranked well behind this priority, so the logic of doing it again and again came into question. Zheng He himself was an outsider in Chinese politics, a Muslim, a eunuch, and not even Chinese (he came from an ethnic minority population and had Persian ancestry as well). His career hinged entirely on the emperor's favor. When Yongle died in 1424, factions came to power that did not favor overseas voyaging.

Those factions eventually prevailed. Voyaging was costly and did not contribute to the security or virtue of the empire, nor much to its prosperity. Repairs to the Grand Canal, finished in 1411, made seafaring less important to the Ming state and Chinese society, since shipping could flow more safely on the canal than on the sea. Yongle's successor judged the oceanic voyaging wasteful and ended it in 1424. Under a later emperor, Zheng He and the eunuch faction prevailed one last time and launched a seventh voyage (1431–1433), again reaching Africa. But Zheng He died en route home, and his remaining supporters lost influence. The Ming eventually broke up the great fleet and sold it for fuelwood. By 1480, the skills needed to build such great ships had vanished.

The geographical and other knowledge accumulated on Zheng He's voyages found its way into Chinese charts, maps, and books. But it did not vastly expand, or fundamentally alter, Chinese understanding of the world. It temporarily lubricated the wheels of commerce that connected China to the Indian Ocean trading ports, but only for a few decades. The **Ming voyages** left scant enduring legacy.

The scale of the Ming maritime effort before 1433 suggests that the Chinese had the ships and skills to sail

Ming Giraffe Giraffes are native to Africa, but here one appears as an illustration in a Ming manuscript, indicating the reach of Chinese maritime voyaging during the Ming period. Like other luxury goods, exotic animals could be brought back from voyages as status objects and prizes.

Chinese Geographical Knowledge This map made by the cartographer Wang Qi in 1607 indicates the extent, by then, of Chinese knowledge of the wider world. Centered on China and the Pacific Ocean, it offers a remarkably accurate depiction of Eurasia, Africa, the Americas, and Antarctica.

around Africa to Europe, or south to Australia, or across the Pacific to the Americas. But they had no good reason to try to reach Europe. They didn't yet know Australia or the Americas existed. So, instead, they sailed familiar waters in grand style with enormous government support. Then, in 1433, they stopped.

EUROPEAN VOYAGING, 1400–1700

At the same time that the Ming were gliding into the Indian Ocean, western Europeans were probing the Atlantic. Some of them dreamed of sailing to the Indian Ocean too. They lacked the massive state support that Zheng He had enjoyed, and the states that helped them could mobilize only a tiny fraction of the resources the Ming could. These mariners were lucky if they could cobble together a tiny flotilla.

But European mariners usually had a good idea of where they were heading. Navigational skill had accumulated slowly but surely over the centuries in Atlantic Europe. In Iberia especially, the practical experience of sailors combined with Arab mathematics and astronomy to improve the art of navigation. By the thirteenth century, European sailors used the compass to find their direction on cloudy days. By the fourteenth, they had translated Arabic texts on the use of astrolabes to help determine latitude. Soon they were authoring their own manuals on astrolabes—the English writer Geoffrey Chaucer penned one—and building the devices themselves. But even perfect navigational skill would have meant little without seaworthy ships.

Portuguese Caravel Caravels like this one were the relatively small sailing ships used by Portuguese and other European explorers on long-distance voyages. This mosaic appears near a sixteenth-century villa outside Lisbon, the Portuguese capital.

Like the Chinese, Atlantic Europeans rapidly refined their ship designs. More frequent connections in the fourteenth and fifteenth centuries between sailors in the North Atlantic and the Mediterranean yielded a hybrid in hull design and rigging. Shipbuilders combined the economical hull structure typical of Mediterranean ships—in which planks were nailed to ribs rather than to one another—with the stern-post rudder invented in the

Portolan Charts This innovation in cartography helped explorers to navigate the routes between ports. A 1571 portolan chart of West Africa shows numerous ports along the coastline, with crests indicating the powers—especially Portugal, the red and white shield—that controlled them.

Baltic. This led to stronger, cheaper, and more maneuverable vessels. In addition, mariners supplemented square sails typical of northern waters with Arab lateen sails to create the so-called fully rigged ship, which could sail effectively regardless of the wind's direction. With these advances, European sailors could dispense with oars and oarsmen and rely entirely on the wind. Ships became cheaper to operate because much smaller crews needed less food, water, and pay. So by the early fifteenth century, European shipwrights knew how to make sturdy, swift, and cheap ships, capable of carrying lightweight cannon and sailing anywhere even in heavy weather. Their ships were far smaller than those of Zheng He, but no less seaworthy. And by 1500, they built ships large enough to carry heavy cannon capable of battering down walls or sinking any ship afloat.

Atlantic European mariners, unlike Zheng He, had incentives to gamble on sailing the open seas and to begin to unlock the secrets of the world's winds. And once they started, unlike the Ming, they did not stop.

EUROPEAN MARINERS' MOTIVES Atlantic Europeans launched onto the high seas primarily in quest of wealth, fame, and the greater glory of their God. They started by sailing south into unfamiliar waters, looking for

Iberian Art A wooden sculpture decorating a late-fifteenth-century altarpiece in the Cathedral of Granada shows the last Muslim king leaving Granada with his followers, after the Spanish Reconquista in 1492.

a practical route to West African gold or Asian spices and silks, the most valuable trade goods they knew of. Merchants from Italian city-states such as Venice and Genoa had tapped into these trades, acquiring gold in Morocco or Tunisia and spices in Egypt or Syria, after the goods had changed hands many times. Merchants who could get these goods closer to the source could buy them for less and make a fortune by cutting out several middlemen.

The search for glory and fame also propelled European navigators. Fifteenth-century Europeans, especially Iberians, were steeped in a culture of adventure and chivalry as proper male pursuits. Owing in part to the centuries-long **Reconquista**—in which Christians retook Iberia from Muslim rulers—Iberian books, songs, poems, and folk tales celebrated the deeds of heroes who took daunting risks and either triumphed or, if they died young, at least won lasting fame. Young males eager to vault several rungs up the social ladder learned that they could do so through acts of reckless heroism.

The Atlantic Europeans' third reason for taking the risks of oceanic seafaring was simultaneously religious and political. It appealed especially to Christian rulers, for whom victories against Muslim states meant more glory, political legitimacy, and support from the Pope. Any European voyager who could find Christian allies in Africa or Asia might tip the balance of power in favor of Christian kingdoms against Muslim foes. Helping to find sea routes that deprived Muslim states of their trade

revenues served the same purposes. If successful, quests for Christian allies might set the stage for renewed conquest of the Holy Land, in the tradition of the Crusaders of a few centuries before. For Iberians, voyaging south along the African Atlantic coast seemed an extension of the Reconquista and the loot and glory it provided. Indeed, the Portuguese had begun to attack Muslim strongholds in Morocco as early as 1415.

LEARNING THE ATLANTIC After about 1200, European and Moroccan mariners sailed hundreds of miles west into the uncharted Atlantic. By the fourteenth century, if not before, some stumbled across the Canary Islands, Madeira, and the Azores. The Canaries' population, called the **Guanches**, descended from North

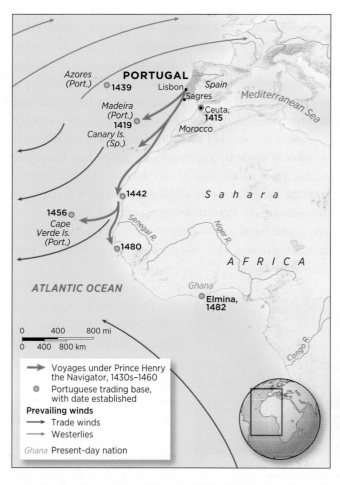

Early Exploration of the Atlantic, 1400–1480 In the fifteenth century, Iberian mariners figured out how to use the winds to venture far out into the Atlantic and get home safely. This accomplishment took navigation well beyond the familiar practice of hugging coastlines, and eventually led to successful crossings of the Atlantic and the discovery of routes linking the Atlantic and Indian Oceans.

African Berber settlers who had arrived in about 1000 BCE. Madeira and the Azores were uninhabited.

By the early fifteenth century, Europeans were attempting settlement of these islands, which in the Canaries required Spain to undertake military conquest of the Guanches. They fought fiercely, but their long isolation meant the Guanches had never acquired metallurgy: they used only stone, bone, and wooden weapons. Moreover, with no experience of infectious diseases by now familiar to Spaniards, they suffered repeated epidemics. The conquest of the Guanches, begun in 1402, ended in 1496. Many isolated peoples around the world would soon share their fate.

Shuttling to and from the new settlements in these little archipelagoes helped European sailors grow accustomed to the open Atlantic. The Canaries were crucial because they served as the entrance ramp to the northeast trade winds, which would prove to be the highway to the Americas.

At the same time as they were learning about, and starting to settle these archipelagoes, European sailors were also edging down the coast of Africa. A pair of Italian brothers, the Vivaldis, tried to circumnavigate Africa in 1291—but they were never heard from again. Others, mainly Portuguese, followed more cautiously. The northwest coast of Africa offered little fresh water, and the northeast trade winds, which made outbound journeys simple, made it hard to get back home to Portugal. Improved ship design helped with that problem, as did the gradual discovery that sailors could follow the trade winds as far south as the Canaries and then swing north to the latitude of the Azores and catch the prevailing westerlies to get home. This was the first step in learning the oceanic wind pattern.

AFRICAN COASTS Portuguese efforts along the African coast quickened when in 1415 an army captured the Moroccan port of Ceuta. One of the leaders of that expedition, a prince known generously as Henry the Navigator, began to organize and support systematic voyaging along the coasts of Atlantic Africa in the 1430s. Henry was a seeker after honor and fame, which he once said were life's highest goals after salvation. He had strong religious convictions, influenced by chivalric notions of crusades against infidels. He also took astrology to heart and interpreted it to mean he was destined for great deeds. Henry the Navigator only put to sea two or three times in his life, but he siphoned off some of the modest resources

of a threadbare dynasty in a poor country to pay for sea voyages along the northwest African coast, hoping to get at the source of West African gold.

The Portuguese voyages along the northwest coasts of Africa formed part of a larger, haphazard program that was full of failures. Several Portuguese sailors tried heading west from the Azores, out into the Atlantic, but either were pushed back by the westerly winds or lost at sea. Others tried to cross the Sahara on foot, but none returned. Henry encouraged military assaults on strongholds in Morocco, most of which failed.

All these efforts were dwarfed by the simultaneous voyaging of Zheng He, who commanded far greater resources than any Portuguese sea captain ever did. The tiny size of its investment, perhaps, explains why the Portuguese Crown did not give up and put a stop to the whole enterprise, as the Ming did with Zheng He's journeys. In any case, the Portuguese kept at it, even after Henry's death in 1460, despite meager returns on their investment for half a century.

Henry the Navigator A fifteenth-century painting depicts Henry the Navigator, the prince who sponsored Portuguese voyages along the coast of northwest Africa and to Atlantic islands.

Elmina Castle The basement of the Portuguese fort of Elmina, in present-day Ghana, was originally built in 1482 as a pen to hold the enslaved people who were traded on the West African coast.

The Cantino Planisphere This Portuguese map was drawn by hand in 1502. Its rendering of the African coastline is especially detailed, an indication of how quickly and how well Portuguese mapmakers and navigators accumulated geographical information.

By the 1480s, their efforts began to pay off. Sailors reached the West African coast of what is now Ghana and established a fort—called Elmina—through which they traded for gold. Soon they found they could buy slaves on the coast and export them from Elmina to Iberia, or the sugar plantations of the Canaries and Madeira in a lucrative supplement to the gold trade. After nearly a century of meager returns, the Portuguese monarchy now had a profitable toehold in African trade. Soon every kingdom in Atlantic Europe would be sponsoring sea captains trying to get in on African commerce. One captain would also try, as several luckless Portuguese had before, to sail to China by heading west across the Atlantic.

COLUMBUS CROSSES THE ATLANTIC In 1477, a ship broke up in a storm off the southern coast of Portugal. Almost everyone aboard drowned, but a 23-year-old sailor swam ashore. That sailor was **Christopher Columbus**.

Columbus was the son of a weaver from Genoa in northern Italy. He was a bit of a dreamer, easily lost in popular literature with its tales of adventure. He turned to the sea as a teenager, escaping the narrow horizons of an artisan's life in Genoa. As a sailor, he first roamed the Mediterranean and then made forays into the Atlantic. He became a trader too, and sometimes made lush profits in walrus tusk, whale blubber, and other items. After he washed up in Portugal in 1477, he went to Lisbon, where he had a brother working as a mapmaker. Through his brother, Columbus met people who told all sorts of tall tales about what lay over the western horizon.

Columbus was working in the sugar trade, shuttling between the eastern Mediterranean and the eastern Atlantic, when in the 1480s he began to peddle schemes for a voyage further west. Sometimes he said he would find new islands, as profitable as the Canaries or Madeira. Sometimes he said he would sail to China, which he claimed was a "few days" away. He had learned of the equatorial trade winds blowing to the west from Africa's northwest shores, and of the westerlies (blowing to the east) at higher latitudes. These prevailing winds, he figured, would allow a round-trip voyage to China. They would also allow him, the weaver's son, to join the titled aristocracy, which seems to have been his primary ambition. Columbus was at heart a social climber, willing to take great risks in his quest for status, wealth, and glory.

Like any would-be entrepreneur, Columbus pitched his schemes to anyone who would listen. He failed to convince the Portuguese monarchy to invest in his plans, so he tried Spain, where he proved more persuasive. Funded by Italian bankers residing in Spain, he secured permission from Ferdinand and Isabella, the king and queen of Castile (the largest region of Spain), to sail under their flag. The story that Queen Isabella pawned her jewels to finance the voyage is, sadly, mere whimsy. Some of her courtiers did invest in the voyage, using funds confiscated from Jews recently expelled from Castile.

Columbus promised the investors that he would forge a route to and from China by sailing west with the trade winds and then back home with the westerlies. He figured that Japan, which he had read about in Marco Polo's book of travels, lay about 2,500 miles (4,000 km) west of Spain. His estimate was off by about 10,000 miles. Had he calculated correctly, he would have stayed home.

Instead, he gathered sailors into three little ships, and set out on the well-worn route to the Canary Islands. From there he ventured west into the open sea, seeing no land for 35 days before coming to an island, perhaps Watlings Island in the Bahamas.

What he found looked nothing like Japan or China. Far from sporting silken robes, the locals stood stark naked and seemed unashamed of it. They had dugout canoes but no ships, and huts instead of palaces. Still hopeful, Columbus quickly moved on and in two weeks was in Cuba. He later stopped at the island of Hispaniola, where he met the more familiar trappings of complex society—dense populations, intensive agriculture, trade networks, and rumors of great kings. On Hispaniola, someone presented him with a few lumps of gold, something he could bring back for his investors. Upon his return home, he insisted to his backers that he had found a direct route to islands off the coast of Asia—and he probably believed it.

The Spanish Crown rewarded him with the title Admiral of the Ocean Sea and granted him broad powers to operate as he saw fit on subsequent voyages. He returned three more times to the Caribbean, even reaching the mainland shores of South and Central America. He engaged in slave trading (of people indigenous to the Caribbean), bloody reprisals, and several sorts of atrocity

in his eagerness for gold. His conduct met with rebukes among his followers and back in Spain. He hanged several Spaniards who defied his authority. A Spanish woman who reminded everyone that the Admiral of the Ocean Sea was the son of a weaver had her tongue cut out.

Columbus's final years were filled with lawsuits, bankruptcy, imprisonment, and bitter disappointment that he had found few riches and had not made it to China. He died in 1506, still convinced he had reached the doorstep of the Great Khan. No one else in history has had so many streets, squares, schools, and hotels named after him for making such a big mistake.

Columbus was wrong and he was brutal, but he was nonetheless a central historical figure. His voyages inaugurated a new age of connection among worlds long separate.

Soon after Columbus returned from the second of his four transatlantic voyages, another Italian, Giovanni Caboto, was also proposing voyages to China across the Atlantic. John Cabot, as he is known, approached merchants in Bristol, England, who were growing rich on the whale and walrus trade of the North Atlantic, and enlisted support from the English court. In 1497, he made it across

Columbus's Landfall In this 1493 engraving from *La lettera dell'isole*, Columbus's first account of his voyage, King Ferdinand observes from afar as Columbus and his crew land on an island in the Caribbean. The island's indigenous inhabitants appear to flee.

the Atlantic to Newfoundland and back in a tiny ship, about 3 percent the size of Zheng He's flagship. His crew numbered about 18. Among the treasures Cabot reported, mostly fanciful, were the very real and stupendously rich cod fisheries off of Newfoundland. Like Columbus, he recruited more investors, fitted out more and bigger ships, and crossed the Atlantic a second time. Unlike Columbus, he never came back. Nevertheless, from soon after Cabot's time, Europeans would sail regularly to the Newfoundland fishing grounds, creating an enduring link—something that Viking voyages to Newfoundland, some 500 years before, had not done.

DA GAMA SAILS TO INDIA In 1497, the same year that Cabot sailed, the Portuguese court sponsored an expedition of four ships and 170 men under the command of a low-ranking provincial noble named **Vasco da Gama**. A few years before, a Portuguese captain, Bartholomew Dias, had sailed from Lisbon to the shores of South Africa and returned safely. Dias discovered the belt of westerly winds in the Southern Hemisphere that enabled ships to sidestep adverse currents and ride into the Indian Ocean from the South Atlantic. Trusting this information, da Gama sailed way out into the South Atlantic to catch the westerlies and made it safely to the tip of South Africa and into the Indian Ocean. He worked his way up Africa's southeast coast and soon found evidence, in the form of Indian cloth and glassware, that he was where he hoped to be—in the Indian Ocean.

The ultimate prize, a practical route to and from the rich trade of Asia, lay almost within da Gama's grasp. He and his men resorted to piracy and the kidnapping of local pilots to help them find their way along East Africa's coast. On the shore of what is now Kenya, they found a pilot who showed them the easiest route to **Calicut**, a trading city on the coast of India, where the Portuguese hoped to find—as one of da Gama's captains put it—Christians and spices.

The Portuguese expedition under da Gama had two main goals. The Portuguese Crown hoped to win glory, papal favor, and some practical political advantage by finding Christian allies somewhere in the Indian Ocean world, friends who would help in struggles against Muslim monarchs of North Africa and Southwest Asia. The Crown also hoped to boost its finances by trading in spices, peppers, cloves, nutmeg, and more, items that were plentiful in India but scarce and expensive in Europe.

Some Italian traders had done well in the spice trade, linking Venetian markets, through Egypt or Syria, with producers in India and further afield in Southeast Asia. The Portuguese hoped to command this trade by sailing around Africa and going directly to the source of spices. Da Gama encountered no politically useful Christians in Calicut, but he found plenty of spice traders.

Da Gama and his crew did not linger long in India. Their trade goods didn't interest the merchants of Calicut. The local prince wanted da Gama to pay customs fees like any trader, whereas da Gama regarded himself as a royal emissary and above such requirements. After three disappointing months, the Portuguese left, kidnapping a few Indians and sailing back toward Africa. Portuguese-Indian relations were off to a rocky start.

Da Gama left in a huff, pointing his ships' prows into the teeth of the summer monsoon. The route that had taken three weeks with the winds at his back now took him four months on the return. Half the crew died before they reached Africa, and only 55 remained alive when da Gama returned to Lisbon more than two years after departing. He had sailed more than 25,000 miles (40,000

Vasco da Gama A sixteenth-century Flemish tapestry illustrates the moment of encounter between da Gama and his men and the people of the Indian trading port of Calicut—which actually looked much less like a European fortified city than this artist imagined.

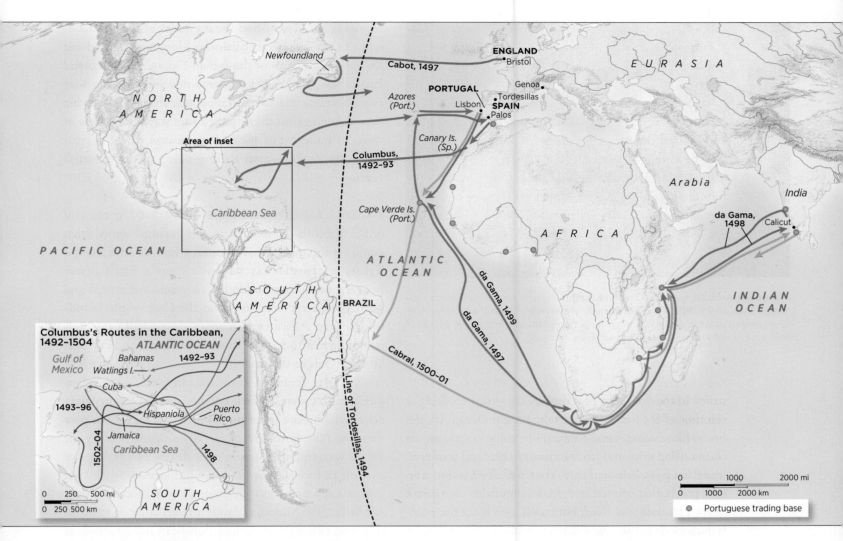

Navigation in the Atlantic and Indian Oceans, 1492–1500 This map shows the new routes pioneered by Columbus, Cabot, da Gama, and Cabral, which began the process of tying together the coasts of Europe, the Americas, Africa, and South Asia. The Line of Tordesillas, established in 1494, divided all "new" lands between Portugal and Spain.

km), equal to the circumference of the Earth. He had confirmed the understanding of the winds of the South Atlantic and had pioneered a practical, if slow, route between western Europe and South Asia. And he had brought back enough spices to inspire investors, especially the Portuguese Crown, to send him back again.

In subsequent voyages, da Gama helped set up a lasting Portuguese presence in India and East Africa. It consisted of small trading enclaves, always fortified, sometimes under the protection of local rulers and sometimes at odds with them. The rivalries among neighboring rulers on both the Indian and African coasts ensured that da Gama, and later Portuguese as well, could always find allies. Da Gama committed acts of great cruelty, especially against Muslims making the pilgrimage to

Mecca. He understood his mission to include piracy against Muslim shipping and did not mind making enemies. (He was not beloved by his own men either—at least, not after he ordered them to rinse their mouths with their own urine to combat scurvy, a gum disease resulting from vitamin shortage, one that often beset sailors on long voyages.)

Initially, the Portuguese commercial presence did not matter much to Indians and Africans, who continued their business much as before. But to Portugal, a poor kingdom of fewer than a million people, the occasional trading voyage to India meant infusions of riches, especially for the Crown. The trade to the Indian Ocean also affected Portuguese culture and self-image. Portuguese monumental architecture developed a distinctive style,

Manueline Architecture The Jerónimos Monastery in Lisbon, on which construction began in 1501, is a characteristic example of Manueline architecture. The braided pattern encircling the midsection of the column at the center of this double arch is intended to evoke ships' ropes.

called Manueline after Manuel I (r. 1495–1521), the king at the time of the first voyages to the Indian Ocean. It celebrates those voyages and nautical life, using artistic motifs from sailing ships and from Indian temples and mosques. The Portuguese national saga, known as *The Lusiads*, is an epic poem, first printed in 1572. It is modeled on ancient epics, especially the *Iliad*, but based loosely on the experiences of da Gama and other sea captains.

One of the voyages to India missed its target. In 1500, on his swing out into the Atlantic in search of the Southern Hemisphere's westerlies, Pedro Álvares Cabral and his fleet of 13 ships accidentally bumped into Brazil. Cabral claimed it for Portugal, despite the fact that people already lived there. After a brief look around, he continued on across the South Atlantic, around Africa, to India. Like da Gama, he ran into trouble in Calicut and engaged in a vengeful massacre before heading home in 1501.

Sailors such as Columbus, da Gama, and Cabral made the years 1492–1501 as pivotal as any decade in world history. Mariners from Atlantic Europe learned how to ride the winds back and forth between Europe and America, between Africa and America, and between Europe and South Asia. They found viable routes across the open ocean linking coastlines of continents formerly out of touch with one another.

The discovery of the oceans did not stop in the 1490s.

Mariners had now solved the mysteries of the wind system of the Atlantic, as others had long ago figured out the monsoon winds of the Indian Ocean. But the broad Pacific was another matter. Its winds and currents were even more essential to master, because the Pacific is so big that sailing against the wind is a sure way to die at sea of thirst or hunger. No one had any reason to try to cross the entire Pacific—until the beginning of the sixteenth century.

MAGELLAN CROSSES THE PACIFIC At the end of the fifteenth century, Spain and Portugal signed what could be the most presumptuous treaty of all time, the **Treaty of Tordesillas** (1494). It drew a line halfway between the American lands Columbus had visited and Portuguese territories known as the Cape Verde Islands off the West African coast. Spain claimed all new lands (meaning new to Spaniards) west of the line, and Portugal all new lands to the east.

With the Treaty of Tordesillas in place, once Portuguese vessels were trading on the Indian Ocean, Spain acquired a motive for trying to cross the Pacific: to gain direct access to precious spices. No one knew how big the Pacific was, and many thought the distance from America to the East Indies—the islands of Indonesia where by 1515 Portuguese merchants were buying spices directly—could not be far. The Molucca Islands, in particular, where nutmeg and cloves grew, excited European imaginations as if they were diamond mines. The Treaty of Tordesillas gave Spain claim to lands west of the Americas, which, if the claim extended far enough, would include the spice islands.

A Portuguese adventurer and dreamer named Fernão de Magalhães, or **Ferdinand Magellan**, tried and failed to convince authorities in Lisbon that it would be easier to reach the **Moluccas** by finding a route south of South America and then sailing west to Asia. He imagined that if there really was an ocean to the west of the American landmass, it was a small one. No one in Portugal would listen. So, like Columbus before him, he took his idea to the Spanish court. Eager to claim the Moluccas and their spices, the Spanish Crown encouraged bankers to invest in Magellan's plans.

So, in 1519, Magellan sailed out into the Atlantic with five ships, 250 men (about 1 percent the size of Zheng He's crew), and the most fanciful ideas of how to find the

CONSIDERING THE EVIDENCE

Portuguese Reasoning about Skin Color

As Portuguese ships explored the oceans, they also recorded observations about geography and people that contradicted traditions handed down from classical scholars. The Portuguese sea captain Duarte Pacheco Pereira (1460–1533) discussed some of these contradictions in his manuscript *Esmeraldo de Situ Orbis*. Pereira had voyaged nearly everywhere the Portuguese reached.

He defended Portuguese forts in India, governed Elmina off the coast of West Africa, and captured a French pirate in the Atlantic. He was also the first person to mention Brazil in a navigation book. In the following excerpt, he draws on personal observations to reconsider the classical Greek assumption that skin color was determined by latitude.

[D]uring the many years we have sailed and operated in this part of the Ethiopias of Guinea [i.e., West Africa], experience has taught us how to take the height of the sun and its declination in order to tell the degrees of latitude by which each place is separated from the Equator and one of the poles. And we have found that this promontory lies directly over the Equator, and have discovered that in this place the days and nights throughout the year are equal. . . .

Many of the ancients said that if two lands lie to the east and west of one another, both would have the same degree of sun and would be in all things alike. As to their equal share of the sun this is true, but such is the great variety employed by the majesty of nature in her work of creation and procreation that we find, from experience, that the inhabitants of this promontory of Lopo Gonçalves and of the rest of Guinea are very black, whereas the people who live beyond the Ocean Sea to the west (who have an equal amount of sun with the blacks of Guinea) are brown, and some almost white. These are the people who live in the land of Brazil. . . . If any want to claim that these are protected from the heat of the sun because there are many trees in that region, I would say that there are also many trees as great and as thick in this land of Guinea on the eastern side of the ocean. And if any should say that they

are black because they go around naked and that the others are white because they go clothed, I would say that both of them . . . go around just as they were born. So we can say that the sun does not affect one more than the others. Now it only remains to find out if they are both descended from Adam.

Source: "Duarte Pacheco Pereira Tries to Come to Terms with 'Difference,'" in Malyn Newitt, ed., *The Portuguese in West Africa, 1415–1670: A Documentary History* (Cambridge, 2010).

QUESTIONS FOR ANALYSIS

1. What evidence does Pereira rely on to challenge the conclusions of "the ancients"?
2. After dismissing possible explanations for the differences in skin color between people in Africa and those in Brazil, what direction does he suggest for future research?
3. Does this excerpt suggest that the Portuguese of Pereira's time considered people whose skin color differed from theirs to be inferior in any way?

---

spice islands. Magellan's crew mutinied twice before they even got to the Pacific. Then things went south in a hurry. Magellan thought he could cross from South America to the spice islands easily, but he had been on the ocean for 14 weeks, out of food and fresh water, before his men sighted Guam—they had sailed across an ocean with hundreds of inhabited islands and missed them all. One of the crew explained their suffering:

We only ate old biscuit reduced to powder, full of grubs and stinking from the dirt, which the rats had

made on it when eating the good biscuit and we drank water that was yellow and stinking. We also ate the ox hides . . . also the sawdust of wood, and rats which cost half-a-crown each, moreover enough of them were not to be got.

On Guam, Magellan guessed he was just off the shore of China. He was 2,500 miles (4,000 km) from it. He next blundered into the Philippines, where he got mixed up in a local war and died in battle.

Magellan's surviving crew kept going west, sailing

through the islands of Indonesia, where they picked up a cargo of spices, and into the Indian Ocean, around Africa, and home to Spain. The trip had taken three years, and only about 10 percent of the crew survived. They were the first humans to circumnavigate the globe—although they had intended only to find a route to the Moluccas and spices.

It took many decades before anything practical came of Magellan's quixotic quest. Magellan had showed how big the Pacific really was, and that it—like the Atlantic—had trade winds blowing east to west. Some 40 years later, another captain showed how one could cross the Pacific west to east, from Asia to America, by riding the westerlies, found at the same latitudes as those of the Atlantic. By 1570, Atlantic Europeans had deciphered the wind system of the Pacific too.

WEAVING A MARITIME WEB

Every coastline in the world was now more accessible than ever before to those who knew the secrets of the winds. While Magellan sailed the wide Pacific, other mariners in less dramatic fashion brought more of the world into a tighter web of connections. Portuguese captains began to visit China and Japan, following routes that Asian sailors had used for centuries. From the East African coast, Portuguese adventurers pushed inland, expanding a previously

small-scale trade in slaves and ivory in Mozambique and making contact with fellow Christians in Ethiopia. These Portuguese travels followed the beaten paths of Asian and African traders.

While European sailors were gathering up knowledge of routes and coasts in Africa and Asia, as far as Australia and Japan, others were adding further information from the Americas. Columbus had begun the process, but dozens of others, mainly Spaniards, followed. They sailed the coastlines, probed the river mouths, and, despite language barriers, absorbed what they could from indigenous American informants. By 1520, they had accumulated a good knowledge of the Caribbean and South American coasts. It took much longer for mariners to figure out the coasts of North America, but by 1620 sailors, mainly English and Dutch, had charted the eastern shoreline all the way north to the fogbound and iceberg-strewn coasts of Hudson Bay. To their dismay, they established that here too there was no good route to the riches of Asia. That dream died hard. As late as the 1630s, Jean Nicolet, a French fur trader, walked and canoed through Wisconsin wearing flowing Chinese robes in hopes of meeting someone who knew the way to China.

Gradually, mariners filled in the remaining blank spots on their maps. Dutch and English ship captains charted the coasts of New Zealand and Australia in the seventeenth century. But finding New Zealand's indigenous Maori

Namban Screen This six-fold Japanese screen from around 1600 likely illustrates the arrival of a Portuguese merchant ship in Japan. Portuguese sea captains began to visit Japan in 1543, bringing Christianity, guns, and Chinese silks and porcelain. They bought thousands of Japanese slaves to sell in Macao, Goa, or other Portuguese enclaves until the trade ended soon after 1600.

Magellan's Circumnavigation The Genoese cartographer Battista Agnese made this map of the world in 1540, showing the route Magellan took across the Pacific and Indian Oceans. The extent of Portuguese and other European navigation enabled Agnese to produce detailed renderings of the world's coastlines.

unwelcoming and the Aborigines poor, they ignored these lands for another 150 years. In the eighteenth century, European sailors refined their knowledge of Pacific shores and blundered into most of the inhabited Pacific islands, including the remotest outposts of Polynesia in Easter Island and Hawaii. They charted the American coastlines from Alaska to Chile. By 1780, every significant coast of every ocean had been mapped, and every important island located. For all intents and purposes, the discovery of the winds and the oceans was complete.

European mariners failed in their quest to find a direct route from Europe to Asian spices and failed to find powerful Christian allies against Islamic polities. But they succeeded at something they did not consciously attempt, which was to unite the world's coasts and harbors into a single network and to build geographical knowledge so that any competent navigator, with the right equipment and ship, could go anywhere on the sea with a reasonably good idea of where he was and what lay ahead. The confidence with which merchants had long sailed the South China Sea, the Arabian Gulf, or the Mediterranean, European merchants (and for a long while only European ones) now extended to the deep oceans.

BIOLOGICAL GLOBALIZATION, 1492–1800

One of the most important consequences of the discovery of the oceans and their prevailing winds, and the establishment of regular traffic linking the world's shores, was a surge in **biological globalization**. This process reshuffled the continents' flora and fauna, bringing both searing new epidemics and useful new food crops to many peoples. It changed the world's demographic balance and altered political and economic fortunes. By and large, it eased life for millions in Eurasia and Africa, and ended it prematurely for millions in the Americas and Oceania. It provides an excellent example of the fact that in world history major consequences often flow from events in ways that no one intended or foresaw.

As earlier chapters have noted, over the centuries people moved plants, animals, and microbes around the world. Sometimes they did it on purpose, like the first settlers of North America who brought dogs with them, or the Polynesians who ferried crops and animals to uninhabited Pacific islands. Sometimes they did it by accident, like

Waldseemüller World Map Created by German mapmaker Martin Waldseemüller in 1507, this map was the first to encompass the full American Hemisphere. It was also the first—on the lower portion of South America—to mention the name "America."

the anonymous people who brought the plague bacillus out of Central Asia in the fourteenth century. Biological exchange has long been an important part of history, with powerful effects on food supplies, disease burdens, and the availability of useful animals.

The pace of biological exchange sped up whenever web connections boosted trade and migration. So, for example, when the Roman and Han Empires were at their height in the first and second centuries CE, and trans-Eurasian trade and travel reached a temporary peak along the Silk Roads, so did biological exchange. China acquired camels, donkeys, and grapes. Mediterranean peoples added cherries, apricots, and walnuts to their gardens and diets. When commerce quickened in the Arabian Sea after 800 CE, the exchange of crops among India, East Africa, and the Mediterranean picked up speed.

Biologically, as in other respects, the Americas had remained a realm apart from these Old World web exchanges. Aside from the import of the dog (from Siberia about 15,000 years ago) and the export of sweet potato (to Polynesia about 1,000 years ago), the American hemisphere before 1492 exchanged nothing consequential with the wider world. American plants and animals included

many unknown elsewhere—tobacco, armadillos, and grizzly bears, for instance. Australia and New Zealand, even more isolated, each hosted flora and fauna—eucalyptus trees, kangaroos, and moas, for example—found nowhere else on Earth.

After the voyages of Columbus, mariners linked almost every nook and cranny of the humanly habitable Earth into a biologically interactive web. The world's oceans no longer served to isolate ecosystems from one another. Biological borders disappeared as plants, animals, and pathogens scattered wherever ecological conditions permitted. They went wherever people took them, and sometimes even further on their own.

Columbus inaugurated regular exchanges of plants, animals, and microbes across the Atlantic in 1492. On his second voyage, he deliberately brought a ship full of species new to the Americas and brought home to Spain some biological souvenirs. Over the next few centuries, his followers did the same in an ongoing process known to historians as the **Columbian Exchange**. The most conspicuous result was that indigenous Americans acquired hundreds of new plants and animals from Eurasia and Africa, as well as a dozen devastating diseases formerly unfamiliar to them. At first, between 1492 and 1700, the spread of diseases was the most important part of biological globalization, mainly because of their horrific impact on the peoples of the Americas.

DEADLY DISEASES

Upon arrival, transatlantic travelers coughed and sneezed billions of deadly microbes into the air that people in the Americas breathed. Among these microbes were the pathogens (viruses, mainly) that cause smallpox, measles, mumps, whooping cough, and influenza. All of these had become fairly widespread in the Old World web. From West Africa to East Asia, they were usually endemic, childhood diseases, sometimes now called crowd diseases (discussed in earlier chapters), that killed huge numbers of small children. But in the Old World web, most adults were survivors, and either resistant or fully immune to most or all of these infections. In addition to the crowd diseases, the Columbian Exchange brought some lethal vector-borne African diseases to the Americas. The two deadliest were yellow fever and falciparum malaria (the worst form of **malaria**), both spread by mosquitos.

In the Americas in 1492, none of the 40 to 70 million people had any prior experience with, and therefore no acquired immunity to, any of these diseases. Their immune systems did not instantly "recognize" and neutralize the exotic pathogens. This vulnerability was compounded by the weakening of their nutrition and health by Atlantic European colonization—which, as we'll see, included loss of farmlands, enslavement, and forced migration.

The cascade of unfamiliar pathogens in the midst of conquests brought suffering and death on the largest scale. Here is how one survivor in Mexico recalled it:

> The illness was so dreadful that no one could walk or move. The sick were so utterly helpless that they could only lie on their beds like corpses, unable to move their limbs or even their heads. A great many died from this plague, and many others died of hunger. They would not get up to search for food, and everyone else was too sick to care for them, so they starved to death in their beds.

In many communities, the social fabric dissolved under this onslaught. People lost all hope. Few wanted to bring children into a world such as theirs had become,

dominated by sickness and pain, and few were healthy enough to do so.

The scale of epidemics and death was gigantic. Between 1492 and 1650, populations in the Americas fell by 70 to 95 percent in one of the largest-scale demographic disasters in world history. The sharp decline in population in the Americas had many consequences that we will meet repeatedly in the chapters ahead.

The Americas had little in the way of lethal infectious disease that transferred to Africa and Eurasia. The first migrants to arrive in North America (23,000 to 15,000 years ago) had passed through northeastern Siberia and Alaska during an ice age. The brutal cold probably killed off some pathogens. And since they left Siberia when no animals but dogs had been domesticated, the human infections derived from herd animals (e.g., smallpox, measles, influenza) had not yet appeared. So the first Americans arrived relatively free from infection.

Once in the Americas, people did not domesticate any herd animals other than alpacas and llamas, which seem, by chance, not to have hosted pathogens that evolved into agents of human disease. If Eurasia and Africa acquired any new diseases from the Americas at all (syphilis is the leading candidate, but the evidence is far from conclusive), they had trivial consequences. So, as regards disease, the Columbian Exchange was a notably one-sided affair.

The one-sidedness of the health consequences of the Columbian Exchange led Europeans who witnessed this devastation to see divine purpose at work. Francisco de

Epidemics in the Americas This illustration of Aztecs suffering and dying from the smallpox brought by Spanish colonists appears in the *Florentine Codex*, a sixteenth-century treatise written by a Spanish missionary and his Nahua informants about the Spanish conquest of Mexico in 1519–1521.

Aguilar, who was present when Spaniards and their indigenous allies conquered the Aztec capital of Tenochtitlán in 1521, wrote: "When the Christians were exhausted from war, God saw fit to send the Indians smallpox, and there was a great pestilence in the city." More than a century later in New England, John Winthrop, the first governor of the Massachusetts Bay Colony, saw the disaster as divine endorsement of the seizure of land: "For the natives, they are neere all dead of small Poxe, so as the Lord hathe cleared our title to what we possess."

USEFUL ANIMALS

The Columbian Exchange was almost as one-sided with respect to domesticated animals. People transported turkeys and guinea pigs from the Americas to other continents, but nowhere did they become important. Alpacas and llamas never prospered outside their native Andes, although scattered populations do exist elsewhere. Indigenous Americans had little in the way of domesticated animals, and those they had did not travel well.

In contrast, Eurasian and African animal species flourished when transported to the Americas. Cattle, goats, sheep, pigs, and horses were the most important animal immigrants. They all found empty niche space in the Americas, especially cattle and horses on the vast grasslands of both North and South America. The new animals provided new sources of hides, wool, and animal protein. Horses and oxen made plowing feasible in the Americas for the first time, allowed transportation with wheeled vehicles, and, together with donkeys and mules, provided a greater variety of pack animals. Animal-powered transport extended the potential of commerce and economic specialization, which over centuries raised overall production levels considerably.

In addition to economic growth, the new animals brought unwelcome frictions to the Americas. They munched and trampled crops, provoking quarrels between herders and farmers of the sort familiar in Africa and Eurasia but almost unknown in the Americas before 1492. In this respect, the Columbian Exchange helped make the Americas a bit more like the rest of the world, where such quarrels had long been routine.

In North America, the introduction of horses upset the political order. The indigenous peoples of the prairies, from Texas to Manitoba, acquired horses from newly Spanish Mexico in the seventeenth century, and some of them quickly mastered riding and horse breeding. On horseback, they became far more adept as bison hunters, solving any subsistence problems as long as the bison lasted. Moreover, those with horses easily inflicted military defeats on those without. Peoples such as the Sioux and Comanche eventually built considerable empires on the basis of mounted warfare, as Mongol and Malian horsemen had recently done in Asia and Africa. In this respect too, the Americas became less distinctive, more like the rest of the world, thanks to the Columbian Exchange and biological globalization.

KEY CROPS

The Columbian Exchange was more evenhanded when it came to crops. The Eurasian staples of wheat, rye, barley, and rice flourished in the Americas. Some of the new crops could survive in cold and dry landscapes where the indigenous crops fared poorly: wheat grows better than maize in North Dakota and Saskatchewan. Others, such as rice, transplanted from both Asia and Africa, required heavy labor in order to produce bumper crops. Rice became a plantation crop in the Americas, worked mainly by enslaved Africans. Aside from grains, the Americas also acquired citrus fruits, grapes, and figs from Eurasia, and millets, sorghums, yams, bananas, okra, and watermelon from Africa. So the new crops extended the possibilities of American agriculture somewhat and allowed a more varied diet. But in many places they brought only a small improvement in nutrition, because people in the Americas already had maize or potatoes (or both) and plenty of fruits and vegetables.

New drug crops changed the Americas at least as profoundly as the new food crops. Sugar, both a mild drug and a food, is originally from New Guinea. It was as a commercial crop in South Asia, China, and the Mediterranean. Iberians brought it to Brazil and the Caribbean in the sixteenth and seventeenth centuries where, as we shall see, it became the mainstay of a plantation economy based on African slave labor. Coffee, from Ethiopia and Arabia, also became a plantation crop in the eighteenth century. We will see the full importance of these crops in a later chapter when we consider the plantation system in the Americas.

The Americas' contributions to global cuisine included the staples maize, potatoes, sweet potatoes, and cassava, together with tomatoes, cacao, peanuts, pumpkins, squashes, pineapples, and a handful of other food crops. Some of these crops had revolutionary consequences in sizeable regions of Africa and Eurasia. Potatoes, for example, which nicely suited soil and climate conditions from Ireland to Russia, led to a spurt of population growth in northern Europe after 1730.

MAIZE This staple had a broader impact than potatoes. It did well in conditions as varied as those of southern Europe, southern and central China, and much of Africa. **Maize** allowed new lands to be brought under cultivation, because it prospered where grains and tubers would not. It soon undergirded population growth and famine resistance in China and southern Europe. But nowhere was it more influential than in Africa, where today it remains the single most important food crop. In the two centuries after 1550, maize became a staple in Atlantic Africa, from Angola to Senegambia. Different maize varieties suited the several different rainfall regimes in Africa and improved African peoples' chances of surviving drought.

While maize helped feed generations of Africans, it had bleaker consequences too. Maize stores much better than millets, sorghums, or tubers, the traditional crops in most of Africa. It thus allowed chiefs and kings to maximize their power by centralizing the storage and distribution of food. In the West African forest zone, south of the Sahel, maize encouraged the formation of larger states than ever before. The Asante kingdom, for example, embarked on a program of military expansion after the 1670s, spearheaded by maize-eating armies that could carry their food with them on distant campaigns. Maize also served well as a portable food for merchant caravans, which contributed to commercialization in Atlantic Africa, including an expansion of existing slave trades. Slave traders could operate over longer distances if they, and their human property, had an easily portable food supply that stored well. Maize in Africa increased the practicality of the slave trade. As we shall see, it helped make slaving an intercontinental business, linking Europe, Africa, and the Americas.

Maize in Africa This small brass statue, a porcupine making off with a maize cob, was used by the Akan people (in today's country of Ghana) as a counterweight when weighing gold dust. It dates from the seventeenth or eighteenth century, by which time maize was well established in West Africa.

Cassava in Africa This illustration of the cassava plant appears in a French book about Caribbean plants from 1688. Originating in the Americas, cassava became a crucial crop in West Africa and Angola, where it was well suited to the climate, soils, and the needs of farming communities.

CASSAVA Also known as manioc, **cassava** was the Americas' other great contribution to African agriculture. Native to Brazil, cassava is admirably suited to drought and poor soils, and resistant to many insect crop pests. It too did well in many parts of Africa, and like maize provided a portable, storable food that underlaid state formation and expansion in West Africa and Angola. Cassava, like potatoes, need not be harvested at a particular season but may be left in the ground for weeks or more. So it is an ideal crop for people who might need to run away for their own safety and abandon their fields—for example, people routinely subject to slave raiding. In this respect, it had the opposite effect of maize: it helped peasantries to flee and survive slave raids, while maize helped slavers to conduct raids and wars.

THE HUMAN WEB

The Columbian Exchange

1492-1800

KEY

⬅ Organisms spreading from the Old World to the Americas

➡ Organisms spreading from the Americas to the Old World

Organisms

measles Pathogen

horses Livestock

maize Food and fiber crop

sugar Drug crop

Population decline due to introduction of pathogens

▢ 90% or more

▢ Less than 90%

Areas of greatest impact of livestock and crops

▢ Horses

▢ Food and fiber crops

▢ Drug crops

NORTH AMERICA

horses

Rocky Mts.

Colorado R.

Mississippi R.

Appalachian Mts.

grains

cotton

coffee
sugar

Mexico

sugar

EUROPE

potatoes

Danube R.

maize

maize

influenza, measles, mumps, smallpox, whooping cough
cattle, goats, horses, pigs, sheep
barley, oats, rye, wheat,
citrus, cotton, figs, grapes
sugar

syphilis?
cassava, maize, potatoes, avocadoes, cacao, chili peppers,
peanuts, pineapples, pumpkins, squashes, sweet potatoes, tomatoes
tobacco

Senegambia

horses

malaria, yellow fever
rice, millets, sorghums, bananas,
cotton, okra, watermelon, yams
coffee

cassava
maize

Nile R.

Arabia

Niger R.

AFRICA

Ethiopia

Congo R.

PACIFIC OCEAN

Andes Mts.

Amazon R.

sugar

coffee
sugar

SOUTH AMERICA

Brazil

sugar

ATLANTIC OCEAN

cassava
maize

Angola

Zambezi R.

▼ Argentina, wagon caravan and herd of cattle crossing a swamp, 1818.

Andes Mts.

Paraná R.

coffee
sugar

horses

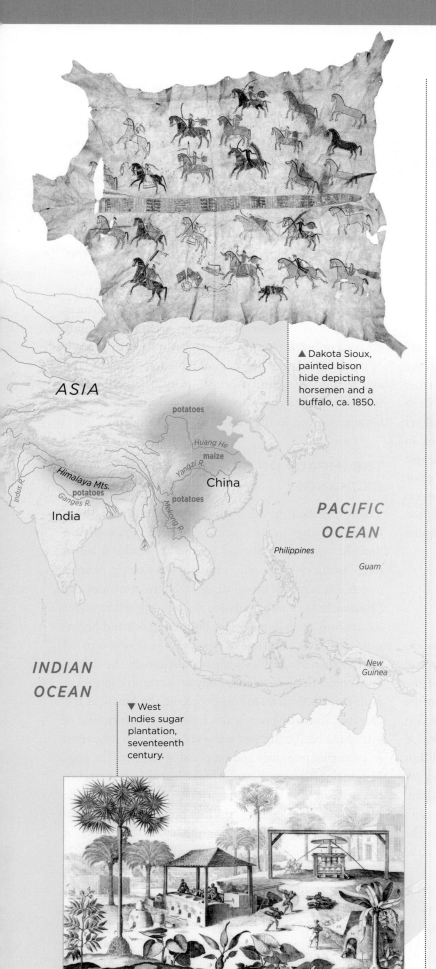

▲ Dakota Sioux, painted bison hide depicting horsemen and a buffalo, ca. 1850.

ASIA

potatoes

Huang He

maize

Yangzi R.

China

Himalaya Mts.

potatoes

Ganges R.

Indus R.

potatoes

Mekong R.

India

PACIFIC OCEAN

Philippines

Guam

INDIAN OCEAN

New Guinea

▼ West Indies sugar plantation, seventeenth century.

THERE WAS THEN NO SICKNESS; THEY HAD NO ACHING BONES; THEY HAD THEN NO HIGH FEVER; THEY HAD THEN NO SMALLPOX; AT THAT TIME THE COURSE OF HUMANITY WAS ORDERLY. THE FOREIGNERS MADE IT OTHERWISE WHEN THEY ARRIVED HERE.

"

THE BOOK OF CHILAM BALAM OF CHUMAYEL, CA. 1530–1550

BETWEEN 1492 AND 1800, mariners tied together the shores of the Atlantic into an especially vibrant part of the emerging Global web. Their voyages created an Atlantic world, similar in many respects to the Indian Ocean world, another lively part of a larger web, built long before. But in one respect—the Columbian Exchange—the Atlantic world had no true parallels in world history.

The Columbian Exchange of plants, animals, and lethal pathogens was the biggest pulse of biological exchange in world history. Anytime that webs extended across vast distances, people—intentionally and accidentally—carried some species to new homes. When the Silk Roads opened, for example, China acquired grapes, sorghum, donkeys, and camels from Southwest Asia. But no other such episode approaches the Columbian Exchange, which suddenly united biological communities that had been separate for 50 million years.

The impacts of the Columbian Exchange included drastic changes in population, agriculture, and the economies of the Americas, Africa, and Europe. For some people, such as indigenous Americans, the Columbian Exchange brought disaster in the form of new diseases. For others, such as southern Europeans or southern Africans, it brought a new, high-energy food crop: maize. The introduction of maize and cassava to African agriculture and diet was so important that for Atlantic Africa, at least, it makes sense to think in terms of pre-Columbian and post-Columbian phases, just as scholars routinely do for the Americas.

Questions for Analysis

Based on this feature and your chapter reading, consider the following questions:

1. Why did some peoples suffer and some peoples benefit from the Columbian Exchange?

2. What regions within the Atlantic world felt the strongest impacts of the Columbian Exchange?

The impact of American food crops on Africa was so great that it makes sense to think of African history, especially Atlantic African history, as divided into pre-Columbian and post-Columbian phases—as is normally done for the Americas. Maize, cassava, and a cornucopia of other crops from the Americas, including peanuts, pineapple, chili peppers, sweet potato, avocado, cacao, and a dozen others, gradually re-fashioned African cuisine and agriculture. This was the second time in African history that imported crops made a big difference—recall the impact of bananas, acquired from Southeast Asia, many centuries before.

African farmers took to the new American crops eagerly, seeing them as either useful additions or even replacements for their old ones. The greater variety of food crops provided a form of insurance against crop failure due to insect pests or bad weather. Maize had the further attraction that birds usually find it too much trouble to poke through the husks to get at the grain. Birds don't bother with cassava either. Ripe millet and sorghum, in contrast, provide tempting targets for birds, and people must defend these crops day and night if they wish to enjoy a harvest. The American crops brought a slow expansion of farming, state making, and perhaps even population growth in Africa after 1650—despite the demographic effects of the transatlantic slave trade.

BIOLOGICAL GLOBALIZATION IN THE PACIFIC

The Columbian Exchange was the largest-scale, fastest, and most important set of intercontinental biological transfers in world history. But it was only part of the surge in biological globalization that followed upon the navigational exploits of Columbus's generation. A modest transpacific exchange resulted from traffic that followed Magellan's voyages, at first affecting chiefly the Philippines. That exchange intensified in the wake of later sea captains' travels throughout the world's largest ocean. The Pacific islands themselves, rather than the ocean's rim, felt the greatest effects, and as in the Americas the most striking result was sharp depopulation in the wake of repeated epidemics.

Guam, for example, in the seventeenth century became a Spanish outpost on the route between the Philippines and the Americas. Its indigenous population, the Chamorro, whose ancestors had arrived some 3,000 years

before, fell by about 90 percent within a century—mainly from the impact of smallpox, measles, tuberculosis, and other new diseases, although violence and loss of lands raised the Chamorros' vulnerability to infections. Guam also acquired many new plants and animals, such as cattle, hogs, chickens, rice, maize, citrus trees, and a Mexican shrub tree called tangantangan. The latter grew widely on Guam, especially in lands no longer farmed because of the population disaster.

In the eighteenth and nineteenth centuries, other Pacific islands and Australia experienced similar biological disruptions when put into sustained contact with the wider world. In every case, the demographic consequences overshadowed all others. Population declines of roughly 90 percent befell many archipelagoes, primarily a result of newly introduced diseases combined with loss of land and resources. A similar grim history befell aboriginal Australians after 1788 when contact with the wider world became routine, as the next chapter will explain.

THE IMPACT OF BIOLOGICAL EXCHANGE

Taken together, the whirlwind of intercontinental biological exchange in the centuries between 1492 and 1800 brought astounding changes around the world. It led to long-lasting demographic catastrophes among peoples unfamiliar with the crowd diseases. In the Americas and Oceania, indigenous population size typically fell for about six or seven generations before bottoming out and beginning to recover. This rate of recovery was slow compared to the experience of Eurasian populations in the face of most epidemics. That is testimony to the terrible impact of multiple infections assaulting peoples in the Americas and Oceania. In many cases, it also reflects the significance of loss of the best lands, enslavement, and forced migration in escalating mortality and suppressing fertility. The population disasters were a part of biological globalization, but they were not just biological processes: they arose from the interaction of biological and social processes. They represent a penalty of isolation from the bigger webs of world history, a theme we have encountered before.

The surge in biological exchange eventually improved the quantity and reliability of food supplies almost everywhere. Farmers had more crops to choose from and so more regularly raised those best suited to their soils and climate. This process slowly reduced the frequency of starvation and the toll of epidemics (because well-fed bodies survive most diseases better than malnourished bodies). The world's population almost doubled between 1500 and 1800, from about 500 million to about 950 million, and a big reason was improved nutrition thanks to food-crop globalization.

One agreeable way of thinking about the whole (admittedly often grim) subject of biological globalization in the wake of Columbus is to contemplate food. Can you imagine Italian food without tomatoes? Or Polish cuisine without potatoes? What would the South African diet be without mealie maize, or West Africa's without peanuts? Cuba's without rice, or Argentina's without beef? New Zealand's or southern China's without sweet potatoes? What would Korean kimchi taste like without chili peppers? If we are what we eat, then the Columbian Exchange and biological globalization not only shaped empires and demography but also helped to make us what we are.

THE BEGINNINGS OF A GLOBAL WEB

The oceanic voyaging of the fifteenth and sixteenth centuries united continents into a single Global web for the first time in human history. The web-making process—at work from the very earliest human settlements onward—had developed an extended, multilayered fabric of connections across Eurasia and North Africa. Significant webs had developed also in the Americas, and smaller, local ones elsewhere. But for thousands of years before 1492, the Americas had largely stood apart from Africa and Eurasia, notwithstanding the brief Viking and Polynesian visits. Now the history of the Americas unfolded in continuing connection with the Old World web. Similarly, after the secrets of oceanic navigation spread and mariners sailed regularly among all the world's inhabited shores, the islands of the Pacific, the coastlands of South Africa, and a few other spots around the world became—like the Americas—linked as never before to the new Global web now in formation.

The oceanic voyaging also tightened linkages within the Old World web. In some cases, the tighter links proved temporary, as with Zheng He's voyages to India and East Africa between 1405 and 1433. But in others they endured much longer, as with Portuguese ties to African

coasts, India, and the spice islands of Southeast Asia. So the three centuries after the 1490s saw a sudden spurt in web building, one that transformed human history and inaugurated a global age in which we still live.

The spinning of the first truly Global web had many consequences. The most enduring and important of these was the biological globalization that reshuffled the distribution of economically significant plants and animals around the world and brought devastating infections to the Americas and Oceania. Another important consequence flowed from the fact that it was mainly Atlantic Europeans—not Chinese, Africans, Polynesians, or anyone else—who first fully deciphered the oceanic winds and currents. As a result, they were the first to sail the seven seas and learn of new long-distance trade possibilities. They also found new opportunities to conquer peoples less militarily formidable than themselves. The role of Europeans, especially seafaring Atlantic Europeans, in influencing world history rose to new levels. Over the prior millennia, only rarely could such a small minority of humankind exercise such outsized influence upon world history as Atlantic Europeans would wield in the three or four centuries after 1492.

The penalties of isolation for societies with few or no connections to the Old World web were now felt as never before. These societies typically hosted a narrower range of infectious diseases than did peoples in the web that enveloped Eurasia and North Africa. More specifically, they had no prior exposure to several highly transmissible and dangerous pathogens, such as measles, influenza, and smallpox, and so, unlike populations in the Old World web, had not converted these into endemic infections. That left them vulnerable to shattering epidemics when European ships arrived with these and other unfamiliar pathogens. In addition, isolated peoples possessed less formidable weaponry than existed in China, India, or Europe, using less metal, no firearms, and no horses. These societies had not previously needed institutions and technologies that equipped them to deal with the challenges posed by seafaring, disease-bearing, horse-riding, well-armed strangers.

The weaving of the first truly Global web proved transformational in other respects too. It continued the long-standing process by which cultural diversity narrowed. The major religions, especially Christianity and Islam, spread to new ground. They became slightly more diverse themselves as a result, because in every case they adopted some local features, but they reduced the overall diversity of religion with their conversions in Asia, Africa, the Americas, and Oceania. The spread of Arabic, Spanish, and English also, on balance, reduced the variety of languages spoken around the world, even if the English spoken in Australia or Barbados was not the same as that spoken in London. Many languages would gradually go extinct in the centuries after oceanic voyaging linked up the world. The next few chapters will detail the formation of the Global web and how it affected political, economic, and cultural life.

CONCLUSION

The world in 1400 included one big web and several smaller ones. The Old World web was the big one, containing the majority of humankind and stretching across Eurasia and North Africa from Senegal to Japan. A smaller one existed in the Americas, and local ones existed in several places around the world. In the course of the fifteenth century, however, this longstanding pattern underwent a major reorganization.

Beginning early in the fifteenth century, Chinese and Atlantic European mariners undertook oceanic voyages that brought the world together as never before. The most decisive changes came with the European, mainly Iberian, voyaging. From 1460 onward, sailors brought an increasing number of African maritime ports (e.g., Elmina) into direct contact with communities of the Old World web. From 1492 onward, they brought the Americas and the Old World web together on a sustained basis. From the early sixteenth century onward, they brought an increasing number of Pacific islands into enduring touch with the Old World web. So those mariners, in seeking fortune and glory for themselves and their monarchs, unintentionally created the first truly Global web.

Biological globalization in some respects was the deepest of all the Global web's consequences, affecting as it did the lives and deaths of hundreds of millions of people during the sixteenth and seventeenth centuries. Exchanges of food crops resulted in changes to agriculture and diets and, in more cases than not, improvements in nutrition. People in Africa and Eurasia acquired maize, cassava, and potatoes from the Americas, while those in the Americas acquired wheat, rye, barley, and new varieties of rice. Exchanges of domesticated animals brought horses, cattle, pigs, sheep, and goats (to name only the most significant) to the Americas. These plant and animal exchanges were important in the sixteenth century and remain so today.

The other major component of biological globalization was the exchange of disease pathogens. It was extremely one-sided—and extremely costly to peoples of the Americas and Oceania. Its toll varied from case to case, but generally was on the order of one-half to nine-tenths of each populations affected. The population catastrophe, made more costly by violence, loss of lands, and other stresses, generally lasted for the first 150 years after sustained contact with peoples of the Old World web.

The oceanic voyaging of the fifteenth through the seventeenth centuries did not start biological globalization, which can be traced back many thousands of years. But it launched the biggest and most consequential spurt of it in world history.

CHAPTER REVIEW

KEY TERMS

Zheng He (p. 507)

Ming voyages (p. 508)

Reconquista (p. 510)

Guanches (p. 510)

Christopher Columbus (p. 512)

Vasco da Gama (p. 514)

Calicut (p. 514)

Treaty of Tordesillas (p. 516)

Ferdinand Magellan (p. 516)

Moluccas (p. 516)

biological globalization (p. 519)

Columbian Exchange (p. 520)

malaria (p. 521)

maize (p. 523)

cassava (p. 523)

Go to INQUIZITIVE to see what you've learned—and learn what you've missed—with personalized feedback along the way.

REVIEW QUESTIONS

1. What were the main trading routes in Eurasia and North Africa in the fifteenth century?

2. What were the three smaller trade networks that existed apart from the main Eurasian and North African trading routes?

3. In what two ways were the Ming voyages exceptional?

4. Identify the three main reasons European explorers sailed west into the Atlantic Ocean during this period.

5. Why was knowledge of the Atlantic Ocean's wind patterns essential for sailors?

6. What was Columbus looking for when he journeyed across the Atlantic?

7. How did the Treaty of Tordesillas spur Spanish exploration of the Pacific Ocean?

8. Why was the transfer of malaria and yellow fever to the Americas so deadly?

9. How did North American prairie peoples, such as the Sioux and the Comanche, use horses to build empires?

10. Which crops that were indigenous to the Old World web became significant plantation crops in the Americas?

11. How did maize support the growth of larger states in West Africa?

12. In what two ways did the global exchange of crops improve food supply around the world?

13. Explain the major consequences of biological globalization in the sixteenth and seventeenth centuries.

FURTHER READING

Judith A. CARNEY, *Black Rice: The African Origins of Rice Cultivation in the Americas* (2002). A detailed study of how African rice got to the Americas.

Alfred W. CROSBY Jr., *The Columbian Exchange: Biological and Cultural Consequences of 1492* (1972). A classic analysis that essentially invented the idea of the Columbian Exchange of plants and animals.

Edward L. DREYER, *Zheng He: China and the Oceans in the Early Ming Dynasty, 1405-1433* (2007). The best general treatment of the Ming voyages.

Felipe FERNÁNDEZ-ARMESTO, *Pathfinders: A Global History of Exploration* (2006). A general (and well-written) history of exploration, with several chapters on European maritime efforts from 1400 through 1800.

Charles C. MANN, *1493: Uncovering the New World Columbus Created* (2012). An accessible account of the global consequences of forging the first Global web.

Linda A. NEWSOM, *Conquest and Pestilence in the Early Spanish Philippines* (2009). A careful analysis of how some of this chapter's themes worked out in one archipelago.

Biological Globalization: Movement, Disease, and Impacts

ONE OUTCOME OF THE DISCOVERY of the oceans and new connections among the continents was biological globalization. As part of this process, pathogens and disease vectors traveled together with people and goods wherever they went. And as a result, epidemics of old and new diseases caused catastrophic human losses and changed entire cultures, societies, and histories.

Different diseases have different symptoms and effects, and therefore they were perceived differently by the various societies that experienced them. The image and documents that follow introduce three communicable diseases: plague, smallpox, and syphilis. Drawn from accounts that were left to us from survivors of the diseases and observers of their effects, these sources offer a glimpse into people's experiences, fears, and imaginations. They also inform us about how these diseases intersected with the social, economic, and political aspects of the societies where their outbreaks occurred.

SOURCE 15.1

The Plague Visits Avignon, 1347

When people speak about catastrophic health events throughout history, plague often comes to mind first. The suffering that it caused, and the human toll that it claimed over centuries, terrified people worldwide. Plague is an infectious disease caused by the bacterium *Yersinia pestis*. Once it invades the lymph system, it triggers the appearance of buboes, or swellings, in the infected person's armpit, neck, or groin, lending the disease its name—bubonic plague. The carrier of *Y. pestis* is a flea hosted by rodents such as marmots and rats. As trade expanded over land and sea, fleas and rats traveled with people on ships or in caravans, usually hidden among their belongings.

Disease historians identify three plague pandemics in world history: the Justinianic Plague (541–755), the Black Death (1330–1743), and the Third Plague (1894–1910). The following anonymous letter, sent from the Pope's court in Avignon (southern France), describes the Black Death. (The papacy was headquartered in Avignon rather than Rome from 1309 to 1376.)

A huge mortality and pestilence started in September 1347, as I have seen in a copy of a letter written by a canon and cantor of St Donatian, who was at the time in the company of a cardinal, his master, at the Roman Curia and sent the letter to his colleagues in Bruges, to give them the news by way of warning. It recounts how terrible events and unheard of calamities had afflicted the whole of a province in eastern India for three days. On the first day it rained frogs, snakes, lizards, scorpions and many other similar poisonous animals. On the second day thunder was heard, and thunderbolts and lightning flashes mixed with hailstones of incredible size fell to earth, killing almost all the people, from the greatest to the least. On the third day fire, accompanied by stinking smoke, descended from heaven and consumed all the remaining men and animals, and burnt all the cities and settlements in the region.

The entire province was infected by these calamities, and it is surmised that the whole coast and all the neighbouring countries caught the infection from it, by means of the stinking breath of the wind which blew southwards from the region affected by plague; and always, day by day, more people died. Now, by God's will, it has reached our coasts and, as some people believe, in this way. On 31 December 1347 three galleys loaded with spices and other goods put into the port of Genoa after being storm-driven from the East. They were horribly infected and, when the Genoese realised this, and that other men were dying suddenly without remedy, the ships were driven from the port with burning arrows and other engines of war. For there was no one who had dared to touch them or do business with them who did not immediately die....

To be brief, at least half the people in Avignon died; for there are now within the walls of the city more than 7000 houses where no one lives because everyone in them has died, and in the suburbs one might imagine that there is not one survivor. Therefore the pope bought a field near Notre-Dame des Miracles and had it consecrated as a cemetery. By 14 March 11,000 bodies had been buried there, and that is in addition to those buried in the churchyards of the Hôpital de Saint-Antoine and the religious orders and in the many other churchyards in Avignon.

Source: *The Black Death*, trans. Rosemary Horrox (New York: Manchester University Press, 1994).

- Did the author actually see all the events he describes in this account? What can we infer from the images he reports?
- Was the disease local? What does this account tell us about people's understanding of the progression of a communicable disease like plague?

SOURCE 15.2

◀ Saint Rocco, Patron Saint of the Sick

Have you heard of Saint Rocco, patron saint of the sick? He is depicted in this painting revealing a bubo on his inner thigh—one of the distinct symptoms of bubonic plague. The cult of Saint Rocco dates to the time of the Black Death in Italy in the fourteenth century. People prayed to saints like Rocco to intercede with God on behalf of the sick.

Source: *The Black Death*, trans. Rosemary Horrox (New York: Manchester University Press, 1994).

- Describe the components of the painting. What does the painting display, and what does it seem to represent?
- What does this painting tell us about the ways in which people understood catastrophes like the ones caused by plague?

SOURCE 15.3

An Indigenous View of Smallpox in Mexico, 1500s

Smallpox (eradicated globally as of 1980) was a dreadful disease caused by the virus *Variola*. Breath-borne, highly contagious, and virulent, it spread fastest where people were crowded together. Those who survived it developed lifelong immunity. In big cities and other large, interactive populations, if the virus was present smallpox became a childhood disease because almost all adults were survivors and therefore immune. But when smallpox reached communities that hadn't previously hosted the disease, it was deadly among adults and children alike.

Smallpox came to Mexico with Cortés's expedition of 1519. The document below, the work of an indigenous informant, represents native Mexicas' experience with the disease. This narrative is drawn from Chapter 29 of the *Florentine Codex*, which was compiled by the Spanish friar Bernardino de Sahagún between 1558 and 1575 from interviews conducted in the Nahuatl language with elders in Central Mexico.

Here it is told how, at the time the Spaniards left Mexico, there came an illness of pustules of which many Mexicas died; it was called "the great rash" [smallpox].

[Even] before the Spaniards appeared to us, an illness broke out, a sickness of pustules. It began in Tepeilhuitl, and it spread over the people as a great destruction. Large bumps spread on people; some were entirely covered—on the face, the head, the chest, etc. [The disease] brought great desolation; a great many [people] died from it.

People with the illness could not walk, they could only lay in their dwellings and sleeping places. They could not move; they could not stir; they could not change position, nor lie on one side, nor face down, nor on their backs. And when they stirred, they screamed. The pustules that covered people caused great desolation; a great many people died of them, and many just died of hunger; [for] no one took care of others any longer.

On some people, the pustules were widely separated, and they did not suffer greatly, nor did many of them die of it. But many people's faces were marred by it; their faces or noses were pitted. Some lost their eyes; some were blinded.

At this time, the pestilence lasted sixty days, sixty fateful days. It began in Cuatlan, where it became so well established that nothing could stop it, and it spread in the direction of Chalco. And many were disabled or paralyzed by it, but they were not disabled forever. It broke out in Teotleco, and it abated in Panquetzaliztli. The Mexicas were greatly weakened by it.

And after this, the Spaniards came; they marched from Tezcoco. They appeared from the direction of Quauhtitlan and stopped at Tlacopan. There, they gave out assignments and divided themselves. Pedro de Alvarado was made responsible for the road coming to Tlatelolco, and the Marquis [Cortés] went to Coyoacan. Here, he took charge of the Acachinanco [road], which led to Tenochtitlan. The Marquis considered that those of Tenochtitlan were valiant warriors.

And at Nextlatilco, or Iliacac, the war first began. The [Spaniards] quickly reached Nonoalco, with the [Mexica] warriors pursuing them. None of the Mexicas died; then the Spaniards turned back. The warriors fought in boats; the warboatmen threw darts at [the Spaniards]. Then [the Mexicas] entered [Nonoalco]. Subsequently, the Marquis sent [his soldiers] toward Tenochtitlan, following the Acachinanco [road]. Many times they fought, and the Mexicas confronted him.

Source: Bernardino de Sahagún, *Historia General de las Cosas de Nueva España*, trans. Nancy Fitch (American Historical Association).

- What does the narrator consider important about smallpox?
- How could the Mexicas be "greatly weakened" by smallpox and only "after this the Spaniards came" to Tenochtitlán?

Source: Cotton Mather, *Magnalia Christi Americana: Or, the Ecclesiastical History of New-England From Its First Planting in the Year of 1620, Unto the Year of Our Lord, 1698* (Hartford: Silas Andrus, 1820).

- How does the author interpret the affliction of the Native Americans in particular? Do a little research on Cotton Mather: In what way does his interpretation here reflect his background?
- How differently did smallpox affect the indigenous population as compared to the English Puritans?

SOURCE 15.4

Smallpox and the Colonization of New England, 1630

As noted above, smallpox was deadly among adults and children alike in communities that hadn't previously hosted the disease. The document that follows reflects such a case—the outbreak of smallpox in New England in 1630, ten years after the first English settlement there. It gives us an idea about the disease's impact on the indigenous communities in New England, mostly Wampanoag, and about the English settlers' understanding of its effects. It is drawn from the *Ecclesiastical History of New-England*, published in 1702 by Puritan clergyman Cotton Mather.

Being happily arrived at New-England, our new planters found the difficulties of a rough and hard wilderness presently assaulting them: of which the worst was the sickliness which many of them had contracted by their other difficulties....

But there were two terrible distresses more, besides that of sickness, whereto this people were exposed in the beginning of their settlement: though a most seasonable and almost unexpected mercy from Heaven still rescued them out of those distresses. One thing that sometimes extremely exercised [exerted] them, was a scarcity of provisions; in which 'twas wonderful to see their dependence upon God, and God's mindfulness of them....

Another thing that gave them no little exercise [exhausted or troubled them], was the fear of the Indians, by whom they were sometimes alarmed. But this fear was wonderfully prevented, not only by intestine [internal] wars happening then to fall out among those barbarians, but chiefly by the small-pox, which proved a great plague unto them, and particularly to one of the Princes in the Massachusetts-Bay, who yet seemed hopefully to be Christianized before he died. This distemper getting in, I know not how, among them, swept them away with a most prodigious desolation, insomuch that although the English gave them all the assistances of humanity in their calamities, yet there was, it may be, not one in ten among them left alive; of those few that lived, many also fled from the infection, leaving the country a mere Golgotha [from the Bible: a place of suffering and death] of unburied carcasses; and as for the rest, the English treated them with all the civility imaginable; among the instances of which civility, let this be reckoned for one, that notwithstanding the patent [right granted by the English king] which they had for the country, they fairly purchased of the natives the several tracts of land which they afterwards possessed.

SOURCE 15.5

Poem on Syphilis, or "the French Disease," 1530

Syphilis, a sexually transmitted disease caused by the bacterium *Treponema pallidum*, is of unknown origin. The main theories are known as the pre-Columbian and the Columbian hypotheses. The pre-Columbian hypothesis argues that syphilis was widespread in both hemispheres before Columbus's voyages, but perhaps with different symptoms. The Columbian hypothesis holds that sailors in Columbus's fleet brought the affliction to Spain when returning from the Caribbean in 1493. Currently, scholars are examining fossil and paleopathological evidence (the latter involves the study of past disease from human remains) to evaluate both hypotheses. The documents that follow recount the disease's origin and impact as interpreted by writers in Italy and Persia.

The poem below is by Girolamo Fracastoro (1478–1553), a poet, scholar, and physician in Verona, Italy. His work *Syphilis sive Morbus Gallicus* (1530) explains why Fracastoro called the disease *morbus Gallicus*, or "the French Disease." Syphilis appeared in Italy in the mid-1490s at the same time as a French invasion of the peninsula.

> Through what adventures this unknown disease
> So lately did astonisht Europe seize,
> Through Asian coasts and Libyan cities ran,
> And from what seeds the malady began,
> Our song shall tell: to Naples first it came 5
> From France, and justly took from France his name,
> Companion of the war—
> ....
> A shepherd once (distrust not ancient Fame)
> Possest these downs, and Syphilus *his* name.
> He first wore buboes dreadful to the sight, 10
> First felt strange pains and sleepless past the night;
> From him the malady receiv'd its name,
> The neighboring shepherds catcht the spreading flame:
> Yet observation rightly taken draws

This new distemper from some newer cause; [15]
Nor reason can allow that this disease,
Came first by commerce from beyond the seas;
Since instances in divers lands are shown,
To whom all Indian traffic is unknown:
Nor could th' infection from the western clime [20]
Seize distant nations at the self-same time;
And in remoter parts begin its reign,
As fierce and early as it did in Spain.
What slaughter in our Italy was made
Where Tiber's tribute to the oceans paid; [25]
Where Po does through a hundred cities glide,
And pours as many streams into the tide.
All at one season, all without relief,
Receiv'd and languisht with the common grief.
Nor can th' infection first be charg'd on Spain, [30]
That fought new worlds beyond the western main.
Since from Pyrene's foot,[1] to Italy,
It shed its bane on France, while Spain was free.
As soon the fertile Rhine its fury found,
And regions with eternal winter bound: [35]
Nor yet did southern climes its vengeance shun,
But felt a flame more scorching than the sun.
The palms of Ida[2] now neglected stood,
And Egypt languisht while her Nile o'erflow'd;
From whence 'tis plain this pest must be assign'd [40]
To some more pow'rfull cause and hard to find.

___

[1] The foot of the Pyrenees Mountains on the eastern side.
[2] Southern part of Palestine, south of Judea.

___

Source: Girolamo Fracastoro, *Syphilis, or, A poetical history of the French disease written in Latin by Fracastorius*, trans. Nahum Tate (London: Printed for Jacob Tonson, 1686).

- **What does the poet want us to understand about syphilis?**
- **How does he explain the geographical spread of syphilis?**

___

SOURCE 15.6

A Persian Monograph on Syphilis, "Risala-I-Atishak," 1569

The excerpt below is drawn from a treatise on syphilis compiled by Hakim Imad-al-Din Mahmud Ibn Masud bin Mahmud, one of the most famous of medieval Persian physicians. From Shiraz, in what is today southwestern Iran, he was a cosmopolitan scholar who wrote in Persian and Arabic and lived several years in India. He completed his treatise on syphilis in 1569.

An European Prescription for Átishak [syphilis]: Mercury, lentiscus, castor, yellow sulphur, incense five drachms,[1] walnut shells two drachms, Chinese zedoary five drachms, well tried infusion of purslane . . . rose water one drachm, lemons nine drachms. With these make pills each the size of a filbert nut. Let the patient take one each morning for three days. But I maintain that this method is too dangerous and is not in accordance with scientific methods. The administering of the electuaries [medicine] that I have already described is a better line, for from them no danger can ensue. And God knoweth all. . . .

The disease is the most infectious of all diseases but does not spread rapidly. Infection is more likely to follow sexual intercourse with one suffering from *átishak* than after simple association. It is caused by the vapors in the hot bath passing from the body of one to the body of another or by the sweat or by contamination of the dressing gown or by clothes much more readily than by mere meeting or inspiration [respiration]. . . .

The Potent Powder: Grind up, put through a sieve, and carefully store cinnamon, fennel, lentiscus in equal parts. . . . I maintain that this is a well known and proved pill which is used in Constantinople, Europe, India and other places. If required as an elixir it can also be made into one. And in my opinion if made with oils and employed as an ointment the gain is greater and the advantages more general and by the will of God it will be entirely free from danger.

___

[1] A unit of weight formerly used by apothecaries, equivalent to 60 grains or one-eighth of an ounce.

___

Source: C. Elgood, "Translation of a Persian Monograph on Syphilis, entitled Risala-I-Atishak by Imad-Ul-Din Mahmud Bin Mascud Bin Mahmud-Ul-Tabib," *Annals of Medical History* 3, no. 57 (1931): 465–486.

- **Are there any clues here about the origin of the disease?**
- **What can we infer from this text about the movement of disease and medicine around the world at this time?**

___

QUESTIONS FOR COMPARISON

1. From these documents, what hypotheses can you offer about the relationship(s) between religion and disease?

2. The viewpoints represented here, aside from an anonymous European one, are Mexica, Italian, New England Puritan, and Persian. What is similar and what is different about their understandings of disease? Are these effects best explained by the cultures of the authors or by the nature of the diseases they describe?

3. Most of the texts here comment, directly or indirectly, on the geographical source of a disease. Why might that have mattered to these authors?

CHRONOLOGY

1441
Portuguese begin selling
Africans as slaves

1482
Portuguese mariners
establish Elmina in
West Africa

1524
Waves of epidemics
begin in the Andes

1580s
Yermak spearheads
fur trade in Siberia

1652
Dutch East India
Company founds
outpost at Cape of
Good Hope

1713
Smallpox epidemic kills
up to 90 percent of Khoi

ca. 1780–1810
King Kamehameha
unites Hawaii

1519
Hernán Cortés attacks
Tenochtitlán

1519–ca. 1860
The transatlantic slave trade

1532
Francisco Pizarro
overthrows Inka
Empire

ca. 1600–1694
Palmares maroon community
in Brazil

1680
Pueblo kill or expel all Spanish
in what is now New Mexico

1689
Russian and Chinese Empires
sign treaty dividing Siberian
and East Asian spaces

1788–1868
Britain sends convict
settlers to Australia

Disruption

AFRICA, THE AMERICAS, SIBERIA, AND OCEANIA

1492 to 1850

T rucanini, who died in 1876, was one of the last of the Tasmanians. She was witness to a grim and frequent process in world history.

Tasmania is an island 150 miles (240 km) off the southern coast of Australia. People first arrived there about 40,000 years ago, when lower sea levels allowed them to walk there from Australia. When rising sea levels divided Tasmania from the Australian mainland around 6000 BCE, the Tasmanians were cut off. For nearly 8,000 years, until a few centuries ago, they had no known contacts with the rest of humankind. They gradually lost the skills to catch fish, make bone tools, and even to make fire. Their technological decay is striking evidence of the costs of isolation in small groups.

In 1642, a Dutch sea captain, Abel Tasman, sighted the island that bears his name but did not disembark. British whalers began to use it as a base in 1798, ending the long isolation of Tasmania, and in 1803 British authorities decided to locate a penal colony there. At that time, there were about 5,000

1807–1845
Musket Wars in New Zealand

1840
Treaty of Waitangi

1898
United States
annexes Hawaii

1845–1872
Intermittent
land wars
between Maori
and *pakeha*

1876
Trucanini
dies

***A Linen Market with a Linen-Stall and Vegetable Seller in the West Indies,* ca. 1780** Agostino Brunias's finely detailed paintings of Caribbean market scenes capture the social gradations of Creole society through the clothing worn by his subjects. Whites and free persons of color wear fine European styles with African accents such as colorful head wraps. Enslaved people wear almost nothing. The textiles for sale at these weekly markets drew buyers and sellers into the Global web of trade.

FOCUS QUESTIONS

1. What were the major effects in Africa of joining the Global web?

2. What were the major effects in the Americas of joining the Global web?

3. What major changes came to Siberia once it was integrated into the Old World web?

4. How did entry into the Global web affect Oceania and Australia?

to 15,000 Tasmanians in existence. By 1830, only some 300 remained. The British prisoners and their keepers had brought new diseases, casual attitudes to murderous violence, and weaponry far superior to what the Tasmanians could muster. Most of Trucanini's family was abducted, enslaved, or killed. She became an outlaw in her 20s and was shot in the head and imprisoned, but she lived into her 60s. Meanwhile, British officials gathered the last of the Tasmanians together with the stated intent of protecting them, but influenza and other infections continued to wreak deadly havoc. With the death of Trucanini, a 40,000-year-old language and culture died as well, after a mere three-quarters of a century of contact with the outside world.

This chapter presents the ways in which peoples previously outside the Old World web found themselves rapidly enmeshed in the Global web in its formative centuries. The processes behind these new connections were simultaneously political and military, economic and technological, religious and cultural, biological and demographic. In most cases, they involved episodes of great brutality. The focus here is on sub-Saharan Africa and the indigenous populations of the Americas, Siberia, Australia, and Oceania. Later chapters will take up the story of how

this globalizing, web-expanding process played out within the former Old World web itself.

Entry into the expanding global web for peoples long isolated was always hard, and sometimes fully as disastrous as for Tasmanians. Most peoples suffered demographic losses due to **disease disasters**, violence, and declines in fertility. Most also experienced wrenching cultural and political changes, and yet somehow made the adjustments necessary to survive in their new worlds as participants in the Global web. They had a lot to learn about operating in new and larger economic and political contexts, and the people who knew most about global contexts often preferred to kill or enslave them rather than instruct them.

The opening of the oceans to navigation, and the sudden spread of information, diseases, migrants, and much else, redistributed power and wealth dramatically. Just about everyone sought to take advantage of the changing situation, including the peoples of Africa, the Americas, Australia, Oceania, and Siberia, although they were rarely well placed to do so. The people best positioned to seize the opportunities of the globalizing world were those who had the fullest information about routes, goods, prices, technologies, languages, and religions. These were the people who traveled the seas themselves—mainly but not exclusively Atlantic Europeans.

European sailors, soldiers, settlers, merchants, and missionaries often knew, or knew how to find out, roughly how much a pound of pepper would fetch in Lisbon markets or whether customers in Calicut preferred pearls over ponies. This enabled them to trade more profitably than others could. They also knew, or could make educated guesses, whether or not their weapons would give them an edge against other peoples, and so whether attacking them might be foolish or not. There was of course much they did not know, and they made many miscalculations. But on average they had a more global perspective than anyone else, and they took advantage of that where they could.

The Last Tasmanians In the mid-nineteenth century, British authorities took this studio photograph of four of the last surviving Tasmanians, dressed in British fashions. Trucanini is seated on the far right.

Atlantic Europeans were only the latest example of people in position to exploit the information advantages of web connections. Ancient Carthaginians usually knew more about distant markets and new technologies than anyone in Spain, and they too took advantage of that when they could. The same was true of the Chola merchants and kings in south India in their relations with landlocked neighbors, or of Arabs with respect to East Africans living inland from the Swahili coast. The difference here is one of scale: the Atlantic Europeans enjoyed information advantages over many peoples around the world and could, more consistently than anyone else, harvest information from every continent.

And information advantages were only part of their edge. Atlantic European mariners were in effect the Mongols of the sea. Like horse nomads, they didn't always have military advantages over potential rivals, but thanks to their mobility they could choose when and where they might wish to fight, when and where they preferred to flee. With their big shipboard cannon, they could attack enemies from a safe distance, as horse nomads could with their bows. Like the mobile Mongols, they could, when it suited them, engage in acts of unspeakable cruelty, knowing they could get away safely, never to return and face the consequences. This is not to suggest that either Mongols or seagoing Europeans were by nature crueler than anyone else, only that they could indulge in cruelty and escape retribution more easily than others who lacked superior mobility. And, like the Mongols, Atlantic Europeans' conquests, massacres, co-optations, and absorptions of other peoples helped prepare the way for unprecedented consolidation of webs of economic, cultural, and biological interaction.

It is important to recognize that this process of globalization, even if on balance it led to European domination of large parts of the world, reshuffled fortunes in complicated ways. In Africa and the Americas especially, some rulers, clans, and peoples found ways to turn the linkages presented by European seafaring to their advantage. Some, for example, monopolized European trade goods and got rich. Others managed to control access to imported European firearms and turn them against their neighbors. Still others translated support from Christian missionaries into prestige and power. And some, such as the kings of Kongo in West Central Africa, did all of the above, if only for a while. Trucanini and the Tasmanians, mainly because of the penalties of isolation in small groups, did none of the above.

AFRICA AND THE GLOBAL WEB

Sub-Saharan Africa in 1400 already had considerable links to the Old World web, across the Sahara and via the sailing routes of the Indian Ocean. Only the southernmost reaches and a few pockets here and there remained truly isolated from the wider world. However, after 1450, as trans-Saharan travel became more common and Portuguese mariners began to visit its coasts, nearly every part of Africa tightened its connections to what was rapidly becoming a Global web. The process, as usual, was a rough one, featuring war, empire building, epidemics, and enslavement, as well as heightened trade and cultural exchange. The main components of the process included, first, the gradual and ongoing spread of Islam through the northern half of Africa, which in places was coupled with wider use of the Arabic language. Second, in a few locations, small colonies of European settlers took root, creating altogether new societies, most notably at the southernmost tip, the Cape of Good Hope. Third, Africans, especially those living near the coasts, became increasingly active in maritime trade circuits, not only of the Indian Ocean (ongoing for centuries) but also of the Atlantic. The largest part of this commerce was the transatlantic slave trade.

ISLAM IN AFRICA

Islam, as we have seen, spread from its Arabian homeland into North Africa, largely by conquest, during the seventh century. It subsequently seeped into sub-Saharan Africa along two main paths: by sea to the Swahili coast and across the desert into the western and central Sahel (the southern edge of the Sahara). In both cases, Islam's spread in Africa usually occurred not by conquest but through efforts of merchants, rulers, and missionaries—categories that overlapped in many cases.

Merchants from North Africa and Arabia brought their varieties of Islam with them when visiting Sahelian towns or Swahili ports. Since they generally stayed for months and interacted daily with locals, they had plenty of opportunity to demonstrate the attractions of Islam to urban Africans. Merchants in Africa, as in South, Southeast, and Central Asia, often found it both agreeable and convenient to adopt Islam. Many were naturally curious about an unfamiliar religion and welcomed instruction. For many African traders, Islam's tenets held genuine appeal. The Qur'an portrays commerce and merchants (Muhammad was one, after all) in a favorable light. It spells out suitable practices for contracts, money lending, and other business procedures. In addition, treating visiting Muslims and Islam with respect was good for business. Converting to Islam was even better, as it smoothed

relations by binding all parties together with the same concepts of law spelled out in shari'a.

Rulers, too, often found advantage in becoming Muslim and proclaiming themselves sultan or emir. They too, no doubt, embraced Islam out of genuine conviction. But doing so could also improve their political position, providing prestige through connections to distant centers of power and learning. Having literate people around was always helpful to monarchs, so Muslim scholars often found employment at African courts. Islam also suited rulers by offering justification (or spiritual compensation) for hierarchy and inequality—as all durable religions do. Kings and chiefs needed less raw power or personal charisma if their poor subjects believed it was God's plan that they should be poor subjects.

The experiences of East and West Africa illustrate the economic and political factors at work in the spread of Islam. In East Africa, the influence of Islam was already widespread before 1400. After 1500, the Portuguese incursions on the Swahili coast that began with Vasco da Gama inadvertently helped promote Islam, which provided a rallying point for resistance to Portuguese attacks. By

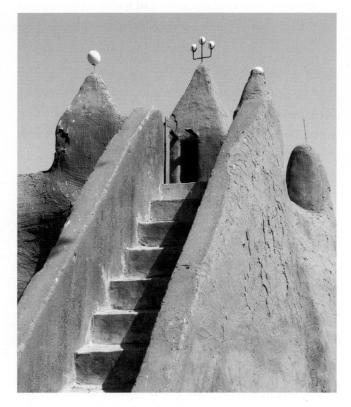

Islam in Africa This eighteenth-century Bambara mosque in present-day employs local architectural traditions in service of Islamic practice.

the seventeenth century, growing trade links with Muslim Oman tightened Swahili cultural connections to the Arabian Peninsula. Swahili and Omani forces drove the Portuguese out of East African coastal cities between 1650 and 1730, opening the door to a wave of immigrants from southern Arabia. Omani merchants, generally trading cloth for ivory and slaves, took up residence on the coast, especially its offshore islands such as Zanzibar. Clerics and holy men, often Sufi mystics, came too. The Omanis gradually extended their operations into the East African interior. Everywhere they went, they interested locals in their religion.

In West Africa, Muslim traders crossing the Sahara had found a welcome reception since at least the eighth century, as we have seen in the history of Ghana and Mali. The Songhai Empire, a successor to Mali that took shape in the 1460s and 1470s, became an active promoter of Islam. Its founder, Sunni Ali, based his new state at Gao and soon conquered the other Niger River trading cities, including Timbuktu and Jenne. By most accounts, he practiced multiple religions, was an indifferent Muslim, and clashed with the Islamic scholars of Timbuktu. But under a later king, Askia Muhammad (r. 1493–1528), Songhai used all available means to spread Islam. A firm Muslim, Askia Muhammad supported Islamic scholars, built mosques, encouraged conversion, and launched wars against unbelievers. His success helped spread Islam widely in the West African Sahel and to revive Timbuktu as a major center of Islamic learning. A Moroccan army, invading across the Sahara with muskets and artillery, ended the Songhai Empire in 1591, and returned home with the Islamic books and scholars of Timbuktu. But smaller successor states continued to promote Islam in West Africa.

To the east, in the central Sudan, smaller Muslim states, most notably Bornu in the sixteenth through the eighteenth centuries, promoted Islam much as Songhai had done. South of the Sahel, in West Africa's forest zone, Muslim traders (called Dyula or Juula in West Africa) served as informal ambassadors of Islam. Muslim communities developed along the trade routes. Where trade and states did not figure prominently, Islam had less impact in West Africa before 1800.

Merchants and rulers both, when accepting Islam, did not necessarily renounce their former ways. From their point of view, Islam was one of several spiritual options. Many continued to celebrate traditional feasts; venerate

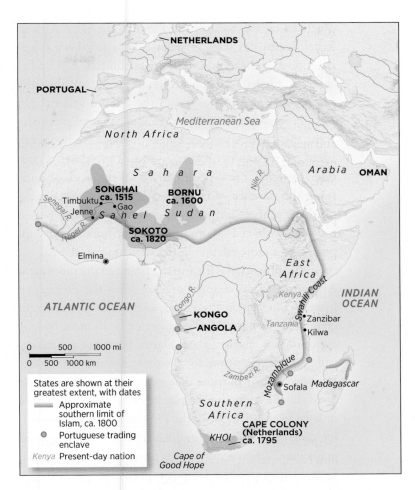

Africa: The Spread of Islam and the European Presence, 1450–1800 Connections between Africa and other parts of the world strengthened in the centuries after 1450. Many Africans along the Swahili Coast and across the Sahel embraced Islam, typically modifying its practices to suit their own traditions. Meanwhile, European mariners, especially Portuguese and Dutch, set up fortified trading posts (and in the Dutch case, an entire colony) in places along coastal Africa.

stars, sun, moon, and ancestors; or call upon spirits long familiar to them. Like Sunni Ali, rulers especially might find it politically prudent to become bicultural, both Islamic and non-Islamic, for different audiences and occasions.

Wherever Islam spread in Africa, it acquired local characteristics: just as parts of Africa were Islamized, Islam was in those places Africanized. African Muslims built mosques out of mud brick in the western Sahel or of coral on the Swahili coast. Muslim African women rarely dressed as modestly as women did in Islam's heartlands.

Such adjustments to Islam offended purists. Ibn Battuta, the great world traveler, was one of many outsiders irritated by the unorthodox, Africanized versions of Islam practiced on the Swahili coast and in the West African Sahel. Centuries later in what is now northern Nigeria, a poet, scholar, and reformer, Uthuman dan Fodio, launched a rebellion against rulers he judged insufficiently Islamic and went on to found the Sokoto caliphate in 1804. He condemned the local sultans as unbelievers who "raise the flag of a worldly kingdom above the banner of Islam." His daughter, Nana Asma'u (1793–1864), a considerable scholar and poet, carried on the work of purifying the practice of Islam in West Africa, organizing Qur'anic schools for girls and women. Tensions persist today between champions of Islamic orthodoxy and supporters of a more adaptable and Africanized Islam.

In the process of Africanizing Islam, many prominent African Muslims claimed descent from the Prophet or from his inner circle. Prestigious ancestors were important credentials in most African societies, as in most Islamic communities. Even if these claims were not genealogically correct, over time some won acceptance and therefore served their purpose. For example, the ruling house of Mali, the sprawling empire in West Africa, claimed descent from Bilal, one of the Prophet's faithful companions and originally an Ethiopian slave. In these ways and many more, Islam acquired new forms and features drawn from African traditions and practices.

EUROPEAN AND CHRISTIAN INFLUENCES ON COASTAL AFRICA

While Islamic and Arab influence trickled into both East and West Africa, after 1440 Portuguese and then Dutch influence crashed into coastal Africa. In 1482, Portuguese mariners established a fortified post called Elmina on West Africa's coast. Their impact was greater still farther south, in the region of Kongo and Angola, and on the Indian Ocean coasts of Mozambique. Dutch involvement in Africa focused on the area around the Cape of Good Hope.

KONGO AND ANGOLA Just south of the mammoth Congo (or Zaire) River's mouth, Portuguese seagoing expeditions encountered a welcoming king, whom they called the *manicongo*. Founded late in the fourteenth century, his kingdom contained over half a million people. In the 1490s, Portuguese missionaries convinced a *manicongo* to convert to Catholicism, which he understood as adding yet one more cult to those he already oversaw. His

son learned to speak, read, and write Portuguese, adopted European dress, and took the Portuguese name Afonso. The Portuguese helped Afonso, not a legitimate heir to the throne by Kongo custom, seize power in conflicts with his brothers. Subsequently, **King Afonso** (r. 1506–1543) ruled, with the help of Portuguese advisors, military officers, and technology, using muskets against neighboring peoples whose weaponry did not include firearms.

Part of the Portuguese interest in Kongo was religious, and in King Afonso they had an eager partner. While Askia Muhammad was using his power in Songhai to spread Islam in West Africa, King Afonso made Catholicism the state religion in Kongo, using it to bolster his shaky legitimacy as ruler. He built churches and required his provincial governors to take baptism. The Pope named King Afonso's son Henrique, who had studied theology in Portugal, bishop of Kongo. Thereafter, missionaries from Portugal poured into the kingdom, although most of them quickly died from malaria, yellow fever, or other unfamiliar diseases. Those who survived disappointed a later king of Kongo, who wrote to the Pope complaining that Portuguese priests "have no preoccupation other than enriching themselves . . . [and] take no interest in gaining souls for heaven." Nonetheless, Catholicism gradually blended with local traditions and became the dominant religion in Kongo.

Eventually the kings of Kongo and Portugal fell out, and Portuguese interest in West Central Africa shifted south to Angola. Here too Portugal allied with a local king, called the *ngola*, which became the name for the country. Portuguese helped him in his political struggles and in exchange won the right to preach Catholicism and conduct trade. Soon several local leaders accepted baptism, although they often kept their old ways as well. Rumors of vast

Christianity in West Central Africa A bronze crucifix from sixteenth- or seventeenth-century Kongo demonstrates how Christianity had become an integral part of Kongolese artistic and cultural tradition.

CONSIDERING THE EVIDENCE

The Perils of Trade in Kongo

After Afonso I defeated his half-brother to gain control of Kongo, he emulated the Catholic king of Portugal. Though Kongolese, Afonso appointed officials with Portuguese titles, corresponded with the Pope, and requested priests to conduct Christian Mass with wine and grain imported from Portugal. He also bolstered his prestige by distributing merchandise imported from Portugal that he paid for with ivory, copper, and enslaved men and women who had supported his political rivals. Although Afonso initially benefited from the slave trade, the following letters between him and King João III of Portugal show that he had reservations about the trade. In the end, Afonso agreed with King João III that the slave trade should be continued, but he appointed officials to witness every sale in an effort to ensure that merchants would not capture and sell his own subjects.

Letter of the King of Kongo to [King of Portugal] Dom João III, 1526

[O]ur kingdom is being lost in so many ways...; this is caused by the boldness your...officials give to the...merchants who come to this kingdom to set up shops with merchandise...that we forbid, which they spread...in so great abundance that many vassals that we held in our obedience elevate themselves [i.e., are no longer obedient] by obtaining those things in greater quantities than we possess. With those things we had kept them content, and subjected under our vassalage and jurisdiction, so now there is great damage to the service of God as well as for the security and orderliness of our kingdoms and state.

And we cannot reckon how great this damage is, since these same merchants each day take our native people, sons of the land and sons of our nobles and vassals, and our relatives, because the thieves...steal them with the desire to have the things and merchandise of this kingdom that they covet.... [O]ur lands are entirely depopulated.... [W]e do not need...merchandise, other than wine and bread for the holy sacrament. For this we are asking of Your Highness...not to send either merchants or merchandise, because our will is that in these kingdoms there is no trade in slaves nor outlet for them.

Letter of Dom João III to the King of Kongo, 1529

You say in your letters that you do not want there to be any slave trade in your kingdom because it is depopulating your land.... I am told of the great size of Kongo and how it is so populated that it appears that not a single slave has left it. They also tell me that you send to buy them [slaves] outside [the country] and that you marry them and make them Christian....

If...as you request,...there shall not be any trade in slaves in your kingdom, I will still want to provide wheat and wine for use at Mass, and for this only one caravel [ship] a year will be necessary.... However,...it would be more praiseworthy to draw each year from the Kongo 10,000 slaves and 10,000 *manilhas* [copper bracelets] and as many tusks of ivory.... If you do not want anyone to bring merchandise to Kongo, this would be against the custom of every country.... [A]nd if a *fidalgo* [noble] of yours rebels against you and receives merchandise from Portugal, where will be your power and greatness....

Sources: "Letter of the King of Kongo to D. João III, 6 July 1526," trans. Jared Staller, in *Converging on Cannibals: Terrors of Slaving in Atlantic Africa, 1509–1670* (Athens, OH, 2019); "The Slave Trade Is Good for the Kongo, Extract from a Letter of Dom João III to the King of Kongo, 1529," trans. Malyn Newitt, in *The Portuguese in West Africa, 1415–1670* (Cambridge, 2010).

QUESTIONS FOR ANALYSIS

1. How did trade in merchandise and enslaved people threaten Afonso I's rule?
2. What arguments did the king of Portugal use to convince the king of Kongo to continue trading?
3. Do these letters indicate that these kings dealt with each other as equals?

---

silver mines proved unfounded, and efforts to establish Portuguese immigrants as farmers failed miserably, mainly the result of the disease environment.

So in Angola, as in Kongo, the Portuguese turned to the economic activity that yielded the most reliable profit: slaving. They encouraged wars and slave raids. Local kings (and one highly successful queen, known as Nzinga or Njinga), seeking Portuguese support and military expertise, eagerly enslaved their enemies. They sold war captives to Afro-Portuguese slave traders, the sons of Portuguese men and African women. As we shall see, Angola became one of the biggest sources of slaves sent to the Americas. Kongo too became a major exporter, originally as a royal monopoly of King Afonso. By 1660, half the population of Kongo were slaves captured from neighboring peoples.

The Portuguese also brought new strains of smallpox to Kongo and Angola. Sub-Saharan Africans had previous experience with the virus, and many peoples regularly used inoculation (the practice of deliberately infecting bodies with weak strains of a pathogen in hopes of triggering immunity without a serious case of disease). But apparently mariners brought a new variety, for major epidemics struck the region in the years 1625–1628 and 1655–1660. Some evidence suggests that tuberculosis and a form of pneumonia also hit Angola in the seventeenth century. For Kongo and Angola, inclusion into the Global web meant new diseases, one additional religion, and much more trade, enslavement, and warfare.

MOZAMBIQUE The Portuguese also took a strong interest in Mozambique. Unlike Angola or Kongo, Mozambique—on Africa's Indian Ocean shore—had a long involvement in maritime trade circuits. When da Gama passed by in 1498, its seaborne trade was in the hands of Swahili, Arab, and Indian merchants based in the coastal towns of Sofala and Kilwa. Sea power enabled Portuguese merchants to take control of Sofala's gold and ivory exports. The Portuguese occasionally sent military missions inland, hoping to seize the goldfields of the Zimbabwe plateau, but these efforts always met with disaster in the form of African armed resistance and deadly disease.

The Portuguese Crown issued land grants to Portuguese settlers, who made themselves into local lords and merchants. Their connections to India and Europe—market knowledge and military hardware proved most useful—gave them an edge in dealing with Mozambican populations. Unlike Kongo and Angola, Mozambique's commerce consisted mainly of gold and ivory until after 1700. Meanwhile, Christian conversion made little headway there, and indeed many Portuguese and Afro-Portuguese abandoned Catholicism for either Islam or local African religious culture.

THE CAPE OF GOOD HOPE From the 1620s onward, the Portuguese had a seafaring rival, the Dutch, seeking toeholds in southern Africa. They conquered, and briefly held, some Portuguese coastal outposts in the 1630s and 1640s. Then, in 1652, the Dutch East India Company—a quasi-governmental trading company known by its Dutch

initials as the VOC—founded a base at the Cape of Good Hope. It originated as a way station for ships headed from Dutch ports to the East Indies (mainly Java), supplying water, fresh fruit, vegetables, wine, and meat to desperate crews—the death rate among sailors on these long voyages ran at 15 to 20 percent. The Cape grew into a full-fledged colony of settlement. Here, unlike in most of tropical Africa, there was no malaria or yellow fever, and foreigners could flourish. While Portuguese traders and missionaries frequently died soon after arrival in Kongo or Mozambique—mainly from mosquito-borne diseases—Dutch settlers at the Cape survived about as well as their relatives at home.

The Africans who lived at the Cape, hunters and cattle keepers called the **Khoi**, numbered perhaps 50,000 to 100,000 in 1652. At first, the Khoi and the Dutch found they could coexist: the Dutch would buy any extra cattle the Khoi could raise and would pay the Khoi to work on their farms. But soon the Dutch were claiming more land and seeking more labor. The Khoi recognized the threat and attacked the Dutch in 1659 and 1673—unsuccessfully.

The Dutch VOC began to import slaves, mainly from Madagascar, Indonesia, and India in the seventeenth century, and from Mozambique in the eighteenth. This arrangement set the Cape on the path toward a sharply stratified society in which concepts of race mattered fundamentally. By 1700, the colony officially contained some 4,000 people—not including the Khoi, whom officials didn't bother to count. During the next century, population surged because of slave imports, immigration from Europe (often French or German), and social norms of early marriage and big families. With European women scarce, marriage often crossed racial lines, making the Cape not just racially stratified but also racially complex. By the mid-eighteenth century, the whites came to call themselves Afrikaners.

For the Khoi, despite new goods and opportunities, the Dutch colony proved a disaster. They lost control of the best lands to the newcomers. They lost their autonomy if they integrated themselves into Dutch society as laborers. In 1713, a large proportion of them lost their lives in a smallpox epidemic at the Cape. Within weeks, the virus killed a quarter of the Dutch colonists, many of whom had enjoyed rural childhoods without exposure to smallpox and so remained vulnerable as adults. All the Khoi were equally vulnerable, and about 90 percent died in the epidemic of 1713–1714, a mortality rate possible only because of widespread malnutrition. Further epidemics in 1755, 1767, and the 1780s burned through the remaining Khoi population. Little of their way of life survived, and Dutch settlers moved into the interior of South Africa with less resistance than ever before. They also imported more slaves to do the work the Khoi no longer could: the disastrous decline of indigenous population inspired an expanded slave trade, a pattern we will see again. By 1800, the Cape region contained about 20,000 settlers, maybe 25,000 slaves, and very few Khoi. In the taverns of Cape Town, which one VOC official described as the "mother of all scandalous practices," one might hear Malay, Tamil, Arabic, Portuguese, German, Dutch, and a dozen other languages. But one was unlikely to hear Khoi. The Cape settlement was an island of cosmopolitan, globalized, and sharply unequal society, now thoroughly enmeshed in the Global web.

THE TRANSATLANTIC SLAVE TRADE

The most visible, and for world history the most important, way in which large parts of Africa joined the Global web was through the slave trade. In Africa as in most lands, slavery had been a fact of life long before 1400. Africans became slaves if captured by slave raiders or in war, if they couldn't pay their debts, or if their family or lineage gave them away as compensation for harm done to another family or lineage. In some societies, enslavement was also punishment for certain crimes. Most children of slaves were legally free (a big difference from many other slave systems), but these children could perform useful labor for slave owners. Slave owners in Africa preferred women and children for working in the fields, tending animals, making cloth, and doing domestic chores. Above all, they valued young women, for labor, sex, and reproduction. Only in a few places were male slaves more valued than females, such as the salt mines of the Sahara.

African slave exports already had a long history. During the eighth and ninth centuries, as we've seen, landowners in Abbasid Iraq purchased many thousands of Africans from what is now Ethiopia and Somalia. Between 1400 and 1900, perhaps another 5 to 6 million Africans were enslaved for sale to Indian, Southwest Asian, and Mediterranean markets.

DIMENSIONS OF THE TRADE The size and significance of African slave exports changed when merchants

connected Africa's coasts to plantations of the Atlantic world. Portuguese sailors seized Africans beginning in 1441 and sold some of them on islands such as Madeira—500 miles (800 km) west of Morocco—where sugar plantations were developing. Meanwhile, Moroccan entrepreneurs organized sugar-and-slave plantations and purchased labor brought by trans-Saharan slave caravans. The success of sugar plantations worked by enslaved Africans in Morocco and Madeira inspired larger-scale imitation, first on the island of São Tomé off the coast of Kongo.

In 1518, the king of Spain authorized the first direct slave trading voyages from Africa to the Americas, and the first recorded voyage arrived in Puerto Rico in 1519. The population catastrophe in the Caribbean that we saw in the previous chapters was already well under way. The Spanish interest in transatlantic slaving arose from concern that

Abdul Rahaman ibn Sori A prince in what is now Guinea, in West Africa, Abdul Rahaman was captured in a local war in 1788. His captors sold him to British slave traders, who sold him to the owner of a Mississippi plantation, where Rahaman worked for 38 years. He was freed at age 67, through the intervention of a Moroccan sultan and the U.S. president, on the condition that he return to Africa, which he did shortly before his death.

Slavery and Sugar Enslaved Africans work a sugar mill in the Dutch Caribbean in the seventeenth century. The grinding mill shown was a dangerous machine that could easily injure or kill its operators.

The Middle Passage The conditions aboard slave ships on the Middle Passage are evident in these illustrations: an engraving from the 1780s shows the configuration of a British ship, the Brooke, that made 11 voyages carrying enslaved Africans to the Caribbean. Here it shows 454 people crammed into the ship's hold, the legal maximum according to British regulations of the time. On one occasion, however, the Brooke is recorded as having carried 609 enslaved Africans. The average mortality on Middle Passage voyages was 10–15%. To the right is a watercolor made in 1846 by a British naval officer who assisted in the capture of an illegal slave ship. Both show enslaved men and women packed together in inhumane conditions.

mines and agricultural estates in the Caribbean might languish for lack of labor. In this way, the misfortune of the Americas became the misfortune of Africa.

The first transatlantic slaving voyages to Brazil's sugar plantations began in 1534. Thereafter, the size of the transatlantic trade grew rapidly. Before long, the African coast from Senegal to Angola was exporting slaves across the Atlantic, and by the late seventeenth century the coasts of Mozambique and Madagascar were as well.

The **transatlantic slave trade**, the largest forced migration in world history, lasted until about 1860. In all, some 12 to 14 million enslaved people departed Africa's shores, of whom about 85 to 88 percent—10 to 11 million—survived what is called the **Middle Passage** across the Atlantic. The survival rate improved over the centuries, but the voyage remained hazardous to the end, especially lengthy crossings. The average trip required about two months at sea, after which food and fresh water often ran short. A three- or four-month trip usually killed a large proportion of both slaves and crew. Slaves were kept belowdecks, usually naked, packed like "books on

a shelf," as one observer put it. Men were often kept in chains for most of the voyage, women usually not. Sanitation was negligible. Dysentery was the foremost killer on the Middle Passage, but violence and other diseases took their toll as well.

Slaves attempted uprisings on perhaps as many as 1 in 10 slave ships. Ottobah Cugoano, born in what is now Ghana, survived the Middle Passage in 1770 en route to the Caribbean and remembered a planned uprising: "And when we found ourselves at last taken away, death was more preferable than life, and a plan was concerted amongst us, that we might burn and blow up the ship, and to perish all together in the flames; but we were betrayed by one of our own countrywomen, who slept with some of the head men of the ship, for it was common for the dirty filthy sailors to take the African women and lie upon their bodies; but the men were chained and pent up in holes." Successful shipboard uprisings were rare.

Of the 10 to 11 million Africans who survived the Middle Passage, about 44 percent landed in Brazil, another 40 percent in the Caribbean, and 4 percent in what would become the United States. The remainder were scattered among Mexico, Colombia, and other parts of mainland Spanish America. Among Africans sold across the Atlantic, about two-thirds were male and one-third female. Children accounted for one-fifth to one-quarter.

During the seventeenth century, the transatlantic slave trade outstripped the size of the combined trans-Saharan, Red Sea, and Indian Ocean slave trades, and cumulatively between 1400 and 1900 was twice as large. The transatlantic traffic peaked in the 1780s at nearly 87,000 slaves per year. It gradually became illegal, outlawed by various countries beginning in 1807, but a secondary peak occurred in the 1820s at 86,000 annually.

THE SLAVING BUSINESS The transatlantic slave trade was big business. In 1750, about one-third of the British merchant fleet took part. For Portugal it was even bigger. Portuguese slavers bought about 5.7 million Africans to carry to Brazil; British slavers purchased about 3.3 million, mainly for the Caribbean; French about 1.4 million; Spanish 1 million; Dutch half a million; and U.S. slavers about 300,000. The leading ports that financed and organized the slave trade were Rio de Janeiro and Salvador da Bahia, both in colonial Brazil, where Portuguese merchants dominated trade; Liverpool, London, and Bristol, all in England; and Nantes, in France. In West African states such as Oyo or Dahomey, capturing and selling slaves was the main source of mercantile wealth. European slavers, with their newfound global reach, had much to offer African dealers. Cloth from India became the chief West African import, supplemented by iron, copper, guns, tobacco, liquor, and cowrie shells collected in the Indian Ocean. Ottobah Cugoano, enslaved at age 13, recalled that he was sold for "a gun, a piece of cloth, and some lead."

A slaver visiting the coast of what is now Nigeria in about 1680 noted that one could buy a male slave for about the same price as 40 baskets of plantains. Cowrie shells came to serve as money in parts of West Africa, and by 1720 about one-third of slaves bought on West Africa's coasts were purchased for cowries. To acquire the cloth and cowries from the Indian Ocean world, European merchants generally sold silver mined in the Americas. The slave trade evolved into a large-scale business linked to trade circuits spanning three oceans and several continents.

The cloth, cowries, and other items on offer provided reason enough for African rulers and entrepreneurs to capture and enslave millions. In Africa, as we saw in Chapter 8, ambitious men normally sought prosperity in the form of people—wives, children, servants, slaves—as was typical of places where land was abundant and people scarce. Accumulating large numbers of dependent followers meant status, power, wealth, and security. To achieve such a following, paradoxically, it made sense to sell slaves, especially males. Women and children were usually more sought after as slaves within Africa, fetched higher prices than men, and were less likely to try to escape. If an African entrepreneur could accumulate slaves cheaply through capture or could buy them at a good price and then sell them for guns, iron, cloth, cowries, or horses, then he could use these goods to attract more followers and either purchase or raid more effectively for more slaves. He could reinvest in his business with little risk of diminishing returns because European slavers and American markets maintained a voracious demand for yet more slaves. And he could use his growing wealth to support more wives, father more children, and build his retinue and status: in short, he could sell people overseas in order to accumulate more useful people.

ESTIMATED VOLUME OF THE SLAVE TRADES FROM AFRICA, 1400–1900

	1400–1599	1600–1699	1700–1799	1800–1899	TOTAL
TRANSATLANTIC	199,000	1,523,000	5,610,000	3,371,000	10,703,000
TRANS-SAHARAN	675,000	450,000	900,000	1,099,000	3,124,000
RED SEA	400,000	200,000	200,000	505,000	1,305,000
INDIAN OCEAN	200,000	100,000	260,000	380,000	940,000
TOTAL	1,474,000	2,273,000	6,970,000	5,355,000	16,072,000

Sources: Nathan Nunn, "The Long-Term Effects of Africa's Slave Trades," data appendix (2007), http://scholar.harvard.edu/files/nunn/files/empirical_slavery_appendix.pdf; "Trans-Atlantic Slave Trade Database, SlaveVoyages, https://www.slavevoyages.org/voyage/database

Note: The reliability of the transatlantic estimates is much greater than that for the other slave trades. These figures represent disembarkations: those who arrived alive.

African Slave Trades, 1400–1900 Over these 500 years, roughly 16 million sub-Saharan Africans were enslaved and exported. Brazil, the Caribbean, and Egypt purchased the most Africans. West Central and West Africa supplied the most. The width of the arrows in this map is proportional to the number of people sold on each route.

African slave traders were overwhelmingly men, but women also took part in the business. European slavers visiting West Africa often formed alliances with local merchant families by marrying "wives of the coast," if

only temporarily in most cases. As European slavers died or moved away, wives of the coast found replacements, new European men, who needed the business connections these women and their families provided. Most

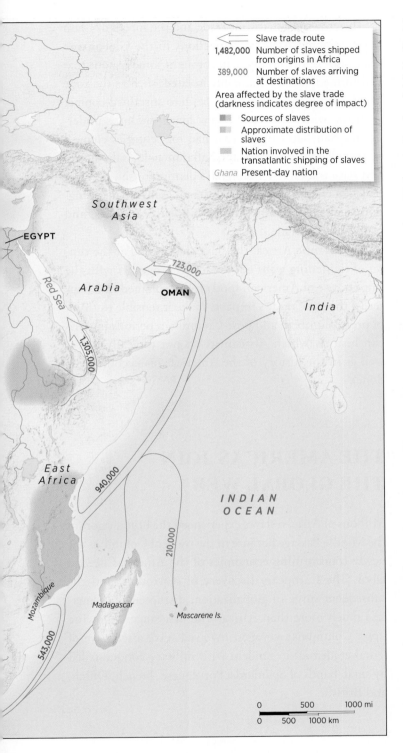

Legend:
→ Slave trade route
1,482,000 Number of slaves shipped from origins in Africa
389,000 Number of slaves arriving at destinations
Area affected by the slave trade (darkness indicates degree of impact)
▪ Sources of slaves
▪ Approximate distribution of slaves
▪ Nation involved in the transatlantic shipping of slaves
Ghana Present-day nation

Robin John. They were elite men of the Efik people, living at the mouth of the Cross River (in today's Nigeria). They made a fine living seizing and buying Africans, usually Igbo-speakers, and selling them to English ship captains. They spoke, wrote, and read English, and when dealing with English slavers they dressed as English gentlemen and followed English manners and customs. In 1767, to their horror, an English captain seized them, crossed the Atlantic, and sold them to a French doctor in the Caribbean. They soon escaped, but instead of freedom they found themselves sold again, this time in Virginia. After further misadventures brought them to England, a judge ruled them free men. They took ship back home to Cross River, where, well acquainted with the horrors of the Middle Passage and American slavery, they returned to their old business and sold thousands more Africans into the Atlantic slave trade. There was no surer way to sustain elite status on the West African coast than to deal in slaves.

CONSEQUENCES IN AFRICA The impact of the slave trade on the population of Africa is a controversial subject among historians. In the 1780s, at the height of the trade, 87,000 slaves crossed the Atlantic annually—roughly 0.1 percent of Africa's estimated population of 75 to 125 million. However, for each slave who stepped off a ship in the Americas, two Africans had been enslaved, and one had died en route to the African coast or on the Middle Passage. So on account of the transatlantic slave trade, Africans in the worst years stood a 1/500 chance of being enslaved. On a continental basis, the transatlantic slave trade probably did not have much impact on the size of Africa's population, but at certain times and places, such as Angola between 1750 and 1850, the demographic effects were substantial.

The transatlantic slave trade also spurred the growth of slavery within Africa. During the centuries of the slave trade, far more

Signares *Signares* was the French word for "wives of the coast," local West African women married to French slave traders. Many *signares* owned houses and operated businesses in their own right, and they often established independent households when their husbands died or returned to France. This elegant *signare* was painted in the 1840s by Abbé David Boilat of Senegal, who was himself the son of a *signare*.

wives of the coast were content to remain informal wives or married according to local practices. But some insisted that representatives of a Christian church recognize their marriages.

Two men who knew the slave trade inside out were Little Ephraim Robin John and his nephew Ancona Robin enslaved Africans lived out their lives within Africa than were transported across the Atlantic. The typical fate of an enslaved African was to be traded (or given to someone) somewhere else within Africa. But the export trade provided strong incentives for slavers to build their businesses in order to reap economies of scale. The more people they seized, the more slaves became available in Africa, and the more uses were found for them.

The transatlantic slave trade had other major impacts on Africa. Politically, it encouraged the development of larger and more militaristic states. Stateless societies with weak defenses, such as the Igbo of what is now southeastern Nigeria, suffered as a result. Igbo farmers had to take weapons with them into their fields and lock children in fortified places at night. Predatory states prospered, such as Asante (Ashanti) and Dahomey in West Africa, which specialized in seizing people from less militarily adept neighbors. One state that refused to export male slaves, the kingdom of Benin after 1516, built up a slave army to defend itself.

Economically, the slave trade encouraged predatory people—African warlord-entrepreneurs who invested in guns, horses, and violence. This diverted effort and investment from other endeavors that might have proven more socially useful than slaving. It also promoted commercialization, adding traffic to long-distance trade routes. As we have seen, the slave trade also affected African agriculture, making both maize and manioc more appealing crops.

Culturally, the slave trade hastened the spread of Islam in Africa. By law, Muslims may not enslave fellow Muslims, so in those areas where slave raiders were mainly Muslims, such as the western and central Sahel, people fearing enslavement had strong incentives to become Muslim themselves. Socially, the slave trade was divisive. Some people became extremely rich and powerful by conducting it; ordinary people who didn't became more fearful and mistrustful. To this day in many parts of Africa, people remember whose ancestors were slave traders and whose were slaves.

The effects of the slave trade were geographically uneven, as the map on pages 546–47 shows. Peoples within reach of armed horsemen, as in the Sahelian regions, were at great risk. The region most affected was Atlantic Africa, from Angola to Senegal—and within that, Angola itself and West Africa from what is now Ghana across to Cameroon. People living deep in central African rain forests remained almost fully out of reach.

The growth in maritime trade and the spread of Islam helped tighten Africa's connections to the Global web after 1450. Both developments brought some regions that had formerly been remarkably isolated, such as the zone around the Cape of Good Hope, into sustained contact with the wider world. The new maritime links undercut the Sahelian empires that had for centuries enjoyed a stranglehold on the trans-Saharan gold, salt, horse, and slave trades. After Songhai's demise in 1591, no great Sahelian empire arose again. Instead, many smaller kingdoms emerged, competing for influence, subjects, and trans-Saharan trade.

For Atlantic Africa, the slave trade stood at the center of tightening webs of interaction. Together with the importance of American food crops explained in Chapter 15, the slave trade's impacts make it sensible to think of pre-Columbian and post-Columbian periods in African history (which Africanists do not typically do) as well as in the history of the Americas (as is commonly done).

THE AMERICAS JOIN THE GLOBAL WEB

Millions of African slaves experienced the brutal rigors of the Middle Passage because in the wake of Columbus the newly transforming economies of the Americas needed labor. The European discovery of sea routes, and the subsequent surge in globalization, disrupted the Americas much more than Africa. The first stage, following upon Columbus's voyages, involved wave after wave of lethal epidemics in tandem with military conquests led by small bands of Spaniards, Portuguese, French, Dutch, and British.

DISEASE AND DEPOPULATION: REGIONAL VARIATIONS

As we saw in Chapter 15, the crowd diseases brought to the Americas by European mariners proved extremely lethal to native populations, who had no protection via prior exposure. Here we will take a closer look at the post-Columbian catastrophe, considering some of the considerable regional variations in the Americas.

THE CARIBBEAN People in the warm coastlands of the Caribbean had the worst of it. The more densely populated islands, such as Hispaniola, where pathogens could most easily find new bodies to infect, suffered losses of more than 99 percent within three or four generations. In 1492, the **Taíno** (as the indigenous population of this part of the Caribbean is called) on Hispaniola numbered several hundred thousand. By 1514, only 26,000 were recorded. By 1550, perhaps 5,000 Taíno remained.

Spanish violence and enslavement of the Taíno added to the deadly effect of unfamiliar diseases. Some Spaniards would stop at nothing in their efforts to find gold or seize farmland. Others, meanwhile, tried to convert Taíno to Christianity, which caused divisions within Taíno communities. Their social structures fell apart. Death of spouses, separations, and demoralization led birth rates to plummet. Young Taíno women became wives or concubines of Spaniards. The net effect of the Spanish efforts to make money on Hispaniola and save Taíno souls was to compound the disease disaster and hasten the demographic decline. On Hispaniola and several other islands, Taíno society, language, culture, and identity virtually disappeared—much as would happen later to the Tasmanians with whom this chapter began.

Immigrants from Europe and slaves from Africa came to dominate Hispaniola demographically, and its culture—religion, language, food, dress—evolved, like so many others, as a blended, or creole, culture. Pottery shows how rapid this process was on Hispaniola: in 1515, most pots bore the marks of Taíno potters. By 1530, none did, and the island's pottery was made by Africans. The demographic story on other big—but less populated—Caribbean islands such as Cuba, Jamaica, and Puerto Rico was broadly similar.

MESOAMERICA AND THE ANDES The major centers of indigenous population—Mesoamerica and the Andes—suffered smaller losses in proportional terms than the Caribbean, but in absolute terms they lost more population than anywhere else in the Americas. Repeated battering from epidemics and disruption of family routines, village life, and the political order cost each region roughly 90 percent of its population within a century. In Mesoamerica, where perhaps 15 to 20 million people lived in 1492, the disaster began in 1519 when a Spanish adventurer, Hernán Cortés, and a band of a few hundred

Cortés and the Aztecs A pictographic Aztec chronicle recorded the events of the conquest of Tenochtitlán. In the illustration, Cortés—shown on horseback carrying a large cross—and his troops arrive in the Aztec capital and slaughter the local inhabitants.

Spaniards rallied some neighboring enemies of the Aztecs, notably the Tlaxcalans, in an assault on Tenochtitlán. A raging smallpox epidemic scythed down the locals but left Spaniards—normally immune as survivors of childhood bouts with the virus—unscathed. Epidemics recurred time and again, birth rates fell, and by 1620 Mesoamerica held fewer than a million people.

In the Andes, waves of epidemics began in 1524, preceding the arrival of Spaniards. A civil war over succession to the throne divided the Inka Empire when in 1532 a distant kinsman of Cortés named Francisco Pizarro led a band of 168 men into the Andes. The combined effect of epidemic and civil war enabled Pizarro to engineer a coup d'état, overthrowing the Inka Empire. For a hundred years after Pizarro, the indigenous population continued to plummet, from perhaps 12 to 15 million in 1532 to under 1 million by 1630.

The demographic disaster in the Americas was least severe in those regions where people were few and pathogens could not easily leap to new bodies. The Arctic is one such example, where the toll of disease was smaller (closer to 50 percent) and came later, in the eighteenth and nineteenth centuries. The Mapuche of southern Chile, whose armies kept Spanish conquistadores at bay, as they had done with the Inka before, also seemed to have survived better than most.

ECOLOGICAL, SOCIAL, AND ECONOMIC FACTORS The demographic catastrophe varied in its intensity from place to place partly for ecological reasons. Malaria, a warm-weather disease carried by mosquitos and introduced from Africa, became entrenched in some parts of the Americas but not others. Higher elevations and higher latitudes, which are colder than lower ones, hosted fewer mosquitos and less malaria.

The variable severity of the population catastrophe also had to do with social factors. In some cases, the ravages of introduced diseases began before European conquerors or settlers turned up, as in the Andes. In New England, in the years 1616–1619, epidemics took a terrible toll before the first English settlement at Plymouth Rock (1620). More often, however, social chaos created by European settlement compounded the effects of epidemics, as in Hispaniola during the early sixteenth century.

Warfare, loss of lands, and enslavement magnified the population losses. Wars of conquest were widespread. Although small in scale, these wars generally involved indigenous Americans on both sides, as in Mexico and Peru. In addition, indigenous peoples when hit by epidemics often sought to recover their losses by seizing people, normally women and children, from their neighbors. The Iroquois, for example, who began to suffer heavily from epidemics in 1645, launched attacks on the Huron starting in 1648 partly to replenish their own numbers.

Almost everywhere in the Americas, sooner or later, indigenous peoples lost their best farmland to encroaching Europeans. That created additional problems of food supply and brought the demoralization that people typically experience when forced from their homes. Hunger and demoralization both can weaken disease resistance.

In many parts of the Americas, forced labor and enslavement added to the toll. Recent estimates suggest that between 1500 and 1800, some 2 to 4 million indigenous people were enslaved. Although slavery had existed in the Americas for millennia, its scale increased just when the population was collapsing. This was no accident: population collapse created intense demand for labor, filled by both the transatlantic slave trade from Africa and the enslavement of indigenous peoples.

In particular, the newly developing mining and plantation economies (of which more below) relied on forced labor, both African and indigenous. Spanish rule in South America continued the Inka practice of the **mita**, the forced labor draft imposed on Andean peoples, using it

Forced Labor in the Americas Across the Americas, European settlers enslaved indigenous people and imported enslaved people from Africa. In this 1522 Spanish illustration, enslaved indigenous people are being forced to lay the foundations for the Spanish capital of Mexico City.

to provide workers for silver mines—where high mortality prevailed. Silver mines in Mexico, pearl fisheries off the coast of Venezuela, and early plantations in what would become the southeast of the United States also drew upon enslaved indigenous people. Charleston, South Carolina, in the seventeenth century even exported some indigenous slaves to plantations on the Caribbean island of Barbados.

Enslavement of indigenous people was repeatedly prohibited by European authorities. The Spanish banned such slavery throughout their empire early in the sixteenth century, but with important exceptions—for peoples judged cannibals, such as the Caribs (of the eastern Caribbean), or for those like the Mapuche of Chile, whose resistance to Spanish rule was especially fierce. Spanish law also permitted slavery for everyone already enslaved. This created incentives for indigenous peoples to capture and enslave their neighbors and sell them, legally, to Spanish mining or plantation enterprises.

Where Spanish authorities tried hardest to save indigenous Americans' souls, death rates were especially high. Catholic missions throughout Spanish America clustered them together in agricultural villages to hasten their conversion to Christianity. Clustering, however, sped the transmission of most infectious diseases. The California missions begun in 1769, for example, suffered population losses that exceeded 90 percent within 50 years. Here too, few babies were born to take the place of the dead and dying.

EFFECT ON CLIMATE All in all, the fate of indigenous Americans after 1492 was among the most dismal chapters in world history. The experience of depopulation and displacement was shared with Tasmanians, the Khoi of southern Africa, and several other peoples around the world. But the scale of the population disaster was larger in the Americas than anywhere else—large enough, perhaps, to affect the Earth's climate.

The loss of population in the Americas from 1492 to 1700 may have deepened the chill of the Little Ice Age. Where some 40 to 70 million people had once lived, in 1700 fewer than 5 million remained. Former farmland became forest over broad patches of the Americas. As the forests grew, they absorbed carbon dioxide from the atmosphere, lowering its concentration and weakening (ever so slightly) the greenhouse effect. This (along with big volcanic eruptions and reduced energy output from the sun) may help explain why the coldest spells in the Little Ice Age occurred between 1590 and 1710.

NEW EMPIRES

The arrival of Europeans and the disastrous depopulation in the Americas had political consequences that varied from place to place. Where large empires had existed, as in the Andes and Mesoamerica, new, Spanish-led ones instantly replaced them. Where smaller-scale political structures had existed, as in most of the Americas, guerilla resistance was more common, and European control took far longer to establish.

The largest-scale conquests took place in Mexico and Peru. In both cases, small bands of conquistadores allied with big local armies, such as the Tlaxcalans who joined Cortés. Locals often outnumbered Spaniards in the armies of conquest by 100 to 1. So, in effect, in 1521 indigenous Mesoamericans used Cortés and his band to overthrow a hated Aztec Empire. Indeed, Tlaxcalans in the mid-sixteenth century considered that they, not Spaniards, had conquered the Aztecs. Similarly, in Peru, Spanish conquistadores made common cause with dissident

subjects of the Inkas. When "Spanish" conquerors later marched into Chile, their armies consisted mainly of former Inka soldiers, and when Spaniards led armies into Guatemala or fought the Chichimecs in northern Mexico, it was mainly Aztecs and Tlaxcalans who followed.

In Mesoamerica, when Cortés and his indigenous allies overthrew the Aztec state, he proclaimed the Viceroyalty of New Spain. Pizarro created a Viceroyalty of Peru. In some ways, these two Spanish colonial states were just the latest successors in native imperial traditions that stretched back centuries. The Spanish in Peru, for example, not only continued the Inka forced labor system, but they also maintained the reciprocal exchange networks among lineages (ayllus) that had underpinned Andean society under the Inkas and the Moche before them. The Viceroyalty of Peru fought on the same frontiers as had the Inkas a century before, using mainly Inka soldiers.

In Mexico, the Spanish also rebuilt an empire on Aztec foundations. Tribute payments from surrounding districts, formerly sent to Aztec Tenochtitlán, now went to the same place—Spanish Mexico City. The Spanish governed together with indigenous elites, splitting tribute revenues and other perks of power. They did not exact tribute from the Tlaxcalans, their coconquerors. In Mexico, as in Peru, the Spanish were too few to conquer and govern alone. Spaniards supplied superior armament and global knowledge; indigenous elites supplied local knowledge and manpower. Together, Spanish and local elites could rule the rapidly declining mass of the population.

Where indigenous polities were small or absent, Europeans encountered more enduring resistance to their rule. The Mapuche of southern Chile and the Maya of Mexico's Yucatán Peninsula, for example, who did not have much in the way of states, fought long and hard against Spanish control. Unlike the populations of Peru and central Mexico, they had no tradition of deference to any imperial authority. For centuries, they succeeded in keeping themselves independent of Spanish rule in most respects, and when that failed they often mounted rebellions. In general, indigenous revolts happened more often in northern New Spain and in the southern Andes. In what is now New Mexico in 1680, the Pueblo rose up against Spanish authority and either killed or expelled all Spaniards for the next 12 years. The biggest uprising, however, took place in the heart of the Andes, around Cuzco in 1781–1783, led by a descendant of the Inka royal family, Túpac Amaru II. It failed, at a cost of more than 100,000 lives. Nonetheless,

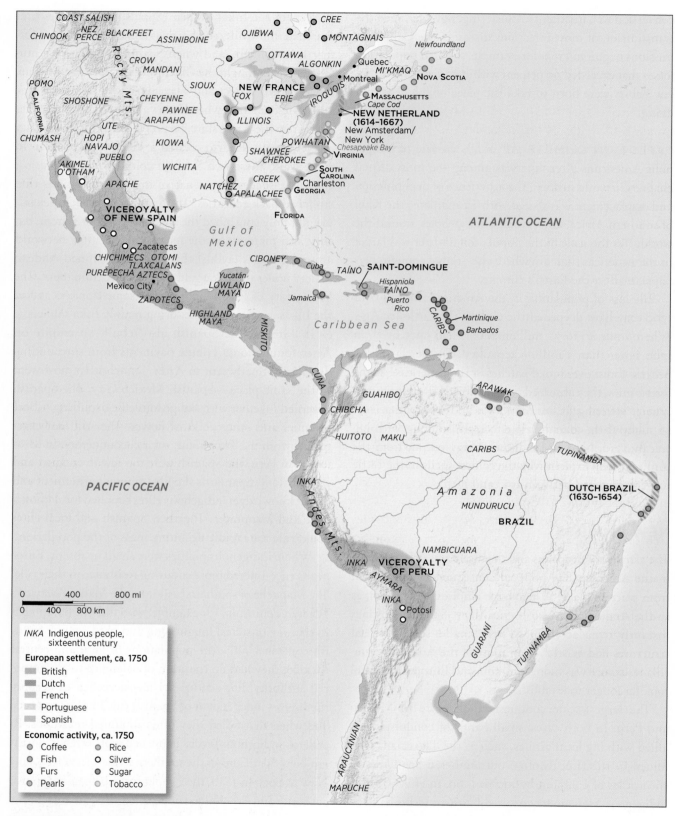

European Presence in the Americas, ca. 1750 By 1750, most of the land in the Americas was claimed by one or another European state. However, the degree to which they actually controlled American territory varied greatly. Where indigenous people remained numerically dominant, as in the heart of North America, they often exercised economic and territorial power, and European claims carried little weight. The new export economy of furs had a longer reach and was a collaboration between indigenous people and Europeans.

the Spanish Empire in America was a patchy one with firm control only in a few centers.

The other European empires in the Americas were much smaller than the Spanish. Portugal claimed Brazil but controlled only stretches of coastline and their immediate hinterlands as late as 1600. When the Dutch decided to take a bit of Brazil for themselves in 1618, Portugal could not prevent it. Almost all of Brazil remained under indigenous authority into the eighteenth century, when gold and diamond strikes brought a wave of European immigrants. The Dutch Empire was smaller still, confined to a few small Caribbean islands, the tiny settlement of New Netherland (now New York), and for 30 years a corner of Brazil. And the Dutch surrendered New Netherland to Britain in 1667.

Like the Spanish and Dutch, both the French and British claimed some Caribbean territories. They founded colonies on several small islands and some of the big ones, such as Jamaica, that Spain could not hold. In North America, they took gradual control of the eastern seaboard from the dwindling indigenous populations. The French settled at Quebec after 1608 but struggled to populate their colony, called New France, with farmers. By 1750, New France had only about 50,000 people despite high birth rates. Very few French wanted to move to New France. British settlement began in 1607 in Virginia and 1620 in Massachusetts, and soon spread everywhere from Georgia to Nova Scotia. These colonies grew quickly, expanding to the Appalachian Mountains by 1750, at which time big families and streams of immigrants accounted for a population of nearly 2 million, some 20 percent of whom were enslaved. In economic and strategic terms, Caribbean islands such as Jamaica and even tiny Martinique were worth a lot more than the North American colonies—because of the money made selling sugar from slave plantations.

SETTLEMENT AND TRANSOCEANIC ECONOMIES

The population catastrophe in the Americas played havoc with economic life and increased the scale of slavery. Labor grew ever scarcer outside of North America's eastern seaboard, and ambitious businessmen despaired over how to mine ores or raise crops without sufficient labor. The motive behind both the transatlantic African and indigenous slave trades was to provide cheap labor for the economies of the Americas. European laborers crossed the Atlantic too, a few as slaves, many as indentured servants—meaning they had to work for no wages for a set period, often seven years. But up to 1820, roughly four enslaved Africans came to the Americas for each European migrant, whether indentured or free. It wouldn't be until about 1880 that the cumulative number of European arrivals in the Americas equaled the number of enslaved Africans who survived the Middle Passage.

African and European migrants, sometimes together with indigenous populations, built a new economy in the Americas. The new connections to transatlantic markets, and in some cases new crops or technologies, presented novel opportunities. All the European powers hoped to find precious metals, as the Spanish did in great quantities. Where that failed, the new empires sought other ways to realize the economic potential of the Americas for their own benefit.

FISHERIES AND FURS One opportunity lay in the world's richest cod fisheries, from Cape Cod to Newfoundland. From the 1520s onward, British, French, and Basque (and eventually American and Canadian) fishermen, free men working for wages, caught thousands of tons of cod annually. Most of it was salted or dried and shipped to Europe for sale. On the mainland of North America, at least its northern half, hundreds of millions of beavers provided another way to make money. Indigenous Americans had long hunted and trapped fur-bearing

Cod Fisheries Fishermen process cod on Newfoundland in this eighteenth-century illustration. After bringing the fish ashore, they gut and dry them, and then pack them in salt to preserve them for the journey to other parts of North America and Europe.

animals on a modest scale. An export trade began around 1630, funneled through Montreal and New Amsterdam (New York after 1667) to Europe, where beaver coats and hats adorned the prosperous classes. Indigenous people still did most of the trapping, but they now sold most of their fur harvest to French, Dutch, or British merchants. Agents for European fur merchants, especially those based in New France, eventually ranged far into the interior of North America, often marrying into indigenous communities in arrangements broadly parallel to those with wives of the coast in the African slave trade. By 1800, the North American fur trade extended as far west as the Rocky Mountains. To the east, beavers were growing scarce, and their tens of millions of ponds, equal in area to 10 times North America's Great Lakes, dried up.

THE PLANTATION ZONE Another transatlantic economy, even more lucrative than the cod fisheries or fur trade, took root in the warmer regions, from the Chesapeake south to Brazil. This became the **plantation zone** of the Americas, the destination of the great majority of enslaved Africans shipped across the Atlantic. In the Chesapeake, where English settlement began in 1607, the moneymaking crop was tobacco. In South Carolina and Georgia, a rice plantation economy flourished after 1690. It was based on slave labor and to some extent on slave know-how: Africans from rice-growing regions transplanted their cultivation techniques.

The heart of the plantation zone lay in the Caribbean and northeastern Brazil, where sugar became the most rewarding plantation crop. Unlike fishing, fur trapping, or even tobacco farming, sugar cultivation only made sense on a large scale. Sugarcane juice had to be crystallized within days after the cane was cut, which required elaborate machinery to press juice out of the cane and boiling houses to convert the cane juice to sugar crystals. Because it called for hefty capital investment, sugar production became a business dominated by big planters with connections to European merchant houses. Dozens of Caribbean islands, including British Barbados and Jamaica, Spanish Cuba, and French Saint-Domingue (part of Hispaniola), produced sugar, as did Portuguese Brazil. From 1650 to 1800, sugar islands were the second-most valuable possessions in the Americas. Sugar plantation workers suffered the highest mortality rates anywhere in the plantation zone. Millions of Africans died on these plantations. Planters bought millions more to take their places.

SILVER Precious metals formed the most valuable sector in the transatlantic economy. Cortés and Pizarro sought gold and silver, and found both in envy-provoking quantities. They and their successors used all the tools they had—imagination, guile, technology, brutality—to coax more gold and silver out of Mexico and Peru. Spanish authorities organized large-scale silver mining in Zacatecas, Mexico, and at **Potosí** in the Andes. Potosí alone yielded 40,000 tons of silver between the 1540s and 1780s. It temporarily became one of the world's largest cities, despite an elevation well over 13,000 feet (4,000 meters).

By 1600 at Potosí, some 20,000 indigenous people—both wage workers and mita forced laborers—mined, processed, and minted silver into coins. Wage workers were well paid by local standards, but their lives were brutal and short on account of harsh conditions, frequent accidents, and poisoning from the mercury used in the refining process. Potosí mineworkers performed heavy labor in darkness relieved only by candlelight. They breathed air laced with dust that over time brought on silicosis and other lung diseases. Many of them spent their shifts carrying 55 lb. (25 kg) sacks of ore up rickety ladders, climbing more than 650 feet (200 meters)—no wonder they wouldn't work without a wad of coca leaves in their cheek to dull their pain, hunger, thirst, and minds. Andean peasant communities held the equivalent of funerals for young men drafted for the Potosí mita, knowing what lay ahead.

By 1608, the mita could no longer deliver enough indigenous workers, and mine owners bought enslaved

Silver Mines The Flemish engraver Theodor de Bry had never been to the Americas, but his depiction of silver mining at Potosí indicates the difficult physical conditions that forced laborers endured there.

Africans for work at Potosí. They generally toiled above ground in transport or refining. Life expectancies were so short for miners, and slaves so expensive, that employers preferred to see mita recruits do as much as possible of the lethal work belowground. One Spanish friar wrote in 1628, "Every peso coin minted in Potosí has cost the lives of ten Indians who died in the depths of the mines." This exaggerated the toll but underlines the human cost of the silver business.

Mule caravans and coastal shipping carried most Mexican and Andean silver to port cities for transport through the Caribbean to Spain. Some went directly from Mexico to Manila in the Philippines. Much of the silver that Spain extracted from the Americas eventually found its way to China or India, as we shall see in a later chapter.

AGRICULTURE People couldn't eat furs or silver: agriculture fed almost everyone from French Quebec to Spanish Chile. Indigenous peoples everywhere grew their own food when they could avoid being dragged off to plantations, mines, or missions. They raised newly introduced livestock species such as sheep, goats, and cattle. In seventeenth-century New Mexico, for example, the Navajo economy combined sheep herding with farming and raiding. Indigenous farmers sometimes added Old World crops to their gardens too. Settlers from Pennsylvania to New England to Quebec also raised their own food, often planting American maize alongside European varieties of wheat. Farther south, in the plantation zone, the richer European settlers obliged slaves to do all farmwork. Poor families in the plantation zone, whatever their racial identity, worked the land themselves. In Spanish America, settlers created big agricultural estates (*haciendas*), and the Crown granted them the right (an **encomienda**) to conscript indigenous laborers for all farmwork.

By and large, everyone ate local food. But by 1750, locally raised food might well consist of crops and animals that had been introduced from other continents in the Columbian Exchange and integrated into the farms and fields of the Americas.

HYBRID SOCIETIES

With lucrative transatlantic (and in cases transpacific) export economies linking them to Africa, Europe, and Asia, the Americas developed creole societies and cultures that blended elements from distant places. The changing languages of the Americas were a good measure of broader social and cultural change.

CREOLE LANGUAGES AND CULTURES Many indigenous tongues spoken in 1492 gradually died out as the number of speakers dwindled. By 1800, perhaps one-third of the roughly 25 million people living in the Americas spoke an indigenous language. Maybe one-tenth—generally, people born in Africa—spoke an African language. The majority spoke a European language, although sometimes not as their native tongue. In the plantation zone especially, new, creole languages developed that typically combined features from European and African tongues. (Most people in the Caribbean today speak one or more creole languages.) Haitian Creole, or Kreyòl, combined mainly French vocabulary with grammar based on West African languages. Papiamento, spoken in Aruba, Bonaire, and Curaçao, is a blend of Portuguese, Spanish, Dutch, and indigenous languages.

Similar blending took place in religious beliefs and practices. By 1800, most people in the Americas practiced one or another form of Christianity, but in ways that might have raised eyebrows in Christianity's homelands. European colonization in the Americas included substantial efforts at conversion and religious education, especially in lands controlled by Catholic kingdoms such

Missionaries This eighteenth-century manuscript illustration celebrates Spanish Dominican friars for their missionary efforts among indigenous people of Michoacán (Mexico). At the top, a friar gathers his congregants in a church away from attacking demons.

as Portugal, Spain, or France. Indeed, Christianization served as a primary justification for empires in the Americas. Catholic empires tended to entrust religion to one or several orders of the Catholic Church, such as the Jesuits, Franciscans, or Dominicans. Members of these orders built missions in French Canada, Portuguese Brazil, and throughout Spanish America, especially in frontier regions: Texas had 30 missions and California 21. Priests and friars, more than officials of the state, brokered the relations between indigenous and European societies in the Catholic domains.

The missions proved divisive in indigenous communities. Some welcomed the strange ideas about morality, sin, prayer, and God. Others strongly preferred their own ways, resisting conversion and resenting those who urged it. Missionaries often suffered high on-the-job mortality rates: in New Mexico over the course of the seventeenth century, about 40 percent of Franciscans were killed by the people they were trying to convert, the Pueblo. In lands controlled by the mainly Protestant British and Dutch, Christianization of the indigenous population carried a far lower priority.

Those attracted to Christianity generally preferred to meld the old with the new, to adopt Christian forms and belief selectively and mix them with their own practices—as Africans did with Islam or Chinese with Buddhism.

In the plantation zone, African religions entered the mix and often dominated it. Vodun, a polytheistic religion with a prominent role for female deities, was imported by enslaved Fon- and Ewe-speakers from West Africa. It took root in the Caribbean, Brazil, and Louisiana, acquiring new features, often from Catholicism, in each locale. People of African descent created new religions, such as Santería in the Spanish Caribbean or Candomblé in Brazil. Both are based on West African spiritual practices but with components adapted from Christianity or indigenous traditions. Yoruba religion played an especially large role in shaping religious practice in the plantation zone. Its tradition of orishas—spirits that guide people to live properly and help win favor from Olorun, the Yoruba creator god—blended fluidly with Catholicism's emphasis on saints. Enslaved Africans adjusted their spiritual lives to fit the challenges of plantation society.

SHIFTING SOCIAL HIERARCHIES The social structures of colonial societies in the Americas were complex and shifting hierarchies. Status depended on a long roster of variables. Gender and age mattered here, as everywhere else. Legal status (i.e., slave or free) and wealth mattered a lot in the Americas, as almost everywhere else. Skin color and presumed ancestry mattered more here than almost anywhere else because the Americas were one of the few places (the Dutch settlement at the Cape of Good Hope was another) where people from multiple continents and with notably different superficial characteristics (e.g., skin color) coexisted.

Every society calculated social status differently because so many variables were involved. For example, in the eighteenth century in the French plantation colony of Saint-Domingue (Haiti today), the social pyramid featured slaves—roughly 90 percent of the population—at the bottom. Above them stood free Blacks of African birth; free Blacks of Caribbean birth; *gens de couleur libres,* or free people of mixed African and European ancestry; poor whites; and at the top, prosperous whites. However, in some contexts wealthy gens de couleur libres might outrank poor whites. A lengthy vocabulary existed to distinguish among people depending on ancestry.

In Brazil, Mexico, or Peru, even more complex hierarchies existed, because—unlike in Saint-Domingue—indigenous populations survived in large numbers. Many

New Social Hierarchies The Italian-born painter Agostino Brunias, who lived on Dominica and St. Vincent in the eastern Caribbean, completed this canvas, *Free Women of Color with Their Children and Servants in a Landscape,* in the late eighteenth century. It depicts three wealthy mixed-race women, front and center, with their retinue. We can't be sure who in their retinue might be free and who enslaved, except for the lighter-skinned boys, who are presumably the children mentioned in the painting's title.

people had African, indigenous American, and European ancestors in every imaginable proportion, all captured in a correspondingly detailed vocabulary. In all three of these societies, slaves were on the bottom and wealthy Europeans on top of the social pyramid, but what lay in between was more complicated, and more fluid, than in Saint-Domingue.

New France and New England had different social hierarchies from the rest of the Americas. In 1750, New England had about 350,000 people, of whom roughly 330,000 were free, Christian, and of European descent. About 13,000 were of African descent, slave or free, and half as many were indigenous. Social distinctions beyond those of age and gender rested mainly on wealth, the prestige of one's ancestry, and one's religious sect. But in New France and farther west, around the Great Lakes, there were only 70,000 French people in 1750 and about 1,200 of African descent. Indigenous Americans outnumbered everyone else until about 1830. Many indigenous groups retained their old social structures, with hierarchies based on age, gender, ancestry, and achievement. But increasingly, they took part in market transactions with frontier settlers—providing furs and hides, for example—and as a result became part of larger societies in which they occupied subordinate roles.

INDEPENDENT GROUPS Some peoples in the Americas managed to keep their distance from the new European empires. The Mapuche and Maya, and the so-called Plains Indians of North America, successfully resisted encroaching empires until the nineteenth century, as did the peoples of the Northwest coast. But even these groups experienced some rearrangements of their social hierarchies. With war and trade more common, specialists in these pursuits could more easily gain status. Many peoples in Amazonia evaded contact with outsiders altogether for centuries (some of them even until this day) and probably underwent no sharp changes in their social structures.

Communities of escaped slaves, called maroons in the English-speaking colonies, secured their freedom for decades, often in mountains or jungles. Brazil had many such communities, called *quilombos*. The largest, Palmares, was home to 30,000 refugees from slavery and lasted from about 1600 until 1694, when Portuguese forces overwhelmed it with an artillery assault. Other such communities were much smaller, mostly composed of young men eking out a living hunting, fishing, and sometimes raiding plantations from which they had fled.

Maroons were not the only ones who temporarily escaped the reach of the new empires. Until about 1730, many coastlands of the Americas hosted pirates who operated on the margins, preying on merchant ships and occasionally on settlements. Most were Europeans themselves, usually runaway sailors fleeing the harsh discipline of naval or merchant vessels, but perhaps one in three was African or of partly African descent. In general, piracy flourishes when a lucrative maritime trade springs up without powerful naval states nearby. The spurt of seaborne trade in the wake of Columbus and da Gama provided such an opportunity, and pirates multiplied in the Caribbean, the Mediterranean, the Indian Ocean, and in East Asian waters. Pirates in the Caribbean enjoyed considerable success from the 1570s until the 1720s, by which time European navies became too large and efficient for piracy to flourish.

The entanglement of the Americas in the growing Global web was an extremely disruptive process. It entailed the dismantling of the pre-Columbian American webs of interaction—mainly through the massive loss of indigenous populations, but also through compulsory labor, forced migration, and other hardships. Meanwhile, merchants, migrants, missionaries, and others forged new linkages both within the Americas and between the Americas and the wider world of Atlantic Europe, Atlantic Africa, and East Asia. A true Global web was spun in the centuries after Columbus, for the first time in the history of the world. The newly refashioned Americas provided much of the thread in the form of silver, sugar, furs, fish, and other commodities traded far and wide.

SIBERIA ABSORBED

Expansion of the Old World web proceeded by land as well as sea. One of the largest territorial expansions took place in Siberia. Nearly the size of South America, Siberia (now Russian territory) lies between the Arctic Ocean to the north and the steppe of Central Asia and Mongolia to the south. It is stunningly cold during its long winter. In 1500, most of it was tall forest or shrubby, coniferous, and often swampy forest called taiga. Getting around within Siberia was a challenge, and getting anything useful out of it was no easier. A strong motive would be required to tempt outsiders to tackle Siberia.

The indigenous population numbered only a few hundred thousand in 1500. They were divided into about a hundred linguistic groups, and most followed a variety of shamanistic religions. Some, in southern Siberia, were influenced by Buddhist beliefs acquired from Mongols, whose empire had included parts of that region. Siberians drew their living from the forest: fishing, hunting, trapping, and reindeer herding. In southern Siberia, they also raised what crops they could in the brief growing season and traded occasionally with the steppe peoples to their south.

FUR: A LUCRATIVE EXPORT

The main thing outsiders wanted from Siberia was fur, just as in northern North America. Several million foxes, ermines, squirrels, and sables, all with thick pelts, wandered the woods and swamps. For centuries, a tiny proportion of those pelts went to rich buyers in China or the Baltic lands and Russia. In the sixteenth century, as elites in East Asia and eastern Europe grew wealthier, demand quickened for Siberian furs. Eventually this demand and export trade provided the motive for outsiders to try to control Siberia.

The outsiders who took this step were Russians and Cossacks. Russians were Slavic-speakers who in 1480 had won independence from the Mongol Golden Horde and formed a state called Muscovy, centered on Moscow. Muscovy grew as Mongol power waned, and its leaders aimed to "gather all the Russias" into a larger empire at the expense of neighbors. The ruler Ivan IV (r. 1553–1584) championed this enterprise. He declared himself tsar (derived from the word *Caesar*), or emperor of Russia, in 1547 and remained in power until his death in 1584. He ruled some 8 to 12 million people and rarely missed an opportunity to flay or boil an enemy alive.

Cossacks were mainly peasants or serfs (or their descendants) who managed to run away from estates in what is now Russia and Ukraine. Beginning in the fifteenth and sixteenth centuries, they settled in the river valleys of the steppes north and east of the Black Sea, forming their own self-governing communities. They were roughly analogous to the maroons in the plantation zone of the Americas. Cossacks lived by farming, raiding, and piracy on rivers and the Black Sea, or by hiring themselves out as mercenaries. In the sixteenth century, Cossacks were often enemies of the Russian state but sometimes were hired as protectors of Russian frontiers against Tatar raiders from the steppe. At all times, they were military specialists. Their population was probably no more than 100,000 in 1600.

The spearhead of the process by which Siberia joined the Global web, and the Russian Empire, was a Cossack named **Yermak**. He was successful as a river pirate, but in about 1580 he became the equivalent of a conquistador. It was not silver that drew him into Siberia, but fur. An entrepreneurial family with close ties to the tsars, the Stroganovs, hired Yermak to expand their fur trade from Siberia. To do so he had to battle through a Tatar khanate in southwestern Siberia, a legacy of Mongol rule. With a band of about 800—just a few more than the Spaniards Cortés led against Tenochtitlán—Yermak defeated the Tatars, thanks to guns and riverboats provided by the Stroganovs. Within a couple of years, Yermak and his roughnecks had reached the Ob River. They sent back enough furs to please the Stroganovs and Tsar Ivan, who—sensing a business opportunity—removed the price he had put on Yermak's head and became his biggest supporter.

Yermak died in 1585 in a scrap with Tatars, but his success inspired Cossacks and Russians to stream into Siberia. By 1640, they had built wooden forts at key portages and river junctions across Siberia all the way to Pacific Ocean shores. The conquest of Siberia paid handsome rewards for Russia. Soon one-tenth to one-third of the tsar's revenues came from the sale of furs. Yermak became a hero in Russia, memorialized over time with postage stamps and public statues.

Like Spain's conquistadores, Yermak and his successors enjoyed the advantages of living inside the world's biggest web. They had the latest military technologies, thanks to the Stroganovs and the tsars. They knew how to build boats that could operate on Siberia's rivers, and how to put small cannon on their boats. They knew the market price of trade goods—tobacco, alcohol, flour—as well as that of furs. At least some of them could read and write, enabling them to communicate and coordinate the actions of scattered groups over vast distances. And by virtue of childhood exposure, they carried immunities to the standard crowd diseases, which indigenous Siberians generally did not.

Siberian Fur The crown of Tsar Ivan V from the seventeenth century was adorned with fur as well as precious stones, an indication of the significance of Siberian fur to the Russian monarch.

Muscovy, Russia, and Siberia, 1400–1800 The expansion of Muscovy and Russia included the incorporation of what is now Siberia, beginning with the incursions of the Cossacks and Russians led by Yermak starting around 1580. Motivated by a quest for furs, by 1640 Russians had built scattered forts across Siberia to the Pacific shores. By 1730, Russians had crossed the Bering Strait and extended their fur trade to Alaska.

THE RUSSIFICATION OF SIBERIA

The Russian conquest carried hard consequences for the native populations of Siberia. In 1600, they numbered over 300,000 people, with 120 languages among them. After Yermak's intrusions, many Siberians died from exposure to unfamiliar diseases. One group, the Yukagir in eastern Siberia, lost two-thirds of their population to diseases, probably smallpox in the main. By 1700, the Yakut and Tunguz peoples had lost 80 percent of their population of a century before. As in the Americas, brutal treatment compounded the effects of diseases. Cossacks, following Yermak's lead, demanded tribute in the form of furs from all adult males (an arrangement with no parallel in the North American fur trade). As the indigenous Siberian population fell, Cossacks and Russians required more tribute from

each man. Many resisted Cossack and Russian demands, and countless ambushes, skirmishes, and battles resulted. Atrocities abounded. The patriarch of Moscow, the top religious official of the Russian Orthodox Church, complained in 1662 that Russian men were neglecting their Christian duties, mistreating native Siberian women, even buying and selling them. In the end, a few thousand Cossacks and Russians subdued a few hundred thousand indigenous Siberians over 5 million square miles of forest and taiga. Together, they trapped and skinned millions of sables, ermines, and foxes—and helped make the Russian tsars richer and more powerful than ever before.

Over time, Siberia entered the Global web and became increasingly Russian. Military and political control came first. Creole versions of Russian gradually developed and occasionally took the place of indigenous languages.

Russian Orthodoxy joined the several forms of shamanism formerly practiced, creating blended religious practices. Siberia in the seventeenth and eighteenth centuries was creating new hybrid cultures with ever-stronger Russian components. By 1795, Siberia's population surpassed 1 million, mostly Russian in language and culture. Many Siberian women took Russian or Cossack husbands, and their children often preferred the identity of their fathers, which conferred more advantages in life. In later centuries, mainly after 1860, millions of Russians migrated to Siberia, swamping what remained of the indigenous peoples, their languages, and their religion, so that Siberian culture became highly Russified.

Russians and Cossacks pushed farther eastward. Clashes with China led to a 1689 treaty that divided vast, uncharted Siberian and East Asian spaces between the Russian and Chinese Empires. By the 1740s, Russians were seeking furs in Alaska. Within decades, they mobilized indigenous Alaskans—Aleuts, mainly—to hunt fur seals along the Pacific coast from the Aleutian Islands south to San Francisco Bay. Russains used the same techniques as in Siberia, demanding tribute and taking hostages. Unfamiliar diseases and Russian guns struck down Aleuts, whose population fell by 80 percent from 1740 to 1800. Only a few hundred Russians settled in Alaska, mostly on the coast. Like Siberia, these North American shores joined the world's web—painfully—through Russia's fur trade.

Russifying Siberia In this engraving found in a seventeenth-century Russian chronicle, Russian magistrates conduct business in the Siberian city of Tyumen. Founded in 1586 on the site of a previous Tatar settlement, Tyumen was the first Russian city established in Siberia.

OCEANIA AND AUSTRALIA ENMESHED

Probably the most isolated peoples in the world in the years between 1500 and 1750 were those living on the continent of Australia and the islands of Remote Oceania. In Australia, as we have seen, people had arrived at least 50,000 years ago and learned to manage a challenging environment. The archeological evidence suggests that by 1750 they numbered 500,000 to 1 million. The islands of Remote Oceania acquired human populations as early as 6,000 years ago in some cases and as recently as 750 years ago in others. The most populated archipelagoes, as of 1750, were Hawaii and New Caledonia, each with perhaps 400,000 people; Fiji with 150,000; and Tahiti and New Zealand, each with maybe 100,000. Taken together, the population of Australia plus all the Pacific Islands in 1750 came to less than 4 million people.

ANOTHER DISEASE DISASTER

Except for some island chains of Near Oceania (meaning New Guinea, the Bismarck Archipelago, and the Solomon Islands) where malaria lurked, Pacific islands, like Australia, harbored few infectious diseases. By global standards, people lived unusually free from infection. That did not mean they lived especially long: droughts, storms, tsunamis, and other natural hazards took a considerable toll. The islanders' minimal experience with infectious disease had long been a blessing, but in the late eighteenth century it became a curse.

In the 1760s, European mariners, especially British and French, began to sail the Pacific more frequently. They increasingly found commodities that, with their knowledge of distant markets, they could sell: sealskins, whale oil, sea cucumber (a delicacy in China), and sandalwood (a luxury in China). Sustained contact between Pacific Island populations and Europeans began between 1767 and 1778 in most cases, and in Australia starting in 1788.

In every case, the contact brought demographic catastrophe. Unfamiliar diseases had similar effects as in the Americas, Siberia, and among the Khoi of South Africa. The precise scale of these disasters is uncertain, but it appears that the Marquesas Islands were among the hardest hit, losing about 96 percent of their population between roughly 1770 and 1920. Small archipelagoes, where everyone was in regular contact with everyone else, allowed infectious diseases to spread quickly. Epidemics hit again and again, sometimes killing a quarter or a third of an island's people each time. As late as 1875, a measles outbreak in Fiji carried off one-third of all remaining Fijians.

Larger archipelagoes, with more dispersed populations, fared somewhat better but still suffered disastrous losses. New Zealand lost about half its Maori population between 1769 and 1870. Australia probably lost more than half of its Aboriginal people between 1788 and 1900. No one had much in the way of useful medicine to combat the epidemics.

Part of the demographic catastrophe, in the Pacific as in the Americas, resulted from falling birth rates. This too had something to do with disease. The arrival of European (and after 1780, American) sailors spurred a sex trade that spread venereal diseases far and wide from Hawaii to New Zealand. These infections made many women infertile. Sometimes women voluntarily took sailors as lovers while a ship anchored offshore, receiving gifts they valued and, as they saw it, enhancing their *mana*, or spiritual prestige, through sex with powerful strangers. Sometimes they did so under duress, compelled by fathers, brothers, or husbands to trade sex for iron nails, liquor, guns, or other treasured items. In New Zealand by the 1820s, Maori clans fought wars with one another to capture and enslave women. The captors then sold these women's favors to visiting sailors for guns to fight rival clans more effectively.

Just about everywhere in the Pacific, as in Siberia and the Americas, indigenous populations fell for about 150 years after the onset of first contact with the wider world. Then they stabilized and slowly began to grow. Despite this recovery, in many cases, most notably Australia, New Zealand, and Hawaii, immigrant peoples came to outnumber indigenous populations.

CHRISTIANITY AND TRADE GOODS

Contact with the wider world brought much more than disease and disaster to Oceania and Australia. Christianity was a popular import. Catholic and Protestant missionaries flocked to many Pacific islands, and although easily horrified by local attitudes to clothing (too little) and sex (too much), in time they proved highly successful in making converts. Missionaries had invisible allies

in the murderous microbes they and others brought with them: everyone could see that newcomers suffered far less from disease, and many islanders concluded that the Christian God offered better protection than their own deities could. Missionaries also had highly visible, if inadvertent, allies in the sailors and whalers who vividly demonstrated Christianity's seven deadly sins. Within a century of contact, almost all Pacific Islanders and most Australian Aborigines had accepted Christianity, although they adapted their new religion to their own traditions and circumstances, as converts normally do.

Trade goods and introduced plants and animals proved as popular as Christianity. European mariners brought such useful novelties as iron fishhooks and farming tools, guns, cattle, horses, goats, and sheep. Pacific peoples traded for these goods and increasingly took up wage work specifically to get them. The new tools and animals increased the economic potential of island (and Australian) landscapes.

AUSTRALIA

In Australia during the eighteenth century, the Aboriginal population of half a million to 1 million divided into roughly 250 groups, each with its own language. According to one of the first foreigners ever to meet them, Captain James Cook in 1770, "They may appear to some to be the most wretched people on earth, but in reality they are far happier than we Europeans. They live in a tranquility which is not disturbed by the inequality in condition: the earth and the sea of their own accord furnish them with all things necessary for life." Cook may have failed to recognize social inequalities among Aboriginal Australians, which surely existed, even if muted by the standards Cook knew from his Scottish-English upbringing. Protocols governed intergroup behavior in Australia, usually keeping conflict under control.

However, no protocols could protect Aboriginal Australians from what came their way starting in 1788: a fleet, the first of many, bearing more than 1,000 settlers backed by the British government. Most of the settlers were convicts. Transportation of convicts continued until 1868, totaling 160,000 settlers in all, of whom about 15 percent were women. Once in Australia, a few were freed, and one rose to become a judge. Free migrants—mostly English, but one-quarter of them Irish—came in larger numbers

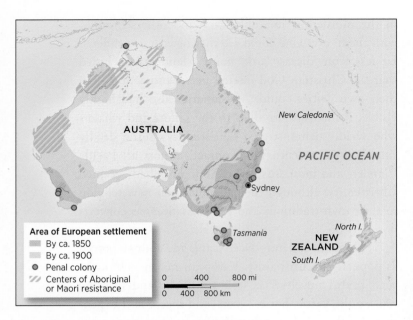

Australia and New Zealand, ca. 1770–1900 Aboriginal Australians had to adjust to British settlement from 1788 onward, as did Maori in New Zealand from about 1800. They often found trade goods attractive, and Christianity too. But like indigenous Americans, native Siberians, and the Khoi in South Africa, they suffered greatly from imported diseases and from attacks by better-armed newcomers. Within a century, both lands were demographically dominated by the newcomers and were securely part of the British Empire.

by the 1820s, and the population spilled out of the original settlements near Sydney onto the tablelands of the interior. Squatters, as Euro-Australians who helped themselves to land were called, pushed Aboriginals off the best lands, often violently.

Over the next century, skirmishes and wars between settlers and Aborigines claimed about 27,000 lives, 90 percent of them Aboriginal. The Aboriginal Australians fought with spears and shields; the newcomers had muskets and, soon, artillery. Scattered guerilla wars flared up now and again, but the tide flowed in favor of the settlers. Outright massacres occurred too. As in Siberia, South Africa's Cape, and the Americas, the toll of disease and the disparity in military technology made the difference.

By 1850, the rising population of Euro-Australians outnumbered the falling one of Aboriginal Australians among the continent's half million residents. Aborigines increasingly lived in the dryer or more tropical parts of the country that the immigrants did not want. Having lost the best lands, many Aborigines made their peace with the settlers and worked as cooks or stockmen (cowboys) on cattle or sheep stations (ranches). Aboriginal women often married (often informally) immigrant men, especially in the early years of settlement when British women were scarce. Australia now had sprawling wheat fields, millions of sheep and cattle, and a prosperous wool export trade. All this seemed right to most Euro-Australians: as one settler asked in 1845, "which has the better right—the savage, born in a country, which he runs over but can scarcely be said to occupy... or the civilized man, who comes to introduce into this... unproductive country, the industry which supports life...?" Aboriginal Australians, of course, thought they had the better right, but they lacked the power to enforce it. By 1850, the southern continent

Cook's Voyages This watercolor appears as an illustration in James Cook's account of his voyages. It shows his ship, the *Endeavour*, anchored on the east coast of Australia on his first voyage in 1770.

Treaty of Waitangi This painting, by New Zealand government artist L. C. Mitchell, is from 1949. It shows the signing of the 1840 Treaty of Waitangi that led to the establishment of British rule over Arotearoa—the Maori term for New Zealand. Some 500 Maori chiefs signed the Maori-language version of the Treaty. Arguments about the translation, which was done by missionaries, have led to disputes ever since.

Maori Culture A nineteenth-century illustration of a Maori warrior carrying a musket is suggestive of the destructive impact that European firearms had on Maori society.

had undergone a radical transformation, similar in its broad outlines to the fate of the Americas and Siberia, if different in the particulars.

NEW ZEALAND

In New Zealand (Aotearoa), the entry into the Global web also came suddenly and wrenchingly. As we've seen, Maori—Polynesians who settled New Zealand in about 1280—lived as farmers, fishers, foragers, and hunters, in groups that since 1500 or so had become more competitive and often warlike. They had had no significant interactions with peoples from outside New Zealand and its tiny offshore islands for many centuries. In 1642, the Dutch sea captain Abel Tasman sighted New Zealand, stayed for a few hours, and was driven away by Maori. In 1769, two French ships visited briefly. Settlers began to dig in around 1800, at first living among, and more or less as, Maori. But by 1840, organized colonization was under way, and the

pakeha (as people of European origin are termed in New Zealand) population ballooned to half a million by 1885. Maori population continued to fall due to introduced diseases and violence until about 1890.

As in the Americas, Siberia, and Australia, the local population in New Zealand alternately welcomed and resisted the settler presence. Some Maori went to work on sailing ships to see the wider world. Many more traded eagerly for exotic goods such as iron nails (useful as chisels for the Maori tradition of wood carving), blankets, and guns. Maori also adopted pig raising and potato farming, markedly improving their nutrition by making new animals and plants their own.

Maori took up firearms with both enthusiasm and desperation. Martial prowess had long been important to male Maori. Now their internal wars became deadlier. As in Africa during the time of the Atlantic slave trade, it often became necessary to acquire guns to defend oneself against others already equipped with them. In the early nineteenth century, Maori with guns terrorized Maori without guns until the point came when all surviving Maori peoples had guns. In the process, 20,000 to 40,000 were killed in the so-called Musket Wars (1807–1845), and many thousand women and children were captured and enslaved. Women captives, as noted above, could be put to use in the sex trade to acquire more guns and ammunition. Maori also turned their weapons on visiting whalers and sealers. On one occasion in 1821, they captured six Americans and forced some to eat others (according to Joseph Price of Wilmington, Delaware, who survived this ordeal, his shipmates "tasted very much like roasted pork").

It comes as no surprise that Maori rarely welcomed newcomers. For half a century after contact in 1769, Maori exposure to the wider world came mainly via two sorts of men: Australian convicts eager to shed their pasts and gamble on a rough life skinning seals on New Zealand's shores, and sex-starved British, Australian, and American whalers. Many encounters ended in deadly skirmishes.

But over time, as the newcomers came to include more and more missionaries and even families, Maori found more to welcome. As elsewhere, in New Zealand many in the indigenous population concluded that the Christians' God was powerful and merited worshipping. They embraced Christianity with remarkable gusto from the 1830s. Missionaries' Christian messages made sense to many Maori, who witnessed the conspicuous sinfulness of visiting whalers and sealers.

In 1840, in the **Treaty of Waitangi**, most Maori chiefs agreed to put down their weapons and become British subjects in return for guarantees of their land. Large-scale British settlement soon followed, and treaty or no treaty, Maori and *pakeha* engaged in intermittent land wars (1845–1872) that ultimately ended Maori independence and confirmed New Zealand's future as a British settler colony. Epidemics, warfare, and dispossession, together with new trade opportunities and a new religion: the entry of New Zealand into the Global web bore a family resemblance to the experiences of Australia, Siberia, and the Americas.

HAWAII

Before contact, Hawaii's roughly 400,000 people lived—mainly on a diet of taro, yams, sweet potatoes, and fish—in a handful of small and competitive kingdoms long

isolated from the rest of the world. After Captain Cook and British sailors turned up in 1778, Hawaiian kings sought to exploit the opportunity presented by the strangers' tools and weapons. One king, Kamehameha, scored a brilliant success when he murdered all but one of a ship's crew and invited the sole survivor to instruct his warriors in the arts of using firearms and sailing European vessels. His soldiers learned well, and between the 1780s and 1810 he defeated all his rivals and unified Hawaii

Hawaiian Monarchy An official portrait shows Queen Liliʻuokalani sitting on her throne in 1892, shortly before Americans deposed her.

as a single monarchy. Unlike the chiefs of New Zealand's rival clans, **King Kamehameha** managed to keep tight control over imported weaponry and so could vault himself into supreme power over his fellow Hawaiians. He ruled as an autocrat, made a fortune on sandalwood exports, banned human sacrifice, and imposed peace.

Despite the peace, his subjects diminished in number. Whalers, traders, and sailors brought the same infections to Hawaii that ravaged the rest of the Pacific. Venereal diseases, probably previously unknown, spread widely and lowered birth rates. The indigenous Hawaiian population plunged to about 75,000 in 1850 and 40,000 in 1890. As this demographic catastrophe unfolded, many Hawaiians came to wonder whether their old ways were best and whether their familiar gods could still protect them.

After King Kamehameha died in 1819, missionaries arrived in force and met with much success. The most politically ambitious of the deceased king's 22 wives, Kaʻahumanu, adopted a Protestant faith. She served as regent for her son, King Kamehameha II, and did her best to suppress both indigenous Hawaiian religion and Catholicism until her death in 1832.

Settlers came late to Hawaii—mainly after 1850—but by 1870 they outnumbered indigenous Hawaiians. They brought cattle, sugarcane, and a new export economy that bound Hawaii mainly to U.S. markets. Sugarcane in particular required labor, which came in the form of nearly 50,000 Chinese immigrants and tens of thousands more Japanese, Koreans, Filipinos, and Portuguese. Hawaii too became a hybrid society and culture. Newspapers in Chinese appeared in 1881. The quintessential Hawaiian musical instrument, the ukulele, was first made in about 1880 by Portuguese immigrants. In the 1890s, American businessmen resident in Hawaii deposed the reigning monarch, Queen Liliʻuokalani, and ended the Hawaiian monarchy. The United States annexed the islands in 1898.

Between the 1760s and 1850, the Global web ensnared the Pacific world from Australia to Hawaii. Formerly isolated peoples now found themselves in regular contact with the wider world, thanks to European mariners often seeking goods for Chinese, European, or U.S. markets. The roughly 4 million people affected entered a new epidemiological world full of dangerous new diseases. They entered a new cultural world dominated by European outlooks, languages, and Christianity, to which many Pacific peoples were strongly attracted. They also entered a political realm in which their small numbers, limited state organization, and stone- and wood-based military technologies put them at an acute disadvantage.

CONCLUSION

When people from Eurasia crossed the seas to the Americas, southern Africa, Australia, and Oceania and pierced the forests into the interior of Siberia, they created the first truly global web. In demographic and political terms, this process proved a disaster for indigenous peoples. In cultural terms, it was a disaster for people who preferred the old, familiar ways. Introduced crowd diseases wrought havoc for five or six generations. People lost hope and initiative. Social networks, institutions, collective memory, and expertise were all eroded or entirely lost. Some peoples—like the Tasmanians with whom this chapter began—were effectively wiped out, and stray survivors attached themselves to new families, tribes, and groups.

In southernmost Africa, the Americas, and Siberia, the creation of the Global web entailed the destruction of indigenous political orders. Empires such as those of the Aztecs and Inkas crumbled. New polities took their place,

usually dominated by Europeans but sometimes run by opportunistic locals, such as Hawaii's King Kamehameha.

In Africa north of the Cape settlement, the new links to oceanic trade and the Global web had political consequences too, but less radical ones. States rose and fell, and on balance more militaristic states prospered in the new situation, which brought with it the risks and opportunities of the expanded slave trade. But basic political formats held up better in Africa than elsewhere. So did the population, despite the slave trade. In much of Africa, as in most of Eurasia, crowd diseases were familiar childhood diseases that rarely caused massive epidemics. The main reason for this was that so much of Africa had participated in the Old World web and shared in its infections for centuries already. The Khoi in southernmost Africa were an exception.

Vast cultural changes resulted from the formation of a globalizing web. These normally led to hybrid, **creole cultures**, with varying mixtures of traditions from Europe and from local populations. In the plantation zone of the Americas, the mix also included a large share of African culture—religion, languages, foodways—carried across the Atlantic in slave ships. And in Hawaii it included strong infusions of East Asian cultures, carried across the Pacific mainly by immigrant laborers.

The economies that underpinned all the societies in question also underwent radical restructuring. Ocean-going trade reached almost every coast and navigable river. New market connections inspired stepped-up (or altogether new) production or extraction of furs in Siberia and North America, slaves and ivory in Africa, wool in Australia, sealskins in New Zealand, whale oil throughout Polynesian waters, fish from the northwest Atlantic, sugar from the plantation zone of the Americas and from Hawaii, and silver from the Andes and Mexico—just to name a few. The growing scale, scope, and pace of commerce created opportunities for survivors, at the same time that unprecedented demographic disasters were unfolding.

Such demographic, political, cultural, and economic tumult around the globe added fuel to the dynamics of change in the heartlands of Eurasia, to which we turn next.

CHAPTER REVIEW

KEY TERMS

disease disasters (p. 536)
King Afonso (p. 540)
Khoi (p. 542)
transatlantic slave trade (p. 544)
Middle Passage (p. 544)

Taíno (p. 549)
mita (p. 550)
plantation zone (p. 554)
Potosí (p. 554)
encomienda (p. 555)

Yermak (p. 558)
Treaty of Waitangi (p. 564)
King Kamehameha (p. 564)
creole cultures (p. 565)

Go to INQUIZITIVE to see what you've learned—and learn what you've missed—with personalized feedback along the way.

REVIEW QUESTIONS

1. Why were Atlantic Europeans in the best position to take advantage of the opportunities that the globalizing world offered?

2. Identify the three main components of the process of globalization in Africa.

3. What motivated merchants and rulers in East and West Africa to convert to Islam?

4. How did the Portuguese economic and religious presence in Angola and Kongo differ from that in Mozambique?

5. Explain the major political, economic, cultural, and social impacts of the slave trade in Africa.

6. What interrelated factors contributed to demographic catastrophes in the Americas?

7. Compare and contrast the Spanish conquest in the Americas in large empires versus smaller polities.

8. How did silver grease the wheels of global commerce?

9. What happened to the native Siberian population after becoming part of the Russian Empire and the world's largest web, and why?

10. What caused birth rates in the Pacific to plummet following sustained contact with Europeans?

11. How did European military technology affect Maori and Hawaiian society and politics?

12. What were the overarching cultural and economic changes that globalization caused?

FURTHER READING

James BELICH, *Making Peoples: A History of the New Zealanders from Polynesian Settlement to the End of the Nineteenth Century* (1996). The first several chapters recount the Polynesian and contact-era history of New Zealand with insight, wit, and verve.

J. H. ELLIOTT, *Empires of the Atlantic World: Britain and Spain in America 1492-1830* (2006). A work by a master historian on the Spanish and British Empires in the three centuries after Columbus.

David ELTIS and David RICHARDSON, *Atlas of the Transatlantic Slave Trade* (2010). The authoritative source on the size, sources, and destinations of the slave trade. See also the website based on the same research: http://www.slavevoyages.org/

Janet M. HARTLEY, *Siberia: A History of the People* (2019). A readable overview, with good chapters on the Russian absorption of Siberia.

Grace KARSKENS, *The Colony: A History of Early Sydney* (2009). A detailed and thoughtful study of the early encounter between settlers and Aboriginal Australians.

Andrés RESÉNDEZ, *The Other Slavery: The Uncovered Story of Indian Enslavement in America* (2016). The author shines a spotlight on a neglected aspect of the history of the Caribbean, Mexico, and the U.S. Southwest.

John F. RICHARDS, *The Unending Frontier: An Environmental History of the Early Modern World* (2003). A massive study of environmental change, 1450-1800.

Randy J. SPARKS, *The Two Princes of Calabar: An Eighteenth-Century Atlantic Odyssey* (2004). A story that explores how the Atlantic slave trade worked in the late eighteenth century.

John K. THORNTON, *A Cultural History of the Atlantic World, 1250-1820* (2012). An excellent transatlantic history, with a broad sense of what counts as "cultural."

Firsthand Accounts from the Middle Passage and Life in Slavery, ca. 1770–1830

AMONG THE MAJOR CONSEQUENCES OF THE formation of a truly global web was a vast expansion of the scale of slavery, especially in the Atlantic world. The transatlantic slave trade reached its peak in the 1780s, just as abolition movements were getting organized. Partly as a result of abolitionism, a small handful of eyewitness accounts of the slave trade were published, many of them authored by refugees from slavery. The excerpts below provide four perspectives on enslavement, the Middle Passage, and/or the experience of slavery in the Americas. One was written by a white abolitionist who had worked on slave ships. Two were written by men who were enslaved in Africa, survived the Middle Passage, and toiled for years in slavery. One was written by a woman who was born into slavery on an island in the heart of the Atlantic.

SOURCE 16.1

The Middle Passage of Olaudah Equiano, ca. 1756

According to his autobiography, Olaudah Equiano—whose life story appears at greater length in a later chapter—was born in the village of Essaka, probably in Iboland (Nigeria), around 1745. He was captured, enslaved, and taken across the Atlantic to the Caribbean. He later managed to buy his freedom in England and became a key figure in the movement to abolish slavery and the slave trade. In 1789, he completed *The Interesting Narrative of the Life of Olaudah Equiano*. The passage below is an excerpt from this work.

One day, when...only I and my dear sister were left to mind the house, two men and a woman got over our walls, and in a moment seized us both, and without giving us time to cry out or make resistance they stopped our mouths and ran off with us into the nearest wood. Here they tied our hands and continued to carry us as far as they could till night came on, when we reached a small house where the robbers halted for refreshment and spent the night....I was now carried...through many different countries....All the nations and people I had hitherto passed through resembled our own in manner, customs, and language: but I came at length to a country the inhabitants of which differed from us....Thus I continued to travel, sometimes by land, sometimes by water, through different countries and various nations, till at the end of six or seven months after I had been kidnapped I arrived at the sea coast.

The first object which saluted my eyes when I arrived on the coast was the sea, and a slave ship which was then riding at anchor and waiting for its cargo. These filled me with astonishment, which was soon converted into terror when I was carried on board....I was now persuaded that I had gotten into a world of bad spirits and that they were going to kill me. Their complexions too differing so much from ours, their long hair and the language they spoke (which was very different from any I had ever heard) united to confirm me in this belief....When I looked round the ship too and saw a large furnace or copper-boiling and a multitude of black people of every description chained together, every one of their countenances expressing dejection and sorrow, I no longer doubted of my fate; and quite overpowered with horror and anguish, I fell motionless on the deck and fainted. When I recovered a little I found some black people about me, who I believed were some of those who had brought me on board and had been receiving their pay; they talked to me in order to cheer me, but all in vain. I asked them if we were not to be eaten by those white men with horrible looks, red faces, loose hair. They told me I was not.... Soon after this the blacks who brought me on board went off and left me abandoned to despair.

...I was soon put down under the decks, and there I received such a salutation in my nostrils as I had never experienced in my life: so that with the loathsomeness of the stench and crying together, I became so sick and low that I was not able to eat, nor I had the least desire to taste anything. I now wished for the last friend, death, to relieve me; but soon, to my grief, two of the white men offered me eatables, and on my refusing to eat, one of them held me fast . . . and tied my feet while the other flogged me severely. . . . I feared I should be put to death, the white people looked and acted, as I thought, in so savage a manner; for I had never seen among my people such instances of brutal cruelty, and this is not only shown towards us blacks but also to some of the whites themselves. One white man in particular I saw, flogged so unmercifully with a large rope near the foremast that he died in consequence of it. . . .

At last, when the ship we were in had got in all her cargo . . . [we] were all put under deck so that we could not see how they managed the vessel. The stench of the hold while we were on the coast was so intolerable loathsome that it was dangerous to remain there for any time, and some of us had been permitted to stay on the deck for the fresh air; but now that the whole ship's cargo were confined together it became absolutely pestilential. The closeness of the place and the heat of the climate, added to the number in the ship, which was so crowded that each had scarcely room to turn himself, almost suffocated. This produced copious perspirations, so that the air soon became unfit for respiration from a variety of loathsome smells, and brought on a sickness among the slaves, of which many died. . . . The shrieks of the women and the groans of the dying rendered the whole scene of horror almost inconceivable. . . .

One day, when we had a smooth sea and moderate wind, two of my wearied countrymen who were chained together (I was near them at the time), preferring death to such a life of misery, somehow made through the nettings and jumped into the sea: immediately another quite dejected fellow, who on account of his illness was suffered to be out of irons, also followed their example; . . . the ship's crew . . . were instantly alarmed. [They] g[o]t the boat out to go after the slaves. However two of the wretches were drowned, but they got the other and afterwards flogged him unmercifully for thus attempting to prefer death to slavery. In this manner we continued to undergo more hardships than I can now relate . . . [until] at last we came in sight of the island of Barbados.

Source: Olaudah Equiano, *The Interesting Narrative of the Life of Olaudah Equiano, or Gustavus Vassa, the African. Written by Himself* (London: Printed for and sold by the author, n.d.).

- **How was Olaudah Equiano captured? Who were the parties involved in his enslavement? Why was Equiano forced to eat?**
- **Why would the ship's crew have punished the enslaved men who jumped into the sea?**

SOURCE 16.2

Doctor Alexander Falconbridge on the Middle Passage, 1780s

Alexander Falconbridge (ca. 1760–1792) worked as a physician on four slaving voyages in the 1780s. Next to nothing is known about his early life, but he was presumably born in Britain. After his four slave trade voyages, he became an abolitionist in the late 1780s. Subsequently he wrote an account, published in 1788, of the British slave trade from West Africa to the Americas as he had known it. He and Olaudah Equiano probably knew each other, as they were active in London's abolitionist circles at the same time. Falconbridge died in 1792 in Sierra Leone (West Africa), apparently from alcohol poisoning.

After permission has been obtained . . . the captains go ashore . . . to examine the Negroes . . . and to make their purchases. The unhappy wretches thus disposed of are bought by the black traders at fairs, which are held for that purpose, at the distance of upwards of two hundred miles from the sea coast; and these fairs are said to be supplied from an interior part of the country. Many Negroes, upon being questioned relative to the places of their nativity, have asserted that they have travelled during the revolution of several moons (their usual method of calculating time) before they have reached the places where they were purchased by the black traders.

At these fairs, which are held . . . generally every six weeks, several thousands are frequently exposed to sale who had been collected from all parts of the country. . . . During one of my voyages, the black traders brought down, in different canoes, from twelve to fifteen hundred Negroes who had been purchased at one fair. They consisted chiefly of men and boys, the women seldom exceeding a third of the whole number.

When the Negroes . . . are shown to the European purchasers, they first examine them relative to their age. They then minutely inspect their persons and inquire into the state of their health; if they are inflicted with any disease or are deformed or have bad eyes or teeth; if they are lame or weak in the joints or distorted in the back or of a slender make or narrow in the chest; in short, if they have been ill or are afflicted in any manner so as to render them incapable of much labor. If any of the foregoing defects are discovered in them they are rejected.

As soon as the wretched Africans, purchased at the fairs, fall into the hands of the black-traders, they experience . . . those dreadful sufferings which they are doomed in future to undergo. . . . Nor do these unhappy beings, after they become the property of the Europeans (from whom, as a more civilized people, more humanity might naturally be expected) find their situation in the least amended.

Near the mainmast a partition is constructed of boards which reaches athwart the ship.... It is about eight feet in height and is made to project about two feet over the sides of the ship.... It serves to keep the different sexes apart; and as there are small holes in it, where blunderbusses are fixed and sometimes a cannon, it is found very convenient for quelling the insurrections that now and then happen....

About eight o'clock in the morning the Negroes are generally brought upon deck. Their irons being examined, a long chain, which is locked to a ring-bolt fixed in the deck, is run through the rings of the shackles of the men and then locked to another ring-bolt fixed also in the deck. By this means fifty or sixty and sometimes more are fastened to one chain in order to prevent them from rising or endeavoring to escape....

The diet of the Negroes while on board, consists chiefly of horse beans boiled to the consistency of a pulp; of boiled yams and rice and sometimes a small quantity of beef or pork. The latter are frequently taken from the provisions laid in for the sailors. They sometimes make use of a sauce composed of palm-oil mixed with flour, water and pepper.... Yams are the favorite food of the Eboe [Ibo]...and rice or corn of those from the Gold or Windward Coast; each preferring the produce of their native soil....

They are commonly fed twice a day; about eight o'clock in the morning and four in the afternoon.... Their allowance of water is about half a pint each at every meal....

Upon the Negroes refusing to take sustenance, I have seen coals of fire, glowing hot, put on a shovel and placed so near their lips as to scorch and burn them. And this has been accompanied with threats of forcing them to swallow the coals if they any longer persisted in refusing to eat....

On board some ships the common sailors are allowed to have intercourse with such of the black women whose consent they can procure.... The officers are permitted to indulge their passions among them at pleasure and sometimes are guilty of such excesses as disgrace human nature....

I will give one instance, as it serves to convey some idea, though a very faint one, of their terrible sufferings.... I frequently went down among them .... The deck, that is the floor of their rooms, was so covered with the blood and mucus which had proceeded from them in consequence of the flux [dysentery] that it resembled a slaughter-house. It is not in the power of the human imagination to picture a situation more dreadful or disgusting. Numbers of the slaves having fainted, they were carried upon deck where several of them died and the rest with great difficulty were restored....

They are ever on the watch to take advantage of the least negligence in their oppressors. Insurrections are frequently the consequence; which are seldom expressed without much bloodshed. Sometimes these are successful and the whole ship's company is cut off. They are likewise always ready to seize every opportunity for committing some acts of desperation to free themselves from their miserable state and notwithstanding the restraints which are laid, they often succeed.

Source: Alexander Falconbridge, *An Account of the Slave Trade on the Coast of Africa* (London: Printed by J. Phillips, George Yard, Lombard Street, 1788).

- Does Falconbridge's account contradict Equiano's in any respects? If so, where? Whose voice deserves greater trust on which subjects?
- Falconbridge was a medical man, although we don't know what training he may have had. How—if at all—should that affect the way we read his text?

SOURCE 16.3

The Story of Omar ibn Said, ca. 1770–1831

Omar ibn Said (ca. 1770–1864) was a highly educated Muslim born around 1770 in what is now modern Senegal. Captured, enslaved, and sold across the Atlantic, he arrived in Charleston, South Carolina, in 1807, just as the United States was about to outlaw the importation of slaves. His journey to Fayetteville, North Carolina, presumably on foot and perhaps on the run from slave-catchers, was more than 200 miles. The Jim Owen he mentions was a planter, congressman, militia general, and brother of the governor of North Carolina.

In 1831 Omar ibn Said wrote a short autobiography in Arabic; it was published in English translation in 1925 and is excerpted here. Among the interesting aspects of the text is its ambiguity about his religious commitments. Scholars are uncertain as to whether or not he became a Christian. He wrote several other works in Arabic as well.

My name is Omar ibn Seid.... I sought knowledge under the instruction of a Sheikh called Mohammed Seid, my own brother, and Sheikh Soleiman Kembeh, and Sheikh Gabriel Abdal. I continued my studies twenty-five years, and then returned to my home, where I remained six years. Then there came to our place a large army, who killed many men, and took me, and brought me to the great sea, and sold me into the hands of the Christians, who bound me and sent me on board a great ship and we sailed upon the great sea a month and a half, when we came to a place called Charleston in the Christian language. There they sold me to a small, weak, and wicked man called Johnson, a complete infidel, who had no fear of God at all. Now I am a small man, and unable to do hard work so I fled from the hand of Johnson and after a month came to a place called Fayd-il.[1] There I saw some great houses (churches). On the new moon I went into a church to pray. A lad saw me and rode off to the place of his father and informed him that he had seen a black man in the church. A man named Handah (Hunter?), and another man with him on horseback, came attended by a troop of dogs. They took me . . . to a place called Fayd-il, where they put me into a great house from which I could not go out. I continued in the great house (which, in the Christian language, they called *jail*) sixteen days and nights. One Friday the jailor came and opened the door of the house and I saw a great many men, all Christians, some of whom called out to me, "What is your name? Is it Omar or Seid?" I did not understand their Christian language. A man called Bob Mumford took me and led me out of the jail, and I was very well pleased to go with them to their place. I stayed at Mumford's four days and nights, and then a man named Jim Owen, son-in-law of Mumford, . . . asked me if I was willing to go to a place called Bladen. I said, Yes, I was willing. I went with them and have remained in the place of Jim Owen until now.

[. . .]

Before I came to the Christian country, my religion was the religion of "Mohammed, the Apostle of God—may God have mercy upon him and give him peace." . . . I gave alms every year, gold, silver, seeds, cattle, sheep, goats, rice, wheat, and barley. I went every year to the holy war against the infidels.[2] I went on pilgrimage to Mecca, as all did who were able. My father had six sons and five daughters, and my mother had three sons and one daughter. When I left my country I was thirty-seven years old; I have been in the country of the Christians twenty-four years.

Formerly I, Omar, loved to read the book of the Koran the famous. General Jim Owen and his wife used to read the gospel, and they read it to me very much—the gospel of God, our Lord, our Creator, our King, He that orders all our circumstances . . . according to his power.—Open thou my heart to the gospel, to the way of uprightness.—Thanks to the Lord of all worlds, thanks in abundance. He is plenteous in mercy and abundant in goodness. For the law was given by Moses but grace and truth were by the Jesus the Messiah.

I reside in this our country by reason of great necessity. Wicked men took me by violence and sold me to the Christians. We sailed a month and a half on the great sea to the place called Charleston in the Christian land.

[1] Fayetteville, North Carolina

[2] This refers to annual campaigns that African Muslims conducted against other Africans, often in effect slave-raiding expeditions.

Source: "Autobiography of Omar ibn Said, Slave in North Carolina, 1831," ed. John Franklin Jameson, *The American Historical Review* 30, no. 4 (July 1925).

- How was Omar ibn Said originally captured? What was his religious and social background?
- What aspects of his enslavement does he seem to remember the most? What moments seem to have made the greatest—and the least—impressions on him?

SOURCE 16.4

Mary Prince's Experience of Slavery, ca. 1800

None of the surviving firsthand accounts of the Middle Passage were written by women. But Mary Prince (ca. 1788–1833), an enslaved woman born on the mid-Atlantic island of Bermuda, dictated her autobiography in 1831 to Susanna Strickland (because Prince herself could not write). Prince's narrative provides us with insight into the post–Middle Passage experience of enslavement. The excerpt here focuses on the experience of being sold, which Mary Prince underwent four times in her life. Most of the events recounted here took place when she was 12 years old, in about 1800. When one family took her to London in 1829, Prince managed to slip the bonds of slavery and found shelter with abolitionists. Her book sold widely, but she vanished from the historical record after 1834.

I was born . . . in Bermuda, on a farm belonging to Mr. Charles Myners. My mother was a household slave. . . . I was bought along with my mother by old Captain Darrel, and given to his grandchild, little Miss Betsey Williams. . . .

Mrs. Williams was a kind-hearted good woman, and she treated all her slaves well. She had only one daughter, Miss Betsey, . . . who was about my own age. I was made quite a pet of by Miss Betsey, and loved her very much. . . . This was the happiest period of my life; for I was too young to understand rightly my condition as a slave, and too thoughtless and full of spirits to look forward to the days of toil and sorrow.

[. . .]

My master, however, was a very harsh, selfish man; and we always dreaded his return from sea. His wife was . . . much afraid of him; and, during his stay at home, seldom dared to show her usual kindness to the slaves. . . . I was truly attached to her, and, next to my own mother, loved her better than any creature in the world. My obedience to her commands was cheerfully given: it sprung solely from the affection I felt for her, and not from fear of the power which the white people's law had given her over me.

I had scarcely reached my twelfth year when my mistress became too poor to keep so many of us at home; and she hired me out to Mrs. Pruden, a lady who lived about five miles off . . . in a large house near the sea. I cried bitterly at parting with my dear mistress and Miss Betsey, and when I kissed my mother and brothers and sisters, I thought my young heart would break, it pained me so. But there was no help; I was forced to go. Good Mrs. Williams comforted me by saying that I should still be near the home I was about to quit, and might come over and see her and my kindred whenever I could obtain leave of absence from Mrs. Pruden....

[...]

At this time Mrs. Williams died. I was told suddenly of her death, and my grief was so great....

...I was then sent back to Mr. Williams to be sold. Oh, that was a sad sad time!... "Mary, you will have to go home directly; your master is going to be married, and he means to sell you and two of your sisters to raise money for the wedding." Hearing this I burst out a crying....

[...]

The black morning at length came; it came too soon for my poor mother and us. Whilst she was putting on us the new osna-burgs [coarse fabrics] in which we were to be sold, she said, in a sorrowful voice (I shall never forget it!), "See, I am shrouding my poor children; what a task for a mother!"... [M]y mother called the rest of the slaves to bid us good bye.... When I left my dear little brothers and the house in which I had been brought up, I thought my heart would burst.

...We followed my mother to the market-place, where she placed us in a row against a large house.... I, as the eldest, stood first, Hannah next to me, then Dinah; and our mother stood beside, crying over us. My heart throbbed with grief and terror so violently, that I pressed my hands quite tightly across my breast, but I could not keep it still, and it continued to leap as though it would burst out of my body. But who cared for that? Did one of the many by-standers, who were looking at us so carelessly, think of the pain that wrung the hearts of the negro woman and her young ones? No, no! They were not all bad, I dare say, but slavery hardens white people's hearts towards the blacks; and many of them were not slow to make their remarks upon us aloud, without regard to our grief—though their light words fell like cayenne [pepper] on the fresh wounds of our hearts. Oh those white people have small hearts who can only feel for themselves.

At length the vendue [auction] master, who was to offer us for sale like sheep or cattle, arrived, and asked my mother which was the eldest. She said nothing, but pointed to me. He took me by the hand, and led me out into the middle of the street, and, turning me slowly round, exposed me to the view of those who attended the vendue. I was soon surrounded by strange men, who examined and handled me in the same manner that a butcher would a calf or a lamb he was about to purchase, and who talked about my shape and size in like words—as if I could no more understand their meaning than the dumb beasts. I was then put up to sale. The bidding commenced at a few pounds, and gradually rose to fifty-seven.[1]...

I then saw my sisters led forth, and sold to different owners. ...When the sale was over, my mother hugged and kissed us... begging of us to keep up a good heart, and do our duty to our new masters. It was a sad parting; one went one way, one another, and our poor mammy went home with nothing.

---

[1] About £4,000, or $5,000 in 2023 money.

Source: *The History of Mary Prince, a West Indian Slave, Related by Herself* (London: Published by F. Westley and A. H. Davis, Stationers' Hall Court, 1831).

- How does Mary Prince describe her relationship with her parents and siblings? How did she relate to the families she was sold to? What influence did she have on the white people whom she served?

- Judging from this excerpt, what moments does Prince seem to remember the most? How does she describe these moments?

QUESTIONS FOR COMPARISON

1. Only one of these accounts was authored by a woman. Considering all four accounts together, what similarities and differences can be identified in the experiences of men versus women who suffered the pain and humiliation of enslavement?

2. What prominent themes emerge in these narratives, and what responses are they intended to provoke?

3. Falconbridge made four voyages just before he wrote his book. Equiano and Omar each made one voyage several decades before writing their texts. How does knowing this background affect the way you read the three accounts?

4. Falconbridge was a free man, a figure of authority on slave ships. Equiano and Omar were enslaved. How does knowing this affect the way you read the three accounts?

CHRONOLOGY

1430–1450
Johannes Gutenberg develops
moveable type and printing press

ca. 1450
Safavis embrace
Shi'a Islam

1469–1539
Lifetime of Nanak

1472–1529
Lifetime of Wang Yangming

1501
Ismail establishes a
Safavid state in Iran

1514
Nicholas Copernicus writes
down his heliocentric system

1517
Martin Luther writes Ninety-Five Theses

1540
Founding of the
order of Jesuits

1542
Reestablishment
of the Inquisition

1555
Treaty of Amasya;
Peace of Augsburg

Sikhs abandon pacifism and begin military tradition

ca. 1580
Reaction against
Wang Yangming's
followers

1587–1629
Reign of Shah Abbas I

1597
Christianity is banned
in Japan

1606

1603
First academy
of science is
founded in
Rome

1608
Invention of
the telescope

1618–1648
Thirty Years' War

ca. 1620
Peak of
European
witch
hunts

17

Cultural Upheavals

RELIGIOUS AND INTELLECTUAL MOVEMENTS

1500 to 1750

1687
Newton publishes his *Mathematical Principles of Natural Philosophy*

1724
Christianity is banned in China

1702
First daily newspaper is published

A round 1545, a Japanese samurai named Anjirō killed someone in a brawl. His remorse led to the introduction of Christianity into Japan. Although sorry for his deed, Anjirō chose to flee and live as an outlaw. In 1547, he met a Portuguese sea captain in the port of Kagoshima on Japan's southern island of Kyushu—Portuguese sailors had recently started looking for trade opportunities in Japan. The sea captain suggested that Anjirō might feel better about his crime if he consulted a priest, specifically a Spanish Jesuit named Francis Xavier. The **Jesuits** were a newly founded (1540) order of priests within the Catholic Church dedicated to evangelizing non-Catholics and to rigorous education.

Francis Xavier worked as a missionary throughout the Portuguese Empire in Asia. Anjirō met him in 1547 at Malacca, the cosmopolitan city on the Malay Peninsula where shipping passed between the Indian Ocean and the South China Sea. While Xavier explained to him the merits of Catholicism, Anjirō—in broken Portuguese—convinced Xavier that the people of Japan

Religious Conflict Dozens of Christians are beheaded and burned at the stake during a backlash against European Christian missionaries in sixteenth-century Japan. The period saw religious upheaval around the world, as new sectarian movements and stronger global connections caused different traditions to come into contact—and conflict—for the first time.

FOCUS QUESTIONS

1. Why was this a period of intellectual upheaval?

2. How were the Renaissance, the Reformation, and the Scientific Revolution disruptions of European culture and society?

3. How did the Safavids enable Shi'a Islam to triumph in Iran?

4. What factors led to the rise of Sikhism in India?

5. How did China's Confucian traditions change in the sixteenth century?

6. How did ruling elites attempt to roll back new religious and intellectual movements?

7. Why was the intellectual upheaval of the period uneven across Eurasia?

might be willing to try a new religion. Together they went to Goa, the Portuguese enclave in India, where Anjirō studied Catholic theology and the Portuguese language at a Jesuit college. In 1548, he was baptized a Christian. Then they returned to Malacca, boarded a Chinese pirate ship (the only boat they could find heading to Japan), and arrived at Kagoshima in 1549, intending to convert Japan to Catholicism.

Japan was fragmented politically and religiously at the time. Buddhism was the primary spiritual path, and several different Buddhist sects competed for followers. They also competed with ritual-rich Shinto, Japan's oldest religion.

Anjirō and Xavier drew crowds in Kagoshima. Anjirō translated the Christian concept of God as *Dainichi*, one of the Japanese terms for the Buddha. That and the fact that they had come from India, the home of the Buddha, added to the interest Japanese

took in their preaching. The Japanese at first understood Catholicism as another version of Buddhism coming straight from the Buddha's homeland.

Xavier and Anjirō met with a warm reception from the local authorities until, two years into their missionary work, Xavier concluded that Anjirō's translation did not convey the true nature of God. He started using the Latin word *Deus* instead and began to denounce Dainichi as a creature of the devil. His reception in Kagoshima cooled quickly.

Xavier left Kagoshima for the capital city of Kyoto, where he hoped to convert the emperor. But he never received an imperial audience, and in 1552 was recalled by the Jesuits to Goa. He died en route. Anjirō, meanwhile, lost most of his following in Kagoshima, forsook missionary work, and returned to a life of crime, taking up piracy. He died at sea.

Nonetheless, his followers won many converts, and by 1579 some 130,000 Japanese came to call themselves Christians. The oceanic voyaging of the Portuguese, together with Anjirō's remorse and Xavier's ambition, brought new ideas to Japan, shaking up its spiritual and political order.

Forging the Global web was a disruptive and destructive process, but also a creative one. As we saw in Chapter 16, joining the web wrought havoc on peoples in Africa, the Americas, Siberia, and Oceania, but in time generated new, hybrid societies and cultures. Within the Old World web, the process was disruptive and creative too, not least in the realm of ideas. During the centuries from 1500 to 1750, the convergence of the webs helped drive major challenges to established patterns of thought, leading to new religions, schisms in old religions, new paths within old philosophies—and to the beginnings of modern science. These are the subjects of this chapter.

INFORMATION FLOWS AND INTELLECTUAL FERMENTS

With the advent of oceanic voyaging and the simultaneous quickening of commerce, information moved farther and faster than ever before. Although shipping had carried ideas and information around for millennia, the linking of formerly separate worlds after the 1490s enabled Confucian and Daoist thought to filter (faintly) into Europe, Christianity to take root in China, and Islam to reach Brazil and coastal South Carolina. Sometimes these exchanges were the work of elites operating at the highest rungs of society, such as the Jesuits who brought European cartography and cannon-making skills to the Ming imperial court in China. In other cases, they involved humbler folk, such as the enslaved West Africans who carried Islam to the Americas.

This swirl of new information from around the globe challenged existing systems of thought. In one important realm, astronomy, new and disruptive information also came from beyond the globe. When glasses makers in northern Europe invented telescopes, starting around 1608, it soon became possible to see the craters of the moon and the rings of Saturn. Heavenly bodies, it turned out, were rather different from what people had long imagined. By 1625, microscopes were also in use in northwestern Europe. Soon people could see all sorts of unexpected things, such as corpuscles in blood, crystals in frost, and cells in plant tissues (named cells because they reminded their discoverer of monastic quarters). Telescopes and microscopes, like the Americas and the coasts of Africa, furnished Europeans with unfamiliar observations. Wherever it came from, new information often proved difficult to fit into prevailing religions and philosophies. That inspired great intellectual efforts to reconcile the new data with the old systems, sometimes convincing, sometimes not.

In this situation, the authority of existing intellectual traditions, religions included, weakened. New versions of truth had an opening. The odds of a new religion, a new wrinkle in moral philosophy, or a new paradigm in science attracting a following improved sharply. This intellectual and cultural ferment took place in several places around the world, but in Europe more than anywhere else. As we've seen, Atlantic Europeans were the ones who completed the linking up of the world's shorelines through oceanic navigation and so came into possession of wider knowledge of the world sooner than others. And they were the ones who first developed the telescope and the microscope, exploring worlds as yet unknown to anyone else.

Two other developments, one global and one mainly European, helped create widespread intellectual ferment during these centuries. The first was faster urbanization. As we have seen at many points already, cities served as hothouses for ideas because people could interact so easily with so many others. Between 1500 and 1750, commerce (among other things) drove the growth of cities, especially port cities, almost everywhere. Here people could rub shoulders with strangers from other continents and exchange their understandings of medicine, metallurgy, morality, and everything else. Most of the time, no doubt, language barriers and preference for familiar ideas prevented meaningful exchange. But every now and then they did not. The second development was entirely new, and its impact for centuries was focused within Europe: the **printing press**.

INFORMATION TECHNOLOGY: THE PRINTING PRESS

Around the years 1430–1450, a few people including Johannes Gutenberg, a goldsmith and gem cutter in the German town of Mainz, started work on casting metal type for use in printing. At that time, printing involved the use of woodblocks, painstakingly carved by skilled woodworkers. Gutenberg gradually developed moveable and reusable type, better ink, and a better press. His invention, one of the most consequential in world history and one of the first for whom we know the name of the primary inventor, made possible the ever-cheaper transmission of information.

Gutenberg was not the first to come up with moveable metal type. Chinese in the Song dynasty had used bronze plates to print paper money. Similar technology filtered into Korea in the thirteenth century. But metal type was not a useful advance over woodblock printing when writing in Chinese, because one needs to make thousands of characters to create a text. When Korea introduced an alphabet with only 24 letters in the 1430s, it made more sense to use moveable metal type. That led to a small flurry of publishing there. But literacy was rare in Korea, and some of the elite resisted the new alphabet, preferring the traditional Chinese characters. So even with moveable type, Korea experienced no revolution in reading, publishing, or the circulation of information: the prior invention of moveable metal type in East Asia had none of the consequences that Gutenberg's did. Given the trans-Eurasian traffic in the wake of the Mongols, it's conceivable that Gutenberg was inspired to experiment with casting type after hearing of the Korean innovation—but there is no evidence for that. This case is a reminder that it is not always the first invention of something that matters.

In Europe, conditions different from Korea's led to an explosion in printing once Gutenberg had shown the way. By 1500, 236 towns in Europe had at least one printing press. Venice alone had 417 printers. Over 30,000 different titles were published, coming to about 20 million books in all, in at least a dozen languages. The first presses using the Cyrillic (for Russian and some other Slavic languages)

alphabet debuted in 1483, and in 1501 the first ones using Greek. Regular newspapers appeared by 1605, specializing in business news. The first women's magazine started publication in 1693 (in England), and the first daily newspaper in 1702. By 1753, British readers bought 20,000 newspapers daily, each copy probably read by several people. By 1800, European presses had released some 2 million different book titles.

Europeans carried this new device overseas. (The typical press, made of wood, was 6 to 8 feet high and weighed several hundred pounds.) Spanish Mexico acquired a press by 1539, Portuguese Goa (where Anjirō studied) had one by the 1550s, and the Spanish Philippines by 1593. Jesuits brought one to Japan in 1590. The first in English North America was set up by Elizabeth Glover, a widow with five children, in 1638 upon her arrival in Massachusetts.

At first, even printed books were expensive. Gutenberg's printed Bible, published in 1455, cost about a year's wages for an ordinary laborer. But gradual improvements in the alloys of lead used in the oil-based ink together with cheaper paper kept pushing the price of printed material

Moveable Type Sets of metal type like that at left—from Korea in the fourteenth century—had been developed to print text in Chinese characters as early as the late thirteenth century. But moveable type was more transformative in Europe, where it enhanced texts like the Bible. At right is a page from a fifteenth-century Bible, printed and subsequently hand-illuminated.

downward. Cheaper books raised the demand for education: literacy rates began to climb.

In Gutenberg's time, only 5 to 15 percent of adult Europeans could read. Two-thirds or more of those were male. By 1500, however, the literacy rate had begun to climb, and by 1650 it reached about 25 to 50 percent. In the Netherlands and Britain, and in New England too, it was slightly above 50 percent; in Sweden and Italy, just below 25 percent. The gender gap remained wide until the twentieth century. The market for books and pamphlets ranged from the Bible (easily the best seller) and texts of Christian instruction, such as catechisms, to manuals of farming and mining and light entertainments of every sort.

Scribes and manuscripts did not disappear. They coexisted with print technology for a few centuries. Yet printing was truly revolutionary, lowering the costs of information while improving its accuracy by reducing copying errors.

For centuries, the printing revolution encompassed only Europe and European outposts. The great states of Asia preferred to rely on scribes and hand copying of texts. For written languages that used thousands of ideographic characters rather than alphabets, such as Chinese, moveable type did not seem an advantage. Muslim authorities until the eighteenth century generally thought that the sacred language of the Qur'an should only be copied by hand, that printing it would amount to desecration. In many settings, scribes and literate elites regarded printing as a challenge to their position. Rulers feared—correctly—that printing would make ideas harder to control.

EUROPE: EXTREME TURBULENCE

As we've seen in previous chapters, it was primarily Atlantic Europeans who made the voyages that forged the Global web. So it was primarily in European societies that the global harvest of new information arrived first, sped forward by the printing press. These circumstances colored three great disruptions in the intellectual sphere of early-modern Europe, major developments that we now call the Renaissance, the Protestant Reformation, and the Scientific Revolution. The first deeply affected European thought but did not travel well beyond Europe's shores.

The second involved far more people than the others, brought fierce conflict, and motivated spasms of violence. The third involved only a tiny few but brought far larger, and more global, consequences in the long run.

THE RENAISSANCE

In an earlier chapter, we saw how exposure to Arab and Byzantine Greek learning helped to stimulate new thinking in twelfth- and thirteenth-century Europe, especially challenges to longstanding Christian dogmas within the newly invented institution of the university. Knowledge of Arabic and Greek gave access to bodies of thought from the ancient world that were otherwise out of reach. Political and military pressure on the waning Byzantine Empire motivated many learned Greeks to seek safe spaces in Italian universities in the early fifteenth century, bringing

Renaissance Art The Italian artist Carlo Crivelli made this painting of the Annunciation for a church altarpiece in 1486. The painting includes artistic motifs such as the use of perspective as well as small scenes of everyday life, both hallmarks of Renaissance art.

Cathedral of the Dormition Built by the Italian architect Aristotele Fioravanti in the years 1475–1479, this Moscow cathedral was one of many magnificent buildings that Italian architects designed and constructed across Europe during the Renaissance.

perspectives, and manuscripts, previously unknown there. The growing fascination with ancient Greek and Roman wisdom brought what historians since the nineteenth century have called the Renaissance, meaning a rebirth of ancient learning. Of course, ancient learning was never dead. It was alive and well in Greek and Arab lands. But in western Europe, much had vanished, and it is from that perspective that the term *Renaissance* makes sense.

The heart of the Renaissance was a reengagement with the literatures, histories, philosophies, and art of the ancient Greeks and Romans. Their emphasis on human affairs and human achievement—as opposed to more spiritual matters—found a ready audience among the literate classes and their wealthy patrons. Plato and Cicero came back into style. Translations of the histories of Herodotus and Thucydides appeared, as did the work of ancient playwrights. Sculptors imitated the ancients' marble statuary, with its emphasis on accurate human form.

The **Renaissance** began in Italy, especially in the city-state of Florence. The political fragmentation of

northern Italy probably helped the movement along because local dukes and princes supported artists, architects, and scholars in their competition for political prestige. By the mid-fifteenth century, Italian architects and scholars were in demand elsewhere in Europe too. In Hungary, Poland, and even Russia, rulers hired Italians to build magnificent buildings, such as the Cathedral of the Dormition in Moscow's Kremlin. Aided by the printing press, Renaissance texts—literature, history, philosophy—circulated swiftly in sixteenth- and seventeenth-century Europe. Styles of Renaissance art, using geometry to achieve perspective and depicting everyday life as well as traditional subjects such as Bible scenes and stories of saints, spread almost as quickly.

Renaissance ideals, especially humanism—the view that human affairs were worthy of careful study and suitable themes for art and literature—also took root in the Netherlands, the German lands, France, England, and beyond. Erasmus of Rotterdam, educated and employed at universities in Paris, Cambridge, Turin, Oxford, and Leuven (now in Belgium), used his extraordinary talents in ancient languages and well-honed powers of reason to produce more coherent translations of the New Testament and to call the Catholic Church to account on some of its inconsistencies. Even the study of politics took on a humanistic tone as writers such as Niccolò Machiavelli, a diplomat in Florence in the early sixteenth century, sought to depict political life as it really was rather than in relation to ideal worlds. The Renaissance affected European elites strongly, especially those who read Latin, and to some extent those in lands elsewhere controlled by Europeans. It did not resonate deeply anywhere else—unlike the upheavals in Christianity, which had more widespread repercussions.

RELIGION: PROTESTANT AND CATHOLIC REFORMATIONS

By 1500, the Catholic Church in Europe had met and mastered many challenges. Since the so-called Great Schism in 1054, when the Church of Rome and the Orthodox Church parted ways, Catholics had developed many theological innovations. The church authorities regarded most of these innovations as heresies. It usually succeeded in stamping them out or confining them to remote mountain districts, often using armed force provided by secular rulers. However, in 1517 Martin Luther (1483–1546) launched a new heresy that proved too popular to uproot. It evolved into a new branch of Christianity, several new branches in fact, collectively called Protestantism.

LUTHER AND PROTESTANTISM Luther was born to middle-class parents. His father leased and operated mines in a part of Germany known as Saxony. His parents' ambitions for young Martin extended to sending him to the University of Erfurt. He completed his degree by age 21 and entered law school at his father's insistence. He hated it, dropped out, and seeking deeper truths, decided to become an Augustinian friar. His father was outraged, considering that path a waste of a good university education. Martin, however, recalled the University of Erfurt as "a beer hall and whorehouse" and preferred to devote himself to confession, prayer, and pilgrimage.

But Luther was not done with education. His Augustinian mentors encouraged him to study theology, and after acquiring a few university degrees, Luther joined the theology faculty at the newly founded University of Wittenberg just before his thirtieth birthday. He remained employed there all his life.

In his schooling, writings, preaching, and teaching, Luther developed two main ideas. One was the primacy of scripture over the traditions of the church. So, for example, Luther noted that celibacy for priests has no basis in the Bible (it became required practice in the late fourth century CE). Nor, he argued, did the ritual of confession, or the concept of purgatory—in Catholic theology, an anteroom to heaven in which all but the sinless souls must linger for as long as it takes to burn away their sins. He came to regard these (and much else) as obstacles to the proper practice of Christianity. Rather than follow traditions unsanctioned in the Bible, believers should, Luther said, read scripture themselves and decide for themselves just what it meant. To make that easier, he translated the Bible into German, finishing in 1534. In effect, said Luther, Christians should be their own priests.

The second idea is known as justification by faith alone. This meant that salvation of one's soul could result only from a full embrace of the Christian faith and the gift of divine mercy. For Luther, true Christianity was an inward commitment. He took issue with the church's position that one could ensure salvation through "good works," such as donating money to the church, although he thought that people who had that inward commitment would likely want to perform good works. Luther held fast to these two ideas, arguing for his beliefs with both skill and ferocity.

Earlier reformers—heretics to the Catholic Church—had foreshadowed some of Luther's ideas. Jan Hus, a university rector in Prague (in today's Czech Republic), challenged the privileges of the clergy and the church's quests for money. Hus also preached a more intimate, personal commitment as the core of Christianity. In 1415, he was burned at the stake at the command of a bishop. Hus and his followers had drawn much of their outlook from John Wycliffe, who preached, taught, and wrote mainly at Oxford University. He oversaw the first translation of the Bible into English, completed in 1382. Wycliffe railed at the wealth and power of the clergy and Papacy, recommending a more personal Christianity and the primacy of scripture over church and tradition. The Pope denounced him, and the head of Oxford University had him imprisoned for his views. Wycliffe died of natural causes in England in 1384, but in 1431 a pope ordered that his corpse be dug up and burned, as befitted a heretic.

Luther's 95 Theses This modern photo shows the main door of the All Saints church in Wittenberg (Germany), built in 1490–1511 and restored in the 1890s. When Wittenberg acquired a university in 1506, this church served as its chapel, and this doorway functioned as a bulletin board for students and teachers. According to legend, Luther nailed his 95 theses to this door on October 31, 1517, although if he affixed them at all he probably would have used paste. Whether he posted them here or not, they went viral—sixteenth-century style—and ignited resistance to the Catholic hierarchy that evolved into the Protestant Reformation.

Luther found it particularly offensive that the church, in need of money to pay for the building of St. Peter's Basilica in Rome, had sent churchmen around Europe offering promises of expedited salvation in exchange for donations. This practice, not so different from the deals forged between holy men and the Gupta kings in India (noted in Chapter 12), was called the sale of indulgences. The practice was invented in the 1090s to persuade people to join the Crusades. Wycliffe and Hus had each condemned it. The sale of indulgences was never official policy, but it had become routine procedure by Luther's time. In effect, the gates of heaven were treated like a tollbooth. Sinners who paid could escape a painful term in purgatory. The most successful salesmen of indulgences promised that even the most unspeakable sins could be wiped away for a suitable fee.

Reformation The Oude Kerk ("Old Church") in Amsterdam became Calvinist after the Reformation reached the Netherlands in 1578. This seventeenth-century painting indicates some of the Protestant characteristics of the decor, including a relative lack of ornamentation and a prominent raised pulpit at the left of the nave.

Luther wrote up his objections, in Latin, in a document now called his Ninety-Five Theses. This was not quite the undertaking it might seem: most of his theses were only a sentence long. He did not seek to challenge the church directly, but the implications of some of his theses aroused the ire of Rome. Number 86, for example, which he described as a shrewd question of lay people, read: "Why does the Pope, whose wealth today is greater than the wealth of the richest Crassus, build the basilica of St. Peter with the money of poor believers rather than with his own money?"

Legend has it that Luther nailed his theses to the door of the cathedral at Wittenberg in 1517. The door often served as a bulletin board. Whether the story is true or not (it probably is not), he did allow friends to translate his text into German and print it in early 1518 as a pamphlet. By 1519, it had circulated all over Europe.

Here it is important to note the political landscape surrounding Luther and his ideas. Germany was not a unified state but a mosaic of dozens of small states, most of them offering a cautious allegiance to the Holy Roman Empire. The Holy Roman Empire was nominally the successor to Charlemagne's kingdom of the ninth century, but in fact it was a loose collection of duchies and principalities whose rulers enjoyed great autonomy. It also comprised about 100 self-governing "free cities," not subject to any duke or prince. The Holy Roman Empire's territory had been shrinking for centuries (and would continue to do so until it was wiped off the map in 1806). It was, however, usually the political force most inclined to serve the interests of the Pope. The political fragmentation of Germany made it hard for authorities to do anything, such as executing Luther, unless every prince, duke, and free city agreed.

By Luther's day, the Papacy had plenty of experience in handling upstarts and heretics. It gave Luther a few chances to recant his positions, which he refused, most dramatically in 1521 at the Diet of Worms (not a college meal plan, but an assembly of officials of the Holy Roman Empire held in the town of Worms). Luther stood his ground, and soon the Pope excommunicated him from the church, calling Luther a "wild boar in the vineyards of the Lord." The Pope's political allies called for Luther's murder. Luther responded to efforts to muzzle him by taking more radical positions, including denying the legitimacy of the Papacy altogether and calling the Pope the antichrist and "servant of the devil." He denounced several important church rituals as unchristian. This was a quarrel that could not be patched up.

Despite having enemies in high places, Luther lived on, in effect an outlaw protected by German princes who liked his ideas, and by his university. He produced his German-language edition of the Bible, wrote many hymns and pamphlets, read a translation of the Qur'an and supported its publication (on the grounds that its errors should be held to scrutiny), and in his last years wrote violent screeds against Jews, few of whom he had ever seen. Always bullheaded, by the end of his life he zealously courted controversy and confrontation.

The printing press and spreading literacy, discussed above, made it more difficult for the church to extinguish an appealing heresy. Luther's many pamphlets found receptive readers all over Europe, and he became a celebrity professor. Even an organization as vast and staffed with talent as the church could not keep Luther's ideas in check.

Variations on Luther's themes soon appeared in Swiss cities. In Zurich, a Catholic priest, Ulrich Zwingli, preached a message similar to Luther's and won over the town leaders. In Geneva, John Calvin took up Luther's

Religious Geography of Europe, 1555–1650 Beginning in the early sixteenth century, the Protestant Reformation added new Christian sects that by 1555 (main map) had acquired millions of followers in western and central Europe. But, as the inset shows, by 1650 the Catholic Reformation, supported by powerful rulers such as the Habsburgs and the kings of France, had won back certain populations. Some lands remained thereafter a patchwork of religions, with multiple Christian minority sects.

cause and gave it his own spin based on the gloomy idea that everyone's fate—heaven or hell—was predestined, and no amount of good behavior (or donations to the church) could improve one's odds of salvation. Bad behavior such as blasphemy, witchcraft, adultery, or heresy, in contrast, brought a parade of executions by drowning, beheading, and burning in Calvin's Geneva after 1536. Calvin's uncompromising formula, much influenced by St. Augustine, claimed to be the sole authentic form of Christianity. It spread further than Lutheranism in the sixteenth century, taking root in parts of Switzerland, France, Britain, Germany, and the Low Countries.

Emigrants from these lands carried it to South Africa and North America in the seventeenth century.

Various groups of Protestants (the term was in use by 1530) formed in pockets across Europe. Those who embraced it tended to be more urban and literate than average. Cities with printing presses were particularly likely to turn Protestant. But village peasants too, especially in Germany, often found **Protestantism** appealing. They felt its emphasis on "God's law" justified their revolt in 1524–1525 against taxes and levies imposed by princes and the church. Luther disavowed the revolt, and it was crushed.

In general, Protestants shared the view that salvation rested on personal commitment to God and that the Catholic Church had grown stale, stolid, and corrupt, standing as a barrier between individuals and God. Several rulers embraced this new creed, finding it appealing in its own right and often advantageous in political terms—it provided grounds for confiscating church and monastic property, a tempting target. Many German princes had chosen Protestantism by 1530. By 1560, the rulers of Denmark, Sweden, England, and Scotland had become Protestant and encouraged or obliged their subjects to follow suit. In France, maybe 10 to 20 percent of the population was Protestant, and in German lands closer to 80 percent. Most of the German speakers in Poland—a sizeable minority there—were as well. Protestantism in the mid-sixteenth century seemed an unstoppable force in Europe north of Italy, Spain, and Portugal.

THE CATHOLIC REFORMATION Yet between 1550 and 1620, the Catholic Church did manage to check the spread of Protestantism. Indeed, the church and its allies regained some lost ground, winning back people in the southern part of the Netherlands (now Belgium) and a good share of Germans. The Catholic Church nearly stamped out Protestantism in Poland and France, and it crushed the followers of Jan Hus in Bohemia (now part of the Czech Republic). Part of its success came through war. Popes had armies in those days, and so did the house of Habsburg, a firmly Catholic family that held the Spanish and Austrian thrones, as well as a few other duchies and provinces.

The Protestants could not unify their resistance. Splinter sects popped up constantly, much to the annoyance of Luther and Calvin, none more hated than the Anabaptists, found mainly in German-speaking lands. They held that only adults who understood Christian commitment, and not infants, should be baptized in the faith. Some Anabaptists regarded polygamy, pacifism, and communal property (as opposed to private property) as acceptable. Protestant sects and princes quarreled fiercely among themselves over fine points of doctrine and over political advantage, which made it harder to fight effectively against Catholic powers. Struggles abated somewhat after an agreement of 1555, the Peace of Augsburg, in which Catholic and Lutheran rulers in central Europe agreed on the principle that rulers should be free to require either Catholicism or Lutheranism of their populations.

The church also undertook major reforms in response to the Protestant Reformation. Beginning in the 1540s, in a movement called the **Catholic Reformation** (or the Counter-Reformation), the church cleaned up its act considerably. No more libertine popes, living in luxury, fathering children, and making a mockery of Christian morals. Bishops and abbots cut back on high living. The church grew more centralized and standardized, settling on a single required script for Mass, for example. Popes became more powerful over bishops and priests, abbots and monks. The Papacy reestablished its Inquisition (1542), an office tasked with rooting out heresy, and created the so-called Index of Banned Books (1559). The Index stopped work in 1966.

The church also went global. While Luther and Calvin were diverting souls in Europe from Catholicism, missionaries found fertile fields for the salvation of different souls overseas. In the first half of the sixteenth century, Catholic priests ventured to the Americas, Africa, India, China, Japan, and almost everywhere in between. Religious orders such as Augustinians, Dominicans, and Franciscans came to specialize in converting unbelievers around the world, usually focusing their efforts on the poor. The Jesuits also took to evangelical work, generally working from the top down, trying to convert rulers and courts. They led the rollback of Protestantism in Poland, helped lead it in Germany, brought Catholicism to Japan, and were especially active in China.

By 1620, the Catholic Church had revitalized itself and stopped the Protestant surge. Divisions in Europe—intellectual, cultural, political—became more entrenched. Vicious religious wars only deepened cleavages and resentments, culminating in the Thirty Years' War (1618–1648) in western and central Europe, which reduced population there by as much as one-third. As the French mathematician and philosopher Blaise Pascal noted in the 1650s, people "never do so much harm so happily as when they do it through religious conviction." The convulsions in religious life in sixteenth-century Europe created divisions and sectarian identities that live on to this day—less lethally—in Europe itself, wherever European migrants have settled, and wherever Christian missionaries made converts.

All durable religions develop schisms and rival sects that get tangled up in struggles for wealth and power. Islam's two largest factions broke apart soon after Muhammad's death, and both Sunni and Shi'a communities subsequently fragmented into many subgroups. Buddhism's two leading forms, Theravada and Mahayana, also fragmented into smaller sects. Christianity splintered into several churches early in its history. While every schism and sect is unique, the human capacity for religious innovation and reform makes the process common.

WITCH HUNTS The competition between Catholicism and Protestantism proved Pascal's point in another respect. It fueled a craze for witch trials. Accusations of witchcraft—typically understood as working with the devil to obtain supernatural powers to use against neighbors or family—had been rare in Europe until 1550, by which time they reached a few hundred annually. The next century, however, brought a flurry of accusations, trials, and executions, reaching a peak in about 1620 with more than 5,000 trials and 2,000 executions annually. In total, between 1500 and 1700, about 40,000 to 60,000 people were hanged, drowned, or burned as witches, often after confessions extracted with torture. Of these, 75 to 80 percent were women, usually over 40 years of age, although in parts of northernmost Europe—Iceland, Finland, Estonia, and Russia—the majority of those accused and killed were men.

Historians still struggle to explain why the **witch hunts** arose and why they stopped. Nearly nine-tenths of the executions took place in Germany (about 42 percent), Switzerland (35 percent), or France (10 percent), mainly in areas where Protestants and Catholics were vigorously competing for allegiance. One way a ruler could demonstrate the logic of accepting his (or, in rare cases, her) preferred religion was to encourage trials and convictions of witches, so as to appear committed to defending the people against the devil's mischief. King James VI of Scotland personally oversaw some cases and published a book in 1597 about witchcraft, which explained the justice of persecuting witches in a Christian community. (Shakespeare borrowed liberally from this book in writing *Macbeth*). Countries with little Catholic-Protestant rivalry saw far fewer cases. Staunchly Catholic Portugal, Spain, and Italy together accounted for only 6 percent of witchcraft executions.

The fact that the majority of victims were women, in Protestant and Catholic lands alike, requires a different explanation, one anchored in demography. A rise in the proportion of unmarried women likely played a big role. Unmarried women, especially those not under the authority of an adult male, seemed a threat to the sanctioned

Witch Hunts A 1555 German leaflet included this vivid woodcut of three witches—one of whom is evidently possessed by a demon—being burned at the stake, perhaps to elicit sympathy for the witch-hunting cause.

social order. The ongoing religious struggles contributed to the visibility of unmarried women: Protestant rulers often seized convents' property and pushed nuns out into society at large.

THE SCIENTIFIC REVOLUTION

While both the Renaissance and the Reformation were gathering pace, shaking up the European intellectual landscape, the **Scientific Revolution** began. The term itself is controversial among experts, some of whom see the gradual pace of change in scientific thinking as reason to avoid the term *revolution*. But if significance rather than pace is the key criterion, then the term is warranted.

Two deep principles spurred the Scientific Revolution. The first was accepting that religious scripture and ancient texts did not contain everything worth knowing after all. The logic of accepting this principle strengthened as unfamiliar and baffling information arrived from overseas. Neither scripture nor the ancients had said anything about the existence of manatees and llamas, or hurricanes and typhoons. The second deep principle was the embrace of mathematics and a quantitative culture. In most fields of scientific endeavor, the book of nature was written in the language of mathematics, as the Italian astronomer Galileo put it.

The Scientific Revolution began roughly around 1500, although it is possible to find evidence of new directions in science before that. It too began mainly in northern Italy, like the Renaissance, but quickly leapfrogged to towns, especially university towns, all over Europe. Again, urbanization, universities, printing, and the challenge of new information from overseas helped to create and sustain the Scientific Revolution. So did political fragmentation, in the sense that it was hard for anyone to crush ideas they didn't like when people could easily move to another city or duchy. In addition, the widespread use of Latin helped advance the Scientific Revolution because scholars all over Europe, whatever their native tongue, wrote and read the language.

Historians sometimes say the Scientific Revolution ended around 1700, because many of the fundamental principles of modern science had by then been articulated. But in one sense the Scientific Revolution has never stopped, because its core procedures and deep principles have remained behind scientific inquiry ever since.

One final factor behind the Scientific Revolution deserves emphasis. Europeans in 1500 had no great body of scientific wisdom to protect against new ideas and information. In this they were like the Arab intellectuals after the early Islamic conquests of the seventh and eighth centuries who suddenly came into possession of philosophy and science from India, Persia, and the Greek and Jewish worlds. This situation had led to daring new syntheses, as Arab thinkers tried to reconcile discordant ideas and data and fit them to their own religion. Their emirs and sultans had not felt required to quash this new thinking, because it offered no threat to them or their supporters. Something similar happened in Europe after 1500. Novel ideas, some of them ancient but new to Europeans, jostled together. New observations from distant continents, and even some from distant planets, challenged old wisdom. But European intellectuals and rulers rarely felt they needed to protect existing ideas (at least, scientific ones) from competitors. And thanks to political fragmentation, intellectual protectionism, when tried, did not fully succeed.

Systematic observation and experimentation lay at the heart of the Scientific Revolution. Scientifically minded men (and a few women) increasingly sought to find the true essence of things by careful study and designed experiments, rather than relying on the church's teachings or the theories of Aristotle and his interpreters. They sought, like many before them, to understand the workings of the heavens, the nature of matter, the secret of human health—but with different methods.

The Scientific Revolution was not antireligion. Every one of its prominent figures considered himself a Christian. Many of them were priests. Most of them sought to reveal God's glory by uncovering the perfection of creation in the precise, regular, harmonious workings of the universe. They aimed to read the book of nature alongside the book of scripture, as early Christian writers had put it. The seventeenth-century English scientist Robert Boyle regarded the study of God's creation as a form of religious worship and enjoyed conducting experiments on Sundays. Boyle's father was the second-richest man in England, so Robert could afford to study chemistry and physics every day of the week. He also took the trouble to learn Arabic, evidence of its standing as a language of science.

Since the early nineteenth century we have divided science into fields called disciplines, but no one did that in the sixteenth and seventeenth centuries. Many thinkers ranged across fields, considering all of science to be one. But to see its long-term impact, it is helpful to look at a few particular fields before returning to the whole.

ASTRONOMY AND HELIOCENTRISM Let's begin with astronomy. In 1500, most people supposed that the sun moved around the Earth, because that's what their eyes told them every day. Ancient Greek philosophers, notably Ptolemy, had explained how and why that was so (although one or two ancient Greeks had suggested the Earth might move around the sun instead). Careful observation of the movements of planets and stars raised questions about Ptolemy's system. One of those puzzled by discordant observations was a Polish-German student in northern Italy, known by his Latinized name as Nicholas Copernicus (1473–1543). He knew Latin and Greek, as well as Polish, German, and Italian, giving him access to a wide intellectual heritage. In 1514, he wrote up an alternative explanation based on a **heliocentric system** in which planets spin around the sun. He tinkered with it for decades, while working in Poland as a cathedral administrator. Just before his death, he overcame his fears of persecution and his perfectionist tendencies and published his work in 1543. In it he cited both ancient and recent Islamic astronomers and was clearly influenced by both.

Copernicus's heliocentric system did not catch on quickly. It violated common sense as well as the wisdom of the ancients. Nor did it arouse the ire of the church, as Copernicus had feared. It was useful for astrologers because it simplified calculations about future positions of the planets. Astrology was a prestigious branch of science

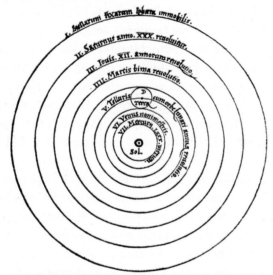

NICOLAI COPERNICI

net, in quo terram cum orbe lunari tanquam epicyclo contineri
diximus. Quinto loco Venus nono menfe reducitur. Sextum
denics locum Mercurius tenet, octuaginta dierum fpacio circu
currens, In medio uero omnium refidet Sol. Quis enim in hoc

pulcherrimo templo lampadem hanc in alio uel meliori loco po
neret, quàm unde totum fimul pofsit illuminare? Siquidem non
inepte quidam lucernam mundi, alij mentem, alij rectorem uo-
cant. Trimegiftus uifibilem Deum, Sophoclis Electra intuenté
omnia. Ita profecto tanquam in folio re gali Sol refidens circum
agentem gubernat Aftrorum familiam. Tellus quocp minime
fraudatur lunari minifterio, fed ut Ariftoteles de animalibus
ait, maximã Luna cũ terra cognationẽ habet. Concipit interea à
Sole terra, & impregnatur annuo partu. Inuenimus igitur fub
hac

Astronomical Revolution In his 1543 book *On the Revolution of the Spheres*, Copernicus published his theory of a solar system in which (as this diagram indicates) the planets revolved around the sun.

in those days. When Elizabeth I of England chose a day for her coronation, she consulted a mathematician and an astrologer. So did the Pope when choosing an auspicious day for laying the cornerstone of the St. Peter's Basilica in Rome in 1506. It took some 200 years, and many further observations and refinements of Copernicus's system, before all serious students of the heavens had abandoned Ptolemaic astronomy.

The three scientists whose work did the most to confirm Copernicus's heliocentric view were Johannes Kepler (1571–1630), Galileo Galilei (1564–1642), and Isaac Newton (1643–1727). Kepler, whose major works were published between 1609 and 1627, used careful mathematics to show that planets revolved around the sun in elliptical, not circular, orbits. That helped resolve some discrepancies between observations and Copernicus's theories, although

it took decades to become accepted. Kepler lived in German cities and, although he considered himself a proper Christian, had to overcome occasional persecution at the hands of Lutheran churchmen, Catholic authorities, and political leaders alike. His mother, Katharina Guldenmann, was tried for witchcraft.

Kepler's contemporary, Galileo, lived in northern Italy and provided detailed observations of the planets using homemade telescopes. In 1615, Catholic officials warned him to stop writing in favor of the heliocentric view, and in 1632 they put him on trial. He officially recanted when faced with the prospect of torture. His works were banned by the church, but this did not stop their spread.

Two generations after Kepler, Isaac Newton, a professor of mathematics at Cambridge University in England, clinched the case for heliocentrism. In the 1660s and 1670s, he formulated his laws of motion and gravity, accounting in detailed mathematical proofs for the movement of planets, comets, the tides, and much else. He too considered himself a devout Christian and maintained that his work, published by 1687, laid out the elegance and beauty of God's creation as revealed by mathematics. England's official Anglican Church did not bother trying to dispute or suppress his work. The scientific battle launched by Copernicus in 1543 was over, and heliocentrists had won. The church abandoned its objections to heliocentrism in 1835.

CHEMISTRY AND EXPERIMENTATION As astrology was to astronomy, so was alchemy to chemistry. The greatest motivation behind experiments and new thinking in chemistry during the Scientific Revolution was the hope that cheap metals could be transformed into valuable ones—for example, lead into gold. Boyle dabbled in alchemy and claimed to have seen other metals changed into gold. Alchemy, unlike astrology, did not carry much prestige and was often scorned at universities, although Newton, at Cambridge, was fascinated by it. It had no classical pedigree from ancient Greeks or Romans, it was messy, and its practitioners had reputations as con men.

But, working on their own, sometimes in their own kitchens, sixteenth- and seventeenth-century chemists developed a tradition of experimentation and precise recording of results. We now consider most of the ideas they advanced to be wrong, but their methods proved enduringly useful. One prominent chemist, physician, and astrologer was the Swiss-born Philippus Aureolus

Theophrastus Bombastus von Hohenheim, who, understandably, preferred to go by the name Paracelsus (1493–1541). He entered and quickly exited six universities before earning a degree at Ferrara, in northern Italy, in 1516. Along the way, he developed the view that all disease results from too much of either sulfur, mercury, or salt, three chemicals that he considered central to all matter. Disdaining ancient wisdom in favor of experimentation, he claimed that "my shoe buckles are more learned than Galen and Avicenna [Ibn Sina]." Although often wrong in his conclusions, his insistence on experimentation to show the medical uses of chemicals and minerals helped establish genuinely scientific methods. More than any other branch of science, it was chemistry that generated the methodology of experimentation.

MEDICINE Unlike chemistry, medicine was among the prestigious subjects and professions. It too underwent major revision, in both methods and concepts. The most important new methods paralleled changes everywhere in science: greater reliance on observation and experiment, and less deference to ancient authors. The most significant new concept was the principle of the circulation of the blood, detailed by the Englishman William Harvey.

Harvey (1578–1657), the son of a small-town mayor, entered Cambridge University at age 15. After studying medicine for six years, he moved on to northern Italy (like Copernicus and Paracelsus before him), where he learned the fine points of dissection of human cadavers

Anatomical Innovation William Harvey's 1628 book *On the Motion of the Heart and Blood in Animals* was accompanied by detailed diagrams illustrating how the heart pumped blood throughout the body.

and live animals. In 1628, now a prosperous physician in London, Harvey published his book on the circulation of the blood, showing that the heart pumped blood through arteries into capillaries, and that veins returned the same blood to the heart. Like Copernicus, Harvey showed what others had earlier guessed—notably, Ibn al-Nafis in thirteenth-century Cairo. He built on assertions made by medical men in Italy and Egypt, using systematic observation, in this case based on dissections. In his work, as in Copernicus's, we can see the circulation of knowledge between the Islamic and Christian worlds, made possible by the longstanding connections of the Old World web.

INSTITUTIONS AND CONNECTIONS Every field of science, from astronomy to zoology, experienced some upheaval during the Scientific Revolution. Those most influenced by the global harvest of information and ideas were probably botany and zoology, due to the large number of strange species attested to in distant lands. Ideas and principles from China, India, and the Islamic world, as well as observations made elsewhere, brought challenges to received wisdom in Europe.

The links between science and technology were weaker in those days than ours, but nonetheless the new scientific outlook filtered into fields such as mining, cartography, navigation, and clock making. In particular, more precise mathematics and a culture of quantification helped these fields develop. Technical advances in these fields helped, in turn, promote commerce and connections both within Europe and between Europe and other lands, contributing to the tightening of the Global web.

The Scientific Revolution was a permanent revolution: it continues to this day. Part of the reason for that is the institutionalization of scientific inquiry that began in the late seventeenth century. Academies of science sprouted first in Italy. An 18-year-old from a wealthy family in Rome founded the first one in 1603, but it folded in 1630 upon his death. More durable academies, enjoying royal support, were created in London (1660) and Paris (1666). Others followed in the eighteenth century in Uppsala (Sweden), Berlin, St. Petersburg, and Philadelphia. Meanwhile, networks of scientists solidified, based on correspondence and travel from one city or university town to another, and eased by the shared use of Latin. Carl Linnaeus, the eighteenth-century Swedish botanist who developed a system for naming, ranking, and classifying organisms, maintained a correspondence with nearly a

Mining Technology This woodcut, from a mining manual published in Switzerland in 1556, illustrates the technological sophistication developing in sixteenth-century Europe. It shows a waterwheel turning the camshaft of a stamping mill, used to crush rock and extract minerals. Considerable engineering expertise and practical geometry went into building these machines. Such technology, adopted in Spanish America, facilitated silver-mining booms in Mexico and the Andes.

thousand people. Such networks, combined with print technology, prepared the way for publication of scientific journals, the first of which appeared in England in 1665 and is still going strong. These academies, networks, and journals helped to entrench the Scientific Revolution in European thought and society by 1700. In later centuries, similar institutions would underpin science around the world, helping make modern science a global undertaking.

THE WORLD OF ISLAM: A SHI'A REFORMATION

The intellectual world of Islam, like that of India and China, underwent less turbulence than Europe in the centuries between 1500 and 1700. Its cities were less affected by newly forged links to distant lands than Seville or Amsterdam were. Its religious and scientific establishments by now had a great deal of established belief, practice, and knowledge to protect from novelty. But nonetheless,

human creativity, the rise of commerce, and the advance of urbanization helped bring about some intellectual realignments in Islamdom. The most important of these was the success of the Shi'a branch of Islam in Iran.

SHI'ISM

Shi'ism is almost as old as Islam itself. Its followers regard descendants of Muhammad through his daughter Fatimah and his son-in-law Ali to be especially endowed with religious and political authority. Only members of Muhammad's lineage could provide proper earthly guidance.

In the early years of Islam, Sunni caliphs crushed Shi'a factions in battle, and they survived only as a tiny minority. For 800 years Shi'ism suffered frequent persecution from Sunni rulers, who regarded it as heresy, and its followers often kept their convictions secret. Many Shi'a felt disdain for power, authority, and sometimes wealth, seeing virtue in humility and commitment to justice. Among the few rulers to embrace Shi'ism, the most important were the Fatimids in Egypt (909–1171) and the Buyids in southern Iran and Iraq (934–1048). But they did not impose it upon their populations. Iran in 1450 had very few Shi'a Muslims.

Shi'a Islam triumphed in Iran for political reasons. In the chaotic conditions of the late fourteenth century, following the decline of Il-Khanid Mongol overlords in northern Iran, charismatic religious leaders competed for influence. They won followers through demonstrations of religious power and military success. Most of them were Sufis.

Sufism (see Chapter 13) is an umbrella term for philosophical, theological, and literary traditions within Islam that emphasize a mystical, intense, and personal engagement with God. Sufi leaders, who usually called themselves sheikhs, did not need much formal education in Islamic theology or law. They attracted followers by convincing people that they had a special connection to God. They flourished in regions where states, law, and the *ulema* (the learned interpreters of Islam) were weak. Sufi sheikhs liked to say that "Sufis learn from God, the ulema from books." They built solidarity with their followers through rituals involving dance and music—attractions that had no place in more formal versions of Islam. They sometimes added distinctive practices in order to stand out from the competition. As from time to time with various sects in Christianity, Jainism, and Buddhism, these practices could include extreme self-denial and the acceptance of self-inflicted pain. The Riffaiyya, a Sufi sect whose followers lived mainly in Egypt and Syria, felt they could improve their relationship with God by biting the heads off living snakes, thrusting iron spikes into their own bodies, and climbing into hot ovens. Theirs was probably the most eccentric set of practices among hundreds of Sufi brotherhoods. Sufi sheikhs usually required unquestioning obedience from their followers, so Sufi organizations were very hierarchical.

As Iran (and neighboring parts of Anatolia and the Caucasus) became more chaotic in the fourteenth and fifteenth centuries, Sufi movements increasingly coalesced

Sufi Warriors A history book from seventeenth-century Iran shows Safavi soldiers (with their distinctive red headgear) fighting Sunni troops in the conflict that saw Ismail and his descendants assume control over Iran.

into orders or brotherhoods, often for self-protection. To the extent they could provide protection, they attracted more followers. The most successful, by 1450, were the Safavis, a Sunni and Sufi brotherhood. They organized herders, former soldiers, and anyone else willing to pledge loyalty into a formidable warrior band, distinguished by their red headgear, which earned them the name *kizilbash* ("red head").

SAFAVIDS AND SHI'ISM IN IRAN

At some point after 1450, the leader of the Safavis decided to embrace Shi'a Islam, perhaps to mark his leadership off from the competition. He began to claim descent from Ali. His grandson Ismail—at age 14—led kizilbash warriors to several victories and in 1501 established a dynastic state with the northwestern Iranian city of Tabriz as its capital. By 1510, Ismail had taken over all of Iran and much of Iraq as well. He declared himself the Hidden Imam—in Shi'a theology, the messiah who will return at the right moment to bring justice to humankind. Ismail sought to cloak himself in the mantle of prestigious religious and political figures to enhance his legitimacy as ruler:

> My name is Shah Ismail.
> I am on God's side, the leader of warriors.
> My mother is Fatima, my father Ali.
> I too am one of the twelve Imams. . . .
> Know that I am the true coin of Haidar [i.e., Ali]
> Ever-living Khezer, and Jesus son of Mary.
> I am the Alexander of the people of this era.

Before he died in 1524, Ismail set about converting the entire population to Shi'a Islam, something prior Shi'a rulers had not attempted. He had to import scholars from afar because Iran had so few Shi'a. His son, Tahmasp, who ruled for 52 years (r. 1524–1576), took this program further. He closed brothels, taverns, and gambling dens and forbade shaving beards. He banned music from his court. The **Safavids** (Safavis were a Sufi brotherhood, Safavids was a ruling dynasty) executed or exiled Muslims who overtly resisted their religious program and instituted harsh penalties for rule-breakers—a bit like Calvin's Geneva, but on a larger scale.

As with many an embattled theocracy, relations with hostile neighbors made the Safavids sterner at home. They faced a powerful foe in the Ottoman Empire to the west, a champion of Sunni orthodoxy with whom they fought for most of the first half of the sixteenth century. They also fought another Sunni polity to their northeast, the Uzbeks. Despite a difficult military situation, the Safavids obtained a peace treaty with the Ottomans that recognized them as Shi'a Muslims rather than heretics or unbelievers. The Treaty of Amasya, signed in 1555, also secured the right of shahs in Iran to enforce the religion of their choice within their domains—coincidentally, the same year as the Peace of Augsburg, which cemented similar rights for central European rulers. Both agreements soothed half a century of deadly religious rivalry by granting opponents legitimacy and allowing monarchs to impose their religions upon their subjects. The Safavids eventually endorsed forced conversion of Jews, Zoroastrians, and most Christians in their quest for uniform religious purity—and political security. The Safavids even turned on Sufis and massacred thousands.

SHI'ISM UNDER THE SAFAVIDS Under Safavid rule, Iran experienced a philosophical and religious reorientation. State power was at the center of it. The most effective of Safavid rulers, Shah Abbas I (r. 1587–1629), enjoyed great economic and military success, and supported artists and thinkers, at least of the sort he preferred—not Sufi sheikhs, whom he preferred to execute. He built a new capital at Isfahan, in west-central Iran, with lavish mosques and palaces. He supported painters, especially

Safavid Iran, 1500–1630 The Safavid dynasty, originally from the southwestern shores of the Caspian Sea, imposed its Shi'a form of Islam as thoroughly as it could within its domain. This sharpened conflicts with Sunni rulers on its borders—notably the Ottomans and Uzbeks, with whom the Safavids warred frequently. The Treaty of Amasya (1555) reduced tensions with the Ottomans. Ottoman strength prevented the Safavids from reviving the formula—Iranian horsemen plus Mesopotamian tax revenues—that had underpinned Achaemenid, Parthian, Sassanid, Abbasid, and Il-Khanid power.

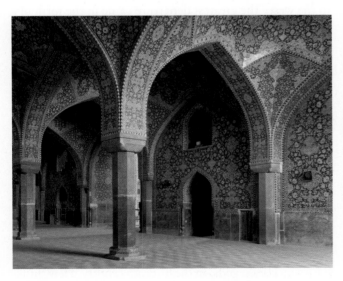

Isfahan Shah Abbas's capital featured magnificent new buildings. The Shah Mosque, on which construction began in 1611, is pictured here. It remains famous for its extraordinary decorative tilework.

the miniaturists who became all the rage in Iran and northern India (Shah Tahmasp had been trained to paint in this tradition). Shah Abbas I also encouraged Shi'a theologians, who worked out a new religious orthodoxy that provided some much-needed glue for Safavid society and equally needed legitimacy for the state.

The most prominent of these theologians was Sadr ad-Din Muhammad Shirazi (or **Mulla Sadra**, 1571–1640). He was born to a courtly family and moved to the capital of Isfahan for study as a young man. He developed unorthodox ideas that resulted in many years of exile to a village, where he began his writing career, trying to reconcile Sufi emotion and intuition with a more reasoned and intellectual Islam. A provincial governor who liked Mulla Sadra's message installed him as the head of a school in Shiraz, in southwestern Iran, where he built an arts and sciences curriculum. An English traveler who passed through in 1629 wrote: "Shyraz has a colledge wherein is read Philosophy, Astrology, Physick, Chemistry and the Mathematicks; so as 'tis the more famoused through Persia."

Mulla Sadra wrote prolifically on deep metaphysical and theological issues, squaring mystical Sufi impulses with the thought of earlier Muslim philosophers such as Ibn Sina (Avicenna). Like Luther, he leaned toward a personal, reflective engagement with the world and with God, and taught that one must live by the principles one's philosophy reveals. He died in Basra while en route to Mecca to perform his seventh hajj. He may fairly be considered the most influential Shi'a philosopher and, despite his early troubles with the authorities, the most important intellectual of Safavid Iran.

THE WIDER ISLAMIC WORLD The reformulation of Shi'a belief and its adoption as the state religion in

Iran was the most important intellectual current within the Islamic world in these centuries, but it was far from the only one. Iranian refugees from Safavid persecution brought many new wrinkles in philosophy, art, and literature to northern India, including the tradition of miniatures in painting. Scholars in Timbuktu, which had some 150 Qur'anic schools in the sixteenth century, brought ideas and practices from Egypt to West Africa, often when returning from a hajj to Mecca. The annual practice of pilgrimage drew pious Muslims from West Africa to Southeast Asia together in Mecca, where they mingled for weeks or months, prayed together, and debated the fine points of religion. Muslim traders traveled far and wide, bringing their particular beliefs in their saddlebags. The quickening of commerce and the growth of cities, especially port and caravan cities, led to faster circulation of ideas and more friction among faiths and sects. Political turmoil in the Islamic world, as we will see in the next chapter, encouraged rulers to embrace legitimating ideologies, including religion above all, as the Safavids did when embracing Shi'a Islam.

West African Scholarship Scholars in Timbuktu in the sixteenth and seventeenth centuries created tens of thousands of manuscripts that recorded knowledge from across the Islamic world. This page is from a sixteenth-century Qur'an.

SIKHISM IN INDIA: THE BIRTH OF A NEW RELIGION

New information and ideas from afar affected intellectual life in South Asia too, but not as disruptively as in lands to the west. The greatest departure came in the form of a new religion, now called **Sikhism**. It is rooted in Hindu and Islamic traditions, but it fostered several innovative twists all its own.

As we've seen, Islam had first come to India in the eighth century. By 1000, it had emerged as a powerful political force, the religion of conquerors and rulers from Central Asia. Thereafter, its followers jostled with India's more numerous followers of Hinduism, sometimes congenially, sometimes violently. Some thinkers emphasized the compatible features of the two religions to try to achieve a synthesis. This became a little easier with the rise of Sufism within Islam. Sufi sheikhs acquired saintlike status, and their tombs attracted worshippers, similar to the shrines of the many Hindu gods. In the fifteenth century, a few thinkers arose in northwestern India claiming that Hinduism and Islam were two approaches to the same sacred truth.

NANAK'S TEACHINGS

The most influential of these was Nanak (1469–1539). He was born into a Hindu family of a merchant caste near Lahore, in Punjab, in today's Pakistan. He had a Muslim teacher, however, and showed keen interest as a youth in theology, philosophy, and poetry. He learned Sanskrit, the ancient language of the Hindu Vedas, as well as Arabic and Persian, giving him access to vast learning—not so different in this respect from his contemporary, Copernicus. His father tried to install him in positions as an accountant, his own line of work, but Nanak found keeping track of money tedious compared to the timeless questions of religion, righteousness, and truth. So, like Luther, he disappointed his father and sought elusive truths rather than a safe career. At age 27, he experienced a vision in which God told him that he, Nanak, was to be the prophet of the true religion. Nanak summarized his new message in the phrase "there is no Muslim, there is no Hindu." He left a wife and children to begin a long journey that purportedly took him all over India and to Tibet and Arabia. Everywhere he discussed the big questions about truth, existence, reality, and divinity, refining his message as he went.

Nanak's followers became known as Sikhs ("disciples" in the Punjabi language). They accepted his message that Hindusim and Islam are really one, and several other tenets that gave Sikhism a special character. Sikhs, like Muslims, accepted that there is but one God, the creator of all things. In contrast to most Indian religions, Sikhism held that God's supreme creation is humankind and other living creatures are lesser beings. So Sikhs have no problem with eating meat, which followers of other Indian religions often avoid. Sikhism did accept reincarnation, more or less along the lines of Hinduism's principle of karma.

Nanak explicitly rejected the elaborate ceremonies of both Hinduism and Islam, just as Protestants scrapped much Catholic ritual. He preferred a more ascetic, personal, plain approach to God, without priests and their arcane knowledge. He regarded religious commitment as something one accepted as an adult, which Sikhs mark with a simple ceremony, rather than something one is born into—again, like some branches of Protestantism. Nanak rejected caste as well and preached an egalitarian creed in which the same moral codes applied to all regardless

of birth, family, and status. He extended this to gender, claiming men and women were equal before God. Nanak also preached a strict pacifism, in line with some strains of Hindusim and a few sects of Protestantism. The parallels with Protestantism are not mere coincidence. Nanak and Luther both reacted against religions that seemed to them too ornate, remote, attentive to worldly concerns, and devoted to the self-interest of priests and officials.

THE DEVELOPMENT OF SIKHISM

Nanak Guru (meaning "leader") died in 1539, but his religion lived on. He left behind an enormous number of hymns, which with a few additions are collectively called the **Adi Granth** (meaning "the first book"), the scripture for Sikhs. It is written mainly in Punjabi, not Sanskrit, and so was accessible to most any literate person in Nanak's part of India, as the translations of the Bible by Wycliffe and Luther made Christian scripture accessible to people who had not studied Latin, Greek, or Hebrew.

Subsequent gurus modified Nanak's teachings, most notably in response to persecution of Sikhs by Muslim princes in the early seventeenth century. After one guru

Adi Granth A copy of the Sikh scripture from around the years 1660–1675 is illuminated with a simple geometric and floral pattern. Written in the vernacular language Punjabi, it was widely accessible to literate people in northwestern India.

Golden Temple Constructed in the 1570s, the Golden Temple at Amritsar became the most important site of worship for Sikhs. An anonymous Indian artist painted this watercolor of the temple around 1840.

was tortured to death in 1606, his son, Guru Har Gobind, the sixth guru, abandoned pacifism and started a Sikh military tradition that survives to this day. Any Sikh male of any background could become a member of a warrior class, called *singhs* ("lions"). They became famous for their valor in battle, which ensured the survival of Sikhism against many threats. Soon Sikh warriors were working as mercenaries here and there throughout South Asia.

Sikhism survived and flourished in north India. It held special attraction for women and low-caste Hindus, for whom it promised some degree of liberation. It also appealed to cosmopolitan urban and merchant groups, who had some exposure to the diversity of religion in the Indian subcontinent and Indian Ocean world. It made a sufficiently good impression on the most powerful Muslim ruler of India, the Mughal emperor Akbar (r. 1556–1605), that he donated land for what would become the most important Sikh shrine, the Golden Temple in Amritsar, in the 1570s.

Ideas and information from the Americas or Oceania contributed nothing to the ferment from which Sikhism evolved. Instead, Sikhism represents an innovation favored by the tightening of the existing Old World web, rather than its expansion. Increased trade and urbanization created a social milieu in which Sikhism prospered. The constant frictions between Islam and Hindusim provided the spark that inspired Nanak in his quest for reconciliation.

CHINA AND JAPAN: CONFUCIAN REFORMATION AND IMPORTED CHRISTIANITY

In East Asia, as in India, Iran, and Europe, intellectual life had a long and refined formal tradition. Here too the new linkages of the sixteenth century jolted established ideas.

WANG YANGMING

In China since the late Song dynasty (960–1279), a coherent ideology held sway among the intellectual elite, one historians now call **neo-Confucianism**. It built on the ancient sages, Confucius and Mencius, but added an even stronger emphasis on self-cultivation and study in the quest for moral rectitude. It formed the core of the civil service examination, so every ambitious young man sought to master this philosophy in hopes of winning a prestigious place in the bureaucracy. Neo-Confucianism survived the downfall of the Song, the Mongol invasion of China, and the Yuan dynasty set up by the Mongols (1279–1368), and it was flourishing under the Ming dynasty (1368–1644).

But in the early sixteenth century, just when Luther and Nanak were shaking up Europe and India, a Chinese philosopher, **Wang Yangming**, mounted a challenge to the reigning ideology. He did not seek to repudiate Confucianism, but to improve upon it, so he too is called a neo-Confucian thinker.

Wang Yangming (1472–1529) was born to a family of the bureaucratic and intellectual class. His father had come in first in the civil service examinations in 1481, and Wang himself did well too, earning degrees at age 19 and 26 when many other men studied into their thirties trying to pass the examinations. He served in the imperial government in middling roles until he offended the palace eunuchs in 1506. For his transgressions, Wang was publicly flogged and banished far from the capital.

Exile and isolation proved productive for Wang, as it would for Mulla Sadra in Iran. During his three-year banishment, Wang developed his distinctive brand of neo-Confucian thought. His fortunes revived, and he won government appointments in southern China, where he distinguished himself as a military commander by

CONSIDERING THE EVIDENCE

A Hymn by Kabir in the *Adi Granth*

India had no shortage of holy men when Guru Nanak founded the community that would become the Sikh religion. *Pirs*, *bhagats*, *mullahs*, *sants*, *qazis*, *swamis*, Brahmins, *pandits*, and gurus; these devotees all defended their doctrine and practices with arguments from the Hindu Vedas and the Muslim Qur'an, just as Protestants and Catholics turned to the Bible for support in their debates. Yet, both Hinduism and Islam also inspired mystics who tired of orthodox religion and the sectarian squabbling it inspired. They rejected rational arguments and the external rituals of fasting, prayer, and pilgrimage as being inferior to an intense, internal devotion to God. Kabir, for instance, was a weaver born in the early fifteenth century to Muslim parents who became the disciples of a Hindu holy man. He lived hundreds of miles away and decades before Guru Nanak, but the Sikh gurus who compiled the *Adi Granth* as their faith's scripture decided to include over 500 of Kabir's songs alongside their own teachings. As shown in the following hymn, Kabir taught that both Hinduism and Islam point to the same God, but everyone needs a personal guru to awaken them to the presence of God in their own hearts.

If Allah lives in a mosque,
to whom belongs the rest of the land?
Hindus say His name dwells in an idol:
I see the truth in neither.

Allah, Ram, I live by Your name.
Be merciful, O Sain. (Rest)

The south is Hari's abode; Allah's camp
is in the west. Look inside your own heart—
inside your heart of hearts—
there is His abode, His camp.

Brahmins fast twice a month twenty-four times;
qazis fast in the month of Ramadan:
Neglecting the remaining eleven months,
they search for treasure in one month.

Why go and bathe in Orissa?
Why bow heads in a mosque?
You're a thug at heart.
Why pray and go on a *hajj* to the Ka'aba.

All these men and women—
they are Your forms.

Kabir is the infant of Ram-Allah;
everyone is my guru, my *pir*.

Kabir says, "Listen, O men and women,
seek only one shelter:
Repeat His name, O mortals.
Only then will you swim across."

Source: *Songs of Kabir from the Adi Granth*, trans. Nirmal Dass (Albany, 1991).

QUESTIONS FOR ANALYSIS

1. Does Kabir want Hindus and Muslims to stop praying or fasting, or is he more concerned about their intentions during worship?
2. How do Kabir's critiques of both Hindus and Muslims help him find the common ground of both faiths?
3. Which lines in Kabir's hymn would have appealed to the Sikh gurus who compiled the *Adi Granth*?

crushing rebellions. He maintained an active scholarly career while holding official posts and holding forth to many admiring students.

Wang Yangming rejected one of the main tenets of the neo-Confucianism of his youth, which treated knowledge as available only through dedicated study. Although himself a champion at book learning, Wang began to argue that true knowledge could not be separated from action and experience. Indeed, he maintained, one did not need book learning to understand truth and morality. Ordinary people, Wang claimed, could as readily obtain wisdom and act ethically as the most learned of scholars. He believed "the nature of all humans is good" and that anyone, however humble, had innate knowledge and could attain moral perfection. All that stood between people and moral perfection was selfish desire, so freeing oneself from that was key. One can see undertones of Buddhist philosophy, familiar to many Chinese intellectuals, in his logic.

This viewpoint was revolutionary in the context of the Confucian tradition and made Wang in effect a traitor to his class. His confidence in ordinary folk led him to maintain that "all the people filling the street are sages"—a heretical thought in China. His philosophy bore some resemblance to Lutheranism or Sikhism, which held that people could achieve spiritual perfection on their own without guidance from priests.

Wang's philosophy attracted many adherents during the sixteenth century. Advances in printing helped spread his (and others') ideas by lowering prices of books. Young strivers of modest means found his message liberating. Wang Yangming study groups proliferated for decades after his death. His philosophy won admirers in Japan too. In retrospect, he stands among the most influential thinkers in the Confucian tradition.

Wang Yangming's revision of neo-Confucianism was only one strand in the tapestry of Chinese thought and belief, but it was the most influential and enduring. Other developments included a Buddhist revival among elites that spread in the late sixteenth century with support from an empress, and the arrival of Christianity, brought by missionaries beginning in 1583.

CHRISTIANITY IN CHINA AND JAPAN

In China, Christianity came mainly with the Jesuits, of whom about 900 made the perilous trip from Europe. In the early seventeenth century, they met with some success, converting three high officials and thereby acquiring some protection. The Jesuits generally concentrated on the top rungs, the high literati, of Chinese society and used technical knowledge to get hearings. Ming dynasty officials showed keen interest in Jesuit skills in map making and cannon casting.

In general, however, Christianity was a hard sell to the Confucian literati. They had spent decades mastering a philosophical-religious system that carried immense prestige in China and had no need to exchange it for another. As a practical matter, Christian morality was often a sticking point, as many Chinese literati had concubines in their households. At a maximum, Christianity won over about 1 percent of the Chinese population, and the proportion fell after the late seventeenth century when the Jesuits tried to embrace a new dynasty of conquerors from Manchuria, the Qing. The Jesuits achieved some success with the Qing imperial household, especially that of the

Christianity in China A sixteenth-century engraving shows the Jesuit missionary Matteo Ricci (left) and Xu Guangqi, a Chinese scholar who converted to Christianity. The two men are depicted in a church, illustrated with a mix of Chinese and Jesuit iconography.

great emperor Kangxi (r. 1661–1722), but they never found broad adherence among the Chinese elite.

Christianity also took root in Japan, as we saw at the start of this chapter. European Christians first arrived, shipwrecked on southern islands, in 1543, and missionaries, mainly Spanish and Portuguese, arrived in 1549, beginning with Francis Xavier and Anjirō. As in China, missionaries in Japan focused first on the upper classes, especially the great landowners called *daimyo* who in the sixteenth century dominated the country. Francis Xavier considered the Japanese to be "of very good manners, good in general and not malicious." Most Japanese, however, regarded missionaries, and other Europeans, as "southern barbarians" and wanted little to do with them except perhaps trade. Missionaries found it convenient to double as importers of exotic goods. Japan was among the world's most urbanized societies, which made the business of conversion a little easier because missionaries could reach bigger audiences in cities. Japan's political divisions also helped the missionaries: no single authority could ban the southern barbarians from all of Japan.

Mission efforts—staffed mainly by Japanese who had already embraced Christianity—converted some 2 to 3 percent of Japan's population, or 200,00 to 300,000 people, by 1590. Christians lived in every province. Hundreds of churches opened. Even some of Christianity's less appealing practices caught on, such as self-flagellation with whips as a way to compensate for sin. But after 1590, rulers of an increasingly unified Japan, including men who had formerly shown some interest in Christianity, tried to prevent conversion. Eager to minimize foreign influence, the government officially banned Christianity in 1597 and again, more effectively, in 1614. Churches were torn down, missionaries expelled, Christian communities conquered by force of arms, and roughly 4,000 converts executed. By 1640, Christianity in Japan was on the edge of extinction, surviving only as an underground religion.

In China, by 1580 a concerted reaction against Wang Yangming's followers took shape, and many were imprisoned or executed. Catholicism in China also provoked official reaction. The Jesuits backed a losing candidate in an imperial succession struggle, and the winner, the Yongzheng Emperor, banned Christianity in China in 1724.

The Scientific Revolution, compared to the several religious movements discussed in this chapter, provoked less official reaction. Galileo and Kepler both met with hostility from church authorities, but Galileo had initially found support from the Pope and the Jesuits when attacked by the Inquisition. Only after he went to some lengths to offend the Pope was he forced to renounce his views and confined to house arrest. But most of the new science did not trouble the church, and indeed much of it was conducted by churchmen or devout Christians like Boyle and Newton. About half the mathematics professors in seventeenth-century Europe were Jesuits.

In any case, the political divisions within Europe made the suppression of new ideas ineffective in comparison with comparable efforts in Safavid Iran, China

REPRESSION AND PERSECUTION

Reactions against novel religious and intellectual movements, like the suppression of Christianity in Japan, were routine among elites and rulers wedded to existing faiths and ideologies. The most secure rulers, however, showed great interest in diverse religions—rather like the Mongol court in the thirteenth century. Among these were Shah Abbas I in Safavid Iran, and two whom we'll see more of in the next chapter—Akbar the Great in Mughal India and Mehmet the Conqueror in the Ottoman Empire. But their successors, often feeling less secure in their power, generally organized clampdowns and persecutions. In Europe, Catholic authorities revitalized the Inquisition in the sixteenth century and supported religious wars against Protestants, and Protestant kings did their best to persecute Catholics. In Iran, the Safavids eventually attacked just about all religious groups and movements other than their preferred version of Shi'a Islam. Sunni Muslims, Sufis, Christians, Jews, and Zoroastrians all felt the consequences. In India in the early seventeenth century, the Sikhs went from being pacifists to militarists in response to assaults from Muslim princes.

Anti-Christian Reaction Dozens of Christians—including several European missionaries—are beheaded and burned at the stake in this seventeenth-century Japanese illustration of the turn against Christianity in unified Japan that started in 1597.

after 1580 or Japan after 1590. Religious disunity flourished in Europe, as in India, as did rival schools of scientific thought, and no prince, however determined, could change that. In Europe, moreover, easy access to information, a result of the spread of the printing press and the shared use of Latin among scholars, also made it hard for authorities to clamp down.

INTELLECTUAL UPHEAVAL: PARALLELS AND CONTRASTS

The entire process of intellectual upheaval in Eurasia was uneven in three main respects. First, as we have seen, it was geographically uneven, affecting Europe more than the rest of Eurasia, and within Europe some parts more than others. Part of the unevenness within Eurasia had to do with Europe's political fragmentation and Atlantic Europe's greater involvement in global circuits than

anywhere else. Much of the unevenness within Europe had to do with local circumstances, such as the fact that Calvin took refuge in Geneva rather than somewhere else.

Second, everywhere the intellectual upheaval affected cities, and especially trading cities, more—or at least sooner—than the countryside. Remote mountain villages in Asia were less likely to be buffeted by the currents of Sikhism or neo-Confucianism than were the cities, where new ideas arrived more frequently and were likelier to win followers.

Third, intellectual upheaval was socially uneven. Although the religious transformations of the Reformation(s) and the conversion of Iran to Shi'ism rippled through all levels of society, and the spread of Sikhism touched the lower classes first and foremost, much of this turbulence shook only the elite. Illiterate Chinese peasants, with the rarest of exceptions, did not know that Wang Yangming and his followers considered them equally as capable of moral perfection as the most learned Confucian scholar. Polish peasants remained

Women Scientists The German entomologist and botanist Maria Sibylla Merian, shown here in a 1679 portrait alongside one of her detailed color paintings of butterflies and caterpillars, was one of the women whose work contributed to the Scientific Revolution.

entirely unaware that Copernicus was charting a new map of the heavens. English peasants did not know that Newton was formulating an elegantly precise mathematical account of the force of gravity. They and their counterparts, 90 percent of the population of Eurasia, had hungry children, sick babies, tired muscles, fickle weather, ravenous tax collectors, and a hundred other things on their minds every day. Although they worried about what might follow upon death, wondered whether or not to do what priests told them to do, and even contemplated the mysteries of divinity, they generally could not spare much time for moral philosophy or mathematical equations.

There is a fourth respect in which the intellectual and religious turbulence of these centuries was uneven, but consistently so across Eurasia. None of the great religious reformers, philosophers, or scientists mentioned in this chapter were women. Some European women did make contributions to scientific work, such as Margaret Cavendish (1623–1673), an English duchess who wrote poetry, plays, and several works on moral philosophy. She undertook scientific experiments and was once—controversially—permitted to attend a meeting of the Royal Society. (The Royal Society, founded in 1660, composed of eminent scientists, was and is dedicated to the advancement of knowledge.) Maria Sibylla Merian (1647–1717) was a German entomologist and botanist who published the first detailed work on caterpillars and their metamorphosis into butterflies. She also undertook a self-funded scientific expedition to South America and produced a landmark study of the insects of Suriname.

But the truth is none of them were anywhere near as influential as Copernicus, Galileo, Harvey, or Newton. No women in Iran, India, or China had anything like the impact on religion or philosophy of Mulla Sadra, Nanak, or Wang Yangming. We can be sure that some women were just as interested in truth, the heavens, health, alchemy, morality, and divinity as any man—as the record of more recent centuries shows. But fewer women than men could act upon an interest in these and other intellectual matters. Women were less likely to be able to read than were men, and in most places far less likely. They were much more likely to face discouragement from family and society if they showed inclination toward deep thinking. A French aristocrat, Martine Berterau, who published a book on mining engineering, was charged with witchcraft, as was her husband.

Women were often forbidden to be members of universities, madrasas, and academies. When in 1678 the University of Padua awarded a PhD to Elena Cornaro, a Venetian noblewoman, the university promptly revised its statutes to prevent women from taking degrees. The Swedish aristocrat Eva Ekeblad in 1748 was elected to the Swedish Royal Academy of Sciences for her successful distillation of alcohol from potatoes. But in 1751, she was demoted to honorary membership, on the principle that full academicians should be men. The rare exception was Laura Bassi, the second woman anywhere to earn a doctorate, which she did in 1732 at age 20 from the University of Bologna in Italy. That same year, she was appointed there as a chaired professor of physics. She taught science for the next 45 years and conducted experiments in electricity—meanwhile bearing 12 children. But by and large, women could not and did not hold positions like Bassi's, and whatever their inclinations and talents, they did not influence intellectual agendas and paths in major ways. So the religious schisms and revivals, the philosophical twists and turns, the Scientific Revolution—as well as all the efforts to suppress these novel ideas—were overwhelmingly the work of men.

CONCLUSION

The Eurasian landmass in the sixteenth and seventeenth centuries experienced unusual intellectual and religious turbulence. Ideas, ideologies, and religions are of course changing all the time. But sometimes they change faster and more radically, and this was such a time. This turbulence always had important local causes bound up in the politics and social changes of particular places, such as the demographic trends that magnified Europe's witch craze or the fragmentation of Japan that gave Christian missionaries an opening. But it also had larger, looser causes connected to both the expansion and the consolidation of what was becoming the Global web.

Those general causes included the difficulty of making sense of new data within old systems of thought. Observations from distant continents after 1492, and from distant planets after 1608 (the date of the invention of the telescope), called old wisdom into question and set curious minds to work. This particular source of intellectual turbulence was strongest in Europe, because Europe was much more involved in overseas linkages to hitherto isolated lands than was anywhere else in Eurasia. And the telescope and microscope were European inventions.

At the same time that new information was flooding into the minds of Europeans, the flow of ideas and information more generally sped up. In Europe, the printing press played a big role in that. But everywhere in the sixteenth and seventeenth centuries, even in those parts of Eurasia least affected by seaborne commerce to the Americas, the pace of trade, travel, and urbanization crept upward. More people came into more frequent contact with strangers bearing exotic notions. While new ideas were usually shunned, from time to time they appealed to people who explored them and sometimes adopted them. Or, more often, adapted them into their prior schemes of religion and thought, and in so doing altered those schemes.

Despite their local causes and distinctive characters, these new intellectual and religious movements—many of them—shared some common features. In most of them

one can find an emphasis on personal responsibility and personal approaches to truth or God, with minimal mediation from priests, as in Lutheranism, Sikhism, and to some extent the Shi'a movement in Iran. One can find an appeal to the value of experience, as in Wang Yangming's thought, Protestantism, Sikhism, and the Scientific Revolution. These common threads reflect not so much interaction among these movements, but similar reactions to dissatisfaction with the entrenched, institutionalized, stolid religions and ideologies, all of them seemingly slow to adapt to changing times.

Most of these intellectual and religious innovations survive into the twenty-first century. Today, in retrospect, we can say that the most important among them was the Scientific Revolution, as it laid the foundations for the technological transformations that distinguish modern times. At the time, however, the religious upheavals seemed most important. They meant more to more people. And they helped animate the political struggles of the early modern centuries, to which we turn in the next chapter.

CHAPTER REVIEW

KEY TERMS

Jesuits (p. 573)

printing press (p. 575)

Renaissance (p. 578)

Protestantism (p. 581)

Catholic Reformation (p. 582)

witch hunts (p. 583)

Scientific Revolution (p. 583)

heliocentric system (p. 584)

Shi'a Islam (p. 587)

Safavids (p. 588)

Mulla Sadra (p. 589)

Sikhism (p. 590)

Adi Granth (p. 591)

neo-Confucianism (p. 592)

Wang Yangming (p. 592)

Go to INQUIZITIVE to see what you've learned—and learn what you've missed—with personalized feedback along the way.

REVIEW QUESTIONS

1. How did new geographic and scientific discoveries lead to the weakening of existing intellectual traditions?

2. Why was the printing revolution mainly confined to Europe and European colonies for many centuries?

3. What was the source and the main emphasis of the Renaissance?

4. What political and technological conditions helped Luther and his ideas evade Catholic persecution?

5. What principles formed the basis of the Scientific Revolution, and what procedures were at its heart?

6. What measures did the Safavids introduce to transform Iran into a Shi'a theocracy?

7. Whom did Sikhism attract, and why?

8. Why was conversion to Christianity unpopular in China and Japan?

9. Why was it more difficult for authorities to clamp down on new ideas in Europe than it was in China, Japan, and India?

10. What were the three main ways in which intellectual upheaval in Eurasia was uneven?

11. What common features did new intellectual and religious movements share, and what widespread trends did these commonalities reflect?

FURTHER READING

Rula Jurdi ABISAAB, *Converting Persia: Religion and Power in the Safavid Empire* (2015). A work that focuses on the Shi'a clerics imported into Iran by the Safavids.

Daniel H. BAYS, *A New History of Christianity in China* (2011). Chapter 2 discusses the Jesuits in the sixteenth century.

H. Floris COHEN, *The Rise of Modern Science Explained: A Comparative History* (2015). An excellent and readable study.

Carlos M. N. EIRE, *Reformations: The Early Modern World, 1450–1650* (2016). A massive, insightful work with a focus on Europe.

Philip J. IVANHOE, *Ethics in the Confucian Tradition: The Thought of Mengzi and Wang Yangming* (2002, 2nd ed.). A dense but thorough exploration of Wang's ideas.

Colin P. MITCHELL, *The Practice of Politics in Safavid Iran: Power, Religion, and Rhetoric* (2011). A work of serious

scholarship rather than an introductory text, but the author contextualizes religion well through the time of Shah Abbas I.

James POSKETT, *Horizons: The Global Origins of Modern Science* (2022). The first few chapters explain how various world regions took part in the Scientific Revolution.

Lawrence M. PRINCIPE, *The Scientific Revolution: A Very Short Introduction* (2011). A perceptive look into the mindset of the time.

Lyndal ROPER, *Martin Luther: Renegade and Prophet* (2017). The 500th anniversary of Luther's Ninety-Five Theses inspired several new biographies, of which this serious but readable account might be the best.

Nikky-Guninder Kaur SINGH, *The First Sikh: The Life and Legacy of Guru Nanak* (2019). A very lively biography with a focus on Nanak's songs and poems.

New Paths to Enlightenment, Wisdom, and Truth

IN EVERY PERIOD OF WORLD HISTORY, some people were (and are) wrestling with timeless questions. A very few of them, such as the Buddha, Confucius, Jesus, and Muhammad, came up with answers that millions of others find compelling. In the early sixteenth century, a generation of thinkers arrived at creative revisions and repudiations of earlier answers. They provided the basis for a major strand of neo-Confucian thought, for Protestant Christianity, and for Sikhism. Based in India, China, and Germany, Nanak Guru (1469–1539), Wang Yangming (1472–1529), and Martin Luther (1483–1546) were contemporaries—but knew nothing of one another. Yet they had something in common: they thought ordinary people, without elaborate education and training, could find truth, wisdom, and enlightenment within themselves and within their personal relationship to God. Catholic priests, Hindu brahmins, and Confucian literati did not—they claimed—have a monopoly on truth. Another thinker, Galileo Galilei (1564–1642), was from a later generation, but he too thought priests had no monopoly on truth. He too recommended a new and different path to truth and wisdom: through scientific observation.

SOURCE 17.1

Verses from the *Adi Granth*, Sikh Scripture, early sixteenth century

As the chapter explains, Nanak Guru founded the Sikh religion after experiencing a vision in 1496. He and later gurus composed an enormous volume of hymns, verses, and prose that together form the scripture of Sikh religion. The first book, the *Adi Granth*, is mainly the work of Nanak. The extract below is from two hymns, composed by Nanak Guru in response to a question about whose disciple he was and to an invitation to become a Hindu yogi (holy man). In this translation, the capitalized words "Thou," "Thy," "Thyself," and "Beloved" refer to God.

What is the Scale? What the weights? What weighman
    shall I call for Thee?
Who is the guru from whom I should receive instruction
    and by whom I should appraise Thy worth?
O my Beloved, I know not Thy limit.
Thou fillest sea and land, the nether and upper regions; it
    is Thou Thyself who art contained in everything.
My heart is the scale, my understanding the weight, Thy
    service the weighman I employ.
I weigh the Lord in my heart, and thus I fix my attention.
Thou are the tongue of the balance, the weight, and the
    scales; Thou Thyself art the weighman;
Thou Thyself beholdest, Thou Thyself understandest;
    Thou Thyself art the dealer with Thee.

A blind man, a low-born person, and a stranger come but
    for a moment, and in a moment depart.
In such companionship Nanak abideth; how can he, fool
    that he is, obtain Thee?

At this point, Nanak's audience urged him to become a yogi to find truth and obtain the benefits of their Hindu religion. Nanak composed another hymn in reply:

Religion consisteth not in a patched coat, or in a Yogi's staff, or in ashes smeared over the body;
    Religion consisteth not in earrings worn, or a shaven head, or in the blowing of horns.[1]
    Abide pure amid the impurities of the world; thus shalt thou find the way of religion.
    Religion consisteth not in mere words;
    He who looketh on all men as equal is religious.
    Religion consisteth not in wanderings to tombs or places of cremation, or sitting in attitudes of contemplation.
    Religion consisteth not in wandering in foreign countries, or in bathing at places of pilgrimages.

---

[1]Yogis were known for blowing deer-antler horns.

Source: M. A. MacAuliffe, *The Sikh Religion: Its Gurus, Sacred Writings, and Anthems*, Vol. I (Oxford: Clarendon Press, 1909).

- **What is Nanak Guru's judgment on the customs of yogis?**
- **Where, according to Nanak Guru, should one look for enlightenment and truth?**

Martin Luther on the Spiritual and Bodily Natures of Man, 1520

Martin Luther (1483–1546) was a German priest, professor, and theologian. His radical conceptions of Christian duty and the route to salvation launched the Protestant Reformation. His views, together with his contempt for many practices of the Catholic Church, earned him the Pope's wrath and, in 1521, excommunication from the Church. The selections below come from a short treatise that appeared in German and Latin in 1520, "On the Freedom of a Christian." In it Luther takes pains to cite the chapter and verse of the Bible from which he draws his quotations and arguments. He begins with a paradox: A Christian man is the most free lord of all, subject to none. A Christian man is the most dutiful servant of all, and subject to everyone. The excerpt below refers immediately to these statements.

Although these statements appear contradictory, yet, when they are found to agree together, they will make excellently for my purpose. They are both the statements of Paul himself, who says, "Though I be free from all men, yet have I made myself servant unto all" (1 Cor. ix. 19), and "Owe no man anything, but to love one another" (Rom. xiii. 8). Now love is by its own nature dutiful and obedient to the beloved object. Thus even Christ, though Lord of all things, was yet made of a woman; made under the law; at once free and a servant; at once in the form of God and in the form of a servant.

Let us examine the subject on a deeper and less simple principle. Man is composed of a twofold nature, a spiritual and a bodily. As regards the spiritual nature, which they name the soul, he is called the spiritual, inward, new man; as regards the bodily nature, which they name the flesh, he is called the fleshly, outward, old man. The Apostle speaks of this: "Though our outward man perish, yet the inward man is renewed day by day" (2 Cor. iv. 16), The result of this diversity is, that in the Scriptures opposing statements are made concerning the same man; the fact being that in the same man these two men are opposed to one another; the flesh lusting against the spirit, and the spirit against the flesh (Gal. v. 17).

We first approach the subject of the inward man, that we may see by what means a man becomes justified, free, and a true Christian; that is, a spiritual, new, and inward man. It is certain that absolutely none among outward things, under whatever name they may be reckoned, has any weight in producing a state of justification and Christian liberty, nor, on the other hand, an unjustified state and one of slavery. This can be shown by an easy course of argument.

What can it profit the soul, that the body should be in good condition, free, and full of life; that it should eat, drink, and act according to its pleasure; when even the most impious slaves of every kind of vice are prosperous in these matters? Again, what harm can ill-health, bondage, hunger, thirst, or any other outward evil do to the soul, when even the most pious of men, and the freest in the purity of their conscience, are harassed by these things? Neither of these states of things has to do with the liberty or the slavery of the soul.

And so it will profit nothing that the body should be adorned with sacred vestments, or dwell in holy places, or be occupied in sacred offices, or pray, fast, and abstain from certain meats, or do whatever works can be done through the body and in the body. Something widely different will be necessary for the justification and liberty of the soul, since the things I have spoken of can be done by any impious person, and only hypocrites are produced by devotion to these things. On the other hand, it will not at all injure the soul that the body should be clothed in profane raiment, should dwell in profane places, should eat and drink in the ordinary fashion, should not pray aloud, and should leave undone all the things abovementioned, which may be done by hypocrites.

And, to cast everything aside, even speculations, meditations, and whatever things can be performed by the exertions of the soul itself, are of no profit. One thing, and one alone, is necessary for life, justification, and Christian liberty; and that is the most holy word of God, the Gospel of Christ, as He says: "I am the resurrection and the life; he that believeth in me shall not die eternally" (John xi. 25); and also (John viii. 36) "If the Son shall make you free, ye shall be free indeed," and (Matt. iv. 4) "Man shall not live by bread alone, but by every word that proceedeth out of the mouth of God."

Let us therefore hold it for certain and firmly established, that the soul can do without everything, except the word of God, without which none at all of its wants are provided for. But, having the word, it is rich and wants for nothing; since that is the word of life, of truth, of light, of peace, of justification, of salvation, of joy, of liberty, of wisdom, of virtue, of grace, of glory, and of every good thing. It is on this account that the prophet in a whole psalm (Ps. cxix.), and in many other places, sighs for and calls upon the word of God with so many groanings and words.

Source: Martin Luther, *First Principles of the Reformation or the Ninety-Five Theses and the Three Primary Works of Dr. Martin Luther Translated into English* (London: John Murray, Albemarle Street, 1883).

- What must a Christian do to attain salvation, according to Luther?
- How does the doctrine of duality of body and soul help Luther make his case?

Wang Yangming on Genuine Investigation, 1525

Wang Yangming (1472–1529) was a philosopher, a high-ranking bureaucrat, and a successful military commander under China's Ming dynasty. He developed a strand of neo-Confucian thought that won many admirers. It emphasized the merits of experience and practical knowledge, claiming that ordinary people without book learning could find their own path to virtue and wisdom. In fact, everyone possesses innate morality and merely needs to activate it. His ideas provoked some objections from other scholars but remained influential for centuries. Here he explains the unity of knowledge and action, and he makes a case for the value of intuition.

Inquiry, deliberation, discrimination, and practice are all to be considered as learning. Learning and practice always go together. For instance, if the individual says that he is learning filial piety, he will certainly bear the toil of his parents, take care of them, and himself walk in the path of filial piety. After that he may speak of learning filial piety. Can he who merely says that he is learning filial piety, therefore be said to be learning? He who learns archery must certainly take the bow and fit the arrow to the string, draw the bow and shoot. He who learns writing must certainly straighten the paper and take the pen, grasp the paper and dip the pen into the ink. In all learning of the Empire, there is nothing that can be called learning unless it is carried out in practice. Thus the beginning of learning is surely practice. The earnest one, being sincere and honest, has already practiced his learning. Making his practice sincere and earnest, he does not cease from his work.

Since doubt must arise in connection with learning, inquiry is necessarily present. Making inquiry, the individual learns and practices. Since doubt arises there is deliberation. Deliberating, he learns and again practices. Being in doubt, he also begins to discriminate, and thus both learns and practices. When discrimination is clear, deliberation careful and sincere, inquiry discerning, learning competent and skillful, and application constant, practice is earnest. It does not mean that after study, inquiry, deliberation, and discrimination, one first is ready to practice.

For this reason I hold and say that seeking to be able to do anything is learning; seeking to dissipate any doubt connected therewith is inquiry: seeking to understand the underlying principles is deliberation; seeking to get at the essence is discrimination; seeking to carry out its genuineness in action is practice. Any discussion of the situation that splits the task gives us these five stages. If the whole affair is united, it is one. This is the substance of my saying that mind and principles are one; it is the task of mutually developing knowledge and practice. This is the real point at which my sayings are different from those of later scholars.

You have especially selected study, inquiry, deliberation, and discrimination as the method whereby the principles of all things are to be thoroughly investigated, but you fail to reach the point of earnest practice. This means that you consider study, inquiry, deliberation, and discrimination as knowledge, but in this investigation of principles do not include practice. Is there a single instance in the Empire in which a person has learned without practice?

[. . .]

Man alone knows what is meant by being enticed by the influence of things, but is unable to carry on self-investigation with full sincerity or to carry out vigorously the law of reciprocity. He stops with recognizing his body as the person and external objects as things, and forthwith separates things and himself into two distinct realms, so that in last analysis his person represents but one thing among ten thousand. How, then, can he extend his knowledge to the utmost, be sincere in purpose, rectify his mind, cultivate his person, regulate his family, govern the kingdom, and tranquilize the empire, in order to complete and exhaust the doctrine of the Great Learning." Therefore it is said that the task is exhausted in extending knowledge to the utmost through the investigation of things.

[. . .]

The devotees of stupid abstraction and empty tranquility are unable to investigate the fundamental principles of the mind, as things and affairs are experienced. Thus what they attain is not the original intuitive knowledge of good. . . . That they continually make use of vacuity and tranquility shows that because they desire these, they cannot govern home, state, or Empire. . . .

[. . .]

The intuitive faculty is in man's mind. It has pervaded all generations of the immemorial past, filled heaven and earth, and was in no wise [way] different from what it now is. It knows without any cogitation. Constantly and easily it knows dangerous paths. It is able to act without learning. Constantly and easily it knows what things tend to hinder its progress. It strives first for heaven-given principles and does not trespass them. How much more is this true in the instance of men, of spirits, and of gods? . . .

The superior man learns for his own sake. He has not thereby considered or been anxious that others may deceive him, but perseveres rather in not deceiving his own intuitive faculty. He has not been anxious that others may not believe him, but perseveres in believing in his own intuitive faculty. Not deceiving himself, he keeps his intuitive faculty free from pretense and hypocrisy, and thereby is sincere. Being sincere, he is intelligent. Having faith in himself, his intuitive faculty is in doubt regarding no one and is therefore intelligent. Being intelligent, it is sincere. Intelligence and sincerity develop *pari passu* [at the same pace], and for this reason the intuitive faculty constantly realizes and constantly reflects. Since it constantly realizes and constantly reflects truly, it is like a suspended bright mirror. Whenever a thing appears before it, it cannot conceal beauty or ugliness. How is this? Not deceiving but always sincere, it does not permit anything to deceive it. If it is deceived, it realizes it. Being itself faithful and sincere, it does not permit anything in which it does not believe; and in case it does not believe it, it is conscious thereof. This means that it easily knows the dangerous path and whatsoever hinders its progress.

Source: Wang Yang-Ming, *The Philosophy of Wang Yang-Ming*, trans. Frederick Goodrich Henke (Chicago: The Open Court Publishing Co., 1916).

- According to Wang, what is the ultimate purpose of inquiry and investigation?
- In Wang's opinion, what prevents people from acting properly, appropriately, and morally?

SOURCE 17.4

Galileo Galilei Responds to Critics of Scientific Observation, 1614

Galileo (1564–1642), who is known by his first name, was an Italian scientist who studied medicine and mathematics but whose main contributions came in physics, mechanics, and astronomy. He was among the first to use a telescope to examine the stars, planets, and moons. His observations inclined him to think that the astronomer Nicolaus Copernicus (1473–1543) had been correct: the Earth moves around the sun rather than vice versa. These views brought Galileo into conflict with the Catholic Church, which at the time held firmly to the Ptolemaic theory that put the Earth at the center of the universe.

Below Galileo explains some of his reasoning in an excerpt from his autobiography. Ultimately, in 1633, a church court found him "vehemently suspect" of heresy, and under pressure he recanted. He spent the rest of his days under house arrest, and some of his writings were banned. (In 1992, the church recanted and removed the ban from his works.)

[T]he intention of the sacred Scriptures is to give to mankind the information necessary for their salvation, and which, surpassing all human knowledge can by no other means be accredited than by the mouth of the Holy Spirit. But I do not hold it necessary to believe that the same God who has endowed us with senses, with speech, and intellect, intended that we should neglect the use of these, and seek by other means for knowledge which they are sufficient to procure us; especially in a science like astronomy, of which so little notice is taken in the Scriptures, that none of the planets, except the sun and moon, and, once or twice only, Venus under the name of Lucifer, are so much as named there.... [I]n the discussion of natural problems we ought not to begin at the authority of texts of Scripture, but at sensible experiments, and necessary demonstrations: for, from the divine word, the sacred Scripture and nature did both alike proceed, and I conceive that concerning natural effects, that which either sensible experience sets before our eyes, or necessary demonstrations do prove unto us, ought not upon any account to be called into question, much less condemned, upon the testimony of Scriptural texts....

Again, to command the very professors of astronomy that they of themselves see to the confuting of their own observations and demonstrations, is to enjoin a thing beyond all possibility of doing; for it is not only to command them not to see that which they do see, and not to understand that which they do understand, but it is to order them to seek for and to find the contrary of that which they happen to meet with. I would entreat these wise and prudent fathers, that they would with all diligence consider the difference that is between opinionative and demonstrative doctrines; to the end that well weighing in their minds with what force necessary inferences urge us, they might the better assure themselves that it is not in the power of the professors of demonstrative sciences to change their opinions at pleasure, and adopt first one side and then another; and that there is a great difference between commanding a mathematician or a philosopher, and the disposing of a lawyer or a merchant; and that the demonstrated conclusions touching the things of nature and of the heavens cannot be changed with the same facility as the opinions are touching what is lawful or not in a contract, bargain, or bill of exchange. Therefore, first let these men apply themselves to examine the arguments of Copernicus and others, and leave the condemning of them as erroneous and heretical to whom it belongeth; yet let them not hope to find such rash and precipitous determinations in the wary and holy fathers, or in the absolute wisdom of him who cannot err, as those into which they suffer themselves to be hurried by some particular affection or interest of their own. In these and such other positions, which are not directly articles of faith, certainly no man doubts but His Holiness hath always an absolute power of admitting or condemning them, but it is not in the power of any creature to make them to be true or false, otherwise than of their own nature, and in fact they are.

Source: Galileo Galilei, *Life of Galileo Galilei: With Illustrations of the Advancement of Experimental Philosophy.* (Boston: William Hyde & Company, 1832).

- What is the appropriate way to seek truth, according to Galileo?
- In his view, who should have authority in matters of astronomy, and why?

QUESTIONS FOR COMPARISON

1. How do these four thinkers relate to established religious and intellectual authority in their respective worlds? In what ways do their writings offer radical challenges--or merely make modest suggestions?

2. Is there any evidence in these excerpts that some of these thinkers were concerned with improving society or the state in addition to the self? If so, where?

CHRONOLOGY

1453
Ottomans besiege Constantinople

By 1490
Very large cannon introduced

1508–1519
Emperor Maximilian I's reign

1516–1517
Ottomans defeat Mamluks and conquer Egypt and the Hejaz

1520–1566
Suleiman's reign

1526
Mughals conquer Delhi sultanate

1543
Chinese ship brings Portuguese guns to Japan

1547–1584
Ivan IV's reign

1550s
Habsburgs acquire windfall of silver from Americas

1556–1605
Akbar's reign

ca. 1590
Introduction of disciplined and drilled standing armies

1591
Saadians conquer Songhai in West Africa

1592–1598
Toyotomi Hideyoshi's Korea campaign

ca. 1600
Japan is unified; start of Tokugawa shogunate

1638
Manchus conquer Korea

ca. 1620–1680
Zheng family flourishes

1644
End of Ming dynasty and start of Qing dynasty

1658–1707
Aurangzeb's reign

1662–1722
Kangxi Emperor's reign

1682–1725
Peter the Great's reign

1694
National banks invented

18

University of War

EMPIRES AND POWER

1450 to 1800

1719–1722
Bartholomew Roberts captures 400
ships in the Atlantic and Caribbean

ca. 1750
Qing crush Zunghars

1735–1796
Qianlong Emperor's
reign

Zheng Zhilong and his son were the most successful pirates in world history. Zheng the elder was born to a Chinese gentry family. In 1622, at age 18, unhappy with his schooling, he ran off to Macao (a Portuguese trading post in southern China), where he had an uncle. He learned Portuguese, was baptized a Christian, and soon took up trade and piracy. Sent by his uncle to Japan, he married a Japanese woman, Tagawa Matsu. Their son, Zheng Chenggong (1624–1662), although born and raised in Japan, was sent to study in a Chinese Confucian academy in hopes that he would qualify for the Ming dynasty's bureaucratic elite. But Zheng Chenggong (also known as Koxinga or Coxinga) eventually joined the family business.

Active along the southeastern coasts of China, from Nanjing to Macao, the Zheng family ran an international trade and piracy operation. In 1628, they captured nearly half of the recorded Chinese ships returning from the Philippines laden with silver. A Chinese governor explained why:

> The Zheng pirate gang is very clever and tricky, and good at sea fighting. Their pirate troops...consist mainly of Chinese bandits, with some Japanese

Military Prowess The early Mughal ruler Babur leads his forces in besieging a city—one of the early conquests that enabled the Mughals to accumulate a land empire in Central Asia. Babur's army includes war elephants and cavalry but also guns and, although not pictured here, cannon. Innovations in military technology and tactics transformed warfare and politics throughout Eurasia during the early modern period.

FOCUS QUESTIONS

1. What general conditions contributed to the growth of empires in the early modern period?

2. What were the most important components of the military revolution during this period?

3. What role did firearms play in the consolidation of power in Japan?

4. Why was the Qing dynasty so effective over its first century and a half?

5. How were the Mughals able to create a multireligious empire in India?

6. What policies helped in the expansion of Ottoman rule during this period?

7. What initiatives of Ivan III and Peter the Great strengthened the power of the Russian state?

8. How did the Habsburgs become rulers of the first global empire?

9. What was the "university of war," and how did it strengthen European states?

10. How did smaller states adapt to the changes wrought by the military revolution?

11. How did nomads and pirates fare during this period of growing state power?

and Europeans. Their war ships and weapons are manufactured by the distant barbarians [i.e., the Dutch]. Their ships are tall and solid, and their cannon can hit targets miles away.

From the late 1620s to the 1680s, no one could trade safely on the southeast China coast without permission from the Zheng family. In the 1650s, they employed some 400,000 sailors and soldiers, mostly Chinese and Japanese, but also some Europeans and a 300-man East African bodyguard. Their fleets included 5,000 ships.

The Zhengs and their sea captains raided and traded far and wide in East Asian waters. When the Chinese Empire tried to deny him supplies and bases on the mainland, Zheng Chenggong conquered the island of Taiwan, then held by the Dutch East India Company. His captains controlled 80 percent of the trade to Japan, carried cargoes from Cambodia and Thailand, and raided as far afield as the Philippines. He organized his own bank and minted coins.

The Zhengs were in effect building their own maritime state when Zheng Chenggong died, probably of malaria, at age 39 in 1662. They used all the resources at hand in their quest for power and wealth: Dutch and Chinese shipbuilding skills; Dutch and Portuguese cannon; Chinese and Japanese manpower; their own wide knowledge of East Asian coasts, islands, and waters; and their deep fund of daring. They ultimately lost, crushed by China's improving military in the early 1680s.

The Zhengs were among many such losers in the centuries between 1450 and 1800, often called the early modern period. Pirates, nomads, and the rulers of hundreds of small states, few of them as powerful as the Zheng clan at its height, lost out to larger, imperial states. These empires flourished as they grew more successful at winning over subject people's loyalties, more skilled at tax collection, and above all, more effective in using new technologies and techniques of violence.

This chapter deals with political, military, and economic history in an age of imperial consolidation. It explains how a handful of great powers arose, how they sometimes competed with one another, and how they shared (often unwillingly) technologies and techniques useful to states. In particular, it focuses on Tokugawa Japan, Qing China, Mughal India, the Ottoman Empire, Russia, and the Habsburg Empire. It includes more about military matters than any previous chapter, because in these centuries military innovations came thick and fast, spread throughout the Global web, and carried greater consequences for the global distribution of wealth and power than ever before.

These imperial powers used their improved skills and technologies to destroy hundreds of smaller states, crush pirates like the Zhengs, suppress bandits, and overwhelm tribal peoples—anyone who stood in their way. They took over lands formerly filled with peoples living in principalities, city-states, tribal confederations, or in no state whatsoever. In political terms, the big got bigger. The small polities and the peoples without states became fewer, surviving mainly in nooks and crannies of world politics such as high mountains, barren deserts, or unhealthy swamps—outside the nodes and threads of the Global web. The variety of political formats in which people lived became smaller—another example of how the globalizing web-building process reduced diversity.

	GLOBAL POPULATION	PROPORTION LIVING IN THE
DATE	GLOBAL POPULATION	SIX MOST POPULOUS STATES
1500	438 million	36% (China, Muscovy/Russia, Aztec Empire, Inka Empire, France, Ottoman Empire)
1600	556 million	55% (China, Russia, Japan, Mughal India, Ottoman Empire, Habsburg Empire)
1700	603 million	60% (China, Russia, Japan, Mughal India, Ottoman Empire, Habsburg Empire)
1800	950 million	57% (China, Russia, Japan, Mughal India, Ottoman Empire, France)

PROPORTION OF GLOBAL POPULATION IN THE MOST POPULOUS STATES, 1500–1800

Sources: Colin McEvedy and Richard Jones, *Atlas of World Population History: A Millennial Perspective* (1978), 55–60, 78–82, 137, 166–75, 179–89; Angus Maddison, *The World Economy* (2001), 241–43; Max Roser's website Our World in Data, https://ourworldindata.org/world-population-growth.

EARLY MODERN EMPIRE IN GLOBAL PERSPECTIVE

The main reason that the big political fish gobbled up the small fish in the early modern period is that the economics of power evolved in ways that favored big fish. In almost every part of the world, the costs of projecting power rose, especially for the technologies and techniques of warfare. Big states could bear those costs with less difficulty than small ones.

The history of empire gives us a valuable perspective on these developments. Today, there are very few states conventionally called empires, so it is easy to regard them as abnormal. But between Sargon of Akkad and today—and especially since the formation of the Roman and Han empires roughly 2,000 years ago—most of the world's people most of the time lived in empires. Most empires came and went quickly, even powerful ones such as those of Alexander the Great or Genghis Khan. Only a few endured, such as the Chinese, dynasty after dynasty—and even it experienced interludes of chaos and disunity.

World history shows two main periods when big empires grew bigger. The first occurred between about 600 BCE and 100 CE, when Achaemenid Persia, Mauryan India, Rome, and Han China—to name only a few—emerged and expanded. For the first time, single states controlled big territories, including all the most populous parts of the world. The second period was the one under consideration in this chapter, roughly the period 1450–1800.

Seen within a single national or imperial tradition, these surges in empire may appear to be accidental or the work of extraordinarily great leaders. Seen in world-historical perspective, they appear as parallel processes with some connections uniting them. In the first era of imperial growth and consolidation (600 BCE–100 CE), the challenge of steppe warriors helped inspire people to band together into larger and larger agrarian states in places such as Persia and China.

In the second era (1450–1800 CE), as we shall soon see, the parallels and connections were even stronger, showing the Global web in action. Empires learned military and fiscal techniques from one another, adopted technologies used effectively by others, and in the process came to resemble one another more as time went on. Improved printing technology generally sped the flow of information, including manuals on naval shipbuilding, army maneuvers, and other military topics. The mobility of experts, especially military architects and shipwrights, promoted the spread of information as well. Although rulers in possession of the best military technologies and expertise generally tried to keep it for themselves, by 1600 it had become harder than ever to keep useful secrets of power from one's neighbors.

Population figures help illustrate the growth of big states (see table on page 615). In 1500, about 36 percent of the global population lived in the six most populous states; by 1700, by which time the roster of the most populous states had changed, that proportion was 60 percent. Two main developments explain this trend: the Inka and Aztec Empires had disappeared from the list of most populous states, to be replaced by the Habsburg Empire and Japan, and the big states in Eurasia had gotten bigger.

WARFARE AND ITS PRICE: THE MILITARY REVOLUTION

Every state and society conducted war in its own way, shaped by its own culture, traditions, and constraints. Societies without horses—as in the pre-Columbian Americas, for example—fought on foot. Mongols and other steppe peoples fought on horseback. South Asians often used war elephants. Some states had navies, but most did not. The reasons for war also differed, and often went no deeper than a monarch's quest for glory. But states also fought in the name of religion—or at least their ruler's religion. Most wars were also fought for control over land or people, and the wealth and prestige that control might bring. Vikings and the kings of Kongo often fought to acquire slaves for sale. And, as we've seen, the Aztecs fought to acquire captives for sacrifice.

All these approaches to warfare had proven effective in their specific settings. Now, however, with the formation of the Global web, several new and useful technologies and techniques of fighting spread widely, replacing some of the local variations. War elephants and big armored horses, for example, gradually became obsolete.

In the years between 1450 and 1800, war grew more expensive and complex just about everywhere. Historians call this development the **military revolution**. It happened at different times, and at different paces, in different places. Many trends underpinned the military revolution. Here we will touch on six.

BIGGER BATTALIONS, HIGHER TAXES

In the seventeenth century, French soldiers had a saying: "God is on the side of the bigger battalions." The first reason warfare became so costly was the expansion of the scale of military operations, with larger armies and, in some cases, navies. In the sixteenth and seventeenth centuries, big empires spent 60 to 90 percent of their state budgets on their armed forces. (Today, the U.S. government spends about 15 to 20 percent of its budget on its military.) By 1700, several states around the world had learned how to organize, equip, and field armies of more than 100,000 men, and a few, mostly Atlantic European states of modest size, boasted battle fleets of dozens of large ships each studded with 40, 50, even 100 heavy cannon.

A second trend was the availability of greater funding for war. More revenue supported more expensive forms of warfare for kings, but costlier forms of warfare also required monarchs to find more funding. Usually, this entailed making taxation more efficient. It often also involved financial practices that made it easier for states to borrow money, either through the invention of national banks (beginning in 1694), the courting of private bankers, or the practice of tax farming—an arrangement in which an entrepreneur advanced money to a ruler in exchange for permission to extract taxes in the future.

The vast expansion of commerce around the world beginning in the sixteenth century (detailed in the next

Military Revolution A sixteenth-century Dutch etching, *The Battle of the Moneybags and the Strongboxes*, satirizes the centrality of money to warfare.

Oceanic Navies States that built oceangoing fleets in the early seventeenth century included Japan (left) and the Ottoman Empire (right), whose galleys suited the calmer waters of the Mediterranean and Red Seas.

chapter) enlarged the tax base for monarchs. It also made it feasible for kings and emperors to demand taxes in the form of money, rather than in rice, maize, or labor. The monetization of taxes enabled rulers to pay more professional soldiers and buy more equipment.

Despite these innovations and opportunities, most successful monarchs teetered on the edge of bankruptcy in wartime. They had to negotiate, often in a hurry, with rich people in hopes of getting cash to pay troops. This financial desperation proved a consistent check on monarchs' power, and it gave people with ready cash, such as big merchants and bankers, great leverage with which to pursue their own interests. In short, the rise of trade and finance—again, the Global web in action—made the military revolution affordable for a fortunate few monarchs, with the effect of often putting rulers at the mercy of bankers.

NAVIES AND ARTILLERY

A third trend of the military revolution that made war more complex and expensive was the emergence of oceanic navies. Local navies operating close to home had existed for more than 2,000 years, but oceanic navies were novel. As we saw in Chapter 15, Ming China built one beginning in 1405 but abandoned it after 1433. Over the next four centuries, China's navy stayed close to home, patrolling rivers, canals, and inshore waters, battling pirates such as the Zhengs but not sailing the open sea. Atlantic European states, however, began to build oceangoing navies and kept expanding and improving them.

Their main innovation, pioneered by the Portuguese, was to build ships big and sturdy enough to serve as gun platforms for heavy cannon. Building, maintaining, and operating such ships were expensive and took great expertise. The workhorse of the British Royal Navy in 1780, the 74-gun ship, cost 10 times as much to build as the largest factory in Britain. But such ships allowed monarchs to project power—through bombardments—anywhere on Earth within reach of the sea. This capacity more than anything else accounts for the rise to global power of five small Atlantic European states: Portugal, Spain, France, the Netherlands, and Britain.

Other Eurasian and North African states built navies too but usually with galleys and small craft, not oceangoing cannon platforms. An exception was Japan between about 1600 and 1635: it built a few hundred armed merchant vessels that each carried about six or eight cannon, used mainly in trading with Southeast Asia. But these ships were small, and in any case in 1635 Japan stopped making them. The Ming by 1637 had naval vessels with as many as 28 cannon, but tiny ones.

Most rulers preferred not to compete at sea and to focus their efforts on land. An English doctor wrote of Aurangzeb, the last of the powerful emperors of Mughal

War Junk This early seventeenth-century image shows a war junk of the Ming dynasty. Warship design in China did not keep pace with that of other parts of the world in the early modern centuries, mainly because China's military priorities lay primarily on its northern, landward, frontier.

India, in the 1670s, "If the King's Fleet be but ordinary, considering so great a Monarch . . . , it is because he minds it not; he [is] contenting himself in the enjoyment of the *continent* [India], and styles the Christians Lions of the Sea; saying that God has allotted that Unstable Element for their Rule." Heavy cannon mounted on sturdy ships enabled "Christians"—more precisely, Atlantic Europeans—to become the lions of the sea.

A fourth trend was the development of **field artillery and fortification**. Beginning in the early fifteenth century, armies lugged cannon into battle. By the 1490s, they used cannon so large that teams of horses or oxen, or a couple of elephants, might be needed to haul them around. By 1650, smaller, nimbler, but more numerous field artillery pieces had proved more effective. To counter the power of such weapons, military architects built new kinds of fortresses with thick walls—those at the fortress of Kumbhalgarh in northwest India, built in the fifteenth century, were 15 feet (4.5 m) thick. The new fortresses had to be big, bristling with artillery, and designed according to geometric principles. It often took 20 years to construct one. In Italy, both Michelangelo and Leonardo da Vinci used their architectural skills designing fortresses before succeeding as artists. The new fortresses also needed garrisons, supplies, and plenty of cannon of their own, all of which made them extremely costly. But the cost of not building them, if one's neighbors had capable field artillery, was surrender.

Ottoman Drill A painting shows Ottoman troops from the era of the sixteenth-century sultan Suleiman in battle. It took years of drilling to achieve coordination among the ranks of artillery, infantry, and cavalry attacking in formation.

STANDING ARMIES

A fifth trend came later, in the 1590s: the formation of disciplined and drilled standing armies. Most monarchs before 1590 recruited men for fighting only when they needed them. They paid military entrepreneurs to raise armies of mercenaries. When there was no war brewing, monarchs didn't want to pay for an army. From the 1590s onward, this system began to give way to one of standing, professional armies that rulers had to pay in times of both war and peace.

The main reason for this change was the effectiveness of drilled and disciplined infantry armed with reasonably accurate muskets—long, smoothbore guns developed in the sixteenth century. Dutch and Ottoman war captains pioneered drill, apparently independently of one another. They found, as had Japanese and others, that musket fire was devastatingly effective in volleys. They arranged

musketeers in parallel lines (ranks) and taught them to fire, reload, and fire on command. While one rank fired, another was busy reloading. To do this quickly, without injuring one's fellows, and while one's closest comrades were being wounded and killed, required iron discipline. To achieve it, Dutch captains obliged their troops to drill endlessly on parade grounds until their choreographed motions were second nature. Close-order drill took years to master, so men had to be housed, fed, and clothed in peacetime at government expense. If unpaid, these men could turn their violent skills against civilians or kings.

A sixth trend underlying the military revolution was the development of a more sophisticated logistical apparatus. With bigger armies and navies, someone had to come up with more horses, oxen, mules, camels, elephants, and their food; and more iron, steel, bronze, tin, wood, leather, and saltpeter (used in gunpowder) to be made into weapons and other war materiel. More men had to be transported to the right places at the right times, and in the right proportions of infantry to cavalry to artillerymen, not to mention cooks, gunsmiths, engineers, and muleteers, camel drivers, or elephant handlers. All these animals, supplies, and people had to get across rivers, over mountains, or through deserts on schedule. Creating, maintaining, and deploying a big military machine required a military bureaucracy, made up of literate and numerate people with desk skills usually despised by men-at-arms.

To summarize, the innovations that made up the military revolution consisted of a hardware package of ships, cannon, muskets, gunpowder, and fortification, and a software package of improved financial systems, military engineering, infantry drill, and logistical bureaucracy. Rulers adopted those innovations that they could afford and that addressed the specific threats they faced.

Let's look at a few examples of states that to one degree or another adopted the innovations of the military revolution to become more powerful. This approach focuses on the winners in military competition. Some of the many losers are mentioned along the way, but there were many more that aren't.

THE TOKUGAWA CONSOLIDATION OF POWER IN JAPAN

An archipelago of perhaps 12 to 18 million people in 1500, Japan was politically fragmented. Any semblance of unity had vanished by the late fifteenth century, and thereafter numerous warlords fought one another for territory, resources, influence, and glory. None could count on the allegiance of, or extract taxes from, more than a couple of million people. But within 140 years, Japan became a unified country. The process was bloody.

Locked in ruthless competition, Japan's warlords were open to innovations that might give them an edge. After 1500, their armies grew in size, and they turned increasingly to unskilled foot soldiers—ordinary peasants with no training or socialization in military culture. Warlords learned to integrate massed infantry into battle tactics. Sieges and elaborate fortification became the

rule. Samurai (an elite warrior class that took shape in the twelfth century) infantry and horsemen, formerly the cutting edge of Japanese warfare, now played smaller roles.

THE INTRODUCTION OF FIREARMS

In 1543, a Chinese pirate ship introduced Portuguese guns to Japan's vortex of violence. Guns required little training or skill to use, and so were well suited to the ordinary infantryman. Soon there were hundreds of thousands of firearms in Japan, and every warlord had to have plenty of them and figure out how to integrate them into his tactics.

In order to obtain guns, many warlords sold slaves. For centuries, Chinese, Japanese, and Korean pirates had been enslaving and selling coastal villagers. Now, Japanese warlords turned to slave exports, especially of young women, to Portuguese merchants, who in turn sold them in China or in Portuguese trading posts such as Macao (in China) or Goa (in India). The Portuguese slave trade from Japan probably involved a few hundred people annually until the trade was outlawed soon after 1600. Many more slaves remained in Japan. As in West Africa and New Zealand (discussed in earlier chapters), in Japan more guns meant more enslavement.

NOBUNAGA AND HIDEYOSHI

The most successful warlord at exploiting the political potential of guns was **Oda Nobunaga**, whose battlefield successes unified the southern half of Japan by 1580. He arranged his gunmen in tight formations to maximize their firepower, and perhaps—accounts are unclear on this—invented the tactic of volley fire. Nobunaga and his successors unified Japan by mobilizing hundreds of thousands of peasants and giving them guns manufactured by Japanese smiths. For a few decades, Japan made more guns than any other country in the world. A great change was taking place in Japan, a country where formerly only exquisitely trained warriors—samurai—could win battles. This change in the social foundation of war loosely resembled the transition in the ancient world from aristocratic warriors armed with bronze armor and weapons to mass armies using iron.

Oda Nobunaga's career exemplifies a pattern that would become increasingly common after 1500. As the Global web connected distant regions, ambitious rulers time and again borrowed useful techniques and technologies from

Japan Invades Korea This painting shows an assault on a defensive position held by Hideyoshi's army in Korea in the 1590s. When Ming forces entered the war in Korea, Hideyoshi had to retreat to Japan.

afar. They mastered them, modified them as needed, integrated them into local culture, and used them to smash or enslave rivals and neighbors, and to build empires. The pattern was not new: the adoption of horses or iron in earlier times sometimes had had similar effects. From the sixteenth century onward, the adoption of guns produced this result in many cases around the world, including, as we saw, with King Kamehameha in Hawaii.

Upon Nobunaga's death in 1582, **Toyotomi Hideyoshi**, a former foot soldier and servant who had risen up the ranks through extraordinary success in war and diplomacy, took power. In 1592, he decided to invade Korea and then China with 160,000 soldiers, a quarter of them gunmen. At first, Japanese armies succeeded in Korea, where guns remained rare. Hideyoshi, who had tried to restrict the export of Japanese slaves in 1587, now eagerly enslaved and sold thousands of Koreans to Japanese and Portuguese buyers. In the end, Ming China sent an army to Korea, and it became clear that Japan's sea power was not up to the task of supplying an overseas army against a large force. In 1598, Hideyoshi's Korea campaign ended in retreat. This war was the largest anywhere in the sixteenth-century world.

At the same time that his soldiers ravaged Korea, Hideyoshi was defeating rival warlords in Japan. By his death in 1598, he had just about unified the country. That task was completed by his successor, a samurai, Tokugawa Ieyasu, who crushed rival forces loyal to Hideyoshi's young son. Only the sparsely populated northern island, Hokkaido, remained outside his realm.

ESTABLISHING THE TOKUGAWA SHOGUNATE

By 1600, Tokugawa Ieyasu stood supreme over a unified Japan. In 1603, he acquired the title of shogun (roughly: top general), which meant he was the de facto ruler of Japan. His descendants continued in that role until 1868 in a dynasty called the **Tokugawa shogunate**. With the country unified after 1600 and peace imposed (except on Hokkaido), Japan ceased to be a center of military innovation. Hideyoshi, despite his common origins, had begun the process of restoring samurai to their former status by banning peasants from owning weapons in 1588. Under the Tokugawa, that became entrenched policy, and only samurai could own and use weapons. The shoguns with their new military policy after 1600 reversed the social, democratizing—but bloody—revolution that helped bring them to power.

The process of consolidation continued into southernmost Hokkaido. There an indigenous population called

The Unification of Tokugawa Japan, 1580–1603 The Japanese archipelago was politically fragmented for most of its history. But in the late sixteenth century, local warlords found ways to use guns effectively, destroy rivals, and create—by 1600—a politically unified Japan in the heavily populated islands of Honshu and Kyushu. The northernmost island, Hokkaido, became part of Japan only later.

Tokugawa Shogunate A painting on silk from the seventeenth century illustrates the importance of the samurai to the Tokugawa shoguns' rule. It shows the shogun at court, surrounded by samurai from the 16 most noble families.

the Ainu, who had only rudimentary technology by Japanese standards, resisted Tokugawa control until about 1700. War and newly introduced diseases reduced their numbers to about 25,000 by 1800, and eventually ethnic Japanese from the southern islands colonized Hokkaido, swamping the Ainu demographically.

The Tokugawa shoguns consolidated their power before 1600 by using new technologies and techniques of war. After 1600, they kept the peace, and kept themselves in power for 250 years by using time-honored tactics including threats of force and keeping regional elites either content or cowed. They encouraged a neo-Confucian ideology that emphasized the authority of men within families and deference to powerful men. Successful monarchs elsewhere did similar things.

THE QING CONSOLIDATION IN CHINA

China's Ming dynasty (1368–1644) ruled over a quarter of the world's population, perhaps 175 million people. As we have seen in earlier chapters, it launched great oceanic voyages under the command of Zheng He and presided over a buzzing hive of intellectual activity, including the neo-Confucian revival associated with Wang Yangming. The Ming also found ways to profit from expanded international trade opportunities (see Chapter 19) brought by European sailing ships. Sales of silk and porcelain for silver from Japan and Mexico fueled an economic expansion that extended from 1520 to 1580. Ming armies could

coordinate movements of 200,000 men and, as they showed when battling Hideyoshi in 1592, could transport 400 artillery pieces over 300 miles of rough terrain. In general, despite droughts, rebellions, and frontier struggles with pastoral peoples to the north, the Ming governed well enough to remain in power for 200 years.

THE FALL OF THE MING

But by 1600, their troubles were mounting. The Ming's campaign against Hideyoshi in Korea in the 1590s depleted the treasury. Adverse climate change—the long spells of drought and cold of the Little Ice Age, especially after 1614—brought more famines and cut state revenues. At the same time, the overseas supplies of silver dried up when mining output in Spanish America and Japan fell, starving Chinese commerce of its medium of exchange and making it harder for anyone to pay their taxes—which by law had to be paid in silver. In the palace, rivalry flared between the eunuchs and the gentry. By the 1630s, China was fracturing, and civil war loomed.

Then things went from bad to worse for the Ming: an enterprising steppe leader from Manchuria, Nurhaci, and his son, Hong Taiji, united many of the tribes of the eastern steppe, forged a new ethnic identity (called Manchu), built an efficient army in ways that recalled Genghis Khan, conquered Korea (1638), and threatened China. When one Chinese faction invited the Manchus to help, they helped themselves, occupying Beijing and refusing to leave. The last Ming emperor hanged himself from a garden tree in 1644, a sorry end for one of China's great dynasties.

THE QING CONQUEST

The Manchu elite renamed themselves the Qing, ruling China as the **Qing dynasty** until 1911. But first they had to consolidate their power, eliminating pockets of Ming loyalists in battle. Then they had to win over elite Chinese, the literati, without whom routine administration and tax collection was next to impossible. The literati, who admired elegant handwriting more than good horsemanship, normally considered the Qing repugnant foreign barbarians with undistinguished ancestry and strange customs. Male Qing shaved the front part of the top of their heads and wore a long braid, a style they made a legal

The Qing Empire, ca. 1600–1800 From their homeland in eastern Manchuria, the Manchu expanded militarily in the steppe and woodlands of northeastern Asia. They intervened in a power struggle in China's declining Ming Empire, and between 1644 and 1683 they took over most of the Ming territory. As rulers of China, they took the name Qing and for over a century proved militarily effective, expanding their empire westward.

requirement for all Han Chinese men. It took most literati families several generations to overcome their resentment of Qing rule.

The Qing faced two main military challenges during their first century in power. One was the naval power of the pirate king and Ming loyalist Zheng Chenggong and his clan, with whom this chapter began. The Qing finished them off by 1683. The other was the perennial problem of Chinese dynasties: confederations of steppe nomads to the north. In the late seventeenth and early eighteenth centuries, a subset of the Mongols, the Zunghars, forged large confederacies, threatening the security of northern China. At the same time, Tibetans to the southwest showed signs of hostility to the Qing and supported their fellow Buddhists in Mongolia.

The Qing's answer to the challenge from the steppe came in the form of army campaigns to the north and west, which, combined with devastating smallpox epidemics, decisively broke Mongol power in the 1750s. Soon thereafter, they added more territory, including the desert and oasis lands in the far northwest now known as Xinjiang, and the high plateau of Tibet. The Qing campaigns doubled the territorial size of their empire and secured their frontiers. They also made their empire more multicultural, multilingual, and multiethnic than the Ming or most previous Chinese empires. By 1800, it counted some 350 million people, roughly a third of the global population.

The Qing also fought expansionist campaigns in the south, against Burma and Vietnam, but with no success.

Kangxi as Sage A 1699 portrait of the Kangxi Emperor emphasizes his classical learning. It was important to the Qing, a foreign dynasty, to gain the support of Chinese intellectual and bureaucratic elites.

Mountain terrain and rain forest hamstrung the Qing cavalry. Malaria killed many thousands of Qing soldiers. Combined with stern resistance, these factors—after multiple failed campaigns—persuaded the Qing that southern expansion was not worth the cost.

The Qing were led by two long-lived, vigorous, conscientious, clever, and ruthless emperors, conventionally reckoned among the greatest in Chinese history. The Kangxi Emperor, who reigned for some sixty years (r. 1662–1722), was the first Qing emperor born and raised on Chinese soil rather than in Manchuria. His grandson, the Qianlong Emperor, reigned from 1735 to 1796, abdicating at age 85 to not outdo his grandfather. Of the 265 years of Qing dynastic rule, about 125 took place under these two men. They were both cultivated, multilingual, highly literate political wizards—and mercilessly brutal when it suited them. The Kangxi Emperor, for example, welcomed foreign Jesuits to his court, but he also obliged the people of Fujian Province to evacuate the entire coastal district in his effort to undermine the Zheng family. The Qianlong Emperor spoke six languages, took a deep interest in Tibetan Buddhism, and hired Italian and French Jesuits to build palaces—but also ordered the extermination of Zunghar Mongols as a people in 1755.

STATECRAFT AND MILITARY INNOVATION

The Qing consolidation of power and expansion of empire owed something to the Eurasian military revolution, but much less than the Tokugawa did. The Ming had already used guns and adapted them into their military system— gunpowder was a Chinese invention, after all. As early as 1400, about 10 percent of Ming soldiers used firearms.

By the time of the war against Japan in Korea (1590s), the Ming had a formidable field-artillery force.

Yet guns and artillery mattered much less in China than in Japan. Siege artillery did not work well in China, because cities typically had earthen walls thick enough to stop cannonballs. Neither guns nor artillery were much use against China's main enemies, the Mongols, whose ponies enabled them to scamper out of range quickly. So although firearms were invented in China and used by both the Ming and the Qing, the Chinese did not always bother to keep pace with other states in firearm quality. In 1644, when the Qing took power, the best muskets, according to the Chinese, were Ottoman, and the best cannon were Portuguese. Like the Ming before them, the Qing studied cannon making with Jesuit teachers skilled in European casting techniques. But they did not rely on firearms to the extent that other early modern empires did.

The Qing's military secret sauce, more than new technology, was new technique. Even before they came to power, Nurhaci and Hong Taiji had organized their steppe warriors into units, called banners, that cut across kin lines and strengthened centralized command—just as Genghis Khan had done with Mongol tribes 400 years before. In their campaigns in China, the Qing effectively integrated cavalry, their own strong suit, with infantry, artillery, and siege skills. They learned, from the Ming, to conduct naval warfare along the rivers and coasts. And when

Qing Military Strategy A large eighteenth-century scroll painting illustrates a scene from the imperial hunt, a ritualized court event. Here athletes train in a circle at the center of the camp, as the emperor and numerous spectators look on. Such activities allowed the Qing army to practice logistical precision and preparedness.

Qing Rule This portrait of the emperor Qianlong (r. 1735–1796) emphasizes the Manchu military tradition—horse, bow, and arrows—more than the technologies important in his day.

they chose to attack the Zunghar Mongols in the eighteenth century, they combined canny diplomacy that divided their enemy together with brilliant logistics that enabled them to campaign out on the steppe grasslands without running out of food and water.

The Qing emphasized military virtues in their efforts to influence Chinese culture. They boosted military spending and highlighted military achievements in art and architecture to a degree unusual in China, where cultured people tended to regard military men as uncouth. The Qianlong Emperor in his first year on the throne (1736) stressed the importance of military preparedness even in peacetime.

Keeping the military paid was a high priority for the Qing. They knew their own rise to power rested in part on disaffected Ming army units rising in rebellion. So they boosted the military's budget, even while lowering taxes overall. They improved the efficiency of tax collection. They also encouraged "voluntary" contributions of silver from big merchants, who knew better than to refuse. And they encouraged the military to go into business for itself to bolster its finances.

All these initiatives, more than new technologies, helped the Qing consolidate their power and expand their empire. They did not disdain foreign military technology. But their most effective statecraft and military innovations came locally, from within China and the Qing homeland of the eastern steppe, and not from contact with the wider world. This was unique among the great powers in the early modern centuries.

THE MUGHAL EMPIRE IN INDIA

The Mughal Empire took shape in the early sixteenth century in northern India. Its founders, Muslims from Central Asia, identified with the Turkic and Mongol (hence *Mughal*) warriors of the steppe. After taking a beating

from an Uzbek emir in Central Asian warfare, they invaded northern India and, after four failed attempts, conquered the much-decayed Delhi sultanate in 1526. A forceful emperor, Abu'l-Fath Jalal ud-din Muhammad Akbar (usually just called **Akbar**, which in Arabic means "the great one"), stabilized the Mughal state and launched it on a path to expansion. He took power as a teenager in 1556 and reigned to his death in 1605, almost as long as Kangxi or Qianlong. Soon the Mughal Empire controlled, although loosely, most of South Asia—like the Mauryans (fourth to second century BCE) and the Gupta (fourth to sixth century CE) before them.

No state in a thousand years had been able to unify as much of South Asia as the Mughals. Akbar ruled over perhaps 60 million people. A century of geographical expansion later, his great-grandson, Aurangzeb, ruled about 120 million, about 20 percent of the world's total. At its height, the Mughal Empire was the second most populous state in the world, trailing only China, and controlled all but southernmost India.

MUGHAL MIGHT

Mughal success rested in part on military innovations. Like the Qing, they found effective combinations of old

Mughal Conquests The Mughal emperor Akbar owed his military success in part to the combination of old and new technologies: on the one hand, war elephants and horses, seen here (left) crossing the Ganges in a 1600 manuscript; on the other, advanced siege artillery, shown here (right) being used to attack a hill fort in central India in 1568.

and new. Warfare in India for five centuries before the Mughals had hinged on foot soldiers, mounted archers, war elephants, and sieges. Indians also used bamboo rockets fired from iron tubes. Guns first arrived, via Central Asia and Iran, in about 1450 but were not yet effective enough to catch on widely—although some armies in parts of Central India used large cannon by 1520. Then, in the 1520s, the Mughals introduced larger quantities of guns and cannon in their north India campaigns and figured out how to combine these new weapons with cavalry archers. Akbar recruited skilled gunsmiths from the Ottoman Empire and Europe to improve the quality of his weaponry, and soon Mughal firearms experts were making excellent muskets and cannon. To maintain a military edge, the Mughals also had to ensure access to horse-producing regions in Central Asia—and deny it to enemies. Lacking enough good grassland, India itself could not raise enough horses. The Mughals imported up to 16,000 annually from Afghanistan, giving them the effective cavalry that their Indian rivals lacked. By 1560, in the early years of Akbar's reign, the Mughals had honed the combination of cavalry, infantry, and artillery—and added to that a mastery of both siegecraft and fortification. After 1580, firearms spread widely in India, including among enemies of the Mughals. But by this time, Akbar had a growing empire and more money than any rivals, money with which he could hire more warriors, elephant handlers, and gunsmiths than anyone else. Superior numbers of men, horses, and elephants—as well as technology and tactical skill—contributed to Mughal military success.

The Mughals also learned to use the navigable rivers, especially the Ganges and Indus, to move their military machinery around. In the watery landscapes of Bengal, which in the monsoon season could become a maze of swampy creeks and ponds, they conducted warfare from boats. On rivers and inshore seas, they used gunboats in support of the army. They never built a navy capable of projecting power on the high seas—recall Aurangzeb's willingness to concede the oceans to the "lions of the sea." At all times, the Mughal navy was subordinate to their army.

The careful integration of infantry with firearms together with cavalry, field artillery, siegecraft, and armed riverboats made the Mughals more formidable at war than any South Asian rival. In Akbar's time, and throughout the seventeenth century, the Mughals generally bested those who resisted them. They met staunch resistance from some Indian rulers, however, such as those of the sultanate of Ahmadnagar in west-central India. In the late 1590s, its armies were led by a female regent, Chand Bibi, who beat back Mughal attacks on her capital for four years. Despite the Mughal conquest of Ahmadnagar city, resistance continued under the leadership of an Ethiopian slave, Malik Ambar. Born in Africa, sold by his impoverished parents to Arabs, and shipped to Iraq, Arabia, and finally India, Malik Ambar became a slave soldier and through skill and guile rose to be the leading minister of Ahmadnagar by 1607. He masterminded guerilla resistance to Mughal expansion for two decades before his successors succumbed to the superior power of the Mughals. Just about everyone else in South Asia also bowed before Mughal power sooner or later.

Malik Ambar An anonymous artist made this portrait of the Ethiopian slave-turned-military-leader near the end of his life, in about 1620.

MUGHAL CONSOLIDATION

The Mughals needed all the raw power they could amass, because as Muslim invaders in an overwhelmingly Hindu land, they faced a legitimacy problem. Akbar addressed this not only with military force, but with a tolerant religious policy as well. Although illiterate himself, Akbar supported scholars and libraries. Like some Mongol khans and the Kangxi Emperor in China, he seems to have been genuinely curious about and—usually—tolerant of multiple religions. He enjoyed discussions with Sufis, Jesuits, Jains, and Buddhists. When the Mughals had first arrived in South Asia in the 1520s, they allowed only Muslims to serve in their military. Then Akbar recruited Hindus too and relaxed other forms of religious discrimination. He suspended the normal Islamic policy of taxing non-Muslims at higher rates, allowed Hindu landowners to hold high office, welcomed Hindus at his court, celebrated Hindu holidays such as Diwali, and married a Hindu woman, Mariam-uz-Zamani (one of his 14 wives). The Mughal religious policy, with a few adjustments in

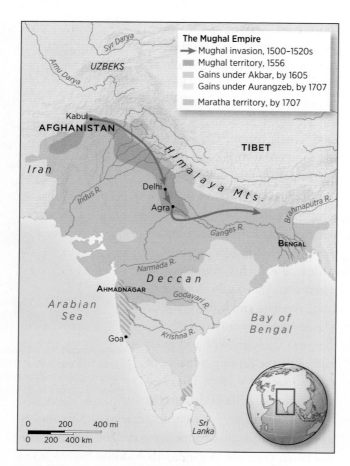

The Mughal Empire, ca. 1500–1707 The Mughal dynasty, originally from Central Asia, became one of the great powers of the early modern world. Once they dominated the fertile Ganges basin, they had the resources to bring most of South Asia under their control. By 1600, their territorial success rivaled that of the Gupta dynasty a thousand years earlier. But by 1700, other polities, such as the Maratha states, were adapting to the Mughals' technologies and techniques, and their empire was in retreat.

favor of Islamic orthodoxy, remained in effect until the time of Aurangzeb (r. 1658–1707).

Like every early modern state, the Mughals needed huge sums to pay for their military. Like every successful early modern state, the Mughals made tax collection more efficient. They also raised money by negotiation with, and occasional intimidation of, local elites, typically landowners who took a share of what the toiling peasantry produced. Under Akbar, they centralized taxation and also encouraged foreign trade, benefiting from customs duties. As they conquered new territories, they used the plunder to win their subjects' loyalty. They could dole out conquered lands to reliable followers, who gave a share of their income to the Mughals.

As long as new conquests kept coming, this system

worked admirably—as a similar one had worked for the Roman Republic and Empire long before. The early Mughals rarely lacked for money, and this underwrote their military and political success. Shah Jahan, who ruled from 1627 to 1658, was able to field an army of a million men and pay for a glorious mausoleum, the Taj Mahal, built to honor his favorite wife, Mumtaz Mahal, who died while giving birth to her fourteenth child in 1631. When Emperor Aurangzeb (the sixth of Mumtaz Mahal's children) went on campaign in Afghanistan in the 1670s, he brought 300 camels carrying gold and silver to cover his expenses.

MUGHAL DECLINE

In Aurangzeb's later years, the Mughal Empire weakened. Having imprisoned his father and defeated his brothers on the battlefield, he took the throne at age 29. Aurangzeb sought legitimacy by burnishing his credentials as a Muslim ruler. By all accounts, he was pious and knew the Qur'an by heart. His religious devotion—and misguided political calculation—led him to adopt a policy that emphasized Sunni orthodoxy and instituted Islamic law (shari'a) throughout his empire. He forbade construction of new Hindu temples, permitted destruction of some existing ones, and imposed higher taxes on non-Muslims. This departure from Mughal tradition alienated Hindus, Sikhs, Jains, Shi'a Muslims—as well as everyone who enjoyed music, dancing, drinking, or gambling.

As a result, the Mughal state faced more frequent rebellions and tax revolts. Eventually, it could not control its southern frontiers. In a region called the Deccan, Hindu warriors known as Marathas gradually rolled back Mughal control. Starting in the 1660s, a successful guerilla captain, Shivaji Bhonsle, built up a Maratha state, including a navy. His state building was a rough equivalent to that of the Zheng family on the southeast coasts of China. But whereas the Qing ultimately vanquished the upstart Zhengs, the Mughals could not overcome the Marathas, despite the efforts of Aurangzeb, who personally campaigned against them for 25 years. Aurangzeb's absence from the empire's heartlands in north India led elites there to experiment with keeping bigger chunks of revenue for themselves, and central control, never very strong, weakened.

After Aurangzeb's death in 1707, with the empire

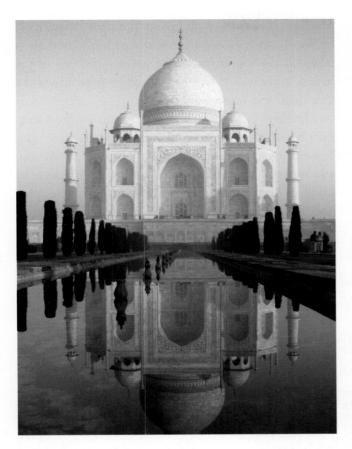

Taj Mahal The huge scale and opulence of the monument Shah Jahan built for his favorite wife indicates what a large treasury he and other Mughal rulers amassed through conquest and taxation.

under less able successors, the Mughal retreat gathered pace. Princes and warlords broke free and carved out their own states. In 1739, Nader Shah, a former slave from northeastern Iran who had just overthrown the Safavid dynasty and made himself shah of Iran, sacked Delhi. He massacred tens of thousands, looted the city, and carried off the Mughals' peacock throne. By 1770, the Marathas controlled half of India. India became more politically fragmented, and the Mughals held only small parts of the country until their final collapse in 1857.

Like the Qing in China, the Mughals were originally foreign invaders who built a formidable multiethnic and multireligious empire within 40 years. Also like the Qing, they focused their efforts on their landward frontiers, leaving the sea to others, and took advantage of innovations in the military sphere to expand their territory. But unlike the Qing—more like the warlord Oda Nobunaga in Japan—their innovations included major elements adopted from abroad, notably firearms. They integrated artillery and muskets into their existing military traditions while monopolizing the import of horses, helping them to dominate South Asia for two centuries and to survive for three.

THE OTTOMAN EMPIRE

While the Mughals lasted some 300 years, the Ottomans, another Turkic and Muslim dynasty that traced its origins to Central Asia, lasted over 600. Their success rested on factors important to the Mughals as well: canny integration of new weaponry into existing military culture, liberal religious policy, and healthy finances.

The Ottomans began as a community of Turkish-speaking mobile pastoralists, followers of a tribal chieftain named Osman. In the fourteenth century, they began to enjoy military success in northwest Anatolia against Byzantine Greeks in the fourteenth century. They may have benefited politically from the bubonic plague pandemic of 1346–1351, which probably killed urban and agrarian populations faster than it did pastoralists. In any case, the Ottomans gradually expanded their domain in Anatolia and the Balkans at the expense of the Byzantine Empire and several smaller polities. By 1453, under a 21-year-old sultan known as Mehmet the Conqueror, they successfully besieged Constantinople, the best-fortified city in all Europe. That brought the Byzantine Empire to its knees, and within eight years its last remnants disappeared.

The Ottomans made Constantinople, also called **Istanbul**, their capital and exploited its geographic location astride the straits connecting the Black and Mediterranean Seas. They now controlled one of the world's most lucrative trade routes. Their conquests continued after 1453, notably in the Balkans and along the Black Sea coasts.

OTTOMAN EXPANSION

Then, between 1514 and 1526, Ottoman good fortune multiplied. Battlefield victories stabilized their eastern frontier with the Safavids of Iran, the Shi'a dynasty with whom the Sunni Ottomans competed for power and prestige. With that frontier secured, in 1517 they conquered Egypt and the Hejaz, the strip of Arabia where Mecca and Medina lie. This was a double windfall for the Ottomans.

Egypt yielded reliable surpluses of grain and revenue. The Ottomans used Egypt, as Achaemenids, Romans, Byzantines, and others had before them, as a means to feed their armies and cities, and to help finance wars and administration. By some calculations, conquering Egypt doubled the revenues of the Ottoman state. On top of that, when drought afflicted the eastern Mediterranean region and crops failed, those of Egypt did not—because the Nile flows from the mountains of Ethiopia, where rain is more reliable and determined by different weather systems. So Egypt not only provided grain and revenue, it also provided insurance against the droughts common in the other lands of the Ottoman Empire.

Taking over the holy places, Mecca and Medina, might have doubled the prestige of the Ottomans. Soon Ottoman sultans (as their leaders were called) took the title of caliph, proclaiming themselves the successors of the Prophet Muhammad and the spiritual leaders of all

Muslims. Not all Muslims agreed. But nonetheless, most Sunni Muslims—always a majority within Islamdom—regarded the Ottoman caliphs as the guardians of the Islamic community. This newly won prestige helped the Ottomans rule more easily.

Moreover, a long spell of good rains in the Ottoman heartland of Anatolia, around the years 1520–1590, boosted livestock herds, grain harvests, the population, and imperial revenues. Whereas both the Qing and the Mughals had to import horses, the Ottoman lands produced all the horses, grain, timber, and important mineral ores that the empire's population and military might need.

These circumstances contributed to the notable success of the empire's longest-reigning sultan, Suleiman (r. 1520–1566), who consolidated Ottoman control over vast territories and added several more—most importantly, Iran and Hungary. Both yielded grain surpluses in most years, and Hungary also provided great herds of

The Expansion of the Ottoman Empire, ca. 1320s–1683 From their beginnings in northwest Anatolia early in the fourteenth century, the followers of Osman—the Ottomans—expanded their domain for three centuries into southeastern Europe, Southwest Asia, and North Africa. Under sultans such as Mehmet and Suleiman, the Ottomans wielded the techniques and technologies of power effectively, becoming one of the great powers of Eurasia.

Ottoman Conquest A sixteenth-century account of the sultan Suleiman's military victories shows his ranks of cannon and infantry besieging a Christian fortress. Through such military precision, the Ottomans swiftly expanded their empire.

horses and cattle. Controlling Hungary meant the Ottomans could use the Danube River as a transport artery to tighten their hold on southeastern Europe. Controlling the Tigris and Euphrates Rivers enabled them to move troops and supplies easily along their eastern frontier with Safavid Iran.

The Ottoman Empire reached its territorial peak in the late sixteenth and seventeenth centuries. Stretching from Iraq to Algeria and from Yemen to Hungary, it contained nearly 30 million people, about 7 percent of humankind.

OTTOMAN CONSOLIDATION

Like that of the Mughals, Ottoman political success rested on military, financial, and religious power. Like the Qing and the Mughals, the Ottomans integrated firearms into their military culture. They used guns as early as the 1390s and artillery by the 1420s. They quickly mastered the fine points of siege warfare and fortification, demonstrated in the capture and rebuilding of Istanbul

in 1453. They recruited an elite infantry force, called the **janissaries**, from Christian communities of the western Balkans. The janissaries were taken from their homes as boys, trained in the arts of war and administration, and deployed, nominally as slaves of the sultans, in the army or bureaucracy. Although slaves, many of them rose to powerful positions. As gun-wielding infantry (by 1560 more than half of the janissaries carried firearms), they played a key role in many battlefield triumphs, such as the defeat of the Safavid army, which did not yet use guns, in 1514. Most states equipped their least skilled soldiers with guns, because they did not take much practice to use. The Ottomans did the reverse, arming their elite soldiers with muskets. By the 1560s, the janissaries had developed the technique of volley fire with muskets, like Hideyoshi's troops. To equip their forces, the Ottomans built up military industries and produced high-quality artillery and small arms. They blended all their military innovations with cavalry, their traditional strength.

The Ottoman military machine grew bigger as well as more efficient. During the reign of Suleiman, the artillery corps tripled in size. Until the 1690s, the Ottomans could usually put more men, horses, and weapons in the field than any of their enemies. They also built a big navy of galleys propelled by oarsmen, suited to the conditions of the Mediterranean and Black Seas but also active in the Indian Ocean, at times as far afield as Mombasa and Malacca. As everywhere, fielding such an expanded and well-equipped military was extremely expensive.

THE TAX SYSTEM

Like every other empire, the Ottomans sought to tighten up their tax system. Mehmet the Conqueror (r. 1451–1481) attempted to centralize taxation and bureaucracy, and to take a bigger chunk of the revenues of provincial elites. He even tried to impose fixed prices on items bought and sold in the markets, which proved hard to enforce. The local elites, often quite different from one province to another, proved resilient. With the scale and cost of warfare expanding so quickly during the sixteenth century, Mehmet and his successors had to strike bargains with them.

The fiscal windfall of expansion, especially the conquest of Egypt, helped. But the state also turned increasingly to tax farming—selling to private entrepreneurs the right to collect taxes from Ottoman subjects. And the

CONSIDERING THE EVIDENCE

An Ottoman Register in Ukraine

In addition to training janissaries to run its war machine, the Ottoman Empire hired thousands of scribes and tax farmers to keep money flowing. Census takers (*muharrir*) determined tax levels by interviewing farmers, traders, herders, bakers, ferrymen, and even alcohol distillers to estimate what they produced in a normal year. Then they wrote everything in duplicate registers: one for the imperial archive in Istanbul and one for local officials to reference. The excerpt below is from a register for the Ukrainian province of Kamaniçe near the Black Sea, which the Ottoman Empire seized from the Polish-Lithuanian Commonwealth in 1672. The imperial government wanted to protect its productive settlements on the nearby Black Sea.

The introduction to the register begins with two lists. The first list describes collections from tax farmers reserved for the Ottoman sultan: poll taxes from Christian and Jewish immigrants, fees from a boat toll, and prepaid taxes on fishponds. The second list, shown below, summarizes the collections from tax farmers that the *beylerbeyi*—the governor—would retain. Although additional taxes pushed annual revenue to over 5 million silver coins (*akçe*), this amount was not nearly enough to pay the 6,000 soldiers garrisoned in the border province. So, each year, the empire subsidized military salaries with nearly 13 million *akçe* from the central treasury in Istanbul until it abandoned Kamaniçe in 1699.

The domains of the *beylerbeyi* [governor] of the province of Kamaniçe

[Tax collections] from market dues on horses, mules, oxen, sheep, goats, and others in Kamaniçe... Žvanec', and... Mohyliv: yearly 54,000 [silver coins]

[and] from weighing and measuring fees in Kamaniçe, except for the rent of the buildings [where the weighing and measuring was done]: yearly 42,000

[and] income from coffee-roasting in Kamaniçe: yearly 19,000

[and] from market tolls, coffee-houses, candle works, slaughterhouses, sheep [herders], eating houses, cook-shops with dye-houses and others in Kamaniçe and from the fair-brokers' fees in Žvanec': yearly 52,200

[and] from the head-broker's fee in the "black" market... [and the] head-broker's fee in the horse and cattle [market] in Kamaniçe...: yearly [scribe did not record amount]

[and] from the fees of the [drivers] of oxen, sheep, goats and with the pasturage and passage fee [collected] from the [drivers] in Žvanec': yearly 25,300

[and] from the [unclaimed] property devolved upon the imperial treasury, left by ordinary subjects and state servants except for *janissaries,*... and from the property of missing and absent persons, stray and run-away [slaves, arrested and sold in auction] in [Kamaniçe] with the fee from the [wineries] and distillery kettles and with the cask fee in Žvanec' and... Mohyliv: yearly 50,000

Source: Dariusz Kołodziejczyk, trans., "Appendix 1: Translation of the Beginning of the *Defter*," in *The Ottoman Survey Register of Podolia (ca. 1681), Defter-i Mufassal-i Eyalet-i Kamaniçe* (Cambridge, MA, 2004).

QUESTIONS FOR ANALYSIS

1. What products and activities did the Ottoman Empire tax?
2. Besides adding a new revenue stream, what could have motivated the Ottoman Empire to tax coffee and alcohol production?
3. Why would the Ottoman Empire conquer territory that provided less revenue than it cost to maintain?

Ottomans in the sixteenth century encouraged the monetization and commercialization of the economy, which enabled them to collect more revenue in cash rather than in produce—always preferable for governments. After territorial expansion and plunder stopped, the sultans had to become more efficient to keep solvent.

THE MILLET SYSTEM Ottoman religious policy helped reduce the costs of ruling. From the beginning, the sultans happily recruited Christians into their military and bureaucracy. They valued loyalty wherever they found it. They welcomed tens of thousands of Jewish refugees from Spain, expelled in 1492 by Ferdinand and

Isabella. Mehmet the Conqueror was genuinely curious, like Akbar, about religions other than Islam and at times tried to present himself as a worthy successor to Byzantine (Christian) emperors. Although they taxed non-Muslims at higher rates, the Ottomans by and large left Christian and Jewish communities to adjudicate their own affairs until the nineteenth century. Sometimes called the **millet system**, this tolerant religious policy, like Akbar's, made the empire a bit easier to govern.

With these measures, the Ottomans managed to stay afloat, to field and finance a military equal to foreign challenges and internal rebellions through the end of the seventeenth century. After a defeat by the combined forces of the Habsburg Empire and Poland-Lithuania in 1683, their position relative to their neighbors and rivals weakened, and after the 1770s the tide was running against them. They could not keep up with their neighbors, especially Russia and the Habsburgs, and their neighbors more often formed coalitions against them. The empire shrank after every lost war. But the Ottomans, like the Qing, lasted into the early twentieth century. So did the Russian Empire.

IMPERIAL CONSOLIDATION IN RUSSIA

Russia is another case of **imperial consolidation** and territorial expansion at the expense of weaker neighbors. In earlier chapters, we saw how the Muscovite princes served as clients of Mongol khans for a while, and how, in the sixteenth century, the Russian state sponsored expansion into Siberia. The conquest of Siberia and its fur trade bolstered Russian state revenues almost as much as the conquest of Egypt helped Ottoman finances. By 1600, Russia was a large and—in ethnic and religious terms—highly diverse state, indeed an empire. It was, however, sparsely settled, with a population of only 10 million.

While the princes of Moscow, who after 1547 took the title **tsar**, were underwriting Siberian expansion, they also took large parts of Ukraine and the Muslim lands of the lower Volga. These were more fertile than their home region around Moscow. This territorial expansion helped boost the population to about 14 million in 1700. During the next century, natural increase and further territorial expansion helped propel it to 40 million. By 1800, the tsars ruled about 5 percent of the global population.

The early tsars faced difficult conditions—the harsh climate of the Little Ice Age, frequent famines and rebellions, and formidable neighbors such as Poland-Lithuania to the west and Muslim khanates to the east and south. Their response was to grab all the power they could. That meant forcing regional elites, mainly landed aristocrats called *boyars*, to knuckle under to the tsars. The tsars drew upon their revenues from the fur trade, the plunder from newly conquered lands, politically astute marriages, and the legitimacy conferred by the Russian Orthodox Church to build a remarkably centralized state over their sprawling domain.

IVAN IV

Much of that was the work of Ivan IV (later called Ivan the Terrible by detractors). He reigned as tsar for nearly four decades (r. 1547–1584) and brought the nobility to heel. He oversaw conquests (and defeats), required military service of his population, wrapped himself in the mantle of the Russian Orthodox Church, married at least seven times, reportedly killed his son and heir in a tantrum, and spent lavishly on war and monumental architecture—following in many ways the age-old emperor's playbook.

But Ivan IV was also an innovator. He helped set up the first printing press in Russia. He sought overseas contacts, especially with England. Most important in the context of this chapter, he built up a huge army and an armaments industry to match. His engineers and craftsmen manufactured countless guns and cannon, and his officers (selected for talent rather than ancestry) refined the blending of infantry, cavalry, and artillery into a cohesive force. Russian engineers even invented mobile fortifications, made of wood, which could be dragged or floated here or there as needed, like a set of giant Lincoln Logs. In conquering the lower Volga, Ivan made that great river into a Russian transport artery, like the Danube in the Ottoman Empire. It gave Russia easy access to the Caspian Sea and trade with Iran. After Ivan died—while playing chess—his successors often struggled to keep the nobility in line and the state intact.

PETER THE GREAT

A later tsar, Peter the Great (r. 1682–1725), was equally innovative. After surviving murderous power struggles within the imperial family, now the Romanovs, Peter inherited an unstable country as a 17-year-old. He studied military matters, mathematics, and navigation keenly as a teenager, grew to be 6′8″ (2.03 m) tall, and scorned the soft, courtly life. After becoming tsar, he took the extraordinary step of visiting western Europe, and at one point he worked as an apprentice carpenter in a Dutch shipyard to learn the ins and outs of shipbuilding. As an English politician of the seventeenth century so brilliantly put it, "A prince who will not undergo the difficulty of understanding must undergo the danger of trusting." Peter studied hard, undergoing the difficulty of understanding, fearing there were few he could trust.

Like Ivan before him, Peter felt the need to strengthen and expand Russia. Like Ivan, his reforms put Russia through great stress but left the country more formidable than before. He too put the boyars on a short leash, modernized the military, and nourished military industries. (He also killed one of his sons.) Like the Qianlong Emperor in China, he encouraged a military culture, especially among the elite of society. He built Russia's first real navy and introduced drill into the army. He reined in the power of the Orthodox Church, which had grown politically powerful under weaker tsars, winning for himself the right to appoint bishops. In building a new capital, called St. Petersburg, he gave Russia an outlet to the Baltic Sea, as Ivan's conquests had accomplished on the Caspian Sea. Access to the Baltic brought better trade connections with all of northern Europe and enabled the use of the navy in wars with Russia's Baltic neighbors

such as Sweden. Reveling in his conquests, Peter formally declared Russia to be an empire, which indeed it was.

Despite initially controlling little in the way of natural resources beyond timber and furs, the Russian state flourished politically under the tsars. The dedicated and energetic ones found ways to mobilize the population and resources of the country, increase tax revenues, control regional elites, and integrate military innovation—especially guns, cannon, army drill, and ships—into the cultural fabric of Russia, all in the service of their own power and Russia's.

THE HABSBURG EMPIRE: THE FIRST GLOBAL POWER

The **Habsburgs**, a clan of modest nobles from southwest Germany and Switzerland, managed to join the winner's circle of Eurasian empires through their mastery of the new technologies and techniques of power. In the thirteenth century, good fortune in war added Austria to their domains. Silver from mines in the Austrian Alps helped finance their further ambitions. In the fourteenth century, through war and strategic marriages, they garnered new territories here and there in central Europe, creating a patchwork empire with Vienna as its capital. Between 1477 and 1526, they enjoyed a run of excellent political marriages, which brought them Burgundy (a sizeable piece of France), territories in the Low Countries (today's Belgium and the Netherlands), northern Hungary, and Bohemia (the Czech lands). These were comparatively productive provinces. Through another marriage, they inherited the kingdom of Spain, a comparatively poor land with about 6 million people.

With Spain came its overseas empire in the Americas and the Philippines. This was worth little at first, but in the 1550s silver began to cascade out of Mexico and the Andes. The windfall was analogous to what the Ottomans enjoyed after taking Egypt, with its vast surpluses of grain. By the mid-sixteenth century, the Habsburgs were the strongest dynasty in Europe and a power on the global stage. With territories in Europe, the Americas, and Asia (the Philippines), the Habsburgs count as the first true global power in history, the first empire on which the sun never set.

St. Petersburg The Summer Palace in St. Petersburg, built in the early eighteenth century on the banks of the Neva River where it flows into the Baltic Sea, suggests the grandeur that Peter the Great imagined for his new imperial capital.

SOFT POWER

The Habsburgs became justly famous for finding marriage partners for their eligible princes and princesses that brought new territories to the empire. An irritated king of Hungary wrote of them, "What kingdoms Mars gives to others, Venus gives to thee." The grand master of strategic matchmaking was Emperor Maximilian I (r. 1508–1519), who used marriages—his own, his children's, and his grandchildren's—to add Spain, Bohemia, northern Hungary, and a few other useful slivers of Europe to the Habsburg collection. He would have been delighted with his daughter-in-law Anna, who bore 15 children, potential political assets all, before she died at age 44.

In addition to marriages, the Habsburgs used image-making to good effect. As rulers of a hodge-podge of territories, they had to work hard to win their subjects' loyalty. They became champions of the Roman Catholic faith, sometimes militantly so. They paid painters, sculptors, architects, and composers to create art that boosted the reputation of the dynasty. Patronage of the arts was expected of rulers in Europe, as in India or China, and the Habsburgs cannily played that role. In another effort to amass prestige, several of them contrived to be elected as Holy Roman Emperor, linking themselves to the legacy of Charlemagne, who had ruled much of Europe and was the first to hold this office. They used every form of soft power to try to burnish their image, inspire loyalty or awe, and thereby reduce their reliance upon brute force to rule.

HARD POWER

But they could not neglect hard power. They were full participants in the military revolution of Eurasia. The Spanish branch of the Habsburgs built an oceanic navy in the sixteenth century and took part in all the innovations of marine warfare. They also oversaw the creation of infantry units called *tercios* that combined musketeers and pikemen to become Europe's most feared soldiers. Pikemen wielded long spears and were effective in protecting musketeers from cavalry charges. In the Austrian domains, Maximilian took a special interest in developing a formidable body of infantry, the *Landsknechte*, German mercenaries who fought in most central European Habsburg campaigns. Until about 1650, the Habsburg army still consisted largely of units recruited by private entrepreneurs and rented out to monarchs, but like the Ottomans and the Mughals, they fielded ever-larger armies. Habsburg military architects and commanders mastered the expensive business of building fortresses and the use of field artillery. Their many wars with the Ottomans, France, and other powers gave them reason to keep up to date on military technology and technique.

The Habsburgs needed all the military power and money they could get to wage war. There were rebellions to stamp out. There were religious wars to fight, against Protestants and against Muslims, to protect the interests of Catholicism. And there were dynastic wars to fight in the interest of the Habsburg family. Through the sixteenth century, these wars more often than not went well for the Habsburgs. After 1620 or so, they went less well, and the dynasty reeled from crisis to crisis, almost collapsing a few times. But fortunately for the Habsburgs, their most formidable neighbor, the Ottomans, also faced many crises after 1620.

A PATCHWORK EMPIRE

The patchwork character of most of their empire made the Habsburgs more dependent than most rulers upon the consent of their elites. They could not easily launch aggressive wars, unlike the Ottoman sultans or Qing emperors. They could rally all the many kings, princes, dukes, and

Habsburg Patrons Habsburg Archduke Leopold Wilhelm (in hat) appears in this 1647 painting in his own art gallery, surrounded by artists and their works. Habsburg patronage of the arts helped burnish their prestige.

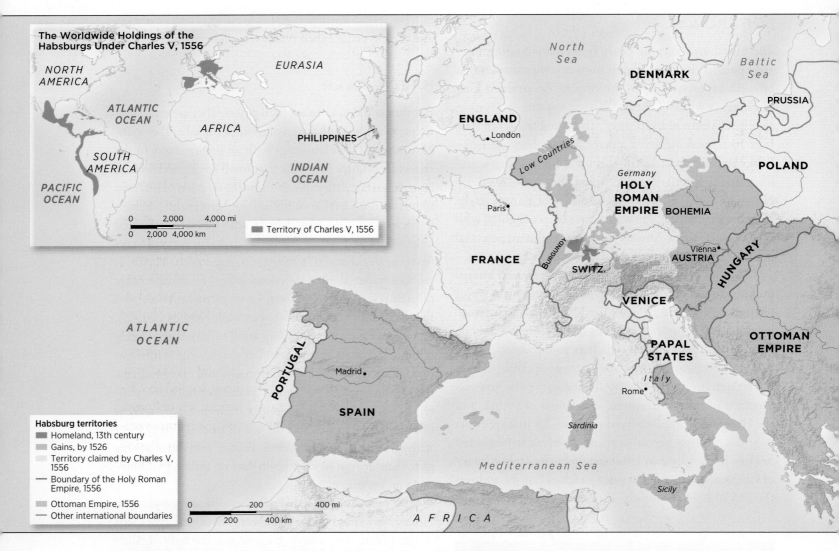

The Growth of Habsburg Territories, Thirteenth through Sixteenth Centuries The Habsburgs built an empire consisting of unusually scattered territories throughout central Europe, soon supplemented in the sixteenth century by others in western Europe, the Americas, and the Philippines. The Habsburgs, like the other great powers of the early modern world, adopted most of the innovations of the Eurasian military revolution to acquire their new lands and defend a stable frontier against their great rival, the Ottomans.

counts—nominally their subjects—for defensive wars and could often build coalitions among neighbors to resist the Ottomans or France when those states threatened Habsburg lands. After the 1520s, the Spanish and the Austrian parts of the dynasty ruled their domains separately, more like allies than a single state. The Habsburgs never achieved the cohesion within their empire that smaller European states, or the Qing, the Ottomans, or Russia's Romanovs, managed.

Nonetheless, between the 1530s and 1556, Charles V, both king of Spain and Holy Roman Emperor, almost became emperor of all Europe. Several of the world's other

big concentrations of population were undergoing violent unification in the sixteenth century: Japan, India, and, under the Ottomans, the eastern Mediterranean. China remained unified, and when it fragmented in the early seventeenth century, the Qing soon put it back together again. The Habsburgs made a bid to be the unifiers of Europe. They tried to crush Protestant princes in Germany, drive the Ottomans back in southeastern Europe, and defeat a rival dynasty, the Valois, in France. Charles V financed, directed, and in cases personally fought in these campaigns. In the end, his enemies made common cause against him, and he could not pull it off. He abdicated his thrones in 1556 and died three years later. The Habsburgs remained a major power in Europe until 1918, but never again could they realistically consider creating a pan-European empire.

THE UNIVERSITY OF WAR AND THE RISE OF EUROPE

Nor could anyone else create a pan-European empire. Europe remained a cockpit of pitiless political competition. It was, as one Dutch observer put it, a **"university of war."** In this respect, it resembled the China of the Warring States period (771–256 BCE) before its first unification, or, on a much smaller scale, the independent, rivalrous Greek city-states of the fifth century BCE. These were terrible circumstances in which to live. War, pillage, and epidemics (many of them associated with armies at war) flourished in Europe.

MILITARY COMPETITION AND STATE POWER

One result of this constant military competition was a gradual growth in the power of surviving European states. Many small ones disappeared, absorbed by the Habsburgs, the Ottomans, the French, the English, the Swedes, the Prussians, or the Russians. But, despite Charles V's best efforts, none of these successful states could destroy all others, establish an empire across the entire region, enforce peace at home, and confine warfare to its frontiers, as did the Qing in East Asia, the Mughals in South Asia, and the Ottomans in the lands around the eastern Mediterranean. Europe, in the sixteenth through the eighteenth centuries, was out of step with the other major population centers of Eurasia because competition among near equals prevailed.

This university of war provided strong incentives for every ruler to maximize the efficiency of revenue collection and military operations. Those who were not successful in these tasks were typically crushed by their neighbors. This brutal pressure lasted for centuries— unlike the situation for the Qing and the Mughals, whose success at unification and expansion meant they no longer had to compete with equals. By 1750, this unusual circumstance enabled a handful of European states— Spain, France, the Netherlands, Prussia, Habsburg Austria, and Britain—to attain world-class efficiency in taxation and fighting.

POLITICAL FRAGMENTATION AND GLOBAL REACH

As we've seen, world history includes several examples of regions divided politically and engulfed in ceaseless warfare. But early modern Europe was unique in the combination of political fragmentation with global reach, global knowledge, and low information costs because of printing. Their maritime prowess and their role in weaving the first Global web gave Europeans access to information from all over the world. They quickly learned of best practices in use elsewhere. If Italian architects showed there was a better way to build a fortress, other Europeans learned about it quickly. If Ottoman commanders showed there was a better way to combine light cavalry, field artillery, and disciplined infantry, Europeans learned about it quickly. The terrible experience of incessant war in Europe during the sixteenth through the eighteenth centuries provided states strong incentives to learn and adapt. And so they did, most importantly in naval warfare, at which

The Costs of Conflict This image, taken from a French book published around 1490, shows a seated provincial lord, accompanied by his accountants, receiving a tax payment in the form of a bag that is presumably filled with coins. Such lords forwarded a share of their tax haul to kings, who, in early modern times, spent most of their revenue on their militaries.

they outclassed other states. These early modern advances helped set the stage for European global power in the nineteenth and twentieth centuries.

THE RISE OF BIG STATES: LEADERSHIP OR CIRCUMSTANCE?

The early modern centuries raise a question that has long divided historians: how much importance should be given to individuals in shaping history? It may seem that the big empires prospered because they had a run of great emperors—Kangxi and Qianlong, Ivan IV and Peter the Great, Akbar and Aurangzeb, Mehmet and Suleiman, Maximilian I and Charles V—all men of intellect, vision, ambition, and political savvy. Seen from the perspective of a single state or empire, that conclusion appears hard to dispute.

But if one steps back and takes a world history perspective, another possibility appears: it could be that the greatness of these emperors owed mainly to the situations of their rule. They all came to power when circumstances, especially those connected to the exercise of military power, favored big states. So they could expand at the expense of little states more easily than at most times in history. While easy conquests lasted, these emperors had the prestige, revenue, land, and armed power to keep their subjects in line and negotiate with regional elites through strength—and with generosity if they wished. So the extraordinary and sustained political success of an Akbar, Suleiman, or Kangxi can in part be explained by the circumstances of their historical moment.

RESPONSES OF SMALLER POWERS

While the Qing, the Mughals, the Ottomans, the Russians, and the Habsburgs became the biggest of the big fish, they did not devour all the little fish. Smaller states could survive by playing the great powers off against one another, although this was a hazardous game that required skill and luck. To succeed, the small fish had to embrace at least some parts of the military revolution—streamlining tax collection and improving their bureaucracies and militaries. Let's look briefly at some that did—and some that didn't.

IRAN AND SOUTHEAST ASIA

Some were successful. The Safavids in Iran, sandwiched uncomfortably between the Ottomans and the Mughals, faced enormous pressure to keep up with their neighbors' military innovations. They had to transition from a strictly cavalry-based military (defeated by the gun-using Ottomans in 1514) to one that used a fuller arsenal of the military revolution: gun-wielding infantry, field artillery, and fortresses, as well as cavalry. And they had to raise all the money they could to finance campaigns, which they accomplished in part by promoting and taxing long-distance trade in silks, silver, and porcelain through their territory. The Safavids survived in power until 1736.

Smaller powers elsewhere survived, and often grew larger and more powerful, by modernizing their militaries and boosting their revenues. In Southeast Asia, Vietnam, after suffering invasion by the forces of Ming China early in the fifteenth century, adopted firearms and used them effectively against its neighbors. Other small kingdoms such as Burma and Thailand took shape and prospered at the expense of their immediate neighbors. In Burma, firearms and centralization of taxation helped to build the Toungoo dynasty (1510–1752) into the largest empire in the history of Southeast Asia for a few decades (ca. 1540–1580). In the late seventeenth century, a kingdom in Thailand briefly attained similar success after imitating Burmese military methods and securing access to weaponry from European merchants trading in the Indian Ocean.

KONGO AND MOROCCO

In Africa, a few states such as Kongo and Morocco took advantage of new opportunities presented by firearms to build their power. Kongo, as we've seen, was a major participant in the transatlantic slave trade. Through contacts with Europeans, mainly Portuguese, the kings of Kongo maintained a privileged position (not quite a monopoly) on imported guns. That gave them the power to attack and enslave neighboring peoples and to make their kingdom the most powerful in southern Africa in the seventeenth century.

In Morocco, in the sixteenth century, ambitious dynasts called the **Saadians** used revenues from trans-Saharan trade and sugar plantations to build their power. They studied Ottoman military tactics and acquired firearms and, from England, cannon. They demolished a

Moroccan Battles A seventeenth-century engraving shows Moroccan troops (right) facing off against Portuguese opponents (left) during the unsuccessful 1578 Portuguese invasion.

Portuguese assault in 1578 and in 1591 sent an expedition across the Sahara to the middle Niger to crush Songhai, the last of the great West African Sahel states. As we've seen, the Songhai Empire had ruled for about a century and centralized its bureaucracy and military, but it did not adopt firearms. Gunpowder weapons proved decisive in the 1591 encounter between the Saadian and Songhai armies.

The Moroccans, well aware of their military advantages, were probably aiming to control the West African goldfields and perhaps to create a caliphate to rival the Ottomans. They achieved neither. Moroccan troops died quickly of diseases along the Niger, and although they held the cities for many years, they could not quash resistance and never came close to the goldfields. Unable to corner West Africa's gold, one Saadian ruler, al-Mansur, set his sights on Spanish America's silver. In 1601, he proposed to England's Queen Elizabeth I that they should join forces and divide Spain's American empire between them. His plan came to nothing. Mastery of firearms enabled the Saadians to unify Morocco, destroy enemies across the Sahara, and dream of greater conquests—but firearms alone, without sea power, could not make those dreams come true.

From Morocco to Vietnam, the same broad pattern among smaller states prevailed. Prudent adoption of new technologies and techniques of warfare allowed an edge, even if temporary, in military formidability. That enabled ambitious rulers to extend their domains. Obtaining such

an advantage was much easier in times of flux, when technologies and techniques were changing faster than usual. The resulting states and empires were often fleeting, as neighbors formed coalitions or adopted new and effective military techniques and technologies themselves.

This broad pattern was a smaller-scale version of the pattern among the great Eurasian powers from the Qing to the Habsburgs: the big got bigger because they were better able to realize the potential of expensive new technologies and techniques. They could exploit economies of scale in, for example, building ships or cannon that small-scale rulers could not.

THE COSTS OF MAINTAINING TRADITION: POLAND AND EGYPT'S MAMLUK SULTANATE

The costs of not following the trend are illustrated by the case of the Polish-Lithuanian Commonwealth (Poland for short). Poland took shape in the fifteenth century, officially merged with the Grand Duchy of Lithuania in 1569, and enjoyed its greatest power in the mid-seventeenth century. Its kings were elected by members of the nobility, who tenaciously guarded their liberties from central control. The Polish military relied on cavalry composed chiefly of nobles, which proved effective against Muscovy, Sweden, and the Ottomans, if less so against Tatar raiders. The Polish nobility kept alive traditions of chivalry long after other states had built up large infantries composed of peasants and had invested in fortresses, artillery, and navies. Polish elites long resisted these trends: they did not wish to help pay for fortresses and ships, nor did they want to see common foot soldiers or the architects of fortresses siphon off any prestige or glory. One nobleman dismissed siege warfare as "mole's work." Nobles particularly did not want to see the king equipped with a standing army, rightly fearing that kings with armies would trample upon their liberties.

Unfortunately for the liberty-loving Polish elites, by 1690 their military did not match, in size or technique, that of Russia or the Habsburgs, and gallant cavalry charges could not make up the difference. Their decentralized, consensual political system prevented the military and fiscal reforms that might have preserved their state. Between 1772 and 1795, Poland's neighbors—Russia, Prussia, and Habsburg Austria—partitioned it three times, wiping Poland from the map (until 1918).

The Polish nobility was not alone in clinging to cherished traditions. Slave soldiers of the Mamluk sultanate, based in Egypt, did so too with similar consequences. In the thirteenth century, Mamluk forces had defeated the Mongols (1260) and become the most powerful military in the Islamic world. The sultans' soldiers mastered archery, swordsmanship, and horsemanship. But their success with these weapons, which required skill, training, and strength, led them to scorn firearms, which were easier to use. Some Mamluk sultans understood the value of guns and cannon, but none could ever get hold of enough of them to equip masses of peasant-soldiers. When one sultan organized a corps of infantry with muskets in 1498, the Mamluk cavalry attacked it. In 1516–1517, Ottoman armies using all manner of firearms crushed the Mamluks and took Egypt. The Mamluk and Polish-Lithuanian cases show the dangers of failure at military modernization in a time of rapid change—in both cases partly attributable to the success of elites, whether slave-soldiers or nobles, at older methods of combat.

NOMADS AND PIRATES IN A WORLD OF EXPANDING STATES

The broad pattern of centralization and expansion of state power through fiscal and military reform was hard on smaller states, but harder still on nomads and pirates. On the world's grasslands and seas, nomad confederations and pirate gangs were for many centuries important political and military forces. But between 1650 and 1890, their power was decisively broken by the armies and navies of agrarian states. Nomads and pirates still existed afterward, but never again exercised much influence in history.

NOMAD POWER

Nomads—or more properly, mobile pastoralists—had operated on the grassy steppes of Asia and North Africa for millennia, and as we have seen time and again, they interacted both peacefully and violently with settled, agrarian populations and states. They often enjoyed considerable political and military power, thanks to their mobility and their capacities for surprise attack and tactical retreat. They could, when unified, defeat great empires. During the tenth through the thirteenth centuries, steppe pastoralists took over China, North India, and Iran, and North African pastoralists did roughly the same in Morocco and Egypt.

But by the seventeenth and eighteenth centuries, settled agrarian states were reinventing themselves and the nomads could not follow suit. Mobile peoples could not develop more efficient tax collection, manufacture cannon, build elaborate fortifications, or add navies to their arsenals. They became increasingly dependent upon agrarian empires and less menacing to them. Their fighters more often served agrarian kings and emperors as auxiliary cavalry in exchange for cash, cloth, food, or weaponry. The Russians and Ottomans, for example, made good use of steppe peoples such as the Tatars. The Ming and the Qing hired Mongols to do some of their fighting for them. But the steppe warriors sometimes proved disobedient and dangerous allies, leading decision makers in Beijing or Istanbul to conclude that it would be wiser to crush pastoralists than to continue to keep them in service and supplied with weaponry.

So, roughly between 1700 and 1850, hundreds of campaigns, small and large, took place from Manchuria to Morocco in which emperors and kings sent their armies against pastoralists and nomads. They built strings of forts in the steppes and deserts. Their armies at times managed to surround or trap a group of nomads and disarm them, slaughter them, or sell them into slavery. Guns played a role in this—although nomads often had guns too—but logistics, money, and manpower played larger ones. The Saadians, Ottomans, Russians, Safavids, Mughals, and Qing all mounted intermittent wars against nomads and pastoralists. The last large-scale confederacy of nomads was that of the Zunghars in Mongolia, about 750,000 people, which Qing forces crushed militarily and then slaughtered in the 1750s.

On a smaller scale, and in a compressed time frame, a similar saga played out in the Americas. With the introduction of horses and guns, after 1800 peoples such as the Comanche and Lakota Sioux created mobile and militarized ways of life that bore some resemblance to that of steppe peoples in Asia. The Comanche and Lakota Sioux were not pastoralists on any scale; they did not keep livestock except horses. They lived more by hunting than stock raising. But they each became a political force in North America and terrorized settled, farming

Nomads (Left) A large-scale painting executed collaboratively by Chinese and European painters shows Qing forces decisively defeating the nomadic Zunghars in their camp. (Right) In the United States in 1876, Lakota Sioux, Cheyenne, and Arapaho forces defeated U.S. troops at the Battle of the Little Bighorn, as this 1900 image by Lakota artist Amos Bad Heart Buffalo records—but they ultimately lost the war.

peoples—mainly other indigenous Americans—with frequent, brutal raids.

In South America, horse cultures arose in northern Patagonia during the seventeenth and eighteenth centuries among peoples such as the Tehuelche. They took to hunting guanacos (close relatives of llamas) and rheas (big flightless birds), raising cattle and sheep, and raiding neighboring settlements. They used lances, guns, and a weapon called the bolo, two stones tied together with a hide rope, in hunting and warfare. The basis of their newfound power, as for the Comanche and Lakota Sioux, was the mobility conferred by horses.

The age of nomad (or seminomad) power in the Americas came late compared to Asia and North Africa, beginning only in the eighteenth or nineteenth century. It ended in the second half of the nineteenth century, when the armies of settled agrarian societies—Argentina, Chile, Mexico, the United States, and Canada—crushed the last remnants of nomad power in world history. This echo of the Qing obliteration of Zunghar power brought to a close a 3,000-year epoch in world history in which nomads and mobile pastoralists were a force to be reckoned with.

The relentless competition among agrarian states, their swift exchange (often unwilling) of information about the technologies and techniques of warfare, and their growth in size and capacity—all directly or indirectly resulting from the tightening of the Global web—spelled the end for nomads. They could not keep up with their agrarian neighbors, and their courage, horsemanship, and marksmanship no longer mattered.

PIRATES

Pirates played a far smaller role in world history. They probably existed even earlier than mobile pastoralists, from soon after the beginning of waterborne trade. Conditions generally suited pirates best when and where long-distance seaborne trade flourished, navies were weak, and at least a few good bays or inlets with minimal population could serve as bases. Access to markets was also important for piracy: when pirates grabbed a cargo of porcelain or sugar, they couldn't use much of it themselves and needed to sell it for money or swap it for what they wanted.

The early centuries of the Global web were a golden age for pirates. The linking up of the world's coastlines by European mariners led to a vast expansion in long-distance maritime trade. Port cities everywhere did a thriving business, and stolen cargoes could find ready buyers. Navies remained too small to patrol the world's oceans, leaving extensive safe space for pirates. Navies were so weak that in wartime they often inadvertently created pirates by recruiting sailors to assault enemy shipping—they were called privateers. In peacetime, privateers were out of work, and many chose to stay afloat as pirates. The distinctions between pirate and privateer were sometimes fuzzy.

THE CARIBBEAN AND INDIAN OCEAN Although pirates might roam anywhere, they preferred certain locations. The Caribbean met their requirements nicely, and from the 1550s to the 1720s it was a hotbed of piracy and privateering. Spanish ships bearing silver exports from Mexico passed through the Caribbean, attracting pirates and privateers such as the Dutch privateer Piet Heyn, who captured a silver fleet off of Cuba's coast in 1628. Bartholomew Roberts, a Welsh-born pirate, captured 400 merchant ships in the Atlantic and Caribbean between 1719 and 1722. In the early eighteenth century, about one-third of pirates were Africans or of African descent, and at least two—Mary Read and Anne Bonny—were women.

The Indian Ocean, from Madagascar to the Red Sea to the Straits of Malacca, also presented pirates with splendid opportunities. These were exploited both by interlopers from the Atlantic, such as the Scottish-born Captain Kidd, who built a base in Madagascar, and by locals, such as the Arakan (or Magh) pirates based on the shores of Burma who feasted on Bengali shipping and coastal settlements. Even better hunting grounds for pirates lay in the South and East China seas. The largest-scale pirate operation was that of the Zheng family on the southeastern coasts of China from Nanjing to Macao, the story of which began this chapter.

THE BARBARY PIRATES From the sixteenth century onward, the North African cities of Algiers, Tunis, and Tripoli hosted large-scale pirate operations. The Mediterranean suited pirates because of its abundant shipping and lively slave markets where captives could be sold. Christians and Muslims raided and enslaved one another regularly. In North Africa, with Ottoman encouragement, local officials, called *beys*, organized pirate/privateer forces to prey on shipping and coastal settlements mainly in Spain and Italy. The Barbary pirates, as they are known, sought cargoes and Christian captives to sell in North African markets. By one estimate, over the years from 1500 to 1800 they seized and enslaved about 1 million captives. On occasion, they ventured farther afield, raiding Iceland in 1627, where they captured 400 people for sale in North Africa; Ireland in 1631; and even the coast of Argentina in 1720. The Barbary pirates were at the height of their power in the early and mid-seventeenth century. Moroccan rulers offered similar support for pirates/privateers operating in eastern Atlantic waters from their base in Salé.

Christian kingdoms such as Spain and France encouraged European piracy and privateering against North African shipping and ports, and by 1630 they used their navies against the Barbary pirates with some effect. But they did not yet have the power to close them down. Piracy flared up in the 1780s and 1790s, and now the targets included

Barbary Pirates A sizeable Barbary fleet appears off the coast of Nice, in the western Mediterranean, in this 1558 illustration. As was typical for Barbary fleets, its commander was an Ottoman bey: Hayreddin Barbarossa. He was responsible for many naval victories against Spain.

American merchant ships in the Mediterranean. For several years, the U.S. government paid protection money to get the pirates to desist—as much as 20 percent of the U.S. federal budget in 1800. The United States launched attacks in 1805 and 1815, and a British-Dutch force bombarded North African ports in 1816. By 1830, the naval power of their foes had become too great and the Barbary pirates were just about out of business.

The same fate befell pirates elsewhere. The Mughals routed pirates from their coastal lairs, mainly in Bengal and Burma, in the seventeenth century. British naval power largely eliminated pirates in the Caribbean by 1730. Everywhere around the world, from Taiwan to Jamaica, pirates were hunted down. Piracy did not entirely disappear—indeed, a few pirates are active today in the Arabian Sea and Southeast Asian waters—but they never again attained anything like the power and wealth of the Zhengs or the beys of North Africa. Like the mobile pastoralists, the pirates of the world ran afoul of the ever-growing power of big empires.

CONCLUSION

The turmoil of the early modern centuries may seem a confusing blur of wars won and lost, dynasties rising and falling, states and empires appearing and vanishing, but there is a general pattern behind it. If one steps back from the details, it is possible to see a brutal political shakeout in which a few polities prospered and many disappeared. This pattern showed up more strongly in Eurasia than elsewhere, but it can also be found on smaller scales in places such as Hawaii and Morocco. As the technologies and techniques of war and power grew more complex and costly, the big got bigger, usually at the expense of the small. A handful of empires dominated Eurasia, and increasingly—a development without precedent in world history—the whole world.

The history of war and empire in these centuries reveals two other significant developments. First is the eccentricity of Europe. Despite the Habsburgs' best efforts, no state could build a pan-European empire. The other great centers of population in Eurasia—China, North India, and the Ottoman lands—all became the seats of gigantic empires far stronger than most of their frontier neighbors. Europe's peculiarity led to relentless competition—the university of war—and, in the long run, to stronger, more efficient, more formidable states, especially with respect to naval power. It also led to exceedingly difficult times for ordinary people caught up in the maelstrom. This peculiarity, combined with the access Atlantic Europeans had to information and commercial opportunity all over the world, helps to explain the rise of European power, specifically Atlantic European power, in the global political arena.

The second notable development was the destruction of nomad power and the marginalization of piracy. In the eighteenth and early nineteenth centuries, the big states developed sufficient capacity—logistics more than firepower—to abandon their cautious and at times cozy relations with nomads and pirates and instead to crush them. This simplified international politics, by reducing the role of nonstate actors and leaving the stage increasingly to a smaller number of bigger players.

Part of the reason for the general pattern of consolidation of power around the world came from a quickening of world trade in the early modern centuries. Ships and caravans carried valuable goods and money—often, silver from the Americas or Japan. Any ruler could take a cut, and those located at choke points on long-distance routes could take big ones. In the next chapter, we will see how this came to pass by turning to the new global economy made possible by the formation of a truly global web.

CHAPTER REVIEW

KEY TERMS

military revolution
  (p. 608)

field artillery and
  fortification (p. 610)

Oda Nobunaga (p. 611)

Toyotomi Hideyoshi
  (p. 612)

Tokugawa shogunate
  (p. 612)

Qing dynasty (p. 613)

Akbar (p. 616)

Istanbul (p. 619)

janissaries (p. 621)

millet system (p. 623)

imperial consolidation
  (p. 623)

tsar (p. 623)

Habsburgs (p. 624)

university of war (p. 627)

Saadians (p. 628)

pirates (p. 631)

Go to INQUIZITIVE to see what you've learned—and learn what you've missed—with personalized feedback along the way.

REVIEW QUESTIONS

1. What is the main reason that large imperial states were able to destroy hundreds of smaller states during the early modern period?

2. What six trends making up the military revolution caused warfare to become more complex and expensive?

3. How did Oda Nobunaga and his successors use guns to unify Japan?

4. Identify the Qing's most successful military innovations, and explain what was unique about these initiatives.

5. What military, religious, and economic techniques did the Mughals employ to consolidate power?

6. Describe how Istanbul, Egypt, the Hejaz, Mesopotamia, and Hungary contributed to Ottoman power.

7. What social, political, and military reforms did Ivan the Terrible and Peter the Great introduce in Russia?

8. What were the main forms of soft power the Habsburgs employed to expand their power in Europe?

9. How did constant political competition in Europe affect successful European states?

10. Explain the main technologies and techniques that small states adopted in order to survive.

11. What was the contribution of the elite class to the downfall of Poland and the Mamluk sultanate?

12. Why did the relationship between nomads and agrarian states change during the early modern period?

13. What was the chief reason for the loss of power among pirates?

14. What two significant developments does the history of war and empire in the early modern period reveal?

FURTHER READING

Tonio ANDRADE, *The Gunpowder Age: China, Military Innovation, and the Rise of the West in World History* (2016). An authoritative comparison of China and Europe.

Jos GOMMANS, *Mughal Warfare: Indian Frontiers and High Roads to Empire, 1500–1700* (2002). This remains the most careful assessment of the military revolution in India.

Xing HANG, *Conflict and Commerce in Maritime East Asia: The Zheng Family and the Shaping of the Modern World, c. 1620–1720* (2015). The standard work on the Zheng family enterprise.

Peter A. LORGE, *The Asian Military Revolution: From Gunpowder to the Bomb* (2008). A handy summary of cases in South, Southeast, and East Asia.

Alfred J. RIEBER, *The Struggle for the Eurasian Borderlands: From the Rise of Early Modern Empires to the End of the First World War* (2014). One of a few comparative studies of multiple empires—the Qing, Mughal, Safavid, Ottoman, Russian, and Habsburg.

Brian SANDBERG, *War and Conflict in the Early Modern World, 1500–1700* (2016). A work that is attentive to questions of organization and culture as well as technology.

Douglas E. STREUSAND, *Islamic Gunpowder Empires: Ottomans, Safavids, and Mughals* (2011). An accessible summary of its subject.

Joanna WALEY-COHEN, *The Culture of War in China: Empire and the Military under the Qing Dynasty* (2006). A very readable and compact study, emphasizing cultural sides of the Qing military buildup.

The Exercise of Power

IN THE EARLY MODERN CENTURIES (ca. 1450–1800), much of Eurasia underwent political centralization, largely through warfare, resulting in larger states and empires. Monarchs and their advisers had good reason to contemplate what principles and rules made the difference between success and failure in statecraft. In the excerpts here, rulers and advisers from two recently enlarged states, France and Japan, and two from sprawling empires, the Ming and the Mughal, set down their ideas about how best to exercise power. Note that the text describing the Ottoman army, state, and customs was written by a foreign ambassador and does represent, at least not directly, the viewpoint of the Ottoman sultan.

SOURCE 18.1

Excerpt from the August Ming Ancestral Instruction

In 1368, the Ming established a new dynasty on the ruins of the Yuan. The Yuan were of Mongol ancestry, and the Ming were proudly Chinese. The founder of the Ming dynasty, the Hongwu Emperor, wrote a book of instructions for his successors, published in 1393. It has 13 sections advising on how to manage finance, run a palace and harem, observe rituals and protocols, administer public works, deal with various sorts of barbarians, and much more. These instructions continued to guide the conduct of the Ming state until its downfall in 1644.

The paragraphs below explain why the Hongwu Emperor abolished the position of prime minister and warn his successors against taking their personal safety for granted. In the latter discussion, ten *zhang* is the equivalent of 32 meters, or about 105 feet.

From ancient times policy was discussed among the three dukes [*san gong*] and the duties of government were divided among the six ministers, but a prime minister was never established. The Qin began the establishment of a prime minister and fell soon thereafter. The Han, Tang, and Song continued the practice. Although there were some virtuous prime ministers, many of them were evil men who monopolized power and confused administration. Now our dynasty has abolished the prime minister and established such offices as the five chief commissions, the six ministries, the Censorate, the Office of Transmission, and the Grand Court of Revision to manage the affairs of the realm. They parallel one another and dare not to seek to dominate each other. It is the court which provides overall control of government affairs. That is why there is stability. From now on, when my descendants become emperors, they absolutely shall not establish a prime minister. If there are officials who dare to memorialize requesting such establishment, civil and military officials shall immediately submit accusations. The offender shall be put to death by slicing and his whole family executed.

[...]

The ruler, even when living in safety, still shall constantly be on guard. At no time during the day or night may you be careless. Then you will not be spied upon, and the state will not be lost. If you take your safety for granted and forget to take precautions, then evil persons will be able to plot. Neither your life nor your state can be protected. You must be prepared day and night as if you were going into battle with clear orders given. In the day, watch people's speech and actions and at night, patrol to strictly enforce the prohibition on entry so that evil persons will be unable to gain admission. Though persons be trusted as your own flesh, in meeting with them during the day or night you still shall be alert in your mind. It is better to be prepared even though nothing happens. If you want your retainers to withdraw so as to consult privately with trusted persons on affairs of state, your accompanying eunuchs and armed bodyguards shall only withdraw to a distance of ten *zhang*; they shall not go too far. For example, when in the Yuan dynasty Yingzong was killed in the night it was just because his retainers and eunuchs had withdrawn too far away and the imperial ladies were also not home. Consequently there was this tragedy. You must be highly vigilant.

Source: Edward L. Farmer, *Zhu Yuanzhang and Early Ming Legislation: The Reordering of Chinese Society Following the Era of Mongol Rule* (New York: E. J. Brill, 1995).

- What seems to be the main worry of the Hongwu Emperor?
- According to this text, what is the advantage to an emperor in not having a prime minister?

SOURCE 18.2

Excerpt from the Turkish Letters, 1555–1562

The author, Ogier Ghiselin de Busbecq (1522–1592), from what is now Belgium, was an illegitimate son of a minor aristocrat and his mistress. Busbecq's intellectual skills took him to Italian universities, after which he became a diplomat for the Austrian Habsburgs. In this capacity he was sent to the Ottoman capital in the 1550s and negotiated a treaty with Ottoman officials under Sultan Suleiman the Lawgiver, then at the height of his power. Busbecq was a careful observer, and his letters provide one of the best depictions of the Ottoman court and state. But among his purposes was the intent to alarm Christians about Ottoman military capabilities. He exaggerates in some respects, such as when discussing the dietary fussiness of Christian soldiers. Here he describes what he judged was the basis of Ottoman power.

At Buda I made my first acquaintance with the Janissaries; this is the name by which the Turks call the infantry of the royal guard. The Turkish state has 12,000 of these troops when the corps is at its full strength. They are scattered through every part of the empire, either to garrison the forts against the enemy, or to protect the Christians and Jews from the violence of the mob. There is no district with any considerable amount of population, no borough or city, which has not a detachment of Janissaries to protect the Christians, Jews, and other helpless people from outrage and wrong.

[...]

The Turkish monarch going to war takes with him over 40,000 camels and nearly as many baggage mules, of which a great part are loaded with rice and other kinds of grain. These mules and camels also serve to carry tents and armour, and likewise tools and munitions for the campaign.... The invading army carefully abstains from encroaching on its magazines [containers of supplies] at the outset; as they are well aware that when the season for campaigning draws to a close, they will have to retreat over districts wasted by the enemy, or scraped bare by countless hordes of men and droves of hungry animals, as if they had been devastated by locusts; accordingly they reserve their stores as much as possible for this emergency. Then the Sultan's magazines are opened, and a ration just sufficient to sustain life is daily weighed out to the Janissaries and other troops of the royal household. The rest of the army[1] is badly off, unless they have provided some supplies at their own expense.... On such occasions they take out a few spoonfuls of flour and put them into water, adding some butter, and seasoning the mess with salt and spices; these ingredients are boiled, and a large bowl of gruel is thus obtained. Of this they eat once or twice a day, according to the quantity they have, without any bread, unless they have brought some biscuit with them.... Sometimes they have recourse to horseflesh; dead horses are of course plentiful in their great hosts, and such beasts as are in good condition when they die furnish a meal not to be despised by famished soldiers.

From this you will see that it is the patience, self-denial and thrift of the Turkish soldier that enable him to face the most trying circumstances and come safely out of the dangers that surround him. What a contrast to our men! Christian soldiers on a campaign refuse to put up with their ordinary food, and call for thrushes, becaficos [a small bird esteemed a dainty, as it feeds on figs and grapes], and suchlike dainty dishes! ... It makes me shudder to think of what the result of a struggle between such different systems must be; one of us must prevail and the other be destroyed, at any rate we cannot both exist in safety. On their side is the vast wealth of their empire, unimpaired resources, experience and practice in arms, a veteran soldiery, an uninterrupted series of victories, readiness to endure hardships, union, order, discipline, thrift and watchfulness. On ours are found an empty exchequer, luxurious habits, exhausted resources, broken spirits, a raw and insubordinate soldiery, and greedy quarrels; there is no regard for discipline, license runs riot, the men indulge in drunkenness and debauchery, and worst of all, the enemy are accustomed to victory, we to defeat. Can we doubt what the result must be? The only obstacle is Persia, whose position on his rear forces the invader to take precautions. The fear of Persia gives us a respite, but it is only for a time.

No distinction is attached to birth among the Turks; the deference to be paid to a man is measured by the position he holds in the public service. There is no fighting for precedence; a man's place is marked out by the duties he discharges. In making his appointments the Sultan pays no regard to any pretensions on the score of wealth or rank, nor does he take into consideration recommendations or popularity, he considers each case on its own merits, and examines carefully into the character, ability, and disposition of the man whose promotion is in question. It is by merit that men rise in the service, a system which ensures that posts should only be assigned to the competent. Each man in Turkey carries in his own hand his ancestry and his position in life, which he may make or mar as he will. Those who receive the highest offices from the Sultan are for the most part the sons of shepherds or herdsmen, and so far from being ashamed of their parentage, they actually glory in it, and consider it a matter of boasting that they owe nothing to the accident of birth; for they do not believe that high qualities are either natural or hereditary, nor do they think that they can be handed down from father to son, but that they are partly the gift of God, and partly the result of good training, great industry, and unwearied zeal; arguing that high qualities do not descend from a father to his son or heir, any more than a talent for music, mathematics, or the like; and that the mind does not derive its origin from the father, so that the son should necessarily be like the father in character, our emanates from heaven, and is thence infused into the human body. Among the Turks, therefore, honours, high posts, and judgeships are the rewards of great ability and good service. If a man be dishonest, or lazy, or careless, he remains at the bottom of the ladder, an object of contempt; for such qualities there are no honours in Turkey!

This is the reason that they are successful in their undertakings, that they lord it over others, and are daily extending the bounds of their empire. These are not our ideas, with us there is no opening left for merit; birth is the standard for everything; the prestige of birth is the sole key to advancement in the public service.

---

[1]This refers to soldiers assembled in a general mobilization, not regular army troops. They were not paid; instead, they lived off of plunder.

Source: Charles Thornton Forster and F. H. B. Daniel, *The Life and Letters of Ogier Ghiselin de Busbecq*, Vol. I (London: C. Kegan Paul & Co., 1881).

- According to Busbecq, what made the Ottomans so powerful?
- In Busbecq's text, is it possible to detect signs of a strategy for centralization of power on the part of Ottoman sultans? If so, what might that strategy be? If not, why not?

SOURCE 18.3

Excerpt from the Mughal *Akbarnama*, 1590s

Akbar (1542–1605) was the true architect of South Asia's Mughal Empire. In addition to building and running an Islamic empire, he supported artists and intellectuals at his court. Among them was Abul Fazl, an adviser and courtier whom Akbar charged with writing a chronicle of the emperor's reign. Abul Fazl used Mughal court documents, interviews, and personal observation to compose the *Akbarnama*, which he wrote in Persian, the court language of the Mughals, in the 1590s. It has three parts. The first two are biographies and chronicles of events. The third describes India's religions, customs, geography, economy, and so on. It also includes Abul Fazl's record of Akbar's own remarks on various subjects, including those on statecraft presented here. Whether Akbar actually said these things is uncertain. It could be that the words represent, instead, what Abul Fazl thought Akbar wanted everyone to think Akbar had said.

A monarch is a pre-eminent cause of good. Upon his conduct depends the efficiency of any course of action. His gratitude to his Lord, therefore, should be shown in just government and due recognition of merit; that of his people, in obedience and praise.

The very sight of kings has been held to be a part of divine worship. They have been styled conventionally the shadow of God, and indeed to behold them is a means of calling to mind the Creator, and suggests the protection of the Almighty.

[...]

A monarch should not himself undertake duties that may be performed by his subjects. The errors of others it is his part to remedy, but his own lapses who may correct?

Sovereignty consists in distinguishing degrees of circumstance and in meting out reward and punishment in proportion thereto.

[...]

What is said of monarchs, that their coming brings security and peace, has the stamp of truth....

In the reciprocity of rule and obedience, the sanctions of hope and fear are necessary to the well-ordering of temporal government and the illumination of the interior recesses of the spirit; nevertheless a masterful will, never suffering the loss of self control under the dominance of passion, should weigh well and wisely the measure and occasion of each.

Whoever walks in the way of fear and hope, his temporal and spiritual affairs will prosper. Neglect of them will result in misfortune.

Idleness is the root of evils. The duty of one who seeketh his own welfare is to learn a profession and practise it. It is imperative in prefects never to be remiss in watchfulness.

[...]

Tyranny is unlawful in everyone, especially in a sovereign who is the guardian of the world.

[...]

A king should abstain from four things: excessive devotion to hunting; incessant play; inebriety night and day; and constant intercourse with women.

Although hunting suggests analogies of state policy,[2] nevertheless the first consideration is to be sparing in the destruction of life. Falsehood is improper in all men, and most unseemly in monarchs. This order is termed the shadow of God, and a shadow should throw straight.

A king should not be familiar in mirth and amusement with his courtiers.

A monarch should be ever intent on conquest, otherwise his neighbours rise in arms against him.

The army should be exercised in warfare, lest from want of training they become self-indulgent.

A king should make a distinction in his watch over the goods, the lives, the honour and the religion of his subjects. If those who are led away by greed and passion will not be reclaimed by admonition, they must be chastised.

[...]

The words of kings resemble pearls. They are not fit pendants to every ear.

---

[2]For rulers of Mongol ancestry, like the Mughals, hunting served as practice for warfare.

Source: *The Ain I Akbari by Abul Fazl – I – Allami*, trans. from the Original Persian by Col. H. S. Jarrett (Calcutta: The Asiatic Society of Bengal, 1894).

- Is it possible to detect a strategy of rulership in Akbar's sayings? If so, what does it consist of?
- What are the ideal attributes of a ruler, according to Akbar?

Excerpt from Laws of Military Households, 1615

Tokugawa Hidetada was the second shogun, formally in power from 1605 until 1623, when he abdicated in favor of his son. But he retained real power until his death in 1632. He ran a militarized state that he had helped his father to create through warfare against contenders for the shogunate. Here he sets forth a code of conduct for the Japanese landowning nobility, the daimyo, and the lesser warrior aristocrats, the samurai. Later shoguns reissued these rules, with modifications, for generations. The word domain is used here to refer to lands owned by the daimyo.

1.—Literature, arms, archery and horsemanship are, systematically, to be the favourite pursuits.

Literature first, and arms next to it, was the rule of the ancients. They must both be cultivated concurrently. Archery and horsemanship are the more essential for the Military Houses. Weapons of warfare are ill-omened words to utter; the use of them, however, is an unavoidable necessity. In times of peace and good order we must not forget that disturbances may arise. Dare we omit to practise our warlike exercises and drill?

2.—Drinking parties and gaming amusements must be kept within due bounds.

In our Instructions it is laid down that strict moderation in these respects is to be observed. To be addicted to venery [sex] and to make a pursuit of gambling is the first step towards the loss of one's domain.

3.—Offenders against the law are not to be harboured in the (feudal) domains.

Law is the very foundation of ceremonial decorum and of social order. To infringe the law in the name of reason is as bad as to outrage reason in the name of the law. To disregard the law (laid down by us) is an offence which will not be treated with leniency.

4.—Throughout the domains whether of the greater or lesser Barons (*Daimyo* and *Shomyo*) or of the holders of minor benefices, if any of the gentry or soldiers (*shi* and *sotsu*) in their service be guilty of rebellion or murder, such offenders must be at once expelled from their domain.

5.—Henceforth no social intercourse is to be permitted outside of one's own domain, with the people (gentry and commoners) of another domain.

6.—The residential castles in the domains may be repaired; but the matter must invariably be reported. Still more imperative is it that the planning of structural innovations of any kind must be absolutely avoided.

7.—If in a neighbouring domain innovations are being hatched or cliques being formed the fact is to be reported without delay.

Men are always forming groups; whilst, on the other hand, few ever come to anything. On this account they fail to follow their lords or fathers, and soon come into collision with those of neighbouring villages. If the ancient prohibitions are not maintained, somehow or other innovating schemes will be formed.

8.—Marriages must not be contracted at private convenience.

Now, the marriage union is a result of the harmonious blending of the *In* and *You* (*i.e.*, the *Yin* and *Yang* of Chinese metaphysics, the female and male principles of nature). It is therefore not a matter to be lightly undertaken. It is said in the "Scowling" passage of the (Chow) Book of Changes: - "Not being enemies they unite in marriage." Whilst (the elders are) thinking of making advances to the opponent (family), the proper time (for the marriage of the young couple) is allowed to slip by. In the "Peach Young" poem of the Book of Odes it is said: - "If the man and woman, duly observing what is correct, marry at the proper time of life, there will be no widows in the land." To form cliques by means of matrimonial connections is a source of pernicious stratagems.

9.—As to the rule that the Daimyos shall come (to the Shogun's Court at Yedo) to do service.

In the *Shoku Nihon ki* (*i.e.*, The Continuation of the Chronicles of Japan) it is recorded amongst the enactments:
"Except when entrusted with some official duty no one (dignitary) is allowed at his own pleasure to assemble his whole tribe within the limits of the capital, no one is to go about attended by more than twenty horsemen, etc." Hence it is not permissible to lead about a large force of soldiers. For Daimyos whose revenues range from 1,000,000 *koku* down to 200,000 *koku*, the number of twenty horsemen is not to be exceeded. For those whose revenues are 100,000 *koku* and under the number is to be in the same proportion.

10.—There must be no confusion in respect of dress uniforms, as regards the materials thereof.

The distinction between lord and vassal, between superior and inferior, must be clearly marked by the apparel. Retainers may not, except in rare cases by special favour of their lords, indiscriminately wear silk stuffs, such as *Shiro-aya* (*i. e.* undyed silk with woven patterns), *Shiro-Kosode* (*i. e.* white wadded silk coats), *murasaki-awase* (*i. e.* purple silk coats), lined *murasaki-ura* (*i. e.* a silk coat lined with purple); *nori* (*i. e.* white gloss silk), *mumon* (*i. e.* a silk coat without the wearer's badge dyed on it), *Kosode* (a coloured silk wadded coat). In recent times retainers and henchmen (soldiers) have taken to wearing rich damasks and silk brocade. This elaborate display was not allowed by the ancient laws and it must be severely kept within bounds.

11.—Miscellaneous persons are not at their own pleasure to ride in palanquins [one-passenger carriages lugged by four or six bearers].

There are families who for special reasons from of old have (inherited) the privilege of riding in palanquins without permission from the authorities; and there are others who by permission of the authorities exercise that privilege. But, latterly, even sub-vassals and henchmen of no rank have taken to so riding. This is a flagrant impertinence. Henceforward the Daimyo of the provinces, and such of their kinsfolk as are men of distinction subordinate to them, may ride without applying for government permission. Besides those the following are receiving permission, viz. vassals and retainers of high position about their lords; doctors and astrologers; persons of over sixty years of age; and sick persons and invalids. If ordinary or inferior henchmen (*sotsu*) are allowed to ride in palanquins it will be considered to be the fault of their lords.

12. —The samurai throughout the provinces are to practice frugality.

Those who are rich like to make a display, whilst those who are poor are ashamed of not being on a par with the others. There is no other influence so pernicious to social observances as this; and it must be strictly kept in check.

13.—The lords of the great domains (*kokushu*, lit., masters of provinces) must select men of capacity for office.

The tenor of the foregoing rules must be obeyed.

Keicho, 20th year, 7th month (August 24th, September 23rd, 1615).

Source: *The Tokugawa Legislation*, trans. John Carey Hall (Yokohama, Japan: 1910).

- Judging from these rules, what seems to be the shogun's greatest worries?
- Why might shoguns be concerned about clothing and who gets to ride in a palanquin?

SOURCE 18.5

Excerpt from Louis XIV's Advice to His Son, 1660s

Louis XIV, king of France, officially reigned for 72 years, from 1643 to his death in 1715. After regents held the reins of power in his childhood, he took personal control in 1661 at age 22. He worked hard to gather power into his own hands and to tame the French nobility and the authority of bishops. He expanded France's tax revenues and its military, and through military successes he expanded the nation's territory while weakening its neighbors. He out-lived all his sons, and on his deathbed his heir was his five-year old great-grandson. In the 1660s, when still young, he foresaw power struggles after his own death and prepared a document for his son, in which he explained some of his approach to wielding power.

The Chancellor received a like order, that is to say, to sign nothing with the seal except by my command, with the exception only of letters of justice, I let it be understood that whatever the nature of the matter might be, direct application must be made to me when it was not a question that depended only on my favour; and to all my subjects without distinction I gave liberty to present their case to me at all hours, either verbally or by petitions.

...I resolved at all costs to have no prime minister; and if you will believe me, my son,...the name shall be banished for ever from France....

To effect this, it was necessary to divide my confidence and the execution of my orders without giving it entirely to one single person, applying these different people to different spheres according to their diverse talents, which is perhaps the first and greatest gift that Princes can possess.

And for this art of knowing men, which will be so important to you...in all the occasions of your life, I will tell you, my son, that it is one that may be learnt, but cannot be taught.

Source: King Louis XIV, *A King's Lessons in Statecraft: Louis XIV, Letters to His Heir*, trans. Herbert Wilson (New York: Albert & Charles Boni, 1925).

- What does Louis XIV seem to consider the main risk for kings?
- What is his strategy for maximizing royal authority?

QUESTIONS FOR COMPARISON

1. Which of these texts recommends gathering as much power as possible into the hands of the ruler, and which recommends relying on subordinates?

2. None of these texts emphasizes defending a state/empire against foreign attack. Should that be interpreted as evidence that other concerns ranked higher for these authors? Or that defense of the realm was such an obvious duty that it went without saying? Or something else? Explain.

3. Most of these texts stress vigilance and self-discipline as essential characteristics for a ruler. What implications can be drawn from that?

CHRONOLOGY

1490s
Portuguese mariners settle São Tomé

1511
Portugese defeat the Muslim sultanate of Malacca

1520s–1540s
Silver strikes in Japan

1530s
Portuguese introduce sugar plantations in northeastern Brazil

1545–1558
Silver strikes in Mexico

1555
English Muscovy Company founded

1550s
Sultans of Aceh begin to compete with Portuguese spice merchants

1570s
Ming China requires everyone to pay taxes in silver

1560s
Ming China rescinds foreign trade band

1590s
Brazil leads world's sugar production

1602–1799
Dutch East India Company (VOC)

1609
Bank of Amsterdam founded

1621
Japanese silver production peaks

By 1640s
Sugar and slavery boom in Caribbean

1684–1715
Shipping from south China to Manila triples

The First Global Economy

1500 to 1800

JAKOB FUGGER (1459–1525) and Virji Vora (ca. 1590–1670) knew how to make money. When Fugger died, his net worth was equivalent to about 2 percent of Europe's total annual economic output. Vora's trading partners reckoned he was the richest man in the world. Both men had acquired the knowledge and contacts to take full advantage of two recent changes that came with the formation of a truly global web: rulers' growing need to borrow money for wars (discussed in Chapter 18) and the expanding scale of long-distance trade.

Fugger was the tenth of 11 children in a merchant family in Augsburg in southern Germany. At age 14, he was sent to represent his family's business in Venice, and he ended up living there for 14 years. Most of his older brothers died young, and he took over the family business, shifting its focus from textiles to mining. He invested in copper and silver mines all over central Europe and traded copper to markets as far away as Russia and India. He also invested in a successful voyage from Portugal to India that returned with cargoes of spices. But his core business was mining, and he eventually controlled most of Europe's copper output.

Global Trade Set within the Dutch East India Company's fort in its capital, Batavia (present-day Jakarta, Indonesia), this 1661 painting by a Dutch artist shows a market of global goods. Merchants from China, Bengal, Europe, and Batavia itself meet to buy and sell—just one of countless instances in which trade knitted the Global web closer together.

1720
British Parliament forbids the wearing and use of imported calico cloth

1760
Tacky's War in Jamaica threatens plantation regime

ca. 1750
China has enough silver in circulation to satisfy demand

1750–1800
Laborers' wages in Beijing, Delhi, and Florence bottom out

FOCUS QUESTIONS

1. What broad factors drove the increases in world population and economic growth between 1500 and 1800?

2. What evidence is there that economic growth in this period mainly benefited elites?

3. How did the spice, cotton, and silver trades help integrate the global economy?

4. What was the significance of the new business formats that emerged during this period?

5. Which world regions experienced commercial revolutions, and why?

Banking became another core business for Fugger. He made loans to dukes, emperors, and popes. He financed the rise of the house of Habsburg. He paid for the Pope's Swiss guards. Fugger earned interest on his loans and also the cooperation of the powerful, which he used to win control over more mines throughout Habsburg Europe. Mining, banking, and political influence underpinned Fugger's success.

A similar formula worked for Virji Vora a century and a half later. Trade, banking, and political influence underpinned his prosperity. He lived in Surat, in northwest India, and was probably a Jain. He first appears in the written record in 1619 and for the next half-century figured prominently in Indian commerce of almost every variety. Commodity trading was a core business for Vora. Documents record him either buying or selling cloth, silver, gold, mercury, lead, pearls, diamonds, rubies, ivory, tea, opium, indigo, coral, and many kinds of spices. His agents had offices in eight Indian cities and as far afield as Malacca in Southeast Asia and the shores of the Persian Gulf and the Red Sea. He was a master at cornering a market—buying up the entire supply of a certain

good and then reselling it on his own terms. He dominated trade with English, Dutch, and French merchants, who often complained of his business tactics.

Like Fugger, Vora was also a banker. He lent money to aristocrats of the Mughal court and to Mughal provincial governors. He lent to European traders, even while he competed with them. Like Fugger, he translated his banking role into favors from politically powerful people, both Mughal officials and those of the English East India Company.

Both Fugger and Vora became immensely rich at a time when—as we shall see—most people around them were poor and getting poorer. These men exploited their knowledge of distant markets and prices and their connections with rising political powers, taking advantage of opportunities presented by changes in the world economy.

This chapter takes up economic history in the sixteenth to the eighteenth centuries. It begins with some data about global population, economic growth, and welfare. It emphasizes the big changes—for example, the rise of long-distance trades in spices, cotton, and silver. It also emphasizes the innovative features of the world's economy, including business and financial organizations such as large-scale slave plantations, joint-stock companies, and banks. In focusing on long-distance trade and innovation, the chapter tilts toward the European experience, because Europeans, mainly Atlantic Europeans, specialized in intercontinental trade and in innovative business organizations. This was no accident: long-distance trade encouraged novel business formats, and novel business formats eased long-distance trade.

For all this economic history to make sense, we need to remember three points in particular. First, that for several millennia before 1500, Southwest Asia was the region most connected to the world's largest web—the Old World web. That region stood at the crossroads of connections among the northern half of Africa, South and Southeast Asia, Europe, and the Mediterranean. It lay close to the steppe corridor of Eurasia. But after the 1490s, as we've seen, all that changed, and Atlantic Europe became the best-connected place on Earth.

The second point to remember is that Atlantic European mariners and merchants had forged most of the intercontinental connections after 1490. This gave them an information edge that translated into more available technologies for adoption and more opportunities for profit based on knowledge of prices in different markets. This information edge, combined with the military advantage of shipboard cannon, goes far toward explaining the rising prominence of Atlantic European societies and states in global economic history after 1500. Atlantic Europeans were not richer than everyone else in 1500. But they, more than anyone else, changed the course of economic history in the three centuries after 1500. And, very gradually, their societies began to grow richer faster than others around the world. To put this another way, Atlantic Europeans took the lead in forming the Global web and knitting it together with trade. They derived greater wealth and power from it than anyone else between 1500 and 1800.

The third point to remember is that despite the long-distance trade and economic innovations, most people between 1500 and 1800 lived much as their ancestors had for centuries. Whether in China, Russia, West Africa, Scotland, or Peru, most people lived in villages, farmed for a living, ate most of what they produced, and rarely ventured far from home. Their economic existence—indeed, their entire existence—was precarious. It depended on the weather and the harvest, as well as the health of their animals (if they had any) and of the able-bodied members of their families. If they were free people, as most were, they turned over a bit of what their hard work produced to landlords or tax collectors, or both. The unfree—whether slaves, serfs, indentured laborers, or in some other bonded status—turned over most of what their work produced to lords and masters. Some of these people, both free and unfree, did additional work on the side, especially in the slack seasons of the farming year, perhaps making cloth or cutting timber. Few of them used money regularly, knew about the business empires of men like Fugger or Vora, or were aware of the commercial webs spanning the globe.

Of course, most people's lives were not exactly the same as their ancestors'. They might raise different crops or animals, perhaps ones newly introduced via the Columbian Exchange. Some technological improvements took place on farms during these three centuries—perhaps most importantly, in the means of draining swampland. A slightly larger proportion of farming families sold some of their harvest or even all of it. A few million people worked to produce spices, cotton, silk, sugar, tea, tobacco, or some other agricultural commodity that someone else traded to distant markets, a way of life rare among their ancestors. And a small but growing proportion did no farmwork and specialized in other tasks, such as spinning cotton or mining silver. But for most people alive before 1800, the routines of life changed little and slowly and remained centered on farming. Nonetheless, this chapter will focus on the new developments in economic life that changed the course of world history.

WORLD POPULATION AND THE GLOBAL ECONOMY

Despite some terrible demographic catastrophes, in the three centuries between 1500 and 1800 the global population more than doubled. Although slow by recent standards, this growth was faster than in any previous era of world history. Improvements in agriculture and food supply helped spark the **population surge**. The Columbian Exchange enabled farmers to raise crops well suited to their local environments that had not been available before, such as maize in Africa or wheat in the Americas. Minor improvements in agricultural technology or practice in some parts of the world also helped. But there were no transformative technical breakthroughs in food production anywhere.

A second reason for the surge was what one historian has called the "microbial unification of the world." As travelers spread pathogens around the globe, the resulting diseases at first had terrible consequences, most notably in the Americas. But over time, populations developed resistance to a wider array of infections than before. More infections became childhood diseases, endemic in communities and only rarely sparking epidemics. No one understood it at the time, but this process of biological adjustment was speeding up by 1700 or 1750.

As more infections became endemic, they killed children without immunities even if hard-won antibodies now protected more disease-experienced adults. As before, families knew to expect about half their children would die of disease before reaching adulthood. So they did their best to produce plenty of them. Fertility rates stayed high in most societies, while mortality diminished slightly between 1500 and 1800. Before 1800, medical improvements remained trivial everywhere in their demographic impact.

The table below gives a rough idea of the trajectory of world population growth over these three centuries. Bear in mind the figures are educated guesswork.

The sixteenth century, as we have seen, was catastrophic for many indigenous peoples. But elsewhere, as best we can judge, populations grew despite repeated epidemics and famines. In Europe and China, where the estimates are more reliable than elsewhere, that was clearly true. Population levels recovered from the losses of the fourteenth-century, such as the plague pandemic, and kept growing briskly.

But the seventeenth century saw slower growth due mainly to enormous disasters. In the Americas, the effects of imported and unfamiliar diseases such as smallpox, measles, influenza, and malaria were still making themselves felt. More broadly, the seventeenth century brought the chilliest and driest years of the Little Ice Age. The years between 1618 and 1697 were ones of recurrent crisis in food supplies, the result mainly of a cluster of volcanic eruptions and their "dust veils." Sharp cold snaps and repeated droughts led to crop failures and starvation, resulting in more epidemics (worsened by malnutrition) and more warfare than normal. Political violence spiked in China, where the invading Manchus battled the collapsing Ming dynasty; in Ottoman lands, unsettled by

internal rebellions; and in Europe, with its bloody religious wars and rebellions. In Gujarat and the Deccan, in India, an official Mughal chronicle described severe famines:

> [A] perfect drought prevailed. . . . High and low were clamouring for their bread and dying from sheer exhaustion. . . . The streets and marketplaces were so thronged by the immense number of corpses that [one] could scarcely make [one's] way through them.

Moreover, infanticide and suicide apparently peaked in several societies around the world during the seventeenth century. On a global basis, the 1640s were probably the worst decade for humankind since the plague pandemic of the 1340s.

A POPULATION LANDMARK

The eighteenth century, in contrast, brought faster population growth than our species had ever before experienced. China more than doubled its population, a result partly of the spread of American food crops such as sweet potatoes and maize, but also of a reduction in deadly epidemics and political violence. In the Americas, the ravages of introduced diseases abated, and millions of immigrants— mostly enslaved Africans—arrived. Europe's population increased by roughly 50 percent, with Ireland's growing the fastest. It more than doubled to about 5 million, fueled by the introduction of the potato from the Americas, a crop that suited Irish conditions well and allowed a family to survive—in poverty—on a small patch of land. The populations of India, Southwest Asia, and Africa grew more slowly—in Africa's case, probably by very little compared to China, the Americas, and Europe. Nobody knew it at the time, but in the eighteenth century the world began its modern rise of population that is still ongoing.

GLOBAL POPULATION GROWTH, 1500–1800		
DATE	**GLOBAL POPULATION**	**AVERAGE ANNUAL GROWTH RATE (ROUNDED)**
1500	438 million	
1600	556 million	0.25% (1500–1600)
1700	603 million	0.1% (1600–1700)
1800	950 million	0.6% (1700–1800)

Source: Angus Maddison, *The World Economy: Historical Statistics* (2003), 256.

From about 1750, if not a decade or two before, growth rates tilted upward at steeper and steeper rates through the late twentieth century, as we will see.

THE SIZE OF THE WORLD ECONOMY

The size of the world economy, the total value of goods and services produced, is called the **gross world product**, or GWP. We have only educated guesses of GWP, but by 1500 those estimates become more reliable.

So let's look at the numbers. The table below uses index numbers, with GWP in 1500 set at 100. (GWP in later years is presented relative to GWP in 1500—so a value of 150 in the year 1700 means the economy was 50 percent larger than in 1500.) In today's money, the size of the world economy in 1500 was about U.S. $250 billion, equivalent to that of Utah, Portugal, or New Zealand in 2023.

The world economy more than doubled in size between 1500 and 1800. It grew by about one-third in the sixteenth century, probably a record at that time. The seventeenth century, marked by crop failures, epidemics, and mass violence, posted a far weaker rate, but the eighteenth century showed resurgent growth.

The growth rates in GWP resemble those in global population. They should: most economic growth was merely the result of more people living and working. But some of it derived from small technical advances in farming and from more important ones in textile manufacturing, mining, and other arenas. A larger spur to economic growth came from the efficiencies of specialization and exchange, whereby more people than before were doing what they did best and trading the fruits of their labor for goods that others produced. After 1500, long-distance trade flourished as never before, quickened by the gradual extension of the Global web into almost every nook and cranny of the globe.

GROSS WORLD PRODUCT, 1500-1800

DATE	SIZE	AVERAGE ANNUAL GROWTH RATE (ROUNDED)	
1500	100		
1600	133	0.3%	(1500–1600)
1700	150	0.1%	(1600–1700)
1800	250	0.7%	(1700–1800)

Source: Elaborated from Angus Maddison, *The World Economy: Historical Statistics* (2003), 259.

THE DISTRIBUTION OF ECONOMIC BENEFITS

But the gains from expansion of trade and technical improvements mainly benefited a fortunate few. There are several ways to estimate how well off people were in the past. Two of the better methods use data on people's heights and incomes. They suggest that although societies collectively grew slightly richer between 1500 and 1800, most people did not.

INCREDIBLE SHRINKING HUMANS

Changes in the average heights of populations are a good indication of changes in the childhood nutrition and disease burden in a society. Well-fed and healthy children reach their genetic height potential. Malnourished ones ravaged by chronic disease don't. The raw data on stature generally come from archeology (skeletons) or, more often, records of military recruits. Let's consider some data from around the world on average heights.

The largest sample available comes from northern Europe: Scandinavia, the Netherlands, and Britain. These data in the table on page 646 show that on average northern Europeans shrank from medieval times until the late eighteenth century by nearly 3 inches (7.5 cm), with the fastest declines in the seventeenth through the eighteenth centuries. By 1800, northern Europeans were smaller than at any time before or since. This loss of stature is extreme in the annals of human height history. Populations in southern Germany (Bavaria), the Habsburg Empire, and northern Italy also shrank a bit between 1730 and 1780. We don't have earlier data for them.

In Russia, matters were apparently similar. The average height of military recruits, most of whom would not have come up to Peter the Great's armpit, fell during the eighteenth century by 2 inches (5 cm). These were glorious times for Russia's rulers and its elites, who managed to corral the benefits of a growing economy and territorial expansion, but times of grinding hunger and economic hardship for regular people. Russia, like many other places, grew richer as a whole and on average, yet at the same time more miserable for most people.

In Mexico, data on army recruits suggest the male population was shorter in 1840 than in 1740 by an average of 1.6 inches (4 cm). Argentine male heights shrank by

AVERAGE MALE HEIGHTS IN SAMPLES FROM NORTHERN EUROPE

PERIOD	AVERAGE HEIGHT
Ninth to eleventh century	173.4 centimeters (just over 5′8″)
Twelfth to fourteenth century	171.5 cm
Seventeenth to eighteenth century	167.5 cm
Eighteenth century	166.2 cm (just under 5′5″)

Source: Richard H. Steckel, "Health and Nutrition in the Pre-Industrial Era: Insights from a Millennium of Average Heights in Northern Europe," in *Living Standards in the Past: New Perspectives on Well-Being in Asia and Europe*, ed. Robert C. Allen, Tommy Bengtsson, and Martin Dribe (2005), 242.

Note: 1 inch = 2.54 cm

about half as much in the same years. In both countries, the population and economy grew while stature declined.

In Korea, the only East Asian society for which we have data prior to 1800, army recruits on average grew taller through the sixteenth century and the beginning of the seventeenth, despite the devastating Japanese invasion of the 1590s. But during the late seventeenth and early eighteenth centuries, recruits lost 1.6 inches (4 cm) in height on average.

All these cases of declining average heights reflect poorer nutrition and heavier burdens of stunting diseases. The main reason for these trends was probably lower protein supply for children. Urbanization may also have played a role: city folk everywhere averaged an inch or two shorter than their country cousins, again a reflection of nutrition and disease.

Army recruit records only pertain to men. If we had more data for women, they would probably show just as much, or even more, loss of stature during the period from 1500 to 1800. In most cultures, when families were short of food, they usually gave more to boys than to girls—as remains true today where food is scarce.

In British North America, the history of stature tells a different and happier story about nutrition and welfare. The population of European descent grew taller on average between 1710 and 1810, by about 0.8 inches (2 cm). British army recruits born and raised in North American colonies towered over their cousins born in Britain, by about 3 to 5 inches (7.5 to 13 cm) on average, an indication of the superior nutrition and health in the lands that would become the United States and Canada. Enslaved

people's average heights fell slightly before 1800 in the United States, but from 1800 to 1840 average male slave heights climbed 1.5 inches (4 cm) to 5′8½″, suggesting they benefited from improving nutrition in those decades.

Meanwhile, the nutrition experience of indigenous North Americans was mixed. Skeletons show that the Iroquois, Cherokee, Delaware, and Ottawa all grew taller, by about 2 to 3 inches (5 to 7.5 cm), between 1650 and 1800. President Thomas Jefferson, in 1804, upon meeting a delegation of Osage from the Kansas plains, wrote that they were "certainly the most gigantic men we have ever seen." While it is hard to imagine this reflected better nutrition, given the rough fate of indigenous North Americans in these years, it is either that or else short people and their genes (but not tall people) were ruthlessly weeded out by violence, hunger, and disease over 150 years—which is unlikely.

Improved protein supply probably played a role. To judge by their skeletons, the equestrian buffalo hunters of the plains were the tallest and healthiest populations anywhere in the Americas. Indeed, by the mid-nineteenth century, Plains Indians were the tallest people in the world for whom data exist, probably a reflection of a meat-rich diet. In contrast, indigenous Americans, especially males, who clustered around Spanish missions in California shrank in average height. That probably registers a change of boys' diet toward cereals and away from meat. Just as human populations in the deeper past shrank when they transitioned from hunting and foraging to farming, so,

Stature and Nutrition North American Plains Indians owed their tall stature to a protein-rich diet centered on game like buffalo. They were distinctive for their height as well as their nomadic hunting lifestyle, as this nineteenth-century romanticized painting by a German American artist suggests.

perhaps, the buffalo hunters of the plains grew in stature from an increasingly protein-rich diet.

While we don't have data yet for Africa, China, and India before the nineteenth century, it appears that the global trend—to which North America was an exception—was that people grew smaller even as economies grew larger. The benefits of expanding economies (outside of North America) seem to have flowed over-whelmingly to elites—while the standard of living for most people fell between 1500 and 1800.

FALLING INCOMES FOR WAGE LABORERS

The evidence on incomes for ordinary city folk supports this discouraging conclusion. In Beijing, Delhi, London, Amsterdam, and Florence (where long-term data exist), laborers' real incomes climbed during the fourteenth and fifteenth centuries. The plague pandemic of the 1340s had yielded one silver lining for survivors: the resulting scarcity of people drove wages up. Unskilled laborers earned three to four times what they required for subsistence in 1450, which meant each one could support a small family. But in the late fifteenth century, laborers' incomes began a long slide, which in Beijing, Delhi, and Florence bottomed out around the years 1750–1800. At that point, a laborer barely earned enough to feed one mouth, which meant in families everyone had to work. In Amsterdam and London, laborers' incomes slipped rather less; they climbed a bit in the seventeenth century, before falling again in the eighteenth. Everywhere, the constraints of an economy based on human and animal muscle meant that the great majority of people lived close to subsistence levels. Britain's North American colonies, again, were an exception to the dismal trend. In the mid-eighteenth century, unskilled free laborers in Boston and Phila-delphia earned four or five times what they needed for subsistence—more than anywhere else in the world for which data exist.

Why did ordinary people grow poorer while economies grew faster than ever before? At any time of large-scale economic reorganization, some people are better situated to benefit from change than others. Most of the economic growth from 1500 to 1800 created rewards for those involved in trade, finance, and government. Ordinary peasants and laborers, outside of a few favored locations

The Laboring Poor Peasants and laborers—ordinary people—were hit hardest by major environmental, demographic, and economic shifts. A seventeenth-century French painting depicts the realities of subsistence life for a peasant family: ragged clothing and a few empty pots and bowls.

such as eastern North America, saw their economic position weaken as their numbers grew.

TRADE

The burst of oceanic voyaging after the 1490s linked markets as never before. This created opportunities for buying cheap in one market and selling dear in another. To do this optimally, one needs more market knowledge than competitors have—exactly what the people who made the voyages acquired. These voyagers were mainly Atlantic Europeans, not the maritime traders of the East China Sea or the Indian Ocean, nor the caravan merchants of Iran or Central Asia, who by and large did not go global.

Certain trades, such as cotton, rewarded market knowledge more than others. You needed to know a lot to not lose your shirt in the cotton business. On the production side, some varieties of cotton plants produced better fiber than others. Spinners and weavers had several techniques for making yarns and cloths of different quality and cost. Different dyestuffs and printing methods produced an array of colors and patterns. And at every stage, spinners, weavers, and other workers had varying skill levels. So "cotton" amounted to dozens of different products.

On the demand side, communities of consumers had particular preferences, and these might change over time.

Cotton Production Technological advances and market know-how enabled Europeans to compete in the global cotton trade. In this painting, mid-seventeenth-century French peasants spin cotton on a spinning wheel and weave it into cloth on a large frame loom within their own cottage—the typical form of cotton production at the time.

During the early modern centuries, most Chinese markets valued plain white cotton. West African markets preferred vivid hues, while Latin American consumers paid more for floral motifs. But beneath these generalizations, specific villages and individuals had different preferences. Knowledge of these complexities helped people make money in the long-distance cotton trade. This favored literate people and those who actually did the voyaging and trading: they accumulated broader knowledge faster.

Atlantic Europeans had another important edge in long-distance trade, noted in the previous chapter. Their sturdy ships, built to withstand Atlantic gales, accommodated heavy cannon. European merchants active in oceanic trade almost always carried serious armament. They could fight back against pirates and hope to prevail. They could engage in piracy themselves when it suited them, attacking, say, Bengali or Malay ships and seizing their cargoes. They could threaten to bombard port cities until local princes and merchants offered their goods at lower prices. Well-armed ship captains could sell "protection" to the less well armed, allowing them to live in peace for a price. These twin advantages, in information and seaborne firepower, went a long way toward enriching Atlantic Europe's merchant classes.

Before 1500, the Indian Ocean world, from southern China to the Swahili coast, was the central arena of long-distance seaborne trade. The sea lanes of the Atlantic, the Baltic Sea, the North Sea, and the coasts as far south as Senegal were busy too, but not on the same scale. Regular transatlantic traffic began in the wake of Columbus, as we've seen, and the slave trade extended it to African coasts as far south as Angola and Mozambique. Almost all Atlantic trade took place in ships owned and operated by Atlantic Europeans. By the 1550s, this burgeoning Atlantic trade was increasingly linked to the Indian Ocean commerce. European merchants gradually got involved in the trade circuits of Indian Ocean and East Asian waters, although never outstripping Asian trading communities.

Three commodities accounted for a sizeable chunk of world trade during the early modern centuries: spices, cotton, and silver. While many other things (as well as millions of people) were traded, these three played central roles in tightening the commercial webs of the world, linking far-flung regions.

SPICES AND THE SPICE TRADE

Cooks have flavored food with spices for several thousand years. When people thought that good health rested on a proper balance of hot and cold influences, spices such as pepper, ginger, and cinnamon acquired reputations as health foods. (In fact, many spices are rich in micronutrients and antioxidants.) The lands that produced the most spices were the islands of Southeast Asia. Spices featured prominently in local diets, but more than 2,000 years ago they had also become staples in long-distance trade to

The Spice Trade The long-distance spice trade of the early modern centuries continues in the twenty-first century, supplying markets like this one in the Turkish city of Istanbul. It is called the Egyptian market, because in the sixteenth century spices came to Istanbul via Egypt.

The Spice Trade, ca. 1600 The spice trade had flowed along the maritime routes of the Indian Ocean world for millennia. The main production zones were Southeast Asian islands such as the Moluccas and Bandas, and eventually southwestern India. The biggest markets by 1600 were China, India, Southwest Asia, and Europe. Before the Portuguese voyages around the southern tip of Africa, spices had arrived in Europe overland via Ottoman territories. By 1600, the Ottomans were losing that trade to seagoing European merchants. The sultans of Aceh kept their grip on the trade passing west from the spice islands through the Straits of Malacca until 1600.

both India and China. Ancient Rome imported spices too, as did, later on, the Muslim caliphates based in Damascus and Baghdad, and Byzantine markets in Constantinople. Eventually, spices, especially peppers, were grown in south India as well as Southeast Asia. In addition to peppers, the most marketable spices included nutmeg, cinnamon, and cloves, valued for their flavor and purported medicinal value. The port cities of the Indian Ocean world, from Malacca to Basra, all had spice bazaars.

In 1400, China and India remained the chief markets for spices. Europe's supply, maybe 2,000 tons annually, came mainly via Egypt to Venice. Vasco da Gama sought a route to the Indian Ocean around Africa in the 1490s, with the backing of the Portuguese Crown, in part to cut out the middlemen in the **spice trade** and get to the source—Southeast Asia and India. An all-sea route lowered the price of spices in Europe, boosting demand. After da Gama's return in 1498, Lisbon soon became one of the world's great spice markets.

The best spices grew wild on islands such as the Moluccas and the Bandas, now parts of Indonesia. Much of the trade flowed through the port of Malacca, a great trading city with perhaps 100,000 people by 1500. Superior firepower enabled the Portuguese to defeat the Muslim sultanate of Malacca in 1511 with a force of only 1,200 men. This strategic conquest was the most important step in the Portuguese quest for a commanding position in the spice trade. Tomé Pires, a Portuguese who visited Malacca in 1511, wrote that one could hear 84 languages spoken on its streets on any given day. Its connections with northwest India were so strong that Pires wrote: "Melaka cannot survive without Cambay, nor Cambay without Melaka." Portuguese merchants now carried increasing shares of the trade not only to Lisbon but also to markets in India and China. The Portuguese language became the lingua franca of the spice trade. Superior market knowledge and naval firepower permitted tiny Portugal to engage in "pepper imperialism," as one historian called it.

The spice trade initially brought spectacular profits for merchants who survived the dangers of long sea voyages. When da Gama first arrived in India, the market price of pepper there was 4 percent of the price in Europe. In the Moluccas, spices could be had for 1/700 the Lisbon price. In the years from 1500 to 1630, an average of seven

Women in the Marketplace An engraving from a Dutch book of the late seventeenth century shows women involved in market transactions on the island of Java. In Southeast Asia, women often took part in market trading.

Portuguese ships set out each year for Asian spice markets. Storms, shipwrecks, and pirates claimed an average of three, but the surviving four brought magnificent profits.

The quantities of spices going to China, India, and Islamic lands remained greater than those headed to Europe. In the pepper trade, perhaps a quarter or a third went to Lisbon, while the rest found its way to Asian markets, often in Portuguese ships. For cloves, more expensive and profitable than pepper, the proportion (for the sixteenth century) was roughly 90 percent to Asia and 10 percent to Europe.

After 1550, the sultan of Aceh (on the northern end of Sumatra) sought to control the spice trade. With allies in Gujarati traders and even more distant Ottoman sultans, Aceh's sultans became formidable competitors for Portuguese merchants after 1550. With the sultans on their side, Ottoman merchants managed to garner a sizeable slice of the spice trade between 1560 and 1600. But Aceh and Ottoman traders acquired more competitors after 1590, when Dutch merchants, and soon English merchants too, tried to get a share of the business. By 1620, the Dutch and English between them sent about 10 ships laden with spices back to Europe annually, more than

twice what Portugal managed. The more competitive market meant less profit for everyone, but Dutch data show the spice trade returned an annual profit averaging 27 percent from 1602 to 1650. By the late seventeenth century, Amsterdam prices were only about 5 times Malacca prices for pepper and 15 times for cloves. The fabulous profits of the early years of the spice trade were gone forever. But more people were able to enjoy spices' flavors and healthful effects.

With their market knowledge and shipboard cannon, Portuguese, Dutch, and English merchants won a growing share of the world's spice trade after 1511. They cut Egyptian and Venetian middlemen out of the trade to Europe. By 1615, English merchants were trading pepper to Ottoman markets in the eastern Mediterranean, where a century before Venetians had purchased pepper to sell in Europe. Portuguese, Dutch, and English traders also carried spices from Southeast Asia to Japan, China, and India, competing with Malay, Gujarati, and other Asian merchants on their home turf. The spice trade continued to grow into the eighteenth century. But its relative importance in global trade dwindled as cotton became the staple of the long-distance trade between the Indian Ocean world and the Atlantic.

COTTON AND THE COTTON TRADE

Cotton grows only in lands where there are at least 200 frost-free days per year and either 20 inches (50 cm) of annual rainfall or irrigation water. The earliest evidence we have of cotton cultivation comes from the ancient Indus valley about 5,000 years ago. Its cultivation spread outside of India to Southwest Asia and Egypt mainly during the era of Islamic expansion, the eighth through the tenth centuries. But world production remained centered on India. Chinese farmers in the southeastern province of Fujian grew cotton too. When the Ming decided to accept cotton as a means of paying taxes in the fourteenth century, the crop spread widely in southern China.

Before 1450, cotton was raised, spun, and woven into cloth and traded chiefly in India and China. It was grown mainly on small farms, spun into thread by women and children in villages, and woven into cloth usually by men in village workshops. During the fifteenth through the seventeenth centuries, India's cotton farming and manufacturing were concentrated in the regions of Gujarat and Punjab, in northwest India, which specialized in cheap

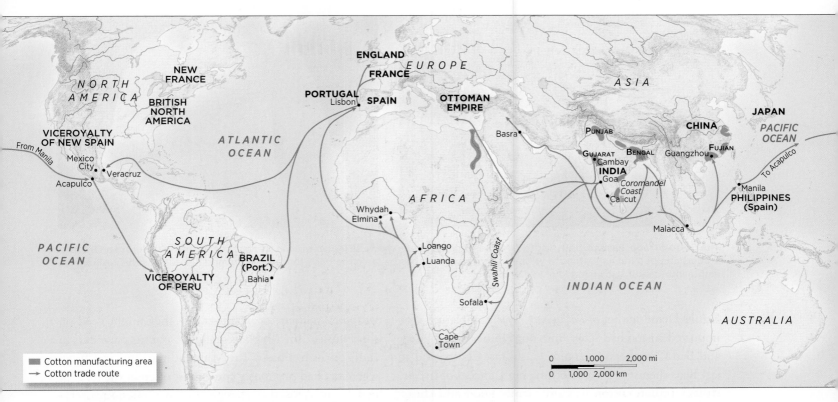

The Cotton Trade, ca. 1700 Cotton grew well in several zones around the world in 1700, but India was the biggest producer. With markets almost everywhere, cotton was one of the first truly global trade commodities. The seaborne circuits shown here include both transatlantic and transpacific routes to markets in the Americas. Southeast Asia, both East and West Africa, the Ottoman lands, and Atlantic Europe were also major importers of cotton.

cottons; in Coromandel, in the southeast; and in Bengal, in the northeast. Coromandel and Bengal specialized in fine muslins and high-quality printed cloth such as calicoes and chintzes.

High-quality cotton, like silk, was well suited for long-distance trade. It was lightweight and durable, and it could be folded or rolled into nearly any shape. In the fifteenth century it was valued from Japan to Spain to East Africa. Merchants traded it by land and sea, including along caravan routes of Asia, many of which were "cotton roads" as much as "Silk Roads." In the mid-seventeenth century, Iran imported 25 to 30 thousand camel loads of cotton annually from India.

As with spices, it was European oceanic merchants who most conspicuously expanded the scope of the world cotton trade. They carried it to new markets in Africa, Europe, and the Americas. They also competed with Asian traders carrying cotton from one Asian port to another.

In the course of the sixteenth century, the Atlantic slave trade came to involve cotton. West Africans already had a taste for Indian cottons, available at considerable cost via trans-Saharan routes from North Africa and Egypt. Between 1500 and 1800, some 50 to 60 percent of African imports in the slave trade were Indian cloth offered by Portuguese, Dutch, or English merchants. Of the roughly 8 million Africans bought for shipment to the Americas in those centuries, over 4 million were purchased with Indian textiles.

People in the Americas also bought Indian cotton goods. Cotton cloth, like Chinese silk and porcelain, crossed the Pacific to Spanish America via Manila and Acapulco. But it also came through Spain's ports and across the Atlantic. Women in Mexico City wore fine calicoes from India. According to one eighteenth-century account, even enslaved women in Veracruz (Mexico) wore skirts of embroidered muslin. Portuguese merchants sold Indian cotton cloth in Brazil.

European markets eventually bought more Asian cottons than did either Africa or the Americas. The Portuguese trade to Indian Ocean ports had initially focused on spices, but by 1620 textiles—mainly cotton—made up 60 percent of it (by value). In 1708, the English man of letters

The Cotton Trade Painted cloth from the Madras region of India shows an Indian woman (center) conversing with European traders. Traders shipped Indian textiles to western Europe, where they became the basis for luxury commodities such as this fashionable eighteenth-century gown made of Indian muslin.

Daniel Defoe (author of *Robinson Crusoe*) complained that imported cotton had "crept into our Houses, our Closets and Bed Chambers, Curtains, Cushions, Chairs, and at last Beds themselves were nothing but Calicoes or Indian stuffs." Indian cotton was sufficiently good and cheap that it menaced Europe's wool and linen business and put thousands of weavers out of work. Responding to weavers' riots and complaints voiced by men such as Defoe, France and Britain enacted tariffs and outright bans on Indian cloth imports, starting in the 1680s. In 1720, the British Parliament passed a law forbidding the use or wearing of imported calico cloth.

These protectionist measures spurred domestic cotton manufacturing industries in England and France, using imported raw cotton. By the 1760s, European cotton mills could compete successfully against Indian producers in African and American markets. Cotton was now a global business—one that, as much as anything else, brought the Indian and Atlantic Oceans into a unified trading world, providing a strong strand in the Global web.

SILVER AND THE SILVER TRADE

Silver became another major global trade commodity, but with a difference. It served primarily as money, whereas cotton was most often used for clothing and only occasionally as money. There were two main reasons for silver's expanded role. First, governments, always in need of revenue, found it advantageous to demand that taxes be paid in silver as opposed to grain, cotton, livestock, labor, or anything else. Silver gave them the flexibility to pay for

weapons, soldiers, or whatever else they might need on short notice. The Mughals gradually put tax payments in India on a silver basis. The Ming did the same in China, where tax had previously come most often in the form of rice. In the 1570s, they changed the laws to require everyone, even peasant families, to pay taxes in silver. A huge proportion of the world's population now needed silver.

The second reason for the rise of silver as a global commodity was that it solved a problem of mistrust that hampered long-distance trade. When people don't know

Silver Production An illustration of the *patio* process shows workers at a mine in Mexico refining silver on an industrial scale—producing the pure silver that was increasingly fueling the global economy. Transmission of the most efficient mining and ore-refining technologies of the day boosted silver output around the world.

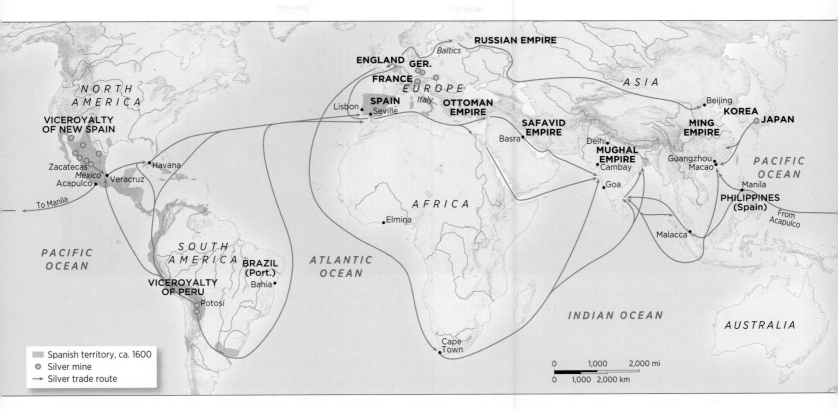

The Silver Trade, ca. 1600 Silver became a truly global commodity in the sixteenth century. The main silver-mining zones were in Japan, central Europe, and Spanish America—especially in Zacatecas (in Mexico) and at Potosí. Silver was crucial to the Spanish Empire's finances. However, it commanded a higher price in India and China than anywhere else, so silver flowed across land and sea to the Mughal and Ming Empires. Silver was so prized in China that it could bear the high transport costs across the length of Asia by overland caravan.

and trust one another, they need money that everyone trusts. In practice, the cash of the early modern world, as before, came in the form of precious metals such as gold, silver, and copper. In long-distance trade, silver emerged as the best option because copper wasn't valued enough, gold was too rare, and paper money or promises of future payment were unreliable.

The silver needed to keep governments going and long-distance trade humming came mainly from Spanish America, central Europe, and Japan. New silver strikes took place in Japan in the 1520s through the 1540s, in Mexico during the years 1545 through 1558, and the biggest of all—as we've seen—at Potosí (in today's Bolivia), high in the Andes, in 1545. In Japan, Chinese and Korean mining technology adopted in the 1550s improved the yield of silver veins. In the Americas, the latest German technology was applied in Mexico in the 1550s and at Potosí in the 1570s. Japan's mines adopted it, via Mexico, by 1580, leading to a peak in production from 1602 to 1630.

These technologies, especially the so-called **patio**

process in Spanish America, made it easier to separate silver from its surrounding rock, so lower-grade ores became worth mining. Japan in the sixteenth century mined about 30 percent of the world's silver, and in the seventeenth century about 15 percent. Spanish American mines produced a good deal more, and Potosí alone accounted for 60 percent of world silver production between 1550 and 1650. The transmission of technology along international circuits helped advance a silver mining boom on three continents. The effects enabled some monarchs to spend as never before and tightened the Global web through the enhanced use of silver in global trade.

FINANCING THE SPANISH AND JAPANESE STATES The rising tide of silver production floated the Spanish and Japanese states and tempted them to overreach. Despite Spain's small population (about 7 million) and poverty of natural resources, it became a great power in Europe and controlled much of the Americas and the Philippines after the mid-sixteenth century. In Europe,

Spanish Power A painting depicts the river port city of Seville at the height of Spanish power in the late sixteenth century. Seville's port played a key role in the silver trade that contributed mightily to the Spanish Crown's vast wealth.

the Spanish Crown—a branch of the Habsburg dynasty from 1519 to 1700—used its silver bonanza to fight endless wars and champion the Catholic effort to roll back Protestantism. Spanish monarchs also committed to continual warfare against the Ottomans (and Muslims more generally) in the Mediterranean. A Spanish friar writing in 1638 put it this way: "Potosí lives in order to serve the imposing aspirations of Spain: it serves to chastise the Turk, humble the Moor, make Flanders tremble and terrify England." By law, the Crown was entitled to one-fifth of all silver production in the Spanish Empire. At times, upward of 40 percent of Spain's government revenue came from Potosí alone.

The silver mountain's bounty peaked in the 1590s and slipped sharply after about 1640. Spanish kings managed to spend all the silver that crossed the Atlantic on royal account and then some. When pinched for funds after production started to fall, they sometimes grabbed private traders' silver as it came ashore. Felipe IV (r. 1621–1665) said, "Nothing do I regret more than having to seize silver." But he did it anyway to fight wars.

Similarly, in Japan, the military entrepreneurs who unified the country—Oda Nobunaga, Toyotomi Hideyoshi, and Tokugawa Ieyasu—financed their campaigns against rival warlords with silver. They converted the mines into a state monopoly exploiting convict labor. Silver revenues also helped pay for Hideyoshi's unsuccessful invasion of Korea in the 1590s. Like Habsburg Spain (and, for that matter, like Athens of the fifth century BCE),

Tokugawa Japan's hard power rested largely on military force supported by the yields of silver mines while they lasted. By 1640, Japan's silver production had shrunk to half its peak levels of 1621.

PROMOTING ECONOMIC GROWTH IN CHINA AND INDIA Most of the silver that was mined in Spanish America and Japan traveled around the world and eventually went to China or India. When both the Ming and the Mughals insisted on silver for tax payments in the sixteenth century, silver became more valuable in those lands than anywhere else. Anyone who could survive the risks of trading across the seas could do well exchanging silver for Indian cotton cloth and pepper, or Chinese silk and porcelain. As a Portuguese official in Macao put it in 1630, "When the Chinese smell silver, they will bring mountains of merchandise."

In the same year, a Ming scholar and official remarked that silver acquired through foreign trade resulted in massive exports, thereby ensuring "employment for weavers, potters, and merchants, whose waxing affluence augured higher standards of living for all." Around 1600, the kilns at the southern town of Jingdezhen employed more than 10,000 workers making ceramics for the court and for export. Meanwhile, silver imports boosted India's massive cloth exports and therefore employment for India's spinners and weavers. Silver flows helped to bolster both the Chinese and Indian economies—and world trade.

Chinese Ceramics The export of Chinese luxury goods, like this intricate Ming-era painted and enameled porcelain box, brought the silver needed for coinage and tax payments in China.

Merchants sent Japanese silver to China, often in Dutch or Portuguese ships because Japanese were officially forbidden to trade with foreigners. American silver flowed along many pathways. Some bullion crossed the Pacific via Acapulco to Manila in the Philippines, and on to China from there. In this way, Chinese silk and ceramics entered markets in Mexico and Spanish America generally. The bulk of American silver, however, crossed the Atlantic, usually via Cuba's main port of Havana, to Seville in Spain. But it did not rest there long. Some of Spain's incoming silver went to repay loans from Italian and German bankers, including the house of Fugger. After the 1560s, plenty of it went to finance Spain's army, which was at war with the Dutch. Once delivered to bankers or the Spanish army, American silver flowed through Ottoman lands, the Baltic, and Russia, or traveled in European ships sailing around Africa, always heading for India and China as if pulled by a magnetic attraction.

For two centuries, nothing produced in the rest of the world, except at times European cannon, interested Chinese and Indian merchants as much as silver. But by 1750 or so, China had enough silver in circulation to satisfy demand and reduce its price to about the same as the world price. Silver flows slowed and no longer quickened global commerce.

Silver, cotton, and spices: they could be produced only in some places but were in demand everywhere. They formed the lifeblood of global trade between 1500 and 1750, and they exemplify the process by which merchants connected far-flung markets in a global commercial web. Tea, sugar, silk, gold, ivory, and many other items—even dried fish—were traded across the oceans as well. So were millions of slaves. At any given time after 1550, hundreds of ships were sailing on well-traveled routes, linking ports such as Guangzhou, Manila, Cambay, Goa, Basra, Cape Town, Elmina, Seville, Amsterdam, London, Bahia, Havana, Acapulco, and many others. Year after year ships and cargoes sailed, tightening the web of global commerce.

NEW BUSINESS FORMATS: PLANTATIONS, COMPANIES, BANKS

The quickening pace of global commerce invited creative entrepreneurs to invent or refine the institutions through which they did business. Three of the most important in the early modern centuries were plantations, trading companies, and banks.

PLANTATIONS

An enslaved African on the Caribbean island of Barbados was quoted in 1676 as saying, "The devil was in the Englishman that he makes everything work; he makes the Negro work, he makes the horse work, the ass work, the wood work, the water work and the wind work." But it was not the devil that inspired Englishmen on Barbados to try to force everyone and everything to make sugar. It was the opportunity to get rich by selling sugar grown, harvested, and processed by enslaved labor on plantations.

Plantations are large-scale commercial farming operations with labor forces of dozens, or even thousands, of people—sometimes free wage workers, sometimes unfree laborers, and often both. They have existed here and there since ancient times. But the interconnected commercial world that developed after the 1490s improved

Sugar Plantations In this early nineteenth-century scene representing a sugar plantation in Antigua, a British Caribbean colony, enslaved men and women prepare the ground for planting. The world's sugar trade rested on the plantation system and slave labor. The windmill provided the power for a mill where mechanical rollers squeezed cane juice from harvested sugarcane.

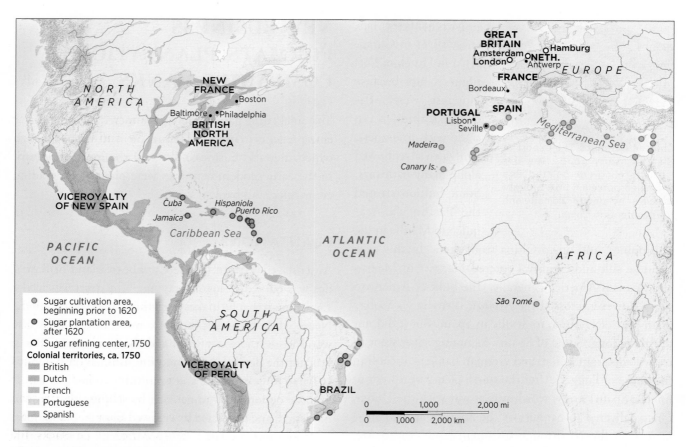

The Sugar Industry, ca. 1750 People had been cultivating sugar for millennia, but it became a major commodity, produced on plantations with slave labor, in the Mediterranean world around 1000 CE. In the sixteenth century, Portuguese and Spanish entrepreneurs brought sugar plantations into the Atlantic world, first to islands such as Madeira, the Canaries, and São Tomé, then across the ocean to the Caribbean and coastal Brazil. Sugar refining was concentrated in Hamburg, Amsterdam, and London, with smaller centers elsewhere in Europe and in British North America, especially Boston and Philadelphia.

the economic logic of plantations. When many markets were within reach, the rewards to large-scale production (known as **economies of scale**) multiplied. Nothing worked better as a plantation crop than sugar.

Sugar is a grass native to Southeast Asia. It will grow in tropical and subtropical latitudes where temperatures are warm for most of the year. It needs either abundant rain or irrigation, and fertile soils. In the harvest season, it needs a burst of labor. Its economies of scale came in the processes of milling and refining, in which juice is squeezed by rollers from sugar cane and then boiled into a goopy mass that dries into crystals. To make sugar pay, one needed to make big investments in land, labor, machinery, buildings, and other infrastructure. Sugar is rarely a small farmer's crop, and for the last thousand years it has been mainly a plantation crop.

Sugar was grown on a modest scale in China and India in ancient times. By 650 CE, it had appeared in Iraq and

Egypt. By 800, its cultivation had spread to several Mediterranean islands, southern (Islamic) Spain, and river valleys of Morocco. In the Muslim lands of the Mediterranean, enslaved captives—mainly from Christian Europe—formed the backbone of the sugar labor force. In Morocco by 1450, entrepreneurs and emirs imported enslaved West Africans across the Sahara to work on sugar plantations. Portuguese and Spaniards bought Africans to work sugar on Atlantic islands such as Madeira, the Canaries, and São Tomé.

THE SPREAD OF THE SUGAR PLANTATION São Tomé, in the Gulf of Guinea, pointed the way toward a large-scale slave-and-sugar complex. Portuguese mariners settled the formerly uninhabited island in the 1490s. Its volcanic, nutrient-rich soils and rainy climate proved ideal for sugar. By the 1550s, the island's economy focused so tightly on sugar that it raised too little food for its population. Merchants brought food from Portugal, a month away by sail. The plantations required a constant influx of people—slaves from Kongo on the mainland of Africa, and settlers, often unwilling migrants whom the Portuguese Crown was happy to deport: mostly Portuguese Jews, debtors, and criminals. For nearly half a century, São Tomé served as the leading example of a new business format, the large-scale slave plantation.

In the 1530s, Portuguese businessmen took the plantation format to the northeast of Brazil. There they found good soils and climate for sugar cultivation, but a shortage of labor. They tried enslaving the indigenous population, but extremely high death rates from disease and maltreatment convinced them that the answer to their problem was massive imports of enslaved Africans. By the 1590s, Brazil led the world in sugar production. By the 1640s, the tandem of sugar and slavery was booming in the Caribbean too, where planters on Spanish, French, British, and Dutch islands all raised cane in quantity. Some Caribbean planters at first tried using enslaved Scots and Irish, but too few could be found. Next came indentured European laborers, who were bound to work for a fixed number of years in exchange for free passage across the Atlantic. But too few volunteered (or could be kidnapped), and once in the Caribbean they died fast from diseases such as yellow fever and malaria. So, as in Brazil, Caribbean planters turned to Atlantic Africa, where local merchants sold people in great numbers at advantageous prices. Thereafter, for 200 years, Brazil and the Caribbean led the world in sugar exports and slave imports.

SUGAR AND PLANTATION SLAVERY The **slave-and-sugar plantations** in Brazil and the Caribbean were a novel form of enterprise, far larger and more efficient than their predecessors in São Tomé or the Mediterranean. The plantations, at least on the smaller islands of the Caribbean such as Barbados, imported most of their food from afar, as had São Tomé—so they could specialize on one product, sugar. Plantations usually held between 100 and 500 slaves, and sugar districts supported the densest rural populations anywhere in the Americas. They were all located near the seacoasts because sugar was an export crop, destined for European markets in Lisbon, Seville, Bordeaux, Antwerp, Amsterdam, or London—and after 1730 or so also North American ones such as Baltimore, Philadelphia, or Boston. They were often enormously profitable for planters.

Sugar profits rested on a double exploitation. Sugar monoculture depleted soil nutrients, so planters periodically had to move to fresh fields, usually to forested land. In time, often about 50 to 75 years, plantations on smaller Caribbean islands became unprofitable due to nutrient loss, and the sugar industry gradually shifted to bigger islands such as Jamaica, Hispaniola, and Cuba. The big islands had more land and forests that, when burned, released nutrients into the soil from which bumper crops could spring for a few years.

The exploitation of people was more consequential. From 1550 to 1850, about half of the nearly 11 million Africans shipped across the Atlantic went to sugar plantations in Brazil and the Caribbean. The majority became field slaves who worked long hours in labor gangs overseen by armed men. During the harvest and milling seasons, men, women, and children worked around the clock with scant rest. A combination of strenuous work, brutality, and a lethal disease environment made sugar plantations notoriously unhealthy and contributed to the short life expectancy of enslaved people on these plantations: shorter than anywhere else in the Americas, averaging about 10 years after arrival for those born in Africa. (Free blacks' life expectancy was marginally longer, indentured Europeans' slightly shorter.) Among those enslaved on sugar plantations, deaths outstripped births until the mid-nineteenth century. So, after more than two centuries of continuous slave trading that brought 5.5 million Africans to Brazilian and Caribbean sugar plantations, their total population in 1790 stood at about 2 million people, 90 to 95 percent of them enslaved.

Brutality stood at the core of sugar-plantation society. Masters and overseers resorted to violence and the threat of violence as the chief means of enforcing discipline among the labor force. Thomas Thistlewood, an overseer on a Jamaican plantation starting in 1750, left a diary in which he detailed the various punishments and tortures he inflicted. His diary also recounts sexual exploitation of enslaved women. Thistlewood's conduct was not unusual for overseers and slave masters. Their brutalities were calculated to make slaves choose obedience over defiance. That calculation worked most but not all of the time.

Occasionally, enslaved people risked everything on attempts to escape or rebel. In 1760, some 1,500 slaves, led by Akan-speakers from what is now Ghana, tried to take over the island of Jamaica. **Tacky's War**, as it is called, lasted a few months and shook the foundations of the plantation regime on that island. As we've seen, in northeast Brazil a community of fugitives, Palmares, managed to defend its independence from about 1600 to the 1690s. The greatest of all slave risings took place in the 1790s in the French sugar colony of Saint-Domingue, as we will see in Chapter 20. By and large, on the smaller islands successful escape was less likely and recapture was more common than on bigger islands or in Brazil, where large and sparsely populated forests beckoned those yearning to flee the plantation.

Other crops in the Americas, notably tobacco, cotton, rice, and indigo, would also be produced on the plantation model. The particulars varied from place to place and from crop to crop. But plantation owners all used slave labor, relied heavily on terror for labor discipline, systematically sought economies of scale, and filled distant markets with their products. By the mid-eighteenth century, some of the richest men in the world made their money this way.

CHARTERED JOINT-STOCK COMPANIES

The commercial opportunities of the Global web offered economies of scale in long-distance trade as well as in cash-crop production. Just as the slave plantation brought new levels of efficiency, human suffering, and profit to the business of sugar production, so the joint-stock company did for oceanic trade.

Intercontinental shipping was risky business. Storms, pirates, disease outbreaks, and other hazards could ruin any voyage. To make business sense, ventures needed to be big: big enough to fight off pirates, negotiate bulk discounts on trade goods, and ensure that *some* ships would surely survive a storm. Despatching a fleet made better business sense than sending a lone ship.

To achieve economies of scale in long-distance trade, merchants found ways to cooperate and pool their resources. Traders and businessmen had done this for millennia, usually with family members or close friends because mutual trust was crucial. These kin-based concerns could be gigantic, like the Zheng family operations along the coast of China or the merchant empire of Virji Vora in India.

COMPANY ORIGINS During the sixteenth century, more anonymous forms of partnership developed to spread and share the risks of long-distance trade. Some

Stock Exchanges The Dutch painter Emanuel de Witte made this painting of the Beurs, or Amsterdam stock exchange, in 1653. Investors met in this busy courtyard to trade shares in increasingly popular and profitable joint-stock companies.

were chartered companies, granted monopoly rights over certain trades by governments. Others were joint-stock companies in which hundreds or thousands of investors might own shares, as in modern corporations. Some were both, such as the English Muscovy Company, founded in 1555, or the Levant Company, chartered by England's Queen Elizabeth in 1581 to conduct trade with Ottoman lands. All had professional managers. This was a business model that could expand to indefinite size more readily than the kin-based business empires of the Zhengs or Virji Vora.

The English pioneered **chartered joint-stock companies**. France and the Netherlands soon followed, and during the eighteenth century Spain, Denmark, and others did too. One of these organizations, the Hudson's Bay Company, begun in 1670 to handle the fur trade in Canada, still exists, albeit in much different form. The gold standard of chartered joint-stock trading companies was the **Dutch East India Company (VOC)**, founded in 1602, which we've already encountered in South Africa and in East Asian waters.

THE DUTCH EAST INDIA COMPANY (VOC) The VOC was a chartered joint-stock company, formed to share the risk of voyages to the spice islands of Indonesia. Voyages in the seventeenth century from Amsterdam to Indonesia and back typically took 200 to 300 days outbound, and more than 300 on the return. About 3 to 5 percent never returned, far better than the 40 percent rate for Portuguese ships in the sixteenth century.

The VOC proved a spectacular success for nearly 200 years. Between 1602 and 1796, the company sent nearly 5,000 ships around Africa to the Indian Ocean. They brought back some 2.5 million tons of trade goods and exchanged countless cargoes between Asian ports. Detailed records for a 300-ton ship, the *Ceulen*, which sailed from Java to Amsterdam in 1697, reveal something of the business. In addition to a crew of 105 seamen and 30 soldiers, it carried a cargo of Japanese copper, tin from Thailand, ceramics from China, aromatic wood, saltpeter, tea, ginger, nutmeg, cloves, cardamom, bird's nests, cotton, silk yarn—and black pepper equal to the ship's weight. The *Ceulen* was small as VOC ships went, less than one-third the size of a typical East Indiaman, as the biggest ships were called. The VOC's most lucrative trade was buying Indian cloth, usually with silver, and selling it for spices destined for European or Chinese markets. It also earned tidy profits carrying silver, silks, and other goods between Japan and China when those two countries discouraged their own subjects from venturing to sea. At its height, it employed 32,000 people in Asia and the Netherlands.

As part of its strategy, the VOC captured port cities. Many, such as Malacca in 1641, were seized from the Portuguese. The VOC built others, such as Cape Town, founded in 1652. It held dozens of fortified posts and at times had as many as 100 heavily armed merchant ships cruising Indian Ocean waters. By 1669, it had 50,000 employees, 10,000 soldiers, and a navy of 40 warships. It constituted a privately funded, state-sanctioned, maritime empire devoted to commercial gain, a smaller version of the Zheng family business empire but with more global reach and governmental support.

The VOC captains enjoyed a military edge in the Indonesian archipelago. VOC forces were frequently outnumbered, but rarely outgunned. Wherever they could maneuver their big floating fortresses, they could concentrate firepower enough to destroy a city in hours. To found their center of operations on Java, they destroyed a local town and rebuilt it as Batavia in 1619. In an effort to monopolize the clove and nutmeg trades in the 1620s,

VOC Conquests This detail of an illustration of VOC forces assaulting a local sultanate in the spice islands (part of Indonesia today) indicates the violent methods that the VOC often used to establish a foothold in lucrative trading locations.

VOC soldiers attempted to kill the entire population of the Banda Islands and replace them with loyal settlers. They tried to burn all pepper vines and clove or nutmeg trees not under their control to undermine their competition. They took part in a slave trade in Southeast Asia that specialized in the sale of women from the island of Bali.

In general, the VOC's business model consisted of using force or the threat of force to extract favorable terms of trade—preferably a monopoly—from local rulers and merchants. The approach was backed up with merciless punishment of anyone who traded with rivals. The centrality of violence to its business is captured in a letter from the governor general of the Dutch East Indies, Jan Pieterszoon Coen, in 1614 to the directors of the VOC. Coen, the man later responsible for the effort to exterminate the Banda Islanders, wrote: "You gentlemen ought to know from experience that trade in Asia should be conducted and maintained under the protection and with the aid of your own weapons, and those weapons must be wielded with the profits gained by the trade. So trade cannot be maintained without war, nor war without trade." Murderous violence half a world away was part of the price for adding a tasty pinch of nutmeg to millions of cakes, sauces, and glasses of cider.

This business strategy worked brilliantly for Coen and the VOC. Before it was liquidated amid a morass of corruption in 1799, the VOC averaged roughly 18 percent annual profit on the totality of its business. Other companies imitated its formula, most notably the English East India Company (EIC). But in its entire career, 1600 to

Dutch Colonists Some merchants settled down in VOC colonies—such as the Dutch merchant Pieter Cnoll, who managed trade in Batavia, the capital of the Dutch East Indies. Cnoll is shown here with his half-Dutch, half-Japanese wife, their children, and their servants.

1857, the EIC managed to carry only about one-fifth the goods traded by the VOC.

BANKS

As long-distance trade grew in volume and reach, businesses more often needed to finance their operations by borrowing money. They borrowed to mount large trading ventures that could realize economies of scale. They also borrowed to cover the period between their purchase of goods and the subsequent sale of those goods, which might be years in trade between Europe and Southeast Asia or China. So the demand for private finance grew dramatically after 1500.

New institutions evolved quickly in response to this demand and governments' constant need for cash to pay military expenses. Most notable among these institutions were modern banks, bond markets (in which people traded governments' debt), and stock exchanges (in which people traded shares of companies). All these institutions helped both governments and merchants get cash when they needed it and earn a return on their money when they didn't need cash.

LENDING AT INTEREST Of these institutions, the most important were banks. To have a flourishing banking sector, societies first had to discard the idea that lending money at interest was immoral. Hindu, Buddhist, Islamic, and Christian scripture and tradition include objections to the practice of charging interest, or too much interest, for loans. Jewish law prohibits lending at interest to fellow Jews, although not to others. Plato, Aristotle, Cicero, the Buddha, Jesus, Muhammad, and Aquinas all denounced lending at interest, and Confucius disdained money-grubbing of all sorts. Luther got his start railing against usury, and early Protestants generally regarded lending at interest as sinful. So robust banking required cultural change.

In Europe, the moral objections and legal prohibitions against lending at interest weakened in places such as northern Italy, where small family banks emerged as early as the thirteenth century, and Barcelona (northeastern Spain), where a city-owned bank appeared by 1381. Elsewhere in Europe, those objections eroded during the sixteenth and seventeenth centuries. The intellectual climate, in which old truths were subject to renewed questioning, combined with economic changes that heightened the demand for finance; probably both contributed to this cultural trend. Lending at interest gradually lost its taint among Protestants, and eventually Catholics as well, despite repeated papal pronouncements about the evils of usury.

The Bank of Amsterdam, founded in 1609, was the first modern bank. It attracted depositors, cleared debts, offered quick transactions, and maintained public trust by reliably allowing anyone to withdraw a deposit on demand. In 1609, at least 800 different coins circulated

Banking The Bank of Amsterdam, the first modern bank, was originally located inside the Amsterdam town hall—shown here in a 1672 painting.

CONSIDERING THE EVIDENCE

On the Circulation of Blood and Money

Usually, the value of a commodity drops when more of it is in circulation. However, as the gold and silver mined in the Americas became more plentiful in Europe, their value increased because more people demanded cold hard cash instead of accepting bartered goods. Some people even began shaving small slivers of metal off of coins before passing them on. Bankers and loan sharks simply lent the money they had in return for a larger amount of money later. Today, that difference is known as interest, but European theologians and politicians saw it as the sin of usury (i.e., lending at interest) that should be banned, or at least regulated. It seemed right to be paid for a hard day's work or a risky investment in overseas trade, but making money from money struck Christians and Muslims alike as immoral.

For the Italian scholar Bernardo Davanzati, usury was just one of the mischiefs people could make with money. In a 1588 lecture on coins, he described money as the lifeblood of states to illustrate why money must circulate to retain its value. Although a scientific description of blood circulation eluded Europeans until William Harvey published his research on the subject in 1628, it was commonly understood that blood moved through the heart and lungs to nourish the rest of the body. Over a century after Davanzati delivered his lecture, a British philosopher named John Toland translated it into English, introducing Davanzati's ideas to a new generation of thinkers and bankers on the other side of the continent. As the center of banking moved from Italy to England, so did the demand for ideas about how to deal with money problems.

Some grave and famous Authors have call'd Money the Sinews of War and Government; but, in my Opinion, it may be more properly stil'd the Second Blood thereof. [F]or as Blood, which is the Juice and Substance of Meat in the natural Body, does, by circulating out of the greater into the lesser Vessels, moisten all the Flesh, which drinks it up as parch'd Ground soaks Rain Water; so it nourishes and restores as much of it as was dri'd up and evaporated by the natural Heat: In like manner, Money,... does, by circulating out of the richer Purses into the poorer, furnish all the Nation.... From the poorer it returns again into the richer Purses; and thus circulating without Intermission, it preserves alive the Civil Body of the Common-wealth. Hence... every State must have a quantity of Money, as every Body a quantity of Blood to circulate therein. But as the Blood stopping in the Head or the larger Vessels puts the Body naturally into a Consumption, Dropsy, or Apoplexy, etc. so [if] all the Money be only in a few Hands, as in those of the rich for Example, the State falls unavoidably into Convulsions, and other dangerous Distempers.... We ought therefore to set a high Value upon the living Member of the Common-wealth, and to preserve it from those Mischiefs which usually befal it, when not carefully look'd after; such as Counterfeiting, Monopolizing, Simony [buying religious privileges], Usury, and the like, already decri'd, and known everywhere. But,... I shall now confine my Discourse only to ... debasing of Coin.

Source: Bernardo Davanzati, *A Discourse upon Coins,* trans. John Toland (London, 1696).

QUESTIONS FOR ANALYSIS

1. How is the circulation of money in a state like the circulation of blood in a body?
2. Why does Davanzati think that concentrating money in a few hands is dangerous?
3. Can you think of a reason why in the 1690s, after more than a century, a British thinker might bother to translate an Italian text on money?

in Amsterdam, including copper, silver, and gold coins from dozens of countries as far away as Japan. Doing business amid this diversity of money—like conducting conversations in 800 languages—was enormously inefficient. The city council of Amsterdam sought to solve this problem by creating a new bank that kept accounts of merchants' deposits and converted them to a single standard, at first a tally of who owed whom how much of an abstract accounting unit, called bank money. This practice reduced transaction costs and attracted yet more business to Amsterdam. The city required merchants to use the bank for all big transactions. Soon the bank routinely lent out more money than it held, a practice typical of modern banks called **fractional reserve banking**. This

Financial Power A detail of an illustration of Jacob Fugger's lavishly decorated house in Augsburg shows visitors bowing before the powerful merchant. Fugger is a key example of someone who leveraged the opportunities presented by long-distance trade and rulers' need for loans to amass vast wealth.

innovative practice had the effect of creating money in the form of credit; although if all depositors demanded their money at the same time, the bank would be unable to pay. To avoid this problem, any bank engaged in this practice had to maintain a solid reputation, as the Bank of Amsterdam did for nearly 200 years. Fractional reserve banking helped lubricate the wheels of commerce by making credit more easily available to merchants.

BANKNOTES AND CREDIT Banknotes boosted commerce too. The Bank of Amsterdam did not issue paper money. Other banks had tried and found customers mistrustful, often rightly so. Banks sometimes would print too many notes and then refuse to honor them. But the Bank of Sweden, in the 1670s, and then the Bank of England, founded in 1694, managed to win public trust in banknotes. They successfully lobbied for government monopoly rights on printing banknotes and issued them only in modest quantity. Both fractional reserve banking and the use of paper money—if trusted—expanded the amount of money in circulation and reduced the transaction costs of commerce.

Banks often found that their best customers were kings. As we've seen, the spiraling costs of warfare, navies, and standing armies put pressure on royal treasuries. Borrowing was one of the few solutions monarchs could find.

If the costs of, say, five years of military campaigns could be spread out over the next 50 years, then the need to raise taxes would not be so sharp, making tax revolts less likely. Early modern monarchs had every reason to wish to see healthy banking systems in their countries. The Habsburgs had relied heavily on the banking house of Fugger to attain and retain power.

In practice, northwestern European monarchs, and the Dutch Republic, had the most extensive banking systems to draw upon. Creditworthiness became a strategic asset for states: in the eighteenth century, bankers lent the British government money at half the rate they charged the French Crown. Indeed, the British government's reputation for repaying debts enabled it to spend as much on war in the eighteenth century as could the far larger Qing empire: it could borrow at low rates, and the Qing could not borrow at all. Banks kept kings and governments solvent, and kings and governments, if they paid their debts, helped keep banks profitable. Governments without access to banks or deemed poor credit risks by bankers struggled financially.

Large-scale plantations, joint-stock companies, and banks were among the new business formats that developed in response to the opportunities and challenges presented by the Global web. Partnerships and family-run businesses survived, of course. But they could not take full advantage of potential economies of scale in production, commerce, and finance that resulted from the newly global reach of ships, the connections among far-flung markets, and the frequent need for ready cash on the part of kings and merchants.

GLOBAL LINKS AND COMMERCIAL REVOLUTIONS

In eastern Canada in about 1680, a Mi'kmaq told a French priest, "In truth, my friend, the beaver does everything to perfection. He makes for us kettles, axes, swords, knives, and gives us drink and food without the trouble of cultivating the ground." By trapping beaver and selling fur, Mi'kmaqs and other indigenous Americans could buy an array of useful goods produced across the Atlantic in Europe. A Khoisan raising cattle in South Africa or a Dayak in Borneo gathering sandalwood might have

Chinese Commercial Revolution In this 1696 painting, a peasant and a water buffalo prepare the soil for rice planting. The poem in the upper left praises the farm tool depicted, which flattens the ground. New, intensive agricultural practices enabled late Ming and Qing China to become more commercialized.

said much the same thing. They all found advantages in taking part in global commerce, selling something they were good at producing in order to buy other things they could not easily produce. People had taken part in such exchanges for millennia before 1500. But now more people did so more often and over longer distances.

During the early modern centuries (1500–1800), the world's trade networks fused into one giant, but patchy, commercial web. Regular shipping linked places that had previously been isolated, such as some Pacific islands or southernmost Africa. Strong links emerged across the Atlantic where none had existed before, such as the trade routes between Mexico and Spain, or Angola and Brazil. New shipping lines also spanned the Pacific between Acapulco and Manila. Moreover, strong links developed where only weak ones had existed before, such as between South China and the Philippines or between Atlantic Europe and West Africa.

These links and shifts to a more commercial orientation touched some places more than others. The commercial transformation ran deepest in coastal China and Atlantic Europe, at the two ends of the Eurasian landmass.

CHINA

Between 1550 and 1800, China underwent a second **commercial revolution**. The first one had occurred during the Song dynasty (960–1279). The second one, under the late Ming and then the Qing, was something of an economic miracle. China doubled its population without impoverishing it. This was achieved partly by conquest of new lands, not only in Mongolia and Tibet (economically not all that helpful) but also in western Sichuan and other southwestern lands populated by non-Han minorities. China absorbed, killed off, or pushed out these peoples and put their lands to more intensive use with state-of-the-art agricultural technologies. This resulted in more rice paddies and millet fields, and less swampland, forestland, and grassland—consequently a bigger economy and more tax receipts for the emperors.

But even more than frontier conquest and territorial expansion, China built its economy through increased commercialization of both agriculture and manufacturing. Regions came to specialize more in certain products, such as tea or cotton, and to import their food from elsewhere in China or even from Vietnam. Most of this specialization and exchange took place within China. But some of it linked up to foreign markets, especially for silk and porcelain, swapped for silver.

The Ming and Qing governments held ambivalent views about foreign trade. Sometimes they tried to ban it, and sometimes they encouraged it. In the 1560s, the

Chinese Manufacturing Chinese goods manufactured in large industrial workshops, such as those in the town of Guangzhou, could be traded worldwide. Guangzhou's manufacturing district is shown here in an 1807 painting.

Ming rescinded an earlier ban, helping to create a surge in foreign trade. Restrictions returned, but under the Qing between the 1680s and 1760s foreign trade again generally met with official approval and grew swiftly. Shipping from South China to Manila tripled from 1684 to 1715, to some 20 ships per year. Silver imports increased nearly sixfold between 1728 and 1800, and manufacturing exports increased by a similar proportion. By 1800, some 10 percent of Chinese grain, 25 percent of cotton, 90 percent of silk, and 95 percent of tea was produced for markets, whether domestic or foreign. Only a few other spots in the world matched this degree of commercialization.

ATLANTIC EUROPE

One was Atlantic Europe, which also underwent a commercial revolution. Here, as in China, frontier expansion played a role. Some settlement and agricultural expansion took place in drained wetlands in Europe, especially in England, the Netherlands, and along Baltic shores in Prussia and Poland. But the main thrust came overseas. The plantation zones of Brazil and the Caribbean were under the control of Atlantic Europeans. By the 1690s, smaller plantation regions were taking shape in South Carolina (rice) and around the shores of Chesapeake Bay (tobacco). Most of the wealth squeezed from plantations enriched Atlantic Europeans.

But as in China, the heart of the commercial revolution in Atlantic Europe took place at home. Ever-larger shares of agricultural harvests went to nearby markets. In Atlantic Europe as a whole, the proportion of people working the land in 1500 was about 75 to 80 percent—less in the Netherlands, more in Iberia. By 1750, that proportion had fallen to about 60 percent, and in England and the Netherlands was well under half. Manufacturing (mostly textiles) and services made up the rest, both attuned almost entirely to market production. Market towns sprouted and financial centers, such as Antwerp, Amsterdam, and London, flourished. By 1600, even bulk items were traded over long distances, such as grain from Poland to Amsterdam or to north Italian cities.

This slow but steady march toward market societies in China and Atlantic Europe distinguished them from most of the rest of the world. Elsewhere, except in the plantation zones and India's cotton districts, markets and commercial production existed in pockets but did not pervade societies. This did not mean ordinary people in Atlantic Europe and coastal China were better off than those elsewhere. By and large they were not. But their societies were richer and included more prosperous families, generally merchant families and owners of agricultural estates. In Atlantic Europe, but less so in China, rulers became more responsive to the wishes of commercial elites. In the Dutch Republic, in fact, the rulers and the commercial elite were the same people.

OTHER REGIONS IN THE GLOBAL ECONOMY

India's connections also expanded after 1500, thanks above all to the cotton trade. They now reached to the Americas and West Africa, although rather thinly. The older links to Southeast Asia, East Africa, and Southwest Asia only strengthened, although some of the actual connecting was now done by European merchants, including the VOC. In general, India's position with respect to the world's webs changed less than coastal China's or Atlantic Europe's: it had long been tightly linked throughout the Indian Ocean trading world, by foreigners—Malays, Persians, and Arabs, mainly—as much as by Indian merchants, and that remained true after 1500, although the foreigners involved now sometimes included Europeans. Those parts of India where cotton growing, spinning, and weaving were concentrated—Gujarat and Bengal especially—became yet more commercial in orientation. So did Kerala, in the southwest, where peasants and landowners found that raising peppers for export and buying food was a preferable strategy to subsistence food production.

Europe east of the Elbe River also underwent a shift to a more commercial economy after 1500 or 1550. Landowners in Prussia, Poland-Lithuania, and Russia developed big grain-producing estates and sold their harvests to cities around the Baltic and in Atlantic Europe. Like the plantations of the Americas, these estates relied on forced labor. Peasants—called **serfs**—who were legally tied to the land and not free to leave increasingly were required to work several days a week on their landlord's estate. In Russia, serfs could also be bought and sold, and their legal status differed little from that of slaves in Brazil or the Caribbean. Landlords also monopolized the right to make alcohol from excess grain and sell it. Commercialization in eastern Europe was agrarian: it did not lead to rapid urban growth but to the proliferation of big estates, each one a world unto itself but with ties to ports and through them to overseas urban markets—again like the plantations of the Americas.

Southwest Asia before the 1490s had stood at the center of the Old World web, a crossroads of trade, travel, and information flows. Under Ottoman control by 1550, this region together with Egypt had long been among the most commercialized in the world—since the cloth workshops of ancient Sumer. By 1800, it was still closely linked to neighboring lands, and by sea to the Indian Ocean's ports. But the biggest flows of world trade now passed it by. The relative importance of caravan trade across the steppe lands of Asia declined, even if absolute quantities did not. Trade and information flows elsewhere in the world—across the Atlantic, for example, or between China and Southeast Asia—grew far faster than anything involving Southwest Asia. Its economic importance in the world dwindled, and its former advantages in access to information about distant markets and foreign technologies disappeared. In a sense, Atlantic Europe dethroned Southwest Asia between 1500 and 1800.

One indication of that change is the change in connections in which Africa was enmeshed. Before 1500, Africa's strongest linkages by far were with Southwest Asia, both by land via Egypt and by sea. But in the course of the next few centuries, while these older connections persisted, stronger ones developed linking Africa to Atlantic Europe and to India, mainly in the form of the slave and cotton trades.

Nonetheless, the bulk of Africa's economies, devoted to farming and pastoralism, bore little connection to the outside world except for the gradual spread of American food crops. Most families produced for themselves. Few sought to maximize production in the ways that Chinese or Indian cotton-producing peasants did in response to market incentives. The African entrepreneurs attuned to distant markets were mainly slave traders or in the elephant-hunting and ivory export business. They were just as ruthless profit-maximizers as Dutch VOC traders or Gujarati cotton merchants, but this culture of commercialism was a rarity in Africa. Where the violence and commercial opportunities of the slave trade did not intrude, African economic life was more stable, less dynamic and disruptive, and less market oriented than in either coastal China or Atlantic Europe.

The Americas, in contrast, became much more powerfully and disruptively connected to the wider world between 1500 and 1800. The plantation zones, the mining

The Fur Trade An 1845 watercolor depicts a white trapper, his indigenous wife, and their family navigating the waters of interior North America. Mixed families like this worked at the source— beaver ponds—of what was a transatlantic trade in furs.

regions, and the northern lands devoted to the fur trade were thoroughly enmeshed in the commercial web that now spanned the globe. By 1800, even some small-farming districts, such as those of southern New England, were substantially market oriented and took part in a transatlantic economy that extended not only to Atlantic Europe but to the Caribbean and West Africa too. Many of the indigenous peoples had also linked up to market economies, whether through the mines of the Spanish Empire, the fur trade of French North America, or a deerskin trade that thrived in the Carolinas in the eighteenth century. Only a few people in 1800, maybe 2 to 4 million in all the Americas, conducted their economic lives locally without reference to distant markets.

This patchiness of the global economic web carried consequences that we will return to in later chapters. The most momentous of them flowed from the fact that by the late eighteenth century the most connected place of all—not the happiest, not the most just, not the best in any moral sense, but the most connected—was Atlantic Europe.

CONCLUSION

In the three centuries after 1500, a true global economy developed for the first time in world history. Like all economic shifts, it benefited some and hurt others.

During these centuries, the world population and the world economy more than doubled in size. Some people, like Jakob Fugger and Virji Vora, became unimaginably rich by taking advantage of new opportunities in trade and banking. Most people, however, grew poorer over these centuries, as evidenced by data on both shrinking average heights and falling wages.

The most dramatic economic change in these centuries was the rise of transoceanic trading in commodities such as spices, cotton, and silver. All three had existed for many centuries on smaller scales, but now all three expanded in size and scope, flowing along the new circuits of global commerce. New business formats arose in response to the globalizing economy and to the growing financial distress of rulers. Plantations, joint-stock companies, and modern banks all fit the new realities. They could mobilize resources on a scale unavailable to most family businesses and partnerships.

The new global economy rewarded those people who could gather the most information about conditions, prices, and politics around the world. Such people could buy cheap and sell dear in different markets. Or they could lend money wisely—rather than to a prince about to be defeated or a merchant about to go broke. Such people might live almost anywhere, including in Augsburg and Surat, like Fugger and Vora. But, increasingly, they were likelier to be found in Atlantic Europe. Flows of information and goods combined to make Atlantic Europe's economy, by 1800 and probably by 1750 if not 1700, more innovative, dynamic, and disruptive than that of anywhere else, including the other parts of Europe. The next century and a half of world history, from roughly 1750 until 1918, may be seen in many ways. But one of those ways is as an age of Atlantic European preeminence.

CHAPTER REVIEW

KEY TERMS

population surge
  (p. 643)

gross world product
  (p. 645)

spice (p. 649)

cotton (p. 650)

silver trade (p. 652)

patío process (p. 653)

economies of scale
  (p. 656)

slave-and-sugar
  plantations (p. 657)

Tacky's War (p. 657)

chartered joint-
  stock companies
  (p. 658)

Dutch East India
  Company (VOC)
  (p. 658)

fractional reserve
  banking (p. 661)

commercial revolution
  (p. 663)

serfs (p. 664)

Go to INQUIZITIVE
to see what you've
learned—and learn what
you've missed—with
personalized feedback
along the way.

REVIEW QUESTIONS

1. What accounts for the rising prominence of Atlantic European societies in global economic history after 1500?

2. Why did the global population more than double between 1500 and 1800?

3. What spurred the massive growth of the world economy between 1500 and 1800?

4. Why did most ordinary people around the world grow smaller in stature while economies grew faster than ever before?

5. In what ways did European oceanic merchants change the scope of the spice and cotton trades?

6. Explain the two main reasons for silver's expanded role.

7. How and why did sugar profits rest on the exploitation of environments and people?

8. Describe the novel tactics merchants used to reduce the risks of long-distance trade beginning in the sixteenth century.

9. Who relied heavily on banks, and why?

10. What were the similarities and differences between the commercial revolutions in China and those in Atlantic Europe?

11. Compare how the global economic connections of India, eastern Europe, Southwest Asia, Africa, and the Americas changed after 1500.

12. What was the most dramatic economic change between 1500 and 1800?

FURTHER READING

Robert C. ALLEN, Tommy BENGTSSON, and Martin DRIBE, eds., *Living Standards in the Past: New Perspectives on Well-Being in Asia and Europe* (2005). A good source of information about consumption, wages, nutrition, and height for Eurasian populations.

Rafael DOBADO-GONZÁLEZ and Alfredo GARCÍA-HIERNAUX, eds., *The Fruits of the Early Globalization: An Iberian Perspective* (2021). This is a collection of essays by economic historians, with a lot on the silver and cotton trades.

Femme S. GAASTRA, *The Dutch East India Company: Expansion and Decline* (2003). Perhaps the best of several histories of the VOC.

Arturo GIRALDEZ, *The Age of Trade: The Manila Galleons and the Dawn of the Global Economy* (2015). An accessible account of world trade, and especially good on silver.

Geoffrey C. GUNN, *History without Borders: The Making of an Asian World Region, 1000–1800* (2011). A seriously scholarly economic history of the connections among Japan, China, and Southeast Asia.

Wim KLOOSTER, *The Dutch Moment: War, Trade, and Settlement in the Seventeenth-Century Atlantic World* (2016). A general study of the Dutch activities in North America, Brazil, and Africa with plenty on the economy.

Lodewijk PETRAM, *The World's First Stock Exchange* (2014). Explains how Amsterdam developed modern financial institutions in the seventeenth century.

Marjorie SHAFFER, *Pepper: A History of the World's Most Influential Spice* (2013). An enjoyable popular history of the early modern spice trade.

Zheng YANGWEN, *China on the Sea: How the Maritime World Shaped Modern China* (2012). The early chapters deal with the Ming and Qing regulation of overseas trade.

The Global Coffee Trade

COFFEE, A GOOD FRIEND TO MANY A STUDENT over the centuries, became a globally traded commodity after 1500—just like spices, sugar, silver, and cotton. The coffee tree or bush is native to northeastern Africa. By the fifteenth century, if not before, it was grown in Arabia. Muslim pilgrims to Mecca developed a taste for it, which they carried home. Within a century, markets for coffee emerged widely throughout the Muslim world, and soon after in Europe and the Americas. Together with coffee came the coffeehouse, a public space where people might converse, transact business, enjoy music, play chess or backgammon, and hear the latest news and gossip.

Sometimes religious and political authorities objected to coffee drinking or coffeehouses. Officials in Cairo tried suppress the consumption of coffee in 1511. In Venice in 1615, clergy condemned coffee as an invention of Satan and appealed to the Pope to ban it. (Pope Clement VIII sampled it, liked it, and gave it his blessing.) An Ottoman sultan in the 1620s decreed penalties for public coffee drinking: first, a beating; for a second offense, death via being sewn in a bag and tossed into the Bosporus. In 1675, coffeehouses in Britain were briefly banned as "seminaries of sedition." Eighteenth-century monarchs in Sweden and Prussia also tried to prevent coffee drinking in their countries.

SOURCE 19.1

The Introduction of Coffee to Cairo and Mecca from Yemen, mid-1500s

The most important early text on coffee was written by the Arab scholar Abd al Qadir al Jaziri around 1558. His view was that "where coffee is served there is grace and splendor, friendship and happiness." Below he offers a version of coffee's emergence as a popular drink in southwest Arabia—first among Sufis who needed to stay wakeful during all-night spiritual exercises, and then among the broader population. Islamic religious authorities had to decide whether the new drink, called *qahwa*, would be permissible or not. They issued legal judgments, called *fatwas*, on coffee.

COFFEE, COFFEEHOUSES, AND THE OPPOSITION

At the beginning of this [the sixteenth] century, the news reached us in Egypt that a drink, called *qahwa*, had spread in the Yemen and was being used by Sufi shaykhs and others to help them stay awake during their devotional exercises, which they perform according to their well-known Way (*'alā ṭarīqatihim al-mashhūra*). Then it reached us, some time later, that its appearance and spread there had been due to the efforts of the learned shaykh, imam, mufti, and Sufi Jamāl al-Dīn Abū 'Abd Allāh Muḥammad ibn Sa'īd, known as al-Dhabḥānī.... We heard that he had been in charge of the critical review of *fatwā*s in Aden, which at that time was a job whose holder decided whether *fatwā*s were sound or in need of revision, which he would indicate at the bottom of the document in his own hand. The reason for his introducing coffee, according to what we heard, was that some affair had forced him to leave Aden and go to Ethiopia, where he stayed for some time. [There] he found the people using *qahwa*, though he knew nothing of its characteristics. After he had returned to Aden, he fell ill, and remembering [*qahwa*], he drank it and benefited by it. He found that among its properties was that it drove away fatigue and lethargy, and brought to the body a certain sprightliness and vigor. In consequence, when he became a Sufi, he and other Sufis in Aden began to use the beverage made from it, as we have said. Then the whole people—both the learned and the common—followed [his example] in drinking it, seeking help in study and other vocations and crafts, so that it continued to spread.

[When we heard all this,] I wrote to one of our brothers in God, one of the people of learning and religion in Zabīd [a town in the Yemen], the jurist Jamāl al-Dīn Abū 'Abd Allāh Muḥammad ibn 'Abd al-Ghaffār Bā-'Alawī ... asking that he inform me of which of the people of learning and faith, people whose opinions are respected, drank it, and of its first appearance.... He answered: "I asked a group of elders in our country [about the appearance of coffee], the oldest of whom at present is my uncle, the jurist Wajīh al-Dīn 'Abd al-Raḥmān ibn Ibrāhīm al-'Alawī—a man over ninety—and he told me ... 'I was at the town of Aden, and there came to us some poor Sufi, who was making and drinking coffee, and who made it as well for the learned jurist Muḥammad Bā-Faḍl al-Ḥaḍramī, the highest jurist at the port of Aden, and for ... Muḥammad al-Dhabḥānī. These two drank it with a company of people, for whom their example was sufficient.'"

It is possible that al-Dhabḥānī was the first to introduce [coffee] to Aden, as he is reputed [to have done], or it is possible that someone else introduced it, but it is associated with him because it was he who was responsible for its emergence and spread. Al-Dhabḥānī died in the year 875 [A.D. 1470–71].

Source: Ralph S. Hattox, *Coffee and Coffeehouses: The Origins of a Social Beverage in the Medieval Near East* (Seattle: University of Washington Press, 1996).

- **According to this account, what were the attractions of coffee for the Sufi sheikh al-Dhabhani?**
- **Why might the introduction of coffee have been controversial?**

SOURCE 19.2

Controversy and Coffee Consumption in Istanbul, ca. 1570-1630

Istanbul, or Constantinople, was the capital of the Ottoman Empire and one of the world's biggest cities in the sixteenth and seventeenth centuries. Early in the sixteenth century, the Ottomans conquered the Arabian Peninsula and Egypt, strengthening their ties to the Arab lands. Appreciation of coffee, and unease about its consumption, spread quickly to Ottoman cities, especially Istanbul. The following account, written around 1635, is translated from the work of a major Ottoman historian, Ibrahim Pecevi (ca. 1574–1650). Pecevi was a careful chronicler of his own times and took pains to inform himself about earlier eras. (In the reading, *fetvas* is another word for *fatwas*. And Sultan Murad III was sultan of the Ottoman Empire from 1574 to 1595.)

Until the year 962 [1555], in the high, God-guarded capital city of Constantinople, as well as in the Ottoman lands generally, coffee and coffee-houses did not exist. About that year, a fellow called Hakam from Aleppo, and a wag called Shems from Damascus came to the city; they each opened a large shop in the district called Tahtalkale, and began to purvey coffee. These shops became meeting-places of a circle of pleasure-seekers and idlers, and also of some wits from among the men of letters and literati, and they used to meet in groups of about twenty or thirty. Some read books and fine writings, some were busy with backgammon and chess, some brought new poems and talked of literature. Those who used to spend a good deal of money on giving dinners for the sake of convivial entertainment, found that they could attain the joys of conviviality merely by spending an asper or two on the price of coffee. It reached such a point that all kinds of unemployed officers, judges and professors all seeking preferment, and corner-sitters with nothing to do proclaimed that there was no place like it for pleasure and relaxation, and filled it until there was no room to sit or stand. It became so famous that, besides the holders of high offices, even great men could not refrain from coming there. The Imams and muezzins and pious hypocrites said: "People have become addicts of the coffee house; nobody comes to the mosques!" The ulema said: "It is a house of evil deeds; it is better to go to the wine-tavern than there." The preachers in particular made great efforts to forbid it. The muftis, arguing that anything which is heated to the point of carbonization, that is, becomes charcoal, is unlawful, issued fetvas against it. In the time of Sultan Murad III, may God pardon him and have mercy on him, there were great interdictions and prohibitions, but certain persons made approaches to the chief of police and the captain of the watch about selling coffee from back-doors in side-alleys, in small and unobtrusive shops, and were allowed to do this.... After this time, it became so prevalent, that the ban was abandoned. The preachers and muftis now said that it does not get completely carbonized, and to drink it is therefore lawful. Among the ulema, the sheykhs, the viziers and the great, there was nobody left who did not drink it. It even reached such a point that the grand viziers built great coffee houses as investments, and began to rent them out at one or two gold pieces a day.

Source: Bernard Lewis, *Istanbul and the Civilization of the Ottoman Empire* (Norman: University of Oklahoma Press, 1963).

- **According to this source, why did coffee become popular in Istanbul?**
- **How did religious and political authorities respond to the sudden popularity of coffee? What does Pecevi seem to think about their responses?**

SOURCE 19.3

A European Visitor to Coffeehouses in Iraq, ca. 1605

Below is an excerpt from the travel book of Pedro Teixeira (ca. 1570–1650), a Portuguese adventurer and writer who traveled to China as a teenager; to India, Persia, and Southwest Asia in his thirties; and to Amazonia in his sixties. The excerpt below is from his account of Baghdad, astride the Tigris River, where he stayed early in the seventeenth century when the city was an Ottoman provincial capital. Teixeira finished his book, written in Portuguese, in 1610.

Amongst other public buildings, as I have said, is a coffee-house. Coffee is a vegetable of the size and appearance of little dry beans, brought from Arabia, prepared and sold in public houses built to that end; wherein all men who desire it meet to drink it, be they great or mean. They sit in order, and it is brought to them very hot, in porcelain cups holding four or five ounces each.... It is black and rather tasteless; and, although some good qualities are ascribed to it, none are proven. Only their custom induces them to meet here for conversation and use this for entertainment; and in order to attract custom there are here pretty boys, richly dressed, who serve the coffee and take the money; with music and other diversions. These places are chiefly frequented at night in summer, and by day in winter. This house is near the river, over which it has many windows, and two galleries, making it a very pleasant resort. There are others like it throughout Turkey and Persia.

Source: *The Travels of Pedro Teixeira; with His "Kings of Harmuz," and Extracts from His "Kings of Persia,"* trans. and annotated by William F. Sinclair, with further notes and introduction by Donald Ferguson (London: The Hakluyt Society, 1893).

- **Does it seem that Teixeira thought his Portuguese readers had encountered coffee before? Why or why not?**
- **What kinds of people drank coffee in Baghdad at this time, and were they the same sorts of people as were drinking it in Istanbul at the same time? Explain your response.**

SOURCE 19.4

The French Coffee Trade in Yemen, 1708–1709

Jean de la Roque (1661–1745) was the son of a merchant credited with introducing coffee to France in 1644. During the years 1708–1713 he twice traveled to the Arabian Peninsula to buy coffee in bulk, sailing from France all the way around Africa to get there. In the sixteenth through the nineteenth centuries, the port of Moka in Yemen, then under Ottoman control, flourished on account of its coffee trade. It is the source of the word *mocha* used to describe a variety of coffee.

Local traders gathered coffee grown both in Arabia and across the Red Sea in Ethiopia for export. De la Roque's account, *A Voyage to Arabia the Happy*, was published in French in 1716 and in English in 1726. (Arabia Felix, meaning "lucky Arabia" or "happy Arabia," was the name given to the southwest corner of the Arabian Peninsula by ancient Romans.)

[...]

I now return to the principal design of our Voyage, which was the buying up and lading of coffee for Europe. For this reason it may be necessary to give you some knowledge of the country that produces this far-fetched commodity....

[...]

The kingdom of Yemen only, of all the countries in Arabia, produces the coffee-tree, nor is it here to be found in great abundance, except in three principal cantons or divisions, namely Betelsaguy, Senan or Sanaa, and Galbany, from the name of three cities in the mountains; Sanaa passes for the capital of all the country....

We might at Aden have had the Galbany and Sanaa coffee, and without going far for it; but neither of them is so much esteemed as that of Betelsaguy. This consideration, and the hopes of finding coffee cheaper there, carried us to Moka: where having entered into a treaty with the governor, settled ourselves in a house in the town, and provided for the safety of our ships, we went to Betelsaguy, and took a house in that city also, for the better carrying on our trade, and getting the coffee....

In this city there is a large bazaar, or market for coffee, which takes up two great courts, having covered piazzas. Hither the Arabians of the country round about bring their coffee in sacks ...one camel carrying two sacks.

...[Y]ou must always pay ready money for what you buy, for the Arabians never trust; they make their payments in Mexican piasters.[1]...

They daily bring down coffee from the mountains to Betelsaguy.... The country people have got the way of bringing but little coffee when the price is not such as they would have it.

At Betelsaguy they buy up all their coffee for Turkey, the Turkish and Egyptian merchants come thither for that purpose, and load great quantities upon camels ...from hence it is conveyed to a small port on the Red Sea,...and stowed in boats, which carry it...to [Jidda], the port of Mecca.

From hence the coffee being put on board the Turkish vessels is brought to Suez, the last port lying at the bottom of the Red Sea....Here it is again laid upon camels, and transported into Egypt, and the other provinces of the Turkish Empire by the several caravans, or through the Mediterranean. And from Egypt has been brought all the coffee consumed in France, till we undertook this voyage to Arabia.

Our buying up of coffee made the market grow dearer [more expensive] every day, besides that the arrival of our ships at Moka had raised the price, which was high before, by reason of the great demands of the Egyptian and Turkish merchants.

As to the price in general, things are much altered; and it is easy to see that the consumption of coffee was never so great as it is at this present; for not above five and twenty years since, you might have had [coffee] weighing seven hundred and fifty pounds for ten or twelve piasters, for which you must give now at the rate of a hundred and fifteen, and sometimes more.

---

[1] In the early modern centuries, in many parts of the world the most trusted money was Mexican silver coins, widely regarded as likely to be pure silver.

Source: *A Voyage to Arabia the Happy by Way of the Eastern Ocean and the Streights of the Red-Sea* (Printed for G. Strahan at the Golden-Ball and R. Williamson near Gray's Inn-Gate, Holborn 1708).

- What evidence is there in this account that the coffee trade by 1708 had become a flourishing international business?
- What impact on Moka's coffee market did de la Roque's activities have?

SOURCE 19.5

Coffee in England, 1721

By 1650, London had some 300 coffeeshops. In England as elsewhere, coffee and coffeeshops became popular quickly—and also aroused objections on the part of religious and political authorities. In one of the first English-language treatises on coffee, *The Virtue and Use of Coffee, with Regard to the Plague and Other Infectious Distempers*, published in 1721, Richard Bradley (1688–1732) gave an account of its introduction into England. Bradley, a self-taught botanist, Cambridge University's first-ever professor of botany, and a member of the Royal Society, wrote books on gardening, cooking, the plague, and medicine. Alas, he greatly exaggerated coffee's medicinal powers.

And thus was the use of coffee first introduced amongst us. The cheapness of it, with the conveniences in this way of meeting (being preferable to those in taverns and ale-houses) soon increas'd its drinkers; and other coffee-houses were set up in most parts of the kingdom: so that, in a few years, it did not only gain a general esteem with us, but also became one of the most valuable commodities imported by the East-India and Turkey Companies.

We may here observe, that King Charles II, finding the daily increase of coffee-houses, and that at those places people were apt to talk too freely of the state, endeavour'd the suppressing of them: but the judges being consulted, they declared it could not be done by law; and only ended in laying a tax on them.

[...]

...It is an effectual remedy against worms in children; so that if the mother drinks frequently of it when she is with-child, the infant will not be troubled with worms, during its first years. 'Tis allowed to be a strong antihypnotick, greatly dissipating sleepy vapours, and fumes of wine.... The Dutch physicians commend the use of it in intermitting fevers, and hold it to be good against infection; and it is apparently the opinion of all physicians who have yet wrote concerning the plague, that such bodies whose spirits are the most overcome by fear, are the most subject to receive infections. And again, that the spirits must be refresh'd only by such liquors, or preparations, as will not promote inflammations. And of this nature, say they, is coffee, which by a right use supports the vital flame, and defends the body from pestilential infection....

The immense quantity of this fruit, which is yearly exported from this one country [Arabia] to other parts of the world, is almost incredible; which, as we are informed, is computed to be about a million of bushels, one year with another: and although it may seem unreasonable to believe, that this country alone should produce it in so great abundance (considering how small a quantity can be gathered from each single tree), yet with as much surprise we may admire how it is possible, that even the number of bushels I have mentioned should be sufficient to answer the vast demand for it; since it is certain, that besides the general esteem it has gained all over Europe, it is not less requested throughout Africa and Asia.

Hence we may reasonably conjecture what vast riches must be amass'd by these Arabs, seeing they are the proprietors of this commodity, and thereby command so great a part of the wealth of the most opulent countries.... But so prudent are its masters, that on no account will they suffer either plant or seed of it to come alive out of their dominions; taking great care to destroy the germinative faculty of those berries they send abroad, and inflicting the most severe punishments on such as shall attempt the transportation of any plants of it.

But notwithstanding this their extraordinary care and caution to preserve this plant peculiar to themselves, the Hollanders, some years ago, found means to furnish themselves with it, and have made a plantation of it about Batavia, in the island of Java, which has already produced some tons of fruit. From this plantation they have lately brought two trees to Amsterdam, which, by the skill of their ingenious gardener, flourish and bear fruit in such perfection, that several hundred plants have been raised there from seeds, ripened at that place; and which, from time to time, they transmit to Surinam, and such places in the West-Indies as are in their possession.

Source: Richard Bradley, *The Virtue and Use of Coffee, with Regard to the Plague and Other Infectious Distempers* (London: Printed by Eman, Matthews at the Bible in Pater-noster-row; and W. Mears, at the Lamb without Temple-Bar, 1721).

- According to Bradley, why did King Charles II want to ban coffee shops?
- What evidence can we find here of coffee as a global business?

QUESTIONS FOR COMPARISON

1. Considering the Islamic and Christian worlds together, what seem to be the main reasons that authorities were often tempted to ban coffee and coffeehouses?

2. What characteristics of coffee and coffeehouses led to it becoming a commodity traded across oceans? What properties, if any, did coffee share with silver, cotton, spices, and sugar?

PART 5

REVOLUTIONS

1640 TO 1920

The weaving of the Global web between 1450 and 1800, the subject of Part 4, had several revolutionary consequences. Some of them, such as the formation of a global economy and the advance of commercialization, were part of the process of web building itself. Others, no less revolutionary, were not. Part 5, which includes Chapters 20 through 24 and deals with the years 1640 to 1920, takes up some major transformations that followed—and to some degree, resulted from—the spinning of the Global web. They were all interconnected and overlapping.

Destruction of the Roehampton Estate, January 1832 An episode in the Jamaican slave revolt of 1831–1832, when some 60,000 enslaved people rose up against local planters and the British Army.

TRANSFORMATIONS: POLITICAL, ECONOMIC, SOCIAL

The first of these major transformations involved politics and violence. Several political revolutions reverberated throughout the world during these centuries, rearranging hierarchies but never—revolutionary rhetoric notwithstanding—eliminating them. The most consequential of these political revolutions took place around the shores of the Atlantic Ocean, in West Central Africa, western Europe, eastern North America, and Spanish America. They all shared some general features, although they led to different outcomes. Together, they established ambitions for self-rule that have resonated around the world ever since. They are the subject of Chapter 20.

The second transformation was, and remains, the most important: the industrial revolutions, the first of which took place in England. Several more followed, all of which changed the ways things were made, affected living conditions and health, reshuffled geopolitical relationships, and brought new impacts on the environment. At the heart of this economic transformation was a shift in energy regime—specifically, the widespread adoption of fossil fuels, beginning with coal. Industrialization included important changes in transport and communications, such as railroads, that sped up connections in the Global web. This transformation is the focus of Chapter 21.

The third transformation partly flowed from the second: it was a pair of liberations helped along by industrialization. The first of these, a partial liberation from disease and early death, translated into giant improvements in human health and life expectancy between 1750 and 1950. The other liberation was the abolition of legal slavery and serfdom, which began in the late eighteenth century. For thousands of years, most societies had recognized forced labor systems such as slavery or serfdom as legal and just. Then, from about 1780 to 1920, almost every society changed its laws on this. Some came to regard slavery or serfdom as immoral or a sign of backwardness. Others, such as the southern states of the United States, abandoned slavery only by force, after losing a war over it. But one way or another, slavery and serfdom were abolished, a dramatic departure from the patterns of the deeper past. In a sense, it is as if history was speeding up. Social changes—and big ones fundamental to the human condition, such as health and freedom—were now coming thick and fast, as Chapter 22 shows.

Chapter 23 considers nationalism and imperialism between 1800 and 1920. Both of these major developments were also helped along by industrialization. Nationalism, which is at root a sense of shared identity among the people of a nation-state, or people hoping to create one, was rare or nonexistent before 1600. After 1790, however, it emerged in several settings, and by 1900 was felt strongly by hundreds of millions of people around the world. Its emergence strengthened some countries, such as Japan, but weakened ethnically diverse empires, such as the Ottoman Empire. Nationalism together with industrialization made some societies far more formidable than others in economic and military terms. The strong took advantage of the weak, acquiring new territories and incorporating them as subordinate colonies in a political system that is often called modern imperialism. The Global web came to include ever more direct political relationships, as the most industrialized states—including Britain, France, and other European states, the United States, and Japan—built overseas empires in Asia, Africa, and the islands of the Pacific.

Empires provoked resistance. So did nationalism when it seemed to trample on other forms of identity. Several kinds of resistance, especially rebellions and political revolutions, shook the world between 1850 and 1920—the subject of Chapter 24. It first considers several uprisings against imperial power in the nineteenth century, from small-scale examples in the U.S. West and the Brazilian backcountry to giant struggles such as the Taiping Rebellion, the Indian Rebellion, and the U.S. Civil War. The chapter moves on to a threesome of large-scale political and social revolutions in the early twentieth century, in China, Mexico, and Russia.

In Part 5, we see some of the indirect effects of the formation of the Global web. Old certainties, such as the acceptability of slavery or of monarchical rule, came in for questioning. Old hierarchies and social orders sometimes now seemed unjust—or merely unfavorable to new coalitions of people who were acquiring the wealth, power, and ambition to change them. Meanwhile, industrialization and changes in health and labor regimes profoundly affected millions of people worldwide. Social and economic changes, such as the rise of commercial classes or the formation of an urban working class, were coming faster than ever. The foundations of longstanding political orders shook and often crumbled as a result, opening the door to new kinds of politics. That crumbling began in the Atlantic world.

CHRONOLOGY

1576
Establishment of
Portuguese trading
colony at Luanda

1649–1660
Commonwealth
and Protectorate
in Britain

1641–1649
British Civil Wars

1641–1660
Garcia II reigns
in Kongo

1661–1685
British Restoration

1665–1709
Fragmentation of
power in Kongo

1707
Union of Scotland
and England

ca. 1684–1706
Lifetime of
Beatriz Kimpa
Vita

1688–1689
Glorious Revolution

ca. 1743–1803
Lifetime of
Toussaint
L'Ouverture

Bourbon Reforms begin in Spanish America

1756–1763
Seven Years' War

1763–1765
Pontiac's War

Continental Congress assembles

1767
Britain imposes new
taxes on American
colonies

1764

1774

1775–1781
American
Revolution

1780–1783
Revolt in Andes led
by Túpac Amaru II

1793–1798
British troops fight Haitian revolutionaries

1790
Uprising in Sainte-Domingue

1789–1799
French
Revolution

1789
American
Constitution
adopted

1791–1804
Haitian
Revolution

1793
Jacobins end
elections;
French royal
family is executed

The Best and Worst of Times

ATLANTIC REVOLUTIONS

1640 to 1830

1799–1815
Napoleon Bonaparte heads French government, becomes emperor

1807–1814
Napoleon Bonaparte occupies Spain

1815
Spanish king sends large army to Colombia and Venezuela

1825
Formal recognition of Brazilian independence

1826
Spain's American empire is reduced to two islands

O n July 14, 1789, a crowd of 900 artisans and workers attacked a 400-year-old prison in eastern Paris. The Bastille, as it was known, had once held important political prisoners, including aristocratic enemies of French kings such as the satirical author Voltaire. As prisons went, it was a nice place, complete with a library—it held 389 books in 1787—a garden, and curtained windows in most cells. In the eighteenth century, the French Crown used the Bastille in its attempts to control unruly publishers—as a place to store books it had banned and printing presses it had seized. The Bastille had acquired public notoriety in part through banned, and therefore prized, memoirs of prisoners such as Henri Latude, a soldier and mathematics student who had done time for, among other things, sending a box of poison to the mistress of King Louis XV. But by the summer of 1789, the Bastille's best days were behind it: the expense of keeping it up seemed too great to those in charge of French finance, who hoped to close it. Its 82-man garrison guarded only four counterfeiters, two madmen, one nobleman accused by his family of sexual depravity—and 250 barrels of gunpowder. It was the gunpowder the crowd of 900 was after.

Atlantic Revolutions Haitian revolutionary guerilla fighters battle against French troops. The Haitian Revolution was one of a wave of revolutions that swept the Atlantic world in the late eighteenth century.

FOCUS QUESTIONS

1. In what ways was the Atlantic world becoming more densely connected after 1600?

2. What were the key similarities between the revolutions in Kongo and Britain in the seventeenth century?

3. What tensions between Britain and its American colonies led to the American Revolution?

4. What were the major outcomes of the French Revolution?

5. In what ways was the Haitian Revolution a distinctively Atlantic revolution?

6. What tensions contributed to the wave of revolutions in Spanish America?

7. What features did all of these Atlantic revolutions share?

At the cost of several dozen lives, the crowd fought its way into the Bastille, killed its governor (prison warden), liberated its surprised prisoners, and seized the gunpowder—igniting an urban uprising in Paris. The uprising grew into a revolution, and its opening act, the storming of the Bastille, became the pre-eminent symbol of liberation in France. A sharp-eyed businessman got permission to tear down the prison and sell its fragments, which then were taken on tours of France as icons of the toppling of an unjust despotism. July 14, Bastille Day, has been France's national holiday for over 140 years. But the Bastille was only one of several symbols, and the French Revolution only one of several Atlantic revolutions. Something was afoot around the shores of the Atlantic. This chapter explores six revolutions around the Atlantic and tries to explain both what they shared and each one's particular elements.

THE ATLANTIC WORLD IN GLOBAL PERSPECTIVE

As we've seen in recent chapters, a Global web formed in the centuries after 1500 as oceanic trade, travel, and biological and intellectual exchanges knitted the world together as never before. The process affected coastal communities, especially port cities, more than anywhere else. But it touched every society and every state involved in oceanic links.

The Atlantic world was forging new connections faster than anywhere else after 1600. New circuits of Atlantic trade reshuffled fortunes and misfortunes. Men and some women of modest origins became rich by trading slaves, sugar, cottons, indigo, wine, fish, and other goods. Those lifted by the new commerce wanted liberty to make more money faster than before, liberty in some cases to practice minority religions, and liberty in the form of guarantees against arbitrary measures by old political elites. To secure these liberties, they sought a greater political voice. Many of them, ironically, were slaveowners or slave traders who would never consider liberty for slaves.

The quests for new liberties developed alongside new political ideas. These ideas, often about freedom, sovereignty, and the sharing of power, spread with ships, sailors, and merchants from port to port. Coffeehouses and taverns, customhouses and dockyards witnessed arguments about tyranny and liberty. Where people could read, cheap pamphlets and newspapers as well as word of mouth served to spread the new political principles. Even if merchants, sailors, cobblers, peasants, and enslaved people did not agree on just what liberty or freedom might mean, increasing numbers of them felt that they had a right to more of it.

Outside the Atlantic world, the new oceanic connections proved less politically disruptive, for several reasons. In some cases, such as in Qing China or Mughal India, oceanic trade accounted for a smaller proportion of the economy as a whole than in most Atlantic societies. Some merchants grew rich in these lands, as we saw in Chapter 19; but overall they were few and weak compared to the thousands of landlords living off of rents paid by peasants, and the ruling elites living off of taxes or war loot. As long as these landlords could control their laborers and in turn supported the state, the basic arrangements of political life endured. Newly rich merchants had a tough time banding together as an interest group against such well-entrenched incumbents—landowners, bureaucrats, military castes, and imperial courts. Instead, they gradually joined the old elites, if they did not come from those groups to begin with.

In general, merchants around the Indian Ocean and the South China Sea were already plugged in to the circuits of power, the result of centuries-long negotiations with kings, sultans, emperors, and their bureaucrats. They had mastered the arts of securing political favors through generous gifts to rulers and savvy marriages of their daughters to princelings. They could reach their goals within the system and rarely wished to overthrow it.

Although they faced many challenges, the ruling elites in Tokugawa Japan, Qing China, Mughal India, and the Ottoman, Russian (Romanov), and Habsburg Empires proved adept enough at adjusting to a globalizing world to avoid revolutions before 1840. In these places, the underlying principle of monarchical rule survived intact. These ruling elites contained, co-opted, or destroyed rival coalitions of power in their own domains more successfully than did several of the old elites in the Atlantic world.

In some Atlantic societies, the new pressures and opportunities coming from the new circuits of commerce and ideas proved enough to spark revolution. In others, they didn't. To understand why, let's zoom in on specific Atlantic societies.

KONGO AND BRITAIN, 1640–1709

In the decades after 1640, the kingdom of Kongo in West Central Africa and the British kingdoms of England and Scotland experienced revolutions. After costly civil wars and eras of religious strife, by 1710 merchant elites in both settings had sharply reduced royal power and expanded their own.

CIVIL WAR AND REVOLUTION IN KONGO, 1640–1709

Kongo, as we've seen, was an African kingdom formed in the fourteenth and fifteenth centuries and centered on the south bank of the Congo River. Its subjects were mainly from an ethnolinguistic group called Bakongo and spoke a language called Kikongo. After 1483, its kings forged ties with Portuguese mariners to bolster royal power. That led to sustained trade links, Christianization of the royal lineage, expansionary warfare, and occasional reliance on Portuguese military power. It also led to one of the best-documented histories anywhere in sub-Saharan Africa before 1800. The Kongo elite left Portuguese-language documents from about 1520 onward, and European missionaries and traders who learned local languages, and took part in Kongo life, wrote down their observations and experiences beginning in about 1580, giving us a richer understanding of history here than in most places in Africa.

MONARCHY AND THE SLAVE TRADE Kongo kings maintained diplomatic relations with Catholic countries of Europe and with the Papacy. Their power rested on their ability to use Portuguese trade goods, including firearms, to maintain a military, win prestige, and buy and raid for slaves. The Kongo state also controlled other exports such as ivory and copper, and it maintained the firm loyalty of lineage heads who themselves controlled, at least loosely, the labor of the common people. Most of those people farmed cassava and maize, American food crops first acquired via Atlantic trade. The geographic base of royal power was the fertile, productive, and densely populated vicinity of the capital, São Salvador (today's M'banza-Kongo, in northernmost Angola). It was, by African standards, an unusually centralized state, thanks to the concentrated resources and population around the capital.

The **Kongo monarchy** was not hereditary but, in theory, elective. In practice, each time a king died a power struggle took place, often bringing brief civil wars, the winner of which became king. To stay alive and in power, kings had to

The Kingdom of Kongo, ca. 1640
One of many African kingdoms, Kongo took shape in the fourteenth and fifteenth centuries. Its rulers strengthened their grip through participation in Atlantic trade, especially by acquiring firearms from Portugal. When Portugal established a base at Luanda in 1576 and expanded its slave trade to Brazil, it gradually destabilized Kongo.

Portuguese Kongo By the late seventeenth century, the Portuguese colony based in Luanda in northern Kongo was itself a large planned city, as this image from the period suggests. Figures in the foreground highlight the centrality of the slave trade to the city's economy.

negotiate a challenging diplomatic and military landscape. They faced problems of internal cohesion, as in any kingdom, and border troubles, mainly to the east and south.

One particular challenge for Kongo's kings was to protect their subjects from enslavement. A large part of the kings' legitimacy and support depended on it. One king in the 1580s went so far as to ransom some of his subjects who had been enslaved and shipped to the offshore Portuguese sugar island of São Tomé. In Kongo society, subjects explicitly expected kings to protect them; if kings could not, their authority collapsed.

In this regard, the establishment in 1576 of a Portuguese trading colony just south of Kongo, at Luanda, created an enduring problem for Kongo kings. Portuguese slavers would happily buy subjects of Kongo. To protect their subjects, the kings needed income, weapons, and loyal followers—and to get all that, they had to continue to trade slaves on their own account. They tried hard to get them from neighboring societies or from the ranks of rebels within Kongo, and not from their own loyal subjects. They had succeeded in this while Kongo was expanding at the expense of neighbors, but by the 1590s, when expansion slowed and then ceased, kings of Kongo found it harder to trade people for the weapons they needed.

After 1590, most royal reigns in Kongo were short, and

many more Kongo subjects were captured in civil wars or rebellions and enslaved. Then a particularly skilled and lucky king, Garcia II, took over in 1641. When he acceded to the throne, his subjects spelled out their expectations: "You shall be king, be no thief, neither covetous nor revengeful, but be a friend of the poor: You shall also give alms for the release of prisoners or slaves." He ruled over roughly half a million people, most of them speakers of the Kikongo language. Garcia, a graduate of a Jesuit school in the capital city of São Salvador took power by force and constantly had to fight rebels to maintain his kingdom. His success represented a high point in the history of the Kongo monarchy. The stability of his reign allowed trade to prosper, boosting the fortunes of some of his lieutenants and supporters. Part of that trade was in people, generally captured or purchased on the frontiers of the kingdom. Like earlier kings of Kongo, Garcia II traded in slaves himself. On one occasion, he sold 700 slaves to the Dutch in exchange for an attack on Portugal's Luanda colony.

FRAGMENTATION OF POWER Things fell apart for Kongo soon after the death of Garcia II in 1660. His successor renewed war with Portuguese forces—made up mainly of African soldiers serving the Portuguese colonial governor in Luanda—and was killed together with most of his high-ranking followers in 1665. Various contenders for power emerged, many of them men who had become empowered and enriched by trade during Garcia's reign. For decades, none could vanquish all rivals, and Kongo fell into civil war. Neighboring states took advantage of the chaos to try to put their puppets on the throne. São Salvador was sacked several times.

The fragmentation of power had something to do with Kongo's Atlantic connections. Rival factions competed for alliances with the Portuguese and briefly with the Dutch. They tried to use European missionaries to

Kongo and the Atlantic This portrait of Kongolese diplomat Miguel de Castro shows him wearing Dutch garb. The portrait speaks to Kongo's embeddedness within the Atlantic world during the period.

bolster their authority. They struggled to win advantageous positions in the trade for foreign goods such as cloth, iron, and guns. That inspired them to try to monopolize exports of slaves, ivory, and copper. During the violent decades of fragmentation (1665–1709), the number of slaves exported from Kongo increased sharply, and Kongo warlord-entrepreneurs increasingly financed their quests for political power by capturing and selling their fellow Bakongo—which had rarely happened before the kingdom fell apart. In 1701, one Kongo warlord wrote a letter to the Pope asking permission to sell Kongo Catholics so he could afford to defend his territory. (There is no record of any papal response.) At this point, the old prohibition in Kongo against enslaving subjects of the kingdom had vanished, and all were at risk.

BEATRIZ KIMPA VITA'S MOVEMENT FOR REUNIFICATION A young woman inspired by a Christian saint tried to bring the chaos in Kongo to an end. **Beatriz Kimpa Vita**, born in about 1684 to a prominent Kongo family, sought to reunite the kingdom. Women had long played behind-the-scenes roles in Kongo politics, and after the breakdown of the kingdom following 1665, some took more direct parts in the ensuing power struggles. Beatriz was apparently a high-spirited youth who preferred to think for herself. Two early marriages did not work out, and in her late teenage years she became more interested in faith than husbands. She had some training in local religious traditions, but by 1700 or so felt more attracted by Catholicism. She soon felt possessed by the spirit of St. Anthony, a medieval Portuguese priest and the patron saint for the recovery of lost goods or people. She believed that Christ was unhappy with the fragmentation of Kongo and preached that it must be reunited. She approached two claimants to the throne, one after the other, but both declined her help. So she decided to do it herself.

She convinced thousands that God spoke through her and that all should work for the reunification of Kongo. She took the unorthodox view that Jesus, Mary, and other central figures in Christianity were all Bakongo, which offended European missionaries but won supporters in Kongo. By 1705, she and her followers had taken up residence among the ruins of São Salvador, where she established herself in the wreckage of the cathedral. One rival sent an army against her, but she converted its commander

and the wife of the would-be king who sent it. She had become a major force in Kongo politics by age 21, commanding strong loyalties among masses of poor people and an increasing number of prosperous ones.

Beatriz Kimpa Vita did not, however, command much of an army. Her religio-political movement threatened all other aspirants to power in Kongo, and in 1706 one of them launched his forces against her. She was captured, declared a witch and a heretic, and burned at the stake. Her followers were defeated in battle, and 30,000 of them sold into the Atlantic slave trade. By 1709, a much weaker Kongo was nominally under the control of a new king. In reality, the king had little authority, and local rulers held sway. Kongo became a highly decentralized polity with power residing in provincial families and warlords, not in the court or the king in São Salvador. Civil war, partly a routine power struggle and partly an outgrowth of changes brought on by Kongo's participation in the Atlantic world, especially the slave trade, destroyed the old kingdom of the Kongo and gave rise, after decades of violent anarchy, to a new, different, and weaker state. This was a revolution that constrained royal authority sharply and shifted power to local elites.

Beatriz Kimpa Vita and St. Anthony This brass pendant of St. Anthony of Padua was cast by a Kongo artist around the time that Beatriz Kimpa Vita sought to reunite the Kongo kingdom. St. Anthony was one of the most popular saints in the Catholic kingdom of Kongo, and he inspired Beatriz Kimpa Vita's reunification movement.

The old political principle undergirding the legitimacy of kings, one that obliged them to see to the security and welfare of their Bakongo subjects, was gone. After 1665, no one was secure, and anyone in Kongo might be enslaved. The political contract between ruler and ruled had changed. Kongo's troubles had loose parallels elsewhere.

THE BRITISH CIVIL WARS AND REVOLUTION, 1640–1707

Another land beset by religious strife and civil war was England. Here again **rising merchant classes** enriched by Atlantic trade were at the center of events. And here again they and their allies upset the structures of power, weakened kingly authority, and in the process put their country through a bloodbath. A charismatic religious zealot tried to unite the country—and briefly succeeded rather better than Beatriz Kimpa Vita in Kongo.

These events are traditionally called the English Civil War (or Civil Wars), lasting from 1641 to 1649, followed by the Commonwealth and Protectorate (1649–1660), the Restoration (1660–1685), and the Glorious Revolution (1688–1689). But because Scotland and Ireland took such a large part in these struggles, it makes more sense to see them as British Civil Wars or a British Revolution. At issue was how much power monarchs should have, whether there should be monarchs at all, and how much religious liberty to allow Britons, as well as the proper relation of Scotland and Ireland to England.

England and Wales in 1600 counted about 4 million inhabitants, mostly Protestant in religion. Both were ruled by a long-lived queen, Elizabeth I, who reigned with a strong hand, although not quite the iron fist favored by her father, Henry VIII. She consolidated the position of the Protestant religion in England, giving rise to what would become the Church of England (Anglicanism), headed by herself. Elizabeth lasted 44 years on the throne, providing stability. But she died, unmarried and childless, in 1603, the last monarch of the Tudor dynasty.

Her throne passed to her cousin James, a Scottish king from the Stuart dynasty, long in power in Scotland. James had keenly awaited this moment, because Scotland was a small kingdom with under a million inhabitants, most of them dirt-poor, and most of them Protestants

Elizabeth I of England Painted in 1588 at the height of her reign, this portrait depicts Elizabeth I surrounded by symbols of her country's rising naval power and its increasingly global reach.

of a Calvinist sort called Presbyterians. As James I of England, he would rule a much larger and richer kingdom. Ireland, recently conquered by England, came with his inheritance. Ireland was also poor, with a population of 2 million, almost all Catholics. The three kingdoms had long histories of warfare among them, and many of their subjects had strong attachments to their preferred sect of Christianity.

James balanced the interests of his three kingdoms reasonably successfully for a while, although a Catholic conspiracy tried to blow him up in 1605. In his later years, when he was drinking heavily and his health was slipping, he indulged his taste for arbitrary rule and alienated elites who felt entitled to a larger voice in political matters. He was a learned man, conversant in Latin and French, and liked to lecture everyone within earshot on the "absolute prerogative of kings." His biggest problem was finance: he needed the consent of **Parliament**—a legislative assembly partly elected by property owners (House of Commons) and partly composed of hereditary nobles (House of Lords)—to raise enough revenue. In 1625, James died, and his son Charles took the throne with a firm belief in the right of kings to rule as they pleased.

KING VERSUS PARLIAMENT Charles I (r. 1625–1649) came to power at age 24 and had not learned to play well with others. He quarreled with Parliament, which in 1628 officially forbade taxation without its consent. No one was willing to lend to the Crown. Desperate for money, Charles resorted to seizing property and selling it. To many of his subjects, he appeared too sympathetic to Catholics—his wife, a French princess, was one. He was less popular than his father, who had been less popular than Elizabeth. The monarchy's stock fell further when Charles tried to force the Scots Presbyterian Church to adopt a new prayer book based on Anglican tradition. Many Scots rose in rebellion. Now in urgent need of armies and money, Charles I could no longer ignore Parliament.

His timing could hardly have been worse. The entire seventeenth century in Britain was marked by rising prices and stagnant standards of living. Fuelwood and coal prices climbed especially fast. And the 1640s were one of the coldest decades of the Little Ice Age in Britain, with bad harvests and pervasive hunger. Ordinary people had plenty to complain about.

So did the more comfortable ones elected to Parliament. A torrent of complaints, mainly about royal

Sectarian Warfare in Ireland English anti-Catholic sentiment led to propaganda like this image, which suggested that Irish Catholics were routinely massacring Protestants—including women—at the instigation of their priests.

overreach, flooded the body when it met in 1640. Many in Parliament were Puritans, zealous Protestants who felt that bishops and royal power over the church were illegitimate. Compromise did not come easily to them. When an Irish rebellion flared up in 1641 and the king needed even more money and men, he could not get the cooperation he wanted. Soon both he and members of Parliament were recruiting their own armies, and by 1642 they were at war. The king set up his headquarters in a college of Oxford University.

Warfare now ravaged England as well as Ireland and Scotland. Allegiances were chaotic. Every county had its own civil war. Government control over religion vanished, and Ranters, Muggletonians, Diggers, Levellers, Quakers and—most of all—Adamites, fundamentalist nudists who held that true Christianity required wearing no more clothing than did Adam and Eve. But in general, English Catholics sided with the king, and Puritans with Parliament. The people of London, and the urban middle classes, tended to support Parliament. Royalists, as those loyal to the Crown were called, seemed to be getting the upper hand in the early 1640s, but Scottish armies helping the forces of Parliament turned the tide. King Charles was captured and in 1649 was tried for treason and publicly beheaded, maintaining to the end the right of kings to rule unhindered and that no court could try a king for any crime.

THE COMMONWEALTH

The victors set up a republic called the Commonwealth of England. It soon slid into military dictatorship, ruled by Oliver Cromwell. Cromwell, a parliamentarian and Puritan, distinguished himself in warfare against the royalists. Confident that God endorsed his every move, he was among those who signed the death warrant of King Charles. He led a brutal suppression of Ireland in 1649–1650 and managed to subdue Scotland by 1653. By force of arms he had achieved what kings could not: a unified Britain under the near-absolute power of one man. But his religious zealotry alienated all those who did not share his Puritanism. His persecution of Catholics in Ireland and Scotland bordered on genocide. After a while, many who had opposed Charles I and welcomed a republic began to think kings weren't so bad after all. The wars and their attendant epidemics and famines, between 1639 and 1653, cost England about 4 percent of its population, Scotland 6 percent, and Ireland a staggering 40 percent.

When Cromwell died of malaria in 1658, the republic gradually fell apart. After an interval of chaos, Parliament invited the son of the beheaded king to rule over England, Scotland, and Ireland as Charles II. He took the throne in 1661. His followers dug up Cromwell's body and beheaded it on the anniversary of the beheading of Charles I. Cromwell's severed head remained on display in London until 1685.

THE RESTORATION

The principle of monarchy was restored and endures to this day in Britain. But Parliament and the propertied classes it represented—landowners, merchants, lawyers, and others—had successfully asserted

Death Warrant of Charles I A detail of the death warrant that was signed by representatives of Parliament in 1648. Oliver Cromwell was among the 59 signatories.

their privileges. The monarchy from then on was weaker than it had been in Elizabeth's time, and it would weaken further. Cromwell's political revolution had been overturned, but the result was a decentralization of power. As in Kongo, the British Civil Wars weakened central authority; unlike Kongo, Britain restored internal peace—and exported only a few thousand of its people to the Americas as forced laborers, mostly Irish and Scottish vagrants and rebels.

King Charles II lived until 1685, devoting at least as much attention to his mistresses as to affairs of state. His younger brother, James II, was a Catholic, and his succession brought a new crisis. Once on the throne, James showed signs of trying to reestablish a more centralized monarchy and of treating religious minorities, chiefly Catholics, with toleration. But Protestant elites, fearful of what James might do, invited a Dutch aristocrat, William of Orange (who was married to James II's eldest daughter, Mary), to invade the country. Eager to improve the Dutch position against France in European geopolitics, William accepted the invitation, overthrowing his father-in-law in 1688–1689.

THE GLORIOUS REVOLUTION William's English allies, members of the Protestant elite, intended to prevent James II from solidifying royal power at their expense. In effect, they wanted to preserve the principles established in the wars between Parliament and king in the 1640s. Their remarkable act of conspiracy and treason became known as the **Glorious Revolution**. Almost bloodless, in sharp contrast to the wars of four decades before, it consolidated the position of Protestants in England and Scotland and the strength of Parliament with respect to monarchs. Parliament made it illegal for Catholics to ascend the throne, a law not changed until 2013. Partly to ensure that no Catholic could come to power and partly to rescue Scottish finances, in 1707 the parliaments of Scotland and England merged, forming the United Kingdom of Great Britain, ruled ever since by a single government seated in London. So Scotland lost its independence, joining Ireland as a lesser partner to England in the U.K.

The British Revolution, spanning the period 1640–1707, ultimately established the principle that Parliament ruled over England and Scotland. Kings and queens increasingly became symbols, sovereign only in name, while their ministers and the (adult male property-owning) people's representatives in Parliament governed. The British Revolution resulted in the triumph of both mercantile elites and landed gentry, but above all of Protestants, especially Anglicans, at the expense of Catholics, who were denied the right to serve in Parliament or as officers in the military. These arrangements at first inspired some rebellions, especially among Catholics in Scotland, which ended in 1746. The settlement of 1707 provided the basis for a stable polity in Great Britain for centuries to come.

NORTH AMERICA, 1750–1790

The British Civil Wars and Revolution left most British subjects with the impression that property-owning adult males should enjoy some political rights, and that government should be based on consent of the governed. Many who left Britain for North America brought these convictions with them. The literate and best-connected among them also kept in touch with friends and relatives in Britain, and a few, mostly merchants, had ties with other lands as well. As a result, they knew something of the political debates and struggles ongoing in Europe over the proper forms of government and the extent of royal power.

North America in 1750 remained home to a substantial, if falling, indigenous population, almost all of whom lived west of the Appalachians. These trans-Appalachian lands were claimed by Britain or France, but not yet occupied by either power except for a few small wooden forts. Despite their shrinking population, indigenous Americans remained in command here.

By 1750, North America's eastern seaboard was dominated demographically by European (mainly British) settlers and, south of Pennsylvania, enslaved people, all but a few of whom were at least partly of African descent. The region was dominated politically by Great Britain and included 14 British colonies, stretching from Nova Scotia to Georgia (Britain added Florida in 1763). The colonies' population was about 1.3 million—but growing fast. Migrants kept pouring in from Britain, and, to a lesser extent, Germany and elsewhere. Land was cheap, and free people, usually with enough to eat, were remarkably healthy. Families with 6 to 10 children were common. Even the most downtrodden, the enslaved population of the plantation colonies (South Carolina and Virginia chief among them), was growing through natural increase, reaching about 230,000 in 1750. French settlements along the St. Lawrence River, called Quebec or Canada, counted about 60,000 people, also growing quickly. Virginia was the biggest of all these colonies, with nearly half a million people in 1750, 40 percent of whom were enslaved.

In 1750, no one supposed that any of these colonies would soon become independent. None of the mainland colonies, not even Virginia, was as important to Britain as Jamaica or even tiny Barbados, with their profitable sugar plantations. The North American colonies were squabbling constantly. But within a quarter-century, 13 of them would be fighting for freedom from British rule.

GROWING TENSIONS WITH BRITAIN

Broad economic and social changes would lead some Americans to aspire to independence from Britain. Many of these changes came from Atlantic connections. Not only did colonists share in some of the political ideas in circulation in Britain, but trade links created prosperous elites with ambitions. In the southern colonies, rice and tobacco plantations, based on slave labor, supported a class of rich planters who considered themselves every bit as good as English aristocrats. In New England, New York, and Pennsylvania, successful merchants and professionals, including some whose fortunes came from slave trading, increasingly thought of themselves as equal to their counterparts in England and deserving of the same political rights.

That situation alone probably would not have led to anything much, but in 1754 a 22-year-old Virginian unintentionally started what would become the first global war. In the summer of that year, authorities in London instructed the colonies in North America to coordinate an effort to check French expansion west of the Appalachians. The colonial assembly in Virginia decided to send its militia, commanded by a youthful George Washington, into what is now western Pennsylvania. After he attacked a French post, Britain and France declared war on one another and eventually fought on three continents and the high seas in the Seven Years' War (1756–1763, sometimes called the

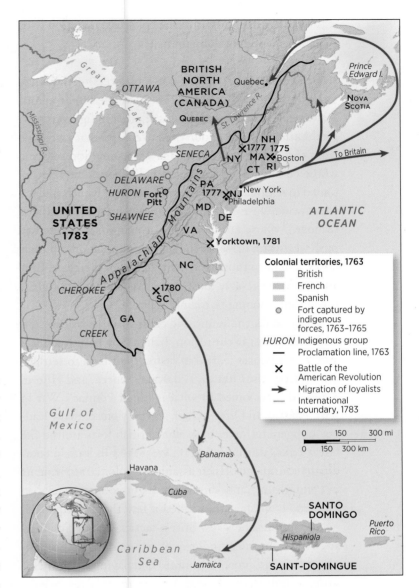

North America, 1750–1783 The peace settlement of the Seven Years' War (1756–1763) left Britain in nominal control of all eastern North America. France ceded all its territorial claims there, and Spain traded Florida for the return of Havana in Cuba and Manila in the Philippines. Indigenous populations, most of them west of the Appalachian Mountains, had no voice in the settlement. The grievances of American colonists grew steadily during the late 1760s and led to the American Revolution, which effectively ended with the siege of Yorktown. Thirteen of the British mainland colonies became independent as the United States. Spain recovered Florida for another 35 years, and thousands of loyalists fled the United States for British colonies in Canada or the Caribbean.

French and Indian War in the United States). Britain's superior sea power and better state finance enabled it to prevail, acquiring from France nominal title to lands west of the Appalachians.

But British victory led to new tensions in North America. Most of the British colonies soon felt that Britain was treating them unfairly. The colonials' irritation with Britain focused on two main issues.

INDIGENOUS LANDS First was access to the lands in the interior of North America, populated by Iroquois, Shawnee, Cherokee, and dozens of other indigenous peoples. Authorities in London tried to control that vast space from the Gulf Coast to Canada with some 500 soldiers, whose conduct alienated many indigenous chiefs accustomed to reasonably smooth relations with French traders. Meanwhile, the Euro-American population of the eastern seaboard, whose numbers were growing fast, wanted to push westward, drive the indigenous populations off their lands, and farm those lands or profit from their sale. Britain wanted to reserve most of the lands for their original inhabitants, hoping to maintain peace.

A large indigenous uprising confirmed the British concern over unrest in the region. Irritated by British soldiers and in some cases fearful of losing their land to settlers, groups from the Ottawa, Delaware, Seneca, and Huron, among others, joined in what is called Pontiac's War in 1763. Pontiac, an Ottawa chief, was only one of many leaders. Indigenous forces took eight British forts around the Great Lakes during the years 1763–1764 in loosely coordinated campaigns. Their assaults on colonial settlements in Pennsylvania and Virginia brought counterattacks on indigenous villages that killed a few thousand people, many in grotesque ways. British tactics included deliberately trying to infect indigenous populations with smallpox at Fort Pitt (now Pittsburgh) and paying a bounty for scalps of indigenous Americans over age 10, a response to the scalping of white children.

The conflict was a military standoff, but Pontiac and his followers won a significant political victory. In the early months of the struggle, the British issued a proclamation that designated North America, from the Appalachians to the Mississippi River and from Florida to Quebec, as an "Indian reserve." Negotiations ended **Pontiac's War** in 1764–1765, confirming indigenous rights to lands west of the Appalachians.

For many colonists, especially in Virginia, Pennsylvania, and New York, the settlement seemed a betrayal of their rights and interests by a distant king. The Crown, as they saw it, had taken the side of savages who had massacred hundreds of colonists, rather than allowing British subjects to occupy western lands. The king, or at least his ministers, had larger strategic interests to consider, and those were incompatible with colonial expansion sure to inflame indigenous resentment.

BRITISH TAXES The second issue was taxes. The British government in 1764 began to impose new taxes on the American colonies to help pay debts incurred in winning the Seven Years' War. After all, its armies and navy had protected the colonists from assaults by the French and their indigenous allies. Many colonials, however, saw the matter differently. After 1763, there was no French threat anymore. With no further need for British protection, the colonists didn't want to pay for it, especially considering that they had no representation in the British Parliament that decided upon taxes. This irritation at new taxes was gradually framed as a matter of principle: British subjects in North America should have the same rights as British subjects in Britain and therefore should be taxed only by their consent, by representative assemblies of their own choosing. "No taxation without representation" became a popular slogan.

Colonial Americans organized boycotts of sugar, tea, and official stamps newly required on newspapers, pamphlets, playing cards and other items on which Britain hoped to collect new taxes. Some proclaimed that they would be no better than slaves if they permitted themselves to be taxed with no say in the matter. In Boston especially, they rioted now and again, on one occasion dumping valuable cargoes of tea into the harbor in what became known as the Boston Tea Party. In 1768, the British government chose to send two army regiments to Boston to keep the peace. Ben Franklin, the Boston-born, Philadelphia-based printer and all-purpose intellectual, warned that this was as prudent as "setting up a smith's forge in a magazine of gunpowder."

And so it was. Frictions in Boston flared up into violence in the early 1770s. Along the coasts, the British Royal Navy fell into conflict with merchants and fishermen. British governors tried to keep colonists out of the "Indian reserve" but with little success. Virginia's governor, Lord Dunmore, complained that he could not "restrain the Americans [who] do and will [move west] as their avidity and restlessness incite them." Farmers in North Carolina who called themselves the Regulators refused to recognize British courts and tried to establish their own system of justice. From Massachusetts to Georgia, colonists who before 1763 could agree on nothing now agreed that they deserved the full "rights of Englishmen" and should not be taxed without their consent.

In 1774, their representatives came together in a new assembly called the Continental Congress. They petitioned Parliament to reconsider several of its policies. But fighting broke out around Boston in the spring of 1775 between local militias and British regiments, leading to six years of warfare.

THE AMERICAN REVOLUTION

The **American Revolution** (1775–1781) was a revolutionary war and a civil war. It was a revolutionary war in that the American forces—mainly poor men—were led by elites who sought fundamental political changes. In the summer of 1776, representatives of 13 colonies gathered in Philadelphia as the Second Continental Congress. The representatives cited grievances going back to 1764 and principles that separated just government, with the consent of the governed, from "absolute despotism." The second sentence of their Declaration of Independence reads: "We hold these truths to be self-evident, that all men are created equal, that they are endowed by their Creator with certain unalienable Rights, that among these are Life, Liberty and the pursuit of Happiness." The author of these words, Thomas Jefferson, owned about 200 people on his plantation in Virginia.

The American Revolution was a civil war in that about

Declaration of Independence An early draft of the Declaration of Independence, handwritten by Thomas Jefferson.

15 to 20 percent of Americans were loyalists who wanted to remain within the British Empire. Rebels and loyalists occasionally indulged in bloodbaths, especially in the Carolinas. It was an unpopular war in Britain, where most of the population wanted peace and favored making concessions to get it—as Britain had recently done in Pontiac's War.

KEYS TO AMERICAN VICTORY The war was a close contest. The Americans won because the fighting was an ocean away from Britain and because France, Spain, and the Netherlands all joined in against Britain. They provided the Americans with much of the money and engineering expertise they needed, 80% of the weaponry, and almost all the naval power. Their entry sapped political support for the war in Britain. The British Crown was mainly concerned about preserving its colonies in the Caribbean, its position in India, and its naval superiority in the waters close to Britain. The rebellious lands from Georgia to Massachusetts just weren't worth that much in comparison.

The Americans also won because their leaders, in particular George Washington, knew to fight a patient war. He avoided major battles, which the better-trained, better-armed, and better-disciplined British Army was almost sure to win. When he did get trapped in battle, he normally lost. His volunteer army sometimes threatened to melt away. Most of his foot soldiers had signed on for a cash enlistment bonus or the promise of land after

Revolution in North America In this French engraving, New Yorkers tear down a statue of King George III following approval of the Declaration of Independence in July 1776.

the war, and not for principles of representative government. Keeping them together as an army was a remarkable feat. In 1781, Washington had to shoot the ringleaders of mutinous New Jersey troops, who were owed money that Congress could not pay.

Washington also had the wisdom to require inoculation against smallpox for every man in the Continental Army when an epidemic was threatening to destroy it. Diseases killed about 10 times as many men as did combat in the war, so reducing losses to infection made a big impact.

Major combat operations ended in 1781. The French navy coordinated with both the French and the Continental armies to pin the bulk of the British forces in a swampy, malarial spot at Yorktown, Virginia, where they surrendered. When a peace treaty was negotiated confirming American independence in 1783, some of Washington's followers urged him to declare himself king and establish a monarchy. Instead, Washington resigned his commission and retired to his Virginia plantation.

Only 13 British colonies had joined the war. The Caribbean island colonies, such as Jamaica and Barbados, and the northernmost—Nova Scotia, Prince Edward Island, and Quebec—chose to remain British. Seventy thousand loyalists fled during and after the war, mainly north to what would become Canada. They took about 2,000 slaves with them.

OUTCOMES OF THE REVOLUTION

Those who remained in the newly independent United States had many differences among them. It took years of politicking before Americans could agree on the governing principles underlying their new country, formalized in a constitution adopted in 1789. Based on the belief that just government required the consent of the governed, it established a federal structure balancing the authority of a central government against that of constituent states. It also carefully divided power among three branches of government: a judiciary, a legislature, and an executive—a president, the first of whom would be Washington, coaxed from retirement. Its first 10 amendments, called the Bill of Rights, added in 1791, guaranteed certain liberties for citizens, such as the freedom of religion, the freedom of speech, the right to bear arms, and the right to a jury trial. Voting rights were left up to the states, most of which

allowed only property-owning adult white males, about 6 percent of the population, to vote. The U.S. Constitution, while far from the first in world history, sparked a rage for written constitutions. Within 50 years, several dozen were adopted, mostly in Europe and the Americas.

WOMEN'S RIGHTS Political rights for women hardly crossed men's minds. In early 1776, while Boston-based lawyer John Adams was away in Philadelphia hatching plans for rebellion from Britain, Abigail Adams tried to alert her husband to an oversight. She wrote to him:

> I long to hear that you have declared an independency—and by the way in the new Code of Laws which I suppose it will be necessary for you to make I desire you would remember the ladies and be more generous and favourable to them than your ancestors. Do not put such unlimited power into the hands of the husbands. Remember, all men would be tyrants if they could.

When her husband replied and dismissed her concerns, in another letter (with the inconsistent capitalization normal in the eighteenth century) she added:

> I can not say that I think you very generous to the ladies for whilst you are proclaiming peace and goodwill to men, emancipating all nations, you insist upon retaining absolute power over wives. But you must remember that arbitrary power is like most other things which are very hard, very liable to be broken.

Neither the Declaration of Independence nor the Constitution reflected Abigail Adams's views. In general, the American Revolution left the matter of women's political rights untouched, despite the participation of women in the boycotts of the 1770s and the support they gave the Continental Army as cooks, nurses, and washerwomen—indeed, a few had even managed to serve as soldiers by disguising themselves as men.

Abigail Adams Born in 1744, Abigail Adams was one of the revolutionary era's most influential women. In a letter to her husband, John Adams, she urged the Continental Congress to "put it out of the power of husbands to use us as they will."

COMPROMISING ON SLAVERY The Revolution was no more revolutionary on the issue of slavery, although it came in for more discussion than did women's rights. After much debate and difficult compromise, the framers of the Constitution decided to permit slavery where it already existed and to allow the continuation of the Atlantic slave trade until 1808. States, however, were free to make their own rules, and Vermont and Massachusetts, where slavery was rare, soon passed laws making it illegal. But the states where most of the new republic's half a million enslaved people lived passed no such laws, and those states' political strength ensured that the federal government could not either. Jefferson in 1782 had written that slavery was an "unremitting despotism" and that "I tremble for my country when I reflect that God is just." But he did not free any of the roughly 200 people he held in bondage. Ironically, slavery lasted in the United States until 1865, long after it had ended in the British Empire, against which Americans had fought for freedom.

FRANCE, 1780–1815

The **French Revolution** led to the formation of another republic at the expense of another monarch. It led to deeper changes in France than had the American Revolution in the United States. The revolutionaries in France overthrew the principle of monarchy, proclaimed the sovereignty of the people, established a secular republic, killed a king, seized most of the property of the Catholic Church, legalized divorce, established freedom of religion, abolished slavery throughout the French Empire, and overturned all they could of feudalism. They even instituted a new calendar. The French then undid most of this.

ORIGINS OF THE FRENCH REVOLUTION

The origins of the French Revolution make up one of historians' favorite puzzles. Like all the revolutions considered in this chapter, the French Revolution had deep and tangled roots. Some of them were intellectual, anchored in what is called the Enlightenment. Some were socioeconomic, based in slow changes in French society. Other, shallower, roots were financial, and even climatic.

THE ENLIGHTENMENT The European Enlightenment took shape in the early eighteenth century. Its center lay in France, but participants lived in most parts of Europe, from Poland to Spain and from Italy to Scotland. It was, in essence, an intellectual movement involving a few thousand well-educated people, although to some extent their ideas affected others, even people who could not read or write—the majority everywhere. In France, its chief targets for reform—or perhaps for elimination—were the twin institutions of monarchy and church. To supporters of the Enlightenment, both seemed out of date and obstacles to human progress. The ideals of the Enlightenment included reliance on reason and science, wider political liberty, and religious toleration for Christians of all sorts and often for Jews. Its exponents were thinkers such as François-Marie Arouet (1694–1778), who mocked the institutions and traditions of France under the pen name Voltaire; Denis Diderot (1713–1784), who tried to compile all knowledge in a 28-volume encyclopedia, published between 1751 and 1778; and Immanuel Kant (1724–1804), a German philosopher who claimed that morality derives from reason. Its sponsors were mainly wealthy patrons, often women who organized "salons" dedicated to discussion of political questions as well as to philosophy, art, and literature. The most prominent was Suzanne Necker (ca. 1737–1794), a Swiss Protestant of modest origins. An intellectual in her own right, she was particularly interested in hospital reform and the question of whether divorce should be legal. She married a successful financier and ran a Paris salon in the 1770s and 1780s that attracted the most active thinkers, writers, and artists.

Salons In this engraving from the eighteenth century, Suzanne Necker is shown seated with her daughter at one of her famous Parisian salons, listening to a writer read his work aloud. The spaces created by *salonnières* such as Necker helped Enlightenment ideas develop and spread.

SOCIOECONOMIC CHANGES The intellectual currents of the Enlightenment flowed together with socioeconomic changes in France. In the late eighteenth century, the French, like other Europeans, divided their society legally, politically, and culturally into three "estates." The clergy constituted the First Estate, about 0.5 percent of the population of 28 million as of 1789. It owned 10 percent of the farmland and pastureland in France and had the right to impose taxes (tithes) on peasants. The nobility made up the Second Estate, about 1 to 2 percent of the French public. They owned about 25 percent of the productive land and enjoyed exemption from most taxes. The Third Estate included everybody else—except the landless poor, who were outside this system altogether. Peasant farmers made up most of the Third Estate, which paid almost all the taxes and had the least political influence in France. They owned at most 40 percent of the useful land in France, usually in small plots. Urban artisans and professionals were also in the Third Estate; many urban families owned farmland too. There was little social mobility in this system: only rarely did anyone change their status as a member of one or another estate. This system of social and political hierarchy, all subject to the authority of the French king, is often called the Old Regime.

In the eighteenth century, France became more urbanized. Atlantic trade played some role in this shift, especially in western France. Cities such as Bordeaux and Nantes rose to prominence on Atlantic trade, including the slave trade. Merchant and professional classes grew in number, strength, and ambition. They resented the grip on social status and political influence held by the nobility. For many in these classes, church, monarch, and especially tax-collector seemed hostile to their ambitions.

Meanwhile, the French aristocratic elite—the nobility and the top ranks of the clergy—began to divide against itself by 1770. Like all elites, it had always had its fault lines. But now some came to share doubts about the Old Regime system, particularly about the efficiency of the monarchy, which wasted money on luxury, employed incompetent bunglers, and lost most wars. Voltaire recommended following the Chinese example and staffing government offices not with well-connected aristocrats but with smart young men selected by examination. Many among the elite thought the Catholic Church suffocated society and culture. Others thought that aristocratic lords (often, their own friends and relatives) did the same to agriculture and the economy by resisting innovations, whether in crop rotations or technologies.

OTHER PRESSURES Other pressures were slowly building in the lower echelons of society. France's

Food Riots One of the catalysts of the French Revolution was a poor harvest and astronomically high food prices. The price of bread inspired hundreds of women of all social classes to march on the royal palace of Versailles in 1789, as illustrated in this engraving.

population grew from 20 million to 28 million between 1700 and 1789. Land was growing scarce, and much of it was already owned by nobles and the church. The prospects for poor peasants and urban laborers were getting bleaker.

This might have come to nothing without short-term financial and climatic stresses. The French Crown, like most monarchies, had perpetual money woes worsened by the costs of war. After 1778, French involvement in the American Revolution drained the French Treasury. Neither bankers, nobles, nor the Catholic Church would lend money to the king except at the most exorbitant interest rates. In France, the body with the authority to vote for taxes was the Estates-General, composed of representatives of the Old Regime's three estates. No French king had consulted it for over 170 years. When the king, desperate for revenue, summoned the Estates-General in 1789, he ignited a political wildfire, blown this way and that by swirling winds beyond anyone's control.

To add to the pressures, in the 1780s bad weather brought meager harvests and widespread hunger. An Icelandic volcano erupted in 1783–1784, spewing dust into the atmosphere and blocking sunlight. Its effect lasted two or three years, reducing harvests and raising grain prices in northern Europe. In 1788, drought—and then a cold winter—hit France. Ordinary people normally spent about half their income on food, but by 1789 that was up to 90 percent. Now people who had never heard of Voltaire or discussed ideas of sovereignty rioted over bread prices and clamored for lower taxes—the last thing King Louis XVI wanted. The food crisis brought poor people—men and women—together as nothing else could and briefly made them a political force in France.

THE EARLY REVOLUTION

The French Revolution began when the Estates-General met in 1789. Its members understood that they, like England's Parliament in 1641, had bargaining power because the king needed money desperately. Soon the Third Estate declared itself to be a National Assembly, embodying the will of the people. Some clergymen joined it. The king tried offering some concessions, but in the summer of 1789 he fired his most reform-minded ministers, a signal that he hoped to face down the Third Estate. Then the poor artisans, clerks, and petty shopkeepers of Paris stormed the Bastille, hungry people rioted in other cities, and peasants began to attack the property of their landlords and the church. The Revolution was under way, and no one knew where it would lead.

THE DECLARATION OF THE RIGHTS OF MAN AND CITIZEN
In August 1789, the National Assembly decided to abolish the feudal privileges of the clergy and nobility. All citizens of France would now be legally equal. No more tax exemptions for the nobility. No more dues owed by peasants to nobles or tithes to the church. The Assembly adopted an extraordinary document entitled the Declaration of the Rights of Man and Citizen, which borrowed from Enlightenment thought and from the American Declaration of Independence. The first of its 17 articles proclaims that "men are born and remain free and equal in rights." The third states that "the principle of sovereignty resides essentially in the nation," meaning adult males.

Some French women objected to being excluded. In the fall of 1789, one group wrote a pamphlet intended for the National Assembly asking why 13 million females should be the slaves of 13 million males (they underestimated the national population slightly). In 1791, Olympe de Gouges, a woman of modest origins from the southwest of France who had moved to Paris and become a playwright, a political intellectual, and a fierce opponent of the enslavement of Africans, wrote a counterblast that she called the Declaration of the Rights of Woman and Citizen. Although de Gouges won little popular support among either men or women in her call for equality, women soon achieved the right to divorce husbands and to equality in matters of inheritance. But they still could not vote or hold office.

Men did a little better with political rights in the first years of the Revolution. At first, only men over age 25 who paid taxes were allowed to vote—about 4 to 5 million Frenchmen, around 15 to 18 percent of the population. By 1792, almost all males over age 21 could vote. But in 1793, they elected representatives, most of them young men, who allowed no further elections.

TARGETING CHURCH AND MONARCHY
Securing political rights was only one part of the Revolution. In the late fall of 1789, the National Assembly confiscated most of the lands and buildings of the Catholic Church and sold them. It forced most clergy to retire and made the rest employees of the state. It made Protestants and Jews equal citizens with Catholics. The church in France eventually recovered some of its property, but never the power it lost in 1789.

From 1789 to 1791, the National Assembly ruled France in uneasy harness with King Louis XVI. But the king, sensing his position weakening, attempted to flee the country. He was caught, tried, and executed. This earned the revolutionaries many enemies within France and throughout Europe. By early 1792, revolutionary France was at war with the monarchs of Austria and Prussia.

Execution of the King A key event of the radical phase of the French Revolution was the execution of the deposed king, Louis XVI, at the guillotine, in early 1793.

A RADICAL TURN

Now the Revolution entered a much more radical and violent phase. The wars against foreign monarchies required unity among the French. But unity could not be achieved by consensus, as many sympathized with the dead king and the dispossessed church, especially in the provinces. So the revolutionaries sought unity through compulsion. The executive machinery of government (called a Legislative Assembly in 1791–1792 and the National Convention in 1792–1795) was increasingly dominated by men called **Jacobins**, mostly middle class, many of them lawyers, who were prepared to take drastic measures to prevent the Revolution from collapsing. They often allied with the urban poor, usually called *sans-culottes* because they wore trousers rather than the more fashionable knee breeches. The Jacobins ended elections in 1793 and ruled with an iron hand.

JACOBIN REFORMS Jacobin members of the revolutionary government sought to change almost everything. Sometimes they aimed to improve the human condition, sometimes to save the Revolution from its enemies, sometimes to destroy one another in their competition for power. One of them, Louis Antoine de Saint-Just, a 26-year-old law school dropout and poet, declared that "everything that is not new in a time of innovation is

July Days of 1793 In a span of about 11 months in 1793–1794, when it seemed that foreign enemies and royalists might combine to crush the French Revolution, its leaders orchestrated a deliberate reign of terror. It led to about 20,000 political executions of citizens deemed enemies of the people, either for their conduct or their social position. Here a guillotine is set up under an ancient Roman arch in the provincial town of Orange.

pernicious." The Jacobins instituted a tax reform whereby the wealthier paid more, a popular move. They created a mass army through conscription, an unpopular one. They tried to create a new religion, sometimes called the Cult of the Supreme Being, based on concepts of civic virtue and an abstract God who preferred reason to faith. They promulgated a new calendar in which the beginning of the Republic in fall 1792 became Year I. It divided years into 12 months, each of three 10-day weeks. No longer would ordinary people get one day in seven off; the calendar was never popular. Days were divided into 10 hours, and hours into 100 minutes of 100 seconds, part of an effort to replace tradition with reason. The Jacobins instituted the metric system of weights and measures. They banned aristocratic fashions such as men's powdered wigs and women's velvet dresses. They abolished slavery in France and French colonies. They encouraged people to destroy statues of kings and bishops and melt them down to be turned into weapons for the army. And they made it clear they would tolerate no dissent. By late 1793, citizens who did not have a "certificate of public virtue" issued by the state could be arrested on sight. The unfortunate Madame de Gouges, suspected of disloyalty to the Revolution, was among those guillotined in Paris.

THE COMMITTEE OF PUBLIC SAFETY The Revolution now reached a stage that historians call the Terror. The government, dominated by a so-called Committee of Public Safety, itself soon dominated by a 34-year-old lawyer, Maximilien Robespierre, found enemies everywhere. Robespierre, who liked to be called "the Incorruptible," was a man of principle at any cost. In early 1794, he wrote that "the spring of government during a revolution is virtue combined with terror: virtue, without which terror is destructive; terror, without which virtue is impotent. Terror is only justice prompt, severe and inflexible; it is . . . a natural consequence of the general principle of democracy, applied to the most pressing wants of the country." Saint-Just, the poet, told the deputies of the Convention that "a nation creates itself only upon heaps of corpses."

He and Robespierre did their part to build those heaps. The Committee of Public Safety ordered the arrest of half a million people and had some 20,000 executed. Everyone now lived in fear. Some 150,000 people, mostly nobles and clergy, fled France, many of them for America. Rebellions in the countryside, prompted by conscription as much as anything else, cost tens of thousands of lives.

Ambitious revolutionaries denounced one another, hoping to climb the slippery pole of political power at one another's expense. Robespierre turned on his friends and comrades at the slightest suspicion of dissent. As one observer put it, "Like Saturn [of ancient mythology] the revolution devours its children." In the summer of 1794, the Terror reached a climax, with public executions in Paris averaging about two dozen daily.

Unfortunately for Robespierre, Saint-Just, and the Committee of Public Safety, the military situation for France improved, weakening their main justification for relentless execution of their political enemies. In a few dramatic days, they lost much of their support in the Convention and, together with their closest supporters, lost their heads at the guillotine in July 1794.

The Convention created a new government called the Directory (1795–1799), which excluded men under age 30 from office. It faced many challenges, from hunger riots to coup d'état conspiracies to rampant inflation. Political turmoil declined but did not disappear. The Directory reinstituted elections but was appalled when royalists won. Some of its members in 1799 mounted a coup against their own government. They installed a military man, **Napoleon Bonaparte**, who gradually made himself a dictator—in the name of liberty and equality.

NAPOLEON BONAPARTE: EXPANSION AND OVERREACH

Bonaparte (1769–1821), who had served in France's revolutionary army, rose from obscurity through talent and ambition. He made his name by crushing a royalist rebellion in Paris in 1795 and became a general at age 26. He won a string of astounding victories against foreign armies beginning in 1796.

The revolutionary republic had been at war since 1792. While fighting for its life against reactionary foreign monarchs, it was nonetheless pursuing traditional French foreign policy, conquering and occupying the same neighboring lands that French kings had previously tried to subdue. Under Bonaparte, however, the French army roamed farther afield and with startling success, especially in Italy, Austria, and Germany. Everywhere it went, Bonaparte's army tried to set up new governments. They were supposedly embodiments of universal principles proclaimed by the Revolution, but in practice mainly puppets of Napoleon, sometimes ruled by his relatives.

Napoleon's Russian Campaign A dramatic 1808 painting depicts the bleak aftermath of the 1807 Battle of Eylau in East Prussia. Napoleon appears at the center on horseback, while bodies lie piled in the snow and farms and villages burn in the distance.

They always found local people who joined them enthusiastically against their own kings and princes. In this way, Bonaparte's armies and agents rewove the fabric of European politics, spreading some of the ideals and practices of the French Revolution.

Bonaparte's military success was part genius and part system. He knew his business well and was especially effective in coordinating field artillery with infantry and cavalry. Thanks to conscription and the size of the French population, he usually had a bigger army than his enemies. Big armies were hard to feed, but Bonaparte found that his could live off the land, buying or stealing food from farms and villages. This worked well as long as the army kept moving and operated in the agriculturally richer parts of Europe that produced enough surplus food.

Bonaparte's system failed when his armies entered poorer lands without much surplus food. Unfortunately for him, for France, and for the Revolution, Bonaparte could not stop attacking other countries, even poor ones with slender surplus. He had a bottomless need for glory. And he rightly feared what would happen, to him and to France, if he discharged a million men with military skills. When he attacked Spain in 1807, his army became bogged down in endless antiguerilla operations. When he invaded Russia in 1812, his army of 600,000 dwindled to 25,000 within months through starvation, typhus and other diseases, and an unexpectedly stiff resistance

From French Revolution to French Empire, 1789–1814   The government guiding the French Revolution declared war on Austria and Prussia in April 1792, igniting more than two decades of warfare. Under Napoleon Bonaparte, the French set up sympathetic rulers in Italy, Germany, Spain, and Poland, but none survived his downfall. The inset shows the location of key sites in revolutionary Paris.

from Russians. As the French novelist Victor Hugo put it, Bonaparte was "conquered by his conquests."

These and other disasters undermined his political support at home, and by 1814 he had to abdicate the imperial throne he had earlier awarded himself. In France, the nobility soon recovered most of its former lands, and the monarchy and church returned atop society, although less powerful than before 1789. Some changes, such as the Napoleonic law code, remained in force. In Europe, all the revolutionary governments installed by Bonaparte's army were overthrown, and monarchs across Europe climbed back onto thrones—even in France in 1814. But in most cases, they had to share power with legislatures.

The Revolution was dead, politically and militarily defeated, but it lived on in the hearts and minds of millions of people in Europe. The ideas it unleashed, however imperfectly brought into practice, retained some of their appeal. Revolutions and republics since 1789 have drawn inspiration from the French experience. And the stated political principles, like those of the American Revolution, remain compelling to billions of people today who cherish freedom, justice, and equality before the law—even if everyone understands these concepts differently.

HAITI, 1780–1804

The French Revolution proved inspirational in the French colony of Saint-Domingue (today's Haiti), where a revolution exploded in 1791. Like the French Revolution, the Haitian Revolution attacked a hierarchical social and political order. But in contrast to the French revolution, race and slavery were at the center in Haiti.

A PLANTATION COLONY: SUGAR, COFFEE, SLAVES

Acquired in war from Spain in 1697, Saint-Domingue soon became France's most valuable colony. Its lowland plains proved excellent for raising sugar, and its hills equally good for less profitable crops such as coffee. By the 1780s, Saint-Domingue had 8,000 plantations. It produced nearly half the sugar and coffee harvested in the Atlantic world. Thirty ships a week used its ports, carrying its products to France and bringing in human cargoes from Africa.

Of its population, about 550,000 in all, nearly 90 percent was enslaved. Two-thirds had been born in Africa, the remainder in the Caribbean. In the 1780s, some 30,000 enslaved Africans arrived annually, largely from Kongo. Two-thirds were male. They worked mainly on the plantations. About 5 percent of Saint-Domingue's people were free blacks or people of mixed African and European ancestry, called gens de couleur libres. Some of them were rich planters and slaveholders—indeed, they owned one-quarter of the colony's slaves—but most were artisans, petty merchants, or laborers. Another roughly 5 percent of the total population were whites, mainly born in France, 80 percent of whom were men. Some were rich planters, others wage laborers. All whites enjoyed legal privileges based on skin color, such as the right to bear

arms or to hold political office. Almost all hoped to get rich and get back to France. Few succeeded.

Saint-Domingue was a tinderbox of unfulfilled ambitions. Whites wanted political representation in Paris, much as in British North America colonists a few years earlier had wanted representation in London. They wanted to be free to trade their sugar and coffee anywhere, not just to France. The gens de couleur libres wanted equality with whites. The enslaved wanted freedom. Word of the revolution unfolding in France in 1789 provided a spark. The first uprising involved the gens de couleur libres in 1790, led by one of the richest men in the colony. Colonial authorities crushed it.

TOUSSAINT AND THE HAITIAN REVOLUTION

A far bigger one, involving at its outset about 100,000 slaves, erupted in the summer of 1791. It took the whites and gens de couleur libres by surprise. Most slave risings in the Americas failed before they started because someone betrayed the plans in advance. Somehow, this one, the biggest of all, was kept secret.

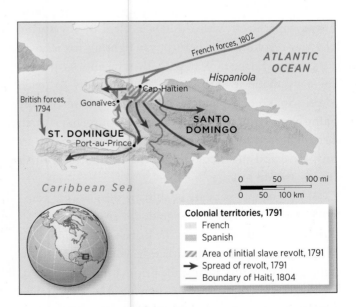

The Haitian Revolution, 1791-1804 Enslaved Africans, and others of African descent, engineered the largest slave revolt in world history beginning in 1791, turning the French sugar colony of Saint-Domingue into a new country, Haiti, by 1804. The uprising began on sugar plantations in the north and prospered especially in difficult, mountainous terrain where guerilla warfare was practical. French armies, arriving in force in 1802, controlled the ports but could not crush the revolution in the countryside. What little remained of them departed in 1804.

Toussaint L'Ouverture The leader of the Haitian Revolution appears in uniform on horseback—cast in the role of a heroic general—in a French engraving from the period.

The primary leader of the revolution, **Toussaint L'Ouverture**, was born into slavery in the north of Saint-Domingue, probably in 1743. He grew up handling animals and became an expert horseman. He also learned the healing arts. His owner freed him when Toussaint was about 30, and as a free man he sometimes owned enslaved people himself. He spoke French, Ewe (the West African language of his father), and the French-based creole (*kreyol*) that was the lingua franca of Saint-Domingue. He was a practicing Catholic and learned to read and write as an adult. It turned out that as a middle-aged man he had remarkable physical stamina, courage in the face of death, and the smarts and flexible principles of a master politician. By 1792, he was one of the top commanders of the slave insurrection.

French planters in Saint-Domingue could not get much help from France against the uprising. Many Jacobins sympathized with the rebels. And by the spring of 1792, revolutionary France was fighting for its own survival in Europe. War with Britain and its powerful navy made it hard for the French army to reach Haiti. So French planters invited Britain to occupy Saint-Domingue and crush the slave insurgency, which Britain agreed to attempt lest the uprising spread to its own slave and sugar colonies in the Caribbean. British troops arrived in 1793.

After a couple of years of shifting allegiances, Toussaint organized an army that gradually swelled to 20,000 poorly equipped men to fight the British occupation. Like Washington a generation earlier, he could not afford to fight set-piece battles against the British army and knew it. He fought a guerilla campaign, moving as needed, attacking when he saw an opening, and prudently allowing yellow fever to scythe down his enemy.

Toussaint recognized that he had an ally in yellow fever. Most of his men had acquired immunity to the lethal disease either in Africa or in Saint-Domingue, where just about everyone faced it in childhood. Virtually no one in the British Army had ever encountered it. Two-thirds of the British soldiers who landed in Saint-Domingue died of it. Those who survived left in 1798.

FRENCH INTERVENTION The French then tried to undo the revolution in Saint-Domingue. A peace treaty with Britain opened the seas to French navigation in 1802, and soon Bonaparte's brother-in-law, leading an army about 65,000 strong, arrived. Bonaparte gave instructions to defeat the insurgents, then reinstall the plantation system and slavery. Things went well at first for the French. But Toussaint and his ragtag army ("naked as earthworms," as he put it) had other ideas and knew time was on their side. He drew inspiration from the slave revolt of Spartacus two thousand years before (Toussaint owned books on Roman history). His troops, many of whom had prior military experience in Africa, tried to pin the French down in the unhealthy lowlands while keeping the mountains to themselves. Although Toussaint was captured in 1802 and died the following year in a French prison, his strategy worked again.

Toussaint's followers stunned France and the world by winning their revolutionary war against an army—Bonaparte's—that had humbled the kings of Europe. The French had spared no effort and still lost. Once again, the Haitians used their ally, yellow fever, which killed about 75 percent of the French army. The Haitians lost many as well, to combat, disease, and massacres (of which there were many on all sides). But they could recruit more Haitians, which the French found difficult to do after it was revealed that Napoleon had relegalized slavery in the French Caribbean.

AFTERMATH The **Haitian Revolution** triumphed by 1804. It ended both French colonial rule and legal slavery in Haiti. It was, perhaps more than any other, an Atlantic revolution. Some of its animating ideas came from the revolutions in North America and France. Nearly a thousand gens de couleur had fought in the American Revolution against Britain. Between 1789 and 1804, events in Haiti and France directly affected one another. Some of the Haitian Revolution's soldiers came from the civil wars in Kongo, via the slave trade. And its victors would soon give advice and arms to revolutionaries in what is now Venezuela.

The Haitian Revolution, like the French one, devoured its children. Toussaint's most prominent lieutenant,

Haitian Revolution A French engraving dramatizes the combat between enslaved workers and slaveowners. Fire was a crucial weapon for Haitian rebels.

Jean-Jacques Dessalines, organized massacres of the remaining French and of his political rivals—and declared himself emperor. His own troops killed him in 1806. His successors, also leaders of the revolution, fought one another in civil wars, created regional despotisms, and, without calling it slavery, reestablished forced labor on plantations where they could.

Toussaint and his followers had pulled off the largest slave rebellion in history, won wars against two of Europe's great powers, and established the second independent republic in the Americas. But the Haitian Revolution still left the great majority of Haitians poor and powerless.

SPANISH AMERICA, 1765–1825

Spanish America underwent a set of revolutions in the early nineteenth century. They were anticolonial, like the American and Haitian revolutions, and resulted in several new republics. They led to abolitions of slavery and in places a degree of popular rule. But in most cases, they resulted in unstable autocracies or military rule.

A DIVERSE SOCIETY

At the end of the eighteenth century, Spanish America included most of South America, all of Central America, and North America as far north as Texas and California—plus several Caribbean islands. Social and economic conditions were extremely diverse over this vast terrain. Some 13 to 15 million people lived there. About 5 million lived in the Viceroyalty of New Spain (today's Mexico), with smaller centers of population elsewhere.

Ever since the conquests of the sixteenth century, people of Spanish birth (*peninsulares*) or Spanish descent (*criollos*, or creoles) dominated Spanish American society politically and economically. They held all public offices, filled the officer corps of the military, and staffed the top positions in the Catholic Church. They made up most, though not all, of the merchant class. Most parts of Spanish America included indigenous populations—usually the demographic majority except in the Caribbean; enslaved people, mostly Africans; free Blacks; as well as large and growing communities of mixed descent. *Mestizos* were of Spanish and indigenous ancestry; *mulattos* of African and European descent; *zambos* of African and indigenous parentage. These groupings were fluid around the edges, and to some extent people could claim whatever status they wanted if they could make others believe it. These designations mattered, partly because of social prejudices and partly because of law: various privileges were reserved for *peninsulares* and *criollos*, and various legal handicaps for people of African descent, whether free or enslaved.

By 1760, the Spanish Empire in America was about 250 years old. This empire was essential to Spain's standing in Europe and the world, the source of about a quarter of its revenues. From Spain's viewpoint, its American empire had two great vulnerabilities. First, it was threatened by rising British military power. Second, its merchants objected to a monopoly trade system that required them to trade only with Spain. They wanted to trade with foreigners too. The rise of Atlantic commerce tempted them with opportunities they were legally forbidden to take.

THE BOURBON REFORMS

Spain's failures in the Seven Years' War (1756–1763), including a defeat at its major port of Havana, led to

Race in Spanish America Intermarriage between people of indigenous, European, and African heritage in Spanish America created new categories of racial difference and hierarchy. Many images from the period show families of mixed racial heritage, such as these eighteenth-century paintings of families in everyday scenes.

reforms coming from Madrid beginning in 1767. Known as the **Bourbon Reforms**, after the name of the ruling family in Spain, these were intended to strengthen the empire. Their backers had read Enlightenment thinkers and preferred reason to tradition as a guide to action. They were, in effect, technocrats, convinced they could make Spain's rule more efficient and productive, but in cases also idealists, hoping to improve human welfare. Under these reformist influences, the Crown allowed more cities to trade with Spain but cracked down on illegal trade with other empires. It reserved a larger proportion of political appointments for Spaniards at the expense of criollos. And it tried to curtail the power of the Catholic Church, most notably by expelling all Jesuits from the Americas in 1767.

With these reforms, the Crown hoped in particular to strengthen colonial defenses, pump up the economy, and increase the wealth flowing to Spain through new taxes and other means. The Bourbon Reforms, like most dynamic reform programs, pleased some and irritated many—rather like the reforms Britain enacted (new taxes and restrictions on westward migration) in the wake of the Seven Years' War.

TÚPAC AMARU'S REVOLT Almost nobody liked the higher taxes. In 1780, a giant tax revolt broke out in the Viceroyalty of Peru, in the Andes. It was led by an elite, Jesuit-educated mestizo, **Túpac Amaru II**, a descendant of the Inka Empire's ruling family. He proposed a return to the supposedly good old days of the Inka Empire. He promised justice, an end to oppression by Spaniards, and the elimination of all distinctions based on ethnicity. He also called for fully free trade. His wife, Micaela Bastidas, was one of several indigenous women who helped organize the rebellion. She took charge of military logistics.

This revolutionary agenda provoked firm and at times ruthlessly violent responses from Spanish authorities, which in turn made Túpac Amaru and his followers more radical still. Many of them concluded that the only route to justice involved full independence from Spain and the murder of all Spaniards. The revolt lasted until 1783 and cost the Viceroyalty of Peru about 10 percent of its population. It was suppressed with maximal cruelty, including a gruesome public execution of Túpac Amaru. Of the 73 leaders killed by Spanish authorities, 32 were women.

Túpac Amaru's failed revolution frightened everyone committed to the future of the Spanish Empire in the Americas. It had almost deprived Spain of the wealth of the Andean silver mines. Ministers in Madrid and their agents in the colonies, trembling with relief, redoubled their commitment to reform.

Túpac Amaru's Failed Revolution
The revolutionary leader Túpac Amaru was memorialized on Peruvian currency in the late twentieth century. Although his revolution failed in the 1780s, it became a part of later conceptions of Peruvian national identity.

Indigenous Americans elsewhere in the Spanish Empire found little to like in the Bourbon Reforms. They lost some legal protections. The Crown's efforts to unshackle the economy led to new opportunities for entrepreneurs, especially on the frontiers, such as northern Mexico. To exploit those opportunities, businessmen needed laborers, and they found ways to require poor people, usually indigenous, to work for them in mines, on ranches, and on farming estates. Debt peonage was one such technique, whereby poor people were encouraged to borrow money and obliged to pay off their debts through labor.

The reforms also increased the scope for slavery in Spanish America. In the 1770s, the Crown opened the Atlantic slave trade to all merchants. For three decades, the traffic boomed and over a million Africans were condemned to the mines of Mexico, the plantations of the Caribbean, and elsewhere in Spanish America. An internal document of the Spanish government from 1802 acknowledged that "the opulence of [Spanish] America . . . could not exist without the slave trade."

The criollo, or creole, elites found plenty to dislike in the Bourbon Reforms too. They lost access to many political offices, which were now open only to men born in Spain. Those creoles who had enjoyed privileged positions in the old monopoly trade system—the merchant guilds of Lima, Mexico City, and Havana, for example—lost out when the Crown permitted more free trade.

TENSIONS OVER TRADE

The Crown's experiment with freer trade was perhaps its most destabilizing step. Formerly only a few merchant guilds in Spanish America could legally conduct transatlantic trade, and only with the merchant guild in Cadiz, a city in southwestern Spain. These rules, although widely flouted by smugglers, severely constrained the chances to make money in commerce. Beginning in 1765, the rules grew looser. By 1789, nine Spanish cities were allowed to trade with almost anyone in Spanish America, but no one was permitted to

trade with foreigners. This program worked, but in a sense too well. Some creole merchants prospered mightily but grew ever more frustrated by their reduced political voice.

As in Haiti, by 1790 few in Spanish America found political arrangements to their liking. All sorts of suggestions arose for reworking relations with Madrid. A very few thought that independence from Spain was the best course. One such was Francisco Miranda (1750–1816), from what is now Venezuela. He had fought with Spanish forces in Florida against Britain in the American Revolution. In the 1790s, he fought for the Revolution in France and became a marshal of the French army. His military service, wide travels, and very wide reading led him to the conclusion

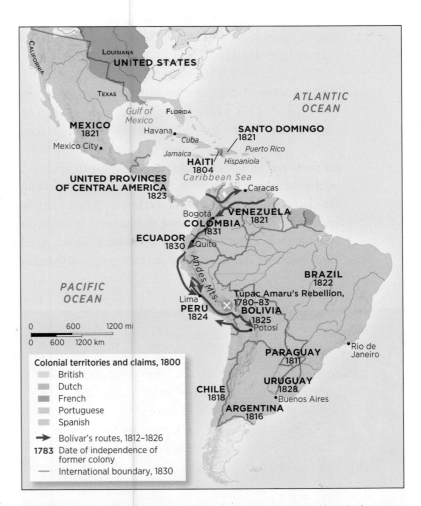

Spanish America, 1800–1830 In 1800, most of the American hemisphere was claimed by European powers, the greater part of it by Spain. Nevertheless, indigenous peoples actually controlled sizeable parts of both continents; moreover, the United States was already an independent country, and Haiti would soon be. Spanish rule was shaken by the revolt led by Túpac Amaru in the Andes in the 1780s, and further uprisings against Spanish rule began in 1808, centered on what is now Mexico, Venezuela, Colombia, and Peru. By 1826, 17 new republics had emerged from the ruins of the Spanish Empire in the Americas.

that Spanish America ought to be free from Madrid's control. Miranda, tireless though he was in his efforts, had little direct effect on the politics of Spanish America while making his tour of revolutions around the Atlantic, and few others shared his view about independence.

GEOPOLITICAL SHIFTS

In the 1790s, matters grew more urgent as the wars of the French Revolution at times cut into Atlantic commerce. This deepened discontent among creole merchants in Spanish America. It hurt the Spanish Crown, which needed the revenues from its American possessions. Everyone concerned was still searching for a new compromise between Spain and Spanish America, a new version of the empire, when in 1807–1808 Napoleon Bonaparte's armies marched into Iberia.

King Fernando VII abdicated the Spanish throne. Bonaparte eventually installed his brother Joseph as the new king of Spain, which few Spaniards welcomed. Having lost Saint-Domingue in 1804, Bonaparte might have had his eye on the silver mines of Spanish America. He got, instead, six years of vicious guerilla war in Spain.

Now Spain and Spanish America were cut off from one another more than ever. This created a power vacuum in Spanish America, giving rise to countless factions. In cities such as Caracas, Bogotá, and Buenos Aires, local elites began to debate politics with the vigor of Jacobin

Exodus from the Town of Caracas The wars for independence in Spanish America took an especially brutal form in Venezuela, featuring ruthless civil war and frequent massacre. This painting from 1913 represents the flight from Caracas in 1814 of 20,000 civilians who had sided with Bolívar's cause and feared slaughter at the hands of a royalist army.

clubs in Paris. Many wanted liberties of the sort Bonaparte often promised and rarely delivered, such as freedom from censorship, and fully free trade. From 1808 to 1814, the situation was fluid, although few yet thought in terms of independence.

In 1814, Bonaparte's army left Spain in defeat. King Fernando VII returned to power and immediately tried to turn back the clock and restore Spain's hold over Spanish America. Many of the elites in Spanish America, now accustomed to greater liberties, especially in foreign trade, objected to the king's plans and embraced independence as a goal. Others, however, remained loyal to Spain. Civil wars soon erupted between revolutionaries and loyalists. As in North America in the 1770s, clumsy royal policy brought matters to a head quickly, converting reformists into revolutionaries.

Spain's efforts to bring its American colonies back into the fold failed spectacularly. In 1815, the king sent a large army to what is now Colombia and Venezuela, where, like the European armies in Haiti, it suffered searing epidemics of yellow fever and malaria. More than 90 percent of the army never came home. Combat took place also in Mexico, Peru, and Chile, and around the city of Buenos Aires, but it involved small armies of a few thousand.

BOLÍVAR AND THE SPANISH AMERICAN REPUBLICS

Revolutionary leaders, such as **Simón Bolívar** (1783–1830), a wealthy, aristocratic creole from Venezuela, forged coalitions of creole elites, free Blacks, and mestizos. Bolívar was educated in Spain and France in his youth and admired Enlightenment ideas as well as the French and American Revolutions. He supported women's political rights and made one woman, Manuela Sáenz, a general in his army. During a period of exile, he went to Haiti and learned about the revolution there. Bolívar and other revolutionaries often promised freedom to any enslaved person who joined the rebel forces.

Spain had little power to deploy in the Americas. Loyalists in Spanish America, although numerous in the upper ranks of society, could not drum up much support among the common people. Bolívar's and other ragtag revolutionary armies trudged far and wide across Spanish America, showing a determination that Spain's troops lacked. In addition, the revolutionaries enjoyed British support. The Royal Navy made it difficult for Spain to carry men and or decades—whereas it lasted until 1874 in Puerto Rico and 1886 in Cuba. Spain, exhausted by recurrent warfare and with its American empire reduced to two islands, was finished as a world power and even as a great power within Europe.

THE ATLANTIC REVOLUTIONS IN BROADER PERSPECTIVE

Other Atlantic societies, such as Spain, Portugal, and Brazil, also underwent revolutionary changes. Bonaparte's 1807–1808 invasion of Spain and Portugal created conditions that led not only to independence across the Atlantic but to struggles in Iberia. After French forces left Spain in 1814, monarchists supported restoration of royal rule, while liberals sought either republics or constitutional monarchies with representative legislatures. By the 1830s, after 20 years of instability, both Spain and Portugal emerged as constitutional monarchies.

Meanwhile, Brazil won its independence from Portugal. In 1807, the Portuguese Crown and court moved from Lisbon to Rio de Janeiro and governed the Portuguese Empire from that Brazilian city. When the king and court returned to Lisbon in 1822, they lacked the power to keep Brazil under their control. A prince, Dom Pedro I, declared Brazil an independent monarchy, with constitutional limits upon royal power. After a few small battles, the Portuguese gave up, confirming the independence of Brazil in 1825.

ATLANTIC CONNECTIONS

All of these revolutions, from Kongo and Britain in the late seventeenth century to Spanish America and Brazil in the early nineteenth, had their own local causes. At the same time, they all shared Atlantic roots: the reshuffling of fortunes resulting from expanding Atlantic commerce proved destabilizing almost everywhere around the ocean's shores. Rising merchant classes increasingly objected to the monopoly on state power held by monarchs and their traditional allies.

By and large, the Atlantic revolutions brought **political decentralization** of two sorts. First, they undermined

South American Revolutionary Movements Representatives in a new revolutionary assembly voting in July 1816 to declare Argentina's independence from Spanish rule.

supplies across the Atlantic. Fighting waned after 1826, and soon Spain gave up entirely. Only Cuba and Puerto Rico remained of Spain's American empire.

Bolívar was hoping to achieve a united states of South America. Instead, seventeen new republics were born from the ruins of the Spanish Empire in America. Confederations in Central America, in northern South America, and between Argentina and Uruguay fell apart a few years after independence. Bolívar expressed his disappointment with this fragmentation when he wrote that all who had served the revolution had only "plowed the sea."

In most of the newly independent republics, creole factions feuded for power. In most cases, the new rulers reduced the sway of the church, leaving the military often as the only institution with any power or prestige. Military dictatorships were frequent. Only Chile managed some measure of stability in the coming decades. Indigenous populations generally found the revolutions did nothing for them. But the republics, whether dictatorships or not, abolished slavery within a few years

CONSIDERING THE EVIDENCE

A Revolutionary's Letter from Jamaica

The revolutions in North America, France, and Haiti inspired revolutionaries in Spanish America, including Simón Bolívar (1783–1830). Bolívar was Spanish by descent, but his birth in South America made him part of the creole class that the Spanish Empire excluded from political offices after the Bourbon Reforms of 1767. For Bolívar, who had studied Enlightenment writings in Europe as a young man, the tyranny of imperial rule was distressing. He felt that if Americans like him could rule, instead of distant Spain, they could build a better future by unifying the provinces of South America. While living as an exile in Jamaica in 1815, he set down his reasons for revolting against Spain in a letter to a British gentleman.

I consider the actual state of America as when, after the collapse of the Roman Empire, each member constituted a political system in conformity with its interests and position, but with this great difference: that these scattered members reestablished the old nationalities with the alterations required by circumstances or events. But we, who scarcely keep a vestige of things of the past, and who, on the other hand, are not Indians nor Europeans, but a mixture of the legitimate owners of the country and the usurping Spaniards; in short, we, being Americans by birth and with rights equal to those of Europe, have to dispute these rights with the men of the country, and to maintain ourselves against the possession of the invaders. Thus, we find ourselves in the most extraordinary and complicated predicament....

Americans, under the Spanish system now in vigor, have in society no other place than that of serfs fit for work, and, at the most, that of simple consumers; and even this is limited by absurd restrictions, such as prohibition of the cultivation of European products; the monopoly of certain goods in the hands of the king; the prevention of the establishment in America of factories not possessed by Spain; the exclusive privileges of trade, even regarding the necessities of life; the obstacles placed in the way of the American provinces so that they may not deal with each other, nor have understandings, nor trade. In short, do you want to know what was our lot? The fields, in which to cultivate indigo, cochineal, coffee, sugar cane, cocoa, cotton; the solitary plains, to breed cattle; the deserts, to hunt the wild beasts; the bosom of the earth, to extract gold, with which that avaricious country was never satisfied.

We were never viceroys or governors except by very extraordinary reasons; archbishops and bishops, seldom; ambassadors, never; military men, only as subordinates; nobles, without privileges; lastly, we were neither magistrates nor financiers, and hardly merchants. All this we had to accept in direct opposition to our institutions....

I desire more than anybody else to see the formation in America of the greatest nation in the world, not so much as to its extension and wealth as to its glory and freedom.

Source: Guillermo A. Sherwell, *Simón Bolívar (el Libertador): Patriot, Warrior, Statesman, Father of Five Nations; A Sketch of His Life and His Work* (Washington, D.C., 1921).

QUESTIONS FOR ANALYSIS

1. For Bolívar, what restrictions in the Spanish system justified revolution?
2. Are Bolívar's grievances against Spanish rule any different from those that led British North American colonies to rebel 40 years previously?
3. How do Bolívar's references to rights, slavery, and commercial restrictions reflect the influence of earlier revolutions?

highly centralized kingdoms such as Kongo, Britain, and France. Second, they dissolved some of the bonds of transatlantic empires by giving birth to newly independent countries in the Americas. In Kongo and England, the revolutions were in effect national in scale, reducing royal authority and empowering commercial elites. In France, the revolution began that way, but it became international when Bonaparte invaded much of Europe and Saint-Domingue as well. In the Americas, the revolutions were anti-imperial, with the effect of creating newly independent countries, generally republics in place of colonies subject to European monarchs.

This pan-Atlantic movement did not sweep all before it. Many West African polities, even some deeply involved in Atlantic trade, managed to survive—partly because they were not so centralized to begin with. Several Caribbean sugar islands such as Jamaica and Barbados, as well as Cuba and Puerto Rico, remained colonies long after the era of Atlantic revolutions. So did the British colonies in eastern Canada, such as Quebec and Nova Scotia.

Nonetheless, the Atlantic record of revolution after revolution, establishing new principles of sovereignty, contrasts sharply with most of the rest of the world, where older polities and older principles held up better. In the big centers of population, such as China, north India, or Southwest Asia, the effects of oceanic commerce were less sudden and disruptive. Existing institutions and elites withstood whatever revolutionary pressures bubbled up, even if specific dynasties came and went. Not so around the Atlantic.

The Atlantic revolutions had direct links in the form of mobile ideas and personnel, and interlocking events. The concepts of limited royal sovereignty that animated the British Revolution filtered into British North America, France, and at least indirectly into Saint-Domingue and Spanish America. Similarly, the principles embodied in the American Declaration of Independence and France's Declaration of the Rights of Man and Citizen were influential in the revolutions in Haiti and Spanish America.

People such as Francisco Miranda moved from revolution to revolution. Many of the fighters in Toussaint's armies in Haiti came from Kongo, bringing not only military skills but ideas about proper exercise of power. Similarly, thousands of Frenchmen fought in the American Revolution, and many of them just a few years later took part in the French Revolution. And a few thousand veterans of the wars of the French Revolution fought for independence in Spanish America.

In some cases, the events of the Atlantic revolutions, as well as personnel and ideas, were interlinked. The French and the Haitian Revolutions, overlapping in time and both involving the French Empire, directly affected one another. The French Revolution, via Bonaparte's invasion of Spain, opened the political vacuum in Spanish America that ultimately brought independence there. And French involvement in the American Revolution deepened debts that pushed the French king to summon the Estates-General, setting in motion events he would regret.

DIFFERENT OUTCOMES

For all their common roots and interconnections, the Atlantic revolutions produced differing results. Some decentralization occurred everywhere, but each situation had its own character. Kongo became more unstable, violent, and enmeshed in the slave trade. Britain achieved considerable stability after 1689. So too did the United States after a rocky start, although the issue of slavery would bring civil war a few decades later—as we shall see. In France, the revolution collapsed into dictatorship, and in 1815 a restoration of royal power followed Bonaparte's exile. Haiti also collapsed into dictatorship and then a very unstable republic. In Spanish America, unstable republics alternating with intervals of military dictatorship became the norm.

The Atlantic revolutions also brought different results for the most disenfranchised members of society. Women took part in various ways, most visibly in Kongo, France, and North America. Some of them hoped that revolution would usher in a new age for women. None of the revolutions immediately changed the political circumstances of women, although in New Jersey the state constitution allowed unmarried women who owned property to vote between 1797 and 1807. After that, New Jersey restricted voting rights, as in most U.S. states, to adult white males. In France, Bonaparte actually restricted women's rights more narrowly than before 1789.

Enslaved people also took part in several of these revolutions, most prominently in Haiti and Kongo but also in the birth of the United States and in Spanish America. The revolutions produced the abolition of slavery in Haiti and most parts of Spanish America. In the United States, some northern states abolished slavery after the Revolution, but it took the Civil War to achieve this on the national scale. France abolished slavery, but then Bonaparte reinstated it, and it lasted until 1848 in the French Empire. In Kongo, slavery survived until the kingdom ended in the 1850s.

The American Revolution and those in Spanish America also had important implications for indigenous populations. Both Britain and Spain imposed constraints on the exploitation of indigenous peoples, in particular checking the seizure of their lands. The revolutions lifted most of those constraints, inviting settlers to stream westward into the Midwest and, after 1810 or so, into the Deep

South—sometimes bringing enslaved people with them. In Mexico and most of South America, for half a century (ca. 1820–1870) the newly independent states were too weak militarily to impose their laws on most indigenous communities. But by the late nineteenth century, as we will see, the legacy of the revolutions in Spanish America and Brazil proved deeply unfortunate for remaining indigenous peoples.

The Atlantic revolutions helped to reshuffle fortunes in a geopolitical sense too. The big winners eventually proved to be Britain, France, and the United States, which in the nineteenth and twentieth centuries would play enlarged roles in international politics. The biggest losers were Spain and Kongo, both of which emerged weaker than before.

REVOLUTIONS AS EXPERIENCE

The Atlantic revolutions, like most revolutions, had two additional important things in common. First, the outcomes just described were never inevitable, and they rarely resembled what revolutionaries intended. They all took place in fluid situations in which old beliefs, customs, institutions—and usually treasuries and armies—grew weaker. People began to imagine new futures of all sorts, but not necessarily the futures they got. In Kongo, Beatriz Kimpa Vita did not get a united Kongo but a weakened one. Abigail Adams and Olympe de Gouges hoped for political rights for women, but did not get them. Bolívar wanted a united South America, not a handful of unstable republics.

The Atlantic revolutions were also miserable experiences for most people. Although many people felt hope, liberation, and exhilaration, many also felt fear, anxiety, betrayal, and worse. Mass executions, massacres, and torture, as well as the more routine sufferings of war, famine, and disease, abounded. While history is rightly concerned with causes and consequences of major events, it is well to remember what it was like to live through them.

CONCLUSION

From 1640 to 1830, the Atlantic world took a new and different path. It underwent an especially rapid expansion of commerce, faster than it had before and faster than anywhere else in the world at the time. This change brought new pressures from new social groups that upset political arrangements all around the Atlantic. Every revolution had its own particular causes, of course, but they all owed something to the economic and social changes common around the Atlantic.

In Britain, the United States, and Spanish America, these revolutions led to a decentralization or disappearance of royal power, greater self-rule, and more representative political institutions such as legislatures or parliaments. Even where such formal institutions did not develop, as in Kongo, royal power weakened and merchant groups, including Kongolese slave traders, won greater political voice. In France and Haiti, the revolutions brought a temporary decentralization of power followed by dictatorship.

The extension of self-rule in the Atlantic revolutions did not go so far as to include women, men without property, or indigenous Americans. The revolutions in Spanish America did lead to the abolition of slavery, but freed people remained marginal citizens with limited, if any, political rights. And in the United States, slavery long outlasted the Revolution.

In the long run, however, the trend established by the ideas, principles, and rhetoric of the Atlantic revolutions led to more open, equal, and democratic societies, both around the Atlantic and eventually in many countries around the world. In cases, it took a century or more before women, poor men, indigenous people, and people of African descent in the Americas enjoyed legal equality with other citizens. That it happened at all is testament to the strength of the ideals voiced by the makers of revolution in Kongo, Britain, the United States, France, Haiti, and Spanish America.

CHAPTER REVIEW

KEY TERMS

Kongo monarchy (p. 677)
Beatriz Kimpa Vita
  (p. 679)
rising merchant classes
  (p. 679)
Parliament (p. 680)
Glorious Revolution
  (p. 682)

Pontiac's War (p. 684)
American Revolution
  (p. 685)
French Revolution
  (p. 687)
Jacobins (p. 690)
Napoleon Bonaparte
  (p. 691)
Toussaint L'Ouverture
  (p. 694)

Haitian Revolution
  (p. 694)
Bourbon Reforms
  (p. 696)
Túpac Amaru II (p. 696)
Simón Bolívar (p. 698)
political decentralization
  (p. 699)

Go to INQUIZITIVE to see what you've learned—and learn what you've missed—with personalized feedback along the way.

REVIEW QUESTIONS

1. What liberties did the rising merchant classes seek during this period?
2. On what principle did the legitimacy and power of Kongo kings rest?
3. In what ways was the fragmentation of power in Kongo linked to its Atlantic connections?
4. What were the main sources of conflict between Charles I and Parliament?
5. What political and religious arrangements did the British Civil Wars and Revolution cement?
6. Describe the disagreements between American colonists and the British government over land access and taxes.
7. What principles did the American Constitution include, and whose rights did it exclude?
8. Explain the intellectual and socioeconomic changes that contributed to the start of the French Revolution.
9. Why and how did the French Revolution enter a violent phase?
10. What features did the Haitian Revolution share with the American and French Revolutions, and what feature was different?
11. How did Toussaint L'Ouverture fend off British and French armies during the Haitian Revolution?
12. Whom did the Bourbon Reforms irritate, and why?
13. How did Napoleon Bonaparte's takeover of Spain contribute to Spain's loss of control over most of its colonies in the Americas?
14. What were the common roots and interconnections of the Atlantic revolutions?
15. What were the effects of the Atlantic revolutions for women, enslaved people, and indigenous Americans?

FURTHER READING

Laurent DUBOIS, *Avengers of the New World: The Story of the Haitian Revolution* (2005). A crisp narrative by one of the top historians of the subject.

Patrick GRIFFIN, *The Age of Atlantic Revolution: The Fall and Rise of a Connected World* (2023). On the eighteenth century only, but a good example of the advantages of a transatlantic perspective.

Brian R. HAMNETT, *The End of Iberian Rule on the American Continent, 1770-1830* (2017). A handy synthesis of independence in Brazil and Spanish America.

Woody HOLTON, *Liberty Is Sweet: The Hidden History of the American Revolution* (2021). A sweeping story that focuses on ordinary people.

Jonathan ISRAEL, *The Expanding Blaze: How the American Revolution Ignited the World, 1775-1848* (2017). A detailed look at the political ideas of the American Revolution as translated into Europe and Latin America.

Wim KLOOSTER, *Revolutions in the Atlantic World: A Comparative History* (2018, 2nd ed.). Provides brief narratives together with an analysis that emphasizes Atlantic dimensions.

Peter McPHEE, *Liberty or Death: The French Revolution* (2016). A general summary of the French Revolution, unusually sympathetic to Robespierre.

Dorindra OUTRAM, *The Enlightenment* (2019). A short but wide-angle look at intellectual changes and their social roots.

Janet POLASKY, *Revolutions without Borders: The Call to Liberty in the Atlantic World* (2015). Explores the circulation of ideas among revolutionary societies.

John K. THORNTON, *The Kongolese Saint Anthony: Dona Beatriz Kimpa Vita and the Antonian Movement, 1684-1706* (1998). A careful study of Beatriz with helpful background on Kongo politics and religion.

Women and Atlantic Revolutions

THE ATLANTIC REVOLUTIONS CONSIDERED IN THIS CHAPTER were mainly led by men. But women contributed in various ways to all of them—sometimes as intellectuals authoring appeals to reform or revolution, sometimes by mounting the barricades, sometimes by sewing shirts for soldiers, sometimes by handling finances. (Women also resisted each of these revolutions, siding with forces that sought to prevent social and political changes.)

In the selections below we see examples of women, both as individuals and in groups, contributing to revolutionary change: as leader of a prophetic movement in Africa, as fundraiser and patriot in the United States, as military logistics manager and political strategist in South America, and as a group of petitioners to the French king. None of these societies sanctioned women playing prominent and overt political roles. But in all of them, women seized the chance presented by instability and uncertainty to insert themselves into politics, one way or another.

SOURCE 20.1

Dona Beatriz's Hymn, ca. 1705

After 1665 the Christianized kingdom of Kongo, in west-central Africa, fractured into warring factions. Forty years later, Dona Beatriz Kimpa Vita, a 21-year-old Bakongo woman influenced by Catholic messages, sought to reunite it. Charismatic and persuasive, she convinced many followers that Italian priests allied with Kongo warlords had concealed the true history of the church; that St. Anthony—conventionally a medieval Portuguese priest—and key figures such as Jesus, Mary, and St. Francis were actually Bakongo; and that St. Anthony had revealed the truth to her.

In the text presented here, Dona Beatriz converts Catholic teachings into something akin to Bakongo nationalism. She changes a Catholic hymn to the Virgin Mary, "Salve Regina," into a hymn to St. Anthony. An Italian priest heard it recited in Kikongo (the language of Bakongo) and wrote down an Italian version, which survives in the Vatican Archives; it is here put into English. While inevitably something has been lost in the two translations, we can still puzzle out some of what Dona Beatriz is saying.

> "Hail" you say without knowing why.
> "Hail," you recite without knowing why.
> "Hail," you beat [perhaps as in a drum] without knowing why.
> God wants the intention, God grasps the intention.
> The marriage ceremony serves no purpose, God grasps the intention. ₅
> Baptism serves no purpose, God grasps the intention.
> Confession serves no purpose, God grasps the intention.

> Prayer serves no purpose, God wants the intention.
> Good works serve no purpose, God wants the intention.
> The mother with her son on lap, if it hadn't been for St. Anthony what could they do? ₁₀
> St. Anthony is merciful,
> St. Anthony is our remedy,
> St. Anthony is the restorer of the Kingdom of the Kongo.
> St. Anthony consoles us about [the difficulty of entering] the kingdom of heaven.
> St. Anthony is the gate to heaven. ₁₅
> St. Anthony holds the keys to heaven.
> St. Anthony stands above the angels and the Virgin Mary.
> St. Anthony stands second only to God.

Source: Archivio "De Propaganda Fide" (Vatican, Rome), Scritture Originali nelli Congregazione Generali, vol. 576, folio 304v. Printed in Teobaldo Filesi, Nazionalismo e religione nel Congo all'inizio del 1700 (Rome: ABETE, 1972).

- Why might Dona Beatriz want to tell her followers that they don't understand the Christian prayers they've been reciting and that the Catholic sacraments (such as baptism and confession) are useless?
- Why might tens of thousands of Bakongo people find her message appealing?
- In this hymn, how is she using religion for political aims?

SOURCE 20.2

The Sentiments of an American Woman, 1780

The text below was written in part or perhaps entirely by Esther de Berndt Reed (1746–1780). Born in

London, at age 23 she married a law student from New Jersey with whom she crossed the Atlantic to Philadelphia in 1770. By 1775 she was a strong supporter of political rights for Americans. By 1780 she had become the mother of five children, and her husband had become a prosperous lawyer and prominent political figure who worked as a secretary for George Washington. As the American Revolution unfolded, she founded the Ladies Association of Philadelphia, which raised money and sewed clothes for the Continental Army. After her death, from dysentery, similar women's associations devoted to the cause of the American Revolution sprang up in other cities.

On the commencement of actual war, the Women of America manifested a firm resolution to contribute as much as could depend on them, to the deliverance of their country. Animated by the purest patriotism they are sensible of sorrow at this day, in not offering more than barren wishes for the success of so glorious a Revolution. They aspire to render themselves more really useful.... Our ambition is kindled by the fame of those heroines of antiquity, who have rendered their sex illustrious, and have proved to the universe, that, if the weakness of our Constitution, if opinion and manners did not forbid us to march to glory by the same path as the Men, we should at least equal and sometimes surpass them in our love for the public good. I glory in all that which my sex has done great and commendable. I call to mind with enthusiasm and with admiration, all those acts of courage, of constancy and patriotism, which history has transmitted to us:...the zeal and the resolution of Deborah, of Judith, of Esther!...Rome saved from the fury of a victorious enemy by the efforts of Volumnia, and other Roman ladies: So many famous sieges where the Women have been seen forgetting the weakness of their sex, building new walls, digging trenches with their feeble hands; furnishing arms to their defenders, they themselves darting the missile weapons on the enemy, resigning the ornaments of their apparel, and their fortunes to fill the public treasury, and to hasten the deliverance of their country; burying themselves under its ruins; throwing themselves into the flames rather than submit to the disgrace of humiliation before a proud enemy.

[...]

We know that at a distance from the theatre of war, if we enjoy any tranquility, it is the fruit of your [Continental Army soldiers'] watchings, your labours, your dangers. If I live happy in the midst of my family...it is to you that we owe it. And shall we hesitate to evidence to you our gratitude? Shall we hesitate to wear a clothing more simple; hair dressed less elegant...? Who, amongst us, will not renounce with the highest pleasure, those vain ornaments, when she shall consider that the valiant defenders of America will be able to draw some advantage from the money which she may have laid out in these; that they will be better defended from the rigours of the seasons, that after their painful toils, they will receive some extraordinary and unexpected

relief; that these presents will perhaps be valued by them at a greater price, when they will have it in their power to say: *This is the offering of the Ladies*. The time is arrived to display the same sentiments which animated us at the beginning of the Revolution, when we renounced the use of teas, however agreeable to our taste, rather than receive them from our persecutors.... Let us not lose a moment; let us be engaged to offer the homage of our gratitude at the altar of military valour.

Source: "The Sentiments of an American Woman," *The Pennsylvania Magazine of History and Biography* 18, no. 3 (1894): 361–66.

- According to this document, what could American women do to help support the American Revolution?
- Why might the author frame this call to patriotism in the contexts of the ancient Hebrews and Romans?

SOURCE 20.3

Micaela Bastidas's Letters to Her Husband, Tupac Amaru, 1780–1781

In 1780–1781, a major rebellion against Spanish rule shook the Andes. An elite indigenous merchant, descended from the Inka royal line, took the name Tupac Amaru II, symbolizing his claim to leadership of the uprising. His wife, Micaela Bastidas (1745–1781), although probably of Spanish parentage, took an energetic part in the revolt. She organized recruitment, arms, and finances for the rebel army of about 6,000 fighters. In particular, she cajoled and threatened local leaders whose loyalties to the cause wavered. As the rebellion collapsed in 1781, she was captured and, like her husband and son, gruesomely executed. A large trove of her captured papers has survived, giving some insight into her roles in the uprising.

Some words may need explaining: *cacica* and *cacique(s)* are terms for indigenous leaders; *Justicia Mayor* is a position similar to sheriff; Chepe is Michaela's affectionate name for her husband; *alcades* are town mayors; *yerba* is a South American tea; *reales* are coins.

1. Letter from *Cacica* Tomasa Titu Condemayta to Micaela Bastidas about Fears of Capture and Tupac Amaru's Absence

Señora Doña Micaela Bastidas.—Tungasuca.—My very dear Lady.—I hereby inform you as I have been surely informed, that those from Cuzco are determined to get out to the provinces and Chumbivilcas this Monday.

That individual who you left or put in place as *Justicia Mayor* in Livitaca, Juan Zubizarreta, left with all his people for Cuzco, but was apprehended in Paruro. And in this manner they [loyalists] have come from Quiquijana from the ravines, from everywhere to surround us. They know that the Inca is far away and with this lack of protection they want to ambush us. I do not know what we can do. Be mindful so that they do not descend on your Mercy.

I have been very worried by Don José's (Tupac Amaru's) tardiness; I hope God will bring him back safe as soon as possible.

In Corma, 500 sheep and some cows have been seized from Bedoya, who has been against us, for which Pedro Antonio will account, and in this I suppose Your Mercy will give me counsel and advise me when you arrive. May God conserve the health that Your Mercy desires, and I beg that you will keep and protect us with your power. Acos, December 9th, 1780.—I kiss your hand—Your humble vassal.

—Tomasa (Titu Condemayta)

2. Letter from *Cacica* Tomasa Titu Condemayta to Micaela Bastidas on the Difficulties of the Situation and Being a Woman

Señora Doña Micaela Bastidas.—My most beloved lady. I received yours [letter] and have taken due notice of its content. I have to say that here among our Band we are so close [intimate] that just for being a woman, I have done much to defend my position; that Don Marcos (de la Torre) is so fresh that he presumes I go about putting on airs.

And under these circumstances I do not know what to do; I am so at a disadvantage just by being a woman, and despite this I did what was needed and all I could in Los Altos, and thus you can see my situation. Also, I warn Your Mercy that you will not be able to get out of Acos or Acomayo, as we are in a bad spot. I warn you so that you can choose a better leader like Don Julián Escalante, who is young and more educated than Marcos . . . so that we have somebody who can motivate us, and you can name Marcos as a sergeant.

And please, Your Mercy, will not permit us to be ruined; already two people have not returned, and I am being very careful; and I do not know when you will be coming here. . . . Your humble.

—Tomasa (Tiru Condemayta)

3. Letter from Bastidas to Tupac Amaru about Problems and Betrayal

Chepe: I just received information as to how those [loyalists] from Cuzco departed for three different places, and one of them is Catca, whose people (based on trusted information) have been wiped out. Sucacagua and the others have betrayed us, as indicated in the attachment; and thus I am not myself, because we have very few people. You have ignored my letters, trying to deliver me to the bulls' horns, but do not allow them to take my life, for your absence has been the reason for all this. On Monday, which is tomorrow, they will enter in Quiquijana and then Acos and the surrounding villages on the same day; so, speed up your march.

May God keep you for many years.—Tungasuca, December 10th, 1780.

—Your *Mica*

4. Bastidas Gives Orders to Apprehend a *Cacique* Who Betrayed Them

COMMISSION.—Don Diego Berdejo is commissioned to go to Quiquijana as soon as possible, and with the help of the people and their *alcaldes,* apprehend Francisco Sucacahua for contradicting the orders of my husband, Don José Gabriel Tupac Amaru, and bring him to this town of Tungasuca, well guarded and protected; preventing him from asking the *caciques* of Combapata and Checacupi for help, who will also be dealt with, under the threat that if they do not carry them out [the orders] they will severely be punished.—Tungasuca, December 10th, 1780.

—Doña Micaela Bastidas

[. . .]

54. Letter from Her Brother to Micaela Bastidas

Sra. Doña Micaela Bastidas.—My most beloved, sister of my heart.—I received Your Honor's [letter] dated 28th of the current month, where you warn me to be careful of my enemies; I do not relent, I am always very careful and always successful.

I received six blocks of cheese, sugar, rice and tea *yerba* for which I am most grateful. I am not sending the bread, as we do not seem to find any. I am keeping the four *reales* with me, so I can order it to be kneaded and will send it soon.

Please ask Your Honor the Inca to send us *piedra de fusil* [rocks specially rounded for the mortar or cannon] which we are badly missing, and to God, whom I beg to protect Your Mercy for many years.—Quiquijana, March 29th, 1781. Your Honor's brother.

—Antonio Bastidas

Source: *The Tupac Amaru and Catarista Rebellions: An Anthology of Sources,* ed. and trans. Ward Stavig and Ella Schmidt, introduction by Charles F. Walker (Indianapolis, IN: Hackett Publishing Company, 2008).

- What duties and responsibilities of Micaela Bastidas do these letters attest to?
- From letters #3 and #4, which she dictated, what would you judge to be her main concerns as of December 1780?

SOURCE 20.4

Petition of Women of the Third Estate to the King, 1789

As the text explains, early in the French Revolution the summoning of the Estates-General allowed segments of the French public to air concerns and grievances. Soon thereafter, members of the Third Estate (mostly peasant farmers and urban artisans and professionals) declared itself to be a National Assembly representing the will of the people.

The petition below was delivered in January 1789, six months before the assault on the Bastille. At the time, women had no political rights and could not legally assemble. But in this time of tumult, some women—we don't know how many or just who they were—took the opportunity to express their views of the plight of women in France and suggest some remedies. They addressed their petition not to the Estates-General, but directly to King Louis XVI. (In the text, "five or six *sous* a day" would equal about a tenth of a workingman's daily wage.

Sire,

At a time when the various orders of the state are busy with their interests, when everyone is trying to assert his titles and his rights, when some people are worrying about recalling centuries of servitude and anarchy, when others are making every effort to shake off the last links which still bind them to the imperious remains of the feudal system, women—continual objects of the admiration and scorn of men—women, wouldn't it be possible for them also to make their voice heard amidst this general agitation?

[...]

The women of the Third Estate are almost all born without fortune; their education is very neglected or very defective: it consists in their being sent to schools at the house of a teacher who himself does not know the first word of the language he is teaching. They continue going there until they are able to read the service of the Mass in French and Vespers in Latin. Having fulfilled the first duties of religion, they are taught to work; having reached the age of fifteen or sixteen, they can make five or six *sous* a day. If nature has refused them beauty, they get married without dowry to unfortunate artisans, lead aimless, difficult lives stuck away in the provinces, and give birth to children they are incapable of raising. If, on the contrary, they are born pretty, without culture, without principles, without any idea of morals, they become the prey of the first seducer, commit a first sin, come to Paris to bury their shame, end by losing it altogether, and die victims of licentious ways.

Today, when the difficulty of subsisting forces thousands of them to put themselves up for auction, when men find it easier to buy them for a spell than to win them over forever, those whom a happy penchant inclines to virtue, who are consumed by the desire to learn, who feel themselves led by a natural taste, who have overcome the deficiencies of their education and know a little of everything without having learned anything, those, to conclude, whom a haughty soul, a noble heart, a pride of sentiment cause to be called *prudish*, are forced to throw themselves into cloisters where only a modest dowry is required....

Also, several, solely because they are born girls, are disdained by their parents, who refuse to set them up, preferring to concentrate their fortune on the head of a son whom they designate to carry on their name in the capital; for it is good that Your Majesty understands that we also have names to keep up. Or, if old age finds them spinsters, they spend it in tears and see themselves the object of the scorn of their nearest relatives.

To prevent so many ills, Sire, we ask that men not be allowed, under any pretext, to exercise trades that are the prerogative of women—such as seamstress, embroiderer, *marchande de mode*, etc., etc.; if we are left at least with the needle and the spindle, we promise never to handle the compass or the square.

We ask, Sire, that your benevolence provide us with the means of putting to use the talents with which nature will have furnished us, notwithstanding the impediments which are forever being placed on our education.

[...]

We ask to be enlightened, to have work, not in order to usurp men's authority, but in order to be better esteemed by them, so that we might have the means of living out of the way of misfortune and so that poverty does not force the weakest among us, who are blinded by luxury and swept along by example, to join the crowd of unfortunate beings who overpopulate the streets and whose debauched audacity is a disgrace to our sex and to the men who keep them company.

[...]

We implore you, Sire, to set up free schools where we could learn our language on the basis of principles [and] religion and ethics.... May our hearts be formed there; may we be taught above all to practice the virtues of our sex: gentleness, modesty, patience, charity; as for the arts that please, women learn them without teachers. Sciences?... they serve only to inspire us with a stupid pride, lead us to pedantry, go against the desires of nature, make of us mixed beings who are rarely faithful wives and still more rarely good mothers of families.

Source: *Women in Revolutionary Paris, 1789–1795: Selected Documents*, trans. with notes and commentary by Darline Gay Levy, Harriet Branson Applewhite, Mary Durham Johnson (Chicago: University of Illinois Press, 1980).

- **What do the petitioners regard as the main grievances of women?**
- **What are the remedies they seek?**

QUESTIONS FOR COMPARISON

1. How do the women represented in these texts justify involving themselves in political struggles?

2. Is there any evidence here that women experienced or understood revolutions and turmoil differently than men did? Explain your response.

CHRONOLOGY

1733
"Flying shuttle" is introduced in Britain

1790
Cotton mill makes use of steam engine for first time in Britain

1770s
First steamships are built in France

1769–1785
James Watt registers six patents on steam engines

1780s
Water-powered loom is developed

1791
Alexander Hamilton writes tract supporting tariffs

1794
Cotton gin is patented

1804
First locomotives go into use in coal mines in Britain

1825
First railway carrying passengers and general freight operates in Britain

1838
Steam-powered vessels begin scheduled Atlantic crossings

1840s
Long-distance telegraph is patented

1848
Worker uprisings in Milan, Berlin, Vienna; *Communist Manifesto* is published

1853
American fleet invades Japan; Lowell girls successfully lobby for shorter work day

1853–1856
Crimean War

1867–1868
Meiji Restoration

1871
German unification

1872
Compulsory education for girls and boys is introduced in Japan

1875
German Social Democratic Party is founded

1879
French socialist party is founded; Canada launches National Policy to promote industry

1882
Japan's first modern cotton mill is set up

1886
Canada's first transcontinental railway opens

1889
Hull House is set up in Chicago

21

Fossil Fuels and Mass Production

INDUSTRIAL REVOLUTIONS AROUND THE WORLD

1780 to 1914

The world is too much with us; late and soon,
Getting and spending, we lay waste our powers;—
Little we see in Nature that is ours;
We have given our hearts away, a sordid boon!

—William Wordsworth, ca. 1802

[The steam engine] has armed the feeble hand of man with a power to which no limits can be assigned; completed the dominion of mind over the most refractory qualities of matter; and laid a sure foundation for all those future miracles of mechanical power which are to aid and reward the labours of after generations.

—Sir John Sinclair, 1825

The first four lines of Wordsworth's sonnet express regret about the changes brought by Britain's **Industrial Revolution**. He felt people had become overly concerned with money and had spoiled nature's

1894–1895
Sino-Japanese War

1903
Trans-Siberian Railway
opens

1901
Japanese Social
Democratic Party
is founded

1900
British Labour Party
is founded

1905
Revolution of
1905 in Russia

Industrial Britain This print depicts a scene at the heart of the Industrial Revolution, in the town of Stockport in Britain's West Midlands region around 1845. Chimneys belch coal smoke into the air, large factory buildings are visible in the background, and a steam train from London crosses a viaduct above the town.

FOCUS QUESTIONS

1. In what ways was the Industrial Revolution an energy revolution?

2. Why did England experience the first Industrial Revolution?

3. How did the aims and technologies of industrialization spread across the globe?

4. What were the important global effects of the industrial revolutions?

beauty. Sinclair, in contrast, praised the potential of industrial technology and brimmed with confidence in the benefits to come. Wordsworth (1770–1850) and Sinclair (1754–1835) were contemporaries and lived only a few miles apart—the former in England and the latter in Scotland. Together, they capture some of the key features of the British Industrial Revolution: it shattered longstanding limits on production and wealth, while fundamentally changing society and nature. It was the most significant revolution in modern history.

The term *Industrial Revolution* entered the English language in the 1880s and refers to two main changes in manufacturing methods. The first was the transition from muscle and hand tools to machinery driven by inanimate power—at first water power and then coal-burning steam engines. The second change was the transition from household- or workshop-scale production to factory-scale production. What made these transitions truly revolutionary was steam power, which vastly expanded the levels of production and consumption a society could achieve. What made steam power work was the energy locked up in coal.

The concept of the Industrial Revolution is sometimes used only for the period from about 1770 to about 1870, and sometimes only for the case of Britain. This chapter, however, deals with the origins and course of industrial revolutions globally up to 1914, emphasizing in particular the experiences of Britain, Germany, the United States, Canada, Russia, and Japan. In following the story to 1914, this chapter includes what historians sometimes call the Second Industrial Revolution. In some cases—notably the United States, Britain, and Germany—after 1870 new industrial techniques dramatically improved the efficiency and scale of production of steel, chemicals, oil, and electricity. This surge of technological change after 1870 relied more heavily on science and educated engineers than did the early Industrial Revolution. A large proportion of the important technologies of today—automobiles, aircraft, turbines—made their debut between 1870 and 1914 in the Second Industrial Revolution.

The Industrial Revolution began in Britain, but it had global consequences. It transformed economies through the production of cheap, mass-produced goods, and it vaulted Britain, a small island nation, to the first rank of economic powers for the entire nineteenth century. It transformed societies through the formation of a new urban class of factory workers and the expansion of a middle class of accountants, lawyers, teachers, secretaries, and factory managers. It transformed politics by creating a newly rich class of entrepreneurs who eventually claimed a share of political power in accordance with their wealth. It also led to groups of workers claiming a share of power through union activism and politics, although that happened more slowly. It transformed the environment too, by generating unprecedented quantities of air and water pollution from factories, and by equipping people with powerful new tools that made it more profitable than ever before to dig new mines, turn forests into cotton fields, or kill 30 million North American bison for their hides.

The Industrial Revolution was the most momentous change in human history since the Neolithic Revolution some 10,000 years ago. As we've seen, the

Neolithic Revolution—the domestication of plants and animals and the advent of farming—opened the way to densely settled populations, cities, hierarchical societies, and eventually states. The Industrial Revolution opened the way to a high-energy society based on fossil fuels such as coal or oil. Over decades, the use of fossil fuels in industry and transport boosted economic growth so that it usually outpaced population growth, enriching at least a segment of every society around the world. It opened the way to greater inequality, as some people could now amass wealth on a scale unavailable even to pharaohs, sultans, kings, and emperors in previous times. It opened the way to fossil-fuel combustion and carbon emissions to the atmosphere in quantities sufficient to change the Earth's climate. And it opened the way to outcomes we haven't yet seen or imagined, because industrialization is still ongoing.

Although both the Neolithic Revolution and the Industrial Revolution were momentous turning points in world history, they were very different. For one thing, people independently transitioned from hunting and foraging to farming in at least seven places around the globe, and with different sets of crops and animals in each case. In contrast, there was only one independent transition from agrarian to industrial society, in Britain. Every subsequent transition has drawn directly or indirectly upon the British experience. By the time of the Industrial Revolution, unlike the situation in 9000 BCE, the world was so bound together by the connections of the Global web that one transition was enough: sooner or later, the example of the British Industrial Revolution influenced every corner of the world.

Compared to the Neolithic Revolution, industrialization spread at a lightning pace. What germinated in British soil could not, however, simply be transplanted to other lands. In every case geography, culture, legal systems, and much else were different from Britain's. Rather, the ambition to imitate Britain's Industrial Revolution spread to many other peoples, some of whom managed to pull off their own industrial revolutions.

The interconnectedness of the Global web made the ambition to imitate Britain an urgent one from a business point of view. Once Britain could mass-produce inexpensive goods, the increasingly unified world economy created ruthless competition for businesses everywhere else. They needed to modernize and mechanize quickly to survive. There was a geopolitical urgency to industrialization too. As British society and the British state quickly grew in wealth and power after 1800, some people in other societies recognized that they needed to follow suit to avoid domination. This recognition created enormous internal stresses within societies and states, as reformers eagerly sought to industrialize their societies while traditionalists fought to preserve the old ways that, as they saw it, had served their societies so well for so long.

The circuits of the Global web proved highly efficient in transmitting the ambition to industrialize. They proved reasonably efficient in transmitting specific technologies, whether power looms or locomotives, from one setting to another. But the underlying knowledge of how to build and maintain machinery, or how to manage a factory and a supply chain, traveled less well. And the interlocking social, political, economic, and technological systems that enabled industrialization to develop, grow, and survive amid the social tensions it provoked—those systems developed only here and there. Some countries, such as the United States or Japan, built such interlocking systems fairly quickly and rode the wave of industrialization with a success that surprised all observers. Other countries, such as Egypt, tried and failed. A few countries, mainly those with minimal traditions of formal education and meager natural resources, did not try at all.

The industrial revolutions changed the nature of older global linkages, especially in terms of economic specializations and economic power. More than ever before, some regions specialized in raw material production—cotton, iron ore, leather—while others concentrated on making these raw materials into shirts, ships, and shoes. By and large, those regions focused on raw material production found themselves poor and weak in relation to those that performed the more skilled, complex, and profitable tasks of industrial production.

So the industrial revolutions of the period 1780–1914 created a more differentiated world, but also a more unified one. It became more differentiated because social inequality within societies, and economic and military gaps between societies, grew spectacularly, and they continue to grow to this day. But it also became more unified because the connections among people, institutions, and societies grew thicker than ever before, thanks to new technologies of transport and communications, new market linkages, and much else brought about by industrialization, patchy though it was.

AN ENERGY REVOLUTION

In every case around the world, industrial revolutions featured **textiles and metallurgy** above all else. In most societies, spinning thread and weaving cloth was routine work for women and girls. In some societies, men also wove, especially in the slack months of the agricultural calendar. Other handicrafts, such as leather working or furniture making, were typically male pursuits, followed both in village households and in town workshops. This local, small-scale manufacturing was conducted with muscle power or occasionally with help from a water mill or windmill. Many of these businesses—leather working or beer brewing, for example—could not scale up to factory mass production easily.

But textiles and metallurgy could scale up. Mills, forges, and factories, in which relatively unskilled laborers worked at machines powered by flowing water or by steam engines, suited the tasks of making cloth and iron.

So these industries were usually in the vanguard of industrialization. By 1870, with the Second Industrial Revolution, factory-scale production was successfully applied to a wider range of activities, creating new key industries such as steel, chemicals, and electricity. To scale up, almost every industry required inputs of energy far beyond what human and animal muscle could provide. So underlying the newly mechanized industries lay a special resource vital to the British Industrial Revolution and important to all of them: coal.

COAL AND STEAM

At its heart, the Industrial Revolution was an energy revolution. At first, the textile and iron industries in Britain scaled up to factory production with waterwheels that conveyed the energy of flowing water to power looms and furnaces. Steam engines weren't efficient enough yet. But over time, the best riverside locations for water-powered mills were taken, and steam engines improved. So by the 1830s, new mills typically used steam power.

Steam power came from **coal**. The central feature of the energy revolution was the development of new ways to use the chemical energy contained in coal and, later, in other fossil fuels such as oil or natural gas. The use of fossil fuels for heat energy wasn't new. In north China during the Song dynasty (960–1279), for example, coal had fueled a metallurgical industry that flourished for over a century. In the Dutch lands

Water Power Harnessing the energy of flowing water made possible factory-scale textile production in Britain. An illustration of an early textile mill from eighteenth-century England emphasizes the large waterwheel used to power the mill's machinery.

from the fourteenth century onward, people used peat (semifossilized remains of bog moss) to fuel brewing, salt making, sugar refining, and other energy-intensive pursuits. From the sixteenth century, Londoners used coal for home heating and for enterprises such as glass-making that needed heat energy.

STEAM POWER **Steam engines**, however, could convert the chemical energy of fossil fuels into mechanical energy rather than simply into heat energy. They used coal fires to heat water into steam. The expansion of hot steam, and its contraction as it cooled, served as the motor force behind pistons, shafts, and belts that carried power to looms, pumps, or wheels. Coal worked its transformations only because of steam engines.

For centuries, people in Ptolemaic Egypt, the Ottoman Empire, Italy, France, and possibly China had experimented with rudimentary steam engines, but they were only curiosities. In eighteenth-century Britain, which had a developed coal industry already, steam engines proved more useful. The first steam engines built there were so fuel-hungry that they could only be used at the mines themselves, where chunks of coal lay around unused. Only Britain had enough coal mines, and a strong enough market for coal, to make it worthwhile to improve steam engines. Between 1712, when Thomas Newcomen revealed an early model, and 1812, steam engines mainly worked to pump water out of coal pits. After 1733, all British coal mines had one. That made mining easier and coal cheaper, and in turn motivated people to tinker more with steam engines. Engineers introduced many small improvements to steam engines, making them 10 times more fuel efficient (1712 to 1812).

The most famous of these engineers was **James Watt** (1736–1819), a Scot born into an educated family and trained to make mathematical instruments. He learned German and Italian to gain access to practical mechanical knowledge. While employed to maintain instruments at the University of Glasgow, he registered six patents on steam engines between 1769 and 1785. Watt had no head for business, but he found partners who did. Together, they designed, built, and marketed much more efficient steam engines starting in the 1780s. They also sued everyone else who built good steam engines until their key patent ran out in 1800.

The first cotton mill to make use of a steam engine opened in Manchester, England, in 1790. Water power still

Steam Engines James Watt's new, more efficient steam engine, depicted heraae in a technical illustration, used the pressure generated from steam to drive a series of pistons and shafts, which in turn could operate machines in factories and mines.

remained more efficient for most factories until the 1830s, but by 1870 steam engines reigned supreme and water power was effectively extinct in British manufacturing.

THE POWER OF FOSSIL FUELS

This shift in Britain represented the beginning of a global energy transition to fossil fuels. The Neolithic Revolution had allowed people to harvest perhaps 10 to 100 times as much energy, in the form of edible plants, as they could when foraging and hunting. Farming allowed more people to exist, but most of them had to work harder to get enough to eat than did hunters and foragers. Despite farmers' expanded energy harvest, energy regimes based on the annual flow of sunshine into plant tissues kept almost everyone poor. Coal, and fossil fuels generally, made it possible for the first time ever for more than a tiny fraction of people to avoid poverty.

Coal is not an annual flow, like sunshine into plants, but a stock. It is the residue of ancient plants, the equivalent of solid sunshine. Burning it provided access to the bounty of about 500 million years' worth of photosynthesis. Machines that could transform coal's energy into motor power burst the boundaries of the old economy, permitting the creation and accumulation of previously unimaginable wealth—as Sinclair foresaw. Since about 1870, humankind has obtained more energy annually from coal than all the green plants on Earth could capture from the sun.

In short, fossil fuels, combined with machinery and know-how, enabled industrial production far faster and far greater than even the hardest workers could manage using only human or animal muscle. This ended the necessity of mass poverty, to which all previous societies were condemned. That was the most important social consequence of the Industrial Revolution.

But the energy in coal scarcely made everyone rich. The wealth created by burning vast quantities of fossil fuels to make goods more efficiently normally went only to some people, such as factory owners, especially in the early decades of industrialization. So a second major consequence of the adoption of coal, and of the industrial revolutions more generally, was an expansion of inequality. This combination—simultaneous increases in both wealth and inequality—is routine in world economic history, but rarely did it come so suddenly as during the industrial revolutions.

THE INDUSTRIAL REVOLUTION IN BRITAIN

England, specifically the north of England, was the birthplace of the Industrial Revolution. Why not in Europe's long-standing centers of textile manufacturing, such as Flanders (in today's Belgium) or northern Italy? Or the textile districts of India, such as Gujarat or Bengal? Or Ottoman Egypt? Or China's manufacturing heartlands? England in the seventeenth century was still a backwater within Europe. It was among the least urbanized lands, and innovations in its economy often required importing Dutch or Italian expertise. So why was England the site of this economic revolution?

WHY ENGLAND?

A short answer is fateful coincidence. England by 1700 had cheap coal and expensive labor. So it made more economic sense in England than anywhere else to find ways to use less labor and more coal in order to create goods. A fuller answer involves trends in English agriculture, urbanization, transport, and public policy—and it begins with farming.

AGRICULTURE AND URBANIZATION England underwent a gradual agricultural modernization after 1650. Technical improvements doubled cereal yields per acre between 1650 and 1900. By the 1750s, England was exporting about 7 percent of its grain harvest. More efficient farming also fed urbanization. Fewer people were needed as farmworkers. In human terms, this often led to underemployment and hunger in villages. In economic terms, it meant labor was freed to work in nonagricultural sectors. Young people streamed from farms into cities, seeking work. England was urbanizing faster than anywhere else in the world for two centuries after 1650. Industrialization did not launch England's spurt in urbanization; it sped up a trend already in motion.

Urbanization and industrialization each promoted the other. Cities, as always, served as hothouses of information exchange and innovation. Industrialization rested on technical advances in machinery, and those happened more often when mechanically inclined people with restless minds could easily find one another, share ideas, and either work together or compete with one another. Industrialization fostered urbanization, but the connectivity of city life also fostered industrialization.

IMPROVED TRANSPORTATION INFRASTRUCTURE Improvements in rural transport also spurred industrialization. The growth of towns and the increase in farm production required better roads and canals to move more food to cities. Firewood, bales of wool, and other bulky items could find bigger markets if better transport links existed. So landowners and merchants paid people to build and maintain roads and canals. Coal use also provided incentive to dig canals: if moved in carts pulled by animals, coal's price doubled within 10 miles, even on the best roads.

Before 1750, Britain had few good roads. In 1703, the ruts and potholes along a 50-mile stretch of road out of London caused the horse-drawn carriage of future Habsburg emperor Charles VI, at that time merely a king of Spain, to overturn 12 times. The young king survived.

After 1750, British and immigrant Irish laborers constructed thousands of miles of new canals and roads. Between 1750 and 1850, they quadrupled the extent of Britain's navigable inland waterways. By 1770, Britain had 15,000 miles (25,000 km) of turnpikes, or privately maintained roads, and almost everyone lived within a day's walk of one. What had been a four-day ride between

Water Transportation A nineteenth-century painting shows construction of a canal in southwest England. Canals joined Britain's inland waterways into a single system, enabling raw materials, manufactured goods, and people to travel much more efficiently around the country.

London and Holyhead before 1787 took little more than one day by 1837. This infrastructure development, roughly analogous to what Song China (960–1279) had done with its canals, dramatically increased the connectivity of Britain. It became one of the most internally integrated parts of the Global web—as Song China had been within the Old World web. By 1820, even before railroads, the dense transport network moved people, goods, and information more swiftly around Great Britain than almost anywhere else.

The British government spent willingly on transport infrastructure. After the political tumult of 1640 to 1689, the English nobility and merchant elite who dominated Parliament gradually grew accustomed to taxing themselves and empowering government ministers to attend to the national interest. That occasionally included building a turnpike or a canal across landowners' property against their wishes. Moreover, in an effort to pacify rebellious Scots, the British government invested in military road and bridge building throughout Scotland in the 1730s and 1740s.

PROTECTIONIST TARIFFS The British state took other steps that contributed to the Industrial Revolution, if sometimes by accident. Parliament imposed tariffs on imported cloth from India and erected other tariff barriers to protect British manufacturers. The government clarified property rights and patent laws. After the 1790s,

innovators could patent not just new inventions but also improvements to existing ones. In addition, during decades of warfare against revolutionary France (1793–1815), the government became an important customer for large-scale production runs of certain manufactures, such as military uniforms and weaponry. James Watt drew on changes in cannon design to make key improvements in steam engines. So British government policy on transport infrastructure, tariffs, intellectual property rights, and patent law—and its frequent wars—helped promote the Industrial Revolution without any intention of revolutionizing anything.

LABOR COSTS AND TECHNOLOGICAL CHANGE
None of these changes would have brought on the Industrial Revolution had it not been for coal and high wages. After 1680, wages in England climbed, then stagnated from 1700 to 1740, then climbed again. By 1780, wage labor in England was more expensive than just about anywhere else in Europe—or the world. High labor costs created persistent incentives for employers to find ways to substitute machinery for labor.

As a result, almost every manufacturing process in England underwent labor-saving technological changes, which often, in turn, inspired more technological change. The textile industry provides the best examples. The "flying shuttle," introduced in 1733, doubled the productivity of weavers, who now wanted more cotton yarn than hand-spinners could make. This created pressure to invent a more efficient spinning process, which happened in the 1760s with the "spinning jenny" and in the 1770s with the "spinning mule." One person operating a "mule" in 1830 could spin as much cotton into thread as 350 skilled women working by hand with spinning wheels. With spinning machines churning out yarn and thread by the mile, incentives now grew to make weaving even more efficient. Tinkerers developed a water-powered loom in the 1780s, and despite active opposition from skilled weavers, by 1800 some 2,000 power looms were installed in Britain. Skilled weavers were out of luck and out of work by 1857, when 250,000 power looms wove more cloth than tens of millions of hand-weavers could have made.

Other British industries, from iron making to lens grinding, underwent technological change, motivated by the entrepreneurial desire to save on labor costs. Thousands of mechanics and tinkerers learned the intricacies of the new machinery and found ways to make improvements.

Textile Machinery The "spinning jenny" (left) sped up the process of making yarn or cotton thread. The "spinning mule" (right) accelerated production far more by using water to power hundreds of spindles at once. Substituting machinery for labor was central to the British Industrial Revolution.

Educated scientists still played only a small role in these technological advances.

This blend of circumstances and policies might have been enough to start the Industrial Revolution in Britain, but only coal kept it alive. Many other places had coal, but Britain had large quantities of cheap, transportable coal that lay near riverbanks and natural harbors.

BRITISH COAL

As we've seen, the first important industrial use of coal was in the mines themselves. Once the easiest surface deposits of coal had been exploited, what remained lay deep underground in pits, where water threatened to swamp miners. Coal-powered steam pumps working night and day prevented the Industrial Revolution from drowning in infancy. This was the only major technical improvement in mining between 1780 and 1914. It remained hard labor throughout.

A vigorous coal miner scraped 200 to 300 tons per year from the earth. By 1840, some 200,000 men, women, and children labored in the coal pits. Women and girls accounted for about 4 percent—in Scotland perhaps 20 percent—of the underground labor force before 1840. They usually worked as "beasts of burthen" (as one Scottish reformer put it), dragging coal hewn from the rock by their husbands or fathers. In the 1840s, Parliament made it illegal for women to work underground. Most male coal miners first entered the pits between ages 7 and 13 and worked until death or disablement. In 1900, Parliament

forbade boys younger than 13 from working down in the mines. By 1880, half a million Britons were miners, and by 1910 one million. Their hard labor enabled British manufacturing to escape its former constraints.

By 1700, if not before, brewing, glassmaking, brickmaking, metal smelting, and tile making had all switched from firewood to coal except in a few remaining well-wooded parts of Britain. Half of England's energy use came from coal, a situation unique in the world. After 1700, British coal use rose briskly, from 3 million tons annually to 30 million in 1830 and four times that by 1870, by which time hundreds of different industries relied on coal and steam power.

Using coal enabled Britain to keep less land in forest and more in farming. The 5 million tons of coal burned in 1750 took the place of fuelwood (or charcoal) that would have required forests covering one-third of Britain's surface area. By 1820, coal yielded energy equivalent to the British Isles if entirely forested. Several Britains covered in forest could not have provided as much energy as the 125 million tons of coal burned in 1870. Britain's coal deposits were in effect a subterranean forest, providing a resource equivalent to extra land.

Coal substituted for labor as well as for wood. In 1840, steam engines in Britain did the work of about 1 million adult men, and in 1880 about 100 million. At the time, Britain's total population was 34 million, of whom maybe 8 million were adult men. So by 1880, it was as if Britain had 12 times as many laborers as it actually had.

Until the 1830s, few recognized what coal was doing to Britain. The brilliant economists Adam Smith, Thomas Malthus, and David Ricardo all supposed that economic growth could never last long because the supply of natural resources (they termed it *land*) was limited. By the 1860s, however, everyone could see what was happening. As the economist W. S. Jevons put it in 1865: "Coal in truth stands not beside, but entirely above, all other commodities. It is the material source of the energy of the country—the universal aid—the factor in everything we do. With coal almost any feat is possible; without it we are thrown back into the laborious poverty of early times." Jevons put his finger on it. Coal, and the ability to convert its energy into motion that could do work and make things, lay at the heart of Britain's Industrial Revolution.

BRITISH INDUSTRIES

The power of coal and steam engines transformed almost every part of British industry in the decades after 1830. Of these, the most important to world history were cotton, iron, and transport.

COTTON A large part of the work that coal did was powering machines that made cotton cloth. In 1700, Britain hardly spun any cotton and imported finished cloth from India. British cotton manufacturing was uncompetitive with India's because British wages were too high and skills too low, and because raw cotton had to be imported since the plant would not grow in Britain's climate. British weavers, who made mainly woolens and linens, objected to the foreign cotton cloth. To protect the woolen industry and its weavers, Parliament restricted the import of Indian woven cotton cloth, although not raw cotton. That policy helped English cotton manufacturers by eliminating Indian competition.

The tariff on imported cotton cloth gave entrepreneurs an incentive to find ways to weave more raw cotton into cloth in Britain and to adopt the new devices—flying shuttle and power loom—that would reduce labor costs. In a few decades, British cotton manufacturing became internationally competitive: by 1810, cotton cloth accounted for nearly half of British exports. By 1830, cotton mills employed half a million workers in Britain and accounted for about 8 percent of the national economy. Overall, between 1770 and 1840, British imports of raw cotton climbed 100-fold, and the cost of cotton clothing fell by 85 percent. The cotton industry became increasingly steam powered after 1830, produced half the world's cotton cloth by the 1850s, and held a central place in Britain's industrial landscape for the next century.

IRON The energy in coal had an even greater impact on the iron industry, which became as important as cotton to Britain's economy and far more important to British military power. Iron making was fuel-intensive. It took 10 acres (4 hectares) of English woodland to make enough fuel to make a ton of iron in the eighteenth century. Fuel constraints made the industry uncompetitive against imported iron from forest-rich Sweden and Russia, where fuelwood was far cheaper. Coal, together with some technical improvements that made it easier to remove impurities in the iron-making process, revolutionized the British iron industry.

In the century after 1788, British iron production climbed 130-fold, and Britain, instead of importing iron, became Europe's largest producer and the world's largest exporter. Massive iron foundries sprang up near coalfields. Iron replaced wood as the key material in construction of everything from tools to bridges to ships. By 1815, with its flourishing iron industry, Britain produced millions of guns annually and all the cannon needed for the world's biggest navy. By 1890, British shipyards built naval vessels for several countries and some 80 percent of the world's seagoing ships of all sorts.

RAILWAYS The iron and coal industries gave rise to locomotives and **railways**, another key sector of the

British Iron Shipbuilding, with its reliance on high-quality iron, was one of the industries that coal power revolutionized. An 1854 illustration shows dozens of metalworkers forging an iron ship's hull at a London dockyard that built ships for the Royal Navy.

Railways Spectators cheer in this 1829 illustration as a steam locomotive designed by inventor Robert Stephenson wins a race against another engine. "Stephenson's Rocket," which could travel at the astonishing speed of 30 miles per hour, was ultimately chosen to power the Liverpool-Manchester railway.

British Industrial Revolution. The first locomotives were used underground in coal mines, in 1804. The first railway to carry passengers and general freight opened in 1825. A railway line between the port of Liverpool and the cotton-manufacturing center of Manchester opened in 1830. Newspapers reported in detail on this maiden voyage, not least because the first train to make the journey ran over a member of Parliament, killing him. Despite this inauspicious debut, the Liverpool and Manchester railway quickly proved a commercial bonanza, carrying half a million passengers in its first full year of operation, and many thousands of tons of cotton and coal. A frenzy of railway construction followed, undertaken by private companies employing tens of thousands of poor men with picks, hammers, and shovels, so that Britain quadrupled its total railway track between 1850 and 1880. Railways linked the country together more thoroughly than canals ever could, making Britain the world's most interconnected country, the thickest patch of the Global web.

STEAMSHIPS Meanwhile, seaborne navigation tightened Britain's links to the rest of the world. Steamships were first built in France in the 1770s. The first to become a commercial success plied North American waters—the Hudson River in 1807 and the St. Lawrence in 1809. In the next few decades, steamships came to rival and then replace most sailing ships on rivers and in coastal waters.

Oceanic steam navigation took longer to take hold because it required carrying so much coal. Scheduled Atlantic crossings with steam-powered vessels began in 1838. Sailing vessels still dominated the routes between Britain and Asia until the opening of the Suez Canal (in Egypt) in 1869, because steaming around Africa required too much expenditure on coal. The Suez Canal shortened the route between Britain and India by about 4,000 miles (6,400 km), making it practical for steamships. By 1870, new oceangoing ships were usually steam powered. Only on the longest routes—between Britain and China, for example—did sailing ships still outcompete steam vessels into the 1890s.

Steamships lowered freight rates at sea, as railways did on land. Between 1840 and 1910, British seaborne freight costs fell by 70 percent, the result mainly of the switch to steamships and continuing technical improvements such as the screw propeller, in regular use by the 1860s. Railways and steamships, built of iron—iron that was made with coal—knitted Britain together and tied it ever more tightly to the rest of the world.

BRITISH SOCIETY

Industrialization brought a social revolution to Britain. In 1750, most of the work done in Britain, as in most societies, was farmwork, and most people lived in villages. By 1850, half the British population of 27 million lived in cities, and millions worked in coal mines, textile mills, iron foundries, or factories.

The conditions of life and work in the new industrial cities took a steep toll on the health of factory workers. An early recruit, Titus Rowbotham, however, went to work in Manchester's cotton mills at age 18. In 1801, looking back on his life, he said of textile mill workers like himself: "Their intellect is enfeebled. . . . They are more like grown up children. . . . The long hours of labour, the high temperatures of the factories, produce lassitude and excessive exhaustion. The operatives . . . seek to sustain life by the excitement of drink." Before labor reforms in the 1840s, most cotton mill workers were younger than Rowbotham, between ages 10 and 18, and labored 12-hour days on repetitive tasks. Factory bosses preferred young workers, who were easier to train and—in most cases—easier to control. Some textile work required fine motor skills

Child Labor As an 1844 lithograph demonstrates, British mine owners relied on the small bodies of children to transport coal through extremely narrow tunnels underground. Children could spend as many as 12 hours a day, 6 days a week, underground.

and small hands, for which employers preferred girls. Most boys were fired by age 16 because as their fingers grew, they lost some of their nimbleness. So most mills employed more females than males. Many workers went deaf due to the din or developed lung diseases because of cotton dust.

Labor in coal mines made factory work look like leisure. Child labor was commonplace in the tight spaces underground. Sally Fletcher, age 8, testified to a government committee in 1841 that she had worked in a coal pit since age 5 and had never been to school. "I cannot read or write. . . . I go to work between six and seven o'clock in the morning. . . . I sometimes go home at three o'clock. Sometimes six." Her job was pushing small wagonloads of coal along a 400-yard (365 m) underground passage. In 1842, one-third of coal miners were teenagers. Few miners could still work by age 40. On-the-job accidents and lung diseases from the long-term effects of breathing coal dust ended many a working life. One flood in a coal mine in 1838 drowned 26 miners, the eldest of whom was 17 and the youngest 7 years old. In an average year before 1850, half a percent to one percent of the workforce died on the job. No one kept track of the numbers maimed.

THE WORKING CLASSES The new forms of work in mines and factories created new social classes in Britain. Over a generation or two, millions who toiled at looms and lathes, or worked as household servants, gradually came to see themselves as members of a vast "**working class**," amounting to about 40 to 45 percent of the English population by 1850. Unlike farmworkers, they worked shifts defined by the clock, not the light of the sun. At work they were subject to the discipline of bosses, not their parents or older siblings. The din, drudgery, and danger of factory or mine work dominated their lives for 10, 12, or 14 hours a day. They lived and worked in crowds. Manchester in the 1840s had a population density higher than any big city in the world today except Dhaka (in Bangladesh). Its working-class districts were a warren of dingy alleys and open sewers.

The term *working class* might better be *working classes* because a person's condition and prospects could vary. Fortunate working-class men learned a skill that ensured employment and a wage sufficient to support a family. With luck, some could rise to positions of management, overseeing the work of others. Women typically held poorer-paying jobs with fewer prospects of advancement. The most common job for women in nineteenth-century Britain was domestic service, doing housework and child care for someone else, but many worked in factories or mines too. Daughters expected to contribute their wages to their parents' household. If they married, they might quit factory work. If they became mothers, they usually did quit.

The least fortunate members of the working classes rarely found work and lived on city streets, slept under bridges, dressed in rags, and scrounged for food. In London, thousands of sharp-eyed, nimble-fingered, hungry children, called mudlarks, lived by scavenging buttons, nails, and other saleable items from city sewers and the muddy banks of the river Thames. Orphans and widows often could survive only by stealing or by selling their bodies for sex.

Britain's working classes lived and worked on the verge of disaster. If they annoyed an overseer, they might lose their job—which meant going hungry. Their jobs were dangerous and ruined their health. Like everyone, rich or poor, they also worried about lethal diseases—much more dangerous than anything else in their lives.

You might wonder why anyone agreed to work in factories or mines in industrial Britain. The answer is that millions of young people had no better option. Farms now needed fewer workers. Spinning and weaving within the home was hopeless in the face of factory competition.

Teenage girls could become domestic servants; boys could join the army or the navy. They could gamble on life in Canada, Jamaica, or Australia as indentured servants. But these and other options looked no better to most young people than a hard life in the factories or mines.

THE MIDDLE CLASSES A notch above the working classes in industrial Britain's evolving social hierarchy stood a lower middle class, also growing, some 10 to 15 percent of the population by 1850. Its members were shop clerks, nurses, teachers, pharmacists—jobs for which at least some education was required. Their work included little dirt or danger, but their wages remained modest. Women in these jobs usually quit upon marriage or motherhood. Lower-middle-class families typically rented rather than owned their homes but might have books and even a piano in them.

Industrial Britain also generated a more prosperous upper-middle class. Factories and mines, if large enough, required managers and professionals. Accountants, engineers, purchasing agents, lawyers—these and other growing professions permitted hundreds of thousands of men (and a few thousand women) to earn enough for a comfortable life in the new industrial society. Men in these positions could expect to own their homes, pay school fees to educate their children, support small-scale charities, and enjoy deference, at least outwardly, from members of the working classes. Their wives did not need paid work. They could expect to manage a house with domestic servants and might devote their time to civic causes, music and art, their church, and their children—unless they assigned all child care to servants. The prosperous middle classes also included middling entrepreneurs, who might own a single mill or small factory. They rejoiced in a good year and feared bankruptcy in a bad one. These middling entrepreneurs were usually but not always men: about 10 percent of British businesses were owned by women between 1780 and 1850. That figure included widows who took over the business affairs of dead husbands, and women who owned small bakeries or butcher shops rather than mills or factories.

INDUSTRIALISTS Higher up the social pyramid of industrial Britain stood a new class of rich factory and mine owners. Some came from modest origins, such as John Rylands (1801–1888), born in a village near Manchester and recipient of a grade school education. He started work as a weaver and soon founded a textile manufacturing company with his brother and father. Rylands, who allegedly worked 19-hour days, became the first cotton millionaire in Manchester and, despite giving substantial sums to charities, died very rich. Wealth did not insulate him from personal tragedy, though: he buried all of his seven children. Manchester was an unhealthy city, even for its richest citizens. More typical of this new class—in his social origins—was Joseph Chamberlain (1836–1914). His father was a businessman who could afford to educate his son to age 16, at which point Joseph became an apprentice in his father's warehouses. But at age 18 he moved to Birmingham, started work in his uncle's brass screw–manufacturing business, became a partner, and at age 37 retired immensely wealthy and launched a career in politics, fighting for social reforms.

The traditional uppermost elite in British society, the landed aristocracy, often resented the wealth of industrialists such as Rylands or Chamberlain. But times were changing, and new money was taking over. Aristocrats who found themselves strapped for money often chose to marry a son or daughter into a prosperous industrial family to restore their fortunes.

FAMILY LIFE Industrialization changed family life as well as social structure in Britain, particularly the condition of young people. When young people went to work in factories and mines, they partly escaped the authority of their parents. During working hours, they became subject to the authority of male bosses, which women sometimes found hazardous. In their scant free time, young industrial workers became freer from parental supervision than village youths could expect to be.

If they held a job, people could marry young. Age at first marriage for British men dipped to about 26, and for women fell from about 26 in the early eighteenth century to about 23 in the mid-nineteenth, and lower still in the industrial cities. Despite younger marriage, out-of-wedlock births became far more common in the industrial towns than in rural villages—a reflection of the greater independence of industrial youth from parental supervision.

ENVIRONMENTAL IMPACTS AND HEALTH

In 1837, the German chemist Justus von Liebig visited England. He described the country between Leeds and Manchester as "one big smoking chimney." Soot and cinder blanketed the iron-making region north of Birmingham by 1840, earning it the name the "Black Country." In London, a million chimneys spewed sulfur dioxide and soot into the air. In Manchester in 1900, the pH of rain averaged 3.5—somewhere between the acidity of tomato juice and that of wine. A perpetual haze of coal smoke enveloped all the industrial towns. Just as the sun famously never set on the British Empire, it never really rose on countless alleys and tenements. Lung diseases became common complaints, especially among miners and millworkers who breathed coal or cotton dust day and night. By one modern estimate, health problems provoked by air pollution around 1900 reduced Britain's total economic output by one-quarter.

Water quality was no better. Rivers and canals everywhere served as industrial sewers. The water of the river Calder made a "tolerably good ink" in 1864, according to a government commission. Another commission, in 1869, described a river flowing through Manchester as:

> caked over with a thick scum of dirty froth, looking like a solid, sooty crusted surface.... Wherever a yard or two of the scum was cleared away, the whole surface was seen simmering and sparkling with a continual effervescence of smaller bubbles ... showing that the whole river was fermenting and generating gas. The air was filled with the stench of this gaseous emanation many yards away. The temperature of the water was 76 F, and that of the air 54 F.

For a few generations, industrialization had catastrophic effects on British health. In the "Black Country," average life expectancy fell by six years between 1820 and 1840. While the industrial working classes grew in number, they shrank in stature. Between 1800 and 1850, army recruits and prisoners—the only populations systematically measured—lost an average of 1 inch in height. The average male in 1850 stood 5'4" (163 cm) tall, and the average female 5'0" (152 cm). The shortest came from industrial cities, and the tallest from the counties farthest from the centers of industry. Some combination of poor nutrition, heavy work, and frequent disease accounted for the stunted stature of industrial workers.

After 1850, these grim conditions gradually improved. Industrial workers' wages began to inch upward. Life expectancy in Britain lengthened, and after 1870 it never again dipped below 40 years. Health improved more quickly after 1890 through improved medical understanding of infectious disease. By 1900, the Industrial

Air Pollution The toxic smoke of copper foundries fills the sky of the copper-producing region of Cornwall in southwest England in this late nineteenth-century engraving. Air pollution was a feature of life throughout industrial Britain, leading to widespread respiratory illness and other health problems.

Revolution had clearly improved the average health and well-being of the British population, now 38 million, nearly four times its size in 1800. Twenty-year-old army recruits in 1900 averaged nearly 5'6" in height (168 cm) and 130 lbs (60 kg).

While sacrificing the health of tens of millions of workers, the Industrial Revolution enriched and empowered Britain as a nation-state. It made Britain the "workshop of the world." Britain's manufacturing exports in 1840 stood at about 50 times their level as of 1700. Efficient production of coal, cotton, or iron underpinned hundreds of huge personal fortunes. And the Industrial Revolution enabled Britain to construct a military machine that helped make a little island into a great power. The rest of the world took notice.

INDUSTRIAL REVOLUTIONS AROUND THE GLOBE

Britain strove to keep the Industrial Revolution to itself. Parliament passed laws making it illegal for people who knew industrial secrets to go abroad. Authorities vigorously hunted down foreign industrial spies, hundreds of whom prowled British factory towns. The government tried hard to enforce intellectual property rules. But nothing worked. Industrial secrets leapt to the European continent and beyond.

The technologies and organizational techniques of industrialization first escaped to continental Europe. Thousands of European towns had supported small-scale handicraft production of textiles since medieval times. As in Britain, by 1800 water power provided the primary energy source for new mills and factories. Clusters of textile mills sprang up where ambitious entrepreneurs found suitable rivers for water power, undercutting household-scale spinning and weaving.

But quickly, coal became king in much of continental Europe as it had in Britain. A long carboniferous crescent, as important for the early industrial age as the Fertile Crescent had been for the early history of agriculture, underlay parts of Britain, northern France, Belgium, Germany, the Czech lands (Bohemia), and what is now southern Poland (Silesia). By 1820, northern France and Belgium had developed steam-powered textile mills and metallurgical industries. Businessmen soon brought coal-fired industry to coalfields farther east, such as those in Germany's Ruhr region. It also sprouted in port cities, or in cities astride rivers where ships and barges could bring coal at low cost: Hamburg, Rotterdam, Vienna, and Bilbao, for example. Germany's Industrial Revolution outstripped all others in continental Europe.

GERMANY

Germany, as we shall see, was a country cobbled together from a welter of small and middling states. Upon unification in 1871, its population was about 40 million—and rising fast. It was still mainly an agrarian nation, but with an industrial sector poised for rapid growth.

The first steam engine in German lands had fired up in 1789. The first railroads opened in the late 1830s, using British locomotives. But industrial production remained tiny for decades, most of it in textiles and rarely using steam power. Some obstacles had to be addressed first. German agriculture needed to provide enough surplus to feed big urban populations. States had to enact social and political reforms that allowed peasants freedom to migrate to cities and fill industrial jobs. But by the 1850s, these and other obstacles were sufficiently overcome that

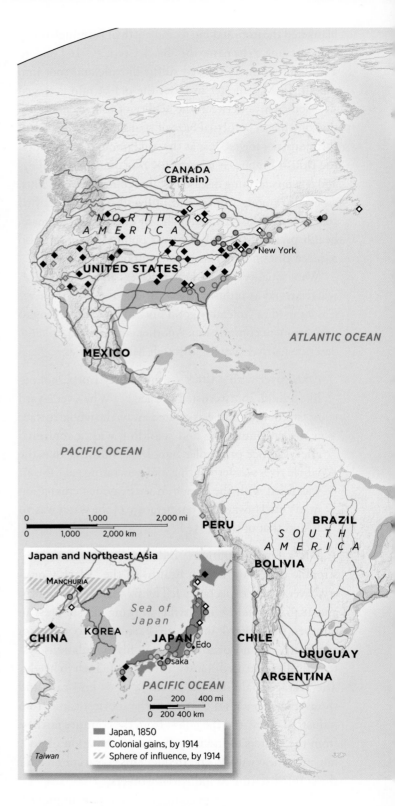

the high-quality coal of the Ruhr in Germany was fueling a flourishing metallurgical industry. Workers flocked to the Ruhr for jobs, making it a European melting pot. Berlin was also rapidly developing textile and metallurgical industries.

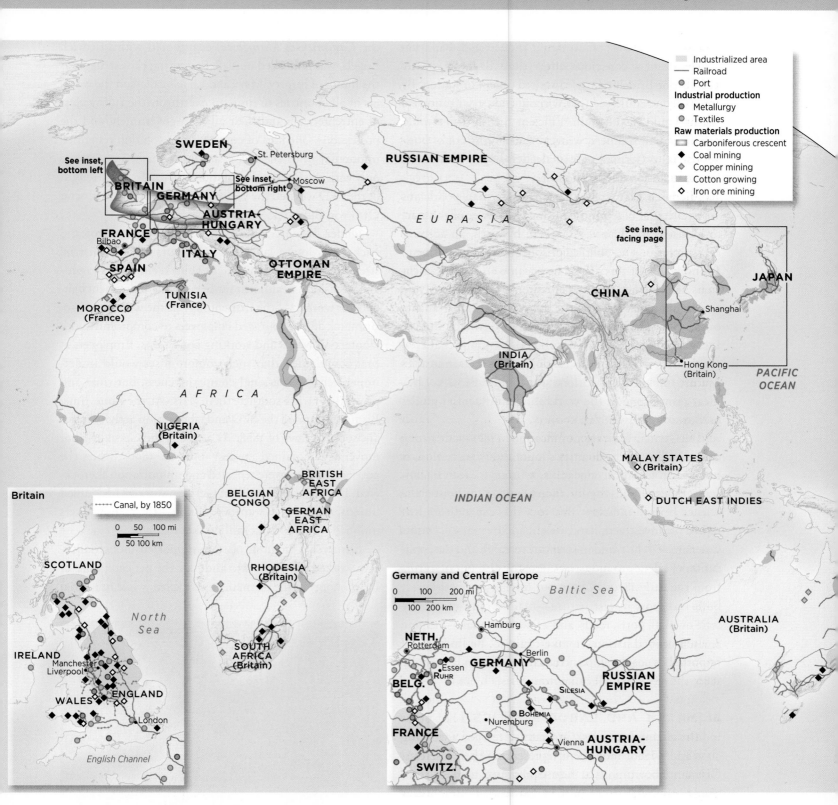

The Global Impact of Industrialization, ca. 1914 Industrialization gave rise to a global economy that was both more geographically differentiated than before—into zones of industrial production and zones of raw material production—and also more tightly knitted together through long-distance trade. Cotton mills, steel mills, and factories as of 1914 were concentrated in Japan, Europe (including Britain), and eastern North America, but the raw materials necessary for industrial production were scattered among all the continents. Railroads, ports, and oceangoing ships handled enormous quantities of raw materials to keep factories and mills supplied. In Europe's case, one crucial raw material—coal—came from one of the world's giant coalfields, the carboniferous crescent, stretching from Scotland to Silesia.

STATE SUPPORT Germany's Industrial Revolution was more of a conscious effort than Britain's, partly because the British example inspired urgent imitation. By 1850, anyone could see that without industrialization no society could rival Britain. Efficient British firms would drive German spinners, weavers, and smiths out of business. Several German political leaders hoped to use state power to do something about it.

Friedrich List (1789–1846) gave German politicians an intellectual blueprint for using the power of the state to industrialize. List was German by birth, an accountant, professor, and political prisoner before emigrating to Pennsylvania in 1825. There he became an American citizen, a landowner, newspaper editor, coal merchant, and author of a book praising the protectionist trade policies of the U.S. government. Returning to Germany in 1833, List wrote newspaper articles and books urging that German states form a customs union, protect their industries against foreign competition, and build railroads. List's ideas proved one of the world's most influential guides on how to industrialize a country.

The German state after unification in 1871 made strong contributions to the country's rapid industrialization. It invested in technical education. It funded research institutes, especially in physics and chemistry, to bolster the science behind industry. By 1900, this expenditure had repaid the investment handsomely, and by many accounts Germany led the world in scientific research and the application of science to industry. Germany also put up tariffs from the early 1870s to keep out foreign competition. It built transport infrastructure—mainly railways (partly state owned), ports, roads, and a few new canals—helping create a unified national market. In 1850, Berlin had still imported its coal by ship and canal-barge from Britain. By 1880, the city's coal all came from Silesia by rail.

BISMARCK AND LABOR POLITICS Like other industrializing countries, Germany developed a working class and a labor movement representing their interests. German labor unions at first represented workers from single industries, such as the cigar-workers union that formed in 1865. The unions joined their efforts to support industrial workers in a political party known by its German initials, the SPD (Social Democratic Party), born in 1875. More radical workers—a tiny minority of the whole—supported the revolutionary ideals of the German journalist Karl Marx, whose powerful pamphlet,

the **Communist Manifesto**, coauthored with Friedrich Engels, was published in 1848. Presenting class struggle as the motor of history, Marx and Engels called on the workers of all countries to unite to overthrow the ruling class of entrepreneurs and their allies in government and the professions. The idea of communist revolution remained unpopular until the 1870s, attaining major importance only with the Russian Revolution of 1917. But the strength of the SPD worried the German chancellor and aristocrat Otto von Bismarck.

Under Bismarck, the German state used carrot and stick to promote labor peace in pursuit of industrial strength. The state provided, or obliged employers to provide, pensions, health insurance, and unemployment benefits for workers—the first country in the world to do so. Bismarck also encouraged employers to compromise with laborers on wages and working conditions. Employers at first complained that such compromises would undermine their international competitiveness, but time and protective tariffs soothed their fears. At the same time, Bismarck banned the SPD and labor union activity in his antisocialist laws of 1878. As a result, the German labor movement remained modest until the 1890s, when the antisocialist laws were repealed and unionization skyrocketed. By 1904, fully 1 million German workers had joined unions, and by 1913, some 2.5 million—the metalworkers union alone had half a million members.

Bismarck's program of state-supported industrialization worked. Between 1850 and 1913, the per capita size of the economy in the German lands tripled, while industrial

German Industrialization Workers in the Krupp factory in Essen ca. 1900 inspect the steel train wheels that the factory manufactured. The steel industry and the expansion of the German railway network allowed it to rival Britain for industrial dominance.

growth quintupled. As in Britain, cities sprouted from next to nothing. Essen, in the Ruhr, was a big village of 3,000 people in 1831, and in 1913 an industrial city of 300,000. The major surge in German industrialization came after unification in 1871, with heavy industry in the vanguard. Iron ore production jumped ninefold between 1870 and 1913, while coal output quintupled. Germany's total railway mileage, still smaller than Britain's in 1870, was double its rival's by 1910. The growth of railways created a huge and reliable market for Germany's iron and steel industries.

The German version of industrial revolution favored giant firms. In 1870, almost all German industrial workers still toiled in tiny enterprises, no bigger than a family. But soon large firms came to account for nearly half of industrial employment. By 1913, Krupp, an iron, steel, and weapons manufacturer in Essen, employed 77,000 people. Siemens, an engineering firm based in Berlin and Nuremberg, employed 57,000 people.

THE UNITED STATES AND CANADA

The United States at its birth was an agrarian country, with 95 percent of its population living on the land. Many of its leaders preferred it that way, but not **Alexander Hamilton** (ca. 1755–1804). As secretary of the Treasury in 1791, Hamilton wrote a tract advising that the new nation should protect its small and inefficient manufacturers from foreign—mainly British—competition. Tariffs would, he claimed, enable American manufacturers to survive and grow, taking advantage of an ever-larger domestic market. Hamilton's vision served as the chief inspiration for U.S. trade policy for more than a century, during which time the United States became an industrial powerhouse. Hamilton's program also served as an inspiration for Friedrich List's ideas.

A nation of only small-scale industry in 1790, the United States had, as Hamilton saw, strong growth potential. It had plentiful timber, good soil, coal, iron ores, and other minerals. Its population was among the fastest-growing in the world: from 4 million in 1790, it leapt to 17 million in 1840 and 63 million by 1890.

High wages (by international standards of the time) throughout the U.S. economy strengthened the economic logic of both slavery, prevalent in the southern states, and labor-saving machinery. To get labor-saving technology, American businesses and officials tried to lure British craftsmen versed in the secrets of the textile and iron-working industries to break British law and bring their knowledge to America. Samuel Slater had worked in the textile business for years when he left England for Rhode Island in 1789. Rather than risk arrest for carrying plans of the latest textile mill technology, he committed it all to memory. He set up a cotton mill for a merchant family (that had founded Brown University) but felt ill-treated and soon set up his own. In the following decades, thousands of others emigrating to the United States brought British industrial technology with them.

American entrepreneurs such as Francis Cabot Lowell also went to Britain to learn what they could. A Bostonian with an inherited fortune, he traveled to Manchester and Scotland in search of the secrets of cotton manufacturing. He learned enough—how to power a loom using waterwheels or steam engines—to set up a large-scale cotton mill in Waltham, Massachusetts.

Not all of the imported expertise for U.S. industrialization came from Britain. One of the nation's first large-scale factories was the gunpowder works established by refugees from the French Revolution, the Du Pont family. Pierre du Pont, a watchmaker's son, had done stints in Parisian prisons in the 1790s. Du Pont fled revolutionary France with his family, emigrating to the United States in 1799. One of his sons founded a gunpowder factory in 1803 using water power from Delaware's Brandywine River and chemistry expertise he brought from France. It evolved into one of the giant firms in U.S. industry.

THE AMERICAN SYSTEM The U.S. weapons industry was especially important to world history. Together with clock making, the arms industry developed the practice of manufacturing with interchangeable parts. Instead of a single craftsman making an entire musket or grandfather clock, this system relied on semiskilled workers using machine tools to mass-produce components that other workers could assemble into a final product. This method, pioneered in British naval shipbuilding, required less skill, lowered production costs, and—crucially for weapons—eased repair. All musket triggers, for example, were so close to identical that a musket with a broken trigger was not junk; it just needed a new trigger.

The virtues of the system of interchangeable parts in weapons manufacture became clear during the War of 1812 with Britain, and the principle was widely followed in other U.S. industries by 1850. Guns and clocks, and eventually almost everything else, were not designed to last, but instead to be cheap to make and easy to fix. The use of interchangeable parts in mechanized production was often called "the American system" of manufacturing.

SOUTHERN COTTON, NORTHERN TEXTILES, AND AMERICAN SLAVERY Americans also developed technologies beyond those they acquired from overseas. Perhaps most important were the cotton gin and the telegraph. The **cotton gin** (short for "engine"), patented in 1794, helped remove the seeds from cotton fiber, making it ready to spin. It eliminated a bottleneck in cotton manufacture and was crucial for the rise of mechanized cotton production in the United States as well as in Britain. It was equally crucial in spreading cotton cultivation and slavery in the U.S. South—the cotton industry could not flourish without abundant raw cotton. Samuel Morse patented the long-distance telegraph in the 1840s. It helped tie the country together by sending information at the speed of electricity from telegraph office to telegraph office. Such near-instant communication suited the needs of railroads and eventually became an important military technology as well.

By 1830, the United States had a robust textile industry based in New England. Francis Cabot Lowell had opened his first mill in Waltham in 1814, followed by several more in Lowell, Massachusetts, outside of Boston. At

U.S. Cotton Enslaved people work a cotton gin on a plantation in the American South. The raw cotton that enslaved people grew and processed on southern plantations was spun and woven into cloth in factories in the northern United States and Britain.

first the American textile industry relied on water power, but, like Britain's, it gradually shifted to coal and steam. Also like Britain's, it relied heavily on female labor, and on cotton grown—before the Civil War—on slave plantations in the southern states. In 1860, about 70 percent of the 4 million enslaved African Americans worked on cotton plantations producing the raw material for New England's—and Europe's—cotton industry.

INDUSTRY AND GOVERNMENT SUPPORT Meanwhile, the U.S. metallurgical industry churned out rails, locomotives, farm tools, and guns, among other goods. The iron industry began to take off in the 1840s in Pennsylvania, where high-quality coal was abundant. U.S. coal output jumped 13-fold and iron ore 16-fold between 1870 and 1913. Immigrants from Europe flocked to American coal mines, iron foundries, and by 1880 big steel mills in cities such as Pittsburgh and Cleveland. Led by iron, steel, and railroads, total U.S. industrial output leapt 8-fold in the years 1870–1913. The United States and Germany were the tigers of the world economy in those decades, fed by their industrial revolutions.

The U.S. government took deliberate steps to advance its Industrial Revolution, although not as directly as the state in Bismarck's Germany. Tariffs protected young and inefficient industries from foreign competition. Cotton cloth, for example, received tariff protection in 1816. The patent system and legal system rewarded innovation and investment—as in Britain. The law provided for a limited liability corporation, widespread among U.S. states by 1860, which enabled investors to pool their resources without fear of becoming liable for a company's debts. Congress and the Patent Office supported Morse financially while he was improving the telegraph. The federal government gave millions of acres of public land to railroad companies and, beginning in 1862, to the states to encourage the creation of agricultural, technical, and engineering colleges and universities.

ECONOMIES OF SCALE The most distinctive feature of the American Industrial Revolution was its exploitation of economies of scale. After the Erie Canal opened in 1825 and railroads crisscrossed the country by 1870, the United States was sufficiently connected that it essentially formed one big, fast-growing national market. U.S. industries got very good at mass production of cheap goods. Several million American families could afford to buy clothing, furniture, and tools made in factories. That prosperity, a result of both high workers' wages by the standards of the time and a thriving middle class, helped to enlarge the market and reward manufacturers in their quests for economies of scale.

The size of the U.S. market and the scale of production also favored bigger business organizations. American entrepreneurs, like their counterparts in Germany, created gigantic companies and conglomerates that employed tens of thousands of people. At one point in the nineteenth century, the DuPont company employed 10 percent of the population of the state of Delaware. By 1890, the United States had surpassed Britain in total industrial production to become the global leader, the result mainly of the size of its domestic market.

Chinese Labor in Canada　Chinese workers build the trackbed of the Canadian Pacific Railway. In 1882 alone, some six thousand Chinese immigrants arrived to work on the Canadian Pacific in British Columbia.

CANADA　Industrialization came more slowly to Canada than to the United States. For most of the nineteenth century, Canadians imported most of their industrial goods from either the United States or Britain. Until Confederation in 1867, Canada was a set of British colonies largely governed from London. Britain sought to keep its edge in industrial production, and so Canada had few manufacturing enterprises. Less than a quarter of its population lived in cities, and industrial production, such as it was, took place mainly in rural areas where sawmilling, leather tanning, and blacksmithing were practical. But after 1867, Canada—with about 3.5 million people and abundant natural resources—acquired more authority over its own affairs.

It soon launched a **National Policy** (1879) intended to promote industry. Tariffs on foreign goods boosted enterprises such as textiles, shoes, pulp and paper, meat-producing, and steel, mainly in Quebec and Ontario. Nova Scotia also developed coal, steel, and shipbuilding. A political emphasis on railroad building—Canada's first transcontinental railroad opened in 1886—helped inspire rail and locomotive works, as well as iron ore and coal mining.

A growing labor supply, as well as abundant raw materials and prudent national policy, also helped Canada to industrialize. By 1890, its population was climbing fast, the result of booming immigration from Britain, continental Europe, and—to British Columbia—China, combined with slowed emigration to the United States. Many immigrants settled in industrial centers, as did many native-born farm youths. By 1910, when the national

population reached about 7 million, some 3 million lived in cities and towns, and half a million worked in industry. Many Canadian industries exported to the much larger market in the United States; some were branch plants of U.S.-owned firms. Canada was well on its way to becoming an industrial society, deeply integrated with the U.S. and British economies.

RUSSIA

Like the United States and Canada, Russia had natural resources well suited to launching an industrial revolution. It had abundant coal and iron. During the nineteenth century, it conquered Central Asian lands that would prove suitable for growing cotton. Russia's social base, however, was less promising. Part of Russia's elite was attuned to western European trends and accustomed to borrowing ideas from abroad. But the rest of the population was poorly prepared to support industrialization—partly because it was too poor to buy much. Unlike in Britain or the United States, the middle class, and the market for anything beyond basic goods, were small.

As of 1850, some two-thirds of Russia's roughly 68 million people were serfs, some owned by the state and others bound to lands owned by the nobility. Most had only rudimentary education, if any. Few were legally free to migrate to cities or jobs. Russia's largest industrial cluster was around the city of Łódź (pronounced [Woodge]) in Russian-controlled Poland. The city hosted hundreds of small textile mills in 1850, most of them owned by German businessmen. At that time, almost no one imagined that a Russian Industrial Revolution was either possible or desirable.

Russia's existing industrial plant was old and small. The weapons industry, developed originally under Ivan IV and Peter the Great, was antiquated by the 1850s. The country had only one real railroad line, opened in 1851 between Moscow and St. Petersburg. Despite long-standing efforts to import technology and expertise from abroad, which included an offer to James Watt to move to Russia, the Russian Empire in 1850 remained overwhelmingly agrarian.

Then Russia lost a war in humiliating fashion. Russia's military performed embarrassingly in the Crimean War (1853–1856) against the Ottoman Empire, France, and Britain. The defeat clarified matters for Russian elites: they needed to reform and strengthen their country in a hurry. Their anxieties made more of them sympathetic to new ideas such as the abolition of serfdom (see Chapter 22) and the industrialization of Russia.

The ambition to industrialize faced many obstacles. Before 1880, the country lacked engineers, compared to Britain or Germany, and technical training was rare. The legal system made it awkward to create businesses. Transport infrastructure was creaky. By 1880, it still had only about 13,000 miles (21,000 km) of railroad—about one-seventh the U.S. total. But in the 1880s and especially the 1890s, Russian industrialization gathered steam. Industrial output expanded at 8 percent per year in the 1890s, and the rail network more than doubled between 1880 and 1905. Russia was late getting started by the standards of Germany or the United States, let alone Britain, but it made up ground fast. From low levels in 1870, Russian coal output climbed 40-fold by 1913, and industrial production 9-fold.

The crowning achievement of Russia's Industrial Revolution was the opening of the **Trans-Siberian Railway** in 1903, financed mainly by the state. Construction began in 1891 and required 90,000 laborers, many of them convicts, army conscripts, or migrants from Korea and China. When finished, the iron road crossed bogs, mountains, and hundreds of rivers over about 5,700 miles (9,200 km) from Moscow to the Pacific Ocean. The railroad opened much of Siberia and its natural resources to Russian settlement and use.

GOVERNMENT SUPPORT The Russian Industrial Revolution was very much a revolution from above. It

Trans-Siberian Railway Like Canada's transcontinental railroad, the Trans-Siberian Railway was a feat of engineering that connected widely separated regions of a vast territory. A photographer recorded the railway's first locomotive traveling along the shores of Lake Baikal in 1900.

could scarcely have succeeded without determined government support, stronger than that in the United States or Germany. That support resulted largely from the efforts of **Sergei Witte** (1849–1915). Born into a noble family, Witte aspired to an academic career in mathematics. Instead, he made his early mark in railroad management and entered government service in 1888. In a political career spanning nearly three decades, and inspired in part by Friedrich List's ideas, Witte promoted railroad building and the creation of technical schools, together with tariffs to protect Russian industry. Guided by Witte, the Russian government welcomed foreign investment (except on the Trans-Siberian project) and technical experts, financed the sale of Russian industrial goods to neighboring countries without much industry (such as China and Iran), and fostered heavy industry by purchasing locomotives, rails, and military hardware. No one else in Russia—or for that matter in Germany, the United States, Britain, or Japan—played a larger role in advancing industrialization than Witte.

JAPAN

Japan blazed its own trail to industrialization. It involved more labor and less machinery, because in Japan labor was cheap and, initially, machines and mechanical expertise were scarce. As much or more than the Russian, American, and German cases, the Japanese Industrial Revolution was nourished by state support.

Like Russia, Japan in 1850 seemed an unlikely candidate for industrialization. Its economy remained agrarian, although Japan was unusually urbanized: perhaps 10 percent of Japanese lived in cities in 1700, and 20 percent—of about 34 million—by 1870. With its countryside crowded after 1720 or so, couples tried hard to limit their family size, and population growth proceeded slowly for about five generations. Japan had some accessible coal, but not much iron ore. Japan seemed to lack the incentive and most of the wherewithal for an industrial revolution, although its highly productive agriculture could feed cities.

MEIJI REFORMS But in 1853, Japan received a shock when a well-armed American fleet steamed into Edo (Tokyo) Bay and demanded diplomatic relations, a commercial treaty, and the rights to build a coaling station. The government—the Tokugawa shoguns in power since 1603—had for 200 years sought to minimize contact with the rest of the world. Now some of the elite realized that Japan's power was inadequate and its national security was at risk. This provided motivation for reforms, just as the defeat in the Crimean War did for Russia. The efforts of the Tokugawa deepened divisions, and a civil war in 1867–1868 brought the **Meiji Restoration**, which reinstated rule by emperors. A new elite took power in Meiji Japan (1868–1912) that was committed to pursuing the knowledge and technologies that made foreigners so threatening. Occasional bombardments of Japanese ports by British, French, Dutch, and American naval ships seeking better trade deals emphasized to the leaders of Meiji Japan the urgency of strengthening the country.

Japan's population was unusually literate and accustomed to hierarchy, group loyalty, and discipline. Millions of women were used to long hours spinning thread in their homes. Japan had the makings of a productive working class. But it needed efficient technology, which the government set out to acquire. Japan's coastal shipping routes and longstanding commercial traditions allowed the makings of a national market by 1868. That appealed to ambitious entrepreneurs who were eager to build industrial enterprises.

No one was more ambitious than **Eiichi Shibusawa**. He was born in 1840 to a prosperous farm family and studied Confucian classics. After an eye-opening trip to view efficient, modern factories in France, he came home during the chaotic fall of the Tokugawa. Called to government service in the Ministry of Finance, he used his office to help start hundreds of companies in textiles, shipping, sugar refining, beer brewing, paper manufacture, hotels, banking, insurance, and railroads. Shibusawa moved among elite businessmen and high government officials who showed remarkable determination to bring an industrial revolution to Japan. They sometimes differed on the means, but rarely on the end: a prosperous, strong, industrial Japan. Most also hoped to get richer in the process.

TEXTILES AND HEAVY INDUSTRY As in Britain, Germany, and the United States, textiles led the way in Japanese industrialization. In 1870, Japan was importing vast amounts of cloth from British factories, which produced cheaper and better cottons than could Japanese households. Then, in 1877, a Japanese student at the University of London agreed to the suggestion from a total stranger—Shibusawa—that for the sake of Japan he should abandon his study of economics and instead learn the cotton business. So young Takeo Yamanobe headed to Manchester, learned all he could, and in 1882 came home to help Shibusawa set up Japan's first modern cotton mill, in Osaka. It soon prospered, drawing imitators into the business. By 1890, Japan was producing almost all its cloth in its own factories and had begun exporting to neighboring countries. Its factories generally worked differently from those in Europe, often using human muscle to power machinery instead of steam engines—because labor was cheap.

The biggest industrial sector in Meiji Japan by employment was textiles, but Japan's place in the world depended

Japanese Industrialization This woodblock print from 1875, by Utagawa Hiroshige III, entitled "Steam Train between Tokyo and Yokohama," captures the novelty of Japan's first train line. It opened in 1872, connecting the capital city to its port. It used British technology, which was common in the early phase of Japan's industrialization.

The Metallic Web

1800-1920

IN 1800, THE FASTEST ANYONE could move was atop a galloping horse at about 30 mph (48 kph)—and that only for a couple of minutes. Horse travel averaged about 5 mph (8 kph). Boats or ships traveled at the speed the wind propelled them, which at times meant no movement at all. It might take 6 to 18 months for messages to get back and forth between Java and Amsterdam.

Between 1800 and 1844, three new technologies sped up global movement: the railway, steamship, and telegraph. Metallic webs soon spanned the globe: steel railway track, copper telegraph wires and undersea cables, and iron steamships. Telegraph messages from Java to Amsterdam and back took a few hours. Overland journeys from New York to San Francisco in 1850 took 6 months, but by 1870 only one week by rail. Transatlantic crossings by sail in 1800 had taken about a month on average; by 1880, steamships took a week.

The metallic web made the world feel smaller. The isochronic areas shaded on the map show, for instance, the broad swathe of Eurasia reachable from London in five days. Even those millions around the world who as late as 1900 had never seen a locomotive, steamship, or telegraph wire—mainly villagers in the areas shaded purple in South America, Africa, and Asia—found their lives changed by people, businesses, and governments who used these technologies every day.

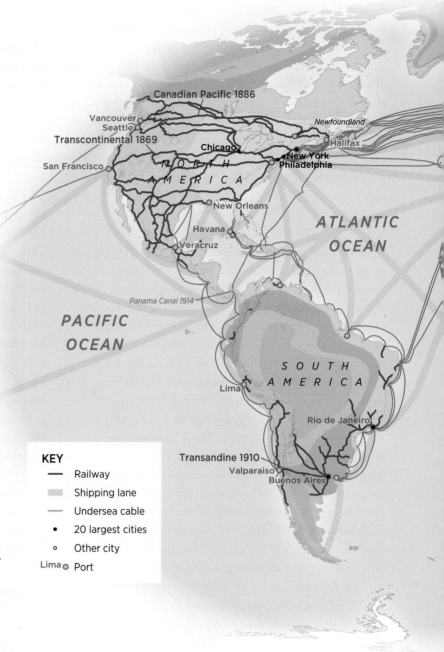

KEY

- —— Railway
- ▨ Shipping lane
- — Undersea cable
- • 20 largest cities
- ○ Other city
- Lima ○ Port

Questions for Analysis

Based on this feature and your chapter reading, consider the following questions:

1. What parts of the world remained least globally connected in 1900, to judge by the isochronic regions and the railway networks?

2. Within Africa and Asia, South Africa and India had unusually dense rail networks. Why?

> **"**
>
> THE WHOLE SURFACE OF THIS COUNTRY [WILL SOON] BE CHANNELED FOR THOSE NERVES WHICH ARE TO DIFFUSE, WITH THE SPEED OF THOUGHT, A KNOWLEDGE OF ALL THAT IS OCCURRING THROUGHOUT THE LAND, MAKING, IN FACT, ONE NEIGHBORHOOD OF THE WHOLE COUNTRY.
> **"**

SAMUEL F. B. MORSE, 1914 , ON THE IMPACT OF THE TELEGRAPH ON THE UNITED STATES

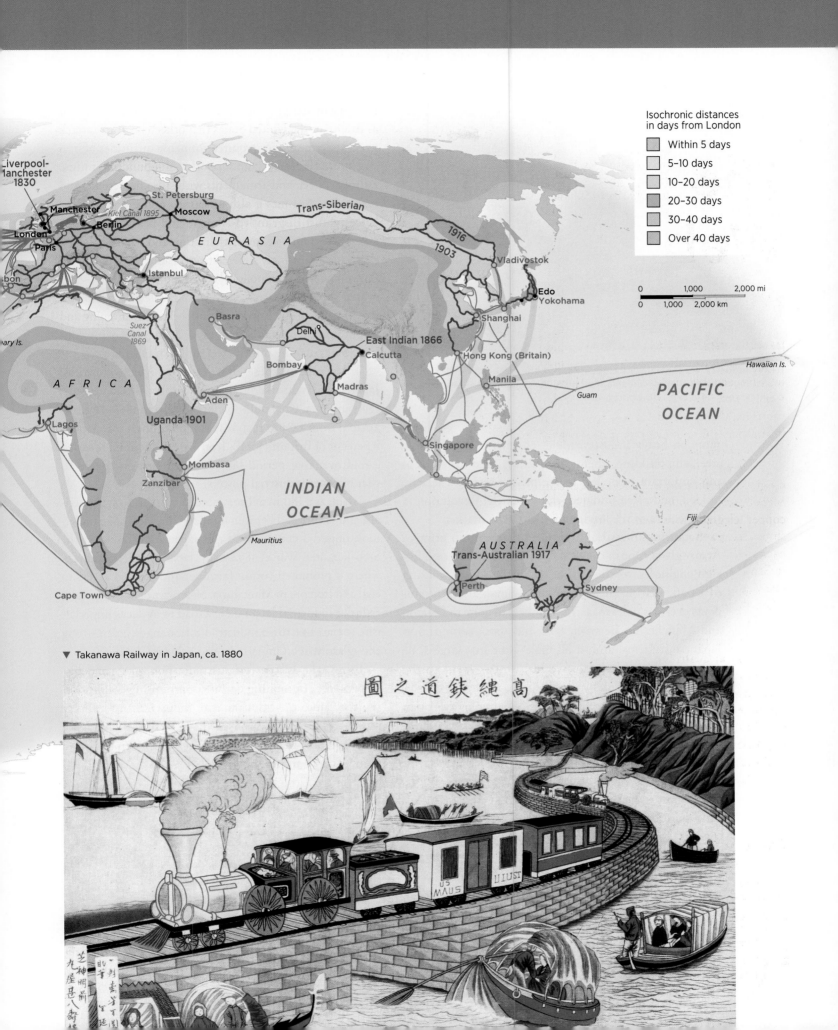

Liverpool-
Manchester
1830

Manchester

London
Paris

St. Petersburg

Kiel Canal 1895

Berlin

Moscow

Trans-Siberian

EURASIA

Istanbul

1916

1903

Vladivostok

*Suez
Canal
1869*

Basra

Delhi

East Indian 1866

Calcutta

Shanghai

Edo
Yokohama

Hong Kong (Britain)

Hawaiian Is.

AFRICA

Aden

Bombay

Madras

Manila

Guam

PACIFIC
OCEAN

Lagos

Uganda 1901

Mombasa

Zanzibar

Singapore

INDIAN
OCEAN

Mauritius

Fiji

AUSTRALIA
Trans-Australian 1917

Cape Town

Perth

Sydney

▼ Takanawa Railway in Japan, ca. 1880

圖之道銕縷高

Heavy Industry As Japan rapidly industrialized, the state built major industrial manufacturing works—like this steel plant in Fukuoka in the south of the country, seen here in a 1910 photograph.

more on heavy industry. Meiji reformers regarded iron, steel, shipbuilding, chemicals, mining, and railroads as too important to be left to the private sector. The state guided, and often initiated, the Industrial Revolution in these sectors, while leaving textiles to the market.

Acquiring industrial expertise became a top priority. At any given time in the 1870s and 1880s, some 2,000 foreign engineers, mechanics, or technicians were working in Japan, sharing their knowledge. Japan also sent students overseas to learn, as Yamanobe had done in London and Manchester. Between 1868 and 1900, some 11,000 Japanese students, almost all male—the first large-scale study-abroad initiative in world history—went to the United States, Germany, and Britain, mainly to master the latest industrial techniques and technologies. Japan also imported foreign technology directly and encouraged engineers to build similar, perhaps better, models, adapted to Japanese conditions.

The Meiji reformers also changed Japanese conditions to fit a more industrial society. They imposed compulsory education for girls and boys in 1872 and adopted patent law in 1885, prompting inventors to improve machinery. They founded engineering schools and sponsored industrial exhibitions. They adopted the metric system of measure, the 24-hour day, and a Westernized calendar.

MILITARY CONSIDERATIONS As in Germany and Russia, military considerations played a major role in the government's choices. Japan, its leaders came to believe,

needed a modern military to deter powerful countries such as Britain or the United States that otherwise might attack it. A modern military required immense quantities of iron and steel. The Meiji state supported shipbuilding, mines, railroads, steel, and armaments with subsidies, credit, and tax breaks. At times it also unleashed police or army violence against disgruntled laborers and peasants—whose taxes helped finance industrialization and whose irrigated rice fields increasingly suffered from deadly water pollution. Firms nurtured their political connections to get their share of state support, an arrangement that favored big businesses like Mitsubishi and Kawasaki, both originally shipping and shipbuilding companies. By 1890, both were giant conglomerates owning mines, steel mills, and factories.

The results of these efforts pleased Meiji reformers. Japan's total industrial production climbed 6-fold between 1870 and 1913. Coal output, close to zero in 1868, climbed 20-fold from 1883 to 1913, reaching 21 million tons (about 8 percent of Britain's total). Iron ore production increased 4-fold over that period but remained tiny compared to that of other industrial powers.

Japan, as it industrialized, needed ever more raw materials, and nature hadn't given it much. The Meiji state undertook imperial conquests at the expense of China in the Sino-Japanese War of 1894–1895. Japan acquired Taiwan, where it promoted cotton farming, and secured access to coal and iron ore in Manchuria. Shortages of key raw materials put industrial Japan on the road to overseas imperialism; at the same time, industrialization made Japan strong enough to win an imperialist war against China.

By 1914, Japan's swift industrialization, a case of deliberate policy triumphing despite unpromising conditions, vaulted it into the front ranks of industrial and military powers. That success aroused the curiosity, and envy, of people all over the world for whom Meiji Japan became a model and an inspiration.

INDUSTRIALIZATION: COMMONALITIES AND COMPARISONS

The industrial revolutions in Germany, the United States, Canada, Russia, and Japan had important things in common. Information flowed easily through the Global web by 1850, so it was easy to learn from the prior British example. All five countries rejected free trade and a fully free market in favor of protection of their industries and government promotion of transport infrastructure. Their leaders were well acquainted with the ideas of Alexander Hamilton and Friedrich List, and adapted them to their own circumstances. The Russian and Japanese governments, late to start pushing industrialization, took the most active roles. Four countries benefited from a large domestic market, providing manufacturers with potential economies of scale. (Canada had a small domestic market but access to U.S. customers.) Good transport systems and integrated national markets were a requirement for large-scale industrialization. And it helped to have additional accessible markets—for example, in the form of overseas empire or neighbors with few efficient industries of their own.

Four countries (not Canada) also shared a reliance on military industry. The first large-scale industrial system of interchangeable parts came in American armories charged with military production during the War of 1812. The first high-precision mass production took place in Portsmouth, England, in a factory designed during the Napoleonic Wars to produce hundreds of thousands of standardized pulleys for naval ships. What motivated the Englishman Henry Bessemer to find a new way to make steel in the 1850s was the problem of making big artillery pieces more durable. German steelmaking, especially that undertaken by Krupp's firm, was first devoted to tableware but by 1865 to weaponry. The programs of industrialization in Russia and Japan, at least the large sectors devoted to metallurgy, were calculated to make their countries militarily strong.

The tables below show the growth of heavy industry in various countries worldwide. Note the early start but modest growth in France; the surge in the United States after 1860 and in Russia after 1880; and the general dominance of the United States, Britain, and Germany.

DEINDUSTRIALIZATION

All these industrial revolutions sparked a related process: **deindustrialization**, the disappearance of old handicraft industries that could not compete for long with mechanized production. It too began in Britain. Hand-weavers, for example, working at home, eventually had to find other work after steam-powered textile mills were up and running. Village smiths, whose hoes and horseshoes could not compete with those churned out by iron foundries in Birmingham, had to do the same. Industrial cities put village industries out of business. This also happened in France, Belgium, and Germany after factory systems took root there, taking decades in each case.

ANNUAL COAL OUTPUT, 1820–1900 (IN MILLION TONS)

	BRITAIN	GERMANY	FRANCE	RUSSIA	JAPAN	UNITED STATES	CANADA
1820	~25	1	1	n/a	n/a	0.3	n/a
1840	43	4	3	n/a	n/a	2	n/a
1860	88	19	8	0.3	n/a	18	0.3
1880	149	59	19	3	0.8	72	1
1900	229	150	33	16	7	245	5

Sources: B. R. Mitchell, *International Historical Statistics: Europe, 1750–2005* (2007), 464–66; *Africa, Asia & Oceania, 1750–2005* (2007), 375; *The Americas, 1750–2005* (2007), 327–28.

ANNUAL IRON ORE OUTPUT, 1840–1900 (IN MILLION TONS)

	BRITAIN	GERMANY	FRANCE	RUSSIA	JAPAN	UNITED STATES	CANADA
1840	n/a	0.4	1	n/a	n/a	n/a	n/a
1860	8	1	3	n/a	n/a	n/a	n/a
1880	18	5	3	n/a	0.2	7	n/a
1900	14	13	5	6	0.3	28	0.1

Sources: B. R. Mitchell, *International Historical Statistics: Europe, 1750–2005* (2007), 490–91; *Africa, Asia & Oceania, 1750–2005* (2007), 397; *The Americas, 1750–2005* (2007), 341.

Handicraft Industry A mid-nineteenth-century watercolor shows a South Asian woman spinning thread by hand, one of the traditional crafts that was threatened worldwide by industrialization.

Soon deindustrialization was a near-global trend. By 1830, millions of spinners, weavers, and metalsmiths working in China, India, Iran, or Algeria were feeling the impact of British factory competition. A Bengali widow in 1828 reported that she had taken up spinning when her husband died, but her business quickly evaporated. She said that previously:

> weavers would come to my doorstep to buy the yarn ... and they would immediately advance as much cash money as I wanted. As a result, we did not have any anxiety about food and clothing.... Now ... the weavers have stopped coming to my doorstep to buy my yarn, [and] even when I send it to the [market] they will not buy it at one-fourth the former price.... I ... have learned that the weavers are using English yarn now.... When I examined the yarn I found it better than mine.

She was not alone in her misfortune. In 1835, the governor-general of British India wrote: "The bones of the cotton weavers are bleaching the plains of India."

Misfortune befell spinners and hand-weavers wherever factory cloth could be sold. Isfahan, in Iran, in 1890 had only 10 percent as many silk looms as in 1830 because British cotton took market share from Iranian silk. Spinners

and weavers from China to Chile faced similar challenges. The table below shows some of the geographical relocation of industry in the nineteenth century.

By the mid-nineteenth century, Britain's factories produced so much so cheaply—and often of such good quality—that handicraft industries worldwide met the same fate as Indian and Iranian textiles. British iron, steel, pottery, and even coal were competitive on every continent. The innovations of the Industrial Revolution conferred an enormous advantage on British industries, especially those that were energy- or knowledge-intensive. By 1870, industries in the United States and continental Europe came to share that advantage, contributing to more deindustrialization. Industrialization not only changed peasants into workers in Britain, Germany, Russia, or Japan; in much of the world it changed handicraft workers into peasants or paupers.

ECONOMIC SHIFTS AND POLITICAL POWER IN THE GLOBAL WEB

The efficiency of modern industrial production and transport launched a geographical reorganization of the world's economy. Lands with limited prospects for industrialization came to specialize in mainly food and fiber crops. The cheapest way to produce such crops was usually on plantations with forced labor. As we saw in Chapter 19, plantations spread widely before 1800, especially in sugar zones of the Americas. Now, with industrialization and cheap transport, they spread farther. Sugar plantations sprouted on Pacific islands such as Fiji and Hawaii. Rubber plantations took root in Southeast Asian lands such as Malaya and Vietnam. Cotton plantations developed in African regions such as the Nile delta or Tanganyika. The largest-scale case occurred in the U.S. South before the Civil War. Planters deepened their commitment to cotton production and slavery in response to the demand for raw cotton from British and New England mills. After the Civil War, despite the abolition of slavery, the trend toward cotton strengthened in the southern states.

The increase in raw material production extended beyond plantation landscapes. Australia and Argentina found niches producing wheat, wool, and leather, although each developed some light industry too. The advent of refrigerated shipping in the 1870s enabled the North American plains, the Argentine pampas, and other

CONSIDERING THE EVIDENCE

Rage against the Machines

The capitalists who owned textile mills and the laborers who worked in them often disagreed about the benefits of steam power. Capitalists claimed the machines made life easier for workers by saving them from the time and labor of monotonous tasks; workers focused on how machines reduced the number of available jobs. Great Britain and other states initially defended the interests of the less numerous capitalists against the demands of the much larger population of workers. Without a sympathetic ear in government, some workers organized violent riots to destroy the machines that threatened their livelihoods. In the following excerpt from a newspaper in Leeds (in northern England), an anonymous contributor describes a confrontation in 1812 between a "furious mob" and mill owners who had recently adopted steam power.

Middleton, April 22, 1812.

On Monday...afternoon, the Mills of Messrs. Daniel Burton and Sons...about five miles from Manchester, were attacked by a furious mob, not from any dislike personally to the proprietors,...but from using a species of looms worked by *power*, as it is called, that is by steam, and by the use of which manual labour is materially diminished....Mr. Emanuel Burton and [about 50] men...posted themselves in the works, determined to resist any attacks....After breaking the windows, the mob fired several shots into the Factory, and endeavoured to force an entrance; in this they did not succeed, and Mr. Burton and his party fired about 50 blank cartridges...to intimidate and disperse [the mob]...; but [they] found [it] necessary to fire upon them with ball, when five of the rioters were shot dead, and a number were desperately wounded, two...have died of their wounds. Seeing their companions fall around them, the assailants became panic-struck, and...they dispersed.

...Early on Tuesday morning a much more numerous mob...assembled....Finding that a detachment of the Scotch Greys [a cavalry regiment of the British Army] had been brought to protect the works, the mob...burnt [Mr. Emanuel Burton's mansion] to the ground.

Encouraged by their success, they repaired to [the mill], when an engagement between the mob and the cavalry took place, [four rioters were] shot dead upon the field, besides a great number wounded, and 17 of the most active of the insurgents taken prisoners....It was observed that all the rioters were strangers at Middleton, and that [Middleton's] labouring classes...took no part in the engagements.... This simple narrative of facts cannot be read without mixed emotions of horror and regret. For many years the military of this country have been solely employed against our foreign enemies; but now, unfortunately, they are under the necessity of acting against their own misled countrymen, and the tranquillity of the country is only imperfectly preserved even at the point of the bayonet!

Source: "Riots," *Leeds Mercury*, April 25 1812, in British Library Newspapers.

QUESTIONS FOR ANALYSIS

1. Why do you think the narrator needed to explain what "steam power" was and why it made people angry in 1812?
2. Does the narrator seem to have more sympathy for the "labouring classes" or the mill owners?
3. Why would the British government give a military regiment (which was accustomed to fighting foreign wars) an assignment to defend the private property of a mill owner?

---

grasslands to specialize in beef or mutton, transported by rail and ship to distant markets.

The rails and steam that stood at the center of the industrial revolutions helped to knit the world economy into a tighter web than ever before. In the early modern centuries, as we've seen, certain goods such as silver, spices, and sugar were traded across oceans. Bulk goods, with few exceptions, did not reward the cost of long-distance transport. But by the 1840s, that was changing fast. Cheap cloth, grain, timber, and coal could now yield profit if carried by steam-propelled trains or ships. Ever-larger spaces functioned more or less as single markets—where tariffs permitted.

Industrialization also changed the distribution of military and political power around the world. Britain, already on its way to becoming a great power before its Industrial Revolution, became the world's strongest power by 1840. It used its leverage to force weaker

APPROXIMATE SHARE OF GLOBAL INDUSTRIAL PRODUCTION, 1800–1900

	BRITAIN + EUROPE	CHINA + INDIA
1800	25%	50%
1850	37%	30%
1900	60%	12%

Source: Elaborated from Kaoru Sugihara, "Global Industrialization: A Multipolar Perspective," in *The Cambridge World History*, ed. J. R. McNeill and Kenneth Pomeranz, Vol. 7 (2015), 123.

countries to lower tariffs on British goods and to expand its overseas empire. Germany too, after unification (1871), emerged as a great power within Europe and, by the late 1880s, as an imperial power in Africa and the Pacific. France, although early to begin industrialization, could not keep pace with Britain and Germany, and by the 1870s no longer matched them in military power. The United States, Canada, and Russia accelerated their overland expansions with their newfound industrial might, and the United States took up overseas empire after 1898 as well. As we've seen, Japan's Industrial Revolution helped thrust that nation into the East Asian mainland as an imperial power from the 1890s.

Meanwhile, Mughal India vanished and Qing China languished. Their militaries, still formidable in the mid-eighteenth century, by 1840 proved helpless in the face of British gunboats and artillery. Britain controlled most of India by 1860 and, together with other industrial powers, parts of China as well. After 1870, peoples without industrial weaponry generally soon lost their independence—and some disappeared altogether. Rarely in world history had so much political and military power concentrated in so few spots. Now, in the nineteenth century, those who had pulled off industrial revolutions found themselves far more formidable than those who hadn't, and usually converted their advantages into conquest and empire. We will examine this theme more closely in Chapter 23.

SOCIAL CONTRACTS AND INDUSTRIAL SOCIETY

The energy revolution and economic transformation that industrial societies experienced deepened their inequalities. This cast new doubt on the social contracts on which those societies had formerly operated. Social contracts—the phrase was popularized by the French Enlightenment thinker Jean-Jacques Rousseau—are not real contracts. They are shared understandings of what is fair in terms of the distribution of wealth, income, opportunity, and political voice. They always reflect the distribution of political power and are reinforced by laws, customs, and policies.

The social contract of industrial society had to incorporate the new urban and professional upper-middle classes into ruling elites that formerly had comprised aristocrats, landowners, and big merchants. Between 1830 and 1900 in every industrialized country, the upper-middle classes obtained rights to vote and hold public office, to join prestigious schools and clubs—in short, to acquire substantial political power and social standing.

It was harder for industrializing societies to agree on the proper standing of the working classes. The older elites included a few people who sympathized with workers, but most were reluctant to share power, or even the right to vote, with people they considered their social and cultural inferiors. Also, workers could never unify behind a single set of aims. Some advocated for individual self-improvement, emphasizing the virtues of sobriety, hard work, and thrift. Others despaired of achieving improvement in this world and placed their hopes in a better life to come in the next. Many, however, came to think that political action provided their best hope.

REFORM   In political terms, workers were divided on the question of reform or revolution. Reform, meaning working within established institutions to achieve gradual improvements in working conditions and political rights, rested on the belief that progress was possible. In industrialized Europe, this outlook drew strength from Enlightenment ideology. Some of the poor, and as we've seen some middle-class observers such as Marx and Engels, rejected reform as a strategy for workers and advocated revolution. Workers' resentments sometimes boiled over into riots or rebellions. French workers took major roles in uprisings in 1830, 1848, and 1871. Workers in Milan, Berlin, Vienna, and other cities joined in revolutions in 1848—chaotic events that involved unstable coalitions with many agendas. In Russia, urban workers played a central role in an insurrection called the Revolution of

1905. But most attempts at revolution failed, sometimes in rivers of blood, and none managed to put the working class in power.

Reform efforts were more successful than revolution in renegotiating social contracts to the advantage of the working classes. There were several keys to the success of labor reform movements: the level of organization, the strength of alliances with the middle classes, and the continuing threat of bloody revolution or economic disruption.

LABOR ACTIVISM The most important key to the success of working-class reform was organization. Where they created labor unions, workers could negotiate more effectively with employers and put pressure on politicians. In 1824, the British Parliament repealed the Combination Acts that prohibited unions and strikes. In the ensuing decades, trade unions successfully drove parliamentary reforms of working conditions and the use of child labor. The unions also supported efforts to expand suffrage to all adult males.

The main weapon available to workers was the threat of a strike. In certain industries, such as coal or railroads, workers had considerable leverage, because the entire industrial economy depended on their labor. In 1877, for example, U.S. railroad workers went on strike in response to reduced wages. State governors called out militias, and violence broke out in several cities, obliging the federal

Trade Unions Speakers rally a crowd of striking mineworkers in Ludlow, Colorado, in 1914. By joining a union, workers could collectively demand better working conditions. But governments often opposed unionization: the Colorado National Guard violently ended this particular strike, resulting in the deaths of 21 people.

government to send in the army. Roughly 100 people were killed. The strikers returned to work, but the railroad companies soon offered pensions and better wages in hopes of preventing further strikes. In imperial Russia, where unions remained illegal, miners and steelworkers in the Donbass region struck or rioted nearly 200 times between 1870 and 1900. In Japan, strikes were few until the advent of labor unions in 1897, after which textile workers and miners used their only weapon to extract modest improvements in conditions and wages. On a much larger scale, in 1912 nearly 1 million unionized British coal miners struck for a minimum wage. Because factories, railroads, and the navy could not operate without coal, the miners had real power; after 37 days, the national government intervened, and the miners got a minimum wage.

ALLIANCES Another key to the success of labor reform was alliances with sympathetic members of the ruling elites or middle-class reformers. Every industrial country included people who were appalled at the squalor of urban working-class neighborhoods and the greed of many factory owners. In Britain, for example, Joseph Chamberlain, the industrial millionaire who turned to politics, became mayor of Birmingham and worked to deliver better schools, public libraries, clean water, streetlights, and other improvements to the entire city, including its working-class tenements. Others, such as the intellectuals Beatrice Webb and Sidney Webb and their colleagues in the Fabian Society (est. 1884), supported public education, shorter working hours, a minimum wage, and nationalized health care. Bismarck, as we've seen, agreed to provide health insurance and other benefits to German workers.

In Chicago, Jane Addams and other educated, well-to-do women set up Hull House in 1889 as a center for research into the plight of the city's poor, especially women and children, and advocated for improved education, housing, health care, and working conditions. By 1913, the United States had 413 **settlement houses**, as these institutions were called. In Japan, middle-class reformers such as the professor Kanai En called attention to the widening social gulf, lamenting that "since the coming of factory organization . . . there is an estrangement between managers and workers." They supported legislation, passed in 1911, that outlawed labor for those under age 12 and shortened the working day to 12 hours for women and children over

Settlement Houses Chicago children pose for a photograph outside Jane Addams's Hull House in 1908. Settlement houses like Hull House pioneered new methods of social work among the urban poor.

age 12. These reform efforts were all linked to one another. Bismarck's program influenced the Fabian Society. Hull House, based on a London settlement house called Toynbee Hall, was itself the model for a settlement house in Tokyo set up by American and Japanese women in 1919. Russian reformers established a settlement house in Moscow in 1905.

EXPANDING SUFFRAGE Some of these allies of the working class, and many workers too, called themselves liberals or socialists. Roughly speaking, liberals favored individual freedoms, constitutional checks on rulers, and often some legal protections for society's most vulnerable members. At the core of liberal movements and political parties were the urban middle classes. **Socialists** placed stronger emphasis on empowering the working classes—in some cases through cooperatives and unions, in others through workers' ownership of factories, farms, and mines. Both liberals and socialists generally wanted to end aristocratic privileges, curtail religion in public life, and broaden political participation. Most sought to reform, rather than smash, existing political systems.

An important focus of political reform was expanding the right to vote. Workers in the early decades of industrialization were not allowed to vote. But through the allied efforts of workers and middle-class liberals, universal male franchise became law in France in 1848, in Germany in 1871, and in Japan in 1925. In Britain, it came in steps

between 1868 and 1918. In the United States, adult white males could generally vote by 1856, with exceptions in particular states. African American men generally could not vote until ratification of a constitutional amendment in 1868; even then, their voting rights were often denied in the southern states for another century.

Everywhere that workers were winning the right to vote, they and their middle-class allies formed new political parties focused on advancing the welfare of the working classes. The German Social Democratic Party (SPD) was founded in 1875, the French socialist party in 1879, the British Labour Party in 1900, and a Japanese Social Democratic Party in 1901. By 1910, they were all important forces in the day-to-day politics of their countries, part of the political system. The United States, in contrast, never developed a successful political party explicitly devoted to the interests of workers. The main workers' party in Russia, the Russian Social Democratic Workers' Party, founded in 1898, did not seek reform within the Russian political system but, instead, strove to overthrow it.

WOMEN AND YOUTH In Britain, the United States, and elsewhere, women launched suffrage movements in the nineteenth century, but they achieved few political rights until the twentieth (see Chapter 25). But with industrialization, wage work in factories altered the fabric of women's lives. They now had a little money to spend and sometimes a wider network of friends in their coworkers, usually other women much like themselves, to whom they could turn in time of need. Women also organized to advance their own interests in response to new pressures brought by industrialization. In the early years in Lowell's mills, for example, young women made what for the time were good wages and were offered free evening educational classes. By the late 1830s, however, Lowell's mills slashed wages to match competition from other entrepreneurs. The Lowell girls, as they were known, resisted by going on strike and organizing a union. By 1853, they managed to convince the mill owners to reduce the work day to 11 hours.

In Japan, teenage girls made up most of the labor force in textile mills and worked in miserable conditions. They often lived in dingy dormitories and labored long hours for little pay. Women coal miners, usually older and married to male miners, fared worse. One observer commented: "Returning black and grimy from a day's

Young Women Workers An engraving shows young women working at weaving machines in the textile mills of Lowell, Massachusetts. Factory work increasingly became a sector that employed young, unmarried women, which gave them access to independent income and a new form of social independence away from home.

work in the pits with their husbands, they immediately had to start preparing meals . . . [and] nursing their babies. . . . [N]o man would be found helping with what were designated as women's tasks."

In the early Meiji years, activists sought a new social contract for women. They argued that the new Japan needed educated, independent women in order to compete in the international arena. Their main impact came in 1872, when four years of compulsory education was required for girls as well as boys. But by the 1890s, the Meiji state had banned women from all political activity and passed new legislation confining them to traditional roles, summarized in the slogan "good wife, wise mother." The most successful women's organization in Meiji Japan, the Patriotic Women's Society established by Okumura Ioko, which had half a million members by 1905, worked to prepare soldiers for overseas deployments and console families whose sons never returned from war. That suited the Meiji state perfectly.

For working-class teenagers and children, the industrial revolutions brought more independence from family supervision and, for some, the first formal schooling. They spent more of their time with other youths, whether in cotton mills, in schools, or on the streets. Many children worked long hours in mills or mines. Increasingly, some attended school. Industrial societies from France to Japan to Canada created systems of public education between 1830 and 1880, changing the nature of childhood. In many cases, education for girls came later than for boys. In Catholic lands, girls' education was often entrusted to

nuns rather than public employees. In addition to reading, writing, and arithmetic, schools taught the young to accept adult discipline, preparing them for life in the workplace. But in every industrial city, many unemployed children roamed the streets while their parents toiled in factories or as domestic servants.

More time spent together with their age-mates led the young in industrial cities to create their own culture—and led dismayed adults to try to shape it. British boys in growing numbers turned to sports such as soccer. In nineteenth-century Britain, and other countries too, young men in many working-class trades—masons, carpenters, smiths, tailors—regularly took to the road, tramping from town to town, looking for work, singing songs, and forging bonds of youth before settling into full adulthood. In many cities, teenage gangs sprang up. Concerned adults organized wholesome organizations and clubs, such as the YMCA and YWCA, founded in London in 1844 and 1855, respectively, or the Girls Club Union, begun in London in 1880. Churches of every denomination began creating youth groups starting in the 1880s. The industrial revolutions forced renegotiation of social contracts between generations and within families as well as among social classes.

INDUSTRIALIZATION AND THE GLOBAL ENVIRONMENT

The industrial revolutions altered nature as well as human society. In the industrialized lands, the sharpest impacts came in the form of air and water pollution, as we saw in Britain. The iron and steel centers of the Ruhr or Pittsburgh or Osaka (Japan), and hundreds of other cities, were also enveloped in smoky haze day and night. Their rivers became toxic currents contaminated by chemicals from dyeworks, bacteria from meatpacking plants, and coal soot raining down from chimneys and smokestacks. Efforts at pollution control remained rare until the twentieth century, although filtration, which turned dirty water into drinkable water, made considerable progress in industrial cities between 1850 and 1920 and sharply reduced the burden of disease.

The environmental impacts of the industrial revolutions reached beyond industrialized landscapes. They were global, transmitted via long-distance trade in commodities. The fibers, minerals, and lubricants needed for industry often came from far afield. The suitability of bison hide as leather belting in textile mills helped drive the North American bison hunt that reduced herds of 30 million to a total of about 500 animals between the 1830s and 1880s. Farmers in New Zealand burned ancient forests to make room for sheep pasture to provide wool for Britain's textile mills. The piano keyboard industry, which needed ivory, drastically depleted the East African elephant population between 1840 and 1930. Industrial demand and cheap transport brought about these fast and furious ecological changes.

Last, but perhaps most important in the long run, the burning of billions of tons of coal added more greenhouse gases to the atmosphere. This had no discernible effect on climate during the nineteenth century, and no one was concerned by it at the time. But these greenhouse gas emissions began, in a small way, the process of desta-bilizing climate that is still ongoing today. Some of the carbon dioxide from the chimneys of early coal-burning factories in 1830 remains in the atmosphere nearly 200 years later, warming the Earth. Some of it is now in the oceans, raising their acidity.

CONCLUSION

Here's an indication of how extraordinary the British Industrial Revolution was: in 1845, raw cotton grown in India was carried by oxcarts to ports, put on ships to sail around Africa to Britain, there spun into thread, woven into cloth, put back onto ships to sail around Africa again to ports in India, off-loaded and carried to Indian markets by oxcarts—and that cloth would be better and cheaper than cloth made in Indian villages.

The industrial revolutions in Europe, North America, and Japan shook up the world in several ways. They tightened linkages of the Global web, mainly through railroads, steamships, and telegraph lines, bringing grad-ual political, economic, and cultural changes that later chapters will explore. They freed societies from the old constraints and near-universal poverty of an energy regime based on muscle and wood, as steam engines enabled conversion of the chemical energy in coal into motion and power. They reordered social relations by cre-ating urban industrial working classes and expanding the middle classes. The industrial revolutions altered family dynamics. They created new inequalities of unprecedented size within societies by bringing untold wealth to a few and much-needed wages to many, along with new forms of hardship and exploitation. They also reshuffled inter-national relations, creating a handful of great powers in Europe, North America, and Japan out of formerly small or peripheral states. And they recast the ongoing relation-ships between human societies and the natural world, accelerating the use of resources such as iron, lead, or copper ores and fibers such as cotton or wool, and pouring out pollution—including greenhouse gases.

All these changes are still with us. By 1900, they shaped the lives of almost everyone in industrial countries, affect-ing work, consumption, social groupings, travel habits, and much else. Today, lives everywhere, even in remote villages, are shaped by the industrial revolutions of the years 1780–1914.

CHAPTER REVIEW

KEY TERMS

Industrial Revolution
(p. 709)

textiles and metallurgy
(p. 712)

coal (p. 712)

steam engine (p. 713)

James Watt (p. 713)

railways (p. 717)

working class (p. 719)

Friedrich List (p. 724)

Communist Manifesto
(p. 724)

Alexander Hamilton
(p. 725)

cotton gin (p. 726)

National Policy (p. 727)

Trans-Siberian Railway
(p. 728)

Sergei Witte (p. 728)

Meiji Restoration (p. 729)

Eiichi Shibusawa (p. 729)

deindustrialization
(p. 733)

settlement houses
(p. 737)

socialists (p. 738)

Go to INQUIZITIVE
to see what you've
learned—and learn what
you've missed—with
personalized feedback
along the way.

REVIEW QUESTIONS

1. What two main changes in manufacturing methods defined the Industrial Revolution?

2. What were the key industries of the Industrial Revolution, and why were they well suited to new manufacturing methods?

3. What combination of fuel and technology made up the energy revolution at the heart of the Industrial Revolution?

4. How did expensive labor and plentiful coal in Britain contribute to the start of the Industrial Revolution?

5. How did energy from coal change the cotton and iron industries in Britain?

6. Describe each tier of the social hierarchy of industrial Britain.

7. What measures did the German state introduce to spur industrialization?

8. Why was the U.S. weapons industry especially important to world history during this period?

9. What obstacles to industrialization did Russia face, and how did it overcome them?

10. What was the role of the Meiji government in Japan's industrialization?

11. Why, after transport and communication technologies changed slowly for millennia, did the technologies of the metallic web come in a cluster between 1800 and 1850?

12. Compare and contrast the level of state involvement in industrialization in Britain, the United States, Germany, Russia, and Japan.

13. What important features did the industrial revolutions in the United States, Germany, Russia, and Japan have in common?

14. How did the Industrial Revolution lead to deindustrialization among handicraft industries?

15. In what ways did industrialization change military and political power around the world?

16. What were the most important keys to working-class labor reform, and what was the main alternative to reform?

17. Identify and describe the main environmental impacts of industrialization and long-distance commodity trade.

FURTHER READING

Robert C. ALLEN, *The British Industrial Revolution in Global Perspective* (2009). A summary statement by one of the foremost economic historians.

Gareth AUSTIN and Kaoru SUGIHARA, eds., *Labour-Intensive Industrialization in Global History* (2013). The best way to get access to Sugihara's important take on industrialization in East Asia.

Boris B. GORSHKOV, *Russia's Factory Children: State, Society, and Law, 1800–1917* (2009). On the child labor experience and the controversies it aroused.

Emma GRIFFIN, *A Short History of the British Industrial Revolution* (2010). A very handy summary of the story and the controversies among earlier historians.

Eiichi SHIBUSAWA, *The Autobiography of Shibusawa Eiichi: From Peasant to Entrepreneur*, trans. Teruko Craig (1994). The life story of the "father of Japanese capitalism."

Robert C. H. SWEENY, *Why Did We Choose to Industrialize? Montreal, 1819–1849* (2015). A detailed study of one city contextualized in the world history of industrialization.

Barrie TRINDER, *Britain's Industrial Revolution: The Making of a Manufacturing People* (2013). A thorough examination of the subject with endless interesting detail.

Peer VRIES, *Averting a Great Divergence: State and Economy in Japan, 1868–1937* (2019). An analysis of the state's role in Japanese industrialization.

Richard WHITE, *The Republic for Which It Stands: The United States during Reconstruction and the Gilded Age, 1865–1896* (2019). A general history with a lot on industrialization and its consequences.

E. A. WRIGLEY, *Energy and the English Industrial Revolution* (2010). The most accessible version of the ideas of this master historian.

The Emergence of the Industrial Working Class in Britain

INDUSTRIALIZATION AND THE FACTORY SYSTEM TOOK hold first in Britain, beginning in the late eighteenth century. Within three generations, most Britons lived in cities and several million had left farm and village life to become laborers in factories, mills, or mines. The sources gathered here shed some light on that massive social change—the motives behind migration, the experiences of factory and mine labor, and what it all meant for the structure of society. Although industrialization and the formation of an industrial labor force took place first in Britain, throughout the nineteenth century broadly similar changes occurred on the European continent, in eastern North America, in parts of Russia, and in Japan as the technologies of mechanization and the idea of a *working class* spread through the Global web.

SOURCE 21.1

Benjamin Franklin to Joshua Babcock, 1772

The American printer, publisher, inventor, and politician Ben Franklin (1706–1790) lived for about 16 years in London, working as an agent and lobbyist for the colony of Pennsylvania. During that time Franklin visited Ireland and Scotland in 1771, spending about six weeks in each. He wrote about what he saw in letters to his friend Joshua Babcock (1707–1783), a Rhode Island physician and politician who in his youth had studied medicine in Britain. In the letter excerpted here, Franklin draws stark contrasts among the living conditions of landlords and laborers in Ireland, Scotland, and New England—and then extends the comparison to "every Indian" in the American colonies.

I have lately made a tour through Ireland and Scotland. In these countries a small part of the society are landlords, great noblemen and gentlemen, extremely opulent, living in the highest affluence and magnificence: The bulk of the people tenants, extremely poor, living in the most sordid wretchedness in dirty hovels of mud and straw, and clothed only in rags. I thought often of the happiness of New England, where every man is a freeholder, has a vote in public affairs, lives in a tidy warm house, has plenty of good food and fuel, with whole clothes from head to foot, the manufacturing perhaps of his own family. Long may they continue in this situation! But if they should ever envy the *trade* of these countries, I can put them in a way to obtain a share of it. Let them with three fourths of the people of Ireland, live the year round on potatoes and buttermilk, without shirts, then may their merchants export beef, butter and linen. Let them with the generality of the common people of Scotland go barefoot, then may they make large exports in shoes and stockings: And if they will be content to wear rags like the spinners and weavers of England, they may make cloths and stuffs for all parts of the world....

Had I never been in the American colonies, but was to form my judgment of civil society by what I have lately seen, I should never advise a nation of savages to admit of civilisation: For I assure you, that in the possession and enjoyment of the various comforts of life, compar'd to these people every Indian is a gentleman: And the effect of this kind of civil society seems only to be, the depressing multitudes below the savage state that a few may be rais'd above it. My best wishes, Dear Sir.

Source: From Benjamin Franklin to Joshua Babcock, 13 January 1772, National Archives, London.

- This letter concerns rural villagers. What can it help us understand about the British Industrial Revolution?
- By "savages" and "Indian" Franklin meant Native Americans. Why might he refer to them in making his point?

SOURCE 21.2

The Testimony of Mill Worker Elizabeth Bentley, 1832

Elizabeth Bentley, born in the north of England in 1809, was one of about 40 workers who gave testimony about factory conditions to a parliamentary committee in 1832. Michael Sadler, who chaired the committee, concluded that textile factories were dens of immorality, ill health, and abuse. But his colleagues judged that he had chosen an unbalanced roster of witnesses and declined to legislate on the evidence he gathered. In 1833, however, another committee interviewed a wider array of witnesses and did so under oath. While its conclusions were less strident than Sadler's, they inspired the so-called Factory Act of 1833. It limited the employment of 14- to 18-year-olds in textile mills to 72 hours per week and that of 9- to 13-year-olds to 54-hour weeks; and it banned the factory employment of children under age 9—except in the silk industry, where small fingers were especially useful. What became of Elizabeth Bentley after age 23 is unknown.

Elizabeth Bentley, called in; and Examined.

What age are you? — Twenty-three.

What time did you begin to work at a factory? — When I was six years old.

What kind of mill is it? — Flax-mill.

What was your business in that mill? — I was a little doffer.[1]

What were your hours of labour in that mill? — From 5 in the morning till 9 at night, when they were thronged.

What were your usual hours when you were not so thronged? — From 6 in the morning till 7 at night.

What time was allowed for your meals? — Forty minutes at noon.

Had you any time to get your breakfast or drinking? — No, we got it as we could.

And when your work was bad, you had hardly any time to eat it at all? — No; we were obliged to leave it or take it home, and when we did not take it, the overlooker took it, and gave it to his pigs.

Do you consider doffing a laborious employment? — Yes.

Does that keep you constantly on your feet? — Yes, there are so many frames, and they run so quick.

Suppose you flagged a little, or were too late, what would they do? — Strap us.[2]

Are they in the habit of strapping those who are last in doffing? — Yes.

Constantly? — Yes.

---

[1]In flax mills doffers removed full bobbins and replaced them with empty ones, a repetitive task performed by the youngest girls.

[2]Bodily punishment with a lash or whip

Source: *Readings in European History since 1814*, eds. Jonathan F. Scott and Alexander Baltzly (Appleton-Century-Crofts, Norwalk, CT, 1930).

- **Is there any evidence here that the interviewer, Mr. Sadler, is "leading the witness" toward the answers he wants? If so, where and how?**

- **Do the interests of Elizabeth Bentley and Mr. Sadler coincide or diverge in this inquiry? Explain your response.**

SOURCE 21.3

Child Laborers in British Coal Pits, ca. 1840

In 1842, an anonymous author published a book on child labor in British mines based on testimony recorded by a royal commission. The commissioners estimated that in various districts as many as one-third of the mineworkers were younger than age 18. Many boys and girls began work at age five as "trappers," which meant sitting alone in the dark for 12 hours controlling trap doors. At age seven or eight they graduated to pushing and pulling carts filled with coal through shafts too narrow and low for adults or horses. Older children carried baskets of coal on their backs up as many as nine consecutive ladders. The commission reported that in the safest mines in Britain, each year on average 1 in every 340 persons died in accidents—most of them children.

It is but fair to state, however, that there is, in this county, a growing feeling against employing very young children in the mines; and there is a rule laid down at Worsley...prohibiting the employment of male children under 10 years of age, and females under 12. Another fact to be noticed is, that the disposition evinced by many of the colliers to carry their children into the mines at so early an age, arises out of the inadequacy of their own earnings to support their families, and also out of the legal restriction that now exists against sending them to the neighbouring factories.

[...]

While the evidence is overwhelming, that in the Yorkshire district children are to be found in the coal-mines regularly at work at the ages of five, six, and seven, it is clear, from a careful perusal of the whole of the depositions, that this fact could never have been brought to light by the examination of the coal owners only. It is in general with extreme reluctance that this class of witnesses acknowledge that children begin to work in the pits even as early as seven years of age....

[...]

In Scotland, the employment of girls and women in the ordinary underground work of the coal-pits is even more extensive than in any part of England....Of the employment of girls and women in the coal-mines in the east of Scotland, Mr Franks [one of the commissioners] says:

"...The *coal-bearers* are women and children employed to carry coal on their backs in unrailed roads, with burdens varying from [75 to 300 lbs]. It is revolting to humanity to reflect upon the barbarous and cruel slavery which this degrading labour constitutes...."

[...]

William Tranter, ground-bailiff, in Coal Brook Dale, says:

"In the coal-mines some boys are employed in bringing the coals in small carriages, called dans, to the horse-road, and others in pitching them into the carriages drawn by the horses. The mines are too low for men to do such work. Some of them are two feet in thickness.... The boys crawl on their hands and knees."

When a child has to drag a carriage loaded with coals through a passage "not more than 18 inches in height," some ingenuity is required to get his body and the carriage through this narrow space.... But an expedient has been adopted with a view of facilitating this labour, of which the sub-commissioner [Tranter] gives the following description: "A girdle is put round the naked waist, to which a chain from the carriage is hooked and passed between the legs, and the boys crawl on their hands and knees, drawing the carriage after them."...

[...]

In the coal mines, in which the seams of coal are thin, the children almost universally hurry[1] on all-fours with the belt and chain.

In some parts, girls are quite as commonly employed in dragging coals in this manner as boys.... "One of the most disgusting sights I have ever seen," says the Sub-Commissioner, "was that of young females, dressed like boys in trousers, crawling on all-fours, with belts round their waists, and chains passing between their legs, at day pits at Hunshelf Bank, and in many small pits near Holmfirth and New Mills. It exists also in several other places."

[...]

The persons employed in coal-bearing are almost always girls and women.... The coal-bearers have to carry coal on their backs....

[...]

Agnes Moffatt, seventeen years of age: "Began working at ten years of age. Works twelve and fourteen hours daily. Father took sister and I down; he gets our wages. I fill five baskets; the weight is more than 22 cwt [2,200 lbs]; it takes me five journeys.... It is no uncommon thing for women to lose their burthen [load], and drop off the ladder. ...Margaret McNeil did a few weeks since, and injured both legs.... The lassies hate the work altogether, but they cannot run away from it."

---

[1] In Yorkshire mines, "hurry" meant to haul carts of coal from the coal-face.

Source: *The Condition and Treatment of the Children Employed in the Mines and Collieries of the United Kingdom* (London: William Strange, 1842).

- **Judging by the evidence gathered by the royal commission, what were the reasons that small children worked in mines in early nineteenth-century Britain?**
- **How reliable can we suppose the evidence of a royal commission on child labor in British mines would be? Does this excerpt seem to show any sign of systematic bias on the part of the commissioners? Explain your response.**

SOURCE 21.4

Manifesto of the Communist Party, 1848

In 1848, Karl Marx and Friedrich Engels published a pamphlet called the Communist Manifesto. Marx was a German journalist with a scholarly bent. Engels, also German, did not need to work because he was born into a prosperous cotton mill– owning family, but he served grudgingly in the family business while studying philosophy and writing political tracts in his spare time. The authors' knowledge of workers came mainly from Engels's employees in an English mill.

The Manifesto is partly a call to revolution, ending with the admonition "Workers of the world, unite! You have nothing to lose but your chains." But it is also an analysis of changing structures of society brought about by the early phases of industrialization, as in the excerpt here. The Manifesto has sold more than 500 million copies since 1848. "Proletariat" means the class of wage-laborers; "bourgeoisie" means the class that includes owners of factories, investors, and members of professions such as law and medicine.

Modern industry has converted the little workshop of the patriarchal master into the great factory of the industrial capitalist. Masses of labourers, crowded into the factory, are organised like soldiers.... Not only are they slaves of the bourgeois class, and of the bourgeois State; they are daily and hourly enslaved by the machine, by the overlooker, and, above all, by the individual bourgeois manufacturer himself....

The more modern industry becomes developed, the more is the labour of men superseded by that of women. Differences of age and sex have no longer any distinctive social validity for the working class. All are instruments of labour, more or less expensive to use, according to their age and sex.

[...]

The lower strata of the middle class—the small tradespeople, shopkeepers, and retired tradesmen generally, the handicraftsmen and peasants—all these sink gradually into the proletariat, partly because their diminutive capital does not suffice for the scale on which Modern Industry is carried on, and is swamped in the competition with the large capitalists, partly because their specialised skill is rendered worthless by new methods of production. Thus the proletariat is recruited from all classes of the population.

The proletariat goes through various stages of development. With its birth begins its struggle with the bourgeoisie. At first the contest is carried on by individual labourers, then by the workpeople of a factory, then by the operative of one trade, in one locality, against the individual bourgeois who directly exploits them. They direct their attacks not against the bourgeois conditions of production, but against the instruments of production themselves; they destroy imported wares that compete with their labour, they smash to pieces machinery, they set factories ablaze, they seek to restore by force the vanished status of the workman of the Middle Ages.

[…]

But with the development of industry, the proletariat not only increases in number; it becomes concentrated in greater masses, its strength grows, and it feels that strength more. The various interests and conditions of life within the ranks of the proletariat are more and more equalised, in proportion as machinery obliterates all distinctions of labour, and nearly everywhere reduces wages to the same low level. The growing competition among the bourgeois, and the resulting commercial crises, make the wages of the workers ever more fluctuating. The increasing improvement of machinery, ever more rapidly developing, makes their livelihood more and more precarious; the collisions between individual workmen and individual bourgeois take more and more the character of collisions between two classes. Thereupon, the workers begin to form (Unions) … to keep up the rate of wages; … Here and there, the contest breaks out into riots.

Now and then the workers are victorious, but only for a time. The real fruit of their battles lies, not in the immediate result, but in the ever expanding union of the workers. This union is helped on by the improved means of communication that are created by modern industry, and that place the workers of different localities … into one national struggle between classes. But every class struggle is a political struggle. And that union, to attain which the burghers of the Middle Ages, with their miserable highways, required centuries, the modern proletarian, thanks to railways, achieve in a few years.

This organisation of the proletarians into a class, and, consequently into a political party, is continually being upset again by the competition between the workers themselves. But it ever rises up again, stronger, firmer, mightier. It compels legislative recognition of particular interests of the workers, by taking advantage of the divisions among the bourgeoisie itself. Thus, the ten-hours' bill in England was carried.[1]

Altogether collisions between the classes of the old society further, in many ways, the course of development of the proletariat. The bourgeoisie finds itself involved in a constant battle. At first with the aristocracy; later on, with those portions of the bourgeoisie itself, whose interests have become antagonistic to the progress of industry; at all time with the bourgeoisie of foreign countries. In all these battles, it sees itself compelled to appeal to the proletariat, to ask for help, and thus, to drag it into the political arena. The bourgeoisie itself, therefore, supplies the proletariat with its own elements of political and general education, in other words, it furnishes the proletariat with weapons for fighting the bourgeoisie.

[…]

Of all the classes that stand face to face with the bourgeoisie today, the proletariat alone is a really revolutionary class. The other classes decay and finally disappear in the face of Modern Industry; the proletariat is its special and essential product.

[…]

… The advance of industry … replaces the isolation of the labourers, due to competition, by the revolutionary combination, due to association. The development of Modern Industry, therefore, cuts from under its feet the very foundation on which the bourgeoisie produces and appropriates products. What the bourgeoisie therefore produces, above all, are its own grave-diggers. Its fall and the victory of the proletariat are equally inevitable.

---

[1]An 1847 Act of Parliament that limited female and teenage textile workers labor to ten hours per day.

Source: *The Encyclopedia of Social Reforms*, 2nd ed., ed. William D. P. Bliss (London: Funk & Wagnalls Company, 1897).

- According to Marx and Engels, the proletariat will inevitably overthrow the bourgeoisie and rule society. Why do they think so?
- How, according to Marx and Engels, did the proletariat come into being?

QUESTIONS FOR COMPARISON

1. Does anything said by actual workers—Elizabeth Bentley or any of the children laboring in British coal mines—support the class analysis of Marx and Engels?

2. These sources all have something to say—directly or indirectly—about the role of women and girls in industrialization. Are the sources consistent in this regard, or in tension with one another? Why or why not?

CHRONOLOGY

1670s
Objections to slavery arise in Quaker community in Barbados

late seventeenth century
Kangxi Emperor requires smallpox inoculation in imperial lineage

1758
Philadelphia chapter of Quakers formally denounces slavery

1773–1774
Emelian Pugachev's rebellion in Russia

1787
Thomas Clarkson, Quakers, and evangelicals form abolitionist committee in Britain

1798
Edward Jenner publishes account of cowpox experiment

1800–1860
Slave population in American South quintuples

1801
Toussaint L'Ouverture abolishes slavery in Haiti

1802–1805
Spanish Empire establishes vaccination program

1807
Britain bans slave trade; Prussia ends serfdom

1808
United States bans slave trade

1812
José Aponte leads slave revolts in Cuba

1817
Cholera begins to spread worldwide; Spain bans slave trade

1823
Jack Gladstone leads Demerara revolt; Anti-Slavery Society forms in Britain

1831
Samuel Sharpe leads slave revolt in Jamaica; autobiography of Mary Prince is published

1834
Britain abolishes slavery

1835
Malê revolt in Brazil

1845–1847
Famine kills 12 to 15 percent of Ireland's population

Cattle disease kills almost all herds in East and southern Africa

1848
France's final abolition of slavery

ca. 1850
Germ theory of disease develops; sanitation reform begins

1850–1880
Migrant flows of indentured labor peak

1853
Britain requires smallpox vaccination for all children

1861
Emancipation of serfs in Russia

1865
United States abolishes slavery

1870s
Slave imports peak in Egypt

1873
Puerto Rico abolishes slavery

1886
Cuba abolishes slavery

1888
Brazil abolishes slavery

1890s

22

Two Liberations

THE VITAL REVOLUTION AND THE
ABOLITIONS OF SLAVERY AND SERFDOM

1750 to 1950

C hristine of Mecklenburg-Güstrow devoted a quarter of her long life to bearing and burying her children. She was born in 1663 to a noble family in a reasonably healthy part of Germany. The daughter of a duke, she married a count when she was 19 and gave birth to twins 8 months later. Both twins died the day they were born. Over the next 22 years, Christine bore 21 more children (she had four pairs of twins). Of her 23 children, 12 died before age 5. Of those who made it to age 5, all survived to age 38 and four saw their 70th birthdays. Christine herself succumbed in 1749 at age 85. Seventeen of her children had already died.

Christine was unusual for her time. She was a noblewoman, she married young, she lived long, and she bore about four times as many children as the average woman of that era. But she was far from unique. England's Queen Anne, born two years after Christine, made every effort to provide the realm with an heir. She had 18 pregnancies that led to 5 births. Only one of her babies reached age 2—only to die at age 19. She had the benefit of the best diet and medical care available in her era—as did Christine.

Even though she was unusual in some ways, Christine's career as a mother tells us a few things about health history in her day. Despite being prosperous

1902–1904
Cholera kills 200,000 people in the Philippines

1910
China abolishes slavery

1924
Turkish Republic abolishes slavery

1918
Flu pandemic kills more than 50 million people

1928
Iran abolishes slavery

Destruction of the Roehampton Estate, January 1832 An episode in the Jamaican slave revolt of 1831–1832, when some 60,000 enslaved people rose up against local planters and the British Army.

FOCUS QUESTIONS

1. What made the Vital Revolution such a dramatic departure in human history?

2. What major developments contributed to the abolition of slavery in the nineteenth century?

3. How did the abolition of serfdom come about?

4. What brought the use of indentured labor to an end?

and reliably well fed, more than half of her children died young, probably all victims of disease. Even a family as comfortable as hers could not consistently keep children healthy and alive. That was equally true in Mecklenburg, Mozambique, and Mongolia—and the London of Queen Anne. In most of the world, just as it took two adults to generate a birth, it took on average two births to make an adult.

Christine's family story also shows us that people who made it past age 5 had a good chance of making it to 40. After age 40, life grew more precarious quickly. Even though global life expectancy at birth was only about 25 or 30 years, people age 10 to 40 stood the lowest risk of dying—on average. Warfare and childbirth could raise the risk of death for people in the prime of life. But in general, death stalked the very young and those over age 40.

A lot has changed since Christine's day. Consider this: for the first 10,000 generations in human history, the average life expectancy of *Homo sapiens* populations was about 25 years. In the last 10 generations since Christine's death (1749), it has nearly tripled. It now stands a little above 73 years—slightly higher for women and lower for men. Japanese people can expect to live the longest, on average about 85 years, and people in the Central African Republic the shortest, about 54 years. This lengthening of life expectancy has brought a new inequality around the world. In Christine's day, life expectancy in the least healthy lands might have stood around 25, and in the healthiest around 35. Now the gap between richest and poorest countries is 32 years of life expectancy, three times longer—although in percentage terms the gap remains about 40 percent. The gaps between the richest and poorest within specific societies today are much smaller than those between countries—roughly 2 to 10 years, depending on the society in question. Whether these gaps have grown or shrunk since Christine's day is unclear.

So industrialization, the focus of the previous chapter, was far from the only process at work changing the world after 1750. This chapter takes up two broad themes, each of which had some links to industrialization but both of which were, in their own right, major historical forces shaping the modern world.

The first of these is sometimes called the Vital Revolution, because it deals with basic biological facts of life such as disease, health, and longevity. On average, human health and life expectancy improved steadily after 1750. For ordinary people, this change might have been the most important revolution of them all, even if at the time no one noticed it—because it was slow and incremental. It is a curious paradox that the most important processes changing the lives of ordinary people might go unnoticed. It is also testimony to the advantages of hindsight—of historical perspective.

The second of these important historical shifts was the decline of forced labor—a broad category. Forced labor ranged from chattel slavery, a lifetime status as human property in which people were bought and sold and their children were slaves by birth, to milder forms of bonded status that were temporary and not heritable. In some systems of forced labor, especially in Africa, the Islamic world, and Brazil, manumission—the granting of freedom—was more common than in others. In eastern Europe, serfs were bound to labor for the lords who owned the land they worked; serfs could also be their masters' legal property. In some cases, such as in the Americas and the Arab lands, forced labor carried with it a strong racial component, as we will see. In the rest of the world, that was less often the case. This chapter will focus on slaves and serfs, but even these categories were broad and variable: there could be a world of difference between a life spent cutting Cuba's sugarcane and another life weaving Central Asia's carpets.

Between the 1790s and 1920s, slavery as a legal institution in all its variety almost disappeared around the world. And between 1800 and 1870, the eastern European practice of serfdom vanished, and elsewhere other forms of forced labor waned. (Serfdom is explained in detail below.) New labor arrangements and new hierarchies took the place of slavery and serfdom. Unlike the Vital Revolution, this historical shift was easily visible to contemporaries—because it was sudden, controversial, and contested.

These two fundamental changes help mark the modern world off from what came before. For all of human history before 1750, a third or a half of all babies born did not make it to their fifth birthday. That was the normal human condition. But in the nineteenth century, and more conspicuously in the twentieth, that changed with the Vital Revolution. More people survived infancy and more lived to ripe old age. In broad terms, since 1750 life expectancy has tripled in the healthiest societies and doubled in the least healthy.

Until recently, forced labor was also a normal part of the human condition, although perhaps only for the last 5,000 years or so. Just about every agricultural society had one or another form of forced labor. Just about every agrarian culture regarded forced labor as acceptable, natural, and normal. Then, at the end of the eighteenth century, that attitude began to change. People who were held in bondage increasingly found allies elsewhere who opposed slavery or serfdom, and together they forced an end to legal forced labor—even if illegal forced labor survives in the shadows of the world economy to this day.

Justifications for Slavery Those who wanted to defend chattel slavery often relied on images of Africans as childlike, savage, or otherwise mentally and psychologically unfit for freedom—as in this 1833 American cartoon, which is critical of abolitionists.

One can judge the improvements in health and longevity, and the abolition of forced labor, as human triumphs and important examples of progress in modern world history. One can also judge the remaining inequalities in health and longevity, and the lingering legacies of slavery and serfdom, as continuing injustices. The study of world history enables each of us to assess these issues for ourselves and arrive at informed conclusions.

THE VITAL REVOLUTION

Like the Industrial Revolution, the **Vital Revolution** was a gradual development with no clear starting date. It began earlier in some places (such as France and Sweden) than in others (such as China and Japan). It could be temporarily reversed: in many cities of Britain, as we've seen, health worsened with industrialization. But whenever it began, within a century it brought a giant change in the human condition.

Just as the Old Regime preceded the French Revolution, what we can call a **biological old regime** preceded the Vital Revolution. It was broadly similar around the world. For most people, life was nasty, sickly, and short. Rich and poor alike were preoccupied with their health and, particularly in the case of women, with the health of their families. And there was a lot to fret about. Poor people had to worry about not getting enough to eat, and everyone had to face the risks of many dangerous diseases, few of which anyone could prevent or treat effectively. It is hard for those of us who have grown up with vaccines, antibiotics, and other powerful tools of modern medicine to imagine the insecurity of life and health under the biological old regime. But let's try.

THE BIOLOGICAL OLD REGIME: HEALTH AND NUTRITION BEFORE 1800

Before 1800, everywhere from China to Chile and Iceland to India, most people were sick much of the time. The crowd diseases, such as smallpox, measles, or mumps, were the most dangerous. They all had spread widely around the world by 1700. Wherever populations were dense enough and large enough to sustain them, they appeared as endemic diseases, always present and afflicting mainly babies and toddlers. Older people had already encountered and survived them, developing disease resistance in the process. Sometimes, however, such as in more isolated places, the crowd diseases appeared as epidemics, which arrived suddenly, from afar, and could affect people of all ages. Smallpox and measles were the worst of the crowd diseases. Both were breath-borne and spread easily from person to person. Both were extremely dangerous to people who had never had them before. In Iceland in 1707, for example, smallpox returned after a 35-year absence and killed about 30 percent of the population—most of them younger than age 35. Other important crowd diseases, although less lethal than smallpox or measles, included influenza and whooping cough (pertussis).

Many other infections besides the crowd diseases caused misery.

Childhood Illness A Chinese painting from around 1800 shows a little girl covered in the distinctive sores of smallpox, one of the common crowd diseases often contracted in infancy or early childhood.

Gastrointestinal infections raged wherever people lived in settled communities, and these illnesses were often fatal to babies. Typhoid was one such disease, usually spread by bacteria in contaminated water. In warm weather—and in many places it was always warm enough for typhoid—it could rip through a community, killing up to 10 percent. Cholera, another mainly waterborne disease, was more deadly. Before 1800, it probably existed only in South Asia, but after the 1810s cholera occasionally attacked communities around the world. Where wastewater and drinking water were not carefully kept apart, which before 1800 was almost everywhere, waterborne diseases took a dreadful toll.

AT-RISK POPULATIONS Cities were especially unhealthy. In 1608, a Chinese observer described Beijing, then the world's biggest city, writing:

> The houses in the capital are so closely crowded together that there is no spare space, and in the markets there is much excrement and filth. People ... live together in disorderly confusion, and there are many flies and gnats. Whenever it becomes hot it is almost intolerable. A little steady rain has only to fall and there is trouble from flooding. Therefore malarial fevers, diarrhea and epidemics follow each other without stopping.

European cities were no better. In the early eighteenth century, Tsar Peter the Great's family lived mainly in Moscow and the new city of St. Petersburg. Of his 14 children, 11 died before age seven. London between 1550 and 1800 recorded more deaths than births every year. In 1750, the average life expectancy for newborns was 19. Only a steady inflow of thousands of migrants each year kept the city going. Every sizeable city had a similar murderous effect due to its intense disease environment. As a German physician put it in 1796, cities were the "open graves of humankind." Before 1800, only about 3 percent of humankind lived in cities. The proportion could not have been much higher without the human race dwindling toward extinction—because urban conditions before 1850 inflicted such a harsh penalty. Japanese cities in the sixteenth through nineteenth centuries seem to have been the least deadly, a result of cultural attitudes about cleanliness, the absence of livestock in cities, and government policies on the handling of wastes and the provision of drinking water. By 1800, about 10 percent of Japanese lived in cities.

Some plantations imposed a health penalty comparable to that of cities. Sugar plantations seem to have been the worst, deadlier than tobacco, coffee, or cotton plantations, owing to both dangerous labor tasks such as feeding cane-rolling mills and a particularly harsh disease environment. On Caribbean sugar plantations in the eighteenth century, where most of the population was enslaved, three people died for every two who were born.

Everywhere, children whose immune systems had not yet been strengthened by surviving infections faced particularly daunting risks, as Christine's misfortunes in motherhood attest. The most dangerous age for babies began the day they were weaned of breast milk, which carried some immunity protection loaned, so to speak, by mothers. Children were also especially likely to suffer from diarrhea and gastrointestinal ailments, as they are today. The wide range of lethal diseases was the main reason that 35 to 50 percent of children around the world did not live to age five.

In some cultures, the risks babies faced also included infanticide. Unwed mothers often abandoned or drowned their babies. Families sometimes did the same when they judged that the addition of a new child was disadvantageous. The best-documented case is probably Qing China, where in the eighteenth-century infanticide (already practiced for more than 1,500 years in China) was common. In some parts of the country, such as the lower and middle Yangzi, infanticide claimed about half of all newborns. Girls were especially vulnerable. Across the empire, roughly 20 to 25 percent of baby girls were deliberately killed before their first birthday. Even the imperial lineage, among the most prosperous segments in Qing society, killed about 10 percent of their baby girls. In Chinese families, elders decided when young people should marry, when they should have children, how many children there should be, and whether or not to kill unexpected babies. They left less to chance than families in most other parts of the world.

Adult women faced at least one health danger that children and men did not: childbirth. The evolution long ago of our big brains and big heads came at a price that mothers pay. Before 1800, about 1 to 3 percent (reliable figures are scarce) of births killed the mother via hemorrhage or infection. By 1880, the risks of childbirth began to diminish in Finland, the country for which we have the earliest systematic data, and by 1940 just about everywhere else. The biggest cause of this improvement was the

Dangers of Childbirth In this 1882 engraving, a Swiss doctor applies an early blood transfusion technique to treat the hemorrhage of a woman who has just delivered twins.

recognition that those assisting with births—midwives, nurses, and doctors—should wash their hands. Today, worldwide, about 0.2 percent of births are fatal to mothers, but in Africa it is 0.5 percent while in Australia and New Zealand about 0.007 percent.

MALNUTRITION AND FAMINE The health risks of the biological old regime included malnutrition and starvation. As we have seen, during the worst decades of the Little Ice Age in the seventeenth century, cold and drought ruined many a harvest. Even in less challenging times, bad weather sometimes destroyed crops. In India, where a bad monsoon meant crop failure, a drought during the years 1630–1632 cost at least 3 million lives in the area around Gujarat. Over the next 200 years, sizeable killing famines appeared somewhere in India about once a decade, on average. In Ireland in 1845–1847, a potato disease led to a famine that killed 12 to 15 percent of the population. Because most people around the world lived close to the bone, even modest harvest shortfalls—the sort that came one in every three or five years—usually brought hunger.

Peoples who lived from herding or otherwise depended on animals suffered hunger and malnutrition too. When drought dried up pastures, the cattle, sheep, and other grazing animals died in droves, depriving people of milk, cheese, and meat. Without animals, herders found it difficult to trade for other foodstuffs. Animal epidemics (called epizootics) could have the same deadly effect as drought. Where farming involved plows pulled by oxen, horses, or water buffalo, as in most of Eurasia, the loss of animal traction paralyzed plowing. The worst episode we know about came in the 1890s, when a cattle disease wiped out 80 to 95 percent of the herds in East and southern Africa. The result was starvation that killed as much as one-third of the population of Ethiopia and twice that proportion among the cattle-keeping Maasai of East Africa.

Famine meant different things for different people, of course. The rich and powerful could usually find a way to get the food they needed—by buying or seizing it. Ordinary families had to ration food, which brought painful decisions. All else equal, women survive food deprivation slightly better than men, but all else was often not equal within families. In most cultures, parents preferred to feed boys over girls when they could not feed everyone. In Africa and China, where the prestige of the elderly was high, grandparents might eat more and younger people less when there was not enough for everyone. Babies and toddlers were often the first to suffer malnutrition. Parents knew that their older children were more valuable, not only because they were already more useful around the home but also because they were likelier to survive. So when families faced the cruel choice of feeding only some children, it made sense to feed the older ones.

Malnourished people suffered more from diseases because a consistently poor diet had weakened their immune systems. So, in the biological old regime, disease and hunger often went hand-in-hand, and death was front and center in life.

IMPROVING GLOBAL HEALTH

After 1750 or so, health started to improve and life spans lengthened. To understand how this happened, let's first review the facts on the macro scale, beginning with global population. As the table below shows, global population grew just about everywhere after 1650. The increase started slowly, at less than 0.1 percent per year, but by 1750 in some places, such as China, it had gathered pace. Between 1850 and 1950, global population doubled, meaning it had achieved an annual growth rate of 0.7 percent.

DECLINING MORTALITY Global population was increasing because people lived longer as death rates fell. The largest component of the drop in death rates was declining infant and child mortality. Crisis mortality (from famines or epidemics) also fell sharply, although this happy trend contributed less to the bigger demographic picture. A still smaller reason behind the overall trend was that fertility rates in some places increased a bit, mainly because people married a year or two younger.

Mortality, especially of infants and children, fell partly because of better nutrition. That improvement came to some degree from the Columbian Exchange, in which people brought crops from one continent to another (as we saw in Chapter 15). Potatoes in northern Europe, maize in Atlantic Africa, and wheat in Canada or Argentina: each of these introduced crops, well suited to their new locations, raised farming output. Refined techniques, such as the adoption of crop rotations that restored nitrogen to soils, boosted farm yields in western Europe and elsewhere. Moreover, the worst of the Little Ice Age had passed by 1750, so bad weather brought killer famines less often. Last, the distribution of food improved in many places, thanks to better transport networks and in Qing China to government policies. The Qing maintained state granaries, which absorbed roughly 5 percent of their empire's annual harvest. These enabled the government to distribute grain wherever it might be needed. All these developments helped to check the ravages of hunger and reduce the frequency of starvation after 1750.

The death toll from disease also began to fall after about 1750. Better nutrition and healthier immune

ESTIMATED WORLD POPULATION, 1650–1950

YEAR	GLOBAL POPULATION	URBAN POPULATION	PERCENTAGE OF GLOBAL POPULATION IN EURASIA	PERCENTAGE IN AFRICA	PERCENTAGE IN AMERICAS	LIFE EXPECTANCY AT BIRTH (GLOBAL AVERAGE IN YEARS)
1650	630 million	15 million	80%	16%	1–2%	[no data]
1750	770 million	20 million	83%	13%	2–3%	approx. 27
1850	1.2 billion	100 million	84%	8%	5%	[no data]
1950	2.5 billion	800 million	77%	9%	13%	approx. 45

Smallpox Inoculation Chinese doctors pioneered a technique for inoculating patients against smallpox in the sixteenth century. They used a needle to expose patients to a small sample of a smallpox scab, as illustrated in this undated Chinese print.

systems contributed to this outcome, but a larger factor was an accidental by-product of the microbial unification of the world, an effect of the interactions in the Global web. After a few centuries of more frequent contact among the various parts of the world (ca. 1500–1750), pathogens had become endemic just about everywhere they could. As a result, big epidemics—and crisis mortality—gradually became less common. In northern Europe, for example, between 1680 and 1780 mortality crises almost disappeared—a big change in what people could expect in life. Plague disappeared from Europe, making its final appearance in Russia in the 1770s. Other diseases that formerly had killed adults and children alike as epidemics became endemic and only killed small children. The average life got healthier and longer.

CONTROL OF SMALLPOX Some of the reduced burden of disease was not accidental but the result of conscious efforts such as **smallpox inoculation**: deliberately putting a tiny bit of infected scab into a cut or scratch on the skin. In most cases, inoculation brought on a mild case of smallpox yet conferred lifetime immunity. In about 2 percent of cases, inoculation proved fatal; but those odds easily beat taking one's chances with the disease. The earliest good evidence for inoculation comes from sixteenth-century China. In the late seventeenth century, one of the Qing rulers, the Kangxi Emperor, began to require inoculation against smallpox in the imperial lineage. When inoculation became routine in the imperial families, infant and child mortality fell from about 40 percent (before 1740) to about 10 percent (by 1830). Smallpox inoculation grew in popularity among ordinary people too, helping to account for the doubling of the Qing Empire's population between about 1720 and 1820.

By the mid-eighteenth century, many people in Eurasia and Africa had learned about inoculation. It was practiced in Mughal India and the Ottoman Empire, although to what extent is unclear. Some Africans inoculated against smallpox too. In early eighteenth-century Boston, an enslaved African named Onesimus explained to his legal owner, the prominent Puritan preacher Cotton Mather, that he had undergone inoculation and that many Africans did so. In Mather's version of Onesimus's words, "People take Juice of Small-Pox; and Cutty-skin, and Putt in a Drop." Strong evidence for the effectiveness of inoculation comes from the Mexican mining center of Guanajuato, where the practice was introduced during a 1797 smallpox outbreak that was especially hard on the indigenous Otomi population. About 20 percent of the uninoculated died but only 1 percent of those who underwent the procedure. By 1800, smallpox inoculation of babies helped lengthen lives, reduce mortality, and raise the population in many lands. The interconnectedness of the world after 1500 helped smallpox inoculation to spread widely.

After 1796, an even better method of smallpox control came to light: vaccination. In that year, an English dairymaid, Sarah Nelmes, consulted a country doctor, Edward Jenner, about a rash on her hands. Jenner, a university graduate trained in medicine, thought she had cowpox, a mild cattle disease. He had heard that people who milked cows rarely got smallpox, and Sarah Nelmes's hands gave him the opportunity to conduct an experiment. He scraped pus from her rash and put a drop into two scratches he made on an eight-year-old boy. The boy felt poorly for a couple of days, then recovered quickly.

Jenner's Smallpox Vaccine European anti-vaccination sentiment is evident in this British cartoon from 1802, which found absurd the notion that anything found in cattle could give patients immunity to a human disease.

Why Do Humans Live So Long?

Three hundred years ago, average human life expectancy around the world was 25 to 30 years, similar to that of our closest cousins, chimpanzees. It was the same 3,000 years ago and 30,000 years ago. But over the last 300 years, something unprecedented happened in human history and probably in the history of life on Earth. Our lives—on average—got longer, slowly at first, but amazingly fast after 1920 or so. Global human life expectancy is now 73 years, and only five or six animal species live longer.

How can we account for this startling change? Demographic, medical, and agricultural historians disagree, but some patterns are clear. A huge part of modern longevity, maybe half of it, comes from the reduction in child mortality, which is defined as death before age five. In the bad old days, nearly half of all deaths were among children under age five. By 1990, that had fallen to one-quarter, and today it is 10 percent.

More reliable food supplies played a big role in boosting longevity from the eighteenth century onward. Today, killing famine strikes far less often than centuries ago, mainly because of higher farm yields and better food transport and storage. Improved sanitation helped after about 1880, slashing the toll from waterborne diseases such as typhoid, especially in cities. Medical care improved beginning around the same time, and it improved dramatically after the introduction of antibiotics in the 1930s. Vaccination checked many viral infections, most importantly eradicating smallpox by 1980. It also seems that violent death—from warfare, murder, and accident—is a smaller risk today than in centuries past, although that reduction has had a much weaker effect on longevity than disease control and changes in nutrition. Nowadays, heart disease, stroke, and cancer are major killers. Three centuries ago, far fewer people lived long enough to suffer these diseases.

How long might the trend continue? On average, Japanese people live 12 years longer than the global average, so there is still room for improvement. But we are unlikely ever to match Greenland sharks and bowhead whales, each of which has a life expectancy of over 200 years.

QUESTIONS FOR DISCUSSION

1. How might family life, especially relationships between parents and children, have been different in a world in which nearly half of all children died before age five?
2. What major differences did the jump in longevity make in our lives, from planning for an education to health care?

Jenner, himself a smallpox survivor, next infected the boy with smallpox and exulted when no symptoms appeared. Jenner repeated the experiment on others and then in 1798 published an account of his work. Today, Jenner's medical ethics would earn a prison sentence, but the British government in 1802 awarded him a princely sum for his experiment.

Jenner's experiment gave rise to the first vaccination programs in history. Vaccination, using cowpox virus, was less risky than inoculation, which used real smallpox virus. In 1853, Britain made vaccination against smallpox mandatory for all children.

The spread of inoculation and then vaccination spelled the beginning of the end for the smallpox virus, the greatest killer of human beings ever known. The growing interconnectedness of the Global web spread vaccination around the world faster than it had inoculation. In the Spanish Empire between 1802 and 1805—only a few years after Jenner published his results—authorities established a vaccination program that saved millions of lives. The decline of smallpox between 1750 and 1900 played a large role in lengthening life expectancy and reducing the fear of disease in general. In 1978, mass vaccination campaigns finally eradicated smallpox, the first such success in human history.

SANITATION REFORM Sanitary improvements after 1850 had a parallel effect to the spread of smallpox vaccination. In cities especially, clean water had always been scarce, and dirty water killed millions. By the second half of the nineteenth century, scientists and doctors in western Europe figured out the role of bacteria in many infections, developing what is sometimes called the **germ theory of disease**, and successfully lobbied for waterworks that carefully separated wastewater from drinking water. These measures were expensive, and public officials often resisted on the grounds of cost. But the results, in the form of reduced death and illness from typhoid and cholera between 1880 and 1930, were so spectacular that the news spread almost everywhere. Chicago, for example, lost 6 percent of its population to cholera in 1854 and suffered repeated typhoid epidemics in the 1880s. But by 1920, waterborne disease killed almost no one in Chicago. Just about every city in western Europe, the United States, Canada, and Japan paid the price for cleaner water in money so as to no longer pay the price of dirty water in lives.

Sanitation reform did not spread uniformly. Some cities continued to run the risks of waterborne disease, partly for reasons of cost. Cities without access to banks and lenders simply could not pay for waterworks. In addition, many people doubted the novel germ theory of disease, without which there is no obvious logic to paying for sanitary measures and waterworks. So the spread of effective sanitation around the world took more than a century—and indeed is still incomplete.

The control of smallpox and the emergence of sanitation were the most important steps in checking the ravages of disease between 1750 and 1950. But there were many more breakthroughs. The germ theory opened the door to research on the specific organisms—pathogens—behind infections. Medical research and public health programs

led to successes in reducing the impact of tuberculosis, yellow fever, polio, and several other killers (1885–1960). All these developments saved lives, improved health, and set the stage for a golden age of health and longevity after 1950—a subject for a later chapter.

COUNTERTRENDS: CHOLERA AND THE 1918 FLU

Two great exceptions bucked this rosy trend. One was the globalization of cholera after 1817, and the other was the great influenza pandemic of 1918. Both show how the tightening of the Global web brought hardships as well as benefits in health. That tightening converted many infections into endemic, childhood diseases through the microbial unification of the world, which on balance was an improvement for humankind. But it also unleashed searing pandemics—worldwide epidemics—which now spread faster and farther than ever before.

CHOLERA   Cholera escaped South Asia in 1817. It is a bacterium, transmitted from person to person via contaminated water or, more rarely, food. Untreated, it can kill half of those who contract it. Its course is swift, with only a few hours between first symptoms and death. This speed, combined with gruesome symptoms, inspired particular dread. People fled at the rumor of cholera. Authorities put up quarantines, forbidding entry into cities or countries, when they suspected cholera among travelers. But in 1817, cholera made it to Russia and in 1820 to southern China and Java. In the following decades it traveled all over the world, killing tens of millions and hitting cities especially hard.

Faster and more frequent travel changed cholera from a local to a global scourge. It was an occasional companion of South Asian Muslims making the annual *hajj* in the nineteenth century; in 1863, it killed 30,000 pilgrims in Mecca. Once British soldiers took control of parts of India in the 1760s, they carried cholera to ports around the British Empire. For example, Quebec City, in British Canada, suffered frequent cholera epidemics between 1832 and 1854 generally brought by soldiers and sailors relocated from India. In the 1850s, it killed 200,000 in Caribbean port cities. After 1860, cholera gradually came under control wherever efficient sanitation was practiced. But elsewhere, its destruction continued, claiming 270,000

Sanitation Reform An 1880 diagram illustrates a design for an elaborate new water supply and waste management system under the streets of Paris. By increasing access to fresh drinking water and separating fresh water from wastewater, it dramatically reduced deaths from waterborne illnesses.

Cholera Epidemics An 1883 illustration from a British newspaper shows inhabitants fleeing a Cairo neighborhood during a cholera outbreak. Fear of the disease was such that even news of an outbreak was enough to inspire unrest.

in Russia in 1892 and 200,000 in the Philippines in the years 1902–1904. By 1925, however, public health authorities and sanitation infrastructure had cholera in check. At the same time that faster transport was spreading cholera to all inhabited continents, better water sanitation—wherever such expensive investments were made—was stopping its ravages.

INFLUENZA Influenza was harder to control. It is a virus, or a series of viruses, in circulation among pigs, birds, humans, and a few other species. It spreads via coughs, sneezes, and contact. Usually, the flu is an inconvenience and kills well under 0.1 percent of those who contract it. But it mutates quickly, and from time to time produces a new and deadly strain. This is what happened in 1918.

In late 1917, a new strain evolved somewhere, perhaps on the farms of the American Midwest, perhaps in China, perhaps near the battlefields of World War I in western

Europe—there is as yet no clear evidence for its origin. Unlike most forms of the flu, the **1918 flu pandemic** was most severe among people in the prime of life. It killed primarily people between ages 15 and 40, so it was especially dangerous in communities such as universities and armies. Pregnant women and malnourished people were the most vulnerable of all.

When millions of soldiers dispersed in late 1918 at the end of World War I, they helped spread the virus all over the world. About 500 million people suffered from it, and upward of 50 million died—roughly 3 percent of the global population and several times the toll of World War I. In India alone, it killed about 15 million, about 5 percent of the total population. On some Pacific islands, it killed 10 percent or more: 22 percent of Samoans died within two months. It killed 2–4% of Mexicans, who were in the throes of a civil war (1910–1920), and a little under 1 percent of Americans (some 675,000) and Canadians (50,000). Japan imposed rigorous quarantines and kept mortality to 390,000 (about 0.7 percent of the population). After peaking in late 1918, the flu died out within months for reasons that remain unclear.

Cholera outbreaks and the 1918 flu pandemic were deadly exceptions to the general rule. They were both diseases of globalization in the sense that improved transport and stronger interconnections eased their spread. But the stronger trend was the Vital Revolution, in which mortality fell and lives lengthened. The Vital Revolution spread around the world too, through the Global web's

Influenza in 1918 Volunteer nurses tend invalids in a makeshift flu ward at a concert hall in Oakland, California, in 1918. So many people worldwide contracted the illness that it was not possible to care for them in standard medical facilities.

circuits of information about crops, inoculation, vaccination, sanitation, and other practices that either improved nutrition or limited the toll of infectious diseases. That is the main reason why people on average now live nearly three times as long as their ancestors did before 1800. No other trend mattered more to more people than the Vital Revolution after 1750.

THE ABOLITIONS OF SLAVERY AND SERFDOM

Forced labor is an old human tradition. Legal codes designating some people as the property of others go back to ancient Mesopotamia. The Greek philosopher Aristotle thought that some people are by nature slaves and others free. Ibn Sina (Avicenna), the great physician and philosopher of eleventh-century Persia, agreed. He extolled the wisdom of God (Allah), who had "placed, in regions of great heat or great cold, peoples who were by their very nature slaves, and incapable of higher things—for there must be masters and slaves." Scholars found justifications for slavery in all major religions. The English philosopher-statesman Thomas More included slavery in the imaginary ideal society of his novel *Utopia* (1515). Slavery and other forms of bondage were widespread until 250 years ago, and few people viewed slavery as immoral or unnatural (although in South Asia both Ashoka and Akbar banned slave trading). Strange as it may seem today, many who escaped slavery themselves worked on slaving ships transporting Africans to plantations in the Americas. In Russia, serfs who had escaped to freedom themselves sometimes bought serfs. In some societies, forced labor was rare. In others, including those in Korea, Southeast Asia, Central Asia, the Ottoman lands, Russia, West Africa, Brazil, the Caribbean, and the United States, among many others, slavery or other forms of unfree labor were common.

In some places, slavery was a racial institution. In the Americas after 1492, enslaved people were almost all of African or indigenous descent, or at least partly so, and slaveholders usually of European descent. There were also many free Blacks in Brazil, the Caribbean, and the United States, but they were often subject to discrimination derived from prevailing ideas connecting race and slavery. A similar racial outlook had taken hold even

earlier in North Africa and Southwest Asia. As we've seen, Arabs imported enslaved sub-Saharan Africans and came to associate black skin with slavery, notwithstanding the common presence in Arab lands of white slaves imported from southern and eastern Europe. But elsewhere, slavery and other forced labor regimes had little or nothing to do with concepts of race. In Russia, both owners and serfs were normally Russian. In China, both enslaved and owners were usually Han Chinese. In Korea, where at times between the fifteenth and nineteenth centuries enslaved peasants accounted for nearly one-third of the population, both were Korean. And in sub-Saharan Africa, both were equally African.

However, enslavers and enslaved in Africa and Asia often came from different ethnic or religious groups. In Central Asia, slaveholders were generally Muslims and speakers of Turkic languages, while many if not most of the people they enslaved were Hindus from India. In China, Muslims from Central Asia and Vietnamese were common among the enslaved population. In maritime Southeast Asia, enslaved captives were usually taken on one island and sold on another that differed in language or religion. In nineteenth-century Ethiopia, Christians generally enslaved Muslim war captives, and Muslims typically enslaved Christians. These differences—in

American Chattel Slavery There were 4 million enslaved people of African descent living in the American South before the U.S. Civil War. A mid-nineteenth-century photograph shows enslaved men, women, and children picking cotton on a plantation.

ethnicity, language, religion, or race—may have helped people believe that slavery was part of the natural order of things. But in Russia and Korea, where such differences did not exist, the commitment of both society and state to forced labor was no weaker.

Unfree labor and its abolition bore a complex relationship to the processes of globalization and industrialization. Recall that globalization both extended the ravages of some diseases while encouraging the spread of practices that led to longer and healthier lives—the Vital Revolution. A similar paradox exists with slavery: the Global web eased the spread of the trade in human beings, but it also propelled ideas, information, attitudes, and practices that curtailed slavery. To make sense of the paradox, we need to zoom in.

THE EXPANSION OF SLAVERY AND FORCED LABOR, 1750–1850

Industrialization, as we saw in Chapter 21, quickened the demand for fibers, ores, and lubricants needed in factories. Clever entrepreneurs saw reward in expanding operations in the mines, forests, and plantations that produced cotton, copper, palm oil, and a hundred other raw materials. To do so they usually needed more labor, which they sometimes hired for wages and in other cases bought. During the first roughly 75 years of industrialization, until about 1850, market-savvy landowners and businessmen had strong incentives to deepen their reliance on forced labor.

THE AMERICAS   In the American South, between 1800 and 1860 the enslaved population quintupled to 4 million. This was the largest enslaved population in any single polity in modern world history, although much smaller than that of the Roman Empire. About 12 percent of the U.S. population in 1860 was enslaved, and about 45 percent in the South. The biggest reason for the expansion of U.S. slavery lay in the growing appetite for raw cotton in the textile mills of New England and Britain. Slave labor also underpinned the production of tobacco in Virginia and Maryland, rice in South Carolina and Georgia, and sugar in Louisiana. But cotton, grown from Georgia to Texas, stood at the heart of the slave economy of the United States.

Elsewhere in the Americas, a similar expansion of slavery took place after 1780. Sugar, tobacco, cotton, and

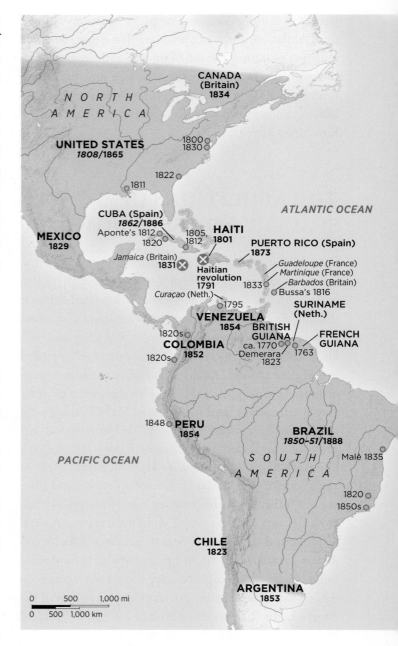

coffee were the main plantation crops in the Caribbean and Brazil. As we saw in Chapter 20, half a million enslaved Africans labored in the French colony of Saint-Domingue in 1790. The British Caribbean colonies—Jamaica, Barbados, and several others—by 1830 had 1.5 million. In Cuba, the enslaved population grew from 30,000 to 290,000 between 1750 and 1870. In 1840, more than 2.5 million Brazilians, about 20 percent of the total population, were enslaved. As in the United States, they were almost all African or of at least partially African descent. They worked in every sphere from whaling to mining

Resistance to Slavery and Abolition of Slavery, ca. 1750–1950 Slavery was legal and common across much of the world in 1750. In the Atlantic world, slave uprisings became more frequent after the rebellion in Haiti (1791–1804), weakening the support for slavery in Europe and the Americas. Beginning with Denmark in 1803, the European nations whose merchants—together with those of Brazil, Cuba, and the United States—conducted the transatlantic slave trade made it illegal. The abolition of legal slavery began soon after in the Atlantic world and was complete by 1888. Partly through pressures applied by Britain, legal slavery was abolished throughout Asia and Africa later in the nineteenth and twentieth centuries.

and on plantations. They also worked in cities—cooking, washing clothes, laying bricks, tanning leather, and doing other tasks, many of them dirty or dangerous. In contrast to the United States, where the sex ratio in the enslaved population was about even by the nineteenth century, it remained primarily male in the Caribbean and Brazil, where imports rather than natural increase accounted for

growth and slave dealers selected males specifically for plantation work.

OTHER REGIONS The eighteenth- and nineteenth-century expansion of forced labor was no less remarkable outside the Americas. In Southeast Asia, growers of sugar, peppers, and other goods used slave labor on an expanding

Slavery in Zanzibar A photograph of an enslaved boy in the sultanate of Zanzibar around 1890. Potent images such as this furthered the cause of abolition.

scale, contributing to a boom in slave raiding and slave trading in the islands of Indonesia between 1770 and 1840. Slavery surged on several Indian Ocean islands, such as Mauritius and Réunion, where after 1780 French planters increasingly bought East Africans for newly created sugar and cotton plantations. Unfree labor, long common in Africa, expanded after 1780 as powerful men took advantage of new opportunities, first in South Africa and then, by 1850 or so, in West and East Africa too. In both latter regions, African entrepreneurs built new plantation economies using slave labor, notably for palm oil in the Niger delta and cloves in Zanzibar. The peanut farms of Senegal owned by Wolof merchants also relied on slave laborers, mostly women, imported from what is now Mali. On the Arabian shores of the Persian Gulf as well, slavery increased sharply after 1820. Here the rise of export industries of dried dates and pearls led to heightened demand for slaves, most of whom came from East Africa on ships owned by merchants based in Oman or Zanzibar. Egypt, which turned to cotton production increasingly after 1805, experienced an upsurge in slavery too; its slave imports peaked in the 1870s. Precise numbers are lacking for Southeast Asia, the Indian Ocean islands, and Africa, but a reasonable guess is that among them the enslaved population reached 10 to 15 million—and rising—as of 1850.

Slavery or bonded labor as a legal category and common practice existed elsewhere in the nineteenth century too—in Central Asian khanates, the Ottoman Empire, and India, and on a modest scale in China and Korea. In the Russian Empire, the numbers of serfs also increased as a result of population growth. As we shall see, Russia's forced laborers numbered about 50 million in 1860, some 70 percent of the total population.

By and large, slavery and forced labor flourished only in certain circumstances. One was where labor was scarce and opportunities to make money beckoned to powerful people. They could profit from mines or plantations only if they could amass enough labor. Another circumstance conducive to slavery was where warfare yielded abundant captives. If numerous, such captives were cheap and could profitably be put to work at almost anything. Such circumstances were common enough around the world before 1800, and they grew more so as markets developed for fibers, ores, sugar, coffee, dates, peanut or palm oil, and in the Russian case, grain. The evolution of the global economy ensured a market for any healthy captive. That is why slavery and other forms of forced labor expanded in the first half of the nineteenth century.

During the nineteenth century, as before, a large share of forced laborers were female. In Africa, Ottoman lands, Central Asia, and probably China, they were the majority. Their labors included household chores such as cooking, cleaning, and caring for children, as well as spinning and other textile work. In Africa, they often did farmwork. And, as was typically the case for enslaved women and serfs throughout history everywhere, their duties often included sex with their owners.

Even as slavery, serfdom, and forced labor expanded around the world between 1750 and 1850, they came under attack as never before. In retrospect, this may seem inevitable, normal, and proper. But at the time it was extraordinary. A practice that religious and political authority had sanctioned for millennia almost overnight became increasingly seen as immoral, impractical, and contrary to divine will. How did this happen?

ABOLITION OF THE SLAVE TRADE IN THE ATLANTIC WORLD

Systematic moral objections to slavery originated where the practice was strongest, in the Atlantic world. Even slaveholders such as Thomas Jefferson could harbor moral objections to slavery. He most certainly feared the consequences of allowing it to continue, which, he thought, might lead to violent uprisings by enslaved people. In his *Notes on the State of Virginia* (1785), he wrote:

> Indeed I tremble for my country when I reflect that God is just: that his justice cannot sleep for ever.... The spirit of the master is abating, that of the slave rising from the dust, his condition mollifying, the way I hope preparing, under the auspices of heaven, for a total emancipation, and that this is disposed, in the order of events, to be with the consent of the masters, rather than by their extirpation.

> R UN away from the fubfcriber in *Albemarle*, a Mulatto flave called *Sandy*, about 35 years of age, his ftature is rather low, inclining to corpulence, and his complexion light; he is a fhoemaker by trade, in which he ufes his left hand principally, can do coarfe carpenters work, and is fomething of a horfe jockey; he is greatly addicted to drink, and when drunk is infolent and diforderly, in his converfation he fwears much, and in his behaviour is artful and knavifh. He took with him a white horfe, much fcarred with traces, of which it is expected he will endeavour to difpofe; he alfo carried his fhoemakers tools, and will probably endeavour to get employment that way. Whoever conveys the faid flave to me, in *Albemarle*, fhall have 40 s. reward, if taken up within the county, 4 l. if elfewhere within the colony, and 10 l. if in any other colony. from
> THOMAS JEFFERSON.

Fugitives from Slavery Thomas Jefferson, who owned over 600 enslaved people throughout his life, circulated this advertisement for a fugitive from slavery in the *Virginia Gazette* in 1769. The reward offered for returning Sandy to Jefferson ranged between $600 and $3,000 in today's money. While attempts to overthrow slavery were rare, attempts to escape it, such as Sandy's, were common.

Moral objections anchored in Christianity, together with fear stirred by slave uprisings of which the Haitian Revolution (discussed in Chapter 20) was the most prominent, help explain the abolition of slavery in the Americas. In two cases, Haiti and the United States, abolition triumphed through war. In other cases, abolition prevailed politically—as a result of shifting opinion organized through political parties. Let's zoom in to see how this transformation happened.

The first organzied movements for abolition came in lands where slavery was not central to society: the northern United States, Britain, and France. But in all three of those lands, profits from slavery and the transatlantic slave trade were economically significant and enriched a segment of society with much to lose if slavery vanished. And in all three, information about the horrors of the slave trade and slavery was readily available by 1750. Antislavery activists in Britain and America, and to a lesser extent those in France and elsewhere, were regularly in touch with one another through correspondence, by reading one another's published writings, and occasionally in person. They were all familiar with the arguments against slavery voiced by thinkers of the Enlightenment, such as the Baron de Montesquieu, who extolled liberty and condemned slavery as bad for enslaved and enslaver alike.

QUAKER OPPOSITION The organized antislavery movement began among **Quakers**, a small Protestant sect

originating in seventeenth-century England. Quakers defied social convention, avoided alcohol and fine clothes, refused military service, and were regarded as peculiar by everyone else. Many Quakers, like other religious minorities, were conspicuously successful in business. Before 1750, many of them in North America owned people, and some were slave traders. But within the Quaker community religious and moral objection to slavery emerged, first in Barbados in the 1670s and more prominently in England and colonial America by the 1750s. Quakers regarded all warfare as immoral, and so trading in or owning African war captives ran contrary to their principles. Moreover, their interpretation of Christianity stressed humility, simplicity, and the fundamental equality of all human beings. This view of the moral duties of Quakers gradually won out among the Philadelphia chapter— by far the biggest in North America—which formally denounced slavery in 1758. Several Philadelphia Quakers visited London to convince their brethren of the Christian duty to end slave trading and slavery. By 1774, all Quaker meetings (as their communities are called) in Britain and North America had agreed that one could not both be a Quaker and also own people. In 1790, Quakers petitioned Congress—in vain—for an end to slavery throughout the United States.

Quaker Abolitionists John Woolman, shown here in an anonymous and undated portrait, was a Quaker abolitionist who in 1758 persuaded his fellow American Quakers to oppose slavery.

BRITISH ABOLITION OF THE SLAVE TRADE

Quakers and their allies proved more effective in Britain. Britain was deeply invested in slavery. British merchants ran the biggest slave trade in the world in the late eighteenth century. Britain's empire included Caribbean slave plantation colonies—Barbados, Jamaica, and others— exports from which were worth five times those of all British North American colonies combined in 1773. The Church of England owned enslaved people in the Caribbean. Adam Smith, author of *The Wealth of Nations*—a defense of free markets—lamented in 1763 that although wage labor would be more efficient, "the love of dominion and authority over others will probably make [slavery]

British Abolitionism The abolitionist ceramics entrepreneur Josiah Wedgwood manufactured medallions bearing an image of a manacled, enslaved man and the phrase "Am I Not a Man and a Brother?" This image became closely associated with the abolitionist cause in Britain and the United States.

perpetuall." Smith was wrong on both counts as regards the British Empire: slavery remained more efficient than wage labor until abolished, and it proved anything but perpetual.

CLARKSON AND WILBERFORCE

Quakers started the British antislavery movement. Barred from serving in Parliament because they were not Anglicans, to change any laws they needed allies and spokesmen from within the Anglican elite. They found one in **Thomas Clarkson**, who in 1785, as a 25-year-old fresh out of Cambridge University, entered a Latin essay contest with no loftier intention than winning a prize. But the contest's question was about the justice of slavery, and Clarkson, a good student, read everything he could find on the subject, won the prize, and in the process came to the conclusion that slavery was unchristian. From the evangelical wing of the Anglican Church himself, Clarkson became a tireless pamphleteer, researcher, and activist in the cause, sometimes risking his life on the docks of port towns to gather information about the British slave trade. Clarkson and friends, mostly Quakers and evangelicals, formed an abolitionist committee in 1787 and decided to focus their efforts on legal reform, in Parliament, and to target the slave trade first, leaving slavery itself for later.

Clarkson helped recruit a sitting member of Parliament to the cause in 1787. William Wilberforce was sickly and half blind, but rich and well connected. He also had attended Cambridge University, where he specialized in gambling and drinking before becoming an evangelical Christian. At Cambridge he became close friends with William Pitt, who in 1783—at age 24—had become prime minister. Wilberforce, the same age as Pitt and a year older than Clarkson, became the parliamentary voice of antislavery, denouncing the slave trade as contrary to God's will and a source of moral corruption. By some accounts, including Pitt's, he was the silkiest public speaker in Britain.

The movement organized by Clarkson, Wilberforce, and their colleagues took shape in the late 1780s. With the zeal and stamina of youth, they documented and publicized both the cruelties of the slave trade and the debauchery of slave traders and their crews.

CUGOANO AND EQUIANO

Freedmen such as Ottobah Cugoano and Olaudah Equiano added their voices to the anti–slave trade movement at the same time. About a dozen of them formed the **Sons of Africa**, an abolitionist committee in London closely allied with that of Clarkson and Wilberforce, although Cugoano especially argued ardently for immediate, rather than gradual, abolition of both the slave trade and slavery. Cugoano had been born in West Africa around 1758, captured as a young teenager, sold into slavery, and shipped to the British Caribbean, where he worked on a plantation for two years. Then his Scottish owner brought him to England, where he learned to read and write, became a Christian, and won his freedom. While it is unclear whether or not Equiano was born in West Africa in 1745 (as he wrote in his autobiography), he worked as an enslaved sailor as a teenager, traveling all over the Atlantic world on British ships. For a decade, he was sold by one ship captain to another. In London, he was baptized as a Christian in 1759. A Quaker slaveholder from Philadelphia allowed him to trade on his own account in the Caribbean, and Equiano earned enough (about $7,000 in today's money) to purchase his freedom in 1766. His travels continued, taking him to Arctic and Ottoman shores. He even agreed to serve as an overseer on a slave plantation in Central America, using his Igbo language ability to watch over enslaved Igbo whom he had helped purchase in Jamaica. That venture failed. Equiano settled in London in 1777 and soon took up the cause of abolition. Both Equiano and Cugoano wrote detailed accounts of their experiences, helping convince readers of the moral depravity and injustice of slavery and especially the slave trade. The descriptions of their ordeals had an air of authenticity about them that the youthful, privileged, and white-skinned Wilberforce and Clarkson could never provide.

Olaudah Equiano A detail of the frontispiece of Olaudah Equiano's eighteenth-century account of his life. Equiano's antislavery activism as a freedman in the Atlantic world played an important role in rallying support for abolitionism.

ACTION IN PARLIAMENT In 1787, both the anti-slavery and proslavery factions in Parliament held about 40 seats. They debated the humanity of Africans, whether slavery was supported in the Bible, and the economic value of the institution. Opponents of the slave trade published reams of moral argument and statistical data, distributed pamphlets, organized mass petitions to Parliament, and raised funds. They penned plays, novels, and especially poems against the slave trade. They presented more than 100 petitions against the slave trade to Parliament, signed by about 12 percent of Britain's population. They persuaded Pitt, as prime minister, to denounce the slave trade in Parliament. They pointed out that Denmark ended its slave trade in 1803. They pointed to the violence and destruction of the Haitian Revolution as the consequence of continued slave trading. Within two decades, they achieved a shift in public opinion against the slave trade. All this was necessary, but it was not enough: every attempt to pass a law banning the slave trade failed—until 1807.

Then Wilberforce, by now a veteran of 23 years of parliamentary intrigues, took advantage of changed political circumstances. A weak, coalition government that needed abolitionist votes took office in 1806. Wilberforce framed abolition of the slave trade as a patriotic measure that would hurt Napoleon Bonaparte's effort to reestablish profitable French Caribbean colonies after the Haitian Revolution. In 1807, he shepherded an abolition bill through Parliament, carrying the House of Commons by a vote of 283–16.

Banning the British slave trade was a dramatic beginning of the end for slavery. Without the transatlantic slave trade, slavery could not long continue in the Caribbean, because except on Barbados, slave populations there registered many more deaths than births. Wilberforce and his colleagues expected that with their legislative victory, slavery in the British realm would fade away.

OTHER SLAVE TRADE ABOLITIONS Other countries around the Atlantic soon followed the British example. The U.S. government made slave imports illegal in 1808, the first year permitted by the Constitution. That act carried lesser implications, however, because it did not endanger slavery in the United States. Slave populations in the United States since about 1730 had grown by natural increase (more births than deaths), so slavery could persist there without the transatlantic slave trade.

In the next 20 years, the Netherlands—a minor participant in the slave trade—and France both prohibited slave trading. Spain announced abolition of its slave trade in 1817 but did not enforce it until 1867. The Catholic Church denounced the slave trade in 1839. Britain began to use its navy, the world's largest, to intercept slave ships on the high seas and return captives to Africa, usually to Sierra Leone, a British colony established largely for this purpose. Some 100,000 Africans disembarked in Sierra Leone this way. The recaptives, as they were called, had come from all over Atlantic Africa, spoke dozens of different languages, and had to forge a new society in Sierra Leone. The tiny Haitian navy between 1811 and 1819 also captured three slave ships and liberated more than 800 people.

The strength of the slave markets in Cuba and Brazil kept the slave trade alive after 1830. Both still imported thousands of Africans annually—in Brazil's case, up to 60,000. A large share of these came from Yorubaland in West Africa, where frequent warfare during the decline of the Oyo Empire resulted in streams of captives sold into the Atlantic trade. This surge in the slave trade helped lead to its demise.

The large and growing concentrations of Yoruba-speakers in both Cuba and Brazil led to an upsurge in slave revolts. Whereas Equiano had tried to use Igbo language and identity to establish a slave plantation in Central America, others later used Yoruba language and identity to build solidarity among the enslaved and plan uprisings. A few revolts occurred in Cuba in 1812, which according to authorities were organized by **José Aponte**, a Yoruba-speaking freedman, carpenter, and artist. He was also a former militia officer whose scrapbook, found by police, contained homages to both Toussaint L'Ouverture and George Washington. After 1825, Cuban elites increasingly questioned the slave trade, alarmed by the continued frequency of revolts, which climaxed with several in 1843–1844, the biggest of which was sparked by an African-born Yoruba-speaker called Carlota. Elites also feared the "Africanization" of Cuba's population, and the patrols of the British Royal Navy. Spanish slavers and some Cuban planters resisted for a while, but Cuba's slave trade wound down in the 1850s and became illegal in 1867.

In Brazil, where the scale of the slave trade was much larger than in Cuba, it ended sooner, in 1850–1851. Slave uprisings averaged about one per year from 1810 to 1830 and climaxed in the Malê revolt in 1835, involving some

600 Africans—again, mostly Yoruba-speakers. Fear of further revolts played a role in shifting the opinion of Brazil's political elite. So did attacks on Brazilian and Portuguese slavers by the British Royal Navy. As in Cuba, intellectual and political elites gradually concluded that the slave trade was bad business and banned it. Like Wilberforce, they anticipated that without the slave trade, slavery would die out.

ABOLITION OF SLAVERY IN THE ATLANTIC WORLD, TO 1832

The abolition of slavery in the Atlantic world, as opposed to the slave trade, came later and involved not only legislation but two major wars. The first of these, the Haitian Revolution of 1791–1804 (see Chapter 20), brought the first large-scale abolition of slavery and raised hopes for abolition throughout the Atlantic world. The second, the American Civil War (1861–1865), put an end to slavery in the largest slave society of the Atlantic—and made it clear to all that slavery's days were numbered.

Even before the Haitian Revolution, movements for the abolition of slavery met with some minor successes in the Atlantic world. Since 1606, it had been legal in Scotland for mine owners to hold miners—fellow Scots—in lifelong bondage. If they ran away, they were subject to "torture in the irons provided only for colliers and witches and notorious malefactors." But in 1775, Scotland banned enslavement of new recruits to the coal mines. In 1777, during the American Revolution, Vermont banned slavery, and Massachusetts did so in 1783. Other New England states followed suit. In 1780, Pennsylvania enacted a gradual abolition that finally brought slavery to an end in the state in 1847. Efforts to abolish slavery gathered pace in British Canada, influenced by British agitation, and the first legal step took place in 1793. These acts of abolition did not resonate loudly because none of these places had many slaves.

SLAVE UPRISINGS AND THEIR POLITICAL CONSEQUENCES Saint-Domingue, in contrast, had nearly half a million enslaved laborers when the Haitian Revolution erupted in 1791 (see Chapter 20). Toussaint L'Ouverture, who had been both enslaved and an enslaver himself, abolished legal slavery in 1801. The revolution in Haiti showed that the enslaved could conceivably end slavery themselves. It convinced slaveholders everywhere that they courted economic ruin and vengeful massacres if slavery ended through revolution rather than legal abolition. The Haitian Revolution, because of its scale and violence, resonated throughout the circuits of the Atlantic world, an inspiration to some and a terror to others.

Meanwhile, the revolutionary French government in Paris decided in 1794 to end slavery everywhere in the French Empire. French antislavery activism, a modest movement compared to that in Britain, had less influence on the 1794 abolition than did fears that the uprising in Haiti might spread to nearby French sugar and slave colonies such as Guadeloupe, Martinique, and French Guiana. But principle supported political calculation: slavery, after all, was clearly incompatible with the "rights of man" and other ideals of the French Revolution. The 1794 abolition, however, proved incomplete and fleeting. It was never implemented in Martinique, Senegal, or France's Indian Ocean colonies. And in 1802, Bonaparte reinstated slavery throughout the French Empire and would have restored it to Haiti had his army there not been defeated. He restored slavery, using force where necessary, to prevent French Caribbean planters from surrendering their islands to Britain, his archenemy, which they seemed ready to do in order to preserve slavery. And he did it to please his wife, Josephine, whose family owned a plantation on Martinique.

Bonaparte, however, could not stop the momentum of Atlantic abolition. The Haitian Revolution inspired slaves elsewhere to test their chains in a series of uprisings. In addition to the revolts in Cuba and Brazil—word of which also ricocheted around the Atlantic—several broke out in British slave colonies. One took place in 1816 on Barbados, led by an enslaved African known as Bussa. Some 400 rose in rebellion, only to be crushed by a British army regiment (composed of Black soldiers). About 270 were killed (as was one soldier). A far larger revolt occurred at Demerara, in British Guiana. For a few days in 1823, some 10,000 enslaved workers followed the call to freedom issued by one **Jack Gladstone**. Gladstone and his father, an African named Quamina, had learned of discussions of emancipation in Britain. Both were literate and, as carpenters and coopers, relatively privileged slaves. Quamina was a deacon in the local church and by all accounts deeply pious. Jack Gladstone (his surname was that of his owner, the father of future British prime minister William Gladstone) believed that legal abolition had already passed in London and that the Demerara planters were conspiring

Slave Revolts A lithograph shows a Jamaican plantation set on fire during the major slave revolt that Samuel Sharpe led in the British colony in the years 1831–1832.

to hide the fact. This conviction lay behind his call to freedom and what was until then the largest slave revolt in the British Empire. Two British regiments vanquished the rebels, killing about 250.

A still larger revolt caught fire in Jamaica in 1831, involving perhaps 60,000 enslaved people, one-fifth of Jamaica's total. It too was led by a slave preacher, Samuel Sharpe, a deacon in the Baptist church; the revolt is sometimes called the Baptist War. Sharpe's lieutenants were mainly from the slave elite—smiths, masons, coopers, and coachmen. They were all born in the Caribbean. As at Demerara and on Barbados, rumors of emancipation swirled around Jamaica, leading to the false belief that London's Parliament had already voted for slavery's abolition. Sharpe called for a slave strike during the sugar harvest season, which led to widespread burning of the crop. In sporadic violence, 14 whites and several hundred insurgents were killed. Planters managed to suppress the rising with decisive help from maroons—fugitives from slavery who had escaped to Jamaica's mountains—and the Jamaica garrisons of the British Army.

The growing frequency and size of slave revolts in the British West Indies (and elsewhere in the Caribbean) quickened the debate on abolition of slavery in Britain. The planter lobby wished to see the activities of missionaries curtailed, because rebel leaders in Demerara and Jamaica were educated Christians, schooled by missionaries. In Jamaica, proslavery factions attacked missionaries and burned several mission churches. The effect was to reduce political support for slavery within Britain. The fact that very few whites had been killed in these uprisings, unlike in Haiti, supported the argument of abolitionists that freed people would be capable of restraint and would not massacre their former tormentors. They were proved right.

ABOLITIONS OF ATLANTIC SLAVERY, 1833–1888

The first truly large legislated abolition of slavery came in the British Empire. The groups that had lobbied for abolition of the slave trade mostly disbanded after 1807. Cugoano and Equiano were long dead. Few favored a swift end to slavery. Even Wilberforce in 1807 wrote that enslaved Africans were unready for freedom and "to grant it to them immediately, would be to insure not only their masters' ruin but their own." Instead, Wilberforce and his circle thought slaveholders should improve conditions on plantations and provide Christian instruction to prepare for the day when slavery would peter out, which in the absence of the slave trade time alone would bring.

Once again, events changed opinion. The Demerara revolt in 1823 created new support for the immediate abolition of British slavery. Over the next eight years, abolitionists, once again led by religious minorities such as Methodists, Congregationalists, Baptists, and Quakers, printed and circulated nearly 3 million antislavery tracts. They—Clarkson, Wilberforce, and a younger generation

Abolitionist Propaganda A 1791 cartoon illustrating one of William Wilberforce's antislavery speeches in Parliament brought to life some of the most gruesome horrors of slavery in the West Indies. It shows an overseer murdering an enslaved person in a vat of boiling sugarcane juice.

more inclined to push for immediate abolition—formed the Anti-Slavery Society in 1823 and beginning in 1825 sponsored a monthly periodical, the *Anti-Slavery Reporter*. They helped prepare and publish, in 1831, the autobiography of Mary Prince, born into slavery in Bermuda and sold several times in the British Caribbean. The book sold out three printings in its first year. In the years 1828–1830, some 5,000 petitions asked Parliament to end slavery. Over 98 percent of Britain's 233,000 Methodists signed at least one. News of the 1831–1832 slave revolt in Jamaica (the Baptist War) and the proslavery attacks on churches there strengthened support for immediate abolition. About 20 percent of Britain's entire adult male population signed antislavery petitions in 1833. The petitions also included one that was half a mile long, with the names of 350,000 women on it. Women could not vote in Britain, but they could sign petitions.

The antislavery faction in the House of Commons expanded when non-Anglicans became eligible to sit in Parliament in 1828. Two years later, an election brought to power the Whig Party, keen on reforms of many sorts, including abolition. In 1832, the Whigs succeeded in broadening the franchise to include some of the upper middle class and then won a large majority in another election. They used the victory to pass the **Slavery Abolition Act**, which took effect in 1834. As with the abolition of Britain's slave trade in 1807, sustained agitation, a shift in public opinion pushed along by slave uprisings, and a political realignment in Parliament combined to bring about the legislation that ended legal slavery in the British Empire.

The terms of slavery's abolition included compensation—in effect a bribe—for 44,000 slaveholders. Their ranks included many of the richest Britons, as well as dozens of members of Parliament and the archbishop of Canterbury. The price equaled 40 percent of the British government's annual budget, requiring a special loan from the Rothschild banking house. The British Treasury provided about $5,000 per freed person in today's money. The largest payout went to the father of William Gladstone. Not a penny went to those who had been held in bondage. In fact, they and their descendants, as taxpayers in the British Empire, helped to pay off the loan, which was liquidated in 2015.

Moreover, British abolition was gradual, taking four years. But as of 1838, all formerly enslaved people in the British West Indies, Mauritius, South Africa, and British territories elsewhere (except India, Ceylon, and the tiny South Atlantic island of St. Helena) were free, a little under 1 million people. British India officially ended slavery in 1860.

Abolition within the British Empire inspired abolitionists elsewhere. In the northern United States, abolition gathered momentum in the 1830s, at the same time that slavery was growing more entrenched in the cotton South. An anti-slavery society formed in 1833. Abolitionists such as William Lloyd Garrison offered moral, religious, and economic arguments in countless lectures, pamphlets, and editorials, drawing freely on the works of British abolitionists. Refugees from slavery such as Frederick

Frederick Douglass Douglass, who escaped slavery in Maryland, became one of the most influential advocates of abolition in the United States.

Douglass did the same, with the added weight of firsthand knowledge of slavery's grim realities as he had lived them in Maryland before his escape to freedom in 1838. The 1852 publication of Harriet Beecher Stowe's melodramatic novel *Uncle Tom's Cabin*, which sold more copies in the United States than any book other than the Bible, also won support for abolition.

Opponents of slavery's expansion into western territories of the United States formed the Republican Party in 1854. Abolitionists and proslavery factions both realized that if freedom was the rule in new states entering the union, then over time Congress would become more anti-slavery and abolition would prevail. The new party won the 1860 election, putting Abraham Lincoln in the White House without carrying any southern states. Abolitionism in the United States proved influential enough to threaten restrictions on slavery that to slaveholders and their supporters seemed dangerous to their prosperity.

In the end, it required an all-consuming war between North and South to end slavery in the United States. When 11 southern states seceded in the wake of Lincoln's election, the president resolved to go to war to keep the union intact. In the Civil War (1861–1865), the North enjoyed superior resources and military manpower and prevailed after four years of grinding combat. Meanwhile, hundreds of thousands liberated themselves by escaping either to the North or to Union army encampments. About 180,000 Black people served in the Union army, including two of Douglass's sons, providing 10 percent of its manpower by war's end. Some 60 percent were refugees from slavery. Lincoln in 1863 issued the Emancipation Proclamation, a military order that declared "all persons held as slaves" in rebel-held territory "forever free." Complete abolition came only with the war's conclusion and the **Thirteenth Amendment** to the Constitution, both in 1865. Altogether, some 600,000 soldiers died in the Civil War, about 40,000 of them Black people, liberating 4 million people—the single largest slave emancipation in world history.

The end was now near for Atlantic slavery. It remained mainly in some Caribbean sugar islands and Brazil. The success of beet sugar—5 percent of the world's sugar market in 1840 and 50 percent in 1880—weakened sugarcane planters everywhere by cutting their sales. Dutch Caribbean colonies—Suriname and Curaçao were the largest—abolished slavery in 1863. An abolition society formed in 1858 in Puerto Rico, a Spanish colony. An uprising there in 1868 included abolition among its goals. Shifts in Spanish politics led to the abolition of slavery in Puerto Rico in 1873, freeing 30,000 people over the next three years. Cuba, which had some 370,000 enslaved people (27 percent of the island's population), did the same in 1886, ending the long history of slavery in the Spanish Empire.

Brazil was the second-largest slave society in the Americas after the United States. By 1800, slavery was important in many economic sectors, including mining, manufacturing, and domestic services, as well as plantation farming. So a broad coalition of businesspeople defended slavery. But by 1850, rapid immigration of poor Europeans was making wage labor an increasingly practical alternative to slavery. It made good business sense to manumit (grant freedom to) enslaved workers, especially the old, sick, or injured, and to hire free labor instead. By the 1880s, businesspeople ceased resistance to abolition, which finally arrived in Brazil in 1888, freeing about 1.7 million people, or 17 percent of the overall population. The Pope issued a general denunciation of slavery in the same year.

ABOLITIONS OF SLAVERY BEYOND THE ATLANTIC

The Atlantic world by the late eighteenth century was by head count the world capital of slavery and slaving, but it was not the only region where bonded labor, after prevailing for centuries, now came under assault. Abolitionism went global, an example of an idea spreading around the web, crossing cultures, and effecting changes on every inhabited continent.

In many cases, the abolition of slavery struck local elites as desirable, even necessary, to make their countries modern and competitive. The example of abolition by Britain, the world's most powerful country by 1850, was highly influential. In cases such as Cuba and Brazil, the rapid growth of population, which reduced labor shortages and thereby undercut the economic logic of slavery, swayed elites. With enough potential laborers, wages would be low enough to keep mines and plantations profitable. In this way, the trends of the Vital Revolution, outlined in the first section of this chapter, helped advance the cause of abolition.

Slavery was abolished on the Pacific coasts of Spanish America beginning in newly independent Chile in 1823. Peru, where African slavery had been important in mining and agriculture for more than two centuries, enacted abolition in 1854. France reabolished slavery in its empire in 1848, within weeks after a revolution overthrew a monarchy and established a republic led by reformers hostile to slavery. Some 250,000 people in the Caribbean, Senegal, and the Indian Ocean sugar islands gained their freedom, but not all instantly. As in the British and Dutch cases, liberation in the French Empire came gradually, and some legal labor obligations to former slaveholders remained in effect for a few years. In East Asia, Korea—where slavery had once been common—joined the trend in 1894, under pressure from Japan. China, where slavery had existed for many centuries but was never important, officially abolished it in 1910. Thailand did so in 1915.

In the Ottoman Empire, slavery had long been a crucial social institution. The status of slave is recognized in the Qur'an and Islamic law, which stipulates that slave status cannot be inherited and Muslims cannot be enslaved. In Ottoman lands, most of the enslaved were women, used as concubines, household servants, and textile workers. Some came from Circassia and the Caucasus, but by the nineteenth century most hailed from Sudan or Ethiopia. Outside pressure made a difference here, as in Korea. After about 1850, Britain in particular used its influence to induce the Ottoman sultans to restrict the import of enslaved people, beginning with enslaved whites (from Circassia and the Caucasus). Later, the Royal Navy intercepted slave ships sailing from East Africa, reducing slave imports and slave populations in Ottoman lands. The Ottoman sultans could not, however, formally

Abolition of the Slave Trade British Royal Navy sailors are shown chasing and capturing a slaving ship off the coast of East Africa in this 1877 painting. After deciding to support the abolitionist cause, the British state began to actively combat the slave trade.

abolish slavery. As caliphs—successors to the Prophet Muhammad—they had the duty to prevent revisions to the divine word of Allah. After the fall of the Ottoman Empire, the Turkish Republic formally banned slavery in 1924. In Iran, rulers responding to British pressure abolished slavery in 1928.

In Africa, European pressure was even more direct. African slavery had expanded notably after 1850: British suppression of the Atlantic slave trade lowered slave prices within Africa, as we've seen, and made it economically attractive to African entrepreneurs to create new plantations, raising peanuts, cloves, or oil palms using enslaved labor. In the West African Sahel, a series of wars launched by Muslim reformers, who felt that African rulers did not fully abide by the rules of Islam, generated streams of captives. The enslavement of many thousands of these captives, in places such as what is now northern Nigeria, raised the enslaved proportion of the total population to a third or a half. By some estimates, after 1850 there were more enslaved people in Africa than in all the Americas, which then had about 7 to 8 million.

In the next few decades, as we shall see in Chapter 23, almost all of Africa fell under European colonial rule. Christian missionaries flocked in and, as in the British West Indies early in the nineteenth century, began to agitate against the evils of slavery and slave trades. This agitation normally struck African elites as unwelcome, presumptuous, and culturally ignorant. For them, as for so many

people for so long, slavery was normal and natural. In the early decades of colonialism in Africa, European authorities often went along with slavery, even if they did not like it and missionaries hated it. In most parts of the continent, they could only rule with the help of Africa's slaveholding elites, and the continuation of slavery was one of the prices they were willing to pay for that cooperation. Moreover, colonial authorities often judged that slavery within Africa was not so oppressive—an argument advanced by African slave traders themselves. In any case, the colonial authorities made an uneasy truce with slavery for a while.

Enslaved Africans, however, often took a different view. Many sought to liberate themselves by running away, often to Christian missions. In the 1890s, this movement

FORMAL ABOLITIONS OF SLAVERY

JURISDICTION	DATE
Vermont	1777
Massachusetts	1783
Chile	1823
New York	1827
Mexico	1829
British Empire	1834
Danish West Indies	1846
French Empire	1848
Colombia	1852
Argentina	1853
Peru	1854
Venezuela	1854
Portuguese Empire	1858
Dutch Empire	1863
United States	1865
Cuba	1886
Brazil	1888
Korea	1894
Zanzibar	1897
China	1910
Thailand	1915
Iran	1928
Northern Nigeria	1936
Ethiopia	1942
Saudi Arabia	1962
Mauritania	1981

Note: These represent final, formal abolitions. In some cases, such as the French Empire, slavery was abolished, reinstated, and abolished again. In many cases, abolition was a drawn-out process involving gradual steps.

Demanding Freedom and Dignity in West Africa

After abolition, enslaved men and women often had to take the initiative to demand their freedom. For example, Abina Mansah gained her freedom by leaving the household where she was enslaved in the Gold Coast Protectorate of Great Britain (now part of Ghana). She had been captured as a young girl during a war between her people and the Asante kingdom. A few years later, a man named Yowahwah bought her to be his wife. When they visited the Gold Coast together on business in 1876, Yowahwah secretly sold her to a man named Quamina Eddoo. Abina only became aware that she had been sold after Eddoo demanded that she marry one of his other dependents. This deception and disregard for her dignity as a married woman convinced her to flee and seek assistance from British colonial courts. Leaving Eddoo's household freed her from those who treated her as a slave, but she also decided to press charges against Eddoo for purchasing her. The trial transcript reveals what slavery and freedom meant to her and other enslaved women in West Africa as they asserted their new status after abolition.

Yowahwah brought me [to Gold Coast] from [Asante]. I was his wife.... [H]e handed me over to [be with Eddoo], and said that he was going back and would return.

About ten days after, [Eddoo] gave me two cloths and told me that he had given me in marriage to one of his house people.... I asked him how ... he had given me in marriage to one of his people. On this I thought that I had been sold and I ran away.... The defendant [Eddoo] said that if I did not consent to be married ... he would tie me up and flog me. ... If the defendant had not given me in marriage, I could not have formed any idea that he had purchased me.... I thought I was a slave, because when I went for water or firewood I was not paid....

I did not know that I was free.... I heard that [the colonial government] had said we were all free. Yet I had been sold and I had no will of my own and I could not look after my body and health: that I am a slave and I would therefore come and complain....

If [Eddoo's sister] said to me "go for firewood" and I said "I won't go," she said "If you don't you will be tied and flogged," and I said "Now all are free. I also am free. I claim freedom." That was why I ran away.... [Eddoo's sister said:] "You are your master's slave." [W]hen she said this I sat down and said I did not like this and I made up my mind to come away.

Source: Trevor R. Getz, *Abina and the Important Men*, 2nd ed. (Oxford, 2015).

QUESTIONS FOR ANALYSIS

1. What are the different reasons Abina Mansah gives for why she ran away?
2. Why does Abina equate freedom with the ability to "look after my body and health"?
3. How did people who had been enslaved assert their dignity, despite the servile status that slaveholders and others forced upon them?

became a torrent in West Africa. Their escapes, in some respects parallel to the actions of enslaved African Americans fleeing to Union army camps during the American Civil War, weakened the elites on whom colonial authorities intended to rely. So, making a calculated decision that went hand-in-hand with their moral views, both British and French colonial rulers changed their allegiances and began to pressure African elites to abandon slavery. This was a case of simultaneous abolition from below and above. Formal, legal abolitions began in 1905. The biggest took place in northern Nigeria in 1936, when about 1 to 2 million people became officially free, and in Ethiopia in 1942, when roughly 3 million were liberated.

As everywhere, the passing of laws did not instantly end an age-old institution. Slavery persisted illegally in many parts of Africa. It was abolished in what is now Mauritania when that was officially French territory but survived well enough that independent Mauritania abolished it again in 1981. The table at left indicates the date of legal abolition in 26 jurisdictions around the world.

The largest abolition took place in the United States, freeing 4 million people. The next largest were Ethiopia and then either northern Nigeria or Brazil—the numbers are too unreliable to be sure. In total, the many acts of abolition freed about 15 to 25 million people.

THE ABOLITION OF SERFDOM

The largest of all labor liberations took place in Russia. In 1861 and the years following, the Russian state freed 23 million serfs held by landlords, 25 million state peasants owned by the imperial government, and nearly 2 million crown peasants owned by the tsar's family. Together, they accounted for more than two-thirds of Russia's population of roughly 74 million people. This momentous event followed on prior abolitions of serfdom in central and eastern Europe, all much smaller than Russia's.

SERFDOM AND REFORM IN EASTERN EUROPE AND RUSSIA

Serfdom in Europe had a long history, existing in one form or another for 1,500 years. In Europe east of the Elbe River, it became widespread in the fifteenth and sixteenth centuries, when markets for grain developed and landlords wanted to secure labor for their expanding agricultural estates. Serfdom consisted of a package of legal obligations that peasants—serfs—were by law and custom obliged to furnish to lords. The package usually included obligatory labor on the lords' estates and, often, delivery of produce to lords' households, fees for using the lords' grinding mills, and permission from lords to marry, leave an estate, or take up a trade. In many cases, serfs were in effect owned by lords. In others, serfs were legally bound to land owned by lords, the state, or the

Serfdom An eighteenth-century Russian artwork shows Cossacks brutally abusing enserfed farm laborers, who had no protection from such maltreatment.

royal family. In some cases, serfs paid money in place of furnishing labor to lords.

By and large, forms of serfdom were milder in the Habsburg lands and Prussia, and harsher in Poland-Lithuania and Russia. Serfs in the latter lands had no legal recourse against exploitation, were subject to brutal punishments, and differed little in status from chattel slaves. Individuals or families could be bought and sold—indeed, whole villages of serfs could be bought and sold. Lords routinely used enserfed women for sex. In fact, in Russia, serfs differed from slaves mainly in that serfs were required to pay taxes and serve in the army. That inspired some of them to sell themselves into slavery until, in 1723, slavery was abolished in Russia to prevent that escape route from serfdom. In Prussia, the Habsburg lands, Poland, and Russia, the landlord class, church, and state all supported serfdom until at least 1750, and while they did, there was little serfs could do to improve their condition, let alone end serfdom.

THE IMPACT OF THE ENLIGHTENMENT AND FRENCH REVOLUTION In the late eighteenth century, the ideals of the Enlightenment undermined the agreement of lords, church, and state about serfdom. Voltaire, Kant, Adam Smith, and other influential writers denounced the institution as inhumane, contrary to the principle of liberty, and inefficient besides. Monarchs in Prussia, the Habsburg Empire, and Russia by 1780 tended to agree with the intellectual challenge to serfdom and changed their minds about its legitimacy. But they did little about it, bowing instead to the interests of landlords.

The Enlightenment changed some minds, but it took the French Revolution to change the politics of serfdom in eastern Europe. French armies under Bonaparte proclaimed an end to serfdom wherever they found it. In the case of Prussia, disastrous defeats at the hands of Bonaparte's free peasant armies in 1807 inspired the king to abolish serfdom in hopes of modernizing his country—and converting Prussia's serfs into more motivated peasant soldiers. Some 25 tiny German principalities abolished serfdom between 1807 and 1852. The Habsburg Empire did so between 1848 and 1853, generously compensating landlords for the loss of free labor.

RUSSIA In Russia, the morality and utility of serfdom had also come into question. In her memoirs, the tsarina Catherine the Great (r. 1762–1796) wrote that serfdom was both immoral and inefficient, even while she entrenched it by awarding newly acquired Polish serfs to loyal nobles. By the 1790s, a few courageous intellectuals such as Aleksandr Radischev had begun to denounce it (he likened serfdom to Caribbean slavery), risking exile or prison. Like their counterparts elsewhere, educated Russians absorbed Enlightenment ideals of liberty and equality, and gradually came to see serfdom as a backward institution that dragged their country down. But landowners usually did not see how they could manage their estates without it: they considered serfdom an inevitable evil. As with slavery, moral opposition was necessary for the abolition of serfdom, but far from sufficient to get it done.

The Russian reformers were aware of the ongoing saga of abolition of forced labor in the Atlantic world. Some, like Radischev, saw resemblances between serfdom and slavery. In the early nineteenth century, Russian emperors often used the word for slave (*rab*) to describe serfs. The novelist Ivan Turgenev referred to serfs, whom he often depicted in a favorable light in his short stories, as "our own blacks." Many in Russia's elite were moved by the gripping scenes in Harriet Beecher Stowe's *Uncle Tom's Cabin*, which was translated into Russian in 1857 and struck a chord. The Atlantic examples of abolition, often in the background of debate, did not make the issue of emancipation any easier for Russians but perhaps a little more urgent.

As often happens, war made matters more urgent still. Back in 1812, Russia's army, with help from winter and typhus, had expelled Bonaparte's army of 600,000 soldiers. In contrast, during the Crimean War (1853–1856), Russia could not defeat 60,000 British and French soldiers encamped on the Crimean Peninsula (which juts into the Black Sea). The great Russian novelist Leo Tolstoy, who served as an officer in Crimea, wrote that Russia did "not have an army but a mob of oppressed disciplined slaves." Defeat in Crimea and the performance of an army composed mainly of serfs convinced Tolstoy and thousands of others that his country was administratively, technologically, and economically backward compared to Britain and France.

ALEXANDER II AND MEMORIES OF PUGACHEV

A new tsar, **Alexander II**, came to power in 1855 determined to enact reforms that would modernize Russia and restore it to the first rank of European powers. Among his top priorities was military reform—in particular,

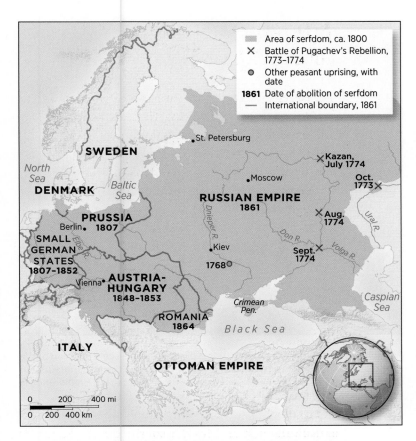

The Abolition of Serfdom in Eastern Europe and Russia, ca. 1800–1861 The abolition of serfdom freed tens of millions of peasants, beginning in German lands and moving eastward to Russia and Romania. The largest of all abolitions of legal forced labor in world history occurred in Russia.

providing the army with more educated, patriotic conscripts than could be found among the serf population. He especially wanted a reserve system such as several European countries had devised, in which soldiers in peacetime would go home but could be called up quickly when war broke out. This was far cheaper than maintaining a full-size standing army in peace and war. But no Russian tsar or noble wanted serfs with military skills on the loose in their home villages, and for good reason. To get a cheaper and better army, Alexander would have to get rid of serfdom.

Alexander and Russian reformers rightly feared serfs with military skills. As in the Atlantic world, uprisings of the oppressed in Russia caused shudders among the elite. Just as every slaveholder in the early nineteenth-century Atlantic world knew of the Haitian Revolution and its furious violence, so every Russian lord was aware of the vast rising in the years 1773–1774 led by a Cossack named Emelian Pugachev. In the middle of a war against the

Pugachev's Rebellion Chaos unfolds in a dramatic large-scale painting of the Battle of Kazan, fought between Pugachev's forces and the Imperial Russian Army in July 1774. Pugachev himself appears at the center, challenging a frightened nobleman.

away with serfdom felt they were riding the tiger: it was dangerous either to stay on or to get off.

In 1856, Alexander II convened a committee, drawn from the landholding elite, to craft a program of **emancipation for serfs**. Invoking the ghost of Pugachev, he stated in his instructions that "the existing condition of owning souls [serfs] cannot remain unchanged. It is better to begin to destroy serfdom from above than to wait until that time when it begins to destroy itself from below. I ask you, gentlemen, to figure out how all this can be carried to completion." After five years, the committee produced recommendations that informed the 1861 statute of emancipation of the serfs, a 360-page small-print document. The tsar was so worried that the terms of liberation might disappoint the serfs that he arranged for it to be read out on the first day of Lent, when Orthodox Christians are expected to abstain from alcohol. In theory, it allowed former serfs to own property, engage in trade, move freely, marry as they pleased, sue in courts, and vote in newly created local elections.

Ottoman Empire, Pugachev, a low-ranking army officer, led a ragtag rebel army of tens of thousands of Cossacks and serfs on a sustained rampage. They looted estates and took important cities such as Kazan on the Volga River, promising freedom to all serfs and death to landlords—of whom they killed about 3,000. It took all that the Russian state could do to defeat Pugachev, who was betrayed by associates and executed in 1775.

Fears of another Pugachev were stoked every year by news of serf uprisings somewhere in Russia. The office responsible for Russia's internal security recorded 712 revolts between 1826 and 1854, or roughly one every two weeks. As with the abolition of slavery in the Caribbean, fear of uprisings provided a strong motive for abolition of serfdom.

THE POLITICS OF RUSSIAN ABOLITION

For Alexander II and reform-minded Russians, the problem of abolition was practical: how to enact it without alienating either the serf owners or the serfs. In this respect as well, the situation paralleled that of the abolition of slavery. Even those masters who wanted to do

Emancipation of the Serfs Alexander II's proclamation announcing the emancipation of the serfs was read aloud in churches throughout Russia in March 1861. This illustration shows a crowd listening to the proclamation at the Dormition Cathedral in Moscow.

But the landlords who crafted the statute had not neglected their own interests. The government paid them handsomely for the loss of their serfs and some of their land. The emancipation provided former serfs with some land but required them to pay for it—except the few who accepted tiny plots called paupers' allotments. Since they had no money, serfs in effect had to buy land on credit from the state by paying a "redemption tax" over the next 50 years. Until they met their payments, former serfs faced many restrictions on their freedom and often remained tied to their village. In many cases, the restrictions lasted the rest of their lives. The landlords kept about two-thirds of the land—usually, the best. As with the abolitions of slavery, the fine print in the deal did not live up to the hopes of those liberated, because legal constraints and obligations lingered on for many years. Peasant unrest remained a feature of Russian rural life in the decades following the abolition of serfdom.

But the mere fact of liberation, of enslaved people and serfs—some 60 to 80 million people in all, most of them Russian, but many either African or of African ancestry—carries world-historical importance. Thousands of years after forced labor became widespread, enshrined in law codes, and routinely judged normal, natural, and divinely sanctioned, it was prohibited almost everywhere.

INDENTURED LABOR

Temporary labor bondage, however, persisted. In 1840, six years after the abolition of slavery in the British Empire, a future prime minister, Lord John Russell, wrote that the growing business of **indentured labor** was in danger of becoming "a new system of slavery." Indentured labor systems had existed for a long time. In the Atlantic world from the seventeenth century through to the 1830s, some 450,000 indentured laborers came from Europe to work in the Americas. Some early ones worked on sugar plantations in the Caribbean. Others worked as domestics, artisans, or farm laborers. A second and larger stream of indentured laborers, mainly from India and China, arose in the nineteenth century. It began as a trickle in response to the end of the slave trade and rose to a torrent with the end of slavery.

Russell's remark notwithstanding, the legal terms of indentured labor were not the same as those of slavery. The main differences were that indenture was a voluntary arrangement and applied for a fixed number of years, usually between two and eight. But often, trickery or coercion lay behind an indenture contract. Unworldly villagers in India or China fell for sunny promises made by labor recruiters. And until their contract expired, indentured laborers often faced some of the same hardships characteristic of slavery and serfdom: they could not legally leave their employment or marry without permission from their employers, and they often faced corporal punishment if they failed to satisfy their bosses. Indentured laborers, unlike almost all slaves or serfs, drew a wage, although a lower one than planters or mining companies would have had to pay without indenture—which is why the system existed.

INDENTURED MIGRANTS

Between 1830 and 1920, about 2 million indentured laborers left India and China for hard work as plantation laborers or miners in the Caribbean, Peru, Hawaii, Mauritius, South Africa, or Southeast Asia. Smaller flows came from Japan, several Pacific islands, and parts of Africa. Some Europeans, mainly Portuguese, also signed up as indentured laborers. Indians accounted for the majority, about 1.4 million—much more than that if one adds in more local migrations to nearby Ceylon, Burma, or Malaya. Chinese indentured migrants numbered about 500,000. Pacific Islanders and Africans each accounted for about 100,000. Most of the Africans were recruited from among the recaptives in Sierra Leone. Others were rescued from a slave ship in the Atlantic only to be indentured for labor in the Caribbean. Japanese indentured migrants numbered about 85,000, and Europeans 56,000. The flows, boosted by each famine or war in Asia, peaked between 1850 and 1880.

The chief destinations for Indians were sugar plantations in Mauritius, the British Caribbean, South Africa, and Fiji (the Pacific archipelago), and for Chinese, the plantations of Cuba or the mines of Peru. For Japanese, the likeliest destinations were plantations in Hawaii and Peru.

Most indentured laborers were men, about 95 percent in the case of Chinese, maybe 75 percent for Indians. The first indentured Japanese in Peru, a shipload of 790

Indentured Labor After the abolition of slavery, unfree labor still contributed to the global movement of peoples—such as these Indian indentured workers in British Jamaica (left) and Chinese indentured workers in Spanish Cuba (right).

who arrived in 1899, were all men, destined for sugar-cane plantations. Single men, if they stayed after their indenture expired, usually married local women if they married at all.

Crossing the oceans in sailing ships with hundreds of other labor migrants was risky. Voyages typically took from one to six months. The death rate for the roughly 150,000 Chinese shipped to Cuba (1847–1873) averaged about 3 percent. For Indians sailing to the Caribbean, it

Indian Laborers in Trinidad Between 1847 and 1917, nearly 150,000 Indians went to Trinidad as indentured laborers, and 90 percent remained there all their lives. Most were men in their 20s from northern India, destined for sugar plantations and bonded for five years. Here we see Indian families, which accounted for a small minority of indentured migrants.

was about 2 percent. Meanwhile, during the last decades of the transatlantic slave trade (1811–1867), mortality in the Middle Passage was 6 percent. (For reference, the death rate for free people traveling from Britain to New York in these decades was 1 percent, and the annual risk of death on the roads of the United States today is about 0.01 percent.) All the death rates for indentured migrant voyages fell over time, so that after 1880 all averaged under 1 percent.

Many of these indentured migrant laborers, especially the Indians, returned home. About one-third of Indians who went to Jamaica, Suriname, or Mauritius went home after their term was up. And more than two-thirds of those who went to Thailand or Malaya did so. Many indenture contracts included promise of a return trip. But even for those whose arrangements did not include that promise, it was often possible eventually to earn enough money for the passage home. By the late nineteenth century, information about global travel was more abundant than before, and its price lower, making return voyages for indentured laborers likelier.

THE END OF INDENTURED LABOR

Indentured labor, although not the same as slavery, served the same purpose, keeping plantations and mines in business. It disappeared, gradually, because mines and plantations could increasingly find enough cheap labor on the free market. After 1870, tens of millions of free people—Europeans, Indians, and Chinese predominantly—left home to cross the oceans in search of employment. Accelerating population growth brought more youths into labor markets. Their sheer numbers reduced labor shortages and lowered free-market wages to the point where indentured labor no longer made economic sense for anyone even in the less thickly populated regions. By 1914, it was, for all intents and purposes, finished. And with it, a long era in human history in which unfree labor was legal and common came—almost—to an end.

Unfortunately, one has to include "almost." Legal slavery lasted in a few countries—Saudi Arabia, Ethiopia, Mauritania, for example—well into the twentieth century. Colonial rulers in Africa—the same ones who had legally abolished slavery in many cases—in the 1920s and 1930s organized temporary forced labor brigades for work in mines, plantations, or on railroads. Certain totalitarian regimes—Nazi Germany and Soviet Russia, among others—reestablished slave labor by other names for a few years or decades. As we will see, about 18 million people worked in Soviet forced labor camps between 1929 and 1953. North Korea uses 200,000 enslaved laborers in its manufacturing and agricultural economy today. And various forms of illegal slavery persist in 2023, involving as many as 50 million people (0.6 percent of humankind). Dozens of countries traffic in sex slaves, typically young women lured by false promises of good wages far from home.

CONCLUSION

Over the period 1750–1950, humankind underwent two great liberations. The first liberation was from a biological old regime that had featured frequent disease, famine, and early death. As a result of scientific advances, deliberate policies, and some good fortune, the biological old regime was banished in a Vital Revolution that saw life expectancy lengthen and child mortality shrink dramatically. By 1950, far fewer parents had to bury most of their children, as Christine of Mecklenburg, Queen Anne, Peter the Great—and billions of anonymous mothers and fathers—had done. For the fabric of ordinary people's

lives, this stands among the biggest changes in modern history, although the benefits of the Vital Revolution remain unequally distributed. The revolution might continue, but it might also prove reversible: there is no guarantee we can always keep infectious diseases in check.

The second great liberation involved less fortune and more human will. The various abolitions of slavery and serfdom around the world, from 1777 to 1981, represent another sea change. Serfdom had existed for centuries, and slavery for millennia. Until the end of the eighteenth century, few voices objected to the practice of forced labor, even if many objected vehemently to their own exploitation. But then, starting in the 1770s and 1780s, a groundswell of dissent began to build. It rose up in eastern Europe against serfdom while mounting in the Atlantic world against slavery. Slavery's abolition rested in part on the skill and commitment of antislavery activists. But it also rested on the actions of the enslaved themselves, who launched rebellions that in one case—Haiti—directly forced the end of slavery and in others, such as Brazil, Cuba, and the British Caribbean, helped tip the political balance against slavery. Serfs too, with their frequent uprisings, hastened the abolition of serfdom in Russia.

Looking more deeply, one can see other forces at work in the end of forced labor. One was the general rise in population that gathered pace after 1750, the result of the early stages of the Vital Revolution. Forced labor in most contexts made economic sense when and where labor was scarce and therefore, in a free market situation, expensive. Slavery and serfdom kept labor costs low. At great cost in human suffering, they made plantations and other enterprises profitable. When the population grew, labor at free market prices grew cheaper, undermining the economic logic of forced labor. This process proved most important to abolition in Brazil and Russia. It was not central in the British West Indies, where the population was not growing and slavery remained profitable until the day of abolition. Nor was it relevant in the United States, where slavery remained profitable despite rapid population growth until the Civil War ended it.

A second force at work was intellectual. Enlightenment thinkers after 1750 increasingly advanced ideals of liberty and attacked slavery and serfdom as unjust and inefficient. Their ideas won many followers in influential circles from Brazil to Britain to Russia. At the same time, religious thinking shifted against slavery—less so against serfdom. While for centuries, established churches had supported slavery, in the eighteenth century a few branches of Protestantism came to see slavery as a moral evil and repugnant to God. Quakers, Methodists, and evangelical Anglicans stood in the forefront of antislavery in Britain and the United States, and used their networks to promote abolition.

Another influential force was the prestige of British example. In the nineteenth century, thanks mainly to the power conferred on it by the Industrial Revolution, Britain enjoyed an influence all out of proportion to its size. When it threw its weight behind antislavery, that commitment reverberated around the world. The tightened webs—which British steamships, railroads, and telegraph lines helped tighten even more—ensured that millions on every continent knew the moral and economic arguments against slavery. Many of them gradually found themselves persuaded. Others, whose minds were less susceptible to gentle suasion, knew by 1820 that the British Royal Navy would punish them for slave trading and, by about 1870, that British foreign policy would penalize them for maintaining slavery.

All these broad currents—population growth, shifting intellectual currents, and the weight of British example—depended on the tightening links in the Global web forged over the course of the eighteenth and nineteenth centuries. The spread of inoculation, sanitation, and vaccination occurred as speedily as it did only because millions learned quickly about the success of these practices and changed their behavior accordingly. So too with the spread of ideas opposed to slavery and serfdom and of information about slave or serf uprisings. Globalization has its dark sides, many of them noted in this book. But globalization also contributed to the Vital Revolution and the decline of regimes of forced labor.

The twin liberations were linked, momentous, and simultaneous. The growth of population resulting from the Vital Revolution reduced the economic logic of forced labor. The end of the deliberate deprivations of slavery and serfdom helped improve health and longevity for tens of millions. The two liberations were part of a new era of revolutions in which big changes happened faster and more globally. The Industrial Revolution, Vital Revolution, and abolition of forced labor took a century or two to affect the whole world—a blink of the eye compared to the spread of domestication, cities, writing, or gunpowder in previous eras.

CHAPTER REVIEW

KEY TERMS

Vital Revolution (p. 749)
biological old regime (p. 749)
smallpox inoculation (p. 753)
germ theory of disease (p. 754)

1918 flu pandemic (p. 756)
Quakers (p. 761)
Thomas Clarkson (p. 762)
Sons of Africa (p. 762)
José Aponte (p. 763)
Jack Gladstone (p. 764)

Slavery Abolition Act (p. 766)
Thirteenth Amendment (p. 767)
Alexander II (p. 771)
emancipation for serfs (p. 772)
indentured labor (p. 773)

Go to **INQUIZITIVE** to see what you've learned—and learn what you've missed—with personalized feedback along the way.

REVIEW QUESTIONS

1. What health risks, including specific risks for women and children, characterized the biological old regime?
2. What accidental and deliberate changes caused the death toll from disease to drop after 1750 or so?
3. What do cholera and the 1918 flu pandemic demonstrate about globalization and disease?
4. Explain the link between race and slavery, and discuss where this connection was most prominent.
5. Why and where did slavery expand between 1750 and 1850?
6. Why did the 1807 British ban of the slave trade endanger slavery more than the 1808 U.S. ban?
7. Describe the key driving forces of the abolition of the slave trade in Britain, the United States, Cuba, and Brazil.
8. What was the broader impact of the Haitian Revolution on abolishing slavery?

9. Compare and contrast the main reasons for the abolition of slavery in the British Empire, the United States, the Caribbean sugar islands, and Brazil.
10. Why did elites outside of the Atlantic world find the abolition of slavery appealing?
11. Why did African slavery expand after 1850?
12. Identify the links among the Crimean War, Alexander II's military reforms, and the emancipation of the serfs.
13. What did the abolition of serfdom mean for former serfs?
14. Who constituted the second and larger stream of indentured laborers, and where were they mainly working?
15. Explain the chief forces that caused the decline of forced labor during this period.
16. Identify the links between the Vital Revolution and the decline of forced labor.

FURTHER READING

William BYNUM, *The History of Medicine: A Very Short Introduction* (2008). The most convenient way to get the basic story on medicine's role in improving health, but confined to the western world.

David Brion DAVIS, *Inhuman Bondage: The Rise and Fall of Slavery in the New World* (2006). An overview by one of the most prominent historians of slavery; includes historiographical context providing a sense of what others have had to say.

Dale T. GRADEN, *Disease, Resistance, and Lies: The Demise of the Transatlantic Slave Trade to Brazil and Cuba* (2014). Emphasizes the role of slave revolts and pressure from the British navy in changing elite opinion against the slave trade.

Adam HOCHSCHILD, *Bury the Chains: The British Struggle to Abolish Slavery* (2005). A lively popular history, with excellent sketches of the principal actors.

Peter KOLCHIN, *Unfree Labor: American Slavery and Russian Serfdom* (1987). Still the only extended study that puts both these systems of forced labor in direct comparison.

Kris MANJAPRA, *Black Ghost of Empire: The Long Death of Slavery and the Failure of Emancipation* (2022). An important argument about the means and terms of emancipation in the Atlantic world.

David NORTHRUP, *Indentured Labor in the Age of Imperialism, 1834–1922* (1995). The best overview of the subject.

James C. RILEY, *Rising Life Expectancy: A Global History* (2001). A handy synthesis of the Vital Revolution.

Manisha SINHA, *The Slave's Cause: A History of Abolition* (2016). A comprehensive history of abolition in the United States, with some attention to Britain, and due recognition of slaves' roles.

Emilia Viotti da COSTA, *Crowns of Glory, Tears of Blood: The Demerara Slave Rebellion of 1823* (1994). A classic in-depth study of one of the key revolts.

Smallpox and Inoculation

UNTIL ITS ERADICATION IN THE 1970S, the smallpox virus ranked among the greatest killers of human beings. In non-immune populations, it usually killed about 30 percent of those infected and blinded many more. Survivors, however, were immune ever after. At some unknown time and place, someone figured out that deliberately infecting people with attenuated (weakened) virus typically brought on a mild case yet conferred lifelong immunity. Inoculation, as this procedure is called, was not foolproof: about 2 percent of those inoculated died. But where smallpox was a daily threat, these odds were appealing. So knowledge and practice of inoculation spread, and by 1750 it was evident in many parts of Eurasia and Africa. The excerpts presented here give some idea of that process.

SOURCE 22.1

Lady Mary Wortley Montague and Ottoman Practices of Smallpox Inoculation, ca. 1717

Mary Pierrepont (1689–1762) was born into the English aristocracy. She was self-educated, yet a published poet at age 15. At 24 she eloped with Edward Wortley Montague. She soon contracted smallpox, which had already killed her brother; but she survived and spent her late twenties in the Ottoman capital, Istanbul, immersing herself in the life of her new home while her husband served there as ambassador. Eager to save her young son from smallpox, she inquired into inoculation, which was common in Ottoman lands. The British Embassy doctor in Istanbul had written a short treatise on it in 1713, and Lady Mary Wortley Montague wrote of it in a letter to her friend Sarah Chiswell in 1717. The excerpt below is taken from that letter. Lady Mary arranged to have a Greek woman inoculate her five-year-old son in 1718, and he survived. After returning to London, Lady Mary used her society connections and growing celebrity status as a writer to spread the acceptance of inoculation.

A propos of distempers, I am going to tell you a thing, that will make you wish yourself here. The smallpox, so fatal, and so general amongst us, is here entirely harmless, by the invention of ingrafting, which is the term they give it. There is a set of old women, who make it their business to perform the operation.... People send to one another to know if any of their family has a mind to have the smallpox; they make parties for this purpose, and when they are met (commonly fifteen or sixteen together) the old woman comes with a nut-shell full of the matter of the best sort of smallpox, and asks what vein you please to have opened. She immediately rips open that you offer to her, with a large needle (which gives you no more pain than a common scratch), and puts into the vein as much matter as can lie upon the head of her needle, and after that, binds up the little wound with a hollow bit of shell, and in this manner open four or five veins. The Grecians have commonly the superstition of opening one in the middle of the forehead, one in each arm, and one in the breast, to mark the sign of the cross; but this has a very ill effect, all these wounds leaving little scars, and is not done by those that are not superstitious, who choose to have them in the legs, or that part of the arm that is concealed. The children or young patients play together all the rest of the day, and are in perfect health to the eighth. Then the fever begins to seize them, and they keep their beds two days, very seldom three. They have very rarely above twenty or thirty [pustules] in their faces, which never mark, and in eight days time they are as well as before their illness.... Every year thousands undergo this operation, and the French ambassador says pleasantly that they take the smallpox here by way of diversion, as they take the waters in other countries. There is no example of any one that has died in it, and you may believe I am well satisfied of the safety of this experiment, since I intend to try it on my dear little son. I am patriot enough to take pains to bring this useful invention into fashion in England, and I should not fail to write to some of our doctors very particularly about it, if I knew any one of them that I thought had virtue enough to destroy such a considerable branch of their revenue, for the good of mankind. But that distemper is too beneficial to them, not to expose to all their resentment the hardy wight [person] that should undertake to put an end to it. Perhaps if I live to return, I may, however have the courage to war with them. Upon this occasion, admire the heroism in the heart of your friend, etc. etc.

Source: Lady Mary Wortley Montague, *Letters of Lady Mary Wortley Montague, Written during Her Travels in Europe, Asia, and Africa; to Which Are Added Poems by the Same Author* (Bordeaux: Printed by J. Pinard, Laurels Street no. 5, 1805).

- Why does Lady Mary think inoculation might encounter resistance in England?
- What likely obstacles to the adoption of this practice in England does she not mention here?

SOURCE 22.2

Inoculation in North Africa, ca. 1700

Smallpox outbreaks in London in the 1720s sparked interest in Lady Mary Wortley Montague's knowledge of inoculation, in Cotton Mather's information about the practice among Africans, and in several other people's views as well. Debate raged about the risks and rewards of inoculation, just as it has in our day about various vaccinations. One of those confident in the procedure was the Tripolitan ambassador to London, known in English as Cassem Aga. (Tripoli after 1711 formed a semi-independent state, only nominally under Ottoman control; its rulers maintained their own diplomatic corps.) Cassem Aga wrote the following passage in Arabic, and it was published in this translation in 1729. By "wild Arabs" he probably meant pastoralists.

My opinion being asked relating to the inoculation of the small-pox, I will mention in a few words what I know of it. If anyone hath a mind to have his children inoculated, he carries them to one that lies ill of the smallpox, at the time when the pustules are come to full maturity. Then the surgeon makes an incision upon the back of the hand, between the thumb and fore-finger, and puts a little of the matter, squeezed out of the largest and fullest pustules, into the wound. This done, the child's hand is wrapp'd up with a handkerchief to keep it from the air, and he is left to his liberty 'till the fever arising confines him to his bed, which commonly happens at the end of three or four days. After that, by God's permission, a few pustules of the smallpox break out upon the child. All this I can confirm by a domestick proof: for my father carried us, five brothers and three sisters, to the house of a girl that lay ill of the smallpox, and had us all inoculated the same day. Now he that had most of us all, had not above twenty pustules. Otherwise this practice is so innocent, and so sure, that out of a hundred persons inoculated not two die; whereas on the contrary, out of a hundred persons that are infected with the smallpox the natural way, there die commonly about thirty. It is withal so ancient in the kingdoms of Tripoli, Tunis and Algier, that nobody remembers its first rise: and it is generally practised not only by the inhabitants of the towns, but also by the wild Arabs.

Source: "Cassem Algaida Aga Paper Relating to the Inoculation of the Small-pox, as It Is Practised in the Kingdoms of Tripoli, Tunis, and Algier," in: J. G. Scheuchzer, ed., *An Account of the Success of Inoculating the Small-Pox in Great Britain, for the Years 1727 and 1728* (London: J. Peele, 1729).

- How does this account differ in its details of the inoculation procedure in North Africa as opposed to Lady Mary's account of the procedure in Istanbul? What conclusions can be drawn by comparing the two accounts?
- Does this account narrow the range of possibilities about where inoculation originated? Why or why not?

SOURCE 22.3

Practices of Smallpox Inoculation in Africa and Boston, 1716–1721

The report on inoculation produced by the British Embassy physician in Istanbul (see Source 22.1) was published by London's Royal Society in 1713 and came to the attention of a Boston clergyman named Cotton Mather. He wrote a letter (excerpted in Selection 1 below) to the Royal Society in 1716 recording the remarks of an enslaved African, Onesimus, given to him in 1706 by his congregation. The "Guramantese" whom he mentions are probably Coromantee (from modern-day Ghana) or Garamantes (from southern Libya). Late in 1716, Onesimus purchased his freedom and disappeared from the historical record.

Subsequently, Boston experienced a smallpox epidemic in 1721. Three years later Mather wrote a book about diseases (excerpted in Selection 2 below) in which he commented on inoculation methods among Boston's African-born population. Mather urged inoculation for all. However, all but one Boston physician refused to inoculate anyone. Dr. Zabdiel Boylston, the exception, inoculated 248 people, including Mather's son. Six of his patients died, or 2.5 percent. In the rest of Boston, 14 percent of those infected died of smallpox.

[1] Enquiring of my Negro-man Onesimus, who is a pretty intelligent fellow, whether he ever had the smallpox; he answered, both, *Yes*, and *No*; and then told me, that he had undergone an operation, which had given him something of the smallpox, & would forever preserve him from it; adding, that it was often used among the Guramantese, & whoever had the courage to use it, was forever free from the fear of the contagion.

[2] I have since met with a considerable number of these Africans, who all agree in one story; that in their country grandy-many die of the smallpox. But now they learn this way: people take juice of smallpox; and cutty-skin and put in a drop; then by-and-by a little sicky, sicky: then very few little things like smallpox; and nobody die of it; and nobody have smallpox anymore. Thus in Africa, where the poor creatures die of the smallpox like rotten sheep, a merciful GOD has taught them an infallible preservative. Tis a common practice, and is attended with a constant success.

Source: Kathryn S. Koo, "Strangers in the House of God: Cotton Mather, Onesimus, and an Experiment in Christian Slaveholding" (Worcester, MA: The American Antiquarian Society, 2007).

- **Why might Bostonians and Boston doctors have avoided inoculation during the 1721 epidemic?**
- **According to Mather, who was responsible for inventing inoculation?**

Kangxi Emperor's "Family Instructions" on Smallpox, ca. 1720–1730

Smallpox ravaged the Qing Empire (1644–1911) in its early years. People who had not lived through it and become immune were justifiably afraid to visit Beijing. The Kangxi Emperor (1654–1722), who had been selected among his brothers partly because he'd survived smallpox, encouraged the Chinese folk-medicine practice of inoculation, which had been in use since at least the 1570s. (A Chinese medical text explained how to do it: "Use slowly dried scabs, grind them into a fine powder, and blow it into the child's nostrils by a suitable tube.") Kangxi arranged to have parts of his army ("the Forty-nine Banners") and his family inoculated, something in which he took pride—as this excerpt makes clear. He wrote this late in life, and it was first published, in Chinese and Manchu, in 1730.

At the beginning of our dynasty, when anyone was attacked by smallpox, people made use of a thousand precautions, and this disease was very greatly feared. The method of inoculation having been brought to light during my reign, I had it used upon you, my sons and daughters, and my descendants, and you all passed through the smallpox in the happiest possible manner. The Forty-nine Banners of the Mongolians, and even the Chiefs of the Khalka people [in outer Mongolia], have made use of inoculation, and all of them were perfectly healed. In the beginning, when I had it tested on one or two people, some old women taxed me with extravagance, and spoke very strongly against inoculation. The courage which I summoned up to insist on its practice has saved the lives and the health of millions of men. This is an extremely important thing, of which I am very proud. Old men used to consider it a necessary precaution never to go into houses where the smallpox was. They did not even dare to pronounce its name, just as they abstained from many expressions which they regarded as of bad augury. But nowadays people take no notice at all of that sort of thing.

Source: Xuanye (Kangxi Emperor), *Ting xun ge yan* ("Family Instructions"), 1730. The Manchu edition is "Han i araha šengdzu gosin hūwangdi i booi tacihiyan i ten i gisun," B24 in Jun Matsumura, *A Catalogue of Manchu Materials in the Library of Congress: Xylographs, Manuscripts, Archives* (Tokyo: University of Tokyo Press Production Center, 1999).

- What can be inferred from the fact that the emperor arranged for the inoculation of his (many) sons and daughters?
- Is the emperor's statement that inoculation "saved the lives and the health of millions of men" convincing? Why or why not?
- Should his insistence on the value of inoculation be taken to mean there was strong resistance in Qing China to the practice? Why or why not?

QUESTIONS FOR COMPARISON

1. Judging from these accounts, which seems more likely: that inoculation originated in one place and spread along the pathways of the Global web, or that it developed more than once in different places? Explain your response.

2. Based on these documents, how would you summarize the arguments in the early eighteenth century for and against smallpox inoculation?

EUROPE
FOR 1870
Prepared by, in Paris.
HADOL
Published by L. Prang & Co's
Chromo Publishing House
BOSTON. MASS

IRELAND
BRITAIN
NORTH SEA
NORWAY
SWEDEN
BALTIC SEA
ATLANTIC OCEAN
HOLLAND
DENMARK
HOLSTEIN
BELGIUM
PRUSSIA
FRANCE
SWITZERLAND
AUSTRIA
PORTUGAL
SPAIN
CORSICA
SARDINIA
ADRIATIC SEA
ITALY
TURKEY IN EUROPE

CHRONOLOGY

1795
France makes
La Marseillaise
its national anthem

1818
Hongi Hika begins importing
guns and potatoes to
New Zealand

1819
British found Singapore

Abdelkadir leads Algerian uprising

1829
Establishment
of nation-state
of Serbia

1830s

1832
Establishment of
nation-state
of Greece

1847
French capture and
exile Abdelkadir

ca. 1840
Peak of Comanche Empire's economic
and military strength

1858
Start of the
British Raj

1859
Charles Darwin publishes
The Origin of Species

1860s
Italian unification

1867
Canadian Confederation;
kingdom of Hungary is granted
limited independence

1871
Algerian
uprising

1876–1878
Major famine
in India

1878
Establishment of
nation-state of
Romania and Bulgaria

1884–1885
Berlin
Conference
partitions
Africa

1888–1892
Drought and famine
in Ethiopia kill half
of population

1889
Adoption of
Meiji constitution;
rinderpest arrives
in East Africa

1894–1895
Japan defeats China
in war and takes Taiwan

1896
Menelik II's army defeats
Italians at Adowa

23

Nationalism and Imperialism

TIGHTENING THE GLOBAL WEB

1800 to 1930

I n 1890, on the Makonde Plateau in what is now southern Tanzania, in East Africa, there lived a merchant-prince and slave trader named Machemba. Leader of a people known as the Yao, he was among a handful of African and Afro-Arab warlords prospering from a growing trade in people and ivory that linked the East African hinterland to its seacoast and beyond to markets in Arabia, India, and Europe. Germany had just laid claim to a big slice of East Africa—Tanganyika—and needed cooperative African leaders who would support German authority. Hermann von Wissmann, a distinguished army officer who had spent several years in Africa, invited Machemba to do so. Machemba had his own ideas:

> I have listened to your words but can find no reason why I should obey you. I would rather die first.... If it should be friendship that you desire, then I am ready for it, today and always; but to be your subject, that I cannot be. If it should be war you desire, then I am ready, but never to be your subject. I do not fall at your feet, for you are God's creature just as I am.... I am Sultan

A Satirical Map of Europe, 1870 Drawn from a French perspective, this satirical view of the geopolitical situation in Europe in 1870 uses stereotypes to represent nations and their relationships. Britain holds Ireland on a leash, Prussia kneels on Austria, and France draws a sword to defend itself against Prussia. The map reflects the view that nations had shared cultural or ethnic identities—a view that flourished in an era of rising nationalisms.

1898
Spanish-American War; United States takes Spain's colonies and annexes Hawaii

1899
Rudyard Kipling publishes "The White Man's Burden"

1900
Australian Federation

By 1910
All local Indonesian rulers submit to the Dutch

1910
Japan annexes Korea

1912
Italy takes Libya from Ottoman Empire

1918
Collapse of Habsburg Empire; Aladura churches in Nigeria take shape

1930s
Development of Yamato race theory

here in my land. You are Sultan there in yours. Yet listen, I do not say that you should obey me: for I know that you are a free man. As for me, I will not come to you, and if you are strong enough, then come and fetch me.

Disappointed but not surprised, Wissmann came to fetch Machemba. The Germans assembled an army of Africans, some from as far away as Zululand (South Africa) and Sudan, trained and equipped by German veterans of European wars. It took nine years to defeat Machemba and a few more to subdue all of Tanganyika.

Machemba, in his defiance, had not appreciated that Wissmann had behind him the resources of an industrialized country of 50 million people. Even when he learned the full measure of German power, he could do little to preserve his independence. For his part, Wissmann didn't know much about Machemba and the Yao, who proved to be resourceful guerilla fighters. But when he learned, there was plenty he could do to them.

Encounters of this sort, featuring unequal levels of resources and knowledge about the world, became especially frequent in the nineteenth century. Thanks mainly to industrialization, some societies and states, including Germany, were in a position to use overwhelming power thousands of miles from home. It proved a temptation hard to resist.

Between 1826 and 1919, about a quarter of the Earth's land surface changed hands politically. People inspired by the ideologies of **nationalism** and imperialism, and in most cases empowered by industrialization, helped to redraw the political map of the world through violence and negotiation. These ideologies, in effect, made some peoples and states stronger and others weaker, rearranging the world political order.

Nationalism and imperialism were the most powerful ideologies changing world politics between 1800 and 1930. Other important political ideas, such as democracy, socialism, or pan-Islamism (the view that Muslims should be politically unified), had fewer global consequences. Nationalism and imperialism loomed so large because they traveled well from one cultural setting to the next. People everywhere found the idea of nationhood appealing. And most people in powerful societies approved of imperialism too.

This chapter begins with nationalism, explaining the concept, where it mattered, why it arose when it did, and what difference it made. It then considers imperialism, outlining why it reached such heights during the nineteenth century, what forms it took, and where it mattered most. As we shall see, nationalism and imperialism sometimes overlapped in mutually reinforcing ways, and sometimes worked at cross-purposes. Both encouraged people to emphasize their differences, but both brought peoples into closer interactions and tighter webs.

NATIONALISM AND NATION-STATES

Nationalism—perhaps the single most powerful ideological force in modern centuries—is difficult to define. It is a set of ideas, beliefs, and attitudes that exalts the virtues of a community claiming distinctive characteristics and, in most cases, a bounded territory. The characteristics that provide solidarity can be shared language and culture, shared ethnicity and ancestry, or shared political and civic values—or some combination of them.

Scholars often distinguish between ethnic nationalism and civic nationalism. The first applies to groups, such as Japanese, that get their sense of solidarity from a common language, ethnic identity, or ancestry. The claim to common ancestry can be, and usually is, fanciful. But if people believe it, the effect is the same as if it were true. The second, civic nationalism, applies to nations whose sense of solidarity comes from common acceptance of a set of institutions and political values. The United States is a good example: the ideals articulated in the Declaration of Independence and the U.S. Constitution, though never fully realized, remain an inspiration and a source of identity for Americans. In practice, ethnic nationalism and civic nationalism often overlap.

Nationalism begins with human biology but doesn't end there. A craving to belong to a group is one of the deepest human desires. Our fellow apes seem to feel it too. In the long hominin and human career, this desire conferred strong advantages. People could forage, hunt, and defend themselves better as groups than as lone individuals. Over hundreds of thousands of years, our brains evolved to make us long to belong to groups.

But human biology has no bearing on just which groups we wish to belong to. It could be a hunter-forager band, a high school debate team, or the community of Green Bay Packers fans known as Cheeseheads. Membership in groups, however large or small and whatever their practical advantages, delivers psychic rewards. For some people at least, nationalism offers a satisfying sense of solidarity with a large community, enabling people to feel part of something greater than their family or village.

Modern nationalism, especially ethnic nationalism, has a strange relationship to history. It rests on simplifying myths and outright falsehoods. Nationalists typically emphasize glorious, ancient, and unified pasts—airbrushed pasts. Modern Mongolian nationalism harkens back to the conqueror Genghis Khan, overlooking his gory massacres. Mexican nationalism invokes the Aztecs, overlooking their ruthless rule over the ancestors of millions of today's Mexicans. As the French scholar Ernst Renan wrote in 1882,

"Forgetting, I would go so far as to say historical error, is a crucial factor in the creation of a nation."

Nationalism prospered in some circumstances more than others. Ethnic nationalism arose most easily where ethnic, linguistic, cultural, and religious diversity was minimal and a unified state already existed—as in nineteenth-century Japan. Nationalism also developed strongly where ethnic minorities in multiethnic states felt persecuted: Poles in the Russian Empire or Afrikaners in South Africa. The idea—whether accurate or not—of a peasantry deeply rooted in the ancestral soil, as in modern Korea or France, also helped foster ethnic nationalism. People who felt their nation was specially chosen for some divine purpose or that their nation was unfairly victimized—or both—also found nationalism appealing.

Another circumstance that favored the development of nationalism was urbanization. As we've seen, cities grew larger and more numerous during the nineteenth century, especially in industrializing countries. Tens of millions of people uprooted from villages felt the need to belong to a community, and so were all the more receptive to nationalistic messages. Those messages might take the form of journalism, heroic novels, poetry, or painting—or stirring patriotic music adopted as national anthems. France in 1795 designated *La Marseillaise* as a national anthem, launching an international trend. Vietnam chose one in 1802, Argentina in 1813, Peru in 1821, and Japan in 1888. The United States adopted its national anthem in 1931. City populations, because clustered together, were easier to reach with nationalist music, art, or journalism.

Nationalism's adherents preferred states whose borders matched those of an ethnic or linguistic group, whether Germans or Koreans or Bengalis. They often claimed that any state with borders that did not correspond to a nation—a multinational state—was illegitimate. Their ambitions almost always required some political reengineering: nationalism served to unite peoples into a single nation-state in some cases and in others to grind multicultural empires into pieces. Let's look at some examples.

FRANCE

Many scholars think France provides the earliest example of genuine nationalism. While France became a kingdom over the span of many centuries, only its elite felt French before the 1790s. The masses generally felt attachments

French Nationalism An 1880 lithograph shows the Place de la Bastille in Paris decorated with French flags in honor of France's July 14 national holiday. A national day, imagery connected with a national flag, and national history grounded in founding events such as the storming of the Bastille are all characteristic nationalist symbols.

to their family, village, region, religion, and perhaps to their king. But in the course of the French Revolution and especially Napoleon Bonaparte's foreign wars (see Chapter 20), more and more people within France came to feel increasingly French. Some were moved by the ideals of the Revolution—liberty, equality, and fraternity (perhaps better translated as solidarity). When the French established a republic that supposedly represented the will of the people, many of them felt they had laid the foundation for a better political community.

In the 1790s, leaders of the French Revolution tried to drum a sense of Frenchness into the uneducated peasantry—80 percent of the population. One tactic was requiring the use of standard (Parisian) French throughout the country, a policy employed off and on ever after. Another, used in the desperate 1790s, was killing people who declined to identify themselves with the French nation.

Two decades of warfare, from 1792 to 1815, helped forge a French nation. Military service in a national army made soldiers feel French. Supporters of the Revolution and Bonaparte devised symbols, ceremonies, and rituals to convey the meaning of French identity to people who could not read: a national flag to match the anthem, for example, or parades and funerals for heroes of the French nation. Army service exposed young men to standard French, no matter which tongue they spoke at home.

After Bonaparte's final defeat in 1815, subsequent rulers of France, even monarchists who hated everything else about the French Revolution, cultivated nationalism. Throughout the nineteenth century, French elites hammered home the nationalist message, using the newly created countrywide public school system, the army, and the press to deepen the popular sense of French national identity. After 1871, the government, now called the Third Republic, tried again to impose a standard French language on the country. Ordinary French citizens learned to feel that theirs was a special nation, committed to ideals such as liberty and equality. They were also taught to consider themselves blood descendants of the formidable ancient Gauls, in whom various admirable traits were conveniently found. At the same time, they identified with the glorious legacies of the Romans, Charlemagne, and, more recent, Bonaparte. French nationalism was, and is, mainly civic nationalism, based on the ideals of the French Revolution, but it also has had, and still has, an ethnic basis for many French people.

JAPAN

Japanese nationalism was based mainly on a sense of ethnic solidarity. It had deep roots, but it matured in the late nineteenth century when Japanese leaders worried, with ample reason, that their country might be colonized by Britain or another industrial power. They made a concerted effort to industrialize, as we've seen, and to foster nationalism and a sense of Japanese exceptionalism. They calculated that these efforts would rally the masses to make sacrifices for the state, which they believed was essential to Japan's continued independence.

Around 1875, Japanese leaders started promoting the fiction of common ancestry among all Japanese. By the 1930s, it had developed into **Yamato race theory**, according to which the Japanese were descended from an ancient ancestral people and were different from, and better than, Koreans, Chinese, and other neighbors. Japanese nationalism also had a strong religious component: the elite in Japan typically embraced the ancient Japanese rituals called Shinto in preference to imported religions such as Buddhism. The state supported Shinto shrines and encouraged worship of the emperor as divine. The Meiji constitution, adopted in 1889, instructed Japanese people that their first allegiance was to the state. Japan's nationalists emphasized the respects in which the country was

Japanese Nationalism Japanese efforts to support Shinto as the national religion resulted in the persecution of Buddhists. An 1874 illustration shows Shinto priests burning Buddhist scriptures, over the tears and protests of a Buddhist monk.

unique and especially how it was, as they saw it, more disciplined, energetic, and warlike than China.

As elsewhere, public education in Japan helped get the message to the masses. After 1870, an older tradition of Confucian learning was replaced by a more practical, nationalistic curriculum, and by 1900 almost every Japanese boy and girl attended school. Each university student had to swear an oath promising to "offer [myself] courageously to the state." Urbanization and increasing literacy also helped nationalism take root.

Japan's nationalism emphasized military virtues. By 1890, sailors and soldiers were instructed to see Japan as a "sacred nation protected by the gods." Civilians were encouraged to revere the armed forces as embodiments of the warrior spirit of the Yamato race. As we will see, after Japan's defeat in World War II, the character of its nationalism underwent a radical makeover, dropping militarism in favor of a narrative of victimization and pride in economic progress.

CANADA

Canadian nationalism, in contrast, had (and has) no ethnic basis and little military emphasis. In 1850, Canadians inhabited a handful of British colonies with two distinct ethnic and religious populations. In Quebec, especially in the countryside, almost everyone spoke French and followed the Catholic religion, a consequence of French colonization and settlement dating back to 1608. In what

are now the Maritime Provinces and Ontario, most people spoke English and were Protestants. The process of building a Canadian identity and nation took shape with Confederation in 1867, the fusing of the various colonies into a self-governing country through negotiations and an act of the British Parliament. The British North America Act reserved Canadian military and foreign affairs for Britain to control but left domestic matters to Canadians.

FIRST NATIONS AND ASSIMILATION The biggest challenge in creating a Canadian nation was reconciling differences between the Anglophone and Francophone communities—something Canada is still working on. Few Canadians had any intention of including First Nations, as the indigenous populations of Canada are now called, in their political community. For two centuries after European settlement, Canada's First Nations had slowly lost land in the east but lived alongside Euro-Canadians as trading partners in a very thinly populated landscape. Wars between France and Britain in North America, especially between 1756 and 1815, featured First Nations involvement, which in every case turned out badly for them. After those wars ceased, First Nations seemed to Euro-Canadians increasingly like obstacles to expansion rather than potential allies and trading partners.

By 1870, First Nation populations had fallen to a few tens of thousands through loss of land, malnutrition, and savage epidemics in the 1780s and 1830s. Through treaties in the 1870s, Canada confined First Nations to "reserves" that lacked good farmland. First Nations leaders accepted these treaties, in effect making them wards of the Canadian state, in order to obtain medicines, manufactured goods, and education for the young. A program of government-funded residential schools, normally run by Catholic or Protestant churches, aimed to assimilate First Nations into Canadian Anglophone or Francophone culture and, as it turned out, destroy children's indigenous identities. After 1894, attendance was compulsory for children between ages 7 and 16. Between the 1870s and 1970s, about 150,000 First Nations children attended these schools, intentionally isolated from the language and culture of their families, undergoing what Canadian governments now call cultural genocide. Before the 1950s, students died—of disease, hunger, abuse—at two to five times the rate of children in the general population. Yet many members of First Nations did assimilate to some extent; 6,000 volunteered for the armed forces in World War I. Creating Canadians was a harsh process for First Nations.

The great champion of Confederation and Canadian nationalism was a Scottish-born lawyer, John A. Macdonald, who beginning in 1867 served 19 years as prime minister. Despite a weakness for whiskey and bribes, he energetically sought to forge a nation from the newly confederated parts of Canada. He encouraged railroad building on a transcontinental scale and pursued a form of economic nationalism, trying to keep American imports to a minimum, to build a truly national economy. He favored the settlement of western farmlands as far as the Pacific. When some 350 Métis—French-speaking people of partly indigenous descent in Manitoba and Saskatchewan—decided they didn't want to be part of Canada, in what is called the North-West Rebellion (1885), Macdonald sent Canadian militia to crush them. He then insisted on the execution of Louis Riel, the charismatic Métis leader. By 1905, western and prairie regions had been organized into Canadian provinces, and the country stretched from the Atlantic to the Pacific.

CANADIAN NATIONALISM, BRITAIN, AND THE UNITED STATES The unintentional help of the colossus to the south helped make the idea of Canada work. Part of nationalism's appeal rested on fears that the United States might try to conquer Canada, using the giant army

Residential Schools Indigenous students attend class at a Catholic residential school in the Northwest Territories in northern Canada. The forced assimilation of First Nations people through the residential schools weakened their communities and cultures, with effects that persist to the present day. Several dozen recently discovered unmarked graves around some of these schools attest to the high mortality among children obliged to attend.

that had won the U.S. Civil War in 1865. Ragtag bands of Irish Americans called Fenians, mainly Civil War veterans, burned to right the wrongs Britain had done to Ireland: they invaded British Canada twice in 1866 and killed several Canadian militiamen. The U.S. purchase of Russian Alaska (1867) only added to Canadian concerns. Invasion fears subsided after 1871, when a hapless group of 35 Fenians misjudged the location of the border and attacked northern Minnesota by mistake.

But realistic anxieties about American economic and cultural power persisted, strengthening an often slender sense of national solidarity among Canadians. French Canadians, centered in Quebec, had since the eighteenth century harbored resentments about their absorption into the British Empire and into a Canada dominated politically and economically by Anglophones. When Britain expected Canadian money and men for distant wars, this came to a head and helped some French Canadians develop a defiantly Canadian, anti-British form of nationalism. So Canadian nationalism was—paradoxically enough—based on fears and resentments directed at the United States and Britain, Canada's closest cultural cousins and political allies. It was and is for the most part a civic nationalism crafted to overcome the ethnic and religious diversity characteristic of Canada from the outset.

GERMANY

German nationalism, like its Canadian equivalent, served to weld together a country. German nationalists fused many smaller political units together to make a new country, but at the same time they set Germany off from the larger cultural unit of German-speakers. Most Austrians and Swiss also spoke varieties of German, but they remained outside of Germany.

Like Japanese nationalism, German nationalism emphasized ethnic and linguistic solidarity. The notion of a common language involved more wishful thinking than it did in Japan. In 1800, the many forms of spoken German were often mutually unintelligible. Few people imagined a country uniting all Germans.

But when Bonaparte destroyed the Holy Roman Empire in 1806, he united several little German duchies and principalities into a rickety political structure called the Confederation of the Rhine. He then demanded soldiers and taxes, arousing fierce resentment and helping German-speakers to see their collective interest and identity more clearly. Parallel efforts following conquests by Bonaparte in Spain, Italy, the Netherlands, and elsewhere helped to inspire nationalisms in other regions of Europe. After Bonaparte's final defeat in 1815, some Germans tried and failed to unite Germany politically. But they did manage to establish a customs union called the *zollverein*—basically a free-trade zone—that gradually tightened the economic bonds among its members.

German cultural nationalism prospered too. Literature, music, and painting extolled the supposed special merits of Germanness, such as the canvas by Philipp Veit that presents Germany in the form of a medieval woman. German scholars and schoolmasters found inspiration in the hardihood and virtue of the wild Germanic tribes described by the ancient Roman author Tacitus, and they encouraged modern Germans to see themselves as a single people, descendants of the ancient tribes. As in Japan, in Germany some nationalists by 1880 understood German ethnicity as a matter of race. They argued that Germans stood superior to all other "races"—a view that, as we shall see, attracted more followers after 1918.

BISMARCK AND GERMAN UNIFICATION

The development of German nationalism and the political unification of Germany went hand in hand. Uprisings against princes and kings in 1848 briefly led to an all-German parliament and an effort by some of the urban middle classes to create a united German republic or at least a constitutional monarchy. Although the revolution failed and the principalities, dukedoms, and kingdoms of the German Confederation survived, the prospect of a united German nation proved inspirational. Soon the aristocrat and chancellor of Prussia (the biggest German state), Otto von Bismarck, saw a way to make nationalism serve his ends. In small wars and strong-armed negotiations, he fused patches of predominantly German-speaking lands to Prussia, creating a politically unified country by 1871. Bismarck deliberately left German-speaking Austria out of this union to ensure that his Prussia would dominate Germany. Ironically, in the process of unification Germany acquired minority populations who spoke Polish, Lithuanian, Danish, or French. They did not feel at all German, although with time many of their children did.

At every step, Bismarck encouraged the development of a German national identity, using the same tools—schools, army, press—as in France or Japan. Industrialization and urbanization helped put more people within reach of messages urging them to think of themselves as German rather than as, for example, Swabian or Silesian. Bismarck's version of German nationalism emphasized military virtues and promoted the army and navy as symbols of national strength. He and his successors encouraged Germans to think in terms of national greatness and geopolitical strength, which many Germans eagerly embraced until it brought their country to ruin in two world wars.

German Nationalism Philipp Veit's *Germania* (1848) imagined the German nation in the form of a beautiful woman in supposed medieval dress—appealing to a myth of a common ethnic German identity that stretched back centuries.

NATIONALISM AS A SOURCE OF STATE POWER

As these four examples show, there were many routes to nationalism and to a nation-state. Where ethnic, linguistic, and religious divisions were weak, and where a unified state already existed, as in Japan, nationalism was an easier project than in France, where nationalism was born of revolution and war. In Germany and Canada, deep Catholic-Protestant divisions proved an obstacle, and nationalist leaders such as Bismarck and Macdonald had to deploy formidable political skills to create a nation-state.

Nationalism could confer great power upon states. If people accepted the notion that they were, say, French, then a government of the French people could get tax revenues and military conscripts with less resistance than if people did not agree they were French. Nationalism helped justify bigger military budgets. Nationalism could discourage workers from calling strikes that would weaken the state. It could prepare people psychologically to let the state manage schooling of the young or use citizens' private property for railroad-building programs—both of which (schools and railroads) helped governments foster nationalism even more. Nationalism, in short, could make states much stronger, both with respect to their own citizens and against foreign countries. It reduced the difficulties of governing—as long as the state's citizens felt that they belonged to one nation and that the state championed the interests of the nation. Consequently, rulers in such states loved to encourage nationalism—and still do.

NATIONALISM AND MULTIETHNIC EMPIRES

Nationalism could also weaken states. The best examples were big multiethnic polities of the nineteenth century such as the Habsburg, Russian, or Ottoman Empires. These **multiethnic empires** all included many linguistic and religious groups, as well as millions of people who might be just as fluent speaking Czech as German or equally fluent in Turkish and Greek. Nationalists, although often educated and multilingual themselves, wanted people to declare themselves as members of one or another nation, and wanted separate states for each nation—or at least a state for their own nation.

THE HABSBURG EMPIRE The Habsburg Empire, dominated by German-speaking Austrians, comprised many ethnic minorities, including Hungarians, Czechs, Slovaks, Poles, Italians, Romanians, Serbs, and Croats, among others. Its multiethnic character made it especially vulnerable to nationalist divisions. After 1815, many members of these groups gradually concluded that they should be recognized as nations. They did not necessarily want to be fully independent but sought autonomy within the Habsburg framework, which the rulers—themselves mostly German-speaking Austrians—were slow to offer. So nationalistic minorities increasingly considered the imperial state an unjust yoke. Nationalist uprisings peppered the empire from 1848 onward. The Habsburgs responded with attempts to impose German in schools and for all official business, provoking more unrest.

Eventually, the Habsburgs relented and allowed more cultural expression and some political autonomy among certain minorities. In 1867, the historic kingdom of Hungary won independence except in military matters and foreign policy—a similar status to the one Canada achieved within the British Empire in the same year. The arrangement for Hungary incited other minorities who felt their nationality was just as worthy of special status.

Polish Nationalism in the Russian Empire A Polish painter depicts Polish nationalist rebels fighting Russian troops at an arsenal in Warsaw in November 1830, during the central battle of the Polish nationalist uprising of 1830–1831.

To compound matters, once Hungarians acquired power over their internal affairs, they ruthlessly repressed Romanians, Croats, and other minorities in their part of the empire. Habsburg efforts to counter minority nationalism and foster a unifying imperial identity yielded only modest results. Until its collapse in 1918, the Habsburg Empire struggled to contain minority nationalisms.

THE RUSSIAN EMPIRE The Russian Empire faced a similar problem. Although most of its subjects spoke Russian and adhered to the Russian Orthodox faith, it had a dozen or more sizeable ethnolinguistic groups and some religious minorities. Poland, as we have seen, was partitioned during the eighteenth century among Prussia, the Habsburg Empire, and Russia, leaving Poles with no country of their own. That circumstance led to a robust nationalism, at least among urban and educated Poles, creating a recurrent problem for Russia. Polish nationalism inspired major rebellions in the years 1830–1831 and 1863–1864. Ukrainians, who lived in both the Russian and Habsburg Empires, developed a cultural nationalism around language and history from the 1840s onward. Russian authorities tried to blunt Polish, Lithuanian, Ukrainian, and other nationalisms, often forbidding the use of these languages and imprisoning poets and professors. Such repressive measures, part of a general program of Russification, typically inflamed minority nationalist sentiment still further.

In Russia, religious divisions often strengthened minority nationalisms. In the first census (1897), some

70 percent of the tsar's subjects were counted as Russian Orthodox, which left roughly 40 million followers of minority religions. For most Poles, Catholicism was a sacred point of pride. In Finland and the Baltic provinces, Lutheranism was woven into people's sense of identity, as was the Armenian Apostolic Church for Armenians. In the western parts of the empire, the census showed Russia with more than 5 million Jews, few of whom identified strongly with the empire. The Caucasus and Central Asia were home to 14 million Muslims, who firmly resisted efforts at conversion to Russian Orthodoxy. The Russian Empire's promotion of Orthodoxy, which included banning several other religions, added to the irritation of religious minorities, providing them another reason to feel Polish, Estonian, Armenian, or Uzbek. As in the Habsburg Empire, in Russia the imperial state never found a way to subdue surging minority nationalisms.

THE OTTOMAN EMPIRE The multicultural and multiethnic Ottoman Empire also suffered from the rise of nationalisms. As in Russia, religious identities and national ones often bolstered one another. Muslims accounted for the great majority of Ottoman subjects—about 75 percent in 1906, the first year for which good census data exist. Some 14 percent were officially Greek Orthodox in religion, although not necessarily Greek in language or identity. In the nineteenth century, Greeks, Serbs, Romanians, Bulgarians, and other linguistic and religious minorities of the empire grew more restive, convinced that they constituted nations. They each had their own increasingly national form of Orthodox Christianity, with priests and bishops who occasionally stirred up nationalist sentiments. From the beginning of the nineteenth century, the Ottomans faced one rebellion after another in the Balkans, often led by graduates of French or German universities who had witnessed the impacts of nationalism and pined for national independence.

Although nationalist consciousness was mainly an elite concern, armed rebellions helped establish new nation-states such as Serbia (1829), Greece (1832), Romania (1878), and Bulgaria (1878). All were mainly Orthodox in religion, but with substantial Muslim minorities. All were keenly nationalistic at birth, eager to expand their territories so as to embrace all their "unredeemed brethren"—to use the language of the time. Arab nationalism was a worrisome sleeping giant for Ottoman authorities,

Grateful Hellas In 1858, Theodoros Vryzakis, whose father was hanged by Ottoman authorities at the outset of the Greek War of Independence in 1821, painted this canvas. Titled *Grateful Hellas*, it portrays Greece as a woman. Vryzakis studied art in Germany, where he might well have seen the 1848 painting *Germania* (on page 789), which offers a similarly romantic nationalist message. The surrounding faces here are of heroes from the Greek War of Independence.

because so much Ottoman territory—the Levant, the Arabian Peninsula, and much of what is now Iraq—was inhabited by Arabic-speakers. But into the early twentieth century, only a few intellectuals and merchants had developed much sense of Arab national identity.

In the early twentieth century, the Ottoman state increasingly turned to a policy of Turkification, broadly parallel to Russification. All branches of government were increasingly required to use only the Turkish language. Muslim minorities, such as Arabs and Kurds, were urged to consider themselves Turks. (Kurds are an ethnolinguistic group living in what is now southeastern Turkey, northeastern Syria, northern Iraq, and northwestern Iran.) Christian minorities, such as Armenians and Greeks living in Ottoman lands, were encouraged to convert to Islam and speak Turkish. Turkification brought scanty results and irritated many of those who were its targets—again, roughly parallel to Russification.

MINORITY NATIONALISMS The Russian and Ottoman empires became masters at meddling in one another's affairs by inciting minority nationalisms. Russia encouraged Greek, Serbian, and Bulgarian nationalisms, supporting publications, welcoming exiles, or supplying weapons for uprisings. To some extent, this policy rested on a shared Orthodox Christianity, but often it emerged from Russian geopolitical calculation. Russia's leaders hoped that vigorous minority nationalisms would weaken their historical foe. In turn, the Ottomans, especially after 1908, promoted nationalisms and Muslim identity among peoples of the Russian Empire in the Caucasus region and Central Asia. Britain and France, and eventually Germany too, meddled in Ottoman and Russian ethnic politics, at times encouraging nationalism among minorities. Nationalism provided a new weapon for geopolitical struggles, one that undermined multinational empires but not nation-states.

Minority nationalisms also made it difficult for multinational empires to allow subjects more political voice. The emperors and elites in the Habsburg, Russian, and Ottoman Empires feared—quite reasonably—that permitting more representative institutions would inflame ethnic passions and weaken their own grip on power. So they experimented with political reform, but only tentatively, and overall held fast to the principle of autocracy. Nation-states, in contrast, could, and did, enhance their popularity and legitimacy by allowing more citizen representation in politics—for example, by allowing more people to vote. In this way too, nationalism strengthened the hand of the state in Germany, France, and Japan, but weakened it in the multinational empires.

IMPERIALISM

Empires have existed for 44 centuries, ever since Sargon of Akkad in ancient Mesopotamia. For most of that time, they have been regarded as normal and natural. They could be large, like the fourteenth-century Mongol or the fifteenth-century Inka empires, but they usually comprised contiguous territories.

But in the sixteenth and seventeenth centuries, as we have seen, truly oceanic empires emerged with the Iberian conquests in the Americas. By 1700, the Atlantic European states—Portugal, Spain, France, the Netherlands, and Britain—all had substantial seaborne empires, held together by commerce and naval power. This marked the beginning of a new era in the long history of empire, one in which naval power and commercial dominance mattered as much as armies.

European overseas empires in 1830 covered about 6 percent of the Earth's land surface and held about 18 percent of its population. Then a surge of imperialism, mainly on the part of western Europeans and Japanese, changed the world's map as well as its politics, economy, cultures, and much else. By 1914, European and Japanese overseas empires controlled about 39 percent of the Earth's land surface and about 33 percent of its population.

Seaborne empires on which the sun never set now spanned the globe. Imperialism after 1870 was so pervasive, and different enough from what had come before, that historians often call it the **new imperialism**. They might better call it industrial-strength imperialism, because what made it so pervasive and different was, first and foremost, the industrialization of some parts of the world—western Europe, Japan, the United States—but not others. That created huge gaps in power and wealth, a situation that invited imperialist attitudes and actions.

TECHNOLOGIES AND IMPERIALISM

Just as the Americas were breaking free of European control (1776–1830), several European states were growing more powerful through the effects of industrialization and nationalism.

Industrial societies, Britain and France foremost among them, developed new technologies useful for building empires. Steamships, at first small, shallow-draft gunboats, proved excellent at projecting military power on coasts and up navigable rivers. They first saw duty quashing rebellions along the St. Lawrence River and the shores of Lake Ontario in Canada in 1837–1838. Over the next 50 years, gunboats chugged up and down the Niger, Ganges, Mekong, and Yangzi, helping Europeans trade, fight, and negotiate treaties on favorable terms. Steam-powered gunboats on the Waikato River gave British forces a major advantage in wars with Maori that led to the entrenchment of British rule in New Zealand. Big steam-powered oceangoing ships became practical

Industrial Empire An 1890 illustration advertises a steam-powered British gunboat, designed for use on inland waterways. New technologies such as steamships aided European empires' efforts to forcibly consolidate power and protect trade routes in overseas colonies.

in the 1870s, which cut transport times and permitted "sailing" routes independent of prevailing winds. That made it easier for industrial powers to quickly project military force overseas.

At least as important as industrial sea power were new, improved, and cheaper guns. Over the course of the nineteenth century, European and U.S. gun manufacturers multiplied the killing power of their products, ranging from pocket-sized pistols to large artillery pieces. This opened a chasm between the effectiveness of their armies and those of peoples without modern guns. While the Zulu of South Africa, the Maori of New Zealand, or the Lakota Sioux in North America could trade for guns, and learned to repair them, they did not have the capacity to mass-produce them. They could win occasional battles against industrial states, but not wars. As the British writer Hilaire Belloc put it in 1898, referring to an early version of a machine gun:

Whatever happens, we have got
The Maxim gun, and they have not.

The couplet captured the gulf in military technology between the armies of European imperialists and the forces arrayed against them in Africa or Asia.

Other new technologies further widened that gulf. The telegraph, in use from the 1840s, radically cut the time needed to transmit messages over long distance. After 1870, the British government could exchange messages with its representatives in India in five hours instead of five months. Over the next 30 years, Britain laid submarine telegraph cables across the world's oceans, linking its empire in a communications web far superior to anything available to anyone else. Aspiring imperial powers tried to imitate Britain's network. For military and commercial purposes, the telegraph was a crucial tool of imperialism.

So was a growing ability to check the ravages of malaria through the mass production of a drug, quinine. Use of quinine, extracted from the bark of a tropical tree called

Military Technology British marines stationed in South Africa at the end of the nineteenth century demonstrate the use of a Maxim machine gun, which proved effective in wars of imperial conquest in Africa, including Hermann von Wissmann's campaign to establish German rule in East Africa.

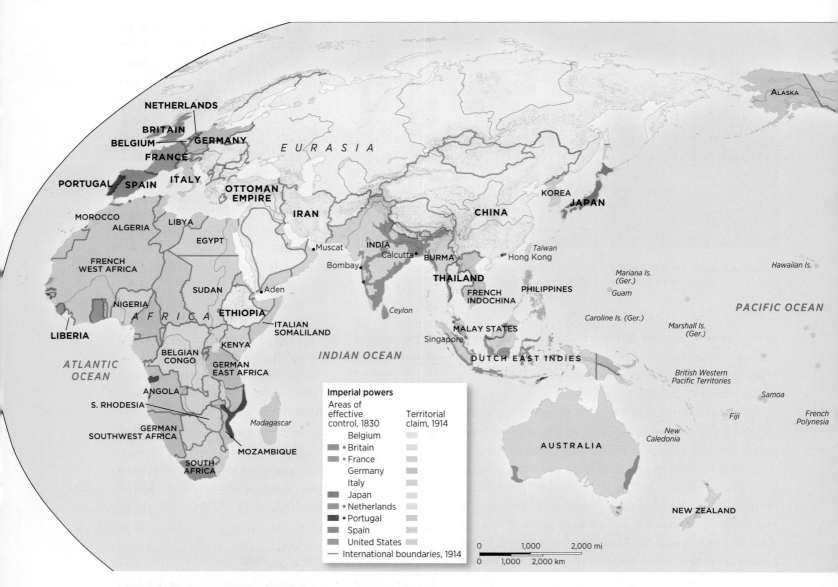

Colonial Empires in 1830 and 1914 Between 1830 and 1914, European powers, the United States, and Japan acquired the capacity to extend or create colonial empires cheaply. That capacity depended largely on industrial strength and the ability to mass-produce weaponry, steamships, quinine, and other tools of empire.

cinchona, dates back centuries. Malaria had long menaced people from malaria-free zones who tried to visit, let alone conquer and occupy, most of Africa, South Asia, and Southeast Asia. People born and raised in malarial lands, on the other hand, usually carried strong resistance to the disease. But quinine, mass-produced by the 1850s, could make anyone resistant. Chemical industries capable of mass-producing quinine, together with ships, guns, and telegraph networks, were all part of the surge in power that industrialization afforded to a handful of societies in the nineteenth century.

NATIONALISM IN SUPPORT OF IMPERIALISM

If industrialization provided new hardware suited to empire building, nationalism offered new popular support. Nationalism contributed to the capacity of states such as Britain, France, Japan, and Germany to indulge in imperialism. The same held for Italy, unified by committed nationalists by 1870 and eagerly imperialist by the 1890s. All cases of imperialism enabled by modern industry were supported by populations fired by nationalism.

From about 1500 onward, European states had competed with one another overseas, mainly in the Americas. Now, in the nineteenth century, with growing global connections, they did so everywhere else—in Africa, Asia, and the archipelagoes of the Pacific. European statesmen came to think in terms of global competition. With nationalistic journalists, business lobbies, and religious establishments all urging action lest their country be left behind, governments sometimes leapt into imperial ventures without much idea of what they were getting into.

This particular motive, geopolitical rivalry, proved strong in the case of Germany. It had no tradition of overseas empire when Bismarck came to power in the newly unified state in 1871. By the 1880s, however, Germany, pushed by nationalistic lobbies, competed for influence and territory in Africa and the Pacific, plunging into imperial ventures for fear that its rivals were getting ahead. Russia and Britain waded deeper into Central Asia after 1870 mainly to prevent the other from dominating it.

CULTURES OF IMPERIALISM

Nationalism and imperialism fed off each other. Nationalistic feeling made it easier for people to support imperialism; at the same time, successful imperialism made many people feel more nationalistic. The British in particular developed a sense of themselves as an imperial people, fit to rule over others, and gradually wove that self-image into their culture. In the later nineteenth century and well into the twentieth, they created celebratory literature, theater, music, public ceremonies, honors, and medals—in short, a **culture of imperialism**. It helped them feel more British, as opposed to merely English, Scottish, Welsh, or Irish. It helped them take pride in their country, as opposed to focusing on their social class or religion. And it helped them support a more nationalistic British policy.

In the 1870s, the British even invented a new word for a particularly pushy foreign policy based on faith in one's own superiority: jingoism. It came from a popular ditty sung in pubs, the refrain to which went:

> We don't want to fight but by Jingo if we do
> We've got the ships, we've got the men, we've got the money too . . .

Rudyard Kipling was an influential exponent of this British culture of imperialism. His poetry, short stories,

This support often took the form of an ideology that explicitly justified imperialism. The French developed the *mission civilisatrice* ("civilizing mission") according to which it was France's special destiny to bring civilization—Christianity, sanitation, antislavery, self-discipline, and so forth—to peoples of the world who lacked it. Such an outlook helped to legitimize the human and financial costs of conquests. Every other imperial power created some version of the same self-serving ideology, according to which their nation must shoulder the moral obligation—rarely met in practice—to lift up downtrodden and often darker-skinned masses in Africa or Asia through imperial rule.

Nationalism promoted imperialism in another important way: through the geopolitical logic of imperial rivalry.

and novels were extremely popular in his day, and are still read—and made into movies—more than a century later. Kipling, who was born in India and spent much of his life there, wholeheartedly endorsed British imperialism. He emphasized the duty of racially superior peoples (as he saw it) to rule the rest in his 1899 poem "The White Man's Burden," which begins this way:

> Take up the White Man's burden—
> Send forth the best ye breed—
> Go bind your sons to exile
> To serve your captives' need
> To wait in heavy harness
> On fluttered folk and wild—
> Your new-caught, sullen peoples,
> Half devil and half child.

The first step towards lightening

The White Man's Burden

is through teaching the virtues of cleanliness.

Pears' Soap

Popular Imperialism Late nineteenth-century British advertising and popular culture often appealed to imperialist and nationalist sentiment. This advertisement references Kipling's poem "The White Man's Burden" and the idea of the civilizing mission in order to sell soap.

The culture of imperialism and confidence in national fitness to rule over others developed as strongly in Britain as anywhere. But to a lesser extent, it existed by the 1880s in the United States, France, Germany, Italy—and was developing rapidly in Japan.

SOCIAL DARWINISM AND PSEUDOSCIENTIFIC RACISM The European, U.S., and to some extent Japanese cultures of imperialism drew strength from three particular late nineteenth-century trends. One was pseudoscientific racism. In 1859, Charles Darwin published his masterwork on biological evolution through natural selection, *The Origin of Species,* with its emphasis on competition and the survival of the fittest. Others soon extended his concepts to subsets of the human species in a doctrine now called **social Darwinism**, which held that some people—usually either nationalities or "races," but sometimes socioeconomic classes—were more fit, in Darwin's sense, than others. If Europeans and their biological descendants in North America, South America, South Africa, Australia, and New Zealand were economically and militarily successful, the thinking ran, it was ultimately because they were a superior breed of human, fit and foreordained to rule the rest of humankind—all inferiors. A British viceroy of India, Lord Curzon, in 1900 wrote, "All the millions I have to manage are less than schoolchildren." Sometimes Europeans and their descendants around the world thought that white people in general formed an inherently superior "race." But especially in Germany and Britain, the notion of a superior breed of human suited for imperial rule was often applied to a single nationality understood to be a "race." Cecil Rhodes, an English business magnate and politician who made a fortune in South Africa, put it confidently in 1877:

> I contend that we are the finest race in the world and that the more of the world we inhabit the better it is for the human race. . . . Africa is still lying ready for us it is our duty to take it. . . . It is our duty to seize every opportunity of acquiring more territory and we should keep this one idea steadily before our eyes that more territory simply means more of the Anglo-Saxon race, more of the best, the most human, most honorable race the world possesses.

Social Darwinism and pseudoscientific racism proved especially popular in Germany, the United States, Britain, and the British dominions of Australia, New Zealand, South Africa, and Canada. The supposedly unfit breeds of humankind included all Africans, Asians, and indigenous peoples and usually Europeans such as Slavs, Greeks, Italians, Jews, and Irish.

At the same time, Japanese intellectuals developed their own version of social Darwinism. A prolific professor and colonial official, Nitobe Inazo, who had studied at U.S. and German universities, justified Japanese imperialism by arguing that Koreans were not suited to self-government and it was Japan's responsibility to bring modern civilization to Korea. Japanese intellectuals adapted social Darwinism to encourage the belief that the Japanese were a distinct biological race, inherently superior to Koreans and Chinese—if not everyone else too.

Disdain for other peoples is of course routine in world history. Chinese and Mongols typically considered one another inferior, as did French and Germans. Rival religious groups regularly vilified one another. What was different about social Darwinism was its resort to science for supposed proof of the notion that humankind is composed of biologically distinct races, of which some are better than others. That gave pseudoscientific racism a seemingly impressive intellectual basis for nearly a century, but in the end made it brittle because it was susceptible to scientific disproof via genetics. Racism flourishes on every continent today, but it no longer appeals to science.

CONCEPTS OF MANLINESS AND MUSCULAR CHRISTIANITY Beyond social Darwinism, the culture of imperialism also drew upon anxieties about manliness. In industrializing and urbanizing societies such as Japan, Britain, Germany, France, and the United States, some people came to think men now spent too much time doing unchallenging chores at desks or workbenches. They were growing soft, losing their resourcefulness and hardihood. It seemed less worrisome if women lacked these qualities because they were not considered suitably feminine virtues. Challenging duties in the great outdoors might prevent the enfeeblement of males, and so conquest and empire were, so to speak, a cure for this societal disease. The U.S. president Theodore Roosevelt was among the more eloquent spokesmen for this anxious view, and he dedicated himself to restoring to American men a suitable vigor and valor.

Muscular Christianity A 1900 photograph shows a French Pères Blancs missionary preaching in what is now Mali.

Curing a loss of manliness could go hand in hand with advancing the cause of one's preferred religion. The culture of imperialism also drew upon developments within European and North American Christianity in the nineteenth century—specifically, the advent of what was called muscular Christianity. The phrase became common by the 1870s, embraced by Protestants and Catholics alike as an ideal. Roosevelt was one among many advocates in the United States. Britons, Germans, and French had their own versions. The best places to exhibit muscular Christianity were distant, physically challenging lands such as Africa, where, amid hardships, certain disciplined, forceful, and energetic men might spread the gospel. Christian missionary societies enjoyed unprecedented support in the late nineteenth century, typically working within the frameworks of one or another empire. New ones, such as France's Pères Blancs ("White Fathers"), were founded to focus on Africa. Muscular Christianity wasn't confined to missionaries. Soldiers could exemplify it too. A British author in 1901 delighted in "the Englishman going through the world with rifle in one hand and Bible in the other."

INTELLECTUAL RESPONSES The culture of imperialism provoked a variety of intellectual responses in Africa and Asia, including everything from self-doubt to defiance. An anti-colonial politician from the Dutch East

Indies, E.F.E. Douwes Dekker (also known as Setyabudi), noted the psychological impacts of the culture of imperialism in 1912: "There is nothing we need so much as self-assurance... we must feel... a strong sense of our own worth, a realization that we are not inferior to anybody." In an assessment written in 1950, Aimé Césaire, a poet and essayist from Martinique, wrote of colonized people around the world: "I am talking about millions of men in whom fear has been cunningly instilled, who have been taught to have an inferiority complex, to tremble, kneel, despair." As we shall see in Chapter 27, colonized peoples in the course of the twentieth century rebuked the culture of imperialism in winning independence.

Industrialization, nationalism, and cultures of imperialism, in varying mixtures, created strong coalitions in favor of imperialism in western Europe and Japan, and a modest one in the United States. But the main incentive for the so-called new imperialism was simply that by 1870, for a handful of countries, Britain first and foremost, industrialization, supplemented by nationalism, made imperialism increasingly cheap and easy. So it was both more practical and tempting.

THE BRITISH IN INDIA, 1818–1914

Britain focused its imperial efforts primarily on South Asia—all of which was generally called India. British influence in India remained largely in the hands of the East India Company, or EIC, which held a monopoly on external trade and maintained its own armed forces. The EIC had conquered small parts of India beginning in the 1750s, even before Britain's Industrial Revolution. In the early nineteenth century, it acquired much more territory and power through war and diplomacy, leaving it in control of most of India by 1818. Meanwhile, the British Crown took Ceylon in 1815 and parts of Burma starting in 1824, among other territories. Then, after a major uprising and civil war in India in 1857–1858 (discussed in the next chapter), the British state terminated both the once-mighty Mughal Empire and the EIC, and in 1858 claimed control over most of India. Nearly 600 "princely states" remained, which had formerly paid tribute to either the Mughals or the EIC. They were all militarily weak, and their rulers had to bend to British wishes on every important matter, even though Britain did not rule them directly.

British Rule in India During the Indian Rebellion of 1857–1858, Sikhs, like these infantrymen, stayed loyal to Britain. The common imperial policy of divide and rule worked well in India.

The princes, variously called *rajputs, maharajas, nawabs, sultans,* or *emirs,* were part of the local elite through which Britain ruled. In 1880, the ratio of Britons to Indians in India was only about 1 to 250,000. The large standing army of British India consisted overwhelmingly of Indians, called *sepoys,* who enforced British rule. So, of necessity, British rule relied on the cooperation of Indian elites, including princes, big landowners, and the religious authorities of both Hinduism and Islam. For these men (and they were all men), British rule—sometimes called the **British Raj**—offered many advantages, helping to firm up their authority, including the property rights of landowners. But it brought frustrations too, as when, despite their distinguished ancestry, great wealth, or deep learning, they were treated as inferior beings by—as they saw it—ignorant commoners without princely blood whose only distinction was being British.

IMPERIAL STRATEGY: DIVIDE AND RULE In addition to finding willing partners among the elite, British rule relied on divisions in South Asian societies. All imperial states practiced the policy of divide and rule; five aspects of India's diversity made this policy especially effective there. First, India had been politically fragmented since the decline of the Mughal Empire in the early eighteenth century. Second, India, although mainly Hindu in religion, had large Muslim, Buddhist, and Sikh minorities. Third, within the Hindu majority, longstanding caste identities discouraged people from making common cause. Fourth, Indians spoke hundreds of different languages and wrote in several different scripts. And fifth, British authorities recognized certain groups in India as "martial races," such as Sikhs or the hill peoples of Nepal called Gurkhas, suitable for army and police work. Men from the "martial races" were encouraged to see themselves as better than others and to sign up for duty controlling other Indians on behalf of the British Raj. Only by learning—partly from Mughal examples—to exploit these divisions could 140,000 Britons in India (as of 1900) dominate 300 million Indians. The ratio of ruled to colonial rulers was more than 2,100:1.

ECONOMIC EFFECTS   In 1840, John Sullivan, an official of the EIC, wrote: "The Englishman flourishes, and acts like a sponge, drawing up riches from the banks of the Ganges, and squeezing them down upon the banks of the Thames." Yet British rule in India had limited economic effect on the bulk of the people. Roughly 80 percent were peasants, raising rice or wheat for their families and village markets. Their yields were among the world's lowest, their risk of crop failure and famine, usually from droughts, among the world's highest. British rule affected their routines only rarely before 1914, even if some of them now paid taxes and rents to British, rather than Indian, officials. A big exception came during a major famine in the years 1876–1878, when colonial policy prioritized grain exports over relief efforts, contributing to the death of 5 to 6 million Indians.

British rule made a much bigger difference for those Indians in cities or connected to export agriculture, and for the long-term direction of India's economy as a whole. Beginning in the 1840s, British engineers laid out thousands of miles of railroads and upgraded port facilities. The new infrastructure helped extend the domain of market relations into Indian society. Together with British efforts to standardize law throughout India, and the spread of English as a common language, the new infrastructure promoted market integration within India and the integration of Indian markets with those elsewhere in the British Empire. Many Indian merchants and landowners took advantage of these market opportunities. The politician Jawaharlal Nehru expressed the ambivalence that many other Indians felt about the infrastructure acquired under the Raj: "I am all in favor of . . . the latest methods of transport, but . . . as I rushed across the Indian plains, the railway, that life-giver, has almost seemed to me like iron bands confining and imprisoning India." Overall, the Indian economy grew slowly under British rule.

The biggest change in economic life under the Raj resulted from the policy of free trade, both within the empire and with the world at large. As Chapter 21 explained, that proved devastating in the short run for Indian weavers and cloth manufacturers, who could not compete against the mass production of British factories. For decades, India's economy shifted in the direction of raw material production, typically of fibers such as cotton and jute—jute fiber is used to make burlap bags for transporting commodities such as rice and cotton. By the 1870s, however, Indian and British businessmen in the leading cities of Bombay and Calcutta (now Mumbai and Kolkata) began to build textile mills; and for a while, until the rise of the Japanese cotton industry by 1900, they did very well selling to China. Jamsetji Tata, for example, from the Parsi religious minority in Gujarat, made a fortune in cotton exports, and in 1907 his heirs started India's most successful steel business. This pattern, in which some found ways to profit handsomely from the changes brought by imperialism while the bulk of the population did not, proved characteristic of modern empires as a whole.

For its economic contributions, its military manpower, and its strategic position in the Indian Ocean world, India remained the jewel in the crown of the British Empire. How Indians reacted to, and ultimately overthrew, British rule is taken up in later chapters

THE FRENCH IN ALGERIA, 1830–1914

Algeria was as important to France as India was to Britain. Located in the Maghreb region of North Africa, Algeria was overwhelmingly Sunni Muslim in religion and mainly Arabic-speaking. It had been loosely governed by Ottoman sultans since 1516 but in practice ruled since 1710 by local authorities called *deys*. Several of the deys practiced piracy and the ransoming of Christian captives, attracting angry attention from French officials. Disputes over debts and ransoms, and an alleged insult to a French diplomat in Algiers, triggered a French assault on Algeria beginning in 1830. In the coming decades, Algeria became—officially—part of France, although in all but

Algiers Cathedral This colorized photograph from 1899 shows the Catholic cathedral of Algiers. Its architecture blends traditional Islamic and Christian features. Its visitors, however, would have overwhelmingly been European colons, because very few Muslim Algerians converted to Catholicism.

name it was a colony. Boatloads of European settlers, Italian and Spanish as well as French, flooded in. The French army pushed the locals off the best lands, sometimes with ruthless violence, turning them over to settlers—called *colons* in French North Africa. The big cities, such as Algiers and Oran, soon had more colons than Muslim Algerians. The Muslim Algerian population fell during the early decades of French rule, the result of dispossession, disease, and violence. It recovered to about 3 million in 1862 and 4 million in 1900. The colons numbered 650,000 by 1900.

The French conquest initially provoked violent rebellions. The biggest, led by a Sufi scholar named **Abdelkadir**, won over most of Algeria in the 1830s. But when the full force of the French military was brought to bear, Abdelkadir's uprising ended in his capture and exile in 1847. Another rebellion in 1871 lasted a few months, after which French rule remained secure, although punctuated by small-scale violence, until the 1950s.

COLONS AND FRENCH RULE With hundreds of thousands of colons living in the cities and on the best lands, French rule relied less on a cooperative local elite than did British control in India. Nevertheless, cultivating cooperation was a useful imperial strategy everywhere, and the French worked hard at it. They claimed to be civilizing Algeria and encouraged Algerians to embrace French language and culture, and to accept Christianity. Those who did so could become French citizens. Many learned French, but only about 3,000 abandoned Islam.

Like every other imperial power, the French in Algeria followed the strategy of divide and rule. Dealing with an overwhelmingly Muslim population, the French exploited distinctions based on language between Arabic-speakers (about 75 percent) and Berber-speakers (25 percent). Berber is a language, or set of languages, long spoken in North Africa, but since the arrival of Arabs in the eighth century

mainly confined to mountainous areas. The French also played up more local tribal identities among both Arabs and Berbers, and, like the British in India, recruited some groups reputed to be warlike—such as the highlanders known as Zwawa or Zouaves—for army and police duty. This strategy of divide and rule helped France to maintain control until the 1950s.

ECONOMIC IMPACT The economic impact of French imperialism in Algeria was considerable. The colons by and large did better than they could have hoped for had they stayed in Europe. A few Algerians who worked with the French also found rewarding niches in the new imperial economy. The majority of Algerians found little or no economic benefit in French rule, especially the peasants and herders who lost their land and the weavers suddenly

French Expansion in North Africa, 1830–1914 Beginning in 1830, Algeria was conquered by France and became its most important overseas possession. Algerians resisted militarily in the 1830s and 1840s, and again in an uprising in 1871. But French power advanced steadily southward, extending well into the Sahara desert by 1900.

put in direct competition with power looms in French industrial cities. The size of Algeria's economy grew considerably under French rule, but the redistribution of land and wealth away from Muslim Algerians and toward colons was more conspicuous—and accounts for the vigor of Algerians' resistance and their later efforts to overthrow colonial rule, discussed in Chapter 27.

FORMS OF IMPERIALISM: SETTLER COLONIES

Algeria and India exemplify an important contrast in modern imperialism: colonies with settlers and those without. Algeria was a **settler colony**. Its European population varied between 10 percent and 30 percent of the total. French policy put settler interests foremost, but not always fully to their satisfaction. The colons often wanted yet more land and more restrictions placed on Muslim Algerians. The authorities in Paris, and French officials in Algeria, did not always agree with the colons. The situation resembled that in British North America before the American Revolution, when colonists wanted to take more indigenous land and officials in London did not fully cooperate. Settler colonies always featured conflicts over land, and consequently more violence, than those without settlers. In addition to Algeria, the best examples of settler colonies—after the independence of the Americas—include Australia, New Zealand, South Africa, and to a lesser extent Morocco, Kenya, and Southern Rhodesia (now Zimbabwe). Japan's colonial empire, discussed below, also featured partial settler colonies.

Australia, New Zealand, and Canada were settler colonies, but with a big difference. Unlike the situation in Africa or East Asia, in these lands the indigenous populations were, as we've seen, drastically reduced in numbers by disease and violence. They were driven off not just the best lands, but almost all productive lands, and in the nineteenth century they were swamped demographically by European settlers. With such a small proportion of indigenous people left in the population in these colonies, almost everyone, except the French in Quebec, traced their ancestry to Britain and had kinfolk there. These ties enabled Australia, New Zealand and Canada to negotiate more and more self-government and autonomy, beginning in the 1840s. Canada, as we saw earlier

in this chapter, won substantial independence at Confederation in 1867. Australia achieved much the same in 1900, when several colonies united in what Australians call Federation. Both Canada and Australia became fully self-governing in 1931. New Zealand's transition from colony to nation had many little steps, spanning the period 1852–1947, and nothing comparable to Confederation or Federation. These were settler colonies that, in the heyday of imperialism, stopped being colonies—but only because their populations had become predominantly British and therefore were judged capable of self-rule by authorities in London.

India, in contrast, attracted very few European settlers. Malaria and other dangerous diseases discouraged migration, and so did the absence of free land. Other destinations, especially North America, appealed more to potential migrants. The British presence in India, therefore, was mainly administrative and military. Almost no expropriation of land took place. During the period of industrial imperialism, roughly 1850–1960, the majority of colonies around the world were, like India, exploited economically but scarcely settled by colonizing populations. Almost all African colonies fell into that category.

THE PARTITION AND CONQUEST OF AFRICA, 1874–1914

In 1870, sub-Saharan Africa remained extremely diverse politically. Many people lived in kin groups without any state ruling them. Some lived in small statelets, others in full-blown states with kings, taxes, and armies. A few lived in small imperial states, such as the Zulu kingdom in South Africa. The only places not under African control were southernmost South Africa, British since 1815; the thinly administered Portuguese colonies of Angola and Mozambique; and a few small coastal outposts.

THE BERLIN CONFERENCE Between 1874 and 1890, European powers carried out the **partition of Africa** among themselves. At first it was a haphazard process in which European states unilaterally claimed chunks of African territory, often merely to prevent a rival from seizing them. But in the years 1884–1885, at Bismarck's insistence, European diplomats gathered at the so-called Berlin Conference and agreed on who should get which territories. They also agreed to ban trading in slaves, guns,

Berlin Conference An 1885 French cartoon shows delegates to the Berlin Conference as the German chancellor, Otto von Bismarck, slices a cake—representing the cavalier way in which Bismarck proposed to carve up Africa among the European powers.

and alcohol in their territories. The first agreement held up better than the second.

MILITARY CONQUEST AND CATTLE DISEASE

Once these six powers had carved up Africa on the map, they set about conquering it on the ground. For centuries, African militaries, combined with a lethal disease environment, had kept outsiders at bay except in the far north and far south of the continent. From the 1870s, however, armies working for European states increasingly fared well in battle in Africa. Improved medicine and guns—and in the case of Britain, the availability of Indian troops—all helped to change the military balance. The bigger and more militarized African states might win major battles against European forces now and again, as the Zulu kingdom (1879) and Ethiopia (1896) did, but the tide had turned very quickly in favor of Europe's armies. Those armies were led, trained, and equipped by Europeans. The rank-and-file soldiers were overwhelmingly Africans. So, in a sense, African soldiers in the service of European states conquered Africa. It took until about 1914.

As in the conquest of the Americas centuries before, European imperialists in late nineteenth-century Africa

had an extraordinarily powerful ally in the form of disease—in this case, a cattle disease. Rinderpest broke loose in Asia in the 1860s and 1870s and arrived in East Africa from India in 1889. Over the next 12 to 15 years, in many regions it killed as much as 95 percent of the cattle and some goats, sheep, and wildlife too. The plague extended from the savannas of East and southern Africa to the Sahel in West Africa. Cattle were the main form of wealth in these lands and a major source of food. Millions of Africans starved to death in the 1890s. In the pastoral and farming societies of East and southern Africa, men had to accumulate cattle before they could hope to marry. With rinderpest rippling throughout the continent, this became a forlorn hope. For many young men, serving as a soldier and helping to conquer Africa on behalf of colonial armies was the best remaining option.

The rinderpest plague stands among the greatest disasters in modern African history. It made European conquest much easier, as Lord Frederick Lugard, a leading British empire builder, recognized: "[Rinderpest] has favored our enterprise. Powerful and warlike as the pastoral tribes are, their pride has been humbled and our progress facilitated by this awful visitation." Indeed, one wonders: Would European societies have willingly paid the price in blood and treasure for colonization that African resistance—without rinderpest—would have exacted?

Even as rinderpest sapped the will and capacity of Africans to resist conquest, armed opposition and rebellions flickered on and off for two decades. In the West African

Conquest and Disease South African settler colonists stand in a field strewn with cattle carcasses in 1897 during the rinderpest outbreak. They have shot the infected animals to prevent transmission of the disease, whose economic effects were felt much more harshly by native South African farmers than by settlers.

Sahel, local rulers fought off French authority until 1898. In what is now Zimbabwe, armed resistance to British rule lasted until 1897. In German Southwest Africa (Namibia today) in the years 1904–1905, rebellion brought especially vicious responses—sometimes labeled genocide—almost obliterating a people called the Herero. As we will see, in Ethiopia, African armies succeeded in fending off colonialism. Elsewhere in Africa, however, by 1914, armed resistance had faded away, and opposition to colonialism took other forms.

COLONIAL AFRICA TO 1930

Colonial states in Africa were threadbare and flimsy. Governments in Europe did not wish to invest in infrastructure, education, or almost anything else for Africans. Neither did private businesses, except where mining was involved. So, until the late 1940s, African colonies did not get much in the way of roads or railroads, except lines connecting mines to ports. They got only rudimentary schools, generally run by missionaries. At times, colonial officials restricted the educational work of missionaries, fearing it would raise the hopes and skills of Africans so much that they would become harder to rule. The colonial court systems were also threadbare, with the administration of justice entrusted to favored African elders.

Imperial power in colonial Africa worked through local elites. The strategy was generally to find cooperative Africans and enhance their authority. This normally meant empowering male elders; making them responsible for organizing labor brigades, tax collection, and military conscription; and rewarding them when they did so. Machemba, the Yao leader in Tanganyika with whom this chapter began, refused just such an offer.

Colonial rule also relied on large lineage and language groups, labeled tribes. By assigning tribal identity to everyone, whether or not they considered themselves Xhosa, Masai, Hausa, and so forth, colonial administrators emphasized social divisions, making colonial rule easier. Such identities existed to some extent before colonial rule in Africa, but because they suited administrative needs, colonial rulers generally tried—and succeeded in—strengthening them. In particular, colonial authorities found it useful to recruit soldiers and police from among those groups they regarded as "martial tribes," such as Bambara-speakers in what is now Mali or Kamba in east-central Kenya. This recruitment policy, pioneered by the British state in its approach to clans in Scotland and refined in India, encouraged some—males, at least—to prize their distinction from nonmartial, lesser peoples.

ECONOMIC EXPLOITATION The economic approach of the imperial powers, at least until the 1930s, was ruthlessly extractive. They intended to make money from mining or commercial agriculture. Each colony was to pay for its own administration and ideally contribute revenue to its colonizer. Monetized, taxable economic activity such as commercial farming helped attain this goal; subsistence farming or herding did not. In West Africa, colonial rulers encouraged cocoa, palm oil, peanuts, cotton, and other cash crops. In South Africa and the copper belt of central Africa, colonial authorities invited private companies to develop mining and offered to provide migrant workers for the mines by organizing labor recruitment drives. In South Africa, that sometimes required recruiting young men from hundreds of miles away, housing them in barracks, and policing them carefully.

In the Congo, where Belgium's King Leopold II claimed a personal fiefdom, economic extraction took a notoriously brutal form. Private companies paid the king for the right to harvest rubber from the forests, with no

Imperial Economies A photograph from the 1920s shows workers laboring in a tin mine in British Nigeria. Mining was the foremost extractive industry in colonial Africa.

constraints on how they did it. They relied on forced labor and created a police force encouraged to kill men who refused to collect rubber. Sometimes they held women hostage until their husbands brought in enough rubber. In one case, 55 women were hanged because their husbands did not meet a production quota. The Belgian parliament considered the abuses sufficient to take control of the Congo away from the king in 1908.

Supporters of imperialism cloaked this economic exploitation in altruism. Confident in the righteousness of their religion and the superiority of their culture, colonial rulers convinced themselves and their publics back home that imperialism was good for Africans and Asians. Britain's secretary of state for colonies in 1897, Joseph Chamberlain (the former Birmingham industrialist we encountered earlier), voiced this conviction: "We now feel that our rule over these territories [British colonies in Africa and Asia] can only be justified if we can show that it adds to the happiness and prosperity of the people, and I maintain that our rule does." Chamberlain, and tens of millions of others in Europe, sincerely believed in the uplifting effect of colonial rule. Few Africans agreed.

CHRISTIANITY IN AFRICA Many Europeans counted Christianity as the primary blessing conferred by colonial rule. As we've seen, Christianity had ancient roots in Ethiopia and won many converts in Portuguese-influenced Angola after 1500. But elsewhere in Africa it figured little, if at all. In 1900, about 6 to 9 million Africans, of a total population of 80 to 90 million, considered themselves Christians. By 1930, missionary work and the spread of hundreds of independent African churches had boosted the Christian population to about 20 million. (Today, African Christians number about 400 million.)

By 1910, some 10,000 Christian missionaries—Catholics and at least 10 varieties of Protestants—were at work in Africa. Their most lasting impact came through mission schools, which attracted Africans who wanted to learn to read and write, and perhaps get a post in the colonial bureaucracy. Instruction in literacy came with instruction in Christianity. Enslaved people, women, poor men, refugees from wars, and the young were especially likely to embrace Christianity. In most African societies, young men had to prove themselves before they could hope to marry and take fully adult roles, while older and richer men could marry several women. Christian missionaries denounced polygamy and, through literacy, offered the hope of rapid

Missionaries in Africa A German nun teaches reading and writing to children enrolled at a mission school in South Africa in this 1912 photo. Mission schools were one of the most visible presences of Christianity—and of European power and cultural influence—in colonial Africa.

advancement to younger men. For young women who preferred to marry someone of their own generation, it offered hope too. In some respects, the success of mission Christianity was a youth revolt against the authority of African male elders.

Many Africans joined independent churches outside of missionary control. Interactions with missionaries under colonialism inspired novel versions of Christianity. Some independent churches accepted polygamy, which mission churches never could. Some promised to counter the evils of witchcraft and sorcery, in which most Africans believed, whereas mission churches denied such malevolent powers existed. Some offered rewarding roles for women as spiritual leaders and faith healers. And all emphasized certain sides of the Christian tradition that spoke to millions of Africans, such as healing the sick. In some respects, the success of independent churches was a revolt against missionary control over Christianity and against colonialism in general. The most successful independent churches developed in Nigeria, South Africa, and the Belgian Congo.

The Aladura churches in Nigeria took shape during the 1918 influenza epidemic. A young Anglican schoolteacher, Sophie Odunlami, had a vision in which God told her that faith alone could heal the sick. She and others began to preach against traditional African religions, polygamy, and European medicine, claiming healing powers through God and blessed water. Within a decade, they gathered disciples and thousands of followers who set up churches.

In South Africa, the most popular independent churches were those called Zionist. They followed the teachings of faith healers from Zion, Illinois (a northern suburb of Chicago), notably John Lake. Lake moved to South Africa in 1908 to escape the wrath of parishioners after an attempted exorcism left two dead. His preaching skills brought him followers who quickly organized several Zionist churches. Migrant workers in South Africa's mines carried African Zionist faith and practices back to their home villages all over southern Africa.

The most enduring of the independent African churches arose in the Belgian Congo. **Simon Kimbangu**, raised at a Baptist mission in western Congo, felt called as a prophet in 1921, and followers credited him with many healing miracles at a time when epidemics were ravaging central Africa. His popular preaching quickly aroused suspicions among Belgian authorities, who imprisoned him for the last 30 years of his life. But disciples spread his message of faith healing, nonviolence, monogamy, and sobriety—and added their own notions of Kimbangu's divinity and the injustice of Belgian rule. By the end of the colonial era in 1960, half a million people had embraced Kimbanguism (as do roughly 20 million today). Independent churches—the Africanization of Christianity in the context of the partial Christianization of Africa—constituted the most important and enduring cultural response to colonialism in Africa.

ISLAM IN AFRICA Islam, like Christianity, prospered as a result of colonial rule. As we've seen, Islam also had deep roots in the northern half of Africa. Colonial rulers often found prestigious Muslim clerics useful in their efforts to control subject populations. French authorities in Senegal supported Malik Sy, who in 1902 set up a *zawiya* (as Islamic schools are called in West Africa) and urged his fellow Muslims to accept French rule and to serve in the French army. Colonial rule inadvertently promoted Islam. Village families often could not pay taxes demanded by colonial authorities and sent their young men to towns, mines, or plantations where they could earn a wage. In these unfamiliar settings, Islamic brotherhoods often offered these youths community and hospitality. Muslim clerics in West Africa who needed workers for their peanut farms employed many such young men, who often became disciples as well as laborers. They carried Islamic practices with them when they returned to their native villages. In these ways, colonial rulers, although intending nothing of the sort, expanded the domain of Islam in West Africa.

Colonial rule changed African religious life as much or more than it did African economic life. While Africans had long been receptive to innovation in spiritual matters, now they had a wider range of examples to choose from. Selective borrowing led to great creativity and novelty, as well as to the spread of established forms of both Christianity and Islam.

EUROPEAN IMPERIALISM IN SOUTHEAST ASIA AND THE PACIFIC

Europe's imperial powers fastened colonial rule on Southeast Asia and the Pacific Islands at the same time that they partitioned Africa. The Dutch East India Company (VOC) had dominated much of island Southeast Asia since the sixteenth century. The trading company went bankrupt by 1800. The Dutch monarchy then stepped in and tried to tighten its grip on the archipelago. That required repeated warfare from the 1820s to 1910, by which time all local Indonesian (the term came into use in the 1880s) rulers had submitted to the Dutch. Export trade in spices and plantation crops formed the basis of the Dutch colonial economy. Meanwhile, in 1819 the British founded Singapore, a port at the southern tip of the Malay Peninsula. They gradually took over most of Malaya, which had the world's best tin deposits and was well suited to rubber tree plantations—both tin and rubber were important to British industrial production. Islam had been the majority religion in these lands since the sixteenth century; neither the Dutch nor the British tried hard to convert Indonesians or Malays to Christianity.

The French conquered much of mainland Southeast Asia starting in 1858. Initially intending only to protect French Catholic missionaries from persecution by Vietnam's Nguyễn dynasty, French armies, with gunboats and industrial weaponry, soon claimed the kingdoms of Vietnam, Cambodia, and Laos—all formerly in the orbit of China. Vietnam became a principal rice exporter and eventually home to rubber plantations too. Many of its elite families, who had long served Vietnamese monarchs, nimbly pivoted to work with French authorities. As in Indonesia and Malaya, few Europeans migrated to Vietnam; in 1913 locals outnumbered the French 700 to 1.

Most Vietnamese were Buddhists. The Catholic Church, which had been present for 200 years and was the spiritual home of perhaps 3 to 5 percent of Vietnamese, proved a valuable ally of colonialism: most Vietnamese Catholics welcomed French rule. France rewarded them, and the church, with land grants and other favors. In mainland Southeast Asia, only Thailand (or Siam, as it was then) remained outside of European empires. Its kings carefully played off the French against the British and preserved a precarious independence.

Before leaving Southeast Asia, it is well to note the inability of the Qing dynasty to keep European powers out of what Chinese had long considered their own backyard. As we shall see, China after 1850 careened from crisis to crisis, leaving power vacuums along its edges.

In the Pacific, the French, Germans, and British claimed several archipelagoes in the late nineteenth century. Islanders could not resist effectively. Their populations were too small and, in most cases, falling fast due to introduced infections. Their stone and wood weapons, supplemented by a few imported muskets, were no match for what European navies could bring to bear. So European rule came swiftly. France used New Caledonia as a dumping ground for convicts and political prisoners after 1864. British Fiji and German Samoa became plantation islands. None of these islands mattered economically to their colonizers. But in an age when naval ships needed coal, Pacific ports carried strategic value as **coaling stations**. Whatever their value, the cost of controlling Pacific islands was so low by European standards that using them to park coal or grow coconuts was reason enough to keep them. Missionaries won more converts to Christianity than they had in Southeast Asia, partly because there was no Islam to contend with.

IMPERIAL LATECOMERS: ITALY, JAPAN, AND THE UNITED STATES

Italy, unified only in the 1860s, was a latecomer to overseas imperialism. By the 1880s, boatloads of poor Italians migrated every year to the United States, Brazil, or Argentina. Italian nationalists hoped to build an empire of settlement in Africa, where Italian emigrants could contribute to Italy's strength. Ambitious statesmen found it irresistible to bring up the Roman Empire as an example to follow, and to exhort Italians to greatness through conquest. Italy first tried to get hold of Tunisia in North Africa but lost out to France. It did manage to obtain part of Somalia in the 1880s.

But that hardly signaled greatness worthy of descendants of the Caesars. Taking advantage of drought, rinderpest, and a resulting famine that killed about half of Ethiopia's 7 million people (1888–1892), Italy launched an invasion of Ethiopia in 1896. At the Battle of Adowa, Ethiopian armies killed or captured three-quarters of the Italian force, securing Ethiopia's independence for the next 40 years. Italy managed to take Libya from the Ottoman Empire in 1912 with the help of the first aerial bombing campaigns in world history. Italy's empire was small, thinly populated, of little economic value, and controversial within Italy.

Japan and the United States were also latecomers to overseas empires. Both had some background in territorial expansion. Japan in the eighteenth and nineteenth centuries had expanded northward, conquering and settling Hokkaido at the expense of the indigenous Ainu people. Smallpox, dispossession, and violence reduced the Ainu population from about 80,000 in 1800 to 15,000 by 1880. The United States had expanded westward at the expense of Native Americans. Their numbers fell from about 600,000 in 1800 to 250,000 in 1890. Both Japan and the United States became industrial powers with modern weaponry, increasingly nationalistic populations, and vocal lobbies eager for imperial ventures. In the 1890s, both became seaborne empires, although on far smaller scales than Britain or France, exploiting regional military superiority based on industrializing earlier than their neighbors.

Japanese imperialists began calling for overseas expansion in the mid-1870s, believing that to fend off foreign imperialists Japan had to become imperialist itself. An opportunity came with the Qing dynasty's continuing crises, allowing Japan to defeat China in war in 1894–1895. Japan took over Taiwan and began to play a larger role in Korea. Japan's expansion worried Russia, which was eagerly exploiting Qing weakness to extend its influence in Manchuria. These simultaneous imperial efforts brought on the 1904–1905 Russo-Japanese War, which ended with the Russian navy at the bottom of the sea. When Japan fully annexed Korea in 1910, it ruled a seaborne empire with a population only somewhat smaller than that of its home islands. As in Southeast Asia, China's feebleness invited others to seek imperial expansion in Northeast Asia.

Japan's government encouraged emigration to its colonies. Taiwan, under Japanese rule until 1945, was partly

Russo-Japanese War A Japanese illustration celebrates a Japanese military victory against Russian opponents in 1904. Winning the Russo-Japanese War enabled Japan to consolidate its presence as an empire in Northeast Asia.

a settler colony: some 5 to 10 percent of the total population was Japanese. Only a few hundred thousand Japanese moved to Korea, accounting for roughly 1 percent of the peninsula's population. But Japanese settlers took over half the farmland by the 1930s and obliged Korean farmers to work as tenants, bringing a key feature of settler colonies to Korea. Japan also resorted freely to deadly military force to suppress political resistance in Korea, especially in 1919–1920.

The United States became an overseas imperialist power in 1898. With the Monroe Doctrine (1823), the United States had tried to discourage European powers from extending their sway in the American hemisphere. In 1898, it intervened in a Cuban nationalist rebellion against Spain, which expanded into the Spanish-American War. Victorious, the United States took over Spain's colonies in the Philippines, Puerto Rico, Guam, and—briefly—Cuba, meanwhile annexing the Hawaiian Islands, partly to secure the ocean route to the Philippines. The newly acquired territories and populations were small compared to the continental United States and, in the Philippines, where a nationalist guerilla resistance lasted until 1903, cost considerable blood and treasure to keep. Suppressing the Filipino insurrection cost the U.S. army 10 times as many lives as did the Spanish-American War. Overseas imperialism delivered no conspicuous advantages to the United States except naval outposts, and as in Italy it was controversial

domestically. The new overseas empire thrust the United States into world affairs as never before.

Almost all the overseas empires took an interest in China. At times after 1840, it seemed likely to be partitioned like Poland or Africa—but it wasn't. That story appears in the next chapter.

LAND EMPIRES

It is customary to use the word *imperialism* in modern history for empires that stretched overseas, but empires existed on land as well. One could use the term *empire* for nineteenth-century Canada, the United States, Brazil, and Argentina: they all used industrial technologies and nationalist ideologies to support westward extension of their rule over indigenous peoples. Indeed, even an indigenous people, the Comanche, used rifles, an industrial technology, to help build a **land empire** in North America. In Africa, Ethiopians used modern firearms and a growing sense of nationalism, to create a land empire of their own. The biggest land empire was Russia's.

RUSSIA: THE WORLD'S BIGGEST LAND EMPIRE

Through war or diplomacy in the eighteenth century, Russia had already acquired what are now called the Baltic States—Estonia, Latvia, Lithuania—as well as Crimea, parts of Poland, Belarus, and Ukraine. In 1809, it acquired Finland in a peace treaty. Emerging victorious in war against Napoleon Bonaparte, Russia accelerated its territorial expansion between 1812 and 1864. It conquered territories in the Caucasus—the region between the Black Sea and Caspian Sea—home to Georgians, Armenians, Circassians, and Chechens. In the Baltics, Poland, and the Caucasus, the Russian state tried hard to spread Russian language, culture, and the Russian Orthodox religion—policies called Russification. It banned the use of Polish in schools and offices, and converted some Catholic churches into Russian Orthodox ones. Growing Russian nationalism spurred the belief, in elite circles, that it was Russia's destiny to rule over lesser peoples on its periphery.

Between 1860 and 1885, the tsar's armies also conquered vast swaths of steppe and desert in Central Asia. Like

Russia's Land Empire, 1800–1900 Russia had built an empire in thinly populated Siberia beginning in the sixteenth century. During the nineteenth century, it began to use the tools of industrial imperialism to expand into the Caucasus region and Central Asia at the expense mainly of Islamic khanates. This brought millions of Muslim subjects into the Russian Empire. As the Trans-Siberian Railway progressed eastward, Russia was also able to tighten its hold on southern Siberia and eventually the Pacific coast, which in the years 1904–1905 brought conflict with Japan.

other imperialists, they exploited advantages conferred by modern rifles, telegraph systems, and a growing railroad network. Dotted by oases, the region was inhabited by Muslim and mainly Turkic-speaking groups such as Uzbeks and Kazakhs. Russia also tightened its grip on Siberia, taking large swaths of Manchuria from the Qing in 1858–1860 and then building the Trans-Siberian Railway beginning in the 1890s. It gave up on overseas empire when it sold Alaska to the United States in 1867.

Russia acquired both headaches and assets in the process of extending its land empire. Its expansion, and its Russification attempts, inflamed nationalism among minorities and inspired repeated uprisings in Poland and Islamist rebellions in the Caucasus. Outside the Caucasus, Russia managed to find Muslim clerics willing to operate under Russian authority. They took care of meting out justice and family matters, while encouraging the empire's 14 million Muslims (as of 1897) to accept Russian

rule and pay their taxes—as Malik Sy did with French rule in Senegal. The state also continued its efforts to get nomads to settle down and become reliable taxpayers. It invested in irrigation in Central Asia, hoping to create a viable cotton industry. Despite all its internal tensions and military defeats in the Crimean War (1853–1856) and the Russo-Japanese War (1904–1905), Russia built the world's largest land empire—after 1880 enabled by its industrialization.

SECONDARY EMPIRES: COMANCHE TEXAS AND ETHIOPIA

Any state with weaker neighbors could take up imperial expansion. In the nineteenth century, the advent of mass-produced weaponry made it easier for a king or chief to monopolize military power in his neighborhood and use it to build a regional empire. The phenomenon is sometimes known as secondary empire, because a key source of power—industrial weaponry—was not internal but acquired from abroad, usually from armaments factories in Europe or the United States.

COMANCHE TEXAS, 1730–1870 Between 1730 and 1850, a Comanche empire flourished on what is now the southern plains of the United States—roughly central and west Texas, plus bits of Oklahoma, Kansas, Colorado, and New Mexico. The Comanche, one of many peoples called Plains Indians, based their political power on access to horses and guns. They were recent migrants to the plains, having arrived in the seventeenth century from what is now Utah and western Colorado at more or less the same time that horses galloped onto the scene. Horses had revolutionized North American plains life starting around 1680. Spanish traders introduced horses via New Mexico, and the Comanche quickly mastered the arts of riding and raising horses. With the mobility that horses gave them, the Comanche became more efficient bison hunters—and more effective fighters against their neighbors.

The Comanche numbered about 40,000 people in 1780, with herds of about 300,000 horses. Between 1779 and 1782, smallpox epidemics halved their number, but they rebounded quickly by capturing women and children from neighboring peoples and assimilating them into Comanche society. Although few in number by the standards of imperial peoples, the Comanche were lords of the vast grassland of the southern plains.

The **Comanche Empire**'s political success rested on guns as well as horses. Spanish authorities in Mexico prohibited the trade of guns northward to Amerindian peoples, but the French based in Louisiana did not; nor did the Americans who bought Louisiana from France in 1803. The Comanche secured a near-monopoly position in the gun trade on the southern plains, allowing them to exert military power unmatched in their neighborhood. They seized captives from agricultural peoples such as the Pueblo in New Mexico. After 1820, when Mexico was becoming independent from Spain, the Comanche raided deep into Mexico, taking horses, mules, and women and children to keep or sell.

Successful raiding over broad territories enabled the Comanche to trade profitably. They sold people, horses, and mules from Mexico to Pawnee, Arapaho, and Cheyenne of the central plains (today's Kansas and Nebraska)

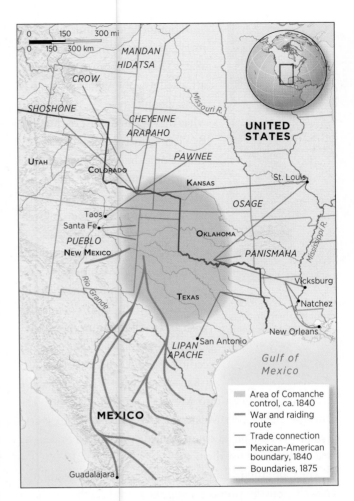

The Comanche Empire, ca. 1800–1850 After 1780, horses and guns gave the Comanche advantages over their neighbors. They mounted raids deep into Mexico, especially during the period 1820–1845, and maintained long-distance trade with several other indigenous peoples and with white Americans along the Mississippi River. This Comanche way of life ended between 1850 and 1875, defeated by U.S. forces and repeated epidemics.

or to white Americans in the Louisiana Territory. Comanche traders came to know which markets preferred which kinds of horses and who would pay the most for captives. They exploited their mobility to acquire broader market knowledge and prospered as a result.

They occasionally captured white children and raised them as Comanche. In 1836 in east Texas, Comanche raiders seized 10-year-old Cynthia Ann Parker, who gradually became Comanche. She married Peta Nocona, leader of the Nokoni band and one of the most successful of Comanche war captains in the 1850s. Among their children was the last independent Comanche leader, Quanah Parker.

Quanah Parker The last independent Comanche leader was photographed in 1892. He is seen standing outside his house with his wife, Tonasa.

Comanche economic and military strength peaked around 1840. They demanded tribute and attacked anyone who did not pay. Most people gave the Comanche what they wanted most of the time. By 1840, 10 to 25 percent of Comanche people had been kidnapped from indigenous communities in Mexico and enslaved or assimilated as wives or adopted children. In 1846, the Mexican authorities in the northern state of Chihuahua complained of the Comanche: "We travel the roads . . . at their whim; we cultivate the land where they wish and in the amount they wish." Comanche attacks in the years preceding the Mexican-American War (1846–1848) made it easier for U.S. forces to drive deep into Mexico and win that war. The resulting treaty cost Mexico nearly half its territory and put the Comanche lands fully inside the United States—a great misfortune for them.

The Comanche Empire came to an end for several reasons, the most important being the arrival on the southern plains after 1848 of the U.S. army backed by an industrializing economy and a population of 23 million. Suffering from repeated smallpox, measles, and cholera epidemics and military defeats, the Comanche population slipped to about 20,000 by 1850. The Comanche struggled against U.S. forces, which emboldened Comanche enemies such as the Osage. After the U.S. Civil War (1861–1865), the big and battle-hardened U.S. army reduced the Comanche to a shadow of their former glory. In 1875, the last of the remaining 3,000 Comanche straggled onto Indian reservations in Oklahoma, led by Quanah Parker.

ETHIOPIA, 1870–1913 Ethiopia, a land of fertile mountains and barren deserts in northeastern Africa, is another example of a secondary land empire built on monopoly access to imported weaponry. It was home to a mainly Christian population with a literate elite aware of Ethiopia's ancient heritage as the land of Aksum, an empire of the fourth century CE. For centuries before 1850, however, Ethiopia had been disunited, and its various peoples fought among themselves and against Muslim sultanates in neighboring lands. From the 1850s, external threats, especially from Egypt, helped Ethiopians come together across linguistic and cultural lines, a process begun by a warlord who united much of Ethiopia by force. Calling himself Tewodros II, he and his successors sought to prevent foreign encroachments and make their country more formidable—much as Japan's leaders were doing after the Meiji Restoration. The surest route, in Ethiopia as in Japan, was judicious borrowing of techniques and technologies of power from elsewhere. In the 1870s, a successor of Tewodros managed to get large quantities of modern British weapons, which he used to subdue all rivals within Ethiopia, fend off an Egyptian attack, and assault his nearest neighbors. Ethiopia was becoming an empire.

The master empire builder of Ethiopia was **Menelik II**, who took the throne in 1889. Menelik claimed descent from King Solomon and the queen of Sheba (of Old

The Expansion of Ethiopia, 1850–1910 Access to modern weaponry underpinned the imperial expansion of Ethiopia, achieved at the expense of neighboring Muslim peoples. Under Menelik II, the Ethiopian military destroyed an Italian invasion in 1896, one of the few resounding defeats delivered to European imperial armies during this period.

CONSIDERING THE EVIDENCE

Ethiopian Imperialism through Russian Eyes

Alexander Bulatovich first arrived in Ethiopia in 1896, as part of the Russian Red Cross. The medical mission was charged with offering aid during the conflict between Italians and Ethiopians that culminated in the Battle of Adowa. When the rest of the delegation left, Bulatovich stayed to explore the western regions that Ethiopia had recently conquered and to record the customs of the Oromo people who lived there. When he returned to Ethiopia again the following year as part of Russia's diplomatic delegation, he joined several thousand Ethiopian soldiers on a military expedition to claim territory between the Nile River and the Red Sea. Emperor Menelik had claimed this region to preempt British and French encroachment, but it was much farther than Ethiopia had previously extended its reach. In Bulatovich's journal of the expedition, published in 1900, he wrote the following introduction to justify Ethiopia's conquests.

Menelik is only carrying out the traditional mission of Ethiopia as the propagator of culture and the unifier of all the inhabitants of the Ethiopian Mountains and of the related tribes in their neighborhood, and only makes a new step toward consolidating and developing the power of the black empire....

[W]e Russians cannot help sympathizing with his intentions, not only because of political considerations, but also for purely human reasons. It is well known to what consequences conquests of wild tribes by Europeans lead. Too great a difference in the degree of culture between the conquered people and their conquerors has always led to the enslavement, corruption, and degeneration of the weaker race. The natives of America degenerated and have almost ceased to exist. The natives of India were corrupted and deprived of individuality. The black tribes of Africa became the slaves of the whites.

Clashes between nations more or less close to one another in culture bring completely different results.

For the Abyssinians [Ethiopians], the Egyptian, Arab, and, finally, European civilization which they have gradually adopted has not been pernicious: borrowing the fruits of these civilizations, and in turn conquering and annexing neighboring tribes and passing on to them her culture, Abyssinia [Ethiopia] did not obliterate from the face of the earth, did not destroy the uniqueness of any one of the conquered tribes, but rather gave them all the possibility of preserving their individual characteristics.

Thus Christian Abyssinia [Ethiopia] plays an important role in world progress as a transmission point of European civilization to wild central African peoples.

The high civilizing mission of Abyssinia [Ethiopia], its centuries-old, almost uninterrupted struggle for faith and freedom against the surrounding Moslems [Muslims], the nearness of her people to the Russian people in creed, won for her the favor of the Russian people.

Source: Alexander Bulatovich, *Ethiopia through Russian Eyes: Country in Transition 1896–1898*, trans. Richard Seltzer (Lawrenceville, NJ, 2000).

QUESTIONS FOR ANALYSIS

1. What "political considerations" and "human reasons" motivated the Russians to support Ethiopia's imperial expansion?
2. Why does Bulatovich think Ethiopians are better than Europeans at transmitting "European civilization" to Africans?
3. How does Bulatovich's description of Ethiopia's "role in world progress" reveal European stereotypes about Africa?

Testament fame) and maintained he was the rightful heir of the ancient emperors of Aksum. Through diplomacy and force, he increasingly brought the various peoples in and around Ethiopia (Amharic- and Oromo-speakers were the biggest groups) into a single imperial state. Aware of the partition of Africa under way in the late 1880s, he was determined to keep newly enlarged Ethiopia under Ethiopian—and his—rule.

Menelik adapted foreign techniques and technologies that bolstered his own power. In the early 1890s, as rinderpest was ravaging the pastoral societies in and around Ethiopia—Menelik himself lost 250,000 head of cattle—he forged a friendship with a Russian cavalry officer sent by the tsar to build a Russian-Ethiopian bond. Nikolai Leontiev brought advisors and weapons for Menelik's army, including 30,000 modern rifles and a few dozen artillery pieces. Menelik's army even acquired a few machine guns. With this armament, Menelik's forces sliced to ribbons the Italian army men at Adowa in 1896.

Menelik continued to exploit his access to foreign weaponry and skills after scattering the Italians. He campaigned against any neighbor bold enough to resist his armies, which now numbered a few hundred thousand men. His conquests to the south and east doubled the size of Ethiopia and left longstanding memories of atrocities and enslavement. Menelik was grateful enough to his Russian friend that he created a new titled rank in Ethiopia and made Leontiev a count.

While in some respects an old-fashioned conqueror, Menelik II was also a relentless modernizer. Starting in 1894, he worked to bring Ethiopia its first railroad line. He introduced electricity and a telegraph and telephone system. In addition to foreign technologies, Menelik borrowed foreign institutions that he thought would make Ethiopia stronger. He started public schools, a postal service, and a formal bureaucracy including a judiciary using the principle of jury trials.

By the time of Menelik's death in 1913, Ethiopia stood alone as a fully independent polity in Africa. He had ruled for a quarter-century over an empire the size of Texas, made possible by the judicious introduction of foreign technologies and skills.

OTHER SECONDARY EMPIRES

Secondary empires of the sort built in Ethiopia and Texas were many but fleeting. The Maori leader Hongi Hika in New Zealand studied European military and agricultural methods before importing guns and potatoes to New Zealand's North Island in 1818. He used the guns to defeat rivals who had none, enslaving captives whom he put to work raising potatoes for his armies. For a decade, he ruled a secondary empire. Simultaneously, under Radama I the Imerina kingdom in the highlands of central Madagascar launched an empire, using a British-trained army. Imerina youth were sent to Britain to learn the techniques of industry, and for several decades the Imerina ran their own armaments industry, producing muskets and cannon. They conquered most of Madagascar by 1850, enslaving hundreds of thousands.

On an even larger scale, the Albanian leader Mehmet Ali created a secondary empire in northeast Africa. As Ottoman governor of Egypt, he first took it under his own control, then reformed his army along European lines and created a new Egyptian arms industry. He used his new military machine to conquer Sudan in the 1820s. Ranjit Singh and his family did something similar in the Punjab (northernmost Pakistan and India today) and neighboring slivers of Afghanistan and Tibet between 1810 and 1840. They first created a Sikh-dominated empire out of the many tiny states that arose in the waning years of the Mughal Empire. Then Singh hired several veterans of Napoleon's army to train and command his elite forces. With help from a French officer, he established an armory capable of producing modern rifles and artillery pieces. Singh's empire combined Sikh and European military skills with great success—to the cost of his neighbors.

Secondary empires of a sort had existed long before the nineteenth century, but with industrialization they became easier to create. The gap in formidability between those with modern guns and those without was huge, and modern guns came from only a few places. The Global web enabled transfers of guns and relevant military skills from Britain and Russia to Ethiopia or from French Louisiana and the United States to Comanche Texas. But the world was not yet so well connected that everybody in and around Ethiopia and Texas had similar access to the tools of power. So ambitious, skilled, and lucky warlords who monopolized that access in their own neighborhoods could build secondary empires.

NATIONALISM, IMPERIALISM, AND THE GLOBAL WEB

Nationalism and imperialism further tightened the Global web. Nationalism was infectious and spread along the circuits of the Global web. Its emergence thickened the web—for example, by inspiring people in Japan to pay more attention to military practices in Germany.

Imperialism, for its part, contributed to the more rapid exchange of goods and the extension of market relations into places such as central Africa or Samoa, where they had been weak. It helped spread versions of Christianity in colonized lands. And in parts of Africa and Southeast Asia, it—unintentionally—helped extend the realm of Islam, the religion that appealed most to people who opposed European empire. Most conspicuously, imperialism brought political consolidation. Its forces crushed hundreds of smaller polities around the world, replacing them with a few big empires. Imperialism and nationalism made the world a smaller, more tightly interactive place.

While nationalism and imperialism brought the world into tighter interaction, they also deepened the differences among peoples in two respects. The first was economic status. The imperial powers, already growing richer through industrialization, enriched themselves further through the economic policies of imperialism—although by just how much is controversial among scholars.

Second, imperialism and nationalism emphasized differences among peoples and religions. As ideologies, nationalism sometimes and imperialism always supported racialist outlooks that divided humankind into several "races" arranged in hierarchies based on either skin color or ethnicity. In racial hierarchies, whites deemed darker-skinned people to be inherently inferior. Imperial strategy fostered division to make subject populations easier to rule, underscoring distinctions—perhaps inventing them. Nationalism had contradictory effects: nationalists invited people to bury their class or religious differences and to prize solidarity as a Japanese, Canadian, or Italian nation, but at the same time, they divided humankind into hundreds of nationalities and often claimed these were unchangeable biological categories. With respect to religion, both nationalism and imperialism showed contradictory effects: while helping spread Christianity and Islam, they also helped splinter both religions. Christianity in Nigeria or Vietnam took on local flavoring. Local religion and culture colored Islam too, as it spread in West Africa or Indonesia under European imperial rule. So nationalism and imperialism bound the world more tightly into a Global web; but at the same time, they both emphasized differences within the human species.

CONCLUSION

The ideas and practices of both nationalism and imperialism reshaped the world between 1800 and 1930. Nationalism took root first in revolutionary France but spread easily to other lands. It helped to forge nation-states and to weaken multiethnic empires. Together with industrialization, it combined to make some countries, such as Britain, France, Germany, Japan, and the United States, much stronger. They used that added strength to expand, or to create, overseas empires at the expense of less powerful societies in Africa, Asia, and the Pacific.

Sometimes imperialism took the form of settler colonies in which migrants from Europe or Japan put down roots in conquered lands, as in Algeria or Taiwan. But more often, settlers were few and colonial rule more narrowly focused on economic extraction and religious conversion. The empires of the nineteenth and early twentieth centuries often had profound economic and cultural effects. Among the unintended effects was the emergence of many new examples of nationalism among the colonized peoples. Their political ambitions, as later chapters will explain, made imperialism too costly to sustain.

CHAPTER REVIEW

KEY TERMS

nationalism (p. 784)

La Marseillaise (p. 785)

Yamato race theory (p. 786)

multiethnic empires (p. 790)

new imperialism (p. 792)

culture of imperialism (p. 794)

social Darwinism (p. 795)

British Raj (p. 798)

Abdelkadir (p. 800)

settler colony (p. 801)

partition of Africa (p. 801)

Simon Kimbangu (p. 805)

coaling stations (p. 806)

land empire (p. 807)

Comanche Empire (p. 809)

Menelik II (p. 810)

Go to INQUIZITIVE to see what you've learned—and learn what you've missed—with personalized feedback along the way.

REVIEW QUESTIONS

1. Identify the circumstances that contributed to the rise of nationalism, and explain the difference between ethnic nationalism and civic nationalism.

2. Compare and contrast the emphases of French, Japanese, Canadian, and German nationalisms.

3. In what ways did nationalism confer power upon states?

4. How did nationalism contribute to the weakening of the Habsburg, Russian, and Ottoman Empires?

5. What were the key reasons that imperialism after 1870 was so pervasive and different from the empire building that came before?

6. Name the industrial technologies that contributed to the rise of the new imperialism, and describe their contributions.

7. On what three trends did Europe, the United States, and Japan base their cultures of imperialism?

8. Identify the similarities between British control in India and French rule in Algeria, and explain the main difference between the two.

9. What was the main difference between settler colonialism in Australia, Canada, and New Zealand and that in Africa and East Asia?

10. How did rinderpest facilitate the European conquest of Africa?

11. In what ways did colonial rule in Africa rely on local elites and the assignment of tribal identities?

12. To whom did missionary Christianity appeal in Africa, and why?

13. What products formed the basis of the Dutch, British, and French colonial economies in Southeast Asia?

14. Discuss the main reasons for Italian, Japanese, and U.S. late imperial expansion.

15. On what techniques and technologies did the political success of the Comanche and Ethiopian Empires depend?

16. In what significant ways did nationalism and imperialism tighten global connections, and in what ways did they deepen global divisions?

FURTHER READING

David B. ABERNETHY, *The Dynamics of Global Dominance: European Overseas Empires, 1415–1980* (2000). A political scientist's systematic and comprehensive history of European imperialism.

Alexander BULATOVICH, *Ethiopia through Russian Eyes: Country in Transition 1896–1898* (2000). The 1897—1898 diary of a Russian soldier serving under Menelik II in Ethiopia. A fascinating document.

Cathie CARMICHAEL, Matthew D'AURIA, and Aviel ROSHWALD, eds., *The Cambridge History of Nationhood and Nationalism* (2023). This authoritative two-volume work includes dozens of case studies and thematic essays.

Pekka HAMALAINEN, *Comanche Empire* (2008). A masterpiece of research and analysis.

E. J. HOBSBAWM, *Nations and Nationalism since 1780* (2012, 2nd ed.). A readable and excellent work on languages and their links to nationalisms.

Adam HOCHSCHILD, *King Leopold's Ghost: A Story of Greed, Terror, and Heroism in Colonial Africa* (1999). A detailed narrative of the Belgian king's pillaging of the Congo.

Heather STREETS-SALTER and Trevor R. GETZ, *Empires and Colonies in the Modern World: A Global Perspective* (2016). A broad overview, thematic in structure.

The Heyday of Eugenics

PEOPLE HAD BEEN BREEDING PLANTS AND ANIMALS for specific characteristics for ten millennia before the crystallization of eugenics. Some, including Plato, had recommended that societies should breed humans selectively, too. However, in the late nineteenth century millions of people misunderstood scientific advances in ways that strengthened this sort of thinking. Foremost were Charles Darwin's ideas about evolution through natural selection, which he presented as a matter of fitness for survival and the struggle for existence, first published in 1859; and Gregor Mendel's work in genetics, done at the same time but publicized in 1900. These ideas provided the framework for pseudo-scientific racism and, within that, eugenics.

Eugenics is the idea that the quality of human populations, or the entire human population, could and should be improved by selective breeding. Inferior humans should be prevented from reproducing; superior ones should be encouraged to do so. The idea is based on a firm faith in heredity—indeed, genetic determinism. Its appeal was strong among elites who liked to think their elevated position resulted from the laws of nature. It proved popular in societies controlling empires or aiming to control Indigenous populations. Eugenics was influential mainly around 1900–1935, controversial from the start, and discredited, though not extinguished, in the 1940s.

SOURCE 23.1

The Origins of Eugenics, 1883

Charles Darwin normally took a dim view of attempts to use his ideas to explain the fates of subsets of the human race. But the year after Darwin died, one of his cousins, a versatile and undeniably brilliant British scientist, Francis Galton (1822–1911), formalized his ideas about human variations and coined the term *eugenics*. Galton came from a prosperous gun-making and banking family and was educated in medicine and mathematics. By the time he published the book from which this excerpt is taken, Galton had drawn the first-ever weather maps, pioneered regression analysis, traveled widely and written best-selling travel books, won prizes, and served in prominent roles in learned societies. His standing ensured a wide audience for his views.

We greatly want a brief word to express the science of improving stock, which is by no means confined to questions of judicious mating, but which, especially in the case of man, takes cognisance of all influences that tend in however remote a degree to give to the more suitable races or strains of blood a better chance of prevailing speedily over the less suitable than they otherwise would have had. The word eugenics would sufficiently express the idea....

[...]

Whenever a low race is preserved under conditions of life that exact a high level of efficiency, it must be subjected to rigorous selection. The few best specimens of that race can alone be allowed to become parents, and not many of their descendants can be allowed to live. On the other hand, if a higher race be substituted for the low one, all this terrible misery disappears. The most merciful form of what I ventured to call "eugenics" would consist in watching for the indications of superior strains or races, and in so favoring them that their progeny shall outnumber and gradually replace that of the old one....

[...]

There exists a sentiment, for the most part quite unreasonable, against the gradual extinction of an inferior race. It rests on some confusion between the race and the individual, as if the destruction of a race was equivalent to the destruction of a large number of men. It is nothing of the kind when the process of extinction works silently and slowly through the earlier marriage of members of the superior race, through their greater vitality under equal stress, through their better chances of getting a livelihood.

Source: Francis Galton, *Inquiries into Human Faculty and Its Development* (London: Macmillan, 1883).

- According to Galton, eugenics is "merciful." What is his logic here?
- What unspoken assumptions can be identified in Galton's work?
- According to Galton, how might "an inferior race" become extinct without being killed off?

Alfred Ploetz's "Neo-Malthusianism and Race Hygiene," 1912

Alfred Ploetz (1860–1940), a German physician and biologist who was also a socialist, fled Germany during the persecution of socialists and studied medicine in Switzerland. After returning, he founded a German Society for Racial Hygiene in 1905 and became a central figure in German eugenics. In 1912, when he wrote the words below, he was president of the International Society for Race Hygiene and delivered this paper at the First International Conference of Eugenics. (The attendees included Winston Churchill and the Scottish-born American inventor Alexander Graham Bell.) For most of his life Ploetz admired "[t]he high aptitude of the Jews and their outstanding role in the progress of mankind, considering men such as Jesus, Spinoza, and Marx," but in his final years he changed his mind about them. At age 77, Ploetz joined the Nazi Party. By "Malthusianism" he meant restraint in reproduction.

We shall now turn...to the effect of Malthusianism upon the whole population, the different social strata being considered as units. In general, the well-to-do practice Malthusianism more frequently and more intensively than do the middle class, and the latter more than the poorer class. Since, now, the upper classes contain also racially, on average, the best variations, at least in regard to intellectual traits, Malthusianism shows here the tendency to reduce the average ability in the population.

Just as Malthusianism affects the higher classes more than the lower, from the same causes it is practiced more, on the average, by the more highly cultivated than by the less cultured. The French and Yankees [Americans of English ancenstry] decrease in number. England, Holland, Scandinavia and Germany—the principal seats of the highly endowed North (Teutonic or Germanic) race—show a decreasing birth rate from year to year. Poles, Hungarians, and Russians, on the contrary—the countries with strong Asiatic mixtures—have an extraordinary high birthrate, so that they are everywhere pressing successfully against the West. The preservation of the Nordic race is thus seriously menaced.

In the struggle of the three great races of mankind, Malthusianism is playing a part and it gives no favorable outlook for the white race, in its great combat for lasting supremacy, but a great handicap, especially before the yellow race which in its ancestor worship possesses a strongly effective hindrance to the spread of Malthusianism practices.... However doubtful, therefore, the harmfulness of Malthusianism may be in its effect on the single families, for the people as a whole and for our race it has without doubt a most harmful tendency, lowering the average fitness and ability, and endangering the future of our race.

If we look on all its effects we must conclude that to-day the spreading, unregulated and misdirected Malthusianism has a harmful effect from the standpoint of race hygiene. We should strive to abolish it, but its abolition would, I believe, be wholly impossible.... Mothers hand it on to their daughters, elder sisters to younger ones, fathers to sons, brothers to brothers. Even the Catholic Church has proven itself powerless against it....

[...]

On the positive side, race hygiene must strive, especially through the work of our artists—our dramatists, novelists, painters—to renew in our young men and women the ambition for the advancement, the perpetuity and the increase of their family.... We must instill in our children greater courage to undertake the responsibilities of life, a higher patriotism, a sense of devotion to our race which must face the great combat of the future.... Only then, in the decision between self-centred individualism and service toward a new generation and new forces for their race, will they decide in favour of life.

Source: Alfred Ploetz, "Neo-Malthusianism and Race Hygiene," in *Report of Proceedings of the First International Eugenics Congress*, Vol. II: *Problems in Eugenics* (London: The Eugenics Education Society, 1913).

- According to Ploetz, restraint in reproduction can be good for individual families yet bad for a population as whole. What is his logic?
- According to Ploetz, people who are well off ought to reproduce more than they do. What is his logic there?

Eugenics in Japan, 1893–1918

In the 1890s, Japan began building an empire in East Asia. At the same time, it was debating the appropriate policies toward the Indigenous population of Hokkaido, its northernmost island: the Ainu (of whom between 25,000 and 200,000 exist today). Some Japanese citizens thought the Ainu should be assimilated into Japanese culture and society; others thought that some aspects of Ainu society should be protected, if possible. Below are two opinions influenced by ideas of social Darwinism and eugenics. The first, from 1893, is from the writings of Kato Masanosuke (1854–1941), a newspaper editor and prominent politician (there is a monument to him in Tokyo). The second was written in 1918 by Hiraoka Sadatoro (1863–1942), a career official who rose to the status of provincial governor.

[1] The survival of the fittest is a natural feature of this world. The Ainu race is an inferior race, while our Japanese race is a superior race. The superior race say that the inferior Ainu race will naturally die out . . . and that there is no need to protect them.

[2] The world is a stage upon which the strong devour the weak. . . . As Darwin wrote in *Origin of Species*, the so-called idea of the survival of the fittest is a principle that rules the whole world of nature. From the phrase 'survival of the fittest' it follows that those unadapted for life are oppressed. The Ainu are unadapted members of humanity. . . . The Ainu today have nothing to contribute to the happiness of humanity, consequently their survival or extinction should be left to nature. In particular, artificial preservation through human agency is unnecessary, and moreover, is said to be impossible. Another view [for letting the Ainu die out] argues from the standpoint of the Yamato race. Our country is proud of the purity of our ancient race, and the long-term preservation of this racial purity is our nationalism. . . . If interbreeding with Ainu introduces Ainu blood into Japanese it will violate the movement to preserve our national essence.

Source: "First reading of the Hokkaido Former Natives Protection Act, House of Representatives, 29 November 1893," in *Collected Materials on Ainu History* 3: *Modern and Contemporary Materials* 1 (Sapporo: Hokkaido Utari Kyōkai, 1990); and S. Hiraoka, "On the Disposal of the Ainu Race," in T. Aoyama, *The Different World of the Extreme North* (Tokyo: Nippon Seinen Tsushinsha, 1918).

- According to these authors, why is it *natural* that the Ainu should die out?
- According to these authors, why is it *desirable* that the Ainu should die out?

SOURCE 23.4

G. K. Chesterton, an Opponent of Eugenics, 1922

Eugenics was controversial from the outset. It had both proponents and opponents across the political spectrum. A fierce opponent was the prolific English philosopher, novelist, and literary critic G. K. Chesterton (1874–1936). He lived by his pen, writing journalism and popular detective fiction. He was nominated for a Nobel Prize in literature and honored by the Pope. An Anglican for most of his life, he converted to Catholicism in the year he wrote the book excerpted here. During the 1920s and 1930s he wielded a powerful intellectual influence in the Anglophone world.

There exists to-day a scheme of action, a school of thought, as collective and unmistakable as any of those by whose grouping alone we can make any outline of history. . . . It is a thing that can be pointed out; it is a thing that can be discussed; and it is a thing that can still be destroyed. It is called for convenience "Eugenics"; and that it ought to be destroyed I propose to prove in the pages that follow. I know that it means very different things to different people; but that is only because evil always takes advantage of ambiguity. I know it is praised with high professions of idealism and benevolence; with silver-tongued rhetoric about purer motherhood and a happier posterity. But that is only because evil is always flattered, as the Furies were called "The Gracious Ones." I know that it numbers many disciples whose intentions are entirely innocent and humane; and who would be sincerely astonished at my describing it as I do. But that is only because evil always wins through the strength of its splendid dupes; and there has in all ages been a disastrous alliance between abnormal innocence and abnormal sin. Of these who are deceived I shall speak of course as we all do of such instruments; judging them by the good they think they are doing, and not by the evil which they really do. But Eugenics itself does exist for those who have sense enough to see that ideas exist; and Eugenics itself, in large quantities or small, coming quickly or coming slowly, urged from good motives or bad, applied to a thousand people or applied to three, Eugenics itself is a thing no more to be bargained about than poisoning. . . .

[. . .]

If something which has been discovered at last by the lamp of learning is something which has been acted on from the first by the light of nature, this (so far as it goes) is plainly not an argument for pestering people, but an argument for letting them alone. If men did not marry their grandmothers when it was, for all they knew, a most hygienic habit; if we know now that they instinctively avoided scientific peril; that, so far as it goes, is a point in favour of letting people marry anyone they like. It is simply the statement that sexual selection, or what Christians call falling in love, is a part of man which in the rough and in the long run can be trusted. And that is the destruction of the whole of this science at a blow.

Source: G. K. Chesterton, *Eugenics and Other Evils* (London: Cassell, 1922).

- What is wrong with eugenics, according to Chesterton?
- Chesterton is firmly opposed to eugenics but gracious toward eugenicists. Why might he have chosen that writing strategy?

SOURCE 23.5

Oliver Wendell Holmes, Majority Opinion in *Buck v. Bell*, 1927

In many places with a strong eugenics movement, policy and legislation came to reflect eugenicist views. The U.S. state of Virginia, for example, passed legislation in 1924 permitting the obligatory sterilization of people deemed mentally unfit. The case of one such person, 18-year-old Carrie Buck, worked its way up to the U.S. Supreme Court in 1927. The State argued that she and her family were "feeble-minded" and "promiscuous" and therefore unfit to reproduce. Buck's lawyers argued that her rights to equal protection under the law would be violated were she forced to undergo sterilization while other people were not. The Court upheld the Virginia law by an 8–1 decision, and Buck was sterilized five months later. Two dozen states quickly passed compulsory sterilization laws modeled on Virginia's. Justice Oliver Wendell Holmes, the most-cited legal scholar in U.S. history, wrote the majority opinion.

The judgment finds the facts that have been recited and that Carrie Buck 'is the probable potential parent of socially inadequate offspring, likewise afflicted, that she may be sexually sterilized without detriment to her general health and that her welfare and that of society will be promoted by her sterilization,' and thereupon makes the order. In view of the general declarations of the Legislature and the specific findings of the Court obviously we cannot say as matter of law that the grounds do not exist, and if they exist they justify the result. We have seen more than once that the public welfare may call upon the best citizens for their lives. It would be strange if it could not call upon those who already sap the strength of the State for these lesser sacrifices, often not felt to be such by those concerned, in order to prevent our being swamped with incompetence. It is better for all the world, if instead of waiting to execute degenerate offspring for crime, or to let them starve for their imbecility, society can prevent those who are manifestly unfit from continuing their kind. The principle that sustains compulsory vaccination is broad enough to cover cutting the Fallopian tubes. Jacobson v. Massachusetts, 197 U.S. 11, 25 S.C.t. 358, 49 L. Ed. 643, 3 Ann. Cas. 765. Three generations of imbeciles are enough. . . . Judgment affirmed.

Source: Buck v. Bell, 274 U.S. 200 (1927).

- According to Holmes and the Supreme Court, why was compulsory sterilization justified?
- Holmes was a thrice-wounded Civil War veteran, and at the time he considered this case more than 116,000 American servicemen had recently died in World War I. Could this background have influenced his decision? Why or why not?

SOURCE 23.6

India's Traditions through a Eugenic Lens, 1927

T. N. Roy, the author of the excerpt presented here, was a civil servant in British India specializing in agriculture in Bengal. He was a vigorous defender of India's caste system, which was sometimes blamed for modern India's misfortunes—such as colonial rule. Roy's essay, titled "Hindu Eugenics" and published in the *Journal of Heredity*, argues that the historical superiority of Brahmins had been compromised by genetic contamination by Buddhists, and that Brahmins were originally a "white race." He ends by saying that "the Hindus' downfall" resulted from failure to observe caste distinction "well enough." Here is his opening paragraph.

The greatest eugenic movement that the world has as yet witnessed originated in India. It was the institution of the caste system. That intermarriage between two different races was undesirable was early appreciated in India and hence prohibited. That marriages which originated in lust were not likely to be good marriages was also appreciated by the Hindus. The Hindus not only classified themselves according to parentage, but they classified the different kinds of marriages. The best form of marriage was known as the Brahmanya marriage whose sole object was the improvement of the progeny. The choice of the mate did not rest with the contracting parties but with their elders and guardians. Such marriages were likely in many cases to be unhappy, nay unbearable, if both the contracting parties did not believe in the sanctity of marriage. Marriage was, therefore, and still is, with many Hindus a sacred duty wherefrom all considerations of self and passions were to be excluded. This was effected by religious inculcations, and by moral and social training. Marriages were usually early, sometimes even in infancy, and the married couple had usually to undergo a rather severe training in controlling themselves. Whatever may be said as to the happiness or otherwise of such matings, no one will deny that eugenically such marriages were in some respects of very great advantage.

Source: T. N. Roy, "Hindu Eugenics," *Journal of Heredity* 18, no. 2 (February 1927), 67–72.

- How does Roy use modern eugenics in defense of the ancient caste system?
- What—if any—changes to eugenics ideas does Roy make to fit the Indian context?
- What does it say about the relationship between eugenics and colonialism that Roy, born, raised, and educated under Britain's colonial rule in India, was an enthusiastic supporter?

QUESTIONS FOR COMPARISON

1. Why might eugenics have become a popular idea between 1900 and 1930? Why might it have infuriated critics such as Chesterton?

2. For the period between 1900 and 1930, how would you summarize the links between colonialism and eugenics?

3. What links can you see among industrialization, social class, and eugenics in these decades?

CHRONOLOGY

1813
British state strips
East India Company
of its trade monopoly

1821
Mexico wins
independence
from Spain

1842
Treaty of Nanjing

1839–1842
First Opium War

1848
Mexico loses territory
to the United States

1850–1864
Taiping Rebellion

1856–1860
Second
Opium War

1869–1870
Development of Ghost
Dance among northern
Nevada Paiute

1857–1858
Indian
Rebellion

1876–1910
Porfiriato

1877–1878
Drought in Brazil;
famine in China

1879
Japan takes
Ryukyu Islands

1885
French
seize
Vietnam

1887
Dawes Act opens
indigenous land
to white settlers

1889
Wovoka has first prophetic vision;
Brazil becomes a republic

1890
Massacre of Wounded Knee

1894–1895
Sino-Japanese
War

1897
Brazilian army
defeats Canudos
rebellion

1899–1900
Boxer Rebellion in northern China
1899–1902
Boer War in South Africa

Making the World Modern

CONFRONTING INDUSTRIALIZATION, NATIONALISM, AND IMPERIALISM

1850 to 1920

1913
Yuan Shikai forces
Sun Yatsen
into exile

1905
Revolution of 1905 in Russia
1905–1911
Revolution in Iran

1910–1911
Chinese Revolution

1908
Cixi and Guangxu die;
Young Turk Revolution

I n April 1856 a teenage girl named Nongqawuse, of the Xhosa people in South Africa, was on duty chasing birds from maize fields down by the Gxarha River. As she explained it, she saw two strangers who instructed her to tell her people they must kill all their cattle and destroy all their crops. The cattle and crops were impure, the strangers said, having been raised by the Xhosa people, who practiced witchcraft. She also heard them say that if the Xhosa did this, new cattle would spring up from the Earth, fresh maize would burst forth, and the ancestors of the Xhosa would return from the dead. Joy and justice would prevail in the land.

It was a difficult time for the Xhosa. They were engaged in frequent wars with their neighbors, including the British-run Cape Colony, which was swelling daily with new settlers from Britain. The Xhosa leader, Sarhili, a man of considerable diplomatic talents and now at the height of his powers, was hard-pressed to maintain Xhosa independence. To make matters worse, a terrible cattle plague had struck—a disaster for a cattle-keeping people like the

Civil War in China A battle scene from the Taiping Rebellion, a massive uprising against the Qing dynasty in the mid-nineteenth century.

FOCUS QUESTIONS

1. How were millenarian movements responses to the pressures of state power?

2. How did the Taiping and Indian Rebellions reflect the impact of global connections?

3. What mix of global and local forces fueled the Chinese and Mexican Revolutions?

Xhosa. Many of them were desperate for relief and eager for good news.

For the Xhosa, it was not unusual for spirits to appear from time to time and offer prophecies. But at first no one believed Nongqawuse. Young girls' words did not count for much in Xhosaland. But she told her uncle, Mhlakaza, who went with her to meet the strangers and heard their message for himself. Mhlakaza had at one time worked for an Anglican archdeacon, and he embraced Anglican ideas of redemption and resurrection. Now he convinced King Sarhili to visit the Gxarha. The king also heard the voices, accepted the prophecy, and arranged for the slaughter of his vast herds of cattle. He instructed his followers, some of whom had also gone to hear the strangers' voices, to do the same. Over the next two years, the Xhosa killed about 400,000 of their cattle. They dug up their maize crop. They keenly awaited the day when the new cattle and crops would come and their ancestors would arise.

And then they starved. No new cattle came, no new maize sprouted, and the ancestors did not return to help them oust their enemies. The Xhosa population fell from about 105,000 to 27,000. They lost much of their land too. The Cape Colony's governor, the brilliant and ruthless Sir George Grey, urged British settlers to help themselves to Xhosa land, spelling the end of Xhosa independence. After 1858, they were a subject people in British South Africa.

The Xhosa were one of many peoples in the nineteenth century struggling to make sense of a confusing world. For many, as for the Xhosa, the extraordinary power of modern imperialism cost them land and liberty. For others, the newly unleashed force of nationalism made them feel like foreigners in their own land. For still others, the overnight economic changes brought on by industrialization and new competition turned their worlds upside down.

All these forces, and others too, worked together to confuse, irritate, and arouse millions of people around the world. Old truths came into question. Old ways no longer worked. Young people tuned out the old, seeking new opportunities and new forms of truth. The disruption, disorientation, and dissatisfaction drove many of the millions to seek spiritual solutions, like the Xhosa. Others took up arms. Some did both at once. Some wished to embrace nationalism and industrialization—in short, to compete with the imperial powers at their own game. Others rejected such a course, hoping instead to strengthen their communities without imitating foreign ways. The growing power of industrial societies made these choices increasingly urgent after 1850.

This chapter explores several responses to the pressures people came to feel during the nineteenth century. First, we'll consider a pair of small-scale **millenarian movements**—religious movements in which people expect spiritual or divine intervention to bring about a better world. We'll see how some indigenous North Americans tried to cope with their problems by calling for spiritual aid through the Ghost Dance. Then we'll move to Brazil, to the town of Canudos, where destitute people tried to set up their own new community according to Catholic principles as they understood them. These were religious responses with political meanings, involving tens of thousands of people.

Next we'll turn to a pair of giant rebellions that

involved tens of millions of people. The Taiping Rebellion (1850–1864), also a millenarian movement in some respects, shook Qing China to its foundations, a cataclysm from which the dynasty never recovered. The Indian Rebellion (1857–1858) destroyed both the Mughal Empire and the East India Company, inadvertently bringing more direct British rule over more of the subcontinent and stimulating the first stirrings of Indian nationalism.

Finally, we'll look at a pair of revolutions that occurred between 1910 and 1920, one in China and the other in Mexico. Both of these succeeded in overthrowing a ruling elite in the name of liberty and justice, and of creating nations strong enough to resist foreign encroachments.

Millenarian movements, rebellions, and revolutions happen from time to time. This book has touched on several already. But they came thicker and faster in the late nineteenth and early twentieth centuries, because the pace and prevalence of change was so great and because the changes so unsettled populations around the globe. These three pairs of millenarian movements, rebellions, and revolutions represent a sampling of ways in which peoples confronted, and participated in, the disruptive changes of the period from 1850 to 1920.

MILLENARIAN VISIONS: THE GHOST DANCE AND CANUDOS

Among the many responses to the pressures of imperialism and intrusive state power were efforts to enlist spiritual forces against unwelcome change. These efforts took many forms, such as millenarian movements.

THE GHOST DANCE IN NORTH AMERICA

The nineteenth century brought hard and bewildering times to the indigenous peoples of North America. They were defeated in wars by the U.S. Army and decimated by disease. In the first half of the century, native peoples of the eastern United States were pushed westward or confined to small reservations. First Nations in Canada fared little better despite the rarity of warfare.

After 1850, indigenous peoples of the western part of the continent met similar fates. On their home ground in the Great Plains, the Rocky Mountains, and the Great Basin, they had to deal with vast disruptions to their ways of life. Fur traders offered access to novel goods such as guns and hard liquor. Epidemics raged. Hunters—including many who were indigenous themselves or partly so—obliterated the once vast bison herds to sell hides, leaving the peoples of the Great Plains without their main source of food, fuel, and clothing. The U.S. and Canadian governments kept breaking promises and treaties, turning over more and more land to white settlers. After the end of the U.S. Civil War in 1865, these disorienting trends grew stronger. In 1876, Canada made assimilation of First Nations a formal policy and offered appealing terms for settlers, who poured in. Then, in 1887, the Dawes Act in the United States opened the vast majority of remaining indigenous land to white settlers. Indigenous Americans had to face more soldiers, settlers, and railroads; fuller restriction to reservations (called *reserves* in Canada); and efforts by churches and governments to assimilate their children through special schools and conversion to Christianity.

The disruptions of indigenous life invited intellectual and religious creativity in response. Peoples of the Great Basin and northern Rockies had long had a prophetic tradition that, from the 1830s onward, acquired some Christian overtones through contact with white Americans and Iroquois missionaries from upstate New York.

This prophetic tradition took a new direction among the Paiute in northern Nevada in the years 1869–1870. In a vision, a prophet sometimes known as Wodziwob ("Gray-hair") foresaw that if people followed certain ceremonies, spirits would respond: the vanished game would come back, and the recently departed (of whom there were many after an 1867 typhoid epidemic) would return to life amid joy and plenty. By some accounts, his vision included the idea that the Earth would swallow up the whites whose arrival had brought such misery.

The **Ghost Dance** (or Spirit Dance), as this movement is now called, featured a ceremony built around a circular dance common among indigenous groups of the

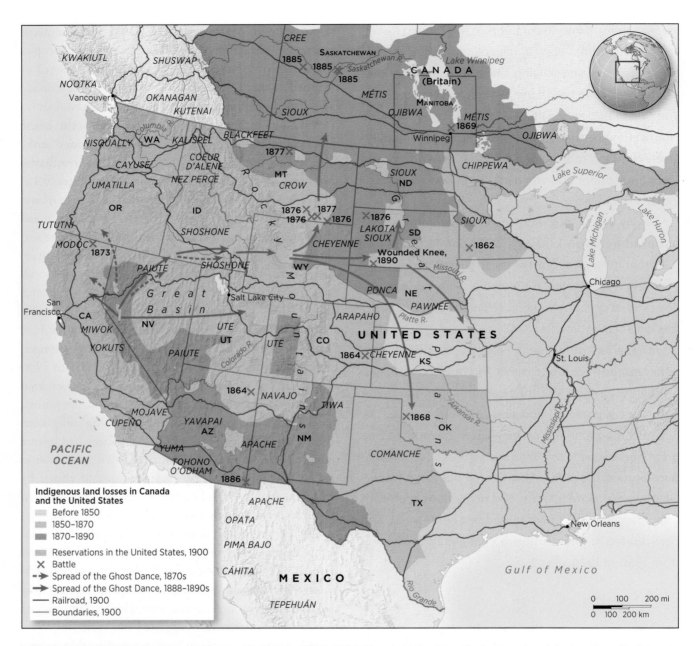

Indigenous North America: Devastation and Response, 1850–1900 The centuries-long displacement and destruction of indigenous communities continued during the late nineteenth century in the United States and Canada. Land losses accelerated, as indigenous peoples lacked the military and demographic power to fight off the U.S. Army and prevent further expansion by land-hungry American settlers, whose numbers swelled, especially along railroad lines. The popularity of the Ghost Dance among several indigenous peoples reflected the desperate position they shared.

West. Men, women, and children held hands, sang, and sidestep-shuffled gently clockwise to a drumbeat. They performed this dance for long hours at night, five nights in a row, to invoke the help of powerful spirits. The ritual dance spread to nearby California and Oregon. But the prophecy failed to come true, and the preaching and dancing died out in these lands by 1873. It survived and

spread in southern Idaho and Utah, where Mormon influence reinforced the prophetic tradition of local indigenous Americans.

Mormons had migrated westward to Utah in the 1840s, bringing a religion that emphasized prophecy. Mormon belief had a special role for indigenous prophecy: as Mormons saw it, one of the lost tribes of ancient Israel had

Ghost Dance In 1890, the leading American magazine, *Harper's Weekly*, published artist Frederic Remington's impression of Lakota Sioux people from the Dakota Territory performing the circle dance ritual that was central to the Ghost Dance movement. Remington based his drawing on sketches from firsthand observers, but he never saw the Ghost Dance himself.

come to North America, and indigenous populations were their descendants. Parts of Mormon doctrine appealed to many Native Americans, and the Ghost Dance prophecies resonated with many Mormons who also looked forward to the restoration of justice and faith. Both groups felt, with justification, persecuted by the U.S. government. Although almost hidden from view, the Ghost Dance survived through the 1870s and 1880s, mainly among peoples in touch with Mormon communities.

WOVOKA'S PROPHECY Then, in 1889, Wovoka ("Axe-man"), a Paiute like Wodziwob, had his first prophetic vision. Having lived for 20 years with a white ranching family of Presbyterians, his visions bore imprints of Christianity. Wovoka believed he had gone to heaven, where everyone he saw was healthy and forever young, enjoying their favorite pastimes. His reputation as a healer and spiritual specialist who could end droughts helped earn Wovoka an audience. In the years 1889–1890, he preached that if Native Americans conducted themselves peacefully and honestly, and performed the Ghost Dance, then the joyful prophecy would come true.

Wovoka's prophecy passed from one people to another. In some versions of the prophecy, white people would be swallowed up by the Earth or drowned in a flood. In others, both whites and Native Americans would live together in peace and health. At some point, Wovoka added the promise that Jesus Christ would return in 1892 to oversee peace on Earth, working through the U.S. president and through Wovoka himself.

Everywhere, the prophecy included the instruction to perform the circle dance for five days and nights. The community dance helped people feel that they were doing something constructive to heal their broken world. It also expressed a growing sense of indigenous identity across tribal lines, a new—we might say nationalist—identity for thousands of people who had formerly seen themselves as Paiute, Shoshone, Ute, Blackfeet, Arapaho, Cree, Ojibwa, and so forth. The shared experience of catastrophic disease, loss of land, and other misfortunes helped the various indigenous peoples of the West feel more "Indian" and express it in the Spirit Dance.

WOUNDED KNEE Among the peoples attracted by Wovoka's prophecy were the Lakota Sioux of the Dakota Territory. Their devotion to the Spirit Dance worried some local U.S. officials, who named it the Ghost Dance. They summoned support from the U.S. Army. A confrontation in 1890 turned violent, resulting in the deaths of 25 members of the U.S. Seventh cavalry and 153 Lakota Sioux, most of whom were women and children. The event, known as the massacre of Wounded Knee, came just short of two years after Wovoka's original vision. It cast a dark shadow over the Ghost Dance movement.

But the Ghost Dance did not die in 1890. It continued to appeal as a way of meeting up with dead friends and kin, and as a means of expressing indigenous identity in an increasingly white world. From Oklahoma to Saskatchewan, indigenous people continued to practice it well into the twentieth century, often secretly. They were trying to revitalize their vanished world.

CANUDOS IN NORTHEASTERN BRAZIL

While the Ghost Dance movement was sweeping western North America, another religious revitalization movement was washing over the northeast of Brazil. It flourished in the thinly populated backcountry called the Sertão, a scrubby land of cattle ranches and erratic rainfall. Its leader was Antônio Maciel.

Maciel was born in 1830 to a moderately prosperous family. But his mother died young and his father took to the bottle, and Antônio went to live with his grandfather, a schoolteacher. In his twenties he married and

CONSIDERING THE EVIDENCE

Messengers of the Ghost Dance

In November 1889, a Cheyenne man named Porcupine traveled by railway, wagon, and foot to "meet other Indians and see other countries." Beginning near Fort Washakie in Wyoming, he passed through indigenous and Mormon communities in Utah before reaching Pyramid Lake in western Nevada, where he stayed with the Paiute communities who had started the Ghost Dance movement. After returning home, Porcupine related the following account of his journey to a Major Carroll of the U.S. Army. Porcupine's description of meeting Christ may refer to an actual meeting with Wovoka, the prophet of the Ghost Dance movement who lived near Pyramid Lake. However, it also resembles a story from the Book of Mormon that claims Jesus Christ visited America after his death. Regardless, Porcupine's account emphasizes the diversity of peoples who embraced the Ghost Dance movement and became its messengers.

All the Indians from the Bannock agency [in Wyoming] down to where I finally stopped [in Nevada] danced this dance.... [T]he whites and Indians danced together.... The people there seemed all to be good. I never saw any drinking or fighting or bad conduct among them. They treated me well on the [railway] cars, without pay. They gave me food without charge, and I found that this was a habit among them toward their neighbors.... I and my people have been living in ignorance until I went and found out the truth. All the whites and Indians are brothers, I was told there. I never knew this before....

The Fish-eaters [Paiute] near Pyramid Lake told me that Christ had appeared on earth again.... [T]hat was why unconsciously I took my journey.... Christ had summoned myself and others from ... fifteen or sixteen different tribes. There were more different languages than I ever heard before and I did not understand any of them....

Just after dark some of the Indians told me that the Christ ... was arrived.... [H]e commenced our dance, everybody joining in, the Christ singing while we danced....

He told us also that all our dead were to be resurrected ...; that we must tell all the people we meet about these things. He spoke to us about fighting, and said that was bad, and we must keep from it; ... and we must all be friends with one another. He said that in the fall of the year the youth of all the good people would be renewed, so that nobody would be more than 40 years old.... He said if we were all good he would send people [to] heal all our wounds and sickness by mere touch, and that we would live forever. He told us not to quarrel, or fight, nor strike each other, nor shoot one another; that the whites and Indians were to be all one people. He said if any man disobeyed what he ordered, his tribe would be wiped from the face of the earth.

Source: "Porcupine's Account of the Messiah," in James Mooney, "The Ghost Dance Religion and the Sioux Outbreak of 1890," in J. W. Powell, ed., *Fourteenth Annual Report of the Bureau of Ethnology to the Secretary of the Smithsonian Institution*, Vol. 2 (Washington, D.C., 1896).

QUESTIONS FOR ANALYSIS

1. What did Porcupine find appealing about the Ghost Dance movement?
2. How did the teachings of the Ghost Dance movement, as described above, promote a shared indigenous identity?
3. What features did the Ghost Dance movement share with other millenarian movements discussed in this chapter?

began work as a teacher. In his mid-thirties, his marriage failed, his career fizzled, and he began to wander the countryside. He dressed in a simple robe, wore a beard and long hair, and reminded people of paintings of Jesus Christ. Everywhere he went, he repaired churches and cemetery walls.

Gradually, he became known for his soaring sermons. Listeners felt as if they were "flying up to the clouds" when he explained that the true path to redemption and salvation required frugality, sobriety, and modesty. People began to call him **Antônio Conselheiro** ("Anthony the Counselor") for the sage advice he dispensed. Listeners started to follow him from village to village.

ANTÔNIO CONSELHEIRO'S QUEST FOR JUSTICE In 1877 and 1878, northeastern Brazil was hit by a searing drought caused by one of the biggest El Niños in recent centuries. (El Niños, as we've seen, are periodic shifts in Pacific equatorial currents associated with both droughts and floods around the world.) Several hundred thousand people died of starvation as crops failed and livestock died. Antônio Conselheiro attracted still more followers among the hungry refugees, who were drawn to his message of social justice and salvation for the righteous poor. His preaching came to include attacks on Protestantism (which was rare in Brazil), alcohol and prostitution, and the evils of slavery. The drought led many slaveholders in northeastern Brazil to manumit people, turning them loose in desperate times with no means of support. A large proportion of Antônio Conselheiro's followers came from their ranks.

In 1893, after 20 years of wandering, Antônio Conselheiro settled down. He chose a mud-hut town, Canudos, in the middle of nowhere. Brazil had abolished slavery (1888) and become a republic (1889). The new state was anticlerical and claimed the right to recognize civil (as opposed to church) marriages. Antônio Conselheiro took vigorous exception to this claim and started to denounce the injustice of the state prominently in his outdoor sermons. He tossed tax edicts onto a bonfire. He encouraged his followers—by 1897 some 20,000 people, mainly women—to form a just community, unconstrained by the new godless laws. He wanted to withdraw from the world of injustice and corruption, but in so doing he was now challenging the Brazilian state. He also promised his admirers that in 1900 Jesus Christ would return to bring about the kingdom of heaven on Earth.

The Brazilian Army attacked Canudos. Three times it failed, as freedmen, servants, and hungry farmworkers with rusty weaponry and no training defended the town. But in 1897, on a fourth attempt, made with tens of thousands of soldiers, machine guns, and field artillery, the army prevailed. All those captured were promptly killed. Antônio Conselheiro had already died—of dysentery.

Tens of thousands of poor, hungry, illiterate Brazilians, hammered by drought, found hope in the message of Antônio Conselheiro, just as thousands of indigenous North Americans put their faith in the Ghost Dance. For both groups, as for the Xhosa in South Africa, the world in the late nineteenth century seemed to be spinning out of control. Nature seemed especially unruly. Powerful people seemed to be conspiring against them. They needed something powerful of their own to restore justice to the world. Millenarian faith answered their needs, even

Antônio Conselheiro's Followers Dozens of Conselheiro's destitute followers who settled in Canudos huddle together. In the background, a line of the rebel soldiers who defended Canudos watches over the group of mostly women and children.

if, in the end, it could not protect them against modern armies with industrial weaponry.

Movements such as these cropped up around the world during the age of industrial imperialism. In hundreds of cases, including the Lakota Sioux, prophets encouraged people to believe that spiritual forces—talismans, amulets, tattoos—could protect them against bullets. They knew they could not match the material power of their enemies. If they were not to give up all hope, they had to place their faith in spiritual power. Yet, whatever its merits, that power could not stop the advances of imperial and national states backed by artillery, machine guns, and railroad networks.

GIANT REBELLIONS, 1850–1864: CHINA AND INDIA

The millenarian prophets who judged that the tide was running against their people could only mobilize a few thousand followers. Far bigger rebellions, involving tens of millions of people, also broke out in the middle of the nineteenth century in China and India. Like the millenarian movements, both rebellions showed the growing impact of global connections, shaped by specific cultures, religions, institutions, and personalities.

THE TAIPING REBELLION, 1850–1864

China in the mid-nineteenth century was ruled by the Qing dynasty, which had taken power from the Ming 200 years before. The Qing had doubled the size of their empire during the eighteenth century and benefited from the stability provided by effective and long-lived emperors. The last of these, the Qianlong Emperor, died in 1799. In the years that followed, the sprawling Qing Empire—with its far-flung territories in Mongolia, Central Asia, and Tibet and its numerous religions, languages, and ethnic groups—became increasingly unsettled.

THE PLIGHT OF THE QING At the time of Qianlong's death, the Qing governed lightly. Tax rates were about a quarter of those in Europe. Most revenues (60

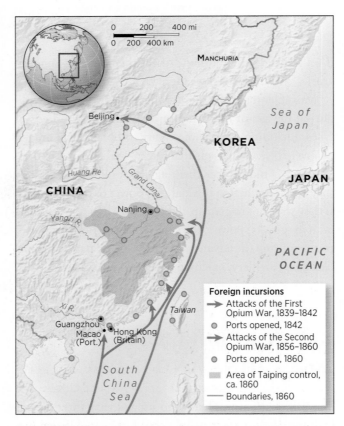

Foreign Incursions and the Taiping Rebellion, 1842–1860 Qing China suffered great disruptions in the middle of the nineteenth century. In the First Opium War, Britain used superior naval forces to force the Qing to open many seaports to foreign trade and made Hong Kong a British colony (1842). In the Second Opium War, Britain and France obliged the Qing to open many more seaports and riverports to foreign commerce. Meanwhile, in central and southeastern China, the Taiping Rebellion brought violence and destruction on a staggering scale. The Qing never fully recovered.

to 70 percent) went to the army, which nonetheless was underpaid and underequipped. The Qing bureaucracy was thin, with roughly 10,000 paid officials, and relied on the goodwill of local landlords for routine administration. That left the state vulnerable to corruption, which flourished, particularly in the 1790s. It also contributed to the development of a large pool of talented men who had passed the civil service exams but could not get a job in government. Many of them became critics of Qing incompetence and corruption, both of which were displayed when a rural revolt, the White Lotus Rebellion (1796–1804), began in central China. At first a largely Buddhist uprising against state corruption, it ended with Qing army units fighting one another in order to continue to draw pay. That drained the Qing treasury dry.

Economic problems facing the Qing worsened early in the nineteenth century. For most of Chinese history, population growth had raised total output and strengthened states because peasants had carved out new farmland from swamps and mountainsides. But now too little land suitable for farming remained. Farm acreage per capita fell by almost half from 1753 to 1812, and continued population growth led only to hunger. In addition, the highly commercial Chinese economy, which had grown accustomed to large infusions of silver for coinage, suffered when the supply of silver diminished in the early nineteenth century. With the wars of independence in Latin America (1808–1830), world silver production fell by about half. After 1810, silver was flowing out of China to pay for imports. Upkeep of canals, dams, roads, and bridges ebbed. By the 1820s, dredging of silt in the Grand Canal was so neglected that the annual supplies of grain from the south to the capital at Beijing rarely arrived. Military morale sagged as Qing revenues plummeted and corruption soared.

Widespread use of opium compounded the Qing plight. An addictive drug that had been introduced by Arab traders a millennium before, opium had been illegal in China since 1729. But its use climbed sharply after about 1820. The British East India Company served as the major supplier, cultivating and purchasing the drug in Bengal and selling it cheaply in southern China. Aware of the growing addiction problem and the resulting outflow of silver to foreign merchants, Chinese officials tried to restrict opium imports in 1838. The British regarded this as an unjust restriction on free trade and used their navy to defeat China in the First Opium War (1839–1842).

Foreign Influence in China French, American, British, and Dutch flags fly over trading posts belonging to those countries in mid-nineteenth-century Guangzhou. The treaty system established after the Opium Wars allowed foreign powers unprecedented levels of influence within China.

The harsh terms of the Treaty of Nanjing ending the war opened several Chinese ports to British trade, obliged China to pay a large cash indemnity to Britain, and ceded Hong Kong "in perpetuity"—among other concessions. The defeat shocked China, and the terms of the treaty outraged most Chinese who learned of them. The prestige and finances of the Qing were nearing rock bottom. Many Chinese concluded that in order for their country to restore its fortunes, the Qing would have to go.

JESUS'S YOUNGER BROTHER Things soon got a lot worse thanks to Hong Xiuquan. Hong (1814–1864) came from a gentry family and an ethnic minority in South China called the Hakka ("Guest Families"). His great-grandfather had been a Qing official and landowner in the southern coastal region of Guangzhou. His family still owned land but had fallen a few rungs. But Hong needed the support of many relatives and neighbors while he pursued that venerable ambition: to pass the civil service exam and pursue a career in government. After many years of study, Hong, now in his mid-twenties, failed the examination three times.

Such failures were common, but Hong's reaction to disappointment was unique. He read Christian missionary pamphlets and, after a stint as a schoolteacher in his home village, began to study Christian doctrines with an American Baptist missionary, Issachar Roberts, in the port city of Guangzhou. Under Roberts's tutelage, as well as the influence of dreams, Hong in 1843 concluded that he was a son of God, the younger brother of Jesus, and responsible for realizing the kingdom of heaven on Earth. Prominent among his instructions was to rid China of

corrupt, foreign rulers—that is, the Qing dynasty, which was originally from Manchuria. Roberts refused to baptize his imaginative pupil, so Hong did it himself.

Hong began to preach a version of Christianity blended with popular spiritual beliefs. He found an audience in the poorest parts of the population—at first, mainly among his fellow Hakka. The economic decline of China and the humiliation of the First Opium War played into his hands. Before long he had inspired a social movement, tinged with Christian lore, dedicated to the overthrow of the Qing, whom he branded as foreign devils. Hong's agenda included the extermination of demon-worship, by which he meant Buddhism and Confucianism. Persecuted by Qing authorities, Hong raised the flag of rebellion in 1850 during a local famine in South China.

REBELLION By 1853, his army had taken cities in the Yangzi valley, the commercial highway of China. They made Nanjing (which means "Southern Capital") their base. Northern thrusts toward Beijing ("Northern Capital") proved unsuccessful—by and large, northerners found Hong's message, soaked as it was in southern culture, unappealing. But for 10 years, the Taiping (meaning "Great Peace") controlled much of the Yangzi valley and parts of southern China.

The Taiping had a distinctive program that in ordinary times would have repelled most Chinese. On the social front, they assaulted the traditions of the Chinese family. They proclaimed that women were equal to men, and they banned prostitution, adultery, concubinage, and indeed all sex outside of marriage. Until 1855, they tried to enforce segregation of the sexes. They proscribed alcohol, opium, and tobacco. On the political side, they invited, and soon compelled, peasants to reject private property and contribute all their possessions to a central Taiping treasury. They instructed everyone to regard Qing officials as foreign devils, and southerners, Taiping rebels especially, as the only uncorrupted Chinese. As for religion and culture, the Taiping preached that Christianity was not an import but had been born in China. They took a militant line against rival faiths, destroying Buddhist and Confucian temples and texts, and killing priests and sages. They were gentler with Islam, a minor religion in the areas they controlled. They disdained the refinement and learning of the Chinese elites that Hong had tried to join.

Despite their puritanical principles, the Taiping leaders indulged themselves in the looting, rape, and gratuitous

The Taiping Rebellion A massive battle between Taiping and Qing forces in the region of Nanjing, the Heavenly Capital of the Taiping leader, Hong Xiuquan. Qing forces prevailed over the Taiping in part through the effectiveness of regional militia organized by talented leaders such as Zeng Guofan (right).

killed more than combat did. Some provinces along the middle and lower Yangzi lost 70 to 90 percent of their population to death and flight. The Qing limped on until 1910.

The **Taiping Rebellion** shows the interplay of internal and external forces in China. Many of its underlying causes were linked to China's changing place in the Global web. The sources of Qing economic weakness involved its dependency on imported Latin American silver and its people's growing addiction to opium from British India. Hong's ideology, a curious mix of local beliefs and Christianity imported from the United States, was as persuasive to downtrodden people eager for hope as the prophecies of Nongqawuse, Wokova, or Antônio Conselheiro. Defeat by a distant nation they disdained as barbarian also undercut the legitimacy of the Qing—before 1839, few Chinese officials had a proper appreciation of the power of Britain's Royal Navy and its modern weaponry. The Qing's failings with respect to the economy, opium, and foreign powers made them all the more vulnerable to nationalistic charges that they were not proper Chinese. China, of course, has always had rebellions. But the character and magnitude of the Taiping Rebellion had everything to do with the global processes corroding the Qing Empire.

violence of conquest. Taiping leaders organized the kidnapping of women for sex duty. They amassed personal fortunes in looted goods, apparently including solid-gold chamber pots. They executed dissenters and massacred millions whose loyalties displeased them.

At first, the Qing armies could offer scant resistance. In 1856, Britain and France launched the Second Opium War, invading north China, attacking Beijing, and burning the emperor's summer palace. They wanted still greater trading privileges in China and the legalization of opium to benefit Britain's merchant class. Meanwhile, three or four other significant rebellions broke out. Amazingly, the dynasty limped on.

In 1860, Britain and France got the trade concessions they wanted from the Qing, and yet more indemnities, and threw their support behind the dynasty. The Taiping, after all, had banned opium and preached a faith that looked like heresy to European Christians. So Qing armies trained and led by American and British officers began to attack the Taiping. At the same time, local gentry leaders such as Zeng Guofan in Hunan raised effective anti-Taiping armies. Now the momentum switched, and the Taiping leaders' quarrels, already murderous, became large-scale purges. Hong died, either from illness or from poison, in 1864. A few months later, the Hunan army finally finished off his die-hard supporters, massacring the population of Nanjing in 1864.

When after 14 years it was all over, at least 30 million of China's 350 to 400 million people, some 7 to 9 percent of the population, were dead. The contemporaneous American Civil War cost 600,000 lives, or 2 percent of the U.S. population. As usual, epidemics and starvation

THE INDIAN REBELLION, 1857–1858

The **Indian Rebellion**—also known as the First War of Independence, Indian Mutiny, Sepoy Rebellion, or Great Rebellion—also showed the impacts of global connections, most obviously of British rule. Since the 1750s, the British East India Company (EIC) had acquired growing authority in parts of India, especially Bengal in the northeast. Before 1857, British rule in India was mainly company rule. The Mughal Empire still nominally ruled north India, but increasingly it served as a façade behind which stood agents of the EIC. By 1803, the EIC—some 600 British merchants and officials protected by an army of 200,000 Indian soldiers—had outmaneuvered or defeated all indigenous powers in India and stood supreme in most of the subcontinent. Until 1813, the company enjoyed a monopoly on trade with India and tried hard to keep out interlopers, including missionaries. But in 1813, the British state, bending to the wishes of merchant and evangelical groups at home, stripped the EIC of its trade monopoly and lifted the ban on missionaries. The British government took an ever-larger role in India and directly controlled about two-thirds of it by 1857, with the rest either under Company control or under local independent Indian rulers.

GRIEVANCES The British—both the EIC and the Crown—enacted reforms that deeply aggrieved the Indian elite through whom Britain governed the country. Among these were changes to the trade and tariff regime that opened up India to foreign competition, including the efficient cotton mills of England. As we've seen, this undercut the business of Indian merchants as well as village spinners and weavers. Reform to the patchwork tax regime awarded the Company most of the revenues from Indian lands and required some landlords to pay tax on lands that had formerly been exempt. A political reform (called the doctrine of lapse) stipulated that any principality without a biological son as heir would henceforth fall to British rule, which meant that sooner or later all of India would be British. In addition, the EIC by means fair and foul annexed chunks of India, leading many princes to suspect that they might be next. In 1856, the Company took over a prosperous polity, Oudh (also spelled Awadh), on the grounds that its ruler was inept and corrupt.

Religion also provided grounds for Indian anxiety and grievance. Christian missionaries proved a particular source of irritation to Indians, all out of proportion to their tiny success in converting Hindus, Muslims, Sikhs, or Jains. Moreover, the EIC army, made up overwhelmingly of Indians, grew restive over call-ups for overseas duty in China, the Crimea, Persia, and Burma. High-caste Hindus, who could not cook according to ritual requirements, risked their caste status as a result of these deployments. In general, elite Muslims and Hindus felt that they—not Christian foreigners—should rule India.

The spark that ignited the Indian Rebellion came in 1857 in the form of new rifle cartridges introduced in the Bengal Army, the largest of the three separate Indian armies run by the EIC. Annoyed by overseas duty and reductions in pay, the Indian soldiers, called *sepoys*, were

The Indian Rebellion, 1857–1858 Large-scale uprisings against British authority took place in the years 1857–1858 in the Ganges plain and in central India. The British-led Indian Army defeated the uprisings militarily, leading to the end of EIC rule and the creation of a British Crown colony of India in 1858. Those states that remained nominally independent had to bow to British wishes on all important matters.

already on edge. The Enfield rifle, a big upgrade over the muskets in use before, required cartridges that would slide down the gun barrel for loading. Rumors spread that the grease used for this purpose was animal fat from both pigs and cows. Since soldiers had to bite off the tip of a cartridge before inserting it in their rifle barrel, Muslims feared defilement by pig fat and Hindus feared breaking taboo against beef. In early 1857, soldiers who resisted orders to use these new cartridges were hanged by EIC military officers, setting off a rebellion.

REBELLION The Indian Rebellion of 1857–1858 was an army mutiny combined with a series of local and regional rebellions. It was never a unified movement under a single command. Several garrisons in northern and central India rose in revolt, joined by about a quarter of the Bengal Army. At its height, the rebels controlled much of the Ganges plain and pockets elsewhere in India.

British Atrocities A painting by a British military artist shows East India Company officers ordering the brutal execution of Indian soldiers who refused to use new rifle cartridges. The soldiers were tied to the muzzles of cannons and killed by cannonballs at point-blank range.

The main goals of the rebellion were the destruction of British rule in India and the restoration of various old regimes. For Muslims, that generally meant returning to the glory days of Mughal power through the person of Bahadur Shah II, the 82-year-old figurehead emperor. Bahadur Shah, who preferred poetry to politics, reluctantly sided with the uprising. For Hindus, the goal was to restore earlier golden ages, when one or another Hindu leader had ruled wisely. Followers of minority religions generally chose not to rebel. Sikhs, for example, proved staunchly loyal to the EIC, preferring it to the prospect of Hindu or Muslim rule.

Local royalty was divided too. Some former rulers tried to reclaim lost power, including **Lakshmibai**, the queen of Jhansi in north-central India. Married at age 13, she was a widow when the EIC invoked the doctrine of lapse, which she regarded as an unjust seizure of her throne. Age 29 when the rebellion came, she gambled on its success and for a few months ruled Jhansi in defiance of the EIC armies. But soon her capital was under siege, her kingdom captured, and her life lost in combat. She has since become a national hero in India, portrayed in movies, TV shows, and video games.

The Indian Rebellion failed because too many Indians, and especially army units, resisted the call to revolt and stayed loyal to EIC army commanders. Had the armies united in revolt, they would easily have driven the British from India. The rebels hoped in vain that Britain's rivals, France or Russia, might come to their aid.

AFTERMATH The rebellion and its aftermath featured all the butchery and gore that are customary in warfare. In one notorious episode, an Indian commander, Nana Sahib, an aristocrat well educated in English and French literature, arranged for 200 British women and children to be chopped up and stuffed down a well in Kanpur—the event is famous in Britain as the massacre of Cawnpore. British officers oversaw vengeful reprisals against Indians, killing men, women, and children indiscriminately. These slaughters continued after the rebellion ceased. The greatest legacy of the rebellion was bitterness on all sides.

The casualties included 11,000 British (most of whom died of disease), several hundred thousand Indians, the Mughal Empire, and the EIC. The rebellion made clear that everything would have to change if Britain were to continue to rule India. India became a Crown colony, and back in Britain Queen Victoria added the title Empress of India. Now Parliament and the India Office in London, represented in India by a viceroy, would rule the country. Hundreds of princely states remained, but all stood subservient to the viceroy. What little had remained of the Mughal Empire in 1857 now vanished into British India, and Bahadur Shah, the last of a line that included great emperors such as Akbar and Aurangzeb, lived out his final years in exile. The EIC lost all its remaining authority. The British Crown took all its assets and liquidated what was left of it in 1874.

Indians often refer to the rebellion as the First War of Independence, emphasizing the first stirrings of Indian nationalism. Although Indians fought one another furiously during the rebellion, thereafter the violence, bitterness, and continuing resentments against foreign rule helped them see their common condition more clearly.

In the aftermath, British rule in India, known as the

Lakshmibai The queen of Jhansi is portrayed wearing white and riding on a white horse, crowned and carrying a crop. All these symbols indicate her status as a hero in the eyes of many Indians for her support of the Indian Rebellion.

British India Students at a school for girls in India during the early twentieth century. The British Raj put schools and other social institutions in place across India, enabling it to consolidate its control over the subcontinent.

Raj, changed its character in ways that hastened the development of nationalism in India. British authority became more bureaucratic and less personalized. It gave more attention to public works, especially railroads, education, and irrigation. It tried harder to regulate justice and health, and it created an India-wide post and telegraph system. It rewarded the many princes who had stayed loyal by allowing them to exercise modest authority and collect enough tax revenue to live in splendor. In general, the Raj made the experience of being ruled more uniform and less localized. In the long run, this helped Indians feel more Indian, as opposed to feeling specifically Muslim, Sikh, or Hindu, or Tamil, Bengali, or Punjabi.

The Indian Rebellion reflected deep distress on the part of many Indians with their situation in the 1850s. The rebels' grievances were different from those that lay behind the Taiping Rebellion in China, and the loss of life far smaller, but at root they had some things in common. One was economic distress resulting from the disruptive impacts of international trade, an example of the blowback from economic globalization. Another was the unintended consequences of Christian missionary activity. A third was resentment against foreign rule.

Resentment against foreign rule took different forms in India and China, but both involved the EIC. Muslim and Hindu elites in India objected to their loss of authority and to the rapid encroachments of the EIC over the previous 100 years. The Taiping resented the foreign origins of China's Qing rulers, in power for 200 years. But part of what led them to despise the Qing was the dynasty's inability to cope with British aggression—specifically, in the First Opium War, which was fought mainly to preserve the Chinese opium market of the EIC. The business interests of the EIC and the military adventures it inspired played a role in both of these giant rebellions.

REBELLIONS AS GLOBAL AND LOCAL

The great rebellions in China and India drew on powerful combinations of macro trends—including nationalism, imperialism, and industrialization—and local institutions, cultures, and leaders. The growing connectivity of the Global web ensured that these were not the only disruptions shaped by the combustible interaction of global and local forces. Pressures from Europe and the United States, as we've seen, helped spur the revolution in Japan known as the Meiji Restoration (1866–1868). Foreign examples of liberal and anticlerical government helped inspire civil wars in Mexico (1857–1867), in which France intervened. Doctrines of nationalism played central roles in wars of unification of Italy and Germany in the 1860s and in the deadliest war in South America's history, in which Brazil, Argentina, and Uruguay pummeled Paraguay (1865–1870).

Even the U.S. Civil War (1861–1865), another momentous rebellion, reflected a combination of global trends, in this case including abolitionism, and local causes. The westward—imperial—expansion of the United States provoked the war over slavery. And as we've seen, slaveholders and their supporters understood that as new free (non-slave) states joined the union, they would eventually tip the political balance in Congress in favor of abolition. To counter the effect of expansion into the West, proslavery forces urged imperial expansion into the Caribbean and twice raised private armies in hopes of adding islands such as Cuba as additional slave states. The industrial power and railroad network of the North helped decide the war, keeping the union intact—at the cost of about 600,000 lives, some 2 percent of the U.S. population. The aftermath of the war featured a more powerful, activist, and nationalist federal government. It amended the Constitution to abolish slavery and extend full political rights to freedmen—although after 1877 most southern states nevertheless sharply curtailed civil and political rights for African Americans. The federal government purchased Alaska from Russia in 1867, sped up the domination and assimilation of indigenous peoples, supported the industrialization of the country, promoted railroad building, and—by 1898—undertook overseas imperialism in both the Caribbean and the Pacific.

Meanwhile, the global forces of nationalism, imperialism, and industrialization grew still stronger. Technological advance continued to tighten the world's connections. The first transatlantic telegraph cable came in 1866. The Suez Canal in Egypt, which connected the Indian Ocean world to the Mediterranean Sea, and the first U.S. transcontinental railroad both opened for business in 1869. The flows of information, goods, and people would only quicken. And so social struggles, although as always largely about local concerns, increasingly reflected international and global influences too.

A common pattern emerged in the societies under pressure from Britain and the world's other leading powers. Some reformers in these societies wanted to strengthen their countries by imitating the most powerful foreign examples, while others thought the way to withstand foreign power was to hold tight to their traditions. In Russia, for example, there were so-called Westernizers such as Sergei Witte who, as we've seen, wanted to make Russia strong by adopting techniques and technologies from industrial western Europe. But at the same time so-called Slavophiles, such as the novelist Fyodor Dostoevsky, argued that Russia's strength lay in its unique

Suez Canal Ships line up to enter the Suez Canal around 1890. The canal connecting the Indian Ocean with the Mediterranean Sea was a major step toward tightening the Global web.

traditions and culture, especially the Russian Orthodox Church. Japan faced similar divisions from the 1850s onward, although there the groups that were inclined to adapt foreign examples won decisively in the policy arena. Muslim states such as Egypt or Iran confronted the same issue in their own ways: should they seek to industrialize and encourage a national identity among their populations, or should they try to strengthen their countries by rallying behind the banners of Islam? These divisions fractured many societies and focused political attention on religion, education, economic policy, technology, and other areas that might help peoples and states become stronger in the face of the severe challenges of the late nineteenth century.

REVOLUTIONS, 1870s–1920: CHINA AND MEXICO

The military defeat of the rebellions in China and India did not resolve the grievances that sparked them. To the contrary, anger and disappointment over the failings of rulers only grew, particularly wherever imperialism, nationalism, or the difficulty of competing against industrial production affected poor families. In places as different as China, Mexico, Russia, and the Ottoman Empire, millions despaired over their prospects in life and came to resent their governments' shortcomings. For peasants, the main issue was usually land. Population growth everywhere reduced the land available per family. In some countries, especially those where governments were attempting reform programs, peasants' tax burdens grew too. Among the educated middle classes, frustration developed at ruling elites that seemed unable to address rising challenges such as the suffering of the peasantry, the lack of opportunity for educated youth, and the growing threat from industrialized and imperialistic states. Observant reformers around the world were concerned by—and often inspired by—the mounting power of Britain, Germany, the United States, or Japan. They wanted their own governments to match that power—typically, by means of military modernization, industrialization, expulsion of foreign missionaries or businesses, and expansion of education. If complacent and corrupt rulers would not rise to the challenge, then the only course was to replace them through revolution.

THE CHINESE REVOLUTION, 1880s–1910s

After the Taiping Rebellion ended in 1864, matters improved—a little—in China. The intense fighting had laid waste to cities and the countryside so that, as one eyewitness put it, "weeds and jungle cover[ed] the land." China's population in 1864, perhaps 350 to 400 million strong, was on average poorer than it had been a century before. In the south and southeast of China, millions gave up on life at home and emigrated to Southeast Asia, the Pacific Islands, and the Americas.

PRESSURES AND GRIEVANCES The Qing government never fully recovered its authority. Without much prestige or money, it could not control the provinces, which gave local officials leeway to pursue their own programs. Governors and provincial officials increasingly used the taxes they raised to build their own military forces and undertake their own reform initiatives in education, infrastructure, industry, and military matters.

These efforts in the provinces are sometimes known as China's self-strengthening movement. It owed little to the Qing court, and much to provincial governors. They typically focused on military industries. In Jiangnan Province (around Shanghai) and in Wuhan along the central Yangzi River, officials worked with private entrepreneurs to set up iron, steel, and weapons industries. Li Hongzhang, who had made his reputation helping to defeat the Taiping Rebellion, built arsenals, shipyards, a steamship company, a telegraph network, and military academies in eastern China's Hebei Province.

These provincial officials were trying to provide the Qing Empire—and themselves—with the tools of modern state power. They saw themselves as following an old saying that originated with Chinese struggles against steppe raiders: "using the barbarians' ways to defend against the barbarians." Now the "barbarians" were not Mongol but European, American, or Japanese. These reformers often wanted to retain Confucian ethics and ideology, or "essence" as they put it, but also acquire the hardware of industrial power.

An illustrative initiative was Li Hongzhang's study abroad program. On the advice of Yung Wing, a Christian convert and the first Chinese graduate of an American university (Yale, class of 1854), Li sent 113 promising boys to high schools in New England to prepare them for administrative posts in his province—a radically different approach from training them in the Confucian classics. They studied those subjects that fit them for high responsibility: science, technology, engineering, math, languages—and, of course, history. In 1881, the program was discontinued when it appeared the boys had grown too Americanized, taking up baseball among other undignified pursuits. To some Qing officials, it seemed that they were losing their Confucian essence in their effort to acquire foreign practical knowledge.

The urgency of self-strengthening grew with time. For sophisticated Chinese, aware of the antiquity of their culture and the majestic power of earlier dynasties, the role of foreign influence was especially irksome. The treaties signed in 1842 and 1860 after the two Opium Wars gave foreigners special rights, called extraterritoriality, which included exemption from Chinese law. Foreign missionaries roamed the country. Foreign businessmen ran new mines, railroads, and factories. Foreigners controlled the maritime customs houses. Foreign gunboats slithered up and down the Yangzi River, enforcing the privileges of foreigners. In 1879, Japan took the Ryukyu Islands, which the Chinese regarded as theirs. In 1885, the French seized control of Vietnam, which the Qing considered to be under their protection. The contest for Vietnam boiled up into conflict, and French ships sank a quarter of the Chinese navy in an hour. By the 1880s, it seemed that at any time Britons, French, Germans, Americans—and, increasingly, Japanese and Russians—might carve up China, as imperialist powers were doing in Africa and Southeast Asia.

The foreign presence was only part of the discouraging situation that set the stage for the **Chinese Revolution**. Opium addiction continued to plague all levels of Chinese society. A terrible famine in the years 1877–1878, caused by the same giant El Niño that brought killing drought to Brazil, cost millions of lives. Japanese silk and Indian tea competed all too well against the Chinese products, undercutting important export trades. More fundamentally, the population kept growing while the available land did not. New crops—maize and sweet potatoes from the Americas—helped somewhat by raising production in areas ill-suited to rice, millet, or wheat. But population growth mainly caused families to grow poorer, more desperate, and more likely to kill their infant girls. Poverty, poor prospects, and a shortage of potential brides encouraged young men to consider radical choices such as banditry, emigration, or rebellion.

The Chinese Revolution, 1905–1911 Foreign pressures exacerbated internal weaknesses, speeding the decline of the Qing Empire and bringing its final collapse. Foreign powers including Russia, France, and Japan exploited the vacuum of power created by Qing weakness, seizing territories that had long been under Qing sway or even part of the Qing state. Qing subjects in Mongolia and Tibet broke away. Qing failings inspired ethnic Chinese increasingly to see their rulers as incompetent foreigners. Many Chinese supported the revolution that began in Wuhan in 1910 and ended two and a half centuries of Qing rule by 1911.

The Qing showed few signs of addressing these challenges. Huge indemnities from lost wars and the cost of suppressing rebellions kept their finances in a desperate state. They sometimes supported, but often opposed, the initiatives taken by talented provincial governors such as Li Hongzhang. In any case, the treaties forced upon them in 1842 and 1860 had deprived the Qing of some of the tools—such as tariffs—used by other countries, including Japan and the United States, to help them industrialize.

Patriotic Chinese did not agree on what to do about these pressing problems. For the self-strengtheners such as Li, China needed to adopt modern weaponry, telegraphs, steamships, and railroads. But it became clear

that this approach required engineering experts, trained managers, bankers, an industrial labor force, and an educational system to match. You could not get the teeth—modern military might—without the tail of a socially and culturally transformed society, one that undercut the authority of fathers, reduced the subservience of women, de-emphasized family ties, and compromised Confucian principles. For most Chinese, even the keen reformers, that was a painful prospect.

An alternative approach, always popular in difficult times in societies with glorious pasts, was to try to return to tried and true ways. Conservatives recommended banning all things foreign and purifying the commitment to

Confucian principles. In most of China, and most of the time at the Qing court, this view prevailed.

FOREIGN PRESSURE AND INTERNAL REVOLT

The contrast with Japan brought Chinese observers further discomfort. As we have seen, foreign aggression in Japan provoked a revolution that put in power an elite dedicated to strengthening the nation. With brisk energy and judicious borrowing from foreigners, they had created an industrial economy, modernized the military, and a reformed education, and embarked on a program of imperialism. Japan, almost overnight, had become both an inspiring example and a direct threat to China. The Chinese view of Japan as a lesser culture, derivative of China, made Japan's ascendance even more painful.

As Chinese elites struggled with their choices, the urgency of the situation grew. Japan's imperialist actions led Koreans to appeal to China for help, which brought on the Sino-Japanese War (1894–1895). China was trounced, its newly built navy sunk. Humiliated, it had to cede Taiwan to Japan and pay yet another large indemnity. The emperor at the time, 24-year-old Guangxu—the only Chinese emperor to learn English—in practice shared power with his aunt, Cixi, known as the Empress Dowager. In 1898, he embarked on a bold program of reforms. His advisors, inspired by Japan's recent history, proposed new universities, railroads, and even a constitutional government. But Cixi, an ardent reformer in her younger days, was now a fierce and formidable conservative and a veteran of court intrigue. She had revealed her priorities in 1893 by using the naval budget to spruce up the imperial summer palace. She engineered a palace coup in 1898, confined her nephew to house arrest, and executed reformers who could not escape China.

In the years 1899–1900, an antiforeign, anti-Christian, and initially anti-Qing uprising by nationalist youths, who called themselves the Righteous and Harmonious Fists, boiled over. Known to foreigners as the Boxers because of their interest in martial arts, they originated during a time of drought and hunger in the northeastern province of Shandong. Their xenophobic movement had a millenarian tinge to it, including a belief that their rituals could make them invulnerable to bullets. They murdered Chinese Christians and foreign missionaries. They looted churches and foreign property throughout northern China and killed the German ambassador. After foreign troops guarding embassies and legations killed several Boxers, Cixi in 1900 declared war on all foreign nations involved in China. Within months, an international force of eight nations, made up mostly of Japanese and Russian soldiers and ships—and partly funded by overseas Chinese eager to end Qing rule—invaded China. Twenty thousand foreign troops crushed the Boxers and Qing forces, and imposed yet another heavy indemnity on China. Russia occupied Manchuria, the homeland of the Qing. Cixi and her nephew Guangxu fled Beijing.

The Qing, it seemed in 1901, could sink no further. The futility of fighting foreign ways became clearer after the Boxers' defeat. Advisers convinced even Cixi that radical reform was required if the dynasty—indeed, China—were to survive. Her government sent thousands of students to

Empress Dowager Cixi The elderly Empress Dowager at court in the 1890s.

Boxer Rebellion Boxer soldiers stand at attention flanking some of the leaders of the movement in 1900.

Japan to observe its modernizing reforms. China abolished the 1,300-year-old civil service examination system; established new schools, including ones for girls; and directed major investment toward military industries.

It was too little, too late for the Qing. Their incompetence in the face of China's humiliations turned many of their most talented subjects, such as **Sun Yatsen**, into revolutionaries. Sun was born in 1866 to a peasant family in Guangdong. At age 13, he followed an older brother to Hawaii, where he received an English-language education at the same school from which President Obama graduated a century later. Having had little exposure to Confucian study, Sun was fully open to the teachings on offer in Hawaii. He was the most notable of the many young Chinese who were concluding that the Qing could not spearhead reform, and that to save China from foreign domination and enduring weakness required overthrowing them.

Sun Yatsen This Guomindang propaganda poster from the 1920s lionizes Sun Yatsen, pictured here between the flags. The caption above reads: "The revolution is not yet completed. Your comrades must continue to make efforts."

SUN YATSEN, REVOLUTIONARY After his schooling in Hawaii, Sun moved to Hong Kong, a British colony, where he studied with missionaries, was baptized an Anglican, and earned a medical degree. Disappointed by Qing weakness, Sun wanted, as he put it in 1894, to see China "do what the Europeans could do." He "tried especially to learn how these countries had grown rich and strong and how they had civilized their people." He thought it especially admirable that in Western countries "the interests of the state and those of commerce flourish together." Building railroads and battleships would not suffice, he thought. China needed to modernize its education system, its agriculture, and its commerce in order to address the root of its weakness. His efforts to energize reform by Qing officials and to gain employment with the government were rebuffed in 1894. If Qing officials refused to embark on suitably thorough reforms, Sun maintained, it was time for a revolution. He left China in 1895 when the Qing put a price on his head, and he did not return for 17 years. Throughout the 1890s and early 1900s, Sun traveled to Southeast Asia, Britain, Canada, the United States, and elsewhere, organizing opposition to Qing rule among overseas Chinese and looking for useful ideas.

Sun devised a revolutionary credo, his Three Principles. The first was a Chinese nationalist position: the Qing—those Manchu barbarians—must go, and real Chinese must rule China. The second principle was that the

imperial monarchy must be replaced by a constitutional republic. This drew on the examples Sun had seen abroad; nothing in Chinese tradition supported this principle. The third was the social principle—influenced by his exposure to European socialism—that everyone should have enough to eat, economic justice should prevail, and peasants should get an education and have a chance to apply their talents. Sun hoped that a China recast along these lines would both recover its proper place in the world and alleviate the suffering of the masses.

For 15 years, Sun's efforts at revolution brought only failures. He raised money and recruits, often collaborating with Chinese students in Japan, for rebellions in Guangzhou in 1895, 1900, 1907, and early 1911. All fizzled. But later in 1911, army officers inflamed by nationalist ideas sparked a mutiny in the central city of Wuhan (Hubei Province). The uprising spread, and many provinces declared themselves independent of Qing rule. Sun Yatsen, however, was on a fundraising trip in Denver. Now middle-aged, he sensed this was the best chance he would get to change China, and after visiting Europe in hopes of enlisting support, he returned home.

REVOLUTION AND REPUBLIC, 1911–1916 Sun's assessment was correct. Both Cixi and Guangxu had died in 1908. She had designated a three-year-old boy as successor to the throne, so power passed to a handful of princes. To suppress the army mutiny, the princes chose a talented general named Yuan Shikai. He saw more promise in the mutineers than in the princes.

An ambitious youth from a distinguished family, Yuan had failed the civil service exams twice, then joined the army. In the 1880s, he made his mark serving the Qing in Korea. As Qing power waned, he built his own army in the 1890s, trained by German officers. His Beiyang ("Northern") Army quickly became China's most effective military force. At Yuan's command, it massacred thousands of hardline Boxers when they rejected Qing authority. In the coming years, Yuan honed the Beiyang Army and helped implement educational and military reforms.

Once given full command to suppress the 1911 mutiny, Yuan decided to join forces with Sun Yatsen and other revolutionaries, and they forced the last Qing emperor, still a child, to abdicate. (A gardener for most of his life, the last emperor—after 2,000 years of imperial rule in China—died in 1967.) Sun was elected president of a new constitutional republic in December 1911. He hoped to reform China along the lines of his Three Principles. Yuan, however, thought a new dynasty would be more agreeable—with himself as emperor. Yuan tossed aside a constitution Sun had written; suppressed Sun's new political party, the Guomindang; arranged for the assassination of many of Sun's associates; and in 1913 drove Sun into exile, in Japan. Various liberations and reforms of 1911 and 1912, including press freedom and representative assemblies, were quickly rescinded. Yuan began to govern like an emperor.

Power in China soon fragmented. Japan made new demands on China in 1915, to which Yuan agreed in return for support of his dynastic dreams. That sparked renewed nationalist outrage and provincial uprisings. Several of Yuan's own Beiyang Army disciples deserted him, and when he died of disease in 1916 at age 56, central rule collapsed. While the republic officially survived in the hands of the Guomindang, China was now fragmented, with dozens of regional warlords competing for power, revenues, and personal survival. Sun Yatsen struggled to unite the country from his base in Guangdong, but he died of disease in 1925 at age 58. Internal warfare continued to plague China for the next 25 years.

The Qing, in power since 1644, had entered a long death-spiral in the 1790s and were finally undone by military defeat and revolution during the years 1895–1912. Confucian ideology, which for 2,000 years had provided a compelling vision of the proper relations among heaven, ruler, and ruled, now stood at a low ebb. Much of the old Qing elite and the Chinese gentry threw their support to the revolution, seeing it as the best bet for the restoration of order and the reconstruction of China. This stood in contrast to elite behavior during the Taiping uprising, when their grandfathers had stood by the dynasty. But in the intervening half-century, the Qing had lost the loyalty of those they most needed.

In the end, the combination of two main challenges undermined the Qing. Population growth and increasing poverty among the peasantry was one, if always slow-moving and rarely commanding urgent official attention. The second challenge was the mounting economic and military strength, and aggression, of industrialized societies, especially Britain, Russia, and Japan. That one was easier to identify and did command urgent attention at the Qing court. But responding to it seemed to require such drastic changes not merely to the state, but to society and family as well, that the Qing policy elite could not agree upon any sustained course of reform. They feared, probably rightly, that enacting radical reforms as the most energetic and imaginative self-strengtheners recommended would provoke widespread rebellion and only hasten the end of the dynasty.

Anti-Qing Rebellion A barber cuts off a boy's queue, or braid, following the overthrow of the Qing dynasty in 1911. The Qing had required all men to wear their hair in a long braid, on pain of death. Cutting off the braids came to be seen as a symbol of liberation.

THE MEXICAN REVOLUTION, 1870s–1920

Similar challenges—peasant poverty and unrest combined with inability to fend off foreign power—fueled the **Mexican Revolution**. Like the Chinese Revolution, it was decades in the making. Mexico had won independence from Spain in 1821 but lost the northern third of its territory to the United States in 1848, the result of the Mexican-American War. After independence, its chaotic political life included repeated bouts of civil war, Comanche raids, and in the 1860s a French invasion. After 1876, its politics stabilized owing to the authoritarian rule of Porfirio Díaz. His rule, 1876–1910, is called the **Porfiriato**.

THE PORFIRIATO, 1876–1910 Díaz, a theology school dropout from a poor family in Oaxaca, fought in the Mexican-American War as a youth and became a hero of the anti-French struggle in the 1860s. He converted his military prestige into a political career and in 1876 came to power by means of a coup. He stayed in power through intimidation, army support, and rigged elections. His policy consisted of three main initiatives beyond doing whatever was necessary to keep power. First, he restored to the Catholic Church some of the lands and privileges it had lost in recent decades when anticlerical factions had ruled Mexico. Second, he recruited foreign investment in Mexico, mainly from the United States, Britain, Germany, and France. He awarded tax breaks and other incentives to firms that owned and operated mines, railroads, plantations, and other big enterprises. Third, he endorsed the dispossession of poor peasants, whose self-sufficient ways did not contribute to national economic growth, and whose small, communal landholdings got in the way of bigger, more efficient, businesses.

Díaz presided over a rapid growth of inequality in Mexico. On his watch, Mexico's economy grew fast, and its richest people prospered mightily. So did many of the foreign firms he invited in. Foreign trade increased ninefold during the Porfiriato, and foreign companies—British, French, and American—built 7,500 miles (12,000 km) of railroads. Investment in mining skyrocketed after Díaz offered tax breaks to foreign companies. It was a good time to be an investor or business leader. But the Porfiriato was a bad time to be poor in Mexico. The standard of living and nutrition for average Mexicans in 1910 was probably lower than in 1810. Wages in the foreign-owned businesses stayed low, and Díaz used armed force to defeat strikes and discourage negotiations for better working conditions.

Peasants, the majority of the population, found less and less land available to them. That trend resulted partly from a rise

Mexican Grievances A 1910 poster celebrates one of the factions opposed to Díaz's rule. It shows (top) Liberal Party members being rounded up by government troops, and (bottom) the same members distributing newspapers and speaking at a rally for factory workers oppressed by Díaz's exploitative policies.

in population from 9 to 15 million between 1876 and 1910. But mainly it came from land concentration: by 1910, about 80 to 90 percent of Mexican land was owned by 1 percent of the population, mostly of Spanish descent and proud of it. The same elite controlled most irrigation water, which in some arid regions was more precious than land. Education did not provide an exit from poverty: most peasants received little or none, and 70 to 80 percent of the population remained illiterate. Most of them were indigenous, called *Indios* in Mexico, and spoke languages such as Mayan or Zapotec.

The vast and widening social inequality, particularly with respect to land, was the primary grievance behind the Mexican Revolution. Young men without land found it harder to marry, support families, and claim the traditional breadwinner role of Mexican males. Between 1850 and 1900, the average height of Mexican males fell by nearly 2 inches (5 cm), strong evidence of worsening nutrition. Waves of labor strikes and peasant rioting after 1905 demonstrated the levels of discontent. A secondary grievance was nationalist irritation at the generous deals offered to foreign businesses in Mexico. The loss of the north in 1848 and the ejection of the French in the 1860s had bolstered Mexican nationalism. So did awareness among the educated classes of the rising tide of nationalism in Europe and the United States. While Díaz did his best to wrap himself in the cloak of nationalism, and he was skilled at such things, he gave away too much to foreign companies to suit many Mexicans and so became—like late Qing emperors in China—an object of nationalist frustration and disdain. These two threads, quests for social justice and Mexican nationalism, ran through the Revolution.

REVOLUTION, 1910–1920 The Mexican Revolution started when Díaz said he would retire and scheduled a presidential election for 1910. When various candidates emerged, he changed his mind and jailed the most promising one, Francisco Madero. A previously apolitical northerner, Madero emerged from a wealthy family with interests in ranching, mining, and cotton. He had ties to Diaz's inner circle. But his education in Paris and at the University of California, Berkeley had persuaded him that a less autocratic system would be better for Mexico—similar to the impact of study abroad in Hawaii in Sun Yatsen's career. After landing in jail, Madero wrote up his political vision, escaped to the United States, and decided to call for the overthrow of the Porfiriato. Amid a bad drought, insurgencies bubbled up all over Mexico. Díaz, now age 80, chose comfortable exile in Paris.

Those insurgencies included two larger ones driven by grievances of inequality. In Morelos, just south of Mexico City, a mestizo peasant, a farmer who probably spoke Nahuatl as well as Spanish, Emiliano Zapata, had been helping villagers retain their land against encroaching sugar plantations. He organized an effective guerilla war against the big landholders and attracted a large following. Meanwhile, in the ranchlands of the far north, Pancho Villa led another uprising made up mainly of cowboys and bandits like himself, at home on horseback. Villa was a tactical magician at organizing cavalry raids, so much so that the U.S. Army studied his techniques. He also had a fine public relations instinct and made a deal with Hollywood producers to have his exploits filmed. He was well connected with gunrunners in the United States who kept his forces supplied. Zapata and Villa both promised land and work to their followers—if they won.

Other insurgent factions were led by urban, middle-class men less flamboyant than Zapata or Villa. But Venustiano Carranza, a politician with a medical education, and Álvaro Obregón, a prosperous chickpea farmer with no education, were the equals of anyone when it came to political guile. They represented more moderate factions, not interested in major redistribution of land or wealth. They favored constitutional government—and focused on crushing their rivals.

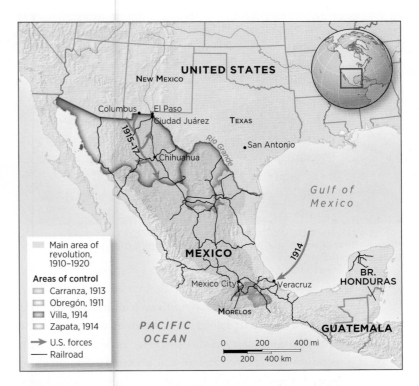

The Mexican Revolution, 1910–1920 Under the rule of Porfirio Díaz, the average Mexican became poorer. Millions lost control of their farmlands, often to foreign companies that Díaz welcomed. Mexico exploded into revolution and multisided civil war in 1910, and the main factions built up regional bases either in the north along the U.S. border or in the highlands south of Mexico City. The largest of the U.S. interventions came first by sea in 1914 and second over land from U.S. states that before 1848 had been part of Mexico.

Francisco Madero A mural in present-day Mexico City celebrates the revolutionary leader. Madero appears seated on a horse and carrying a large Mexican flag, surrounded by supporters ranging from peasants to middle-class professionals.

Mainly through the backing of Zapata's peasant army, Madero, not yet 38 years old, became president late in 1911. But not for long. Madero resisted land redistribution, costing him the support of Zapata's forces, which controlled the food supply to Mexico City. Madero's former lieutenants plotted against him. One of them, a hard-drinking former army officer and math prodigy of indigenous descent, Victoriano Huerta, emerged as president after a coup. Huerta arranged for Madero's murder and established a military dictatorship that lasted about a year. But his forces lost out to other factions, and he took the road of exile.

In the coming years, the various factions fought, joined forces, quarreled, and fought again. Their leaders became warlords, leading private armies, making their own rules, enforcing their will where they could. It became hard to tell the revolutionaries from the bandits and vice versa. Rival armies marched this way and that, carrying off

Mexican Revolution A group of rebel women and girls practice their shooting skills during the Mexican Revolution in 1911.

food and livestock. The contest was a multisided civil war fought by amateur soldiers with modern armaments. The United States intervened twice, once in Veracruz to help pressure Huerta into resigning, and once in the north to punish Pancho Villa for a raid on a New Mexico town. Germany also got involved, negotiating with most of the warlord factions at one point or another between 1914 and 1918. In early 1917, Germany, wanting the United States too distracted to enter World War I, offered to pay Carranza's government if Mexico would make war on the United States. Mexico turned down the offer.

OUTCOME AND AFTERMATH By 1920, when the fighting calmed, more than a million Mexicans—6 percent of the population—had been killed. In proportional terms, this came to three times the death toll of the U.S. Civil War. Another million fled to the United States to escape the violence. If anyone may be said to have won, it would be Carranza and Obregón. They drove out Huerta, murdered Zapata, and bought off Villa, who betrayed his stated principles by accepting a large ranch and pension, which he enjoyed until ambushed and murdered in 1923. Obregón, as the last man standing after Carranza's assassination, became president in 1920, crushed the last Zapata loyalists, and ruled Mexico directly or through a loyal subordinate until assassinated in 1928.

The revolution remade Mexico. The nation adopted a new constitution that brought some land reform; more would come in the 1930s. Big estates were broken up and parceled out to indigenous communities, a radical step that resonated throughout the Americas wherever

Indio and mestizo populations were in the majority—for example, in Central America and the Andes. New labor laws provided for a minimum wage, maximum hours, and—astonishing at the time—paid maternity leave for mothers. The new state stripped the Catholic Church of its lands and privileges, converted churches into public property, and even forbade clerics from wearing their ecclesiastic garb in public. Education was taken from the church and put in the hands of the state. These broad social and economic changes amounted to a fair chunk of the agenda that the followers of Zapata and Villa wanted.

Politically, the constitution and the agreements that ended the fighting guaranteed universal male suffrage and the formal equality of male citizens regardless of wealth or ancestry. It reduced foreigners' economic rights, claiming for the state all minerals, oil, and other natural resources. There wasn't much the revolutionary factions agreed on after ousting Díaz, but undermining the church and foreign businesses met with widespread approval.

The Mexican Revolution was both a social and a national revolution. It took until the 1930s before several of the provisions of the new constitution were put into effect, but eventually the old landed elite lost most of its grip on the country and peasants won access to more land. Although Mexico became a one-party state, its politics after the revolution represented more of the population than during the Porfiriato. The mobilization for revolution and civil war, and antiforeign sentiments resulting from the two U.S. interventions and Germany's meddling, sharpened Mexican nationalism. That found expression in popular culture—food, folk dress, songs—and in economic policy, largely directed against foreign (mainly U.S.) ownership of Mexican assets. Many Mexicans in 1920 agreed with the statement attributed to the former theology student Porfirio Díaz: "Poor Mexico! So far from God and so close to the United States."

So, although fundamentally about land, the Mexican Revolution became something more than that. It was a power struggle among warlords, similar to what happened in China after 1911. (Indeed, one might say Mexico had a revolution and warlord period all at once, whereas China did it in stages.) It was a national struggle to reassert Mexican independence from foreign influence. It was an anticlerical struggle to free the country from the grip of the Catholic Church. And, from the point of view of most ordinary people, it was a terrifying, chaotic bloodbath.

REVOLUTIONS AND GLOBAL FORCES, 1900–1920

The great revolutions in China and Mexico early in the twentieth century were accompanied by several others that resulted from the macro-scale forces of nationalism, imperialism, and the uneven effects of industrialization. In South Africa, between 1899 and 1902, the Boer War, a keenly nationalist uprising against British rule by the Boers—Afrikaans-speaking whites descended mainly from Dutch settlers—led to a settlement in 1910 that, while not called a revolution, in some respects was one. It conceded much more local control and representative government to white South Africans, who quickly stripped Black Africans of the right to own most farmland. In Iran, revolutionaries led by the merchant classes imposed a constitution, parliament, and elections upon the ruling shahs of the Qajar dynasty between 1905 and 1911. The Qajars had seemed unable to resist Russian and British influence. They were all too willing to grant monopolies to foreign companies, concede control of their finances to foreign bankers, and squander the tax revenue they collected from the commercial classes.

In the neighboring Ottoman Empire, nationalist army officers engineered a coup d'état in 1908 called the **Young Turk Revolution**. The Young Turks considered the imperial government incapable of facing up to foreign encroachments on Ottoman territory. As in Iran, they imposed a constitution on the monarch. In Russia, frustration with the tsar's failure to address mass poverty and permit wider political participation led to street demonstrations against the government. Although bloodily suppressed, the demonstrations led to constitutional constraints on the tsar's power in what is known as the Revolution of 1905. We will return to the Ottoman and Russian cases in the next chapter, because their stories are inseparable from that of World War I.

Each of these revolutions was unique, with its own grievances, coalitions, personalities, and train of events. The Chinese and Mexican Revolutions were bigger and bloodier than that of the Young Turks or the Iranian merchants. Yet they all represent the disruptive impacts of nationalism, imperialism, and industrial power upon agrarian peoples.

CONCLUSION

All of the movements, uprisings, and revolutions in this chapter form important parts of national histories in the United States, Brazil, China, India, Mexico, and South Africa. They occurred in very different settings. They were triggered by things as different as greased rifle cartridges and a young Xhosa girl's prophetic vision. But they all took place within the span of a human lifetime (1856–1920) and shared a few overlapping features.

In a general way, all of them resulted from widespread anxieties about ongoing trends. Changes seemed to be coming too thick and fast. People outside the handful of industrialized countries found reason to fear new technologies and new weapons, powerful strangers from afar, and missionaries with new religions. Economic competition from the other side of the world ruined what had once seemed secure livelihoods. Familiar ways, institutions, and rulers no longer seemed up to the challenges of safeguarding their subjects, keeping order, and preventing hunger. In short, the forces of economic globalization, imperialism, and nationalism, circulating through the Global web, were shaking things up in confusing and threatening ways.

In most cases (Brazil was an exception), the perceived threats to a cherished way of life came in part from foreigners. Sometimes those foreigners were settlers, as in the North American West. Sometimes they included Christian missionaries, as in India and China. Sometimes they were representatives of encroaching imperial powers and foreign businesses, as in North America, India,

Boer War Boer soldiers guard an outpost during the Boer War of 1899–1902. British forces prevailed by 1901, but guerilla resistance flickered on until a treaty was reached that promised the Boers self-government within the British Empire.

and China. The degree to which international influences affected daily life and domestic politics was on the increase, a result of tightening travel, trade, financial, and intellectual links within the Global web.

In many cases, the causes for which so many people died took on religious hues. The followers of prophets such as Nongqawuse, Antônio Conselheiro, Wovoka, or Hong Xiuquan found in their faiths an answer to their fears. Many of the Indian rebels of 1857 couched their battles in terms of Hindu or Islamic revivals. Even the revolution of Sun Yatsen carried religious tinges. Sun's program for nationalist China was inflected by his Christian education. The Mexican Revolution was an exception (on the surface), a case in which revolutionaries targeted the church. But at the same time, the appeal of Zapata and Villa to peasants, servants, and ranch hands was of a better world to come, a concept that their Catholic upbringing prepared most Mexicans to embrace.

The great rebellions and revolutions heralded an onrushing era of mass politics and mass mobilizations around the world. The forces of nationalism, imperialism, and industrialization—transmitted along the pathways of the Global web—would affect more lives more forcefully, as the next chapter will show.

CHAPTER REVIEW

KEY TERMS

millenarian movements (p. 822)

Ghost Dance (p. 823)

Antônio Conselheiro (p. 826)

Taiping Rebellion (p. 830)

Indian Rebellion (p. 830)

Lakshmibai (p. 832)

Chinese Revolution (p. 835)

Sun Yatsen (p. 838)

Mexican Revolution (p. 839)

Porfiriato (p. 839)

Young Turk Revolution (p. 843)

Go to INQUIZITIVE to see what you've learned—and learn what you've missed—with personalized feedback along the way.

REVIEW QUESTIONS

1. Describe the feelings and ideas that the Ghost Dance helped indigenous North Americans express.

2. Who was drawn to Antônio Conselheiro's message, and why?

3. What shared experiences caused the Xhosa, indigenous North Americans, and Antônio Conselheiro's followers to put their faith in millenarian movements?

4. Explain the external forces that contributed to the Taiping Rebellion.

5. What economic, political, and religious grievances did Indians under British rule have?

6. How did the British Raj change after the Indian Rebellion, and what were the long-term effects of this shift?

7. What common pattern emerged among reformers in societies under pressure from the world's leading powers?

8. During this period, what were the main grievances of peasants and the educated middle classes around the world?

9. Who led the self-strengthening movement in China, and what were its focuses?

10. Identify and discuss the two challenges that ultimately undermined the Qing.

11. What were Porfirio Díaz's three main policy initiatives, who benefited from them, and which groups did they disadvantage?

12. In what ways did Mexico change socially, economically, and politically after the Mexican Revolution?

13. Compare and contrast the aims and frustrations of rebels in South Africa, Iran, the Ottoman Empire, and Russia.

14. What widespread anxieties and changes contributed to revolutions and rebellions around the world during this time?

FURTHER READING

Michael ADAS, *Prophets of Rebellion: Millenarian Protest Movements against the European Colonial Order* (1979). A work on millenarian movements in East Africa, South and Southeast Asia, and New Zealand.

C. A. BAYLY, *The Birth of the Modern World, 1789–1914* (2004). A very imaginative and thoughtful take on connections around the world.

Man-houng LIN, *China Upside Down: Currency, Society, and Ideologies, 1808–1856* (2006). An in-depth account of China's struggles before the Taiping Rebellion.

Jürgen OSTERHAMMEL, *The Transformation of the World: A Global History of the Nineteenth Century* (2014). A gigantic

book with lots of insight about globalization, imperialism, nationalism. His main emphases are on China and Europe.

Wang GUNGWU, *Anglo-Chinese Encounters since 1800: War, Trade, Science & Governance* (2003). A readable and slender book emphasizing intellectual and technological transfers from Britain to China, mainly through overseas Chinese.

Louis S. WARREN, *God's Red Son: The Ghost Dance Religion and the Making of Modern America* (2017). An authoritative and accessible study.

Odd Arne WESTAD, *Restless Empire: China and the World since 1750* (2012). A highly readable book, and strong on the international dimensions of the decline of the Qing.

The Steam Engine, River Gunboats, and Global Imperialism

BETWEEN 1500 AND 1825, EUROPE'S IMPERIAL POWERS used naval force to impose their will around the world's coastlines. They had much less impact inland. However, that began to change in the 1820s with steam-powered river gunboats that could chug upstream and navigate shallow waters. This invention eased the projection of imperial power into the interiors of Asia and Africa. By the 1830s, gunboats were beginning to glide up and down the Niger, Euphrates, Indus, and Ganges—and in due course all major navigable rivers anywhere. River gunboats played a role in the U.S. wars against Native Americans along the Missouri and Mississippi, as Source 24.1 shows. (They also helped the North invade the South during the Civil War.) Russia used them, on the Volga and the Caspian Sea, against the peoples of the Caucasus region. Brazil used them in the 1860s against Paraguay. These vessels could carry heavy guns, far beyond the capacity of canoes and other rivercraft.

Moreover, steamships had unmatched stamina: "the muscles and sinews of man could not hold out against the perseverance of the kettle," as one British observer put it in 1841. The steam engine, in this application, helped industrialized countries (notably Britain) to defeat and intimidate peoples, mainly in Asia and Africa, who lacked the engineering and metallurgical skills to build steam-powered, iron-hulled gunboats.

SOURCE 24.1

The Steamship *Warrior* in the Black Hawk War, 1832

Black Hawk (1767–1838) was a Sauk leader who in the late 1820s objected to the implementation of a disputed 1804 treaty with the United States that others believed ceded Sauk lands in Illinois. In 1832 he crossed into Illinois from Iowa with 1,100 Sauk, of whom about 600 were women and children. By his account, he hoped to harvest corn. Others thought he aimed to drive out white families, perhaps with British support from Canada. In any case, the U.S. Army sent units north from St. Louis, some 300 miles away, by steamboat; and the governor of Illinois called out the state militia (including 23-year-old Abraham Lincoln). Together with Sauk enemies such as the Menominee, Dakota, and Ho-chunk, they chased and harried Black Hawk's band in the summer of 1832. In the final clash, the Sauk tried to flee across the Mississippi back into Iowa, perhaps under a flag of truce (accounts differ), but the steamboat—the *Warrior*—opened fire.

In Black Hawk's dictated autobiography, published in 1833, he offers an account of this event [1 below]. An Illinois lawyer and politician, Perry Armstrong, whose family had fled Black Hawk's band in 1832, wrote another version [2] in the 1880s.

[1] Myself and band having no means to descend the Wisconsin, I started over a rugged country, to go to the Mississippi, intending to cross it and return to my nation. Many of our people were compelled to go on foot, for want of horses, which, in consequence of their having had nothing to eat for a long time, caused our march to be very slow. At length we arrived at the Mississippi, having lost some of our old men and little children, who perished on the way with hunger.

We had been here but a little while before we saw a steamboat (the "Warrior") coming. I told my braves not to shoot, as I intended going on board, so that we might save our women and children. I knew the captain (Throckmorton) and was determined to give myself up to him. I then sent for my white flag. While the messenger was gone, I took a small piece of white cotton and put it on a pole, and called to the captain of the boat, and told him to send his little canoe ashore and let me come aboard. The people on board asked whether we were Sacs or Winnebagoes. I told a Winnebago to tell them that we were Sacs and wanted to give ourselves up! A Winnebago on the boat called out to us "to run and hide, that the whites were going to shoot!" About this time one of my braves had jumped into the river, bearing a white flag to the boat, when another sprang in after him and brought him to the shore. The firing then commenced from the boat, which was returned by my braves and continued for some time. Very few of my people were hurt after the first fire, having succeeded in getting behind old logs and trees, which shielded them from the enemy's fire.

The Winnebago on the steamboat must either have misunderstood what was told, or did not tell it to the captain correctly; because I am confident he would not have allowed the soldiers to fire upon us if he had known my wishes. I have always considered him a good man, and too great a brave to fire upon an enemy when sueing for quarters.

After the boat left us, I told my people to cross if they could, and wished; that I intended going into the Chippewa country. Some commenced crossing, and such as had determined to follow them, remained; only three lodges going with me. Next morning, at daybreak, a young man overtook me, and said that all my party had determined to cross the Mississippi—that a number had already got over safely and that he had heard the white army last night within a few miles of them. I now began to fear that the whites would come up with my people and kill them before they could get across. I had determined to go and join the Chippewas; but reflecting that by this I could only save myself, I concluded to return and die with my people, if the Great Spirit would not give us another victory. During our stay in the thicket, a party of whites came close by us, but passed on without discovering us.

Early in the morning a party of whites, being in advance of the army, came upon our people, who were attempting to cross the Mississippi. They tried to give themselves up; the whites paid no attention to their entreaties but commenced slaughtering them. In a little while the whole army arrived. Our braves, but few in number, finding that the enemy paid no regard to age or sex, and seeing that they were murdering helpless women and little children, determined to fight until they were killed. As many women as could, commenced swimming the Mississippi, with their children on their backs. A number of them were drowned, and some shot before they could reach the opposite shore.

[2] Like an evil genius or bird of ill-omen, Capt. Throckmorton, with his steamboat *Warrior*, reached the scene of action just as Gen. Henry drove the fugitives into the Mississippi and opened a disastrous and terrible fire upon the poor wretches who were struggling with the waves of the Mississippi. Men, women, and children, some on their ponies but the great portion without aid, were buffeting the rapid stream, to be swept into eternity by the terrific discharges of his heavy guns charged with grape and canister.[1] Many a dusky mother either lashed her infant between her shoulders or wrapped it up in her blanket, seized hold of it with her teeth, sprang into the swift current and struck out for the other shore, fully three hundred rods[2] off, to either sink, never to rise again, or to be mangled and cut to pieces by the shot and shell from the *Warrior*.

---

[1]Ammunition of grape-size balls

[2]300 rods (an antiquated measure) is 1,650 yards—just under a mile.

Source: *Autobiography of Ma-Ka-Tai-Me-She-Kia-Kiak or Black Hawk*, interpreted by Antoine Leclair, ed. J. B. Patterson (Rock Island, IL: J. B. Patterson, 1882); Perry Armstrong, *The Sauks and the Black Hawk War, with Biographical Sketches, Etc.* (Springfield, IL: H. W. Rokker, Printer and Binder, 1887).

- Black Hawk's autobiography was dictated to Antoine Le Claire, a U.S. Army interpreter (whose mother was Potawatomi and whose father was French Canadian). Black Hawk himself was not present when the *Warrior* opened fire. What cautions should we observe in reading this source?
- In what respects do these two accounts differ?
- What was the military significance of the *Warrior*?

The *Nemesis* in China, 1841–1842

The first conflict in which river gunboats determined the outcome was the First Opium War between Britain and China. The iron-hulled *Nemesis*, built specifically for service in Chinese rivers, was 184 ft (56m) long and carried heavy cannon, but it needed only 5 to 6 feet of water in which to chug along. Known as the "devil ship" to the Chinese, a poet noted that it "is moved by the use of burning coal and turns around like a galloping horse" and that its "shape and fashion astonish mankind."

This vessel played a key role in British victories in the Pearl River delta near Guangdong, before contributing to the final campaign up the Yangzi River to Zhenjiang and Nanjing. There, where the Yangzi intersected the Grand Canal, the British could cut "the throat" —as a Chinese official put it—of China, stopping the rice and salt cargoes to the north, the capital, and the Qing imperial court. Because of this threat, Qing rulers instructed their diplomats to accede to British demands.

With gunboats such as the *Nemesis*, 12,000 British sailors and soldiers (many of them Indians) forced the most populous polity in the world to accept humiliating terms in the Treaty of Nanking (1842). The excerpt here is from a British lieutenant's account of the war.

[O]n the morning of the 7th January [1841], the troops destined for the land attack on the fort of Chuenpee[1] having been put on board the *Nemesis*, *Enterprize*, and *Madagascar* steamers, were landed about two miles to the southward of the point of attack, while the *Calliope*, *Larne*, and *Hyacinth*, and *Queen* and *Nemesis* steamers, stood in until abreast of the Chinese batteries, when they dropped their anchors and commenced the action....

[...]

The *Nemesis* had on this day the first opportunity of displaying the great utility of small iron vessels of light draught in river service. After disembarking the whole of the 37th regiment below Chuenpee, she ran alongside the fort and threw shells into the upper fort, until the advance of the troops compelled the shipping to cease firing, when, taking advantage of her light draught, she ran close up to the sea battery and poured through the embrasures destructive rounds of grape as she passed; then pushing on over the shallows into Anson's Bay, into the midst of the war junks lying at anchor, she threw Congreve rockets[2] with startling effect, the very first having set fire to the largest of them, which blew up, with all her crew on board. Aided by a flotilla of boats from the squadron, she proceeded on her course across the bay, setting fire to junk after junk, until the whole fleet, eleven in number, was destroyed, except two which yet remained unhurt, moored to the shore on the far side of the bay; but Captain Hall went over, grappled them, towed them off into deep water, and set fire to them, before the Chinese could sufficiently recover from their surprise and consternation, to offer any resistance to the bold manoeuvre....

[...]

The whole line of the defenses... having now been carried, with the exception of the fort and encampment on the Tycocktow side of the [Pearl] river, the *Nemesis* was sent... with some boats of the *Wellesley* in tow, to expel the Chinese troops who appeared yet to cling to it as a last hope of resistance. But the severe lesson which they had seen their countrymen receive ... had had an effect too impressive to suffer them to dream of opposing their assailants, and upon the marines landing from the boats and entering by the embrasures of the fort, they abandoned the encampment and dispersed over the hills....

[...]

The *Cornwallis*[3] and several of the men-of-war... arrived off the northern angle of the walls of Nanking [Nanjing, on the Yangzi River] on the 5th, the flag-ship being towed and attended by steamers.... The small battery, which had shown symptoms of hostility against the first steamer sent up to reconnoiter, had been since abandoned; a huge white flag waved from the walls of Nanking, over a battery near which the *Cornwallis* lay at anchor, and was recognized as the harbinger of that peace which we had imagined to be yet far distant.

---

[1]Chuenpi, in the Pearl River delta

[2]Explosive but inaccurate artillery used for setting fire to targets, developed in Britain in imitation of Indian precedents. ("The Star-Spangled Banner" refers to their use by the British in the War of 1812.)

[3]A 74-gun naval ship, not a river gunboat. It could not sail up the Yangzi and needed steamers to tow it.

Source: John Ouchterlony, *Chinese War: An Account of All the Operations of the British Forces from the Commencement to the Treaty of Nanking* (London: Saunders and Otley, 1844).

- According to the author, how did the Chinese troops and populace respond to the power of the *Nemesis*?
- What military functions did the *Nemesis* perform aside from firing on Chinese targets?

SOURCE 24.3

The Gunboat *Pioneer* in the New Zealand Wars, 1863

Between 1845 and 1872, intermittent warfare pitted the forces of the British Empire against the Maori of New Zealand (Aotearoa). The intensity peaked in the 1860s with the single largest campaign along the Waikato River, New Zealand's longest. At peak strength, roughly 14,000 British soldiers faced about 4,000 Maori. In the North Island's rugged landscapes crowned with dense vegetation, moving artillery by land proved extremely difficult. Shallow-draft gunboats gliding along rivers magnified British fighting power considerably, as this Australian newspaper account of the impact of the (Australian-built) *Pioneer* suggests. The *Pioneer*, one of several river gunboats operating on the Waikato, was among the first boats anywhere with turret guns, able to fire in any direction without needing to maneuver the entire vessel.

All the obstacles to the movement are smoothed away by the arrival of the *Pioneer* gunboat without accident. She has since been taking up guns and other things to the redoubt at Whangamarino. [S]he went up to Meremere,[1] to see how the land lay and if possible ascertain whether the natives were still in force at that place....

No sooner did the gunboat tie up alongside the landing-place than a tremendous fire was opened upon her from the rifle-pits on the hillside.... The shots, both from the musketry and the cannons, rained upon the *Pioneer* incessantly, and she replied with great vigour, and apparent effect, upon her assailants. No injury whatever was sustained by the vessel, although under fire for two hours and a half. During the firing, a large number of canoes came down the river from Puparata, with not less than 1,000 men on board them. The *Pioneer* saluted them with a few shots....

The experiment . . . showed plainly, in the first place, that the *Pioneer* was admirably adapted for her work; and, in the second, that the numbers of natives now at Meremere are very great—probably not far short of 4,000 men in all.

---

[1]Where strong Maori fortifications stood

Source: The Argus, 18 November 1863 (Melbourne, Australia).

- From this account, what was the military significance of boats such as the *Pioneer*?
- Consider the tone of the Australian newspaper article. What might it indicate?

SOURCE 24.4

The Times of London on Nile Gunboats, 1897

Egypt, long an Ottoman province, became de facto independent early in the nineteenth century. By the 1870s it had built its own empire in northeast Africa; but after a disastrous war with Ethiopia, Egypt was taken over by British forces in the 1880s. They pushed southward, up the Nile, and soon were at war with African armies loyal to a charismatic Sudanese Muslim, Muhammad Ahmad, who had been leading resistance to Egyptian rule since 1871. Ahmad, known as the Mahdi, or "Guided One," massacred a British-led army at Khartoum in 1885. Fighting continued in the years thereafter, inspiring the British Royal Navy to seek specially constructed gunboats for use on the Nile, as reported in *The Times* of London. In this account, "the Egyptian Government" means the British colonial government of Egypt.

Three very interesting little war vessels, about which, doubtless, a good deal will be heard in the not distant future, have lately been constructed at the yard of Messrs. Yarrow and Co. at Poplar. They have been built to the order of the Egyptian Government for carrying on operations on the Nile, from designs prepared in the Constructors' Department at the Admiralty. . . .

The boats are of shallow draught and are built in floatable sections for ease of transport. The first of these vessels was launched some time ago and is by this time probably half-way up the Nile. . . . The vessel now on the Nile . . . is 145 ft. [in length] and her width 24 ft., 6in., whilst the hull proper is no more than 6ft deep. On this shallow, raft-like body is raised a fighting super-structure of imposing proportions. It is protected by bullet-proof armour. . . . The vessel is, in fact, a floating castle, but one that can travel at a speed of over 13 miles an hour. . . . At each end is a 12-pounder quick-firing gun having a wide angle of fire, and on the broadside are four 0.45 in. automatic Maxim guns. . . . At the forward end . . . is a bridge deck, or rather, a raised citadel. . . . This is 14 ft long and contains four more 0.45 in. automatic Maxim guns. . . .

It will be seen that in these vessels the Egyptian Government has secured a most valuable means of attack. Each boat could carry about a thousand troops. . . . If moored in the neighbourhood of a camp they would constitute a citadel beyond the powers of attack of any but the organized forces of a civilized nation.

Source: *The Times*, 7 October 1897 (London).

- What does the author foresee as the purpose of gunboats on the Nile?
- How does this article reflect British confidence in their technological superiority to that of people in the Nile Valley?

QUESTIONS FOR COMPARISON

1. The technological sophistication of steam engines, guns, and gunboats grew tremendously between 1832 and 1897. How is that reflected in these sources?

2. Based on these sources, how would you summarize the links between imperialism and industrial technology?

3. Based on these sources, how would you summarize the political and military powers that gunboats conferred on those who had them?

PART 6

THE GLOBAL WEB

SINCE 1870

The web of connections among societies that helped bring about the revolutions and rebellions discussed in Part 5 grew tighter after 1870. The main engine behind this process was continuing technological change, which sped up and cheapened communication and transport. But several other trends contributed to the growth of the Global web after 1870, such as ideologies that claimed global relevance, the alliance systems of international politics, and the steady march of the English language to its current status as a common international language. All these processes, and others as well, made

Arab Spring With flags upraised, Egyptians rejoice in Tahrir Square following the 2011 resignation of President Hosni Mubarak. Between 2010 and 2012, a series of protests in Arab countries dethroned several governments.

the contemporary world more interactive than ever before—but in fits and starts rather than at a regular pace.

THE PACE OF GLOBAL INTEGRATION

The irregular pace of modern globalization consisted broadly of three phases. The first, from 1870 to 1914, saw rapid extension of links driven above all by new technologies such as railroads, steamships, and telegraphs. The second phase, from 1914 to 1945, showed a mixed record. New technologies such as radio and air travel emerged, speeding flows of information and people. But two world wars and a worldwide economic depression drove several societies to turn inward, fall back on their own resources, and try to be self-sufficient. In economic terms, global integration retreated as flows of international trade and finance slowed. In political and cultural terms, however, there was no retreat. Societies took one another increasingly into account in shaping their own policies and preferences, whether in military matters or music. The third phase, from 1945 to the present, again saw an intensification of the process of globalization, with louder objections to it than ever before. The pace, scale, and scope of international interactions came to exceed those of any previous era especially after about 1980, when computerization and digitization began to take hold.

KEY THEMES

The next five chapters—Part 6 of the book—highlight three main themes. First is the prominence of international politics and war. Ordinary people increasingly could not escape involvement in the affairs of states, especially the many states that took part in major wars. These chapters explore World Wars I and II, the Cold War, and the struggles of decolonization, the primary conflicts that refashioned political, social, and economic life after 1914.

Second is a shift in world power away from Europe. Beginning in the 1490s, Atlantic Europe had slowly attained unusual wealth and power by global standards. With industrialization in the nineteenth century, Europe, North America, and Japan had rapidly attained still greater power, expressed in overseas empires. Between 1945 and 1991, the empires of Japan and the European

states—including the USSR—crumbled sooner and faster than almost anyone expected. A general rebalancing of world wealth and power took place, and indeed is still in motion. The formerly colonized peoples of Africa and Asia won their independence, and those in several Asian countries—first Japan, but then South Korea, Singapore, Taiwan, and to some extent China—became rich almost overnight. This rise of East Asia is the fastest and most dramatic rearrangement of the global economy in world history.

The third general theme is the recurrent backlash against global integration. Immediately after World War I, political and ideological movements—fascism and Soviet communism—arose that intensified nationalism and encouraged economies built on self-sufficiency rather than international trade. The global economy became still more protectionist and fragmented during the Great Depression of the 1930s. While most international linkages were repaired after World War II, and economic and cultural globalization galloped ahead in the following decades, once again it produced discontent. Politics based on sectarian religion made a comeback, for example, and after about 2010 xenophobic nationalism did too. Many millions also blamed economic globalization for rising inequalities in wealth and income.

Chapter 25 takes up international politics, specifically World War I and its aftermath. It emphasizes not only the war itself but also some of the political and ideological movements created or advanced by revulsion at the war and its peace settlements: fascism, communism, and anticolonialism. The chapter also presents suffragism, the campaign to win the vote for women, in the general context of World War I. Chapter 26 treats World War II (1937–1945), explaining the origins, course, and results. Chapter 27 focuses on the intertwined stories of the Cold War and decolonization between 1945 and 1990. Chapter 28 concerns what we might call postcolonial economic history since the 1960s, contrasting the extraordinary rise of East Asian economies with the more mixed results in Africa and Latin America. The East Asian emergence amounts to another basic shift in the geography of power in the global system.

Chapter 29 considers the—equally extraordinary—acceleration of almost every form of globalization since 1980, including international migrations and financial flows. It emphasizes the economy, environment, popular culture, and health and disease and considers some of the political backlash against globalization. The chapter also explores some unintentional effects of the tight Global web, such as the faster spread of emerging diseases including HIV/AIDS, Ebola, SARS, and COVID-19.

CHRONOLOGY

1918–1919
Global influenza pandemic

1920
League of Nations opens

1918–1921
Russian Civil War

1915–1916
Gallipoli campaign

Nov. 7–8, 1917
Bolshevik Revolution

Apr. 1919
Amritsar massacre

June 28, 1914
Gavrilo Princip kills Austrian archduke

Apr. 1917
United States enters
World War I

1919
Treaty of
Versailles is
signed;
Weimar
Republic is
established

1869
The Subjection of Women
is published; Wyoming
allows women to vote

Feb.–Dec. 1916
Battle of
Verdun

1922
Start of Mussolini's rule

1893
New Zealand allows women
to vote in national elections

July 1914
Start of
World War I

July 1916
Battle of
the Somme

Mar. 1918
Treaty of
Brest-Litovsk

1921
Kronstadt rebellion;
Hitler becomes head
of Nazi Party;
formation of Chinese
Communist Party

1915
Italy enters World War I;
Japan issues The Twenty-One Demands

Mar. 1917
Tsar Nicholas II abdicates

Nov. 1918
World War I ends

May 1919
May Fourth Movement

International Politics

WAR, PEACE, AND IDEOLOGIES

1870 to 1940

1927–1928
Stalin consolidates power

1939
Germany attacks Poland

1933
Hitler becomes
chancellor of
Germany

1929
Start of Great
Depression

1930
Gandhi leads
salt march

1935
Hitler
introduces
Nuremberg
Laws

If you could hear, at every jolt, the blood
Come gargling from the froth-corrupted lungs,
Obscene as cancer, bitter as the cud
Of vile, incurable sores on innocent tongues,—
My friend, you would not tell with such high zest
To children ardent for some desperate glory,
The old Lie: *Dulce et decorum est*
Pro patria mori.

Wilfred Owen finished the poem "Dulce et Decorum Est" during the last months of World War I. An infantry officer in the British Army, Owen had witnessed up close the final agonies of soldiers dying from poison gas attacks. Twice wounded and decorated for valor, Owen was killed in action one week before the war ended in November 1918. In quoting Horace, an ancient Roman poet, whose message he calls "The old Lie," Owen expresses his disillusionment with the war and his resentment of its supporters. The Latin line "dulce et decorum est pro patria mori" was familiar to

The Western Front New technologies intensified the brutality of warfare. The American painter John Singer Sargent painted *Gassed* in 1919, after spending several months embedded with British and American troops in France. A line of wounded soldiers, blinded by mustard gas, gropes in search of medical treatment while casualties lie piled around it.

FOCUS QUESTIONS

1. In what ways was World War I a global event?

2. How did fascism and communism advance in the 1920s and 1930s?

3. Why did anticolonial movements gain strength after World War I?

Britain's educated classes and etched into the chapel wall of Sandhurst, Britain's foremost military academy. It translates as: "How sweet and suitable it is to die for one's country."

Among the many strands of global politics in modern times, one that stands out is the extreme violence of modern war. The effort involved in both world wars (I: 1914–1918, and II: 1937–1945) involved complete mobilizations of the resources and populations of the combatant countries, as well as deadly new technologies, including poison gas in **World War I** and the atomic bomb in World War II. The savage destruction and thorough mobilization characteristic of these wars is sometimes called total war.

A second strand is the global scale of politics. The ancient Romans, Mauryans, or Inkas never worried about peoples on the other side of the world. For them, all politics was local or regional. By the early twentieth century, however, policy makers took into account circumstances and events on distant continents as a matter of course. The interconnectedness of the Global web had reached a point at which decisions made in Paris could quickly trigger uprisings in China.

A third is the increased impact of international politics on ordinary people. Centuries ago, millions of people lived beyond the reach of tax collectors and military recruiters, and they had few dealings with any state. No longer. Since 1914, almost no one has lived free from the demands of states. If your country

got into a big war, your life would change, whether you served on the front lines or remained on a family farm. Total war was not the sport of kings, but the concern of all.

A fourth strand is the rise of mass ideological and political movements, including those considered here: fascism, communism, anticolonialism, and suffragism—the effort to secure voting rights for women. Such movements were not strictly new in the twentieth century, but they became much more common than before. This was the result partly of disillusionment with established authorities brought on by World War I, partly of new media such as radio that connected audiences with charismatic politicians as never before, and partly of longer-term trends in urbanization and globalization that reached new heights in the twentieth century. Monarchies and empires fell; traditions and certainties melted into air. People everywhere, whether frightened or inspired by the crumbling of old regimes, searched for a new basis for politics. World War I and the peace settlement that followed shaped all of these developments, so that's where this chapter will begin.

WORLD WAR I AND ITS LEGACIES

World War I, despite its name, was mainly a European war, but its repercussions reached every continent. Its unprecedented butchery and unsatisfactory peace settlement gave rise to resentments and ambitions that shaped life for decades—indeed, to this day.

THE GREAT POWERS, 1870–1914

Great powers are great because they have more people, money, military force, and unity of purpose than lesser powers. In the nineteenth century, industrialization and the emergence of nationalism created a handful of new great powers, several of them mid-sized European states such as Germany, France, and Britain. They joined multicultural empires such as the Ottoman, Russian, and Habsburg—longstanding great powers—atop the greasy pole of international politics. In the years 1914–1918, these powers went to war with one another. Before wading into World War I, let's look briefly at the major participants.

In 1914, the most powerful polity on Earth was the British Empire, thanks to its industry and its navy. Britain's industrial production stood third in the world behind that of the United States and Germany, but counting the industry of the empire—Canada, India, South Africa, Australia—it easily surpassed Germany. Britain's army was tiny, but the British navy was the largest and most effective in the world. The British Isles in 1914 had 42 million people, and with the dominions of Canada, Australia, and New Zealand, the empire included 57 million more—most of them British immigrants or their descendants. To some extent, Britain could also rely on British India, another 252 million people. Britain's population was, by and large, reliably patriotic, although in the Empire, especially India, many resented British rule.

By 1914, the United States had the potential to become the world's second most powerful state. Its population of some 100 million was growing fast—by about 2 percent per year. Although about one in every six Americans in 1914 had been born overseas, their loyalty to the state proved reliable when war came. The country produced two-thirds of the world's oil and led the world in coal, iron, and steel production. It had a tiny overseas empire consisting mainly of the Philippines, Hawaii, and Puerto Rico, as well as a small and inexperienced army, but a sizeable and growing navy. Its political elites generally did not like to think of the United States as a great power but rather as a hemispheric power in the Americas. So the United States had the capacity but not the will to function as a great power in 1914.

If the United States was not the second most powerful state in 1914, then Germany was. Its population of about 67 million was growing by 1.2 percent annually. The majority were enthusiastically patriotic. The sharp divisions between Protestants and Catholics, or among social classes, did not appreciably weaken loyalties to the German fatherland. Its coal, iron, and steel output trailed only that of the United States. Its technological and scientific sophistication was second to none. It had an overseas empire, in Africa and the Pacific, but that added little to German power. Germany's army and navy were large, well

British Imperial Might A British naval convoy in the Atlantic in 1914. A new class of battleships called dreadnoughts constituted perhaps the strongest weapon in the British Empire's arsenal, contributing to its status as the world's greatest power at the start of World War I.

trained, and well equipped, probably the best and second best, respectively, in the world.

A notch below these three, in terms of strength in international politics, stood France and Russia. France had 40 million people and a bit more military manpower and resources available in its overseas empire. Its industrial production and its navy came well behind Britain's or Germany's. Russia's strength lay mainly in its size. It had 175 million people and the resources of a giant territory. Its industrial production was growing rapidly, and the recently completed Trans-Siberian Railway gave access to some of the vast mineral supplies of Siberia. But the loyalty of its minority populations was shaky. Russia's Poles, for example, still prized their Polish identity long after the eighteenth-century partitions of their country placed them inside the Russian Empire. Russia's army was big but poorly trained and equipped. Its navy was no better.

A notch below France and Russia stood Austria-Hungary and the Ottoman Empire. Austria-Hungary, as the Habsburg Empire was generally known after 1867, had 48 million people in 1914, but many of them belonged to ethnic or religious minorities and their allegiance to the state was tempered. The table below gives some idea of the ethnic diversity of Austria-Hungary's army. Industrial production was modest—lots of textiles, but not much iron and steel. Austria-Hungary had no overseas empire and virtually no navy, but an effective army despite its mix of languages. The Ottoman Empire in 1914 had recently lost a lot of territory in little wars in the Balkans and North

LANGUAGES OF THE ARMY IN AUSTRIA-HUNGARY, 1914	
German	25%
Hungarian	18%
Czech	13%
Serbian and Croatian	11%
Polish	9%
Ukrainian	6%
Romanian	6%
Slovak	4%
Slovenian	2%
Italian	2%

Note: Another 4 percent of army recruits spoke other languages.

Source: David Reynolds, *The Long Shadow: The Legacies of the Great War in the Twentieth Century* (2015), 7.

Africa. It had about 19 million people, some 4 million of whom were ethnoreligious minorities—mainly Armenians, Arabs, and Greeks, whose loyalty Ottoman elites often rightly distrusted. Ottoman industry produced little military materiel. The navy was weak. The army, however, was substantial and partly trained by German officers.

ORIGINS OF THE WAR

For more than a century, the question of the origins of World War I has fascinated historians, who still don't agree on an answer. The controversies swirl around the whys of the war, and less around what happened. For the sequence of events to make sense, we have to understand that by 1914 Europe's international system was divided into two big **alliance networks**. One, the Triple Alliance anchored by Germany, included Austria-Hungary and Italy. The other, the Triple Entente, enrolled France, Russia, and Great Britain. The original purpose of these alliance networks was to extend Europe's long peace, begun in 1815 in the aftermath of the Napoleonic Wars and broken only briefly thereafter. Instead, the alliances drew states into a long, devastating war that no one wanted.

On June 28, 1914, a 20-year-old Serbian student, Gavrilo Princip, shot and killed an Austrian archduke on the streets of Sarajevo. Princip was a member of underground Serbian nationalist organizations eager to liberate those Serbs (and other "south Slavs," or "Yugoslavs") who remained under Austro-Hungarian rule. The assassination led to an ultimatum from Austria-Hungary: Serbia must surrender much of its independence or face war. Confident of support from Russia—fellow Slavs who had long supported Serbs—the Serbian government chose war.

In preparing to fight on Serbia's behalf at the end of July 1914, Russia mobilized its vast army against both Austria-Hungary and Germany. Germany, in keeping with its war plans, mobilized its army to attack both Russia to the east and France to the west. When Germany did attack, starting with tiny Belgium en route to France, Great Britain joined the war. By August 4, the two alliance systems—minus Italy, which at first kept out—were at war. In late 1914, the Ottoman Empire joined on the German side, and in 1915, Italy entered the war against Germany and Austria-Hungary despite its treaty commitments to those powers. As wartime coalitions, these two blocs became known as the Central Powers (Germany, Austria-Hungary, the Ottoman Empire) and the Entente or Allied Powers (France, Russia, Britain, Italy). Many smaller nations in Europe joined in too.

So why did the conflict between Serbia and Austria-Hungary bring on a general European war? A short answer includes the cultural climate of nationalism, the political influence of armies in most of the great powers, the rigidity of war plans, and the alliances that bound countries to go to war on one another's behalf. It would also include, more specifically, some key decisions—two above all.

First was the choice made by German leaders to support whatever Austria-Hungary elected to do against Serbia. That made Austria-Hungary's leaders more willing to accept the risk of war with Russia, which they knew might result if they attacked Serbia. Second was Russia's choice to support Serbia, which was not a treaty obligation, with a general military mobilization that threatened both Germany and Austria-Hungary. Russian war plans called for such a broad mobilization, but they might have been overridden by a more forceful, attentive, and imaginative tsar. (Nicholas II once described himself as "without will and without character.") These and other fateful decisions might well have been made differently if diplomats and emperors had understood that in the circumstances of 1914, war would bring little glory and much gore.

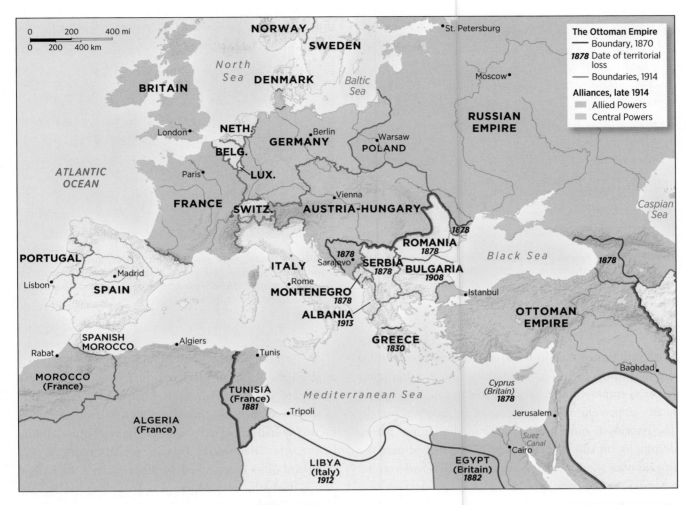

European Alliance Systems and the Ottoman Empire, 1914 Before World War I, the great powers of Europe organized two major alliance systems. One included France, Britain, and Russia. The other enrolled Germany, Austria-Hungary, and Italy. The Ottoman Empire, which lost most of its territories in southeastern Europe between 1830 and 1913, was neutral. When the war began in August 1914, Italy proclaimed neutrality despite its alliances. And by November, the Ottoman Empire, despite its former neutrality, joined with Germany and Austria-Hungary, forming the Central Powers. In 1915, Italy would join the Allies.

THE COURSE OF THE WAR

Fighting began in August 1914 and continued until November 1918, and in a few places beyond that. News of war was welcomed in some cities by cheering crowds and provoked mass enlistments in most of the countries involved. But joy evaporated fast. At first, armies sprinted after one another. Where they met, they discovered the pitiless violence of modern combat. The effect of machine guns on infantry became evident on August 22, 1914, when a French attack against German positions led to the deaths of 27,000 Frenchmen in a matter of hours.

By early 1915, the armies on the western front had settled into lines of trenches. Occasional offensives required men to run across no-man's-land toward enemy trenches amid a hail of bullets and, if all went well, fall upon the enemy. More often, they fell in no-man's-land first. On the eastern front, attacks sometimes won a little more ground, but nonetheless the war became one of stalemate and attrition, in which both sides were losing soldiers faster than they could recruit new ones.

Weaponry as well as soldiers soon ran short. Of the combatants in 1914, only Germany, Britain, and France had military-industrial complexes equal to the situation. Mines and munition factories everywhere hummed around the clock. Labor supply became a bottleneck.

Trench Warfare British Army soldiers hole up in captured German dugouts to shelter during the Somme offensive in 1916. Trench warfare became characteristic of the western front.

Munitions Factories A photograph of the factory floor at a German munitions factory in 1917 shows many women workers. Women even operate heavy machinery, which would have been highly unusual before the war.

With millions of men in the armed forces, women filled the munitions factories. Germany's Krupp armaments factories employed almost no women in 1914, but by 1917 nearly 30 percent of its workforce of 175,000 was female. The enormous industrial capacity of the United States, despite its official neutrality until 1917, helped ease the situation for the Allies. In general, the Allies had a strong advantage in industrial production, food production, and military manpower.

World War I's chief theaters were in Europe, but small-scale campaigns took place in Africa among rival colonies. British forces launched bigger campaigns against Ottoman armies in Palestine and Mesopotamia, using mainly Indian troops. Naval actions occurred in the Pacific and off of Argentina, as well as in European waters.

For four years, all efforts to break the stalemate failed. In 1915, the Allies tried to knock the Ottoman Empire out of the war with an attack in Turkey, at Gallipoli, but they succeeded only in opening a new stalemated front. The Allies abandoned the front within a year—a major setback. In 1916, the Germans decided to "bleed France white" with a sustained offensive at Verdun in eastern France. It gained nothing of note and cost both countries rivers of blood. To relieve the pressure at Verdun, the British and French launched an offensive along the Somme River in northern France in July 1916. It cost Britain 20,000 dead on the first day—more Britons than had died in 15 years of wars against Bonaparte.

By 1917, the gambles grew more desperate. Naval power enabled the Allies to blockade the Central Powers. All could see that Germany and Austria-Hungary would slowly starve, because they did not grow enough food—Germany had imported about one-quarter of its calories before 1914. Meanwhile, Britain, which produced only one-third of its food, relied on supplies from the United States, Canada, and Argentina. This situation led the German High Command to open unrestricted submarine warfare everywhere in the Atlantic, attacking neutral shipping in order to starve Britain. Sustained submarine warfare, new with World War I, sank nearly 4 million tons of merchant shipping within six months, from February through July 1917. German leaders understood that U-boat (submarine) attacks would bring the Americans, with all their men and industrial capacity, into the war against them, but they hoped the attacks would weaken Britain fast enough that the Central Powers could win before American forces tipped the balance. The U-boat attacks drove the United States to join the war against the Central Powers in April 1917.

The Russian Revolution of 1917 (see below) gave Germans new reason to hope. By the fall of that year, Russia had stopped fighting, its soldiers deserting en masse ("voting with their feet," as revolutionary leader Vladimir Lenin put it). In March 1918, Russia, now mainly under Lenin's control, agreed to the Treaty of Brest-Litovsk, surrendering to the Central Powers its 16 westernmost

World War I, 1914–1918 World War I was fought mainly in Europe and Ottoman lands in the Middle East, with smaller campaigns on the high seas and in German overseas holdings in Africa, New Guinea, and China. The western front stretched between Switzerland and the North Sea. The eastern front extended from the Baltic Sea to the Black Sea. Fighting also took place along the Caucasus front, in Ottoman Mesopotamia and Palestine, and in the Balkans. The Allied blockade of the Central Powers, and the German U-boat (submarine) campaigns against Allied and neutral shipping, led to food shortages for civilians.

provinces, including 34 percent of its population, half its industry, and 89 percent of its coal mines. Lenin agreed to this amputation of Russia only because he thought continuing the war would "sign the death warrant of [the revolution's] power within three weeks." The German army now shifted 50 divisions—600,000 men—to the western front and used its numerical superiority to mount one more gigantic offensive. It almost worked—Britain and France were tottering by April 1918. But they drew strength from the American forces pouring into Europe. The prospect of far more Americans yet to come sapped German morale, as did the Allies' blockade: by 1918, German city-dwellers were living on 1,000 calories a day, half of what an adult body needs to maintain itself. Talk of revolution swirled in the cafés, classrooms, and factory floors of Berlin and Vienna. Strikes broke out. In November, the German top military leadership, aware of the worsening odds against them, decided to quit and negotiated an armistice, ending the war.

THE HUMAN COST

In 51 months of war, the combatants lost about 10 million dead and 21 million wounded, of whom 7 million were maimed for life. On average, about 6,000 men were killed per day. Half of France's male population age 18 to 40 was either killed, wounded, or taken prisoner. In Austria-Hungary, 90 percent of those mobilized were either killed or wounded. The United States lost 53,000 killed in battle and another 63,000 to disease—some 0.4 percent of males of military age. Canada lost 54,000 killed in combat and a few thousand more to disease—roughly 3 percent of males 18 to 40 years old. The table below shows the human cost to the major combatants.

Most World War I armies included units drawn from specific regions, so villages and counties could lose almost all their young men in one bloodbath. The Royal Newfoundland Regiment, for example, lost 90 percent of its men (killed or wounded) in a matter of minutes in the Battle of the Somme.

Sooner or later, the slaughter broke the morale of even the best-trained armies. French soldiers in 1917 baaed like sheep going to the slaughter when ordered to attack. Millions of soldiers suffered mental breakdowns, after years living for weeks on end among rats, lice, and mud, regularly enduring artillery bombardments, and, most terrifying of all, occasionally going "over-the-top" into a fusillade of bullets. All except Germany's army mutinied within 35 months. (The American army experienced only 6 months of combat and did not mutiny.) Since armies were among the most revered institutions in Europe in 1914, the evaporation of military discipline left many soldiers and civilians feeling unmoored.

A cruel irony maximized the carnage. In prior wars, infectious disease had prevented soldiers from massing in their millions long enough to butcher one another on such a scale. By 1914, advances in military medicine enabled armies to stay healthy long enough to kill one another wholesale. In another cruel irony, as we've seen, a global influenza pandemic broke out at the war's end, killing some 50 million people in the years 1918–1919.

The horrors of war extended to civilian populations.

WAR CASUALTIES, 1914–1918						
COUNTRY	TOTAL MOBILIZED FORCES	KILLED	WOUNDED	PRISONERS AND MISSING	TOTAL CASUALTIES	CASUALTIES AS PERCENTAGE OF FORCES
ALLIED AND ASSOCIATED POWERS						
Russia	12,000,000	1,700,000	4,950,000	2,500,000	9,150,000	76.3
British Empire	8,904,467	908,371	2,090,212	191,652	3,190,235	35.8
France	8,410,000	1,357,800	4,266,000	537,000	6,160,800	73.3
Italy	5,615,000	650,000	947,000	600,000	2,197,000	39.1
United States	4,355,000	116,516	204,002	4,500	323,018	7.5
CENTRAL POWERS						
Germany	11,000,000	1,773,700	4,216,058	1,152,800	7,142,558	64.9
Austria-Hungary	7,800,000	1,200,000	3,620,000	2,200,000	7,020,000	90.0
Ottoman Turkey	2,850,000	325,000	400,000	250,000	975,000	34.2

Source: https://www.britannica.com/event/World-War-I/Killed-wounded-and-missing

Armenian Genocide Armenian refugees flee Ottoman persecution around 1916. The Ottoman state systematically starved or murdered about 1 to 2 million Armenians during World War I.

In Lebanon, dependent on food imports, one-third of the population starved to death in 1915 when the war interrupted shipping. The Ottoman Turks, suspicious of Armenian loyalties, starved, shot, or bayoneted 1 to 2 million Armenians in 1915–1916 in a genocidal campaign. In German East Africa (today's Tanzania), the war reduced the population by 20 percent, mainly through starvation and disease. Atrocities on scales large and small occurred wherever armies occupied enemy territory, as in eastern France or western Russia.

Life on the home fronts grew ever grimmer as the war dragged on. Food ran short in Russia, Germany, and Austria-Hungary in particular. Civilians had to work extra-long hours in mines, factories, fields, offices, and hospitals. In many countries, currency inflation ate into workers' wages, leading to hardship and strikes.

Women did the work of men in addition to their own. In Britain, 1.4 million women joined the paid labor force between 1914 and 1917. In Austria-Hungary by 1918, 1 million women had done so. Most of the women laboring in armaments and heavy industry during the war had already been workers before 1914, but now they shifted from textile mills to munitions plants. Most of the extra work that women shouldered was not in factories but on farms. Some armies let some soldiers go on leave during harvest season. But in Germany, France, Austria-Hungary, Serbia, and other countries where almost all able-bodied men and

horses were at war, women, children, and the elderly had to do even the heaviest farmwork.

Hundreds of thousands of women volunteered as nurses—some 120,000 in France and 92,000 in Germany. In the United States, about 22,000 did, and 3,000 in Canada. Vera Brittain, a middle-class Englishwoman, put her Oxford education on hold at age 21 to serve as a nurse. Before she returned to her studies, she had spent three hard years amid splintered bodies and shattered minds. She lost her only brother, her fiancé, and her two closest male friends to the war.

German, Austro-Hungarian, and French armies recruited thousands of female prostitutes for regulated army brothels. Unregulated brothels and the demand for prostitutes in general flourished during the war, as millions of men and women were away from the constraints of family and village.

Some women also served in combat. Bulgaria, Romania, Serbia, and Russia allowed women soldiers to fight. Milunka Savić, who took her brother's place in the Serbian Army, was wounded several times, won a handful of decorations for valor, and on one occasion captured 23 Bulgarian soldiers by herself. In Russia in the summer of 1917, a call for volunteers resulted in 5,000 women joining special battalions, the original purpose of which was to try to shame male soldiers into fighting harder. But two of the women's battalions took part in an offensive in July 1917, and one, the so-called Women's Battalion of Death, led by Maria Bochkareva, a 27-year-old of peasant origins, stormed a German trench line successfully.

The mobilization of women for war work was controversial everywhere. It ran counter to prevailing notions of femininity. Skeptics feared that driving ambulances, doing police work, selling train tickets, or building tanks alongside men would corrupt women's morals. After the war, most of the women who had taken on men's roles left their wartime jobs to return to their former lives.

Women at War Maria Bochkareva, posing with medals she earned for bravery in combat in the Russian army. She was wounded several times but survived the war—only to be executed in 1920 as an "enemy of the working class" by Russia's new Bolshevik regime.

THE RUSSIAN REVOLUTION OF 1917

In addition to the human casualties, World War I destroyed most of the political structures of Europe and the Middle East. The defeated Central Powers—Germany, Austria-Hungary, and the Ottoman Empire—all crumbled. So did one of the Allies, Russia. The experience of war stoked Europe's nationalisms and made these multicultural and multinational empires less popular than ever. The experience of defeat—which Russia shared with the Central Powers—destroyed them.

The **Russian Revolution of 1917** stands among the largest political legacies of World War I, partly because Russia was a big country but mainly because it featured an ideology that inspired imitation far and wide. Although it was triggered by World War I and probably would not have happened without it, the Russian Revolution, like those in China and Mexico discussed in the previous chapter, had deep roots.

GRIEVANCES AND REFORMS After the abolition of serfdom in 1861, Russia remained an agrarian country of 75 million. By 1914, its population had grown to 175 million. For the peasantry, freedom from serfdom did not bring freedom from hunger and hard work. For many educated Russians, the conspicuous strengthening of Britain, France, and Germany as industrial and imperial states led, around the period 1860–1900, to worries that their country was falling behind.

What to do? The answers came down to two broad choices. One, that of the conservatives called Slavophiles, was to hold true to Russian ways and shun most innovations and reforms. Novelties such as representative government and factories were not suited to Russia, they thought, and would corrode the social cement of Russian Orthodoxy, faith in tsars, and village solidarity. According to others, often called Westernizers, autocracy and the power of the Orthodox Church held Russia back, and the likeliest route to power and prosperity was reform based on selective imitation of western Europe—as Japan was beginning to show.

These debates grew more urgent in 1881 when a group calling itself the People's Will assassinated Tsar Alexander II. It was one of several groups that sought solutions to Russia's ills through revolution, spurning the slow path of reform. After his father's assassination, Tsar Alexander III outlawed public discussion of many political topics and drove the revolutionaries underground.

Russia's revolutionaries, although few in number and divided among themselves, figured time was on their side. Some put their faith in the peasantry, noting the egalitarian custom in many Russian villages of periodically redistributing land, animals, and tools according to each family's needs. Others, under the influence of the ideas of Karl Marx, thought that real revolution could only come from the industrial working class—or as Marxists put it, the proletariat.

The hour seemed to strike in 1905. The Russo-Japanese War (1904–1905) brought shocking humiliations for Russians. Hungry peasants and workers, restive ethnic minorities, and alienated students all felt mistreated by an incompetent state. The government, now headed by Tsar Nicholas II, unleashed the army on unarmed demonstrators in the capital of St. Petersburg, killing more than 100. Instead of being intimidated, workers, peasants, and dissident middle-class groups known as the intelligentsia became more vocal. Demands rang out for more schools, legislative assemblies, and land for peasants. Peasants themselves wanted reduced rents or ownership of the land they worked. Workers wanted better wages and a voice in factory management. Urban workers invented new citywide workers' councils, called soviets.

These events, sometimes called the Revolution of 1905, led Nicholas—reluctantly—to make concessions, including an empire-wide legislative assembly, called the Duma, whose members would be elected. The first Duma met in 1906 and urged radical land reform. To the tsar and his aristocratic landowning counselors, land redistribution seemed to strike at the heart of Russia's political system.

The tsar summoned a brilliant bureaucrat, aristocrat, and scholar of agriculture, Pyotr Stolypin, to manage the Duma's demands. Stolypin tried to stave off peasant resentment with, as he put it, a "wager on the strong." His reforms favored the richer peasants, easing their route to greater prosperity and property ownership. He wanted to establish a peasant bulwark against revolution. But a young revolutionary who also worked for the secret police assassinated him in 1911, leaving Russia in less capable hands. Even the most capable hands would have been full, given the pressures facing Russia after the outbreak of World War I.

WAR, DEFEAT, AND REVOLUTION From the start of the war in 1914, Germany hammered the Russian army. Russia's economy proved unable to produce enough ammunition, artillery, locomotives—even shoes—for the war effort. Russia's soldiers, justifiably, began to think their government was failing them, treating them as mere cannon fodder while profiteers grew fat from government contracts. Russia mobilized 12 million men, of whom 1.7 million were killed, 5 million wounded, and 2.5 million missing or captured. Only Austria-Hungary's casualty rate was worse.

In this time of crisis, Tsar Nicholas II showed all his many personal weaknesses. He could not control bickering generals. In late 1915, the tsar went to the front to supervise the conduct of the war personally. That invited Russians to hold him directly responsible for military misfortunes. He ignored mounting economic problems on the home front—notably, inflation of food and fuel prices. The tsar's authority melted away.

Mass demonstrations took place in March 1917 (February by the calendar then in use in Russia). Troops called out to tame the riotous crowds refused to fire. Generals and Duma politicians, agreeing that the tsar had become a liability, forced him to abdicate in favor of his brother, who refused the throne. After 300 years of the Romanov dynasty, Russia now had no tsar.

A handful of Duma politicians now formed a Provisional Government that represented mainly the privileged segments of Russian society. In the capital, now called Petrograd, workers and revolutionaries organized into a soviet and claimed authority. Russia had, in effect, two governments, and so no government.

Bolshevik Revolution Rebellious Russian soldiers in early 1917 march in St. Petersburg, carrying a banner that reads "Liberty, Equality, Fraternity" in homage to the French revolutionary slogan.

Through the spring and summer of 1917, the Provisional Government, headed by the moderate socialist lawyer Alexander Kerensky, made two big mistakes. First, it chose to continue fighting, even ordering an offensive in June that became a retreat by July. Second, it postponed land reform. Millions of peasants took matters into their own hands, seizing estates and sometimes killing landlords. Soldiers from peasant families deserted the battlefront in droves so as not to miss redistributions of land. Critics of the Provisional Government promised peace, land, and bread—none of which Kerensky could provide.

LENIN Into this chaotic situation came **Vladimir Lenin**. Born in 1870 to a prosperous provincial family, Lenin became a dedicated revolutionary in his teens after the shock of seeing his brother hanged for trying to build an assassin's bomb. An excellent student interested in physics and math, and a fine chess player, Lenin studied law at university but was expelled for taking part in a demonstration. He responded by studying revolutionary writers, especially Marx, on his own. Thanks to his mother's intervention, he was allowed to take university examinations in 1890, despite not having been a student for years. He passed brilliantly and became a provincial lawyer, devoting every spare minute to preparing for revolution. His activities earned him banishment to Siberia in 1897 and then exile, during which he wrote political treatises. He was in Switzerland in early 1917 when the High Command of the German Army decided to provide him with a special train to neutral Finland. From there, he could take his revolutionary skills to Petrograd and undermine the teetering Russian war effort.

Lenin in 1917 was a middle-aged man in a hurry. He had created a splinter faction, called the Bolsheviks, of a revolutionary Marxist party and dominated it through force of personality and intellectual brilliance. Most Bolsheviks in 1917 hoped to take power soon, some of them optimistic it could happen through elections. Lenin wanted revolution now, by whatever means necessary, using the slogan "all power to the soviets." Within those soviets, the Bolshevik faction prevailed, thanks to tight organization and the fervor of its members.

THE OCTOBER REVOLUTION AND EARLY BOLSHEVIK RULE Lenin ordered an armed insurrection. The Bolshevik Revolution was a coup d'état on November 7–8, 1917 (but sometimes called the October

Vladimir Lenin Lenin addresses Red Army soldiers in Moscow in 1920.

Revolution because of the different Russian calendar). Within 10 days, the Bolsheviks controlled Petrograd and Moscow and had begun to squeeze out other revolutionary factions. Within three months, they were governing alone and had set up a secret police and revolutionary courts to identify, and then imprison or murder, those insufficiently loyal to their party.

Their policies, however, won them the loyalty of many Russians. The Bolsheviks made peace with the Central Powers early in 1918. They ratified the peasants' seizures of land. They stripped away the civil rights of priests, landlords, bankers, and others whom they, like millions of ordinary Russians, deemed exploiters.

Lenin and many Bolsheviks believed that the Duma, and all democracy, was a sham. They believed Russia needed what they called the dictatorship of the proletariat. In practice, that meant a one-party state led not by proletarian workers but by people like Lenin: long-time professional revolutionaries, some of them brilliant intellectuals, well schooled—if self-educated—in German philosophy, British political economy, and the history of the French Revolution. They saw themselves as "the vanguard of the proletariat" and were so convinced of their historical mission that at times they used armed force against workers and peasants in whose name they claimed to rule. They thought they were "building communism," a political system first outlined by Marx that, in theory, was without private property, without exploitation, and in some versions (not Lenin's) without a state.

It took four difficult years for Lenin to consolidate power. In the Russian Civil War (1918–1921), the Bolsheviks—officially called communists by March 1918—created an improvised army to fight opponents of their revolution. Lenin assigned this task to Leon Trotsky, who had planned the coup of 1917. Despite having no military experience, Trotsky built an effective military in the terrible conditions of 1918. He imposed conscription on a war-weary population and hired officers from the old tsarist army against the wishes of almost every Bolshevik. His Red Army prevailed against both left-wing but non-Bolshevik revolutionaries and a loose coalition of counterrevolutionaries backed by foreign powers, including troops from France, Britain, the United States, and—by far the largest contingent—Japan.

By early 1921, Lenin, Trotsky, and the Bolsheviks had essentially won the Russian Civil War and ruled a shattered, bankrupt, impoverished, and territorially shrunken country. Some 8 to 13 million people had died of violence or disease in the turmoil of the years 1917–1921. Another 2 million emigrated. Industrial production stood at 20 percent of 1914 levels. Hunger stalked the streets. The Bolsheviks concluded that they could not let workers run the factories after all, so they imposed hierarchical management. They requisitioned all the grain they could from the peasantry, who responded with strikes. In March 1921, sailors at a naval base, Kronstadt, renowned for its revolutionary ardor against the tsars, rebelled against Bolshevik rule. The Red Army and the new secret police force, the Cheka, crushed them at the cost of many thousand lives, demonstrating—for any who still needed convincing—that the Bolsheviks would brook no dissent. In the years to come, they would try to destroy the surviving elites of prerevolutionary Russia, spread their ideology abroad, and make their country, from 1922 called the Soviet Union or USSR, a powerhouse in world politics.

VERSAILLES AND POSTWAR PARTITIONS

In 1919, in the middle of Russia's civil war, representatives of the victorious powers of World War I gathered at Versailles outside Paris to hammer out a set of peace treaties. The Allies excluded the defeated Central Powers and communist Russia, which had announced it would not pay the tsars' debts. Edith Wilson, the wife of the American

A New Political Geography: Europe, the Middle East, and Africa, 1922 The treaties signed in 1919 and 1920 concluding World War I redrew the boundaries of Europe, European colonies, and the Ottoman Middle East. New countries arose in east-central Europe and in former Russian, Austro-Hungarian, and German territories. New de facto colonies, as well as the new country of Turkey, were created in former Ottoman lands in the Middle East. The Allied powers devising this new political geography tried to respect ethnic identities in Europe, but not in the Middle East or Africa.

president, Woodrow Wilson, told her husband that the assembled diplomats poring over their maps looked like so many little boys playing a game. The president assured her theirs was a serious business. They were redrawing the map of east-central Europe and Southwest Asia, reassigning Germany's overseas colonies, dividing up territories, creating countries, marking borders, and defining peoples. In short, they were doing roughly what an earlier generation of European diplomats had done to Africa at the Berlin Conference of 1884–1885.

REMAKING EUROPE The European powers had carried out the partition of Africa in ignorance, but they undertook the partition of the territories of the Central Powers in a mood of vengeance. French diplomats especially wanted to cripple Germany. The deal imposed on Germany, the **Treaty of Versailles**, explicitly blamed Germany for the outbreak of the war, required Germany to pay huge sums (called reparations) to the victors, and turned some 13 percent of German territory over to either France or newly re-created Poland. It put strict limits on the size of Germany's armed forces. Other treaties, equally vengeful, were signed with Austria, Hungary, Bulgaria, and the Ottoman Empire.

The treaties reflected two other ambitions aside from vengeance. The first was **self-determination**, to use Wilson's preferred phrase. The American president thought that each European nationality ought to rule itself. This would, he hoped, remove an important cause of discontent, helping to ensure future peace. Wilson did not consider Africans and Asians capable of self-rule. Racism of this sort was common in 1919.

The second ambition behind the treaties was, in Wilson's phrase, collective security. He hoped that international institutions might cool the militarism and nationalism that had boiled over into World War I. So the Allies designed an international body, the League of Nations, to prevent war through arbitration. Based in Geneva, Switzerland, the league settled several international disputes during the 1920s. But in the 1930s, it proved helpless in the face of renewed militarism—as we shall see. In a bitter rebuke to Wilson, the U.S. Senate refused to ratify U.S. membership in the league.

World War I and its peace treaties left legacies more durable than the League of Nations. The Romanovs in Russia were not the only longstanding dynasty toppled. In Germany, when the emperor, Kaiser Wilhelm II, fled the country late in 1918, it ended the reign of the house of Hohenzollern, emperors of Germany since 1871 and kings of Prussia since 1701. Now, new political factions battled in the streets of Berlin and Munich. In Munich, a Soviet-style government briefly came to power. In August 1919, after nine months' painful gestation, Germany brought forth a republic, soon called the Weimar Republic after the town where its first constitutional assembly took place. It struggled to gain legitimacy among Germans. The economy careened from hyperinflation of the currency in 1923 and 1924 to economic depression in 1931. The rise of Adolf Hitler to power in Germany, described below, resulted from the inadequacies of the Weimar Republic and stands as one of the legacies of World War I.

In Austria-Hungary, the house of Habsburg also lost its throne after 400 years as a major force in Europe. As in Germany, revolution followed defeat in 1918. Reorganization followed along lines set forth in the treaties negotiated in Paris in 1919, creating new countries in place of the multinational Habsburg state. Austria and Hungary became independent countries. Poland was re-created from Habsburg, German, and Russian territory. Another republic, Czechoslovakia, was cobbled together from Habsburg provinces. The southern Slavs were gathered into a new kingdom, Yugoslavia. All of these countries were small and comparatively weak. Their borders did not perfectly match ethnic geography—no borders could. Most of them soon became nationalist and authoritarian in character, oppressing their minority populations.

The remaking of Europe extended to one minority population of the British Isles. Ireland had long been part of the United Kingdom but often chafed at its subordinate status. Agitation for home rule gathered steam in the decades before 1914. Although some 200,000 Irishmen volunteered for the British Army in World War I (and one-fifth of them died in it), the war presented Irish nationalists with an opportunity to escape British domination. A 1916 uprising in Dublin met with defeat, but an island-wide guerilla war (1919–1921), in which many World War I veterans applied their military skills both for and against independence, resulted in another new European country, the Irish Free State, formalized in 1922.

REMAKING THE MIDDLE EAST After 600 years as a ruling family, the Ottomans, like the Romanovs, Habsburgs, and Hohenzollerns, also lost their empire as a result of World War I. The result was a dramatic transformation of the Middle East—a term that came into occasional use in the late nineteenth century and became common after 1918. Its precise meaning varies, but in this book it refers to Southwest Asia and Egypt.

After weathering all manner of challenges for centuries, the Ottoman state proved unequal to the demands of industrial warfare in the years 1914–1918. The treaty its representatives signed with the Allies in 1919 amounted to the partition of most of the empire among Britain, France, Italy, and Greece. This outraged many Turks, sparking a nationalist revolution led by an army hero, **Mustafa Kemal**. Between 1919 and 1924, Kemal's forces defeated all rivals, repelled a Greek invasion, expelled millions of non-Turks from Anatolia, replaced the Ottoman state with a new Turkish republic, and, most radical of all, abolished the Islamic caliphate.

For more than 1,200 years, caliphs, the earthly leaders of the Islamic faith and the official successors of Muhammad, had guided Muslims. Since 1517, every Ottoman sultan had claimed the mantle of caliph, and most Sunni Muslims, and therefore most Muslims accepted that claim. So it came as a great shock when Kemal's government eliminated the caliphate in 1924.

Kemal drew the lesson from defeat in World War I that the Ottoman Empire had been backward and inefficient, handicapped by an antiquated culture steeped in Islamic tradition. So he pushed through reforms in education and law that secularized Turkey, closing Islamic schools and courts. The Latin alphabet replaced the Arabic. Religious symbols and garb were banned in public. Sisters' inheritances now equaled their brothers', contrary to Islamic law. Women acquired more legal rights as individuals rather than as wards of their fathers or husbands. Polygamy was banned, and women could initiate divorce. From 1930, women could vote and hold office.

This package, often known as the Atatürk Reforms after Kemal's adopted name of Atatürk ("father of the Turks"), was part of a century-long process of reform in Ottoman lands. It was also a legacy of World War I. Kemal's main motivation was to strengthen Turkey as the Meiji reformers had done in Japan. To achieve this, he drew upon the law, culture, and technology of the most formidable states of the day—those of western Europe. Kemal's military record and his success in rallying Turks against foreign invasion gave him the prestige and power to enact far-reaching reforms and harness the nationalism of ethnic Turks.

The territory of the Turkish republic was a mere remnant of the Ottoman Empire. The mainly Arab provinces of the defunct empire, now officially called Mandated Territories of the League of Nations, became de facto colonies of Britain and France. The French got Syria and Lebanon; the British took Palestine, Jordan, and Iraq.

That arrangement stored up trouble for the future. During the war, the British government had promised unspecified land in Ottoman Palestine to Zionist Jews. A nationalist movement of the Jewish people, Zionism grew up partly in response to anti-Semitism in Europe in the late nineteenth century. The Zionist movement aimed to create a Jewish homeland centered on Jerusalem, despite the presence of tens of thousands of Muslim and Christian Arabs who themselves considered Palestine home. British diplomats had also promised independence to Arabs if they rebelled against the Ottomans. And other British diplomats cut a deal with France, promising to divide the

Secularized Turkey A photograph of a Turkish classroom dated to around 1930 shows women students learning to read and write in the Latin alphabet. Most of the women wear Western dress, and many have their hair uncovered: characteristic signs of Atatürk's program of reform.

Arab provinces of the Ottoman Empire between them. So when the peacemakers in Paris in 1919 redrew the map of the Middle East, just about everyone felt betrayed. Their descendants often still do.

The diplomats in Paris rearranged the political geography of Africa and the Pacific as well as the Middle East. Germany's former African colonies, such as Tanganyika, Togo, Southwest Africa, and others, became League of Nations Mandated Territories administered by Britain, France, Belgium, or South Africa. In the Pacific, former German colonies went to Japan, Britain, Australia, or New Zealand. The local populations in Samoa or New Guinea or Togo were not consulted.

SUFFRAGISM TO 1939

While the peacemakers at Versailles were discussing the fine points of the right of self-determination of peoples, women reminded them that the female half of humankind did not enjoy that right. As we've seen, Olympe de Gouges, Abigail Adams, and others had advocated women's political rights in the late eighteenth century with little success. Winning the vote—the goal of **suffragism**—was an essential step in women's quest for political equality. It happened in a surge, like the abolitions of slavery, and World War I provided a big push.

PREWAR SUFFRAGE MOVEMENTS As of 1850, voting was a male preserve in the few countries that permitted it at all. Many voices challenged this arrangement. Their arguments included the notion that denying women the vote was inherently unjust; that women's influence in politics would reduce corruption and war; and, in some cases, such as the United States, that woman suffrage, if confined to a preferred class or race, would reduce the influence of poor people, immigrants, or racial minorities who, if they did not already vote, might do so one day.

During the nineteenth century, women in the United Kingdom and the United States built social movements aimed at winning the vote, often allied with supporters of moral causes such as banning prostitution or alcohol. Many who took up the suffragist cause in the United States were abolitionists or Quakers—including Lucretia Mott and Elizabeth Cady Stanton, who in 1848 organized a women's rights gathering in upstate New York, the Seneca Falls Convention. Stanton held that only the vote would make woman "free as man is free." The convention concluded by issuing a Declaration of Sentiments modeled on the Declaration of Independence. The most influential suffragist publication was John Stuart Mill's *The Subjection of Women* (1869), likely written with substantial input from his wife, Harriet Taylor Mill, who had published on suffragism in 1851. The book was translated into dozens of languages and read by suffragists all over the world. Suffragism, like abolitionism, was an international movement, coursing through the Global web.

By 1890, suffragists and other reformers in a few countries had achieved some important goals such as limits on working hours or the sale of alcohol, improved city lighting or sanitation, more girls' schools, and a woman's right to own property in her own name. But, despite sustained effort and support from many male politicians, they were not significantly closer to securing women's right to vote in national elections.

In Britain, the movement took on an especially militant character between 1909 and 1914. Suffragists, frustrated with 70 years of meager results, tried mass demonstrations, hunger strikes, and sabotage. They

Woman Suffrage On May 21, 1914, British suffrage activist Emmeline Pankhurst was arrested outside Buckingham Palace in London, England.

even exploded a bomb at a prime minister's residence. These efforts, organized by a minority wing of British suffragists led by Emmeline Pankhurst and her daughters, failed in their purpose as of 1914.

EARLY SUFFRAGE When World War I began, about 2 million of the world's roughly 400 million voting-age women could vote in national elections, all of them in four small countries. Not counting places that had provided women the vote and then quickly took it away, such as the state of New Jersey, the first jurisdiction in the world where women could vote was Wyoming. It was a U.S. territory with only 8,000 people in 1869 when one activist—Esther Hobart Morris—convinced the legislature that women would exert a civilizing influence upon the wild west territory. Utah followed suit in 1870 when the federal government threatened to ban polygamy, a common practice in the Mormon-dominated territory. Utah's polygamous men granted women the vote to show that the women of Utah were not oppressed. By 1914, women had won the right to vote in state elections in most other western U.S. states. But not in national elections.

New Zealand was the first country to enfranchise women fully. The foremost leader of the suffrage movement in New Zealand was Kate Sheppard, a Scottish immigrant, wife, mother, and formidable organizer in antialcohol campaigns. She published persuasive arguments in the same vein as Taylor and Mill, adding the idea that expanding the electorate would reduce vote buying and other forms of corruption. Sheppard presented New Zealand legislators with a petition in favor of enfranchising women signed by a goodly share of the country's adult population. She and her allies, who included several of New Zealand's leading politicians, prevailed in 1893. By 1902, Australia had followed suit. Both New Zealand and Australia were composed substantially of immigrants, with men handily outnumbering women. This made woman suffrage less threatening to

Kate Sheppard The influential New Zealand woman suffrage activist posed for this portrait around 1910.

them than it did in most other countries. And, as in Wyoming, many men thought women voters might cleanse the grubby quality of public life.

Finland in 1906 and Norway in 1913 allowed women to vote as a result of nationalist campaigns. Finland, part of the Russian Empire since 1815, won substantial autonomy in 1906, including a legislature. To maximize the Finnish voice within what remained a Russian territory, Finnish men agreed that Finnish women should vote. In Norway, the nationalist quest was for independence from Sweden, and once again women's votes seemed politically useful to men hoping to strengthen Norway's claims for independence. These four countries, all small in population, overwhelmingly rural, and far from the centers of world power and intellectual ferment, were the only ones anywhere that allowed women to vote in national elections before World War I.

Elsewhere, resistance to suffragism was too strong. In Catholic countries of southern Europe, for example, and in Islamic countries such as Iran or those of the Ottoman Empire (where few men could vote), the dominant culture led people to suppose that the position of women in society was divinely ordained rather than politically negotiable. Resistance was also entrenched where men—some men, at least—had long ago won voting rights, as in France, the Netherlands, the United States, and the United Kingdom. Political participation had become a ritual of manhood, one that most men felt would undermine feminine virtues if shared with women. In Britain, one of the most active and effective opponents was Mary Augusta Ward, founder in 1908 of the Anti-Suffrage Society. Mrs. Humphry Ward, as she preferred to be known, showed astute political skills while arguing—paradoxically—that women were unfit for politics.

SUFFRAGE AND WORLD WAR I   In the end, it required major social upheavals—war, invasion, revolution—to splinter the opposition to enfranchising women. World War I provided an opening for suffragist movements, one they were by 1914 fully capable of exploiting.

Between 1914 and 1920, women won the vote in 19 countries, including big and populous ones such as Russia, Poland, Germany, the United Kingdom, Canada, and the United States. Some restrictions applied—so, for example, in the United Kingdom only women over age 30 could vote until 1928, and in the United States

WHEN WOMEN WON THE VOTE (NATIONAL ELECTIONS)	
1893	New Zealand
1902	Australia
1906	Finland
1913	Norway
1915	Denmark, Iceland
1917	Russia
1918	Austria, Canada, Germany, Hungary, Latvia, Lithuania, Poland, United Kingdom
1919	Belgium, Luxembourg, Netherlands (and white women in colonial Kenya, Rhodesia)
1920	Albania, Czechoslovakia, United States
1921	Sweden
1922	Ireland
1923	Burma
1924	Mongolia
1928	Guiana
1929	Ecuador
1930	South Africa (white women only)
1931	Spain (revoked 1939)
1932	Brazil, Uruguay, Thailand
1934	Cuba, Turkey
1937	Philippines (U.S. territory)
1938	Bolivia
1939	El Salvador

Source: Jad Adams, *Women and the Vote: A World History* (2014), 437–38.

the southern states quickly found ways to disenfranchise black women. In Russia, now becoming the communist USSR, women from privileged backgrounds were denied the vote. In Canada, Asian and First Nations women could not vote. But, taken together, more than 100 million women acquired the vote in these seven years. The following table shows the significance of the era of World War I in the history of women's suffrage up to 1940.

In some countries, including the United Kingdom and the United States, the political winds shifted because women's patriotism and sacrifices for the war effort won them enough goodwill—and undermined notions of their unfitness for public life—to get enfranchisement bills passed in all-male legislatures. In others, such as Germany, Austria, and Russia, when the collapse of autocracy in the years 1917–1918 revamped politics in general, opposition

Arguments for Suffrage A California poster in support of woman suffrage from around 1910 suggests that women should be given the vote because they will "clean up" politics by combating bribery, corruption, and social problems.

to women's voting quickly crumbled—despite the efforts of Germany's League to Combat Women's Emancipation, which had a few hundred thousand members (before disbanding in 1920). In all combatant countries, where most young men were away from wives and families for years, moral reformers hoped that enfranchising women would check the spread of drunkenness and prostitution. In Canada in 1917, a prime minister trying to build support for military conscription pushed through a law allowing the vote to women who were wives, mothers, daughters, or sisters of men in uniform. His reasoning, which proved correct, was that they would favor conscription of other men to join their relatives in the Canadian Army in the trenches of France and Belgium.

So among the legacies of World War I was a giant stride toward the political emancipation of women. By 1920, of countries with constitutional government that allowed regular elections, only France and Italy denied the vote to women. (These countries granted women full suffrage in the 1940s.)

THE RISE OF THE UNITED STATES

In addition to sparking revolutions, shattering empires, and accelerating social and political movements, World War I shifted the global balance of power. In broad terms, it weakened Europe and bolstered the United States. This shift showed up in many spheres, from the size of navies

to the pace of industrial innovation. It was most obvious in finance. Britain and France had borrowed heavily from New York bankers and the U.S. government. Anyone seeking big loans in the 1920s now first thought of New York rather than London, Amsterdam, Paris, or Berlin. As the American theologian Reinhold Niebuhr put it in 1930, "We are the first empire of the world to establish our sway without legions. Our legions are dollars."

Bankers aside, Americans proved reluctant to take on the role of the world's leading power. The United States retreated into isolationism in the 1920s, refusing to join the League of Nations, for example. It remained active in the American hemisphere, using its military power freely to intervene in Haiti, Nicaragua, and elsewhere. It kept a world-class navy, equal in size to Britain's. But most Americans preferred to stay out of the world's trouble spots and rely upon broad oceans for U.S. security.

American power—or more precisely, potential power—rested in large part on the fact that the United States had the world's largest industrial sector and pumped two-thirds of the world's oil. The U.S. economy boomed during the war years. After a brief postwar recession, it did so again in the Roaring Twenties, led by the automobile industry, where American innovation was the envy of the world. U.S. car factories exemplified the American system of manufacturing with interchangeable parts pioneered a century previously. Starting in 1913, production managers turned workers into interchangeable parts too by adopting the electrified assembly line. Formerly, carmaking required skilled craftsmen. Now anyone could learn the ropes in a few hours, bolting and welding parts onto car body after car body as they passed by on conveyor belts. By 1925, this technique reduced the time needed for car assembly to one-eighth that required in 1912. Car prices fell to one-third of their former level. To retain workers who hated the assembly line, carmakers had to pay higher wages—indeed, high enough that workers could buy cars. The Ford Motor Company first developed this system of assembly line mass production and higher wages, so it is sometimes called Fordism. Other U.S. industries adopted it. Together with cheap energy in the form of oil, it underpinned the heady growth (nearly 5 percent per year) of the U.S. economy in the 1920s.

The centrality of oil to world politics was another legacy of World War I. By the end of the war, trucks, tanks, aircraft, and submarines had become important instruments of military power, and all used oil derivatives as

American Oil In 1912, this Standard Oil Company refinery in California was the largest in the United States, which led the world in oil output.

fuel. So did an increasing proportion of surface ships. In 1918, Lord Curzon, a prominent member of Britain's War Cabinet, said the "Allies floated to victory on a wave of oil." Oil had become essential to modern warfare and a strategic good of the utmost importance—as it remains today. The American oil industry remained the world's largest and most efficient, boosted by the discovery of big new oil fields in Texas, Oklahoma, and California in 1924.

A further political legacy of World War I was the changed relationship between governments and the governed in many societies. The war dealt a setback to the ideal of restrained government. None of the combatant states trusted the market to provide enough war materiel. All of them relied on government to organize war production to some extent. The German war economy, entirely improvised but carefully controlled by the military, worked miracles in munitions factories, even if it could not adequately feed the civilian population. It made such a favorable impression on Lenin that he used it as his model for Russia once he took power. The combatants only partly demobilized their economies after 1918, keeping government regulation of markets in effect in different ways. World War I advanced a long-term trend, one with several subsequent ebbs and flows, toward bigger government.

THE GREAT DEPRESSION

The Great Depression, the sharpest contraction in the global economy in modern history, began in 1929 with a stock-market collapse in the United States. The economic rise of the United States in the previous decades meant that what happened in New York powerfully affected the rest of the world. The Depression spread quickly, faster

than any previous economic downturn, because of the speed with which information and money now flowed. People tried to pull their money out of banks, many of which failed. Global economic output fell by 15 percent from 1929 to 1932. Agricultural prices fell by as much as 60 percent, and international trade shrank by half.

Countries deeply tied into international circuits of finance or dependent on exports were especially hard hit. Unemployment in Germany, which owed large sums in reparations from World War I, reached 33 percent, and in the United States and Canada, about 25 percent. Australia and New Zealand, dependent on farm exports, suffered heavily. So did countries relying on mining exports, such as South Africa, Peru, Bolivia, and above all Chile, where total economic output fell by half.

In contrast, countries less tied into the international circuits and more structured around peasant food production felt far less distress. China, India, and Japan weathered the crisis comparatively well. Japan's economic contraction was about 8 percent, India's less, and China's less still. The USSR scarcely took part in international trade or financial flows and so was unscathed by the Great Depression, although, as we'll see below, it underwent its own homemade economic crisis in the early 1930s—collectivization.

In the hard-hit countries, families were thrown back on their own resources. Farm families could at least feed themselves. Urban families whose breadwinner lost a job struggled more, selling what they had, scratching out livings as day laborers, peddlers, beggars, or thieves. Couples

Great Depression Unemployed men wait for a hot meal outside a Chicago soup kitchen. In the United States, unemployment in 1932–1933 reached about 25 percent.

had fewer children: the global birth rate fell by 5 to 10 percent between 1930 and 1935.

Governments did not know how to ease the crisis. Before World War I, in a global depression such as that of 1873 or 1893, citizens had not expected governments to do anything. But the record of successful economic management during World War I, when governments had managed prices, wages, and production levels to unprecedented degrees, now made it politically impossible for them to do nothing. A new era of government direction of national economies—another legacy of World War I—dawned. Some tried to boost domestic production and employment by imposing tariffs on imported goods, which often reduced trade and deepened the Depression. Some tried rigorously to balance budgets in hopes of winning reputations for responsible public finance and inspiring investors. That translated into laying off government workers and higher unemployment. The most effective response was increasing public spending, even if it swelled national debt and ran counter to the wisdom of most 1930s economists. At the center of this response was rearmament. Germany and Italy pioneered this path under leaders who looked forward to a new war that would undo the result of World War I.

FASCISM AND COMMUNISM, 1919–1939

The return to peacetime conditions after World War I did not end turmoil around the world. In 1919, political chaos boiled over in cities throughout Europe and from Winnipeg to Sydney, Buenos Aires to Beijing. New ideologies simmered almost everywhere, with fascism, communism, and anticolonialism the most important. All were radical in the sense that their followers wished to see thorough changes in the political order. All thrived upon either disgust at the mass butchery of war or the sordid compromises of the 1919 peace—or both.

FASCISM TO 1939

Fascism was born in Italy during World War I. Italy had joined the war in 1915 on what became the winning side, lured by promises of Austrian territory. But the peace

settlement granted less land than many Italians expected, and nationalists called it a "mutilated victory."

To many Italians, this outcome was a betrayal of the more than 2 million killed, wounded, taken prisoner, or missing in the war. They blamed, among others, a weak government, parliamentary institutions, and cultural and business elites. They wanted an Italian state that would be more forceful, nationalistic, imperialistic, and unified—and less hobbled by debate, division, and deliberation. They wanted action, not words. People who saw matters this way admired the fascist movement.

Fascism, in Italy or elsewhere, had distinctive features. First among them was militant nationalism. Fascists idolized vigor, power, ruthlessness, and war. Their nationalism included a call for regeneration and purification of the nation. Many fascists felt only violence could cleanse their nation of impure elements, by which they usually meant ethnic or religious minorities and immigrants. Fascism also emphasized the cult of the dynamic leader, the man (never a woman) who took bold action and rejected political bickering, compromises, and backroom deals. Fascists scorned multi-party politics and preferred a one-party state—like Lenin and the Bolsheviks.

Fascist movements tried to make a display of national solidarity and strength through theatrical marches and rallies. They adopted uniforms for party members: Blackshirts in Italy, Blueshirts in Spain and Ireland, Brownshirts in Germany. Fascists had their own salutes and catchphrases. Their rallies, often dramatic and emotional affairs, extolled strength and exuded menace toward people judged not genuinely part of the nation. Fascist parties always included youth movements, because the cult of action, vigor, and renewal required young faces.

On the home front, fascists wanted men to wield authority in families and women to keep house and raise strong children. The growing independence of women under wartime conditions often annoyed men—and many women too—who preferred that families live under the authority of an adult male. Fascists wanted men to reassert that domestic authority. Fascist gender politics was an extreme version of a common outlook around the world in the early twentieth century.

Fascists usually offered an economic program that was critical of both capitalism and communism, proclaiming a third way, sometimes called corporatism, involving substantial state direction but mainly private ownership of property. In any case, they claimed to provide an economy that served all the people, not just bosses or workers. Religious policy differed greatly among fascists. Some were scornful of organized religion. Others allied themselves with the Catholic or Orthodox Church. Fascism never amounted to much outside of Christendom, although Chinese nationalists borrowed some of its elements.

ITALIAN FASCISM AND MUSSOLINI The mainspring behind Italian fascism was **Benito Mussolini**. Born in 1883 in a provincial town, his father was a blacksmith with socialist politics, his mother a pious Catholic and former schoolteacher. Benito did well in school and was certified as an elementary school teacher. But in 1902, he left Italy for Switzerland to avoid army service. He read widely, especially in political philosophy, took part in socialist organizations and strikes, and was arrested now and again in both Switzerland and Italy. He thought of himself as an intellectual, and as of age 30 there was nothing about him to suggest he would become Italy's dictator.

Then came World War I. Unlike most socialists, Mussolini eventually argued for Italy's entry into the ongoing bloodbath. He decided that national identity was more important, more natural, than class identity. He volunteered for the army and spent nine months near the trenches, where an accidental explosion left shrapnel in his body. The war years gave Mussolini credentials for political leadership and an audience he otherwise could not have had. In 1919, he formed a paramilitary group in the northern city of Milan that embraced the term *fascist*.

Italy in 1919 was in disarray. Class conflict boiled over into violence between workers and bosses—or thugs hired by bosses—and between peasants and landlords. Fascists claimed to offer a solution, one based on national unity, discipline, and authority. They promised to prevent communism from succeeding in Italy. They denounced deliberation and compromise as weakness. In practice, they advocated crushing labor unions, jailing or exiling socialists and communists, building up the military, entrusting power to a fascist party elite, and grabbing territory from supposed racial inferiors, specifically Slavs, Albanians, and Africans. In 1922, some 30,000 fascists marched on Rome threatening a coup d'état. The king, afraid of civil war, asked Mussolini to form a government.

Mussolini ruled Italy for more than 20 years in an

Mussolini The Italian fascist leader addresses an enormous crowd in May 1936, proclaiming a new Italian empire following Italy's invasion of Ethiopia.

increasingly authoritarian fashion. He excelled at manipulating mass media, including print journalism, his former profession, but also the new media of radio and film. He appealed to all those worried about communism, which included most employers. In this respect, the Bolshevik Revolution was indispensable to the rise of Mussolini. He made an effort to appeal to the church and Catholics, and to those upset by women's autonomy—he presented the memory of his pious mother as the ideal for Italian womanhood. Above all, he appealed to Italian nationalism. After 1922, he squashed or co-opted all opposition and increasingly ruled as dictator, through the Fascist Party.

The anxieties that made Mussolini and fascism attractive to millions of Italians existed elsewhere too. Italy's example—a purposeful government that promoted deeds, not bickering—appealed broadly. Fascist propaganda bolstered that appeal, trumpeting decisive actions such as draining marshes or building highways and dams.

By 1933, when the Great Depression was eroding faith in existing institutions, fascist movements had arisen in a dozen or more countries, mainly in Europe. Even countries with longstanding traditions of representative government, such as France and Britain, had fascist movements. The British Union of Fascists claimed tens of thousands of members in the early 1930s, although it never did well in elections. Nor did fascist groups in France. Fascists came to power in Hungary in 1932 and Spain (after winning a bloody civil war) in 1939. Movements that, while not genuinely fascist, found inspiration in Mussolini's Italy took power in Romania, Poland, Greece, and Portugal. Small fascist movements took shape in some Latin American countries such as Chile and Brazil.

GERMAN FASCISM AND HITLER By far the most important case was Germany, where a fascist party emerged in the 1920s and took power in 1933. They were called National Socialists, or Nazis. The Nazi Party emerged from the chaotic and violent world of postwar Germany. The Versailles treaty, particularly its war guilt clause and reparations, seemed deeply unjust to most Germans, who felt they had neither caused nor lost World War I. Many found it comforting to believe in the "stab in the back," the idea that traitorous politicians working for Jews, communists, or both had sacrificed Germany. One who admired such thinking was the Austrian **Adolf Hitler**.

Hitler was born in 1889 to a modest family—one of six children, three of whom died in infancy. His father was a customs inspector and beekeeper in various small towns along the border between Austria-Hungary and Germany. Hitler's younger brother died in 1900, leaving Hitler sullen and uncooperative, a reaction not so different from Lenin's to the death of his older brother. He quit school at age 16 and went to Vienna, where he was twice rejected for art school. For the next seven years, he eked out a living selling watercolor paintings and sleeping in

Adolf Hitler Hitler giving a campaign speech in a beer garden tent in Munich. The banner urges voters to elect Hitler and the National Socialists, or Nazis, whose party headquarters were in Munich.

homeless shelters. In 1913, he moved to Munich in Germany. When World War I began, he volunteered for the German army and served with distinction, chiefly as a messenger, winning an Iron Cross, for which a Jewish officer recommended him. He was wounded in 1916 and temporarily blinded by mustard gas late in 1918. Hitler loved the camaraderie, commitment, and acceptance he found in the army.

Outraged by the Versailles treaty, Hitler drifted into politics in 1919 in Munich. He joined a fringe group, the National Socialist Party, one of many hypernationalist organizations in Germany. By 1921, he was its leader. He honed a gift for oratory, practicing poses and turns of phrase in front of a mirror. He encouraged the anger and resentment of common people, especially those who felt Germany had been wronged at Versailles. Hitler urged them to believe that Germany's future depended on ridding the country of Jews and communists, and that he alone embodied the will of the people. He promised action, not words—a renewal of German greatness, rather than the squabbling of democracy.

He had a strange charisma, with his frenzied gestures, theatrical poses, and absurd hyperbole. He was a peculiar politician, living simply, avoiding tobacco, alcohol, meat, and the pleasures of the flesh. He was lazy and undisciplined in his work habits, although he went to lengths to project an image of vigor and stamina. For millions of struggling Germans, he seemed like the savior they needed. His early efforts to seize power landed him in jail, and for most of the 1920s he remained a marginal figure in German politics.

Hitler rode to power on a wave of anxiety and anger that grew with Germany's economic setbacks. Hyperinflation wiped out the value of the currency in the years 1923–1924, so that one needed a wheelbarrow full of banknotes to buy a loaf of bread. Then, in 1931, the global depression hit Germany hard.

The Nazi Party started doing well, winning 18 percent of the vote in 1930 and 37 percent in early 1932. Germany's veteran politicians, mainly educated men often from aristocratic backgrounds, thought little of Hitler, a mere Austrian corporal and school dropout. They calculated that they could control him if he became chancellor (more or less prime minister). In early 1933, he took power—because the political establishment offered it to him.

In the next few years, Hitler outmaneuvered both the

Hyperinflation Amid the hyperinflation crisis that hit the Weimar Republic in 1923 and 1924, banknotes became so worthless that children used bundles of them as building blocks.

old politicians and all rivals within his party. He co-opted the military, which shared his contempt for the Versailles treaty restrictions. He gradually purged all institutions of people with insufficient loyalty to himself. He installed Nazis atop all universities, professional societies, and courts, while banning labor unions and political parties other than his own. He was building a totalitarian state—one in which all aspects of life were politicized and displays of loyalty to a dictator and his party were required. It was similar in some respects to what Lenin and his successors had done after the Bolshevik Revolution. But Hitler's consolidation of power served goals very different from Lenin's.

Hitler wanted absolute power in order to return Germany and Germans to great-power status. As a first step, that required unshackling the German military from the terms of the Versailles treaty, and Hitler moved to covertly expand the army and create an air force. It also meant gathering into a larger Germany all of the German-speaking peoples, whether they lived in Austria, the Sudetenland (part of Czechoslovakia), or East Prussia (mostly Lithuania at the time). Hitler wanted to purify what he imagined as the German race, which meant killing or exiling those who in German were called *untermenschen*—people he considered lower racial types, such as Jews, Slavs, and Roma. Last, he wanted to smash Bolshevism, which he connected with Jews. He hoped for another great war, one that Germany would win and that would allow it to set terms for the rest of the world. Like most fringe ideologues, he nurtured revenge fantasies.

None of these ambitions originated with Hitler. Most of them were in circulation in Munich, where he settled in 1919, and some of them in the Vienna of his youth. But Hitler gave them both a modest coherence as a political program and an extreme, toxic, and murderous character. In the early and mid-1920s, his views struck most Germans as too crazy for consideration. But by 1932, as we've seen, 37 percent of German voters supported him.

After Hitler became chancellor in 1933, his popular support strengthened. He undertook a large-scale public works and rearmament campaign, which boosted the economy quickly. Workers found jobs more easily—unemployment was eliminated by 1938—and businessmen made bigger profits. Given the frequent hardship Germans had experienced since 1914, Hitler's economic successes won over millions. Most Germans preferred greater prosperity and renewed national pride to the political liberties Hitler took from them. The segments of society that lent him the strongest support were small farmers, artisans, shopkeepers, university students, and youth in general. As long as the economy flourished, most Germans were content with Hitler, and many of them were enraptured by his charisma, accepting his claim to be the authentic voice of the German people.

The business elite adjusted quickly to Hitler and Nazism. Many large industrial firms, such as Krupp and IG Farben, looked forward to rearmament or massive public works projects, and they donated generously to the Nazi Party. Most employers welcomed Nazi destruction of labor unions. Even some of the refined cultural elite embraced Hitler after he became chancellor. Germany's most distinguished philosopher, Martin Heidegger, joined the Nazi Party in 1933, and as rector (more or less president) of Freiburg University he lavished praise on Hitler. A famous dancer and film star, Leni Riefenstahl, also gushed about Hitler's greatness and made skillful propaganda movies for the Nazi Party.

Despite his genuine popularity among Germans, Hitler and the Nazi Party had plenty of detractors. Most of

German Fascism The filmmaker Leni Riefenstahl played a pivotal role in constructing the iconography of Nazism. Her 1935 propaganda film *Triumph of the Will* featured speeches by Hitler and other Nazi leaders and footage of mass rallies that captured the emotional fervor of crowds so important to fascism.

the political left—socialists and communists—despised him. Many of the more religious Germans, Catholics and Protestants alike, found him too unchristian in his conduct. Some of the old elites regarded him as an uncouth, uneducated upstart who was unfit for the chancellor's office. Hitler ruthlessly repressed his opponents, some of whom were murdered and many more imprisoned.

Hitler's social program, extremely important to him, included building a classless national German community. He thought that to be strong it had to be pure and therefore purged of all those deemed un-German. This view lay behind various racial purification efforts such as the Nuremberg Laws of 1935, which deprived German Jews of citizenship and political rights, banned marriage—and sex—between Jews and Germans, and defined Jewish identity as a matter of ancestry, not religion. Hitler also felt strongly that women ought not to compete with men for jobs but should focus on homemaking and child-rearing. His laws limited women to 10 percent of the places in universities and offered incentives to marriage and motherhood for women considered truly German. Every marrying couple received as a gift a copy of Hitler's political and philosophical ramblings, dictated from prison in the 1920s and published as *Mein Kampf* (*My Struggle*). Nonetheless, many young women found a career and an escape from humdrum village life by joining the Nazi Party and training as a secretary or a nurse.

In his first six years in power, Hitler delivered on many of his economic promises. He failed, however, in his ambition to make Germany self-sufficient in food and fuel, which contributed to his decision to seek more *lebensraum* ("living space") for Germans in 1939—by launching an expansionist war.

COMMUNISM TO 1939

Communists took their cues from Marx and his most influential follower, Lenin. They wanted a political order without private property or capitalism. They entrusted their hopes to hierarchical, disciplined parties that promised revolution and a bright future of equality, harmony, and prosperity. Marx and Lenin touted imagined laws of history assuring the inevitability of such a future. For people raised to believe in a second coming or the arrival of the kingdom of heaven on Earth, **communism** had some familiar features.

As we've seen, Lenin and the Bolsheviks took over Russia during the period 1917–1921, which inspired some people and frightened others around the world. Once the Bolsheviks had consolidated their hold on Russia, they set about spreading communist revolution to other countries, actively supporting tiny communist parties in Europe, China, British India, the United States, and elsewhere. They financed and dominated the Comintern, an international union of communist parties set up in 1919. Thanks in large part to economic calamities, communists in Italy, Germany, Hungary, and elsewhere in Europe attracted followings, arousing fears that fed fascism. And to a lesser extent, the success of fascism in Italy, Germany, and elsewhere fed fears that inspired people to join communist parties. Both movements, although enemies, benefited from the other's existence.

Communist and fascist movements typically shared certain elements: a militant and hierarchical party organization, a cult of the leader, a willingness to use violence in politics, and an emphasis on youth and the future, for example. Both shared the conviction that life would be permanently improved if certain class enemies or national enemies were destroyed.

They differed in important respects too. Communists typically proclaimed equality of the sexes, even if practice was another thing altogether, while fascists claimed either nature or God had subordinated women to men. Fascists could coexist cheerfully with capitalist business and private property, which communists reviled as the root of all evil. Fascism extolled the virtues of war and the solidarity of the nation, whereas communism extolled the virtues of class struggle—specifically of workers against owners and bosses—and the solidarity of the international working class. Fascism found it possible to co-opt churches and coexist with organized religion, whereas communists normally treated religion as an enemy.

Their fortunes differed too. Fascism was an important political movement for a little more than two decades, mainly in Europe. Communism held wider appeal and for a longer period. For 70 years after the Russian Revolution, communism remained an occasional political force in many countries and enjoyed a monopoly on power in a few, the most important of which was the USSR.

SOVIET COMMUNISM AND STALIN   In the USSR, the revolutionary regime in power by 1918 at first wobbled from crisis to crisis. Reconstituting a multinational empire in an age of fervid nationalism was a herculean task. So was quashing the resistance of all those opposed to the revolution. Lenin managed to prevail over these and other challenges. A power struggle followed Lenin's death in 1924, won by **Josef Stalin** (1878–1953). He was a Georgian from the Caucasus, the son of a hard-drinking cobbler father and a deeply religious mother. A fine student at seminary school, he dropped out and took up radical politics as a teenager. He played small roles in the 1917 revolution. But he caught Lenin's eye as a useful, unflinchingly loyal communist, willing to take on any

task. He also had real administrative and organizational gifts. Unlike Hitler and Mussolini, Stalin was hardworking and self-disciplined.

Upon consolidating power in the years 1927–1928 (which involved exiling Trotsky), Stalin set to transforming the USSR. He intended to make it—as all communists wanted—a more industrialized country. He wanted a workers' paradise but also a militarily formidable state. To advance these priorities, he put Soviet support for revolution abroad on the back burner. He promoted a "socialism in one country" policy that sat uneasily with the Marxist theory he and all communists had studied. His most revolutionary act came in agriculture.

To squeeze out the investment funds for industrialization, Stalin pushed through collectivization of agriculture in 1929. His agents forcibly gathered private landholdings into huge farms, run either as collectives or as state farms. The collectives had to turn over quotas of food to the state, which sold it cheaply to industrial workers. Collectivization amounted to taking peasants' land, forcing them into collectives, and seizing much of their grain. Peasants resisted by eating their livestock, destroying machinery, and hiding grain.

Stalin's innovations were more revolutionary than the Russian Revolution of 1917. Let's look first at two areas beyond agriculture: the industrial economy and education. Stalin instituted formal planning of the national economy in 1928. Millions of peasants migrated, some involuntarily, to mines and factories to produce vast

Soviet Reforms A 1921 Soviet propaganda poster quotes the Russian poet Pushkin—"Long live the sun!"—to celebrate the expanded education system bringing social mobility to people from peasant backgrounds across the Soviet Union.

quantities of coal, iron, steel, locomotives, and weaponry. In 1931, Stalin proclaimed—correctly, as it happened—that the USSR had only 10 years to become strong enough to defend itself from foreign attack. He spared no effort to build up the armaments industry. After 1934, the economy grew quickly, owing to forced industrialization. By the late 1930s, the USSR was the world's third largest industrial economy, after the United States and Germany, an astonishing achievement given its overwhelmingly agrarian character in the late 1920s and the disaster that collectivization brought to agriculture.

Thanks to state schools for all children, social mobility became common in Stalin's USSR. The children of peasants routinely became engineers and doctors, army officers and professors. The number of children in school doubled between 1928 and 1933, despite chaos in parts of the country. The number of high school students climbed from 2 million in 1927 to 12 million in 1939. Stalin intended to create a "proletarian intelligentsia," an educated cohort of peasant or worker background—and he did. They proved his most loyal backers.

At the same time, Stalin's program relied on brutal coercion. It did not begin with him. Lenin had unleashed terror without qualms when in power (1918–1922). Ten years later, when peasants resisted collectivization, Stalin ordered the "liquidation" of *kulaks* ("fists," the term used in the USSR to describe prosperous peasants). About 8 million farmers were either killed or sent to forced labor in Siberia in the gulag, a system of slave labor camps scattered in cold and remote parts of the USSR. In 1932 and 1933, poor harvests combined with pitiless requisition of grain led to famines—especially brutal in Ukraine and Kazakhstan—that killed 5 to 7 million peasants.

Stalin responded to these and other misfortunes by unleashing state terror. His secret police, the NKVD, the successor to Lenin's Cheka, arrested and killed millions. He purged the ranks of the Communist Party and the army, and targeted ethnic Poles and Germans. He murdered most of the remaining heroes of the 1917 revolution and anyone who might supplant him. Children of bankers or aristocrats, whose loyalty to the "workers' paradise" was automatically suspect, were shipped to the gulag. So were people who made jokes about Stalin, people denounced by jealous neighbors or by jilted lovers, people who were late to work three times or who stole a hammer from a collective farm. Stalin's terror had a random quality to

Gulags Kulaks (prosperous peasants) perform heavy labor in a Soviet prison camp in 1930. Millions of kulaks died in the forced labor camps.

it. The terror also had a bureaucratic quality. Officials kept records of those whom they shot. In 1937 and 1938, Stalin issued quotas, district by district, of the numbers to be shot. The Bolsheviks had raised extravagant hopes for a new fair, just, prosperous, and classless society. As it became clearer that they could not deliver on their promises, they resorted to ever more urgent witch hunts for wreckers and saboteurs—scapegoats for the disappointments of Soviet communism.

In the gulag, malnutrition, overwork, disease, and brutality had few limits. In all, between 1929 and Stalin's death in 1953, perhaps 18 million people passed through one or more of the 500 camps of the gulag, and 1 to 3 million died there. More were released when on death's door and died within days or weeks after regaining freedom. In all, Stalin's peacetime policies killed about 10 to 12 million Soviet citizens between 1928 and 1941, about 6–8 percent of the Soviet population. Part of the reason behind Stalin's enthusiasm for educating millions of peasant children was that so many doctors, engineers, and accountants had been murdered or imprisoned on his command.

Soviet communism—like Italian fascism and German Nazism—both attracted and repelled people around the world. The overnight industrialization struck many observers as a model path to wealth and power. But rumors of famine, purges, and state terror leaked out, despite the best efforts of Stalin's loyalists to conceal the truth. As of 1939, communism had come to power only in the USSR.

ANTICOLONIALISM TO 1939

Another important political movement that gathered pace after World War I was **anticolonialism**. Asians and Africans, almost all of them subjects of one or another colonial empire, created new ideologies and social movements that helped them focus their resistance. Their experience of World War I, as participants or observers, generally lowered their estimate of their colonial masters. Fewer than ever now accepted British or French claims to represent a higher civilization. The cynicism and duplicity of the peace settlement invited further contempt for the colonial powers. Movements arose calling for self-rule and the end to colonial empires. In most cases it took decades, and another world war, for these movements to bear fruit, but they first came of age during the tumult of World War I and its aftermath.

CHINA AND THE MAY FOURTH MOVEMENT

In China, as we've seen, the Qing dynasty had collapsed during the years 1910–1911. World War I, when it came, at first seemed distant. But in 1915, Japan exploited the European powers' preoccupation with the war to issue an ultimatum, the Twenty-One Demands, calling, in effect, for China to become a de facto colony of Japan.

Many Chinese students and intellectuals responded with defiance. But negotiations between China and Japan resulted in an agreement signed in 1915 by Yuan Shikai—the military man running most of China at this point. The agreement focused popular anger upon the government of China as much as upon Japanese imperialism. Nationalistic intellectuals redoubled their questioning of China's policies and traditions in the New Culture Movement. Hundreds of new publishing houses and journals sprang up in which debates raged about how best to reform China. An example was the magazine *New Youth*, edited by a dean of Beijing University, Chen Duxiu. In a soul-searching essay, "Our Final Awakening" (1916), Chen wrote:

> We...must ask ourselves what is the level of our national strength and our civilization. This is the final awakening....If we open our eyes and take a hard look at the situation within our country and abroad, what place does our country and our people occupy, and what actions should we take?

At the same time that Chen and others were searching for a new basis for Chinese society, the existing government entered World War I in 1917 against Germany. Its leaders hoped to recover the German territorial concessions established in 1898 in Tianjin, a port near Beijing. Some 600,000 Chinese men served the Allied cause in Europe as laborers, most of them in Russia, and more than 30,000 died—almost all in Russia.

In the spring of 1919, the Chinese learned, to their shock, that the Versailles treaty had transferred German concessions in China to Japan. Britain, France, and Italy had made a secret deal, offering Japan the German holdings, to secure its wartime support for the Allies. The diplomats in Paris had ignored the principle of self-determination and instead supported Japanese imperialism. They had discounted the Chinese contribution to the Allied war effort. As in the Arab Middle East, they had made incompatible promises, justified to themselves by the urgency of winning the war.

That spring, university students in Beijing led protests against Japan, the Versailles treaty, the diplomatic missions of the Allies, and the Chinese government that seemed inclined to accept humiliation. Boycotts and demonstrations swept across the country in the May Fourth Movement, named for the day of the first big protests in Beijing. Police arrested over 1,000 students, but thousands more joined strikes and protests. The government soon concluded it could not endorse the Versailles treaty and would have to risk standing up to Japan.

The insulting terms of the Versailles treaty did much to strengthen the cause of anti-imperialism in China.

May Fourth Movement Students protest outside the seat of Chinese government in Beijing's Forbidden City in 1919. The May Fourth Movement, sparked by discontent with the terms of the Versailles treaty, launched a broad examination of Chinese culture and politics.

The treaty's support for Japanese imperialism undermined the appeal of European ways and examples, although one European idea, Marxism, rose in the balance. Many young, educated Chinese in the years 1919–1921 admired the Bolsheviks' swift seizure of power in Russia and their dedication to remaking society. They formed the Chinese Communist Party—of which more in the next chapter.

INDIA

In India, World War I and its aftermath strengthened another nascent anticolonial movement. After the uprisings of the years 1857–1858, British rule had fastened more tightly upon India. Although many Indians resented British power, they knew that the Indian Army, trained and commanded by British officers, would smash any rebellion. But in the 1880s, elite, educated Indians, mostly Hindus, came together to form the Indian National Congress. At first a group that lobbied for a larger Indian role in government, Congress, as it was called, gradually came to function as a political party, at first with British approval. Meanwhile, educated Muslims created their own political organizations, such as the All-India Muslim League formalized in 1906 and soon led by a brilliant London-trained lawyer, Muhammad Ali Jinnah, also a Congress member. The leaders of Congress were products of schools and colleges established by the British to create a class of men—no women—competent to handle the lower rungs of officialdom. The schools also created a cadre of fluent English speakers well acquainted with British traditions, law, literature—and the merits of representative self-government.

Most of these educated Indians expected that India would one day become ready for self-government—perhaps in 50 or 100 years. World War I reduced their patience. Some 1.2 million Indians served the armies of the British Empire, mainly in campaigns against the Ottomans. About 62,000 died in the war. Indian businessmen and landowners contributed a lot of money to the British war effort. They did so in the expectation that in exchange for its blood and treasure, India would win something akin to the self-governing dominion status within the British Empire already accorded to Canada, New Zealand, Australia, and South Africa. Like the Chinese who expected a reward for their contributions to the

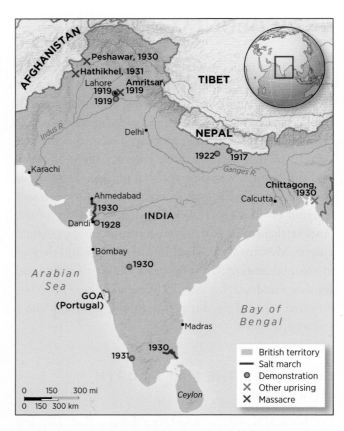

The Indian Independence Movement, 1915–1935 The Indian independence movement, the world's largest decolonization campaign, involved both peaceful protests and violent insurgency. Gandhi and his followers mounted nonviolent campaigns designed to embarrass colonial authorities, such as the 1930 salt march from Ahmedabad to the sea. Other Indians attempted armed insurrection, as in Chittagong, also in 1930. By 1935 India was on the road to self-rule.

Allies in World War I, these Indians were soon keenly disappointed.

After the war's end, British authorities showed no eagerness to extend self-rule to India. It was not the Versailles peace settlement that disappointed Indians. Indeed, India was allowed to send its own delegation to the talks. But early in 1919, when the British government extended its own wartime powers that curtailed freedom of speech and assembly, Indian nationalists reacted with outrage. Protests proliferated. That April, a demonstration in the holy city of Sikhs, Amritsar, ended in bloodshed. A British general ordered his Indian troops to fire into an unarmed crowd, killing some 400 demonstrators and wounding 1,000. Afterward, the British House of Lords formally commended the general who gave the order. To many Indians, the Amritsar massacre showed that Britain would never allow India to enjoy dominion status but would try to rule the country indefinitely.

GANDHI The anticolonial movement in India was already growing impatient when **Mohandas K. Gandhi** returned to India in 1915 and joined Congress. Born in 1869 in Gujarat, he came from a middle-class family and despite a mediocre school record went to study law in London at age 20. Starting in 1893, he spent 21 years in British South Africa defending the rights of the Indian community there. He suffered slights at the hands of white South Africans but remained a loyal subject of the British Empire, even winning a medal for his work organizing Indian medics for the Boer War (1899–1902).

In South Africa, he developed the political tactic called *satyagraha* (translated as "truth force" or "soul force"), which amounted to the practice of nonviolent civil disobedience in the face of unjust treatment. It drew upon Hindu, Jain, and Christian religious traditions. Gandhi also learned from the writings of the American author Henry David Thoreau and the Russian novelist and philosopher Leo Tolstoy, with whom he corresponded. The South African compound where he trained people in *satyagraha* was called Tolstoy Farm. Gandhi's thought combined many influences, a reflection of the growing interconnectedness of the world in his day.

When he arrived in India in 1915, Gandhi encouraged Indians to join the British armed forces, hoping that by showing loyalty Indians would win political independence after World War I ended. His fellow Congress members found him strange. He had abandoned his lawyer's suit and tie for the *dhoti* worn by poor Indians. He ate sparingly and flaunted his frail physique. The Bombay (Mumbai) police considered him "a psychological case." But in 1919, he more than anyone else converted Indian anticolonial nationalism from an elite affair into a mass movement.

The spur was the massacre at Amritsar. Gandhi now proclaimed there could be no cooperation with the British "satanic regime." Since armed resistance to British rule was futile, Gandhi, with his nonviolent tactics honed in South Africa, became the most effective and prestigious leader of anticolonialism in India. He pioneered mass politics, rousing illiterate peasants to the cause of self-rule. Congress chose him as its president in 1920.

Gandhi's program baffled most other Indian nationalists. He argued for a self-sufficient peasant economy and against factories and industrialization. He claimed that British education, of which he was a product, corrupted India and prevented its liberation. He particularly disliked modern science and technology, preferring Hindu traditions. Yet he was no respecter of caste, campaigning for the rights of the lowest of the low in India's caste system, people called dalits ("untouchables"). Gandhi embraced all Indians, Muslim and Hindu alike, and Christians, Jains, and Buddhists too. He spoke out against child marriage, dowry, and the Muslim custom of seclusion of women. He felt India's strength could come from piety and moral righteousness, not factories and armies. He regarded women as natural champions of this cause: "If by strength is meant moral power, then woman is immeasurably man's superior."

His methods included deft use of the weapons of the weak. He lived simply, all the better to be an Indian David against a British Goliath. He went on well-publicized hunger strikes. He and his colleagues in Congress organized marches involving thousands of poor Indians who were trained not to resist violence but to suffer it—in order to seize the moral high ground and undercut British claims to superiority.

To succeed, he had to know his adversary well, and three years of legal education in London helped in that regard. And he required an adversary that was vulnerable to the weapons of the weak, to public shaming and moral truth—one that would not be willing to repeat the massacre of Amritsar time and time again.

Gandhi Followers of Gandhi's civil disobedience movement join him on the 1930 salt march. Gandhi's shaved head and traditional attire signaled his public commitment to a life of simplicity.

Satyagraha: Gandhi's Strategy of Resistance

Before Gandhi returned to India in 1915, he had spent two decades in South Africa, where he led Indian residents in protests against laws that limited their rights because of the color of their skin. It was there that he first distinguished satyagraha from political movements that used violence. Gandhi taught his followers to disobey unjust laws without resorting to physical force—instead, they dared the British governments in South Africa and India to commit violence against them. Through such tactics, they hoped to shame the British Empire into living up to the principles of justice that Gandhi had studied in his legal education in London.

The suffragists had no franchise rights. They were weak in numbers as well as in physical force.... The suffragist movement did not eschew the use of physical force. Some suffragists fired buildings and even assaulted men. I do not think they ever intended to kill any one. But they did intend to thrash people when an opportunity occurred....

But brute force had absolutely no place in the Indian movement in any circumstance,... no matter how badly they suffered, the *satyagrahis* never used physical force. *Satyagraha* is soul force pure and simple, and whenever ...there is room for the use of arms or physical force or brute force, there and to that extent is there so much less possibility for soul force. These are purely antagonistic forces....

[Yet] even a generous friend like Mr. Hosken [an English supporter of Gandhi in South Africa] imagined us to be weak. The power of suggestion is such that a man at last becomes what he believes himself to be. If we continue to believe...we are weak...our resistance would never make us strong.... On the other hand, if we...

offer *satyagraha*, believing us to be strong,... we grow stronger and stronger every day....

Satyagraha and brute force, being each a negation of the other, can never go together.... In *satyagraha* there is not the remotest idea of injuring the opponent. *Satyagraha* postulates the conquest of the adversary by suffering in one's own person.

Source: M. K. Gandhi, *Satyagraha in South Africa*, trans. Valji Govindji Desai. (Madras, 1928).

QUESTIONS FOR ANALYSIS

1. Why did Gandhi reject the idea that satyagraha was weak?
2. How did the woman suffrage movement affect Gandhi's approach to anticolonial resistance?
3. Contrast Gandhi's anticolonial movement with the fascist and communist movements in Italy, Germany, and Russia.

Gandhi's classic act of civil disobedience was the salt march of 1930. By law, the sale of salt was a government monopoly, and Indians had to pay a salt tax. Gandhi exploited this by organizing a 24-day march from his base near Ahmedabad, in western India, to the coasts of the Arabian Sea in order to scoop up natural sea salt in defiance of the law. Tens of thousands of Indians joined him, and several journalists too. As he expected, Gandhi's act of civil disobedience earned him a jail sentence. Some 80,000 others were arrested. The British authorities undermined their own legitimacy in India, Britain, and around the world by arresting so many poor people over salt—just as Gandhi intended. By 1935, Britain had passed new legislation turning many governmental functions over to Indians. India was on the road to self-rule.

European rule in India had begun in the sixteenth century as a result of a quest for valuable peppers, and it would end in 1947 as a result—in part—of Gandhi's salt march. He was able to make the struggle for self-rule a mass movement after 1919, parallel in this respect, but different in every other, to what Mussolini did with fascism in Italy in 1919. He recast a political movement based on novel tactics that fit India's circumstances far better than violent resistance. He made nonviolent civil disobedience into a potent political force.

AFRICA, THE CARIBBEAN, AND PAN-AFRICANISM

In Africa and the Caribbean, anticolonial movements also drew strength from the disillusionment that came with World War I and the peace settlement. Recall that by 1914, European powers, chiefly Britain and France, had colonized almost all of Africa. The Caribbean too was a patchwork of European colonies, with a population mainly descended from Africans who had survived the transatlantic slave trade.

In World War I, several hundred thousand Africans and a few thousand West Indians—as people from the Caribbean are known—served in European armies. Some 400,000 black volunteers and conscripts fought for the French army on the western front and often were assigned the most dangerous tasks. The president of France, Georges Clemenceau, made his views clear in 1918: "We are going to offer civilization to the Blacks. They will have to pay for that.... I would prefer that ten Blacks are killed rather than one Frenchman." Some 30,000 to 70,000 Africans died in the French army in Europe in World War I. The British refused to use African troops in Europe. But, like the French and Germans, they employed large numbers in the campaigns fought in East and West Africa, and a few thousand as laborers in the Middle Eastern theater.

Almost all soldiers and laborers came from the lower ranks of African societies. Those chiefs and kings who by 1914 supported colonial rule encouraged poor men to enlist. They hoped African contributions to the British and French war efforts would result in more political rights, power, and autonomy—for chiefs and kings. These hopes, like Gandhi's during World War I, were disappointed. Policy makers in France and Britain believed that only after centuries of tutelage—if then—would Africans become ready for self-rule.

Soldiers, chiefs, and kings were not the only ones to be disappointed. Africa by 1918 included a small population of men—and far fewer women—equipped with European formal education and a cosmopolitan knowledge of the world. They liked the sound of President Wilson's emphasis on self-determination, until it became clear that neither Wilson nor any of the peacemakers of 1919 intended to apply it to Africa.

PAN-AFRICANISM Many of them found hope in **Pan-Africanism**, an idea that had not won much attention before 1914. The war seemed to present new opportunities. African American intellectuals from the Caribbean and the United States, including the Harvard-trained historian and sociologist W.E.B. Du Bois, called for unified political action among Africans and people of African descent. Many saw anticolonialism in terms of race. In an essay appearing in 1915, Du Bois, after calling for the extension of the "democratic ideal to the yellow, brown, and black peoples," wrote apocalyptically: "The colored peoples still will not always submit to foreign domination.... These nations and races, composing as they do the vast majority of humanity, are going to endure their treatment as long as they must and not a moment longer. Then they are going to fight and the war of the Color Line will outdo in savage inhumanity any war this world has yet seen." To avoid this grim prospect, Du Bois concluded, would require an end to racism and colonialism.

Pan-Africanism The prominent Pan-African movement leader Marcus Garvey is pictured here in a New York City parade in 1922.

Other Pan-Africanists looked forward to the imminent liberation of Africa. Marcus Garvey, a Jamaican who lived in London and later New York, organized a political and cultural movement that celebrated Black identity. He wanted educated people of African descent to return to their ancestral homeland and "assist in civilizing the backward tribes of Africa." In 1920, he proposed to "organize the 400 million Negroes of the world into a vast organization and plant the banner of freedom on the great continent of Africa."

Several Francophone Pan-Africanists shared Garvey's emphasis on culture and identity. In the late 1930s, a black poet from Martinique, Aimé Césaire, and his friend and fellow-poet from Senegal (West Africa), Léopold Senghor, developed a cultural philosophy they called Négritude (literally: "Blackness"). They extolled the qualities of Black people, among which they counted generosity, warmth, spontaneity, and honesty. In their own way, which featured literature as much as politics, they too endorsed the notion of solidarity among people of African background both as an end in itself and as a means to end colonial rule. Both men became leading politicians in later decades.

Pan-Africanism had a strong literary and cultural component. Garvey, Senghor, and others shared the view of Chinese intellectuals of the New Culture Movement: a revitalization of culture was required before political independence could be achieved. Theirs was an elite movement, with no equivalent to Gandhi's outreach to the illiterate masses.

To give Pan-Africanism political weight, Du Bois and others organized Pan-African Congresses in 1919 and 1921, held in Europe. Another took place in New York in 1927. Scores of educated men—no women—from the African diaspora and Africa itself attended. They specifically challenged the continuation of colonial rule in Africa and called for an Africa for Africans.

ANTICOLONIALISM AND THE GLOBAL WEB

Within Africa itself, anticolonialism consisted of more than Pan-Africanism. Every colony had its own groups working toward greater political voice for Africans. In most cases, those groups imagined that one day they would replace the colonial masters themselves and rule independent countries. Indeed, in time this vision—rather than the Pan-African ideal of African unification—would come to pass.

All these movements, in China, India, and Africa (and the African diaspora), had local grievances and causes. But they all shared some commonalities too, first and foremost their anticolonialism. In each case, World War I and the disappointing peace settlement contributed mightily to a sense of disillusionment—and to a sense of new possibilities. The war and the peace showed conspicuously that Europeans were not the morally superior beings they had claimed to be. The rhetoric of self-determination rang hollow when followed by renewed imperialism.

These movements also shared a reliance on European-educated elites. In Africa, as in India, the key to the formation of effective anticolonial groups was colonial education. In the 1920s and 1930s, a new generation with more formal education arrived on the scene in Africa. A symbol of the ongoing change occurred in Gabon (West Central Africa), where a people called the Fang altered one of their rituals: where once spears had been dipped in the water in which baby boys took their first bath, now their parents dipped pencils. Education, they foresaw, was the key to power and status.

In every case, anticolonial leadership came substantially from young men educated in European schools—often, mission schools. While colonial authorities generally wanted the colonized peoples to confine their educations to job training—such as rudimentary office skills—Africans and Indians wanted to study subjects that, as they saw it, fit people for leadership, such as law, philosophy, and history.

There are two lessons here. One is the irony of colonial rulers creating institutions that contributed to the downfall of colonial rule. The other is the power of the swirl of ideas in the decades after 1914. Growing literacy, and then the advent of radio after 1920, made it easier for Wilson's and Lenin's ideas to reach Chinese students, Tolstoy's ideas to reach Gandhi, or Garvey's ideas to reach Black people in Lagos or London. The interconnections of the Global web were now better than ever at spreading ideas and ideologies, offering people everywhere new choices with which to try to fashion their futures and helping people find like-minded allies. The Global web, which had helped to form and strengthen colonial empires in the nineteenth century, now began to undermine them through the flow of ideas, ideals, and ambitions for self-rule.

CONCLUSION

World War I wasn't all that worldwide as a war. The combat took place mainly in Europe and the Ottoman lands of Southwest Asia. But as a political event, World War I was truly global. It inspired the mobilization of people and resources on every inhabited continent. More enduringly, the war's horror and destruction posed strong challenges to existing authority in every sphere. If the leaders and institutions of Europe permitted the slaughter of 10 million soldiers, what argument could there be to leave such leaders and institutions in place? Millions thought it must be better to try something new and different, such as fascism or communism. The peace settlement, with its evident hypocrisies, multiplied the challenges to existing authorities by dashing hopes and breaking promises, especially in Asia and Africa. How could such leaders and institutions be permitted to rule over most of the world's population through colonial empires? Millions thought it must be better to end colonial rule as soon as possible. Considering that men—and only men—had directed a brutal war and an unsatisfactory peace, what argument remained for excluding women from politics? Millions found no convincing argument and agreed that women should vote.

Like the influenza virus in 1918 and 1919, the intellectual and political repercussions of the war and the resulting peace spread quickly around the world—but news and ideas traveled even faster than pathogens. The peace settlement in Versailles gave rise to events in China almost instantaneously in 1919.

Of all the meanings and legacies of World War I and its peace settlement, perhaps the greatest was one that took decades to work itself out: the decline of western Europe in world affairs. It is not that European states necessarily grew weaker as a result of the war and its aftermath, although some did. Rather, the United States and soon the USSR grew much stronger, as did, if less obviously, the enemies of empire in Asia and Africa. The growing strength of the United States and the USSR came mainly in the form of material power such as industrial capacity. The enemies of empire in Asia and Africa gained strength through organization, education, and determination. Their material resources were scant—wholly inadequate for a military challenge to colonial rule. But, as Gandhi showed, sometimes the weapons of the weak are enough to change history.

CHAPTER REVIEW

KEY TERMS

World War I (p. 854)

alliance networks (p. 856)

Russian Revolution of 1917 (p. 862)

Vladimir Lenin (p. 863)

Treaty of Versailles (p. 865)

self-determination (p. 866)

Mustafa Kemal (p. 866)

suffragism (p. 867)

fascism (p. 872)

Benito Mussolini (p. 873)

Adolf Hitler (p. 874)

communism (p. 876)

Josef Stalin (p. 877)

anticolonialism (p. 879)

Mohandas K. Gandhi (p. 881)

Pan-Africanism (p. 883)

Go to **INQUIZITIVE** to see what you've learned—and learn what you've missed—with personalized feedback along the way.

REVIEW QUESTIONS

1. What are four major strands of global politics in modern times?

2. In order of strength, who were the great powers in 1914, and to which alliance network did each belong?

3. Discuss the two key decisions that contributed to the start of World War I.

4. Why did the German High Command begin unrestricted submarine warfare in the Atlantic, and what effect did it have on the war?

5. Describe the various roles that women filled during World War I, and explain what happened to these positions when the war ended.

6. Compare and contrast the policies of the Provisional Government in spring and summer 1917, the Bolsheviks in 1918, and the Bolsheviks in 1921.

7. What were the chief ambitions behind the post-war peace treaties?

8. What longstanding dynasties did World War I destroy, and what governing structures replaced each one?

9. How did World War I lead to the extension of the vote to women in several large and populous countries?

10. Why did Mussolini's fascism seem an attractive choice to millions of Italians after World War I?

11. What were Hitler's ambitions, and what economic and cultural policies did he introduce after 1933 to achieve them?

12. Identify the significant elements that communist and fascist movements shared, and explain their important differences.

13. What agricultural, economic, and educational policies did Stalin advance?

14. How did World War I contribute to the rise of anti-colonialism as a mass movement?

15. What elements did anticolonial movements in China, India, Africa, and the Caribbean share?

16. Explore the global aspects of World War I as a political event.

FURTHER READING

Volker R. BERGHAHN, *Europe in the Era of Two World Wars: From Militarism and Genocide to Civil Society, 1900–1950* (2006). A brief overview of European affairs, with useful sketches of fascism and communism.

Laura ENGELSTEIN, *Russia in Flames: War, Revolution, and Civil War, 1914–1921* (2018). A massive narrative of momentous events, with many insights along the way.

Adrian GREGORY, *A War of Peoples, 1914–1919* (2014). A short overview of World War I, with a chapter on how historians have presented it for the last hundred years.

Erez MANELA, *The Wilsonian Moment: Self-Determination and the International Origins of Anticolonial Nationalism* (2009). A study of the reception of the 1919 peace agreement in Egypt, India, China, and Korea.

David REYNOLDS, *The Long Shadow: The Legacies of the Great War in the Twentieth Century* (2015). A readable and insightful study of the meanings of World War I.

Eugene ROGAN, *The Fall of the Ottomans: The Great War in the Middle East* (2015). An authoritative but readable account of the origins and course of the war itself, with less on its aftermath.

Vladimir TISMANEANU, *The Devil in History: Communism, Fascism, and Some Lessons of the Twentieth Century* (2012). A thoughtful reflection on the origins and character of communism and fascism, mainly in the USSR, post-1945 Eastern Europe, and Germany.

Pan-Africanism, Pan-Arabism, and Pan-Turkism

THE SURGE OF EUROPEAN IMPERIALISM, the turmoil of World War I, and the disappointments of its peace settlement sharpened the resentments and resistance of peoples who judged themselves unfairly colonized, disenfranchised, and discriminated against. Intellectuals from these communities recognized that part of their struggle involved overcoming the old strategy of divide and rule: to avoid being ruled over, they needed to unite. As they saw it, they needed to forge nations out of sects, tribes, lineages, and other groupings to achieve power and respect in the world. They needed to put nationalism to work as their ally—as European powers, Japan, and the United States had done.

Two of the intellectuals represented here were Black men born in the colonial Caribbean who made their adult careers elsewhere. Each employed journalism as a primary tool for their pan-African programs and emphasized the importance of education for people of African descent. The other two intellectuals were born in the Ottoman Empire in its waning days. They witnessed the demise of multinational empires under the impact of national sentiments and hoped to harness that sentiment for the betterment of Arabs and Turks—peoples whom the victors of World War I proposed to subject to European rule, either directly or through the League of Nations.

SOURCE 25.1

The Reverend Edward Blyden on Liberian Independence, 1865

Edward Blyden (1832–1910) was born in the Danish West Indies to free Black parents. He claimed Igbo (in today's Nigeria) ancestry. At age 18, after being rejected by the seminary at Rutgers University (in New Jersey) because of his race, he emigrated to Liberia and made a career as a journalist and educator. He taught Greek and Latin at Liberia College, dabbled in politics, and served as an ambassador. In 1865, a few weeks after the end of the American Civil War and the liberation from slavery of four million Black Americans, Blyden gave a speech marking the anniversary of the foundation of Liberia—a country established in the 1830s and 1840s by African Americans. They hoped both to escape racism in the United States and to bring, as they saw it, superior civilization to Africa. Blyden was the leading intellectual in Liberia, and perhaps all of West Africa, in his day and an early spokesman for pan-Africanism.

ADDRESS

Today we celebrate the eighteenth anniversary of the Independence of Liberia.... We are laying the foundations of empire on this coast.... With all our failings and deficiencies, we are obviously the agents in the hand of the great Ruler [God] in doing an important work. Well, how should the day be spent?

If we had thoroughly solved the problem to which we are committed; if we had firmly established a nation; if we had fairly demonstrated our capacity to achieve and maintain sovereignty and independence; if the mass of our people had risen to the dignity of superior and cultivated life; if we had exalted the general tone and character of the tribes around us; if we were united by the sympathy of one feeling and of one interest; if all asperity and bitterness and ignorant jealousies were unknown among us, and we lived in the warmth and glow of one common cordiality; if, superior to local or individual prejudices, we were combining our energies and our means for the benefit of the whole country; if we were daily developing a stronger attachment to the cause of race, and a more determined zeal for the upbuilding of an African nationality; if we had effectually silenced the cavils of adversaries; then we might devote the day to unbounded festivity; then we could afford to impose no check upon our feelings of gladness and joy. But when we review the years during which we have been numbered among the nations, and see how far behind we are in all the elements of abiding prosperity and usefulness; how little we have done for the cause of Africa's regeneration; how small the quota we have contributed to the comfort and happiness of mankind; this should be to us a day of earnest and solemn thoughtfulness, as well as of joyous demonstrations.

... We must, as a holy and solemn duty, labor to benefit our country. We must not content ourselves with joining the general depreciation and lamentation concerning national decline and ruin. We must, we are in duty bound, to do all we can, by earnest effort and self-denial, to arrest the downward tendency of things. The love of country is a virtue. . . .

And we must cultivate *pride* of race. Longfellow[1] has sung of the "dead past"; but we must allow him such an assertion as a poetic privilege. In *reality*, the past is *not* dead. It still lives in activity, and is wonderful in its influence upon the present. . . . Our antecedents often exert a most depressing influence upon us. We have been so cruelly oppressed, that we have, in a great measure, lost our self-respect. Almost any little untoward event will scare us into the belief that we cannot succeed in our undertaking on this coast. But we must endeavor to shake off the influence of the past. We must have faith in the negro race.

There is something within us, a God-like principle, ever whispering to us the lessons of self-government, and telling us of our sublime origin and high destiny; and, during all that dark and dismal night of oppression and unnumbered woes, that principle remained uncrushed, retained its vital activity; and this day every negro, on every plantation, and in every humble cabin, is hearing its secret whispers. Surely we Liberians should hear and hearken to it. If any man, who has lived in Liberia two years, cannot come to believe in the ability of the negro race, under favorable circumstances, to maintain an organized, regular, and adequate government, that man has mistaken his country; he should at once pack up bag and baggage, and transfer his residence to a more congenial clime. And I go further, and say, if any man, at all acquainted with the history of this country, does not see the hand of God plainly guiding and directing our affairs in all the past, that man would not have seen the pillar of cloud by day and the pillar of fire by night before the Israelites.[2]

[. . .]

Descendants of Africa, in other parts of the world, have been contributing, and are now contributing, by noble deeds, to the vindication of the race. And we cannot, in this connection, refrain from referring, with admiration, to the heroic deeds of our brethren in the United States. Indeed, we should be unpardonably indifferent if we could remain silent and unmoved spectators of such heroism, unlooked for by their oppressors, as they have displayed. We feel proud of their martial deeds and their valorous demeanor. We rejoice with them in their brilliant achievements and magnificent success. They have produced a most wonderful impression upon the minds of those who formerly stigmatized them as idle, vicious, and lazy. Such has been the revolution, in public sentiment, which their prowess has achieved that, whereas in former times, a powerful tide of odium ran against the men who attempted to advocate their right to liberty, and there was a smile of general connivance, if not approbation, given to those who contended for their perpetual servitude; now, the contest is not whether the negro shall be free, but whether he shall be raised to equal political rights and privileges with his former master.

[1] The American poet Henry Wadsworth Longfellow

[2] Blyden is alluding to the Bible's Book of Exodus in which the Israelites were guided out of captivity by the pillars.

Source: Reverend Edward W, Blyden, "Our Origin, Dangers and Duties" (Address before the Mayor and Common Council of the City of Monrovia, Liberia, July 26, 1865).

- **Why, in reflecting on Liberia's independence day, does Blyden speak so much about recent events in the United States?**
- **What appear to be Blyden's reasons for advocating an "African nationality"?**

SOURCE 25.2

UNIA on Pan-Africanism, 1920

In the aftermath of World War I, the Jamaican American political activist Marcus Garvey (1887–1940) sought to rally Black Americans to the cause of pan-Africanism. Many African Americans considered that the United States was not living up to its wartime and postwar rhetoric of fighting for freedom and the self-determination of peoples. Garvey, largely self-educated, lived briefly in London as a young man. In 1914, back in Jamaica, he founded the United Negro Improvement Association (UNIA). But it sparked little interest until he moved it to New York in 1916 and preached a doctrine of Black economic power. Subsequently the UNIA founded the Black Star shipping line to encourage emigration of African Americans to Africa. At a business meeting of the Black Star line in New York in 1920, thousands of delegates of the UNIA adopted the "Declaration of Rights of the Negro Peoples of the World," excerpted here. Days later, a weekly newspaper founded by Garvey and his wife Amy Ashwood Garvey, *The Negro World*, published it. The paper had a circulation of about 200,000 readers in 1920.

Be It Resolved, That the Negro people of the world, through their chosen representatives in convention assembled in Liberty Hall, in the City of New York and United States of America, from August 1 to August 31, in the year of Our Lord one thousand nine hundred and twenty, protest against the wrongs and injustices they are suffering at the hands of their white brethren, and state what they deem their fair and just rights, as well as the treatment they propose to demand of all men in the future.

We complain:

1. That nowhere in the world, with few exceptions, are black men accorded equal treatment with white men, although in the same situation and circumstances, but, on the contrary, are discriminated against and denied the common rights due to human beings for no other reason than their race and color. We are not willingly accepted as guests in the public hotels and inns of the world for no other reason than our race and color.

[...]

3. That European nations have parceled out among them and taken possession of nearly all of the continent of Africa, and the natives are compelled to surrender their lands to aliens and are treated in most instances like slaves.

[...]

9. In the British and other West Indian islands and colonies, Negroes are secretly and cunningly discriminated against and denied those fuller rights of government to which white citizens are appointed, nominated and elected.

10. That our people in those parts are forced to work for lower wages than the average standard of white men and are kept in conditions repugnant to good civilized tastes and customs.

In order to encourage our race all over the world and to stimulate it to overcome the handicaps and difficulties surrounding it, and to push forward to a higher and grander destiny, we demand and insist on the following Declaration of Rights:

1. Be it known to all men that whereas all men are created equal and entitled to the rights of life, liberty and the pursuit of happiness, and because of this we, the duly elected representatives of the Negro peoples of the world, invoking the aid of the just and Almighty God, do declare all men, women and children of our blood throughout the world free denizens, and do claim them as free citizens of Africa, the Motherland of all Negroes.

[...]

3. That we believe the Negro, like any other race, should be governed by the ethics of civilization, and therefore should not be deprived of any of those rights or privileges common to other human beings.

[...]

9. We believe that any law especially directed against the Negro to his detriment and singling him out because of his race or color is unfair and immoral, and should not be respected.

[...]

13. We believe in the freedom of Africa for the Negro people of the world, and by the principle of Europe for the Europeans and Asia for the Asiatics, we also demand Africa for the Africans at home and abroad.

14. We believe in the inherent right of the Negro to possess himself of Africa and that his possession of same shall not be regarded as an infringement of any claim or purchase made by any race or nation.

[...]

16. We believe all men should live in peace one with the other, but when races and nations provoke the ire of other races and nations by attempting to infringe upon their rights[,] war becomes inevitable, and the attempt in any way to free one's self or protect one's rights or heritage becomes justifiable.

17. Whereas the lynching, by burning, hanging or any other means, of human beings is a barbarous practice and a shame and disgrace to civilization, we therefore declare any country guilty of such atrocities outside the pale of civilization.

[...]

22. We protest against the system of education in any country where Negroes are denied the same privileges and advantages as other races.

[...]

25. We further demand free speech universally for all men.

26. We hereby protest against the publication of scandalous and inflammatory articles by an alien press tending to create racial strife and the exhibition of picture films showing the Negro as a cannibal.

27. We believe in the self-determination of all peoples.

28. We declare for the freedom of religious worship.

29. With the help of Almighty God we declare ourselves the sworn protectors of the honor and virtue of our women and children, and pledge our lives for their protection and defense everywhere and under all circumstances from wrongs and outrages.

[...]

37. We hereby demand that the governments of the world recognize our leader[1] and his representatives chosen by the race to look after the welfare of our people under such governments.

[...]

43. We call upon the various government[s] of the world to accept and acknowledge Negro representatives who shall be sent to the said governments to represent the general welfare of the Negro peoples of the world.

[...]

45. Be it further resolved, That we as a race of people declare the League of Nations null and void as far as the Negro is concerned, in that it seeks to deprive Negroes of their liberty.

[...]

47. We declare that no Negro shall engage himself in battle for an alien race without first obtaining the consent of the leader of the Negro people of the world, except in a matter of national self-defense.

48. We protest against the practice of drafting Negroes and sending them to war with alien forces without proper training, and demand in all cases that Negro soldiers be given the same training as the aliens.

49. We demand that instructions given Negro children in schools include the subject of "Negro History," to their benefit.

[...]

54. We want all men to know that we shall maintain and contend for the freedom and equality of every man, woman and child of our race, with our lives, our fortunes and our sacred honor.[2]

---

[1]This refers to Garvey but allows the possibility of other leaders in the future.
[2]This phrase echoes the final sentence of the U.S. Declaration of Independence of 1776.

Source: UNIA, "Declaration of Rights of the Negro Peoples of the World," *The Negro World*, August 31, 1920.

- It was 1920 when this text was written, 55 years after Blyden's speech. What differences between the two documents can you detect that reflect the two different moments in time?
- What revisions to the international system, and Africa's place within it, does the UNIA organization appear to have in mind?

SOURCE 25.3

Sati al-Husri on Arab Nationalism, 1920s

Sati al-Husri (1880–1968) was born to a prosperous Syrian family under the Ottoman Empire. He studied in Istanbul and then for several years served as a teacher in Ottoman lands that were strongly influenced by Greek and Macedonian nationalism. He later studied educational systems in European countries, and came to admire German nationalism. In 1914, the Ottoman government appointed him director of education in the province of Syria. In 1916, during World War I, several Arab leaders rebelled against the Ottoman Empire, and many Arab intellectuals, including al-Husri, turned toward Arab nationalism. At the peace settlement in 1919–1920, the victorious allies divided former Ottoman territories, including ones demographically dominated by Arabic-speakers, into several de facto colonies, called mandates, to be administered by either France or Britain. In 1921, al-Husri moved to Iraq (a British mandate), where he again served as director of education. He used that post to promote Arab national consciousness among the young. The passages below are excerpted from his newspaper pieces of the 1920s.

A common language and a common history is the basis of nation formation and nationalism. The union of these two spheres leads to a union of emotions and aims, sufferings, hopes, and culture. Thus the members of one group see themselves as members of a unitary nation, which distinguishes itself from others. However, neither religion nor the state nor a shared economic life are the basic elements of a nation, and nor is common territory.... If we want to define the role of language and history for a nation, we can say in short that the language is the soul and the life of the nation, but history is its memory and its consciousness.

It is true that the advent of Islam marked a new and significant period in Arab history, but it is wrong to claim that the Arabs before Islam were an uncivilised or primitive people. Historical research has proved the falsity of this view. But even if we leave aside the results of this research and simply examine the Arabic language of this period more closely, it becomes clear to us that this is not the language of a primitive people...on the contrary, it is a language which shows a high capacity for abstraction, which could not have been achieved without the foundation of an intellectual tradition. Thus we must insist that the denial of a pre-Islamic culture and of the existence of a spiritual tradition among the Arabs in no way corresponds to the historical evidence.

Source: Bassam Tibi, *Arab Nationalism: Between Islam and Nation-State* (New York: Palgrave Macmillan, 1997).

- Why might al-Husri argue that language and shared history define a nation, rather than shared religion or a common territory?
- Why might it be important to al-Husri that pre-Islamic Arabs—people alive more than 1,300 years before he wrote—should not be judged a "primitive" people?

SOURCE 25.4

Ziya Gokalp on Pan-Turkism, 1923

Ziya Gokalp (1876–1924) was one of the foremost advocates of pan-Turkism. Born in eastern Anatolia, he studied veterinary medicine in Istanbul but was imprisoned by Ottoman authorities for political activity. He later taught sociology in a secondary school and after 1912 at Istanbul University. He also wrote poetry and essays, the most important of which came between 1915 and 1923, a time of extreme tumult in the crumbling Ottoman Empire and its successor states.

Gokalp contributed to the development of pan-Turkism, first in the form of a supposed essential unity among all Turkic-speaking populations, from the Balkans to Central Asia; and then—after the formation of the Republic of Turkey in the early 1920s—in a narrower form, a nationalism of those Turks who had once been Ottoman subjects. Here, writing in 1923, he reflects upon just what defines a nation.

Turkism means furthering the ascendancy of the Turkish nation. In order to understand the nature of Turkism, therefore, we have to define the nature of the group which we call nation. Let us discuss various theories of nationality.

What, then, is a nation? What kind of unifying force is there that is superior to, and dominant over, racial, ethnic, geographic, political, and volitional forces? Sociology teaches us that this unifying force lies in education and culture; in other words, in the community of sentiments.

It follows from these statements that nation is not a racial, ethnic, geographical, political, or voluntary group or association. Nation is a group composed of men and women who have gone through the same education, who have received the same acquisitions in language, religion, morality, and aesthetics. The Turkish folk express the same idea by simply saying: "The one whose language is my language, and whose faith is my faith, is of me." Men want to live together, not with those who carry the same blood in their veins, but with those who share the same language and the same faith. Our human personality is not our physical body but our mind and soul. If our physical excellences come from our racial traits, our moral virtues come from the society in which we are raised.... Thus, it is absurd to base nationality on lineage. It is only shared education and ideals which are most essential to nationality....

Source: Ziya Gökalp, *Turkish Nationalism and Western Civilization: Selected Essays of Ziya Gökalp*, trans. and ed. Niyazi Berkes (New York: Columbia University Press, 1959).

- According to Gokalp, what are the key characteristics of a nation?
- Gokalp says that a nation is not a voluntary association. Why, in his view, can it not be voluntary? Does that fit with his claims about a nation's key characteristics? Why or why not?

QUESTIONS FOR COMPARISON

1. According to these authors, how does religion matter in the definition of nations or political communities?

2. According to these authors, how does ancestry matter in the definition of nations? Why might they differ on this question?

3. How did major wars—the U.S. Civil War and World War I—affect the ideologies reflected in these sources?

CHRONOLOGY

Nov. 1942–Mar. 1943
Battle of Stalingrad

Aug. 1942–Feb. 1943
Battle of Guadalcanal

June 1942
Battle of Midway

Sept. 1939
Germany invades Poland;
World War II in Europe
begins

Jan. 1942
Wannsee Conference

June 1941
Operation Barbarossa;
war on European
eastern front begins

Aug. 1945
United States drops
atomic bombs on
Hiroshima and Nagasaki;
Japan surrenders

1937
Japan attacks China;
World War II in Asia
begins

Sept. 1943
Italy
surrenders

Apr. 1945–June 1945
Battle of Okinawa

Sept. 1938
Munich
conference

July–Oct. 1940
Battle of Britain
prevents German
invasion of British Isles

Dec. 1941
Japan attacks
United States,
British Malaya,
Philippines;
Pacific War begins

**Oct. 1942–
Nov. 1942**
Battle of
El Alamein

July 1943
Allied
landings
in Sicily

June 1944
Normandy
landings

May 1945
Germany
surrenders

World War II

GLOBAL WAR IN THE GLOBAL WEB

1937 to 1945

We rely upon the loyalty and courage of Our subjects in Our confident expectation that the task bequeathed by Our forefathers will be carried forward and that the sources of the evil will be speedily eradicated and an enduring peace immutably established in East Asia, preserving thereby the glory of Our Empire.

With these words, the high command of the Japanese armed forces concluded its public declaration of war, issued in the name of Japan's emperor, against the United States and the British Empire on December 8, 1941. Attacks had already begun against American bases at Pearl Harbor (it was December 7 in that time zone) and the Philippines, and against British positions in Hong Kong, Malaya, and Singapore. In 1941, Japan was a colonial power in East Asia, controlling Korea, Taiwan, Manchuria, and most of eastern China. The leadership appealed to ordinary Japanese citizens to continue the overseas expansion under way since 1895, and to expel European and American colonial powers from East and Southeast Asia, leaving Japan unrivaled in the region. Confidence in the loyalty and courage of the

Global War, Total War This oil painting of the Battle of El Alamein, by William Francis Long-staff, shows British infantry supported by an American-made Sherman tank, and the smoking ruin of a German mobile artillery piece. El Alamein, in Egypt, turned the tide in favor the Allies in the North African campaign in late 1942.

FOCUS QUESTIONS

....

1. What events led to the outbreak of World War II?

2. What were the main turning points of World War II?

3. What factors had the biggest impact on the outcome of World War II?

4. How did the home-front experience differ between the major Axis countries and major Allied countries?

5. Why was World War II so costly in human terms?

6. How was the postwar order shaped during the war?

emperor's subjects proved well placed, but Japan lacked the economic resources to defeat its foes. Rather than preserve the glory of Japan's empire, the attacks would seal its doom, which came in August 1945 after 43 months of pitiless combat.

This chapter explores the titanic political battles and unspeakable violence of World War II (1937–1945). It was truly a global contest, much more so than World War I or any previous struggle. The Global web had grown so strong that politics spilled across boundaries and oceans with ease. By the end of the war, combat would take place on three continents and three oceans.

By any measure except duration, **World War II** was the biggest war in history. About 140 million men and women served in it. It ranged over more terrain, mobilized more resources, and killed more people than any other war. It also dramatically reconfigured world politics, as had World War I. Sometimes scholars like to lump the two world wars together as one extended conflict (1914–1945). In the European context this makes some sense, because in both wars Germany and its allies fought against a coalition including Russia, Britain, France, and the United States. But whereas World War I took place mainly in Europe, World War II involved major theaters of combat in China, the Pacific,

and North Africa. From the perspective of world history, as opposed to European history, it makes sense to treat the world wars separately.

Three main themes predominate in this chapter. First, World War II featured violence on astonishing scales. It killed five times as many people as did World War I. Ordinary civilians often became targets. This marked a return to an older pattern of warfare in which the distinction between military and civilian was often blurry. As a result, violence during World War II affected women and children more often than in World War I. These were hard and dangerous times—especially if you were Chinese, Japanese, Korean, German, Italian, Greek, or any kind of eastern European, but above all Jewish.

Second, ferocious hatreds sharpened these conflicts and added to the human cost. Sometimes these hatreds were ethnic or "racial," as in the case of Hitler and his supporters, or in the struggles between the Japanese and Chinese or Japanese and Americans. Sometimes they were more ideological, such as that between communists and fascists. While ethnic, racial, and ideological hatreds had long been common, in World War II they became extreme and were often grounds for murder.

Third, this chapter tries to explain why the winners won and the losers lost in the several conflicts that together made up World War II. These struggles, and especially their results, shaped the international political system we live in today, and fundamentally affect all our lives. It is important to grasp why they turned out as they did.

ORIGINS

The origins of World War II are not as complex, accidental, or contested as those of World War I. Most historians agree that its causes lay in the expansionist ambitions of Japan, Germany, and to a lesser extent Italy. Those powers formed a loose alliance in the late 1930s known as the **Axis**. Each was run by an authoritarian clique hostile to pluralist democracy and the rule of law. Each felt shortchanged by the international status quo. Each eagerly ran the risks of provoking large-scale warfare to acquire more territory, resources, and in particular an empire that might match that of France or Britain. Indeed, many of the governing elites of the Axis countries regarded war as something to be sought rather than avoided because, they thought, it was good for a nation to be tested in blood. The fact that almost no one thinks such things anymore is in large part a consequence of the many horrors of World War II.

FASCISM AND HISTORICAL FANTASIES

As we've seen, both Italy and Germany by the 1930s had fallen under fascist dictatorships, led by Mussolini and Hitler, respectively. Each had consolidated his grip on power by 1935 or before, muzzling the press, squashing legislatures, and filling the court system, the military, and key government ministries with loyal fascists. Outraged by the terms of the Treaty of Versailles, both leaders felt that their countries should not shrink from launching wars to achieve a more glorious future for the Italian or German people. In schools and state-run media, Germans and Italians were peppered with messages encouraging them to embrace nationalism and militarism as solutions to almost all problems.

Both Mussolini and Hitler envisioned futures based on nationalistic fantasies. For Mussolini, that glorious future entailed re-creating the grandeur of the ancient Roman Empire. He wanted Italy to dominate the Mediterranean, as the Romans had done, and to populate its colonies in Africa—Libya, Ethiopia, and Somalia—while acquiring new ones. Only a few thousand Italians lived in Italy's African empire, whereas some 16 million had emigrated to other countries such as the United States or Argentina. For Mussolini and other nationalistic Italians, this was an intolerable loss that additional colonies would remedy. For Hitler, overseas colonies were not a priority. Instead, he wanted what he called *Lebensraum* ("living space") for Germans in eastern Europe. He wanted to unite all Germans, including millions living in Poland, Austria, Czechoslovakia, Ukraine, Russia, and elsewhere, into a greater Germany. His understanding of U.S. history, which relied heavily on adventure stories by the popular German novelist Karl May, suggested to him that

Germans could displace or kill Slavs and Jews in eastern Europe and take the land for themselves—as white Americans had done to Indigenous Americans in the nineteenth century. He was convinced that the German people were a biologically pure and superior race but that they faced a mortal threat. He believed they could survive only by means of expansion at the expense of neighbors—specifically, the Slavs and Jews, whom he held responsible for all the misfortunes Germans experienced. Both Mussolini and Hitler concocted mythical pasts to justify their future plans.

Italy was poorly positioned for expansionist warfare. In the late 1930s, it had about 43 million people, most of them undernourished peasants. It had almost no coal or oil and only a small military-industrial complex, and it depended on imports for vital goods. Its armed forces were sizeable but neither well trained—one-third of army recruits could not read—nor abundantly supplied, although the quality of their equipment was good. They also had plenty of experience, fighting in Libya off and on for decades, in the bloody conquest of Ethiopia in 1935–1936, and in the Spanish Civil War in 1936–1939.

Germany included about 67 million people. In 1938, Hitler absorbed his native Austria into the German Third Reich (*Reich* means "empire"), raising the population closer to 80 million. Most of them felt Germany had been unfairly treated by the Allies after World War I, and many agreed with Hitler that their nation in 1918 had been "stabbed in the back" by Jews and Bolsheviks. The Versailles treaty at the end of World War I had officially limited the size of Germany's armed forces, but since coming to power in 1933, Hitler had been building up the military in defiance of these restrictions. By the late 1930s, Germany had a formidable and technologically modern military.

The third Axis power was Japan, with about 70 million people in 1935. Since the Meiji Restoration (1868), Japan had industrialized its economy and modernized its state administration and armed forces with astonishing speed, despite a comparative lack of raw materials. It had defeated China (1895) and Russia (1905) in war and had acquired Taiwan and Korea as colonies. In 1919, it took over some former German possessions in the Pacific through the Versailles treaty. The Japanese people increasingly came to see themselves as a special nationality—indeed, a "race," better than their neighbors if not everyone else. Their leaders, like those in Italy and Germany, used schooling and media to hammer home messages of Japanese racial superiority and victimization by foreigners. In particular, they felt the British, French, Dutch, and American empires (remember that the United States held the Philippines) prevented Japan from achieving its rightful place as the leading power in Asia.

JAPANESE AGGRESSION IN ASIA TO 1937

Like Italy and Germany, Japan wanted to revise the international system. It aimed to expand its empire. But it was thwarted mainly by Britain and the United States, neither of which wished to see Japan or any other nation become pre-eminent in East Asia. Back in 1922, Japan had agreed to a deal that limited the size of the Japanese, British, and U.S. navies—the world's first arms limitation treaty. The agreement fixed Japan's navy at about 60 percent of the size of the U.S. or British fleets, which struck Japanese diplomats as a prudent way to prevent the Americans from outspending everyone else and creating a still more dominant navy. But it soon became clear that U.S. politicians had no interest in bankrolling a giant navy, especially once the Great Depression set in (late 1929). Japanese military officers grew impatient with these and other constraints, and in 1931 they manufactured the so-called Mukden Incident in Manchuria (a region in northeast China twice the size of Texas) to justify seizing it. Army officers dynamited railroad tracks near the city of Mukden, blamed it on Chinese, and used it as an excuse to mount a full-fledged invasion of Manchuria. Rich in natural resources such as coal and iron ore, Manchuria could strengthen Japan's heavy industry, including its weapons industry.

Japanese rulers felt that to fulfill its destiny as a great imperial power and to provide for its growing population, their nation needed more space and resources. Setting up a puppet state in 1931–1932 in Manchuria was a first step. Manchukuo, as it was called, was nominally led by Chinese selected for loyalty to Japan's army. Japanese elites hoped that millions of Japanese peasants would settle there. After 1931, Manchukuo's iron, coal, steel, and railroads served Japanese purposes. Japan's military fought minor campaigns against neighboring parts of north China in 1933 and 1935.

Japan's leaders had bigger plans. They envisioned Japan leading the peoples of East and Southeast Asia in throwing off the shackles of European rule. They offered an anti-colonial ideology, called the **Greater East Asia**

Nanjing Massacre The Japanese Imperial Army entering the city of Nanjing in the winter of 1937–38. For six weeks Japanese troops conducted what is variously known as the Nanjing Massacre or the Rape of Nanjing, killing perhaps 200,000 Chinese, raping perhaps 20,000 women and girls, and looting freely. It was one of worst atrocities of World War II.

Co-Prosperity Sphere, but in reality intended to make all of East Asia subordinate to Japan. Japan's navy was the world's third largest. By the mid-1930s, its army was six times the size of the American army. By the late 1930s, the European colonial rulers of Southeast Asia—Britain, France, and the Netherlands—were, like the USSR, becoming increasingly anxious about the rising power of Germany in Europe and less inclined to devote military resources to Asia. Japan took advantage of that to launch a comprehensive attack on China in 1937.

China made a tempting target for Japan. Its 511 million people (as of 1937) were politically divided. The central government, run by the Guomindang, a party that had evolved out of Sun Yatsen's 1911 revolution, was famous for corruption and unloved by the masses. It controlled only parts of the country. It had virtually no navy and a poorly equipped army. China was a peasant land, with little industry. Yet it had plenty of raw materials that Japan wanted. Japan's assault on China in 1937 was the beginning of World War II.

GERMAN AGGRESSION IN EUROPE TO 1939

The war in Europe began in 1939. In the previous years, Germany had annexed territories with large proportions of German speakers—often eager to be absorbed into Hitler's Reich. France and Britain offered no effective response to German expansion. At the Munich Conference in 1938, they signed over the Sudetenland, a mainly German-speaking region of Czechoslovakia, to Hitler in exchange for a promise that he would seek no more territory. This was part of a policy called **appeasement**, based on the hope that a few concessions might satisfy Hitler. A few months later, in March 1939, Hitler effectively seized the rest of Czechoslovakia, turning the Czech lands into German "protectorates" and Slovakia into a vassal state. The Czech protectorates included a large weapons industry that now fell into Hitler's hands.

France and Britain proved feeble adversaries in the diplomacy of the late 1930s. Both were haunted by the

Nazi Aggression A cartoon published in August 1939 depicts the Nazi threat to Poland. Germany invaded Poland within weeks.

Territorial Aggression in Europe, 1936–1939 Germany, under Hitler from 1933, sought to undo the settlement established in the Treaty of Versailles. Among his early violations of the treaty was the stationing of military units in the Rhineland near the French and Belgian border. He followed with territorial annexations of Austria—cheered by most Austrians—and parts of Czechoslovakia. In April 1939, after a brief battle, Italy's fascist dictatorship under Mussolini converted Albania into a protectorate, fully subservient to Italy.

human losses of World War I and eager to avoid another war at almost any cost, explaining the seductive appeal of appeasement, both psychological and in terms of domestic politics. They had a population of 90 million between them, plus another 520 million, bountiful resources, and considerable industrial capacity in their overseas empires. But compared to Germany's, their armies and air forces were poorly equipped. After the seizure of Czechoslovakia early in 1939, their leaders realized they could not check Hitler's expansionist plans short of going to war.

In August 1939, Hitler's diplomats negotiated a non-aggression pact with the Soviet Union, a stunning reversal of both German and Soviet foreign policy. The agreement reduced Germany's risk of a two-front war against both Soviet Russia and the western Allies, a lesson Germans had learned from World War I. Stalin signed it to buy time to build up his military, which had suffered greatly from his own purges of top commanders. The agreement included secret protocols for yet another partition of Poland—there had been three during the eighteenth century. The German army invaded Poland on September 1, 1939, the start of World War II in Europe. France and Britain agreed that they could not allow Germany to gobble up the remainder of Europe, so they declared war against Germany. Two weeks later, the Soviet Red Army invaded Poland too, seizing the share promised to Stalin in the Nazi-Soviet pact.

THE COURSE OF THE WAR

World War II in effect consisted of four overlapping wars in four different theaters. They began at different times, but all ended in 1945. The first to break out was that between Japan and China in 1937. Most of the fighting took place in China. The second was Germany's war against Poland, Britain, France, and most of the rest of Europe, begun in 1939. Italy joined in May 1940. Fought in Europe, North Africa, and on the waters of the North Atlantic, by the end of 1941 it included the United States, aligned against the Axis powers. The third began in June 1941, when Germany attacked the USSR despite the recent Nazi-Soviet pact. It was fought mainly in the lands between Berlin and Moscow. The last was Japan's war against the United States, the United Kingdom, and Australia in the Pacific and Southeast Asia, begun in December 1941.

The United States, the Soviet Union, and Britain formed the major Allied forces, or **Allies**, opposing the Axis of Germany, Japan, and Italy. Until mid-1942, the Axis—Japan, Germany, and Italy—went from strength to strength. But by 1943, the Allies acquired the upper hand.

JAPANESE ADVANCES IN ASIA AND THE PACIFIC

Beginning in 1937, Japan inflicted huge losses on China and took the richest parts of the country. In late 1940, it conquered French Indochina (now Vietnam, Laos, and Cambodia) and in 1941 reduced Thailand to the status of a dependent ally. Part of Japan's interest in mainland Southeast Asia lay in its rubber and tin supplies, important for military production. Japan's aggression inspired a joint response from the United States, Britain, and the Dutch East Indies colonial authorities—the latter directly threatened by Japanese expansion. In August 1941, at which time the United States supplied 93 percent of Japan's oil, these governments stopped their oil and steel exports to Japan. They hoped to force Japan to give up expansionist warfare.

But the Japanese doubled down instead. The Japanese military elite, already bogged down in China and now anticipating acute oil shortages that would imperil their success there, gambled on a multipronged surprise attack in December 1941. Almost simultaneously, their naval and air forces hit British military bases in Singapore and Hong Kong; the Dutch East Indies; the U.S. colony of the Philippines; and U.S. naval bases at Pearl Harbor in Hawaii and on the remote islands of Midway, Guam, and Wake. The attacks were intended to cripple American and British naval power, giving Japan a chance to seize oil fields in the Dutch East Indies (Indonesia today) and time to win its war in China. Once Japan had firmed up its positions in China and Southeast Asia, the thinking went, the United States and the United Kingdom would acquiesce. The Japanese leaders knew the United States had twice the population of Japan and far more industrial might, but they hoped, and many believed, that Americans were too soft and undisciplined to pay the price of war with Japan. Moreover, as they all knew, a similar surprise attack had worked well for the Japanese military in the Russo-Japanese War (1904–1905). President Franklin Roosevelt responded to the attack on Pearl Harbor by asking Congress to declare war, which it did on December 8, 1941. The Pacific War, as this part of World War II is often called, was underway. Most of Japan's military might, however, remained devoted to its campaigns in China.

Pearl Harbor The USS *West Virginia* was badly damaged in the Japanese attack on Pearl Harbor, December 7, 1941. The battleship was repaired and later re-entered the war in the Pacific.

Japanese Expansion and World War II in Asia and the Pacific, 1931–1945 Japan focused its war effort on China, beginning with the seizure of Manchuria in 1931. After Japan's attacks of December 7–8, 1941, on U.S. and British bases, the war widened to include vast spaces of the Pacific Ocean. This became a war of movement, fought with ships and aircraft. While trying to control vast territories in China with its army, the Japanese military now needed to cover huge expanses of ocean with its naval and air forces. The outcome of the war depended on access to oil, which Japan lacked. After the battles of Midway and Guadalcanal, the Americans turned the tide against Japan. By mid-1944, U.S. aircraft were bombing Japanese cities relentlessly from bases in the Mariana Islands, ending with the two atomic blasts of August 1945.

The United States in 1941 was a sleeping giant. It had retreated from great-power politics after World War I. Its armed forces had shrunk, and its military equipment was obsolete. Its economy was slowly emerging from the Great Depression. But it had the largest industrial capacity of any country in the world. And it had more than 130 million people, who turned out not to be as soft as the Japanese hoped.

THE WAR IN CHINA The war in China (1937–1945) cost about 15 to 20 million lives, 80 percent of them Chinese, most of them civilians. Japan by the end of 1938 occupied most of northern and eastern China, and by mid-1942 all of the major ports. Chinese armies lacked military materiel, and China had almost no navy or air force at all. Once the Japanese occupied the coastal regions, any aid from the Allies had to come either overland from the

USSR, which after 1941 had little to spare, or, after 1941, via American airlift over the Himalayas from Burma to the southwest. Little aid arrived.

In this war, there was no major turning point, only deadly stalemate. China could not effectively counterattack, but it could hope to outlast the Japanese in a war of attrition. Chinese forces retreated to the west, engaged in guerilla operations, and drew Japanese armies further and further inland, away from the ports and bases through which Japan's soldiers could be supplied. The Japanese might have won battles and controlled the major cities and richest parts of the country (at least by day), but they could not get the Chinese to quit. China was too big for Japan to swallow.

After 1940, Chinese strategists learned to avoid big battles in favor of smaller operations in Japanese-occupied areas. The Chinese remained divided between forces fielded by the Chinese Communist Party (CCP), headed by Mao Zedong, and the far larger—but often less effective—armies loyal to the Guomindang, led by Chiang Kai-shek (also transliterated as Jiang Jieshi). After Pearl Harbor, both leaders expected Japan would ultimately lose, which undercut their ability to cooperate. Each one intended to rule China after Japan withdrew. Their forces fought one another frequently, and as Japanese defeat seemed more certain by late 1944, they prepared for all-out civil war.

From the start, atrocities and extreme suffering marked what the Chinese call the War of Resistance. Japanese forces bombed Chinese cities at will. Tens of millions of refugees streamed to the west and south, hoping to escape the Japanese. The Chinese military pursued a scorched-earth policy, trying to leave behind nothing of value to the Japanese. The occupying army, steeped in anti-Chinese racism, treated civilians brutally. Chinese forces showed no mercy to anyone deemed sympathetic to Japan. Hunger, disease, and currency inflation were rampant.

THE WAR IN THE PACIFIC TO 1943 After Japan's attacks of December 7–8, 1941, the Japanese war widened to include vast spaces of the Pacific, from the Aleutian Islands to Australia. The Japanese armed forces thrashed the Allies in the first six months after Pearl Harbor. They drove U.S. forces out of the Philippines. They seized Britain's colonies of Hong Kong, Malaya, and Singapore, as well as the Dutch colony of Indonesia, and bombed northernmost Australia. Their navy sank British battleships, shelled Australia's Sydney suburbs, and attacked and occupied two Alaskan islands. By mid-1942, they had won dominion over almost all of Southeast Asia and the western Pacific, and had plans for more.

Despite these stunning victories, difficulties loomed on the horizon for Japan. Its imperial army treated people in conquered Asian and Pacific Island territories with increasing contempt and cruelty, which weakened Japan politically. As a Japanese officer admitted, the "banner of the Greater East Asia Co-Prosperity Sphere in fact meant only a new Japanese colonial exploitation, a sign advertising beef that is really dog meat." Militarily, the war required moving ships and aircraft over huge distances—therefore using oil—which would prove a severe constraint for oil-poor Japan.

Japanese strategy also required abundant anti-malarial medicines. By invading Southeast Asia and the southwest Pacific in 1940–1942, Japan put its forces within reach of mosquitos that carry the deadliest form of malaria, falciparum. Japan by mid-1942 was running low on anti-malarial medicines such as quinine. The commander of a field hospital for the Japanese army on the island of New Guinea wrote in 1942 that the useful career of a Japanese soldier there was one month—after that, he fell too sick to fight. Of the 300,000 men the Japanese sent to fight in Burma, 60 percent died there, most from malaria. The U.S. and Australian forces initially suffered heavily too, but once committed to war in the Pacific, the United States made a major push to develop new anti-malarial

Chinese Leaders Mao Zedong (left) and Chiang Kai-shek (right) were leaders of the Chinese Communist Party and the Guomindang, respectively. Each led an army against the Japanese, with Mao's guerilla forces proving more effective in mobilizing popular resistance to the invasion.

drugs. By 1943, drugs such as Atabrine proved highly successful in protecting Allied troops, while the Japanese remained vulnerable. Falciparum malaria killed far more Japanese soldiers in the southwest Pacific than did combat.

By late 1942, Allied forces had begun to turn the tide in the Pacific War. They won some naval engagements in 1942, most notably at Midway Island in the middle of the Pacific, where the U.S. Navy blunted a Japanese attack and sank one-third of Japan's aircraft carriers. Japan had to abandon plans to invade additional islands. By the end of the year, the Americans were winning a major land, air, and sea battle on and around Guadalcanal—despite having to rely on old issues of *National Geographic* for information about the island. Despite ferocious combat, most Japanese casualties on Guadalcanal were malaria victims. Meanwhile, Australian and American troops were slowly getting the upper hand in New Guinea. By late 1943, the Americans were island-hopping toward Japan.

AXIS ADVANCES IN EUROPE

Meanwhile in Europe, the Germans also fared well early on. Their enemies were poorly prepared for war. Their innovative combinations of airpower, tank units, and infantry, informally called blitzkrieg, or "lightning war," proved highly effective.

WAR IN THE WEST After defeating Poland in late 1939, the Germans in the spring of 1940 swiftly overran Denmark, Norway, the Netherlands, Belgium, and France. The French defeat took only six weeks, surprising almost everyone. The Germans then occupied northern France and set up a collaborationist regime, often called Vichy France, to govern the south. A small share of the French forces escaped capture and carried on the battle from Britain and from French colonies in Africa.

Britain continued to resist, but it had lost most of its army equipment in a hurried and harried evacuation of France in June 1940. Many in Britain thought it wise to reach a deal with Hitler. But the new prime minister, Winston Churchill, in office since May 1940, refused to consider it.

Britain withstood a sustained German air attack on its port cities and military industries—the Battle of Britain—in the summer and fall of 1940. Londoners crowded into Underground (subway) stations night after night to avoid the worst of German bombing. Industrial workers in munitions factories worked long shifts amid the bomb blasts. The 2,900 fighter pilots of the Royal Air Force, a quarter of whom were not British but Polish, Czech, or Belgian or from Britain's empire, took a sufficient toll upon the German air force that Hitler had to abandon plans for an invasion of Britain. Churchill famously said of the pilots, "Never in the field of human conflict was so much owed by so many to so few."

Meanwhile, late in 1940, Italy attacked Greece. To nearly everyone's surprise, the Greek army bested Mussolini's legions—the first Allied victory in World War II. But the German army made short work of Yugoslavia and Greece in the spring of 1941, leaving the Axis supreme on the European continent. Romania and Bulgaria, intending to side with a winner, both joined forces with the Axis, as Hungary had already done. Then, with most of Europe under his bootheel, Hitler made an epic blunder.

Winston Churchill British prime minister Winston Churchill displays a "V for Victory" during the Battle of Britain in 1940. Churchill was an elderly career politician, nationalistic, imperialist, racist, and stubborn as a man can be. He had an American mother, an aristocratic politician father, a fondness for reading history, and a burning desire to make it. He also had an eloquence that inspired the British public when they needed it most.

OPERATION BARBAROSSA AND STALINGRAD

On June 22, 1941, in Operation Barbarossa—named for a medieval German emperor—Germany attacked the Soviet Union. Hitler believed its mostly Slavic population was subhuman, inferior to Germans, and ripe for conquest—despite Napoleon Bonaparte's disastrous experiences in Russia in 1812. The population of the USSR in 1941 was about 195 million people, many of whom were fervently devoted to its ruler, the dictator Josef Stalin. Many more passively endured Stalinism, while some looked for any opportunity to end the brutal regime. The Soviet military had just undergone a political purge in which Stalin, thinking it would bolster his political

The Battle of Stalingrad   The bodies of German soldiers, as well as broken-down trucks, lie abandoned in the snow near Stalingrad following the decisive German defeat in the winter of 1942–1943. More Axis soldiers died of typhus or hunger than in combat at Stalingrad, an indication of the extent to which the German army's support systems had broken down.

position, ordered many of the best officers killed. But the army was still large and well equipped. Soviet industry was considerable, growing by leaps and bounds, and by the late 1930s it was oriented toward military production. The Soviet Union's vast spaces and few roads made movement difficult for attackers. Its stoic population, accustomed to enduring harsh conditions, proved Hitler's low estimation wrong.

Hitler intended to destroy the USSR and settle its richer lands with German families. The Nazi-Soviet pact of 1939 had bought him time to conquer western Europe first so he would not have to fight on two fronts. Now, in June 1941, he felt the time had come to complete his life's ambition by shattering the USSR, destroying communism, and—of fundamental importance to him—killing the millions of Jews who lived in eastern Europe and the USSR. The Germans assembled the largest invasion force in world history, some 3 million men, which Hitler believed would destroy the USSR within four months.

Stalin—surprisingly—was taken by surprise. It is remarkable that anyone as cynical and calculating as Stalin could have been unprepared for Hitler's double-dealing. But he was. He disbelieved more than 80 intelligence reports of the impending invasion, some correctly giving the exact date. When the attack came, he went into hiding for a couple of weeks while the Soviet army (often called the Red Army until 1946) was in full retreat. For 16 months, the German army pushed eastward, inflicting tremendous damage along the way. In October 1941,

Hitler declared victory, claiming the war was over. But the Soviet state, the Soviet economy, the Soviet people, and the Soviet Red Army did not break. They summoned grim determination, withdrew to the east, and, as their ancestors had done with Bonaparte's legions in 1812, pulled their enemy deeper into Russia. Like the Chinese forces frustrating Japan, the Soviets could lengthen their enemy's supply lines until the invading army became vulnerable to counter-attack. Late in 1942, they checked the German advance.

The epic **Battle of Stalingrad** was one of the war's turning points. The city, on the banks of the Volga River in Russia's southwest, had both strategic and symbolic importance. With control of Stalingrad, the Germans could have prevented oil barges from the Caspian region from chugging upstream on the Volga to supply the Soviet forces around Moscow. That would have stopped the Red Army's tanks and grounded the Soviet air force. Stalingrad carried additional psychological importance because Stalin had named it for himself. Aware that the war's outcome might be decided there, huge German and Soviet armies clashed at Stalingrad between November 1942 and March 1943. In the end, the Soviets encircled and captured the Axis armies, which Hitler had unwisely forbidden to retreat. The Axis lost about 800,000 men killed or taken prisoner. After Stalingrad, Soviet forces began to slowly drive the Germans out of the USSR.

The eastern front, as the Soviet-German war is often called, was the scene of unremitting horror before, during, and after Stalingrad. The Soviet army here consisted of 6 to 9 million men and thousands of women. The Axis forces, about 80 percent German, included Finns, Romanians, Hungarians, and Italians, and by 1942 added hundreds of thousands of Soviet citizens—Russians, Ukrainians, and Lithuanians—who saw the German invasion as their liberation from Stalin's dictatorship. A quarter million Ukrainians served in Hitler's legions (while over 4 million fought in the Red Army). At their mid-1943 maximum, the Axis forces on the eastern front counted 4 million men. This was the decisive theater of the war in Europe, and the largest military campaign in world history. Four-fifths of the German war dead fell here, and more than half of the total Axis casualties in all theaters. In total, about 15 million soldiers of all nationalities died on the eastern front, and another 15 million civilians; another 25 million were homeless because of wartime destruction by 1945.

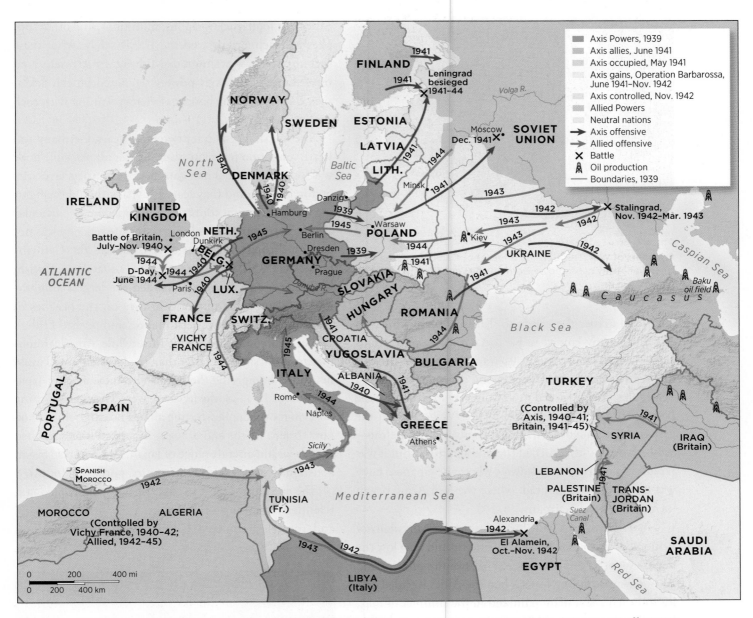

World War II in Europe, North Africa, and the Middle East, 1940–1945 Roughly three-quarters of the German war effort was devoted to the eastern front against the Soviet Union. The German drive eastward was stopped at Stalingrad, after which the Soviet Red Army slowly pushed the Germans back to Berlin. In North Africa, the tide turned against the Axis in 1942 at El Alamein in Egypt, which was followed by the Allied invasion of Italy launched from Tunisia in 1943. In the final year of the war in Europe, another major front opened in France with the Allies' D-Day invasion.

WAR IN NORTH AFRICA AND ITALY Meanwhile, a secondary front developed in North Africa: in Egypt, a semi-colony of Britain; in Libya, claimed by Italy; and in Tunisia, Algeria, and Morocco, all effectively French colonies. This campaign was fought mainly in desert terrain. Civilians, mainly Arabic- or Berber-speaking peoples, were comparatively few, and the scale of brutality inflicted on ordinary people was small compared to the eastern front or China. Italian armies based in Libya attacked British forces in Egypt in late 1940 but were routed. Hitler chose to support his ally, sending an army to Libya early in 1941. It too attacked Egypt and came close to reaching the strategic prize of the Suez Canal, the choke point in the sea route to British India. But in October–November 1942, the German-Italian force was stopped and then, at El Alamein, soundly defeated. The British forces—a large share of which were from India, Australia, or New Zealand—pushed their enemies back

Prisoners of War This German photo shows soldiers of the British Indian Army captured by German units in December of 1943, probably in Italy.

westward across the sands to Tunisia. Meanwhile, an American army landed in Morocco and, despite serious battlefield setbacks, fought its way eastward to Tunisia. The Axis armies lost nearly 300,000 prisoners in Tunisia before the remainder fled to Italy in May 1943, ending the North African campaigns. As in the Pacific and on the eastern front, in North Africa the Axis suffered a defeat—at El Alamein—that turned the tide against it. But it was far less important than Midway, where the Japanese navy was crippled, or Stalingrad, where the Red Army began its march toward Germany.

Nonetheless, Italy had already lost its African colony of Ethiopia to armies of the British Empire and now lost the remainder of its overseas empire. Mussolini's prestige and authority were fading fast. When the Allies invaded Sicily and then the Italian mainland in the summer of 1943, his fellow fascists ousted him from power. A new Italian government quit the war. But once again Hitler chose to rescue his ally, sending an army into Italy to continue the fight against the Allies and placing Mussolini in nominal charge of a puppet state.

THE FINAL YEARS, 1943–1945

In 1943, without any key battle, the Allies also prevailed over Germany on the seas of the North Atlantic. After heavy losses to German submarines, called U-boats, the U.S., U.K., and Canadian navies learned how to protect shipping and hunt the subs effectively. Before the war's end, they sank most of the U-boats, killing 80 percent of their crews. That enabled millions of tons of North

American food, fuel, weapons, munitions, and other supplies to reach Britain and the USSR safely. After these turning points—Stalingrad, Midway, El Alamein, and the Atlantic—the Axis powers remained on the defensive, their now slim chances of victory waning with each passing month.

The war dragged on for two more years. Germany and Japan fought on tenaciously, even after all plausible hope was lost. Their forces had committed countless atrocities on foreign soil, and they feared payback should the fighting reach their own countries. The Japanese in particular almost never surrendered. But desperate tenacity was not enough. In 1943–1944, the Soviets pushed the Germans out of the USSR. On June 6, 1944—D-Day—the British, Canadians, and Americans landed the largest amphibious invasion force in world history on the beaches of Normandy, in northwestern France, and pushed Hitler's armies back toward Germany. Meanwhile, American submarines sank ships far faster than the Japanese could build new ones, hampering the supply and movement of Japanese forces. By 1944, the Japanese were using small fishing boats to move supplies, having almost no cargo ships or oil tankers left. By the end of 1944, American forces reached islands within aircraft range of Japan, and bombers began a sustained assault on Japanese cities, ports, and industry.

The end came at last in 1945. In Europe, by late 1944, relentless bombing of factories, rails, roads, bridges, and tunnels hampered German war production and

D-Day An embedded U.S. Coast Guard photographer took this picture of American soldiers wading ashore onto Omaha Beach during the D-Day landings on the Normandy coast on June 6, 1944.

Hiroshima A trade exhibition hall was the only building left standing near the epicenter of the atomic bomb's explosion over Hiroshima on August 6, 1945. Today, the building's ruins are the site of a memorial park.

movement. The Red Army slugged its way into Germany and took Berlin in April 1945, while the Americans and British fought their way into the western half of Germany. The Germans were running low on fuel, men—400,000 were killed per month in 1945—and the will to fight. They surrendered in May 1945, shortly after Hitler committed suicide.

In the Pacific, the Americans pushed back the Japanese, island by island. The fiercest combat took place on Iwo Jima and Okinawa, where Japanese troops, taught that surrender was worse than death, fought nearly to the last man. Meanwhile, British forces, mainly made up of Indians, began to prevail in Burma. In the summer of 1945, the Americans prepared to invade Japan's home islands, which they expected would cost tens or hundreds of thousands of American lives—and many more Japanese. But before they embarked on that mission, in early August 1945, they dropped an atomic bomb on each of two mid-size cities, **Hiroshima and Nagasaki**, using up their supply of these new weapons. The explosions instantly killed about 105,000 people, 90 percent of them civilians. Radiation poisoning soon killed roughly an equal number. In the same week, the USSR declared war on Japan and attacked in Manchuria, destroying a large but ill-equipped Japanese army in a few days. The Japanese high command chose to surrender in mid-August 1945. Scattered skirmishes continued for a few weeks, and in an indication of the depth of their devotion to duty, two Japanese officers, one in the Philippines and one in Indonesia, hid out in jungles for 29 years, refusing to believe in Japan's surrender until 1974.

WHY THE ALLIES WON

The Axis won almost every battle in the years 1937–1941. But neither time nor space was on its side. The only realistic chance it had was a quick victory before the Allies could bring to bear their enormous advantages in manpower and materiel. Until 1941, the Axis held an edge in military manpower and the quantity and quality of weaponry. But after the Axis attacked both the USSR and the United States, it was heavily out-numbered and soon out-gunned. Its chances of winning shrank, slowly at first and then rapidly after Midway, Guadalcanal, and Stalingrad. Moreover, the Chinese and Soviets could—and did—trade space for time, retreating thousands of miles into their own vast countries, luring the Japanese and Germans far from the bases, ports, and dense rail networks that their militaries needed to operate efficiently. These retreats exposed millions of Chinese and Soviet citizens to endless brutalities at the hands of Japanese and German occupation forces but at the same time made it extremely unlikely the Axis armies could win.

COALITION WAR

The Axis was not only out-numbered and out-gunned but also out-managed. Germany, Japan, and Italy scarcely cooperated and, in the case of Germany and Italy, often worked at cross-purposes. When Hitler occupied Romania in 1940, he did not tell Mussolini, and Mussolini returned the favor when Italy invaded Greece months later—although the two men met in person on the day of the Italian attack. When Italy surrendered to the Allies in 1943, the Germans captured hundreds of thousands of Italian soldiers and took them as slave laborers to Germany. Cooperation between Japan and its Axis partners amounted to little beside occasional information sharing, because their theaters of operations were so distant.

In contrast, the Allies cooperated—not smoothly but effectively. Churchill and Roosevelt met in person 10 times during the war, and they twice met together with Stalin. Their staffs were in regular communication throughout. On the battlefield, in Sicily and France, for example, British and American forces sometimes coordinated their efforts, even if with considerable friction among commanders in the field. The United States and Britain frequently shared secret intelligence with each other and from time to time with Stalin, who rarely reciprocated. Cooperation with China was much weaker, partly because anti-Japanese forces in China were divided against each other.

Even before entering the war itself, the United States provided materiel to its allies through a program called Lend-Lease. Via Lend-Lease, the United States "lent" 17 percent of its military output—guns, aircraft, and trucks, as well as fuel and food—to its two main allies, Britain and the USSR, with little expectation of repayment. (Small amounts of Lend-Lease aid went to France while it remained in the war and to China too.) Most Lend-Lease aid went to Britain, but the top Soviet general, Marshal Georgy Zhukov, said afterward that without American equipment the USSR could not have continued to fight against Germany.

This level of cooperation was a remarkable achievement given the ideological chasm between Stalin on one side and Roosevelt and Churchill on the other. Churchill had long been a vocal anti-communist, but after the German invasion of the Soviet Union in 1941, he concluded a pact with Stalin. He justified his position by saying, "If Hitler invaded hell I would make at least a favorable reference to the devil in the House of Commons." Roosevelt found it even easier to work with Stalin against Hitler and convinced Congress to overcome its anti-communism in order to support the Red Army.

The Allies overcame strategic as well as ideological differences. Roosevelt and Stalin often thought Churchill was more interested in preserving the British Empire than anything else. At their in-person meetings, Churchill consistently argued for military commitments that would safeguard Britain's position in Egypt or India. The biggest tensions in the alliance arose over the American and especially British caution in opening a second front against Germany. With German armies deep in Soviet territory, Stalin wanted his allies to invade German-occupied France in 1942. But U.S. and U.K. commanders did not feel ready to mount an amphibious assault on France, and the Americans sent armies to Axis-occupied North Africa instead. In 1943, at Churchill's insistence, Anglo-American troops assaulted Sicily instead of France. Stalin suspected his allies were content to see his army bear the brunt of German firepower, as they probably were. But the shaky performance of the U.S. Army against German forces in North Africa in 1942 and 1943 strongly suggested it was not yet prepared for an invasion of German-occupied Europe. The tensions pitting the USSR against the United

States and the United Kingdom helped break the wartime alliance and usher in the Cold War, as we will see. But holding the alliance together until victory in 1945, across an ideological chasm and despite strategic differences, was the supreme achievement of Roosevelt, Churchill, and Stalin. It enabled them to make full use of their inherent advantages.

ECONOMIC WAR

The major combatants in World War II mobilized their populations and economies on a scale unique in history. Governments raised taxes, rationed goods, re-allocated workers, and re-organized factories in their determination to prioritize war production.

MATERIAL ADVANTAGES The biggest advantage the Allies enjoyed was their economic strength. In population, the Allies in 1941 outnumbered the Axis by two to one when counting only the major combatants (the USSR, United States, and United Kingdom and its dominions of Canada, Australia, New Zealand, and South Africa on one side and Germany, Italy, and Japan on the other). If one includes India and China among the Allies, the ratio swells to close to seven to one. In 1944, when all combatants were fully mobilized, about 45 million people were serving in the armed forces. Over the course of the war, Germany and the USSR put about 17–18 percent of their populations in uniform; the United States and Britain each mobilized about 11 percent. The following table provides estimates for the total number of men and women mobilized for the armed forces of major combatants at any point during the war. Note the contributions from the British Empire. The figure for Africa refers to troops who fought for either the British or French forces.

The combined economies of the Allies were 2.1 times as large as those of the Axis in 1940—before the United States and the USSR entered the war—and 5 times larger by 1945. In the core years of the war, 1942–1944, total Allied military production outstripped that of the Axis by ratios between 3 to 1 and 10 to 1. This imbalance came in part from the success of the U.S. and U.K. navies in keeping sea routes open, maintaining access to raw materials from Latin America or Africa, while the Axis had to rely on its own resources and those of the lands it conquered. Japan in 1940 had adequate supplies of only 2 of the 32 raw materials its high command deemed essential

POPULATIONS AT WAR										
SIZE OF ARMED FORCES OF MAJOR COMBATANTS IN WORLD WAR II (IN MILLIONS OF MEN AND WOMEN)										
ALLIES								AXIS		
USSR	USA	Britain	India	Canada	Australia	Africa	France	Germany	Japan	Italy
34	16	5	2.6	1.6	1.0	1.3	3.5	18	9	9

to warfare—graphite and sulfur—and not enough metallic ores for steel and aluminum or oil and coal for fuel. By and large, the Axis enjoyed an advantage in the quality of its military goods but suffered an enormous disadvantage in quantity, partly from shortages of raw materials.

The Allies controlled almost all the world's oil, a crucial advantage. The most effective weapons systems in the 1940s—tanks, ships, and airplanes—all ran on oil. Fighting without oil meant moving men and equipment by rail, by draft animal, or on foot, in effect fighting with one hand tied behind your back. In particular, there was no way to fight an effective naval or air war without oil. In 1940, about 90 percent of the world's oil production took place in the United States, the USSR, Mexico, Venezuela, and parts of the Middle East mainly under British control. The Axis produced only 4 percent. Japan's initial conquests in 1941–1942 included oil fields in the Dutch

East Indies (now Indonesia), which produced 25 times as much oil as did the rest of Japan's empire, and the Germans in 1940 took over an oil patch in Romania that supplied Hitler's forces with most of their oil. Hitler tried to engineer a revolution in British Iraq in 1941 in hopes of securing its oil and targeted Soviet oil fields near Baku on the Caspian Sea. But after Stalingrad, he had no hope of adding to German oil supplies, and he later said that his North African campaign failed due to insufficient oil. Late in the war, the German air force could not fly for lack of fuel. Nor could Japan's. With U.S. submarines sinking almost all the oil produced anywhere in the shrinking Japanese empire, Japan's refineries were reduced to making low-quality substitute fuels from potatoes, rice, and pine roots.

U.S. oil fields alone pumped 86 percent of the oil used by the Allies. Roosevelt famously referred to the United States as the "arsenal of democracy," in reference to American weapons production for the Allies' cause. It was also the gas station of democracy.

MOBILIZATION AND MANUFACTURING Economic culture mattered too. For different reasons, both the American and Soviet economies could change almost overnight into effective war economies. The mobilization of the American economy was stunning. Soon after the United States entered the war, one of Hitler's closest comrades, Air Marshal Hermann Goering, scoffed that the Americans were only good at making razor blades. But in fact, the U.S. economy could make mass quantities of anything.

The Detroit area was the center of the world's automobile industry, which had been using electrified assembly lines for three decades. This production technique worked superbly for the mass production of tanks, aircraft, jeeps, and trucks. Chrysler engineers who had never seen a tank in 1940 designed a tank factory that churned out 15 tanks a day by the end of 1941. The U.S. auto industry stopped making cars in 1942 to focus entirely on military

Munitions Workers Women working in a Japanese ammunition factory during World War II. By 1940, Japan had a roughly fifty-year old tradition of employing poor, young, unmarried women in factory work, especially in textile mills and in tasks that required manual dexterity. But work in technologically advanced industries was sharply discouraged until 1943–44, when the shortage of male workers brought a reversal in policy. By 1944, even married women were encouraged to work in war industries, overriding social norms. Of all the major combatants, Japan was the slowest to mobilize female labor for war production.

vehicles and aircraft. The Ford Motor Company alone out-produced Italy during the war. By 1944, Ford workers could assemble a B-24 bomber every 63 minutes. Their counterparts in U.S. shipyards could weld together big cargo ships in eight days. The United States launched 16 warships for each 1 Japan could build, and in 1943 alone launched five times as many aircraft carriers as the Japanese navy possessed. Indeed, American war production alone outstripped that of the Axis from 1943 on. As Roosevelt put it, the United States had a "genius . . . for mass-production."

The United States also had the resources to pay for, and found the labor to undertake, a giant war effort. The government sold billions of dollars of bonds to ordinary Americans and raised taxes across the board—the richest Americans paid a 94 percent income tax. As men left for war, American women streamed into war work in factories, in offices, and on farms. The federal government opened about 30,000 day-care centers to make it easier for young mothers to undertake war work. Five million women joined the paid labor force between 1940 and 1945. By 1943, the majority of workers assembling airplanes were women. Thousands of women, including chemists and physicists, worked to create atomic bombs. Some 350,000 women joined the U.S. armed forces, driving trucks, serving as nurses, or handling paperwork. But overall, women made up a smaller proportion—27–29 percent—of the American industrial labor force during

Women at Work Women aeronautics workers assemble the fuselage of a B-17F bomber at a California factory in 1942. They were some of the millions of women in Allied countries who joined the paid workforce to aid the war effort.

the war than in the United Kingdom (27–32 percent), Germany (27–32 percent), or the USSR (about 60 percent). Labor was less of a constraint on the war effort for the United States than it was for the other major combatants.

The Soviet economy also performed miracles during the war. Since 1918, it had been a command economy in which the government, not market forces, made most major decisions. Since 1929, the government had used five-year plans to run the economy, relying on the enthusiasm of people devoted to Soviet communism and the coercion of everyone else to accelerate industrialization. It specialized in heroic mobilization—building a new steel mill in weeks or a factory in days. This helps to explain why the Soviet economy did not collapse in the years 1941–1942 while the Germans hammered ever deeper into the country, occupying lands that had formerly accounted for one-third of the Soviet economic output. Soviet factory workers packed up everything they could, took it east of the Ural Mountains, and put their factories back together again. Everyone not in uniform or producing food—teenagers, the elderly, political prisoners—was recruited for armaments production. Elizaveta Kochergina was 16 years old in 1941 when she began to "make cartridges for automatic guns. . . . The workday was 12 hours or more. And so it went on for four years. Without any days off or holidays." She and millions of others were subject to ruthless discipline. Workers who slacked off might be summarily shot. The Soviet economy already made widespread use of female labor before 1941 and, unlike the United States, had no great reserve of labor left to mobilize. Nevertheless, the Soviet economy, despite losing many of its most industrialized regions to Hitler's armies and much of its workforce to active military duty, produced more military materiel than Germany in every year of the war.

Both the Americans and the Soviets relied on mass production of simple designs built with interchangeable parts. That made it easier to maintain and repair machinery. Neither the Americans nor the Soviets made high-quality military goods, at least not until 1944. But they could make much more much faster than anyone else. And they could do much of it with comparatively unskilled labor performing simple, repetitive tasks on assembly lines.

The contrast with the German and Japanese war economies was sharp. Both had strong industrial traditions of skilled craftsmen. They built excellent tanks and air-planes; but lacking electrified assembly lines, they could not make them quickly, and repair was difficult. It took prolonged training to learn to make or maintain German or Japanese high-quality equipment. Skilled labor short-ages became a bottleneck in the German and Japanese war economies.

Indeed, general labor shortages hindered the Axis economies. The Axis mobilized almost all young men for military service early in the war. By 1943, it was con-scripting middle-aged men, and by 1945 Germany and Japan were putting untrained 15-year-olds in battle. That left only women, children, and old men for farm or fac-tory work. Both Germany and Japan enslaved millions of men, and some women and children too, from countries they occupied and dragged them into war production. By war's end, one-third of Germany's coal miners and nearly half its farmworkers were forcibly taken from occupied Europe. Japan conscripted roughly 2.5 million Koreans to work in its mines and factories. Upward of 4 million Indonesians were forced to work for the Japanese on Java and throughout Southeast Asia, some 15 percent of whom never made it home again. Forced laborers would slow production or even sabotage it if they were not constantly intimidated. But the Axis had no reserves of loyal labor to call upon.

The Allies benefited more than the Axis from mobi-lizing female labor. In Germany, Japan, and the USSR, about 40 percent of women were already in the paid labor force when the war began. Germany and Japan managed to raise that to about 50 percent, but the USSR achieved 78 percent by 1944. The extent of Soviet reliance on women workers was unique. In the United States and Britain, the proportion of women working outside the home was lower to start with (about 25–26 percent) and climbed to 36–38 percent. So the Allies not only had larger female populations than the Axis but they also increased their labor participation faster. Every major combatant except the United States conscripted women's labor.

SCIENTIFIC WAR

The enormous economic advantages of the Allies told in the long run. But as the war dragged on, the Allies acquired another advantage. They harnessed the brain-power of their populations more effectively than did the Axis powers.

Part of the Allies' success resulted from the flight of scientists from Germany and Europe as the Nazi threat took shape. Before the rise of the Nazis, Germany had by far the world's most advanced centers of physics. Sev-eral great physicists, such as Albert Einstein, were Jewish and left Europe to escape from Nazism. A dozen or more worked on the U.S. atomic bomb project. So did Enrico Fermi, who oversaw the first self-sustaining nuclear reac-tion, which took place in late 1942 under the stadium stands at the University of Chicago. Although a Fascist Party member himself, Fermi had left Italy in 1938 because his wife, Laura Capon, was Jewish, as were several of his research assistants, who were barred from working under new Italian racial laws. Refugees from fascism contributed significantly to scientific war work in the United States and the United Kingdom.

Moreover, the United States and the United Kingdom converted their industrial laboratories, engineering works, and universities to war work. This strategy paid dividends in the form of weaponry, radar, bombsights, antibiotic drugs and much else that helped win the war. The most famous example is the Manhattan Project, the secret, swift, and successful effort to build an atomic bomb that, starting in 1941, tapped scientists and engineers from several American, British, and Canadian universities and U.S. corporations. Together with hundreds of thousands of laborers, they built the engineering and weapons com-plex that developed the bombs used to destroy Hiroshima and Nagasaki.

The Manhattan Project Members of an all-female engineering team operate equipment at a uranium enrichment facility in Oak Ridge, Tennessee, in 1944. Laboratories and other facilities around the United States were dedicated to the effort to develop a nuclear bomb.

A key example of war-related technological development was miniaturized radar. The Allies needed to ferry millions of tons of fuel, food, and munitions across the Atlantic, from North America to Britain and the USSR, running a gauntlet of German submarines. To help do so, they devised radar devices small enough to fit on airplanes. Two British physicists at the University of Birmingham—one of them, Harry Boot, only 22 years old—developed miniaturized radar technology (used today in microwave ovens), and American factories built the units. Before they had them, the Allies were losing ships to German submarines faster than they could build new ones. After they started using micro-radar in airplanes, they could hunt down and destroy submarines faster than the Germans could build new ones. That soon enabled North American farms and factories to keep Britain and the USSR reliably supplied by sea.

In addition to engineering improvements in military hardware, the Allies put to use extraordinary advances in medicine. A good example is the use of DDT, a chemical compound that kills insects. (It was later banned in many countries because of its toxic effects on wildlife.) The Americans mass-produced it and sprayed their troops with it to protect them from lice, which can carry typhus, and mosquitos, which can carry malaria. Thanks to lab work begun by young scientists working with moldy cantaloupes in Peoria, Illinois, the Allies also had a major advantage in the mass production of anti-bacterial drugs such as penicillin, which saved countless soldiers from dying from infected wounds.

More generally, the United States and the United Kingdom, and to a lesser extent the USSR, proved better at learning from mistakes than did the Axis powers. The first requirement of learning from mistakes is admitting them and studying them. Much went wrong for the United States, the United Kingdom, and especially the USSR early in the war, and they could not pretend to themselves they knew how to fight as well as the Germans and Japanese. They had urgent reason to study their failures. After some fatal fiascoes, the Americans got very good at amphibious landings on Pacific islands. After several deadly disasters, the Soviet army learned how to fight tank battles. The Axis proved less able to improve combat performance by learning from failure. The Japanese navy even concealed its loss of one-third of its aircraft carriers at Midway from civilian leaders and the army, which for several months forged its strategy in the false belief that 12 carriers were still available. In general, both the United States and the United Kingdom were more open societies—although this was not true of the USSR—in which information flowed more freely than in Germany or Japan, which also helped people and organizations learn from mistakes.

Finally, the Allies outdid the Axis in codebreaking. With the help of Polish mathematicians and intelligence officers, the British learned the secrets to German encoding machines before the war even began. As the Germans changed their codes throughout the war, British codebreakers got better at deciphering their messages. Britain employed thousands, many of them university students trained in mathematics, classics, or foreign languages, in its codebreaking operation—and used a rudimentary computer. The British codebreakers' successes helped especially in anti-submarine warfare in the Atlantic. The Germans and Italians broke some of the Allies' codes too, which aided them considerably in the years 1940–1942. Through June 1942, the Germans, with Italian help, were reading coded dispatches on British military plans sent to Washington by an American army officer in Cairo. The legendary German general Erwin Rommel, known as the Desert Fox, could read these messages within hours, and his success in North Africa depended on this intelligence.

Navajo Code Talkers Navajo, a Native American tongue spoken in the American Southwest, was not a written language and the U.S. military correctly assumed no one available to the Axis armed forces could understand it. Here two Navajo code talkers serving with a US Marine signals unit operate a portable radio set on the island of Bougainville in the Solomon Islands campaign in late 1943. Several hundred code talkers, using fourteen different Native American languages, served with U.S. forces in the Pacific and European theaters.

But the Germans and Italians could not keep up with periodic changes in the Allies' codes, and by 1943 were usually operating in the dark.

In the Pacific War, codebreaking was also crucial. The Americans could read the main Japanese diplomatic and naval codes from near the beginning of the war. Convinced that their code was too complex to decipher, the Japanese made only small changes that did not baffle codebreakers for long. Right after the Battle of Midway, the *Chicago Tribune* carelessly printed a story indicating that the U.S. Navy knew what to expect from the Japanese, but even then the Japanese refused to believe the Americans could break their code. The Japanese failed to crack any important American codes. For radio communications among combat units, the American forces sometimes used Native American radio operators who had developed codes based on languages such as Navajo or Choctaw, which the Japanese could not understand. Some new words had to be invented: *besh-lo*, or "iron fish," became the Navajo word for submarine. One U.S. officer said the Marines could not have taken Iwo Jima without the Navajo radio men.

In the scientific war as in the economic war, the Allies could draw on much larger pools of talent and resources than the Axis. Most of the Global web was within their reach, if not within their full control. They could get refugee scientists from Europe, rubber from Brazil, or uranium for atomic bombs from the Congo. The Axis could not access talent and resources outside of the much smaller spheres it had carved out for itself.

HOME FRONTS AND MILITARY OCCUPATIONS

World War II reached into lives far from the many battle zones. Total war required the involvement of all citizens, whether on the front lines or at home. Almost every family had to economize, and many had to go hungry. Most lived with constant anxiety, if not for themselves then for loved ones in combat. Millions compromised their morals in ways unthinkable in peacetime to survive. Here we divide the war experience away from the military fronts into two sections: home fronts of the major combatants and zones of military occupation.

HOME FRONTS

Even in those countries most fully mobilized for war, most people experienced World War II not in uniform but on the home front. That experience varied considerably from country to country, and from one year to the next.

AXIS POWERS In Germany, all was relatively quiet on the home front until 1943. Remembering the privations of World War I, German authorities reserved plenty of food and other necessities for civilians until late in the war, when they no longer could. Domestic support for Hitler remained strong, and organized resistance to his regime—extremely dangerous for anyone—was minimal. The most famous anti-Nazi movement was a non-violent and ineffective student group in Munich called the White Rose, almost all of whose members were executed in 1943. Three times military officers organized assassination plots against Hitler, and all three narrowly failed.

By 1943, the veneer of normalcy in Germany was challenged by the presence of 10 to 12 million slave laborers dragged from occupied territories, and by Allied bombing of German cities. Moreover, as we will see, the **Holocaust** was underway: most Germans eventually knew that Jews were disappearing, and many knew they were being killed, but almost no one objected publicly. Either they approved of the mass murder, or they feared—with good reason—for their own position and safety should they protest. In 1944 and 1945, any appearance of normalcy disappeared. Allied bombing intensified. Shortages of food and supplies became frequent. A dark joke at the time went like this: "Enjoy the war, because the peace will be horrible." Anxiety about what was to come when the Red Army entered German lands was common and well founded: Soviet soldiers raped many of the German women they encountered in 1944 and 1945.

Japan's home front was also quiet into 1943. The military exercised tight control and kept any discouraging information, such as the fate of the Japanese fleet at Midway, from the public. Support for the emperor and the war stayed high. By 1944, however, the strain hit home. Amid growing shortages, the government asked women to work in war industries, and half a million "volunteered" before the war's end—they could be fined if they did not. Hiroko Nakamato, whose Hiroshima high school closed in 1943, went to work in an unheated airplane factory where she toiled long hours, slept on the premises,

CONSIDERING THE EVIDENCE

Propaganda for the Japanese Home Front

During World War II, the Japanese government produced films, leaflets, plays, radio broadcasts, and posters to unify the home front. But some of the most effective propaganda was *kamishibai*—that is, one-person performances accompanied by 10 to 30 hand-painted illustrations presented in sequence. Before the war, *kamishibai* artists and writers worked under the direction of managers who rented the illustrations, scripts, and bicycles to performers, who made their money by selling candy. The performers visited the same neighborhoods every day, captivating their young audiences with serialized melodramas and adventure stories. After Japan seized Manchuria from China in 1931, government agencies began writing and sponsoring official *kamishibai* performances at factories, farming collectives, and schools to promote the idea that Japan was liberating, rather than conquering, the rest of East Asia. The *kamishibai* also encouraged adults to support wartime policies—for example, by depositing the money saved by rationing into the country's banks. In the following excerpt, members of a group that grows vegetables speak with their leader, named Sakuta, about the best way to spend the profits from their sales.

Scene 12

Troop member: "Troop Commander, sir! I have run out of face cream; may I purchase some, sir?"

Sakuta: "What? You want to buy face cream? Outrageous! Don't you know that 'Luxury is the Enemy'? Huh?"

Another troop member: "Troop Commander, I would like to buy a pair of socks."..."I would like to eat some bread." ..."I am out of tissues."...

Scene 13

Sakuta: "Stop yelling 'Troop Commander' in my ear! 'I need to buy this, I want that'—you sound like a bunch of whining babies. I am about to make a speech, so listen up."...

Scene 15

Sakuta continues: "...what Japan needs now is not just money; we also have to use goods as carefully as possible. Buying things just because you have some money...weakens our nation."...

Scene 16

Sakuta continues: "The money that you keep in hand belongs just to the person who has it, but...putting money into savings is an expression of loyalty to the nation....

"What would you do if you had children? Would you eat those adorable little kids?

"Or, instead, would you loyally offer them up to the service of the nation? Hmm? It's just the same with money."...

Scene 17

Sakuta continues: "If you don't understand something as simple as this, even children will laugh at you. In fact, the reason I am making this speech is that I heard it from my son who is in elementary school. These days even children understand the importance of savings."

Source: Sharalyn Orbaugh, "Record of the Cheerful Troop," in *Propaganda Performed: Kamishibai in Japan's Fifteen-Year War* (Boston, 2015).

QUESTIONS FOR ANALYSIS

1. Which parts of the script suggest that this *kamishibai* was intended for adults instead of children?

2. How do the writers of this *kamishibai* use references to children to persuade adults that they should contribute to the war effort?

3. Why was it important to Japan and other countries for their people to ration resources, save money, and invest in war bonds?

and got little to eat. Heavy aerial bombing began late in 1944 and intensified thereafter, making the last months of the war a living hell for urban Japanese. Ten million people evacuated cities for the countryside, including 87 percent of Japan's schoolchildren, all separated from their parents. Yet there was no serious resistance to the imperial government or to the war. What little occurred was swiftly repressed.

In Italy, the war was never popular outside of committed fascist circles. Many Italians thought they were fighting on the wrong side, a conviction deepened by witnessing German atrocities in North Africa and eastern

Europe. A steady diet of military defeats sapped morale. Food and other supplies grew short early on. Black markets flourished. Factory workers went on strike. Resistance movements took up arms in the mountains. Millions fled the cities to avoid Allied bombing. In the summer of 1943, after Italy quit the war, Italian factions were fighting one another in a civil war while the Allies occupied the southern part of the country and the Germans the north. The Axis powers' efforts to keep things normal on the home front faltered and then, as the tides of war shifted against them, collapsed.

THE ALLIES In the Allied countries, governments were able to demand greater sacrifices sooner from their populations because they had been attacked by aggressors. In the USSR, Stalin had no choice because the war started so badly. Total and immediate mobilization of manpower, womanpower, and all resources followed quickly upon the German invasion and the sudden loss of millions killed or taken prisoner. Women took over most of the farmwork and much of the factory work. Nearly a million women served in the armed forces, including in combat roles such as tank commander, infantry sniper, and fighter pilot. One regiment of women bomber pilots won 23 medals for its assaults on German bases. No other country deliberately put women in battle. Food shortages were widespread and strict rationing imposed. In Leningrad, which the Germans and their Finnish allies besieged for nearly 900 days, one-third of the population (800,000 people) starved to death.

And yet the Soviet home front did not collapse. Soviet citizens were accustomed to stoic endurance. Many truly idolized Stalin and were prepared to sacrifice for him, for communism, and for their country. His appeals to patriotism helped, which extended to enlisting the Russian Orthodox Church in the war effort, reversing two decades of ruthless Soviet persecution of the church. Well-publicized German brutality made it clear to almost everyone in the USSR that the lesser of the evils available was to work as hard as possible for victory. And for those who doubted it, Stalin's network of informers and secret police stood ready to execute anyone suspected of defeatism, sympathy for the enemy, or insufficient admiration of Stalin.

Soviet Mobilization In the Soviet army, it was relatively common for women to serve in combat roles. The highly decorated Soviet fighter pilot Lydia Litvyak, posing here with her plane, was shot down in the Battle of Kursk in 1943 at age 22.

In the United Kingdom, thorough home-front mobilization was also the rule. Strict rationing prevailed and made everyday life drab—except during German bombing raids, when it was terrifying. Morale at times was shaky, despite Churchill's charismatic leadership. Petty crime spiked during air raid blackouts. In 1940 and early 1941, when Britain suffered several battlefield defeats, many thought—and some said—that making peace with Germany made sense. Women worked long hours in armaments factories, entrusting their children to relatives and friends. In 1941, they were required to register for national (not military) service, working wherever the government judged they would be most useful. The entry into the war of the USSR and then the United States, and stepped-up deliveries of American and Canadian food, fuel, and other supplies, brightened the outlook by late 1943, as did the improving prospect of victory.

The United States instituted rationing too but experienced no serious deprivations nor any serious bombing after Pearl Harbor. Most citizens accepted the necessity for sacrifices, and little compulsion was needed. The government worked with business leaders to mobilize the economy for war production. As we've seen, millions of women took on war work in offices, factories, and the armed forces, but not in combat roles. Hundreds of thousands of African Americans and poor whites left the rural South for jobs in armaments factories or shipyards in the Midwest or California, often competing for housing. In 1943, race riots erupted in five cities, most seriously in

The Tuskegee Airmen African American fighter pilots who belonged to the U.S. Air Force's segregated 332nd Fighter Group pose in front of their plane in 1944. The Tuskegee Airmen, trained in Tuskegee, Alabama, were in great demand by bomber crews, who wanted the best fighter escorts they could get on air raids over Nazi-controlled Europe.

Detroit where 34 died and the army sent in 6,000 soldiers to impose peace. The war against the most uncompromising racists in world history drew heightened attention to racial inequalities at home. Whereas in 1941 only 4,000 African Americans were in uniform, by 1945 about 1.2 million had served, albeit in segregated units and usually in non-combat roles. The United States de-segregated its armed forces in 1948.

RACE AND WAR EFFORTS Racialist thinking shaped—and often weakened—the war efforts of most of the major combatants. The United States, together with Canada, Mexico, Brazil, and Peru, treated most citizens of Japanese ancestry as potential enemies. Most of the Japanese American population on the West Coast, about 110,000 people, was rounded up in 1942 and kept in internment camps for the duration of the war. This was Roosevelt's decision, upheld by the Supreme Court in 1944. In contrast, almost none of the larger Japanese Hawaiian population was interned. German Americans, a much larger population, were sometimes kept under surveillance, and some 11,000 were interned. Almost all Japanese Canadians, about 22,000 people, most of whom were born in Canada, were put into camps and their property sold to help pay for the war. Mexico put 3,500 of its 6,000 Japanese Mexicans in internment camps. Even Brazil, which had more citizens of Japanese descent than any

Nazi Racist Propaganda A Nazi propaganda poster from 1934-35. The images represent a proud, powerful, and courageous German working man on the left, and on the right a prosperous Jew depicted (and described in the text) as ugly. The text is light verse, and refers to the Jew as the biggest scoundrel in the Reich. The pairing was intended to encourage contempt of Jews as urban, unproductive, and un-German, while associating German-ness with vigor and farm work.

Japanese Internment The American photographer Dorothea Lange took this photograph of the Mochida family of Hayward, California, preparing for their removal to an internment camp in May 1942.

other country in the Americas, restricted their movement and put some in a concentration camp when it entered the war in 1942, despite having no coastline on the Pacific Ocean. Allied governments, and probably most of their citizens, regarded Japanese and people of Japanese descent as an alien race and, after the surprise attacks of December 1941, especially untrustworthy. About 22,000 Japanese Americans volunteered for the army, and many fought, often with distinction, in campaigns in Europe. More potential troops and factory workers languished in internment camps.

Britain (and its empire) and to a lesser extent the USSR also hamstrung their war efforts due to racial attitudes. Britain recruited only from those Indian and African populations deemed "martial races," such as India's Sikhs and Gurkhas and Kenya's Kamba. In one of the great disasters of the war, in 1943–1944 British officials declined to take measures to relieve famine in Bengal, costing the lives of about 3 million Indians—and the allegiance of many more. South Africa refused to employ Black Africans, the vast majority of its population, in military roles until losses among white troops left it no choice. New Zealand was slow to mobilize the indigenous Maori. The USSR initially refused to use men from non-Slavic minorities as combat troops until the death toll obliged the army to pour Tajiks, Uzbeks, Turkmen, Chechens, and others into battle. It also deported about 2 million people from Muslim minorities in the Crimea and the Caucasus to Siberia or Central Asia on the grounds—often well founded—that they preferred the Germans to Stalin.

None of the Allies, however, put racism at the center of their war strategy, as Germany and Japan did—to the cost of their war efforts. The Axis underestimated the determination and skill of its foes, especially Russians and Chinese, supposed racial inferiors. The Nazis, fixated on imaginary Jewish racial characteristics, wasted precious manpower and war materiel in their war against the Jews. Each of the Axis powers forfeited vast potential support with their brutally racist treatment of Slavs, Arabs, Chinese, Filipinos, and many others—mainly in the lands their forces occupied.

MILITARY OCCUPATIONS AND RESISTANCE MOVEMENTS

Lands occupied by Axis troops in Europe or East Asia suffered grievously. Their populations organized resistance movements, but these were dangerous, divisive, and of little consequence to the outcome of the war.

EUROPE In German-occupied western Europe, conditions were grim; in eastern Europe, they were horrific. Food, fuel, and other supplies went first to the Germans; everyone else had to make do with what remained. In Greece, some 300,000 people, or 4 percent of the population, starved to death in the first year of German occupation. Germans everywhere found willing collaborators, especially early on when it seemed likely they would win. Collaborators helped to organize German war production, labor drafts, and the deportation of Jews to death camps. Eager collaborators were few, although fascist groups used German or Italian occupation to advance their fortunes. More collaborated out of fear for their jobs, their families, and their lives. Most people tried to stay out of the Germans' way, waiting to see which side would win.

Occupation also incited armed resistance, despite the extreme risks it entailed. It was strongest in Yugoslavia and the conquered parts of the USSR but present on some scale everywhere. Once the Germans attacked the USSR (June 1941), communists throughout Europe organized

resistance movements. When the Germans started rounding up people for forced labor in 1942, many people in occupied Europe chose to join the resistance. After Stalingrad, when it seemed Germany was likely to lose the war, still more people joined. About 15–30 percent of those in occupied Europe's resistance movements were women, often very young. Perhaps one-quarter to one-third of them were killed.

No resistance movement had much military effect until 1944–1945. Yugoslav partisans operating in mountains and forests at times kept two German army divisions tied up. Partisans in the woods and swamps of eastern Europe and, late in the war, in the mountains of Greece, Italy, and France also gave the Germans trouble. Just before D-Day, the French Resistance sabotaged rail lines on a considerable scale. But generally, resistance movements did not want to serve as assistants to the Allies and made only minor contributions to Allied victory. They had their own agendas, which usually included positioning themselves to take power as soon as the German occupation ended. Sometimes this pitted them against the Allies: in late 1944, Greek communist forces were fighting the British Army in and around Athens. Everywhere, resistance fighters were poorly equipped, often hungry, and always divided and mutually suspicious. In both Greece and Yugoslavia, communist and royalist resistance factions fought one another as much as the occupiers.

Everywhere, but especially in eastern Europe, acts of resistance provoked terrible German reprisals, typically featuring the murder of dozens or hundreds of civilians. The Germans made it clear that acts of defiance, sabotage, or violence against them would result in the killing of innocents. They massacred entire villages if a German soldier was killed nearby. When the Polish Home Army resistance group rose in rebellion in Warsaw in August 1944, Hitler ordered the city razed to the ground and all its citizens murdered. About 150,000 were killed. As a result of reprisals, and the fact that resistance members often stole food to survive in the woods or mountains, civilians in occupied Europe often resented resistance fighters as much as those who collaborated with the Germans.

ASIA In the parts of China occupied by Japanese forces, the war years were also exceedingly grim. Major famines afflicted parts of the country, especially Henan Province. In occupied China, millions collaborated with

Filipinos at War Filipino soldiers in early 1942 shortly after the Japanese invasion of the Philippines. About 200,000 Filipinos fought alongside the U.S. Army in the Philippines campaigns of 1942 in which the Japanese triumphed. Over the next three years, Filipinos mounted a substantial guerilla war against Japanese occupation. In all, the war cost about 1 million Filipino lives, most of them civilians.

the Japanese, and millions resisted them. Japanese racial ideology encouraged extremely harsh treatment of Chinese, which over time nourished resistance. Both the Guomindang and the Chinese Communist Party (CCP) mounted small-scale guerilla actions in occupied China. The Guomindang on balance proved less successful at them than the CCP, which did a better job of winning over peasant support and dodging Japanese reprisals. Like the resistance factions in Greece and Yugoslavia, CCP and Guomindang units fought one another. Mao Zedong, the CCP leader, later said that 10 percent of the CCP resistance effort was directed against the Japanese, leaving 90 percent for collaborators and the Guomindang.

Japanese forces were no gentler in Southeast Asia or the Pacific than in China. They seized food from starving locals, bringing 3 million deaths by famine on Java and nearly as many in northern Vietnam. With ship and rail transport serving mainly Japanese military purposes, it became next to impossible to transport food or medicine. In the Philippines, where resistance was widespread during the Japanese occupation

(1941–1945), some 330,000 starved and another 140,000 were massacred—most famously in the so-called Bataan death march in 1942, when about 9,000 captured Filipino soldiers and 1,000 Americans lost their lives. Millions of men and women were forced into slave labor for the Japanese war effort, most notoriously in 1943 on a railway-building project linking Burma and Thailand, on which 90,000 Southeast Asians and 12,000 Allied prisoners of war died. Everywhere, epidemics raged, worsened by malnutrition.

MALTREATMENT OF WOMEN A harsh aspect of life in occupation zones was rape and sex slavery. Millions of women and girls who fell into the hands of marauding soldiers were raped, especially in China, eastern Europe, and, in 1945–1946, in Germany. The Japanese and Soviet armies often condoned rape as a means of terrorizing and humiliating people under their control and as a way to revenge wrongs (real or perceived) done to Japanese and Soviet citizens. When confronted with charges that Soviet soldiers had raped thousands of Yugoslav women in 1945, Stalin answered "what was so awful" about that, considering all that his soldiers had been through. In early 1945, one Soviet officer, Lev Kopelev, tried to stop his comrades from raping German women, resulting in his conviction on charges of "bourgeois humanism" and ten years in a Soviet prison. Estimates of the number of German women raped by Soviet troops range from 200,000 to 2 million.

In another grievous wartime abuse, the Japanese army seized hundreds of thousands of young women in Korea, China, the Philippines, the Dutch East Indies, and elsewhere and forced them to work in military brothels throughout occupied Asia. Most were teenagers. Poor Japanese women were also dragooned into sex slavery. Only about one-quarter of these so-called **comfort women** survived the abuse meted out to them. A few survivors, such as Maria Rosa Luna Henson, a Filipina who was 15 years old when first raped by Japanese soldiers, wrote harrowing memoirs of their sufferings. German authorities also forced women in occupied Europe into brothels serving the German army. They selected many women from concentration camps, mainly Germans who had run afoul of the Nazi regime, Poles, and Ukrainians. The full extent of sexual violence directed at women and girls is among the most difficult aspects of the war to assess because so much of it went unreported.

THE HUMAN COST

The death toll of World War II reached 60 million, more than any war before or since and about 3 percent of humankind at the time. Between half and two-thirds were civilians. In addition to those killed, many millions more suffered bodily or psychological harm that lasted for the rest of their lives. The ravages were greatest in eastern Europe and China. The USSR, Poland, Germany, Yugoslavia, and Greece lost large proportions of their populations. Europe as a whole lost 6 percent of its population. The United States, which made huge contributions in terms of war materiel, paid the lowest human cost of any major combatant—partly because it joined the war later than most but mainly because after Pearl Harbor no combat took place on American soil. The table here reduces the grisly tragedy to numbers and percentages.

WAR CRIMES

War crimes took place on an unprecedented scale. Outside of combat, Germans and their accomplices murdered 10 to 14 million people, including nearly 6 million Jews in the Holocaust (see below). Stalin's henchmen killed at least 1.2 million and perhaps as many as 7 million—the figures are highly controversial. They killed anyone suspected of favoring the Germans, which included many Ukrainians and Poles. In addition, they tried to kill all educated people and military officers in the parts of Poland they controlled. Japanese forces murdered or deliberately starved millions more, most notoriously in the Nanjing Massacre of 1937–1938, in which perhaps 200,000 Chinese civilians were slaughtered and 20,000 women and girls raped. In north China in 1941, the Japanese implemented a policy known as the Three Alls: kill all, loot all, burn all. That resulted in nearly 3 million civilian deaths. In the Philippines, as the Japanese were withdrawing early in 1945, they massacred at least 100,000 civilians in Manila.

Atrocities occur in every war. In World War II, there were more than in other wars partly just because the scale of warfare was bigger. Beyond that, the mobilization of civilians, the activities of partisans, and the reach of modern weaponry made it easy and tempting to ignore distinctions between military and non-military targets. In addition, ideological and racist hatreds hardened conduct, especially on the eastern front and in the theaters involving Japan. Commanders often chose not to restrain their troops but to encourage them to murder prisoners or assault civilians. A cycle of rage and revenge developed in many war zones, in which soldiers witnessed, or heard about, crimes committed against their comrades and took those as justification for crimes of their own.

All armies, and all resistance movements, engaged in atrocities on some scale. But the Germans and Japanese outdid the rest, partly because as invading and occupying armies they had access to tens of millions of enemy civilians, and partly because they were steeped in racist ideology that convinced them their enemies were sub-human and not fit to live. The Allies did not try to exterminate populations that came under their control but, like the Axis, bombed cities without mercy.

The fates of prisoners of war give some idea of the differences in the policies of the combatant powers. Of the 30–35 million prisoners of war, perhaps 6–10 million, most commonly those held by Germany, Japan, or the USSR,

THE HUMAN COST OF WORLD WAR II

	War dead (in millions)	1940 population (in millions)	War dead as a percentage of 1940 population
USSR	25–29	194	13–16%
China	15–20	520	3–4%
Germany	6.9–7.4	70	8–9%
Poland	6	35	17%
Dutch East Indies	3–4	70	4.3–5.7%
India	3–3.5	400	0.8–0.9%
Japan	2.5–3.1	72	3.5–4.3%
Yugoslavia	1.0–1.7	16	6.3–11%
Greece	0.5–0.8	7.2	6.9–11%
France	0.6	42	1.4%
Italy	0.5	45	1.1%
United Kingdom	0.5	48	1%
United States	0.4	132	0.3%
Canada	0.04	11.3	0.4%
Australia	0.04	7	0.6%
WORLD	65	2,300	2.6%

Sources: Gerhard Weinberg, *World at Arms* (1995), 894, and https://en.wikipedia.org/wiki/World_War_II_casualties#Total_deaths_by_country

War's End Japanese prisoners of war on the island of Guam, August, 1945. Japanese soldiers were taught to prefer death to surrender, and to expect to be tortured and murdered if they did. Few Japanese soldiers did surrender until the end of the war.

died of starvation and disease. About 50–55 percent of Soviet prisoners but only 3 percent of Americans or British in German hands died in captivity. Some 27 percent of prisoners taken by the Japanese died, as did 15 percent of those held by the Soviet forces. Only 1 percent of the Italians and Germans captured by the British and American forces did not survive the war. (Very few Japanese became prisoners until the final week of the war, when 600,000 surrendered to the Red Army in Manchuria. Only half ever left Soviet custody.) While many factors are involved here, including the duration of imprisonment and the availability of food and medicine, a large part of the discrepancies in these figures comes from deliberate mistreatment of prisoners, which was more systematic among the Germans and Japanese.

BOMBING OF CITIES

Aerial bombing of cities, regarded by some as a war crime, killed about 1 million civilians, mostly in Germany and Japan. War strategists thought, incorrectly, that they could break civilian morale by bombing cities and terrorizing populations. But the bombing only hardened the popular will to resist. Worst hit were the city of Chongqing, China's wartime capital, bombed at least 268 times in 1938–1941; Britain in 1940–1941; Germany in 1943–1945; and Japan in 1944–1945. Squadrons of bombers burned whole cities to the ground. British bombers burned the north German port of Hamburg in summer 1943, killing 34,000 civilians. In February 1945, the British and American bombing of Dresden, in Germany, undertaken at Stalin's request to relieve pressure on advancing Red Army units, killed about 25,000. In Tokyo in March 1945, one American air raid killed about 85,000. In total, 3 percent of Britain's urban area was turned to rubble by bombing, 40 percent of Germany's, and half of Japan's.

As we have seen, in August 1945 the United States dropped two atomic bombs, one each on the Japanese cities of Hiroshima and Nagasaki. Counting lingering deaths from radiation exposure, the bombs killed roughly 200,000 people. These were the first and so far the last uses of nuclear weapons in warfare. They succeeded in their immediate purpose: to force a Japanese surrender without the heavy losses expected in an invasion of Japan's home islands. President Truman's decision to use them was welcomed by the Allies at the time, but later became highly controversial because of the uniquely devastating power of atomic weapons.

THE HOLOCAUST

The horrific human cost of the war included the near destruction of European Jewry. Hitler intended to kill Europe's entire population of 9 to 10 million Jews, whom he regarded as sub-humans unfit to live in the Germany he hoped to create. Sporadic murders of Jews in Germany, of whom there had been more than 400,000 when Hitler came to power, began before the war. In 1939, when the Germans conquered half of Poland, they murdered many more Jews and tried to collect all the rest into ghettoes—in effect, urban prison camps. Larger-scale systematic murder, carried out by specialized death squads called *Einsatzgruppen*, began with the German invasion of the USSR in June 1941.

Hitler at first planned to win the war quickly and afterward finish off the Jews, but he realized that the fighting would drag on after two events in December 1941: the first Soviet army counter-attack against German forces, and the Japanese attack on Pearl Harbor, which brought the United States into the war. He then decided to kill all of

The Holocaust Emaciated survivors of the Buchenwald concentration camp in eastern Germany, photographed shortly after U.S. troops liberated the camp in April 1945.

Europe's Jews while the war was still under way, and his underlings convened a conference in early 1942 outside of Berlin at Wannsee to plan what they called the "Final Solution to the Jewish question."

At the Wannsee Conference, 15 Nazi officials, nearly half of whom held doctorates in law, worked out the broad outlines of the plan, built around a network of extermination camps. Even after the tide of battle had turned against them in 1943, the Germans devoted manpower and railcars to the transport of Jews from all over Europe to dozens of concentration camps—both labor camps and death camps. The extermination camps' names are synonyms for the deepest abyss in the annals of human morality: Treblinka, Sobibor, Auschwitz.

In all, the Germans and their helpers murdered about 6 million Jews, the vast majority from eastern Europe. Some they worked to death, some they starved to death, some they gassed in specially built death chambers, and most they shot. A quarter of the victims were children. Greece, Yugoslavia, Poland, and Lithuania lost upward of 85 percent of their Jewish populations to the Holocaust, and the Netherlands 80 percent. In those parts of Europe once occupied by Axis forces, only half a million Jews remained alive when the war ended.

THE SCALE OF GENOCIDE The scale of the extermination at first seemed impossible to believe. German propaganda maintained that Jews deported from around Europe were destined for labor camps. Even Jews confined to ghettoes could not believe Germans intended to murder them all: Jakub Poznański wrote in his diary on September 27, 1943, "Persistent rumors circulate about the liquidation of the ghettos.... In my opinion, people are exaggerating, as usual. Even if certain excesses have taken place... that does not incline one to believe that Jews are being mass-murdered." He wrote this 21 months after mass murder of Jews had begun in the Chelmno extermination camp, 30 miles away. Leaders of many of the ghettoes thought that by allowing the Germans to take some Jews to their deaths, they might save the rest. Some Jews trusted God would save them. However, as deportations continued, fewer and fewer Jews could remain in denial about the fate awaiting them.

Sooner or later, everyone in occupied Europe also had a pretty good idea of what was happening to their Jewish neighbors. Most judged—correctly—that it was safest for themselves to do and say nothing. Moreover, most had little sympathy for Jews, especially the many who were refugees. Some, especially local police forces, aided in the deportation of Jews, either because they wished to be rid of them or because they feared—justifiably—German wrath if they did not comply. German executioners often found eager assistants, especially among Croats, Slovaks, Ukrainians, Romanians, Hungarians, and Poles. Croatian fascists even set up their own death camp. In western Europe, where Jews were comparatively few, puppet governments collaborated with the Nazi genocide. The so-called Vichy regime in France sent a quarter of French Jews to their deaths. Denmark, on the other hand,

Warsaw Ghetto After defeating the uprising of 1943, German soldiers round up Jewish residents of the Warsaw ghetto—including many children—for deportation to extermination camps.

The Holocaust, 1939–1945 This map shows a landscape of death and despair. Beginning in 1933, the Nazi Party set up a system of concentration camps, also called labor camps, which held about 21,000 people when World War II began in Europe, in 1939. They held 715,000 at their height, in early 1945. A parallel system of seven extermination camps opened in 1942. (Auschwitz, opened in 1940, was both a labor camp and an extermination camp.) Some 800,000 people died in the labor camps of starvation, disease, and brutality. About 3.1 million died in the extermination camps—most of them Jews. Another 2.6 to 2.9 million Jews were murdered outside the camp systems.

managed to resist demands to deport its tiny Jewish population (8,000) to death camps, and 99 percent of Danish Jews survived. In Italy, about 80 percent (of 50,000) Jews survived, and some Italian generals mustered the courage to defy their ally's instruction to hand over Jews in regions occupied by the Italian army.

DEFIANCE Occasionally Europe's Jews had courageous defenders. Led by a Protestant pastor, one village in the south of France, Le Chambon-sur-Lignon, hid a

thousand or more Jews and helped others escape from France. A Dutch village, Nieuwlande, also inspired by a Protestant clergyman, did much the same. In 1943, when German authorities ordered the mayor of the capital city of the Greek island of Zakynthos to provide a list of the island's Jews and their property, they received a list with two names: the mayor's and that of the island's bishop. Islanders helped all 275 Jews on Zakynthos to hide, and all survived the Nazi occupation. So, improbably, did the mayor and the bishop. The Swedish diplomat Raoul Wallenberg, posted to Budapest, saved thousands of Hungarian Jews by issuing them documents providing the legal protection of neutral Sweden. (The Soviet army seized Wallenberg when it captured Hungary in 1945, and he perished not long after, probably in a Soviet prison.) One Polish diplomat, Jan Karski, working as a courier for the Polish resistance, snuck into the Warsaw ghetto twice, and a Jewish transport camp once, to bring authentic information of the fate of Poland's Jews to the attention of the outside world. He went to London and Washington to explain what he knew to all who would listen, but with little result: the U.S. Supreme Court justice Felix Frankfurter, Jewish himself, told Karski he did not believe him. In any case, Churchill and Roosevelt thought the best way to save lives, whether Jewish or not, was to win the war fast. Karski was not alone: Over 2,500 Poles were executed for trying to help Jews.

The courage of Karski, Wallenberg, and all the rest saved only a few. The vast majority of ordinary people did not wish to run risks for themselves, their families, or their friends to help Jews. Those in positions of political authority, such as Churchill, Roosevelt, Stalin, judged it impractical to attempt to rescue Europe's Jews. Pope Pius XII, who enjoyed a different sort of authority, preferred to maintain good relations with Hitler and stood by when the Jews of Rome were rounded up.

A few tens of thousands of Jews actively fought back against Hitler's extermination campaign, concluding that death was not far off whatever they did, and it was better to die fighting. Whereas most non-Jews could submit to Nazi rule and hope to wait out the war, for Jews submitting meant death, and so their only choice was how to die. As one resistance leader in the Polish city of Kraków put it, "We are fighting for three lines in the history books to make the world know that the Jewish youth did not go like lambs to the slaughter." Some managed to join Polish or Ukrainian guerillas in the forests and swamps of eastern Europe, but few survived more than a few months there due to hunger and disease—and frequent hostility and betrayal on the part of non-Jewish resistance factions. Five short-lived uprisings took place in the death camps themselves, and 18 more in labor camps. Jews rose in rebellion in seven of the major ghettoes. The largest such rising took place in the Warsaw ghetto, which had once held 400,000 Jews. Only 60,000 remained by January 1943, when renewed deportations to the extermination camps were met with violent resistance by about 750 poorly armed Jews who had smuggled in weapons over the previous months. They held off German units for 27 days before being overwhelmed. The Germans then destroyed the entire ghetto and everyone in it.

The mass murder of the Jews was the biggest part of a larger Nazi extermination project. Hitler also regarded Roma (Gypsies), those labeled "homosexuals," and the mentally ill as unworthy to live in his expanded and racially purified Germany. His supporters murdered 200,000–500,000 Roma, 20–50 percent of Europe's Roma population, most of them in the same camps as the Jews. Some 300,000 people judged by doctors to have mental or physical disabilities were also killed in Hitler's efforts to safeguard the German "race." Hitler also regarded most or all Slavs as sub-human. German soldiers, police, and other units murdered millions of civilian Poles, Ukrainians, and Russians. They particularly sought to kill anyone with an education, except those willing to join the German war effort.

Hitler was one of few extreme racists ever to hold sufficient power to put his views into practice. He thought a pure German race existed and deserved to thrive, while Slavs, Roma, and especially Jews were obstacles to German greatness. He wanted to kill, starve, enslave, or expel them all. German voters, politicians, and military men had put him in a position to realize much of his murderous agenda, which he pursued, even at the cost of war aims, until the very end.

AFTERMATH

Wars rarely end crisply upon surrender. After World War II, violence and suffering lingered on for a decade or more in some cases. The psychological toll lasted far longer. In the final weeks of the war and the months following surrender, tens of thousands of high officials in Germany and Japan committed suicide, often killing their families with them. Allied troops liberated the remaining Nazi death camps and their shockingly emaciated survivors, none of whom could ever forget their experience. Nor could millions of soldiers, prisoners, women, and children who had seen the ugly face of war up close.

REFUGEES, VENGEANCE, JUSTICE Tens of millions of war refugees wandered in search of safety, food, and shelter. Many were orphaned children. Japanese struggled to get home from China and Southeast Asia. A quarter of China's population was on the move, people trying to return to villages and towns they had fled to avoid the Japanese army. Fourteen million "displaced persons" in Europe relied on Allied charity. Most were eastern Europeans or former Soviet prisoners who did not want to go home to live under Stalin's control. A fifth of all Germans trudged westward to get away from the Soviet Red Army. They huddled in camps, dependent on Allied food handouts, and often found cold welcomes from their fellow Germans. The last of the displaced persons camps closed in 1957.

Meanwhile, violent clashes continued as people settled scores with those they had come to resent for personal or political reasons. Many thousands who had collaborated with the Germans or Japanese were casually killed. Allied troops occupying former Axis countries sometimes took revenge upon civilians, in the form of theft, rape, and occasionally murder. The Allied governments formally charged 24 top-ranking Nazis and 28 Japanese political and military leaders with war crimes and conducted trials at Nuremberg (1945–1946) and Tokyo (1946–1948). Almost all were found guilty and sentenced to death or prison.

In some of the Axis-occupied lands, such as China, Vietnam, Greece, and Yugoslavia, civil wars had emerged within resistance movements. These continued after the Japanese and Germans went home, gradually becoming, as we will see, battlefronts in the early Cold War.

HUMAN RIGHTS Sorrow and anger at the atrocities and crimes of World War II led to a surge of interest in preventing anyone, especially governments, from committing such injustices again. One form this took was renewed discussion of individual human rights, usually understood to include at a minimum the right to life, freedom of

PUZZLES IN WORLD HISTORY

How Much Do People of Prominence Influence World History?

You can find prominent people throughout this book, but the revolutions and world wars discussed in recent chapters afford an especially good opportunity to weigh the question of how much such people matter to the course of history. For example, without Kate Sheppard's leadership of its suffrage movement, would New Zealand still have launched the international trend of granting women the vote in national elections?

We can't know with certainty the answers to such hypothetical questions. Thinking about them, however, helps us understand why history and, for that matter, current events unfold as they do. Historians today use the word *agency* when talking about how individuals and groups act to advance their interests and ideals on the historical stage. At times, actions like these can push history in one direction or another; in other cases, history is influenced more by larger economic or social structures that are the collective outcomes of countless daily routines of living and working.

With the Global web tying together movements and peoples around the world, the question of agency applies globally as well as locally. Kate Sheppard participated in an international community of advocates for woman suffrage and also organized New Zealand women—she was a key human node at the intersection of global and local networks. At the same time, larger structures have demonstrated global effects: for example, the economic productivity of the Allied powers made a clear difference in the outcome of World War II. How can we weigh the impact of economic power against the strategic decisions made by leaders like Churchill, Roosevelt, Hitler, and Stalin?

QUESTIONS FOR DISCUSSION

1. Using an example, how do you weigh the importance of individual decisions and actions in history?
2. In today's globally connected world, do individual actions have more or less influence than before? Explain the reasoning behind your response.

expression, and equality before the law. The concept had deep roots in western Europe and its offshoots in North America—despite their histories of imperialism, slavery, and disenfranchisement of women. Most cultural traditions in world history, in contrast, understood rights not as held by individuals but as shared by groups such as clans, castes, classes, or tribes. Nonetheless, the principle of human rights held broad appeal—not least in the colonized world, where it lent moral support to independence movements. When the victorious Allies met in San Francisco in 1945 to establish an international body charged with keeping the world at peace, the United Nations, they set up a commission for human rights.

Chaired by Eleanor Roosevelt, widow of the late president, the commission issued a Universal Declaration of Human Rights in 1948, the preamble of which included these words: "[R]ecognition of the inherent dignity and of the equal and inalienable rights of all members of the human family is the foundation of freedom, justice, and peace in the world." All UN member nations voted to adopt the declaration as a statement of principles—with the exception of the USSR and those Eastern European countries now under its control; Saudi Arabia, where slavery was still legal; and South Africa, which had just passed racist laws denying basic rights to its Black majority.

The new emphasis on human rights was subsequently expressed in UN agreements on the rights of refugees (1951), women (1979), and children (1989) and other conventions. The World War II tradition of tribunals—temporary courts—for war criminals, such as at Nuremberg and Tokyo, led to the establishment in 2002 of the International Criminal Court (ICC), based in The Hague in the Netherlands. The ICC and the UN's human rights regime are generally ongoing responses to one of the saddest legacies of World War II and its more recent echoes.

POST-WAR ADJUSTMENTS Over time, a new normal settled in. Tens of millions of soldiers and sailors went home, shedding uniforms for civilian garb. Millions of women gave up factory or office jobs and returned to domestic roles, some willingly, some only because they were fired in favor of ex-soldiers. In some countries, including France and Italy, the wartime contributions of women translated into political rights in the form of suffrage; the United States during its post-war occupation of Japan imposed a new constitution providing for female suffrage. Food and fuel shortages eased in most countries—but slowly. Starvation stalked the USSR in 1946–1947; rationing of some items in the United Kingdom lasted into the 1950s. A few hundred thousand lucky refugees found new homes in the United States or Canada or Australia. Many more spent years or decades in Soviet prisons or displaced persons camps. The scale of death among young men left an enduring gender imbalance in some populations. Among Germans in their twenties in 1946, there were three women for every man. In the USSR, the ratio was likely similar.

In terms of international politics, the new normal was very different from the pre-war world. Two former great powers, Germany and Japan, were defeated, partially destroyed, and now under military occupation by the Allies. Italy, formerly an imperial power if not really a great power, also lay in ruins. The United Kingdom, although victorious, was financially bankrupt and dependent on the United States. The British, French, and Dutch empires, as we shall see, were enfeebled, while restless colonized populations everywhere had acquired new skills and ambitions during the war. The USSR, although triumphant, was exhausted, hungry, and now without the supplies formerly shipped from North America through Lend-Lease. Soviet forces remained in most of the lands

they had taken from the Germans and soon created communist governments to rule them, to the dismay of most Eastern Europeans. China remained at war after the Japanese left, as the Guomindang and the CCP fought until 1949 to control the ravaged country.

The United States, in contrast, with only 7 percent of the world's population, now accounted for half of its industrial production and a quarter of the global economy. It alone had nuclear weapons, and it had the world's biggest air and naval forces by far. It produced most of the world's surplus food and much of its oil. Its science and technology communities, buoyed by the arrival of refugees, were now the world's most dynamic and creative. Never before or since has the United States been as dominant in world politics as in late 1945. Never in the history of the world had any single state exercised greater power relative to all others. It could not last.

CONCLUSION

World War II (1937–1945) took about 60 million lives through combat, murder, disease, and starvation. It ruined many more through wounds or psychological torment. Well over half the victims were civilians. The scale of suffering is the single most important lesson to learn about the war.

The ferocity of the conflict, more obvious in some theaters than others, derived largely from the racism and ideological enmities involved. Governments and military organizations, some much more than others, encouraged savagery, not merely in combat but toward prisoners and civilians. All wars involve war crimes, but none to date match World War II in this regard.

Nor do any wars before or since equal World War II in the scale of mobilization of combatant societies. All the Axis and Allied powers devoted huge portions of their economic, demographic, scientific, and other resources to the war effort. The Allies had more to draw upon.

In that lie the central reasons behind the Allied victory. While the Axis powers had an edge early on and conquered vast territories, they could not match the manpower, resources, and industrial might the Allies could bring to bear once the USSR and United States entered the war. And because the Germans could not vanquish the Soviet Red Army, and the Japanese got bogged down

Indian Troops Britain's Indian Army training in the English countryside in 1942. By the end of the war, the Indian Army was the largest all-volunteer force in world history with a strength of 2.5 million men. They fought in North Africa, Italy, and above all in Burma against the Japanese. Some 90,000 died in the war. Churchill extolled their "unsurpassed bravery" in action.

in China, the Allies were granted the time in which to mobilize fully their formidable war machines. They could enlist far more troops than could the Axis and, even more importantly, could provide them with far more fuel, food, medicine, guns, tanks, ships, and aircraft—not just the razor blades that Goering had mocked.

World War II cast a long shadow. Frictions among its winners led quickly to a new global conflict, the Cold War. The international system today still reflects the victory of the United States and the USSR. Opposition to imperialism, anti-Semitism, and racism and support for human rights all owe much to the war experience and result. So does reluctance to engage in total war and to use nuclear weapons. By now almost no one still living remembers World War II, but the study of history may keep its lessons alive for a while longer.

CHAPTER REVIEW

KEY TERMS

World War II (p. 894)

Axis (p. 895)

Lebensraum (p. 896)

Greater East Asia
Co-Prosperity Sphere
(p. 896)

appeasement (p. 897)

Allies (p. 898)

Battle of Stalingrad
(p. 902)

Hiroshima and Nagasaki
(p. 905)

Holocaust (p. 911)

comfort women (p. 916)

Go to INQUIZITIVE
to see what you've
learned—and learn what
you've missed—with
personalized feedback
along the way.

REVIEW QUESTIONS

1. Describe the shared ambitions and beliefs behind Germany, Italy, and Japan's expansionist pursuits.

2. What four overlapping wars and four theaters made up World War II?

3. What key moments caused the tide of the war to turn against the Axis powers?

4. Compare and contrast the cooperation among the Allied powers with the cooperation among the Axis powers.

5. What economic, natural-resource, and labor advantages did the Allies have over the Axis during World War II?

6. How did racist ideologies affect the conduct of World War II?

7. Which groups did Hitler's extermination program target, and why?

8. Compare and contrast the level of home-front mobilization in Germany, Japan, the Soviet Union, the United Kingdom, and the United States.

9. Explain what happened to people of Japanese ancestry living in the United States and Canada during World War II.

10. In terms of international politics, what was different about the post-war world?

FURTHER READING

Svetlana ALEXIEVICH, *The Unwomanly Face of War: An Oral History of Women in World War II* (2017). Narratives of the lives of women who served in the Soviet armed forces during World War II.

Anonymous, *A Woman in Berlin* (2006). First published in the early 1950s, this diary details the grim experiences of a young woman in the weeks after the Soviet army marched into Berlin.

Mark EDELE, *Stalinism at War: The Soviet Union in World War II* (2021). A compact but comprehensive look at the Soviet Union's participation in World War II.

Paul KENNEDY, *Engineers of Victory: The Problem Solvers Who Turned the Tide in the Second World War* (2013). A clear analysis of how the Allies learned to do things better over the course of World War II.

Halik KOCHANSKI, *Resistance: The Underground War against Hitler, 1939–1945* (2022). The most comprehensive, clear-eyed, and unromanticized survey yet of resistance in occupied Europe.

Evan MAWDSLEY, *World War II: A New History* (2020). Strong on the purely military aspects.

Rana MITTER, *Forgotten Ally: China's World War II, 1937–1945* (2013). A clear account of complex political and military events and their impacts on ordinary people.

Richard OVERY, *Blood and Ruins: The Great Imperial War, 1931–1945* (2021). A thorough study of every aspect of the war.

S.C.M. PAINE, *The Japanese Empire: Grand Strategy from the Meiji Restoration to the Pacific War* (2017). A brief narrative and analysis of Japan's rise and overreach.

Peipei QIU, *Chinese Comfort Women: Testimonies from Imperial Japan's Sex Slaves*, with Su Zhiliang and Chen Lifei (2013). A study based on recent and disturbing interviews of women who survived terrible ordeals.

Srinath RAGHAVAN, *India's War: World War II and the Making of Modern South Asia* (2016). Especially good on the relationship between India's war effort and independence movement.

The Holocaust, Genocide, and Concentration Camps

ONE OF THE CHARACTERISTICS OF WORLD WAR II was the frequency and extent of atrocities against and mass imprisonment of civilians. Some armies abandoned all discipline for weeks or months on end and indulged in looting, raping, and massacring prisoners and noncombatants. Some governments incarcerated thousands or millions of their own citizens in efforts to neutralize groups thought to be potentially disloyal and therefore dangerous. The following selections from documents from the 1940s reflect a small sample of the horrors perpetrated upon civilians. They may help you to understand, at least to some extent, both the experiences of millions caught up in what historians sometimes call "total war" and the diverse policies and conduct of armies and governments in times of stress, fear, and anxiety.

SOURCE 26.1

Rudolf Hoess, Testimony at Nuremburg, 1946

One of the willing mass murderers in the Nazi military bureaucracy was Rudolf Hoess. Born in 1901 and raised a strict Catholic, he joined the German army in World War I at age 14. He was wounded three times and won several military decorations before the 1918 armistice and his return to high school. Not long after graduation, Hoess heard a speech by Adolf Hitler, renounced Catholicism, and joined the Nazi Party. His account of his career running death camps is accurate with the exception of the total murdered at Auschwitz. He exaggerates the toll, which was closer to 1.1 million than 3 million (the Holocaust in total amounted to the murder of about 6 million Jews). Hoess was hanged in 1947 for war crimes.

I, Rudolf Franz Ferdinand Hoess, being first duly sworn, depose and say as follows:

1. I am forty-six years old, and have been a member of the NSDAP [National Socialist German Workers' Party] since 1922; a member of the SS since 1934; a member of the Waffen-SS since 1939. I was a member from 1 December 1934 of the SS Guard Unit, the so-called Deathshead Formation (Totenkopf Verband).

2. I have been constantly associated with the administration of concentration camps since 1934. . . . I commanded Auschwitz until 1 December, 1943, and estimate that at least 2,500,000 victims were exterminated there by gassing and burning, and at least another half million succumbed to starvation and disease, making a total dead of about 3,000,000. This figure represents about 70% to 80% of all persons sent to Auschwitz as prisoners, the remainder having been selected and used for slave labor in the concentration camp industries. . . . The remainder of the total number of victims included about 100,000 German Jews, and great numbers of citizens, *mostly* Jewish from Holland, France, Belgium, Poland, Hungary, Czechoslovakia, Greece, or other countries. We executed about 400,000 Hungarian Jews alone at Auschwitz in the summer of 1944. . . .

6. The "final solution" of the Jewish question meant the complete extermination of all Jews in Europe. I was ordered to establish extermination facilities at Auschwitz in June 1941. At that time there were already in the general government three other extermination camps; Belzek, Treblinka, and Wolzek. . . . I visited Treblinka to find out how they carried out their exterminations, the Camp Commandant at Treblinka told me that he had liquidated 80,000 in the course of one-half year. He was principally concerned with liquidating all the Jews from the Warsaw Ghetto. He used monoxide gas and I did not think that his methods were very efficient. So when I set up the extermination building at Auschwitz, I used [Zyklon] B, which was a crystallized Prussic Acid which we dropped into the death chamber from a small opening. It took from 3 to 15 minutes to kill the people in the death chamber depending on climatic conditions. We knew when the people were dead because their screaming stopped. We usually waited about one-half hour before we opened the doors and removed the bodies. After the bodies were removed our special commandos took off the rings and extracted the gold from the teeth of the corpses.

7. Another improvement we made over Treblinka was that we built our gas chambers to accommodate 2,000 people at one time, whereas at Treblinka their 10 gas chambers only accommodated 200 people each. The way we selected our victims was as follows: we had two SS doctors on duty at Auschwitz to examine the incoming transports of prisoners. The prisoners would be marched by one of the doctors who would make spot decisions as they walked by. Those who were fit for work were sent into the Camp. Others were sent immediately to the extermination plants.

Children of tender years were invariably exterminated since by reason of their youth they were unable to work. Still another improvement we made over Treblinka was that at Treblinka the victims almost always knew that they were to be exterminated and at Auschwitz we endeavored to fool the victims into thinking that they were to go through a delousing process. Of course, frequently they realized our true intentions and we sometimes had riots and difficulties due to that fact. Very frequently women would hide their children under the clothes but of course when we found them we would send the children in to be exterminated. We were required to carry out these exterminations in secrecy but of course the foul and nauseating stench from the continuous burning of bodies permeated the entire area and all of the people living in the surrounding communities knew that exterminations were going on at Auschwitz.

8. We received from time to time special prisoners from the local Gestapo office. The SS doctors killed such prisoners by injections of benzine. Doctors had orders to write ordinary death certificates and could put down any reason at all for the cause of death.

9. From time to time we conducted medical experiments on women inmates, including sterilization and experiments relating to cancer. Most of the people who died under these experiments had already been condemned to death by the Gestapo....

Source: Rudolf Franz Ferdinand Hoess, "Affidavit, 5 April 1946," in *Trial of the Major War Criminals Before the International Military Tribunal, Nuremberg, 14 November 1945–1 October 1946* (Nuremberg, 1949).

- Did Hoess in 1946 seem more remorseful or proud of his work administering death camps?
- Hoess describes doctors as participants in murder. How can you explain such behavior on the part of medical professionals who had taken the Hippocratic oath to "do no harm"?

SOURCE 26.2

A Woman's Experience in the Gulag, 1967

Eugenia Ginzburg, an idealistic communist, university instructor in literature and history, journalist, and 30-year-old mother of two was arrested in 1937 by the Soviet secret police and charged with anti-Soviet terrorism for not denouncing a colleague. She spent two years in various prisons and sixteen years in a labor camp in the far northeast of Russia, one of hundreds in the gulag, as the prison camp system was called. Together with other women charged with political crimes, she did hard labor felling timber in all weather until a sympathetic doctor invited her to serve as a nurse—her chief qualification was that she knew Latin. About 15 million people, or 8 percent of the Soviet

population, entered the gulag, most of them during the late 1930s and 1940s. The arrests in the late 1930s included 35,000 officers of the Soviet Red Army, affecting its performance in combat in WWII.

I only remember the ferocious wind, the forty-degree frost, the appalling weight of the pick, and the wild, irregular thumping of one's heart. At one o'clock we were marched back for dinner. More stumbling in and out of snowdrifts, more shouts and threats from the guards whenever we fell out of line. Back in the camp, we received our longed-for piece of bread and soup, and were allowed half an hour to huddle around the stove in the hope of absorbing enough warmth to last us halfway back to the field. After we had toiled again with our picks and spades till late in the evening, Senka [a guard] would come and survey what we had done and abuse us for not doing more. How could the assignment ever be completed if we spoiled women fulfilled only thirty per cent of the norm? ... Finally, a night's rest, full of nightmares, and the dreaded banging of a hammer on an iron rail which was the signal for a new day to begin.

It was the winter of 1939–c40....

... [O]ur life in the forest became one of famine. "Eighteen per cent—that's all the takings for today," he [another guard] would say gloomily, and with a sidelong glance at his escort, put this figure down against mine and Galya's names.

After receiving the morsel of bread corresponding to our "output" we were led out next day to our place of work, literally staggering from weakness. We divided the morsel into two parts, eating one in the morning with boiling water and the other in the forest, sprinkled with snow.

Source: Eugenia Semyonovna Ginzburg, *Journey into the Whirlwind*, trans. Paul Stevenson and Max Hayward (New York, 1967).

- How did Ginzburg's university education and status as an intellectual help her and hurt her in the gulag?
- What seems to have mattered most to Ginzburg during her imprisonment, judging from this passage in her memoir?

SOURCE 26.3

Franklin Roosevelt, Presidential Proclamation 2525, 1941

Sources 26.3 and 26.4 concern the legal foundation of the United States' internment of Japanese Americans after Pearl Harbor. About 110,000 people, nearly two-thirds of them U.S. citizens, were required to leave their homes for internment camps operated by the U.S. Army in the American West. They lived in isolated locations, often in army-style barracks behind barbed-wire fences, for three years or more. About 4,000 were released to attend college and 22,000 to join the U.S. Army. Court challenges to the internment policy, based on the fact that Japanese Americans were not charged with any crimes yet deprived of their liberty, reached the Supreme Court. In the *Korematsu v. United States* decision of late 1944, the Supreme Court upheld the policy as "a military necessity" by a 6–3 vote. In 1988, Congress passed a law awarding every internment survivor $20,000 as compensation for wrongful imprisonment.

Whereas it is provided by Section 21 of Title 50 of the United States Code ... as follows: "Whenever there is a declared war between the United States and any foreign nation or government, or any invasion or predatory incursion is perpetrated, attempted, or threatened against the territory of the United States by any foreign nation or government, and the President makes public proclamation of the event, all natives, citizens, denizens, or subjects of the hostile nation or government, being of the age of fourteen years and upward, who shall be within the United States and not actually naturalized, shall be liable to be apprehended, restrained, secured, and removed as alien enemies."

PROCLAMATION

Now, Therefore, I, Franklin D. Roosevelt, as *President* of the United States, and as Commander in Chief of the Army and Navy of the United States, do hereby make public proclamation to all whom it may concern that an invasion has been perpetrated upon the territory of the United States by the Empire of Japan.

CONDUCT TO BE OBSERVED BY ALIEN ENEMIES

And, acting under and by virtue of the authority vested in me by the Constitution of the United States and the said sections of the United States Code, I do hereby further proclaim and direct that the conduct to be observed on the part of the United States toward all natives, citizens, denizens or subjects of the Empire of Japan being of the age of fourteen years and upwards who shall be within the United States or within any territories in any way subject to the jurisdiction of the United States and not actually naturalized, who for the purpose of this Proclamation and under such sections of the United States Code are termed alien enemies, shall be as follows:

All alien enemies are enjoined to preserve the peace towards the United States and to refrain from crime against the public safety, and from violating the laws of the United States and of the States and Territories thereof: and to refrain from actual hostility or giving information, aid or comfort to the enemies of the United States or interfering by word or deed with the defense of the United States or the political processes and public opinions

thereof: and to comply strictly with the regulations which are hereby or which may be from time to time promulgated by the President.

Source: Franklin D. Roosevelt, Presidential Proclamation 2525: Alien Enemies—Japanese (1941).

Franklin Roosevelt, Executive Order 9066, 1942

Whereas the successful prosecution of the war requires every possible protection against espionage and against sabotage to national-defense material, national-defense premises, and national-defense utilities....

Now, therefore, by virtue of the authority vested in me as President of the United States, and Commander in Chief of the Army and Navy, I hereby authorize and direct the Secretary of War, and the Military Commanders whom he may from time to time designate, whenever he or any designated Commander deems such action necessary or desirable, to prescribe military areas in such places and of such extent as he or the appropriate Military Commander may determine, from which any or all persons may be excluded, and with respect to which, the right of any person to enter, remain in, or leave shall be subject to whatever restrictions the Secretary of War or the appropriate Military Commander may impose in his discretion. The Secretary of War is hereby authorized to provide for residents of any such area who are excluded therefrom, such transportation, food, shelter, and other accommodations as may be necessary, in the judgment of the Secretary of War or the said Military Commander, and until other arrangements are made, to accomplish the purpose of this order.

I hereby further authorize and direct the Secretary of War and the said Military Commanders to take such other steps as he or the appropriate Military Commander may deem advisable to enforce compliance with the restrictions applicable to each Military area hereinabove authorized to be designated, including the use of Federal troops and other Federal Agencies, with authority to accept assistance of state and local agencies.

I hereby further authorize and direct all Executive Departments, independent establishments and other Federal Agencies, to assist the Secretary of War or the said Military Commanders in carrying out this Executive Order, including the furnishing of medical aid, hospitalization, food, clothing, transportation, use of land, shelter, and other supplies, equipment, utilities, facilities, and services.

Source: Franklin D. Roosevelt, Executive Order 9066 (1942).

• **President Roosevelt, while in many matters a defender of civil rights, ordered the imprisonment of U.S. citizens of Japanese descent. What**

- justification for this policy did his executive order offer?
- These documents are written in dense "legalese." Why?

SOURCE 26.5

The Nanjing Massacre, 1937–1938

In November–December of 1937, the Chinese government and army withdrew from the capital city of Nanjing. After a few days' siege, the Japanese imperial army entered the city, commanded by a prince of the emperor's family. In the next six weeks, the Japanese murdered at least 200,000 Chinese and raped at least 20,000 women and girls. Known at the time as the Rape of Nanking, this was one of the worst atrocities of World War II. In 1948, one Japanese general involved was hanged for war crimes; the prince was granted immunity from trial as a member of the imperial family. The Nanjing Massacre remains a bone of contention in Sino-Japanese relations to this day. The following accounts are among hundreds of testimonials from foreign residents of Nanjing.

222. January 30, a family moved home from the Sericulture Building into a house at 25 Er Tiao Hsiang because of the order to leave the camps [maintained by a committee of foreigners in an effort to protect Chinese]. That night three Japanese soldiers broke down the fence in the back, came around the house and knocked on the front door.... One man carried a sword, one a rifle, and the third was without arms.... They searched the place for money and then the man with the sword raped a 12 year old girl and the other two raped an old woman. The soldiers left about midnight. So the family moved back to camp on the 31st....

223. February 1. This morning at 6:30 a group of women gathered a second time to greet Dr. Bates when he left the University. They told him they could not go home. Last evening Japanese soldiers came and demanded to have a chance to rape the girls. The two girls objected and the soldiers bayoneted them to death. The woman says there is no use going home. If they are going to be killed at home they might just as well be killed at the camp by soldiers attempting to drive them out on February 4....

227. February 1. This afternoon about 2:30 a child came running to our house to tell Mr. Forster and myself that soldiers were after women in a house near us next to Overseas Building. We ran there and were admitted by a Chinese family. They pointed to a bedroom door which was locked but when no response was made to our knocking we smashed the door and found two Japanese soldiers in the room. One was reclining on the bed and the other sitting by the bed. The girl was on the bed between them and the wall. One soldier immediately jumped for his belt and pistol and went out through a hole in the wall. But the other one had his trousers down and was so drunk he could not get away quickly and moreover left his belt so his pants would not stay up. We had to help him out through the hole in the wall. Out on the road he wanted to shake hands. Mr. Forster ran ahead to find a military police while I walked behind the soldier. We delivered him to the two sentries at the opening of Shanghai Road where it joins Chung Shan Lu. We were told that the girl was raped before we got there....

230. January 29, a woman returned home, aged 22. Her husband had been bayoneted by [a] Japanese soldier and died several days before. When she herself returned home to No. 2 Shan Pei Lu on January 29, she was raped by Japanese soldiers three times.

231. January 30, a woman aged 45 returned to her home at South Gate but four Japanese soldiers came to her home, looted and wanted beautiful girls. As a result, they took away her registration card and beat her.

Source: *Documents on the Rape of Nanking*, ed. Timothy Brook (Ann Arbor, MI, 2002).

- These testimonials were among the evidence used in war crimes trials after Japan's surrender. What might have led courts to consider them as credible evidence?
- Historian Jonathan Spence wrote that there can be no explanation of the behavior of the Japanese army at Nanjing, whereas historian Hans van de Ven thought that failures in the Japanese logistical system, brutalization and exhaustion of Japanese troops in training and fighting, and a breakdown of discipline were the "main causes." Do you agree with either judgment?

QUESTIONS FOR COMPARISON

1. How can you account for the prevalence of the imprisonment, injury, and slaughter of civilians in World War II?

2. Perpetrators of war crimes in World War II sometimes claimed their actions were justifiable for military reasons. Is there reason to believe imprisonments and atrocities improved military performance?

3. What are the main differences among these instances of imprisonment and atrocity?

4. To what extent does racism appear to be a factor in the conduct of governments or armies in their treatment of civilians?

CHRONOLOGY

1949
Stalin acquires
nuclear weapons;
NATO is formed;
Mao Zedong establishes
People's Republic of China

1956
Uprising in Hungary
crushed by Soviet
Red army

Oct. 1962
Cuban
missile crisis

1975
End of Vietnam War

1947
India wins
independence
from Britain

1949
Indonesia becomes
independent from
the Netherlands

1956
Suez Crisis shows
weakness of Britain
and France

1968
Soviet invasion of
Czechoslovakia

1975–2002
Angolan Civil War

1979–1989
Soviet-Afghan
War

1945
Start of
Cold War

1948
Berlin
airlift

1950–1953
Korean War

1961
Construction
of Berlin Wall
begins

1962
End of Algerian
war for independence

1945–1949
Chinese Civil War

1954
Vietnam is
divided between
north and south

1955
Bandung conference
of non-aligned nations

The Cold War and Decolonization

1945 to 1991

N o Kum Sok was born in 1932 in the harshly ruled Japanese colony of Korea. Unlike most Koreans then, he had plenty to eat. In his childhood, No's family had books and magazines with photos of cars and houses that convinced him he would like to live in the United States. No's father, a willing collaborator with the Japanese and a manager in a chemical company, ensured his son learned Japanese, which soon became the only permissible language in all Korean schools. In 1940, Japan decreed that all Koreans must take Japanese names, and at age 8 No became Okamura Kyoshi. By age 13, he identified so strongly with Japan's war effort that he tried to volunteer to be a kamikaze pilot for the Japanese air force (his father intervened). He recovered his Korean name and identity in 1945 when World War II ended and Japan withdrew from Korea. Decolonization had come to Korea, but so too had the Cold War.

The Soviet Red Army occupied northern Korea, and soon installed hand-picked communists to rule a new Soviet zone. No's family, collaborators with defeated Japan, lost everything. His mother sold her furs and hawked snacks on the street to get by. Early in his teens, No began lying about his

1986
Chernobyl
disaster

1991
Collapse of
USSR

Nov. 9, 1989
Fall of the
Berlin Wall

Costs of the Korean War The Korean War resulted in at least 100,000 orphans. These youngsters, huddled in a rail yard in Seoul in 1950, might well be among them. Seoul endured repeated battles and sustained massive damage in 1950–1951.

FOCUS QUESTIONS

1. What competing visions of international security did the United States and USSR advance in the wake of World War II?

2. How was the Cold War waged through ideology and violent conflicts?

3. What led to the collapse of the USSR?

4. What were the causes and results of the third pulse of decolonization?

5. What were the main legacies of decolonization in Africa and Asia?

family background, pretending he didn't know Japanese, and hiding his interest in baseball, which was strongly associated with Japan. He enrolled in the military at age 17 some ten months before the Korean War began. Thanks to a helpful history teacher, he avoided assignment to the North Korean infantry and trained to be a pilot. By age 19, he was the youngest pilot in the North Korean air force. He flew over 100 combat missions. against experienced and well-equipped American pilots, he did his best to avoid dogfights. Throughout his pilot career, he pretended to be a devoted communist, denouncing American imperialism constantly, while secretly hoping to escape North Korea for the United States.

The Korean War ended in 1953 in a cease-fire. Two months later, taking a giant risk, 21-year-old No flew his Soviet-made fighter jet to South Korea and landed at a U.S. Air Force base. Escaping his North Korean squadron was a small miracle but not without consequences. To discourage defections, the North Korean military made it a policy to kill the friends and family of anyone who fled. While American military and intelligence officers were debriefing No and teaching him English, his closest friends and immediate superiors in North Korea were executed.

No finally got his wish, arriving in the United States at age 22. The U.S. government brought him to Washington and used him in propaganda and public relations efforts. In 1957, it arranged his entry to the University of Delaware as a 25-year old freshman engineering major…He changed his name once more, to Ken Rowe. A helpful history professor with political connections got Rowe permanent resident status. He launched a long career in the defense industry, helping to design the hardware with which the U.S. military confronted its Cold War enemies. He died a millionaire in 2023.

From ages 13 to 21, No Kum Sok/Okamura Kyoshi/Ken Rowe was perpetually in danger. His identity, like his name, was in flux. He lived a lie in order to survive. No one in the world experienced decolonization and the Cold War exactly like young No Kum Sok, but hundreds of millions of people found themselves living dangerously as a result of these intertwined phenomena—the subjects of this chapter. And several million, like No's friends, died prematurely because they were in the wrong place at the wrong time.

The **Cold War** was a global strategic and geopolitical struggle linked to capitalist and communist ideologies, rival economic orders, and big changes in military technology. While its main actors were the United States and the USSR, each recruited many countries into rival alliance systems, forming what were often called western and eastern blocs. The conflict dominated international politics between 1945 and 1991. It divided Korea and Germany, and it added a dangerous combustibility to civil wars and other conflicts, each of which had its own logic, in countries such as Greece, China, Korea, Vietnam, Mozambique, Angola, Ethiopia, Somalia, Chile, Guatemala, El Salvador, and Nicaragua. The international system no longer featured multiple great powers but became a "bipolar system," with two superpowers, the United States and the USSR, more formidable than all the rest. The Cold War was simultaneously a struggle between those superpowers and a series of regional struggles in which the superpowers intervened.

Within societies, the Cold War exerted strong pressures. It helped Stalin and his successors justify continuing dictatorship in the USSR. It brought harsh divisions and increased regimentation to life in the United States. The Cold War's pressures were also psychological, as nuclear weapons buildups brought the possibility of instant annihilation. Its tensest moments are the closest the human race has yet come to self-destruction.

The Cold War was also linked to the spurt of decolonization occurring between about 1945 and 1980. Dozens of countries won their independence as empires crumbled in Asia, Africa, the Middle East, and the Caribbean. Many independence movements sought assistance from one of the superpowers during their liberation struggles from European colonial rule, and after independence leaders of new countries often chose to align themselves—or felt pressure to align themselves—with a superpower. At the same time, both the United States and USSR grew increasingly interested these struggles, seeing new potential allies. In pursuing their respective interests, both the newly independent countries and the two superpowers connected these two large-scale political processes—the Cold War and decolonization. The two are coupled in yet another way: the end of the Soviet Union was itself a chapter in the story of decolonization. It liberated six Soviet satellite countries in Eastern Europe, and turned 14 former units of the USSR into independent countries. So the Soviet collapse in 1989–1991 marked both the end of the Cold War and an after-echo of decolonization. For clarity's sake, this chapter will present the overlapping stories of the Cold War and decolonization one after the other rather than at the same time.

COLD WAR ORIGINS: FRACTURES IN THE WORLD WAR II ALLIANCE

Although historians usually date the onset of the Cold War to 1946 or 1947, in some respects, it began before World War II ended. The Allied coalition, although on balance highly successful, showed strain from early on. As noted in the previous chapter, Stalin thought the United States and United Kingdom deliberately delayed opening a second front against Germany. Frictions intensified as peace finally arrived and the victorious Allies began to refashion the world's political and economic systems. As they set about this task, the interconnectedness of the Global web made conflict among them almost impossible to avoid. Policy makers in Washington, London, and Moscow cared about politics, economics, and ideologies in almost every corner of the world, giving them endless opportunities for quarrels.

SECURITY CONCERNS

The most difficult of those quarrels concerned security. After long and terrible years of warfare, each of the victors wanted an international system that would protect its citizens, borders, and interests. The Soviets and the Americans had sharply different ideas of how to achieve that.

SOVIET SECURITY AND EASTERN EUROPE
When World War II ended in 1945, the Soviet army occupied the eastern half of Europe including the eastern third of Germany. Stalin had no intention of leaving the fate of all this territory to its own citizens. His strongest commitment in foreign policy was that the USSR should never again be traumatized by invasion. He wanted all of Eastern Europe, including what was to become East Germany, as a buffer. Northern Iran, which his troops also controlled in 1945 but from which he withdrew, mattered far less to him.

Stalin's position on security, although partly a result of his longstanding paranoia, had a rational basis. The USSR had lost about 18,000 to 20,000 citizens daily during World War II, albeit many of them from Stalin's own brutalities. In mortality terms, this amounted to the equivalent of a Pearl Harbor every three hours for the duration of the war. Aware of massive invasions by Napoleon Bonaparte's forces in 1812 and by Germany in 1914 and 1941, most Soviet citizens would have agreed with Stalin: it was wise to control eastern Europe so any future invasions could be checked before reaching Soviet soil.

Accordingly, Stalin extended the borders of the USSR. In 1945, he annexed small slices of Romania and Czechoslovakia. (He had already annexed the Baltic countries—Latvia, Lithuania, and Estonia—and the eastern half of Poland in 1940–1941). Then, in the years 1946–1948, he found willing puppets—or, in his view, loyal and reliable communists—to govern Poland, Czechoslovakia, Hungary, Romania, Bulgaria, and East Germany. By 1949, he had consolidated a new Soviet empire in Eastern Europe.

Territorial empire was a central feature of Stalin's plans for Soviet security, but he also maintained the wartime economic orientation toward military production and promoted communist ideology abroad, especially in East Asia and Europe. Stalin ordered the removal of huge amounts of machinery to the USSR from Eastern Europe, especially Hungary and East Germany, to bolster Soviet heavy industry. Soviet citizens made do with less in the way of consumer goods, even food, so that more investment could go toward weaponry. Supporting communists as best he could in Korea, China, and Europe also appealed to Stalin: if they succeeded in winning power, they might become reliable Soviet allies.

THE U.S. VISION OF SECURITY The American leadership, however, preferred a different approach to international security. The United States, in comparison to the USSR, had suffered lightly in World War II and had big oceans between it and any potential enemy. Territorial empire held little appeal. Led now by Harry Truman, who became president when Roosevelt died in April 1945, the U.S. government favored a system of collective security anchored by the United Nations (UN), founded in 1945 as an improved version of the League of Nations. Its structure, with a Security Council including only five powers—the United States, the USSR, Britain, France, and China—promised outcomes agreeable to the United States as long as the latter three remained American allies. In any case, the United States had the world's largest navy and air force. Its mobile military was a more flexible instrument, with greater global reach, than that of the USSR, which was composed mainly of infantry and tanks. The UN, combined with the overwhelming power of the U.S. Navy and Air Force and the American monopoly on nuclear weapons, would theoretically ensure international security for all—in forms that suited American interests.

CLASHING VISIONS These incompatible visions of international security defeated any hopes of prolonging Allied cooperation. At a conference in February 1945, held at **Yalta** in Soviet Crimea, Stalin, Roosevelt, and Churchill agreed to divide Germany when the war ended and to give the USSR part of the Japanese island of Sakhalin.

They formally agreed on free elections in the eastern European countries controlled by the Soviet army, but it would become clear that Stalin would only permit elections that returned governments subservient to him. The wartime Allies resumed discussions in July 1945 at Potsdam outside Berlin, but they could agree on little besides details of the treatment of a defeated Germany and the requirement of absolute surrender from Japan. The fate of eastern Europe was the biggest unresolved issue: the United States and the United Kingdom wanted free elections but were not prepared to try to force the Soviet army out of the region.

Truman and Stalin also clashed over China's future. After Japan's defeat, China's warring factions—Mao Zedong's communists against the nationalists, or the Guomindang—stepped up their fighting in the **Chinese Civil War** (1945–1949, discussed below). Each side appealed for outside help and received it, one from the USSR and the other from the United States. The rivalry between the USSR and US also involved Korea. After the Japanese withdrew in 1945, the victorious Allies divided Korea in two, as we saw at the outset of this chapter. So the security ambitions of the two superpowers were fundamentally at odds both in eastern Europe and East Asia.

Even the United States and the United Kingdom, which had collaborated effectively during World War II, discovered that they had postponed some important disagreements. The greatest of these was the future of the British Empire, which Churchill dearly wished to protect but Roosevelt and Truman did not. Drained by war and in need of American money, food, and oil, Britain often had to bow, if grudgingly, to American wishes in matters of security, empire, and decolonization. Diverging geopolitical and security ambitions among the USSR, United States, and United Kingdom fractured the wartime alliance.

THE WORLD ECONOMY

In addition to their differences on international security, the United States and the USSR held incompatible ambitions, rooted in both self-interest and ideology, for the world economy. The United States emerged from the war with the world's most competitive industries and healthiest financial sector. Its leadership supported an international economy with free trade and free flows of capital, lightly regulated by international institutions such as the International Monetary Fund and what would become the World Bank. These institutions anchored the Bretton Woods system, named for the resort in New Hampshire where a conference in 1944 hammered out agreements to manage monetary policy, currency rates, and debt, with the aim of preventing a return of the Great Depression. In light of the Cold War and the presumed appeal of Soviet-style communism to hungry and defeated people eager for new hope, the United States also decided to help rebuild the economies of Japan and West Germany and try to convert its former enemies into economic and political partners.

This capitalist vision did not suit Stalin and the USSR. The Soviet economy was uncompetitive internationally. Its remarkable growth since 1929 had derived from the enormous, inefficient use of raw materials and the ruthless exploitation of labor. It produced little that anyone with a choice wished to buy. Stalin preferred to shield his economy from the pitiless competition of the international market and divide the world into spheres of control, much as the Germans and Japanese had wished to do in the 1930s. In the early stages of the Cold War, the USSR oversaw a miniature form of economic globalization within the territorial empire Stalin had created.

The rival visions of the world economy also had an ideological component. U.S. officials, and American culture generally, endorsed the idea that free markets underpinned other freedoms and were a prerequisite to both prosperity and liberty. This concept had many supporters around the world, especially among those who benefitted the most from market transactions. In contrast, Soviet economic ideology presented free markets as an invitation for the rich to exploit the working classes, as Karl Marx had argued a century before. According to Marx, Lenin, and the official Soviet view, capitalism would inevitably crumble as a result of such exploitation, to be followed eventually by the triumph of communism— heralding prosperity, freedom from exploitation, and social justice. That vision had won new adherents during the mass unemployment of the Great Depression of the 1930s. It also made sense to many in the colonized world who thought free markets in an international economy seemed likely to doom Africa and Asia to everlasting subordination. The United States' and the USSR's opposing ideologies and self-interests made for conflicting plans for the global economy.

Once the Axis menace disappeared in 1945, there was nothing to bind the United States and the United Kingdom to the USSR and much to divide them. So within months after the defeats of Germany and Japan, the victorious Allies were allies no longer. They resigned themselves to grim competition and tried to keep it from erupting into outright war.

THE CHARACTER AND COURSE OF THE COLD WAR

Although the United States and the USSR never engaged each other in actual combat during the Cold War—except on a tiny scale between fighter planes over Korea—they competed fiercely. Each side planned to outlast rather than outright destroy the other, confident that time was on its side. Moreover, nuclear weapons made outright warfare too dangerous for everyone. The Cold War was fought by other means than head-to-head combat.

STRATEGIES

The guiding Cold War strategies of both the United States and USSR were based on outlasting the opponent. The American version of this strategy, called containment, was formulated in 1946 by George Kennan, a U.S. diplomat and student of Russian history. The **containment strategy** rested on the faith that Soviet communism would ultimately collapse if the United States prevented communism from expanding elsewhere. It reflected American confidence that people everywhere would prefer greater political freedom and material prosperity than the Soviet system seemed likely to provide. It also reflected Kennan's view that control of major industrial zones was the key to power in international politics; the United States and its allies controlled four of these zones, while Stalin had only one.

The Soviet strategy rested on a supposed law of history according to Marxism: that capitalism would inevitably collapse under the weight of its own contradictions— specifically due to the rise of a militant, alienated working class that would recognize that its true interest required a revolution to usher in communism. Until that day, the USSR could coexist in peaceful competition with its foes. Not everyone believed this doctrine in the USSR, but everyone pursuing a political career either did or pretended to do so. So although ideologically at odds, and bitter rivals, both the United States and the USSR pursued strategies of patience, believing time was on their side.

Rather than strike militarily, both tried in several ways to hasten the collapse of their foe. They built up their armed forces, including nuclear arsenals, in readiness for actual war. They mounted propaganda campaigns aimed both at their own citizens and people all over the world. They competed for influence, especially in Europe and East Asia. They undertook "covert actions," using spy services to undermine politicians and governments opposed to them. And they supported rival factions in local and regional wars around the world. The most dangerous of these undertakings was their nuclear arms race.

NUCLEAR WEAPONS

Both the United States and the USSR invested heavily in their militaries during the Cold War, including their nuclear arsenals. From 1945 to 1949, the United States enjoyed a nuclear weapons monopoly. Then, thanks to good spies and better physicists, Stalin acquired atomic weapons in 1949. In the same year, communists came to power in China, deepening the United States' anxieties and fueling its enthusiasm for nuclear weapons. Thereafter, the United States and the USSR built thousands of nuclear bombs and missiles, enough to wipe out the human race several times over. Britain (from 1952), France (1960), and China (1964) tested nuclear weapons too, although they never built arsenals anywhere near the size of the Soviet or American ones. Of the roughly 2,000 nuclear tests conducted during the Cold War, about 1,000 were American, 700 Soviet, 200 French, 45 British, and 45 Chinese. Until a treaty banned atmospheric testing in 1963, most tests—about 500—involved nuclear explosions that sprinkled toxic radiation downwind of test sites.

Nuclear weapons reinforced the Cold War strategies of patience. With the development of hydrogen bombs— many times more powerful than the original atomic bombs—by the mid-1950s, everyone knew that all-out nuclear war would annihilate a large share of the human race. The superpowers avoided war in part because their leaders understood that neither country could survive nuclear war. Once armed with nuclear weapons, neither side had any incentive to disarm or use nuclear weapons. The bombs' value lay in what was called **deterrence**— the certainty that any country that launched a nuclear attack would be destroyed in a retaliatory attack. Both superpowers felt it was vital to their security to have giant arsenals of nuclear weapons and, paradoxically, equally vital that the arsenals should never be used.

Nonetheless, at times, the world was a whisker away from self-annihilation. A close call came during the **Cuban missile crisis** of October 1962. In 1959, a revolution led by Fidel Castro had succeeded in ousting a corrupt, pro-American military government in Cuba. After a failed U.S.-backed attempt to overthrow Castro in 1961, the Soviets, eager to prevent another U.S. invasion of Cuba and to enhance their own strategic position, shipped nuclear missiles to the island, only 90 miles from Florida. When U.S. president John Kennedy insisted on the removal of the missiles, two anxious weeks followed in which the world faced the very real possibility of a massive nuclear exchange. In the end, the Soviets chose to avoid the worst and removed their missiles, averting nuclear war.

Several other close calls came as a result of malfunctions in weapons systems. In 1966, a U.S. Air Force plane on a routine flight collided with a tanker plane during a mid-air refueling over the southeastern coast of Spain. It accidentally released four hydrogen bombs, whose non-nuclear explosives detonated, but not the nuclear devices. At least five times during the years 1979–1983, military officers of either the United States or the USSR were briefly convinced that enemy missiles had already launched, typically due to radar or computer malfunctions. They prepared to unleash devastating counter-attacks, but in each case received more accurate information just in time. Despite these brushes with planetary disaster, the nuclear arms race continued amid occasional arms-reduction talks.

The fear of atomic obliteration became part of everyday life during the Cold War. It was the primary way that ordinary people in the USSR, China, the United States, and Europe experienced the conflict. Governments sought to moderate that fear with civil defense systems intended to improve survival chances in the event of nuclear war. These ranged from extra-deep subway systems built after 1950 in the USSR and Eastern Europe to "duck-and-cover" drills for schoolchildren in the United States, adopted in the early 1950s. By the 1960s, several societies had built bomb shelters in public buildings and stocked them with food and water. Switzerland required all citizens to maintain bomb shelters in their homes. Chinese city-dwellers dug (by hand) sprawling underground systems of tunnels and shelters. None of these measures would have helped

The Folimanka bunker Like many cities, in the 1950s and 1960s the Czechoslovak capital of Prague prepared for nuclear attacks that never came by digging and equipping underground bomb shelters. Prague had 768 of them, as deep as four stories beneath street level, with space for 150,000 people. This is the air filtration system of the Folimanka bunker, one of Prague's biggest, with space for 1,300 people and supplies for three days.

much in the event of nuclear war, but they provided some modest comfort for anxious citizens. And that was a large part of the point.

PROPAGANDA

The threat of nuclear attack by a devious enemy featured in both U.S. and Soviet propaganda. The United States sought to portray itself as a shining city on a hill, often using that biblical phrase, in which democracy, freedom, justice, and prosperity prevailed in the land of opportunity. The government underwrote hundreds of documentary films illustrating the merits of U.S. technology or democratic governance. It did its best to emphasize the many dark parts of Soviet life, such as the gulag, the vast network of prison camps for political dissenters; the routine surveillance of citizens; and the lack of political rights and economic freedoms. The U.S. government created offices specifically charged with spreading these messages and set up radio stations, such as Radio Free Europe, that broadcast news to communist countries. They did not need to bend the truth to make life in the USSR or Eastern Europe look grim, although they sometimes did so anyway.

For its part, the USSR's propaganda machinery tried to paint communism as the wave of the world's future and the United States as a menace to peace and justice. The USSR was, or would shortly be, a workers' paradise in which equality was triumphant, the exploitation normal in capitalism was banished, and everyone was content and well fed. Given actual conditions in the USSR and Eastern Europe, this portrayal required routine dishonesty. The obvious gap between daily realities and official pronouncements provided citizens in communist countries with endless opportunities for sarcastic humor. For example: under capitalism, man exploits his fellow man, but under communism it is the reverse. In the long run, as the gap persisted, it undermined what confidence people might have had in official information. But Soviet propaganda succeeded easily when it drew attention to racism and racial segregation in the United States and in British and French colonies—no exaggeration was required to make the routine discrimination and occasional racist violence plain to see. Indeed, one of the reasons the American government eventually came to support civil rights for Black Americans in the 1950s was to reduce the impact of Soviet propaganda. The Soviets also often succeeded with audiences around the world when painting the United States as a militaristic danger to world peace, especially amid American-led wars in Korea and Vietnam (discussed below).

China relied heavily on propaganda aimed mainly at Chinese audiences. The main goal was to win the allegiance of the masses for Mao and the Chinese Communist Party (CCP) and to encourage citizens to betray anyone whose loyalties lay elsewhere. Chinese propaganda also vilified Cold War enemies, mainly the United States until the Sino-Soviet split (see below) and thereafter the USSR as well. Because the target audience was usually

The "Little Red Book" This poster from 1967 exhorts revolutionary workers to unite behind the ideas of Chinese leader Mao Zedong. They are holding up copies of the "little red book" of quotations from Mao. By the 1960s, China was competing with the USSR to support communist revolution around the world.

illiterate, Chinese propaganda relied on simple slogans and plays, and it raised poster-making to a high art.

A DIVIDED EUROPE

The big prizes of the Cold War lay in Europe and East Asia, regions devastated by combat in World War II, in political turmoil in the war's aftermath, and yet potentially valuable because of their location, resources, and industry. In Europe, as Stalin was consolidating power in Eastern Europe in 1945–1949, Truman, countered what he and most Americans regarded as Soviet aggression. He made security guarantees to Greece and Turkey in the **Truman Doctrine** announced in 1946, and he helped Greek nationalists defeat an insurgent communist army in the Greek Civil War, which ended in 1949. He delivered large flows of economic aid to western Europe through the Marshall Plan, begun in 1947–1948. He offered Marshall Plan funds to countries in Eastern Europe too, confident they would be refused; Stalin, as expected, told their leaders to reject the aid. The U.S. government also led the formation of the **North Atlantic Treaty Organization** (NATO, 1949), a military alliance binding the United States, Canada, and most of western Europe, intended mainly to check Soviet ambitions. When NATO embraced West Germany in 1955, the Soviets responded by organizing an alliance system called the Warsaw Pact involving seven Eastern European satellites.

By the end of 1948, the lines in Europe were clearly drawn. Eastern and western Europe were divided politically, ideologically, and militarily by what Churchill called the iron curtain, running from the head of the Adriatic Sea to the shores of the Baltic, and right through Germany. The one exception was Berlin, well within the Soviet zone, which by agreement was divided into an eastern half under Soviet control and a western half occupied by American, British, and French forces. Cold War Europe was tense, occasionally marked by crises but generally stable, after 1948. The biggest of these crises were sparked by tensions in Berlin or by uprisings of Eastern European populations against Soviet domination.

CRISES IN BERLIN, 1948 AND 1961 The first Berlin crisis began in 1948 when Stalin, alarmed by the Marshall Plan and other measures such as the merging of the United States, British and French occupation zones into a single West Germany, ordered a blockade of West

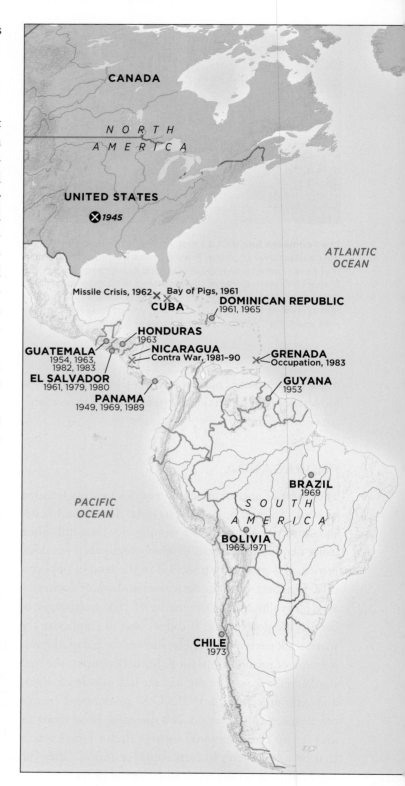

Berlin in hopes that his adversaries would abandon it. The blockade left 2.5 million West Berliners with no sources of food, fuel, or electricity. The United States and the United Kingdom, however, responded with the Berlin Airlift,

The Cold War World, 1946–1991 The Cold War was a global contest in which the world's superpowers—the United States and the Soviet Union—asserted their strength repeatedly in Africa, Asia, and Latin America. The Cold War was particularly tense in Europe, most notably Berlin, and especially violent in East Asia, most notably Korea and Vietnam. The map shows the superpowers' most important military or political interventions, in which they provided arms, money, intelligence, or training to one or another faction in civil wars, coups d'état, or other forms of political struggle.

flying 270,000 loads of supplies into West Berlin over 11 months, earning gratitude from millions of Germans. Stalin concluded his gambit was counter-productive and lifted the blockade.

The second Berlin crisis arose in August 1961. One-fifth of all East German citizens, especially educated youth, had already fled to West Germany. Another 1,500 were leaving every day in Berlin, voting with their feet against communist rule. Encouraged by the Soviet leadership, East German authorities began to build a wall to prevent citizens from leaving. For the next several weeks, incidents at the boundary between East and West Berlin took place almost daily, and a shooting war seemed likely to break out. But cool heads prevailed, and a new reality took hold in Berlin, dominated by a wall that divided families and symbolized the imprisonment of Eastern Europeans within a political system most of them did not want. The two Berlin crises were moments of high anxiety but not violence.

UPRISINGS IN 1953, 1956, AND 1968 Violence flared when Eastern Europeans tried to loosen the Soviet grip on their countries. The first major uprising came in East Germany in 1953. In the 24 largest cities, industrial workers led

The Berlin Wall Children walk along a street in Kreuzberg, West Berlin, in the 1960s. The street was divided in half by the Berlin Wall, whose construction began in 1961.

demonstrations against pay cuts and in favor of free elections. Several hundred thousand people took to the streets and in East Berlin almost toppled the government. Soviet military forces intervened, killing dozens before restoring order. In Poland in 1956, a factory workers' uprising, initially focused on wages and working conditions, met with a similar military response from Polish army units under Soviet command, leaving 50 to 80 people dead. Given that the Soviet system claimed to represent the working classes, revolts led by workers were particularly intolerable to communist party leaders.

A much larger revolt followed later that year in Hungary. Soviet domination there had led to economic decline and strong resentments directed at both the USSR and Hungary's puppet rulers. In October 1956, university students and intellectuals gathered to protest Soviet influence, calling for Hungarian independence. Police fired on the crowds, leading to wider protests and an effort by the Hungarian communist government to enact reforms. These included allowing freedom of expression, permitting political parties other than the communists, dissolving the secret police, and enacting a foreign policy of neutrality. That brought a full-scale invasion by the Soviet army. Some 2,500 Hungarians were killed and another 22,000 imprisoned, while 200,000 escaped to other countries (Many Hungarians expected support from the United Nations or the United States, not least because Radio Free Europe broadcasts told them it would come. It did not, because American leaders feared nuclear war and

The Greek Civil War This photo, from March 1946, shows 24-year-old Elizabeth McNeill (my mother) on Mount Pelion with a band of Greek communist guerillas. Although born in Kentucky, she lived most of her childhood in Greece. Here she was working as an interpreter with the U.S. military attache's office assessing political conditions during the Greek Civil War, in which communist rebels fought a royalist and nationalist government backed by Britain and, after the announcement of the Truman Doctrine in 1947, by the United States. Stalin chose not to support Greece's communists and by 1949 they were defeated.

because the United States, Britain, and France were pre-occupied with a simultaneous drama unfolding in Egypt, the Suez Crisis (covered below).

Czechoslovak efforts at reform in 1968 prompted yet another Soviet invasion. The communist government in Prague, in response to citizen unrest, promised what it called socialism with a human face. In practice, that mainly meant less censorship and more personal and press freedom. That opening, sometimes called the **Prague Spring**, unleashed a torrent of public criticism of the communist system and Soviet domination. The Soviet leadership responded with troops and tanks. They killed between 70 and 140 people despite mostly passive resistance from Czechs and Slovaks.

The brutal suppression of reform efforts in Hungary and Czechoslovakia divided communist parties around the world. Leaders of the USSR's Eastern European satellite states, especially East Germany, eagerly supported the 1968 invasion, knowing that their own power would be at risk if socialism with a human face survived in Czechoslovakia. But the French, Italian, and Finnish communist parties denounced the Soviet invasion of Czechoslovakia. The Chinese foreign minister, Zhou Enlai, compared it to Hitler's invasion of Czechoslovakia in 1939. Albania, a Warsaw Pact member (but not important to Soviet security), withdrew from the alliance in 1968. The USSR never recovered the international prestige it sacrificed in 1956 and 1968 by invading its allies. For Soviet leaders, the forfeited prestige was a price they had to pay. Like Stalin

The Prague Spring Massed demonstrators block Soviet tanks from moving through the streets of Prague in August 1968, during the Prague Spring uprising against Soviet control.

before them, they considered control over Eastern Europe vital for national security.

EAST ASIA AND THE COMMUNIST VICTORY IN CHINA

In East and Southeast Asia, the Cold War began hot with the military victory of the CCP over its Guomindang foes in the years 1945–1949. During the war with Japan (1937–1945), as we've seen, both factions fought one another as much as the Japanese. A quarter of the population had fled Japanese occupied-zones, and now, in 1945, 100 million Chinese tried to walk back home. Famine, banditry, currency inflation, and official corruption plagued the country. The chaos presented an opportunity to anyone who could provide order.

MAO ZEDONG AND THE CHINESE CIVIL WAR

Mao Zedong (1893–1976) was one of the most consequential leaders of the twentieth century. The son of prosperous peasants from the south-central province of Hunan, as a youth he had played a small role in Sun Yatsen's nationalist revolution. While working as a grade-school history teacher in Hunan and then as a librarian at Peking University, he had become interested in socialism, Marxism, and revolution, and he joined the newly formed CCP in 1921.

During the war against Japan, Mao organized guerilla forces and rose to the top of the CCP. In the 1940s, the CCP offered a program shaped by Mao and calculated to appeal to China's 400 million peasants. It resembled the Taiping program of a century before: peasants should take farmland from landlords; social equality should replace Confucian hierarchy; women should live free from male oppression; discipline and morality should replace corruption and decadence; and foreigners should go home. Unlike the Taipings', the CCP program had no Christian components, but it used a different foreign idea, Marxism, to lend it prestige and coherence. Mao's main innovation within Marxism was the argument that peasants could lead a communist revolution, whereas Marx and Lenin had believed only industrial workers could do so.

The message worked: peasants increasingly supported the CCP after 1945, and its armies swelled with recruits from farming villages, half of them teenagers. Peasants under CCP leadership proved to be a determined military force. By the end of 1949, with some modest help from Stalin, the communist forces had driven the Guomindang army to the offshore island of Taiwan. China, now called the People's Republic of China (or PRC) was in the hands of Mao and his lieutenants, and was loosely, and warily, aligned with the USSR.

For Mao and many Chinese, this victory was not only the triumph of the oppressed masses over the upper classes but also of the Chinese people over a century of humiliation imposed by foreign powers, dating back to the Opium Wars of the mid-nineteenth century. As Mao put it in a speech in September 1949, "Our work will go down in the history of mankind, demonstrating that the Chinese people ... have now stood up. The Chinese have always been a great, courageous, and industrious nation. In modern times they have fallen behind due entirely to oppression and exploitation by foreign imperialism and domestic reactionary governments." With the victory of Mao and communism in the Chinese Civil War in 1949, the Cold War became more complex. Now there were two major communist powers, the USSR and the PRC, both anti-American and anti-capitalist, but neither fully trusting the other.

WAR IN KOREA Once China had joined the communist camp in 1949, the United States deepened its involvement in East Asia. A major challenge came in Korea, then a country of about 30 million people. With Japan's defeat in 1945, the status of its former colony was thrown into doubt. Koreans celebrated their independence when Japanese troops left, but by a hasty agreement between the superpowers, as noted above, American forces took control south of the 38th parallel and Soviet soldiers occupied the north. Soviet military occupation was ruthless, especially harsh for the wealthy and for young women. In 1946–1948, nearly a fifth of all Koreans in the Soviet zone headed south of the 38th parallel with whatever they could carry into the American zone. Soviet and American occupying forces sought out suitable Koreans—communists in the north and anti-communists in the south—to help them rule. By 1948, ethnic Koreans had assumed formal power in both north and south, but in each case remained reliant on their superpower patron. Each of the new governments claimed sovereignty over all Korea and denied the legitimacy of the other.

Then, in June 1950, with grudging agreement from both Stalin and Mao, the North Korean leader Kim Il

Sung launched an invasion across the 38th parallel, starting the **Korean War**. The North Korean army did well at first. But the UN resolved to defend South Korea and sent a joint force in July 1950. That UN army, 88 percent of which was American, drove the North Koreans back north, which prompted Mao to send in his battle-hardened Chinese infantry with Soviet air support. It pushed the UN forces south. This retreat, costing many thousands of lives, was the worst moment for the U.S. Army since the American Civil War. The remainder of the Korean War was a battle of attrition until, with Stalin's death in early 1953, new Soviet leaders decided to end the war, overruling Mao and the North Koreans, who still hoped to win. A cease-fire agreement followed. No peace treaty was ever signed, so North and South Korea still officially remain at war today.

Korea suffered tremendous damage as armies rampaged up and down the peninsula. The U.S. Air Force relentlessly bombed North Korean cities—wherever one brick rested on another, according to one American official. By 1952, no significant buildings remained upright in North Korea. The war killed about 7–10 percent of all Koreans, roughly 2–3 million people, mostly civilians. Some 35,000 Americans lost their lives, and perhaps 250,000–400,000 Chinese—including Mao's favorite son, Mao Anying, a decorated war hero killed in a bombing raid.

The Korean War further hardened Cold War divisions in East Asia and indeed worldwide. The United States emerged more concerned about China as a regional threat. China, the USSR, and North Korea, now painfully well informed about the American capacity for bomber offensives, emerged more concerned about what they saw as "imperialist" military superiority. The Korean War boosted economic recovery in Japan, which served as a base for American operations, and brought the United States and Japan closer politically. Yet the Korean War also showed some of the limits to U.S. power. The war had quickly become unpopular among the American population, and the U.S. leadership tried hard to avoid casualties. This led Stalin to say to a Chinese diplomat that "Americans don't know how to fight.... They are fighting with little Korea and already people are weeping in the U.S.A." The United States choice not to use its nuclear weapons and to minimize battle casualties encouraged Mao to consider the United States a "paper tiger." The extraordinarily powerful position in world affairs that the United States had occupied at the end of World War II was already eroding.

WAR IN VIETNAM During the next 25 years it would erode further for many reasons, including the American defeat in the **Vietnam War**. Vietnam had been colonized by France late in the nineteenth century and occupied by Japan during World War II. After the war, France tried to reassert its colonial rule, but in 1954 a Vietnamese force—with some weapons, food, and trucks from the Chinese—crushed the French at Dien Bien Phu. Negotiations followed, and the Geneva Accords of 1954 left Vietnam divided into a communist-nationalist government in the north, led by Ho Chi Minh and aligned with China and the Soviet Union, and an anti-communist state in the south, aligned with the United States. National elections were set for 1956, which seemed sure to result in victory for Ho because his political movement controlled the territory where most Vietnamese lived. Those elections never occurred, because the government of South Vietnam, with U.S. support, refused to take part in a contest it expected to lose. From the mid-1950s onward, the United States crept deeper and deeper into Vietnamese politics and its emerging civil war, supporting an unpopular and corrupt government in South Vietnam to prevent communists from taking over the whole country.

In 1964, after North Vietnamese torpedo boats and a U.S. naval ship clashed off the Vietnam coast, President Lyndon Johnson chose to escalate the struggle. By late 1967, half a million American troops were in Vietnam. The justification for this escalation was the so-called **domino theory**: Johnson worried that if Vietnam went communist, the rest of Southeast Asia would soon follow. The United States and its allies, including the ineffective South Vietnamese government, could not prevail on the ground against determined forces employing guerilla tactics. Ho and the Vietnamese communists recruited millions of peasants, convincing them that communist victory would deliver social justice in the villages and expel foreigners. As in the

Vietnam War Two North Vietnamese women fighters examine wreckage from a downed American plane in 1968. The United States enjoyed vast air superiority and technological advantages, but in this war victory went to the more patient and determined combatant.

Korean War, the United States did most of its damage from the air: it dropped more than three times as much bomb tonnage on Vietnam as it had used in all of World War II. The United States also used chemical defoliants such as Agent Orange on the forests of Vietnam, killing about 10 percent of the country's vegetation.

As it happened, no more dominos fell. The war became unpopular in the United States, especially among young men subject to the draft. The Americans consequently sought an acceptable way out starting in 1968 but could not find one despite years of peace negotiations. In 1973, as U.S. troops left Saigon, the capital of South Vietnam, communist forces began to take control of the entire country. The victors put some 250,000 South Vietnamese who had sided with the Americans into forced labor camps.

Roughly two or three million Vietnamese died in the war between 1954 and 1975—the figures are uncertain and controversial. Another 275,000 Cambodians and 60,000 Laotians lost their lives too. About 59,000 Americans were killed. The war cost the United States dearly in prestige and popularity around the world: it seemed a contest between David and Goliath, with the North Vietnamese showing enormous courage in standing up to a superpower. The war also fueled intense political divisions in the United States between those who wanted to fight on in hopes of victory and those who concluded the war could not be won at an acceptable cost.

Air-Raid Practice Aerial bombing was a routine danger for North Vietnamese during the Vietnam War. Here residents of the capital, Hanoi, prepare to emerge from manholes during an air-raid alert.

After 1975, the Cold War in East Asia stabilized. Crises occasionally flared up, sometimes between Taiwan and the PRC, sometimes on the Korean Peninsula. But none escalated into serious fighting, none had anywhere near the impact of the hot wars in Korea and Vietnam, and none changed the balance of power significantly.

REGIONAL CONFLICTS AND THE COLD WAR

The Cold War intersected with local and regional conflicts beyond Europe and East Asia. The U.S. and Soviet governments backed rival factions in at least 50 local struggles and civil wars, providing weapons, money, training, and other support. The goal was to show resolve and win a new ally, or at least prevent the enemy from winning one. The effects of superpower involvement often included prolonging and intensifying warfare.

WAR IN ANGOLA A major theater was southern Africa, rich in minerals and seemingly up for grabs. In the 1960s and 1970s, Africans sought to end colonial rule in Angola and Mozambique, both Portuguese colonies, and in Rhodesia, a British colony until 1965 and then an independent country run by a tiny white settler minority. Both superpowers judged that at little cost to themselves they could find supporters among southern Africa's independence movements and therefore among its future rulers.

Angola, a colony for nearly 500 years, became Africa's biggest cauldron of Cold War competition. During the 1960s, several rival parties and militias eager to oust Portuguese rule emerged. They found cooperation difficult for two reasons: One of these parties, UNITA, mainly represented the Ovimbundu people of central Angola, and other Angolans feared Ovimbundu domination. The other obstacle was the involvement of foreign powers, whose support enabled groups to fight on even if their popularity within Angola was low. Angola's

War in Angola A poster for the MPLA shows a young mother carrying an automatic rifle—signifying the devotion the faction dsought from ordinary citizens. Supported by the USSR, the MPLA became caught up in a proxy war against the U.S.-backed UNITA.

substantial oil reserves, discovered in 1955, had heightened the interest of foreigners.

When a revolution in Portugal in 1974 led to the sudden end of colonial rule in Angola and the departure of 250,000 Portuguese citizens, fighting among rival anti-colonial factions stepped up. UNITA's main foe was a faction called the MPLA, whose leaders had proclaimed themselves communists. South Africa (then run by its white minority), Israel, and the United States supported UNITA with arms, money, and training, while the USSR, several Eastern European governments, and Cuba backed the MPLA. In the mid-1980s, Cuba sent 40,000 soldiers to Angola to bolster the MPLA. But in 1990 and 1991, as the USSR came apart, the MPLA's position weakened, bringing peace talks.

The civil war continued, at lower intensity, until 2002. In all, about half a million—of 8 million—Angolans were killed, and another 2 to 4 million became refugees. The war was at root an Angolan power struggle, but for 17 years, from 1974 to 1991, it was made much more lethal by the involvement of Cold War powers. Civil wars in two other newly independent southern African nations, Mozambique (1977–1992) and Zimbabwe (1965–1979), attracted foreign involvement along Cold War lines too, but on smaller scales.

WAR IN AFGHANISTAN The USSR, with less capacity to fight overseas wars than the United States, used its own troops sparingly in combat except in neighboring Afghanistan. The Soviet-Afghan War (1979–1989) ranks with Korea and Vietnam among the deadliest of Cold War contests. Afghanistan, on the USSR's southern border, was an extremely poor, mainly Muslim country of 13 million in 1978 when the Afghan Communist Party staged a successful coup ending centuries of unstable rule by Afghan monarchies. Communist rule provoked widespread rebellion, particularly among committed Muslims called *mujahideen* ("those who follow jihad [Islamic struggle]"). When they appeared likely to topple the communist government, the Soviet leadership, without consulting its allies, sent in the Red Army in December 1979. The decision reflected Soviet anxieties about the loyalty of the USSR's Central Asian Muslims: if Muslims could cast off communist rule in Afghanistan, then they might try to do so in the Soviet Union itself. The invasion brought wide condemnation, especially in the Islamic world and also from the United States and China.

Soviet forces fought several bands of mujahideen, most of which enjoyed support from Pakistan, Iran, China, Saudi Arabia, the United Kingdom, or the United States. Over a 10-year span, combat and massacres killed about 1.5 million people, 90 percent of them Afghan civilians. In addition, about 5 to 6 million Afghans fled the violence, becoming refugees in neighboring Iran and Pakistan. After losing nearly 15,000 soldiers, the Soviets withdrew in 1989, leaving Afghanistan in turmoil.

WAR IN LATIN AMERICA Smaller conflicts smoldered in Latin America during the Cold War. Some of them acquired new character and intensity when the United States grew anxious about the possible spread of communism to the American hemisphere. For more than a century, the United States had considered Latin America its own backyard and had often intervened in the Caribbean, installing or supporting friendly governments. By the late 1940s, friendly came to mean anti-communist.

The interventionist habit continued into the Cold War years, notably in Guatemala in 1954. A popularly elected government there had embarked on a program of land reform that U.S. president Dwight Eisenhower interpreted as a step toward communist takeover. He authorized covert action that overthrew the Guatemalan government and installed a reliably anti-communist military dictatorship. Guatemala's new rulers faced recurrent resistance and often responded with lethal force. In the early 1980s, its military government, still receiving U.S. support, tried to destroy the rural base of the resistance and murdered about 200,000 ethnic Maya, the main Indigenous group in Guatemala. Widely seen as genocide, that campaign was the deadliest episode of political violence in Latin America during the Cold War.

Under Stalin, the Soviet Union had not been interested in Latin America, but by the late 1950s that was beginning to change. An opportunity arose when Cuban revolutionary leader Fidel Castro, in need of friends, sought alliance with the USSR. Cuba's alignment with the USSR in 1960–1961 intensified the Cold War in Latin America. Castro's Cuba, with what meager resources it could muster—often no more than words and advice—encouraged revolutionary movements in South and Central America. The U.S. government reacted by supporting coups and often brutal military dictatorships in Brazil, Argentina, Chile, Guatemala, Nicaragua, the Dominican Republic, and elsewhere, hoping they would quash

U.S. Involvement in Latin American In 1970, voters in Chile elected a socialist, Salvador Allende. U.S. President Richard Nixon, worried that Chile might turn communist, instructed his intelligence services to "make the economy scream" in Chile so as undermine Allende's support and create conditions for his overthrow. In this street demonstration in 1973 in Santiago, Chile a crowd calls for the resignation of President Allende. He died a week later, probably by suicide, during a coup d'etat conducted by the Chilean army. During the Cold War, the U.S. achieved regimes to its liking in most of Latin America, but in the process alienated most Latin American populations.

communist influence. Latin American rulers found that as long as they convincingly claimed to be anti-communist, they could receive money and weapons from the United States, reducing their need to appeal to their own citizens. Meanwhile, the U.S. efforts to oust Castro met with no success and indeed boosted his prestige.

The most sustained combat in Latin America's Cold War took place in Central America during the 1980s. As in Guatemala, Nicaragua and El Salvador descended into civil wars in which the United States became deeply involved. In 1979, the USSR waded into Nicaragua's conflict, supplying a newly victorious revolutionary government with money and weapons, in turn ratcheting up U.S. efforts to undermine it. The total loss of life in these Cold War–related conflicts in Central America (1975–1991) came to about 300,000, counting political murders in addition to combat. That amounted to about 1 percent of the total Central American population of about 30 million—about one-sixth the death rate of Angola's war and one-twelfth that of Afghanistan's.

The United States failed in its efforts to unseat Castro in Cuba but more often than not achieved its Cold War goals elsewhere in Latin America. It often employed methods—coups, covert action,—that few North Americans admired and almost all Latin Americans detested. The United States valued the allegiance of Latin American governments much more than did the distant USSR, but in securing that allegiance it deeply alienated most Latin American populations, which would prove a lasting legacy of the conduct of the Cold War in the Americas.

THE COSTS OF WAR Among the reasons that the Cold War tempted the United States and USSR into countries and conflicts near and far is that the superpowers could often off-load much of the human cost. As the Americans and Soviets avoided committing large numbers of their soldiers other than in Korea, Vietnam, and Afghanistan, the economic and domestic political costs of backing factions in Africa, Asia, or Latin America were low, and therefore the temptation to do so was high. Sometimes interventions could be kept secret so that American or Soviet citizens did not know what their governments were doing in distant lands. Paying for weapons and training for the fighters of regimes or rebels in Africa, Asia, or Latin America was easy enough, especially for the more prosperous United States. Meanwhile, governments and rebels around the world grew adept at posing as ardent communists or anti-communists to receive flows of money and weapons. Through their frequent interventions, the United States and the USSR avoided direct conflict between themselves but inflamed conflicts in the poorer parts of the world.

THE COLD WAR IN THE ARCTIC Geographically speaking, the United States and USSR confronted one another most closely in the Arctic. The shortest distance for bombers or missiles from one country to the other was over the Arctic, so the homelands of a variety of Indigenous peoples became hot spots in the Cold War. The superpowers' interventions here were not into existing or emerging regional conflicts, as in Asia, Africa, and Latin America, but into ways of life and delicate ecologies.

The USSR and Canada claimed the bulk of the land in the Arctic, with most of the rest going to the United States (Alaska) and Denmark (Greenland). Norway, Sweden, and Finland completed the roster of Arctic countries. The Arctic contained very few people, and large proportions of them in every area were Indigenous. The Inuit lived in Alaska, Canada, and Greenland; the Dene in Canada; the Sámi in Scandinavia; and the Sámi, Nenets, Yukagir, Chukchi, and many other peoples or nations in territory claimed by the USSR. The ancestors of these various Indigenous peoples had lived in the Arctic for centuries at

The Arctic Cold War and Its Legacies This map, an unconventional projection that puts the North Pole at the center, shows the Arctic as the region geographically separating the Cold War's superpowers. The United States and Canada, but above all the USSR, used the Arctic for nuclear weapons testing and nuclear waste dumping.

least—and often for millennia. Their ways of life featured hunting, fishing, sealing, and reindeer herding for subsistence, and fur sales to acquire goods from afar. With few exceptions, they had some experience of life in the Global web but little power to shape it.

With the onset of the Cold War, the Arctic's Indigenous populations acquired new neighbors. The USSR and NATO each built military bases for aircraft and submarines. They added giant radar installations to warn of possible attacks. Beyond the new military presence, the Cold War powers embarked on new efforts to obtain minerals such as nickel in northern Siberia, uranium in northern Canada, and oil on the north slope of Alaska. New dams were built across northern rivers, especially in Quebec, Siberia, and Scandinavia, with hydroelectric stations and power lines to carry electricity south to larger populations. Hundreds of thousands of military personnel, miners, and technicians of all sorts flooded into the Arctic, often swamping the Indigenous populations numerically. The USSR offered special incentives in the form of higher pay, extra vacations, and better housing to anyone willing to migrate to the Arctic.

For Indigenous populations, this influx proved disruptive but also provided new opportunities. Some of their lands became military reserves, off-limits to them. Soviet, Canadian, and American governments made efforts to undermine their culture and assimilate them into larger nations. Soldiers, sailors, and airmen all too often treated Indigenous women brutally. Oil spills, pipelines, mining slag, smelter smoke, and discarded military equipment stained and littered Arctic landscapes. The United States conducted 3 underground nuclear tests on an unpopulated Alaskan island, Amchitka (1965–1971). Beginning in 1955, the Soviets performed 224 nuclear tests, above and below ground, on a large island with a small population, Novaya Zemlya. In the Arctic, radioactivity accumulated quickly to alarming levels in reindeer—frequently eaten by Indigenous people. But at the same time, the bases and the mines offered jobs and good wages to Indigenous people, particularly for young adults—especially those seeking independence from their elders.

When the Cold War ended, some of the Arctic military installations were abandoned, but most of the disruptions and opportunities the conflict brought to local populations remained. For the Indigenous peoples of the Arctic, the Cold War represents less an interlude defined by political struggle than the dawn of a new era and a means by which they became more firmly enmeshed than their ancestors in the Global web.

THE DECLINE AND COLLAPSE OF THE USSR

In the end, the Cold War was won and lost not so much in Vietnam, Angola, Cuba, or the Arctic but at home. The United States survived the Cold War's pressures but suffered deep divisions over domestic campaigns in the 1950s to purge the army, the State Department, the media, and universities of suspected communists and communist sympathizers. Frictions over the United States intervention in Vietnam in the 1960s also left lasting effects. The USSR, however, came apart under Cold War pressures. The Soviet regime collapsed during the years 1989–1991, leaving Russia and 14 other new countries. Among the many reasons the USSR crumbled were the cost of nuclear competition, the implausibility of much of its propaganda, and the toll of the war in Afghanistan. But the deeper causes were the USSR's failure to build an effective bond with fellow communists in China and its inability to construct an international economy to rival the American-led one.

THE SINO-SOVIET RIFT

The first big problem to arise was the Sino-Soviet rift. In the late 1950s, cracks began to widen between the two communist powers. Mao resented his treatment by the Soviets as a junior partner and preferred his own version of communist ideology, spearheaded by peasants instead of industrial workers.

Mao also came to see Stalin's successors as disappointingly soft on capitalism. When in the years 1959–1961 Soviet premier Nikita Khrushchev tried to reduce Cold War tensions by meeting with American presidents, Mao sensed treasonous compromise. He began to compete with the USSR for influence and admiration among communists worldwide. Chinese and Soviet leaders started denouncing one another at international communist

Cold War Refuse in the Arctic Oil drums and other refuse left behind on Canada's Baffin Island after the abandonment of a Cold War radar installation. Canada and the United States built a string of radar stations in the 1950s across the North American Arctic to warn of any Soviet air attack. Delicate Arctic ecosystems will carry scars like this one for many centuries to come.

congresses. Whereas in 1956 Mao had strongly supported the Soviet invasion of Hungary, by 1968 he denounced the invasion of Czechoslovakia. By 1969, the Chinese and Soviet armies were shooting at one another at points along their long border.

The Sino-Soviet rift cost the USSR dearly. It had to park roughly 20 percent of its military on the Chinese border, far from the food and supplies it needed and therefore expensive to sustain. Moreover, in 1972, when the U.S. government wanted Chinese help to exit the Vietnam War, Mao saw an opportunity to bolster his position against the USSR. In a shocking diplomatic maneuver, China suddenly welcomed warmer relations with the United States, isolating the USSR. The inability to keep China and the USSR in alignment, despite their shared commitment to communism, was a momentous failing for the Soviets.

THE SOVIET ECONOMY AND OIL

Economic troubles, meanwhile, constrained Soviet options. After World War II, the Soviet planned economy grew rapidly while rebuilding, and it sustained its momentum into the 1960s. But then, with few incentives for innovation, it stagnated technologically, except in armaments production and its space program. The Soviet economy's growth rate sagged by 1970. Its industry produced plenty of steel, but few—or shoddy—consumer goods such as toasters, refrigerators, or shoes. Soviet agriculture could not reliably feed the population. The USSR had to purchase food on the international market, including from the United States, and the only way it could do so was by selling oil abroad. That made the Soviet economy highly sensitive to oil price fluctuations. Many Soviet international economic linkages, such as making loans to India or bartering oil for Cuba's sugar, proved a net drain on Soviet resources.

Paradoxically, international capitalism came to the rescue—temporarily. Production in the USSR's giant Siberian oil fields spurted in time for spikes in the world price of oil in 1973 and 1979. For a few years, the USSR, now financially solvent if still technologically stagnant, could afford to import new technology, food, and other goods. With plentiful oil revenues, it could subsidize the creaking economies of its Eastern European satellites, Cuba, Mongolia, and Vietnam. It could send money and

arms to preferred factions in wars in Angola, Mozambique, Nicaragua, and many other countries.

Then, in 1985 and 1986, world oil prices—and Soviet revenues—plummeted. The USSR had to borrow more heavily from foreign banks, which soon grew cautious about further loans. Moscow had grown accustomed to oil money and had no substitute when it dried up. It had to cut back on its overseas adventures and subsidies for Eastern Europe. The legitimacy of the Soviet state, long shaky, was crumbling fast.

GORBACHEV'S GAMBLES In 1985, a vigorous new leader, **Mikhail Gorbachev**, age 54, came to power in Moscow. Although members of his family had suffered in Stalin's gulags, Gorbachev was deeply committed to rescuing communism and the USSR. He idolized Lenin. He had traveled abroad and understood how clumsy the Soviet economy appeared compared to those of its capitalist competitors. Gorbachev's response to the challenges facing the Soviet Union was to gamble on radical reforms. In some respects, his approach resembled those taken by self-strengtheners in the nineteenth century who recognized that their countries could not compete with the rising industrial powers, that time was not on their side, and that only radical economic development could stave off political defeat.

Gorbachev's version of self-strengthening featured twinned policies called *perestroika* ("restructuring") and *glasnost* ("openness"). Restructuring meant decentralization of the state-run economy and slightly more reliance on markets in the interest of improved efficiency. With *glasnost*, Gorbachev permitted much more free expression and circulation of information, hoping to breathe life into the Soviet economy through innovation and technological advances. Gorbachev aligned his foreign policy with these goals and sought to relax tensions with the United States and NATO, negotiating arms reduction treaties with U.S. president Ronald Reagan. He was trying to buy the USSR some time to reform. But his gamble did not work: the medicine killed the patient.

Without a vibrant economy, the Soviet system could not survive a freer flow of information. In 1986, at Chernobyl (in Ukraine, then part of the USSR), a nuclear reactor blew up, spreading lethal radiation far and wide. At first, ignoring glasnost, Soviet authorities tried to cover it up. But the accident was too big to hide. Efforts to contain Chernobyl's contamination cost huge sums just when Soviet monetary resources were shrinking fast. For Ukrainians especially, the Chernobyl meltdown and cover-up underscored the technological backwardness of the USSR and the untrustworthiness of the government.

Gorbachev's glasnost also allowed the expression of hopes and ambitions that did not fit with the Soviet system—most importantly ethnic nationalism. The USSR contained dozens of ethnicities, some with strong but long-underground nationalist traditions. Now Ukrainians, Lithuanians, Armenians, Georgians, and others found ways to express their national identities and—within limits—to denounce Soviet oppression.

EASTERN EUROPE IN THE 1980S

In addition, by the mid-1980s, keeping the lid on in Eastern Europe was getting harder for the USSR, especially in Poland. Poles, East Germans, Czechs, and Hungarians had grown more restive, showing their frustration at stagnant or falling standards of living, acute environmental pollution, and the ever-present surveillance state. The more they learned about life in Western Europe, the more they resented their own lack of freedoms and comforts. Poles in particular organized underground movements that in the 1980s emerged from the shadows to challenge the right of communists to rule. A trade union called **Solidarity**, formed in 1980, battled for workers' causes and urged political change. Within two years, it had become a civic movement and attracted 10 million members (28% of Poland's population). It proved a persistent problem for Polish rulers and their Soviet backers throughout the 1980s.

In 1988–1989, Gorbachev decided to take the lid off before the pot boiled over. He signaled, gradually, that Eastern Europe's communist rulers could not count on the USSR's army to suppress demonstrations calling for greater freedoms. East Germans began to flee to West Germany, Czechs to Austria—and Gorbachev did not send in tanks. Soon the Berlin Wall, the symbol of the imprisonment—as many saw it—of Eastern European populations, was crumbling. The security forces watched the wall fall on November 9, 1989, and did not receive an order to shoot the people of Berlin. Soon all the Soviet satellite regimes in Eastern Europe were falling, with remarkably little violence.

COLLAPSE

By 1991, the USSR itself dissolved. The Russian component declared itself independent of the USSR, and soon the others followed suit. Remarkably, and mercifully, a once-mighty superpower went out with a whimper, not a bang.

The Cold War ended because the Soviet bloc's economic and political performance disappointed its citizens. As decades passed, fewer and fewer could believe in the promised rosy future, and more and more saw that the USSR's performance could not match its rival's. The material comforts and relative freedom of capitalist liberal democracy, for all its flaws, held more appeal to more people than any variant of communism. As this grew ever clearer, it eventually drove Gorbachev to undertake his doomed radical reforms.

Containment worked in that the US-led bloc outlasted its foe. The United States often irked its allies but kept its alliances intact, never suffering an equivalent of the Sino-Soviet rift. Despite the debacle of Vietnam, its military both commanded respect and inspired fear. Its economy flourished thanks to vibrant technological innovation and plentiful energy supplies. In addition, the U.S. civil rights campaigns of the 1950s and 1960s showed to the world a society capable of confronting its own worst features. The United States and its allies had a flexibility and a capacity for reform often absent in the Soviet bloc—as well as far greater financial and energy resources.

The Cold War ended *peacefully* because Gorbachev was prepared to let Eastern Europe go without a fight, which none of his predecessors would have done, and because his reforms ironically discredited the Soviet state at home, bringing the dissolution of the USSR rather than its salvation. Sometimes a single person makes a big difference—especially in autocratic systems—even if in unexpected ways.

End of the Cold War Demonstrators take sledgehammers to the Berlin Wall, which fell on November 9, 1989. Soldiers watch from atop the wall but do not intervene to stop the protesters.

DECOLONIZATION AS A GLOBAL MOVEMENT

With the formation of a truly global web in the sixteenth century, overseas empires had become easier to create and therefore more numerous. But they were not always easy to keep: there were four pulses of decolonization in recent centuries, all of them linked to major international conflicts. A quick backward glance will help put the late-twentieth-century experience in perspective.

OVERVIEW OF DECOLONIZATION, 1776–1991

The first pulse of decolonization came between 1776 and 1826, with the liberation of the Americas from European imperial rule during the Atlantic revolutions (see Chapter 20). This burst of decolonization led to the creation of roughly 20 new countries in the Americas. The term *decolonization* can also be applied to the demise of the Habsburg, Ottoman, and Romanov (Russian) empires during the years 1917–1923, brought on by the intense pressures of World War I. As we've seen, this led to the creation of 8 new countries in east-central Europe and to an independent Turkey. In Russia's empire, decolonization resulting from the Romanov dynasty's collapse in 1917 was temporary: by 1925, Lenin and his successors put most of the empire back together again as the USSR, but the Baltic countries—Latvia, Lithuania, and Estonia—became independent (until 1940). The financial and manpower demands of World War I upon Britain also contributed mightily to the creation of the Irish Free State (Éire) in 1922. After surges of civil disobedience and small-scale guerilla war between 1918 and 1921, Irish revolutionaries negotiated independence from an exhausted United Kingdom. In these two pulses of decolonization, 1776–1826 and 1917–1923, big wars put events into motion. They put pressures on imperial powers, giving anti-imperial forces opportunities they seized.

The third—and biggest—pulse of decolonization, the focus of the rest of this chapter, came between 1947 and 1975. Colonized peoples took advantage of the material pressures that World War II and the Cold War placed on several remaining empires. This time, about 100 new countries emerged, mainly in Africa, Asia, and the Caribbean.

The fall of the USSR was a decolonization story as well as a Cold War story, so the destruction of the Soviet empire constitutes a fourth great pulse of decolonization. When it lost its grip on Eastern Europe in 1989 and then dissolved in 1991, roughly 20 countries acquired independence. Poland, Czechoslovakia, Hungary, Romania, and Bulgaria were officially independent already, but in reality they had been controlled by the USSR in all important matters between the late 1940s and the late 1980s. Fourteen new countries, formerly units of the USSR subservient to Moscow, became independent in 1991.

THE BIG PULSE, 1947–1975

Empires of one sort or another had been common around the world for millennia, but in the twentieth century, empire suddenly—at least on the time scale of millennia—seemed less inevitable and more illegitimate. The mobilizing rhetoric of the Allies in the world wars, championing the self-determination of peoples, had something to do with this change in perspective. So did the sorry record of colonial rule on the ground in Africa, Asia, and the Caribbean. In 1960, the United Nations declared colonialism a violation of human rights.

THE SHIFTING BALANCE OF POWER
The moral legitimacy of empire was slipping after 1945, but more important were the shifts in power relations between the colonized and colonizers. Within many colonies, those people who chafed most under colonial rule increasingly organized themselves into political parties or guerilla bands. Many future leaders of anti-colonial movements learned about law, politics, and economics as students in British or French universities, and they used their new knowledge to advance the cause of independence. So did about 2.5 million South Asians and 750,000 Africans who learned about warfare as soldiers serving the British or French empires in World War II. Anti-colonial movements sometimes made common cause across borders, sharing expertise, weapons, or money. All this gave anti-colonial movements more tools than they had wielded before 1940.

For example, anti-colonial leaders seized upon the Allies' rhetoric of liberation from tyranny in World War II, embodied in the Atlantic Charter of 1941, signed by Roosevelt and Churchill. Its third clause endorsed the principle that all peoples should be free to choose their form of government. Although Churchill did not intend it to apply to the colonized peoples of the British Empire, the text makes no exceptions, and people in Asian and African colonies logically argued that it should pertain to them too. African, Asian, and Caribbean peoples also used the language, symbols, ideologies, and institutions of nationalism, and sometimes race or religion, to combat colonialism. Pan-Africanism (discussed in an earlier chapter), Pan-Arabism, and Pan-Islamism are examples of political movements that had agendas congruent with, although not identical to, anti-colonialism.

While colonized peoples were getting better organized and more committed to ending empires, imperial powers were struggling with resources and resolve. World War II had drained the manpower and treasuries of most of the combatants. Defeat in 1945 destroyed Japan's empire in Manchuria, Korea, and Taiwan. Meanwhile, the effort required for victory in 1945 exhausted both Britain and France. They began to lose the determination necessary to maintain their empires, partly because they were strapped for military manpower and money but mainly because colonized peoples were raising the costs of continued empire. Public support for imperialism gradually faded, dissipating faster in France and Britain after the humiliations of Dien Bien Phu in Vietnam (1954) and the Suez Crisis (1956).

INSPIRATION: DIEN BIEN PHU, SUEZ, BANDUNG

As noted above, the crushing defeat at Dien Bien Phu in Vietnam in 1954 led France to abandon imperial rule in Vietnam. It also undercut French determination to hold on to colonies elsewhere. In showing the weakness of French power, it encouraged anti-colonial movements everywhere to press for independence. Thirty months later, another defeat for European imperialism redoubled their resolve.

The Suez Canal, a strategic and commercial artery of the first importance—most of Europe's oil flowed through it—cut through Egypt but was owned by a company belonging to French and British shareholders. A new Egyptian government led by Colonel Gamal Abdel Nasser, who had come to power in a coup d'état, nationalized the canal in 1956 as part of Nasser's efforts to free Egypt of British influence and establish himself as the foremost leader in the Arab world. A few months later, during the tumult of Hungary's attempted revolution, Israel, Britain, and France launched a surprise attack, intending to take over the canal from Egypt. This proved a major miscalculation. The United States and USSR denounced the

The Bandung Conference In 1955, in Bandung, Indonesia, leaders of 29 countries, representing 54% of the world's population, gathered to denounce imperialism and proclaim their neutrality in the Cold War. Here India's prime minister, Jawaharlal Nehru prepares to speak while Ghana's Kwame Nkrumah, wearing West African dress, and Egypt's Colonel Gamal Nasser in military uniform stand by. Between them, in coat and tie, is Liberia's foreign minister Momolu Dukuly.

attack (a rare show of harmony between the Cold War rivals). When President Eisenhower threatened Britain and France with withdrawal of American financial support, they called their forces home from Suez and resentfully accepted humiliation. The Suez Crisis showed the world that the age of European empire was at an end, and that Britain and France in particular were no longer great powers but dependent on the United States.

In these same years, 1954–1956, an equally dramatic diplomatic inspiration for anti-colonialists took shape. India, Pakistan, Indonesia, Burma, and Sri Lanka, all recently independent, organized a nascent bloc of countries committed to further decolonization and to neutrality in the Cold War. They hosted a conference in 1955 at Bandung, Indonesia, inviting 29 countries hostile to continued colonialism. The resulting declaration condemned "colonialism in all its manifestations," which some took to include the Soviet position in Eastern Europe as well as British and French control in Africa and the Caribbean. In any case, the emergence on the world stage of post-colonial countries taking firm and unified positions on global affairs, criticizing the superpowers, calling for peace, condemning racism, and demanding an immediate end to existing empires encouraged anti-colonial movements everywhere. Dien Bien Phu, Bandung, and the Suez Crisis all show how decolonization was deeply intertwined with the Cold War.

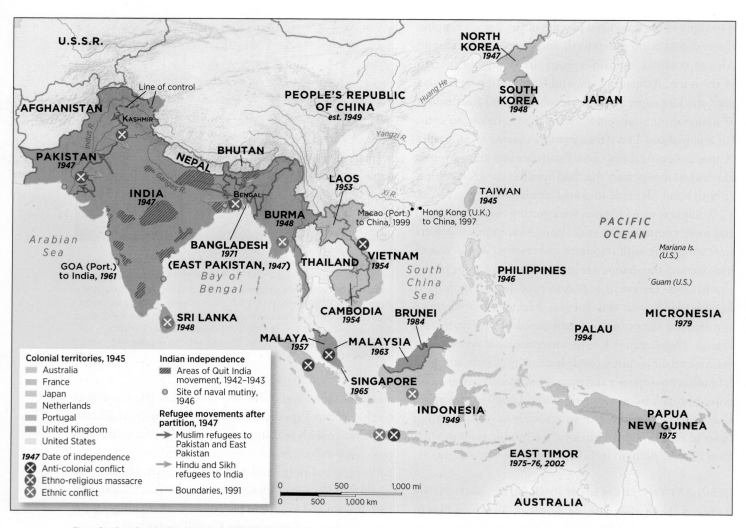

Decolonization in South and Southeast Asia The third pulse of decolonization began in the late 1940s, starting in Asia. Anti-colonial movements in Indonesia and Vietnam won independence by militarily facing down the colonial powers—the Netherlands and France, respectively. Britain's exit from South Asia was negotiated, but the formation of India as primarily Hindu and of Pakistan as primarily Muslim brought intense violence and massive refugee movements. Independence for East Timor and Bangladesh required two phases: first political victory over European colonial powers and then over local powers, Indonesia and Pakistan, respectively.

THE GLOBAL WEB AND DECOLONIZATION

Beyond the impacts of World War II and the worldwide resonance of events such as Dien Bien Phu, Bandung, and the Suez Crisis, three other aspects of the Global web of the mid-twentieth century propelled the **third pulse of decolonization**. The first was economic: Colonial rule in most places depended financially on mines and plantations. The sale of gold, diamonds, and mineral ores and crops such as cotton or jute made the money that bankrolled colonial governments. Those ores and crops normally traveled by rail to seaports for export. So Asian and African rail workers and dockworkers acquired power over colonial economies: if they refused to work, exports and revenues would both cease. By the late 1940s, their

well-organized strikes, often aiming to undermine colonial rule as much as to improve wages, became increasingly common. Some 19,000 rail workers and dockworkers in French West Africa went on strike for several months in 1947–1948. They enjoyed wide support from villagers and townsfolk alike, who helped feed their families while wages were suspended. Rail freight traffic fell by more than half, weakening the finances of colonial rule, forcing compromises, and signaling the political power of organized labor. Such strikes nourished a growing sense of empowerment among colonized populations.

The second aspect of the Global web was military, political, and demographic. Europe's imperial armies consisted largely of Africans and Asians. Britain and France did not have enough young men to militarily maintain empire, especially after the losses of World War II. Algerians, Moroccans, and Senegalese made up most of the French army defeated at Dien Bien Phu. European colonial rule had originally been established by armies recruited from among Africans and Asians, commanded by European officers. But after 1945, fewer Africans and Asians were now willing to serve the cause of empire, and too few Europeans were available to do the job.

The third aspect was cultural and technological: the speed with which information now traveled helped spur the process of decolonization. By the 1920s, newspapers used telegraph networks to report on important events within hours of their occurrence. During the 1930s and 1940s, radio and newsreels (short films of current events) quickly carried news around the world and reached the great majority who could not read. When Indians achieved independence in 1947, Indonesians—and many others—were watching. By the 1960s, television added to the flows of information—and inspiration—so when Algeria won an independence war (1956–1962), everyone was watching. Images of anti-colonial successes coursed through the pathways of the Global web, hurrying the end of empire.

Let's look at a few examples of these factors at work.

ASIAN DECOLONIZATION: INDIA AND INDONESIA

The movements for decolonization in Asia, Africa, and the Caribbean were all connected. Many anti-colonial activists had studied together in their youth in Lisbon or London. Some had attended the same Pan-African congresses or other international gatherings. After 1945, they offered what support they could to one another, as they recognized a common struggle against imperial rule. The advent of the Cold War provided opportunity in that the USSR (and after 1949, China) wanted to see the end of capitalist countries' empires, and the United States wanted the allegiance of colonized peoples around the world. Everyone keen on ending colonialism paid attention to India, the most populous of all the world's colonies.

INDIA At midnight on August 14–15, 1947, some 400 million people cast off British colonial rule for independence as the countries of India and Pakistan. Ceylon and Burma, longtime British colonies administratively linked

to British India, became independent in 1948. (Ceylon changed its name to Sri Lanka in 1972, and Burma changed to Myanmar in 1989.)

As we've seen, anti-colonial nationalism had a deep tradition in British India. After 1919, Gandhi and the Indian National Congress made it a mass movement. After 1935, British legislation put Indians in more and more government posts and set colonial India on a path toward independence. World War II shortened that path.

Indian Independence Residents gather en masse in central Delhi to celebrate the declaration of Indian independence on August 15, 1947.

India contributed mightily to Britain's efforts in World War II. Several million Indians volunteered for military service, and 87,000 of them died in the war. In summer 1945, Britain's Indian Army counted 2.5 million men, the largest all-volunteer army in world history. Most of them had fought against the Japanese in Southeast Asia, some against German and Italian forces in North Africa, and a few in Europe.

Although millions of Indians volunteered to fight for the British Empire, World War II sharpened opposition to British rule in India. Some 40,000 Indians captured by the Japanese chose to switch sides and fight for Japan, or—as they saw it—against the British Empire in Asia. One independence leader, Subhas Chandra Bose, visited Axis leaders in Berlin and Tokyo, and organized Indian forces against Britain. To the British, he was a traitor, to many Indians, a national hero. Most leaders of the Indian National Congress—now operating as a political party—refused to cooperate with the war effort from late 1942 on. Following Gandhi and the British-trained lawyer **Jawaharlal Nehru**, who since the late 1920s had emerged as the second most important figure in the Congress, they demanded immediate independence as the price for their cooperation. Britain's viceroy agreed to promise liberation only after the war. Gandhi called that promise "a post-dated cheque on a crumbling bank," not to be trusted.

Instead, Gandhi called for Britain to "quit India" immediately, despite the risk of Japanese invasion. Britain's wartime prime minister, Churchill, who had served in India as a young man, was determined that India should

Gandhi and Jinnah Gandhi, leader of the Quit India movement, and Jinnah, leader of the Muslim League, pose together for a photograph at talks in Mumbai in 1944. But Gandhi and Jinnah's efforts at cooperation could not avert the violence of partition.

Partition Conflict between Hindus and Muslims over the partition of India led to widespread violence and upheaval. Here police in Calcutta use tear gas to suppress rioters attempting to set fire to a Hindu temple in 1948.

remain British. Relying on loyal police and Indian Army units, the British responded to the Quit India movement by arresting over 100,000 Indians in 1942 and 1943, including Gandhi, Nehru, and all the top leadership of the Congress Party. At the same time, British authorities did little to address a famine in Bengal that killed 2 to 3 million Indians in 1943 and 1944. British rule in India was now shakier than ever.

As World War II wound down, everyone attentive to politics knew independence was coming. The Congress Party tried to represent all Indians, not just Hindus, but many Muslims regarded it as deaf to their interests. Muslims, who formed about a quarter of India's population, had taken the opportunity to fill many administrative positions open by 1943 as a result of the imprisonment of so many Congress Party members. This deepened the divide between the Muslim and Hindu communities. The **Muslim League**, headed by the cosmopolitan and wealthy lawyer Muhammad Ali Jinnah, grew increasingly attached to the idea of a divided post-colonial India, with separate Muslim and Hindu states.

Jinnah and South Asia's Muslims generally feared they would be oppressed by the Hindu majority if independence yielded a united India. Most of them wanted their own state, where they could be in the majority. Many Sikhs (about 3 percent of India's population) wanted their own state too. Many Hindus, however, objected to the idea of a fragmented India and opposed Muslim and Sikh separatist ambitions. Almost everyone wanted

independence, but they could not agree on how to define the independent nation.

Despite their divisions, Indians had succeeded in making India ungovernable for Britain. This became clear in early 1946, when a mutiny among Indian naval units showed that Britain could no longer rely on the loyalty of Indian military manpower. Without it, Britain could not continue as an imperial power in South Asia. By this point, most British politicians were almost as eager for Indian independence as Indians were. Soon the government in London appointed a lawyer who had never been to India to draw a line on the map, based on religious identities, as a border between what were to become two countries.

The lawyer was given a month to draw the line: getting it done fast was more important to all parties than getting it done well. But no line, however well drawn, could have tidily divided Hindu from Muslim from Sikh in India. On August 14–15, 1947, India and Pakistan were born. Nehru, whose appetite for politics far exceeded Gandhi's, became prime minister of India, while Jinnah led Pakistan. Gandhi, the pacifist, was murdered in 1948 by an assassin who considered him too sympathetic to Muslims and Sikhs.

The partition of British India into two countries provoked a bloodbath. Roughly 1 million people died in violent clashes. Another 10 to 17 million became refugees, fleeing to one or another side of the new borders to avoid persecution or worse. India and Pakistan quickly became lasting enemies, fighting three wars since 1947 and perpetually skirmishing over Kashmir, a majority Muslim region claimed by India. Pakistan was born in two parts, one in the Indus valley and one in East Bengal, an arrangement that Bengalis often likened to colonial rule. In 1971, Pakistan's Bengalis seceded, fought a brief independence war with India's help, and created their own country, Bangladesh.

Independence in Burma and Sri Lanka, both formerly part of Britain's South Asian empire, brought conflicts too. It plunged Burma into a brief civil war among factions hoping to rule the new country. Sri Lanka suffered from ethnic division between Sinhalese and Tamil groups, the latter mainly descended from Indian immigrants. That rivalry escalated into civil war in the 1980s. While prior to 1947, most South Asians agreed that Britain must depart and colonial rule must end, after 1947 agreements proved harder to come by. And while each of the successor states was born as a democracy, based on the British model, India alone has consistently retained that form.

INDONESIA Indonesia's path to independence was no less rocky than India's. The Dutch had acquired a foothold on this sprawling archipelago of 13,000 islands in the seventeenth century. By 1940, the Dutch East Indies had 70 million people divided by religion, language, and ethnicity—among other things. Muslims were the most numerous religious community, maybe three-quarters of the population, but many Indonesians were Hindu, Buddhist, Christian, or followers of one of several Indigenous faiths. Indonesia was then and is now one of the most diverse countries in the world, with hundreds of languages spoken and some 600 ethnicities. Nationalism and unity did not come easily there.

Early anti-colonial groups had formed in the 1920s. These included an Islamic group; a communist organization; the Congress of Indonesian Women; and a nationalist political party, the PNI (or Partai Nasional Indonesia). The PNI mainly represented traditional landed elites on the most populous island, Java, but claimed to speak for all Indonesians. Its founder and moving spirit was **Sukarno**, who like most Javanese went by a single name.

On his father's side, Sukarno (b. 1901) came from an aristocratic Javanese Muslim family, but one that had fallen on hard times. His mother was from a high-caste Hindu family. Sukarno trained as an architect and spoke four Indonesian languages as well as Dutch, English, French, Arabic, and Japanese. His greatest talent, though, was political flexibility.

Sukarno made difficult compromises in pursuit of his goals. His agitation for independence in the late 1920s earned him a prison term as a young man. When Japan invaded the Dutch East Indies, he collaborated eagerly with the Japanese occupation (1941–1945), helping recruit millions of Indonesians as essentially slave laborers for work on railroads, bridges, and airfields throughout Japanese-occupied Southeast Asia. Few ever came home. He also helped Japan secure access to Indonesia's natural resources, notably bauxite, from which aluminum is made, and oil. In return, the Japanese helped Sukarno

Indonesian Independence (Left) Sukarno, as president of an independent Indonesia, addresses a crowd of demonstrators in 1950. (Right) Peasants from rural parts of Indonesia—photographed here being trained as guerilla fighters in 1947—were a key component of the opposition to Dutch colonial rule.

denounce Dutch colonialism and spread his version of Indonesian nationalism—and boost his own fame and prestige.

The Japanese occupation took a heavy toll on Indonesia. Malaria flared up, and food requisitioning for Japan's army led to starvation. Thousands of Indonesian women, and dozens of Dutch women, were forced into sex slavery as comfort women for Japanese troops. In 1944 and 1945, roughly a million Indonesians died from these and other hardships. The Japanese departed hastily in the summer of 1945, leaving Sukarno and other prominent collaborators in a tight spot.

With the Japanese going and the Dutch not yet returning, some Indonesian nationalists thought the moment of liberation had come. Sukarno was unsure, but after a fervently nationalist youth group held him hostage for a night, he agreed to declare independence. He also declared himself president.

In September 1945, the Dutch returned, intending to restore colonial rule. They negotiated with many different groups, following the old strategy of divide and rule. They succeeded in rallying people in the outer islands against Javanese domination, Sukarno, and the PNI. Indonesia in the next few years was racked by political violence.

But the Dutch could only turn back the clock in Indonesia with American approval. In 1946, the United States cautiously agreed to the Dutch attempt to restore colonial power in Indonesia. Then, in 1948, the Dutch deployed 150,000 soldiers to impose their will. Sukarno and the PNI responded with guerilla warfare. When the scale of violence became clear, both the UN and the United States denounced the Dutch action and called for a cease-fire. The U.S. government threatened to stop delivering food and fuel to the Netherlands under the Marshall Plan. The Dutch government was too poor and too indebted to defy that threat.

By 1949, with communists about to take over China, American policy makers judged that the best bet for resisting communism—the dominant consideration in Cold War Washington—was a resolutely non-communist independent country. The PNI and Sukarno, despite his wartime collaboration with the Japanese, fit the bill. Once the Americans made it clear they preferred Sukarno to continued Dutch colonialism, the Dutch gave up and negotiated a quick exit from Indonesia.

So in 1949, Indonesia acquired the independence the PNI had claimed since 1945, thanks to the disruptions of World War II, the persistence and opportunism of Sukarno and the PNI, the weakness of the Netherlands, and the intervention of the United States. The PNI and Sukarno now undertook an ambitious experiment in democracy in an ethno-linguistic patchwork of a country. Indonesian nationalism proved too weak to overcome the country's diversity. By 1957, the democratic experiment was on hold and the country was an autocracy, with Sukarno and the army in charge.

AFRICAN DECOLONIZATION

In a broad sense, the story of independence in Africa followed the same lines as in Asia: African anti-colonial nationalists found ways to band together and use what tools they had either to negotiate or to fight their way to freedom. In the late 1940s, France and Britain still intended to keep and develop their African colonies to strengthen their empires. But by 1956–1957, Africans had persuaded them to change their plans.

Let's look at a couple of examples: Ghana and Algeria. Ghana was among the first African countries to achieve independence and among those that took the most peaceful of roads. Algeria was among the last, and it took the most violent road of all.

GHANA The West African peoples of the Gold Coast, as Ghana was called in colonial times, mainly spoke languages of the same group, called Akan. They numbered about 5 million in the 1940s, but they did not think of themselves as Akan, Gold Coasters, or Africans. More local identities, based on clan and village, prevailed. As in Indonesia, national identity did not come easily here.

The British had colonized the Gold Coast beginning in the 1870s and controlled it by 1900. By the 1920s, the Gold Coast economy rested largely on cocoa production. It became Britain's most prosperous African colony—indeed, Britain's model African colony.

For the Gold Coast, the combat zones of World War II were a lot farther away than for India or Indonesia, but the war nonetheless provided a catalyst for independence. Tens of thousands of volunteers from the Gold Coast fought in British armies. To secure fuller cooperation in wartime, British authorities created an advisory body of Gold Coast Africans called the Legislative Council. Its members worked with the British rulers on a new constitution that would delegate some authority to Africans.

Almost everyone still thought British rule in the Gold Coast would last far into the future.

But as the war ended, the Gold Coast came to simmer with discontent. The colonial government infuriated peasant farmers when it killed over 2 million cocoa trees to try to stop a crop disease. Many former soldiers, of whom the Gold Coast counted about 63,000, felt dissatisfied with the reward for their military service in World War II on behalf of the British Empire—they wanted bigger pensions. School graduates also stewed with resentments. The Gold Coast in 1950 enrolled 44 percent of school-age children in school, an extraordinarily high percentage for colonial Africa. But schooling raised hopes for jobs and careers that in the late 1940s too often went unfulfilled. Unemployment climbed. Riots broke out in several towns and cities, particularly in the capital of Accra.

Broad discontent led in 1947 to the formation of a new political party, the United Gold Coast Convention (UGCC), the first in Africa to adopt independence as its stated goal. Its members were British-educated elites, eager to negotiate better terms within colonial structures, eventually leading to self-rule—not unlike the Indian National Congress in its early decades.

The UGCC's gradualist ambitions did not suit one of its members, **Kwame Nkrumah**, who did not wish to wait for freedom. Nkrumah looms large over Ghana's history. Born in 1909, he came from a poor and illiterate family in a seaside village in the southwest of the Gold Coast. He excelled in Catholic schools and in the late 1920s became a schoolteacher himself. But his intellectual gifts soon caught the attention of other West Africans who recommended that he go overseas for further education. With money from relatives, Nkrumah enrolled at Lincoln University near Philadelphia. There he grew interested in Pan-African ideas in circulation among the African American intelligentsia and came to envision an Africa united and free from foreign rule. In late 1945, having gone to London for PhD work in anthropology, he organized a Pan-African congress in England, where he met many prominent African and Caribbean politicians and intellectuals. He gave up his studies for politics, hoping to liberate Africa—beginning with his homeland.

Nkrumah returned to the Gold Coast in 1947 after 12 years abroad. He instantly joined the UGCC and almost as quickly grew impatient with its gradualism. He founded a rival party, the Convention People's Party, to demand immediate independence. He sought to appeal not to the

Kwame Nkrumah Officials of the newly independent Ghanaian government carry the new prime minister, Nkrumah, on their shoulders in celebration in 1957.

intellectuals and well-to-do but to former soldiers, dockworkers, students, market women (as the women who dominate West African open-air markets are called), and other groups he thought he could organize politically. He knew how threadbare Britain was in 1947, and he understood the opportunity at hand.

Nkrumah had studied the arts of political organization, particularly the examples from India, and developed his own program of non-violent agitation—demonstrations, strikes, boycotts—that he called Positive Action. His talents as a political orator and organizer had few rivals within the Gold Coast. Even though the British jailed him, he and his party easily won an election in 1951, the first in African history open to adult male franchise.

At this point, the British authorities either had to work with Nkrumah or face massive unrest in their model African colony. They released Nkrumah from prison and invited him to form a cabinet. In effect, he led a colonial government for the next several years. He and his supporters negotiated an orderly transition to independence, officially achieved in 1957. British policy makers had judged it too difficult to hold on to the Gold Coast. A constitutional handover of power suited them—if power could be handed to someone willing to maintain business and military ties with Britain. Nkrumah could seem such a person when he wished.

Ghana—the name was chosen to honor West Africa's ancient kingdom—was the first sub-Saharan African

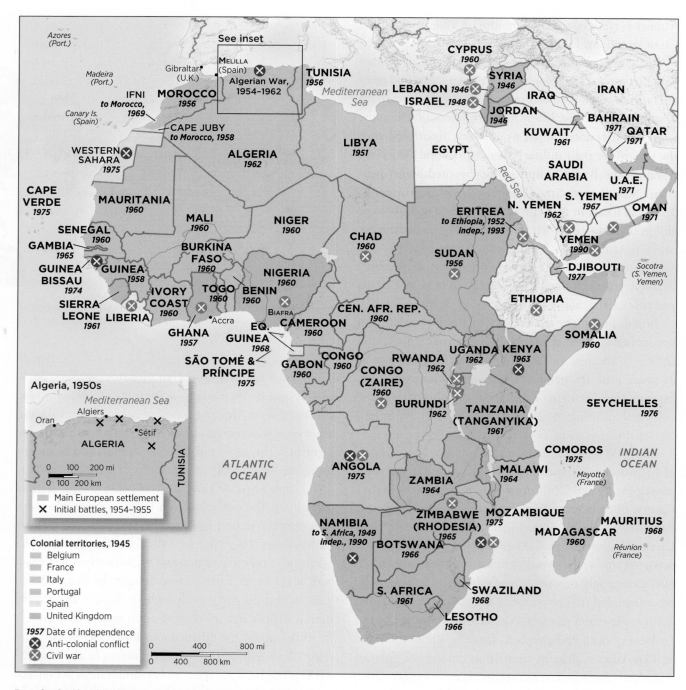

Decolonization in Africa and the Middle East The third pulse of decolonization created almost 50 new countries between 1956 and 1975. Independence involved warfare—particularly in former Portuguese colonies, but also in Algeria, Madagascar, and on a smaller scale, Kenya. Political conflicts with ethnic or religious components were widespread in Africa's newly independent countries and exploded into warfare most lethally in Nigeria, Angola, and Mozambique.

country to slip the bonds of colonial rule. Thanks to the pressure groups organized by Nkrumah and his colleagues, and to British willingness to withdraw, the process happened peacefully, with few disturbances of any size after 1951. A wave of hope and optimism splashed over Ghana and indeed all Africa. As Nkrumah put it

in a speech to a big crowd at the moment of Ghanaian independence, "We are going to demonstrate to the world, to the other nations, that we are prepared to lay our own foundation. . . . We are going to create our own African personality and identity. It is the only way we can show the world that we are ready for our own battles."

The aftermath proved disappointing. Nkrumah hoped the liberation of Ghana would be only the first step toward the independence of all Africa and the formation of a unified African federation: a united states of Africa. Unity proved elusive, though, even within Ghana. Cocoa prices nosedived, and unrest bubbled up. Soon Nkrumah was detaining political opponents and censoring newspapers. By the early 1960s, Nkrumah banned all but his own party and had himself declared "president for life." Unhappy army officers ousted him in a coup d'état in 1966.

The discouraging record of Ghana between 1957 and 1966 was partly a matter of Nkrumah demonstrating the truth of the old saying that "power corrupts." It was also something else: African nationalists—indeed, Asian ones too—promised too much when rallying people against colonial rule. As a motivational tool, it made sense to claim that independence would bring peace, justice, and prosperity. But it set up post-colonial rulers for failure, whether in Ghana or Indonesia, when ordinary people found that independence would not necessarily enable them to get jobs or feed their families.

ALGERIA Algeria's independence struggle took a different, darker form than Ghana's. French armies had claimed Algeria beginning in 1830. Over the next century, thousands of French, Spanish, and Italians crossed the Mediterranean to settle in Algeria. They often benefited from the colonial government's efforts to push native Algerians off their land. As we've seen, Algeria became a settler colony. By the 1950s settlers, known as *pieds-noirs* ("black feet" in French), accounted for 10 percent of the population of 10 million but owned a quarter of the land—including all the best farmland.

Algeria's Indigenous population was overwhelmingly Muslim and mainly Arabic-speaking. Large numbers of them learned French, and some tried to advance within the confines of the colonial system. Thousands made good, but for the majority of Algerians, French Algeria held limited opportunity.

Once again, the war proved galvanizing. There was no heavy fighting in Algeria, but the rhetoric of the Allies—including the right of all peoples to self-determination—was widely heard. At least 200,000 Algerians served with French armies in the years 1943–1945, fighting in Italy and in the liberation of France from German occupation. Their experiences pushed many of them to think hard about how to liberate Algeria from France.

In May 1945, news of Hitler's defeat prompted a celebration in the eastern Algerian city of Sétif. Somehow—accounts differ—shooting broke out and about 100 pieds-noirs were killed. Local police and vigilantes reacted by killing several thousand Muslim Algerians, the great majority of whom had done nothing more than celebrate the Allies' triumph over Nazism.

As the news of Sétif spread, millions of Algerians changed their minds about French rule. Liberation organizations sprouted. In 1954, one of them, known as the FLN (short for "national liberation front" in French), declared a war for independence—a few months after French armies, made up substantially of Algerian soldiers, were defeated at Dien Bien Phu in Vietnam. In Algeria and throughout the French empire, people followed the news from Vietnam and recognized French weakness.

The **Algerian war for independence** (1954–1962) cost a million Algerian lives, about one in every ten. France fought hard to keep Algeria, the most important part of its empire. The French aimed to protect the pieds-noirs, who were in legal fact French citizens, and to preserve strong business and economic ties to Algeria. The forces of the FLN proved equally committed and just as ruthless.

The French Army—bolstered by tens of thousands of Muslim Algerians known as *harkis,* who fought against Algerian independence—fared well in combat. But the FLN would not quit. They outlasted the French, who by 1962 had already given up in Vietnam and had already conceded independence to all their African colonies,

The Algerian War Guards of the French Foreign Legion capturing FLN fighters during the Algerian war for independence. The controversial and bloody war lasted for eight years, with the tenacity of the FLN ultimately achieving independence.

including Algeria's neighbors, Morocco and Tunisia. Fighting on in Algeria was very controversial in France and led to a constitutional crisis and almost to civil war. In the end, a French leader with strong imperialist and nationalist leanings, Charles de Gaulle, decided to quit Algeria in order to save France. The FLN and Algerians had successfully made it clear that the costs to France of continued war would outweigh the benefits of protecting the *pieds-noirs* and preserving French Algeria.

The gruesome war had a gruesome aftermath. Some 800,000 of the million pieds-noirs, told to choose between "a suitcase and a coffin" by the FLN, left Algeria for France. France under de Gaulle refused entry to harkis, leaving them to the mercy of the FLN, whose supporters murdered about 70,000 and brutalized many more, often by cutting off their noses.

VIOLENCE AND LEGACIES OF DECOLONIZATION

Between 1945 and 1975, the process of decolonization swept away the Japanese and European colonial empires. Japan lost its empire in East and Southeast Asia by losing World War II. For the other imperial powers, the fundamental story was that anti-colonial nationalists found ways to raise the costs of continued colonialism above the threshold that populations and politicians in Europe were prepared to pay.

VIOLENT AND PEACEFUL DECOLONIZATIONS

Decolonization proved a violent process in colonies with sizable settler communities, such as Algeria, Kenya, or Mozambique. Madagascar's independence from France also came with a high price in blood, exacted by African troops under French command who suppressed a revolt in 1947 and 1948. The table here shows the size of the military commitments in a few cases of violent decolonization.

In far more cases, decolonization came reasonably peacefully, as in Ghana. This was true in the Philippines, a U.S. territory from 1898 until 1946, and everywhere in the Caribbean. Indeed, the third pulse of decolonization was almost entirely peaceful throughout the American hemisphere. Newfoundland, a self-governing British island colony of 360,000 (mainly) British-descended settlers, voted to become part of Canada in 1948. In the Caribbean in 1945, only Haiti, the Dominican Republic, and Cuba were independent countries. But the winds of change were blowing. Jamaicans organized in labor unions and political parties negotiated their independence from Britain gradually between 1944 and 1962. Trinidad and Tobago also achieved independence via constitutional negotiations. French and Dutch possessions in the Caribbean worked out new arrangements whereby they became more autonomous if still affiliated with their metropoles. Britain and France, by and large, welcomed decolonization in the Caribbean. But part of the reason colonial powers did not fight to keep every colony, whether in the Caribbean, Africa, or Asia, is because they saw—in

CASUALTIES OF DECOLONIZATION, 1945–1975

	PALESTINE, 1945–1948	VIETNAM, 1946–1954	MADAGASCAR, 1947–1960	KENYA, 1953–1963	CYPRUS, 1954–1959	ALGERIA, 1954–1962	MOZAMBIQUE AND ANGOLA, 1961–1975
Number of imperial troops deployed	100,000 British	190,000 French and Africans	30,000 French and Africans	10,000 British and Africans	20,000 British	470,000 French and Africans‡	125,000 Portuguese
Estimated number of people killed (on all sides)	500*	500,000 to 800,000†	30,000 to 50,000	15,000 to 30,000	300	500,000 to up to 1 million	80,000 to 100,000

Sources: Data drawn by author from various sources.

*and another 15,000 to 20,000 killed in a 1948 war between Arabs and Israelis
†This refers to the Vietnamese war against France. The war with the United States killed another 2 million or so.
‡not including *harkis*

Decolonization in the Greater Caribbean Region The third pulse of decolonization reached the Caribbean in 1962, when Jamaica and Trinidad and Tobago won independence. Thirteen new countries emerged, counting the mainland territories of Belize, Guyana, and Suriname. Unlike decolonization in Asia or Africa, in the greater Caribbean no major violence took place. Several territories remain in effect colonies today, such as Puerto Rico, French Guiana, and the Netherlands Antilles (Aruba, Bonaire, and Curaçao).

Vietnam, Kenya, Algeria, and elsewhere—the high price of holding on.

POST-COLONIAL BORDERS

With few exceptions, former colonies kept their colonial borders when becoming independent countries. In most cases, the borders did not fit snugly around any ethnic or language group, ensuring cultural diversity within almost every former colony. In many countries, as in India, diversity led to internal strife. Nigeria, for example, suffered through a secessionist war when the southeastern part of the country proclaimed independence as Biafra in 1967. Biafra collapsed in 1970 amid a famine that killed 2 million, and Nigeria—unlike India—held together. Only a handful of secession movements succeeded; Bangladesh was by far the largest. Brief experiments with federations also took place at the dawn of decolonization, uniting

Egypt and Syria, for example, in the United Arab Republic during the years 1958–1961, or bringing together the West Indies Federation in 1958–1962. None lasted. The borders created during the colonial era largely remain in place today.

NEO-COLONIALISM

Decolonization remains incomplete. A small number of colonies still exist, relics of earlier empires. They are generally little islands or enclaves, economically subsidized by their colonizers. Examples include Spanish Melilla on the coast of Morocco, British Gibraltar, and the U.S. territories of Guam and Puerto Rico.

Decolonization remains incomplete from another point of view as well. Nkrumah and others scorned what they called flag independence, referring to new countries that were formally independent but still economically and

CONSIDERING THE EVIDENCE

Sankara Condemns Neo-colonialism

In 1983, a 33-year-old military officer named Thomas Sankara launched a successful coup against the president of Upper Volta in West Africa, whom he condemned as a French puppet. He promptly re-named the country Burkina Faso, or "Land of Incorruptible People." While the first generation of African nationalists had declared political independence from European colonialism, Sankara and others of his generation sought economic independence from neo-colonialism—the control exercised by the United States, the Soviet Union, and other nations through trade regulations, monetary policy, foreign aid, and loans. Under Sankara's leadership, Burkina Faso supported other countries from Asia, Latin America, and Africa in the Movement of Non-Aligned Countries, which refused to take sides in the Cold War and lobbied for its own interests as part of what was considered an underdeveloped "third world" in the General Assembly of the United Nations. In the following speech to the UN, Sankara expresses support for liberation movements in Palestine, South Africa, Ireland, East Timor, Grenada, Nicaragua, and Afghanistan and decries the exploitation of an international economic order that continues the legacies of colonialism. In 1987, Sankara was murdered by fellow army officers.

I do not intend to enunciate dogmas here. I am neither a messiah nor a prophet. I possess no truths. My only ambition is to...express...the feelings of that mass of people who are disinherited—those who belong to that world maliciously dubbed "the third world"—and to state, even if I cannot make them understood, the reasons that have led us to rise up....

Nobody will be surprised to hear us associate... Burkina Faso with that despised rag-bag, the third world, which the other worlds [i.e., the United States, Europe, and the Soviet Union] invented at the time of our independence in order better to ensure our intellectual, cultural, economic and political alienation. We want to fit in there without at all...accepting that we are a backward world left behind by the West. Rather, we do so to affirm,...as one of the non-aligned countries, our deeply felt conviction that a special solidarity unites the three continents of Asia, Latin America and Africa...[against] political traffickers and economic exploiters....

There must be no more deceit. The new international economic order...can be achieved only if we manage to do away with the old order, which completely ignores us, only if we insist on the place which is ours in the political organization of the world, only if we realize our importance in the world and obtain the right to decision-making with respect to the machinery governing trade, economic and monetary affairs at the world level.

The new international economic order is simply one among all the other rights of peoples...it is a right which can be gained only through the struggle of the peoples. It will never be obtained by any act of generosity by any Power whatsoever.

Source: Transcript of Thomas Sankara's address to the United Nations General Assembly, 20th plenary meeting, Thursday, October 4, 1984, New York.

QUESTIONS FOR ANALYSIS

1. According to Sankara, what "special solidarity" unites the three continents of Asia, Latin America, and Africa?
2. What parts of Sankara's speech would be appealing to "third world" countries but concerning to other countries?
3. How is Sankara's critique of neo-colonialism similar to or different from the grievances that motivated the earlier independence movements in Ghana and Algeria?

politically dependent on their former imperial masters—a situation sometimes called **neo-colonialism**. Chad, for example, once part of French Central Africa, still maintains strong ties to France. French companies dominate Chad's economy, and the French military still props up or overthrows Chadian leaders as it pleases. French armed forces have intervened at least 20 times since 1962 in its former colonies in Africa.

Neo-colonialism could take subtler forms as well. Especially in Africa, post-colonial populations often found they could communicate with their compatriots only in the language of their former colonial masters. In Nigeria and Angola, no practical alternative to English and Portuguese existed, because there were many local languages and choosing one as the national language would invite resentments. Educational systems retained the imprint of imperial states: in India, for example, a British system of high school graduation exams lasted until 1969. In Ivory Coast, education from primary school through university is in French. For many, such as the Kenyan novelist Ngũgĩ wa Thiong'o, who was called James Ngugi at birth, these issues of language and education were fundamental. In the 1970s, he declared he would no longer write in English, only in his native language of Gikuyu, and urged the abolition of the English Department at the University of Nairobi as a necessary step toward the flourishing of authentically African culture. In multiple arenas, from sport to publishing to engineering standards for electrical outlets, post-colonial countries often show continued influences from their former colonizers.

Neo-colonialism was and remains a controversial concept. In Africa and the Caribbean, however, where people often felt either mistreated or neglected by richer, more powerful countries such as France, the U.K., or the United States, the concept seemed to capture their lived experience—and still does.

PEASANTS, POPULATION, AND DECOLONIZATION

Hidden underneath decolonization, and also many of the Cold War struggles in Asia, Africa, and Latin America, was a unique moment in world history in which rural peasant uprisings enjoyed unusual success. From 1945 onward, rapid population growth almost everywhere (explored in the final chapter) worsened prospects for young villagers, who could not expect to inherit enough land to attain their parents' or grandparents' modest standards of living. Their willingness to join armed uprisings grew accordingly. Social solidarity based on centuries of communal rituals, ceremonies, and traditions, now enhanced by a shared sense of deprivation, helped them achieve military effectiveness despite often minimal training and third-rate weaponry. Examples include the peasant forces in the Chinese Civil War, the Greek Civil War, Vietnam, and Afghanistan. They typically used the hit-and-run tactics of guerrilla warfare. They studied one another's successes

and failures as best they could, not always easy for rural people without much education or international experience. They did not always win, but often they did. In this way, changes in the social experience of billions of poor peasants helped to shape some of the macro political trends of the late twentieth century.

By the 1980s, however, this unique world-historical moment was ending. Rural insurgencies were losing their power. Billions of youthful villagers had by now left the countryside for cities. They normally remained poor. But in leaving their villages and kin networks for city life, they lost the solidarity that had boosted the military fortunes of peasant forces. Those remaining in the villages, often the elderly, showed less appetite for gambling on violent uprisings and revolution. At the same time, the governments fighting against peasant insurgencies learned new methods of defeating poor, hungry, ragtag, but determined guerrillas. And they often shared what they learned through linkages among military academies, exchanges among officer corps, and other contacts now routine within the Global web. This helped to tip the balance against rural insurgencies, reducing their rate of success.

CONCLUSION

During the Cold War, humankind came closer than ever before or since to destroying itself with the new technology of nuclear weapons. The decades between 1945 and 1991 witnessed genuinely global struggles. The world had become a smaller place. Great powers could meddle across oceans with ease. Any small conflict had the potential to blow up. Regional power struggles in poor places now attracted superpower support, fueling wars with additional funding, weaponry, and in rare cases such as Korea, Vietnam, or Afghanistan, military manpower. All the interconnections of the Global web, and the technological and economic power they created, made international politics more unstable, unpredictable, and potentially dangerous than before.

The Cold War was a falling out of former allies, a geostrategic battle between the world's two superpowers, an ideological and propagandist struggle between the torchbearers of capitalism and communism, and, more broadly, a contest over the future organization of the world. The American-led bloc favoring internationalism and globalization of the world economy won out. It proved better at creating and maintaining its alliances and partnerships. When the Americans forced their allies, Britain and France, to give up their Suez adventure in 1956, it did not shatter the American coalition; when the USSR and China developed frictions, they escalated into border warfare and persistent rivalry. The American-led bloc also proved better able to satisfy ordinary people, both economically and politically, than the Soviet bloc. The sputtering Soviet economy crashed in the mid-1980s, convincing Gorbachev that only radical reforms could save the USSR. Those reforms undermined it, bringing the Cold War—against all odds—to a peaceful close.

Economic success, and the military strength that success afforded, allowed the United States and its allies to take advantage of the opportunities presented by decolonization and the creation of about 100 new countries between 1945 and 1980. The USSR tried to do so as well, but with poorer results. The spurt of decolonization that coincided with the Cold War happened because colonized people made the continuation of empire cost more than what imperial societies and politicians were willing to pay. It represented the reversal of a trend that began in the fifteenth and sixteenth centuries, and gathered steam with the Industrial Revolution, in which European powers enjoyed dominion over much of the Earth. And it also represented the end—at least for now—of the 4,000 years of world history in which empires were common political forms.

Nonetheless, the international system after decolonization still featured great imbalances between stronger and weaker countries. While by 1980 formal colonialism had almost fully disappeared, the all-too-familiar repressive policies of new, home-grown authoritarian rulers often seemed like colonial rule in new guise. The continuing military, business, and cultural roles of former colonial powers, especially in Africa and the Caribbean, confirmed that sense of mere flag independence. Paths to prosperity and power in the international system proved rocky for all post-colonial countries, but as the next chapter shows, easier for some than for others.

CHAPTER REVIEW

KEY TERMS

Cold War (p. 932)

Yalta (p. 934)

Chinese Civil War
(p. 934)

containment strategy
(p. 935)

deterrence (p. 936)

Cuban missile crisis
(p. 936)

Truman Doctrine (p. 938)

North Atlantic Treaty
Organization (p. 938)

Prague Spring (p. 941)

Mao Zedong (p. 941)

Korean War (p. 942)

Vietnam War (p. 943)

domino theory (p. 943)

Mikhail Gorbachev
(p. 948)

Solidarity (p. 949)

third pulse of
decolonization
(p. 952)

Jawaharlal Nehru
(p. 953)

Muslim League (p. 954)

Sukarno (p. 955)

Kwame Nkrumah (p. 957)

Algerian war for
independence (p. 959)

neo-colonialism (p. 962)

Go to INQUIZITIVE
to see what you've
learned—and learn what
you've missed—with
personalized feedback
along the way.

REVIEW QUESTIONS

1. Discuss the competing United States and Soviet visions
of international security after World War II.

2. What were the guiding Cold War strategies of the
United States and the USSR?

3. In which cities or countries did the biggest crises in
Cold War Europe erupt, and why?

4. What was Mao Zedong's program during the Chinese
Civil War, and to whom did it appeal?

5. What were the main international consequences of the
Korean War?

6. How could a country as poor as Vietnam defeat the
United States in the Vietnam War?

7. Why did the USSR invade its allies Hungary (1956) and
Czechoslovakia (1968)?

8. Why did the USSR lose the Cold War?

9. How did colonized peoples manage to bring colonialism
to an end?

10. Why was decolonization violent in some cases and
peaceful in others?

FURTHER READING

Pierre ASSELIN, *Vietnam's American War: A History* (2017).
A well-researched account of how North Vietnam prevailed
over the United States in the Vietnam War.

Xiaobing LI, *The Cold War in East Asia* (2017). A synthesis
strong on the Chinese role.

Lorenz M. LÜTHI, *Cold Wars: Asia, the Middle East, Europe*
(2020). A regional approach emphasizing local factors as
well as superpower rivalry.

Sunil PURUSHOTHAM, *From Raj to Republic: Sovereignty,
Violence, and Democracy in India* (2021). A detailed look

at how independence worked out in various parts of India,
1946–1952.

Odd Arne WESTAD, *The Cold War: A World History* (2017).
A massive and detailed work by a dean of Cold War
historians.

Vladislav M. ZUBOK, *A Failed Empire: The Soviet Union
in the Cold War from Stalin to Gorbachev* (2007). A good
study of the USSR during the Cold War.

Global Politics During the Cold War

THE COLD WAR AND DECOLONIZATION DOMINATED global politics in the decades after 1945. The documents below include several viewpoints on international issues of the day. The first three are speeches from 1946 to 1947 by Stalin, Churchill, and Truman that demonstrate the transition from the anti-Axis wartime alliance of the USSR, U.K., and United States to the iron-curtain divisions of the Cold War. The 1955 declaration from the Bandung Conference reveals something of the connectedness between decolonization, already in full swing, and the Cold War, as well as some of the fears generated by the intensity of the rivalry between the superpowers. Castro's speech from 1963 reflects the position of the sole communist state in the American hemisphere and its dependence on support from the distant USSR. Together, the documents show that great and small powers alike had friends and enemies on the other side of the world and that politics had become a genuinely global pursuit.

SOURCE 27.1

Joseph Stalin, Speech in Moscow, February 1946

Some 11 months after the defeat of Nazi Germany, Stalin addressed members of the Communist Party of the USSR with his analysis of international affairs, especially the significance of World War II. The speech was broadcast by radio throughout the USSR.

It would be wrong to think that the Second World War broke out accidentally, or as a result of blunders committed by certain statesmen, although blunders were certainly committed. As a matter of fact, the war broke out as the inevitable result of the development of world economic and political forces on the basis of present-day monopolistic capitalism. Marxists have more than once stated that the capitalist system of world economy contains the elements of a general crisis and military conflicts, that, in view of that, the development of world capitalism in our times does not proceed smoothly and evenly, but through crises and catastrophic wars. The point is that the uneven development of capitalist countries usually leads, in the course of time, to a sharp disturbance of the equilibrium within the world system of capitalism, and that one group of capitalist countries regards itself as being less securely provided with raw materials and markets [and] usually attempts to change the situation and to redistribute "spheres of influence" in its own favour—by employing armed force. As a result of this, the capitalist world is split into two hostile camps, and war breaks out between them....

It was on this basis that the anti-fascist coalition of the Soviet Union, the United States of America, Great Britain and other freedom-loving countries came into being and later played the decisive role in defeating the armed forces of the Axis Powers.

That is how it stands with the question of the origin and character of the Second World War....

As far as our country is concerned, for her this war was the fiercest and most arduous ever fought in the history of our Motherland.

But the war was not only a curse. It was also a great school which examined and tested all the forces of the people. The war laid bare all facts and events in the rear and at the front, it ruthlessly tore down all the veils and coverings that concealed the actual features of states, governments, parties, and brought them onto the stage without masks and without make-up, with all their defects and merits. The war was something in the nature of an examination of our Soviet system, of our State, of our Government and of our Communist Party, and it summed up their work and said, as it were: Here they are, your people and organizations, their life and work, scrutinize them carefully and treat them according to their desserts.

This is one of the positive sides of the war....

[T]he war itself has verified the work of our organizations and leaders and has summed it up. It is now much easier for us to examine it, and arrive at correct conclusions.

And so, what is the summation of the war?

There is one principal summation upon which all the others rest....

Now we can say that the war has, refuted all these assertions of the foreign press and has proved them to have been groundless. The war proved that the Soviet social system is a genuine people's system, which grew up from the ranks of the people and enjoys their powerful support; that the Soviet social system is a fully viable and stable form of organization of society.

More than that, the issue is not whether the Soviet system is viable or not, because after the object lessons of the war, no skeptic now dares to express doubt concerning the viability of the Soviet social system. Now the issue is that the Soviet social system has proved to be more viable and stable than the non-Soviet social system, that the Soviet social system is a better form of organization of society than any non-Soviet social system.

Source: Joseph Stalin, *Speeches Delivered at Meetings of Voters of the Stalin Electoral District, Moscow* (Moscow, 1950).

- According to Stalin, what was the significance of World War II?
- What seem to be Stalin's views on capitalist countries?

SOURCE 27.2

Winston Churchill, "Iron Curtain" Speech, March 1946

In July 1945, Churchill had been voted out of office by the British electorate but remained a hero to millions for his role in leading the United Kingdom in World War II and working with Roosevelt and Stalin to achieve victory. In this famous speech, delivered at a small college in Missouri at President Truman's request, Churchill reflects upon the postwar situation and the deterioration of wartime cooperation among the Allies. (He uses *Russian* to mean "Soviet" and *Russia* to mean "the USSR").

A shadow has fallen upon the scenes so lately lighted by the Allied victory. Nobody knows what Soviet Russia and its Communist international organization intends to do in the immediate future or what are the limits if any to their expansive and proselytizing tendencies. I have a strong admiration and regards for the valiant Russian people and for my wartime comrade, Marshal Stalin. There is sympathy and goodwill in Britain—and I doubt not here also—towards the peoples of all the Russias and a resolve to preserve through many differences and rebuffs in establishing lasting friendships. We understand the Russian need to be secure on her western frontiers by the removal of all possibility of German aggression. We welcome Russia to her rightful place among the leading nations of the world. Above all we welcome constant, frequent and growing contacts between the Russian people and our own people on both sides of the Atlantic. It is my duty however, for I am sure you would wish me to state the facts as I see them to you, to place before you certain facts about the present position in Europe.

From Stettin in the Baltic to Trieste in the Adriatic an iron curtain has descended across the Continent. Behind that line lie all the capitals of the ancient states of Central and Eastern Europe. Warsaw, Berlin, Prague, Vienna, Budapest, Belgrade, Bucharest and Sofia, all these famous cities and the populations around them lie in what I must call the Soviet sphere, and all are subject in one form or another, not only to Soviet influence but to a very high and, in some cases, increasing measure of control

from Moscow.... The Russian-dominated Polish Government has been encouraged to make enormous and wrongful inroads upon Germany, and mass expulsions of millions of Germans on a scale grievous and undreamed-of are now taking place. The Communist parties, which were very small in all these Eastern States of Europe, have been raised to pre-eminence and power far beyond their numbers and are seeking everywhere to obtain totalitarian control. Police governments are prevailing in nearly every case, and so far, except in Czechoslovakia, there is no true democracy. Turkey and Persia are both profoundly alarmed and disturbed at the claims which are being made upon them and at the pressure being exerted by the Moscow Government. An attempt is being made by the Russians in Berlin to build up a quasi-Communist party in their zone of occupied Germany by showing special favors to groups of left-wing German leaders. At the end of the fighting last June, the American and British Armies withdrew westwards, in accordance with an earlier agreement, to a depth at some points of 150 miles on a front of nearly 400 miles to allow the Russians to occupy this vast expanse of territory which the Western Democracies had conquered. If now the Soviet Government tries, by separate action, to build up a pro-Communist Germany in their areas this will cause new serious difficulties in the British and American zones, and will give the defeated Germans the power of putting themselves up to auction between the Soviets and the Western Democracies. Whatever conclusions may be drawn from these facts—and facts they are—this is certainly not the Liberated Europe we fought to build up. Nor is this one which contains the essentials of permanent peace.

Source: Winston Churchill, "Sinews of Peace," March 5, 1946.

- What does Churchill mean by the phrase "iron curtain," and why might it have caught on?
- How can one reconcile Churchill's recognition of Soviet security needs in the first paragraph with his denunciation of Soviet actions in central and Eastern Europe in the second paragraph?

SOURCE 27.3

Harry S. Truman, Truman Doctrine, March 1947

Truman had been president for nearly two years when he gave the speech excerpted here. He was trying to convince Congress, dominated at the time by Republicans, to vote in favor of support for anticommunist governments in Greece and Turkey. Both had enjoyed British support in prior years, but that dried up, and Truman wanted the United States to step in forcefully as part of a general effort to stem communism around the world. His speech succeeded in convincing Congress to endorse a more active and more global role than the United States had ever played in peacetime.

One of the primary objectives of the foreign policy of the United States is the creation of conditions in which we and other nations will be able to work out a way of life free from coercion. This was a fundamental issue in the war with Germany and Japan. Our victory was won over countries which sought to impose their will, and their way of life, upon other nations.

To ensure the peaceful development of nations, free from coercion, the United States has taken a leading part in establishing the United Nations. The United Nations is designed to make possible lasting freedom and independence for all its members. We shall not realize our objectives, however, unless we are willing to help free peoples to maintain their free institutions and their national integrity against aggressive movements that seek to impose upon them totalitarian regimes. This is no more than a frank recognition that totalitarian regimes imposed on free peoples, by direct or indirect aggression, undermine the foundations of international peace and hence the security of the United States.

The peoples of a number of countries of the world have recently had totalitarian regimes forced upon them against their will. The Government of the United States has made frequent protests against coercion and intimidation, in violation of the Yalta agreement, in Poland, Rumania, and Bulgaria....

At the present moment in world history nearly every nation must choose between alternative ways of life. The choice is too often not a free one.

One way of life is based upon the will of the majority, and is distinguished by free institutions, representative government, free elections, guaranties of individual liberty, freedom of speech and religion, and freedom from political oppression.

The second way of life is based upon the will of a minority forcibly imposed upon the majority. It relies upon terror and oppression, a controlled press and radio; fixed elections, and the suppression of personal freedoms.

I believe that it must be the policy of the United States to support free peoples who are resisting attempted subjugation by armed minorities or by outside pressures.

The free peoples of the world look to us for support in maintaining their freedoms.

If we falter in our leadership, we may endanger the peace of the world—and we shall surely endanger the welfare of our own nation.

Source: Harry S. Truman, "Address of the President of the United States," March 12, 1947.

- Why might Truman have wanted the United States to expand its role in world affairs?
- Not once in the entire speech does Truman mention the USSR. The only enemies mentioned are Germany and Japan, which both surrendered in 1945. Why might Truman have chosen this rhetorical strategy?

Bandung Conference, 1955

In April 1955, representatives from 29 Asian and African countries, representing more than half of humankind, met for a week in the Indonesian city of Bandung. Leaders of India (Jawaharlal Nehru), Indonesia (Sukarno), and China (Zhou Enlai) played prominent roles in organizing the conference and shaping its agenda. Their aim was to reach agreements on positions concerning the Cold War and decolonization. The text below is the conclusion of the final communiqué of the conference.

DECLARATION ON THE PROMOTION OF WORLD PEACE AND COOPERATION

The Asian African Conference gave anxious thought to the question of world peace and cooperation. It viewed with deep concern the present state of international tension with its danger of an atomic world war. The problem of peace is correlative with the problem of international security. In this connection, all States should cooperate, especially through the United Nations, in bringing about the reduction of armaments and the elimination of nuclear weapons under effective international control. In this way, international peace can be promoted and nuclear energy may be used exclusively for peaceful purposes. This would help answer the needs particularly of Asia and Africa, for what they urgently require are social progress and better standards of life in larger freedom. Freedom and peace are interdependent. The right of self-determination must be enjoyed by all peoples, and freedom and independence must be granted, with the least possible delay, to those who are still dependent peoples. Indeed, all nations should have the right freely to choose their own political and economic systems and their own way of life, in conformity with the purposes and principles of the Charter of the United Nations.

Free from mistrust and feat, and with confidence and goodwill towards each other, nations should practise tolerance and live together in peace with one another as good neighbours and develop friendly cooperation on the basis of the following principles:

1. Respect for fundamental human rights and for the purposes and principles of the Charter of the United Nations.

2. Respect for the sovereignty and territorial integrity of all nations.

3. Recognition of the equality of all races and of the equality of all nations large and small.

4. Abstention from intervention or interference in the internal affairs of another country.

5. Respect for the right of each nation to defend itself singly or collectively, in conformity with the Charter of the United Nations.

6. (a) Abstention from the use of arrangements of collective defense to serve the particular interests of any of the big powers. (b) Abstention by any country from exerting pressures on other countries.

7. Refraining from acts or threats of aggression or the use of force against the territorial integrity of political independence of any country.

8. Settlement of all international disputes by peaceful means, such as negotiation, conciliation, arbitration or judicial settlement as well as other peaceful means of the parties' own choice, in conformity with the Charter of the United Nations.

9. Promotion of mutual interests and cooperation.

10. Respect for justice and international obligations.

The Asian and African Conference declares its conviction that friendly cooperation in accordance with these principles would effectively contribute to the maintenance and promotion of international peace and security, while cooperation in the economic, social and cultural fields would help bring about the common prosperity and well-being of all.

Source: Final communiqué of the Asian-African Conference, April 24, 1955.

- **What appear to be the highest priorities of the leaders at Bandung?**
- **The text mentions the United Nations five times. Why might those represented at Bandung wish to emphasize the UN so?**

SOURCE 27.5

Fidel Castro, Speech at Moscow's Red Square, 1963

Just a few months after the Cuban missile crisis, the leader of the Cuban Revolution, Fidel Castro, visited the USSR. The Soviet leadership showered him with honors and medals, even an honorary doctorate from Moscow State University. Castro, whose government by 1963 relied heavily on the Soviets for economic aid to offset a U.S. embargo on trade with the island country, showed his gratitude in his speech's interpretation of the success of Cuba's revolution.

Many Soviet people ask: How was it possible to accomplish the Cuban revolution? How was it possible to accomplish such a radical change in such a small, economically underdeveloped country, in a country which was under the American yoke? It is quite possible that many Soviet people admire Cuba for this very reason. And perhaps because of this we meet on all sides with warm sympathy and cordiality toward our country.

However, we ourselves shall never forget one circumstance—the Cuban revolution became possible only because the Russian revolution of 1917 had been accomplished long before. Without the existence of the Soviet Union, Cuba's socialist revolution would have been impossible. However, this does not at all mean that the Cuban revolution was accomplished by the Soviet Union. Among their many lies and slanders, the enemies of the Soviet Union have not gone as far as to say that. This means that without the existence of the Soviet Union, the imperialists would have strangled any national-liberation revolution in Latin America. And as they go as far as to crush even bourgeois revolutions, if these revolutions affect their imperialist interests, they would strangle socialist revolutions in Latin America with much greater readiness and hatred. Had the Soviet Union not existed, the imperialists would not even have had to

resort to weapons. They would have strangled such a revolution with hunger. They would have liquidated it using only an economic blockade. But because the Soviet Union exists, it proved impossible to liquidate our revolution. . . .

The courage, patriotism, and healthy spirit of the citizens of the country where socialism has been fully victorious leave not the smallest doubt that the CPSU[1] Program will be fully carried out, [applause] that the present generation of the Soviet people will live under communism, [applause] and that your forward movement cannot be halted by anyone. . . . vFrom the bottom of their hearts the peoples of the entire world, all the peoples of the world, must regard your success as their own.

[1] The Communist Party of the Soviet Union.

Source: Fidel Castro, speech at Red Square, 1963.

- **When Castro refers to "imperialists," who does he have in mind?**
- **Why did Castro go to such lengths to praise the USSR and its people in 1963?**

QUESTIONS FOR COMPARISON

1. To what extent, if any, do these five texts reflect ideological positions held by their authors?

2. Can you detect reflections of changes in the international system between the first three texts, all from 1946 to 1947, and the later ones, from 1955 and 1963?

3. The words "free" and "freedom" appear frequently in these texts (except Castro's). Do these words mean the same or different things to Stalin, Churchill, Truman, and the conferees at Bandung?

CHRONOLOGY

1947
Japan adopts new constitution

1948
Apartheid regime is established in South Africa

1953–1959
Cuban Revolution

1963
Organization of African Union is formed

1964–1985
Brazilian military dictatorship

1965
Singapore becomes independent

1966–1976
Great Proletarian Cultural Revolution

1967–1970
Biafran War

1976
Mao Zedong dies

1978
Deng Xiaoping becomes head of China

1979
Sandinista revolutionaries come to power in Nicaragua

1980
Gwangju uprising

1982
Falklands War

1983
Fall of Argentine dictatorship

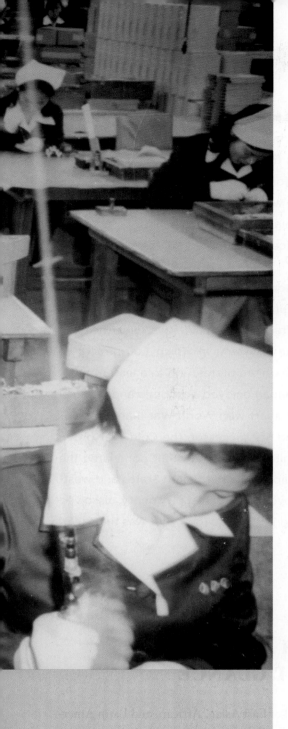

28

Rebalancing the Global Web

AFRICA, LATIN AMERICA, AND THE
RISE OF EAST ASIA SINCE 1960

> It doesn't matter whether the cat is black or white,
> as long as it catches mice.
>
> —Deng Xiaoping (1962)

Deng Xiaoping, the leader of communist China from 1978 to about 1995, was a practical man. His reference to cats is an assertion that ideological stripes matter less than effectiveness. What he wanted to achieve was a transformation of China into a global power, and he did more than anyone else to do so. Deng and his allies within the Chinese Communist Party (CCP) revolutionized China by emphasizing practicality. The resulting changes in East Asia were as great as any since the Qing conquests of the seventeenth century. The changes to the global balance of power were as great as any since the Industrial Revolution in the nineteenth century and the resulting rise of Britain, Germany, and the United States.

This chapter is about the shifting global distribution of wealth and power since about 1960. The biggest change, by far, was the rise to prosperity of several East Asian societies and the geopolitical rise of the biggest of them, China. In contrast, the experiences of sub-Saharan Africa, despite decolonization,

1989
Tiananmen
Square
massacre

1992
China's stock
exchange
re-opens

1994
NAFTA trade
agreement;
South Africa
ends apartheid

1998–2008
Second Congo War

Factory Labor in East Asia The East Asian economic miracles of the late twentieth century relied heavily on female labor outside the home, as in this South Korean factory from the 1970s.

FOCUS QUESTIONS

1. How did the economic rise of East Asia shift the balance of the Global web?

2. Why did East Asian nations experience strong economic advances in the late decades of the twentieth century?

3. What obstacles to economic growth did Africa and Latin America face?

and of Latin America—both regions also featured in this chapter—showed no great leaps forward toward either prosperity for citizens or power within the international system. The chapter aims to explain these three divergent trajectories that directly shape the lives of half the world's population and indirectly shape those of everyone else.

The chapter also highlights the consequences of decolonization and rise of neocolonialism. Just as colonization of much of the world was important to the slow rise of western Europe between 1500 and 1914, so decolonization was a crucial precondition to the sudden rise of East Asia. The first step came with the destruction of Japan's empire in World War II. Liberation from Japanese colonial rule was necessary before South Korea and Taiwan could transform themselves into rich countries. Likewise, Singapore shed British rule before becoming prosperous. Hong Kong, however, became rich while still a British colony—a unique case and the exception that proves the rule. In fact, giving up on territorial empire was crucial to the economic rise of Japan too. The consequences of decolonization in Africa, however, more closely resembled those in Latin America since the nineteenth century: neocolonialism and economic stagnation rather than spectacular economic success. In addition, this chapter notes the differing pace of fertility transitions and the economic mobilization of women. A key source

of modern per capita economic growth is a socio-economic shift in which women bear fewer children and spend less time nurturing children and more in the paid labor force. Where girls' education became a priority, many women found alternatives to youthful marriage and big families. Female labor in factories, fields, and offices contributed to faster economic growth.

In the broadest of strokes, over the past century the distribution of wealth and power within the Global web shifted in three main ways. First, the early twentieth-century system, in which Europe's colonial powers, the United States, and to a lesser extent Germany and Japan enjoyed economic and political dominance, fell apart with World War II and decolonization. Second, its successor, the Cold War order, in which the United States and USSR dominated the political landscape while the United States and western Europe enjoyed the greatest prosperity, dissolved in the 1980s and 1990s. The third shift was the rise of East Asia.

GROWTH SINCE 1960: A GLOBAL GLANCE

To see the record of East Asian, African, and Latin American economies in global context, see the map on page 794. It shows several world regions' changing shares of the global economy since 1960. Note how in recent decades East Asia vaulted upward, while Africa and Latin America did not. Those regions' economies grew at about the same rate as the world as a whole, while East Asia grew much faster, claiming an ever-increasing share of the global economy.

These comparisons are important partly because they help explain disparities in power in the international system. The main reason that East Asian countries—at least China, Japan, and South Korea—are much more powerful now than they were in 1960 is because their economies boomed.

CONSIDERING THE EVIDENCE

Measuring Growth and Inequality

To understand the changing welfare of ordinary people in different parts of the world, a key piece of evidence is GDP per capita. GDP—gross domestic product—measures the total monetary value of all goods and services produced annually within a country, and GDP per capita—essentially average incomes—divides that figure by the population.

In 1960, the average person in China had only 7 percent as much income as the average person in the world: see the first row of Table A below. By 2019, the average Chinese income had grown more than 30-fold from 1960, but the average Latin American's income grew by less than 3-fold, and the average African's had only doubled. These relative growth rates go a long way toward explaining the changes in relative power in the world exerted by countries in these various regions.

Table B will help explain some of the regional differences in per capita income. It shows the percentage of all income earned by women, which reflects two things: how many women participated in the paid labor force and how well they were paid. Here, 50 percent would represent gender parity. Globally, the trend after 1990 was toward less inequality, as women's share of all income climbed from 30 percent to 35 percent.

In China, however, women's share of all income declined, from well above the world's average in 1990 to slightly below it in 2020. That makes the remarkable expansion of the Chinese economy since 1990, explored below, all the more remarkable. Meanwhile, Latin America posted the fastest reductions in gender inequality in income, mostly because more women entered the paid labor force, rather than because their pay increased. In Africa, women took part in paid labor at rates as high as anywhere in the world, but their wages were lower relative to men than those of women anywhere.

QUESTIONS FOR ANALYSIS

1. Which world regions recorded per capita income growth faster than the global average between 1990 and 2019?
2. Among South Asia, Africa, China, and Latin America, which region's per capita income growth rate slowed after 1990?
3. What do these data *not* capture about female labor?

TABLE A: PER CAPITA INCOME BY WORLD REGION, 1960–2019, AS A PERCENTAGE OF THE WORLD 1960 AVERAGE ($3,586)

	WORLD	SOUTH ASIA	AFRICA	CHINA	MENA	LATIN AMERICA	EUROPEAN UNION
1960	100	9	31	7	n.d.	91	n.d.
1990	189	16	36	25	133	162	600
2019	307	52	46	283	206	241	921

Source: Our World In Data, https://ourworldindata.org/search?q=GDP+per+capita.

Note: Figures adjusted for inflation. MENA is Middle East and North Africa. 2019 is used rather than 2020 to avoid skewing by the temporary effect of the pandemic.

TABLE B: FEMALE INCOME SHARE, 1990–2020

	1990	2020
World	30%	35%
China	39%	33%
North America	34%	38%
Latin America	28%	35%
Sub-Saharan Africa	27%	29%
Middle East and North Africa	11%	12%

Source: World Inequality Report 2022, https://wir2022.wid.world/www-site/uploads/2022/03/0098-21_WIL_RIM_RAPPORT_A4.pdf.

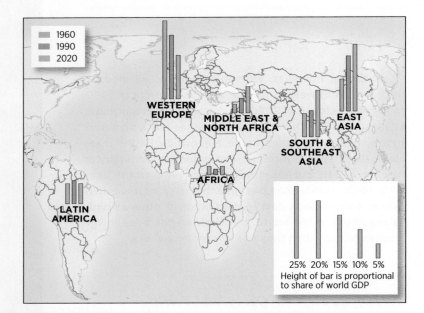

Share of World GDP, 1960–2020 This map shows the rapid redistribution of economic activity around the world since decolonization. Each bar's height represents the share of world GDP for a given region. While in Latin America and Africa, changes were modest, elsewhere they were dramatic. Taken as a whole, this is probably the fastest and largest redistribution of global wealth in world history. Bear in mind that the global economic pie grew 8–9 fold between 1960 and 2020, and global population by 2.6 fold.

THE RISE OF EAST ASIA

The astonishing economic rise of China followed in the wake of smaller East Asian societies. The economic "miracles" of Japan, South Korea, Singapore, Hong Kong, and Taiwan preceded China's and to some extent served as models for it. They all managed sustained economic growth, as measured by GDP, at rates rarely if ever achieved before in world history. Together, the success of the **Asian tiger economies** plus China amounted to the most rapid large-scale economic transformation in world history and, as such, deserves close attention. Each case had national features, as sections below explain, but there were also some important common characteristics.

SOURCES OF RAPID ECONOMIC GROWTH

East Asians often explain the astonishing economic record of several East Asian countries as a product of culture. Singapore's first prime minister, Lee Kuan Yew, never tired of touting "Asian values" of hard work, frugality,

and discipline. There may be some truth in that argument, but East Asian societies with "Asian values" had been poor for centuries and condemned by necessity to hard work and frugality. Something more is needed to explain their modern rise.

An important precondition was peace. Revolutions, civil wars, and international wars ravaged much of East Asia on and off before 1945. China suffered from civil war between 1946 and 1949, and Korea from a civil war that quickly became an international war between 1950 and 1953. But after 1953, with tiny exceptions, peace prevailed in East Asia, although not in Vietnam and elsewhere in Southeast Asia. As we'll see, war in Vietnam actually helped the economies of East Asia.

DEMOGRAPHIC CHANGE Another factor common to the economic success of East Asia was a gigantic **demographic dividend**. The key to a demographic dividend is a fertility transition that offers a window of time highly favorable for economic growth and development. Under the biological old regime, with high fertility and big families, adults—women especially—devoted great effort to child care. When fertility falls, the age structure of a population changes: the ratio of people of prime working age to children and the elderly rises. That shift makes economic growth and development likelier. In addition, with fewer children to support, families find it easier to pay for education. In short, fertility transitions deliver demographic dividends in the form of economic growth, and nowhere—so far—has this ever happened faster than in East Asia after 1950.

The demographic dividend in East Asia was in some cases partly a result of government policy encouraging lower birth rates, as we will see. But since it happened everywhere at almost the same speed and at close to the same time, regardless of policy, it is likely that the choices made by hundreds of millions of couples throughout East Asia were more fundamental than policy. As formal education became more important to securing one's future, couples increasingly preferred to invest more heavily in fewer children.

TECHNOLOGY, THE OPEN ECONOMY, AND LABOR Another factor contributing to the economic rise of East Asia came from technical changes to shipping, the biggest of which was **containerization**. Before the 1950s, ports were the bottlenecks in maritime shipping. Longshoremen filled and emptied ships, which might take weeks for a big freighter. Beginning in the United States in the late 1950s, entrepreneurs started using shipping containers—enormous metal boxes—to hold freight. Containers could go on ships, trains, or trucks, and no one had to "break down" the cargo first. Big cranes plucked containers from ships to shore or vice versa. Labor costs plunged as longshoremen lost jobs. Containerization cut the costs of maritime shipping between the 1950s and 1990s by one-third. Transoceanic shipping times fell by nearly 90 percent. The risk of broken or stolen goods declined, and longshoremen's strikes no longer delayed transport. Shipping times became so reliable that companies—led by the Japanese carmaker Toyota—began what is now known as "just-in-time delivery" of product parts. With parts and products produced on demand and delivered speedily, companies no longer stockpiled anything in warehouses. With no inventories sitting around and tightened supply chains, production costs declined too.

The container revolution was global, but East Asia benefited most. Containerization put the big consumer markets of North America and Europe within reach of the East Asian economies. Export-oriented growth strategies, which all the East Asian tigers adopted, became much more practical when shipping costs plummeted and shipping times became more predictable.

Another general factor contributing to the East Asian economic rise is connected to containerization's success: the comparative openness of the world economy, or at least a big slice of it, since 1950. All of the successful East Asian economies prospered on the basis of exports—the imports of other countries. The United States, historically a protectionist country, by 1950 encouraged free trade and low tariffs everywhere around the world. It had the power to persuade many countries in western Europe and Latin America to lower their trade barriers. This opened the door for export-led growth of the sort the East Asian tigers pursued.

Cheap labor was another important factor. Just as Meiji Japan's industrialization at the end of the nineteenth century took advantage of low labor costs, so it was with all of the East Asian tigers in the late twentieth century. Hundreds of millions of very poor people were willing to work for paltry wages. If they asked for higher pay or better working conditions, their bosses—at least in

The Rise of East Asia since 1960 Certain parts of East Asia recorded unprecedented rates of sustained economic growth especially after about 1960. This was the most important force behind the dramatic reorganization of the global economy in recent decades. Japan led the way, beginning as early as the 1950s, emphasizing manufacturing exports. The smaller economies of South Korea, Taiwan, Hong Kong, and Singapore followed a broadly similar path to prosperity. After 2000, China proved the most dynamic force in the global economy.

South Korea, Japan, and China—could easily find eager replacement workers in rural villages. Hong Kong and Singapore did not have masses of poor villagers, but they could draw on cheap immigrant labor from neighboring China or Malaysia.

North Korea missed out entirely on East Asia's economic surge. Its leadership did not choose export-led industrial growth as its guiding strategy. It preferred to rely on its own meager resources rather than integrate into the international economy. North Korea suffered mass starvation in the 1990s and remains very poor today. Its record shows, among other things, the economic penalty of isolation from the commercial circuitry of the Global

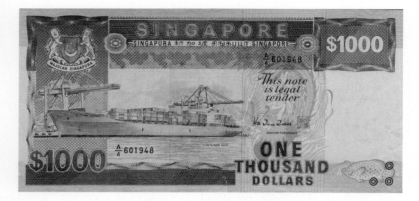

Containerization A 1980s Singaporean banknote shows a freighter filled with shipping containers. The innovation of containerization contributed to immense economic growth in postwar Singapore and other East Asian economies.

web. Self-reliance, in a global economy, has often proved disastrous, especially for small countries.

Let's look more closely at the examples of Japan, South Korea, and China. The story of Taiwan is equally remarkable and similar to South Korea's. Hong Kong and Singapore also engineered economic take-offs, but on the much smaller scale of city-states.

JAPAN

Japan's post-1945 economic miracle was its second. It had pulled one off after the Meiji Restoration of 1868. That one featured rapid industrialization, beginning with textiles and shifting to heavy industry. It continued into the 1930s, little troubled by the Great Depression, with a new emphasis on military production and planning.

Bombing during World War II obliterated about one-quarter of Japan's buildings and infrastructure and slashed its GDP in half (1940–1945). In the immediate postwar years, most people were hungry, and some starved to death. Malnutrition caused the average heights of children to decline. Japan's currency lost almost all value to inflation in the years 1945–1949. But Japan had expertise, traditions, and institutions that, with a few tweaks, could support another economic surge when conditions improved—as they did markedly in the 1950s.

THE U.S. OCCUPATION AND STRATEGIC SUPPORT From 1945 to 1952, the Allies—mainly the U.S. military—occupied Japan and directed its high-level policy. American army officers wrote a new constitution for

Japan, adopted in 1947. Their goals were to eradicate militarism and ensure a stable, democratic, and pro-American Japan. They pushed through land reform that ended the domination of the countryside by big landlords and made Japan into a country of small farmers, a key step on the road to economic transformation.

The new constitution provided for the legal equality of men and women in articles written by Beate Sirota, a 23-year-old American of Ukrainian parentage. She had grown up in Japan and was working for the occupation authorities as a translator when invited to help draft the constitution. Equality of the sexes was a revolutionary concept in Japan and helped bring about a fertility transition and demographic dividend.

Once communists took over China (1949) and the Korean War broke out (1950), U.S. policy toward Japan shifted. Engineering social change seemed less urgent than rebuilding Japan as a bulwark against communist expansion in East Asia. After some missteps, the Americans came to understand that on economic policy they needed to work within Japan's cultural traditions, one of which included cooperation between business elites and government bureaucrats to craft national economic and industrial strategies. After 1949, a new ministry for international trade and industry (MITI) took primary responsibility for creating these strategies. It sponsored research and directed investment funds toward chosen industries. Like the leaders of the Meiji era, postwar Japan's government did not trust the free market to make the best economic decisions for Japanese.

One important factor sustaining the Japanese economic miracle was its role in supplying the U.S. military during the Korean and Vietnam Wars. These efforts needed vast quantities of supplies, and Japan was close to the war zones, especially Korea. A Japanese prime minister referred to the Korean War, a bit callously, as "a gift of the gods."

In 1950, Japan's economy, halved by war's ravages, was smaller than that of Colombia, Costa Rica, or Morocco. Its per capita annual growth after 1950 averaged about 8 percent to 1973, a sustained rate never seen anywhere before and more than twice the global average of those years. During the 1970s, a tough decade for the world economy because of oil price hikes, Japan's economy still grew rapidly and by 1980 was the third largest in the world. Prosperity—in the form of cars, TVs, washing machines, and the like—reached into the villages and formerly poor neighborhoods of big cities. The average income was now 7 times higher than in 1950. Expansion slowed in the 1990s and beyond. By 2020, Japanese incomes were more than 11 times the level of 1950.

Some of the general factors discussed above help explain Japan's economic takeoff. It benefited from a demographic dividend, containerization, and easy access to the U.S. market. At first, its industrial competitiveness also benefited from cheap labor. But under the Allies' occupation, Japanese workers had been encouraged to unionize, which led to rising wages by the mid-1950s. In addition, the supply of poor villagers willing to work for low wages dried up by about 1965, so Japan could not profit for long on the basis of cheap export manufactures such as textiles and toys.

ZAIBATSU AND KEIRETSU Japanese business organizations, especially large, integrated corporate conglomerates, proved especially nimble at exploiting the opportunities of the postwar years. These conglomerates had existed in Japan since the late nineteenth century, when they were called *zaibatsu*. They brought together banks, trading companies, and industries all under the same leaders, often from one family. They had led industrialization in late nineteenth-century Japan, when they emphasized iron, steel, and ship building, and during the years 1937–1945, when they organized war production. The *zaibatsu* tradition was woven into the fabric of Japanese society, culture, and politics.

The Americans had at first tried to break up the *zaibatsu* during the postwar occupation, but the effort withered as U.S. policy shifted to building up Japan to counter communism in East Asia. Called **keiretsu** after 1945, the conglomerates regrouped and led a new campaign aimed at capturing foreign markets in select industries. Their success in some areas was stunning: in 1965, nearly two-thirds of the world's new ships were built in Japan.

Like the zaibatsu of the Meiji era, the keiretsu proved excellent at technological innovation, especially adapting foreign technology to Japanese contexts. The rising wages of Japanese workers in the 1950s tempted companies to give up on labor-intensive approaches. With the encouragement of the MITI, they shared research costs and pooled resources to buy licenses for foreign technology. They sent people abroad to study the latest production techniques—as Japan had done during the Meiji era. In the 1950s and 1960s, the U.S. government eagerly assisted in transferring industrial technology to Japan. Japanese engineers worked small wonders inventing or improving cameras, computers, printers, electronic keyboards, automated teller machines, and hundreds of other common devices.

The keiretsu and other Japanese firms entrenched assembly-line production in Japan and found ways to ensure better quality control than the Americans, the originators of the assembly line. In the 1950s, they succeeded mainly because they made cheaper goods than industry elsewhere could manage, but by the 1970s they did it with high-quality goods: better steel, ships, cars, audio equipment, and TVs than companies elsewhere could make.

The keiretsu and smaller firms also pioneered miniaturization. Postwar Japan was crowded. Its urban apartments were small and its streets narrow. Japanese industry responded with small TVs, refrigerators, and cars that fit Japanese spaces—and similarly crowded societies

Economic Miracle Consumer goods and electronics helped to fuel Japan's economic revolution in the mid-twentieth century. During the 1970s, the Nissan factory near Yokohama could turn out three cars per minute for worldwide export. Workers in a 1960s Tokyo factory assemble components of color television sets, which became common even in poorer Japanese households as prosperity increased.

elsewhere. In pursuing miniaturization, they developed skills and technologies that proved useful in markets such as personal computers, mobile phones, and robotics.

The Japanese economic spurt made Japan an industrial powerhouse and one of the richest societies in the world. Its growth rates slowed from a sprint to a trot during the 1970s and 1980s, and after 1995 to a crawl. Among the reasons for its economic stagnation was an aging population. The public and politicians have so far resisted immigration—which skews young—leaving Japan since 1990 with the world's oldest population. By 2020, 28 percent of Japanese were age 65 or older, and in no other country was the proportion above 23 percent. Japan's total population has been falling since about 2010. In addition, since the 1980s, Japan has also enjoyed less cooperation from the United States, whose automobile and other businesses came to feel threatened by Japan's. And Japan's export sector faced growing competition from South Korea, Taiwan, Singapore, and, by 1990, China.

SOUTH KOREA

South Korea engineered an economic miracle even more extraordinary than Japan's. Whereas Japan already had decades as an industrial society behind it in the 1950s, South Korea had next to nothing. Its few modern industries had served the interests of Korea's colonial master, Japan, which siphoned all the wealth and resources that it could from Korea between 1910 and 1945. In the Korean War (1950–1953), Korean, Chinese, and American armies blasted the peninsula into tatters and left it divided in two. South Korea in the late 1950s had virtually no natural resources, and per capita incomes were lower than those of newly independent Ghana—and of communist North Korea. Yet, by 1990, South Korea was well on its way to becoming one of the world's best-educated and richest populations. How could a former colony ruled so harshly pull off such a self-transformation?

Although harsh, Japanese colonial rule (1910–1945) in Korea left a few useful legacies. The Japanese built the foundations of a modern educational system. They also built roads, railroads and ports, although most of them needed rebuilding after the Korean War. And they trained some Koreans in industrial skills, both as workers and as managers.

The American military occupation of the South beginning in 1945 left another helpful legacy: **land reform**. In

	PER CAPITA GDP
YEAR	**(1950 = 100)**
1950	100
1970	304
1990	1,390
2020	4,492

SOUTH KOREAN PER CAPITA GDP, 1950–2020 (INDEXED TO 1950)

Source: Maddison Project, https://www.rug.nl/ggdc/historicaldevelopment/maddison/releases/maddison-project-database-2018

Note: Per capita GDP refers to the national GDP divided by the national population.

1948, most South Koreans were peasants, renting land from aristocratic landowners called *yangban* who made all important decisions about farming. But by 1956, South Korean peasants owned most of the farmland, grew whatever they liked, and sold as much of their harvest as they wished. Land reform, undertaken under pressure from the U.S. government, was the foundational act of South Korea's economic miracle.

A second step was building a universal education system for both boys and girls. In the 1950s, South Korea's government began an enduring investment in primary and secondary school education that paid off in the decades ahead. In the mid-1950s, school lessons were often held in tents, and teachers had to cope with classes of as many as 100 students. By 1960, almost every child over five years of age spent long hours in newly built schools. Soon South Korea's literacy rates were among the highest in the world. By 1980, its workforce was among the world's most educated.

INDUSTRIAL POLICY AND U.S. SUPPORT Government policy helped in other ways too. In the early 1960s, South Korea's rulers embarked on a series of five-year plans featuring government direction of economic policy but private ownership of most business enterprises. In the latter respect, it was crucially different from communist five-year plans followed in the USSR or China. The government's industrial policy rewarded companies that exported goods. It protected South Korean industry behind tariff barriers. It also increasingly welcomed foreign investment, which came mainly from the United States and Japan.

The United States regarded South Korea, like Japan,

as an important Cold War bulwark against communism in Asia. During the 1950s, the U.S. government paid about 80 percent of South Korea's government budget. From 1946 to 1976, the United States gave twice as much aid money to South Korea as it did to all of Africa. The Vietnam War provided South Korean industry, especially construction firms, with an opportunity to win contracts from the U.S. military—as it did for Japanese firms. And most important of all, the United States opened its market to South Korean exports. For decades, it was the main customer for South Korean manufactures.

ECONOMIC AND SOCIAL CHANGE At first, those manufacturing exports were mainly textiles and shoes. Then, in the 1970s, the South Korean government—ignoring advice from U.S. economists—decided to leave textiles behind and invest in heavy industry such as steel, ships, automobiles, and chemicals, following the Japanese route. By this time, South Korean schools and universities had trained enough scientists and engineers to staff such industries. This gamble on heavy industry worked well, as it had for Japan.

South Korea's leaders were no angels. They had studied the experiences of Meiji Japan and Atatürk's Turkey—both of which fended off foreign domination and used threats, detention, and violence against their own citizens. In 1980, South Korea's military government unleashed the army on peaceful prodemocracy protesters, killing hundreds in the city of Gwangju. Until the late 1980s, South Korea's rulers were authoritarian nationalists whose aim was to strengthen South Korea economically and to reduce dependence on the United States. From the 1990s, when elites recognized they could allow free elections and still expect to retain power, they were democratic nationalists with similar aims.

Throughout its economic surge (1960–1990), South Korea underwent social change that boosted economic growth. Land reform enabled peasants to save enough to educate their children in hopes of upward social mobility. Millions moved from farm to city. And like much of the rest of East Asia in these years, South Korea underwent a lightning-fast fertility transition. In the 1950s, South Korean families averaged more than 5 children. In the decades that followed, partly as a result of government support for birth control, South Korean women changed their ambitions and their lives. Mothers' clubs in thousands of villages spread knowledge of birth control

methods, which were eagerly taken up by South Korean women. In 1975, they averaged under 3 children each, and in 2005, only 1.2. This social change delivered a huge demographic dividend to the economy as the proportion of people in the prime of life climbed.

In addition, during these decades women took up jobs in offices and factories in unprecedented numbers. The investment in girls' education led to very rapid (by world standards) reductions in gender inequality in South Korea (as measured by the UN *Human Development Report*), considerably faster than either Japan or China. Putting more women in the paid labor force and paying them more boosted South Korean economic growth.

South Korea transformed itself from a poor peasant country to a rich industrial one within a generation. Its economy grew by 8 to 10 percent annually from 1960 to 1985, and in the late 1980s it led the world with annual growth rates of up to 12 percent. The explanation for this spurt lies in shrewd industrial and educational policy; a quick fertility transition and big demographic dividend; and the opportunities presented by U.S. strategic support such as massive aid, access to U.S. markets and technology, and U.S. guarantees of security that made South Korea an attractive destination for investment.

CHINA

China's economic rise is the most miraculous of all. It has lifted nearly a billion people out of grinding poverty. It began under the rule of the authoritarian and often brutal Communist Party, which has since embraced capitalism and the unabashed pursuit of private gain. And China engineered its rise without the support from the United States that helped Japan and South Korea.

In longer historical perspective, China's economic transformation looks less miraculous. China—as we have seen—was the first market society, dating back to the Song dynasty (960–1279 CE), with a long tradition of technological ingenuity. Chinese culture was suited to competition in a global economy. But first, China's economy had to survive a century of imperialist exploitation, revolution, war, and Maoist rule.

Concerted efforts to modernize and industrialize China began in the late nineteenth century under the wobbling Qing dynasty. These efforts continued after the revolution of 1910 under Guomindang rule, but the results were modest: in 1936, factories accounted for only

3 percent of China's economic output—compared to 25 percent in Japan. Textiles in the area around Shanghai made up most of that industrial output. The only other industrial cluster in the 1930s was in Manchuria, which was under Japanese control after 1931.

As we've seen, World War II (1937–1945) and the Chinese Civil War (1945–1949) took a terrible toll on China. Violence, disease, and starvation killed about 7 to 8 percent of the population in those 12 years. The standard of living fell to levels of the early nineteenth century. In 1945 and 1946, hyperinflation reduced the currency to near worthlessness. China was among the poorest countries in the world when Mao Zedong and the Chinese Communist Party came to power in 1949. It remained overwhelmingly rural, with only small pockets of industry.

THE ECONOMY UNDER MAOISM Mao Zedong ruled China from 1949 until his death in 1976. His economic policies were ambitious and erratic. He thrived on chaos and used sudden reversals in policy as a political tool to destroy rivals. Given the economic history of China's neighbors since 1950, and that of China itself since Mao's death, it is tempting to conclude that the main impact of Mao and Maoism was to delay the economic rise of China by 30 years.

In the early years of the People's Republic of China (PRC), Mao and his fellow communists aimed to make China stronger, richer, and fairer. Their reforms drew on Chinese precedents and the example of Stalin's USSR, which had stood the test of World War II. So they tried

Chinese Collectivization A 1960 propaganda poster shows farm workers prospering under collectivization. The poster associates collectivization with modern technology: electricity, tractors and other farm machinery, and a factory in the background.

to build a hierarchical communist party, a one-party state, a robust military, and a highly regulated society. They shared the standard communist faith in five-year plans and heavy industry, which they hoped would make China economically and militarily strong and give it a proletariat with which to build communist society. They began with collectivization of agriculture, as Stalin had done.

Collectivization started with the murder of a few million landlords in the early 1950s and the intimidation of the rest. Once the power and authority of the landed gentry were eliminated, the CCP reorganized peasants into communal "work units" that shared land, tools, and animals. Party-appointed leaders of work units decided almost everything for peasant families, including who could marry and who could have children. Peasant families were allowed to keep about 10 percent of the farmland for themselves. Collectivization in China proved unpopular with peasants, as it had in the USSR. In the far South, many slipped over borders to the British colony of Hong Kong or to Burma. The hundreds of millions who remained usually worked much harder on their own tiny plots than on the communal fields—if they could get away with it.

In Japan and South Korea, breaking the hold of landholding elites and turning land over to peasants was a crucial step in launching their economic upsurges. In China, crushing the landlords and turning land over to communal work units was a disaster. At Mao's death in 1976, agricultural efficiency, measured in yields per hectare or per acre, was lower than in 1956. The tiny private plots were the only exceptions: their yields were 5 to 10 times higher than those on collectively farmed land. Agriculture was unable to feed the population: China became a food importer from 1961 to 1996, despite Mao's ambitions for self-reliance.

In embracing heavy industry as a path to growth, Mao was also following in Stalin's footsteps. In what could be the most massive technology transfer in world history, China imported industrial machinery from the USSR and Eastern (Sovietized) Europe in the 1950s. By 1955, two-thirds of China's foreign trade was with the USSR, and Moscow paid for one-third of the projects undertaken in China's first five-year plan (1953–1957). Thousands of Soviet experts flocked to China, giving advice on factory construction, mining, dam building, and much else. Millions of Chinese peasants now became factory workers. In sheer quantitative terms, Mao's program of industrialization was a success. Starting from a very low base, it achieved roughly 11 percent annual growth in industrial output between 1952 and 1978. But the growth in output came only from using more labor, coal, ores, and other raw materials. Chinese industry remained inefficient, wasting energy and raw materials. The quality of goods remained shoddy.

The most spectacularly inefficient—and tragic—of Mao's policies was the **Great Leap Forward** of 1958–1961. To strengthen his hand in domestic politics, Mao decided to make a massive economic push involving both industry and agriculture. Instead of building modern steel mills, for which China did not have the capital or expertise, he required the work units to produce steel in a million "backyard furnaces." For Mao, steel had a symbolic value. He wanted to outstrip British and American production levels and show that he could build a steel industry from scratch even faster than Stalin had done. Even students and faculty at China's elite Peking University had to meet steel quotas. Through heroic effort, China doubled its steel output, melting down doorknobs, bedsprings, bicycle frames, and cooking pots. But steel made this way was usually brittle and useless, a waste of vast quantities of coal, charcoal, and labor, not to mention bikes, beds, and pots.

The Great Leap Forward also featured fiascoes in agriculture. Skeptical of true scientific expertise, Mao maintained that seeds of the same species, even if planted close together, would not compete for nutrients and water. The crops did not cooperate. When food ran short, he demanded that the village work units hand over more grain for the cities, the army, and even for export. Fearing the consequences if they did not deliver, party workers took so much grain that peasants starved. Estimates vary greatly, but between 1958 and 1961 some 20 to 50 million Chinese starved to death—3 to 8 percent of the population of 650 to 700 million. It was by far the worst self-inflicted famine in world history. The Great Leap Forward coincided with a rupture in Sino-Soviet relations, resulting in the expulsion of Soviet advisers and the isolation of China.

THE CULTURAL REVOLUTION Mao's reliance on political mobilization campaigns continued to hamper China's economy. The biggest campaign was the Great Proletarian Cultural Revolution (1966–1976), an effort to rekindle revolutionary spirit and oust some of Mao's

Great Leap Forward Workers manufacture steel in the "backyard furnaces" mandated by Mao's Great Leap Forward, his economic policy of the period 1958–1961.

critics within the CCP. He shut down schools and universities, urging young people to organize themselves as Red Guards and to assault everything old. The Red Guards destroyed temples and texts and attacked elders from teachers to party cadres to their own parents. They beat up foreigners, including Soviet and East German diplomats. They targeted ethnic minorities, killing thousands, especially Mongolians and Tibetans. They inflicted public humiliations on their targets, exhibiting them to jeering crowds. One Red Guard recalled: "We were told that we needed to use violence to destroy a class, spiritually and physically. That was justification enough for torturing someone. They weren't considered human anymore. If they were the enemy, they deserved to be strangled to death, and they deserved to be tortured. This was the education we received."

In 1967 and 1968, Mao called out the army, in some cases to tame the Red Guards and in others to support them. The Cultural Revolution was now virtually a civil war, with 1 to 2 million killed by either the Red Guards or the army. It was also an economic disaster, costing the country about 7 to 8 percent of its GDP in each of 1967 and 1968—a more severe decline than any two-year period of the Great Depression in any major country. By keeping young people out of school for several years and by encouraging them to memorize the quotations of Chairman Mao rather than learn to read and write, the Cultural Revolution cost China in the longer run too. As the economic growth surge swept the rest of East Asia in the 1960s, Mao's policies, whatever their motives, kept China poor and, after the Sino-Soviet split, isolated.

Cultural Revolution Red Guards humiliate victims—forcing them to wear dunce caps proclaiming their crimes—as crowds look on. Humiliation tactics were characteristic of the ideological warfare of the Cultural Revolution.

At the same time, however, Mao laid a foundation for future economic growth. He and the CCP reunified China in the 1940s and then, despite domestic turmoil, kept it together as one country. He succeeded where Gandhi, Nehru, and Jinnah in India failed. In effect, he established a new dynasty—not of a family or lineage as in China's past but of the CCP. National unity would help vault China's economy upward after his death.

Also, in obliterating the landlord class, Mao achieved through murder and brutality what American-imposed land reform achieved in South Korea and Japan. When collectivized agriculture ended after Mao's death, land did not revert to landlords but went to the peasants in long-term leases. His reliance on Soviet machinery and expertise in the 1950s provided industrial skills to a few million Chinese. And as we've seen, Mao thawed relations with the United States in the early 1970s, setting the stage for the full participation of China in the international economy. But it took Mao's death in 1976 and a few other favorable developments for China to embark on its epic rise.

DENG XIAOPING In the years following Mao's death, **Deng Xiaoping** emerged as China's supreme leader—head of the party, the government, and the army. His reorientation of Chinese economic policy led to a genuine great leap forward and a real cultural revolution.

Deng was born in the southwestern province of Sichuan in 1904 to a family of middling gentry status. His father had attended university and played a local role in Sun Yatsen's nationalist revolution. As a schoolboy, Deng became an ardent nationalist, eager to rescue China from weakness, poverty, and humiliation. As a teenager, he joined a work-study program in France, where over a six-year stay (1920–1926) he worked in factories and joined the European branch of the Chinese Communist Party. Like several young Chinese, he saw communism as a way to make China strong. In 1926, Deng went to Moscow to study at a university set up by the Soviets to train Chinese revolutionaries. A year later, he returned to China and began political work.

For the next several decades, Deng rose through the ranks of the CCP. He worked as an ideological enforcer in the CCP's army units during the long struggles against Japan and Chiang Kai-shek's Guomindang party. After the CCP took power in 1949, he served as mayor of a major city, Chongqing, and in many central government posts in the 1950s and 1960s. By and large he supported Mao's policies, but he occasionally ran afoul of Mao anyway and was stripped of his posts more than once. During the Cultural Revolution, he and his family were attacked by Red Guards, his son thrown out of a fourth-story window (he survived as a paraplegic).

Patience and shrewdness were among Deng's hallmarks. He weathered all the storms of Mao's rule and the power struggles after Mao's death. When he took power beginning in 1978, Deng was well over 70 years old and about to embark on a world-changing program of reform to make China strong again.

In 1978, Deng visited Japan and Singapore. At the time, China's per capita income was less than half of sub-Saharan Africa's. Singapore dazzled Deng with a shiny vision of wealth combined with one-party rule and an orderly society—and all overseen by a local population of ethnic Chinese. Thousands of CCP officials visited Singapore after 1978, and Singapore's autocratic leader, Lee Kuan Yew, traveled to China many times. Lee's Singapore had the prosperity of Western countries or Japan and all the advantages of an open, technologically modern economy but no political opposition, no litter or graffiti, and almost no drugs or decadence. Why couldn't China be more like Singapore?

In fact, it could. Deng cautiously allowed the profit motive to operate within limits prescribed by the Communist Party, calling it "socialism with Chinese characteristics." In fact, he was dismantling Maoist socialism and gradually replacing it with capitalism—with Chinese characteristics. Deng's economic reforms unleashed the rise of contemporary China while keeping the CCP's monopoly on political power intact.

DENG'S ECONOMIC REFORMS Deng's first task was replacing the Maoist economy. He allowed peasant families to lease farmland long-term, ending the commune work-unit system. Agricultural production skyrocketed. Between 1978 and 1990, the average Chinese calorie intake doubled, and by 1991 China no longer needed to import food. Between 1979 and 1988, Deng, working with provincial party bosses, created several "special economic zones," at first next door to Hong Kong and across from Taiwan, and invited foreign investment and trade. Small businesses, such as textile workshops, sprouted alongside the older state-owned factories built under Mao. The Pearl River delta—the hinterland of Hong Kong—became, in effect, another Asian economic tiger, similar to Taiwan and South Korea. China's stock exchange, closed since 1949, reopened in 1992.

Whereas Mao had tried to raise production by means of political exhortation and threat, Deng let economic incentives do that work. He allowed local governments to make most of their own decisions about how to invest, produce, and trade. Following the path blazed by the East Asian tigers, he encouraged export-oriented industry and welcomed foreign technology and factory management techniques. Deng unchained the profit motive, claiming that in China markets and socialism were compatible. He translated his earlier remark—that the color of a cat doesn't matter, only that it catches mice—into action: economic growth mattered more than ideological purity. His pragmatic policies sparked an industrial revolution in China, focused on textiles and consumer electronics—as in South Korea and Taiwan. Deng retired in the early 1990s and died in 1997, but his successors steered China along the same path.

Deng was no democrat. He ordered mass executions to encourage obedience and reduce corruption. He maintained oppressive policies toward ethnic minorities such as Uighurs and Tibetans. Whereas Gorbachev in 1989 declined to use the Soviet Army to crush Eastern Europeans' efforts to win greater freedom, Deng in 1989 called out the army against peaceful democracy protesters at Tiananmen Square in the heart of Beijing, leading to a massacre much larger than the one South Korea's army perpetrated in Gwangju in 1980. His commitment to one-party rule was as firm as Mao's.

His ruthless authoritarian streak did not interfere with his liberalization of the economy, the results of which were of world historical importance. By 2004, China was receiving more foreign investment than any other country in the world. Between 1980 and 2020, the economy grew

Tiananmen Square A single Chinese man attempts to block tanks on their way to Tiananmen Square to crush peaceful prodemocracy protests on June 5, 1989. As many as several thousand protesters may have been killed by the Chinese military during the protests.

50-fold, posting annual growth rates of 8 to 11 percent. No big country had ever done this before or even come close. The United States achieved such rates only briefly during World War II.

Comparison between the world's two most populous countries helps show how extraordinary China's economic trajectory was. China and India between 1950 and 1990 were twins in poverty. In both countries, most people barely had enough to eat. After 1990 both got richer, but China did so far faster, so that in 2020 its per capita GDP was roughly five times that of India.

ECONOMIC EFFECTS AND GLOBAL REACH The Chinese government and some Chinese citizens were getting rich. By 2000, government revenues were about 30 times the level of Mao's last years and rising fast. The wealth of the central and provincial governments allowed tremendous investment in infrastructure: China built 54 new airports between 2000 and 2010 and a network of bullet trains covering much of the country. According to World Bank figures, about 800 million Chinese climbed out of poverty between 1990 and 2020. This represents the largest and fastest escape from mass poverty in world history.

By 2015, China was the workshop of the world—as Britain had been called in the mid-nineteenth century. It was the world's largest carmaker, having overtaken the

United States in 2009. It made 90 percent of the world's personal computers and mobile phones, 80 percent of the air conditioners, 70 percent of the solar panels, and 65 percent of the shoes. Its biggest cities—Beijing, Shanghai, Guangzhou—became nodes of the Global web.

Economic prosperity also brought China international prestige and power. By the mid-1990s, China was doubling its military budget every few years and converting uninhabited islands in the South China Sea into military bases. It became a major arms dealer. It offered loans to many governments in Asia and Africa in exchange for control of commercial ports and military bases around the Indian Ocean. It purchased long-term leases on farmland in Africa. Some 10,000 Chinese companies were active in Africa as of 2020, creating new factories, mines, and plantations and building roads, bridges, dams, and hotels. Outside of Lagos, Nigeria, for example, a Guangdong-based firm opened a new industrial zone that its Chinese manager said was "like managing a country. We have our own customs, our own police, our own operations." There is irony in the resemblance of these quasi-imperial arrangements to the autonomous commercial compounds run in Chinese cities by European powers a century before.

By the early twenty-first century, the Chinese state had become a major force not only in East Asia but in global politics as well.

SOURCES OF CHINA'S ECONOMIC SURGE

Deng's economic reforms took advantage of several favorable circumstances with roots in the Mao period. The diplomatic opening to the United States that Mao had engineered in the early 1970s enabled China's return to the global economy. It joined the World Trade Organization (WTO) in 2001, symbolizing its economic reintegration. The Chinese economy also benefited from the millions of overseas Chinese, many of them refugees from Maoism, living in Singapore, Hong Kong, Taiwan, and throughout Southeast Asia. These communities included bankers and entrepreneurs who spoke Chinese, understood Chinese cultural contexts, and were willing to trade with and invest in Deng's China. For the first two decades after Deng's reforms, the majority of investment in China came from overseas Chinese and from South Korea.

Education was another source of China's economic surge. When the CCP took power in 1949, only about 20 percent of Chinese could read. By 1964, thanks to intensive efforts in primary education, about 65 percent could. The Cultural Revolution (1966–1976) slowed progress, so that figure remained about the same in 1980—and women were still much less likely to be literate than men. But by 2018, fully 97 percent of Chinese could read, and the gender gap had almost vanished. By 2020, 8 million Chinese graduated from universities each year, and another 400,000 were studying in U.S. universities.

Additionally, Deng and his successors inherited a growing demographic dividend. During the 1950s and 1960s, Mao urged Chinese to have big families on the theory that a country's strength lies in its people and there could never be too many Chinese. In 1967, Chinese women averaged six births over their lifetime. By 1978, the average had dropped to only three. As the graph shows, it took the United Kingdom 95 years (1815–1910) to reduce fertility from six to three births per woman over her lifetime. The United States took 82 years (1844–1926). China did it in 11—and did not stop there.

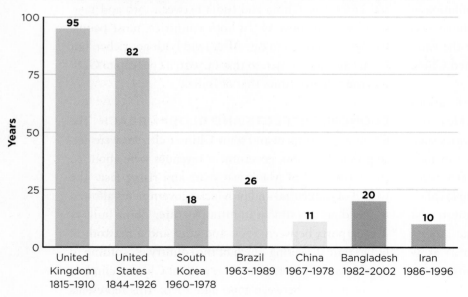

Fertility Declines from More Than 6 to Fewer Than 3 Children per Woman

This bar graph shows the timing and pace of fertility transitions in seven countries. The earlier transitions—in the United Kingdom and the United States—were slower. Those occurring from 1960 on were far faster. Fast transitions created an age structure—lots of people in the prime of life and fewer who were very old or very young—that sped up economic growth for a few decades. China and Iran were among the countries with the fastest fertility transitions in world history.

Source: Our World in Data, ourworldindata.org (data from Gapminder fertility dataset, version 6, and World Bank World Development Indicators).

In the years 1978–1980, with the birth rate already falling rapidly, the CCP abandoned Mao's position on population and imposed a "one-child rule" that penalized families with two or more children. Birth rates continued to slide; by 1990 the average fell to 2 children per woman and by 2000 to 1.6, where it has stayed. It is likely that urbanization and the education of females had more to do with this fall in fertility than did the government restrictions. But whatever the causes, it delivered an enormous demographic dividend. Some economists credit this factor alone with one-quarter of China's economic growth since 1980. Faced with a rapidly aging population, China abandoned the one-child policy in 2016.

So Deng, his allies, and his successors took advantage of some favorable circumstances that, combined with shrewd policies, ignited an era of economic growth in China that fit the earlier regional pattern. While Japan launched the economic rise of East Asia, and South Korea, Taiwan, Singapore, and Hong Kong confirmed it, China—because of its size—completed it.

ENVIRONMENTAL AND SOCIAL PROBLEMS

Economic growth spurts usually come at a price. In the East Asian cases, that price included heavy pollution affecting air, water, and human health. Environmental protection carried a low priority for governments in East Asia while countries were trying to industrialize and escape poverty. Japan suffered many episodes of acute pollution in the 1950s and 1960s. The most famous of these was so-called **Minamata disease**, referring to a seaside bay slathered in mercury from a nearby chemical plant. Many people who ate seafood from Minamata developed nerve damage, and their babies often had horrible birth defects. By the 1970s and 1980s, Japan got around to addressing its environmental health. South Korea and Taiwan followed a similar trajectory. China today is trying to address monumental pollution problems, but air and water pollution still kill a few million Chinese annually.

East Asia's rapid economic growth also produced new frictions and resentments due to social inequality. Some people got very rich while others did not. Japan suffered less strife from this cause than South Korea or China. Today, China is—depending how you measure it—among the most spectacularly unequal societies in the world. In 1978, its top 1 percent of earners took in 6

Minamata Disease　A mother in the village of Minamata in southern Japan holds her 12-year-old daughter, who was born with severe nerve damage due to exposure to the mercury that polluted Minamata Bay.

percent of national income, but by 2020 they received 16 percent. One-quarter of its population remains dirt-poor, and in the interior, away from the more prosperous coasts, that proportion is much higher.

A demographic inequality affects China as well, one that empowers young women and deprives tens of millions of Chinese men of a chance to marry and raise families. Chinese families for centuries have had a strong preference for boys and in difficult times had often sold or killed girl babies. When ultrasound technology became available to monitor pregnancies around 1990, and the government permitted most families only one child, many couples turned to selective abortion in their effort to ensure that they got a boy. As a result, China's population in recent decades developed a shortage of females. The ratio of boys to girls among newborns peaked at 1.22 to 1.0 in 2008, by far the highest in the world. Today, Chinese women of marriageable age are in short supply and consequently enjoy unprecedented choice in selecting partners. Their good fortune comes at the expense of tens of millions aborted because they were female and tens of millions of men unhappily unmarried.

Economic development also brought corruption. Where governments take a strong role in the economy, as in every East Asian economic surge, officials have countless opportunities to accept bribes and kickbacks. Hong Kong and Singapore minimized this problem, largely because those in charge chose to suppress corruption rather than revel in it. Japan tackled the issue and today

How Many Children per Family?

Most cultures, and all those reliant on agriculture, have long encouraged big families. Until the nineteenth century, and in many places well into the twentieth, so many children died young that it made sense to have several. That ensured enough hands for the countless tasks in a farming household, as well as help for its elderly members. The world's major religions, all of which emerged in times when many children died young, all endorse big families.

Kings and emperors agreed that big families were best for everyone. They wanted more taxpayers and soldiers in order to expand their own revenues and power. They generally encouraged people to marry young and discouraged any form of birth control.

In 1800, the average woman in Japan or France had 4 children over her lifetime, and in Russia and the United States about 7. Since then, parents have increasingly come to see family size differently. More families sought to limit the number of children they had, either because they expected more to survive or perhaps because they lived in a city and didn't need children to tend chickens, pick berries, or weed fields. By 1970, the average had fallen to 2.5 in the United States and France and to about 2 in Japan and Russia; by 2010, it was 2 or fewer in all four countries.

Most kings, emperors, and other rulers in the nineteenth and twentieth centuries still promoted big families because they still wanted large populations. Fascist Italy, Nazi Germany, and several communist countries awarded women medals for having many children. Several other countries offered "baby bonuses" or tax incentives to encourage parents to have more children.

China took the opposite position on family size between 1978 and 2016. Its leaders used various rewards and punishments to discourage families from having more than one child. The policy consolidated an enormous demographic dividend. But in 2016, its leadership growing concerned with the aging population distribution, China abandoned that policy. Likewise, Iran in the 1990s aggressively promoted family planning and cut its birth rate in half within 15 years, but in 2012 its supreme leader, Ali Khamenei, proclaimed that birth control was wrong and that Iran needed more Iranians. Japan, South Korea, and Taiwan, which decades ago promoted birth control, now have financial incentives to encourage bigger families—none of which have worked.

Families and rulers used to agree that big families were best. In recent history, their views on the ideal number of children often diverge—and often change.

QUESTIONS FOR DISCUSSION

1. Why did parents change their view of family size after 1800?
2. Why has family size long been a concern of rulers?

---

ranks with Singapore and Hong Kong among the least corrupt societies when it comes to business practices. China, however, has suffered from widespread corruption that, despite occasional crackdowns, often involves top government officials and their families.

Despite these and other dark clouds, almost no one in East Asia regrets the economic transformations of the past two generations. Their full meaning, of course, is impossible to assess because the process is still under way.

REBALANCING IN THE GLOBAL WEB

By the second half of the twentieth century, the Global web was no longer expanding much. It had drawn in just about every population on Earth. But, as always, the web of connections was changing shape, with some pathways carrying more traffic and others slowing down. And just what those circuits carried—political ideas, trade goods, investment funds, cultural fashions, human migrants, and microbes—also evolved.

The rise of East Asia reshaped the Global web. East Asia became one of its most interactive zones. Sometimes called Asia-Pacific, this tightly integrated space centered on the humming economies of China and the neighboring Asian tigers. East Asia also became firmly linked—economically, culturally, and politically—to the United States and to some extent almost everywhere else. Japanese businesses built links to companies based on the Pacific coasts of Canada, the United States, and South America by the 1960s. China and Brazil had almost nothing to do with each other before 1980, but by 2009 China was Brazil's biggest trade partner, importing soybeans and ores and building new ports and railroads in South America. Flows of investment, joint research ventures, diplomatic visits by heads of state, and much else bound them together. South Korea developed strong business connections to the Persian Gulf, pioneering another new strand of the Global web. The rise of East Asia is the single largest shift in the Global web and international politics of the past 50 years.

Glittering Skyscrapers The marina and shore of Tanzania's capital, Dar-es-Salaam, in 2020. In that year, Tanzanians' average income per capita was 165th (out of 192) in the world. Their incomes had doubled since the 1990s, which helps explain the modern office towers and apartment blocks.

THE GLOBAL SOUTH SINCE 1960

Scholars increasingly understand the distribution of wealth and power in the world as a matter of Global North (rich and powerful) and Global South (poorer and weaker). This vocabulary plays fast and very loose with geography: low latitude, that is, closeness to the Equator, correlates with poverty much more than does southern latitude—Australia and New Zealand are rich countries and among the southernmost. Its merit is that it acknowledges a shift in international politics and economics away from the Cold War order. Here we will focus mainly on two regions of the Global South: sub-Saharan Africa and Latin America. While East Asian societies were pulling off an economic miracle unmatched in world history, these two regions hardly changed their position in the international order. They were both comparatively poor and weak in 1960 and by 2020 were a little richer but scarcely any more powerful.

AFRICA IN THE GLOBAL WEB SINCE 1960

Remember from earlier chapters the diversity of Africa. The continent as a whole, including North Africa, now contains more than 50 countries. Sub-Saharan Africa, the focus here, features between 1,000 and 2,000 spoken languages. Some people live or work in glittering skyscrapers in giant cities such as Nairobi or Johannesburg, much as their counterparts in New York or Tokyo do. Others scratch hard livings from the soil in remote villages, much as their ancestors did.

PERSPECTIVES ON ECONOMIC PERFORMANCE
Most observers, including Africans, find the economic record of Africa since 1960 disappointing. Per capita income for the average African has doubled since 1960. But in the same years, average incomes in Latin America tripled, those in South and Southeast Asia grew sixfold, and those in East Asia increased nearly tenfold. South Asians, on average, were slightly poorer than Africans in 1960, but now their incomes are twice those of Africans. From this comparative perspective, Africa's economic record is indeed disappointing. Other world regions, equally poor at the time of Africa's decolonization, have prospered much faster than Africa.

There is another way to look at it. If one considers the postcolonial economic record of Africa in light of the longer past, it looks better. While we have no reliable figures about African economies before the twentieth century, the most informed expert guesses suggest that they grew very slowly, maybe 0.1 percent per year. Against that background, the post-1960 growth record looks fast. So Africans who compared their economic circumstances to those of their ancestors often concluded they were doing well. But those who compared their circumstances to those of other people around the world would conclude the opposite.

One further factor shaped the understanding of postcolonial economic performance in Africa: raised expectations. In the late colonial era, African independence leaders routinely promised that once the shackles of colonialism were thrown off and liberation achieved, citizens would enjoy freedom and prosperity. Those promises made the realities of the next 60 years harder to accept—in most countries.

For, as you would expect, the economic record among African countries after independence varied considerably, as the table below shows. Botswana, for example, was among the poorest parts of Africa in 1960 in per capita income but by 1990 was among the continent's richest and by 2020 the richest of all. It was the only African country whose population enjoyed incomes above the world average. Niger and Madagascar, on the other hand, grew poorer after the end of colonial rule. The most populous country, Nigeria, enjoyed improvements in living standards at about twice the rate of Africa as a whole and indeed a little faster than the global average. That mixed record disappointed everyone who believed their leaders' predictions made at independence.

Inequality is another important measure of economic performance. Here again the African glass is either half-full or half-empty depending on one's perspective. In 1980, the top 10 percent of earners in Africa took in 57 percent of the total income, a level of inequality higher than in any world region except the Middle East. In 2015, African income inequality remained almost exactly the same, whereas it had increased almost everywhere else in the world (especially in Russia and India). So relative to the rest of the world, Africa restrained the growth of income inequality—but at levels that remained high.

STIFLED ECONOMIES What accounts for Africa's postcolonial economic record? Different answers apply in different parts of Africa, but on the whole we can point to three main factors. First, geography in many parts of Africa posed a challenge for taking advantage of modern global connections. Roughly one-third of African countries since 1960 were (and are) landlocked. Only one-fifth of Africans lived within 62 miles (100 km) of a navigable river or the sea (compared to two-thirds in the U.S. and China and nine-tenths in Europe). The African coastline does not have abundant natural harbors compared to most other parts of the world. Within Africa, transport costs were high because navigable rivers, railroads, and paved roads remained few. At independence, three landlocked countries, Upper Volta (now Burkina Faso), Niger, and Central African the Republic had no railroads at all; in 2023 the latter two still had none. These geographical facts had mattered less in prior centuries, when opportunities for long-distance trade were fewer. In the postcolonial world, when the Global web was humming with trade, and ports in Japan, Korea, and China as well as those of western Europe and North America were launching cargo ships round the clock, Africa could play only a small role. None of the world's 50 busiest ports between 2004 and 2020 were in Africa (27 were in East or Southeast Asia). The economic advantages of specialization and exchange were harder to seize for Africans than for East and Southeast Asians, Europeans, and North Americans.

Second, African population growth after 1960 reached such high rates that improving average living standards was extremely difficult. In Kenya, for example, the population in 1960 was about 8 million and by 2022 had reached 55 million. It briefly attained an annual growth rate of 4 percent in the late 1970s and early 1980s. Niger, meanwhile, grew from 3.4 million to 25 million and approached 4 percent annual growth around 2013. (With 4% annual population growth, the average woman bore eight children.) No country in world history has ever improved per capita incomes with population growth at such levels. Part of the difficulty with such rapid demographic growth was that women especially, but adults in general, needed to devote tremendous amounts of time and energy to minding children and babies, leaving less for farming, weaving,

	1960	1990	2019
World	100	189	307
Africa	31	36	46
Botswana	10	101	196
South Africa	107	140	171
Zambia	34	24	38
Tanzania	n.d.	16	30
Ethiopia	n.d.	7	22
Chad	16	12	18
Niger	21	13	15
Nigeria	40	44	70
Ivory Coast	44	53	65
Madagascar	23	16	14

PER CAPITA GDP IN AFRICA, 1960–2019, AS A PERCENTAGE OF THE 1960 WORLD AVERAGE ($3,586)

Source: Our World in Data, https://ourworldindata.org/search?q=GDP+per+capita.

Note: Figures are adjusted for inflation. 2019 is used rather than 2020 to avoid skewing by the temporary effect of the pandemic.

accounting, engineering, or any other form of work that might generate income. Africa's total population growth rate peaked in 1982 (at 3 percent per year). By 2023, it had fallen to 2.3 percent annually, so it matters less. But it still remains a considerable handicap—especially in Angola, Malawi, Uganda, Niger, and Mali, where it remains highest. The demographic dividend that boosted East Asian economies in the 1960s–1990s has not occurred (yet) in Africa outside of South Africa and Botswana.

The main reason behind this decades-long surge of population growth in Africa is a happy one: improved disease control. Public health measures such as vaccination, provision of clean drinking water, creation of clinics, and so forth sharply reduced infant and child mortality and lengthened life expectancy. So death rates declined, while until recently birth rates remained high—causing the surge. If Africa's demographic trajectory follows that of other parts of the world—and all signs suggest it will—birth rates will continue to fall, the growth surge will end, and a demographic dividend will be within reach. Meanwhile, by 2023, the continent of Africa had 1.4 billion people, one-sixth of the world's total and equal to the populations of China and India—both of which it will likely outstrip in the decades ahead.

A third important factor shaping recent African economic performance is the colonial legacy and its durability. African colonial economies were **commodity dependent**, often centered around the export of a single product such as copper, cocoa, or cotton. International prices for these commodities remained high for about a decade after independence, inspiring governments to maintain or even double down on these narrow export sectors. In the 1970s and 1980s, however, prices for most commodities around the world crashed. Copper prices nosedived by 75 percent between 1975 and 1985, for example. Citizens' incomes and government revenues in several African countries, including Zambia (copper), Ivory Coast and Ghana (cocoa), and Chad and Sudan (cotton) plummeted. Escaping this particular colonial legacy, which by and large was stronger in African colonies than Asian ones, proved difficult. Economic diversification, the obvious cure, was elusive. Industrialization, the historical route to prosperity in Europe and East Asia, remained minimal outside of South Africa.

Part of the difficulty in diversifying came from outside the continent. Foreign businesses, banks, and governments sought to preserve these one-commodity export

African Railroads in 2017 This map shows part of the colonial legacy in Africa. The former settler colonies of Algeria and South Africa have the densest rail networks. Somalia, Burundi, Central African Republic, Chad, Niger, Gambia, Guinea-Bissau, Equatorial Guinea—among the world's poorest countries—have none at all. The existing rail lines, mostly built before 1960, helped to perpetuate colonial economic linkages by easing the export of minerals or cash crops. In addition, some countries have rail lines of different gauges (width of track), which has made it difficult to connect different lines into a network.

sectors through lending policies or trade agreements—part of what critics called neocolonialism. Foreign industrial sectors—especially those of France and Portugal—wanted raw materials from Africa, not competition. French governments intervened militarily in former colonies more than 50 times after 1960 to try to shore up or install African rulers with cozy relations with French businesses. And prevailing economic theory—specifically the principle of comparative advantage according to which every producer benefits by focusing on the one thing it does best—told everyone that Gambia's future lay in continued peanut production, not in industrial products. Zambia's lay in copper, Guinea's in bauxite. To get loans from foreign banks and governments, which they needed after years of low commodity prices, African countries had to abide by bankers' prevailing economic ideas and channel investment toward raw material exports.

Countries that discovered major deposits of oil, such as Nigeria and Angola, found that their fortunes improved in the 1970s and early 1980s, when world oil prices spiked. What was good for them was bad for other countries without oil to sell. Then, after 1986, fortunes reversed as oil prices collapsed. Dependence on oil exports was not a colonial legacy, because very little oil had been found in colonial Africa. But it was a variation on the theme of dependence on a single commodity export, making entire countries vulnerable to international prices over which they had little control.

Another constraint affecting large parts of Africa was, and is, the gender imbalance in education and income. All over Africa, adult women earned (and still earn) less than half of what men do, even though almost all of them held jobs. Often these jobs were in the informal economy, sewing at home or selling items on the street. The strongest reason for this gender gap was the disparity in education. However, the most recent trend in southern Africa has been toward greater education for females and, with that, both greater use of the talents of women in the economy and a narrowing of the gender gap in income among younger women.

Several other factors constrained Africa's economic performance after 1960, but in most cases in less enduring ways. In the Sahel and the Horn of Africa, climate shifts delivered devastating shocks, destroying harvests for years on end and bringing recurrent famines, especially in 1968–1986 and again after 2016. Drought is cyclical in much of Africa, and these were not without precedent. They were deeper than any droughts since about 1910, but Africans had long experience rebuilding their herds and replanting crops once rainfall returned.

In many countries, most notably Zaire (now Congo) under President Mobutu Sese Seko (in office 1965–1997), corruption flourished. That also hamstrung economic development. Mobutu's appetite for bribes made him one of the world's richest people while making it harder for businesses to get off the ground in Zaire. Africans invented a colorful word for rich public officials who wear expensive suits and are driven in fancy cars: *WaBenzi*, which means "(Mercedes) Benz people." Political and economic corruption generally went together. Some rulers, often with external support from France, the United States, or the Soviet Union, manipulated (or prevented) elections, jailed rivals, muzzled independent media, and stayed in power for 40 or more years. In Gabon (an oil-rich country in West Central Africa), a father-and-son pair have held the presidency since 1967. Botswana, with the highest per capita income in Africa, is rated the least corrupt by the international NGOs that publish corruption rankings.

Probably more important than drought or corruption was widespread government underinvestment in primary and secondary education. Colonial-era education levels were extremely low. Congo had about 20 university graduates at the time of independence. Postcolonial governments in the 1960s expanded access to education considerably, but after about 1970, when economic times got tougher, they generally chopped education budgets—in sharp contrast to the policies adopted and sustained in postcolonial East Asian countries. Countries such as Niger and Mozambique are so poor in part because since independence only about half of their populations have completed primary school.

Many factors, from inconvenient geography and demographic trends to colonial legacies and unhelpful policies, combined to limit African economic performance since independence. They help to explain why Africa's trajectory looks disappointing if compared to other parts of the world, especially East Asia. But it is wise to remember that for many Africans, especially in rural areas, the comparison to East Asia or Latin America remains less important than the comparison to the lives of their parents and grandparents, which yields a more favorable judgment.

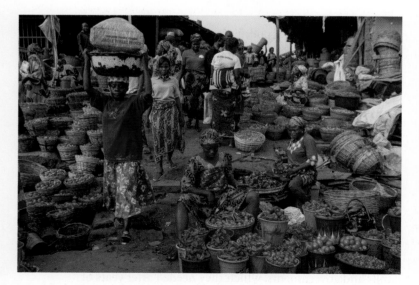

Market Women In parts of Africa, women mainly worked in informal jobs. In this 2015 photo from Ibadan, Nigeria, women sell peppers, greens, and vegetables. Throughout West Africa, so-called "market women" have long played a prominent role in economic life.

FRAGMENTED POLITICS In much of Africa, post-colonial politics compounded economic challenges mainly through the frequency of armed conflict and instability. Here the burden of the colonial legacy was especially heavy. The borders drawn in colonial times amounted to a recipe for both internal conflicts and wars between countries. Borders inherited at independence had little logic to them in terms of languages or religious and ethnic identities among Africans. Every country contained multiple ethnolinguistic groups and religions, making the formation of national identities hard. Sudan, for example, had an Arabic-speaking and Muslim north and a largely Christian south where languages and identities such as Dinka or Nuer prevailed. Chad and Mali also straddled the divide between Islamic and non-Islamic populations. Divisions of these sorts exist widely in the world, but in many cases, national languages and a sense of common identity evolved over centuries (often a bloody process). Most African countries, only about 60 years old, as yet have comparatively weak national identities. That helps explain why in about half of African countries at least one minority population has tried to secede since 1960. Only two have succeeded: Eritrea broke free from Ethiopia in 1993, and South Sudan separated from Sudan in 2011. The costliest attempt in terms of the scale of violence was the Biafran War (1967–1970), in which Nigeria, at the cost of about one million lives, prevented the independence of its southeastern region, dominated by the Igbo people. The Igbo secession was partly about asserting their own identity but also about who would benefit from selling Nigeria's oil, which lies mainly in Igboland.

Inherited borders also contributed to political instability in the form of warfare between states. African countries have fought more than 90 wars with one another since independence. Sometimes they were motivated by grievances connected to the mismatches between borders and religious or ethnic identities. Sometimes war broke out over oil patches or diamond mines. The largest African war raged between 1998 and 2008, involving armies of Congo and Rwanda with occasional participation by troops from Angola, Namibia, Chad, and Zimbabwe, among others—and several local militias. Usually called the **Second Congo War**, it probably cost more than 5 million lives—the world's deadliest conflict since World War II.

Coups d'état also weakened independent Africa. On roughly 200 occasions, members of the armed forces tried to overthrow a sitting government. About half of these coups succeeded. Sudan, independent since 1956, has seen 15 attempted coups and 5 successful ones. Only seven countries have never experienced a coup attempt: Botswana, Eritrea, Malawi, Namibia, South Africa, South Sudan, and Tanzania. Coup attempts were most likely in countries where leaders tried to stay in power for 20 or 30 years. Since 2000, the frequency of coup attempts has fallen.

All these forms of political instability contributed to the economic challenges that Africans faced and also to the weakness of Africa in the international system. Conflict, violence, and mistrust almost always undermine prospects for prosperity, in Africa or anywhere else. One further factor, something that did not happen, should be considered as well. Africa did not unite.

As independence approached, many voices, most prominently Kwame Nkrumah of Ghana, had called for a unified Africa consistent with the ideology of Pan-Africanism (see Chapter 25). A big, united Africa such as Nkrumah envisioned would have been a major force within international politics and the international economy, able to drive favorable bargains on commodity prices, for example. But an Africa fragmented into 50 countries was not. Like Bolívar's call for a united states of South America in the 1820s, efforts to address Africa's political fragmentation in the 1960s came to nothing. A few regional confederations were created, but all quickly broke up. The Organization of African Unity, formed in 1963 and after 2002 called the African Union, was intended to support the status quo, the right of every African leader to govern unmolested by anyone else—within the inherited borders of each country. It did little in the cause of African unity. Moreover, very few leaders once in control of independent countries wanted to surrender the power they had just won to a larger, unified Africa. Ideological differences, sometimes kindled by the Cold War superpowers, made cooperation, let alone unification, difficult. It is of course uncertain that a united Africa could have stayed united, but it was the best hope for Africans to achieve a more favorable distribution of wealth and power in the international system. Africa's 54 members in the UN General Assembly provided a formidable voting bloc—when all could agree—but that was modest consolation for a divided continent.

The one thing that almost all Black Africans agreed upon was the injustice of white supremacist regimes in southern Africa. In 1960, Mozambique and Angola remained colonies dominated economically and politically by substantial populations of white settlers, mostly Portuguese. South Africa, which acquired independence from Britain in stages beginning in 1910, imposed an ideology of **apartheid** ("separateness") in 1948, according to which political rights and most land were reserved for the white settler minority. For whites, about 20 percent of the population in 1948, South Africa was becoming a comfortable democracy; for Black Africans, it was a poor country, full of humiliations and punishments. Southern Rhodesia (now Zimbabwe), Bechuanaland (now Botswana), and Southwest Africa (now Namibia), were similarly dominated by small white minorities and carefully supported by South Africa. So the southernmost quarter of the continent practiced a ruthless white supremacy. Its regimes often enjoyed support from the United States while the Cold War lasted, as we've seen in Chapter 27.

Resistance eventually triumphed. With assistance from other African governments, rebels in Angola and Mozambique overthrew Portuguese rule by 1975 amid great violence. Most whites quickly fled to Portugal or South Africa. Armed rebels in Southern Rhodesia ousted the white settler government by 1980. Gradually, the majority of the white population (never more than 5 percent in Rhodesia) left, under pressure from Zimbabwe's new rulers. In South Africa, white rule lasted until 1994, when the government agreed to free elections for all, ending the white monopoly on political rights.

The end of apartheid and white rule in South Africa came more peacefully than in neighboring countries. It resulted from the sustained political campaigns of the African National Congress (ANC), formed in 1912 and modeled on the Indian National Congress that under Gandhi led India to independence. The ANC, after a massacre of protesters in 1960, created an armed wing that eventually adopted terrorist tactics, although with little success. After 1961, the ANC accepted increasing aid from the USSR, which made it easy for the apartheid regime to appeal to the United States for aid against communism. The struggle continued for another three decades. By the 1980s, the South African state, still supported by the U.S. government, gradually became an international pariah, the target of boycotts and disinvestment campaigns. None truly threatened white rule. But by 1990, as the Cold War ended, Soviet aid to the ANC ceased and U.S. support for the apartheid state waned. In financial peril, both the South African government and the ANC agreed to negotiate. Talks succeeded in large

part because the ANC, now led by Nelson Mandela, chose reconciliation over revenge.

Mandela was a consequential man. Born into an aristocratic Xhosa lineage in 1918, raised in the Methodist church, he studied law and joined the ANC in the early 1940s. He never finished his degree but instead rose through the ranks of the ANC. The installation of apartheid in 1948 provoked his commitment to revolution. After helping organize many protests, boycotts, and strikes and undergoing several arrests, in 1961 he cofounded the militant wing of the ANC. That led to arrest, trial, and a life sentence. Mandela spent the next 27 years in prison, emerging in 1990, now an old man. Despite his prior endorsement of violence against apartheid and despite his life sentence, Mandela in the early 1990s put bitterness aside and negotiated a peaceful demolition of white supremacy and the foundation of a democracy with universal adult suffrage in South Africa.

The end of white supremacy in southern Africa did not solve everything. Civil wars lasted until 1992 in Mozambique and 2002 in Angola. More or less authoritarian, one-party states developed in Mozambique, Angola, and especially Zimbabwe. South Africa became, in effect, a one-party state, and the ANC's commitment to multiracial democracy weakened after Mandela's retirement in 1999. South Africa remained one of the world's most economically unequal societies: most whites continued to live comfortably, while half the African population struggled in stark poverty. A quarter of the white population has emigrated since 1994, and increasing numbers of educated Black Africans have left as well.

Despite these and other problems, the end of white supremacy brought a radical decline in racial injustice and political violence to southern Africa. In Botswana, it helped bring prosperity, based on diamond exports and tourism, and in South Africa it supported a rise in average incomes far faster than in most of Africa. Postcolonial African political history contains many disappointments, but almost all Africans rank the end of racist minority rule in southern Africa, which in 1960 seemed an unlikely prospect, as a triumph.

Africa's deepening integration into global circuits took new forms, including migration. Africans have long been mobile, and colonial-era economies encouraged long-distance (mostly male) labor migrations to mining districts in central or southern Africa. In the first postcolonial decades, upward of 80 percent of African migrants stayed within Africa, usually in countries adjacent to that of their birth. Since 2000, however, that pattern has globalized somewhat. Between 2000 and 2020, only about 55 percent of African migrants remained within Africa. About a quarter went to Europe, a tenth to the oil states of the Persian Gulf, and 7 percent to North America. Here the colonial legacy brought an advantage: many Africans spoke English, French, or Portuguese fluently, easing their entry into societies such as Britain, the United States, Canada, France, or Brazil. As of 2020, about 3 percent of Africans lived abroad, a rate slightly lower than the world average. It came to about 40 million people, mostly young males. Africans left home for the usual range of reasons behind emigration: to find a better life and, especially those from Ethiopia, Somalia, Rwanda, and Congo, to escape dangerous conflict zones. Increasingly, the search for a better life entailed leaving regions ravaged by drought, heat waves, or other forms of changing climate.

Another change in Africa's global integration came in the form of a growing Chinese presence. The early postcolonial period in Africa coincided with the Mao years in China, and relations were mainly diplomatic, symbolic, and rhetorical—although in the early 1970s Chinese workers did help build, and China financed, a railroad from Zambia to the Indian Ocean coast through Tanzania. As of 2000, China and Africa still had minimal trade links, but the relationship soon blossomed. By 2009, China had become Africa's single largest trading partner; in 2015–2020 China accounted for about 15–20 percent of African international trade. Since 2012, China has also been the single largest investor in Africa, replacing the United States. Almost overnight, China became economically important to Africa.

Africa became economically important to China in a more limited way. It accounts for only about 4 percent of Chinese trade, and 0 percent of incoming investment. It now supplies one-third of China's oil, mostly from Angola, and some minerals, including Zambian copper. China also set up rubber, sugar, and tobacco plantations in Africa. In all, about one million Chinese now live in Africa (compared to 232,000 U.S. citizens).

While in the future Africa may become more economically valuable to China, in the early decades of the twenty-first century the dividend for China was mainly political. In 2016, China began construction of a military base in the northeast African country of Djibouti (one of seven countries to have Chinese bases there). Africa's

Confucius Institutes Dozens of Confucius Institutes help Beijing wield soft power by bringing Chinese culture to Africans. Here students at the University of Johannesburg's Confucius Institute, in South Africa, practice their Chinese calligraphy skills in 2023.

54 votes in the UN General Assembly since 2010 have supported China's positions with increasing regularity. All African countries but one now back China's claim to Taiwan, for example. China avoided criticizing African rulers for corruption or human rights abuses, and African rulers returned the favor.

By and large, African states and most Africans welcome the Chinese presence. Violent labor protests against Chinese employers have flared up in Zambia's copper belt and elsewhere, and some Africans see the Chinese initiatives as a form of neocolonialism. Giant loans to African governments put some countries at risk of having to turn assets over to China, as happened to Sri Lanka and Laos. Aware of the accusations of practicing "debt-trap diplomacy," China lately has tried to employ **soft power** in Africa, opening more than 60 Confucius Institutes, whose mission is to tell China's story the Chinese way. By 2018, scholarships to Chinese universities for African students numbered more than 80,000 (about 1,000 are available from the UK). The growing links with China have given Africans more choices in their economic and political partnerships. Whether or not that will help Africa claim a larger share in the distribution of wealth and power in the world remains to be seen. At present, the continent remains poor by global standards, politically fragmented, its countries nearly powerless in the ruthless arena of international politics.

LATIN AMERICA IN THE GLOBAL WEB SINCE 1960

As with Africa and other big regions, the first thing to bear in mind with respect to Latin America is its diversity.

Currently, Latin America—here the phrase refers to South America, Central America, Mexico, and the Caribbean—includes 33 countries, 11 of which had fewer than 1 million people by 2023. Brazil, with 215 million, and Mexico, with 127 million, are the region's demographic giants. Most of the nearly 650 million Latin Americans speak either Spanish or Portuguese, but several million speak indigenous languages, especially in the Andes and Central America. In much of the Caribbean, either English, French, or Dutch is spoken, or creole languages based partly on these European languages and partly on African or indigenous languages. For instance, Haitian creole (or kreyòl), based on eighteenth-century French vocabulary and grammar from West African languages, has more than 10 million speakers. In terms of religion, the majority of Latin Americans have long been Catholics. But in the past 50 years, other forms of Christianity, notably evangelical Protestant sects, have become more popular. So have religions based on West African and Angolan spirituality, such as Santería in Cuba or Candomblé in Brazil. Indigenous religions retain followings as well. In every case, Latin American religion involves some mixture of Christian, African, and indigenous tradition, occasionally with elements from Islam too. When asked about their ethnicity in 2018, 46 percent of Latin Americans said they were mestizo, 27 percent considered themselves white, 11 percent identified as Indigenous, 6 percent as mulatto, another 6 percent as Black (and the remainder as "other"). Big variations exist among countries and in some cases, such as Brazil, within them. Whether in matters of language, religion, or other considerations—such as race, ethnicity, or income level—Latin America, although a convenient phrase, contains diverse multitudes.

Nevertheless, it is possible to hazard a few generalizations about Latin America since about 1980 that help explain the changes and the continuities in the region's place in the world. Here we will focus on demography, the economy, and politics.

POPULATION AND MIGRATION Three main population trends shaped recent Latin American history: slowing growth, urbanization, and migration. In 1960, the Latin American population growth rate was nearly 3 percent annually. By 1987, that had fallen to 2 percent, and by 2017 to 1 percent. Like East Asia, Latin America underwent a fertility transition. In the 1950s–1960s, the average Latin American woman gave birth to 5 or 6 children over

her lifetime. By 2015, the region's fertility rate fell below replacement level (2.1 births per woman), and by 2023 had dipped to 1.9. As in East Asia, this amounted to a fundamental change in women's lives and provided a big boost to standards of living. With fewer babies and children in the population, especially in the decades after 2000, adults—especially women—were able to devote more of their time to education and jobs, yielding a demographic dividend.

The second big demographic trend was explosive urbanization, underway for many decades. In 1950, about 40 percent of Latin Americans lived in cities, already a high proportion by world standards. By 1990, the urban proportion reached 70 percent, and by 2020 about 83 percent—as high as any world region. In 1950, none of Latin America's cities had ranked among the world's biggest 15. By 1990, the global top 12 included Mexico City, Buenos Aires (Argentina), and Brazil's two megacities, São Paulo and Rio de Janeiro. By 2020, although the explosive growth of Asian cities had pushed Buenos Aires and Rio de Janeiro out of the top 12, Lima (Peru) and Bogotá (Colombia) entered the top 30. This heady urbanization occurred largely because hundreds of millions of Latin Americans left the villages of their birth for city life. In most cases, they stayed in the same country.

Life for migrants was often grim. Carolina Maria de Jesus moved from a Brazilian village to the metropolis of São Paulo and lived in its shantytowns (called *favelas* in Brazil) for several decades. She had only a second-grade education and struggled to make a living as a single mother, protect her three children from violence, and avoid falling into the despair that claimed so many of her neighbors. She kept a diary, translated as *Child of the Dark*, which gives an unsparing picture of favela life in the late 1950s, marked by domestic violence, alcoholism, and the constant struggle to put food on the table—which she did by selling paper she scavenged from garbage heaps. Urban hardships did not deter tens of millions of

Carolina Maria de Jesus Carolina Maria de Jesus, who migrated to the hardscrabble favelas of Rio de Janeiro as a young woman, pictured here after her memoir became a successful book.

Favelas Jerrybuilt houses line a hillside in Rio de Janeiro, adjacent to a luxury apartment tower. Rio, like most Latin American cities, exhibits extremes of wealth and poverty, often side by side.

Brazilians from following her from countryside to city in later decades.

The scale and pace of urbanization often overwhelmed the capacity of governments to cope. As in Carolina Maria de Jesus's day, many newcomers to big cities had to build their own housing out of sheet metal, cardboard, and, if they were lucky, cinder blocks. These shantytowns lacked running water, sewer systems, electricity, and subway stops. People who succeeded in finding steady work normally faced daunting commutes of several hours, on foot and in buses. Yet this hard life struck most of them as preferable to staying in the villages. Since 2000, the pace of migration to cities has slackened somewhat, and governments have in most cases begun to catch up with the demand for services such as water and electricity. But Rio de Janeiro still has its gigantic *favelas* and Lima its impoverished *pueblos jóvenes* ("young towns") where perhaps one-third of the city population resides. Among the bleakest is Haiti's Cité Soleil, where a quarter million people live without sewer systems or clean water, often terrorized by armed gangs.

Migration to Latin American cities was part of a larger web of international migration. For centuries prior to 1950, Latin America had been a net importer of people, mainly Europeans and, until 1860, enslaved Africans. But in the 1950s, the region became a net exporter of people. The largest flow was of Mexicans to the United States. In the early twenty-first century, at any given moment about 25–30 million Latin Americans lived outside countries of their birth, roughly 4 percent of the region's population. More than two-thirds of them had moved to the United States, and one-tenth of them to Spain. While Mexico still supplied the largest numbers, the countries most affected by emigration were in Central America—Honduras, Nicaragua, El Salvador—where political instability and violence convinced many to take their chances elsewhere, usually in Mexico or the United States.

Unlike fertility declines, however, emigration—typically of young adults—did not normally help Latin America's economies. But there were exceptions. Small and poor countries, such as El Salvador or Jamaica, that sent large numbers to the United States benefited from the money ("remittances") that emigrants sent home to their families.

After 2014, by far the largest exodus was of Venezuelans flooding out of their oil-rich country. Falling oil prices, economic mismanagement, authoritarian rule, and international sanctions led to hyperinflation and a stunning economic collapse. By 2022, Venezuela's GDP had fallen by about 75 percent from its 2014 level. Unemployment spiked. Violence, crime, and government oppression raged. By 2023, some 7–8 million Venezuelans, about a quarter of the total population, left—often on foot and penniless. Most went to neighboring countries. Flor Peña, for example, fled in 2017. She had been an industrial engineer in Caracas, but when overcrowded hospitals turned away her father as he was dying from a heart attack, she felt that Venezuela's chaos would ruin her family's future. She gathered her husband and children and went to Peru.

Venezuelan Migrants Between 2014 and 2023, about a quarter of Venezuela's 30 million people left home due to economic collapse and mounting violence. These refugees have just crossed into northern Chile (from Bolivia), looking for a new home. By 2023, Chile hosted half a million Venezuelan migrants.

She found work cleaning houses and selling food on the streets of Lima. Peru, however, was overrun with Venezuelan refugees, and Flor's children faced harassment in school. So the family moved on to Mexico City, where she got work waiting tables in a restaurant. Hers is just one of millions of stories of Venezuelan emigrants.

ECONOMY AND INEQUALITY   The economic record of Latin America in recent decades is both the best in its history and disappointing by world standards. As the table shows, since 1960, the world per capita GDP has grown slightly more than 3-fold, but Latin America's only by a factor of 2.6. That rate, however, compares favorably with any previous 60-year period in the region's history. As with Africa, Latin America's performance looks weak if one's yardstick is East Asia, North America, or the world as a whole, but it looks good if it is the region's own deeper past. The table also shows the sharply divergent fates of different countries. Nicaraguans' standards of living have scarcely improved since 1960, while Panamanians and people in the Dominican Republic are about six times better off than their grandparents were. Among bigger countries, Brazil posted the biggest improvement in average living standards, and Argentina the smallest.

PER CAPITA GDP IN LATIN AMERICA, 1960–2019, AS A PERCENTAGE OF THE 1960 WORLD AVERAGE ($3,586)			
	1960	**1990**	**2019**
World	100	189	307
Latin America	91	162	241
Nicaragua	47	35	55
Guatemala	52	76	118
Panama	76	143	420
Cuba	n.d.	139	224
D.R.	38	78	232
Jamaica	n.d.	124	141
Mexico	104	208	274
Brazil	73	172	241
Argentina	205	227	354
Peru	76	76	184

Source: Elaborated from Our World in Data, https://ourworldindata.org/search?q=GDP+per+capita.

Note: Figures are adjusted for inflation. 2019 is used rather than 2020 to avoid skewing by the temporary effect of the pandemic. "D. R." is Dominican Republic.

One of the enduring features of modern Latin American economic life is high levels of inequality. Prior to about 1880, Latin American economic income inequality was at the global average. But it grew more acute over the next 100 years and did not diminish in the decades between 1940 and 1980, as it did in most of the world. Then, after 1980, it expanded dramatically. On account mainly of spikes in world oil prices, Latin American public debt increased tenfold in the 1970s. To secure loans from international bankers, governments had to slash social services, public transport, and education budgets. At the same time, in the 1980s, commodity prices—copper, for example—nosedived. That lowered tax revenues, forcing yet more cuts, all of which affected the poor and middle classes who used social services, public transport, and public education.

By 2000, Latin American inequality was the most extreme of any major world region. The rich often lived behind walls for safety, sent their children to private schools, found tax loopholes, and parked their money in banks overseas to avoid the ravages of inflation. The poor lived either in villages with poor roads and schools or in the shantytowns described above. Since 2000, however, inequality has declined somewhat in Latin America and spectacularly in some countries, such as Bolivia. The main reasons seem to be government policies helping the poor and effects of improved access to education. But today, Latin American economic inequality still ranks with Africa's as the world's most extreme.

Another enduring feature is dependence on commodity exports. Beginning in the colonial period (before 1800), pockets of prosperity developed around the export of silver, diamonds, sugar, and a few other commodities. Later on, copper, coffee, wheat, beef, and timber came to account for most of the region's exports. In the middle of the twentieth century, many Latin American governments deliberately tried to break this long-standing pattern because it led to cycles of boom and bust based on price fluctuations in global markets. It could not sustain a stable economy or society. They pursued import-substitution policies, trying to industrialize and diversify their economies. Brazil, for example, aimed to build a steel industry. But industrialization efforts proved far less successful than in East Asia, and reliance on primary commodities remained widespread. In 2020, about 60% of Latin American exports were commodities. In the case of Venezuela, about 90% of its export revenues came from a single commodity, oil. Only Mexico had broken out of this pattern, thanks in large part to a free trade agreement with the United States and Canada, NAFTA, in force since 1994. That resulted in rapid industrialization in Mexico's northern border region.

High levels of inequality and continuing dependence on commodity exports constrained Latin America's economic fortunes after 1960. Whereas in East Asia the grip of traditional landowning elites was broken, in Latin America they generally survived atop the social pyramid. Landed elites used their power to prolong these twin constraints because they benefited from policies promoting commodity exports and from having many poor and landless peasants whom they employed as cheap labor. Land reform that redistributed farmland to peasants was rare. It succeeded in most of Mexico in the 1920s and 1930s, in much of Bolivia after a 1952 revolution, and in Cuba in the 1960s after Castro's revolution. Although on the political agenda almost everywhere by the 1960s, land reform elsewhere in Latin America was half-hearted, thwarted, or, in the case of Nicaragua, effected in the 1980s after a revolution but then reversed in the 1990s when the revolutionaries lost an election. So a crucial spark to the economic miracles in East Asia was not matched in Latin America. In addition, the demographic dividend provided by reduced fertility came slower and later in Latin America than in East Asia.

Latin America experienced environmental pressures resulting from its economic pathway. Whereas in East Asia rapid industrialization generated acute pollution problems, in Latin America that happened only in a few locations, including Mexico's northern border region after 1994. But pell-mell urbanization and overcrowding brought other problems (shared with cities throughout the Global South), such as poor sanitation. The prominence of mining, especially in Chile and Peru, led to widespread scarring of landscapes. As a consequence of both population growth and foiled land reform, Latin America witnessed rapid deforestation. In both Central America and Amazonia, farmers burned forest in order to plant crops, usually as squatters on land to which they had no legal rights. Between 1960 and 2020, about 15 percent of Amazonian forests went up in smoke.

In one important respect, however, fortune smiled on Latin American economies: like East Asia, but unlike Africa, the region enjoyed a peace dividend. In East Asia, international peace prevailed after the end of the Korean

Deforestation One of the major environmental changes in Latin America, and one with global implications, is the reduction in tropical rain forest. Here a swatch of Amazonian forest burns. While illegal in most of Amazonia, such burning was widespread as a way to prepare land for crops or cattle. Burning Amazonian forest reduces biodiversity and adds carbon to the atmosphere.

War in 1953. No serious civil wars broke out after the end of the Cultural Revolution in China in 1976. In Latin America, while civil wars have raged on and off in recent decades in Colombia, Guatemala, and Nicaragua, no big international wars have occurred since the 1930s. In the Falklands War of 1982, the only one involving big countries, Britain easily defended its South Atlantic island colony that Argentina claims as its own (and calls Las Malvinas). Combat lasted only 74 days, and the losing side, Argentina, lost fewer than 700 dead. This record forms a happy contrast to the blood-drenched period from 1810 to 1920 in Latin America. The peace dividend meant that in recent decades Latin American military budgets (as a proportion of GDP) came to about half the global average, and Latin American economies experienced few interruptions in production and trade flows.

POLITICS AND DEMOCRATIZATION Latin American politics since 1980 shows a sharp shift from the Cold War order. The region underwent a remarkable, if precarious, **democratization** in the 1980s and 1990s. That eased a gradual elimination of civil wars between 1990 and 2016. After 2000, Latin America diversified its linkages within the Global web, specifically by building economic, diplomatic, and cultural ties with China and thereby reducing the relative influence of the United States.

In 1980, most Latin American countries were dictatorships. Of countries with more than 10 million people, only Colombia and Venezuela had democratically elected governments. Perhaps Mexico's also qualified as democratic, although politics mainly took place inside the one party that had held power since the 1920s. Many smaller countries such as Uruguay, Ecuador, the Dominican Republic, Panama, Guyana, and Cuba were also run by dictators. Most dictators were army men supported by the traditional landed elites. During the Cold War, the United States coddled dictators who were firmly anticommunist (as we have seen). They borrowed vast sums from foreign lenders during the 1970s, when credit was cheap, to boost their domestic support with infrastructure projects and popular subsidies for food, water, and electricity.

By 1980, these dictatorships were losing their grip on power. International interest rates rose, and they could not pay their debts, compensate their civil servants, and continue their subsidies. The first to fall was Peru's in 1980. More resoundingly, Argentina's tumbled in 1983, humiliated by its defeat in the Falklands War and by the protests organized by mothers whose children the ruling junta had murdered. Brazil's military dictatorship collapsed in 1985. In short order, dictators stood aside or were pushed aside almost everywhere in the region. The United States withdrew its support for dictators once Soviet power weakened in the 1980s. Without Soviet aid, Castro's Cuba had to curtail its activities, and the communist threat in Latin America vanished. By 2000, when Mexico's ruling party allowed multiparty elections, democracy had triumphed widely, although not in Cuba, where Castro, the last of the dictators, clung to power.

This extraordinary wave of democratization, part of a global trend discussed in the next chapter, eased the gradual elimination of civil wars in Latin America. The peace dividend in Latin America expanded after 1990, when five civil wars wound down. Nicaragua's (1978–1990), El Salvador's (1979–1992), and Guatemala's (1960–1996) ended in large part because Cold War support from the United States or Cuba ended. Peru's (1980–1992) ended with the capture of Abimael Guzmán, a philosophy professor and admirer of China's Cultural Revolution. He and his students masterminded a brutal terrorist insurgency that killed tens of thousands—mostly poor peasants who, understandably, did not wish to join a revolution led by a murderous academic. In Colombia, civil wars and rebellions, often financed by cocaine sales, flickered on and off after 1948. Negotiations brought peace in 2016. While violence remains common in Latin America, especially where illegal drug trades flourish, the end, at least for now,

of civil wars is another remarkable feature of the region's recent political history.

The democratically elected governments that took office in the 1980s at first pursued a free-market agenda that its critics came to call neoliberalism. It was pioneered starting in 1975 under a Chilean dictatorship whose economic advisors had studied at the University of Chicago. But elected governments found that to get fresh loans from the World Bank and other foreign lenders, they had to lift trade tariffs; deregulate their economies; slash subsidies for food, water, and public transportation; and privatize public utilities and state-owned companies. This package of reforms contributed to the sharp rise in economic inequality and the reliance on commodity exports discussed above. It favored the educated classes and internationally competitive businesses such as Chile's copper, Argentina's beef, or Venezuela's oil. But it was hard on poor and indigenous populations, provoking a rise in emigration especially from Central America, Mexico, and the Caribbean.

Neoliberal politics also provoked the formation of coalitions of those who felt they were its victims. In the late 1990s, left-wing parties won power in Argentina, Brazil, Bolivia, Venezuela, and elsewhere. Often called populist, because they sought to appeal to the poor and uneducated and made a point of blaming all ills on the rich and foreigners, they decried globalization, banks, and multinational corporations. They encouraged identity politics wherever indigenous populations were numerous. Harkening back to movements in Mexico and Peru in the 1920s, they forged a renewed ideology of *indigenismo*, harping on Indigenous grievances and asserting Indigenous rights. *Indigenismo* became a potent political force in Mexico, Central America, and the Andean republics, especially Venezuela, Ecuador, Peru, and Bolivia. Once in office, its proponents' policies helped reduce economic inequality but damaged their countries' public finances, credit ratings, and standing with international bankers.

The triumph of democracy over dictatorship in the 1980s and 1990s was wildly popular. But in time, many Latin Americans were frustrated that their elected governments so often undid the work of their predecessors, producing a pendulum effect in politics. Policies changed back and forth every few years, which often felt to voters that they were getting nowhere. The popularity of democracy in public opinion polls dipped slightly. Nonetheless, the routine and peaceful transfer of power from one party to another by constitutional means remains characteristic of Latin America—and a distinguishing feature that marks the post-1980 decades off from the region's longer history. Cuba alone has consistently bucked that trend, although resurgent authoritarian politics in Venezuela, Brazil, and elsewhere suggests that Latin America's extraordinary democratization remains precarious.

In one respect, however, democratization produced a durable change in Latin America politics. The political class, long dominated by landholding elites of European ancestry, widened to include far more women, people of indigenous background, and technocrats with advanced degrees. Chile, Brazil, Argentina, Panama, Guyana, Barbados, Costa Rica, and Nicaragua elected women as heads of state between 1990 and 2010. After 2010, the trend in Brazil and Spanish-speaking Latin America stalled, but the Anglophone Caribbean elected two more female prime ministers, in Trinidad and Tobago (2010) and Jamaica (2012). As of 2022, across the region, 29 percent of cabinet ministers were women, and in Chile and Costa Rica women outnumbered men in cabinet positions. Women held 36 percent of parliamentary seats in Latin America, the largest share of any region in the world. This was a huge change since 1980.

Indigenous political leaders also enjoyed greater success after 1980, although not to the same extent. That is partly because indigenous populations make up a large share of voters only in Central America and the Andes. Peru in 2002 and Bolivia in 2005 elected indigenous men from poor backgrounds as president. Both pursued agendas that emphasized Indigenous rights and empowerment. In Ecuador in 2007, a president of partly indigenous background took office. At the same time, highly educated technocrats also met with electoral success. Since 1995, about a dozen Latin American heads of state have held PhDs, typically in public policy, economics, or sociology, many of them earned in U.S. universities.

Alejandro Toledo, Peru's president from 2001 until 2006, symbolizes the widening of Latin America's political class. He was born in 1946 to a poor Quechua-speaking family in a provincial village, one of 16 children, and worked as a shoeshine boy. U.S. Peace Corps volunteers, impressed by his talents, arranged for him to study in California, where he eventually earned a PhD from Stanford University. He entered Peruvian politics in the 1990s and sought to capitalize on his Indigenous heritage. While campaigning, he occasionally dressed in Inka garb and

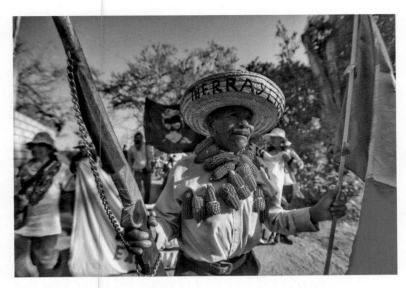

Indigenismo Movement Mexico in 2019 officially counted more than 16 million indigenous persons. Here some of them stride toward a rally for Indigenous rights on the hundredth anniversary of the death of Emiliano Zapata, the partly indigenous leader of the Mexican Revolution.

delighted in referring to himself by an ethnic slur typically used by white Peruvians to insult poor and indigenous ones. He held his inauguration at Machu Picchu, a sacred Inka site. In office, he tried to implement free-market policies while at the same time championing Indigenous rights. Such a political career would have been unthinkable only a few years previously.

LATIN AMERICA IN THE GLOBAL WEB Despite the dramatic changes in Latin American politics after 1980, the region's countries remained comparatively weak internationally. Brazil and Mexico formed only partial exceptions. Latin American nations commanded little authority in international organizations. Their leaders chafed under what they regarded as high-handed, discriminatory, exploitative, and unfair treatment by the United States and, to a lesser extent, the European powers.

After 1980, Latin American countries pursued two main strategies to bolster their economic and political position within the international system. One was regional integration. Between 1973 and 2001, more than a dozen Caribbean countries joined CARICOM, a common market. In the 1990s, Argentina, Brazil, Uruguay, and Paraguay created Mercosur, another common market, which if it were a single country would be the world's sixth largest economy. Neither organization produced dramatic results. Mexico charted a different course, hitching itself to the United States and Canada with the NAFTA agreement, which did boost Mexico's economic fortunes but did nothing to free it from subordination to the United States.

The second strategy was closer connections to China. Since 2001, several Latin American countries have eagerly sought trade agreements and financial help from China, which Chinese leaders welcomed. In 2010, China became the leading trade partner for South America as a whole, replacing the United States. Chile, Peru, Venezuela, and Brazil built particularly strong trade ties with China. The South American countries exported commodities—copper, oil, soybeans—in exchange for Chinese manufactures. This deepened the historical pattern Latin American countries had long tried to escape but in the hope that competition among buyers might raise commodity prices. In addition, the Chinese government offered big loans, especially to Venezuela and Brazil, without any conditions attached about honoring human rights or respecting the environment. China also offered arms deals, joint military training exercises, and sophisticated surveillance technologies for governments wanting to keep their citizens under watch. As in its involvement in Africa, China's embrace of Latin America was intended to win support for its efforts to isolate Taiwan and to offer an alternative to alignment with the United States and its European allies. Latin American countries, by and large, welcomed an opportunity to diversify their commercial and military partnerships and thereby reduce U.S. leverage over them. As with China's involvement in Africa, the connections between China and Latin America are so new that it is hard to see where they might lead.

CONCLUSION

Since 1980, the world has witnessed unusually rapid shifts in the international order. The most important, eclipsing even the meltdown of the USSR in 1989–1991, was the dramatic economic and political rise of East Asia. Decolonization prepared the way. The defeat of Japan's empire enabled it to integrate into the global economy as never before and gave South Korea and Taiwan their chance to engineer their own economic miracles. China's economic transformation owed much to the examples of Japan, Taiwan, and South Korea and at least as much to the end of empire and the subsequent liberalization of global trade and investment flows. Without decolonization, the rise of East Asia would have come much more slowly, if at all.

A new architecture of the international system, shaped by the outcomes of World War II and the ongoing Cold War, favored the rise of East Asia. First, peace prevailed in the region after 1953. Second, the United States provided a security umbrella for Japan, South Korea, and Taiwan, and most of the time they happily accepted it. The U.S. government underwrote a liberal economic order in which the East Asian tigers could export to American markets even if they closed off their own markets. Third, after Mao and Nixon defrosted China-U.S. relations in the early 1970s, even communist China could, and shortly did, enter the liberal economic order. These developments proved highly favorable for trade and investment flows in and out of East Asia.

The rise of East Asia, and China in particular, represents a fundamental shift in the distribution of wealth and power around the world. As in the heyday of the Tang and Song dynasties (roughly the seventh through twelfth centuries), East Asia now became an unusually interconnected space. After 1980, it became the most dynamic part of the global economy, exchanging goods, technologies, and ideas at a feverish pace. And after 2000, its engine, China, engineered the largest shift in global power politics so far in the twenty-first century.

Nowhere else in the world matched the economic dynamism of East Asia. The records of Africa and Latin America reveal some of the difficulties. Although both regions posted economic growth unmatched in their own histories, they could not come close to keeping pace with East Asia. They remained locked into long-standing historical patterns that emphasized commodity exports. Their efforts at diversification and industrialization met only modest successes. Closer cooperation with China in the early twenty-first century seemed only to confirm their reliance on commodity exports. Politically as well as economically, they struggled to shake their enduring subordination to western Europe and the United States. Fundamental changes, such as the end of white supremacy in southern Africa or of dictatorships in Latin America, inspired optimism and brought rewards to millions. But neither Africans nor Latin Americans found a way to fundamentally change their positions in the international order. The tightening links of the Global web, explored in the next chapter, favored some parts of the world over others, and none more than East Asia.

CHAPTER REVIEW

KEY TERMS

Asian tiger economies
(p. 974)

demographic dividend
(p. 974)

containerization (p. 974)

keiretsu (p. 977)

land reform (p. 978)

Great Leap Forward
(p. 981)

Deng Xiaoping (p. 982)

Minamata disease
(p. 985)

commodity dependent
(p. 989)

Second Congo War
(p. 991)

apartheid (p. 992)

soft power (p. 993)

democratization (p. 997)

indigenismo (p. 998)

Go to INQUIZITIVE to see what you've learned—and learn what you've missed—with personalized feedback along the way.

REVIEW QUESTIONS

1. How did demographic factors affect the economic history of East Asia, Africa, and Latin America?

2. Identify the common demographic, technological, and global economic factors that led to the economic success of East Asia.

3. How did the keiretsu contribute to the Japanese economic miracle?

4. What social changes facilitated South Korea's economic surge?

5. What chief agricultural and economic policies did Deng Xiaoping introduce?

6. Identify and explain the main environmental and social problems associated with rapid industrialization.

7. What international developments favored the rise of East Asia?

8. What factors contributed to Africa's economic record since independence?

9. Explain the factors that led to a wave of democratization across Latin America.

10. What patterns have emerged in China's recent political and economic relationships with countries in the Global South?

FURTHER READING

Kent DENG, *China's Political Economy in Modern Times: Changes and Economic Consequences, 1800–2000* (2012). A work presenting lots of data not easily available elsewhere.

Barry EICHENGREEN, Dwight H. PERKINS, and Kwanho SHIN, *From Miracle to Maturity: The Growth of the Korean Economy* (2012). An authoritative and readable book on South Korea's economic transformation.

Alma GUILLERMOPRIETO, *Looking for History: Dispatches from Latin America* (2001). Engaging journalistic account of the texture of life and politics in the 1990s.

Tessa MORRIS-SUZUKI, *The Technological Transformation of Japan: From the Seventeenth to the Twenty-First Century*

(1994). A compelling analysis, strong on how Japanese traditions proved favorable for Japan's postwar surge.

Michael REID, *Forgotten Continent: A History of the New Latin America* (2017). A journalist's assessment of recent political and economic history.

Ezra F. VOGEL, *Deng Xiaoping and the Transformation of China* (2011). A detailed assessment arguing that Deng stands among the titans of twentieth-century history.

Martin WELZ, *Africa since Decolonization: The History and Politics of a Diverse Continent* (2021). An introductory overview but full of insights.

Economic Shifts, 1970–1990

THE INTERNATIONAL ECONOMIC ORDER set up in the late 1940s served its primary purpose of avoiding a return to conditions of the Great Depression of the 1930s. But it showed signs of strain by 1970. Thanks to decolonization, several dozen new countries now existed but had minimal voice within international economic institutions. Over time, changes in the relative strength of various economies made fixed exchange rates and the gold standard hard to sustain. Then inflation started to climb, worsened by hikes in international oil prices in 1973–1974 and 1979–1980. In much of the world—but not in East Asia—economic growth faltered in the 1970s and 1980s, and longstanding assumptions about how best to run national and international economic policy came under scrutiny. The four viewpoints represented here offer a sample of the clashing intellectual and policy responses to this context of global economic turbulence.

SOURCE 28.1

A Call for a New International Economic Order (NIEO), 1974

A decade after the heyday of decolonization, representatives from most of the poorer countries addressed the UN General Assembly to call for a new global economic system. The tripling of world oil prices (1973–1974) hampered their economic prospects and threatened their governments with unrest; in parts of Africa, lethal famines prevailed. Moreover, the poorer countries agreed that the structures of the existing world economy, rebuilt after World War II, unfairly burdened them through neocolonialism. They saw the NIEO as the completion of decolonization.

The NIEO declaration, excerpted here, was adopted without a vote in the General Assembly. It represents an intellectual tradition championed by Argentinian economists and a political effort within the UN led by Algerians. Although it was the most important intellectual challenge to the world economic order since 1945, it gained little traction in terms of policy.

We, the Members of the United Nations,

Solemnly proclaim our united determination to work urgently for THE ESTABLISHMENT OF A NEW INTERNATIONAL ECONOMIC ORDER based on equity, sovereign equality, interdependence, common interest and co-operation among all States, irrespective of their economic and social systems, which shall correct inequalities and redress existing injustices, and ensure steadily accelerating economic and so-cial development in peace and justice for present and future generations, and, to that end, declare:

1. The greatest and most significant achievement during the last decades has been the independence from colonial and alien domination of a large number of peoples and nations which has enabled them to become members of the community of free peoples.... However, the remaining vestiges of alien and colonial domination, foreign occupation, racial discrimination, *apartheid* and neo-colonialism in all its forms continue to be among the greatest obstacles to the full emancipation and progress of the developing countries and all the peoples involved. The benefits of technological progress are not shared equitably by all members of the international community. The developing countries, which constitute 70 per cent of the world population, account for only 30 per cent of the world's income.... The gap between the developed and developing countries continues to widen in a system which was established at a time when most of the developing countries did not even exist as independent States and which perpetuates inequality.

2. The present international economic order is in direct conflict with current developments in international political and economic relations. Since 1970, the world economy has experienced a series of grave crises which have had severe repercussions, especially on the developing countries. The developing world has become a powerful factor that makes its influence felt in all fields of international activity. These irreversible changes in the relationship of forces in the world necessitate the active, full and equal participation of the developing countries in the formulation and application of all decisions that concern the international community.

[...]

4. The new international economic order should be founded on full respect for the following principles:

   (a) Sovereign equality of States, self-determination of all peoples, inadmissibility of the acquisition of territories by force, territorial integrity and non-interference in the internal affairs of other States;

[...]

(c) Full and effective participation on the basis of equality of all countries in the solving of world economic problems in the common interest of all countries, bearing in mind the necessity to ensure the accelerated development of all the developing countries....

[...]

(e) Full permanent sovereignty of every State over its natural resources and all economic activities. In order to safeguard these resources, each State is entitled to exercise effective control over them and their exploitation with means suitable to its own situation, including the right to nationalization or transfer of ownership to its nationals....

(f) All states, territories and peoples under foreign occupation, alien and colonial domination or apartheid have the right to restitution and full compensation for the exploitation and depletion of, and damages to, the natural and all other resources of those States, territories and peoples;

(g) Regulation and supervision of the activities of transnational corporations

[...]

(j) Just and equitable relationship between the prices of raw materials, primary products, manufactured and semi-manufactured goods exported by developing countries and the prices of raw materials, primary commodities, manufactures, capital goods and equipment imported by them with the aim of bringing about sustained improvement in their unsatisfactory terms of trade...;

(k) Extension of active assistance to developing countries by the whole international community, free of any political or military conditions;

(m) Improving competitiveness of natural materials facing competition from synthetic substitutes;

[...]

(o) To give to the developing countries access to the achievements of modern science and technology, to promote the transfer of technology and the creation of indigenous technology

Source: UN General Assembly, Resolution 3201(S-VI), Declaration on the Establishment of a New International Economic Order (6th special session, 1974).

- **Which two or three features of the world economy as of 1974 seem particularly unfair to the authors of this Declaration?**
- **How does the Declaration propose to deal with inequality among countries?**

Ronald Reagan on the U.S. Economy, 1981

Soon after taking office, U.S. president Ronald Reagan gave a televised address on the state of the national economy, excerpted here. After emphasizing how dismal a legacy his predecessors had left, he explained his vision for the restoration of American prosperity. Reagan (1911–2004), together with British prime minister Margaret Thatcher, led the revival of free-market policies both domestically and internationally, thwarting the hopes of backers of the NIEO. The policy initiatives associated with Reagan and Thatcher are sometimes called neoliberalism.

I regret to say that we're in the worst economic mess since the Great Depression.

The Federal budget is out of control, and we face runaway deficits...larger than the entire Federal budget in 1957....

Now, we've just had 2 years of back-to-back double-digit inflation—13.3 percent in 1979, 12.4 percent last year. The last time this happened was in World War I.

...Our income more than doubled in the 25 years after the [Second World] war. We increased our take-home pay in those 25 years by more than we had amassed in all the preceding 150 years put together. Yes, there was some inflation, 1 or 1.5 percent a year. That didn't bother us. But if we look back at those golden years, we recall that even then voices had been raised, warning that inflation, like radioactivity, was cumulative and that once started it could get out of control.

Today this once great industrial giant of ours has the lowest rate of gain in productivity of virtually all the industrial nations with whom we must compete in the world market. Japanese production of automobiles is almost twice as great per worker as it is in America. Japanese steelworkers outproduce their American counterparts by about 25 percent.

We once produced about 40 percent of the world's steel. We now produce 19 percent. We were once the greatest producer of automobiles, producing more than all the rest of the world combined. That is no longer true....

...We're threatened with an economic calamity of tremendous proportions, Together, we must chart a different course.

We must increase productivity. That means making it possible for industry to modernize and make use of the technology which we ourselves invented. And that means above all bringing government spending back within government revenues, which is the only way, together with increased productivity, that we can reduce and, yes, eliminate inflation.

Our basic system is sound. We can continue to meet our responsibility to those who, through no fault of their own, need our help. We can meet fully the other legitimate responsibilities of government. We cannot continue any longer our wasteful ways at the expense of the workers of this land or of our children.

Since 1960 our government has spent $5.1 trillion.... How much better off are we for all that? Well, we all know we're very much worse off.... We must not be timid.... We will unleash the energy and genius of the American people, traits which have never failed us.

Together we can forge a new beginning for America.

Source: Ronald Reagan, "Address to the Nation on the Economy—February 1981" (Washington, DC, February 5, 1981, National Archives).

- **What aspects of the international economy seem to worry Reagan the most?**
- **What is his frame of reference, the source of his ideas for the way the economy ought to be?**

Deng Xiaoping, "We Shall Concentrate on Economic Development," 1982

In 1982, six years after Mao Zedong's death, the new leader of China, Deng Xiaoping, was traveling to Sichuan Province accompanied by Kim Il Sung, the long-time dictator of North Korea. Kim, a staunch ally of Mao, always committed to a version of socialism that emphasized following Kim's doctrines and ideology. Deng explained that under his direction China would pursue a new course—one that emphasized economic results over ideological purity. Deng's novel direction was an implicit rebuke to Kim, so Deng tried to justify his departure from Maoism to his ally. Kim's reaction is not recorded.

Parts of this excerpt need explaining: (1) "Gang of Four" is a nickname for the four party leaders, including Mao's last wife, who took power after Mao's death in 1976; (2) the "two whatevers" is shorthand for a policy of loyalty to whatever policies and instructions Mao had issued; (3) "I would never have come back to work" refers to the fact that Deng had been banished from positions of authority in 1968 during the Cultural Revolution and, after a comeback, was purged again in 1976 by the Gang of Four; (4) "from each according to his ability, to each according to his needs" is a phrase made famous by Karl Marx.

We have just held the Twelfth National Congress of the Communist Party of China. Thanks to that congress, the political situation in our country will be more stable than ever before. This will make it possible for us to concentrate all the more on economic development.

The objective set at the Twelfth National Congress is to quadruple the gross annual value of industrial and agricultural output in 20 years, starting from 1981, that is, by the end of the century. We shall achieve this objective in two stages. In the first ten years, we shall lay a solid foundation and in the second, develop at high speed. Our strategic priorities will be first, agriculture; second, energy resources and communications; and third, education and science. I think the third priority is crucial. We cannot succeed without skilled personnel and knowledge. A grave mistake of the "cultural revolution" was that for ten years it made it impossible to train people. Now we should lose no time in developing education.

At the Twelfth National Congress comrades who had made mistakes were handled with circumspection. After the downfall of the Gang of Four, the comrade in charge of the work of the Central Committee at the time clung to a "Left" political line and put forward a wrong ideological line known as the "two whatevers". As I have said before, if Chairman Mao had still been around, he would never have accepted that line, because it was not in conformity with Marxism-Leninism and Mao Zedong Thought. For one thing, if the "two whatevers" had been followed, I would never have come back to work. I came back in July 1977, nine months after the Gang of Four had been smashed. It was then that I was allowed to attend the meetings of the Central Committee. After my return, I put forward the idea that the essence of Mao Zedong Thought was seeking truth from facts, and that gave rise to a debate about whether practice is the sole criterion for testing truth. At the time, some people opposed the debate. In June 1978 I delivered a speech about this ideological line at an all-army conference on political work. Later, when I was on my way back from a visit to your country, I made similar speeches in the three provinces of Northeast China [Heilongjiang, Jilin and Liaoning].

After about one year of debate, at the end of 1978 we convened the Third Plenary Session of the Eleventh Central Committee. At that session we criticized the idea of the "two whatevers" and put forward instead the slogan "We must emancipate our minds and use our heads." We declared that we had to integrate theory with practice and proceed from reality in everything we did, affirmed that practice was the sole criterion for judging truth and reestablished the ideological line of seeking truth from facts. It was after we resolved the question of the ideological line that we were able to formulate correct new policies. These include, above all, the policy of shifting the focus of our work to economic development, but also rural policies, policies on foreign relations and a complete set of policies on building socialism.

Wherever I went in the three northeastern provinces, I stressed the need to concentrate on economic development. In a country as big and as poor as ours, if we don't try to increase production, how can we survive? How is socialism superior, when our people have so many difficulties in their lives? The Gang of Four clamoured for "poor socialism" and "poor communism", declaring that communism was mainly a spiritual thing. That is sheer nonsense! We say that socialism is the first stage of communism. When a backward country is trying to build socialism, it is natural that during the long initial period its productive forces will not be up to the level of those in developed capitalist countries and that it will not be able to eliminate poverty completely. Accordingly, in building socialism we must do all we can to develop the productive forces and gradually eliminate poverty, constantly raising the people's living standards. Otherwise, how will socialism be able to triumph over capitalism? In the second stage, or the advanced stage of communism, when the economy is highly developed and there is overwhelming material abundance, we shall be able to apply the principle of from each according to his ability, to each according to his needs. If we don't do everything possible to increase production, how can we expand the economy? How can we demonstrate the superiority of socialism and communism? We have been making revolution for several decades and have been building socialism for more than three. Nevertheless, by 1978 the average monthly salary for our workers was still only 45 yuan, and most of our rural areas were still mired in poverty. Can this be called the superiority of socialism? That is why I insisted that the focus of our work should be rapidly shifted to economic development. A decision to this effect was made at the Third Plenary Session of the Eleventh Central Committee, and it represented an important turning point. Our practice since then has shown that this line is correct, as the whole country has taken on an entirely new look.

Between the Third Plenary Session of the Eleventh Central Committee and the Twelfth National Congress, we have blazed a new path: concentrating on economic development.

Source: Deng Xiaoping, "We Shall Concentrate on Economic Development" (speech, transcription by Joonas Laine, September 18, 1982, Marxist Internet Archive).

- **What characteristics of China seem to motivate Deng?**
- **How does Deng intend to demonstrate the superiority of socialism over capitalism?**
- **How does Deng justify his new direction for China?**

SOURCE 28.4

The Japan That Can Say No, 1989

Akio Morita (1921–1999) co-founded the Sony Corporation in 1946 and became one of postwar Japan's, indeed the world's, most successful businessmen. Shintaro Ishihara (1932–2022) was a journalist and ultranationalist politician, famous for making derogatory remarks about foreigners—especially Chinese and Koreans. In 1989 they co-authored a an essay, "The Japan That Can Say No," that caught the attention of a congressman from Michigan, Sander Levin. His district included elements of the U.S. auto industry, which was at that point reeling from Japanese competition. Levin had parts of the essay added to the record of congressional proceedings.

As the world goes smaller, and issues in the world further settle down, whether it be China or Siberia, development will proceed. In order to get the needed access (participation in the market) the most important possibility lies in linear technology. Japan and West Germany are the most advanced countries in this research and development, and the theoretical base of Japanese technology is far superior....

[...]

It is said that Japan contributed to efforts to stop a possible disastrous chain reaction ignited by Black Monday[1] which began in America and soon affected the London stock market as well. At that point, the Japanese Ministry of Finance asked Japanese institutional investors to support prices for a time, which instantly normalized Japanese stock prices. Later, the chairmen of one of the major U.S. banks, who was visiting Japan, told me "it was Japan who put a stop to the chain reaction, and it was the Ministry of Finance who was able to move the Tokyo stock market. The Japanese government now has the clout to sustain Wall Street and the City of London.[2] So-called Japanese guidance is truly powerful."

This gentleman went on to say "we are worried about the fact that the Japanese people are unaware of the fact that they have a significant impact on the world economy." And I believe it is true that Japan's economic status has been much enhanced.

Like it or not, this is the picture held by Americans, and the Japanese people have to recognize it and to behave in accordance with that status in the world community today.

[1] The term for a stock market crash in September 1987
[2] Then the world's biggest financial centers

Source: Hon. Sandler M. Levin in the House of Representatives, Extension of Remarks, November 13, 1989, citing Akio Morita and Shintaro Ishihara, *The Japan That Can Say No* (1989).

- **Judging by this excerpt, what appears to be the point of *The Japan That Can Say No*?**
- **How does the essay reflect the changing position of Japan in the postwar decades?**

QUESTIONS FOR COMPARISON

1. Considering all these sources, what factors made the 1970s and 1980s a key moment for the management of the international economy and economic policy in general?

2. Considering the economic history outlined in this chapter, who would be most pleased with the trends in the world economy since 1980: the authors of the NIEO, Xiaoping, Japanese business magnates, or Reagan? Why?

CHRONOLOGY

2003
US invasion of Iraq

2001
Vladimir Putin ends democracy in Russia

Sept. 11, 2001
Terrorist attacks in eastern United States

1961
Amnesty International
is founded

1980s
HIV/AIDS pandemic begins

1998
Indonesia ends
military rule

1973
End of Bretton Woods system of
currency and debt management

1991
Launch of
Women's World
Cup of soccer

early 1970s
Surge in Indigenous
activism worldwide

1977
Likud Party
rises to power
in Israel

1986
Overthrow of
Ferdinand Marcos
in the Philippines

1996
Rise of the
Taliban

1971
Médecins Sans
Frontières (Doctors
without Borders)
is founded

1974
Formation of
the International
Indian Treaty
Council

1988
Intergovernmental Panel on
Climate Change is founded;
Osama bin Laden founds
al-Qaeda

1997
Kyoto
Protocol

1964
Beginning of
worldwide TV
broadcasts of Olympics

1970s
Eradication of smallpox

1979
Iranian Revolution

1992
Hindu extremists
destroy Babri mosque

2002
Islamist party in Turkey
wins election

A Shrinking World

GLOBALIZATION SINCE 1980

Wangari Maathai was persistent. Born in 1940 in a farming village in the central highlands of Kenya, a British colony at the time, she started school at age eight. A good student, she mastered English, won a scholarship to attend high school, and was selected in 1960 as one of 300 young Kenyans to study in the United States. After studying biology at a small Catholic women's college in Kansas, she won another scholarship for graduate work at the University of Pittsburgh, where she grew interested in grassroots movements to combat the Steel City's notorious air pollution. After further study in Germany and at the University of Nairobi, in 1971 she became the first woman in the history of East Africa to earn a PhD.

Maathai embarked on an academic career in Nairobi while raising a family, but she was drawn to grassroots environmental activism. In her analysis, environmental problems such as soil erosion and water contamination undermined Kenya's economic and social health. She established the Green Belt Movement in 1976, which encouraged women to stand up for their rights and for the environment. She objected when Kenya's autocratic president proposed to build a skyscraper with a giant statue of himself in a public park. Police beat and arrested her more than once. The president said she should behave like a proper African woman, respect men, and be quiet. But she persisted.

Coronavirus Pandemic A Palestinian artist painting a COVID-19 awareness mural, Gaza, March 28, 2020. The Arabic writing at top reads #StayInYourHome.

2007
UN issues Declaration on the Rights of Indigenous Peoples

2011
Arab Spring

2019
COVID-19 pandemic begins

2016
Paris Agreement

2007–2009
Great Recession

FOCUS QUESTIONS

1. What major environmental changes have become evident in recent decades?

2. How have population trends and public health interacted since 1980?

3. What major developments have occurred in global politics since 1980?

4. What major changes has the global economy undergone since 1980?

5. How have music and sports reflected the intense globalization of the period?

6. What limits to global integration have become evident in recent decades?

The Green Belt Movement eventually planted 30 million trees in Kenya. A figure of growing national and international prominence, **Wangari Maathai** was elected to Kenya's parliament in 2002, and two years later she was awarded the Nobel Peace Prize. Before her death in 2011, she had garnered 15 honorary degrees and nearly 50 public service awards in 11 countries. She raised funds all over the world for the Green Belt Movement and for women's rights in Africa. Maathai operated—skillfully and persistently—within a Global web of educational, environmental, and fundraising communities.

The main themes in this chapter are the scale and pace of contemporary environmental change, the ongoing—but imperiled—golden age of human health and longevity, and the meanings of contemporary

Wangari Maathai The founding leader of the Green Belt Movement was also a strong proponent of women's rights in Africa.

globalization for politics, economics, and culture. In many respects, the strands of the Global web since 1980 have grown thicker and stronger, carrying more goods, ideas, data, and microbes than ever before—and at faster speeds. That is a shared human experience, but everyone lived it—and lives it—differently.

It is easy to know what happened in recent decades but hard to know what it means. The Bantu migration, the rise of the Mughal Empire, and the Meiji Restoration happened long enough ago that their consequences have worked themselves out. With a little effort, we can hope to know what they meant in their time and mean for today. But we can't yet know the full significance of recent events or how ongoing trends will unfold. What seems important now may seem superficial in years to come, and what now seems trivial might loom large. Treacherous terrain indeed, but no reason to shy away from trying to understand it.

ENVIRONMENTAL CHANGE: INTO THE ANTHROPOCENE?

According to geologists, the Earth for the last 11,700 years has been in an epoch called the Holocene (from the ancient Greek for "wholly recent"). But since 2000, increasing numbers of scientists have argued that the Holocene is over and a new interval of geological time has begun. They call it the **Anthropocene** to highlight the role of humankind (*anthropos* in Greek) in changing big natural systems, including global climate. Most earth scientists who embrace the concept of the Anthropocene think it began in the middle of the twentieth century.

It is important to bear two points in mind here. First, the Earth's natural systems have always been changing. So, for example, the climate over the past 2.5 billion years has undergone ice ages that come and go as a result of regular changes in the Earth's orbit. Change in the Earth's natural systems is nothing new. What is new, as we shall see, is the scale and pace of change in the recent past, and what lies behind it.

Second, humans have been causing major environmental changes mainly by accident. The concept of the Anthropocene does not mean that humans now control the global environment. Far from it. We influence the global environment, now more than ever, but mainly in ways no one intends and no one fully understands. The Anthropocene is an age of unintended consequences.

CLIMATE CHANGE AND CLIMATE POLITICS

Earth's climate is affected by many variables, including changes in the Earth's orbit, how much energy the sun emits, and how well the atmosphere traps heat. The climate has never been changeless. But in the past 30 to 40 years, it has been changing faster than at any other time in human history.

The main reason for the current pulse of **climate change** is that the atmosphere now traps heat from the sun more efficiently than it has for the last 3 million years. That is a consequence of rising concentrations of the gases that do the trapping, called greenhouse gases, the most important of which is **carbon dioxide** (CO_2). Air bubbles trapped in polar ice caps show that for the entire human career—some 300,000 years—CO_2 levels in the atmosphere have ranged between 180 and 280 parts per million (ppm). For the past 12,000 years, CO_2 concentrations fluctuated a little bit on either side of 280 ppm. That made for unusually stable climate by the standards of the last few million years.

After 1840 or so, CO_2 concentrations slowly climbed above 280 ppm. The causes lay in the burning of forests and fossil fuels for agricultural and industrial expansion. Over the next century, the impact on climate was tiny.

But, after 1950, fossil fuel combustion around the world, but especially in North America and Europe, took off. By 1960, the CO_2 level had climbed to 315 ppm, and by 2020 it topped 417 ppm (see the graph on this page), a level not previously touched in 3 million years and not consistently topped in 16 million years. At 2 ppm per year, the current rate of increase in atmospheric CO_2 levels is roughly 10

times faster than ever before—as far as we know. But there have been times in the deep past (about 500 million years ago, long before any mammals existed) when CO_2 levels stood much higher than today's, and the Earth was a lot hotter. We know about past CO_2 concentrations from measurements taken since 1958 on Mauna Loa, a Hawaiian mountain, and before that from air bubbles trapped in ice cores taken from Greenland and Antarctica.

Adding billions of tons of carbon to the atmosphere and oceans every year amounts to a gigantic unintentional experiment on the planet. Together with other greenhouse gases, the added carbon in the atmosphere has raised average temperatures on Earth by about 2 degrees Fahrenheit (1.1 degree Celsius) since widespread temperature measurement began in the 1880s. As is evident in the graph on the next page, most of that warming took place after 1980. It has also raised the sea level by about 9 inches (23 cm) since 1880, because warmer air temperatures melt glacial ice and warmer sea temperatures expand the oceans' volume. The extra carbon in seawater makes it more acidic—about 30 percent more since 1800. Over the last 500 million years, oceans have grown notably more acidic about 30 times. Four different times, growing acidity drove more than 75 percent of marine animal species into extinction.

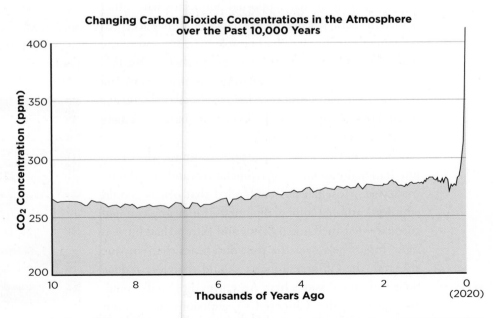

Changing Carbon Dioxide Concentrations in the Atmosphere over the Past 10,000 Years

Through most of human history, the amount of atmospheric CO_2—the main greenhouse gas that helps regulate climate—was fairly stable. The Industrial Revolution in the nineteenth century and the widespread adoption of fossil fuels in the twentieth ended that age of stability. Since 1950 or so, the atmosphere has been changing faster than at any time in many millions of years.

Source: Scripps Institution of Oceanography and NOAA.

Changes in Global Average Surface Temperature, 1850–2018

This chart of global average surface temperature shows a strong warming trend from the 1850s to the present, especially pronounced since 1980. This warming trend is occurring far faster than any known in the deeper past. The main cause of the warming measured here is the atmospheric carbon dioxide trend shown in the figure on page 1009.

Source: Land data prepared by Berkeley Earth and combined with ocean data adapted from the UK Hadley Centre.

Since the 1980s, this gigantic experiment upon the Earth has drawn climate issues into politics. One issue was the validity of the science that points overwhelmingly to human-caused climate change. In some societies, notably Russia, the United States, and Australia, constituencies developed that supported politicians who either denied the existence of climate change or, if they accepted it, claimed that humans had no role in it. In most of the world, however, these arguments got nowhere in the face of strong evidence and near-unanimous consensus among scientists. Only in countries where the fossil fuel industry was politically powerful did the existence of rapid climate change become controversial.

The second focus of climate politics was on what to do internationally about rising temperatures and greenhouse gas levels. Most nations contended that others should emit less carbon. Chinese diplomats, for example, noted correctly that the United States and Europe had burned more fossil fuels over the past 200 years than anyone else and, the Chinese argued, should therefore reduce their carbon emissions first. American diplomats noted, also correctly, that Chinese CO_2 emissions (as of about 2013) were the highest in the world, and they argued that China should curtail its emissions. Poorer countries claimed that they needed to burn more fossil fuel

energy to escape poverty and should be exempt from any limits on carbon emissions. Such differences proved hard to reconcile, resulting in the trends shown in the graphs. The major international agreements that sought to slow climate change—the Kyoto Protocol of 1997 and the Paris Agreement of 2016—had no visible effect on carbon dioxide levels. The U.S. government chose not to ratify Kyoto and temporarily withdrew from the Paris Agreement, refusing to accept restrictions on its greenhouse gas emissions—a position that undermined both agreements.

ENVIRONMENTAL TURBULENCE

Climate change was only one of several global environmental concerns that emerged in the late twentieth century. Biologists documented rapidly accelerating rates of animal and plant extinctions. Over the long history of life on Earth, on average about one in every million species has gone extinct each year. By the early twenty-first century, the annual extinction rate had climbed to several hundred, perhaps several thousand, suggesting that life on Earth was entering a sixth spasm of mass extinction. The previous one, about 66 million years ago, led to the disappearance of

Climate Change A polar bear leaps over melting ice in Svalbard, an island at the northern tip of Norway. Arctic regions have warmed disproportionately, with profound consequences for animals adapted to life in cold, icy conditions.

Climate Change: Emissions and Sea Level Rise, 1751–2016 The international politics of climate change is complicated by the fact that the countries most responsible over centuries for the buildup of greenhouse gases are not necessarily the same as those now emitting the most greenhouse gases. The United States now releases far less greenhouse gas than China but over time has emitted far more. In addition, the countries most likely to suffer from ongoing climate change are often those with low emissions, such as Egypt, Bangladesh, Mozambique, Vietnam, or the Maldives—all of which have densely populated areas just inches above sea level. The key to the future of climate change lies mainly in South, Southeast, and East Asia, where half of humankind lives, tens of millions are at risk of sea level rise, and greenhouse gas emissions are rising rapidly.

dinosaurs. The sixth one, if it is indeed that, is in its early stages, and its consequences so far remain modest. The driving force behind the acceleration of extinction is destruction of habitat, notably tropical forests, which are rich in species diversity. Vigorous efforts at species conservation dating from the 1960s have rescued some creatures, such as whooping cranes, California condors, and grizzly bears—at least for now.

Other acute environmental issues affected people more directly than the loss of species. For example, after the 1980s overfishing brought several of the world's economically important fisheries, such as those of the North Atlantic cod, Peruvian anchoveta, and Pacific salmon, to the point of collapse, fisherfolk were deprived of their

livelihoods. Air pollution in hundreds of cities reached levels sufficient to kill about 5 million people every year, especially in India and China.

Most of these environmental issues were more difficult to address politically than technologically. Reducing air pollution, for example, proved feasible in cities in western Europe, Japan, and North America once citizen activism, between 1965 and 1980, produced enough political will to nudge public policy toward tighter regulations. But in many cases, political will remained weak. Some environmental problems, such as climate change or the accumulation of plastics in the oceans, were slow-brewing, so ignoring them for another year or two seemed unlikely to make matters much worse. Moreover, the economic

CO₂ Emissions A Chinese city enveloped by the dense smog that coal-fired power stations and home coal fires cause in cities across the nation. Particles emitted from burning coal fill the sky beyond, giving it a hazy appearance.

activities behind environmental problems produced winners as well as losers, and winners fought to preserve their gains. Coal miners and coal companies checked the regulation of carbon emissions. Fishermen fought regulations on fishing—even if it meant their catch would shrink with each passing year.

Although it is hard to say what all this global environmental flux may mean in the long run, we can be sure of a few things. First, while human-caused environmental change is not new, the pace, scale, and scope of it in the last couple of generations are unique in human history. Second, global averages, whether of temperature, biodiversity loss, or the reduction in fish stocks, don't reveal much about specific places. Arctic regions, for example, have warmed far more than the tropics in the past 30 years. Hundreds of millions of people within reach of tropical storms in places such as the Philippines, Bangladesh, or the Caribbean had to face more frequent and larger typhoons, cyclones, and hurricanes. Meanwhile, the hundreds of thousands of people in northern Siberia, Scandinavia, Greenland, Canada, and Alaska experienced longer growing seasons and much milder winters.

Just why the world became so environmentally turbulent over the last 70 years or so is easy to explain. Many factors contributed, among them culture. Most people around the world clung to, or adopted, a culture of consumption, preferring more clothes, more furniture, more travel—more of just about everything. Cultural traditions such as Buddhism or Christianity, which historically had

associated virtue and godliness with poverty and asceticism, proved extremely flexible in this regard. So did the Chinese Communist Party, which in the 1950s had trumpeted poor peasants as the most admirable of classes but after 1980, as we've seen, converted to the gospel of wealth. In India, Gandhi's emphasis on simplicity lost out to a political culture that idolized industry, wealth, and power. Bhutan, a tiny kingdom high in the Himalaya, formed an exception: there the government since 2008 tried to measure, and to maximize, gross national happiness rather than gross national product.

Politics reinforced the impacts of consumer culture. Neither elected officials nor dictators thought asking anyone to consume less was good politics. Moreover, leaders concerned with national security normally thought a wealthier society would help fund a bigger military, which would make everyone safer. Rulers for 5,000 years had thought the same way. But now the consequences were different.

At the same time as these notions of consumption and security prevailed, an enormous expansion in energy use made mass consumption much easier. We last looked at energy in Chapter 21, which emphasized the transition to fossil fuels. As late as 1960, however, that transition was mainly confined to North America, Europe, and Japan. Since then, the continuing rise of energy-intensive activities, such as motor vehicle use or the production of nitrogen-based fertilizer, has changed the picture. The world's vehicle fleet (cars, buses, trucks), for example, grew from 250 million in 1970 to 1.4 billion by 2020. Nitrogen fertilizer use rose sevenfold between 1961 and 2020. As the table below shows, the total quantity of energy used globally more than doubled between 1975 and 2015. China, India, and Egypt by 2015 used eight or nine times their 1975 totals.

ENERGY USE SINCE 1975 (IN MILLIONS OF TONS OF OIL EQUIVALENT)

	WORLD	United States	China	Japan	India	Egypt
1975	5,762	1,698	337	329	82	10
1995	8,545	2,117	917	489	236	38
2015	13,105	2,276	3,006	446	685	87

Source: BP *Statistical Review of World Energy*, various years.

About 80 percent of this surge in energy use came in the form of fossil fuels. So this global trend led to considerable increases in urban air pollution, especially in India and China. It also led to more oil spills—notably in the oil fields of Siberia and Nigeria and in the world's shipping lanes, where tankers occasionally ran aground or broke up in storms. And, as noted above, the increased use of fossil fuels pumped carbon into the atmosphere, warming the Earth.

POPULATION TRENDS SINCE 1950

Population growth was another powerful driving force behind environmental change and much else in recent decades. We last looked at the subject in Chapter 22, in the context of the Vital Revolution, which carried the story up to 1950.

POPULATION AND PUBLIC HEALTH

The population history of planet Earth since 1950 is unique, although almost everyone alive has known nothing else and so considers it normal. In the span of one human lifetime (1950–2023) the global population more than tripled, from 2.5 billion to 8.0 billion, growing at well over 1 percent per year. For the previous 10,000 years, the annual rate was closer to 0.05 percent. Put another way, two-thirds of the population growth in all 300,000 years of human history took place after 1950. We now outnumber any other large mammal on Earth, and we account for about 5 percent of the globe's animal biomass (although ants easily outweigh us—because there are so many of them). The graph shows how peculiar the last few decades have been in light of longer patterns.

The key to this unique development has been better public health programs since 1945. One way to think of it is that humankind invented and adopted effective "death control" measures before we adopted much birth control. Improved public health took a giant stride forward in World War II when medical personnel figured out how to administer vaccines and antibiotics to millions of soldiers and sailors. After 1945, similar techniques applied more broadly reduced mortality, especially for infants and children, especially in Asia, Africa, and Latin America. In the late 1970s, international health teams wiped out smallpox, ridding the human race of one of its greatest killers. Even counting deaths caused by the COVID-19 pandemic, the global death rate in 2020 stood at less than half the 1950 rate, mainly through reductions in infectious diseases such as measles, smallpox, and typhoid. The average life expectancy around the world in 2020 exceeded 72 years. In almost every country except India, women outlived men—by five years on (global) average.

Improved nutrition and a rollback of famines also helped boost longevity. More fertilizers and irrigation, better crop breeding and weather forecasting, and a host of other changes to agriculture enabled the global food supply to grow even faster than the global population. In addition, better transport enabled people to move food faster to places where it was in short supply. All these changes reduced the frequency and size of deadly famines. While hundreds of millions of people remained

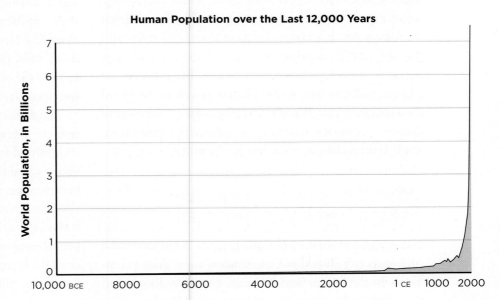

This chart shows the size of the human population over the past 12,000 years. It reached 1 billion around 1820 and 2 billion by 1930. Since 1960, it has grown by 1 billion every 12 or 15 years. Although the rate of growth is now slowing, the record of the recent past through to the present is an extreme departure from the pattern of the longer past.

Source: World population data from the United Nations, the U.S. Census Bureau, and others, found at https://en.wikipedia.org/wiki/Estimates_of_historical_world_population#/media/File:Population_curve.svg.

ESTIMATED LIFE EXPECTANCY IN 2020			
	YEARS		**YEARS**
Japan	85	Mexico	75
Switzerland	83	Egypt	72
Australia	83	Russia	72
New Zealand	82	Indonesia	72
Greece	82	India	69
United Kingdom	81	Pakistan	67
United States	79	Haiti	64
China	77	South Africa	64
Vietnam	76	Uganda	63
Brazil	76	Nigeria	54
Jamaica	75	Central African Republic	53

Source: United Nations Development Program data, found at https://en.wikipedia.org/wiki/List_of_countries_by_life_expectancy

persistently malnourished, after the 1980s mass starvation occurred only in war zones and the hermit country of North Korea.

The consequences of improved public health and food supply played out differently around the world. Richer, more stable countries could provide the means of death control more thoroughly than could poorer or unstable countries, as the table above suggests. Lives are briefest in Africa, which accounts for 32 of the 33 countries with the shortest life expectancy. Even the poorest and most unstable countries, however, now have life expectancies almost twice as long as the richest places in the world two centuries ago. This surge in longevity, a golden age of health by historical standards, is perhaps the most meaningful social change in the last half century.

COUNTERCURRENTS IN PUBLIC HEALTH: EMERGING DISEASES

Recognition of these extraordinary gains in human health and longevity should not overshadow some grim exceptions. In the former Soviet Union, especially Russia and Ukraine, in the 1990s, life expectancy fell by almost five years mainly because of illnesses associated with alcohol and smoking. It has rebounded since. In the United States, where overall life expectancy crept upward after 2000, it stalled after 2010 and fell for the middle-aged white male population due to suicides, alcoholism, and drug overdoses—so-called deaths of despair. It has not yet rebounded.

New infectious diseases also imperiled the golden age of health. The viruses that caused AIDS in the 1980s, SARS in 2003, MERS in 2012, and COVID-19 in 2019 all mutated and leapt successfully from animal to human populations. As more people brushed up against wild and domestic animals more frequently, they gave viruses more opportunities to evolve so as to survive in human bodies. **HIV/AIDS**, genomic evidence tells us, was an infection of chimpanzees until the 1940s, when it first became a human infection. It did not spread much until the 1980s, when growing connectivity within Africa enabled it to travel farther and faster, igniting a global pandemic that had taken some 30 million lives as of 2020. HIV/AIDS was much worse in Africa than elsewhere. In South Africa, for example, it shortened average life expectancy by about 10 years from 1990 to 2005. (It has rebounded since, thanks to medical interventions.) SARS and MERS had killed fewer than 1,000 each as of 2023.

The coronavirus (SARS CoV-2) that causes the disease COVID-19 apparently lived only in bat colonies until late in 2019. It mutated into a human pathogen in or near Wuhan in central China and spread quickly around the world, causing another global pandemic and killing more than 7 million as of mid-2023 by official tallies—probably more like 20–25 million in truth. To prevent far greater death tolls, people worldwide adopted social distancing to slow the virus's spread, which seriously damaged the interconnected world economy.

The devastating health impact of **COVID-19** was the result of four conditions. First, the pathogen itself is easily transmitted from human to human. Normal gatherings, such as weddings, concerts, or religious services, easily became superspreader events. Second, at first nobody carried any resistance or immunity to the disease, because it was new to humans. Third, air travel moved so many people so far and so fast that they carried the virus out of central China to every other country within two months. Every day, about 13 million people flew in airplanes in 2019—about 16 times the daily air traffic in 1970. And fourth, the world's public health systems were—like individual immune systems—unprepared for what hit them. The main exceptions were effectively governed small countries such as Taiwan, South Korea, Singapore (all of which learned from their experiences with SARS), Vietnam, New Zealand, and Iceland. National leaders in China, western Europe, Brazil, and the United States, in contrast, reacted only after the virus had already spread widely within their countries, and their populations—indeed, the entire human population—paid a heavy price. China soon adopted a so-called zero-covid policy, which reduced deaths and infections at the cost of enormous restrictions on hundreds of millions of ordinary citizens.

The same Global web that spread COVID-19 so quickly also checked it. Millions of researchers around the world turned their attention to the virus and shared information with unprecedented speed. Two days after Chinese scientists identified the pathogen, its entire genome was published for all to see. Within three weeks, scientists were at work on new vaccines that targeted specific features of the virus. Within a year, scientists and drug companies had developed, tested, and begun mass production of the novel vaccines—a process that ordinarily takes 5 or 10 years.

It is too soon to say whether COVID-19 and other newly emerging infectious diseases mark the end of the golden age of health or just a temporary setback. None of them equaled the 1918 influenza, which killed perhaps 50 million people worldwide. But more novel diseases are sure to come, because humans so frequently are in contact with animals, such as bats and rodents, that harbor an immense variety of viruses.

FERTILITY DECLINES

Regardless of the impact of emerging diseases, the anomalous moment of supercharged population growth after 1950 is now slowing because birth control is catching up to death control. We touched on the economic significance of fertility declines in East Asia, Africa, and Latin America in the previous chapter. Globally, the rate of population growth reached its maximum in the late 1960s, briefly exceeding 2 percent per year. It now stands at 1.05 percent per year. By 2020, roughly three out of every four women of reproductive age around the world used some form of birth control. About 140 million babies were born that year (and about 55 million people died).

Everywhere, the main reasons behind the downward fertility trend were the spread of formal education for

Viral Epidemics COVID-19 patients fill a temporary hospital erected in a sports center in Wuhan, China, in February 2020. Wuhan was at the center of the first outbreak of COVID-19, when the virus that causes the illness somehow made the jump from bats to humans.

females and urbanization. On average, women with more education prefer not to have large families, and couples living in cities want smaller families than do their country cousins. The places where fertility did not fall much—Afghanistan and parts of Africa, mainly—are places where urbanization and formal education for females made less headway in the past 70 years. In Angola, for example, women with no schooling bore four times as many children as did women with college degrees (as of 2023). But far more women never attended school than attended college in Angola, so its fertility rate stood among the world's highest.

Humans grew bigger as well as more numerous after 1950. The greatest changes came in East Asia, southern Europe, and the Baltic countries. South Koreans topped the list, growing 7 to 9 inches (18–23 cm) taller on average between 1950 and 2015, an indication of better diets especially among the poor. A few populations, mainly in Africa, have not grown taller since 1950. Egyptians and Ugandans have been shrinking since 1990 because of malnutrition.

On average, people grew heavier as well as taller. More sedentary lifestyles and more food have caused the average person to gain weight in just about every country since 1980. In the United States, the average adult in 2020 weighed 20 lbs. (9 kg) more than in 1990. The average human has expanded in size far faster in the past 50 years than ever before.

> FROM MIDNIGHT TONIGHT WE BUNKER DOWN FOR FOUR WEEKS TO TRY AND STOP THE VIRUS IN ITS TRACKS. . . . EVERY MOVE YOU THEN MAKE IS A RISK TO SOMEONE ELSE. THAT IS HOW WE MUST ALL COLLECTIVELY THINK. THAT'S WHY THE JOY OF PHYSICALLY VISITING OTHER FAMILY, CHILDREN, GRANDCHILDREN, FRIENDS, NEIGHBORS, IS ON HOLD. BECAUSE WE'RE ALL NOW PUTTING EACH OTHER FIRST. "

JACINDA ARDERN
PRIME MINISTER OF NEW ZEALAND

MARCH 18, 2020

Reported cases and deaths, by July 1, 2020

Number of reported cases, by country

- 2,600,000
- 1,400,000
- 650,000
- 85,000
- 200

34.8 12 countries with the highest number reported of deaths, in thousands

29.5 10 states of the United States with the highest number of reported deaths, in thousands

KEY

← Initial spread of infection from Wuhan, China, January 1–31, 2020. Arrow thickness indicates approximate number of travellers.

• City with recorded outbreak, by January 31, 2020

Stay-at-home requirements in place, by March 24, 2020

- Required, with virtually no exceptions
- Required, except for daily exercise, food shopping, and essential trips
- Recommended
- None
- No data

The COVID-19 Pandemic

▶ COVID-19 testing site, Wuhan, China, May 2020.

CANADA

NORTH AMERICA

Seattle

ILLINOIS 7.1

MICHIGAN 6.2

MASSACHUSETTS 8.1 From Italy

New York

UNITED STATES 125.2

CONNECTICUT 4.3
NEW YORK 29.5
NEW JERSEY 15.0
PENNSYLVANIA 6.6
FLORIDA 3.7

CALIFORNIA 6.0

LOUISIANA 3.2

ATLANTIC OCEAN

MEXICO 27.8

BRAZIL 59.6

PERU 9.7

SOUTH AMERICA

CHILE

LATE IN 2019, A CORONAVIRUS new to humans burst upon the world, causing a disease called COVID-19 in those infected. The outbreak began in Wuhan, a provincial capital in central China, and spread rapidly within the country aided by travel at the Chinese New Year. The virus then spread around the world and grew to pandemic proportions. By July 1, 2020, global agencies had recorded about 10 million confirmed cases and half a million deaths from COVID-19, with the numbers continuing to rise. The stay-at-home and shut-down orders adopted in many countries and large cities shook the global economy.

The pandemic was entangled in the Global web in three main ways. First, the virus itself moved along every pathway of the Global web. It spread by jet from China to the hubs of the world's airline systems in cities such as Milan, London, and New York. From the hubs it eventually traveled out to every city and town of any size everywhere in the world.

Second, information about the virus and how to combat it spread at electronic speed throughout the Global web. The virus was formally identified in China on January 7, 2020, and its genome was published on the Internet on January 10. Scientists around the world collaborated in the effort to find effective drugs and a vaccine. Strategies for slowing the virus, such as social distancing, stay-at-home requirements, and the use of face coverings, also spread almost instantly, although authorities often delayed implementation at the cost of many thousands of lives.

Finally, the necessary measures to slow the virus resulted in economic hardship wherever web connections were strong. Tens of millions of people lost jobs and billions lost income. The COVID-19 pandemic led to more economic pain than the far deadlier 1918 flu pandemic because economic globalization was stronger in 2020 than in 1918. The world economy in 2020 was built on dense and active international supply chains, trade, and travel. These strong global connections made the world economy more vulnerable to interruption than at any earlier time in world history.

Questions for Analysis

Based on this feature and your chapter reading, consider the following questions:

1. How did the COVID-19 pandemic reveal connections between your life and the Global web?

2. Did the public health emergency of COVID-19 show the need for stronger national and global coordination of response measures or more local autonomy? Explain your response.

URBANIZATION IN OVERDRIVE

While humans have been growing more numerous, and on average bigger, we have also become predominantly urban animals. For most of the last 10,000 years, the typical human habitat was the farming village. A century ago, only about 10 to 15 percent of the world's people lived in cities. By 1950, that figure reached 29 percent, and by 2007 half of all humans were city-dwellers. Today, the figure is 55 percent, about 4.4 billion people in all.

Big cities got bigger. In 1800, only one, Beijing, had more than 1 million inhabitants. By 1950, there were about 70, led by New York, London, Tokyo, and Moscow. By 2020, some 550 cities reached the 1 million threshold, and 35 of those had more than 10 million people. The biggest were in Asia: Tokyo, Delhi, Jakarta, Seoul, Karachi, Shanghai, and Manila all counted more than 24 million in their metro areas.

Two trends drove this spurt of accelerating urbanization. First, as we saw in Chapter 22, city life stopped killing people quite so fast. Between 1880 and about 1950, cities around the world became healthy enough that their birth rates came to exceed their death rates. That trend strengthened after 1950. Meanwhile, streams of migration from the countryside swelled to torrents: population growth and land shortages in the villages drove more young people to seek their futures in cities.

One who went to the big city seeking a better life is the uncle of one of my former students. Alim (not his real name) was born in 1960 in a village in what was then East Pakistan, now Bangladesh. He spent his early years in a corrugated tin hut. His life changed when he was sent to live with a relative whose village had a school. He loved school, did well in it, and began to win scholarships—like Wangari Maathai. Studying electrical engineering at a polytechnic institute allowed Alim to get a job helping the government build an electrical grid in rural Bangladesh. In the 1980s, he tried his hand at business, distributing fertilizer, but ended up in debt. In the 1990s, he moved to the capital, Dhaka, seeking better opportunities because he now had a family to feed. They stayed in the countryside while Alim, feeling lonely and economically insecure, worked in Dhaka. Hundreds of millions of men around the world found themselves in similar predicaments, able to make a better living in the big city than in their native village but still unable to support their families reliably.

The largest and fastest spurt of urbanization in world history took place in China. In 1980, 19 percent of Chinese lived in cities; by 2023, 66 percent did. In Australia, Argentina, Japan, and a few smaller countries, more than 90 percent of people now live in cities. In the United States, 83 percent do. But in South Asia and sub-Saharan Africa, only a third of the people are urbanites, although cities there are growing fast. Around the globe, the urban population is growing at about twice the rate of the total population, a little above 2 percent annually.

It is still too soon to tell the full meaning of this overnight urbanization of the human species. It has contributed to lowering fertility—a social revolution in and of itself. It has also helped raise levels of education, because providing such services is easier where people are close together. On average, it has made people slightly richer. It surely has also made them more acutely aware of inequality, as rich and poor live close together. And it has created opportunities for infectious diseases, such as COVID-19, to flourish in tightly packed neighborhoods.

Urbanization Residents throng the streets of Mumbai, one of the world's largest cities. In 2020, Mumbai had a population of over 20 million.

INTERNATIONAL MIGRATION

The movement from village to city was not the only important migratory flow in recent decades. In 1980, some 100 million people (2.3 percent of the global population) lived in a country other than where they were born. In 2020, roughly 280 million people, or 3.6 percent

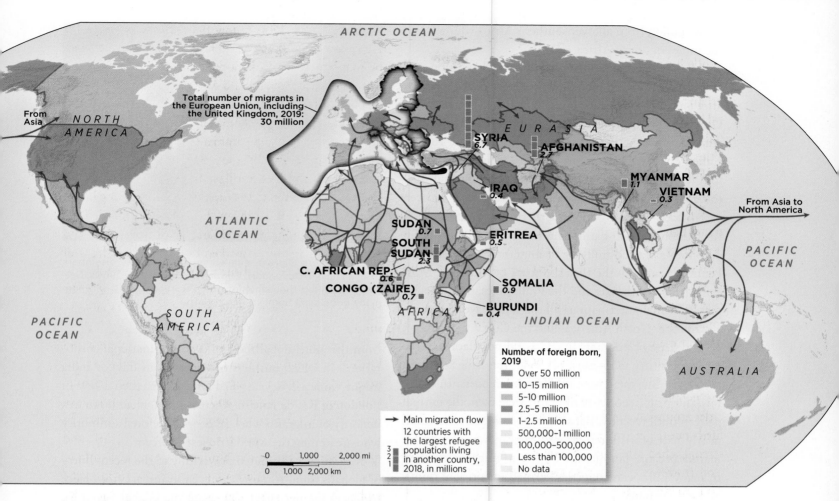

International Migration and Refugee Flows, ca. 2015–2020 The broadest pattern in recent migration history is movement from poor countries to richer ones. Several million people migrated every year in the 2010s, mainly to North America, Europe, the Persian Gulf region, and Australia. Latin Americans went chiefly to the United States, Africans to Europe, and East and Southeast Asians to both North America and Australia. Refugees left war-torn lands, especially Syria, Afghanistan, and several countries of central and eastern Africa. Those leaving Myanmar fled religious persecution rather than war.

of humankind, did so. Some 10 percent were officially refugees who fled war or persecution. The table on the next page shows the five biggest population groups living abroad in 2020.

In 2020, some 51 million **international migrants** lived in the United States. Another 16 million lived in Germany, and 14 million in Saudi Arabia. In 2012, a Gallup poll concluded that 640 million people *wanted* to migrate to another country but couldn't. International migration remains highly restricted, so much of it goes uncounted. Each year since 2010, about 8 to 16 million people have migrated internationally, of whom about one-quarter were going back home.

This surge of migration is best understood in longer context. Between 1840 and 1940, inexpensive, steam-powered transport enabled over 170 million people, mostly young men, to move to another country. The number of international migrants peaked in 1913 and again in the late 1920s at a little more than 3 million per year.

Broadly speaking, there were three main currents of migration in the century before 1940. One involved 55 to 60 million people moving to the Americas from Europe and the Middle East. A second current featured 45 to 55 million Indians and southern Chinese going to Southeast Asia and other rimlands of the Indian Ocean such as Burma and Ceylon (now Sri Lanka). A third current took 45 to 55 million northern Chinese, Koreans, and Russians to Manchuria or Central Asia. But there were smaller flows too, such as the 2 to 3 million Canadians who migrated to industrial cities in the United States and a few million from all over southern Africa who went to the mines of South Africa.

After a downturn during the Great Depression and World War II, international migration revived, especially after 1960. Northern European countries, especially West Germany, began to recruit large numbers of supposedly temporary workers from southern Europe and Turkey. Called guest workers, many of them wound up staying for life. Meanwhile the United States, Canada, and Australia changed their immigration rules, which had been overtly racist, opening doors for more migrants from Asia, the Caribbean, and Latin America. And in the 1970s, an oil boom attracted millions of migrants to the Arabian Peninsula, mainly the tiny countries of the Gulf. Most came from South Asia and the Philippines. So, since the 1970s, the main destinations for migrants have been western Europe, North America, and the Gulf.

The share of migrants in the world population in the quarter-century 1990–2015 was about the same as that in 1890–1915. But there were two big differencess. In 1890–1915, the great majority of migrants were men, the normal pattern until recently. Between 1990 and 2020, however, nearly half of all international migrants were women, mainly because families are likelier to migrate together. In many European countries, a small majority of immigrants are women.

The other big difference is education. Before 1940, the overwhelming majority of migrants were uneducated. Their skill set usually consisted of what they learned growing up in farming villages. Since 1990, in contrast, roughly 20 percent of migrants brought with them university educations and professional training. This change reflects immigration policy, especially in the United States, Australia, and Canada, which gave preference to people with skills expected to be economically useful. It also results

Guest Workers Migrant mineworkers from Turkey disembark from a plane in Düsseldorf, Germany, in 1961. In the 1960s, Germany recruited thousands of guest workers, many of whom made permanent homes in the country.

from the more globalized world of multinational corporations, in which business managers from Italy or India might work a few years in Hong Kong, then a few in London or Rio de Janeiro. There is, then, in addition to a majority of migrants who are poor (as before), a minority who are among the world's richest 1 percent.

Migration contributed powerfully to the recent flurry of globalization. Although uneven in impact from place to place, the net effect was to tie the Global web a little tighter, bringing more people into daily contact with strangers from afar.

POLITICS AND THE GLOBAL WEB

In the decades since the end of the Cold War, the most important global political trends were the rise of China (discussed in Chapter 28), the growing role of international institutions, a revival of religious politics, and a cresting wave of democratization.

INTERNATIONAL INSTITUTIONS

Many of the powerful **international institutions** still with us were created in the 1940s as leaders sought to avoid future crises like the Great Depression and World War II. The most important were the United Nations and

LARGEST POPULATIONS LIVING ABROAD, 2020	
Indians	17 million
Mexicans	11 million
Chinese	11 million
Russians	11 million
Syrians	8 million

Source: United Nations Department of Economic and Social Affairs, www.un.org /development/desa/en/news/population/international-migrant-stock-2019.html the pair tasked with looking after the world economy—the International Monetary Fund and the World Bank. Some others are a little older, such as Interpol, founded in 1923, which facilitates cooperation among law enforcement agencies around the world. Some are more recent, such as the Intergovernmental Panel on Climate Change, formed in 1988 under the authority of the UN, which reports periodically on all aspects of the global climate.

With the rise of problems and challenges that are global in scale, such as international drug trades, human trafficking, and climate change, states around the world came together more often to create such institutions and came to rely on them as never before. The UN grew particularly active after the end of the Cold War, for example, mounting far more peacekeeping operations than previously, helping end 21 civil wars between 1991 and 2017.

The UN's peacekeeping record, however, was mixed. UN forces grew from about 20,000 in 1990 to about 117,000 in 2020, mainly provided by the armed forces of South Asian and African countries. While its interventions in Cambodia (1991–1993) and El Salvador (1989–1995) contributed to lasting peace, it failed to prevent genocide in Rwanda (in East Africa) in 1994 or massacres in Bosnia (part of the former Yugoslavia) in 1995. As of 2022, it maintained 12 peacekeeping operations, 7 of them in Africa. Since the UN, like other international institutions, had no armies, its authority ultimately came from the support of countries—only some of which consistently proved supportive. This problem limited the impact of the UN and at times made people and politicians skeptical of its value.

Also over the last half-century, an increasing number of international nongovernmental organizations emerged to play larger and larger roles. Amnesty International, formed in 1961, sought to protect people against governmental abuses. Médecins Sans Frontières (Doctors without Borders) took shape in 1971 as a volunteer group of medical professionals who donated their services, particularly in war-torn areas. Such outfits, and many like them, gradually became part of the fabric of international affairs. So too (less happily) did criminal cartels, which also responded to global opportunities by internationalizing their businesses—for example, moving cocaine from Peru and Bolivia to high-priced markets in the United States and Europe. In some cases, such as the Russian Mafia since the 1990s, international criminal cartels were informally allied with governments. All these organizations and groups arose in response to a more globalized world and by their actions helped globalize it further.

REVIVALS OF RELIGIOUS POLITICS

A second powerful trend around the world was a revival of religious politics. Most societies throughout world history blended political and religious authority together. Religious politics are as old as religion itself. But during the nineteenth and twentieth centuries, many states had distanced themselves from formal religion, following a tradition born in the French and American Revolutions, both of which put barriers between church and state. Most communist states, including the USSR, China, and Cuba, were officially atheist. But starting in the 1970s, religious politics made a comeback.

POLITICAL ISLAM   The most conspicuous case was the rise of political Islam. Religion had always mattered in the politics of Muslim societies—both Shi'a, who predominated in Iran and Iraq, and Sunni, the majority almost everywhere else. But between the 1920s and 1960s, it mattered less and national and class identities mattered more. Nationalist regimes, often run by military men, held sway in several predominantly Muslim countries, such as Turkey from the 1920s, Pakistan from the 1940s, Egypt from the 1950s, and Algeria after independence in 1962.

By the 1970s, the governments of many Muslim societies seemed to their citizens corrupt and ineffective. Despite decades in office, they had failed to live up to promises of social justice or national wealth and power. Young people in particular felt excluded and ignored. Religious leaders called for more virtuous, godly, and efficient rule. In Iran, mullahs—meaning Muslims learned in Islamic law and tradition—seized power in a revolution in 1979. They overthrew a monarch whom they regarded, with justification, as corrupt and subservient to foreign powers. They installed an Islamic republic, enforcing a Muslim law code and imposing rules about personal conduct and dress—mainly for women—that they deemed consistent with their religious heritage. Despite numerous popular uprisings, often led by university students, Iran's mullahs remained in power as of 2023.

The dominant form of Islamic political revival was party politics. Muslims, like everyone else, had been adapting to electoral systems for decades when the 1979 revolution in Iran added inspiration for a new generation of politically active Muslims. In Turkey, an Islamic party grew prominent in the 1990s and started winning elections in 2002. It gradually reasserted the authority of religion in Turkish society, entrenched itself in power, and undid some of the Atatürk revolution of the 1920s that, as we've seen, had built a secular state. Islamic parties did well in elections in Algeria, Tunisia, Bangladesh, Indonesia, and elsewhere. They typically promised a more just and godly society and, in particular, an end to corruption. They proved adept at providing social services such as food kitchens and support for widows and orphans. They funded school systems intended to instill the teachings of Islam in the young.

In some cases, Islamic politics took extremist, intolerant forms. Religious parties of all sorts often struggle with notions of compromise and negotiation, because some believers consider any compromise with divine will to be immoral. Several factions claiming to represent the will of Allah in the politics of Islamic societies resorted to terrorist violence. The Taliban in Afghanistan, active since 1996, are a leading example, but many others arose across the Islamic world from Mali to the Philippines. In places where repressive monarchs or military rule quashed all forms of opposition, terrorist tactics seemed—to those who adopted them—the only weapon at their disposal. Most Muslim societies by 2010 had some experience with terrorist factions operating in the name of Islam.

Al-Qaeda Rescue workers remove casualties from the wreckage of the U.S. embassy in Nairobi, Kenya, following a 1998 al-Qaeda attack that killed more than 200 people. The Nairobi bombing was one of several international terrorist attacks that Osama bin Laden orchestrated in the 1990s and 2000s.

A small proportion of these factions flourished internationally. The most successful was **al-Qaeda** (its name means "the base" in Arabic), begun in 1998 by a charismatic and wealthy Saudi Arabian and Sunni zealot, Osama bin Laden. He acquired his prestige by helping defeat the Soviet Army in its war in Afghanistan from 1979 to 1989. He based his ideology of militant jihad—as warfare in the name of Islam is often called—on his selective interpretation of the Qur'an. He promoted the notion of a restored Islamic caliphate and encouraged violence against Shi'a Muslims and other minorities within Islam, as well as against non-Muslims.

In the 1990s, after the Soviets left Afghanistan, bin Laden turned to new enemies, especially the United States. At that time, the United States had troops stationed in bin Laden's home country. He regarded foreign armies in Saudi Arabia as an intolerable affront and organized anti-American terrorist assaults. He was the paymaster behind the terrorist attacks of September 11, 2001, that killed nearly 3,000 people in New York; in Arlington, Virginia; and in Shanksville, Pennsylvania. Al-Qaeda also flourished in Iraq after a U.S. invasion in 2003, undertaken in the mistaken belief that Iraq had weapons of mass destruction. The war and subsequent U.S. occupation left Iraq in chaos easily exploited by al-Qaeda. Offshoots of al-Qaeda engaged in terrorism, usually targeting other Muslims, in several countries such as Somalia, Syria, and Yemen. U.S. forces killed bin Laden in Pakistan in 2011, but al-Qaeda lived on. Its franchises and affiliates continued to operate in at least 20 countries, sharing funding, training, and propaganda, regularly using international banks, air travel, the Internet, and other sinews of the Global web.

OTHER RELIGIONS Like Islam, other major religious traditions after the 1970s served as fuel for political ideologies. In India, for example, organizations promoting various versions of Hindu values grew more active. A political party (the Bharatiya Janata Party, or BJP) devoted to making India more authentically Hindu took shape in the 1980s. The BJP, originally dominated by upper-caste men, at first supported a stricter observance of caste distinctions. But since that appealed only to a minority of voters, the party evolved so as to embrace more lower-caste Hindus and to emphasize anti-Muslim rhetoric and the ideology known as Hindutva—the notion that India ought to be dominated by Hindu believers and their values. Its

Hindu Militancy A photograph of the Babri mosque in northern India in 1992, shortly before Hindu extremists destroyed it with the intention of building a Hindu temple on the site.

leaders wanted to see India become more forceful in international affairs, especially in its stance toward its Muslim neighbor Pakistan. Many of its members wished to stop Muslim immigrants from entering India. In 1992, Hindu extremists destroyed the old Babri mosque in Ayodhya, in northern India, with the aim of building a temple to the Hindu god Rama on the site. Deadly riots followed. Various Hindu terrorist cells stood behind bombings of mosques, attacks on Christian missionaries, and assaults on representatives of India's secular state. But as with other cases of religious politics, the primary expression of Hindu political revival was in Indian party politics and specifically the BJP. Since the 1990s, the BJP has been in and out of power, always one of the two biggest parties in Indian politics, and increasingly committed to Hindutva.

Christianity, especially its Protestant evangelical forms, has also been increasingly enlisted in political struggles since the 1970s. Evangelical Christians in the United States, often motivated by social issues such as abortion, overcame their traditional distaste for politics. Evangelical Protestantism also became a political force in several Latin American countries, such as Brazil and Guatemala, from the 1980s onward. In 1960, the Protestant population of Latin America was tiny, but by 2020 some 20 percent of Latin Americans considered themselves Protestants, usually Pentecostalists. They typically pressed their governments to restrict abortion and gay marriage. In Africa too, evangelical Protestant faiths acquired many recruits after 1980. By 2020, they accounted for perhaps 20 to 25

percent of all African Christians. Both Kenya and Zambia elected presidents who identified as evangelical Protestants, and Zambia's, Frederick Chiluba, officially declared his country a Christian nation in the 1990s.

Buddhism too acquired a new political edge. After 2000, in majority-Buddhist countries such as Thailand, Burma, and Sri Lanka, small groups, sometimes called Buddhist fundamentalists, organized militant wings that targeted Muslims and Christians. Many Buddhists in these countries felt that their religion and culture were under threat from foreign values, including those of Islam, Christianity, and the unholy marketplace. They appealed to their governments for laws that would ban uncomplimentary remarks about the Buddha or make it illegal for Buddhist women to marry anyone of another faith. The most strident was a group in Burma that collaborated with the military in the oppression of a Muslim minority population, the Rohingya, many of whom fled to neighboring Bangladesh.

Israel, the only country with a Jewish majority, also developed a more religious politics after the 1970s. Officially a Jewish state since its foundation in 1948, its central political issue was that it claimed land—the land of the ancient Hebrews—that Palestinian Arabs regarded as their own. So Israelis had to choose whether to try to coexist with Palestinians or dominate them, a dilemma complicated by Israel's vulnerability to the often hostile Arab states surrounding it. In its early decades, Israel was led by secular Jews of European background. But in 1977, several religious factions, calling for a more observant society and less compromise with Palestinians, helped put the nationalistic Likud Party in power. Thereafter, religious groups provided crucial support for nationalist parties that consistently did well in Israeli elections. What unified them was the wish for a more aggressive policy toward Palestinians and the so-called West Bank, land that the Israeli army conquered in 1967 but that Palestinians—supported by most of the world—considered theirs. Governments in Israel encouraged Jews to settle in the West Bank, guaranteeing frictions with Palestinians, and used those frictions to justify stricter controls on Palestinians.

Everywhere, globalization created problems that people hoped religion would solve. The sudden ups and downs of a globalized economy cost many people their economic security. When in distress, they felt grateful for the charity and social support that religious groups typically provided. Rapid urbanization uprooted people from their communities, leaving emotional and psychological voids in their lives. Religious groups offered comfort and companionship for those in need. Religion also offered an affirmation of identity for those who felt their culture was under siege by strangers with alien values.

DEMOCRACY CRESTING

One of the signal trends of world politics in the late twentieth century was the **spread of democracy**. We've seen in the previous chapter that some 25 dictatorships collapsed in Africa and Latin America between 1979 and 1994. That was part of a broader trend. In 1974, the world had twice as many authoritarian states as liberal democracies. Then, in the mid-1970s, dictatorships in Portugal, Spain, and Greece fell in near-bloodless revolutions that led to durable parliamentary democracies. The Iranian Revolution, mentioned above, also replaced an authoritarian monarchy with a parliamentary system. In the Philippines, a popular revolution overthrew a dictator in the late 1980s. In 1989 and 1990, Eastern Europe's communist regimes tumbled down with the Berlin Wall, giving way to much more democratic states. Communist Yugoslavia fragmented in the late 1980s, giving rise to six new republics, two of which, Slovenia and Croatia, built more or less democratic political systems by the late 1990s. South Korea and Taiwan, as we've seen, replaced authoritarian regimes with more democratic ones in the 1980s and 1990s. Indonesia ended military rule in 1998.

By 2010, the world had twice as many democracies as authoritarian regimes—a remarkable turnaround since 1974. Durable dictatorships, such as those of Fidel Castro in Cuba, Hosni Mubarak in Egypt, Robert Mugabe in Zimbabwe—or the Communist Party in China—now were the exception.

CONTRIBUTING CONDITIONS Three forces, all connected to late twentieth-century globalization, help explain this upsurge of democracy. First, in Latin America and Eastern Europe especially, governments with large amounts of debt ran into trouble in the early 1980s when interest rates spiked. New loans became expensive, and governments had to impose austerity on their populations. This cost them what little legitimacy they had and strengthened dissent.

Second, the end of the Cold War proved bad news

"People Power" In the Philippines in 1986, a corrupt and brutal regime headed by Ferdinand Marcos fell in 1986 to a "People Power" revolution, ushering in decades of democracy. Marcos portrayed all his opponents as communists, which helped him win U.S. support. But when he rigged an election, massive demonstrations resulted and the Catholic Church, units of the armed forces, and finally the United States deserted him. Corazon Aquino, shown here campaigning in a suburb of Manila, took office and restored power to the legislature in a new constitution.

for dictators. Not only did the collapse of the USSR mean no more Soviet backing for communist dictatorships, but it normally meant the end of U.S. support for anticommunist dictatorships. During the Cold War, as we've seen, the U.S. had propped up dozens of brutal military rulers because they were anticommunist, but in the late 1980s the United States lost interest. Most of these dictators could not stay in power without the weapons and money that had formerly flowed from Moscow or Washington.

Third, the power of example helped propel the spread of democracy. The case of Argentina was inspirational throughout Latin America. The "people power" on display in the Philippines in 1986, when Ferdinand Marcos was ousted, resonated in Southeast Asia. The well-televised scenes of ordinary Germans hacking apart the Berlin Wall in 1989 struck chords everywhere. So did the courage, that same year, of Chinese protesters in a losing battle at Tiananmen Square. Modern communications, especially television news, spread sound and image of these events far and wide, helping motivate and mobilize people who had for years grudgingly accepted their life under authoritarian rule. They accepted it no longer.

AUTHORITARIAN RESPONSES The global wave of democratization crested around 1997–2007. Some autocrats withstood the wave, and eventually new ones partly

CONSIDERING THE EVIDENCE

Social Media in the Arab Spring

On January 25, 2011, over 50,000 Egyptians marched into Tahrir Square in downtown Cairo to demand the resignation of their president, Hosni Mubarak. They accused him of corruption and negligence, but they were also angry at his plans to pass the presidency to his own son in the next election. The protesters overwhelmed police, who assaulted them with tear gas, rubber bullets, and water cannon. To keep the protest going, organizers throughout Egypt used social media to announce and organize events, communicate with one another, and share news independently of the state media. When the government responded by shutting down the Internet and mobile phone networks, the protests gained even more support. By February 11, when the president resigned, the crowds in Tahrir Square alone had swelled to over 250,000 people. As Adel Abdel Ghafar writes in his recollection of the protest, organizing on Facebook could never compensate for getting people out into the streets.

Revolutions are not hatched in smoke-filled rooms or by activists armed with Twitter and Facebook accounts; rather, revolutions are made by everyday people who are no longer afraid. That is the profound change that happened in Egypt on January 25. Egyptians, who had bowed down to their pharaohs for seven thousand years, simply said, no more.

As the riot police approached us with their armor and batons raised high, they noticed that we were not moving, something they had never seen before. The line of soldiers started to slow down until they abruptly stopped a few meters in front of us. For a moment, both crowds stared at each other, polar opposites on an urban battlefield. That moment will be etched in my memory forever; time almost seemed to stand still.

Then the most incredible thing happened. The riot police turned back and started running for their lives. We chased them, captured a few, hit them, and took away their weapons and helmets. They ran back to their lines, psychologically broken. Although they would still fight us in the coming days, we all knew that something profound had just taken place. There was a raised collective consciousness among us. A realization. An epiphany. Simply that we will no longer be afraid. We drew strength, courage, and resolve from one another, from our numbers, and from our conviction. Our small group right there reached that conclusion, just as other Egyptians had reached it across the country that day. And in that moment, the Mubarak regime had lost its most significant weapon: fear. Eighteen days later, the tyrant stepped down.

Source: Adel Abdel Ghafar, "The Moment the Barrier of Fear Broke Down," in *Voices of the Arab Spring: Personal Stories from the Arab Revolutions*, ed. Asaad Alsaleh (New York, 2015).

QUESTIONS FOR ANALYSIS

1. According to Adel Abdel Ghafar, why were the protesters successful this time?
2. How did the Internet help protesters organize support on the streets during the Arab Spring?
3. How were the actions taken by the protesters in Egypt similar to or different from the methods promoted by Gandhi as *satyagraha*?

reversed it. In China, as we have seen, the communist leadership crushed a democratization movement in 1989 and tightened its monopoly on politics, especially after 2013, when President Xi Jinping took control. He extinguished democracy in Hong Kong by 2022. In Central Asian countries such as Uzbekistan or Turkmenistan, the end of Soviet rule led merely to new dictatorships run by men who had formerly served Moscow's will. Some dictators, such as Mugabe or Castro, managed to outmaneuver and outlast their enemies until feeble with age.

In several other countries, experiments with democracy left many citizens unsatisfied, opening the door to an authoritarian resurgence in the early twenty-first century. Ambitious authoritarian politicians learned how to rig elections, intimidate or jail opponents, use social media for propaganda purposes, cut deals with billionaires who owned media empires, and muzzle all independent media. These tactics enabled them to undermine democracy even while often preserving its outward forms. In Russia, Vladimir Putin, who made his career in the USSR's spy services before entering politics, proved a master of this general strategy. In 2001, he ended Russia's chaotic flirtation with democracy and thereafter ruled with the help of billionaire oligarchs whose businesses he protected.

Arab Spring Citizens celebrate in Tahrir Square in Cairo in 2011 following protests that led to the resignation of President Hosni Mubarak. However, democratic government in Egypt lasted only two years.

In the so-called Arab Spring in 2011, democracy protesters challenged several longstanding dictatorships and in Tunisia and Egypt overthrew them. In Egypt and Bahrain, authoritarian rulers recovered, and in Syria, Libya, and Yemen civil wars resulted from popular efforts to topple dictators. In Tunisia, democracy endured for 10 years before a president dismissed parliament and ruled alone. Meanwhile, Turkey, the Philippines, India, Hungary, Poland, Brazil, Nicaragua, Venezuela, South Africa, Sudan, Uganda, and several other countries drifted toward more authoritarian rule in the early twenty-first century.

Three main factors lay behind this revitalization of authoritarianism. One was the rise of China, the best example of an undemocratic state that achieved wealth and power rapidly. China provided economic support for rulers around the world without imposing conditions about human rights or democracy, unlike the United States or the European Union. Another factor was the increasing cooperation among undemocratic rulers, which helped solidify their grips on power. Led by China and Russia, these rulers offered money, weapons, surveillance technology, or other help to prop up authoritarians in Belarus, Turkey, Venezuela, and elsewhere. A third factor was the frequent failure of democracies to protect their citizens from the economic dislocations of globalization. Millions who lost their jobs after a major economic downturn in 2007 and 2008 also lost their faith in democratic systems of government. Authoritarian politicians won support by promising prosperity, crackdowns on

immigrants, or a return to traditional morality. And in 2020, the COVID-19 pandemic enabled many governments to claim emergency powers, which in India, Sri Lanka, Cambodia, Bolivia, Hungary, and elsewhere they used to detain political opponents illegally.

Resurgent authoritarianism did not always go over well. In the early 2020s, street demonstrations, uprisings, and other efforts aimed at checking arbitrary power—often requiring great courage—took place in Turkey, Iran, Tunisia, Myanmar, Cuba, and elsewhere. Even in China and Russia, where state authorities had long honed their skills at repression of dissent, a brave few protested authoritarian rule, risking prolonged imprisonment or death.

THE ROLE OF SOCIAL MEDIA Twenty-first-century politics was also shaped by the rise of the Internet and by social media in particular. Social media are online platforms designed for communication and for sharing, via computers and mobile devices, images, videos, news, stories, and opinions. They include social networking sites such as Facebook, launched in 2004; microblogging platforms such as Twitter (2006) and Tumblr (2007); and platforms used mainly for image and video sharing such as YouTube (2005), Instagram (2010), Snapchat (2011), and TikTok (2017). The most frequented social media networks in 2020 were offered by either American or Chinese companies. Approximately 3.8 billion people—half the human race—used social media in 2020, and some 4.5 billion used the Internet.

The Internet has been used for political purposes practically since its inception, and by the late 2000s prodemocracy movements around the globe were using social media to advance their agendas. As one Egyptian activist of the Arab Spring tweeted in 2011, "We use Facebook to schedule the protests, Twitter to coordinate, and YouTube to tell the world." Popular protests in Turkey, Iran, Russia, the United States, Hong Kong, and many other places did so as well.

At first, governments were outflanked by the online tactics of young, technologically savvy activists. But within a few years, authoritarian governments began to restrict online content and block social media platforms or users. They also arrested people who organized dissent through social media, and they used the platforms themselves to create and spread lies designed to discredit their critics. Their security services used data collected from online communications companies and social media platforms to monitor citizens, improving the efficiency of surveillance operations. In 2017 in Burma, the military used Facebook to incite violence against the Rohingya.

States found that they could use social media at minimal expense to influence political opinions in other countries as well as their own and undertook to sway elections or even incite riots abroad. Putin's Russia demonstrated considerable skill with this tactic, running social media campaigns in about 20 countries' elections. Meanwhile, terrorist organizations such as ISIS (the Islamic State of Iraq and Syria, or Daesh) also found that social media served their ambitions, especially for recruiting volunteers, spreading propaganda, and coordinating attacks. Every new communications technology in world history—writing, printing, telegraph, radio, TV—has carried political consequences, sometimes empowering states, sometimes weakening them. Often, the new technologies at first weaken states by enabling subjects and citizens to share information more rapidly and cheaply, but states eventually learn how to exploit the new tools to buttress their own power.

WAR AND PEACE IN THE TWENTY-FIRST CENTURY

The resurgence of authoritarian rule in the early twenty-first century contributed to a handful of major wars. Unpopular regimes often found foreign wars tempting as a way to justify repression at home in the name of national unity. Some found repression alone could not keep them in power and unleashed military assaults on their own populations.

The deadliest war by far, the Second Congo War (as we've seen) ravaged eastern Congo beginning in 1998. It originated in a succession crisis that became a Congolese civil war but eventually involved armies and militias from nine African countries. Some five million Africans lost their lives before the violence tapered off around 2008. A Syrian civil war evolved out of protests in the Arab Spring of 2011 directed at the dictatorial government of Bashar al-Assad. With help from Kurds based in Iraq, and from the United States, rebel militias almost toppled him. But desperate attacks, some involving chemical weapons, plus help from Russia and Iran

kept Assad in control of parts of Syria. The war (as of mid-2023) has killed half a million and uprooted about 12 million refugees, nearly half of whom fled the country. Smaller civil wars bedeviled Sudan (2003–2008), killing perhaps 300,000, and Yemen (since 2012), where nearly 400,000 lives have been lost.

The U.S.-led invasions of Afghanistan in 2001 and Iraq in 2003 launched lengthy wars. In Afghanistan, the target was the Taliban, which sheltered Osama bin Laden's al-Qaeda. It outlasted the patience of its foes and triumphed in 2021. Roughly 125,000 fighters died in the war, about 96 percent of them Afghans. In Iraq, the invading coalition won a conventional war quickly, destroying the brutal regime of Saddam Hussein. Insurgencies followed, and after the departure of U.S. troops in 2010, civil war. The death toll is highly controversial but probably exceeded 150,000, of whom all but 5,000 were Iraqis.

In 2022, Putin's Russia shattered Europe's peace with a large-scale invasion of Ukraine. He had annexed part of Ukraine in 2014, alleging it had no legitimate historical identity and ought to be part of Russia. His likely motives for the 2022 assault included a wish to restore Russian power to the height achieved during the heyday of the USSR, and, perhaps more important, an anxiety that a democratic and prosperous Ukraine would inspire Russian citizens and oligarchs alike to reject his rule. If Ukraine, which was similar to Russia in many ways, began to prosper like many European countries—and perhaps eventually joined the European Union and NATO—Russians might sour on Putin's rule.

To the surprise of almost everyone, Ukraine, led by a former TV comedian, Volodymyr Zelensky, fended off the invasion. The war settled into a bloody stalemate. NATO countries pumped vast amounts of money and weaponry into Ukraine. Russia received small amounts of help from China. While both sides treated casualty figures as military secrets, after 18 months Ukraine had probably lost 10,000 to 20,000 killed, and Russia 50,000 to 70,000—with no end in sight to the bloodshed.

These seven wars—in Congo, Syria, Sudan, Yemen, Afghanistan, Iraq, and Ukraine—were the deadliest of the early twenty-first century. Most of them involved shifting coalitions of participants and supporters, giving them broader dimensions and reverberating through the Global web politically and economically.

THE GLOBAL ECONOMY SINCE 1980

As usual, political changes were tightly bound up with economic ones. In the previous chapter, we looked at economic performance in East Asia, Africa, and Latin America. Here we consider economic globalization, especially in trade and finance, and trends in inequality. To see the significance of the recent economic integration, it helps to look backward first.

The international economy before 1914 had been knitting itself together rapidly. But with world wars and the Great Depression, the decades between 1914 and 1945 were a time of economic deglobalization. International trade and investment flows fell to levels below those of 1880. So did labor migration. After 1945, the global economy resumed its integration, limited by the Cold War. Indeed, it might be better to say that two rival processes of economic integration began—a communist one under Soviet leadership and a capitalist one anchored by the United States. In the years 1989–1991, the end of the Cold War gave globalization another boost by opening the former Soviet bloc to stronger connections with the capitalist world. The two most important features of this entire process—integration, disintegration, reintegration—were trade and finance.

THE GROWTH OF INTERNATIONAL TRADE

In 1913, about 20 to 25 percent of the world's goods were traded internationally. During the 1930s and 1940s, that fell to about 10 percent. The proportion recovered to 20 to 25 percent by 1980, and then it skyrocketed. In the decade between 2008 and 2017, it reached a plateau of about 55 to 60 percent. Machinery, consumer electronics, and oil have lately topped the list of goods traded across borders.

Why this sudden change since 1980? Part of the explanation is illusion: there are more countries than before. Shoes exported from Russia to Uzbekistan in 1980 were not international trade because both were part of the Soviet Union, but after 1991 and the breakup of the USSR, they were. However, the fuller explanation involves basic changes in the organization of the global economy, the result of several shifts in ideas, policy, business organization, and technology.

FREE TRADE POLICY   In the realm of ideas and policy, the 1980s marked a major shift in favor of **free trade**. The United States and the United Kingdom, led by President Ronald Reagan and Prime Minister Margaret Thatcher, spearheaded efforts to get other countries to liberalize trade. Most big American businesses by now had abandoned their support for high import tariffs because much of their own production took place overseas. Since the United States remained by far the biggest national economy and the most powerful country in the world, its ideas, policies, and preferences carried considerable weight internationally.

A second key policy shift was the effort to reduce barriers to trade within Europe, which dated back to the 1950s. The main idea then was to make western Europe stronger and richer through cooperation and integration so it would not be eclipsed by the Cold War superpowers. But the biggest steps toward free trade in Europe took place in the early 1990s with the formation of the European Union (EU), symbolized by the adoption of a common currency, the euro, which replaced more than a dozen national currencies. Between 2004 and 2013, the EU expanded to include almost all the Eastern European countries of the former Soviet bloc, creating a highly integrated trade zone accounting for about 22 percent of the world economy.

As the policies of free trade spread around the world, multinational corporations got bigger and better at scattering parts of their operations in several countries. For labor-intensive jobs, they chose low-wage countries. Reagan and Thatcher regarded labor unions as obstacles to the economic changes they wished to see, and both succeeded in reducing the power of unions—making it easier for firms to move manufacturing jobs from the United States or the United Kingdom to Mexico, India, or China. Meanwhile, firms put technology-intensive work in countries with a highly educated labor force. They located their pollution-intensive operations in countries with minimal environmental regulation. So by 2015, a Ford truck might be designed in Michigan, have a transmission built in China, contain an engine from Brazil, and be assembled in Kentucky. Most big companies in the auto, petrochemical, pharmaceutical, electronics, and computer industries found ways to cut costs by globalizing their supply chains. When big companies did this, they "traded" internationally with themselves to prepare finished products for market. By 2015, roughly 80 percent of international trade took place inside such global firms.

their jobs or homes. Street protests in the United States and Europe lasted for months, and citizens voted out existing governments in favor of more radical parties, fueling the resurgence of authoritarianism. Countries with no debt loads and those least linked to the world's financial system—China, India, Indonesia, Australia, and several African nations—weathered the crisis comparatively well.

The financialization of the world economy led to a spike in economic volatility. It amounted to a rising tide that lifted some boats but swamped others. It added to the hunger felt around the world for economic stability and security, especially among older citizens who remembered calmer times and who had worked for decades to build savings or acquire a house, only to see their assets swept away in the financial storm. Politicians responded to this hunger with promises of a return to stable jobs and economic security—which none of them could deliver.

HEIGHTENED INEQUALITY

Like every earlier surge in economic globalization, the rapid one after 1980 created winners and losers. Globally, there were more winners than losers, especially in China. In poor countries, roughly 500 to 700 million people with few options found new opportunities in the years between 1980 and 2020. They left their villages to accept low wages and sometimes dangerous working conditions in new factories. They may not have won much, but they were the bulk of the winners from economic globalization. Most of the winnings—a different thing—went to the few people who had the education, skill, connections, and luck to profit from either the growth in finance or the migration of manufacturing from high-wage to low-wage countries. This profit flowed to a few million people around the world, who became superrich.

One of those was the Mexican business magnate Carlos Slim, born in 1940. He was a first-generation Mexican of Lebanese ancestry. He parlayed a modest inheritance into diverse business holdings in Mexico, the rest of Latin America, the United States, and Europe. Slim became one of the world's 10 richest people in the 1990s and was the richest of all for a few years starting in 2010. His fortune came from the heady growth of several manufacturing businesses he owned in Mexico, most of which exported goods to the newly open U.S. market. He owned Latin America's biggest mobile phone company when mobile phones took off. As of 2015, he owned about 200 companies, several of which enjoyed monopolies in their markets. Slim took full advantage of the deregulation of the telecom, insurance, and financial industries, as well as the reduction in barriers to transactions among Mexico, the United States, and other countries. He is among the biggest beneficiaries of economic globalization (and says his favorite subject in high school was history).

The losers from globalization included the tens of millions of people in high-wage countries who saw the market for their skills disappear. In the 1970s, a unionized Chicago steelworker with a grade-school education could support a family by himself, own a home and a car, and even take foreign vacations. But as steel production migrated to South Korea, Mexico, and elsewhere, high-paying jobs of this sort gradually disappeared in the United States, much of Europe, and Japan. Secure industrial jobs also disappeared in Russia and Eastern Europe after 1989 as communist-era factories could not compete internationally. Automation of factory work also replaced high-wage laborers everywhere. In the United States, the proportion of the economy that went to wages and salaries peaked at around 50 to 52 percent between 1945 and 1970, and it fell thereafter as a result of global competition and automation. By 2020, it had slid to 42 percent. Wage earners struggled to find and keep what they considered decent jobs in the globalized economy.

All this reshuffling of income as a result of economic globalization changed patterns of inequality in the world. On most measures, **income inequality** of the global population declined after 1990. Rising wages in China and to a lesser degree India accounted for most of that change. Apart from these cases, there was very little reduction in global inequality.

Income inequality within—as opposed to among—countries was a simpler story. Throughout the twentieth century up to about 1980, a strong trend toward greater equality had prevailed just about everywhere. In the 1970s through the 1980s, that trend leveled off in Europe. In the United States, the United Kingdom, Canada, and Australia, it then reversed direction sharply. Those societies developed megarich classes, known colloquially after 2008 as "the one percent." In the United States in 2021, the top 1 percent got 15 percent of all national income—up from 7 percent in 1980. Most of the countries with the greatest income inequality were poor countries with

Deindustrialization A woman walks past an abandoned steel plant in western Pennsylvania in 2008. In developed countries like the United States, as well-paid industrial jobs disappeared after 1980, income inequality widened dramatically.

superrich elites, such as South Africa, Botswana, and Panama. Those with the least income inequality were mainly in Europe, especially Scandinavia.

Measured by wealth—what people owned, rather than their incomes—inequality widened even more sharply after 1990. By 2015, the richest eight individuals on Earth, including Carlos Slim, owned as much as the poorest 3.7 billion people. Winners in this redistribution of wealth understood it as a consequence of meritocracy and often claimed that anyone who wanted to pursue education and work hard could succeed in free-market economies. But most who lost out, men especially, felt they could not find dignified work in the new economy, work that would underpin status as a respected member of a community, and resented the callous attitudes of the winners.

CULTURAL GLOBALIZATION

Recent decades witnessed globalization in the realm of culture as well as economics. Thanks to technical advances in communication and to the upswing in international migration, people more frequently came in contact with unfamiliar languages, customs, food, and music. This proved unsettling for many people but also sparked a surge of cultural creativity around the world.

Everything from food fusion (such as sushi burritos) to Facebook friendships (15 percent of which were international in 2015) globalized. Men wear baseball caps in Nepal and Namibia. Modern skyscrapers and airports look the same everywhere. Here we'll look at two aspects of the broader cultural trend: music and sports.

MUSIC

Music is one of the cultural forms that travels well through the Global web. People can enjoy it without words or without understanding the words. Until the 1880s, music was always experienced live. It traveled most easily when musicians traveled, bringing, for example, Celtic ballads (from Ireland and Scotland) to North America in the eighteenth and nineteenth centuries. Religious music traveled wherever religions did: Sufi ceremonial music and dance went everywhere that Sufism went, from Morocco to Mindanao (in the Philippines) and every Islamic land in between.

The globalization of music accelerated with the invention of recording technology, beginning in the 1880s, and then radio, in the 1920s. Those technologies took hold first in the richer countries, so in the first half of the twentieth century European and North American music proved the most mobile. Classical music—the symphonies, sonatas, and concertos that Europeans had raised to a high art during the eighteenth and nineteenth centuries—found audiences around the world. Today, more people are trained in classical music in East Asia than anywhere else. European musical styles often traveled in the footsteps of European empire.

In the 1950s, a dramatic change in the history of music took place with recordings marketed exclusively to youth—a growing share of the world's population after 1950, owing to the widespread "baby boom." The change began in the United States and proved lucrative. Young people came to define themselves partly by the music they liked and to mark themselves off from their elders with their musical preferences. This development, combined with cheaper recordings, led to an even faster surge of musical globalization.

The engine room of this musical movement was the American South, the home of jazz and blues. In the late 1950s, when John Lennon and Paul McCartney were Liverpool teenagers, they eagerly awaited the arrival of American ships because sailors brought records made by Black American artists, such as Chuck Berry and Little Richard,

Fela Kuti The Nigerian musician Fela Kuti with his band in 1980. Fela's music, called Afrobeat, was a blend of Yoruba traditions with American rhythm and blues and jazz.

with roots in the South. Lennon and McCartney imitated their sound and soon became the core of one of the most popular musical acts of all time, the Beatles.

The music they learned, at the time called rhythm and blues in the United States, was itself derived partly from West African traditions, including polyrhythmic drumming used in jazz. Black Americans in the 1950s and 1960s had combined those traditions with vocal styles from gospel church choirs. In their lyrics, they replaced gospel music's intense longing for salvation with longing for love and sex. This proved a magic formula, generating a youth music—including soul and rock 'n' roll—that exploded on the scene in the 1960s.

In an ironic twist, the wealth and power of the United States by the 1960s helped spread the cultural influence of its most underprivileged population, Black Americans from the South or from the inner cities of Detroit or Chicago. During the Cold War years, the economic and political clout of the United States was at its height. The U.S. State Department sponsored global goodwill tours by American jazz musicians. U.S. soldiers and sailors stationed around the world served as unofficial ambassadors for American popular music. In earlier centuries, the power and wealth of the Roman Empire had helped spread the tastes and fashions of its aristocrats throughout Europe and North Africa. The prestige of China's Song dynasty had had a similar impact in Korea and Southeast Asia. Now the United States wielded even broader influence, but, in music at least, that influence came not from the elite but from the lower rungs of the social hierarchy.

Musicians all over the world developed their own styles, blending local and international—often American—influences. Brazilians made bossa nova—combining their own tradition of samba with American jazz—globally popular in the 1960s. The South African singer Miriam Makeba melded a style from Johannesburg's dance halls with American pop to create an international hit in the Xhosa language. Other African musicians—perhaps most notably the Nigerians King Sunny Ade, who sang in Yoruba, and Fela Kuti, who sang in Nigerian English—enjoyed international popularity in the 1980s with styles that incorporated instruments from American popular music, such as pedal steel guitar and synthesizers, but relied on West African drumming traditions. Both were at the forefront of what since 1987 has been called world music, a loose category of popular music made by people outside of North America or Europe but influenced by the popular music of the United States.

American country music also went global, finding audiences especially in Europe and Australia. Bal Kishore Das Loiwal, born to a prosperous family in northern India, learned to play and sing country music from records sent home by an aunt who had moved to Nashville, the mecca of country music. He changed his name to Bobby Cash and after 2005 broke into the Australian market as well as creating a following at home, calling himself the Indian cowboy and dressing the part.

One of the world's most popular musical forms by the 1970s was the Jamaican invention called reggae, a blend of older Caribbean styles with American jazz and rhythm and blues. It was associated with the Rastafarian religion, a Jamaican innovation of the 1930s, which revered the Ethiopian king Haile Selassie as a prophet. Reggae's most successful artist was Bob Marley, a global star from the early 1970s until his death in 1981. By the 1980s, Jamaican reggae was popular everywhere.

Few musicians blended as many global influences as Shakira, whose name means "grateful" in Arabic. Born in Colombia, her ancestors came from Spain, Italy, and Lebanon. By her teenage years, she was performing throughout Colombia, singing in Spanish and occasionally in Arabic. She learned from an eclectic mix of music from Lebanon, Latin America, the United States, and the United Kingdom. Her Lebanese dance style translated well to music videos, a format that became popular in the 1980s. In the early 2000s, she began to record in English, expanding

Global Popular Culture Fans cluster around the Colombian pop singer Shakira after she opens a child-care center in Cartagena, Colombia, in 2012. Shakira's performances in Spanish, Arabic, and English made her a global sensation.

her audience. Together with the Haitian-American rapper Wyclef Jean, she recorded the best-selling song of the twenty-first century (so far) in 2006. Asked in 2001 to describe herself, Shakira said: "I'm a fusion between black and white, between pop and rock, between cultures—between my Lebanese father and my mother's Spanish blood, the Colombian folklore and Arab dance I love and American music."

Drake and Rihanna were almost as international in their inspirations as Shakira and even more successful as global stars. Drake, whose Canadian mother had Eastern European Jewish roots and whose father was an African American musician from Tennessee, grew up in Toronto. He helped develop a rap style that proved enormously popular around the world by 2010. Rihanna began singing in outdoor markets in her hometown of Bridgetown, Barbados. She moved to the United States in her late teens and launched a recording career that mixed Caribbean reggae and dancehall styles with American pop, rap, and dance music. By 2020, she stood among the 10 best-selling recording artists ever, the only one among them born after 1960. She became a movie star and, like Drake and Shakira, an entrepreneur with a global following.

Nowadays, thanks to YouTube, Spotify, and their successors, music swirls around the world as never before. Traditions rub up against one another, leading to new forms every year. Rap stars from Korea (Psy, of "Gangnam Style" fame) could become global celebrities overnight. Opera, whose fans usually expect adherence to tradition, also globalized: one of the most admired sopranos of the last 40 years, Kiri Te Kanawa, who sang in Italian and German, as opera singers normally do, was raised in a Maori family in New Zealand.

SPORTS

Modern sports took shape at the end of the nineteenth century with the reincarnation of the ancient Greek Olympic games and the formation of leagues for team sports such as soccer in Britain and baseball in the United States. These became spectacles for crowds as well as competitions for athletes, like chariot racing in the ancient Roman world. All the major global sports developed first in Europe and America and often spread along the trails of empire. Polo, originating in Iran, is the closest thing to an exception. Cricket became popular in South Asia, Australia, and the Anglophone Caribbean—formerly parts of the British Empire. Baseball took root in Mexico and those parts of the Spanish Caribbean with the strongest historical links to the United States, such as Puerto Rico, Cuba, the Dominican Republic, and Panama. It acquired a following in those parts of East Asia where the U.S. presence, especially military, was strong, such as Japan, Taiwan, and South Korea. Basketball by the 1990s spread far and wide, aided by its minimal need of equipment, unlike ice hockey, a Canadian invention played only in cold and prosperous countries, or American football, which won few fans outside North America.

The most global of sports was soccer. Its rules crystallized in Britain during the nineteenth century. Britain's global reach in the nineteenth century brought soccer to every continent. It found especially fertile soil in South America and continental Europe, which to this day produce most of the best male players, lately joined by West Africa. The secret to soccer's global appeal lay in how little one needs to play it: some open space and a ball.

The women's game also originated in Britain, where a public match was played as early as 1895 and one in 1920 drew 53,000 spectators. France and Italy had amateur leagues by the 1930s. But it took until late in the twentieth century before professional women's soccer leagues sprang up, aided by the development of girls' sports programs in schools, the launching of the Women's World Cup in 1991, and the inclusion of women's soccer as an Olympic sport in 1996.

The men's soccer World Cup began in 1930 with only 13 national teams taking part. The first TV broadcasts came in 1954, and soon the World Cup was a global cultural event. Decolonization led to increased participation, so that by 2006 nearly 200 national teams competed for slots in the 32-team tournament. The World Cup attracted more TV viewers than the Olympics or any other sporting competition. Since 2006, the final match of each tournament has been seen live by 10 to 12 percent of humankind. The Women's World Cup, at first a 12-team tournament,

Global Sports A member of the U.S. women's national soccer team plays in a match against Sweden during the 2019 Women's World Cup tournament. The world's most popular sport, soccer is today played on every inhabited continent.

expanded to a 32-team event between 1999 and 2023, also attracting many millions of spectators on TV.

Sports changed less when traveling than did music. The rules of baseball were very much the same in South Korea as in South Carolina. Styles of play differed a bit more than rules, but any innovations that brought competitive advantage spread almost instantly because of modern communications and intense competition. Stable rules through the decades were important to the public appeal of sports, so fans could enjoy arguing whether Walter Payton was a better football player than Christian McCaffrey (he was), whether Serena Williams was better at tennis than Margaret Court (she was), or whether Pelé was better at soccer than Lionel Messi (he wasn't).

Television helped convert international competitions such as the World Cup and the Olympics into global cultural phenomena and arenas of peaceful national competition. The modern Olympics began in Europe in 1896 as a gentlemanly competition, mainly in track and field. Women—at first only golfers and tennis players—began to take part in 1900. With the beginning of worldwide TV broadcasts at the Tokyo games in 1964, the Olympics began to attract global audiences. Decolonization increased the number of teams and competitors and made the Olympics more interesting to Africans and Asians. The increasing participation of female athletes also boosted the popularity of the Olympics. Women runners competed in the 1500 meters beginning in 1972, and the women's marathon debuted in 1984. In the most recent Olympiads, about 42 to 44 percent of athletes were women.

During the Cold War, the Olympics became one of the stages on which the USSR and the United States tried to demonstrate the superiority of their sociopolitical systems. Both supported officially "amateur" athletes for the purpose of winning medals. Sports fans—and politicians too—developed an obsession with medal counts. In East Germany and China, which entered Olympic competition in 1980, governments controlled sports organizations and went to great lengths to use sports to show the vigor of their brand of communism. East German politicians, desperate to outdo West Germany, encouraged the nation's sports federation to administer performance-enhancing drugs to the best athletes, often without the athletes' consent. Some as young as 10 years of age were fed testosterone, steroids, and amphetamines. They did bring home a bumper crop of Olympic medals—at the price of health problems later in life. The Olympics, which officially admitted professional athletes by 1992, remains one of the most politically meaningful sporting events today, even if the intensity of the Cold War years is gone.

The advent of TV in the 1950s and 1960s made many sports into big businesses and enabled some athletes—a few hundred in all—to become exceedingly rich, through endorsements as well as salaries or winnings. In most years since 2000, all of the top 30 earners among athletes were male, generally soccer players in Europe or basketballers in the United States. The top women were always tennis players, with Serena Williams leading the way until her retirement in 2022.

GLOBAL COMMUNITY AND ITS LIMITS

The surge in global connections after 1980 helped create new human communities. People on different continents who previously knew little or nothing of one another more easily made common cause despite distance and cultural differences. To a limited extent, such global communities had existed in previous centuries, for example among bankers who lent one another money across oceans or among mathematicians who corresponded about certain puzzles. In the nineteenth century, organized labor tried to create linkages among workers around the world but with little success. By and large, before 1980, it was mainly the wealthy and well-traveled who took part in any kind of global community. Cheaper communications in the late twentieth century changed that. Now people could find like-minded people easily and cheaply and share their interests, whether in computer games, African art, gambling, or South Korean TV dramas.

INDIGENOUS PEOPLES MAKE COMMON CAUSE
Sometimes these new global communities carried political consequences, as in the case of the growing solidarity among Indigenous people around the world. While the formal definition of **Indigenous peoples** varies from country to country and among and within Indigenous groups, there's no doubt that sizeable Indigenous populations—at least as a proportion of the total population—exist in New Zealand, Australia, Russia, Canada, the United States, Mexico, Brazil, and several other Latin American countries. By some definitions, India, Bangladesh, China, and Japan, among other Asian countries, also include Indigenous populations—although the Chinese government maintains that China has none. Several pastoralist or hunting and foraging peoples in Africa also claim status as Indigenous peoples.

The UN as of 2005 officially recognized more than 5,000 different Indigenous peoples in 72 different countries. In total, they represent a population between 250 million and 600 million, depending on definitions—roughly 3 to 6 percent of all humans. Some live in big

Global Indigenous Activism Members of a South American Indigenous community marching in Glasgow, Scotland, in 2021 on the occasion of a United Nations conference on climate change. Climate stabilization is a priority for many Indigenous populations.

cities, some on ancestral lands. According to the International Labor Organization, about 70 percent of the world's Indigenous population lives in Asia or the Pacific Islands, 16 percent in Africa, 12 percent in Latin America, nearly 2 percent in North America, and 0.1 percent in Europe. All have ancient claims to the lands they inhabit, with distinct cultures and languages, although they are often bicultural and bilingual. Most are now outnumbered by more recently arrived settler populations. A tiny minority, mostly in Amazonia, have no contact with the rest of humankind.

Indigenous peoples around the world shared, and increasingly recognized that they shared, certain concerns. Sheer survival was often one of them. Genocides of Indigenous peoples date back millennia. Since 1980, the largest of them was directed against the Maya by Guatemala's military government in the 1980s. Since then, state violence used against Indigenous peoples has ebbed but not fully disappeared.

Most Indigenous peoples have long held concerns about the survival of their language and culture. Wherever they are in the minority, their children gain advantages by learning to speak the language of the majority, so that over time Indigenous language survival has often been—and will continue to be—threatened. Marie Smith Jones, who died in 2008, was from a fishing community in southeast Alaska and was the last speaker of a language called Eyak. Her nine children were not interested in speaking Eyak, because English was more useful both in southeast Alaska and throughout the Global web. Of the world's 4,000 Indigenous languages in existence, most are now endangered. Many, like Ainu (spoken on the Japanese island of Hokkaido) have only a few dozen speakers left. Thirty or more, most of them in the Americas, Australia, or Russia, have gone extinct since 2010, a rate probably higher than at any time in human history.

Indigenous peoples worldwide also shared concerns about environmental stability. A large proportion of Indigenous populations typically rely directly on plants and animals for their livelihood and are eager to preserve biodiversity in their lands. Some 80 percent of terrestrial species today are found on Indigenous lands, mostly in moist tropical forests. For centuries, however, their lands have proven attractive to outsiders with economic ambitions that endanger environments. For example, the Navajo in the southwestern United States, the Cree and

Dene in Saskatchewan (Canada), the Mirarr in Australia, and the Buryats in southeastern Siberia (Russia) all faced radioactive messes resulting from uranium mining on their lands. Elsewhere, oil drilling, timber harvesting, dam building, or industrial-scale fishing vexed Indigenous peoples. Economic activities like these, which are always environmentally disruptive, imperilled the lands, traditional economies, ways of life, and spiritual paths of Indigenous peoples. They sometimes brought welcome jobs in return. That often divided Indigenous communities between those who valued the jobs and those who preferred to keep environments and old ways intact.

Indigenous peoples have long tried to counter the trends of land loss, cultural assimilation, language death, and environmental decline. The experience of the Ashaninka, who live in the Amazonian rain forest straddling the border between Brazil and Peru, is illustrative. For centuries, they deliberately isolated themselves from the outside world. In the twentieth century, this policy became impractical as the timber and rubber available in their lands now commanded good prices in world markets. By the 1980s, transport in Amazonia, a priority especially for Brazil's government, had improved to the point where ranchers, loggers, and cocaine traffickers moved in to pursue their businesses. The Ashaninka quickly concluded, after massacres at the hands of well-armed loggers and drug dealers, that violent resistance was a losing strategy. As one of them, Benki Piyãko, put it: "We began to study." Young Ashaninka were sent to study law, politics, economics, and languages. They developed the skills needed to win support from NGOs, from sympathetic segments of Brazilian and Peruvian society, and from international sources as well. They secured titles to land, reforested denuded landscapes, dug out new fish ponds, and struggled to preserve their language, culture, crafts, and spiritual understandings. Their response to external threats emphasized foreign practical knowledge combined with key tenets of their own culture. In this respect, it echoed earlier successful responses to a newly threatening world, such as that of Meiji Japan in the nineteenth century.

While Indigenous peoples have always pursued their own specific agendas, since the 1970s they have increasingly forged common cause across continents and oceans. The American Indian Movement (AIM), formed in 1968, originally devoted itself to cultural renewal and employment programs for Native Americans in the United States. A Canadian organization, the National Indian Brotherhood (NIB), took shape in the same year with parallel goals. Similar groupings arose in the Andean region of South America. By 1974, these organizations, led by AIM, joined forces in the **International Indian Treaty Council**, bringing Indigenous peoples throughout the Americas and Pacific together to try to preserve their land rights and cultural autonomy. The early 1970s witnessed a surge in Indigenous activism around the world, fueled in part by recognition of common issues and struggles. Maori battled in New Zealand's Parliament for land rights. Australian Aborigines protested in Canberra. AIM had several tense confrontations with the U.S. federal government between 1969 and 1975. This growing activism and mutual awareness led the Canadian NIB to champion the formation of the World Council of Indigenous Peoples in 1975. It dissolved in 1996 due to internal frictions, whereas the International Indian Treaty Council, once its rival, lives on.

All these organizations sought help from national governments but in the 1970s rarely found it. In response, they turned their attention both to the public at large, hoping to win allies, and to international organizations. In 1982, Indigenous peoples managed to win recognition from the UN, which created a permanent forum for discussion of Indigenous issues in 2000 and issued a Declaration on the Rights of Indigenous Peoples in 2007. That declaration insists Indigenous peoples have the right to self-determination and a voice in the use of natural resources in their ancestral lands. Only a handful of countries have not signed on to the declaration, the most significant of which is Russia, where oil barons and the state profit by pumping up petroleum from beneath lands inhabited by Mansi, Nenets, Dolgan, and others.

The early international efforts at Indigenous solidarity in the 1970s and 1980s arose mainly in the Americas, Australia, New Zealand, and among the Sámi of northern Scandinavia. By the 1990s, Russian groups, mainly from the Siberian Arctic, had begun to form and to seek allies internationally, including at the UN. So did people claiming Indigenous status in Africa, such as Tanzania's Maasai or the Khoisan-speakers in Botswana and South Africa. This globalization of the concept of indigeneity unsurprisingly brought conflict. Some people felt that Indigenous status should belong only to people who suffered from

European imperialism, which would rule out the Ainu in Japan, for example. Others took a broader view of indigeneity. Some felt that working with national governments was the only practical approach, while others thought that collaborating with those they regarded as their oppressors was never justified. The resulting divisions constrained the success of Indigenous people in realizing their agendas. Around the world they often remain poor, politically weak, disdained, and exploited.

Nonetheless, Indigenous solidarity efforts have yielded results that in the 1970s seemed impossible. As more and more Indigenous people "began to study," as Benki Piyãko put it, they found ways to use law and courts to address some of their grievances. In Canada and Australia, large expanses of land have reverted to Indigenous control as a result of court decisions. In Bolivia, where half the population identifies as Indigenous, large regions are now autonomously governed by indigenous groups. In Taiwan, where Indigenous people amount to about 2.5 percent of the population, the government made it harder for mining companies to defile Indigenous land. On a visit to Canada in 2022, Pope Francis apologized to Indigenous peoples for cruelties inflicted on children in Canada's residential schools (which operated between the 1870s and 1997). While victories such as these may seem meager in the balance, they represent the first fruits of a growing global solidarity.

IMAGINARY GLOBALIZATION Strong as they are in light of the past, all these currents of demographic, economic, and cultural globalization are much weaker than most people think they are. A survey of people in 138 countries undertaken in 2015 revealed that on average, people imagind that international migrants make up 30 percent of the world's population, whereas 3.6 percent is about right. Respondents thought that 22 percent of university students came from abroad; the real figure was 2 percent. They thought foreign trade was twice as large as it was. Across dozens of variables, the survey showed that people around the world imagined globalization was about five times more prevalent than it actually was.

The fast pace of cultural and economic globalization after 1980 has had its limits. First of all, many people feared globalization as a threat to their livelihood, their identity, or both. Elections in the United States, Latin America, Turkey, India, and several European countries after 2012 reflected this sentiment. Moreover, there are big and basic obstacles checking globalization. People in Nigeria and Norway have good reason not to dress alike, because it's always warm in Nigeria and often cold in Norway. And it seems most unlikely that anyone other than Icelanders will ever regard fermented shark meat as a delicacy.

The long trend, nevertheless, remains toward greater integration of the Global web. Since its formation in the sixteenth century, it has expanded and tightened despite several setbacks along the way. The COVID-19 pandemic was another setback but hardly a reversal. The web building process has been woven into world history since the earliest times, and it has rebounded from shocks, including world wars and pandemics far deadlier than COVID-19. No one planned it, and many people resent its effects, but almost everyone contributes to the ongoing life of the Global web by pursuing their own economic, intellectual, cultural, and religious interests.

CONCLUSION

From our current perspective, the post-1980 world looks like one of tumultuous change. Climate change sped up dramatically. Population growth slowed down and fertility decreased as women increasingly devoted more time to schooling and paid work and less to child rearing and household chores. Emerging viruses threatened human health on every continent, perhaps heralding a countertrend to the remarkable centuries-long reduction in the burden of disease. Nevertheless, population growth as of 2023 remained more rapid than at any time in human history before about 1940. Humankind became predominantly urban for the first time ever. Politics evolved so as to become more democratic, more religious, and more influenced by global international institutions. The latter trend, combined with changes to the world economy, sparked a countertrend in the form of authoritarian revivals that fed on antiglobalization sentiment. Cheap travel and cheap communications brought a kaleidoscopic swirl of cultural interaction, vividly expressed in music. The same trends made sports into an international spectacle of immense popularity. But to people in 50 or 100 years, the world of 1980 to 2023 will look very different from what it seems to any of us now.

CHAPTER REVIEW

KEY TERMS

Wangari Maathai (p. 1008)

Anthropocene (p. 1008)

climate change (p. 1009)

carbon dioxide (p. 1009)

HIV/AIDS (p. 1014)

COVID-19 (p. 1014)

international migrants (p. 1019)

international institutions (p. 1020)

al-Qaeda (p. 1022)

spread of democracy (p. 1024)

free trade (p. 1028)

information technology (p. 1029)

financialization (p. 1030)

income inequality (p. 1031)

Indigenous peoples (p. 1036)

International Indian Treaty Council (p. 1037)

Go to **INQUIZITIVE** to see what you've learned—and learn what you've missed—with personalized feedback along the way.

REVIEW QUESTIONS

1. What is new about climate change since 1840?
2. Culturally and politically, why did the world become so environmentally turbulent over the last 70 years?
3. What key innovations in medicine and agriculture led to population growth after 1950?
4. What four conditions contributed to the devastating health impact of COVID-19?
5. Explain the main reasons behind the worldwide downward fertility trend since 1960.
6. What two trends drove the spurt of urban growth since 1950?
7. Compare and contrast the characteristics of international migrants in the periods 1890–1915 and 1990–2015.
8. Why have so many international organizations arisen since World War II?
9. What factors caused political Islam to grow in popularity in Muslim societies after 1970?
10. Identify and describe three forces related to late twentieth-century globalization that help explain the worldwide upsurge of democracy.
11. Why did multinational corporations get bigger and globalize their supply chains?
12. Describe the consequences of the financialization of the world economy.
13. Who were the winners and losers of economic globalization after 1980?
14. Compare how music and sports changed when traveling worldwide.
15. What shared concerns motivate cooperation among the world's Indigenous peoples?
16. Discuss the long trend of global integration.

FURTHER READING

Richard BALDWIN, *The Great Convergence: Information Technology and the New Globalization* (2016). An economist's take on recent trends, written informally.

Angus DEATON, *The Great Escape: Health, Wealth, and the Origins of Inequality* (2013). A work that's strong on health trends and the economics of globalization.

Edward Ross DICKINSON, *The World in the Long Twentieth Century: An Interpretive History* (2018). A very useful look at political, economic, and environmental trends.

Najib GHADBIAN, *Democratization and the Islamist Challenge in The Arab World* (2019). A compact look at recent decades in Arab and Islamist politics.

Wangari MAATHAI, *Unbowed: A Memoir* (2006). An account of her path from Kenyan village girl to international environmental activist.

J. R. MCNEILL and Peter ENGELKE, *The Great Acceleration: An Environmental History of the Anthropocene since 1945* (2016). A brief account of global environmental changes since 1945.

Branko MILANOVIC, *Global Inequality: A New Approach for the Age of Globalization* (2016). A book that's packed with data but highly readable (as economists' prose goes).

Paul MORLAND, *The Human Tide: How Population Shaped the Modern World* (2019). Extremely readable assessment of how population growth mattered.

Indigenous Peoples and Politics since 1963

EVER SINCE THEY ABANDONED ARMED RESISTANCE more than a century ago, Indigenous peoples have sought to improve their condition through conventional political means. They have done so within local, regional, and national frameworks. And since the formation of the League of Nations in the 1920s, they have done so through international institutions. That strategy bore fruit in 2007 with the formal adoption by the United Nations of the Declaration on the Rights of Indigenous Peoples (UNDRIP; see Source 29.3).

In the sources gathered here, we see two that directly represent Indigenous voices: an Aboriginal Australian parliamentary petition and a declaration by the International Indian Treaty Council. A third source—the UNDRIP of 2007—includes many Indigenous voices but was ultimately authored by a large team. The final source records the position of the Russian Federation's government with respect to certain articles within a draft of the UNDRIP; in effect, it is a statement defending the interests of the Russian state in response to Indigenous voices.

SOURCE 29.1

Yirrkala Bark Petitions, 1963

In 1963, the Australian government removed 300 km² (109 square miles) of northern Australia, a place called Yirrkala, from a reserve held for the Aboriginal people known as the Yolngu. The intent was to lease Yirrkala to a bauxite mining company. At the time, the global market for bauxite, used to make aluminum, was booming.

The Yolgnu responded with a formal petition, written in both English and the local language, and framed in artwork drawn on bark that depicts Yolgnu legal traditions. The petition asked for a parliamentary inquiry; but the result, upheld in court, found that Aboriginal concepts of land rights were trumped by the principle of *terra nullius*—a historically unfounded doctrine holding that prior to white settlement Australia was an empty land to which no one held rights. Despite the Yolgnu petition's requests, mining at Yirrkala continued. Parliament did, however, recognize the existence of Yolgnu traditional law, recommend that Yolgnu sacred sites be protected, and require that compensation be paid to those whose livelihoods suffered from the impacts of mining. The Yirrkala bark petitions represent a key step toward the ultimate overturning of *terra nullius* in law in 1992.

TO THE HONOURABLE SPEAKER AND MEMBERS OF THE HOUSE OF REPRESENTATIVES IN PARLIAMENT ASSEMBLED.

The Humble Petition of the Undersigned aboriginal people of Yirrkala, being members of the Balamumu, Narrkala, Gapiny, Miliwurrwurr people and Djapu, Mangalili, Madarrpa, MagarrwanaImirri, Djambarrpuynu, Gumaitj, Marrakulu, Galpu, Dhaluangu, Wangurri, Warramirri, Naymil, Riritjingu, tribes respectfully showeth.

1. That nearly 500 people of the above tribes are residents of the land excised from the Aboriginal Reserve in Arnhem Land.

2. That the procedures of the excision of this land and the fate of the people on it were never explained to them beforehand, and were kept secret from them.

3. That when Welfare Officers and Government Officials came to inform them of decisions taken without them and against them, they did not undertake to convey to the Government in Canberra the views and feelings of the Yirrkala aboriginal people.

4. That the land in question has been hunting and food gathering land for the Yirrkala tribes from time immemorial: we were all born here.

5. That places sacred to the Yirrkala people, as well as vital to their livelihood, are in the excised land, especially Melville Bay.

6. That the people of this area fear that their needs and interests will be completely ignored as they have been ignored in the past, and they fear that the fate which has overtaken the Larrakeah tribe will overtake them. [1]

7. And they humbly pray that the Honourable the House of Representatives will appoint a Committee, accompanied by competent interpreters, to hear the views of the people of Yirrkala before permitting the excision of this land.

8. They humbly pray that no arrangements be entered into with any company which will destroy the livelihood and independence of the Yirrkala people.

And your petitioners as in duty bound will ever pray God to help you and us.

I certify that this Petition is in conformity with the Standing Orders of the House 14/8/63 Clerk of the House

Milirrpum	Larrakan	Wawunymarra
Djalalingba	Dhayila	Dhuygala
Manunu	Wulanybuma	Nyabilingu
Daymbalipu	Dundiwuy	Raiyin

[1] The Larrakia people claim land ownership in and around the city of Darwin. In 2016 some of their claims won legal recognition.

Source: Petition of the Aboriginal People of Yirrkala (Yirrkala Bark Petitions), 14 August 1963, Parliament of Australia, House of Representatives.

- **What justifications do the petitioners offer for requesting an inquiry?**
- **Besides the committee of inquiry, what else do the petitioners want?**

SOURCE 29.2

Declaration of Continuing Independence, 1974

In the late 1960s, Native Americans in the United States ramped up their efforts to improve their status and condition in American society. The American Indian Movement (AIM), formed by Indigenous men who had served time in federal penitentiaries, organized an occupation of Alcatraz Island in San Francisco Bay in 1969. Two years later, in 1971, AIM orchestrated an occupation of Mt. Rushmore, a national monument in South Dakota; and in 1973 the group organized an armed occupation of the nearby Pine Ridge Indian Reservation. Against this backdrop, in 1974 the International Indian Treaty Council (IITC) took shape when representatives from 97 tribes or nations of Indigenous people in the Americas and the Pacific came together, again in South Dakota, and pledged to advocate Indigenous rights. That 1974 gathering generated the document excerpted here.

The United States of America has continually violated the independent Native Peoples of this continent by Executive action, Legislative fiat and Judicial decision. By its actions, the U.S .has denied all Native people their International Treaty rights, Treaty lands and basic human rights of freedom and sovereignty....

Might does not make right. Sovereign people of varying cultures have the absolute right to live in harmony with Mother Earth so long as they do not infringe upon the same right of other peoples. The denial of this right to any sovereign people, such as Native American Indian Nations, must be challenged by truth and action....

[...]

...The International Indian Treaty Council recognizes the sovereignty of all Native Nations and will stand in unity to support our Native and international brothers and sisters in their respective and collective struggles concerning international treaties and agreements violated by the United States and other governments.

[...]

We recognize that there is only one color of Mankind in the world who are not represented in the United Nations; that is the indigenous Redman of the Western Hemisphere....

The International Indian Treaty Council established by this conference is directed to make the application to the United Nations for recognition and membership of the sovereign Native Nations. We pledge our support to any similar application by an aboriginal people.

[...]

We, the People of the International Indian Treaty Council, following the guidance of our elders through instructions from the Great Spirit, and out of respect for our sacred Mother Earth, all her children, and those yet unborn, offer our lives for our International Treaty Rights.

Source: International Indian Treaty Council, "Declaration of Continuing Independence," Standing Rock Indian Country, South Dakota, June 8-16, 1974.

- **What is the purpose of this document?**
- **The IITC appeals to the United Nations, not to the United States. Why might it do so?**

UN Declaration on the Rights of Indigenous Peoples, 2008

In 2007, after some 25 years of effort in committees and working groups, an alliance of Indigenous peoples from around the world managed to persuade the UN General Assembly to adopt the 46 articles of the Declaration on the Rights of Indigenous Peoples, excerpted here. It is a legally non-binding document, but its adoption by the UN gives it a certain moral authority that Indigenous peoples try to translate into practical benefits in national and international negotiations.

In 2006, a draft of the Declaration was adopted by the UN's Human Rights Council (47 countries were represented), and Canada and Russia were the only ones to object. (For a statement of Russia's objections, see Source 29.4.) One year later, when the document came before the General Assembly (with all UN members represented), Russia abstained and four countries voted against: Canada, the United States, Australia, and New Zealand—all former settler colonies of the British Empire in which Indigenous claims to land ran up against those of larger populations, and in which court cases concerning land rights could conceivably draw upon the UN Declaration. But between 2009 and 2016, these four concluded that the Declaration did not harm their interests after all and declared their support for it, with Canada being the last to do so.

Article 1 Indigenous peoples have the right to the full enjoyment, as a collective or as individuals, of all 8 human rights and fundamental freedoms as recognized in the Charter of the United Nations, the Universal Declaration of Human Rights and international human rights law.

Article 2 Indigenous peoples and individuals are free and equal to all other peoples and individuals and have the right to be free from any kind of discrimination, in the exercise of their rights, in particular that based on their indigenous origin or identity.

Article 3 Indigenous peoples have the right to self-determination. By virtue of that right they freely determine their political status and freely pursue their economic, social and cultural development.

Article 4 Indigenous peoples, in exercising their right to self-determination, have the right to autonomy or self-government in matters relating to their internal and local affairs, as well as ways and means for financing their autonomous functions.

Article 5 Indigenous peoples have the right to maintain and strengthen their distinct political, legal, economic, social and cultural institutions, while retaining their right to participate fully, if they so choose, in the political, economic, social and cultural life of the State.

Article 6 Every indigenous individual has the right to a nationality.

Article 7 1. Indigenous individuals have the rights to life, physical and mental integrity, liberty and security of person. **2.** Indigenous peoples have the collective right to live in freedom, peace and security as distinct peoples and shall not be subjected to any act of genocide or any other act of violence, including forcibly removing children of the group to another group.

Article 8 1. Indigenous peoples and individuals have the right not to be subjected to forced assimilation or destruction of their culture....

[...]

Article 10 Indigenous peoples shall not be forcibly removed from their lands or territories. No relocation shall take place without the free, prior and informed consent of the indigenous peoples concerned and after agreement on just and fair compensation and, where possible, with the option of return.

Article 11 1. Indigenous peoples have the right to practice and revitalize their cultural traditions and customs. This includes the right to maintain, protect and develop the past, present and future manifestations of their cultures, such as archaeological and historical sites, artifacts, designs, ceremonies, technologies and visual and performing arts and literature....

Article 12 1. Indigenous peoples have the right to manifest, practice, develop and teach their spiritual and religious traditions, customs and ceremonies....

[...]

Article 14 1. Indigenous peoples have the right to establish and control their educational systems and institutions providing education in their own languages, in a manner appropriate to their cultural methods of teaching and learning. **2.** Indigenous individuals, particularly children, have the right to all levels and forms of education of the State without discrimination....

[...]

Article 16 1. Indigenous peoples have the right to establish their own media in their own languages and to have access to all forms of non-indigenous media without discrimination. **2.** States shall take effective measures to ensure that State-owned media duly reflect indigenous cultural diversity....

[...]

Article 25 Indigenous peoples have the right to maintain and strengthen their distinctive spiritual relationship with their traditionally owned or otherwise occupied and used lands, territories, waters and coastal seas and other resources and to uphold their responsibilities to future generations in this regard.

Article 26 1. Indigenous peoples have the right to the lands, territories and resources which they have traditionally owned, occupied or otherwise used or acquired. **2.** Indigenous peoples have the right to own, use, develop and control the lands, territories and resources that they possess by reason of traditional ownership or other traditional occupation or use, as well as those which they have otherwise acquired. **3.** States shall give legal recognition and protection to these lands, territories and resources....

[...]

Article 29 1. Indigenous peoples have the right to the conservation and protection of the environment and the productive capacity of their lands or territories and resources. States shall establish and implement assistance programs for indigenous peoples for such conservation and protection, without discrimination. **2.** States shall take effective measures to ensure that no storage or disposal of hazardous materials shall take place in the lands or territories of indigenous peoples without their free, prior and informed consent....

Article 30 1. Military activities shall not take place in the lands or territories of indigenous peoples, unless justified by a relevant public interest or otherwise freely agreed with or requested by the indigenous peoples concerned....

Article 31 1. Indigenous peoples have the right to maintain, control, protect and develop their cultural heritage, traditional knowledge and traditional cultural expressions, as well as the manifestations of their sciences, technologies and cultures, including human and genetic resources, seeds, medicines, knowledge of the properties of fauna and flora, oral traditions, literatures, designs, sports and traditional games and visual and performing arts....

[...]

Article 33 1. Indigenous peoples have the right to determine their own identity or membership in accordance with their customs and traditions. This does not impair the right of indigenous individuals to obtain citizenship of the States in which they live....

[...]

Article 36 1. Indigenous peoples, in particular those divided by international borders, have the right to maintain and develop contacts, relations and cooperation, including activities for spiritual, cultural, political, economic and social purposes, with their own members as well as other peoples across borders....

[...]

Article 44 All the rights and freedoms recognized herein are equally guaranteed to male and female indigenous individuals.

[...]

Article 46 1. Nothing in this Declaration may be interpreted as implying for any State, people, group or person any right to engage in any activity or to perform any act contrary to the Charter of the United Nations or construed as authorizing or encouraging any action which would dismember or impair, totally or in part, the territorial integrity or political unity of sovereign and independent States....

Source: UN General Assembly, Resolution 61/295, United Nations Declaration on the Rights of Indigenous Peoples (March 2008).

- Does Article 46.1 undermine or contradict any of the previous articles? If so, which ones, and in what ways?
- Which historical experiences of Indigenous peoples are most strongly reflected in the concerns represented here?

SOURCE 29.4

The Official Russian Position, 2006

In 2006, when the UN released the draft document of the Declaration on the Rights of Indigenous Peoples (the final version is excerpted in Source 29.3), the Russian government issued a press release explaining its rejection of the draft Declaration. Russia and Canada were the only countries to vote against it at this stage. Russia, remember, has a considerable Indigenous population, about 260,000 people in all, mainly in Siberia. About 100 different Indigenous languages and identities exist, of which 41 are legally recognized as "small-numbered peoples." They typically practice hunting, fishing, gathering, and reindeer herding. Eleven Indigenous populations have been officially declared extinct. The English-language text presented here is the work of the Russian Foreign Ministry.

PRESS RELEASE OF THE RUSSIAN FOREIGN MINISTRY ON DECISION BY UN HUMAN RIGHTS COUNCIL ON DECLARATION ON RIGHTS OF INDIGENOUS PEOPLES

The first session of the United Nations Human Rights Council in Geneva on June 29 approved the Draft Declaration on the Rights of Indigenous Peoples and forwarded it to the UN General Assembly for consideration.

Thirty Council member states supported the draft, with 12 abstentions and the delegations of Russia and Canada voting against.

As to the motives of our voting on the substance of the document, the Russian delegation was unable to agree with a number of its provisions. It is primarily about the article on the right of indigenous peoples to self-determination, which, unfortunately, is not accompanied by a reservation that it is to be exercised in the framework of national legal systems and with regard for the provisions of the constitutions of countries and cannot be interpreted as a basis for the violation of the territorial integrity of states. If that specification had been made, we could have supported this article. In addition, into contradiction with Russian legislation come the articles on the rights of indigenous peoples to lands, territories and resources. All peoples of the country, not just the indigenous alone, possess such rights.

Also unacceptable to the Russian side was the procedural aspect—the approach of the chairman-rapporteur of the working group of the UN Commission on Human Rights (Peru's representative Luis Chavez), who submitted for consideration by the Council a text not agreed in the Group. Such actions, as is known, are contrary to UN practice.

Russia, like a number of other countries, would have been ready to continue work on the text of the Declaration, but since neither this offer nor our concerns based on Russian legislation were taken into account and the draft itself was put to the vote, we were unable to support the above decision.

Source: Ministry of Foreign Affairs of the Russian Federation, "Press Release of the Russian Foreign Ministry on Decision by UN Human Rights Council on Declaration on Rights of Indigenous Peoples," June 30, 2006.

- **Does it appear that Russia's concerns about the draft resulted in any changes to the final version (which is excerpted in Source 29.3)? Why or why not?**
- **Why might Russia find language about Indigenous rights to self-determination—and to lands, territories, and resources—objectionable?**

QUESTIONS FOR COMPARISON

1. The first three documents, representing Indigenous viewpoints, reflect efforts spanning the period from 1963 to 2007. What changes over time do you see in their tone, goals, and approaches?

2. What inconsistencies, differing emphases, and/or conflicting interests are evident in the first three sources?

3. Considering the varied concerns of Indigenous peoples as expressed in the first three documents, and taking the Russian state's concerns as an example of a government's priorities, is it likely that full agreement will ever be possible between a state's Indigenous residents and its governing structures? Why or why not?

ACKNOWLEDGMENTS

During the years devoted to researching, writing, and revising this book, I have accumulated deep debts to many people. First to acknowledge are those to my former undergraduate and graduate students at Georgetown University who have read parts of the text and suggested improvements: Kwabena Akuamoah-Boateng, Dan Brendtro, Faisal Husain, Adrienne Kates, Michelle Melton, Ani Muradyan, and Michael Samway. Then various classes of History 007 and History 008 in recent years, undergraduates who collectively made thousands of (anonymous) comments on a first draft of the book. Because the book is written for students, their feedback proved enormously valuable. I also wish to thank—enormously—Robynne Mellor and Javier Puente, who worked as teaching assistants in my world history classes and provided their own advice on early drafts of the book. And Benan Grams, then a PhD student—now a professor—provided indispensable help, first with medieval Arabic passages. Then Benan and two other Georgetown PhD students, Yujin Zhou and Leigh Stephens, performed heroic feats on the Making Connections feature, new in the Second Edition. Ari Filler, an undergraduate economics student, helped assemble some data on recent economic history and sketch out some infographics.

I am fortunate to have family members willing to share their unvarnished opinions of my work. These include Katriona McNeill, Jesse McNeill, and Patrick McNeill, Mairead MacRae, Leila Meymand, and especially my late sister Ruth McNeill. Ruth and her husband, Bart Jones, read every word and were not stingy with their advice. My sister taught me to read before I went to school and ever after, it seems, felt a responsibility to improve my facility with the English language. When she read my PhD dissertation, she commented that it could be improved if I added 20 commas per page, and it would hardly matter where I put them. I must have taken her suggestion too strongly, because when she read this book she said I should remove most of its commas. My wife, Julie Billingsley, also read passages and suggested, tactfully, that I should try to make the book more amusing.

Another family member earned my deepest thanks, although he never read a word of this book. In his final years, my father, William McNeill, never failed to ask me when I would finish it, which spurred me along. Debating with him how best to present the big picture in our short coauthored book, *The Human Web: A Bird's-Eye View of World History* (2003), influenced the thinking behind this book more strongly than anything else—other than my years teaching world history.

Several professional colleagues also earned my deep gratitude. Three experienced world history teachers helped shape my understanding of how to introduce the subject to students: Alan Karras of the University of California and Merry Wiesner-Hanks of the University of Wisconsin–Milwaukee, with both of whom I served for several years creating and vetting questions for the Advanced Placement world history examination, and the late Jerry Bentley of the University of Hawaii. Rick Potts of the National Museum of Natural History, an expert in human evolution, helped me avoid missteps in the first chapter. At the Foundation for Civic Space and Public Policy in Warsaw, Poland, Professors Spasimir Domaradzki, Maciej Janowski, Dariusz Kołodziejczyk, and Jan Szemiński critiqued parts of the manuscript, correcting some of my misconceptions especially about central and eastern European history. My colleagues in the History Department and Walsh School of Foreign Service at Georgetown University have contributed to my education in countless ways over the past 30-plus years. Their insights, perspectives, knowledge, and encouragement have enabled me to come to grips with world history in ways unimaginable to me without their help. David Goldfrank and Aviel Roshwald read sections of the book and improved it with their advice.

I wish to acknowledge as well the superb work of a team of colleagues at W. W. Norton, beginning with Steve Forman, who has patiently supervised the entire project from start to finish, read multiple drafts, and made thousands of valuable suggestions—of which I probably should have taken more than I did. Lily Gellman was invaluable in her orchestration of myriad details in the publishing process. Justin Cahill and Angie Merila shepherded the Second Edition into existence, a herculean task. Alice Vigliani, the excellent manuscript editor, improved and tightened my prose and eliminated some of those extraneous commas to which I am now apparently prone. Scott Sugarman also provided superb copyediting for the Second Edition. Charlotte Miller, our outstanding cartographer, created an ambitious map program with insight and vigor and politely tolerated my endless suggestions for revisions. Tommy Persano was creative and resourceful in building the extensive illustrations program. Melissa Atkin brought order to the puzzle pieces of the book as project editor. Anne-Michelle Gallero, our brilliant designer, created a beautiful design for our new Making Connections feature, as well as the eye-popping new cover designs. Sarah England Bartley led the marketing effort along with a terrific team of social science specialists: Cynthia Anderson, Susan Hood, Carrie Polvino, and Julie Sindel. Carson Russell, our media editor, planned and implemented the important digital resources that support the book, along with his colleagues Jenn Jussel and Clara Drimmer. Jane Searle, our production manager, kept this big train running on schedule.

Many thanks as well to the professors who contributed to and helped build our digital resource and ancillary package. The Test Bank was revised by John Handel (University of Virginia), Brian McKnight (University of Virginia at Wise), Bradley Woodworth (University of New Haven), and Ryan Bixby (Three Rivers College). InQuizitive was updated by Daren Ray (Brigham Young University), Holly Hernandez (California State University, Long Beach), Amy O'Hearn (University of California, Berkeley), and Carolina Zumaglini (Council for International Educational Exchange, Buenos Aires). The lecture PowerPoints were touched up by Renee Rodriguez (University of Texas, Rio Grande Valley) and Grace Linden (University of York), and the Check Your Understanding questions were created by Susan Hinely (Stony Brook University).

Reviewers

Other professional colleagues, most of whom I have never met, have also worked wonders for this book. World history teachers and scholars from many colleges in the United States and abroad have read draft chapters and made useful suggestions:

For the Second Edition
Ibrahim Al-Marashi, California State University, San Marcos
Daniel Berenberg, City Colleges of Chicago, Richard J. Daley College
Eugene Berger, Georgia Gwinnett College
Anna Biel, Fulton-Montgomery Community College
Ryan Bixby, Three Rivers College
Scott Black, Buffalo State University

Shannon Bontrager, Georgia Highlands College
Patrick Brennan, Gulf Coast State College
Lee L. Brice, Western Illinois University
Nathan Brooks, New Mexico State University
Holly Canatella, Lock Haven University
Karen Carter, Brigham Young University
Ryne Clos, Community College of Rhode Island and Jefferson Community and Technical College
Nicholas Cunigan, Calvin University
Bradley Camp Davis, Eastern Connecticut State University
Courtney Doucette, State University of New York at Oswego
Lei Duan, Arizona State University and Sam Houston State University
Paul Edison, University of Texas at El Paso
Joshua Fan, University of Texas at El Paso
Amy Forss, Metropolitan Community College
Jessica Gerard, Ozarks Technical Community College
Eric Grube, Boston College
Kenneth Hammond, New Mexico State University
Julie Hofmann, Shenandoah University
Liz Horodowich, New Mexico State University
Yongguang Hu, James Madison University
Joseph Irvin, Jefferson State Community College
John Ivens, Glenville State College
Ronald L. James, Idaho State University
Alison Williams Lewin, Saint Joseph's University
Elaine MacKinnon, University of West Georgia
Anupama Mande, Fullerton College
Judith M. Mansfield, Chemeketa Community College
Kathryn L. Mapstone, Bunker Hill Community College
Stephen McFarland, University of North Carolina, Wilmington
Eva M. Mehl, University of North Carolina, Wilmington
Steven P. Miller, Webster University
Curtis Morgan, Laurel Ridge Community College
Debra A. Mulligan, Roger Williams University
Kenneth Munsell, Central Washington University
Jennifer Nalmpantis, Lakeland Community College
Lance Nolde, California State University, Channel Islands
Jason Phillips, Peru State College
Louis Picone, William Paterson University
Masako Racel, Kennesaw State University
Tony Rafalowski, Jackson State Community College
Liz Elizondo Schroepfer, Virginia Military Institute
Sherri Singer, Alamance Community College
Molly Warsh, University of Pittsburgh
Adam Witten, Kapiolani Community College
William Wood, Point Loma Nazarene University

For the First Edition

Anthony Barbieri-Low, University of California, Santa Barbara

Hayden Bellenoit, United States Naval Academy

David Biggs, University of California, Riverside

Beau Bowers, Central Piedmont Community College, Levine

Kevin Brady, Tidewater Community College, Chesapeake

Gary Burgess, United States Naval Academy

Annette Chamberlin, Virginia Western Community College

Stephen Chappell, James Madison University

Katy Clay, Shippensburg University

Sean C. D. Colbert-Lewis Sr., North Carolina Central University

Phyllis Conn, St. John's University

Judith Davis, Three Rivers College

Peter De Rosa, Bridgewater State University

Eric Dursteler, Brigham Young University

Gregory Ference, Salisbury University

Allen Fromherz, Georgia State University

Denis Gainty, Georgia State University

Jessica Gerard, Ozarks Technical Community College

Rachael Goldman, Rutgers University

Noah Goode, Central Piedmont Community College, Levine

Andrew Goss, University of New Orleans

Candice Goucher, Washington State University

Hans Hägerdal, Linnaeus University

Sarah Hamilton, University of Bergen

Ann Hardgrove, University of Texas at San Antonio

Matthew Herbst, University of California, San Diego

Carsten Hjort Lange, Aalborg University

Stephanie Holyfield, Wesley College

Paul Stephen Hudson, Georgia Perimeter College

John Hyland, Christopher Newport University

Joanna Jury, Georgia State University

Sofia Laurein, San Diego City College

Jess LeVine, Brookdale Community College

Scott Lloyd, University of Arkansas

Anthony Makowski, Delaware County Community College, Marple

Harold Marcuse, University of California, Santa Barbara

Matthew McCoy, University of Arkansas, Fort Smith

Ian Miller, St. John's University

Elizabeth Milliken, Mount Hood Community College

Philip Misevich, St. John's University

Lance Nolde, California State University, Channel Islands

Hosok O, Dixie State University

Annette Palmer, Morgan State University

Alejandro Quintana, St. John's University

Daren Ray, Auburn University

Charles V. Reed, Elizabeth City State University

Thomas J. Rushford, Northern Virginia Community College, Annandale

Ruma N. Salhi, Northern Virginia Community College, Annandale

Christine Senecal, Shippensburg University

Michael Seth, James Madison University

Emily Story, Salisbury University

Barbara Syrrakos, City College of New York

Peter Utgaard, Cuyamaca College

Evan Ward, Brigham Young University

Molly Warsh, University of Pittsburgh

James Webb, Colby College

André Wink, University of Wisconsin

Jennifer Winters, Northern Virginia Community College, Annandale

In a book that aims to explore and make sense of the history of the world from the origins of humans until today, there are sure to be more than a few lapses. Those are all my fault and no one else's.

J. R. McNeill, *Georgetown University*

GLOSSARY OF KEY TERMS AND PRONUNCIATION GUIDE

AH *a* sound, as in *far*
IH short *i* sound, as in *hit*
OO long *o* sound, as in *snooze*
UH short *u* sound, as in *cup*
A short *a* sound, as in *tap*
EE long *e* sound, as in *sneeze*
OH long *o* sound, as in *bone*
EH short *e* sound, as in *very*
AY long *a* sound, as in *say*
EYE long *i* sound, as in *white*
OW diphthong *o* sound, as in *how*
AW diphthong *a* sound, as in *saw*

Emphasis: Syllables in capital letters receive the emphasis. If there is no syllable in capitals, then all syllables get equal emphasis.

1918 flu pandemic: A flu mutation that spread worldwide after World War I, killing more than 50 million people mostly between the ages of 15 and 40. Due to tighter global connections, it spread quickly and widely.

Abbasid caliphate [ah-BAH-sihd KA-lih-fayt]: The Islamic successor state (750–1258) to the Umayyads. Based in Baghdad, the Abbasids consolidated power over most of the Islamic world, profited from widespread trade, supported scholars and artists, and had learned works from Chinese, Sanskrit, Hebrew, Greek, and Latin translated into Arabic and Persian.

Abdelkadir [ab-dehl-KAH-dihr] (1808–1883): A Sufi scholar and the leader of a large revolt against French rule in Algeria, which reached its height in the 1830s. The French captured and exiled Abdelkadir in 1847.

aboriginal Australians: Also known as Aborigines, aboriginal Australians were mobile hunter-foragers. They spoke 200 to 250 related languages and shared consistent animist religious beliefs across the continent.

Achaemenids [ak-KEE-muh-nids] (559–330 BCE): A dynasty that came from what is now southwestern Iran. They conquered all major powers from Egypt to northwest India, making their empire unprecedented in size.

Adi Granth [ah-dee GRAHNTH]: The scripture of the Sikhs. Written in Punjabi, it is a collection of Nanak's hymns, or teachings, as well as some additional hymns.

Adolf Hitler (1889–1945): The fascist head of the Nazi Party who became chancellor of Germany in 1933. Wanting to return Germany to great-power status, he introduced social and economic reforms, including national purification, which targeted Jews, Slavs, and Roma for elimination.

Ahura Mazda [uh-HOOR-uh MAHZ-duh]: A benevolent, all-knowing god, the preferred deity of the Achaemenid dynasty from Darius onward. A priesthood called the Magi led Ahura Mazda worship, which involved outdoor fire ceremonies and sacrifices.

Akbar [AHK-bah] (r. 1556–1605): A Mughal emperor who spearheaded the unification of most of South Asia. He used a combination of horses, guns, and siegecraft along with tolerant religious policy to assert and maintain power.

Aksum: An African state south of Kush that reached its peak between 300 and 500 CE. It traded African products to Egypt, the Mediterranean world, and Mesopotamia, which enabled it to amass wealth and power.

al-Andalus [al-ANN-duh-luhs] (711–1492): The Muslim-controlled part of Spain that the last Umayyad dynast founded in 711 and the Córdoba caliphate ruled from 929 to 1031. Afterward, it remained fragmented until Christian armies defeated it in 1492.

al-Qaeda: An extremist Islamist political faction begun in 1988 by Osama bin Laden that funded the September 11, 2001, terrorist attacks on the United States. It became powerful in Iraq after 2003, and its offshoots have engaged in terrorism targeting other Muslims in several countries.

Alexander II (1818–1881): The tsar of Russia who emancipated the serfs due in part to his commitment to military reform. He wanted a standing army and hoped the abolition of serfdom would lead to a cheaper and better-educated army without the risk of rebellion.

Alexander Hamilton: An American politician who prescribed tariffs to protect U.S. industry when he was secretary of the Treasury in 1791. His recommendations guided U.S. trade policy for a

century and inspired the German economist Friedrich List.

Alexander the Great (356–323 BCE): Born in Macedonia to the king of Macedon, Alexander was one of the most skilled military commanders in history. He continued and completed his father's conquest of the Greek world and claimed the Achaemenid throne, uniting both regions in a vast empire.

Alexandria (founded 331 BCE): A wealthy Mediterranean seaport city during the Hellenistic age that fostered trade linkages among Egypt, Africa, the Mediterranean, and Southwest Asia. It was a center for manufacturing, medicine, mathematics, commerce, and culture.

Algerian war for independence (1954–1962): The conflict between the FLN (Algerian independence fighters) and the French Army, along with its collaborators, over France's colonial presence. It led to Algerian independence; the massacre of Muslim Algerians, known as harkis; and the mass expulsion of French settler-colonists, the pieds-noirs.

alliance networks: Two groups into which the great European powers were divided in order to uphold peace in Europe after the Napoleonic Wars. In 1914, Germany, Austria-Hungary, and Italy belonged to the Triple Alliance, and France, Russia, and Great Britain belonged to the Triple Entente.

Allies: A coalition of countries that fought against the Axis powers in World War II, most prominently the United Kingdom, United States, USSR, and China. The alliance also included many other countries, colonies, and members of the British Commonwealth.

American Revolution (1775–1781): An anticolonial, revolutionary war between 13 British colonies in America and the British government. The colonists won and created the United States, an independent country.

Ancestral Pueblo: Inhabitants of the high-plateau Four Corners area in today's U.S. Southwest who developed a dispersed agricultural society around the ninth century. Their distinctive architectural style of cliff dwellings and ceremonial spaces called *kivas* is evident at their central settlement of Chaco Canyon. Their settlements declined in the twelfth and thirteenth centuries as a probable result of long-lasting drought cycles.

Anthropocene: The proposed new geological age defined by the influence of humans on big natural systems, such as climate. Around 2000, many scientists started to argue that the Holocene ended in the mid-twentieth century and that we are now living in the Anthropocene.

anticolonialism: A mass political and social movement that developed after World War I. Supporters, disillusioned with European rulers and postwar peace settlements, advocated for self-rule and the end of colonial empires.

Antônio Conselheiro [kohn-say-YAY-roo] (1830–1897): A traveling preacher in Brazil who eventually settled in Canudos. He attracted many followers with his sermons on salvation, denunciations of the state, and promises of the imminent return of Jesus Christ.

apartheid: The racial segregation policy of the Afrikaner-dominated South African government starting in 1948 and remaining law until the early 1990s. An ideology of separateness, it ensured that the white settler minority had more political rights and more land rights than the indigenous populations.

appeasement: A foreign policy tactic in which concessions are made to an aggressing nation in the hopes that doing so will prevent further conflict. At the Munich conference in 1938, France and Britain signed over the Sudetenland (a mainly German-speaking region of Czechoslovakia) to Germany in exchange for a promise that Hitler wouldn't annex other territories.

Arabs: At the time of Muhammad's birth, Arabs were a group of polytheistic, loosely connected, mostly nomadic tribes who lived on the Arabian Peninsula and made a living herding, trading, and raiding. In the seventh century, united under Muhammad, they became a formidable military force, conquering lands from India to Spain.

Asian tiger economies: Collective name for the economies of certain East Asian countries—Japan, South Korea, Taiwan, Singapore, and Hong Kong—that experienced massive economic growth after World War II.

Assyrian [uh-SEER-ee-uhn] **Empire** (ca. 911–609 BCE): A large and multicultural empire based in northern Mesopotamia; its power rested partly on raising horses and forging iron tools and weapons.

Augustine (354–430): A North African bishop whose prolific moralistic writings influenced the creation of a more uniform Christianity called Catholicism.

Axis: A loose coalition among Germany, Italy, and Japan. The Axis powers instigated World War II through their expansionist aims and fought against the Allies during the conflict.

Aztecs: People of Central Mexico, mainly speakers of the Nahuatl language, who claimed to have migrated from a mythical place called Aztlan. The term can also mean all those peoples subject to the Aztec Empire, based in Tenochtitlán, now Mexico City, in the fourteenth through sixteenth centuries.

Bantu [BAN-too]: A language group that originated in the area of the modern-day Cameroon-Nigerian border. It is made up of 600 related languages now spoken in East, central, and southern Africa.

Battle of Stalingrad (1942–1943): A brutal, months-long conflict between Soviet and German armies on the eastern front. The German loss of the battle was a major turning point in World War II and part of a broader Axis decline.

Beatriz Kimpa Vita (ca. 1684–1706): A young woman in Kongo who was drawn to Catholicism, became a preacher, and sought the reunification of Kongo. She gained thousands of followers by telling them God spoke through her, but her movement threatened other aspirants to power, and she was burned at the stake as a witch and heretic.

bell beaker ware: Clay containers shaped like an upside-down bell that became popular across Europe and North Africa between around 2900 and 1800 BCE. Used mainly for beer, their widespread presence points to commercial and cultural connections among elites in Europe.

Benito Mussolini (1883–1945): The fascist and authoritarian ruler of Italy who took power in 1922. He manipulated the media, promoted Italian nationalism, and capitalized on Italians' anxieties, particularly about communism, to build support.

Bhakti [BAHK-tee] **movement**: A popular form of Hinduism that emerged in the seventh century in India and appealed to a broad segment of the population. The religion stressed intense, personal devotion to one god (usually Shiva, Vishnu, or Devi) and used local languages (not Sanskrit) spoken by the common people.

Big Bang: The origin of our universe and the start of time, space, and energy. It occurred about 13.8 billion years ago,

and the universe has been cooling and expanding since that time.

biological globalization: A worldwide exchange of plants, animals, and microbes that followed the discovery of the oceans and of which the Columbian Exchange was a part. It led to connections among ecosystems and a change in flora, fauna, and diseases across the world.

biological old regime: Conditions of human health that preceded the Vital Revolution. Deadly crowd diseases, gastrointestinal infections, high infant mortality, malnutrition, and starvation defined it.

bipedalism: The ability to stand and walk upright that evolved 6 million to 4.5 million years ago; a trait that distinguishes hominins from apes and apelike ancestors.

Bourbon Reforms: Changes reflecting Enlightenment thought that the Spanish Crown introduced in Spanish America to revitalize its empire. They included new taxes, strengthened fortifications, administrative reorganization, and freer trade.

British Raj [rahj] (1858–1947): British colonial rule in India, which relied on the cooperation of local Indian elites and the exploitation of existing societal divisions. It reordered the Indian economy with the introduction of free trade and new infrastructure.

bronze: An alloy, or combination, of the two metals copper and tin; used in many cultures for armor and weapons as well as for ornamentation.

Byzantine [BIHZ-ann-teen] **Empire**: The eastern part of the Roman Empire and all that remained of the empire after 476. At its height in the sixth and seventh centuries, it included Egypt, the Levant, Anatolia, and the Balkans; it lasted until 1453.

cabotage: Port-to-port, local trade links. In the Indian Ocean world, shorter-distance cabotage trade in everyday goods supported long-distance trade in luxuries.

Cahokia [kuh-HOH-kee-uh] (ca. 1000–1350): A large indigenous city that was located in the floodplain of the Mississippi River in present-day Illinois and home to mostly farming people. Cahokians engaged in coordinated efforts to build ceremonial plazas and over 100 mounds used mostly for sacrifices and burials.

Calicut: An important commercial port city on the southwest coast of India. Its merchants traded various spices that were highly sought by Arab, Persian, and European merchants.

caravanserais: In Eastern countries, inns along major trade routes that accommodated large numbers of traders, their animals, and their wares.

carbon dioxide: Released by burning fossil fuels, it is one of the most important greenhouse gases. The rise of fossil fuel use since around 1840—especially since 1950 or so—has contributed to increased concentrations of CO_2 in the atmosphere and, in turn, the current pulse of climate change.

Carolingians (ca. 750–843): A dynasty that ruled a comparatively modest and poor state in western Europe and introduced feudalism. The state became an empire during the reign of Charlemagne (r. 768–814) but fell apart after his death.

Carthage: A Phoenician colony on the Mediterranean Sea's North African coast that became a formidable seaborne empire based on commerce. Carthage flourished between approximately 800 and 146 BCE.

cassava [kuh-SAH-vuh]: Native to Brazil, as part of the Columbian Exchange cassava (also called manioc) became a staple food in many parts of Africa. It is drought resistant, does well in poor soils, and remains edible even if left in the ground for long periods of time.

caste system: A hierarchical and hereditary division of society that developed in the Ganges basin. The early caste system split people into four main tiers: Brahmins, Kshatriya, Vaishya, and Sudra.

Catholic Reformation: Also called the Counter-Reformation, a period of major reforms in the Catholic Church undertaken in response to the Protestant Reformation. The Catholic Church became more centralized and standardized; popes, bishops, and abbots cut back on high living; efforts were made to root out heresy and ban certain books.

Celts: A loose grouping of various peoples in Atlantic Europe who spoke similar languages and shared cultural features. They emerged between 1300 and 700 BCE. They migrated south from the Alps and Danube in droves during the fifth to third centuries BCE.

Chaco Canyon: A settlement in northern New Mexico that was likely the center of the broader Ancestral Pueblo region spread throughout the Four Corners area. All roads built by Ancestral Pueblo led to Chaco Canyon, and it was the home of religious and political elites until its collapse due to drought in the twelfth century.

Champa rice: A variety of rice that matures quickly, is drought resistant, and ripens at higher and cooler elevations than other strains. After the Chinese imported it from Vietnam in the eleventh century, it became a reliable food supply that spurred massive population growth.

chariots: Two-wheeled carriages pulled by horses and often used as weapons of war. Chariots appeared first in western Asia around 2100 BCE and were widespread in Eurasia by 1500 BCE.

chartered joint-stock companies: Companies to which governments grant monopoly rights by charter and in which hundreds or thousands of investors own shares. These innovative measures, developed during the sixteenth century, helped share the risks and increase the scale of long-distance trade.

Chinese Civil War (1945–1949): Conflict between the Chinese Communist Party, led by Mao Zedong, and the nationalist Guomindang. The CCP won and created the People's Republic of China.

Chinese Revolution (1880s–1910s): A long revolution that ultimately overthrew the Qing dynasty. Yuan Shikai, an army general, along with Sun Yatsen and other revolutionaries, took advantage of an army mutiny to force the last Qing emperor to abdicate.

choke point: A narrow route providing strategic, affordable passage from one large body of water to another—such as the Straits of Malacca between Sumatra and the Malay Peninsula or the strait between India's southern tip and Sri Lanka. Those who controlled choke points were often able to profit economically and politically.

Chola [CHOH-lah] **kingdom** (ca. 970–1300): A state that arose in southeastern India and ultimately controlled Indian Ocean trade passing along south Indian coasts and Sri Lanka. Partly an alliance of merchant trading guilds, the Chola flourished through commercial and naval activity, and even attacked Srivijayan cities while under the expansionary rule of Rajendra I (r. 1012–1044).

Christopher Columbus: Born in Genoa, Italy, Christopher Columbus secured funding from the king and queen of Castile (a powerful state in Spain) to sail west from Europe and find a route to China in 1492. He instead found islands in the Caribbean and inaugurated a new age of global interconnection.

Cimmerians: Horse nomads from the Russian and Ukrainian steppe who began arriving on the Hungarian plain around 900 BCE, bringing with them steppe traditions. Many waves of nomads and seminomads followed, migrating from the steppes to eastern Europe in subsequent centuries.

city: A large settlement with elaborate divisions of labor, social hierarchies, tightly packed living spaces, open public areas, and large buildings. Trade, exchange, and markets feature prominently in cities.

civil service examinations: The use of written examinations on Confucian ideology to select public administrators in China (and in Korea while under Tang influence). This system fostered cultural unity and an educated elite.

classic Hinduism (begun ca. 400 BCE): An evolution of Vedic traditions of caste, ritual, and sacrifice. Hindus added several new beliefs to Vedic foundations, including the endless migration of souls based on moral conduct, or *karma*.

climate change: Recent, rapid change in Earth's climate patterns that is unprecedented in human history and largely human-caused. It is due mainly to a significant increase in fossil fuel use in the past 30 to 40 years, which created high concentrations of greenhouse gases in the atmosphere and caused Earth's temperature to rise.

Clovis points (ca. 12,000–11,000 BCE): Stone spearheads used throughout North America; their broad dissemination indicates widespread cultural and technological diffusion across the continent.

coal: A fossil fuel made up of ancient plant remains that can be converted into motor power. Cheap, low-lying coal gave rise to the Industrial Revolution in Britain and fueled industrialization around the world.

coaling stations: Pacific ports where imperial powers' naval ships refueled during the late nineteenth century. European powers seized Pacific islands largely for their strategic use as coaling stations and the low cost of controlling them.

Cold War (1945–1991): An ideological and political struggle, primarily between the United States and the USSR, that led to a proliferation of nuclear weapons and pervasive propaganda campaigns. It also intensified conflicts around the world through the two countries' participation in proxy wars.

Columbian Exchange: The transfer of plants, animals, and microbes among Eurasia, Africa, and the Americas following Columbus's initiation of contact.

Comanche [kuh-MAN-shee] **Empire** (1730–1870): The Comanche rule of the southern plains of the present-day United States, resulting from their near monopoly of the regional gun trade and mastery of horses.

comfort women: Hundreds of thousands of women that the Japanese army captured from various places, including Korea, China, and the Philippines, and forced to work as sex slaves in occupied areas.

commercial revolution: The increased commercialization and specialization, coupled with frontier expansion and territorial conquest, that occurred especially in China and Atlantic Europe during the period 1500–1800. In combination, these factors caused the regions' economies to grow and their societies to become richer.

communism: A broadly appealing international movement and political theory based on the ideas of Karl Marx and Vladimir Lenin. Communists opposed capitalism and private property and believed that inevitable revolution would bring about a prosperous, equitable world.

Communist Manifesto (1848): A political pamphlet coauthored by Karl Marx and Friedrich Engels arguing that class struggle propels history. It describes the inevitability of a communist revolution and calls for the working classes around the world to join together in the struggle against the ruling elite.

complex society: A social unit characterized by a large hierarchical society, regulatory institutions, and a complex division of labor. Complex societies often developed states and cities.

Confucius [kuhn-FYOO-shuhs] (Kong Qiu) (ca. 551–479 BCE): A *shi* whose followers wrote down his ideas in the book *Analects*, which emphasized ethical conduct, ritual, social hierarchy, and the importance of scholars.

Constantine (r. 306–337 CE): A Roman emperor who established a second Roman capital in Byzantium (modern-day Istanbul), renamed it Constantinople, and split the Roman Empire into two halves. He converted to Christianity, ultimately making it an imperial, state-supported religion.

containerization: The transition to the use of shipping containers for the transport of goods, which led to decreased shipping and labor costs as well as shorter shipping times. Containers facilitated the connection between East Asian export economies and large North American markets.

containment strategy: An approach guiding U.S. Cold War policy toward the USSR based on defeating it with patience and endurance rather than military strength. The strategy was based on the belief that Soviet communism would collapse if the United States prevented its spread.

cotton: Lightweight and durable cloth woven from the cotton plant. During the early modern period, Atlantic Europeans expanded the trade of cotton to new markets in Africa, Europe, and the Americas, and it became an essential global trade commodity.

cotton gin: A machine, invented in the United States and patented in 1794, that separated cotton seeds from cotton fiber, thereby easing cotton production. It contributed to the rise of cotton manufacturing and the spread of cotton production and slavery in the U.S. South.

COVID-19: An easily transmittable infectious disease caused by the novel coronavirus (SARS CoV-2), which apparently originated in bat colonies before mutating into a human pathogen in or near Wuhan, China, in late 2019. In 2020, COVID-19 quickly spread around the world, causing a global pandemic that killed millions.

creole cultures: Societies in the Americas, particularly in the plantation zone, that blended various features from Africa and Europe to create hybrid cultures, religions, and languages.

crowd diseases: Infections such as smallpox, mumps, or measles that require large populations to stay in circulation. In large populations, these pathogens mostly affect children.

Crusades (1096–1291): Waves of small-scale wars and attacks on the Levant that were motivated by both religious and military aims. Over 200 years, Crusaders of mostly French, German, and English origin established small kingdoms that all fell by the thirteenth century.

Cuban missile crisis (1962): A tense standoff between the United States and the Soviet Union, during which the Soviet Union attempted to position nuclear missiles in Cuba.

culture of imperialism: Celebratory literature, theater, music, and public ceremony that supported the belief in the right and duty of one group to rule over others. It was most prominent in Britain but also existed in the United States, France, Germany, Italy, and Japan.

cuneiform: The earliest known form of writing, cuneiform developed in Uruk around 3400 to 3300 BCE and consisted of scratches made on wedges of clay.

Darius (r. 522–486 BCE): A lance-bearer who staged a coup d'état and became an Achaemenid king. He introduced many innovations that helped him effectively manage the vast Achaemenid territory.

dark earth: Human-made patches of nutrient-rich soil in Amazonia. People used these areas to raise crops that supported thousands of settlements.

deindustrialization: During the Industrial Revolution, the decline of industries that could not compete with the price and quality of factory-made products.

Delhi sultanate (ca. 1206–1400): A military aristocracy established in northern India by Turkic horsemen from Central Asia who fostered an Indo-Islamic culture fusing Indian, Turkic, Persian, and Arabic elements. Its legacy includes palace and mosque architecture, and Urdu poetry—a blend of Hindi and Persian.

democratization: The process by which a society adopts democracy as its mode of government.

demographic dividend: A shift in fertility patterns that aids economic growth and development. Demographic dividends in East Asia after 1950 contributed to the Asian tigers' economic success.

demokratia [day-moh-kra-TEE-uh]: After 508 BCE, a form of government that the Athenian *polis* introduced wherein all citizens directly participated in governance. It was based on an elected ruling council of 500 that was responsible to a larger assembly of all free Athenian men over age 18 who had completed military training.

Deng Xiaoping [DUHNG show-pihng] (1904–1997): The head of China beginning in 1978 and leader of its economic transformation. His economic reforms, which essentially replaced socialism with capitalism, included the end of the commune work-unit system, the reintroduction of profit motives, and the encouragement of export-oriented industry.

deterrence: The certainty that any country that launched a nuclear attack would be destroyed by a retaliatory attack.

dhow [dow]: A type of ship used by Arab seafarers in the Indian Ocean. Dhows featured slanting, triangular sails to efficiently capture the wind and hulls sewn with coconut fiber for maximum flexibility.

disease disasters: As a result of entry into the expanding Global web, the introduction of deadly diseases to previously isolated areas of the world that had no experience with them. In combination with violence and declining fertility, these diseases led to devastating demographic collapses in the Americas, Siberia, many Pacific Islands, and parts of southern Africa.

dolmens: Stacks of stones, erected mainly between 1500 and 500 BCE, that mark burial sites and imply growing social stratification. Although they were built in many places in Eurasia, Korea contains almost half the world's dolmens.

domestication: The genetic modification of plants or animals through human selection or breeding. Domestication enables humans to produce food instead of searching for it.

domino theory: Conjecture among U.S. policy makers that if one country fell to communism, then the countries surrounding it would follow. This theory drove U.S. involvement in the Vietnam War because officials feared that if Vietnam became entirely communist, the rest of Southeast Asia would too.

dreamtime: One of the religious beliefs of aboriginal Australians according to which a distant past linked to the birth of the world when supernatural entities crossed Australia, forming the continent and tracing paths that became "songlines."

Dutch East India Company (VOC): A very successful chartered joint-stock company created to control the Dutch spice trade. During the seventeenth and eighteenth centuries, the VOC's heavily armed ships dominated the Indonesian archipelago as the company used force and violence to gain advantageous trade terms.

economies of scale: Economies of scale occur when a producer's costs per unit of output decline as the scale of the enterprise grows. This condition, which exists only in some industries, such as sugar production, benefits large-scale enterprises.

Eiichi Shibusawa [ay-EE-chee shih-boo-SOW-ah] (1840–1931): A Japanese government official and businessman who was passionate about bringing industrialization to his country. He set up Japan's first modern cotton mill in Osaka with the help of Takeo Yamanobe.

emancipation for serfs (1861): A labor liberation granted by a statute that, in theory, liberated serfs by granting them freedoms they previously lacked. In practice, it introduced many new legal constraints to which former serfs remained subject.

encomienda [ehn-koh-mee-EHN-dah]: Granted by Spanish rulers to colonizers in Spanish America, the legal right to conscript indigenous people as unpaid laborers.

Epic of Gilgamesh: A long poem written down around 2100 BCE in cuneiform and the oldest surviving epic poem in world history. It is about a legendary Uruk king, Gilgamesh, who lived around 2600 BCE.

Eurasian steppe: A broad grassland that stretches from eastern Europe to East Asia.

fascism: A political movement and ideology that formed the basis of Benito Mussolini's and Adolf Hitler's governments. It emphasized militant nationalism, purification of the nation, a cult of the leader, and showy displays of national strength.

Ferdinand Magellan: A Portuguese explorer whom the Spanish Crown funded to find a route to the Moluccas by sailing west from Europe and along the southern coast of South America in 1519. He died in the Philippines after crossing the Pacific, but his crew became the first people to sail around the world and attained knowledge of the vastness of the Pacific Ocean.

field artillery and fortification: Large and heavy mobile guns and cannon deployed in the field, and the highly engineered structures used to defend against them. These elements increased the cost and intricacy of war during the early modern period.

financialization: The rise in the prominence, prevalence, and profitability of finance worldwide due to deregulation and digital technology. It has eased the global flow of money and contributed to increased economic volatility.

firestick farming: Intentional burning of landscapes and methodical use of fire that promotes the growth of edible plants and attracts animals for hunting. Aboriginal Australians employed firestick farming to increase their food supply.

flint maize: A form of maize, developed in the American Midwest around the ninth or tenth century, that matured faster than other varieties and with bigger kernels. It boosted food supplies and enabled North American farmers to subsist mainly on agricultural crops and less on hunting and foraging.

Florentine Codex: A comprehensive catalogue of Aztec history and culture, compiled between 1545 and 1590 by a Spanish priest and his Aztec students. The *Codex* incorporates about 2,000 illustrations of Aztec daily life along with text in Nahuatl expressed in the Roman alphabet.

fractional reserve banking: The practice of banks lending out more money than they have in their reserves in order to create money in the form of credit. The Bank of Amsterdam pioneered this practice, which promoted commerce by reducing its costs.

free trade: Deregulation of trade beginning in the 1980s that Ronald Reagan and Margaret Thatcher spearheaded. Free-trade policy spread around the world, leading to bigger multinational corporations and globalized supply chains.

French Revolution (1789–1799): A political revolution within France aimed at reforming the hierarchical social order. It led to sweeping changes, descended into terror and dictatorship, and was largely reversed when the monarchy was reestablished in 1814.

Friedrich List (1789–1846): An economist born in Germany who wrote newspaper articles and books that guided state-sponsored industrialization. He advocated for protectionist policies and the construction of railroads.

Ganges [GAN-jeez] **basin**: Rich alluvial lands surrounding the Ganges River that supported the development of a new Indian culture and complex society starting around 1500 BCE. It is also known as the Gangetic plain.

Genghis Khan (ca. 1165–1227): Born as Temujin, Genghis Khan was the founder and leader of the Mongol Empire. Under his command, the Mongols conquered territory from China to Ukraine.

germ theory of disease: The scientific theory developed after 1850 that pointed to bacteria's role in infection. It led to sanitation reforms that reduced death and illness from waterborne diseases and paved the way for understanding infections.

Germanic tribes: Groups originating from east of the Danube River and north of the Rhine River in Europe, including Goths, Vandals, and Franks. Beginning in the 370s, the Germanic tribes migrated to Roman territory as they fled from the Huns or when the Romans hired them to fight against other tribes or in civil wars.

Ghost Dance: A spiritual movement that arose in response to disruptions in indigenous North American life during the nineteenth century. Inspired by Wovoka's prophecy, participants performed a community circle dance in hopes that it would bring the return of peace, joy, and plenty.

Glorious Revolution (1688–1689): The nearly bloodless replacement of James II with William of Orange on the throne of England, organized by Protestant British elites. It cemented the increased power of Parliament in relation to the monarchy.

Göbekli Tepe [goh-behk-LEE teh-peh]: A site in southeastern Turkey; likely a religious temple that a sedentary or semi-sedentary group built around 9000 BCE and abandoned by 7000 BCE.

gracialization: The thinning and shrinking of skeletons through evolution. Humans underwent this process as they relied less on their physical strength for survival and as social groups grew.

Grand Canal: A massive public works project, started under the Sui dynasty (581–618), that linked north and south China, promoting unity and enabling emperors to move troops and food quickly and easily.

Great Leap Forward (1958–1961): Mao Zedong's massive and disastrous campaign to improve China's industry and agriculture. He called for citizens to produce steel in their own backyards, the output of which proved to be useless, and introduced new agricultural policies that caused a devastating famine.

Great Zimbabwe (ca. 1250–1450): A city and center of power in southern Africa based on cattle wealth and a thriving gold trade. The rulers at Great Zimbabwe had enough authority and wealth to erect great stone buildings beginning in 1275.

Greater East Asia Co-Prosperity Sphere: A Japanese anticolonial ideology that suggested that East and Southeast Asia could throw off the shackles of European rule by allowing Japan to lead them.

gross world product: The size of the world economy, calculated by using the combined value of all goods and services produced worldwide. Between 1500 and 1800, the GWP almost doubled.

Guanches [GWAHNCH-ihz]: Descendants of North African Berbers, the Guanches were inhabitants of the Canary Islands who fought against Spanish conquest and settlement from 1402 to 1496. Spanish weapons technology and the diseases they carried with them eventually led to the defeat of the Guanches.

Gulf Stream: The counterclockwise movement of North Atlantic currents that warms the climates of western Europe's coastal areas from Portugal to Norway.

Gupta [GOOP-tah] **dynasty** (ca. 330–550): A dynasty that ruled the north of India and supported religious institutions, math, science, and arts. Samudragupta (r. 335–375) and Chandragupta II (r. 375–415) were two successful Gupta kings.

Habsburgs (1282–1918): Originating as Swiss and German nobles, the Habsburgs extended their territory with military force and advantageous political marriages. They built a global empire and became a major European power but were unable to unify Europe.

Haitian Revolution (1791–1804): An anticolonial, political, and antislavery revolution rooted in racial tensions and led primarily by Toussaint L'Ouverture, a former slave. It began with the largest slave rebellion in history and ended in victory, but it left Haiti fractured in its aftermath.

Hammurabi [hahm-uh-RAH-bee] (r. 1792–1750 BCE): A king of Babylon who formed a short-lived empire; he erected a stone monument inscribed with 282 laws that survives today.

Han (206 BCE–220 CE): Emperor Gaozu founded the Han dynasty following Qin rule. Han rulers expanded Chinese territory and promoted Confucian ideology; under their leadership the economy and population grew, and land and maritime trade flourished.

Hannibal Barca (247–ca. 182 BCE): A member of the Carthaginian Barca clan who transformed Carthage's presence in Spain into an empire there. Hannibal led the fight against Rome in the Second Punic War and gained renown for his skills as a military commander.

Harappans [hah-RAP-puhnz] (ca. 2600–1700 BCE): The name of the Indus valley populations and culture; its two largest cities were Harappa and Mohenjo Daro.

Hawaiian kings: Between 1450 and 1700, several Hawaiian chiefs responded to shortages of resources and increased competition by making themselves kings, thereby initiating a ruling class, an administrative bureaucracy, and struggles for succession to the throne. Kings and kingdoms were unique in the Pacific world; no other Polynesians outside of Hawaii had them.

heavy cavalry: One of Darius's military innovations. Instead of wielding only light equipment, heavy cavalry rode on large, strong horses with full armor and weaponry.

Heian [HAY-ahn] **Japan** (794–1185): A period of rule in Japan, based at Heian (modern Kyoto), during which Chinese influence waned, indigenous religious traditions (especially Shinto) became dominant, an aristocratic social order prevailed, and refined courtly life produced the first substantial body of literature written by women anywhere in world history.

heliocentric system: The idea, which Nicholas Copernicus wrote down in 1514, that planets rotate around the sun as opposed to the idea that the sun moves around the Earth. Johannes Kepler, Galileo Galilei, and Isaac Newton built on this work, and the heliocentric system won acceptance in 1687.

Hellenistic age (323–31 BCE): The age of Greek and Macedonian rule in Greece, Egypt, and Southwest Asia. It began after Alexander died and his generals Ptolemy, Antigonus, and Seleucus divided his empire among themselves.

herders: People who live mainly off of domesticated grazing animals that they raise in arid and semiarid grassland and scrubland regions.

hieroglyphs [HEYE-ruh-gliphs]: The primary Egyptian writing system, which eventually contained nearly 1,000 symbols; it began developing around 3000 BCE, possibly influenced by Sumerian cuneiforms.

Hiroshima and Nagasaki: Two Japanese cities and centers of military production onto which the United States dropped nuclear weapons in August 1945. The bombs killed 105,000 people immediately and were the first, and so far only, nuclear weapons used in warfare.

HIV/AIDS: The infectious and deadly disease that spread from chimpanzees to humans in the 1940s and caused a global pandemic beginning in the 1980s. Africa was the hardest hit. As of 2020, the disease had killed 30 million people.

Holocaust: The outcome of a Nazi-led effort to racially purify Germany through the mass murder of groups Hitler deemed inferior, particularly Jews. During the Holocaust, Nazis murdered millions of Jews, as well as Roma (Gypsies), the mentally ill, and the physically disabled.

Holocene: The name given to the roughly 11,700-year period beginning with the end of the Younger Dryas and continuing until today.

hominins [HAWM-ih-nihms]: The term used to describe all humans, extinct human branches, and apelike human ancestors who have lived in the last 7 million years. Fossil hunters have discovered 18 species of hominin so far.

Homo erectus [HOH-MOH ee-REHK-tuhs]: A hominin species that emerged 1.5 million years ago and went extinct 190,000 years ago. *Homo sapiens*, Neanderthals, Denisovans, and Flores Island "Hobbits" are all probably descended from *Homo erectus*.

Homo sapiens [HOH-MOH SAY-pee-uhns]: A type of hominin and the name of our species, human beings. *Homo sapiens* emerged 300,000 to 200,000 years ago in Africa.

Hyksos [HICK-sohs]: A group of people, probably from the area of modern-day

Lebanon, who migrated to and invaded Egypt. They ruled Egypt from around 1700 to 1500 BCE.

imperial consolidation: The general trend during the early modern period of empires growing bigger and more powerful at the expense of smaller powers.

income inequality: The growing divergence in incomes beginning in the 1980s. Globalization caused a vast share of the world's wealth to be concentrated in the hands of the few, creating the megarich class.

indentured labor: Commitment to a fixed period of bonded labor, usually between two and eight years. Although signing indenture contracts was technically voluntary, labor recruiters often used predatory practices to secure laborers.

Indian Ocean monsoon: Regular and predictable alternating winds that made the Indian Ocean relatively easy to sail.

Indian Rebellion (1857–1858): A rebellion that began with an army mutiny and spread to include many regional revolts. The rebels' aims were to get rid of British rule and restore old regimes, but many Indians remained loyal to Britain, and the rebellion collapsed.

indigenismo: This Spanish word refers to an ideology that asserts and demands social and political rights for Indigenous people. It is popular in Latin America, including in Mexico, Central America, and the Andean republics, especially Venezuela, Ecuador, Peru, and Bolivia.

Indigenous: A term applied to populations inhabiting a land from the earliest human settlement or prior to the arrival of colonial settlers. (Note: in this book, when "indigenous" is used as a descriptive term, it is not treated as a proper noun. The term "Indigenous" emerged as an identity label starting in the twentieth century, as Indigenous peoples used the Global Web to form connections with each other and make common cause. It is capitalized in such contexts.)

Indus River: A river 2,000 miles (more than 3,000 km) long that runs from the Himalayan glaciers to the Arabian Sea. The Indus was central to agriculture and trade for the complex Indus valley cities.

Industrial Revolution: A monumental switch to factory-scale production using machinery driven by water power and fossil fuels instead of human muscle and hand tools. It began in Britain in the late eighteenth century and spread to other countries and continents, with global consequences.

information technology: Innovations in information storing, processing, and sharing, particularly via the Internet and computers. IT reduces the costs of transportation and production, aiding in the growth of globalized supply chains.

Inka (ca. 1300–1532): A people whose empire was located in the Andean region, with its capital in Cuzco. Using a combination of military force and cultural influence, it quickly became one of the two largest polities in the Americas prior to 1492.

International Indian Treaty Council: An organization of Indigenous peoples founded in 1974 and dedicated to their sovereignty and self-determination. While beginning in North America, it came to include peoples across the Americas and the Pacific.

international institutions: Governmental, nongovernmental, and illicit organizations that operate internationally due to the rise of challenges, problems, and opportunities that are global in scale. Prominent examples include the United Nations, Amnesty International, and drug cartels.

international migrants: People who live in a country other than that in which they were born. Since the 1970s, the majority of migrants have moved to western Europe, North America, and the Arabian Gulf; by 2019, international migrants made up about 3.5 percent of the global population.

iron: Made from a relatively common ore, iron was cheaper and better than bronze in many ways. However, it required a lot of fuel to smelt and highly skilled ironsmiths to shape it into useful objects.

irrigation: The process of diverting water from lakes, streams, and rivers and supplying it to fields and gardens to ensure crop growth. Irrigation enabled farmers to cultivate land that was otherwise too dry for growing crops.

Islam: A monotheistic religion established in the seventh century whose followers are called Muslims. Its scripture is the Qur'an, which contains God's revelations to Muhammad.

Islamization: The widespread conversion to, and adoption of, Islam. India underwent Islamization beginning in 1000; coastal East African Islamization mostly occurred between the seventh and thirteenth centuries.

Istanbul [ihs-tan-BOOL]: Formerly named Constantinople, it was the capital of the Ottoman Empire from 1453, after Mehmet the Conqueror seized it from the Byzantine Greeks. Istanbul gave the Ottomans control of profitable trade routes and was a launching point for several successful attacks in the Balkans and along the Black Sea coasts.

Jack Gladstone: A slave in British Guiana who led the Demerara revolt of 1823 with his father, Quamina. Gladstone believed that legal abolition had passed in London and called Guiana's slaves to freedom, causing 10,000 slaves to revolt.

Jacobins: A political faction made up of mostly middle-class lawyers who increasingly dominated the government of revolutionary France. They ended elections in 1793, introduced wide-reaching reforms, and ushered in the Terror—a period of widespread suspicion and public executions.

James Watt (1736–1819): A Scottish-born engineer who designed and built more efficient steam engines. He was among a group of engineers who made steam engines more appealing to and useful for manufacturers.

janissaries [JAN-ih-sehr-eez]: Slave soldiers who formed an elite infantry under the Ottoman sultans and developed volley fire with muskets. They were taken as young boys from Christian homes in the Balkans and trained in warfare and administration.

Jawaharlal Nehru [jah-WAH-hah-lahrl NAY-roo] (1889–1964): Instrumental leader of the Indian independence movement and first prime minister of India. Next to Gandhi, he was the second most important figure in the Indian National Congress.

Jenne: An archeological site in West Africa where either a cluster of villages or a city stood by 450 CE. It offers evidence of long-distance trade along the Niger River.

Jesuits: Founded in 1540 in Spain, an order of priests in the Catholic Church dedicated to evangelizing non-Catholics and to rigorous education. During the sixteenth and seventeenth centuries, Jesuit missionaries worked to counter Protestantism in places as varied as Poland, Germany, Japan, China, India, and the Americas.

Jomon culture: A group that became sedentary around 7000 BCE, mostly along the Pacific coast of east-central Japan. They lived off of shellfish, fish, acorns, and chestnuts and were among the first inventors of pottery.

José Aponte [HOH-say uh-POHN-tay]: A Yoruba-speaking freedman who led a slave revolt in Cuba in 1812. This revolt was part of a rise in resistance in Cuba and Brazil due to the growing number of Yoruba-speaking slaves being shipped to these slave markets.

Josef Stalin (1878–1953): The leader of the USSR who consolidated power in the years 1927–1928. He introduced policies of industrialization and collectivization and headed state-led mass terror and brutal coercion.

Julius Caesar (100–44 BCE): A skilled military commander who gained prominence and the loyalty of legions of soldiers, which he refused to disband when the Roman Senate instructed him to. This decision led to civil war, from which Caesar emerged successful and then ruled as dictator from 48 BCE until his assassination four years later.

Justinian (r. 527–565): A Byzantine emperor who built the famous church Hagia Sophia in Constantinople and sought to reconstitute the old Roman Empire by reconquering territories the Romans had once controlled. He was militarily successful, but he drained the empire of money, and his successors lost many of his gains.

keiretsu [kee-REHT-soo]: Large, often family-based Japanese corporate conglomerates made up of banks, trading companies, and industries. They led Japan's post–World War II economic miracle by spearheading technological innovation, assembly-line production, and miniaturization.

Khazaria [kuh-ZAHR-ee-uh] (ca. 640–ca. 970): A Turkic-speaking, multireligious kingdom located in the grasslands of the North Caucasus. Its leaders converted to Judaism in the ninth century.

Khoi [KOH-ay]: African hunters and cattle raisers who lived at the Cape of Good Hope and clashed with Dutch colonists. Many Khoi eventually died, and their culture largely disappeared due to dispossession and disease epidemics.

King Afonso (r. 1506–1543): A king in Kongo, West Central Africa, whose father, also a king, had converted to Catholicism. Afonso learned to speak, read, and write Portuguese, and as king he made Catholicism the state religion in Kongo. His power grew with the help of Portuguese advisers and military technology.

King Kamehameha [kah-MAY-hah-MAY-hah] (r. 1782–1819): A ruler who unified Hawaii by using imported military and sailing technologies that he strictly controlled. His monarchy lasted a century.

Kongo monarchy: Elected rulers of the kingdom of Kongo whose legitimacy and backing largely rested on protecting their subjects from enslavement.

Korean War (1950–1953): A conflict that began when Soviet-backed, communist North Korea invaded U.S.-backed South Korea. Chinese and United Nations forces joined the fight, which became a war of attrition until a cease-fire was agreed to in 1953.

Koryo [KOHR-yoh] (918–1392): A kingdom in Korea that was based on an alliance of aristocratic families known as *yangban*. It was started due to the threat of steppe nomads.

Kwame Nkrumah [KWAH-may n-KROO-mah] (1909–1972): An influential anti-colonial agitator and chief negotiator in the Gold Coast's transition from British colony to the independent country of Ghana. He was Ghana's first leader and ruled in an increasingly authoritarian way until his ouster in 1966.

La Marseillaise [MAHR-say-yehz]: The song chosen as the French national anthem in 1795. It inspired many countries to designate national anthems, which became a part of growing nationalist cultures around the world.

Lakshmibai [lahk-SHMEE-beye]: A local Indian ruler, also known as the queen of Jhansi, in north-central India who continued to rule in defiance of British East India Company armies until she died in combat. She remains a national hero in India.

land empire: An empire that used industrial technologies and/or nationalist ideas to extend control over large areas of land rather than overseas. These empires included Russia, the United States, Canada, Brazil, and Argentina. The Comanche Empire in North America and the Ethiopian Empire in northeastern Africa were secondary land empires.

land reform: In Japan and South Korea, the transition from the majority of peasants renting land from wealthy landowners to the majority owning their own land. Pursued under pressure from the U.S. military during the post–World War II occupation, land reform laid the foundation for Japan and South Korea's economic growth.

Lapita: An Oceanic group that sailed out into the Pacific Ocean from the Bismarck Archipelago around 1300 BCE. They settled most of Remote Oceania, including Fiji, Tonga, and Samoa.

Late Pleistocene Extinctions: The extinction of about 65 percent of the genera of big mammals between 50,000 and 12,000 years ago.

latte stones: Large stone pillars erected on several islands of the Marianas that probably formed the bases of buildings. The Chamorro of Guam began to build latte stones around 1000.

League of Peace and Power: An Iroquois confederacy forged sometime before 1450 among the five Iroquois nations; the League united them and stopped them from warring among one another.

Lebensraum ("living space"): A geopolitical concept developed by the Nazis that argued that territorial expansion in lands where German populations lived, particularly in eastern Europe, was necessary to create a greater Germany and thereby consolidate German national identity.

Legalism: A Chinese political philosophy that emphasized law, punishment, regimentation, and the power of the state. Lord Shang (390–338 BCE), one of Legalism's chief advocates, promoted intimidation as an ideal governing method.

Levant: The eastern Mediterranean coast and its hinterland. It forms the western edge of the Fertile Crescent and is the location of the first strong evidence of farming.

Lucy: Discovered in 1974 in Ethiopia, a fossilized skeleton of a hominin called *Australopithecus afarensis* who lived 4 million to 3 million years ago.

Magdalenian culture: A semisettled group that lived between Portugal and Poland and intercepted seasonal migrations of reindeer for sustenance. Magdalenians painted the famous cave art at Lascaux and Altamira.

maize [mayz]: A staple food crop indigenous to the Americas; also known as corn. Part of the Columbian Exchange, maize flourished in southern Europe, China, and western and southern Africa.

malaria: A disease originating in Africa that is transmitted by mosquitos and was particularly deadly in warm, humid, and populous locations. Malaria spread widely around the world, including to the Americas, as part of the Columbian Exchange.

Mandate of Heaven: A Chinese cultural formula positing the divine authority that allowed kings to rule. It was a provisional legitimacy that rulers had to convince their subjects they maintained.

Manichaeism [man-ih-KEE-iz'm]: A dualistic religion derived from the preachings of Mani around the third century CE. A blend of Christianity, Zoroastrianism, and Buddhism, it emphasized a struggle between good and evil and a code of conduct including nonviolence, fasting, and restraint.

Mao Zedong [MOW tsay-TOHN] (1893–1976): Head of the Chinese Communist Party beginning in World War II and founder of the People's Republic of China. He developed a novel perspective on Marxist theory, arguing that peasants, not just industrial workers, could lead a communist revolution.

Maori [mow-ree]: Polynesians who live in New Zealand. They arrived from central or eastern Polynesia around 1280 and experienced two centuries of peace and prosperity until population growth led to scarcity and warfare at the end of the fifteenth century.

Mauryan [MAWR-yuhn] **Empire** (ca. 321–230 BCE): Indian prince Chandragupta Maurya united the Indus and Ganges valleys for the first time and established the Mauryan Empire; it ended after his grandson Ashoka's reign.

Maya [MEYE-uh] (ca. 600 BCE–900 CE): A complex hierarchical Mesoamerican society that was culturally and linguistically united but politically fragmented. Its rulers amassed wealth through the export of products such as salt, jade, and obsidian, and the Mayan glyphs were the most complete Mesoamerican writing system.

Meiji [MAY-jee] **Restoration** (1867–1868): A political revolution in Japan that ended in the reinstatement of rule by emperor and the introduction of a new elite. Meiji reformers were committed to strengthening Japan and promoting its industrialization.

Menelik II [MEHN-eh-lihk] (1844–1913): Architect and ruler of the Ethiopian Empire who used foreign military technology and skills to conquer surrounding lands and defeat Italian forces at the Battle of Adowa. He also introduced foreign technologies and institutions, such as railroads and public schools.

menhirs: Large oblong stones, standing upright, that began appearing in Europe in about 5500 BCE, marking a shift in spiritual practices that spread across the region. One example is Stonehenge, built around 2500 BCE in southern England.

merchant trading guilds: Formal organizations of groups of traders who worked together to facilitate trade and ease the risks associated with it. An alliance of merchant trading guilds formed the foundation of the Chola kingdom's power (ca. 970–1300).

Meroë [MEHR-oh-wee]: A kingdom in Kush located on the Nile between Egypt and sub-Saharan Africa that reached its peak around the first century BCE. It was the center of iron working in Africa and controlled the export of African goods to Egypt.

Mesopotamia: A largely agricultural region in river valleys of the Tigris and Euphrates where Sumer, Akkad, Assyria, and Babylon were located.

metallurgy: The process of separating metals from ore—the rock in which they are found—and then fashioning metals into objects.

Mexican Revolution (1910–1920): A social and national revolution that remade Mexico. It began when a succession struggle led to the jailing of presidential candidate Francisco Madero, which sparked insurgencies across the country and led to a decade of fighting.

Middle Passage: The months-long journey of slave ships between Africa and the Americas. Slaves were tightly packed belowdecks, usually naked and in chains, and many died due to unsanitary conditions and violence.

Mikhail Gorbachev [mihk-HEYEL gohr-bah-CHUHV] (1931–2022): The reform-minded final leader of the USSR who came to power in 1985. He introduced policies of *perestroika* ("restructuring") and *glasnost* ("openness"), defused international tensions, and pursued nuclear arms reduction treaties but ultimately could not prevent the collapse of the Soviet Union.

military revolution: An increase in the complexity and expense of war between 1450 and 1800. It comprised several innovations in weaponry, defense, technique, and administration.

millenarian movements: Religious movements whose adherents believe that spiritual or divine intervention will transform the world for the better.

millet system: The Ottoman Empire's tolerant religious policy: the Ottomans taxed non-Muslims at a higher rate than Muslims but also welcomed Christians and Jews and left them alone to oversee their own communities.

Minamata disease: The effects of mercury poisoning that those who ate seafood from the Minamata bay in Japan developed due to pollution from a nearby chemical plant. It was one among many acute pollution disasters in the 1950s and 1960s that arose from East Asia's rapid industrialization.

Ming voyages (1405–1433): Seven large maritime voyages arranged by Zheng He under the Yongle Emperor of China during the Ming dynasty. The extent of the voyages and the size of their wooden ships were unprecedented, and they served to project power as far as East Africa.

mita [MEE-tah]: Forced labor draft imposed on Andean peoples by the Inka. Under Spanish rule in South America, the mita provided unfree labor to work in the brutal conditions of the silver mines.

Mohandas K. Gandhi (1869–1948): The Indian anticolonial activist who developed the practice of nonviolent civil disobedience called *satyagraha*. His activism led to a widespread nationalist movement in India and contributed to the end of British rule in 1947.

Moluccas [moh-LUH-kuhz]: Part of the islands of Indonesia, also known as the East Indies, where nutmeg and cloves grew. Because Europeans placed great value on these spices, trade connections to these islands were very attractive to merchants.

monasticism: A way of life long prominent in Christianity and Buddhism that involves voluntary withdrawal from society, including a rejection of marriage and family, in favor of dedication to rigorous spiritual work.

Mongol western campaigns (1219–1260): A series of campaigns beginning under Genghis Khan and carried on by his grandsons Batu and Hulegu. By 1260, Mongol rule stretched from Russia and the Black Sea to Mongolia.

monotheism [MAW-noh-thee-iz'm]: A religious system that espouses a belief in one god, or the oneness of God. Judaism, Christianity, and Islam are all monotheistic religions.

Muhammad [muh-HAH-mehd] (570–632): The founder of Islam, who was born in the city of Mecca in Arabia and had visions at age 40 telling him he was God's prophet. He subsequently gathered a group of followers, called Muslims, and embarked on a successful military campaign in 622, establishing Islam as both a political and a religious movement.

Mulla Sadra [MOO-lah SA-drah] (1571–1640): An influential Shi'a theologian living in Safavid Iran. His writings attempted to reconcile Sufi mysticism with Islamic philosophical traditions and helped create an intellectual foundation for the Safavid theocracy.

multiethnic empires: Polities comprising different linguistic and religious groups and containing many ethnic minorities and multilingual people. The Habsburg, Russian, and Ottoman Empires were all multiethnic.

Muslim League: The organization of Muslims in British India that advocated for the division of postcolonial India into a Muslim state and a Hindu state. Muhammad Ali Jinnah, who became the first head of Pakistan, was its leader.

Mustafa Kemal [MUHS-tah-fah kuh-MAHL] (1881–1938): Leader of Turkey's nationalist revolution and its first president. Also known as Atatürk, he introduced a set of educational and legal policies, the Atatürk Reforms, aimed at strengthening and secularizing Turkey.

Nalanda: A Buddhist monastery in northeast India that was a center of learning and science in the Indian Ocean world, reaching its height in the sixth to the ninth centuries.

Napoleon Bonaparte (1769–1821): A military man who ascended to power in France in 1799 by way of a coup d'état and became a dictator. He won numerous military victories against foreign armies but abdicated in 1814 after a string of disastrous campaigns.

Narmer: The first ruler of Upper and Lower Egypt who completed unification around 2950 BCE; also known as Menes.

National Policy: A Canadian program that was launched in 1879 to stimulate industrialization. It involved the introduction of tariffs on foreign goods and investment in railroads.

nationalism: A set of beliefs, ideas, and attitudes that provides a sense of solidarity for a group. The group usually occupies a defined territory and claims to share language, culture, ethnicity, ancestry, political values, civic values, or some combination of these.

Natufians (ca. 13,000–9500 BCE): Sedentary residents of the Levant who showed the earliest known signs of plant cultivation and farming.

natural selection: The process whereby organisms that are better adapted to their environments pass down advantageous genetic traits through generations.

Neanderthals [nee-ANN-duhr-tawls]: An extinct "cousin" of human beings that lived from 400,000 to 40,000 years ago in Europe, Siberia, and southwestern Asia.

neo-colonialism: A situation in which countries that were former colonies are pressured to rely economically and politically on their former imperial rulers.

neo-Confucianism: An ideology originating in the Song dynasty (960–1279) that emphasized rigorous study and academic learning as the path to morality and righteousness. In the sixteenth century, Wang Yangming—also considered a neo-Confucianist—claimed that book learning was not necessary for obtaining wisdom and acting ethically.

new imperialism: A pervasive and widespread form of empire that arose after 1870 due to the power and wealth gaps that industrialization caused and the popular support that nationalism stirred.

Nile River: A river 4,000 miles (nearly 7,000 km) long that flowed through Nubia and ancient Egypt, bringing precious water and fertile silt.

Norte Chico (ca. 3100–1600 BCE): The collective name for a group of roughly 25 settlements in the Andes. Norte Chico was the earliest complex society in the Andean world, and its elites' power was based on the control of dried fish, a staple in the food supply.

North Atlantic Treaty Organization: A military alliance that bound together the United States, Canada, and most of western Europe to check Soviet ambitions.

Nubia [NOO-bee-uh]: A region south of ancient Egypt and upriver from it on the Nile. Egypt mostly traded with or ruled over Nubia, but on occasion Nubia asserted control over parts of Egypt.

Oceania: The Southeast Asian region that includes the islands in the Pacific Ocean, including Melanesia, Micronesia, and Polynesia. Near Oceania consists of New Guinea, the Bismarck Archipelago, and the Solomon Islands; Remote Oceania reaches as far as Hawaii and Easter Island.

Octavian (Augustus): Caesar's grand-nephew, adopted son, and heir, who became emperor of Rome and changed his name to Augustus. He was a ruthless emperor who ruled for 40 years, consolidated the Roman state, and built a strong administrative foundation for subsequent emperors.

Oda Nobunaga [oh-DAH noh-boo-NAH-gah] (1534–1582): A Japanese warlord who unified southern Japan and may have invented volley fire. He met his political aims by militarizing peasants and arming them with widely produced Japanese guns.

Olmecs: Concentrated in the urban centers of San Lorenzo (ca. 1600–900 BCE) and La Venta (ca. 900–300 BCE) in southern Mexico, the Olmecs were the first Mesoamerican group to develop complex hierarchical societies. They were builders of giant basalt heads and pioneers of pyramid construction in the Americas.

oracle bone inscriptions: The first evidence of Chinese writing, oracle bone inscriptions are questions posed to the gods written on turtle shells and cattle bones. Diviners heated the bones until they cracked and then interpreted the gods' answers using the fragments.

Paleolithic: The period lasting from 2.6 million years ago to 13,000 years ago; the latter part, the late Paleolithic, saw a profusion of cultural change.

Pan-Africanism: The call for Africans and people of African descent to liberate Africa and end racism through unified political action. The movement also supported literary and cultural revitalization.

W.E.B. Du Bois and Marcus Garvey were prominent pan-Africanists.

Parliament: A British legislative body comprising elected officials and hereditary nobles. Following the British Civil Wars and Revolution, Parliament became the chief governing authority in Britain.

Parthians (247 BCE–224 CE): Successors of Seleucid rule that emerged from a group of mobile pastoralists. They were particularly notable for successfully cultivating long-distance trade.

partition of Africa: The dividing up of African lands among Britain, France, Germany, Belgium, Spain, and Portugal between 1874 and 1890. It began as an informal process until the Berlin Conference convened to officially partition the continent in 1884–1885.

***patío* process**: A technology involving the use of mercury to separate silver from its surrounding rock. This process made the task of silver extraction easier in the sixteenth and seventeenth centuries, increasing the value of lower-grade silver ores.

Pax Mongolica (ca. 1260–1350): Meaning "Mongolian Peace," a relatively calm period during which the Mongolian Empire boosted trade along the Silk Road by creating an environment of largely peaceful exchange.

pharaohs [FARE-ohs]: Egyptian kings; there were about 170 pharaohs between around 2950 and 30 BCE.

Phoenicia [fih-NEE-shuh]: The Greek term for the cities on the eastern coast of the Mediterranean, including Tyre. The word *Punic* is derived from *Phoenicia* and is used to describe things Carthaginian.

pirates: Seafaring bandits who took advantage of periods when long-distance trade was widespread and navies were weak. The beginning of global trade was a very lucrative period for pirates such as the Zhengs and those organized by the North African *beys*.

plague pandemic (1346–1351): A disastrous outbreak of plague that is historically unmatched in its death toll. At the time incurable, plague killed 30 to 50 percent of the western Eurasian and North African population and continued to return regularly for centuries.

plantation zone: An area stretching from the Chesapeake to Brazil where the majority of African slaves were used. Plantations grew tobacco, rice, and sugar on a large scale as part of the transatlantic economy.

plebeians [plih-BEE-uhns]: Roman citizens who did not come from elite families. Plebeians were commoners who often performed the same work as slaves, although plebeians were reimbursed for their labor whereas slaves were not.

plow agriculture: The use of large domesticated animals to pull plows—a piece of farm equipment that tills soil. Farmers could cultivate five times more land using plows.

polis [POH-lihs]: A type of city-state developed by the Greeks around 700 BCE that included governance by magistrates, citizenship for adult males, and mandatory military duties for citizen-soldiers.

political decentralization: The weakening of centralized kingdoms and the diminishing of links among transatlantic empires, all as a result of the Atlantic revolutions.

Pontiac's War (1763–1765): An indigenous American uprising against the British. Named after one of the uprising's leaders, it was a military standoff but resulted in the designation of all North American lands between Appalachia and the Mississippi River as an "Indian reserve."

population surge: A nearly twofold growth of the global population in the three centuries between 1500 and 1800.

Porfiriato [POHR-fihr-ee-AH-toh] (1876–1910): The decades of Porfirio Díaz's authoritarian rule in Mexico. During this period, the Mexican economy grew rapidly, as did increasing inequality, due to Díaz's encouragement of foreign investment and support of dispossessing poor peasants.

Potosí [poh-toh-SEE]: Site of large-scale, dangerous silver mining in the Andes under Spanish authorities during the sixteenth and seventeenth centuries; laborers were mostly conscripted indigenous Americans and, later, African slaves who suffered harsh conditions, frequent accidents, and mercury poisoning. Silver was the most valuable transatlantic commodity.

praetorian guard: A select group of 4,500 men that Augustus created to protect the emperor. On five occasions, the praetorian guard assassinated emperors deemed ineffectual or corrupt, including Caligula and Elagabalus.

Prague Spring (1968): A Czechoslovak reform effort that called for less censorship and more freedom during post–World War II communist rule. The Soviets repressed it with a violent military invasion, causing widespread criticism of communism and the USSR.

printing press: A device invented by Johannes Gutenberg in the mid-fifteenth century that involved the use of movable metal type. It allowed for easier, faster, and cheaper production and dissemination of written information.

Protestantism: A branch of Christianity, initiated by Martin Luther (1483–1546), that took issue with the Catholic Church. Luther's writing and preaching emphasized scripture and salvation by inner faith over tradition. Many variations of Protestantism arose, but all denominations generally emphasized the importance of individual relationships with God.

proxy wars: Local conflicts around the world in which the United States and the USSR supported rival factions, with each superpower indirectly engaging the other as part of broader Cold War competition. There were at least 50 proxy wars, including the Korean War, the Vietnam War, the Angolan Civil War, and the Soviet-Afghan War.

Punic Wars (264–241 BCE, 218–201 BCE, 149–146 BCE): A series of three wars between the Romans and the Carthaginians. Rome won all three wars and razed Carthage after the Third Punic War.

pyramids: Monumental tombs, containing provisions for an eternal afterlife, that Old Kingdom pharaohs used conscripted peasants to build. The largest was Khufu's Great Pyramid at Giza.

Qin [chihn] (221–207 BCE): A state, under the ruthless leadership of Shi Huangdi, that conquered the Warring States, expanded to the south, and made unifying reforms that left a legacy of a large and united China.

Qing [chihng] **dynasty** (1644–1911): An imperial dynasty descended from a group of Manchu elites. Using innovative military techniques such as banners (units that cut across kin lines) and improved centralized command, the Qing vastly expanded Chinese territory and power.

Quakers: A Protestant sect originating in England that began the organized antislavery movement. Quaker beliefs stress the fundamental equality of all human beings, and their moral objections were instrumental to antislavery efforts in Britain and the United States.

Queen Boudica: A British queen who led an uprising against the Roman Empire in the years 60 to 61 CE. The Roman army ultimately defeated Queen Boudica and her followers.

railways: Transportation infrastructure that was central to industrialization and an outgrowth of the coal and iron industries. Railways and locomotives lowered transportation costs, connected markets, and linked countries together.

raised-field agriculture: A labor-intensive and very productive early farming technique used in the Americas from today's Bolivia to Mexico. It is a form of amphibious agriculture that involves creating islands in wetlands and raising crops on them.

Reconquista [ray-kohn-KEE-stah]: A centuries-long Christian campaign to retake Iberia from Muslim rulers. Europeans, especially Iberians, viewed sailing expeditions as a way to continue the Reconquista in new lands by spreading Christianity and depriving Muslim states of wealth from trade.

Renaissance (ca. late 1400s–1600s): A fascination among European elites with the intellectual and artistic traditions of the ancient Greeks and Romans. Humanism, the focus on experiences, was a defining feature of the Renaissance.

rising merchant classes: Those of modest backgrounds who traded goods in the Atlantic world and became wealthy. With their newly accumulated fortune, they sought liberties and political voice to ease their commerce and preserve their position.

Russian Revolution of 1917: The overturning of imperial rule in Russia that started with a coup d'état led by the Bolsheviks, a minority Marxist faction. They eventually seized control of the government and set out to reform Russia based on the ideology of communism.

Saadians [SAHD-ee-ihnz]: Dynasts who successfully used guns and cannon to unify Morocco and defeat the Songhai in West Africa. They ultimately were unsuccessful in further attempts to gain wealth and power.

Safavids [SAH-fah-vihds]: A dynasty that originated as a Sunni-Sufi brotherhood but adopted Shi'a Islam and then conquered Iran and most of Iraq. They made Shi'a Islam the state religion, reformulated its theology, and pursued mass conversions.

Sahel: An area of semiarid grassland that stretches east to west on the southern edge of the Sahara Desert. The Senegal and Niger Rivers are in the western Sahel, and ancient Ghana and Mali were located in their floodplains.

Sargon of Akkad: A king who pioneered the political format of empire and united the city-states of southern and central Mesopotamia around 2340 BCE; he built the first professional army, promoted trade, and reigned for about 56 years.

Sassanid [suh-SAH-nid] **dynasty** (224–651 CE): Successors of the Parthians and leaders of the Sassanian Empire who popularized the term *Iran* to refer to Persia. They built up irrigation works, introduced new crops, promoted long-distance trade, and made Iran into a great regional power.

schism [SIH-zuhm]: A formal division generally based on opposing beliefs, especially within young religions. Early Christian schisms involved Arianism, Nestorianism, and Monophysitism. Islam split into Shi'a and Sunni branches soon after its inception.

Scientific Revolution: The adoption of mathematics, observation, and systematic experimentation to understand the world instead of relying solely on scripture and ancient texts, as had been done previously.

Second Congo War (1998–2008): The largest African war involved armies of Congo and Rwanda with occasional participation by troops from Angola, Namibia, Chad, and Zimbabwe, among others—and several local militias. Estimates suggest it probably cost more than 5 million lives—the world's deadliest conflict since World War II.

sedentary: A term that describes people who stay in one place and form settlements instead of moving around.

self-determination: U.S. president Woodrow Wilson's idea that every European nationality had the right to its own, self-ruled nation. This concept was an important feature of the post–World War I peace treaties and an inspiration for anticolonialists.

Seljuk [sahl-JYOOK] **Turks** (ca. 980–1090): A pastoral Sunni Muslim group that rode into Iran, took Baghdad, and conquered Byzantine territory in Anatolia. They spearheaded the lasting Turkification and Islamization of the eastern Mediterranean.

serfs: Peasants who worked as forced labor on large, grain-producing estates for the gentry in Prussia, Poland-Lithuania, and Russia. Landlords of these estates controlled the movement, economic activity, and personal lives of serfs.

Sergei Witte [SAYR-gay VIHT-tee] (1849–1915): A Russian statesman who was deeply involved in the country's industrialization. He directed the government to build railroads, create technical schools, and introduce protectionist tariffs.

settlement houses: During the Industrial Revolution, institutions that elite and middle-class women set up to research and help improve the conditions in which poor and working-class people lived and labored.

settler colony: A form of imperialism in which migrants from a conquering nation establish colonies in conquered lands. Settlers often seek land and dominance, and settler colonies are more violent than colonies without settlers.

shabti [SHAH-tee]: Miniature figurines buried with pharaohs to aid them in the afterlife. Pharaohs sacrificed humans to be their otherworldly attendants until 2600 BCE, after which the use of *shabti* supplanted this practice.

shamanism [SHAH-mah-niz'm]: A broad set of religious beliefs and practices, including direct communication with the supernatural realm and a belief in the existence of a spirit world where the dead live.

Shang dynasty (ca. 1600–1046 BCE): A highly militarized and hierarchical society based in the lower Huang He basin that worshipped the deity Di. During Shang rule, Chinese writing was invented.

shari'a: Meaning "the path" in Arabic, shari'a is the body of Islamic holy law and ethics that governs every aspect of Muslim life. Originally developed on the basis of the Qur'an and accounts of Muhammad's life, it has evolved to form the basis of several schools of Islamic legal practice today.

shi: A cultural elite that emerged under the Zhou and consolidated much of Chinese culture. During the Warring States period, they transformed from being just scholars to also being men of war.

Shi Huangdi [shee HWAHNG-dee] (259–210 BCE): Also known as King Zheng and Qin Shi Huang, Shi Huangdi was a successful military commander who conquered vast amounts of land, put an end to the Warring States period, and began the Qin dynasty. He promoted Chinese unity and created a base of unification for subsequent dynasties.

Shi'a [SHEE-ah] **Islam**: An orthodox branch of Islam that was adopted as the state religion in Iran under the Safavid dynasty in the sixteenth and seventeenth centuries. Followers of Shi'a Islam believe that only members of Muhammad's lineage can hold religious and political authority.

shifting agriculture: A type of farming in which farmers clear land, farm it for a few years, and then move to a new patch of land once soil is depleted; often used in forest zones with poor soils.

Shinto [SHIHN-toh]: Meaning "the way of the gods," Shinto is an indigenous Japanese religion that is animistic and polytheistic. It emphasizes ritual and is based on tradition, folklore, shrines, and monuments.

Siddhartha Gautama [sih-DAHR-tuh GOW-taw-mah]: A Kshatri caste prince, born in the sixth or fifth century BCE, who rejected his privileged background and became the Buddha (the Enlightened One); his followers established the religion known as Buddhism.

Sikhism [SIHK-ihzm]: A religion that developed in India in the sixteenth century based on the teachings of Nanak (1469–1539), who asserted that Hinduism and Islam were one and the same. Nanak rejected elaborate ceremony and the caste system, promoted pacifism, and stressed the importance of humankind over other living creatures and the equality of all people before God.

Silk Road: Relay trade routes that crossed the steppes and deserts of Asia from China to the shores of the Mediterranean; named after one of the most valuable commodities transported on these routes—Chinese silk.

silkworms: Domesticated caterpillars that provided the raw materials for the silk industry in China. Women and girls produced silk, a lucrative trade item, from the threads that silkworms excreted.

silver trade: A major commodity that sustained the global economy and grew increasingly important as more people used it as money. In particular, governments and merchants sought silver to engage more easily in state spending or long-distance trading.

Simón Bolívar [see-MOHN boh-LEE-vahr] (1783–1830): A Venezuelan creole revolutionary leader who fought the Spanish Crown and hoped to found a united states of South America.

Simon Kimbangu [KIHM-ban-goo] (1887–1951): The Congolese founder and leader of the independent African Kimbanguist Church, whom the Belgians imprisoned for 30 years until his death. He preached faith healing, nonviolence, monogamy, and sobriety.

slave soldiers: Slaves used in the military; most had been sold by their families in Central Asia to the armies of caliphs and sultans. A few slave soldiers managed to overthrow their masters and install themselves on thrones. The Ghaznavids and the Turkic horsemen who established the Delhi sultanate were slave soldiers, and they spread the practice of slave soldiery into India.

slave-and-sugar plantations: Profitable, extensive commercial sugar farms in Brazil and the Caribbean that were larger and more efficient than their predecessors. They relied on the brutal exploitation of slaves who worked in notoriously unhealthy conditions and faced a life expectancy shorter than that of slaves anywhere else in the Americas.

Slavery Abolition Act (1834): Passed in Britain, the first large abolition of slavery. When the Whig Party took power in British Parliament, it introduced the act with widespread support from petitioners. It inspired abolitionists around the world.

smallpox inoculation: The intentional infection of humans with a small amount of smallpox to produce immunity.

social Darwinism: The pseudoscientific application of Charles Darwin's ideas to subsets of the human species. Arguing that some humans were more fit than others, social Darwinism appealed to science to support racism and racial hierarchies.

socialists: People who sought to alter social and political institutions with an emphasis on the rights of the working class. They often supported ideas such as strong unions, worker cooperatives, and communal ownership of industry.

soft power: Power derived from cultural and/or economic influence rather than military might or coercion.

Solidarity: A Polish trade union formed in the 1980s that battled for workers' causes and urged political change. Eventually, it attracted 10 million members and posed a persistent problem for Polish communist rulers.

Sons of Africa: A London-based abolitionist organization. It was made up of former slaves, including Ottobah Cugoano and Olaudah Equiano, who wrote detailed descriptions of their experiences as slaves to strengthen the anti-slave trade movement.

spice: The most frequently traded raw materials in the Indian Ocean world. Spices—including nutmeg, cloves, cinnamon, and a variety of peppers—largely came from Southeast Asia and southern India; the greatest importers were China, Egypt, Arabia, and Iran.

spice trade: The exchange of spices that became increasingly widespread in the early modern period and acted as a driving force of global trade. Portuguese, English, and Dutch merchants dominated the spice trade after 1511.

spread of democracy: The shift from the world having twice as many authoritarian states as liberal democracies in 1974 to the reverse by 2010 due to a rise in interest rates, the end of the Cold War, and the power of example.

Srivijaya [sree-VIH-juh-yuh] (ca. 670–1300): A Southeast Asian, Buddhist kingdom based in Sumatra that Indian culture influenced. It controlled the Straits of Malacca, gaining income from taxes on Indian and Chinese shipping.

state: A territorial unit and political community with a formal government. States always have bureaucrats, judges, and soldiers, and usually have ideologies.

steam engine: A machine that converts the chemical energy in fossil fuels into mechanical energy, called steam power. Steam engines powered the defining technologies of the Industrial Revolution and vastly expanded production levels.

steppe nomads: Mobile peoples, including Khitans, Jurchens, and Mongols, who came from the steppe grasslands north of China. Often fighting with the Chinese, they conquered north China three times and all of China once.

suffragism: A mass political and ideological movement that sought to give women the right to vote. It originated in the nineteenth century, and World War I greatly facilitated its progress and success.

Sufi [SOO-fee] **movement**: A form of mystical Islam that sprang up in the ninth century in response to official attempts to enforce orthodoxy. Instead of following scholarly traditions, Sufism promoted a more personal relationship with God and incorporated song, poetry, and dance into its rituals.

Sukarno [soo-KAHR-noh] (1901–1970): Javanese aristocrat, Indonesian independence activist, and founder of the nationalist Partai Nasional Indonesia. He became the first president of Indonesia after collaborating with the Japanese during World War II and then fighting off the return of Dutch colonialism.

Sumer [SOO-mehr]: The region and culture of southern Mesopotamia, located in today's southern Iraq; the early cities Ur and Uruk were in Sumer.

Sun Tzu [suhn-zoo]: Attributed author of *The Art of War*, possibly written in the fifth century BCE or later. The classic work gives insight on military strategy, diplomacy, statecraft, and espionage.

Sun Yatsen [suhn YAHT-suhn] (1866–1925): A physician and revolutionary who opposed the Qing and wanted to reform China in the image of powerful Western countries. He led the Chinese Revolution and became president of China's new constitutional republic until his ouster and exile to Japan in 1913.

Swahili [swah-HEE-lee] **coast**: The coast of East Africa where Arab and Persian traders interacted with local Africans. A distinct Swahili culture and language rooted in Indian Ocean trade developed along this coast.

Tacky's War (1760): An uprising in Jamaica of nearly 1,500 slaves, led by Akan-speaking slaves from what is now Ghana, that lasted for several months before it was brutally suppressed.

Taíno [TAY-noh]: The indigenous population of the Spanish-controlled Caribbean island of Hispaniola. Disease, violence, and enslavement led to a demographic catastrophe among the Taíno.

Taiping [TEYE-pihng] **Rebellion** (1850–1864): A large rebellion led by Hong Xiuquan and his army, the Taiping. Motivated by political, nationalist, and Christian goals, the Taiping managed to control much of the Yangzi valley for 10 years until their defeat and Hong's death.

Tenochtitlán [thuh-NOCH-tee-tlahn]: The large, populous capital of the Aztec Empire, located on an island in Lake Texcoco in the Basin of Mexico.

textiles and metallurgy: The two main industries at the forefront of industrial revolutions around the world. Both cloth making and iron making were well suited to steam-powered mass production.

third pulse of decolonization: The comparatively rapid emergence of around 100 new countries that occurred between 1945 and 1975, mainly in Africa, Asia, and the Caribbean.

Thirteenth Amendment (1865): Introduced at the end of the Civil War, an amendment to the U.S. Constitution that abolished slavery. It led to the liberation of 4 million people, making it the largest emancipation in world history.

Thomas Clarkson (1760–1846): A member of the Anglican elite and a staunch anti-slave trade and abolitionist activist. He allied with the Quakers to publicize the atrocities of the slave trade and was influential in the British abolition of the slave trade and slavery.

Tibetan Empire (ca. 618–842): Also known as Yarlung, the Tibetan Empire was located north of the Himalaya, and its influence spread from India to Mongolia. It was a formidable competitor to the Tang.

Tigris and Euphrates Rivers: Twin rivers that flow into the Persian Gulf; they supported agriculture and trade in Mesopotamia.

Tiwanaku [tee-wahn-AH-koo] (ca. 100–1100 CE): An Andean city and empire that amassed wealth and power through its control of the supply of llamas. The city was a religious center located near Lake Titicaca in what is now Bolivia; its empire and influence reached as far as northern Chile, lowland Bolivia, and the Peruvian Andes.

Tlacélel [tlah-KAY-luhl] (ca. 1398–1480): A successful and influential Aztec king who fortified the cultural legacy and importance of the Aztecs. He invented a glorious Aztec history and strengthened the Aztecs' religious importance by putting them in charge of sustaining the sun god.

Tokugawa shogunate [TOH-koo-GAH-wah SHOH-guh-nayt] (1600–1868): A ruling dynasty in Japan made up of the descendants of Tokugawa Ieyasu, who completed the task of unifying Japan around 1600.

Toussaint L'Ouverture [TOO-sahn LOO-vehr-toor] (ca. 1743–1803): The main leader of the Haitian Revolution. He was born a slave on Saint-Domingue but was freed around age 30, after which he led the Haitian slave insurrection and became a successful commander in the Haitian army.

Toyotomi Hideyoshi [toh-yoh-TOH-mee hee-day-OH-shee] (1537–1598): Oda Nobunaga's successor; a Japanese warlord whose soldiers liberally employed guns and nearly united all of Japan. He invaded Korea, enslaving thousands, but retreated from a failed invasion of China.

transatlantic slave trade (1519–ca. 1860): The transportation by European traders of 12 to 14 million slaves from Africa to the Americas, mainly to work on plantations. This trade constituted the largest forced migration in world history.

transition to agriculture: The switch between human populations finding or cultivating food and settled human populations producing food through domestication. This process occurred in various places independently of one another.

Trans-Siberian Railway: A railway from Moscow to the Pacific Ocean that was completed in 1903. A remarkable feat of engineering and construction, the almost 6,000-mile-long railway built by 9,000 laborers was a defining symbol of the Russian Industrial Revolution.

Treaty of Tordesillas (1494): Spain and Portugal used this agreement to demarcate a line halfway between Columbus's discoveries in the Americas and the Cape Verde islands off the coast of West Africa. It gave all lands west of the line to Spain and all lands east to Portugal.

Treaty of Versailles [vehr-SEYE] (1919): A peace treaty written by the victorious Allies that imposed strict and punitive policies on Germany in the aftermath of World War I. The treaty provoked outrage in Germany due to its reparations and war guilt clauses, as well as among Chinese because it gave German concessions in China to Japan.

Treaty of Waitangi [weye-TANG-ee] (1840): A treaty in which Maori of New Zealand agreed to become British subjects in exchange for land guarantees.

British settlers soon broke this treaty, fought Maori for land, and ended Maori independence.

Truman Doctrine (1947): A declaration by President Truman that promised U.S. political, military, and economic intervention against Soviet influence.

tsar [ZAHR]: The title Russian rulers adopted after 1547. The tsars, particularly Ivan IV (r. 1547–1584) and Peter the Great (r. 1682–1725), built an expansive and centralized Russian empire by modernizing the military and asserting control over the Russian elite.

Túpac Amaru II [too-pak ah-MAHR-oo] (1738–1781): A Jesuit-educated mestizo revolutionary descended from the Inka ruling family. He led a tax revolt in the Andes beginning in 1780 and emphasized justice and the end of ethnic oppression.

Tyre: A merchant town that linked the trade of Egypt, northern Mesopotamia, Syria, and Anatolia and specialized in a highly desirable maroon-purple dye. To expand their metals trade, Tyre's merchants established Carthage as well as several other colonies along the Mediterranean coast.

Umayyad caliphate [oo-MEYE-ahd KA-lih-fayt]: The first genuine Islamic state (661–750), based in Damascus and led by caliphs ("deputies of God") who claimed to be successors of the prophet Muhammad. They expanded their empire through conquests and exerted soft power through monumental architecture such as the Dome of the Rock mosque.

universities: The first opened in Cairo in the tenth century, followed by several in Europe in the twelfth century. European universities, as comparatively free spaces of inquiry and debate, prompted the development of science and art.

university of war: The state of constant military competition and chaos in Europe during the early modern period. These conditions increased the power of successful states and made them skilled in warfare, efficient at tax collection, and able to adapt quickly to innovations.

Vasco da Gama: A low-ranking Portuguese noble who led an expedition in 1497 around the southern tip of Africa and into the Indian Ocean in search of Christian allies and valuable spices for the Portuguese Crown. He helped set up a lasting Portuguese presence in India and East Africa.

Vedas [VAY-duhs]: Four texts, which probably originated as oral traditions, that are the earliest existing examples of literature in Sanskrit and the oldest sacred

texts of Hinduism. The culture of the Ganges basin is called Vedic after them.

vertical archipelago: The system by which Andean clans, called *ayllus*, placed people from a given lineage in communities at each elevation level of the mountains to exploit the resources of the different environments. The Inkas did not invent this system but greatly expanded it.

Vietnam War (1965–1975): A proxy conflict between communist North Vietnam, aligned with China and the USSR, and anti-communist South Vietnam, aligned with the United States. The United States committed hundreds of thousands of troops to the domestically unpopular war, which the North Vietnamese ultimately won.

Vikings: A group of seaborne marauders from Scandinavia that looted, slaved, and conquered nearby territories beginning around 800 CE. They settled land from Russia to Greenland and established several enduring trade links.

Vital Revolution: The steady improvement of human health and life expectancy after 1750. Better nutrition, microbial unification, control of smallpox, and sanitation reform contributed to this shift.

Vladimir Lenin (1870–1924): A Russian-born revolutionary and influential member of the Bolsheviks. He consolidated power by 1921 and was the first leader of the USSR.

Wang Yangming [wang YAHN-mihng] (1472–1529): A Chinese philosopher who challenged prevailing neo-Confucian thought and gained followers by arguing that ordinary people could attain moral perfection through inherent knowledge rather than through book learning.

witch hunts: The spike in accusations of witchcraft between 1500 and 1700, which resulted in the widespread use of torture and execution of accused witches. Unmarried women over age 40 were the main targets.

working class: A section of society, formed during the Industrial Revolution, that comprised factory and mineworkers who performed shift work for wages. Workers' lives at this time were precarious and dangerous, and they were politically divided between seeking reform and inciting revolution.

World War I (1914–1918): A conflict between the Central Powers (Germany, Austria-Hungary, the Ottoman Empire) and the Entente or Allied Powers (France, Russia, Britain, Italy) fought mainly in Europe. Many smaller European nations joined in, as well as ultimately the United States. The war required mass mobilization of populations and resources and led to unprecedented violence and destruction.

World War II (1937–1945): The most expansive and deadliest war in history, fought between the Axis powers and the Allies. It involved four overlapping wars, fought primarily in Europe, China, the Pacific, and North Africa.

Wu Zetian [woo ZAY-shihn] (624–705): The only woman who both ruled China in her own name and was the most powerful person on Earth when in power. Wu was a controversial ruler who was ruthless toward her enemies, adept at foreign affairs, a great patron of Buddhism, and a supporter of commerce.

Yamato race theory: A fictional idea developed in the 1930s. It held that all Japanese people shared a common ancestry to an ancient race that was superior to other nearby peoples, including Koreans and Chinese.

Yalta: The site of a 1945 conference in Soviet Crimea during which Soviet premier Josef Stalin, U.S. president Franklin D. Roosevelt, and British prime minister Winston Churchill agreed to divide up Germany and give the USSR part of the Japanese island of Sakhalin.

Yamato region: A state in the southeast of Japan that began to expand its influence in the 600s. It ruled several rice-producing regions, emphasized military skill, adopted Buddhism, and imported cultural ideas from the Tang.

Yamna: Pastoralists from what is now Ukraine and southwestern Russia who were among the first to master horseback riding and to use wheeled carts. In around 3500 to 2500 BCE, their genes and language replaced many of those of existing Europeans.

Yangzi [YAHNG-zuh] **River**: A river in China whose valley was home to the second transition to agriculture, which occurred about 7000 BCE and was rice-based.

Yermak [yehr-MAHK]: A Cossack who pioneered the expansion of the Russian fur trade into Siberia during the 1580s. His success also spearheaded the introduction of disease and practices of brutality that ultimately killed many native Siberians.

Yoshinogari [yoh-shih-noh-GAH-ree]: A site on Japan's southern island of Kyushu where evidence of weaving, bronze casting, and other crafts has been found, as well as mainland trade goods such as Korean bronze daggers and Chinese bronze mirrors.

Young Turk Revolution (1908): A coup d'état in the Ottoman Empire that nationalist army officers, called the Young Turks, led. They were frustrated with foreign encroachment on Ottoman territory and successfully imposed a constitution.

Younger Dryas (10,900–9700 BCE): A severe cold and dry period that temporarily reversed the process of slow global warming that occurred after the coldest part of the last ice age.

Yuan [yoo-AHN] **dynasty** (1279–1368): The dynasty established by the Mongols after the defeat of the Song by Khubilai Khan. Despite their rough-edged steppe-nomad nature, the Yuan allowed religious diversity, promoted scientific creativity and cultural exchange, and encouraged trade throughout the many lands they controlled.

Zanj revolt (868–883): A massive uprising of slaves from East Africa who worked on plantations in Iraq. One of the most successful slave rebellions in world history, it dealt an immense blow to southern Iraq and ended the practice of plantation slavery in Iraq for around a millennium.

Zheng He [SHENG-hah]: An admiral and an important ally of the Yongle Emperor. He arranged and led the Ming voyages during the fifteenth century.

Zhou [JOH] **dynasty** (ca. 1045–256 BCE): The dynasty that began the process of Chinese unification, developed irrigation, promoted iron farm tools, and began using chariots in war. In 771 BCE, Zhou rulers lost much of their territory; only part of their kingdom, the Eastern Zhou, survived until 256 BCE.

ziggurats [ZIG-uh-rahts]: A pioneering form of monumental architecture, ziggurats are temple-palaces dedicated to local gods.

Zoroastrianism [zohr-oh-ASS-tree-ahn-iz'm]: A monotheistic religion that arose in Persia around the prophecies of Zoroaster sometime between the tenth and sixth centuries BCE. With priests called magi, it emphasized the creator-god Ahura Mazda, human choice between good and evil, and divine judgment.

TEXT CREDITS

MAKING CONNECTION FEATURES

3.2

"The Indus Civilization and the Dilmun, The Sumerian Paradise Land," from *Expedition Magazine*, 1964. Courtesy of the Penn Museum.

3.4

"Letters of Ashurnasirpal II" from *Assyrian Rulers of the Early First Millennium BC I (114–859 BC)*, by A. Kirk Grayson (pp. 207–208, ii 72–76). © University of Toronto Press 1991. Reprinted with permission of University of Toronto Press."

4.3

Excerpts from EA 096 (Egypt), EA 162 (Egypt), EA 367 (Egypt) From AEMW/Amarna at ORACC. Reprinted by permission.

6.2, 6.3, 6.4

Excerpts from "The Account of Dayuan," "The Account of the Southwestern Barbarians," and "The Account of Xiongnu" from *Records of the Grand Historian: Han Dynasty II* by Sima Qian; Burton Watson (tr). Copyright © 1993 Columbia University Press. Reprinted with permission of Columbia University Press.

13.3

"An Abbasid Diplomat Encounters Vikings while Traveling in Russia 921," from *Mission to the Volga* Ahmad ibn Fadlan; James E. Montgomery (tr). © 2017 NYU Press. Reprinted by permission.

15.1

Rosemary Horrox. "The travel of plague to Avignon" in *The Black Death*. Published by Manchester University Press. © 1994. Reproduced with permission of The Licensor through PLSclear.

15.3

Bernardino de Sahagun; Nancy Fitch (tr). Excerpts from *Historia General de las Cosas de Nueva España*. Edited by Francisco del Paso y Troncoso. 4 vols. Madrid: Fototipia de Hauser y Menet, 1905. Reprinted by permission of the American Historical Association.

18.1

Republished by Permission of Brill. Excerpt from "The August Ming Ancestral Instruction" in *Zhu Yuanzhang and Early Ming Legislation* by Edward Farmer, pp. 118–119, 121–122. © 1995. Permission conveyed through Copyright Clearance Center, Inc.

19.1

Hattox, Ralph S. *Coffee and Coffeehouses: The Origins of a Social Beverage in the Medieval Near East*, pp. 14–15, 29. © 2015. Reprinted with permission of the University of Washington Press.

19.2

Republished by Permission of the University of Oklahoma Press. Excerpt from "First Coffee House in Istanbul in 16th Century" by Ibrahim Pecevi; in *Istanbul and the Civilization of the Ottoman Empire* by Bernard Lewis, © 1963. Permission conveyed through Copyright Clearance Center, Inc.

20.3

The Tupac Amaru and Catarista Rebellions: An Anthology of Sources tr. Stavig and Schmidt (Hackett: © 2008), pp. 109–113. Reprinted by Permission of Hackett Publishing Company, Inc.

20.4

From *Women in Revolutionary Paris, 1789–1795*. Copyright 1979 by the Board of Trustees of the University of Illinois. Used with permission of the University of Illinois Press.

26.5

Republished by Permission of the University of Michigan Press. Excerpts from *Documents on the rape of Nanking* by Timothy Brook (ed.), pp. 122–124. © 1999. Permission conveyed through Copyright Clearance Center, Inc.

29.2

Excerpts *from Declaration of Continuing Independence by the First International Indian Treaty Council* at Standing Rock Indian Country, June 8–16, 1974. Reprinted by permission of the International Indian Treaty Council.

PHOTO CREDITS

INDEX

Page numbers in **bold** refer to chapter key terms that are defined in the Glossary section. Page numbers in *italics* refer to illustrations. Page numbers followed by *m* indicate maps.

Abbas I, Shah, 589, 595
Abbasid caliphate. *See also* Islam and Muslims
Abdelkadir, **800**
abolition of slavery, 673
  in Atlantic world, from 1833–1888, 765–67
  in Atlantic world, to 1832, 764–65
  in Brazil, 763–64, 767
  Britain and, 761–63, *762*, 766
  in China, 767
  Clarkson and Wilberforce and, 762, 765–66
  in Cuba, 763
  Emancipation Proclamation and, 767
  Equiano and Cugoano and, 762
  France and, 763, 764, 767
  global spread of, 767–69, *768*
  in Haiti, 764
  in Korea, 767
  morality and, 760–61
  Netherlands and, 763
  in Ottoman Empire, 767–68
  propaganda for, *765*
  in Puerto Rico, 767
  Quakers in favor of, *761*, 761–62
  from 1750–1950, 758–59*m*
  Slavery Abolition Act and, **766**
  Sons of Africa and, **762**
  in South America, 699
  Thirteenth Amendment and, **767**
  in United States, 766–67
abolition of transatlantic slave trade, 760–64
aboriginal Australians, 561–62
aboriginal peoples, 1040
Adams, Abigail, 686, *686*
Addams, Jane, 737, *738*
Adi Granth, **591**, *591*, 591–92, 593, 600
Afghanistan
  Soviet-Afghan War, 944–45
  Taliban in, 1022, 1027
Afonso, King, **540**, 541
Africa and Africans, 778. *See also specific regions and countries*
  anticolonialism in, 882–83
  apartheid in, **992**
  cattle in, *802*, 802–3
  China's presence in, 993, *993*
  Christianity in colonial, *804*, 804–5
  colonialism in, 768, 803–5, *804, 805*, 989
  commercial revolutions in, 665
  conquest and disease in, *802*, 802–3
  corruption in, 990
  coups d'état in, 991
  decolonization of, 956–60, 958*m*
  disease control in, 989
  drought in, 990
  economic exploitation in colonial, *803*, 803–4
  economies in, since 1960, 972, 974*m*, 987–90, *988*
  evangelical Protestants in, 1023
  fragmented politics in, 991–93
  in Global web, since 1960, 987–93

Global web and, 537–48
Islam in, *538*, 538–40, 539*m*, 805
neo-colonialism in, 962–63
oil in, 990
Pan-Africanism and, *883*, 883–84
partition of, 801–3, *802*
per capita GDP in, 987, *988*
population growth in, 644, 988–89
railways in, 988, 989*m*
slavery in, 547–48, 768–69
smallpox inoculation in, 753
transatlantic slave trade and, 543–48, *545*, 546–47*m*
white supremacist regimes in, 991–92
women's education in, 990, *990*
African National Congress (ANC), 992
African Union, 991
agriculture. *See also* diet and nutrition
  in Americas, 555
  Industrial Revolution and, 714, 722
  Mao's collectivization of, 980, *980*
  population surge and, 643–44
  Stalin's collectivization of, 877–78
Ainu people, 806, 1036
Akbar, 592, 595, **616**, *616*, 616–17
Akbarnama, 643
Akio Morita, 1002
Alaska, 560, 788, 834, 1036
Albania, 812, 941
alchemy, 585
Aleuts, 560
Alexander II, **771**, 771–72, 862
Algeria
  Abdelkadir in, **800**
  decolonization of, 959–60
  deindustrialization in, 734
  French imperialism in, 799–801, *800*, 800*m*
  Islam in, 959
  as settler colony, **801**
  war for independence, *959*, 959, 959–60
Ali, Mehmet, 812
Allende, Salvador, *945*
alliance networks, 856, 857*m*
Allies, **898**. *See also* World War II
  casualties of, 917, *917*
  coalition management success of, 905–6
  codebreaking and, *910*, 910–11
  D-Day and, 904, *904*
  home fronts of, 913–15
  in Italy, 904
  Lend-Lease and, 906
  Manhattan Project and, 909, *909*
  material advantages of, 906–7
  mobilization and manufacturing of, *907*, 907–9, *908*
  in North Africa, 903*m*, 904
  oil controlled by, 907
  in Pacific War, 901, 904
  population of Axis compared to, 906, *907*
  scientific advantages of, 909–11
  war crimes and, 917–18
All-India Muslim League, 880
alphabet, Cyrillic, 576
American football, 1034
American Indian Movement (AIM), 1037, 1040

American Revolution, **685**, *685*, 685–87
Americas, 316, 493. *See also* Mesoamerica; North America; South America
  agriculture in, 555
  Christianity in, 555–56
  commercial revolutions in, 665
  cotton trade and, 651, 651*m*
  Creole languages and cultures in, 555–56, **565**
  disease and depopulation in, 548–51
  escaped slaves in, 557
  European voyagers in, 551–53, 552*m*
  fisheries in, 553, *553*
  fur trade in, 553–54, *665*
  in Global web, 548–57
  Habsburg Empire and, 624
  hybrid societies in, *555*, 555–57, *556*
  missionaries in, *555*, 556
  nomads in, 630–31
  plantation zone in, **554**
  population growth in, 644
  race in, 556
  religion in, 556
  settlement of, 553–55
  shifting social hierarchies in, *556*, 556–57
  silver mining in, *554*, 554–55
  slavery and forced labor in, 550, *550*, 757–59
  transatlantic slave trade and, 543–48, *545*, 546–47*m*
  transoceanic economies of, 553–55
  warfare in, 550
Ancestral Pueblo, 551
Andes
  diseases and depopulations in, 549
  Potosí in, 554–55, *653*, 653–54
  Spanish colonization of, 551, 552*m*
  Túpac Amaru II's revolt in, 696–97, *697*
Angola
  civil war in, 944, *944*
  diseases in, 542
  oil in, 990
  Portugal in, 540–42, 944
  slavery in, 541–42, 548
  white supremacist regimes in, 991–92
animal epidemics, 751–52
Anjirō, 573–74, 594
Annam. *See* Vietnam
Anne, Queen, 747
Anthropocene, **1008**, 1008–9
anticolonialism, **879**. *See also* decolonization
  in Africa and Caribbean, 882–83
  in China and May Fourth Movement, *879*, 879–80
  Gandhi and, *881*, 881–82
  Global web and, 884
  in India, 880*m*, 880–82
  Pan-Africanism and, *883*, 883–84
Anti-Slavery Reporter, 766
Anti-Suffrage Society, 869
Antônio Conselheiro (Antônio Maciel), 825–27, **826**, *827*
Aotearoa. *See* New Zealand
apartheid, **992**
Aponte, José, **763**
appeasement, **897**

Arabia and Arabs. *See also* Islam and Muslims
  Islam spread by, 538–39, *539m*
  language of, 800
  nationalism and, 791
Arab Nationalism, 886
Arab Spring, *850*, 1025–26, *1026*
Arctic
  climate change and, *1010*
  Cold War in, *946m*, 946–47, *947*
Ardern, Jacinda, 1016
Argentina, 645–46, *996*, 997, 998
Aristotle, 757
Armenian genocide, 861, *861*
Arouet, François-Marie (Voltaire), 687, 688
art
  Habsburg Empire and, 625, *625*
  Renaissance, *577*, 578
artillery, field **610**, 615, 625
Asante, 548
Ashaninka, 1037
Asia. *See* East Asia; Southeast Asia; Southwest
  Asia; *specific countries*
Asian tiger economies, **974**
Askia Muhammad, 539
Asma'u, Nana, 540
al-Assad, Bashar, 1027
astrology, 584–85
astronomy
  Scientific Revolution, heliocentric system and,
    584–85, *585*
  telescopes and, 575
Atabrine, 901
Atatürk Reforms, 867, 1022
Atlantic Charter, 950–51
Atlantic revolutions (1640–1830). *See also*
  specific countries
  American Revolution, *685*, 685–87
  in Britain, 679–82
  in broader perspective, 699–702
  experiences living through, 702
  French Revolution, 675–76, 687–783, *692m*
  Global web and, 676–77
  Haitian Revolution, *693m*, 693–95, *695*
  in Kongo, 677–79
  in North America, 682–87, *683m*
  outcomes of, 701–2
  political decentralization from, 699–701
  Spanish America and, 695–99, *696*, *697m*
  women and, 702
Atlantic slavery abolition. *See also* abolition of
  slavery
  Brazil and, 763–64, 767
  Britain and, 761–63, *762*, 766
  Cuba and, 763
  to 1832, 764–65
  from 1833–1888, 765–67
  France and, 763, 767
  morality and, 760–61
  Netherlands and, 763
  Quakers and, *761*, 761–62
  United States and, 766–67
Aurangzeb, Emperor, 618
Australia and Australians, 1040
  aboriginal, 561–62
  British convicts in, 561–62
  Christianity in, 561
  disease disasters in, 561
  in Global web, 560–65, *562m*
  Great Depression and, 871
  as settler colony, **801**
  suffragism in, 868–69
  Tasmania and, 535
  World War II refugees in, 923
Austria-Hungary. *See also* Habsburg Empire;
  Nazi Germany
  in alliance networks, **856**, *857m*
  languages in, 855–56, *856*
  reorganization of, 866

  World War I and, 854–61, *859m*, *860*
  World War I origins and, 856
authoritarian responses to democracy, 1024–26
automobile industry, in United States, 870,
  907–8
Avicenna (Ibn Sina), 590, 757
Axis, **895**. *See also* World War II
  casualties of, 902, 904, 917, *917*
  China occupation by, 915–16
  coalition management failures of, 905–6
  codebreaking and, 910–11
  European advances of, 901–4, *903m*
  European occupation by, 915
  fascism and, 895–96
  home fronts of, 911–13
  Japanese aggression in Asia, to 1937, 896,
    896
  in Libya, 903, *903m*
  material disadvantages of, 906–7
  mobilization and manufacturing of, *907*,
    908–9
  Nazi aggression in Europe, to 1939, 896–98,
    897, *897m*
  in North Africa, *903m*, 904
  oil disadvantage of, 907
  Philippines occupation by, 916, *916*
  population of Allies compared to, 906, *907*
  resistance movements against, 915–16
  scientific disadvantages of, 909–11
  war crimes and, 917–18, 921
Aztecs, 549, *549*

Babcock, Joshua 742
Babur, *604–5*
Baghdad, 676
Baltic region, 807
Banda Islands, 659
Bandung Conference, 951, *951*, 966
Bangladesh, 961
banknotes, 662
banks and banking. *See also* economies; global
  economy, 1500–1800
  Bank of Amsterdam, *660*, 660–62
  Bank of England, 662
  Bank of Sweden, 662
  Baring Brothers, 1030
  credit and, 662
  fractional reserve, 661–62
  Fugger and, 642
  global economy and, 660–62
  Great Recession and, *1030*, 1030–31
  international finance, 1029–31
  lending at interest, 660–62
  morality and, 660–61
  Vora and, 642
  World Bank, 935, 998, 1021
Barbados, 657, 761, 763, 765
Barbary pirates, 632, *632*
Baring Brothers, 1030
baseball, 1034–35
basketball, 1034
Bassi, Laura, 597
Bastidas, Micaela, 696, 704
Bastille, storming of, 675–76
Bastille Day, 676
Battle of Adowa, 811
Battle of El Alamein, *892–93*
Battle of Eylau, *691*
Battle of Stalingrad, **902**, *902*
Beatles, the, 1033
Beatriz Kimpa Vita, **679**, *679*
Belgium, 733
Belloc, Hilaire, 793
Benin, 548
Bentley, Elizabeth 742
Berber language, 800
Berlin Airlift, 938, 940
Berlin Conference, 801–2, *802*

Berlin crises of 1948 and 1961, 938, 940
Berlin Wall, 940, *940*
Berry, Chuck, 1032
Berterau, Martine, 597
Bharatiya Janata Party (BJP), 1022–23
Bhonsle, Shivaji, 618
Biafra independence, 961
Bill of Rights, 686
bin Laden, Osama, 1022, 1027
biological old regime, **749**, 749–52
Bismarck, Otto von, 724–25, 789, 801–2, *802*
Black Death, 530
Black Hawk, 846
blues, 1032
Blyden, Edward, 886
Bochkareva, Maria, 861, *861*
Boer War, 843, *843*
Boilat, Abbé David, *547*
Bolívar, Simón, **698**, 698–99, 700
Bolivia, 996, 997. *See also* Andes
Bolsheviks, 863–64, 876
Bonaparte, Napoleon, **691**. *See also* French
  Revolution
  in French Revolution, 691–93, *692m*
  in Germany, 788–89
  Haitian Revolution and, 764
  law of, 692
  nationalism and, 786
  Russian campaign of, *691*, 691–92
  in Spain, 698
Boot, Harry, 910
Bornu, 539, *539m*
Bose, Subhas Chandra, 953
Bosnia, 1021
Boston, 778
Botswana, 988, *988*, 992
Bourbon Reforms, **696**, 696–98
Boxer Rebellion, 837, *837*
boyars, 623
Brazil
  abolition of slavery in, 763–64, 767
  Antônio Conselheiro and Canudos movement
    in, 825–27, *827*
  commercial revolutions in, 664
  dictatorship's fall in, 998
  evangelical Protestantism in, 1023
  favelas in, 995, *995*
  independence of, 699
  music in, 1033
  per capita GDP in, *996*
  plantation zone in, **554**
  Portuguese colonization of, *552m*, 553
  slave-and-sugar plantations in, 657
  transatlantic slave trade and, 543–48, *545*,
    546–47m
Bretton Woods system, 935, 1030
Britain. *See also* Allies; England
  abolition of slavery and, 761–63, *762*, 766
  in alliance networks, **856**, *857m*
  American Revolution and, *685*, 685–87
  apartheid imposed by, **992**
  Australia and convicts from, 561–62
  in Boer War, 843, *843*
  Canada relations with, 788
  child labor in, 718–19, *719*
  cholera in, 755, *756*
  civil wars and revolution in, 679–82
  coal and Industrial Revolution in, 716–17, *733*
  colonization by, *552m*, 553
  commercial revolutions in, 664
  cotton and Industrial Revolution in, 717
  cotton trade and, *651m*, 651–52
  culture of imperialism of, 795–96
  deindustrialization in, 733–34
  environment and Industrial Revolution in,
    720–21, *721*
  in Falklands War, 997
  family life and Industrial Revolution in, 720

fascism in, 873
Ghana decolonization and, 956–59
in Global web after Industrial Revolution, 711
Haitian Revolution and, 694
health and Industrial Revolution in, 721
imperialism in India of, *798*, 798–99
Indian anticolonialism against, *880m*, 880–82
Indian independence from, *953*, 953–55
Indians resisting reforms from, 831
indigenous American conflict with, 684
industrialists in, 720
Industrial Revolution in, *708–9*, 709–21, 735–36, *736*
iron and Industrial Revolution in, 717, *717*, *733*
labor activism in, 737, *737*
labor alliances in, 737
labor costs in, 715
middle classes in, 720
navy of, 609
Nazi attack on, 901
Nazi expansionism unchecked by, 897
North America tensions with, 683–85, *685m*
in Opium Wars, *828m*, 828–30, 835
pirates fought by, 632
Pontiac's War and, **684**
power of, 1914, 855, *855*
protectionist tariffs in, 715
race and, 914
railways and Industrial Revolution in, 717–18, *718*
rising merchant classes in, **679**
Seven Years' War and, 683
Slavery Abolition Act and, **766**
smallpox vaccination in, 753–54
society during Industrial Revolution, 718–20
spice trade and, *649m*, 650
steam engines and Industrial Revolution in, 718
Suez Canal and, 718, 834, *834*, 951
suffragism in, 868–69
Tasmania and, 535–36
taxation of colonies by, 684–85
telegraph and, 793
transatlantic slave trade and, 543–48, *545*, 546–47m
voting rights in, 738
working class in, 719–20
World War I and, 854–61, *859m*, *860*
World War II mobilization in, 913
British, 742
British Columbia, 727
British Empire, 846
British North American Act, 787
British Raj, **798**, 798–99
Brunia, Agostino, *534–35*
Bry, Theodor de, *554*
Buddhism
    fundamentalism and, 1023
    in Japan, 574
    on lending at interest, 660
Bulatovich, Alexander, 811
Bulgaria, 791
Burkina Faso, 962, 988
Burma, 953
    independence and conflict in, 955
    Toungoo dynasty in, 628

Cairo, 676
Calvin, John, 580–81
Cambodia, 943, 1021
Canada
    British North American Act and, 787
    British relations with, 788
    Chinese labor in, 727, *727*
    cholera in, 755
    coal and Industrial Revolution in, *733*
    colonization of, *552m*, 553

First Nations people in, 787–88, *788*, 823
Great Depression and, 871
heights of population in colonial, 646
Industrial Revolution in, 727, *727*
iron and Industrial Revolution in, *733*
Iroquois in, 550
NAFTA and, 997, 1000
nationalism in, 787–88, *788*
National Policy, **727**
1918 flu pandemic in, 756
North-West Rebellion in, 788
as settler colony, **801**
suffrage and, 869–70
United States invasion fears of, 788
World War I casualties of, 860
World War II refugees in, 923
Canudos movement, 825–27, *827*
Cape of Good Hope, 542–43
capitalism, 935, 948
Capon, Laura, 909
carbon dioxide (CO_2), **1009**, *1009*, 1009–12, *1011m*, *1012*
Caribbean islands. *See also specific islands*
    anticolonialism in, 882–83
    cholera in, 755
    colonization of, *552m*, 553
    commercial revolutions in, 664
    Creole languages and cultures in, 555–56, **565**
    decolonization in, 960–63, *961m*
    diseases and depopulations in, 549
    indentured labor in, 773–74, *774*
    pirates in, 631–32
    plantation zone in, **554**
    slave-and-sugar plantations in, 657
    transatlantic slave trade and, 543–48, *545*, 546–47m
CARICOM, 999–1000
Carranza, Venustiano, 841
Cash, Bobby, 1033
Castro, Fidel, 936, 945, 966
Castro, Miguel de, *678*
Catherine the Great, 770–71
Catholic Church and Catholics, 791. *See also* Christianity; Jesuits; missionaries
    French Revolution targeting, 689
    in Ireland, 681, *681*
    missionaries in Africa, *804*, 804–5
    missionaries of, 582
    Peace of Augsburg and, 582
    Protestantism's spread checked by, 582
    Reformation of, 581m, **582**, 582–83
    in Vietnam, 805–6
    witch hunts and, **583**, *583*
Caucasus, 807
Cavendish, Margaret, 597
Central America revolutions, 698–99
Césaire, Aimé, 883
Ceulen, 659
Ceylon, 953
Chad, 962, *988*, 991
Chamberlain, Joseph, 720, 737
Charlemagne, 625
Charles I, 680–81, *681*
Charles II, 681
Charles V, 626–27
chartered joint-stock companies, **658**, *658*, 658–60. *See also* Dutch East India Company
chemistry, Scientific Revolution and, 585–86
Chen Duxiu, 879
Chernobyl nuclear disaster, 948–49
Chesterton, G. K., 815
Chiang Kai-shek, 900, *900*
childbirth, dangers of, 751, *751*. *See also* fertility
child labor, 742
Child of the Dark (Jesus), 994
children
    diseases of, 750, *750*

Industrial Revolution and labor of, 718–19, *719*, 739
infanticide and, 751
Chile
    abolition of slavery in, 767
    Allende in, *945*
    independence in, 699
    Spanish colonization of, 551, *552m*
Chiluba, Frederick, 1023
China and Chinese. *See also* Mao Zedong; Ming dynasty; Qing dynasty
    abolition of slavery in, 767
    African presence of, 993, *993*
    authoritarianism's rise and, 1026
    Axis-occupied, 915–16
    Boxer Rebellion in, 837, *837*
    British Industrial Revolution's impact on, 736, *736*
    in Canadian labor, 727, *727*
    ceramics, *655*
    cholera in, 755
    Christianity in, 594, *594*, 829
    Civil War, 1945–1949, **934**, 941–42
    collectivization of agriculture in, 980, *980*
    commercial revolution in, *663*, 663–64
    communism in, 900, *900*, 941–42
    corruption in, 986
    cotton trade and, 650–51, *651m*
    COVID-19 outbreak in, *1016–17m*, 1017
    deindustrialization in, 734
    Deng Xiaoping ruling, 971, 982–84
    economic reforms of Deng in, 982–85
    economy under Mao in, 980–81
    education in, 984
    extraterritoriality in, 835
    family size in, 986
    fertility in, *984*, 984–85
    firearm origins in, 611
    gender imbalance in, 985
    Great Depression and, 871
    Great Leap Forward in, **981**, *981*
    Great Proletarian Cultural Revolution in, 981–82, *982*
    Guomindang in, 839, 896, 916
    Hakka in, 829
    indentured migrants from, 773–74, *774*
    Latin America ties with, 1000
    May Fourth Movement in, *879*, 879–80
    modernization of, 979–80
    moveable type in, 575–76, *576*
    Nanjing Massacre and, 896, *896*
    navy of, 609
    neo-Confucianism in, 592–94
    New Culture Movement in, 879, 883–84
    in Opium Wars, *828m*, 828–30, 835
    pollution in, 985
    population of, 644
    propaganda of, *937*, 937–38
    Qin dynasty and, 828, *828m*, 829
    Red Guards in, 981
    Revolution in, 823, 834–39, *836m*
    silver trade and, *653m*, 654–55
    Sino-Japanese War of 1894–1895 and, 732
    slavery in, 757
    smallpox in, 750, *750*
    smallpox inoculation in, 753, *753*
    Song dynasty in, 663
    Soviet rift with, 947–48
    spice trade and, 649, *649m*
    sugar in, 656
    Taiping Rebellion in, *820–21*, 823, *828m*, 828–30, *830*
    Tiananmen Square protests and massacre in, 983, *983*
    Treaty of Versailles and, 879–80
    urbanization in, 1020
    Wang Yangming in, 592–94
    White Lotus Rebellion in, 828

China and Chinese (*continued*)
  women's per capita income in, 1990-2020, 973, *973*
  World War II in, 899-900, 915-16
  Zheng family piracy and, 605-6
Chinese Revolution, 823, 834
  Boxer Rebellion and, 837, *837*
  challenges leading to, 835-37
  extraterritoriality prior to, 835
  Japan and, 837, 839
  map of, 836*m*
  Sun Yatsen and, *838*, 838-39
  Yuan Shikai and, 839
cholera, 750, 755-56, *756*
Christianity and Christians. *See also* Catholic Church; missionaries; Protestantism
  in Americas, 555-56
  in Australia, 561
  in China, 594, *594*, 829
  in colonial Africa, *804*, 804-5
  Evangelical, 1023
  Great Schism in, 578, 582-83
  in India, 831
  in Japan, *572-73*, 573-74, 594-95, *595*
  on lending at interest, 660
  Luther and, *579*, 579-82
  Maori and, 564
  muscular, 797, *797*
  in Oceania, 561
  printing press and, 576-77
  repression and persecution of, 595
  slavery and, 757, 761
  in West Africa, *540*, 540-43
  witch hunts and, **583**, *583*
  Wovoka's prophecy and, 825
Christine of Mecklenburg-Güstrow, 747-48
Chrysler, 907
Churchill, Winston, 901, *901*, 905-6, 966
Cicero, 578
Cité Soleil, Haiti, 995
civic nationalism, 785
civilizing mission (*mission civilisatrice*), 795
Cixi, Empress Dowager, *837*, 837-38
Clarkson, Thomas, **762**, 765-66
class. *See also* working class
  fascism and, 873
  middle, 720
classical music, 1032
climate
  depopulation in Americas impacting, 551
  Holocene, 1008
climate change, **1009**
  Anthropocene and, 1008-9
  Arctic and, *1010*
  CO_2 concentrations and, *1009*, 1009-12, 1011*m*, *1012*
  depopulation in Americas impacting, 551
  energy use and, since 1975, *1012*, 1012-13
  mass extinctions and, 1010-11
  politics and, 1009-10
  rising temperatures and, 1010, *1010*
  sea level rise and, 1011, 1011*m*
clockmaking, 725-26
coal, **712**
  economic impact of, 713-14
  in Industrial Revolution, 712-13, 716-17, 733, *733*
  in United States, 726
coaling stations, **806**
codebreaking, *910*, 910-11
cod fisheries, 553, *553*
Coen, Jan Pieterszoon, 659
coffee, 676
coffee plantations, in Saint-Domingue, 693
Cold War, 851, **932**, 966
  Angola civil war and, 944, *944*
  in Arctic, 946*m*, 946-47, *947*
  Berlin Airlift in, 938, 940
  Berlin Wall and, 940, *940*
  costs of, 946
  Cuban missile crisis and, **936**
  divided Europe in, 938-41
  East Asia during, 941-44
  end of, 949, *949*
  global economy and, 934-35
  impact of, 932-33
  Latin America and, *945*, 945-46
  map of world in, 938-39*m*
  NATO and, **938**
  nuclear bombs and, 936-37
  Olympic Games during, 1035
  origins of, 933-35
  Prague Spring and, **941**, *941*
  propaganda in, *937*, 937-38
  Soviet-Afghan War and, 944-45
  Soviet decline and collapse, 947-49
  Soviet security and eastern Europe in, 933-34
  strategies of, 935-36
  United States security and, 934
collectivization
  in China, 980, *980*
  in Soviet Union, 877-78
Colombia, 698, 998, 1033-34, *1034*
colonies and colonization. *See also* anticolonialism; imperialism
  in Africa, 768, 803-5, *804*, *805*, 989
  by Britain, 552*m*, 553
  British taxation and, 684-85
  educational systems of, 963
  empires of, 1830-1914, 794-95*m*
  by France, 552*m*, 553
  in India, 801
  by Netherlands, 552*m*, 553
  by Portugal, 552*m*, 553
  settler, **801**
  by Spain, 551, 552*m*
colons, 800
Columbian Exchange, population surge and, 643-44
Comanche, 630-31
Comanche Empire, **809**, 809-10, 810*m*
comfort women, **916**
Comintern, 876
commerce. *See* trade
commercial revolutions, 662-65, **663**, *663*
Committee of Public Safety, 690-91
Commonwealth of England, 681
communication. *See* languages
communism, **876**
  Bolsheviks and, 864
  in China, 900, *900*, 941-42
  fascism compared to, 877
  Soviet, 876-78, *877*, *878*
Communist Manifesto (Marx and Engels), 724
Communist party, 742, 966
computing, 1029, *1029*
Concentration camps, 926
Confucius Institutes, 993, *993*
Congo, 805, 990-91
Congo War, Second, **991**, 1027
conquistadores, 551
Constitution, United States, 686
containerization, **974**, 974-76, *976*
containment strategy, **935**
Continental Congress, 685
Cook, James, 561, *562*
Copernicus, Nicholas, 584-85, *585*
Cornaro, Elena, 597
corporatism, 872-73
Cortés, Hernán, 549, *549*, 551
Cossacks, 558-60
cotton and cotton trade, **650**
  early cultivation of, 650-51
  as global business, 651*m*, 651-52, *652*
  Industrial Revolution and, 717, 726, *726*, 734

market knowledge for, 647-48, *648*
  transatlantic slave trade and, 651, 651*m*
cotton gin, **726**
courts. *See* law
COVID-19 pandemic, *1006-7*, **1014**, 1014-17, *1015*, 1016-17*m*, 1038
cowrie shells, 545
Coxinga (Zheng Chenggong), 605-6, 614
credit, banking and, 662
Creole languages and cultures, 555-56, **565**
cricket, 1034
Crimean War, 1853-1856, 728, 771
Crivelli, Carlo, *577*
Cromwell, Oliver, 680
Cuba, 758
  abolition of slavery in, 763
  in Cold War, 945
  dictatorship in, 998
  indentured immigrants in, 774, *774*
  land reform in, 997
  per capita GDP in, *996*
  slave uprisings in, 763
Cuban missile crisis, **936**
Cugoano, Ottobah, 544-45, 762
Cult of the Supreme Being, 690
cultural globalization, 1032-35
cultures of imperialism, **795**, 795-98
Curaçao, 767
Cyrillic alphabet, 576
Czechoslovakia, 897, **941**, *941*

da Gama, Vasco, 538, 649
Dahomey, 548
dan Fodio, Uthuman, 540
Darwin, Charles, 796, 815
Davanzati, Bernardo, 661
da Vinci, Leonardo, 610
Dawes Act, 823
D-Day, 904, *904*
DDT, 910
de Berndt Reed, Esther, 704
Declaration of Independence, 685, *685*
Declaration of the Rights of Man and Citizen, 689
Declaration of the Rights of Woman and Citizen, 689
Declaration on the Rights of Indigenous Peoples, UN, 1037
decolonization
  African, 956-60, 958*m*
  of Algeria, 959-60
  Atlantic Charter and, 950-51
  Bandung Conference and, 951, *951*
  borders following, 961
  in Caribbean islands, 960-63, 961*m*
  casualties of, *960*
  Dien Bien Phu inspiration for, 951
  in East Asia, 972
  of Ghana, 956-59
  Global web and, 952-53
  incomplete, 961-63
  in India, 952*m*, 953-55
  in Indonesia and Southeast Asia, 952*m*, 955-56
  in Middle East, 958*m*
  overview of, 950
  peasant uprisings and, 963
  shifting balance of power and, 950-51
  Suez Crisis and, 951
  third pulse of, **952**
  violent and peaceful, 960-61
Defoe, Daniel, 652
deforestation, Latin America, 997, *997*
de Gouges, Olympe, 689, 690
deindustrialization, **733**, 733-34
Demerara, 765
democracy
  Arab Spring and, *850*, 1025-26, *1026*

authoritarian responses to, 1024–26
contributing conditions to spread of, 1024
cresting, 1024–27
in Latin America, 997–99
social media and, 1026–27
spread of, **1024**
democratization, **997**
demographic dividend, **974**
Deng Xiaoping, 971, 1002
  economic reforms of, 982–85
  rise of, **982**
  in Singapore, 982
  violent rule of, 983
deregulation, 1030
Dessalines, Jean-Jacques, 695
deterrence, **936**
de Witte, Emanuel, *658*
Díaz, Porfirio, 839–40
Diderot, Denis, 687
Dien Bien Phu, Vietnam, 951
diet and nutrition. *See also* health
  biological old regime and, 750–52
  heights of population and, 645–47, *646*
Diet of Worms, 580
Directory, France, 691
diseases. *See also specific diseases*
  in Africa after conquest, *802,* 802–3
  African control of, 989
  Americas, depopulation and, 548–51
  of children, 750, *750*
  cholera and, 750, 755–56, *756*
  COVID-19, *1006–7,* 1014–17, *1015,* 1016–17*m,*
    1038
  disease disasters, **536,** 560–61
  germ theory of, 754–55
  HIV/AIDS, **1014**
  influenza and, *756,* 756–57
  in Kongo and Angola, 542
  MERS, 1014
  "microbial unification of the world" and, 644
  Minamata, **985,** *985*
  1918 flu pandemic and, *756,* 756–57
  SARS, 1014
  smallpox control and, *753,* 753–54
Djibouti, 993
Doctors without Borders (Médecins Sans
    Frontières), 1021
Dominican Republic, 996, *996*
domino theory, **943**
Dona Beatriz, 704
Dostoevsky, Fyodor, 834
Douglass, Fredrick, 766, *766*
Drake, 1034
drilled standing armies, *610,* 610–11
Du Bois, W.E.B., 883
"Dulce et Decorum Est" (Owen), 853–54
du Pont, Pierre, 725
Dutch East India Company (VOC), *640–41,* **658,**
    805
  business model of, 659
  in Cape of Good Hope, 542–43
  formation of, 658–59
  slavery and, 542
  success of, *659,* 659–60, *660*
Dyula, 539

early modern period empires, 606. *See also*
    military revolution; Mughal Empire; Ottoman
    Empire
  in Global web, 607–8
  Habsburg Empire, 624–27, *625,* 626*m*
  military competition and state power in, 627
  military revolution in, 608–11
  nomads and, 630–31, *631*
  population distribution in, *607,* 608
  Qing dynasty, 613–16, 614*m,* *615, 616*
  rise of big states, 628
  Russian imperial consolidation, 623–24

smaller powers and, 628–30
Tokugawa Japan, 612*m,* 612–13, *613*
East Africa
  Islam in, 538–39, 539*m*
  slavery in, 760
East Asia. *See also* China; Japan; Korea;
    Southeast Asia
  during Cold War, 941–44
  containerization in, 974–76, *976*
  corruption in, 985–86
  decolonization in, 972
  demographic dividend in, **974**
  economy of, since 1960, 972, 974*m*
  Global web rebalanced with rise of, 986–87
  labor costs in, 975
  pollution in, 985
  rise of, since 1960, 974–87, 975*m*
  women working in, *970–71*
economies. *See also* global economy, 1500–
    1800
  in Africa, since 1960, 972, 974*m,* 987–90, *988*
  Americas and transoceanic, 553–55
  Asian tiger, **974**
  of British imperialism in India, 799
  of China under Deng, 982–85
  of China under Mao, 980–81
  coal's impact on, 713–14
  Cold War and global, 934–35
  colonial Africa and exploitation, *803,* 803–4
  deregulation and, 1030
  in East Asia, since 1960, 972, 974*m*
  of French imperialism in Algeria, 800–801
  global, since 1980, 1028–32
  Great Recession and, *1030,* 1030–31
  income inequality and, 1031–32
  Islam and, 538
  Japan's economic miracle, 976–77, *977*
  in Latin America, since 1960, 972, 974*m,* *996,*
    996–97
  malaria impact on, 550
  Mexico, inequality and, 840
  in North Korea, 975–76
  per capita income in, *973, 973,* 987, *988*
  of Qing dynasty, 828
  of scale, **656,** 726–27, 906–9
  South Korean economic miracle, 978–79
  of Soviet Union, 948–49
  Stalin's strategies on, 935
  of Taiwan, 974, 976
Ecuador, 999
Eddoo, Quamina, 769
education. *See also* writing
  Africa and women's, 990, *990*
  in China, 984
  colonial systems of, 963
  international migrants and, 1020
  in Soviet Union, 878
  women and, 597
Efik people, 547
Egypt
  Arab Spring in, 1025–26, *1026*
  cholera in, *756*
  Mamluk sultanate in, 630
  Ottoman expansion in, 619–20, 620*m*
  slavery in, 760
  Suez Canal in, 718, 834, *834,* 951
Einstein, Albert, 909
Eisenhower, Dwight, 945
elephants, 617
Elizabeth I, 585, 679, *679*
Elmina, 540
El Niño, 826–27
El Salvador, 945, 1021
emancipation for serfs, **772,** 772–73 *780*
Emancipation Proclamation, 767
En, Kanai, 737
encomienda, **555**
Enfield rifle, 831

Engels, Friedrich, 724, 736
England. *See also* Britain
  Charles I against Parliament in, 680–81, *681*
  Commonwealth of, 681
  English Civil Wars in, 679–81
  Glorious Revolution and, **682**
  political decentralization in, 700
  Restoration, 681–82
English East India Company (EIC), 659–60,
    798–99, 828, 830–33
Enlightenment, 687, *687,* 770
enslaved labor. *See* slavery
environment. *See also* climate; climate change
  British Industrial Revolution impact on,
    720–21, *721*
  of Sahel, 990
epizootics, 751–52
Equiano, Olaudah, 567, 762, *762*
Erasmus of Rotterdam, 578
Erie Canal, 726
escaped slaves, in Americas, 557
estates, in France, 687–88
ethics. *See* morality
Ethiopia, 769, 803, 904
  in Battle of Adowa, 811
  Italian imperialism in, 806, 811
  land empire of, 810*m,* 810–12
  Malik Ambar and, 617, *617*
  per capita GDP in, *988*
  Russia and, 811–12
ethnic nationalism, 785
Eugenics, 815
Eurasia, intellectual upheaval in, 596–97. *See
    also specific countries*
Europe. *See also* early modern period empires;
    specific countries
  alliance networks in, **856,** 857*m*
  Axis advances in, 901–4, 903*m*
  Charlemagne's empire in, 625
  Cold War and divided, 938–41
  commercial revolutions in, 664
  Enlightenment in, 687, *687*
  heights of population in, 645, *646*
  imperialism in Southeast Asia and Pacific of,
    805–6
  intellectual upheaval in, 596–97
  lending at interest in, 660–62
  literacy in, 577
  military competition and state power in, 627
  Nazi aggression in, to 1939, 896–98, *897,*
    897*m*
  Nazi occupation and resistance in, 915
  partitions following World War I in, 865*m,*
    865–66
  political fragmentation in, 627–28
  population surge in, 644
  religious geography of, 1555–1650, 581*m*
  Renaissance in, *577,* 577–78
  rise of big states in, 628
  satirical map of, 782–83*m*
  Scientific Revolution in, 583–87
  serfdom in eastern, 770
  Soviet security and eastern, 933–34
  World War I and, 854–61, 859*m, 860*
European Union (EU), 1028
European voyagers
  advantages of, 537
  in Americas, 551–53, 552*m*
  Columbian Exchange from, 643–44
  commercial revolutions and, 664
  disease disasters and, **536**
  global economy and, 643, 648
  globalization and, 537
  in Oceania, 560–61
evangelical Christians, 1023
extinctions, mass, 1010–11
extraterritoriality, in China, 835
Eyak language, 1036

Fabian Society, 737
Facebook, 1026
falciparum malaria, 901
Falklands War, 997
family life
    in British Industrial Revolution, 720
    family size and, 986
    in North America, 682
famine
    biological old regime and, 751-52
    in Ireland, 751
    in North Korea, 975
    in Soviet Union, 923
fascism, **872**
    Axis and, 895-96
    British, 873
    class and, 873
    communism compared to, 877
    corporatism and, 872-73
    gender and, 872
    Italian, 872-74, *873*, 895
    nationalism and, 872
    Nazi Germany and, *874*, 874-76, *876*, 895
favelas, 995, *995*
Fermi, Enrico, 909
Fernando VII, 698
fertility
    in China, *984*, 984-85
    demographic dividend and, **974**
    global declines in, 1015
    in Latin America, 994
    population surge and, 644
    South Korean social change and, 979
field artillery, **610**, 615, 625
Fiji, 806
finance, international, 1029-31
financialization, **1030**
Finland, 751, 791, 869
Fioravanti, Aristotele, *578*
firearms, 611, 617, 621, 630, 725-26, 793, 831,
    857
First Nations people, in Canada, 787-88, *788*,
    823. See also indigenous Americans
First Opium War, 846
fisheries, in Americas, 553, *553*
Fletcher, Sally, 719
flu pandemic, 1918, **756**, *756*, 756-57
food riots, in France, *688*, 688-89
forced labor, 748. See also serfs and serfdom;
    slavery
Ford Motor Company, 870, 908
fortification, **610**, 625
fossil fuels, power of, 713-14
fractional reserve banking, **661**, 661-62
France. See also French Revolution
    abolition of slavery and, 763, 764, 767
    Algerian war for independence with, *959*,
        959-60
    in alliance networks, **856**, 857m
    Chad and, 962
    coal and Industrial Revolution in, *733*
    colonization by, 552m, 553
    cotton trade and, 651m, 652
    deindustrialization in, 733
    Dien Bien Phu defeat of, 951
    Directory in, 691
    Enlightenment in, 687, *687*
    estates in, 687-88
    food riots in, *688*, 688-89
    Haitian Revolution and, *674-75*, 693m,
        693-95, *695*
    imperialism in Algeria of, 799-801, *800*, 800m
    imperialism in Vietnam of, 805-6
    iron and Industrial Revolution in, *733*
    La Marseillaise in, **785**
    mission civilisatrice (civilizing mission) in, 795
    Napoleonic law in, 692
    nationalism in, 785-86, *786*

Nazi expansionism unchecked by, 897
Nazi invasion of, 901
in Opium Wars, 830
Pères Blancs in, 797
political decentralization in, 700
power of, 1914, 855
Seven Years' War and, 683
socioeconomic changes in, 687-88, 736
transatlantic slave trade and, 543-48, *545*,
    546-47m
Vichy, 919-20
voting rights in, 738
witch hunts in, **583**
World War I and, 854-61, 859m, 860
Frankfurter, Felix, 920
Franklin, Benjamin 742
free trade, **1028**
French, 530, 676
French Revolution, **687**. See also Bonaparte,
    Napoleon
    Bastille, storming of, 675-76
    Bonaparte in, 691-93, 692m
    Catholic Church targeted in, 689
    Committee of Public Safety and, 690-91
    Declaration of the Rights of Man and Citizen
        and, 689
    Declaration of the Rights of Woman and
        Citizen and, 689
    Directory following, 691
    Jacobin reforms and, **690**
    Louis XVI's execution in, 689, *689*
    nationalism and, 786
    origins of, 687-89
    political decentralization after, 700
    serfs and, 770
Fugger, Jakob, 641-42, *662*
fur trade
    in Americas, 553-54, *665*
    Siberian, 558, *558*

Gabon, 884
Galileo Galilei, 585, 595, 600
Gandhi, Mohandas K., **881**, *881*, 881-82, 953-54,
    954
Garcia II, 678
Garrison, William Lloyd, 766
Garvey, Marcus, 883, *883*
Gassed, 852-53
Gaulle, Charles de, 960
gay marriage, 1023
gender. See also family life; women
    Chinese imbalance of, 985
    fascism and, 872
    indentured labor and, 773-74
    literacy and, 577
General Assembly, 1002
Genocide, 926
Georgia, 554
Germany. See also Axis; Habsburg Empire;
    Hitler, Adolf; Nazi Germany
    agriculture in, 722
    in alliance networks, **856**, 857m
    Berlin Airlift in, 938, 940
    Berlin Wall in, 940, *940*
    Bismarck and labor politics in, 724-25
    Bismarck and unification of, 789
    Bonaparte in, 788-89
    coal and Industrial Revolution in, *733*
    deindustrialization in, 733
    division of, 934
    East, 938, 940
    fascism in, *874*, 874-76, *876*, 895
    Great Depression and, 871-72
    Holy Roman Empire and, 580
    hyperinflation in, 874, *875*
    Industrial Revolution in, 722-25, *724*, 736
    international migrants in, 1019
    iron and Industrial Revolution in, *733*

labor unions in, 724-25
List and state power in, **724**
nationalism in, 788-89, *789*
power of, 1914, 855
steam engines in, 722
suffrage and, 869-70
Treat of Versailles and, 865-66
Treaty of Brest-Litovsk and, 858-59
voting rights in, 738
Weimar Republic in, 866
West, 938, 940
witch hunts in, **583**, *583*
World War I and, 854-61, 859m, 860
germ theory of disease, **754**, 754-55
Ghana, 548, 769
    decolonization of, 956-59
    Nkrumah and, *957*, 957-59, 991
    UGCC and, 957
Ghost Dance, **823**, 823-26, *825*
Gladstone, Jack, **764**
global economy, 1500-1800, *640-41*. See also
    banks and banking
    banks and, 660-62
    changes in, 642-43
    chartered joint-stock companies in, *658*,
        658-60
    commercial revolutions and, 662-65
    European voyagers and, 643, 648
    falling income and, 647, *647*
    gross world product and size of, **645**, *645*
    heights of populations and, 645-47, *646*
    population surge and, 643-45, *644*
    sugar plantations and, *655*, 655-58, 656m
    trade and, 647-55
global economy, 1980 to present, 1028-32
globalization
    authoritarianism's rise and, 1026
    backlash against, 851
    containerization and, 975
    cultural, 1032-35
    European voyagers and, 537
    imaginary, 1038
    income inequality and, 1031-32
    music and, 1032-34, *1033*, *1034*
    phases and pace of modern, 851
    sports and, 1034-35, *1035*
Global web, 850
    Africa and, 537-48
    Africa in, since 1960, 987-93
    Americas in, 548-59
    anticolonialism and, 884
    Atlantic revolutions and, 676-77
    Australia in, 560-65, 562m
    COVID-19 pandemic spread through, 1015,
        1016-17m
    decolonization and, 952-53
    disease disasters and, **536**
    early modern period empires in, 607-8
    East Asia's rise rebalancing, 986-87
    Hawaii in, 564-65
    Industrial Revolution and, 711, 734-36, *736*,
        739-40
    information flows in, 575-77
    Latin America in, since 1960, 993-1000
    limits of, 1035-38
    nationalism, imperialism and, 812-13
    New Zealand in, 563-64
    Oceania in, 560-65
    pirates and piracy in, 631
    politics and, 1020-27
    Siberia absorbed by, 557-60
Glorious Revolution, **682**
Glover, Elizabeth, 576
Goering, Hermann, 907
gold
    in Mozambique, 542
Golden Horde, 558
Golden Temple in Amritsar, 592, *592*

Goldman Sachs, 1030
Gorbachev, Mikhail, **948**, 948–49
Great Depression, *871*, 871–72
Greater East Asia Co-Prosperity Sphere, **896**
Great Leap Forward, **981**, *981*
Great Proletarian Cultural Revolution, 981–82, *982*
Great Recession, *1030*, 1030–31
Great Schism, 578, 582–83
Greece, modern, 915
    Civil War, *940*
    Great Recession and, 1030
    nation-state establishment of, 791, *791*
Green Belt Movement, 1007–8
Grey, George, 822
gross domestic product (GDP)
    African per capita, 987, *988*
    global per capita, 973, *973*
    global shares of, 1960–2020, *974m*
    Latin American per capita, 996, *996*
    South Korean per capita, *978*
gross world product, **645**, *645*
Guangxu, 837–38
Guatemala, 945, *996*, 1023
gulags, 878, *878*, 926
guns, 611, 617, 621, 630, 725–26, 793, 831, 857
Guomindang, 839, 896, 916
Gutenberg, Johannes, 575
Guzmán, Abimael, 998

Habsburg Empire, **624**. *See also* Austria-
    Hungary
    Americas and, 624
    art and, 625, *625*
    fall of, 866
    growth of, 625–27, *626m*
    heights of population in, 645
    marriages expanding, 624–25
    military revolution and, 625
    nationalism and, 790
    silver and, 624
    Spain inherited by, 624
haciendas, 555
Haiti
    Cité Soleil in, 995
    instability in, 702
    race in, 556, 693
    slave uprising in, 658
    Toussaint L'Ouverture and, *694*, 694–95, 764
Haitian Revolution, *674–75*, 693m, 693–95, **694**, *695*, 764
hajj to Mecca, 590
Hakka, 829
Hamilton, Alexander, **725**
Harvey, William, 586, *586*, 661
Hawaii
    in Global web, 564–65
    Kamehameha in, **564**
    kings in, 564, *564*
    missionaries in, 564
health. *See also* diet and nutrition; diseases; life expectancy; Vital Revolution
    biological old regime and, 750–52
    British Industrial Revolution and, 721
    cholera epidemics and, 755–56, *756*
    COVID-19 pandemic and, *1006–7*, 1014–17, *1015*, 1016–17m, 1038
    HIV/AIDS, **1014**
    1918 flu pandemic and, *756*, 756–57
    population and, *1013*, 1013–14
    sanitation reform and, 754–55, *755*
    smallpox control and, *753*, 753–54
    Vital Revolution improving global, 752–55
Heidegger, Martin, 875
heights of population, 645–47, *646*
heliocentric system, **584**, 584–85, *585*
Henrique, 540

Henry VIII, 680
Henson, Maria Rosa Luna, 916
Herodotus, 578
Hideyoshi, Toyotomi, **612**, *612*
Hinduism
    extremism and, 1022–23, *1023*
    Gandhi and, 881
    Indian independence and, 954
    on lending at interest, 660
    Mughal Empire and, 617–18
    Sikhism and, 590
Hiroshige, Utagawa, III, *729*
Hiroshima and Nagasaki bombings, **905**, *905*, 918
Hispaniola, 549
Hitler, Adolf, 866, **874**, 905. *See also* Nazi Germany; World War II
    appeasement and, **897**
    detractors of, 875–76
    domestic support for, 911
    fascism and, *874*, 874–76, *876*
    historical fantasies of, 895
    Jews and plans of, 895, 918–19
    Lebensraum and, **895**
    military expansions of, 875, 895
    Operation Barbarossa and, 901–2
    racism of, 921
    rise of, 874–75
    social program of, 876
    Stalin surprised by, 902
HIV/AIDS, **1014**
Ho Chi Minh, 943
Hoess, Rudolf, 926
Holocaust, **911**. *See also* Nazi Germany; World War II
    Hitler's plans and, 918–19
    homosexuality and, 921
    map of, *920m*
    resistance in, *919*, 920–21
    Roma in, 921
    scale of genocide of, *919*, 919–20
Holocene, 1008
Holy Roman Empire, 580
homosexuality, Holocaust and, 921
Hong Xiuquan, 829
horses
    in Mughal Empire, 617
    nomads and, 630–31
Hudson's Bay Company, 658
Huerta, Victoriano, 841
human rights, World War II and, 921–22
Hungary. *See also* Austria-Hungary
    fascism in, 873
    Ottoman expansion in, 620–21
    uprising in, 1956, 940–41
Hus, Jan, 579, 582
Hussein, Saddam, 1027
hybrid societies, in Americas, *555*, 555–57, *556*
hyperinflation, in Germany, 874, *875*

Ibn Said, Omar, 567
Ibn Sina (Avicenna), 590, 757
ice hockey, 1034
Iceland, 750
Ieyasu, Tokugawa, 612
Igbo, 548, 762
immigrants and immigration
    indentured labor and, 773–74, *774*
    international, 1018–20, **1019**, 1019m, 1020
    Latin American population trends and, 994–96
    main currents of, before 1940, 1019–20
imperial consolidation, **623**, 623–24
imperialism, 673. *See also* colonies and colonization; land empires
    of Britain in India, *798*, 798–99
    colonial Africa, to 1930, 803–5, *804*, *805*
    cultures of, 795–98

of Europe in Southeast Asia and Pacific, 805–6
of France in Algeria, 799–801, *800*, 800m
of France in Vietnam, 805–6
global impact of, 784
Global web and, 812–13
intellectual responses to cultures of, 797–98
Italian, 806, 811
Japanese, 797, 806–7, 931–32
manliness and muscular Christianity, 797, *797*
nationalism supporting, 794–95
new, **792**
partition of African and, 801–3, *802*
pseudoscientific racism and, 796–97
settler colony and, **801**
social Darwinism and, 796–97
technology and, 792–94, *793*
of United States, 806–7
Inazo, Nitobe, 797
income inequality, **1031**, 1031–32
indentured labor, **773**, 773–75, *774*
India and South Asia. *See also* Buddhism; Hinduism; Mughal Empire
    anticolonialism in, 880m, 880–82
    British imperialism in, *798*, 798–99
    British Industrial Revolution's impact on, 736, *736*
    British reforms resisted in, 831
    cholera in, 755
    Christianity in, 831
    colonialism in, 801
    commercial revolution in, 664
    cotton trade and, 650–51, *651m*
    decolonization in, 952m, 953–55
    deindustrialization in, 734
    firearms introduced in, 617
    fortification in, **610**
    Gandhi and, *881*, 881–82, 953–54, *954*
    Great Depression and, 871
    Hindu extremism in, 1022–23, *1023*
    horses in, 617
    indentured migrants from, 774, *774*
    independence in, *953*, 953–55
    Islam in, 954
    Lakshmibai in, 832, *832*
    Marathas in, 618–19
    Muslim League in, **954**, *954*
    partition of, *954*, 954–55
    population surge in, 644
    Rebellion in, 823, 830–33, 831m, *832*
    Sikhism in, 590–92, *591*, *592*
    silver and, 653m, 655
    Singh's secondary empire in, 812
    spice trade and, 649m, 649–50
    Suez Canal and, 718
    sugar in, 656
    Taj Mahal in, 618, *619*
    urbanization in, 1020
    war elephants in, 617
Indian National Congress, 880, 953
Indian Ocean world
    piracy in, 632
    trade in, 648
Indian Rebellion, 823, **830**, 830–33, 831m, *832*
indigenismo, **998**, 998–99, *999*
indigenous Americans
    Ancestral Pueblo, 551
    British conflict with, 684
    codebreaking by, *910*, 911
    Comanche, 630–31
    Comanche Empire, 809–10, *810m*
    Dawes Act and, 823
    diseases and depopulations of, 550–51
    displacement of, *824m*
    Ghost Dance and, 823–26, *825*
    heights of population of, 646, *646*
    Iroquois, 550
    Lakota Sioux, 630–31, 825

indigenous Americans (*continued*)
  missionaries and, 556
  Navajo, 555, *910*, 911
  pollution and, 1036-37
  Pontiac's War and, **684**
  population decline of, 806
  Wounded Knee massacre of, 825
  Wovoka's prophecy and, 825
Indigenous peoples, 530, 846, **1036**, *1036*, 1036-38, 1040. *See also specific communities*
Indonesia, 649
  decolonization in, 952*m*, 955-56
  Dutch occupation of, 956
  Japanese occupation of, 955-56
  Sukarno and independence of, *955*, 955-56
indulgences, sale of, 579
industrialists, in Britain, 720
Industrial Revolution, 673, **709**, 742
  agriculture and, 714, 722
  in Britain, *708-9*, 709-21, 735-36, *736*
  British society during, 718-20
  in Canada, 727, *727*
  child labor and, 718-19, *719*, 739
  coal in, 712-13, 716-17, 733, *733*
  concept of, 710
  cotton and, 717, 726, *726*, 734
  country comparisons in, 732-40, *733, 736*
  deindustrialization from, 733-34
  environmental impacts of, 720-21, *721*
  family life in British, 720
  fossil fuels and, 713-14
  in Germany, 722-25, *724*, 736
  global impact of, 710, 722-23*m*
  Global web and, 711, 734-36, *736*, 739-40
  health impact of, 721
  iron in, 717, *717*, 733, *733*
  in Japan, 728-29, *729*, 732, *732*
  labor activism and, 737, *737*
  labor alliances in, 737-38
  labor costs and, 715
  middle classes in, 720
  Neolithic Revolution compared to, 710-11
  protectionist tariffs and, 715, 725
  railways and, 717-18, *718*
  rubber and, 734
  in Russia, 727-28
  slavery and, 734
  social contracts and, 736-39
  steam engines and, **713**, *713*, 718, 722, 730, 730-31*m*, 735
  technological changes in, 715-16, *716*
  textiles and metallurgy in, 712
  transportation infrastructure in, 714-15, *715*
  in United States, 725-27
  urbanization and, 714
  voting rights and, 738
  women and, 738-39, *739*
  working class in, 719-20
infanticide, 751
influenza, *756*, 756-57
information flows, in Global web, 575-77
information technology (IT), **1029**, *1029*
Inkas, 549-50
Inoculation, 778
Instagram, 1026
interest, lending at, 660-62
Intergovernmental Panel on Climate Change, 1021
International Criminal Court (ICC), 922
international finance, 1029-31
International Indian Treaty Council, **1037**
international institutions, **1020**, 1020-21
international migrants, 1018-20, **1019**, 1019*m*, *1020*
International Monetary Fund (IMF), 934-35, 1021

Iran
  deindustrialization in, 734
  family size in, 986
  military revolution response in, 628
  polo in, 1034
  Qajar dynasty in, 843
  revolution of 1979 in, 1021-22
  Safavids in, 588-90, 589*m*, 619, 628
  Sufi movement in, 588, *588*
  Treaty of Amasya and, 589
Iraq, 676, 1027
Ireland, 644
  Catholics and Protestants in, 681, *681*
  famine in, 751
  Great Recession and, 1030
  sectarian warfare in, 681, *681*
Irish Free State, 866
iron
  in Industrial Revolution, 717, *717*, 733, *733*
  in Japan, 732
  in United States, 726
Iroquois, 550
Isfahan, 589, *589*
ISIS (Islamic State of Iraq and Syria, or Daesh), 1027
Islam and Muslims
  in Africa, *538*, 538-40, 539*m*, 805
  in Algeria, 959
  Arabs spreading, 538-39, 539*m*
  in East Africa, 538-39, 539*m*
  economic appeal of, 538
  hajj to Mecca in, 590
  in India, 954
  Indian Rebellion and, 832
  jihad and, 1022
  on lending at interest, 660
  Mughal Empire and, 617
  Muslim League and, **954**, *954*
  in North Africa, 538, 539*m*, 805
  political, 1021-22, *1022*
  printing press and, 577
  al-Qaeda and, **1022**, *1022*, 1027
  repression and persecution of, 595
  Russian land empire and, 808
  Safavids and, 588-90, 589*m*, 619, 628
  shari'a and, 618
  Shi'a, 587-90
  Sikhism and, 590
  slavery and, 548, 757, 767
  spread of, 590
  Sufi movement in, 587-88, *588*
  in West Africa, 538-40, 539*m*, 805
Ismail, 588
Israel, 1023
Istanbul, **619**, 676
Italy, 530. *See also* Axis
  in alliance networks, **856**, 857*m*
  in Battle of Adowa, 811
  fascism and, 872-74, *873*, 895
  fortification in, **610**
  imperialism of, 806, 811
  Mussolini ruling, *873*, 873-74
  Renaissance in, 578
  World War I and, 854-61, 859*m*, *860*
  World War II in, 903*m*, 904, 912-13
Ivan IV, 558, 623
ivory, 542
Ivory Coast, *988*

Jacobins, **690**, 694
Jahan, Shah, 618
Jamaica, 552*m*, 553
  Bolívar in, 700
  labor unions in, 960
  per capita GDP in, *996*
  Rastafarian religion in, 1033
  reggae in, 1033

slave-and-sugar plantations in, 657
slave uprising in, *672, 746-47*, 765, *765*
Tacky's War in, 657-58
James I, 680
janissaries, **621**, 622
Japan and Japanese, 815, 926, 1002. *See also* Axis
  aggression in Asia, to 1937, 896, *896*
  aging population in, 978
  Ainu people in, 806, 1036
  Boxer Rebellion and, 837
  Buddhism in, 574
  in China during World War II, 899-900, 915-16
  Chinese Revolution and, 837, 839
  Christianity and missionaries in, *572-73*, 573-74, 594-95, *595*
  coal and Industrial Revolution in, *733*
  comfort women and, **916**
  corruption in, 985-86
  economic miracle in, 976-77, *977*
  family size in, 986
  firearm origins in, 611
  Great Depression and, 871
  heavy industry in, 732, *732*
  Hideyoshi in, **612**, *612*
  Hiroshima and Nagasaki bombings in, **905**, *905*, 918
  home front of, 911-12
  imperialism of, 797, 806-7, 931-32
  indentured migrants from, 773-74
  Indonesian occupation by, 955-56
  Industrial Revolution in, 728-29, *729*, 732, *732*
  internment in United States, 914, *914*
  iron and Industrial Revolution in, *733*
  kamishibai propaganda in, 912
  keiretsu in, 977-78
  Korea invaded by, 612, *612*
  labor activism in, 737, *737*
  labor alliances in, 737-38
  malaria in Pacific War and, 900-901
  Meiji Restoration in, **729**, 732, 739
  Minamata disease in, **985**, *985*
  Nanjing Massacre and, 896, *896*
  nationalism in, 786-87, *787*
  navy of, 609, *609*
  1918 flu pandemic in, 756
  Oda Nobunaga in, 611-12
  Pacific War and, 898-901, 899*m*, 904
  Pearl Harbor attack and, 893-94, 898, *898*
  Philippines occupation by, 916, *916*
  pollution in, 985
  race in, 895-96
  religion in, 573-74
  Russo-Japanese War and, 806, *807*, 862
  samurai in, 612, *613*
  Shinto in, 574, 786
  silver trade and, *653*, 653-54
  Sino-Japanese War of 1894-1895 and, 732
  textiles in, 729
  Tokugawa shogunate unification of, 612*m*, 612-13, *613*
  Treaty of Versailles and, 879-80
  United States occupation of, 976-77
  voting rights in, 738
  women workers in, 738-39
  Yamato race theory and, **786**
  zaibatsu in, 977
Japanese internment, 926
Java, 659
jazz, 1032-33
Jean, Wyclef, 1034
Jefferson, Thomas, 646, 685, *685*, 760, *761*
Jenner, Edward, *753*, 753-54
Jesuits, **573**
  in China, 594, *594*
  in Japan, *572-73*, 573-74, 594-95, *595*
  printing press and, 576

Jesus, Carolina Maria de, 994, *994*
Jevons, W. S., 717
Jews and Judaism
    Hitler's plans for, 895, 918–19
    Holocaust and, **911**, 918–21, *919*, *920m*
    Israel and, 1023
    on lending at interest, 660
    Luther's violent screeds on, 580
    Nazi propaganda against, *914*, 915
    Nuremberg Laws and, 876
    in Ottoman Empire, 622–23
    science and, 909
    in Warsaw ghetto uprising, *919*, 920–21
    Zionist movement and, 867
jihad, 1022
jingoism, 795
Jinnah, Muhammad Ali, 880, 954, *954*
João III, 541
Johnson, Lyndon B., 943
Jones, Marie Smith, 1036
"just-in-time delivery," 975
Juula, 539

Kabir, 593
Kamehameha, King, **564**
kamishibai, 913
Kangxi, 594, 778
Kangxi Emperor, 615, *615*
Kant, Immanuel, 687
Karski, Jan, 920
keiretsu, **977**, 977–78
Kemal, Mustafa, **866**, 866–67
Kennan, George, 935
Kennedy, John F., 936
Kenya
    Green Belt Movement in, 1007–8
    population growth in, 988
Kepler, Johannes, 585, 595
Kerensky, Alexander, 863
Khoi, **542**, 542–43
Khrushchev, Nikita, 947–48
Kidd, Captain, 632
Kimbangu, Simon, **805**
Kim, Il Sung, 942
Kipling, Rudyard, 795–96, *796*
Kochergina, Elizaveta, 908
Kongo, *541*, 704
    Beatriz Kimpa Vita in, **679**, *679*
    civil war and revolution in, 677–79
    fragmentation of power in, 678–79
    instability in, 702
    kingdom of, *677m*
    military revolution response in, 628–29
    monarchy, **677**, 677–78
    political decentralization in, 700
    Portuguese, 540–42, 677–79, *678*
    slavery in, 678
    women in politics of, 679
Kopelev, Lev, 916
Korea. *See also* North Korea; South Korea
    abolition of slavery in, 767
    division of, 934
    firearm origins in, 611
    heights of population in, 646
    Japan imperialism in, 807, 931–32
    Japan invasion of, 612, *612*
    moveable type in, 575–76, *576*
    slavery in, 757–58
Korean War
    casualties of, *930–31*, 942
    course of, **942**
    dangers of, 932
    Japan's economic miracle and, 976
    United States and, 942
Koxinga (Zheng Chenggong), 605–6, 614
Kuti, Fela, 1033, *1033*
Kyoto Protocol, 1997, 1010

labor, 742. *See also* serfs and serfdom; slavery; working class
    activism, 737, *737*
    alliances, 737–38
    Americas and forced, 550, *550*, 757–59
    Bismarck and German politics of, 724–25
    child, 718–19, *719*, 739
    of Chinese in Canada, 727, *727*
    East Asian cost of, 975
    expansion of forced, 758–60
    falling incomes for, 647, *647*
    indentured, 773–75, *774*
    Industrial Revolution and cost of, 715
    international migrants and, 1020, *1020*
    settlement houses and, **737**, *738*
    unions, 724–25, 737, *737*, 875, 960, 1028
    women in, 738–39, *739*
Lakota Sioux, 630–31, 825
Lakshmibai, **832**, *832*
land empires, **807**
    Comanche Empire, 809–10, *810m*
    of Ethiopia, *810m*, 810–12
    of Russia, 807–8, *808m*
    secondary, 808–12
land reform, **978**, 997
languages
    Ainu, 1036
    Arabic, 800
    in Austria-Hungary, 855–56, *856*
    Berber, 800
    Creole, 555–56, **565**
    Eyak, 1036
    German nationalism and, 788
    of indigenous peoples, 1036
    in Latin America, 994
Laos, 943
Latin America. *See also specific countries and regions*
    Chinese ties with, 1000
    Cold War and, *945*, 945–46
    commodity exports in, 996–97
    definition of, 993–94
    deforestation, 997, *997*
    democratization in, 997–99
    economies in, since 1960, 972, *974m*, *996*, 996–97
    evangelical Protestantism in, 1023
    fertility in, 994
    in Global web, since 1960, 993–1000
    indigenismo in, 998–99, *999*
    inequality in, 996
    land reform in, 997
    languages in, 994
    neoliberalism in, 998
    per capita GDP in, 996, *996*
    politics, 997–99
    population and migration trends in, 994–96
    race in, 994
    religion in, 994
    urbanization in, 994–95, *995*
    women's per capita income in, 1990–2020, 973, *973*
Latude, Henri, 675
law
    Napoleonic law, 692
    Nuremberg Laws, 876
League of Nations, 866
Lebanon, 861
Lebensraum ("living space"), **895**
Lee Kuan Yew, 982
lending at interest, 660–62
Lend-Lease, 906
Lenin, Vladimir, 858–59, **863**, 863–64, *864*, 935
Lennon, John, 1032–33
Leontiev, Nikolai, 811–12
Leopold II, 803–4
Levant Company, 658

Liberia, 886
Libya
    Italian imperialism in, 806
    in World War II, 903, *903m*
life expectancy. *See also* diet and nutrition; diseases; health
    modern trends in, 754
    in 2020, 1014, *1014*
    Vital Revolution and, 748
Li Hongzhang, 835, 836
Lili'uokalani, 565
Lincoln, Abraham, 766
Linnaeus, Carl, 586–87
List, Friedrich, **724**
literacy, 577. *See also* education; writing
Little Richard, 1032
Litvyak, Lydia, *913*
"living space" *(Lebensraum)*, **895**
Longstaff, William Francis, *892–93*
Louisiana Territory, 809
Louis XIV, 643, 704
Louis XV, King, 675
Louis XVI, King, 688, 689, *689*
Lowell, Francis Cabot, 725
Lowell girls, 738
Lugard, Frederick, 802
Luther, Martin, *579*, 579–82, 600
Lutheranism, 582, 791

Maathai, Wangari, **1007**, 1007–8, *1008*
Macdonald, John A., 788
Machemba, 783–84
Machiavelli, Niccolò, 578
machine guns, 793, 857
Maciel, Antônio (Antônio Conselheiro), 825–27, **826**, *827*
Madagascar, 812, 960, 988, *988*
Madero, Francisco, 840–41, *841*
Makeba, Miriam, 1033
Malacca, 649–50
malaria
    economic impact of, 550
    falciparum, 901
    medicine for, 901
    Pacific War and, 900–901
    quinine for, 793–94
Malay Peninsula, 805
Mali, 991
Malik Ambar, 617, *617*
malnutrition, biological old regime and, 751–52. *See also* famine
Malthusianism, 815
Malthus, Thomas, 717
Mamluk sultanate, 630
Manchukuo, 896
Manchuria, 896
Mandela, Nelson, 992
Manhattan Project, 909, *909*
manliness, 797
Mansah, Abina, 769
al-Mansur, 629
Mao Anying, 942
Maori, *563*, 563–64, 812, 846
Mao Zedong, 900, *900*, **941**
    Chinese Civil War and, 941–42
    collectivization of agriculture by, 980, *980*
    Great Leap Forward and, **981**, *981*
    Great Proletarian Cultural Revolution and, 981–82, *982*
    legacy of, 982
    propaganda of, 937, *937*
    Sino-Soviet rift and, 947–48
Mapuche, 549, 557
Marathas, 618–19
Marcos, Ferdinand, 1024, *1024*
Marley, Bob, 1033
maroons, 557

Marquesas Islands, 560
marriage, Habsburg Empire's expansion
    through, 624-25. *See also* family life
Marseillaise, La, **785**
Marshall Plan, 938
Mary Wortley Montague, Lady, 778
Marx, Karl, 724, 736, 935, 941. *See also*
    communism
mass extinctions, 1010-11
mathematics, 586
Mauritania, 769
Mauritius, 760
May, Karl, 895
Maya, 557
May Fourth Movement, *879*, 879-80
McCartney, Paul, 1032-33
measles, 750
Mecca, 590, 620, 676. *See also* Islam
Médecins Sans Frontières (Doctors without
    Borders), 1021
medicine
    for malaria, 901
    quinine for malaria, 793-94
    Scientific Revolution and, 586, *586*
Medina, 620
Mehmet the Conqueror, 621-23
Meiji Restoration, **729**, 732, 739
Mein Kampf (Hitler), 876
Menelik II, **810**, 810-12
Merian, Maria Sibylla, *596*, 597
MERS, 1014
Mesoamerica. *See also specific peoples*
    diseases and depopulations in, 549, *549*
    Maya in, 557
    Spanish colonization of, 551, 552m
Metallic web, 730, 730-31m
metallurgy, **712**
Métis, 788
Mexica. *See* Aztecs
Mexican-American War, 810
Mexican Revolution, 823, 834, **839**, *842*
    grievances of, *840*
    Madero and, 840-41, *841*
    map of, 841m
    outcome and aftermath of, 842
    Porfiriato prior to, 839-40
Mexico, 530
    cotton trade and, 651, 651m
    democratization in, 998
    economic inequality in, 840
    heights of population in, 645
    income inequality in, 1031
    industrialization in, 997
    land reform in, 997
    Mexican-American War and, 810
    mining in, 697
    NAFTA and, 997, 1000
    1918 flu pandemic in, 756
    patío process for silver in, *652*, **653**
    per capita GDP in, *996*
    population in, 1876-1910, 840
    printing press in, 576
    Revolution in, 823, 834, 839-42, 841m
    silver trade and, 653, *653*
    smallpox inoculation in, 753
    Spanish colonization of, 551, 552m
Michelangelo, 610
"microbial unification of the world," 644
microscopes, 575
middle classes, Industrial Britain, 720
Middle East. *See also specific countries and*
    peoples
    decolonization in, 958m
    partitions following World War I in, 865m,
        866-67
    women's per capita income in, 1990-2020,
        973, *973*
Middle Passage, **544**, *544*, 567

Mi'kmaqs, 662
military. *See also* war and warfare
    Hitler expanding, 875, 895
    navies and, 609, *609*, 631, 858
    technology, 793, *793*
military revolution, **608**
    costs of, 608, *627*
    field artillery and fortification in, **610**
    Habsburg Empire and, 625
    military competition and state power, 627
    Mughal Empire and, *616*, 616-17
    oceanic navies in, 609, *609*
    Ottoman Empire and, 621
    Peter the Great and, 624
    Qing dynasty and, *615*, 615-16
    smaller powers responding to, 628-30
    standing armies and, *610*, 610-11
    taxation and, *608*, 608-9, 616
    university of war and, **627**
millenarian movements, **822**
    Canudos movement in Brazil, 825-27, *827*
    Ghost Dance and, 823-26, *825*
millet system, **623**
Minamata disease, **985**, *985*
Ming dynasty, 643
    commercial revolution in, 663
    fall of, 613
    navy of, 609, *609*
    population of, 614
    silver trade and, 653m, 654-55, *655*
mining
    Fugger and, 641
    in Japan, 732
    in Mexico, 697
    silver in Americas, *554*, 554-55
    technology, *587*
minority nationalisms, 792
Miranda, Francisco, 697-98
missionaries
    in Africa, *804*, 804-5
    in Americas, *555*, 556
    in Australia, 561
    Catholic, 582
    in China, 594, *594*
    diseases and depopulations from, 550-51
    in Hawaii, 564
    in India, 831
    indigenous Americans and, 556
    in Japan, *572-73*, 573-74, 594-95, *595*
    in Oceania, 561
    Portuguese in Kongo, 540-42
mission civilisatrice (civilizing mission), 795
mita, **550**
MITI (ministry for international trade and
    industry), 976
Mongols, Qing attacks on, 615-16
Monroe Doctrine, 807
morality
    abolition of slavery and, 760-61
    banking and, 660-61
    slavery and, 760-61
More, Thomas, 757
Mormons, 824-26, 868
Morocco
    military revolution response in, 628-29
    Saadians in, 628-29
    sugar plantations in, 656
Morris, Esther Hobart, 868
Moscow, 966
Mott, Lucretia, 868
moveable type, 575-76, *576*
Mozambique, 542, 991-92
MPLA, 944
Mubarak, Hosni, 1025
Mughal Empire, *604-5*. 643
    Akbar and, *616*, 616-17
    consolidation of power by, 617-18, 618m
    decline of, 618-19

firearms used by, 617
Hinduism and, 617-18
horses in, 617
Indian Rebellion and, 823, 830-33, 831m, *832*
Islam and, 617
military revolution and, *616*, 616-17
pirates attacked by, 632
shari'a and, 618
Taj Mahal and, 618, *619*
taxation by, 618
Mulla Sadra (Sadr ad-Din Muhammad Shirazi),
    589, 589-90
multiethnic empires, **790**, 790-92
Mumtaz Mahal, 618
Muscovy, 558, 559m
Muscovy Company, 658
muscular Christianity, 797, *797*
music
    globalization and, 1032-34, *1033*, *1034*
    ukulele, 565
Musket Wars, 564
Muslim League, **954**, *954*
Muslims. *See* Islam and Muslims
Mussolini, Benito, **873**, *873*, 873-74, 895, 905
Myanmar, 953

Nader Shah, 619
NAFTA (North American Free Trade
    Agreement), 997, 1000
Namibia, 803, 992
Nanak, 591
Nanjing Massacre, 896, *896*, 926
Nasser, Gamal Abdel, 951
National Indian Brotherhood (NIB), 1037
nationalism, 673, **784**
    Arab, 791
    Canadian, 787-88, *788*
    civic compared to ethnic, 785
    defining, 784-85
    fascism and, 872
    French, 785-86, *786*
    German, 788-89, *789*
    global impact of, 784
    Global web and, 812-13
    Habsburg Empire and, 790
    imperialism supported by, 794-95
    Japanese, 786-87, *787*
    minority, 792
    multiethnic empires and, 790-92
    Ottoman Empire and, 791
    past influencing, 785
    Russian empire and, *790*, 790-91
    state power from, 789-90
    Ukraine and, 790
National Policy, Canada, **727**
Native Americans. *See* indigenous Americans
Navajo, 555, *910*, 911
navies. *See also* military
    military revolution and, 609, *609*
    piracy and, 631
    in World War I, 858
navigation. *See* oceanic navigation and sailing
Nazi Germany. *See also* Axis; Germany; Hitler,
    Adolf; World War II
    aggression in Europe, to 1939, 896-98, *897*,
        897m
    anti-Jewish propaganda of, *914*, 915
    in Battle of Stalingrad, **902**, *902*
    British defense against, 901
    Czechoslovakia seized by, 897
    defeat and division of, 934
    detractors of, 875-76
    European occupation by, 915
    family size in, 986
    fascism and, *874*, 874-76, *876*, 895
    France invaded by, 901
    Holocaust and, **911**, 918-21, *919*, 920m
    labor unions banned in, 875

Nuremberg Laws and, 876
Operation Barbarossa of, 901–2
Poland invaded by, 897–98
resistance movements against, 915
rise of, 874–75
Soviet non-aggression pact with, 897
White Rose against, 911
Necker, Suzanne, 687
Négritude, 883
Nehru, Jawaharlal, 799, **953**
Nelmes, Sarah, 753
neo-colonialism, 961–63, **962**
neo-Confucianism, **592**, 592–94
neoliberalism, in Latin America, 998
Neolithic Revolution, 710–11
Netherlands. *See also* Dutch East India
    Company
    abolition of slavery and, 763
    Bank of Amsterdam in, *660*, 660–62
    in Cape of Good Hope, 542–43
    colonization by, 552*m*, 553
    commercial revolutions in, 664
    Indonesian occupation by, 956
    spice trade and, 649*m*, 650
    standing armies of, 610
    transatlantic slave trade and, 543–48, *545*,
        546–47*m*
New Caledonia, 806
Newcomen, Thomas, 713
New Culture Movement, 879, 883–84
New England, 530, 555, 557, 683
Newfoundland, 960
New France, 552*m*, 553, 557
new imperialism, **792**
New International Economic Order, 1002
New Jersey, 868
New Mexico, 551, 555, 809
New Spain, 551, 552*m*
Newton, Isaac, 585
New York, 683, 684, 886
New Youth, 879
New Zealand, 846
    disease disasters in, 561
    in Global web, 563–64
    Great Depression and, 871
    Maori in, *563*, 563–64, 812
    music from, 1034
    Musket Wars in, 564
    as settler colony, **801**
    suffragism in, 868–69
    Treaty of Waitangi and, *563*, **564**
Nicaragua, 945, *996*, 996–97
Nicholas II, 862–63
Niebuhr, Reinhold, 870
Niger, 988, *988*
Nigeria, 547–48, 769, 804
    Biafra independence and, 961
    music in, 1033
    oil in, 990
    per capita GDP in, 988, *988*
1918 flu pandemic, **756**, *756*, 756–57
Ninety-Five Theses (Luther), *579*, 580
Nixon, Richard, *945*
Nkrumah, Kwame, **957**, *957*, 957–59, 991
Nobunaga, Oda, **611**, 611–12
No Kum Sok, 931–32
nomads, early period empires and, 630–31, *631*.
        See also horses; immigrants
North Africa, 778. *See also specific countries*
    Barbary pirates in, 632
    Islam in, 538, 539*m*, 805
    Italian imperialism in, 806
    women's per capita income in, 1990–2020,
        973, *973*
    World War II in, 903*m*, 903–4
North America. *See also specific countries*
    Ancestral Pueblo in, 551
    British taxation in, 684–85

British tensions with, 683–85, 685*m*
colonization of, 552*m*, 553
Comanche in, 630–31
falling income in colonial, 647, *647*
family life in, 682
Ghost Dance and, 823–26, *825*
heights of population in colonial, 646
Iroquois in, 550
Lakota Sioux in, 630–31
plantation zone in, **554**
printing press in, 576
revolutions in, 1750–1790, 682–87, 683*m*
transatlantic slave trade and, 543–48, *545*,
    546–47*m*
women's per capita income in, 1990–2020,
    973, *973*
North Atlantic Treaty Organization (NATO),
    938, 1027
North Korea. *See also* Korean War
    defection threats of, 932
    economy in, 975–76
    slavery in, 774
    starvation in, 975
North-West Rebellion, 788
Norway, suffragism in, 869
Notes on the State of Virginia (Jefferson), 760
Nova Scotia, 727
nuclear weapons
    Arctic tests of, 947
    Cold War and, 936–37
    Cuban missile crisis and, **936**
    deterrence and, **936**
    Gorbachev and Reagan treaties on, 948
    Hiroshima and Nagasaki, **905**, *905*, 918
    Manhattan Project and, 909, *909*
    preparation for, 936–37, *937*
Nuremburg, 926
Nuremberg Laws, 876
nutrition. *See* diet and nutrition

Obregón, Álvaro, 841
Oceania. *See also* Australia; Hawaii; New
        Zealand
    Christianity in, 561
    disease disasters in, 560–61
    European voyagers in, 560–61
    in Global web, 560–65
oceanic navies, 609, *609*, 631
oceanic navigation and sailing. *See also*
        European voyagers
    disease disasters and, **536**
    Ming voyages and, 609, *609*
October Revolution. *See* Russian Revolution
        of 1917
Odunlami, Sophie, 804
oil
    in Africa, 990
    Allied control of, 907
    in Arctic, 947, *947*
    Soviet Union and, 948
    United States and, 871, *871*
    Venezuela exports of, 996–97
    World War I and, 870–71
Oliver Wendell Holmes, 815
Olorun, 556
Olympic Games, modern, 1035
Oman, 539, 760
Ontario, 727, 787
*On the Motion of the Heart and Blood in
    Animals* (Harvey), *586*
On the Revolution of the Spheres (Copernicus),
    585
Operation Barbarossa, 901–2
Opium Wars, 828*m*, 828–30, 835
Organization of African Unity, 991
Origin of Species, The (Darwin), 796
Ottawa, 684
Ottoman, 778

Ottoman Empire
    abolition of slavery in, 767–68
    alliance networks joined by, **856**, 857*m*
    Armenian genocide and, 861, *861*
    consolidation of, 621
    Crimean War of 1853–1856 and, 728
    expansion of, 619–21, 620*m*, *621*
    fall of, 866–67
    firearms introduced in, 621
    janissaries and, **621**, 622
    Jews in, 622–23
    military revolution and, 621
    millet system of, **623**
    minority nationalisms in, 792
    nationalism and, 791
    navy of, 609, *609*
    origins of, 619
    power of, 1914, 855–56
    spice trade and, 649*m*, 650
    standing armies of, 610, *610*
    taxation and, 621–23
    World War I and, 854–61, 859*m*, *860*
    Young Turk Revolution in, **843**
"Our Final Awakening" (Chen Duxiu), 879
overfishing, 1011
Owen, Wilfred, 853–54
Oyo, 763

Pacific War, 898–901, 899*m*, 904
Pakistan, *954*, 954–55
Palestine, 867
Palestinians, 1023
Pan-Africanism, **883**, *883*, 883–84, 886
Panama, *996*, 996
Pan-Arabism, 886
Pankhurst, Emmeline, 868, *868*
Pan-Turkism, 886
Paracelsus, 585–86
Paris Agreement, 2016, 1010
Parker, Quanah, 809–10, *810*
Parliament, **680**, 680–81, *681*
partition of Africa, **801**, 801–3, *802*
Pascal, Blaise, 582
Patagonia, 631
patío process, *652*, **653**
Peace of Augsburg, 582, 589
Pearl Harbor attack, 893–94, 898, *898*
peasant uprisings, decolonization and, 963
Pennsylvania, 555, 683, 684
"People Power" revolution, Philippines, 1024,
    1024
People's Will, 862
per capita income. *See* gross domestic product
Pères Blancs, 797
Persia and Persians, 530. *See also* Iran
Peru. *See also* Andes
    dictatorship's fall in, 998
    indentured immigrants in, 773–74
    per capita GDP in, *996*
    pueblos jóvenes in, 995
    Spanish colonization of, 551, 552*m*
    Toledo running, 999
    Túpac Amaru II's revolt in, 696–97, *697*
Peter the Great, 623–24
Philippines, 960
    Axis-occupied, 916, *916*
    cholera in, 756
    "People Power" revolution in, 1024, *1024*
    printing press in, 576
    United States imperialism in, 807
pirates and piracy, **631**
    Barbary, 632, *632*
    in Caribbean, 631–32
    firearm origins through, 611
    in Global web, 631
    in Indian Ocean world, 632
    oceanic navies and, 631
    Zheng family, 605–6

Pires, Tomé, 649
Pitt, William, 762, 763
Piyãko, Benki, 1037, 1038
Plains Indians, 557
plague, 530
plantations. *See* sugar plantations
plantation zone, **554**
Plato, 578
Ploetz, Alfred, 815
Plymouth Rock, 550
Poland
   commercial revolutions in, 664
   military revolution resisted by, 629
   nationalism in Russian empire, 790, *790*
   Nazi invasion of, 897–98
   Nazi resistance movements in, 915
   re-creation of, 865–66
   Solidarity in, **949**
   Soviet invasion of, 898
   uprising in, 1956, 940
   Warsaw ghetto uprising in, *919*, 920–21
political decentralization, **699**, 699–701
political Islam, 1021–22, *1022*
politics
   African fragmented, 991–93
   Bismarck and German labor, 724–25
   climate change and, 1009–10
   global scale of modern, 854
   Global web and, 1020–27
   international institutions and, 1020–21
   Kongo women in, 679
   Latin America, 997–99
   political revolutions, 673
   religion and, from 1970s on, 1021–24
   slave uprisings and, 764–65, *765*
pollution. *See also* climate change; environment
   British Industrial Revolution and, 720–21, *721*
   CO_2 concentrations and, *1009*, 1009–12, *1011m, 1012*
   in East Asia, 985
   indigenous peoples and, 1036–37
polo, 1034
Pontiac's War, **684**
population
   African growth of, 644, 988–89
   of Allies compared to Axis, 906, *907*
   in Americas, 644
   of China, 200–1400 CE, 644
   early modern period empires, distribution of, *607*, 608
   emerging diseases and, 1014–17
   fertility declines and, 1015
   global, 1650–1950, 752, *752*
   global, 1950–2023, 1013, *1013*
   heights of, 645–47, *646*
   of indigenous Americans, 806
   of indigenous peoples, 1036
   international migrants and, 1018–20, **1019**, *1019m, 1020*
   Japan's aging, 978
   Latin American trends in, 994–96
   in Mexico, 1876–1910, 840
   of Ming dynasty, 614
   public health and, *1013*, 1013–14
   surge, **643**, 643–45, *644*
   trends since 1950, 1013–20
   urbanization in overdrive and, 1018, *1018*
Porcupine, 826
Porfiriato, **839**, 839–40
Portugal
   in Angola, 540–42, 944
   Brazilian independence from, 699
   colonization by, 552*m*, 553
   cotton trade and, 651, 651*m*
   firearm origins in, 611
   Kongo and, 540–42, 677–79, *678*
   in Mozambique, 542
   slavery and, 541–43

spice trade and, 649*m*, 649–50
sugar plantations and, 656*m*, 657
Positive Action, 957
Potosí, **554**, 554–55, *653*, 653–54
Prague Spring, **941**, *941*
Price, Joseph, 564
Prince, Mary, 567
Princip, Gavrilo, 856
printing press, **575**, 575–77, *576*, 623
propaganda
   for abolition of slavery, *765*
   Cold War, *937*, 937–38
   kamishibai and Japanese, 912
   Nazi anti-Jewish, *914*, 915
Protestantism and Protestants, **581**
   creed of, 582
   evangelical, 1023
   in Ireland, 681, *681*
   Luther and, *579*, 579–82
   missionaries in Africa, *804*, 804–5
   Ninety-Five Theses and, *579*, 580
   spread of, 581*m*, 582
   witch hunts and, **583**, *583*
Prussia, 663, 664
pseudoscientific racism, 796–97
Psy, 1034
Ptolemy, 584
pueblos jóvenes, in Peru, 995
Puerto Rico, 543, 767
Pugachev, Emelian, 771–72, *772*
Putin, Vladimir, 1027

al-Qaeda, **1022**, *1022*, 1027
Qajar dynasty, 843
Qianlong Emperor, 616, *616*
Qin dynasty, foreign incursions against, 828, 828*m, 829*
Qing dynasty, **613**
   Chinese Revolution and, 823, 834–39, 836*m*
   commercial revolution in, 663
   consolidation of power by, 613–14
   economy of, 828
   empire of, 614*m*
   fall of, 839
   food distribution of, 752
   Kangxi Emperor in, 615, *615*
   military revolution and, *615*, 615–16
   Mongols attacked by, 615–16
   Qianlong Emperor in, 616, *616*
   smallpox inoculation in, 753
   Sun Yatsen and, *838*, 838–39
   Taiping Rebellion against, *820–21*, 823, 828*m*, 828–30, *830*
   warfare of, 614–15
   White Lotus Rebellion against, 828
Quakers, **761**, *761*, 761–62
Quebec, 552*m*, 553, 555, 727, 787, 788
quinine, 793–94

race
   in Americas, 556
   in Haiti, 556, 693
   Hitler's racism, 921
   Japan and, 895–96
   in Latin America, 994
   pseudoscientific racism, 796–97
   slavery and, 757
   in Spanish America, 695, *696*
   voting rights and, 738
   World War II and, *914*, 914–15
   Yamato race theory, **786**
Radio Free Europe, 937
Radischev, Aleksandr, 771
Rahaman ibn Sori, Abdul, *543*
railways, **717**
   in Africa, 988, 989*m*
   British Industrial Revolution and, 717–18, *718*
   in Japan, 732

Metallic webs and, 730, 730–31*m*
Trans-Siberian Railway, **728**, *728*
Rape of Nanking, 926
rap music, 1034
Rastafarian religion, 1033
Reagan, Ronald, 948, 1002, 1028
rebellions, 827. *See also* Atlantic revolutions; millenarian movements; slave uprisings
   Boxer Rebellion, 837, *837*
   as global and local, 833–34
   Indian Rebellion, 823, 830–33, 831*m*, *832*
   North-West Rebellion in, 788
   Pugachev's, 771–72, *772*
   Taiping Rebellion, *820–21*, 823, 828*m*, 828–30, **830**, *830*
   White Lotus Rebellion, 828
Red Guards, Chinese, 981
Red Square, 966
refugees, World War II, 921, 923
reggae, 1033
religion. *See also specific religions*
   in Americas, 556
   European geography by, 1555–1650, 581*m*
   Jacobins and, 690
   in Japan, 573–74
   in Latin America, 994
   Mormons, 824–26, 868
   politics and, from 1970s on, 1021–24
   Rastafarian, 1033
   repression and persecution of, 595–96
   schisms in, 582–83
   Scientific Revolution and, 584
   Shinto, 574, 786
   in Siberia, 560
Renaissance, *577*, 577–78, **578**
Réunion, 760
Revolts in, 704
Revolution of 1905, Russia, 736–37, 843
Rhodes, Cecil, 796
Ricardo, David, 717
Riefenstahl, Leni, 875, *876*
Riel, Louis, 788
Riffaiyya, 588
Righteous and Harmonious Fists, 837
Rihanna, 1034
rising merchant classes, **679**
Roberts, Issachar, 829
Robespierre, Maximilien, 690–91
Robin John, Ancona, 547
Robin John, Ephraim, 547
Roehampton Estate, destruction of, *672*, *746–47*
Roma, in Holocaust, 921
Romania, 791
Rommel, Erwin, 910
Roosevelt, Eleanor, 922
Roosevelt, Franklin, 898, 905–6, 926
Roosevelt, Theodore, 797
Rowbotham, Titus, 718
Royal Society, 597
rubber, Industrial Revolution and, 734
Russell, John, 773
Russia, 1040. *See also* Soviet Union
   abolition of serfdom in, 771*m*, 772–73
   Alexander II in, 771–72, 862
   in alliance networks, **856**, 857*m*
   Bolsheviks and, 863–64, 876
   Bonaparte's campaign in, *691*, 691–92
   Boxer Rebellion and, 837
   cholera in, 755–56
   Civil War in, 1918–1921, 864
   coal and Industrial Revolution in, *733*
   commercial revolution in, 664–65
   Cossacks and, 558–60
   Crimean War of 1853–1856 and, 728, 771
   emancipation for serfs in, 772–73 *780*
   Ethiopia and, 811–12
   family size in, 986

heights of population in, 645
imperial consolidation in, 623–24
Industrial Revolution in, 727–28
iron and Industrial Revolution in, *733*
Islam and land empire of, 808
Ivan IV in, 558, 623
labor activism in, 737, *737*
land empire of, 807–8, 808*m*
Lenin leading, 858–59, 863–64, *864*
minority nationalisms in, 792
nationalism and empire of, *790*, 790–91
People's Will in, 862
Peter the Great in, 623–24
power of, 1914, 855
printing press in, 623
Pugachev's rebellion in, 771–72, *772*
Revolution of 1905 in, 736–37, 843
Russo-Japanese War and, 806, *807*, 862
serfs in, 664, 757–58, 760, 770–72
Siberia conquered by, 559*m*, 559–60, *560*,
     623, 808
St. Petersburg in, 624, *624*
Trans-Siberian Railway and, **728**, *728*
Treaty of Brest-Litovsk and, 858–59
tsars in, 623–24
Ukraine conquest by, 623
Ukraine invaded by, 2022, 1027
Witte and, **728**
World War I and, 854–61, 859*m*, *860*
Russian Orthodox Church, 623, 791
Russian Revolution of 1917, **862**, *863*
     Bolsheviks and, 863–64
     grievances of, 862
     Lenin and, 863–64, *864*
     Treaty of Brest-Litovsk and, 858–59
     World War I and, 862–63
Russo-Japanese War, 806, *807*, 862
Rwanda, 991, 1021
Rylands, John, 720

Saadians, **628**, 628–29
Sadr ad-Din Muhammad Shirazi (Mulla Sadra),
     589, 589–90
Safavids, **588**, 588–90, 589*m*, 619, 628
Sahel
     environment of, 990
     slavery and, 768
Sahib, Nana, 832
sailing. *See* oceanic navigation and sailing
Saint-Domingue. *See also* Haiti
     abolition of slavery in, 764
     Haitian Revolution and, 693*m*, 693–95, *695*
     race in, 556, 693
     slavery in, 693
     slave uprising in, 658
     sugar and coffee plantations in, 693
     Toussaint L'Ouverture and, *694*, 694–95,
          764
Saint-Just, 690–91
salons, 687, *687*
Samoa, 806
samurai, 612, *613*
Sander Levin, 1002
sanitation reform, 754–55, *755*
Sankara, Thomas, 962
Sargent, John Singer, *852–53*
SARS, 1014
Sati al-Husri, 886
satyagraha (truth force), 881–82
Saudi Arabia, 1019
schism, 578, 582–83
science
     Jews and, 909
     mathematics and, 586
     Scientific Revolution, 583–87
     technology and, 586
     women and, *596*, 597
     in World War II, 909–11

Scientific Revolution, **583**
     astronomy, heliocentric system and, 584–85,
          585
     chemistry and, 585–86
     hostility towards, 595
     institutions and connections of, 586–87
     intellectual protectionism and, 584
     medicine and, 586, *586*
     principles of, 583
     religion and, 584
     spread of, 583–84
Scotland, 680, 681. *See also* Britain
scribes, 577. *See also* writing
sea level rise, 1011, 1011*m*
secondary empires, 808–12
Second Congo War, **991**, 1027
Second Continental Congress, 685
Selassie, Haile, 1033
self-determination, **866**
Seneca Falls Convention, 868
Senegal, 548, 760
Senghor, Léopold, 883
September 11th terrorist attacks, 1022
Serbia, 791, 856
serfs and serfdom, **664**, *770*
     decline of, 748–49
     in eastern Europe, 770
     emancipation for, 772–73 *780*
     Enlightenment and, 770
     expansion of, 758–60
     French Revolution and, 770
     in Russia, 664, 757–58, 760, 770–72
     Russian abolition of, 771*m*, 772–73
settlement houses, **737**, *738*
settler colony, **801**
Seven Years' War, 683
Shakira, 1033–34, *1034*
shari'a, 618
Sharpe, Samuel, 765, *765*
Sheppard, Kate, 868, *868*, 922
Shi'a Islam. *See also* Islam
     origins of, **587**
     Safavids in Iran and, 588–90, 589*m*, 619, 628
Shibusawa, Eiichi, **729**
Shintaro Ishihara, 1002
Shinto, 574, 786
shipping, containerization and, 974–76, *976*
ships. *See also* oceanic navigation and sailing
     of Dutch East India Company, 659
     for navies, 609, *609*
     steam, 718, 730, 730–31*m*, 792–93, *793*
Siberia. *See also* Russia
     Cossacks and, 558–60
     fur trade from, 558, *558*
     Global web absorbing, 557–60
     religion in, 560
     Russian conquest of, 559*m*, 559–60, *560*,
          623, 808
     Trans-Siberian Railway and, **728**, *728*
Sierra Leone, 763
signares, 547
Sikh, 600
Sikhism, **590**, 590–92, *591, 592*, 600
silver, **652**
     Americas and mining of, *554*, 554–55
     China and, 653*m*, 654–55
     Habsburg Empire and, 624
     India and, 653*m*, 655
     Japan and, *653*, 653–54
     patío process for, *652*, **653**
     Spain and, *653*, 653–54, *654*
     trade, 652–55, 653*m*
Sinclair, John, 709–10
Singapore, 982
Singh, Ranjit, 812
Sino-Japanese War, 1894–1895, 732
Sirota, Beate, 976
Slater, Samuel, 725

slave-and-sugar plantations, **657**, 657–58
slavery, 567. *See also* abolition of slavery;
     transatlantic slave trade
     in Africa, 547–48, 768–69
     American Revolution and, 687
     in Americas, 550, *550*, 757–59
     in Angola and Kongo, 541–42
     in China, 757
     Christianity and, 757, 761
     decline of, 748–49
     defenders of, *749*
     Dutch East India Company and, 542
     in East Africa, 760
     escaped slaves in Americas, 557
     expansion of, 758–60
     fugitives from, *761*
     history of, 757
     Industrial Revolution and, 734
     Islam and, 548, 757, 767
     in Kongo, 678
     in Korea, 757–58
     Middle Passage and, **544**, *544*
     morality and, 760–61
     in North Korea, 774
     Portugal and, 541–43
     Quakers opposing, *761*, 761–62
     race and, 757
     Sahel and, 768
     in Saint-Domingue, 693
     in Southeast Asia, 759–60
     sugar plantations and, 543, *543*, 655, 657–58
     in United States, 758–59, 763
     in West Africa, 760
Slavery Abolition Act, **766**
slave uprisings
     in Cuba, 763
     in Jamaica, *672*, *746–47*, 765, *765*
     political consequences of, 764–65, *765*
     from 1750–1950, 758–59*m*
Slim, Carlos, 1031, 1032
smallpox, 530, 542, 750, *750*, 778
smallpox inoculation, **753**, *753*, 753–54
smallpox vaccination, **753**, 753–54
Smith, Adam, 717, 761–62
Snapchat, 1026
soccer, 1034–35, *1035*
social contracts, Industrial Revolution and,
     736–39
social Darwinism, **796**, 796–97
socialists, **738**
social media, 1025–27, *1026*
soft power, **993**
Sokoto, 539*m*, 540
Solidarity, **949**
Somalia, 806
Song dynasty, 663
Songhai Empire, 539, 539*m*
Sons of Africa, **762**
South Africa
     apartheid in, **992**
     in Boer War, 843, *843*
     Gandhi in, 882
     Mandela and, 992
     missionaries in, *804*, 805
     music in, 1033
     per capita GDP in, *988*
     Xhosa people in, 821–22
South America. *See also* Andes
     abolition of slavery in, 699
     nomads in, 631
     patío process for silver in, *652*, **653**
     plantation zone in, **554**
     revolutions in, 698–99
     Spanish colonization of, 551, 552*m*
     transatlantic slave trade and, 543–48, *545*,
          546–47*m*
South Asia. *See* India and South Asia
South Carolina, 554

Southeast Asia. *See also specific countries*
  decolonization in, 952*m*, 955–56
  European imperialism in, 805–6
  military revolution response in, 628
  slavery in, 759–60
  spice trade and, 648–49, 649*m*
South Korea. *See also* Korea; Korean War
  economic miracle in, 978–79
  industrial policy in, 978–79
  land reform in, **978**
  music from, 1034
  per capita GDP in, *978*
  pollution in, 985
  social change in, 979
  United States support for, 978–79
Southwest Asia. *See also specific countries*
  commercial revolutions in, 665
  population surge in, 644
Soviet-Afghan War, 944–45
Soviet Union (USSR). *See also* Allies; Cold War;
    Russia
  Afghanistan war with, 944–45
  African National Congress supported by, 992
  in Battle of Stalingrad, **902**, *902*
  birth of, 864
  Chernobyl nuclear disaster and, 948–49
  Chinese rift with, 947–48
  collectivization of agriculture in, 877–78
  communism in, 876–78, *877*, *878*
  decline and collapse of, 947–49
  eastern Europe and security of, 933–34
  economy of, 948–49
  education in, 878
  Gorbachev's gambles in, 948–49
  Great Depression and, 871
  gulags in, 878, *878*
  Latin America and, *945*, 945–46
  Nazi non-aggression pact with, 897
  oil and, 948
  Operation Barbarossa against, 901–2
  Poland invaded by, 898
  propaganda of, 937
  race and, 914–15
  starvation in, 923
  suffrage and, 869
  Warsaw Pact and, 938, 941
  World War II manufacturing in, 908
  World War II mobilization in, 913, *913*
Spain
  Americas, diseases arriving from, 549
  Bonaparte in, 698
  Bourbon Reforms and, 696–98
  colonization by, 551, 552*m*
  conquistadores from, 551
  fascism in, 873
  Habsburg Empire inheriting, 624
  silver trade and, *653*, 653–54, *654*
  Spanish America revolutions, 1765–1825,
      695–99, *696*, 697*m*
  Spanish America trade tensions and, 697–98
  transatlantic slave trade and, 543–48, *545*,
      546–47*m*
  Túpac Amaru II's revolt against, 696–97, *697*
Spanish America revolutions, 1765–1825,
    695–99, *696*, 697*m*
spice trade, 648, 648–50, **649**, 649*m*
sports, 1034–35, *1035*
Spotify, 1034
spread of democracy, **1024**
Sri Lanka, 953, 955
Stalin, Josef, **877**, 966
  Allied cooperation and, 905–6
  collectivization of agriculture by, 877–78
  domestic admiration of, 913
  economic strategies of, 935
  gulags and, 878
  Hitler surprising, 902
  on maltreatment of women, 916

political purge of, 901–2
  reforms and innovations of, 877–78
  territorial expansion of, 933–34
Stalinism, 901–2
standing armies, 610, 610–11
Stanton, Elizabeth Cady, 868
Steam Engine and Industrial Revolution, 846
steam engines, **713**, *713*, 718, 722, 730, 730–31*m*,
    735, 792–93, *793*
steamship, 846
steel, 726, 732, *732*
stock exchanges, 658, *658*
Stolypin, Pyotr, 862
Stowe, Harriet Beecher, 766
St. Petersburg, 624, *624*
Sudan, 539, 991, 1027
Suez Canal, 718, 834, *834*, 951
Suez Crisis, 951
suffragism, **867**
  by country, *869*
  early, 868–69
  prewar movements, 867–68
  resistance to, 869
  World War I and, 869–70
Sufi movement, 587–88, *588*
sugar plantations
  global economy and, *655*, 655–58, 656*m*
  in plantation zone, **554**
  in Saint-Domingue, 693
  slavery and, 543, *543*, 655, 657–58
  spread of, 656*m*, 656–57
Sukarno, **955**, *955*, 955–56
Suleiman, 620–21
Sullivan, John, 799
Sumatra, 650
Sunni Ali, 539
Sun Yatsen, **838**, *838*, 838–39
Suriname, 767
Swahili coast, 538–40, 539*m*
Switzerland, 583. *See also* Habsburg Empire
Sy, Malik, 805
Syphilis, 530
Syria, civil war in, 1027

Tacky's War, **657**, 657–58
Tagawa Matsu, 605
Tahmasp, 588
Taíno, **549**
Taiping Rebellion, *820–21*, 823, 828*m*, 828–30,
    830, *830*
Taiwan
  economic miracle in, 974, 976
  indigenous peoples in, 1038
  Japanese imperialism in, 806–7
  pollution in, 985
  Zhengs conquering, 606
Taj Mahal, 618, *619*
Taliban, 1022, 1027
Tanganyika, 783
Tanzania, 783, 861, *987*, *988*
tariffs, protectionist, 715, 725
Tasman, Abel, 535, 563
Tasmania and Tasmanians, 535–36
Tatars, 558
taxation
  British taxes on colonies, 684–85
  military revolution and, *608*, 608–9, 616
  by Mughal Empire, 618
  Ottoman Empire and, 621–23
  tax farming, 608, 621, 622
technology
  imperialism and, 792–94, *793*
  Industrial Revolution and changes in, 715–16,
      716
  information, **1029**, *1029*
  microscopes, 575
  military, 793, *793*
  mining, *587*

moveable type, 575–76, *576*
  printing press and, 575–77, *576*, 623
  science and, 586
  Scientific Revolution and, 583–87
  telescopes, 575
Tehuelche, 631
Te Kanawa, Kiri, 1034
telegraph, 730, 730–31*m*, 793
telescopes, 575
television, sports and, 1035
Tenochtitlán, 549, *549*
Tewodros II, 810
Texas, Comanche, 809–10, 810*m*
textiles, **712**
  in Industrial Revolution, 712
  Industrial Revolution and changes in, 715, *716*
  in Japan, 729
Thailand, 767, 806
  military revolution response in, 628
Thatcher, Margaret, 1028
third pulse of decolonization, **952**
Thirteenth Amendment, **767**
Thirty Years' War, 582
Thoreau, Henry David, 881
Tiananmen Square protests and massacre, 983,
    983
TikTok, 1026
Timbuktu, 590, *590*
Tokugawa shogunate, **612**, 612*m*, 612–13, *613*
Toland, John, 661
Toledo, Alejandro, 999
Tolstoy, Leo, 881
Toungoo dynasty, 628
Toussaint L'Ouverture, **694**, *694*, 694–95, 764
trade, 676. *See also specific goods*
  British imperialism in India and, 799
  commercial revolutions and, 662–65
  cotton, *648*, **650**, 650–52, *652*
  free, **1028**
  global economy and, 647–55
  in Indian Ocean world, 648
  in Kongo, 541
  NAFTA and, 997, 1000
  silver, 652–55, 653*m*
  Spanish America tensions over, 697–98
  spice, *648*, 648–50, 649*m*
transatlantic slave trade, 567. *See also* slavery
  abolition of, 760–64
  African consequences of, 547–48
  business scope of, *545*, 545–47
  cotton trade and, 651, 651*m*
  dimensions of, 543–45
  Middle Passage and, **544**, *544*
  routes of, 546–47*m*
  signares and, *547*
transoceanic economies, in Americas, 553–55
transportation infrastructure, in Industrial
    Revolution, 714–15, *715*
Trans-Siberian Railway, **728**, *728*
Treaty of Amasya, 589
Treaty of Brest-Litovsk, 858–59
Treaty of Versailles, 864–66, **865**, 879–80
Treaty of Waitangi, *563*, **564**
trench warfare, 858, *858*
Trinidad, 774, 960
Triumph of the Will, 876
Trotsky, Leon, 864
Trucanini, 535–36, *537*
Truman Doctrine, **938**, 966
Truman, Harry, 934, 938
Truman, Harry S., 966
truth force (*satyagraha*), 881–82
tsars, **623**, 623–24
Tumblr, 1026
Tunisia, 806
  Arab Spring in, 1026
  in World War II, 904
Tupac Amaru, 704

Túpac Amaru II, 551, **696**, 696–97, *697*
Turkey. *See also* Ottoman Empire
  Atatürk Reforms and, 867, 1022
  creation of, 950
  migrant workers in, 1020, *1020*
  secularization of, 866–67, *867*
Tuskegee Airmen, *913*
Twitter, 1026
typhoid, 750, 755

Ukraine
  Chernobyl nuclear disaster and, 948–49
  Cossacks and, 558–60
  nationalism and, 790
  Ottoman Empire in, 622
  Russian conquest of, 623
  Russian invasion of, 2022, 1027
  in World War II, 902
ukulele, 565
Uncle Tom's Cabin (Stowe), 766
UNITA, 944
United Gold Coast Convention (UGCC), 957
United Nations (UN), 922, 934, 942, 1002, 1020–21, 1037, 1040
United Negro Improvement Association, 886
United States, 1002. *See also* Allies; Cold War; indigenous Americans
  abolition of slavery in, 766–67
  Alaska purchased by, 788, 834
  American Revolution and, *685*, 685–87
  Ancestral Pueblo in, 551
  automobile industry in, 870, 907–8
  Bill of Rights of, 686
  Canadian fears of invasion by, 788
  civic nationalism in, 785
  Civil War in, 766–67, 833–34
  coal and Industrial Revolution in, 726, *733*
  colonization of, 552*m*, 553
  Comanche Empire in, 809–10, 810*m*
  Constitution of, 686
  containerization and, 975
  cotton and Industrial Revolution in, 726, *726*
  Dawes Act in, 823
  Declaration of Independence of, 685, *685*
  dictators propped up by, 1024
  economies of scale and, 726–27
  Emancipation Proclamation and, 767
  evangelical Christians in, 1023
  falling income in colonial, 647, *647*
  family size in, 986
  Great Depression and, *871*, 871–72
  Great Recession and, 1030–31
  heights of population in colonial, 646
  Hiroshima and Nagasaki bombings and, **905**, *905*, 918
  imperialism of, 806–7
  income inequality in, 1031–32
  Industrial Revolution in, 725–27
  iron and Industrial Revolution in, 726, *733*
  Iroquois in, 550
  Japanese internment in, 914, *914*
  Japan occupied by, 976–77
  Korean War and, 942
  labor activism in, 737, *737*
  labor alliances in, 737
  Latin America and, *945*, 945–46
  Lend-Lease and, 906
  Manhattan Project and, 909, *909*
  Marshall Plan and, 938
  Mexican-American War and, 810
  Monroe Doctrine in, 807
  music from, 1032–33
  NAFTA and, 997, 1000
  oil and, 871, *871*
  in Pacific War, 900–901
  Pan-Africanism and, *883*, 883–84
  Pearl Harbor attack and, 893–94, 898, *898*
  pirates attacked by, 632

post-World War I rise of, 870–71
power of, 1914, 855
power of, post-World War II, 923
propaganda of, 937
protectionist tariffs and, 725
security concerns of, 934
September 11th terrorist attacks in, 1022
settlement houses in, **737**, *738*
slavery in, 758–59, 763
smallpox inoculation in, 753
South Korea supported by, 978–79
steel in, 726
suffragism in, 868–69
Thirteenth Amendment in, **767**
Truman Doctrine in, **938**
Vietnam War and, **943**, *943*
voting rights in, 738
World War I and, 854–61, 859*m*, *860*
World War II manufacturing in, 907–8, *908*
World War II mobilization in, *913*, 913–14
World War II refugees in, 923
Wounded Knee massacre in, 825
Universal Declaration of Human Rights, 922
university of war, **627**
urbanization
  heights of population and, 646
  Industrial Revolution and, 714
  in Latin America, 994–95, *995*
  in overdrive, 1018, *1018*
Utah, 868
Utopia (More), 757

Venezuela, 697, 698, *698*
  migrants from, *995*, 995–96
  oil exports of, 996–97
Vichy France, 919–20
Vietnam
  Catholic Church in, 805–6
  Dien Bien Phu, 951
  French imperialism in, 805–6
  military revolution response in, 628
Vietnam War, **943**, *943*
Villa, Pancho, 841
Virginia, 683, 684
Vital Revolution, **749**
  biological old regime preceding, 749–52
  countertrends in, 755–57
  declining mortality in, *752*, 752–53
  global health improvements in, 752–55
  impact of, 756–57
  life expectancy and, 748
  sanitation reform and, 754–55, *755*
  smallpox control during, *753*, 753–54
Vodun, 556
Volga, 623
Voltaire, 687, 688
von Liebig, Justus, 720
Vora, Virji, 641–42
voting rights, 738, 867–70, *868, 869, 870*
Vryzakis, Theodoros, *791*

Wales, 680. *See also* Britain
Wallenberg, Raoul, 920
Wang Yangming, **592**, 592–94, 600
war and warfare. *See also* military; military revolution; World War I; World War II
  in Americas, 550
  costs of, 608, *627*
  Ireland and sectarian, 681, *681*
  of Qing dynasty, 614–15
  taxation and, *608*, 608–9, 616
  trench, 858, *858*
  in twenty-first century, 1027
  violence of modern, 854
war crimes, in World War II, 917–18, 921
Ward, Mary Augusta, 869
war elephants, 617
War of 1812, 725

Warsaw ghetto uprising, *919*, 920–21
Warsaw Pact, 938, 941
Washington, George, 685–86
Watt, James, **713**, *713*
Wealth of Nations, The (Smith), 761–62
Webb, Beatrice and Sidney, 737
webs, Metallic, 730, 730–31*m*. *See also* Global web
Wedgwood, Josiah, *762*
Weimar Republic, 866
West Africa
  Christianity in, *540*, 540–43
  demanding freedom in, 769
  Islam in, 538–40, 539*m*, 805
  slavery in, 760
  transatlantic slave trade and, 543–48, *545*, 546–47*m*
  writing in, *590*
West Bank, 1023
White Lotus Rebellion, 828
"White Man's Burden, The" (Kipling), 796, *796*
White Rose, 911
white supremacist regimes, in Africa, 991–92
Wilberforce, William, 762, 763, 765–66
Wilhelm, Leopold, *625*
Wilhelm II, Kaiser, 866
Wilson, Woodrow, 865–66
Wissmann, Hermann von, 783–84
witch hunts, **583**, *583*
Witte, Sergei, **728**, 834
women. *See also* gender
  Africa, education and, 990, *990*
  American Revolution and, 686
  Atlantic revolutions and, 702
  comfort, **916**
  East Asia and working, *970–71*
  education and, 597
  Green Belt Movement and rights of, 1007–8
  Industrial Revolution and, 738–39, *739*
  in Kongo politics, 679
  in labor, 738–39, *739*
  in Latin American politics, 999
  in Olympic Games, 1035
  per capita income of, 1990–2020, 973, *973*
  science and, *596*, 597
  as *signares*, 547
  South Korean social change and, 979
  suffragism and, 867–70, *868, 869, 870*
  witch hunts and, **583**, *583*
  in World Cup soccer, 1034–35, *1035*
  World War I and, 861, *861*
  World War II and maltreatment of, 916
  World War II service of, 913, *913*
  as World War II workers, 908, *908*
Women's Battalion of Death, 861
Wordsworth, William, 709–10
working class, **719**, 719–20, 742
  labor activism and, 737, *737*
  voting rights and, 738
World Bank, 935, 998, 1021
World Cup soccer, 1034–35, *1035*
World Trade Organization (WTO), 984
World War I, 851, *852–53*, **854**
  alliance networks and, **856**, 857*m*
  casualties of, *859*, 859–60
  course of, 857–60, 859*m*
  "Dulce et Decorum Est" on, 853–54
  Great powers heading into, 854–56
  legacies of, 866
  navies in, 858
  1918 flu pandemic and end of, 756
  oil and, 870–71
  origins of, 856
  partitions following, 864–67, 865*m*
  Russian Revolution of 1917 and, 862–63
  suffragism and, 869–70
  Treaty of Versailles and, 864–66, 879–80
  trench warfare in, 858, *858*

World War I (*continued*)
  United States' rise following, 870–71
  weaponry and munitions in, 857–58, *858*
  women and, 861, *861*
World War II, 851, **894**. *See also* Allies; Axis
  adjustments following, 922–23
  aftermath of, 921–23
  Axis advances in Europe in, 901–4, 903*m*
  Battle of El Alamein in, *892–93*
  in Battle of Stalingrad, **902**, *902*
  bombing of cities in, 918
  casualties in, 917, *917*
  in China, 899–900, 915–16
  codebreaking in, *910*, 910–11
  course of, 898–905
  D-Day in, 904, *904*
  economies of scale in, 906–9
  final years of, 1943–1945, 904–5
  Hiroshima and Nagasaki bombings and, **905**, *905*
  Holocaust and, **911**, 918–21, *919*, 920*m*
  home fronts during, 911–15
  human rights and, 921–22
  in Italy, 903*m*, 904, 912–13
  Japanese internment in, 914, *914*
  Lend-Lease and, 906
  maltreatment of women in, 916
  military occupations in, 915–16
  in North Africa, 903*m*, 903–4
  Operation Barbarossa in, 901–2
  origins of, 894–98
  Pacific War in, 898–901, 899*m*, 904
  Pearl Harbor attack and, 893–94, 898, *898*
  prisoners in, 917–18, *918*
  race and, *914*, 914–15
  refugees in, 921, 923
  resistance movements in, 915–16
  science in, 909–11
  Ukraine in, 902
  war crimes in, 917–18, 921
  women as workers in, 908, *908*
  women serving in, 913, *913*
Wounded Knee massacre, 825
Wovoka's prophecy, 825
writing. *See also* education
  printing press and, 575–77, *576*, 623
  in West Africa, *590*
Wycliffe, John, 579
Wyoming, 868

Xavier, Francis, 573–74, 594
Xhosa people, 821–22

Yakut, 559
Yalta Conference, **934**
Yamanobe, Takeo, 729

Yamato race theory, **786**
Yemen, 676, 1027
Yermak, **558**
Yoruba, 556, 763
Young Turk Revolution, **843**
YouTube, 1026, 1034
Yowahwah, 769
Yuan dynasty, 643
Yuan Shikai, 839
Yugoslavia, 866, 915
Yukagir, 559
Yung Wing, 835

zaibatsu, 977
Zambia, *988*, 993
Zanzibar, 760, *760*
Zapata, Emiliano, 841
Zelensky, Volodymyr, 1027
Zeng Guofan, 830
Zheng Chenggong (Koxinga or Coxinga), 605–6, 614
Zheng Zhilong, 605–6
Zhou Enlai, 941
Zimbabwe, 803, 992
Zionist churches, 805
Zionist movement, 867
Ziya Gokalp, 886
Zwingli, Ulrich, 580

WORLD POLITICAL MAP

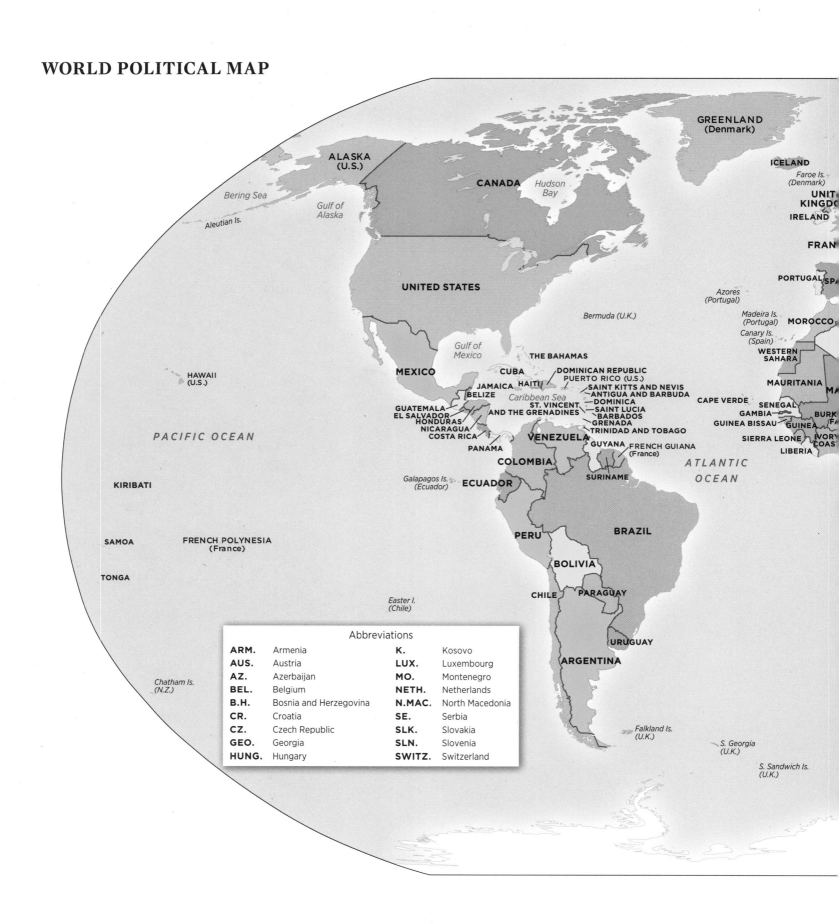

GREENLAND
(Denmark)

ALASKA
(U.S.)

ICELAND

Faroe Is.
(Denmark)

Bering Sea

CANADA

Hudson
Bay

UNIT
KINGDO

IRELAND

Gulf of
Alaska

Aleutian Is.

FRAN

PORTUGAL SPA

Azores
(Portugal)

UNITED STATES

Bermuda (U.K.)

Madeira Is.
(Portugal)

MOROCCO

Canary Is.
(Spain)

Gulf of
Mexico

THE BAHAMAS

WESTERN
SAHARA

HAWAII
(U.S.)

MEXICO

CUBA

DOMINICAN REPUBLIC
PUERTO RICO (U.S.)

MAURITANIA

JAMAICA HAITI
BELIZE

SAINT KITTS AND NEVIS
ANTIGUA AND BARBUDA
DOMINICA

CAPE VERDE

SENEGAL

Caribbean Sea

PACIFIC OCEAN

GUATEMALA
EL SALVADOR
HONDURAS
NICARAGUA
COSTA RICA

ST. VINCENT
AND THE GRENADINES

SAINT LUCIA
BARBADOS
GRENADA
TRINIDAD AND TOBAGO

GAMBIA
GUINEA BISSAU

BURK
FA
GUINEA

SIERRA LEONE

IVOR
COAS

PANAMA

VENEZUELA

GUYANA

FRENCH GUIANA
(France)

ATLANTIC

LIBERIA

COLOMBIA

SURINAME

OCEAN

KIRIBATI

Galapagos Is.
(Ecuador)

ECUADOR

SAMOA

FRENCH POLYNESIA
(France)

PERU

BRAZIL

TONGA

BOLIVIA

CHILE

PARAGUAY

Easter I.
(Chile)

URUGUAY

Chatham Is.
(N.Z.)

ARGENTINA

Abbreviations

ARM.	Armenia	**K.**	Kosovo
AUS.	Austria	**LUX.**	Luxembourg
AZ.	Azerbaijan	**MO.**	Montenegro
BEL.	Belgium	**NETH.**	Netherlands
B.H.	Bosnia and Herzegovina	**N.MAC.**	North Macedonia
CR.	Croatia	**SE.**	Serbia
CZ.	Czech Republic	**SLK.**	Slovakia
GEO.	Georgia	**SLN.**	Slovenia
HUNG.	Hungary	**SWITZ.**	Switzerland

Falkland Is.
(U.K.)

S. Georgia
(U.K.)

S. Sandwich Is.
(U.K.)

ARCTIC OCEAN

NORWAY
SWEDEN
FINLAND
DENMARK
TH.
ESTONIA
LATVIA
LITHUANIA
GERMANY
POLAND BELARUS
CZ. SLK
AUS. HUNG.
WITZ. CR.
SLN. B.H. SE.
ITALY ROMANIA
MO.
K.
N. MAC.
ALBANIA GREECE
MALTA
TUNISIA

RUSSIA

Baltic Sea

Bering Sea

Sakhalin

UKRAINE
MOLDOVA

KAZAKHSTAN

MONGOLIA

BULGARIA GEO.
ARM.
AZ.
Black Sea
Caspian Sea
TURKEY
CYPRUS
SYRIA
LEBANON
ISRAEL
JORDAN
Mediterranean
Sea

UZBEKISTAN
TURKMENISTAN

KYRGYZSTAN
TAJIKISTAN

N. KOREA
S. KOREA
JAPAN
Sea of Japan

IRAN
IRAQ

AFGHANISTAN

CHINA

East China Sea

KUWAIT
BAHRAIN
QATAR
U.A.E

PAKISTAN

BHUTAN

NEPAL

LIBYA EGYPT

SAUDI ARABIA

INDIA

TAIWAN

OMAN

BANGLADESH

NIGER
CHAD
SUDAN

YEMEN
ERITREA

DJIBOUTI

MYANMAR
LAOS
THAILAND
VIETNAM
South China Sea

PACIFIC OCEAN

Arabian Sea

Bay of Bengal

PHILIPPINES

FEDERATED STATES
OF MICRONESIA

MARSHALL
ISLANDS

NIGERIA
CENTRAL
AFRICAN REP.
EQ.
CAMEROON
NEA
GABON
O TOMÉ
AND
ÍNCIPE
CONGO

SOUTH
SUDAN
ETHIOPIA
UGANDA
KENYA
RWANDA
BURUNDI
DEM. REP.
OF THE
CONGO
TANZANIA

SRI
LANKA

CAMBODIA
BRUNEI
MALAYSIA

PALAU

KIRIBATI
NAURU

MALDIVES

SINGAPORE
Sumatra

Borneo

INDONESIA

SEYCHELLES

INDONESIA

New Guinea

PAPUA NEW
GUINEA

SOLOMON
ISLANDS

TUVALU

Java

ANGOLA
ZAMBIA
MALAWI
COMOROS

INDIAN
OCEAN

TIMOR-
LESTE

VANUATU

NAMIBIA
ZIMBABWE
MOZAMBIQUE
MADAGASCAR
MAURITIUS

FIJI

New Caledonia
(France)

BOTSWANA

Réunion
(France)

AUSTRALIA

SOUTH
AFRICA
ESWATINI
LESOTHO

0   1,000   2,000 mi
0   1,000   2,000 km

Kerguelen Is.
(France)

Tasmania

NEW
ZEALAND

SOUTHERN OCEAN

A N T A R C T I C A